PSYCHOLOGY

SIXTH EDITION

Chuck Close is a preeminent U.S. artist and is known mostly for his large portraits based on photographs. He received his B.A. from the University of Washington in Seattle and then graduated with a MFA from Yale University. He has taught art at the University of Massachusetts.

Close's first one-man show was exhibited in 1970 and he was first exhibited at the New York Museum of Modern Art in early 1973. On December 7, 1988, Close felt a strange pain in his chest. That day he went to the hospital and within hours was paralyzed from the neck down. Afterwards Close had to rehab in order to strengthen his muscles; he soon regained slight movement in his arms and could walk only short distances. He has relied on a wheelchair since then.

Today, Close paints with a brush strapped onto his wrist in order to creating large portraits in low-resolution grid squares created by his assistant. Viewed from a distance, these discrete squares appear as a single image which attempt photo-reality, much like the cover of this book.

Close currently lives and paints in Bridgehampton, New York. His works are located in myriad public and private art collections across the globe. His paintings can be seen in such notable public collections as the Museum of Modern Art (NYC), The Metropolitan Museum of Art (NYC), the Tate Modern (London), and Le Centre Pompidou (Paris). The painting on the cover of this book is in the collection of the Walker Art Center, Minneapolis.

PSYCHOLOGY

SIXTH EDITION

PETER GRAY

Boston College

WORTH PUBLISHERS

Permission is acknowledged to reprint the artwork on the pages accompanying the beginnings of chapters: Chapter 1 (page xxviii): Ken Orvidas; Chapter 2 (page 26): Philippe Lardy; Chapter 3 (page 50): Stefano Vitale/lindgrensmith.com; Chapter 4 (page 92): Stefano Vitale/lindgrensmith.com; Chapter 5 (page 136): Gianpaolo Pagni/Rep. By Marlena Agency; Chapter 6 (page 184): Anson Liaw/Images.com; Chapter 7 (page 230): Rafael Lopez; Chapter 8 (page 268): Elizabeth Rosen/Morgan Gaynin Inc.; Chapter 9 (page 308): Jim Tsinganos; Chapter 10 (page 350): Philippe Lardy; Chapter 11 (page 396): Cathy Gendron/theispot.com; Chapter 12 (page 434): Pierre Mornet/Rep. By Marlena Agency; Chapter 13 (page 474): Curtis Parker/Images.com; Chapter 14 (page 510): Stephanie Dalton Cowan/www.daltoncowan.com; Chapter 15 (page 548): Elizabeth Rosen/Morgan Gaynin Inc.; Chapter 16 (page 592): Michael Morgenstern/theispot.com; Chapter 17 (page 638): Illustration by Philippe Lardy

Publisher: Catherine Woods

Acquisitions Editor: Erik Gilg

Development Editor: Valerie Raymond

Marketing Manager: Amy Shefferd

Art Director and Cover Designer: Babs Reingold

Interior Designer: Lissi Sigillo

Art Researcher: Lyndall Culbertson

Associate Managing Editor: Tracey Kuehn

Project Editor: Leo Kelly, MPS Content Services, a Macmillan Company

Photo Research Manager: Ted Sczcepanski

Photo Editor: Cecilia Varas

Photo Researcher: Donna Ranieri

Illustration Coordinator: Eleanor Jaekel

Illustrations: DragonFly Studios, Matthew Holt, and Hans Neuhart

Production Manager: Barbara Anne Seixas

Composition: MPS Limited, a Macmillan Company

Printing and Binding: RR Donnelley

Cover Art: Photograph by Ellen Page Wilson, courtesy PaceWildenstein, New York. © Chuck Close, courtesy PaceWildenstein, New York; Collection Walker Art Center, Minneapolis, Gift of Judy and Kenneth Dayton, 1994

Library of Congress Control Number: 2009940260

ISBN-13: 978-1-4292-1947-1

ISBN-10: 1-4292-1947-5

Worth Publishers
41 Madison Avenue
New York, NY 10010
www.worthpublishers.com

For Diane

About the Author

Peter Gray was a full-time professor of psychology at Boston College for 30 years, where he served his department at various times as Department Chair, Undergraduate Program Director, and Graduate Program Director. He has published research in biological, evolutionary, cultural, developmental and educational psychology; published articles on innovative teaching methods; taught more than 20 different undergraduate courses, including, most regularly, introductory psychology; helped develop a university-wide program to improve students' study and learning skills; and developed a program of research practicum courses. He is now retired from regular teaching, but maintains a position as Research Professor at Boston College. Most of his current research and writing has to do with the value of play, especially free age-mixed play, in children's development. He is author of a popular weekly blog entitled *Freedom to Learn: The Roles of Play and Curiosity as Foundations for Learning,* which can be found on the *Psychology Today website* at https://www.psychologytoday.com/blog/freedom-learn.

Before joining Boston College, Peter Gray studied psychology as an undergraduate at Columbia University and earned a Ph.D. in biological sciences at Rockefeller University. He earned his way through college by coaching basketball and working with youth groups in New York City. As a graduate student he directed a summer biology program for talented high school students from impoverished neighborhoods. His avocations today include long distance bicycling, kayaking, and backwoods skiing. He welcomes sincere comments and suggestions concerning this textbook, from students as well as from faculty, and can be reached by email at grayp@bc.edu.

Brief Contents

Contents

PART 8
Personality and Disorders

Preface

I am addressing this Preface primarily to instructors, but if you are a student reading it, welcome. My intent here is to tell you about my long-standing goals for the book, my specific goals for this edition, the general organization of the book, and the special features of the book that are designed to help students enjoy it and learn from it.

Long-Standing Goals for the Book

The primary purpose of a liberal arts education, in my view, is to gain experience in thinking critically about ideas. Information today is available at everyone's fingertips; we don't need to store a lot of it in our heads. We do, however, need to use our heads to evaluate information and apply it logically to larger ideas. My hope is that students who have been introduced to psychology through my book will, upon hearing of some new idea in psychology, almost reflexively ask, "What is the evidence?" and will feel empowered to think logically and critically about that evidence. As I point out to students in Chapter 1 of this new edition:

> . . . I have done my best to present psychology as a set of ideas to think about, not as a set of facts to memorize. I have tried to give you enough information about each idea, enough of the evidence and logic supporting it, to enable you to have something to think about and argue with. Most of all, I do not want you to read this book as Truth with a capital T. Psychology is a science, and the essence of science is this: We do not accept anything on authority. It doesn't matter *who* says that something is or isn't true; what matters is the evidence and logic behind the statement. Each page of this book is offered for your consideration, not for your unquestioned acceptance.

Even if the goal of the book were merely to teach students the main concepts of psychology, the best means would still be one that stimulates thought. As cognitive psychologists have shown repeatedly, the human mind is not particularly good at absorbing and remembering miscellaneous pieces of information. It is designed for thinking, figuring out, understanding; and it remembers what it understands. In the absence of some knowledge of the logic and evidence behind them, the concepts in psychology are words devoid of meaning.

In this book, critical thinking does not come in separate boxes or in exercises at the ends of chapters. It is—if I have done my job as intended—woven through almost every paragraph of the text. I have entered each domain of psychology to identify its main questions, its main approaches to answering questions, its main discoveries, and the most durable ideas and theories that have resulted from those discoveries. I have striven to describe these in as logically coherent and intellectually stimulating a manner as possible—one that excites students' interest by appealing to their intelligence. My goal throughout has been to depict the science of psychology as a human endeavor in which progress comes through the work of thoughtful, if fallible, people who make observations, conduct experiments, reason, and argue about behavior. I want students to join you and me in *thinking about* behavior—its functions, causes, and mechanisms. In writing each edition of this book, I have constantly imagined myself carrying on a dialogue with an inquiring, thinking, appropriately skeptical student.

One of my dearest aims has been to achieve some small measure of the personal touch that William James accomplished so masterfully in *The Principles of Psychology*— the book that still stands, in my mind, as the best introduction to psychology ever written. While reading James, one constantly senses a mind at work, a mind that is honestly struggling to understand the big issues in psychology and that invites readers into the process. I also confess to sharing two of James's biases: rationalism and functionalism. As a rationalist, I am uncomfortable presenting findings and facts without trying to make sense of them. Sometimes in our teaching of psychology we overplay the methods for gathering and analyzing data and underplay the value of logical thought. I want students always to think about findings in relation to larger ideas and not to get the impression that the discipline is simply a piling of fact upon fact. As a functionalist, I want to know why, in terms of survival or other benefits, people behave as they do.

The functionalist theme runs through the book and is part of the reason the first major unit (following the brief *Background to the Study of Psychology* unit) is entitled *The Adaptiveness of Behavior* and deals with behavioral evolution and learning in back-to-back chapters. Natural selection and learning are the two reasons behavior is functional, and I want students to know something about those processes, and their interaction, right from the start. The functionalist orientation also leads me, throughout the book, to pay more than the usual amount of attention to cross-cultural research and to behavioral processes as they operate in the contexts of people's everyday lives.

Goals for the Sixth Edition

My two main goals in each revision of the book are (1) to keep the book current and accurate, and (2) to make the book more enjoyable and useful to all who read it.

Keeping the Book Current and Accurate

Most of the work and fun of each revision, for me, lies in my own continued learning and rethinking of each realm of psychology. In producing this revision, I skimmed thousands of new research articles and chapters and read hundreds carefully to determine which new developments warrant inclusion in the introductory course. The result was not so much the discovery of new ideas as the determination of how long-standing ideas are playing themselves out in current research and debate. This edition contains approximately 530 new references to research, mainly to works published within the past five years, out of a total reference list of approximately 2,200. By including the most recent research and controversies, I can convey to students the understanding that psychology is a continuously advancing, dynamic, contemporary human activity, not a stale collection of facts.

When I compare this new edition of *Psychology* with my first edition, I see the great progress psychology has made in the past 20 years. What a pleasure it has been for me to keep pace with it! The progress has come on all fronts and is not easily summarized, but it is pleasing to me that the general theme of adaptation, which was central to my initial conception of the book, is even more central to psychology today. Our basic behavioral machinery is adapted, by natural selection, to the general, long-standing conditions of human life. That machinery, however, is itself designed, by natural selection, to be adaptive to the conditions of life within which the individual person develops. An enormous amount of research over the past few years, in all areas of psychology and neuroscience, elaborates on the theme of adaptation. That work is well represented in this new edition.

Here are a few examples of new or expanded discussions, in this edition, that reflect our increased understanding of adaptive mechanisms: Chapter 4 brings our understanding of observational learning up to date with a new section on the role of reflexive gaze following. Chapter 5 extends the already present theme of neuro-plasticity to include new work on the rapidity by which brain structures alter themselves in response to changes in sensory input. Chapter 6 presents new work showing that circulating levels of sex hormones not only influence sexual behavior, but are themselves influenced by the environmental context. Chapter 8 presents new work on memory consolidation, showing how those memories that are most likely to be useful in the future become most durable. Chapter 10 presents new work suggesting that abstract reasoning ability has advanced, from generation to generation, in step with historical changes in the ways that people use their minds in everyday life. Chapters 12 and 16 present new work showing how a particular gene variation may make a person more or less sensitive to stressful environmental occurrences. Chapter 15 includes new work showing that people's beliefs about the modifiability of personality and intelligence actually influence that modifiability. Chapter 16 expands on the already present theme that cultural differences in attitudes toward mental disorders affect the course of those disorders.

Making the Book More Enjoyable and Useful to All Who Use It

A book becomes more useful and enjoyable not by being "dumbed down" but by being "smartened up." The clearer the logic and the more precisely it is expressed, the easier a book is to understand and the more engaging it becomes. With each revision, and with feedback from adopters, students, and editors, I find new ways to make difficult ideas clearer without ignoring their inherent subtlety or complexity. Sometimes this involves a simple change in wording or a minor alteration in the sequence of an argument's elements or a new example or visual illustration that captures the essence of the argument. At other times the change is more fundamental. In this edition, my efforts toward clarity were greatly facilitated by two excellent editors—Valerie Raymond and Mary Trahan. Valerie was reading my manuscript for the first time, as a student would, and helped very much to sharpen the wording. Mary, who is the author of the study guide for each edition, brought her long experience in reading the book from the viewpoint of a student to the task of showing me where students might have difficulty.

In the last (fifth) edition I made some large changes aimed at making the book more accessible to the full range of students. One such change was a reformulated Chapter 1, which became an orientation to the textbook and how to use its study features, as well as an orientation to psychology as a discipline. Another large change was the addition of a new review aid, *hierarchical review charts,* at the end of each major section within each chapter. The value of these charts is described in the "Special Features" section of this Preface and again, more fully, on pp. 1–25 of Chapter 1. Feedback concerning the fifth edition indicates that the new orientation chapter and the review charts have been very useful in helping students to learn from the book, and so these features have been retained and improved upon for this edition.

With each edition, I take personal responsibility for every detail of the book, including all of the illustrations. I am never content to add an illustration simply to brighten up the page; each photograph, drawing, and cartoon must in my mind serve a purpose that is relevant to the text. I have hand chosen all of these and written all of the captions. For this edition I have added more than the usual number of new cartoons, not just for humor but also for their value in stimulating thought. My favorite cartoons are those that in some way poke fun at the very idea I am discussing and in that way help stimulate critical thought about the idea.

General Organization of the Book

Although the content within chapters is considerably revised, the overall organization of the book is essentially the same as it was in the previous edition. For those who are new to the book, I will describe here that organization and something of the logic behind it. The book is divided into eight units, or parts, each of which consists of two or (in one case) three chapters.

Part 1, *Background to the Study of Psychology,* has two relatively brief chapters. Chapter 1, *Foundations for the Study of Psychology,* is an orientation both to psychology as a discipline and to the book. It presents three major historical ideas that underlie contemporary psychology; it outlines the scope of contemporary psychology; and it offers students some advice about studying this book. Chapter 2, *Methods of Psychology,* lays out some general elements of psychological research that will be useful to students in later chapters. (If you prefer a more thorough discussion of statistics than Chapter 2 contains, you might supplement it with the first three sections of the *Statistical Appendix,* found at the back of the book.)

Part 2, *The Adaptiveness of Behavior,* is devoted explicitly to the functionalist theme that reappears throughout the book. Behavior can be understood as adaptation to the environment, which occurs at two levels—the phylogenetic level (through natural selection) and the individual level (through learning). These themes are developed in two chapters that emphasize the interaction of nature and nurture in behavioral adaptation. Chapter 3, *Genetic and Evolutionary Foundations of Behavior,* includes the idea that even behaviors that are most highly prepared by evolution must develop, in the individual, through interaction with the environment. Chapter 4, *Basic Processes of Learning,* includes the idea that learning mechanisms themselves are products of evolution.

Part 3, *Physiological Mechanisms of Behavior,* is concerned most directly with psychologists' attempts to explain behavior in terms of the neural and hormonal mechanisms that produce it. Chapter 5, *The Neural Control of Behavior,* is a functional introduction to the nervous system and to the actions of hormones and drugs. In addition to providing a background that is useful for the rest of the book, this chapter continues the theme of adaptation with an up-to-date discussion of neuroplasticity and brain mechanisms of learning. Chapter 6, *Mechanisms of Motivation and Emotion,* applies the ideas about the nervous system and hormones developed in the preceding chapter to the topics of hunger, sex, reward mechanisms, sleep, and emotionality. Although this chapter centers on physiological mechanisms, it is not exclusively physiological. The discussions of motives and emotions pay ample attention to environmental influences.

Part 4, *Sensation and Perception,* is about the processes through which the brain or mind gathers information about the outside world. It contains Chapter 7, *Smell, Taste, Pain, Hearing, and Psychophysics,* and Chapter 8, *The Psychology of Vision.* The main question for both chapters is this: How does our nervous system respond to and make sense of the patterns of energy in the physical world? In both chapters the discussion of sensory and perceptual mechanisms is placed in a functionalist context. The senses are understood as survival mechanisms, which evolved not to provide full, objective accounts of the world's physical properties, but, rather, to provide the specific kinds of information that are needed to survive and reproduce.

Part 5, *The Human Intellect,* is about the ability of the brain or mind to store information and use it to solve problems. Chapter 9, *Memory and Consciousness,* focuses on the roles of both unconscious and conscious mechanisms in attention, memory encoding, and memory retrieval. The chapter includes an analysis of the multiple memory systems that have evolved to serve different adaptive functions. Chapter 10, *Reasoning and Intelligence,* deals with the cognitive processes by which people solve problems, both in everyday life and on structured tests, and with the measurement of intelligence and controversies associated with such measurement.

Throughout these chapters, the information-processing perspective is highlighted but is tempered by ecological discussions that draw attention to the functions of each mental process and the environmental contexts within which it operates.

In sum, Parts 2, 3, 4, and 5 are all concerned with basic psychological processes—processes of learning, motivation, emotion, sensation, perception, attention, memory, and problem solving—and each process is discussed in a manner that integrates ideas about its mechanisms with ideas about its adaptive functions. The remaining three parts are concerned with understanding the whole person and the person's relationships to the social environment.

Part 6, *Growth of the Mind and Person,* is about developmental psychology. Its two chapters develop the functionalist perspective further by emphasizing the interactions between evolved human tendencies and environmental experiences in shaping a person's behavior. Chapter 11, *The Development of Thought and Language,* is concerned with the traditional topics of cognitive and language development. Chapter 12, *Social Development,* is concerned with the changes in social relationships and life tasks that occur throughout the life span and with ways in which these relationships and tasks vary across cultures. Chapter 12 also sets the stage for the next pair of chapters.

Part 7, *The Person in a World of People,* is about social psychology. Chapter 13, *Social Perception and Attitudes,* is concerned with the mental processes involved in forming judgments of other people, perceiving and presenting the self in the social environment, and forming and modifying attitudes. Chapter 14, *Social Influences on Behavior,* deals with compliance, obedience, conformity, cooperation, competition, group decision-making, conflict, and the social regulatory roles of emotions. A theme of this chapter is the contrast between normative and informational influences. This unit on social psychology is placed before the one on personality and mental disorders because the insights of social psychology—especially those pertaining to social cognition—contribute to modern personality theories and to ways of understanding and treating mental disorders.

Part 8, *Personality and Disorders,* consists of three chapters on topics that students tend to identify most strongly as "psychology" before they enter the course. Chapter 15, *Personality,* has sections on the nature and origins of traits, the adaptive value of individual differences, and the classic theories of personality. Chapter 16, *Mental Disorders,* begins by discussing the problems involved in categorizing and diagnosing disorders and then, through the discussion of specific disorders, emphasizes the notion of multiple causation and the theme that the symptoms characterizing disorders are different in degree, not in kind, from normal psychological experiences and processes. Chapter 17, *Treatment,* offers an opportunity to recapitulate many of the main ideas of earlier chapters—now in the context of their application to therapy. Ideas from Parts 2, 3, 5, and 7 reappear in the discussions of biological, behavioral, and cognitive therapies, and ideas from the personality chapter reappear in the discussions of psychodynamic and humanistic therapies.

Although this ordering of topics makes the most sense to me, I recognize that other sensible arrangements exist and that time limits may prevent you from using the entire book. Therefore, each chapter is written so that it can be read as a separate entity, independent of others. Links are often made to material presented in another chapter, but most of these cross-references are spelled out in enough detail to be understood by students who have not read the other chapter. The only major exception falls in the physiological unit: Chapter 6, on motivation, sleep, and emotion, assumes that the student has learned some of the basic information presented in Chapter 5, on the nervous system. Specific suggestions for making deletions within each chapter can be found in the *Instructor's Resources,* which is available on Worth Publishers' Web site, at www.worthpublishers.com/gray.

Pedagogical Features of the Book

The main pedagogical feature of this or any other textbook is, of course, the narrative itself, which should be clear, logical, and interesting. Everything else is secondary. I have attempted through every page of every chapter to produce as logical and clear a flow of ideas as I possibly can. I have avoided the kinds of boxes and inserts that are often found in introductory psychology texts, because such digressions distract from the flow of thought and add to the impression that psychology is a jumble of topics that don't fit together very well.

I want students to read and think about the ideas of this book, not attempt to memorize bits and pieces of isolated information. Toward that end I have refrained from the use of review lists of terms, presented out of context of the larger arguments, and have developed, instead, study aids that help students to focus their attention on the arguments and think about individual findings and terms in relation to those arguments.

Focus Questions

The most useful study aid in this book—in my judgment and that of many students who have provided feedback—are the *focus questions*, which appear in the margins throughout the text at an average frequency of about 1 question per page. Each question is designed to direct students' attention to the main idea, argument, or evidence addressed in the adjacent paragraphs of text. In Chapter 1 (on pp. 1–25) I spell out more fully the rationale behind the focus questions and offer advice to students for using them to guide both their initial reading and their review of each main section of each chapter. I ask students to develop the habit of reading and thinking about each focus question as they come to it, before they read the paragraph or paragraphs of text that answer that question. Most students, once they get used to this method of study, find that it helps them greatly in focusing their attention, stimulating their thought, and increasing their understanding of what they are reading. I have even had students tell me that the focus questions are so helpful that they find themselves writing their own focus questions in the margins of their other textbooks. I urge instructors to reinforce the value of the focus questions by talking about ways of using them in an early lecture and perhaps also by modeling their use with a think-aloud exercise.

The focus questions also offer instructors a means to make selective assignments within any chapter. The questions are numbered so instructors can easily let students know, with a list of numbers, which questions will be fair game for exams. The multiple-choice questions in the *Test Bank* are keyed by number to the focus questions. When I teach the course I tell students that tests will consist of multiple-choice and brief essay questions that are derived from the book's focus questions. This makes clear what students must do to prepare. If they can answer the focus questions, they will do well on the test.

Hierarchical Section Reviews

Students are not always aware that the information in textbooks is hierarchically organized. Main ideas, or theses, appear as main headings, subordinate ideas pertaining to the larger ideas appear as second order headings, and so on. When students can see the hierarchical structure of a textbook section, they have a foundation for thinking about its content as an organized whole. All of the bits and pieces of the section become chunked, in a logically coherent way, into the single hierarchical structure of the section's overarching argument. The task of studying the section suddenly makes sense and becomes less daunting. The task is not to memorize terms and bits of information but to follow and think about a single argument. In doing so, memory of the specifics comes as an almost incidental by-product.

At the end of each major section of each chapter of this edition, I have provided a *section review,* which depicts explicitly the hierarchical structure that relates the section's thesis to its subordinate ideas and to specific observations and concepts that are relevant to those ideas. The primary purpose of this feature is to help students to review each section before moving on to the next. Here they can see, in one organized picture, the structure of the argument that they have just read. Some students may also find these charts useful as previews. By looking ahead at the section review before reading each new section, students can get a coherent overview, which should help them to read with greater focus and thought.

In Chapter 1 (pp. 1–25), I advise students on how to use the section reviews, but, as with the focus questions, I urge instructors to encourage their use by offering their own advice and, perhaps, by demonstrating in an early lecture how to use them.

Concluding Thoughts and Further Reading

Because the focus questions and section reviews make a traditional end-of-chapter review unnecessary, I end each chapter with a section called *Concluding Thoughts* that expands on the broad themes of the chapter, points out relationships to ideas discussed in other chapters, and sometimes even offers a new idea or two for students to consider as they reflect on the chapter. In many cases these thoughts are aimed at helping students to see connections between ideas from different sections of the chapter, which were not tied together in any of the section reviews.

Concluding Thoughts is followed by a brief section called *Further Reading,* which contains thumbnail reviews of several relevant and interesting books that are sufficiently nontechnical to be read by first-year students. The kinds of students who continue in psychology or in related disciplines, who become the next crop of professors or professional psychologists, are the ones who take most advantage of this feature.

Supplements

A full description of the many supplements that Worth Publishers makes available to users of my textbook follows this Preface, so I will comment here on just three of them that I know well and particularly recommend.

Study Guide

Mary Trahan's study guide, entitled *Focus on Psychology: A Guide to Mastering Peter Gray's Psychology,* is an excellent tool for those students who could benefit from study help even beyond what is provided within the textbook itself. Mary is a cognitive psychologist who has a special interest in applying the insights of her field to the teaching of psychology. The guide is designed to be used in tandem with the reading of each textbook chapter, and its contents are linked to the textbook's focus questions. Students who have used previous editions of the guide have praised it highly. It is not a shortcut to learning or a substitute for reading the textbook. Instead, it structures students' study of the textbook so that they slow down and think, writing out brief answers to questions as they read. Some instructors ask that this supplement be bound as a package with the textbook, so all their students buy both at once. Others make it optional by asking the bookstore to order copies and then leaving it up to students to buy it or not at their discretion. I would suggest that you obtain a copy of this guide from your Worth representative and look at it carefully to see whether you would like it to be required or optional in your course. If you make it optional, your familiarity with the guide can help you decide when to recommend it to individual students who seem to need extra help.

The Instructor's Resources

An extremely useful and extensive set of *Instructor's Resources* has been prepared for use with this textbook. The sixth edition has been updated and improved by Sarah L. Strout of the University of Southern New Hampshire and Rosemarie Sokol Chang of EvoS: The Evolutionary Studies Consortium. For each chapter of the textbook, this manual offers interesting class demonstrations, suggestions for incorporating the Internet and other media into classroom lectures and demonstrations, and ideas for lecture elaborations and class discussions. I have contributed to this manual some general thoughts about teaching introductory psychology and some specific teaching suggestions for each chapter, including specific suggestions for cutting each chapter down for shorter courses. You can access this Web-based manual through Worth Publishers' Web site, at www.worthpublishers.com/gray. It is easily searchable, and you can download any portions of it that you wish to use.

Test Bank

A *Test Bank*, containing approximately 2,000 multiple-choice questions, has been prepared for this edition by Ramona Houmanfar of the University of Nevada at Reno, Lori Bica of the University of Wisconsin, Eau Claire, Mary Trahan, and a team of other psychologists. The questions are keyed to the focus questions in the text, so instructors can easily identify questions that correspond with the focus questions that they have asked students to emphasize in their studies. The Test Bank is available in various computerized versions and in printed form. Creating good multiple-choice questions is always a challenge, and I am greatly pleased by the set of questions that Mary, Lori, and Ramona have put together. Previous editions of the Test Bank have been much praised by its users.

Acknowledgments

Nobody writes a textbook alone. Countless people have contributed directly or indirectly to the development and revisions of this one, of whom I can only list a few here: John Broida, University of Southern Maine, Victor Ferreira, University of California—San Diego, David Z. Hambrick, Michigan State University, Ramona Houmanfar, University of Nevada, Reno, Jennie Jamison, St. Petersburg High School, Alan Lambert, Washington University, Brian Malley, University of Michigan—Ann Arbor, Marc Mooney, University of Minnesota—Twin Cities, Joe Morrissey, SUNY Binghamton, Tony Robertson, Malaspina University, and Tom Rodebaugh, Washington University.

This edition, as I noted earlier, has been much improved by the excellent editing of Valerie Raymond and Mary Trahan. Of the many great editors who have worked with me on earlier editions, I single out Phyllis Fisher for special mention. She worked closely with me on the first edition to help shape my ideas into a successful textbook, and she also helped to improve the book by serving as developmental editor on the third and fifth editions. We have enjoyed many wonderful arguments over the years, and the book has profited greatly from them.

Many others contributed their expertise to the development and production of this edition and deserve my heartfelt thanks. Among them are Elizabeth Widdicombe, President of Worth Publishers, Catherine Woods, Senior Publisher of Worth Publishers, Erik Gilg, Acquisitions Editor, Amy Shefferd, Marketing Manager, Jaclyn Castaldo, Assistant Editor, Babs Reingold, Art Director, Tracey Kuehn, Associate Managing Editor, Cecilia Varas, Photo Editor, Barbara Seixas, Production Manager, Leo Kelley, Production Editor, and Peter Twickler, Media Editor.

This book has also profited from the input, over the years, of more than 300 scholars who have contributed their thoughts to the development of previous editions. Among the many researchers who have made such contributions are (in alphabetical order): Michael Atkinson, Alan Baddeley, Robert Bell, Sharon Brehm, Nathan Brody, Stephen Ceci, Robert Cialdini, Stanley Coren, Martin Daly, Patricia Devine, John Dovidio, Nancy Eisenberg, Anders Ericsson, Bennett Galef, Dedre Gentner, Daniel Gilbert, Norma Graham, Jill Hooley, David Hothersall, Lloyd Kaufman, Philip Johnson-Laird, Annette Karmiloff-Smith, Mark Leary, Joseph LeDoux, Dan McAdams, Matt McGue, Gilda Morelli, William Miller, Susan Mineka, Irene Miura, Darwin Muir, Randy Nelson, Randolph Nesse, Julie Norem, Michael Numan, Hal Pashler, Holly Prigerson, Dennis Proffitt, Robert Rescorla, Emilie Rissman, David Rowe, Shepard Siegel, Robert Siegler, Anne Treisman, Harry Triandis, David Uttal, George C. Van Dyne, Connie Varnhagen, Kevin Weinfurt, and Leslie Zebrowitz.

In closing, I thank my dear wife, Diane Pingeton. Without her support and encouragement I would not have undertaken this revision or seen it through. It is to her that this edition is dedicated.

Peter Gray
Department of Psychology, Boston College
grayp@bc.edu

Supplements and Media

Supplements

For Instructors

Instructor's Resources An extremely useful and extensive set of *Instructor's Resources* has been prepared for use with this textbook. The sixth edition has been updated and improved by Sarah L. Strout of the University of Southern New Hampshire and Rosemarie Sokol Chang of EvoS: The Evolutionary Studies Consortium. For each chapter of the textbook, this manual offers interesting class demonstrations, suggestions for incorporating the Internet and other media into classroom work, and ideas for lecture elaborations and class discussions. I have contributed to this manual some general thoughts about teaching introductory psychology and some specific teaching suggestions for each chapter, including specific suggestions for cutting each chapter down for shorter courses. You can access this Web-based manual through Worth Publishers' Web site, at www.worthpublishers.com/gray. It is easily searchable, and you can download any portions of it that you wish to use. There is also a printed version of this instructor's manual.

For Students

Focus on Psychology: A Guide to Mastering Peter Gray's *Psychology*, by Mary Trahan. The comprehensive study guide helps students develop a thorough and organized understanding of the text, using an active, question-driven approach. It follows the orderly flow of material in each chapter and focuses students' attention on ideas, in keeping with the spirit of the text. The study guide is designed to be used in tandem with the reading of each textbook chapter, and its contents are linked to *Psychology,* Sixth Edition's marginal Focus Questions. Each chapter features an introduction, integrated study material for each section of the chapter, two self-tests with answers, and answers for selected questions. In cases where the study guide does not come packaged with the text, students can purchase it separately.

From the pages of *Scientific American*: *Scientific American Mind*: A Collector's Edition This new magazine explores riveting breakthroughs in psychology, neuroscience, and related fields. It is free when packaged with the text (upon request).

Improving the Mind and Brain: A *Scientific American* Special Issue This single-topic issue from *Scientific American* magazine features 8 articles from the most distinguished researchers in the field. It is free when packaged with the text (upon request).

***Scientific American* Explores the Hidden Mind: A Collector's Edition** In a special collector's edition, *Scientific American* provides a compilation of updated feature articles that explore and reveal the mysterious inner workings of the mind and brain. It is free when packaged with the text (upon request).

Scientific American **Reader to accompany** *Psychology,* **Sixth Edition** Drawn from *Scientific American* and handpicked by Peter Gray, this is a collection of classic articles tied to topics discussed in the text. A brief introduction and series of discussion questions (written by Peter Gray) accompany each article. It is free when packaged with the text (upon request).

Media

Presentation Resources

NEW! Instructor Video Tool Kit Worth Publishers' Video Tool Kit for Introductory Psychology spans the full range of standard topics for the introductory psychology course, combining classic experiments, current news footage, and cutting-edge research. With its superb collection of 120 brief (1 to 13 minutes) clips across two volumes and emphasis on the biological bases of behavior, the Video Tool Kit gives students a fresh new way to experience both the classic experiments at the heart of psychological science, and cutting-edge research conducted by the field's most influential investigators.

ActivePsych: Classroom Activities Project and Video Teaching Modules CD-ROM Set ActivePsych is a series of interactive activities and video clips that will captivate your classroom and inspire student participation, with minimal instructor preparation necessary (just load the CD and launch the activity). ActivePsych includes three components: Classroom Activities Project, providing 30 interactive demonstrations; Digital Media Archive, Second Edition, with approximately 30 short video clips; and *Scientific American* Frontiers Teaching Modules, Third Edition, offering 15 recent segments.

Instructor's Resource CD-ROM This newly customized presentation CD-ROM contains all text art and illustrations, as well as an electronic version of the Instructor's Resource Manual. The CD also includes the PowerPoint® slides described below.

Chapter Art and Outline PowerPoint® Slides for Psychology, Sixth Edition These PowerPoint® slides can be either used as is or customized to fit particular needs. There are two pre-built versions for each chapter—one featuring chapter outlines, the other featuring all chapter art. Also available at www.worthpublishers. com/gray.

Web Sites and CD

Interactive eBook at ebooks.bfwpub.com This fully integrated, flexible, and customizable online version of *Psychology,* Sixth Edition, links the complete text with all student media resources, adding study features such as bookmarks, note taking, and quizzes.

Companion Web site at www.worthpublishers.com/gray A set of resources for students that are free and do not require any special access codes or passwords. The tools on the site include:

- learning objectives that provide enrichment to text topics
- quizzing from PsychSim 5.0, by Thomas Ludwig, Hope College

A password-protected Instructor Site offers a full array of teaching resources, including PowerPoint® slides, an online quiz gradebook, Instructor's Resource Manual, and links to additional tools (WebCT, Blackboard, etc.).

PsychSim 5.0, by Thomas E. Ludwig, Hope College. These 42 interactive simulations involve students in the practice of psychological research and dynamic tutorials or demonstrations.

Focus on Research: PsychInquiry, by Thomas Ludwig, Hope College, and Connie Varnhagen, University of Alberta. This CD-ROM contains dozens of interactive activities designed to help students learn about psychological research and improve their critical thinking.

Course Management/Online Resources

NEW! PsychPortal

Integrating the best online material that Worth has to offer, PsychPortal is an innovative learning space that combines a powerful quizzing engine with unparalleled media resources. PsychPortal conveniently offers all the functionality you need to support your online or hybrid course, yet it is flexible, customizable, and simple enough to enhance your traditional course. The following interactive learning materials contained within PsychPortal make it truly unique:

An **interactive eBook** allows students to highlight, bookmark, and make their own notes just as they would with a printed textbook.

- Tom Ludwig's (Hope College) suite of interactive media—**PsychSim 5.0** and the **Concepts in Action**—bring key concepts to life.

- The **Student Video Tool Kit for Introductory Psychology** includes more than 110 engaging video modules that instructors can easily assign, assess, and customize for their students. Videos cover classic experiments, current news footage, and cutting-edge research, all of which are sure to spark discussion and encourage critical thinking.

Enhanced E-Pack and Course Cartridge To further save time and to provide additional support, the E-Pack and Course Cartridge for Gray's *Psychology*, Sixth Edition, now includes additional, premium student AND instructor resources in one place. Course management solutions are available for WebCT, Blackboard, Desire2Learn, and Angel.

Assessment

Printed Test Bank, by Dr. Ramona Houmanfar, University of Nevada, Reno, and Lori Bica, University of Wisconsin, Eau Claire. Includes over 2,000 multiple-choice and essay questions. Each question is referenced by topic, page number in the text, and appropriate marginal Focus Questions.

Diploma Computerized Test Bank (Windows and Macintosh on one CD-ROM).

Diploma Online Testing at www.wimba.com/products/diploma.

Online Quizzing at www.worthpublishers.com/gray.

i•clicker Radio Frequency Classroom Response System Offered by Worth Publishers, in partnership with i•clicker. Created by educators for educators, this radio frequency system is the hassle-free way to make your class time more interactive. It allows you to pause to ask questions and instantly record responses, as well as take attendance, direct students through lectures, gauge your students' understanding of the material, and much more.

Video/DVD Resources

Digital Media Archive, Second Edition Housed in ActivePsych and edited by Joe Morrissey and Ann Merriwether, State University of New York at Binghamton, the Second Edition offers approximately 30 completely new short video clips, drawn from a variety of sources, and numerous new animations.

Scientific American Frontiers **Teaching Modules, Third Edition** Housed in ActivePsych and edited by Martin Bolt, Calvin College, the Third Edition offers you 15 edited clips from *Scientific American Frontiers* segments produced between 2003 and 2005.

Moving Images: Exploring Psychology Through Film VHS or DVD. Faculty Guide available at www.worthpublishers.com/gray. Edited by Martin Bolt, Calvin College, this new series (drawn from the Films for the Humanities and Sciences series) contains 25 one- to eight-minute clips of real people, real experiments, and real patients, combining historical footage with cutting-edge research and news programming.

Worth Digital Media Archive VHS, DVD, or CD-ROM. Faculty Guide available. This rich instructor's presentation tool contains 42 digitized video clips of classic experiments and research. Footage includes Bandura's Bobo doll experiment, Takooshian's bystander studies, Piaget's conservation experiment, Harlow's monkey experiments, Milgram's obedience studies, and Neisser's selective attention studies.

Psychology: The Human Experience **Teaching Modules** VHS or DVD. Faculty Guide available. This series includes more than 3 hours of footage from the Introductory Psychology telecourse, *Psychology: The Human Experience,* produced by Coast Learning Systems in collaboration with Worth Publishers.

The Many Faces of Psychology Video, created and written by Frank J. Vattano, Colorado State University, and Martin Bolt, Calvin College (produced by the Office of Instructional Services, Colorado State University). VHS or DVD. This 22-minute video introduces psychology as a science and a profession, illustrating basic and applied methods.

Scientific American Frontiers **Video Collection, Second Edition** VHS or DVD. Faculty Guide available. Hosted by Alan Alda, these 8- to12-minute teaching modules from the highly praised *Scientific American* series feature the work of such notable researchers as Steve Sumi, Renée Baillargeon, Car Rosengren, Laura Pettito, Steven Pinker, Barbara Rothbaum, and Michael Gazzaniga.

The Brain Video Teaching Modules, Second Edition Edited by Frank J. Vattano, Thomas L. Bennet, and Michelle Butler, all of Colorado State University. VHS or DVD. Faculty Guide available. This collection of 32 short clips provides vivid examples for myriad topics in introductory psychology.

Background to the Study of Psychology

"Know thyself." These two words were inscribed on the shrine of the Oracle of Apollo, at Delphi, Greece, in the sixth century B.C. Throughout recorded history, human beings have striven to understand the nature of being human, to fathom the mysteries of the human mind and human behavior. Today that endeavor is pursued as a science, the science of psychology. In this first, background unit, we examine some ideas that helped to bring about a science of psychology, and we preview some of the methods that help to make psychology a science.

Foundations for the Study of Psychology

The human being, as far as any human being can tell, is the only creature that contemplates itself. We not only think, feel, dream, and act but also wonder how and why we do these things. Such contemplation has taken many forms, ranging from just plain wondering to folk tales and popular songs, to poetry and literature, to formal theologies and philosophies. A little more than a century ago, human self-contemplation took a scientific turn, and we call that science psychology.

Welcome! Welcome to *Psychology* and to psychology— that is, to this book and to the field of study it is about. I hope you will enjoy them both. The principal questions of psychology are among the most fascinating that anyone can ask: Why do people feel, think, and behave the way they do? In this book you will read of many ways by which psychologists go about trying to answer such questions, and you will discover many dozens of findings and ideas that help to answer them.

It is useful to begin with a formal definition of our subject: **Psychology** is the *science* of *behavior* and the *mind*. In this definition, **behavior** refers to the observable actions of a person or an animal. **Mind** refers to an individual's sensations, perceptions, memories, thoughts, dreams, motives, emotional feelings, and other subjective experiences. It also refers to all of the unconscious knowledge and operating rules that are built into or stored in the brain and that provide the foundation for organizing behavior and conscious experience. **Science** refers to all attempts to answer questions through the systematic collection and logical analysis of objectively observable data. Most of the data in psychology are based on observations of behavior, because behavior is directly observable and mind is not; but psychologists often use those data to make inferences about the mind.

In this opening chapter, I will do three things, all aimed at helping to prepare you for the rest of the book. First, I will present you with a tiny bit of the history and philosophy that predate and underlie modern psychology. More specifically, I will say something about the historical origins of three ideas that are so basic to our science that I refer to them as "foundation ideas for psychology." Second, I will tell you something about the scope of modern psychology, especially about the various explanatory concepts, or levels of analysis, that psychologists employ in their attempts to understand the mind and behavior. Third, I will tell you something about the features of this book and how you might use them to maximize your enjoyment of it and your ability to learn from it. I put that section last, because I thought you might learn more from it after you have read a bit of the book than you would if it came first. If you prefer to read that section first, please do. It starts on page 20.

1
How might the focus questions (such as this one) in the text's margins be used as a guide to reading this book?

◄ There is one feature of the book that I want you to notice right now, however. In the margins of the text, throughout the book, you will find numbered focus questions. The first such question appears in the margin next to the paragraph you are reading right now. These are the questions that I am trying to answer in the text, and they are also good self-test questions. An effective way to study this book is to read and think about each focus question, as you come to it, before you read the adjacent paragraphs of text, which are aimed at answering that question. This method of study will help you focus your attention on the text and understand and remember what you read. If you read with the active intention of answering the focus questions, your mind is less likely to drift, and you are more likely to understand and think about what you read than if you read passively just to "learn" or "absorb" the material. In addition, after reading the whole chapter or a section of it, you might review by rereading each focus question and answering it in your own words.

▉ Three Foundation Ideas for Psychology: A Historical Overview

The founding of psychology as a formal, recognized, scientific discipline is commonly dated to 1879, when Wilhelm Wundt, in Germany, opened the first university-based psychology laboratory. At about that same time, Wundt also authored the first textbook of psychology and began mentoring psychology's first official graduate students. The first people to earn Ph.D. degrees in psychology were Wundt's students.

But the roots of psychology predate Wundt. They were developed by people who called themselves philosophers, physicists, physiologists, and naturalists. In this section, we shall examine three fundamental ideas of psychology, all of which were conceived of and debated before the establishment of psychology as a recognized scientific discipline. Briefly, the ideas are these:

1. Behavior and mental experiences have physical causes, which can be studied scientifically.

2. The way a person behaves, thinks, and feels is modified, over time, by the person's experiences in his or her environment.

3. The body's machinery, which produces behavior and mental experiences, is a product of evolution by natural selection.

The Idea of Physical Causation of Behavior

Before a science of psychology could emerge, people had to conceive of and accept the idea that questions about human behavior and the mind can, in principle, be answered scientifically. Seeds for this idea can be found in some writings of the

René Descartes Descartes's speculations, in the seventeenth century, about reflexes and the interaction of the body and soul in controlling voluntary actions were an important step toward a scientific analysis of human behavior.

Corbis-Bettmann

ancient Greeks, who speculated about the senses, the human intellect, and the physical basis of the mind in ways that seem remarkably modern. But these seeds lay dormant through the Middle Ages and did not begin to sprout again until the fifteenth century (the Renaissance) or to take firm hold until the eighteenth century (the Enlightenment).

Prior to the eighteenth century, philosophy was tightly bound to and constrained by religion. The church maintained that each human being consists of two distinct but intimately conjoined entities, a material body and an immaterial soul—a view referred to today as **dualism.** The body is part of the natural world and can be studied scientifically, just as inanimate matter can be studied. The soul, in contrast, is a supernatural entity that operates according to its own free will, not natural law, and therefore cannot be studied scientifically. This was the accepted religious doctrine, which—at least in most of Europe—could not be challenged publicly without risk of a charge of heresy and possible death. Yet the doctrine left some room for play, and one who played dangerously near the limits was the great French mathematician, physiologist, and philosopher René Descartes (1596–1650).

Descartes's Version of Dualism: Focus on the Body

Prior to Descartes, most dualists assigned all the interesting qualities of the human being to the soul. The soul was deemed responsible for the body's heat, for its ability to move, for life itself. In *Treatise of Man* (1637/1972), and even more explicitly in *The Passions of the Soul* (1649/1985), Descartes challenged this view. He had performed dissections of animals and of human cadavers, was familiar with research on the flow of blood, and began to regard the body as an intricate, complex machine that generates its own heat and is capable of moving even without the influence of the soul. Although little was known about the nervous system in his time, Descartes's conception of the mechanical control of movement resembles our modern understanding of reflexes, which are involuntary responses to stimuli (see Figure 1.1).

Corbis-Bettmann

Descartes believed that even quite complex behaviors can occur through purely mechanical means, without involvement of the soul. Consistent with church doctrine, he contended that nonhuman animals do not have souls, and he pointed out a logical implication of this contention: Any activity performed by humans that is qualitatively no different from the behavior of a nonhuman animal can, in theory, occur without the soul. If my dog (who can do some wondrous things) is just a machine, then a good deal of what I do—such as eating, drinking, sleeping, running, panting, and occasionally going in circles—might occur purely mechanically as well.

In Descartes's view, the one essential ability that I have but my dog does not is *thought,* which Descartes defined as conscious deliberation and judgment. Whereas previous philosophers ascribed many functions to the soul, Descartes ascribed just one—thought. But even in his discussion of thought, Descartes tended to focus on the body's machinery. To be useful, thought must be responsive to the sensory input channeled into the body through the eyes, ears, and other sense organs, and it must be capable of directing the body's movements by acting on the muscles.

How can the thinking soul interact with the physical machine—the sense organs, muscles, and other parts of the body? Descartes suggested that the soul, though not physical, acts on the body at a particular physical location. Its place of action is

▶ – ⟨2⟩
What was Descartes's version of dualism? How did it help pave the way for a science of psychology?
– – – – – – – – – – – – – – – – – – – –

FIGURE 1.1 Descartes's depiction of a reflex Descartes believed that reflexes occur through purely mechanical means. In describing this figure, Descartes (1637/1972) suggested that the fire causes movement in the nearby particles of skin, pulling on a "thread" (that runs "C" to "C" along the back) going to the brain, which, in turn, causes a pore to open in the brain, allowing fluid to flow through a "small conduit" to the muscles that withdraw the foot. What Descartes called a "thread" and a "small conduit" are today called nerves, and we now know that nerves operate through electrical means, not through physical pulling or the shunting of fluids.

FIGURE 1.2 Descartes's depiction of how the soul receives information through the eyes Descartes believed that the human soul is housed in the pineal gland, depicted here as the tear-shaped structure in the center of the head. In describing this figure, Descartes (1637/1972) suggested that light from the arrow enters the eyes and opens pores in structures that we now know as the optic nerves. Fluid flows from the eyes through the opened pores, causing movement in the pineal gland, which, in Descartes's words, "renders the idea" of the arrow to the soul.

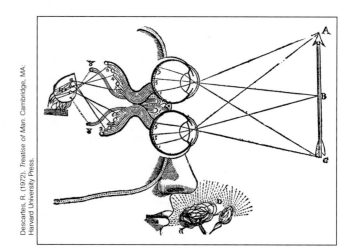

Descartes, R. (1972). *Treatise of Man.* Cambridge, MA: Harvard University Press.

a small organ (now known as the pineal body) buried between the two hemispheres (halves) of the brain (see Figure 1.2). Threadlike structures, which we now call nerves, bring sensory information by physical means into the brain, where the soul receives the information and, by non-physical means, thinks about it. On the basis of those thoughts, the soul then wills movements to occur and executes its will by triggering physical actions in nerves that, in turn, act on muscles. Descartes's dualism, with its heavy emphasis on the body, certainly helped open the door for a science of psychology.

3

Why was Descartes's theory, despite its intuitive appeal, unsuitable for a complete psychology?

◀Descartes's theory is popular among non-scientists even today, because it acknowledges the roles of sense organs, nerves, and muscles in behavior without violating people's religious beliefs or intuitive feelings that conscious thought occurs on a non-physical plane. But it has serious limitations, both as a philosophy and as a foundation for a science of psychology. As a philosophy, it stumbles on the question of how a non-material entity (the soul) can have a material effect (movement of the body), or how the body can follow natural law and yet be moved by a soul that does not (Campbell, 1970). As a foundation for psychology, the theory sets strict limits, which few psychologists would accept today, on what can and cannot be understood scientifically. The whole realm of thought, and all behaviors that are guided by thought, are out of bounds for scientific analysis if they are the products of a willful soul.

Thomas Hobbes and the Philosophy of Materialism

At about the same time that Descartes was developing his machine-oriented version of dualism, an English philosopher named Thomas Hobbes (1588–1679) was going much further. It should be no surprise that an Englishman, not a Frenchman, was first to break from dualism entirely. The church and state were constantly feuding in seventeenth-century England, and inklings of democracy were emerging. Hobbes had been employed as a tutor to the future King Charles II, and he enjoyed royal protection when the latter came to power. When a committee of bishops petitioned that Hobbes be burned to death for his blasphemous book *Leviathan,* Hobbes received instead a stern warning (Hunt, 1993). The church burned copies of his book, but Hobbes, promising not to repeat his heresy, lived to the ripe age of 91.

4

How did Hobbes's materialism help lay the groundwork for a science of psychology?

◀In *Leviathan,* and in a shorter work called *Human Nature,* Hobbes argued that spirit, or soul, is a meaningless concept and that nothing exists but matter and energy, a philosophy now known as **materialism.** In Hobbes's view, all human behavior, including the seemingly voluntary choices we make, can in theory be understood in terms of physical processes in the body, especially the brain. Conscious thought, he maintained, is purely a product of the brain's machinery and therefore subject to natural law. This philosophy places no theoretical limit on what psychologists might study scientifically. Most of Hobbes's work was directed toward the implications of materialism for politics and government, but his ideas helped inspire, in England, a school of thought about the mind known as empiricism, to which we shall soon turn.

Nineteenth-Century Physiology: Learning About the Machine

The idea that the body, including the brain, is a machine, amenable to scientific study, helped to promote the science of physiology—the study of the body's machinery. By the beginning of the nineteenth century, considerable progress had been made in this endeavor, and during that century discoveries were made about the nervous system that contributed significantly to the origins of scientific psychology.

Increased Understanding of Reflexes One especially important development for the later emergence of psychology was an increased understanding of reflexes. The basic arrangement of the nervous system—consisting of a central nervous system (brain and spinal cord) and peripheral nerves that connect the central nervous system to sense organs and muscles—was well understood by the beginning of the nineteenth century. In 1822, in France, François Magendie demonstrated that nerves entering the spinal cord contain two separate pathways: one for carrying messages into the central nervous system from the skin's sensory receptors and one for carrying messages out to operate muscles. Through experiments with animals, scientists began to learn about the neural connections that underlie simple reflexes, such as the automatic withdrawal response to a pin prick, and found brain areas that, when active, could either enhance or inhibit such reflexes.

Some of these physiologists began to suggest that all human behavior occurs through reflexes, that even so-called voluntary actions are actually complex reflexes involving higher parts of the brain. One of the most eloquent proponents of this view, known as *reflexology*, was the Russian physiologist I. M. Sechenov. In his monograph *Reflexes of the Brain*, Sechenov (1863/1935) argued that every human action, "[b]e it a child laughing at the sight of toys, or . . . Newton enunciating universal laws and writing them on paper," can in theory be understood as a reflex. All human actions, he claimed, are initiated by stimuli in the environment. The stimuli act on a person's sensory receptors, setting in motion a chain of events in the nervous system that culminates in the muscle movements that constitute the action. Sechenov's work inspired another Russian physiologist, Ivan Pavlov (1849–1936), whose work on reflexes (discussed in Chapter 4) played a crucial role in the development of a scientific psychology.

The Concept of Localization of Function in the Brain Another important advance in nineteenth-century physiology was the concept of localization of function, the idea that specific parts of the brain serve specific functions in the production of mental experience and behavior. In Germany, Johannes Müller (1838/1965) proposed that the different qualities of sensory experience come about because the nerves from different sense organs excite different parts of the brain. Thus we experience vision when one part of the brain is active, hearing when another part is active, and so on. In France, Pierre Flourens (1824/1965) performed experiments with animals showing that damage to different parts of the brain produces different kinds of deficits in animals' abilities to move. And Paul Broca (1861/1965), also in France, published evidence that people who suffer injury to a very specific area of the brain's left hemisphere lose the ability to speak but do not lose other mental

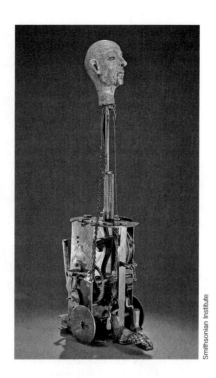

A seventeenth-century mechanical man Mechanical clocks represented the pinnacle of technological achievement of the seventeenth century, comparable to computers today. For amusement, clock-like mechanisms were used to operate robotic, humanoid figures, as illustrated here. Such mechanical men helped to inspire, in Descartes and Hobbes, the idea that actual human beings might also operate by mechanical means, not requiring a non-material spirit to move them.

Smithsonian Institute

5
How did the nineteenth-century understanding of the nervous system inspire a theory of behavior called reflexology?

6
How did discoveries of localization of function in the brain help establish the idea that the mind can be studied scientifically?

Early evidence for localization of function Shown here is the preserved brain of Paul Broca's patient, known as Tan, who lost his ability to speak after suffering brain damage. The damage is in the left frontal lobe, in an area now called Broca's area (discussed in Chapter 5).

Paris Museum

abilities. All such evidence about the relationships between mind and brain helped to lay the groundwork for a scientific psychology, because it gave substance to the idea of a material basis for mental processes.

The Idea That the Mind and Behavior Are Shaped by Experience

Besides helping to inspire research in physiology, the materialist philosophy of seventeenth-century England led quite directly to a school of thought about the mind known as *British empiricism,* carried on by such British philosophers as John Locke (1632–1704), David Hartley (1705–1759), James Mill (1773–1836), and John Stuart Mill (1806–1873). *Empiricism,* in this context, refers to the idea that human knowledge and thought derive ultimately from sensory experience (vision, hearing, touch, and so forth). If we are machines, we are machines that learn. Our senses provide the input that allows us to acquire knowledge of the world around us, and this knowledge allows us to think about that world and behave adaptively within it. The essence of empiricist philosophy is poetically expressed in the following often-quoted passage from Locke's *An Essay Concerning Human Understanding* (1690/1975, p. 104):

> Let us suppose the mind to be, as we say, white paper, void of all characters, without any ideas; how comes it to be furnished? Whence comes it by that vast store, which the busy and boundless fancy of man has painted on it, with an almost endless variety? Whence has it all the materials of reason and knowledge? To this I answer, in one word, from experience. In that, all our knowledge is founded; and from that it ultimately derives itself.

The Empiricist Concept of Association by Contiguity

7

How did the British empiricists explain the origin of complex ideas and thoughts? What role did the law of association by contiguity play in their philosophy?

In keeping with materialist philosophy, Locke and the other British empiricists argued that thoughts are not products of free will but rather reflections of a person's experiences in the physical and social environment. All the contents of the mind derive from the environment and bear direct relationship to that environment. According to the empiricists, the fundamental units of the mind are elementary ideas, which derive directly from sensory experiences and become linked together, in lawful ways, to form complex ideas and thoughts.

The most basic operating principle of the mind's machinery, according to the empiricists, is the law of **association by contiguity,** an idea originally proposed by Aristotle in the fourth century B.C. *Contiguity* refers to closeness in space or time, and the law of association by contiguity can be stated as follows: If a person experiences two environmental events (stimuli, or sensations) at the same time or one right after the other (contiguously), those two events will become associated (bound together) in the person's mind, such that the thought of one event will, in the future, tend to elicit the thought of the other.

As a simple illustration, consider a child's experiences when seeing and biting into an apple. The child receives, from the apple, a set of sensations, which produce in her mind such elementary ideas as red color, spherical shape, and sweet, tart taste. The child may also, at the same time, hear the sound *apple* emanating from the vocal cords of a nearby adult. Because all these sensations are experienced together, they become associated in the child's mind. Together, they form the complex idea "apple." Because of association by contiguity, the thought of any of the sensory qualities of the apple will tend to call forth the thought of all the apple's other sensory qualities. Thus, when the child hears *apple,* she will think of the red color, the spherical shape, and the sweet, tart taste. Or, when the child sees an apple, she will think of the sound *apple* and imagine the taste.

A complex idea To the empiricist philosophers, even as simple a concept as that of "apple" is a complex idea, consisting of a set of elementary sensations—of shape, color, and taste— that become associated in the person's mind through experiences with apples.

The empiricists contended that even their own most complex philosophical ponderings could, in theory, be understood as amalgams of elementary ideas that became linked together in their minds as a result of contiguities in their experiences. John Stuart Mill (1843/1875) referred to this sort of analysis of the mind as mental chemistry. Complex ideas and thoughts are formed from combinations of elementary ideas, much as chemical compounds are formed from combinations of chemical elements.

As you will discover in Chapters 4 and 9 of this textbook, the law of association by contiguity is still regarded as a fundamental principle of learning and memory. More broadly, most of psychology—throughout its history—has been devoted to the study of the effects of people's environmental experiences on their thoughts, feelings, and behavior. The impact of empiricist philosophy on psychology has been enormous.

➤ ------------------------------ 8
What influence has empiricist philosophy had on psychology?

The Nativist Response to Empiricism

For every philosophy that contains part of the truth, there is an opposite philosophy that contains another part of it. The opposite of empiricism is **nativism,** the view that the most basic forms of human knowledge and the basic operating characteristics of the mind, which provide the foundation for human nature, are native to the human mind—that is, are inborn and do not have to be acquired from experience.

Take a sheet of white paper and present it with all the learning experiences that a normal human child might encounter (a suggestion made by Ornstein, 1991). The paper will learn nothing. Talk to it, sing to it, give it apples and oranges, take it for trips in the country, hug it and kiss it; it will learn nothing about language, music, fruit, nature, or love. To learn anything, any entity must contain some initial machinery, already built into it. At a minimum, that machinery must include an ability to sense some aspects of the environment, some means of interpreting and recording those sensations, some rules for storing and combining those sensory records, and some rules for recalling them when needed. The mind, contrary to Locke's poetic assertion, must come with some initial furnishings in order for it to be furnished further through experience.

➤ ------------------------------ 9
Why is the ability to learn dependent on inborn knowledge? In Kant's nativist philosophy, what is the distinction between *a priori* knowledge and *a posteriori* knowledge?

While empiricist philosophy flourished in England, nativist philosophy took root in Germany, led by such thinkers as Gottfried Wilhelm von Leibniz (1646–1716) and Immanuel Kant (1724–1804). In his *Critique of Pure Reason* (1781/1908), Kant distinguished between *a priori* knowledge, which is built into the human brain and does not have to be learned, and *a posteriori* knowledge, which one gains from experience in the environment. Without the first, argued the nativists, a person could not acquire the second. As an illustration, Kant referred to a child's learning of language. The specific words and grammar that the child acquires are *a posteriori* knowledge, but the child's ability to learn a language at all depends on *a priori* knowledge. The latter includes built-in rules about what to attend to and how to store and organize the linguistic sounds that are heard, in ways that allow the child

A fun robot that can learn This computer-driven robot, designed by researchers at the University of California, San Diego, can keep track of some of its previous interactions with children and incorporate them into its future responses to the children. Such machines can learn only the kinds of information that they are programmed to learn. Similarly, according to nativist philosophers, human learning is limited by the information and operating rules that are genetically programmed into the human brain.

Alan Decker/University of California, San Diego

eventually to make sense of the sounds. Kant also argued that to make any sense of the physical world, the child must already have, built into its mind, certain fundamental physical concepts, such as the concepts of space and time. Without such built-in concepts, a child would have no capacity for seeing an apple as spherical or for detecting the temporal contiguity of two events.

The Idea That the Machinery of Behavior and Mind Evolved Through Natural Selection

Kant understood that the human mind has some innate furnishings, but he had no scientific explanation of how those furnishings could have been built or why they function as they do. That understanding came, at last, in 1859, when the English naturalist Charles Darwin (1809–1882) published *The Origin of Species,* a book that was destined to revolutionize biology, mark a new age in philosophy, and provide, along with the developments in physiology, a biological grounding for psychology.

Natural Selection and the Analysis of the Functions of Behavior

10

How did Darwin's theory of natural selection offer a scientific foundation for explaining behavior by describing its functions? How did it provide a basis for understanding the origin of *a priori* knowledge?

Darwin's fundamental idea (explained much more fully in Chapter 3) was that living things evolve gradually, over generations, by a process of natural selection. Those individuals whose inherited characteristics are well adapted to their environment are more likely to survive and reproduce than are other individuals. At each generation, random changes in the hereditary material produce variations in offspring, and those variations that improve the chance of survival and reproduction are passed from generation to generation in increasing numbers.

Because of natural selection, species of plants and animals change gradually over time in ways that allow them to meet the changing demands of their environments. Because of evolution, the innate characteristics of any given species of plant or animal can be examined for the functions they serve in helping the individuals to survive and reproduce. To understand, for example, why finches have stout beaks and warblers have slender beaks, one must know what foods the birds eat and how they use their beaks to obtain those foods. The same principle that applies to anatomy applies to behavior. Through natural selection, living things have acquired instinctive tendencies to behave in ways that promote their survival and reproduction. A key word here is *function*. While physiologists were examining the neural mechanisms of behavior, and empiricist philosophers were analyzing lawful relationships between behavior and the environment, Darwin was studying the functions of behavior—the ways in which an organism's behavior helps it to survive and reproduce.

Application of Darwin's Ideas to Psychology

In *The Origin of Species,* Darwin discussed only plants and nonhuman animals, but in later writings he made it clear that he viewed humans as no exception. We humans also evolved through natural selection, and our anatomy and behavior can be analyzed in the same ways as can those of other living things.

In a book entitled *The Expression of the Emotions in Man and Animals,* Darwin (1872/1965) illustrated how evolutionary thinking can contribute to a scientific understanding of human behavior. He argued that the basic forms of human emotional expressions (such as laughing and crying) are inherited, as are those of other animals, and may have evolved because the ability to communicate one's emotions or intentions to others of one's kind improves one's chances of survival. Darwin's work provided psychology with a scientific way of thinking about all the inborn universal tendencies that constitute human nature. The innate mechanisms underlying human emotions, drives, perception, learning, and reasoning came about gradually because they promoted the survival and reproduction of our

Granger Collection

Charles Darwin Darwin's principle of evolution by natural selection helped provide a scientific footing for psychology. The principle links humans to the rest of the biological world and explains the origin of brain mechanisms that promote the individual's survival and reproduction.

ancestors. One approach to understanding such characteristics is to analyze their evolutionary functions—the specific ways in which they promote survival and reproduction.

If Kant had been privy to Darwin's insight, he would have said that the innate furnishings of the mind, which make it possible for children to learn language, to learn about the physical world, to experience human drives and emotions, and, more generally, to behave as human beings and not as blank sheets of paper, came about through the process of natural selection, which gradually built all these capacities into the brain's machinery. Darwin, perhaps more than anyone else, helped convince the intellectual world that we humans, despite our pretensions, are part of the natural world and can be understood through the methods of science. In this way he helped make the world ripe for psychology.

We have now reached the end of the first section of the chapter, and, before moving on, I want to point out a second feature of the book that is designed to help you study it. At the end of each major section of each chapter is a *section review* chart that summarizes the section's main ideas. The chart is organized hierarchically: the main idea or topic of the section is at the top, the sub-ideas or subtopics are at the next level down, and specific facts and lines of evidence pertaining to each sub-idea or subtopic fill the lower parts. A good way to review, before going on, is to read each item in the chart and think about it. Start at the top and think about the main idea or purpose of the whole section. How would you explain it to another person? Then go down each column, one by one; think about how the idea or topic heading the column pertains to the larger idea or topic above it and how it is supported or elaborated upon by the more specific statements below it. If you are unclear about the meaning of any item in the chart, or can't elaborate on that item

11

How can the section review at the end of each major section of each chapter be used to guide one's thought and review before going on to the next section?

in a meaningful way, you may want to read the relevant part of the chapter again before moving on. Another way to review is to look back at the focus questions in the margins and make sure you can answer each of them.

SECTION REVIEW

Psychology—the science of behavior and the mind—rests on prior intellectual developments.

Physical Causation of Behavior	The Role of Experience	The Evolutionary Basis of Mind and Behavior
➤ Descartes's dualism placed more emphasis on the role of the body than had previous versions of dualism. Hobbes's materialism held that behavior is completely a product of the body and thus physically caused.	➤ The British empiricists claimed that all thought and knowledge are rooted in sensory experience.	➤ Darwin proposed that natural selection underlies the evolution of behavioral tendencies (along with anatomical characteristics) that promote survival and reproduction.
➤ To the degree that behavior and the mind have a physical basis, they are open to study just like the rest of the natural world.	➤ Empiricists used the law of association by contiguity to explain how sensory experiences can combine to form complex thoughts.	➤ Darwin's thinking led to a focus on the functions of behavior.
➤ Nineteenth-century physiological studies of reflexes and localization of function in the brain demonstrated the applicability of science to mental processes and behavior.	➤ In contrast to empiricism, nativism asserts that some knowledge is innate and that such knowledge provides the foundation for human nature, including the human abilities to learn.	➤ Natural selection also offered a scientific foundation for nativist views of the mind.

■ The Scope of Psychology

Psychology is a vast and diverse field of research. Every question about behavior and mental experience that is potentially answerable by scientific means is within its scope. One way to become oriented to this grand science is to preview the various kinds of explanatory concepts that psychologists use.

Varieties of Explanations in Psychology, and Their Application to Sexual Jealousy

Psychologists strive to *explain* mental experiences and behavior. To explain is to identify causes. What causes us to do what we do, feel what we feel, perceive what we perceive, or believe what we believe? What causes us to eat in some conditions and not in others; to cooperate sometimes and to cheat at other times; to feel angry, frightened, happy, or guilty; to dream; to hate or love; to see red as different from blue; to remember or forget; to suddenly see solutions to problems that we couldn't see before; to learn our native language so easily when we are very young; to become depressed or anxious? This is a sample of the kinds of questions that psychologists try to answer and that are addressed in this book.

The causes of mental experiences and behavior are complex and can be analyzed at various levels. The term **level of analysis,** as used in psychology and other sciences, refers to the level, or type, of causal process that is studied. More specifically, in psychology, a person's behavior or mental experience can be examined at these levels:

- *neural* level (brain as cause),
- *genetic* level (genes as cause),
- *evolutionary* level (natural selection as cause),
- *learning* level (the individual's prior experiences with the environment as cause),
- *cognitive* level (the individual's knowledge or beliefs as cause),

- *social* level (the influence of other people as cause),
- *cultural* level (the culture in which the person develops as cause),
- *developmental* level (age-related changes as cause).

You will find many examples of each of these eight levels of analysis in this book. Now, as an overview, I'll describe each of them very briefly. For the purpose of organization of this presentation, it is convenient to group the eight levels of analysis into two clusters. The first cluster—consisting of neural, genetic, and evolutionary explanations—is most directly biological. The second cluster, consisting of all of the remaining levels, is less directly biological and has to do with effects of experiences and knowledge.

Any given type of behavior or mental experience can, in principle, be analyzed at any of the eight levels. As you will see, the different levels of analysis correspond with different research specialties in psychology. In the following paragraphs, I'll illustrate the different levels of analysis and research specialties by applying them to the phenomenon of sexual jealousy. For our purposes here, *sexual jealousy* can be defined as the set of emotions and behaviors that result when a person believes that his or her relationship with a sexual partner or potential sexual partner is threatened by the partner's involvement with another person. One reason for choosing sexual jealousy as the example is that it has, in fact, not been studied very much at most of the levels, so I can describe hypothetical ways of studying it without getting into too much factual detail.

Sexual jealousy in humans Like any common human behavioral predisposition, sexual jealousy can be studied at the neural, genetic, evolutionary, learning, cognitive, social, cultural, and developmental levels of analysis. Here the theme of sexual jealousy is played out by Rita Hayworth, Tyrone Power, and Anthony Quinn in a scene from the 1941 film *Blood and Sand.*

Explanations That Focus on Biological Processes

Neural Explanations All mental experiences and behavioral acts are products of the nervous system. One logical route to explanation in psychology, therefore, is to try to understand how the nervous system produces the specific type of experience or behavior being studied. The research specialty that centers on this level of explanation is referred to as ***behavioral neuroscience.***

◆─────────────**12**
How do neural, genetic, and evolutionary explanations differ from one another? How might each be applied toward an understanding of jealousy?

Some behavioral neuroscientists study individual neurons (nerve cells) or small groups of neurons to determine how their characteristics contribute to particular psychological processes, such as learning. Others map out and study larger brain regions and pathways that are directly involved in particular categories of behavior or experience. For example, they might identify brain regions that are most involved in speaking grammatically, or in perceiving the shapes of objects, or in experiencing an emotion such as fear. Behavioral neuroscientists also study the ways that hormones and drugs act on the brain to alter behavior and experience, either in humans or in nonhuman animals.

To date, no neural studies of jealousy have been conducted with humans, but at least one such study has been conducted with macaque monkeys (Rilling & others, 2004). Researchers made male monkeys jealous by exposing each one to the sight of a female, with which he had previously mated, being courted by another male. During this

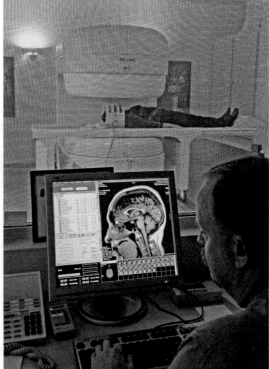

Viewing the active brain In recent years, the field of behavioral neuroscience has advanced greatly, due in part to new techniques for assessing the amount of activity that occurs in specific brain locations as a person performs mental tasks. These neuroimaging techniques are discussed in Chapter 5.

experience, the researchers measured the male monkey's brain activity using a technique called positron emission tomography (PET, described in Chapter 5). The result was a preliminary mapping of specific brain areas that become especially active during the experience of sexual jealousy in male macaques.

A next step, not yet taken, might be to try to increase or decrease jealous behavior in monkeys by artificially activating or inactivating those same areas of the brain. They might also examine people who have, through strokes or other accidents, suffered damage to those brain areas to determine if they have any deficits in the experience of jealousy. These are the kinds of techniques regularly used by behavioral neuroscientists.

Genetic Explanations Genes are the units of heredity that provide the codes for building the entire body, including the brain. Differences among individuals in the genes they inherit can cause differences in the brain and, therefore, differences in mental experiences and behavior. The research specialty that attempts to explain psychological differences among individuals in terms of differences in their genes is called *behavioral genetics.*

Some behavioral geneticists study nonhuman animals. They may, for example, deliberately modify animals' genes to observe the effects on behavior. Others study people. To estimate the extent to which differences among people in some psychological trait is the result of differences in their genes, researchers might assess the degree to which genetic relatedness between people correlates with their degree of similarity in that trait. A finding that close genetic relatives are more similar in the trait than are more distant relatives is evidence that genes contribute to variation in the trait. Behavioral geneticists might also try to identify specific genes that contribute to a trait by comparing the DNA (genetic material) of people who differ in that trait.

People differ in the degree to which they are prone to sexual jealousy. Some become jealous with much less provocation than do others. To measure the degree to which such differences are the result of genetic differences, researchers might assess sexual jealousy in twins. If identical twins, who share all their genes with each other, are much more similar in jealousy than are same-sex non-identical twins, who are no more closely related than are other siblings, that would indicate that much of the variation among people in sexual jealousy is caused by variation in genes. A next step might be to find out just which genes are involved in these differences and how they act on the brain to influence jealousy. So far, none of these types of studies have been done concerning sexual jealousy, but you will read later of such studies of intelligence (in Chapter 10), personality traits (in Chapter 15), and various other mental disorders (in Chapter 16).

Evolutionary Explanations All the basic biological machinery underlying behavior and mental experience, coded by genes, is a product of evolution by natural

Sexual jealousy in ducks Ducks, such as these blue-winged teals, form monogamous pair bonds, at least for the duration of the breeding season. When an intruder encroaches, the member of the pair that is the same sex as the intruder drives the intruder away. Such jealous-like behavior helps to keep the mated pair intact.

© Cliff Beittel

selection. One way to explain universal human characteristics, therefore, is to explain how or why they came about in the course of evolution. The research specialty concerned with this level of analysis is called ***evolutionary psychology.***

Some evolutionary psychologists are interested in the actual routes by which particular behavioral capacities or tendencies evolved. For instance, researchers studying the evolution of smiling have gained clues about how smiling originated in our ancestors by examining smile-like behaviors in other primates, including chimpanzees (discussed in Chapter 3). Most evolutionary psychologists are interested in identifying the evolutionary functions—that is, the survival or reproductive benefits—of the types of behaviors and mental experiences that they study. You will read in later chapters about evolutionary, functional explanations of many human behavioral tendencies, drives, and emotions.

Evolutionary psychologists have examined the forms and consequences of human jealousy in some detail to identify its possible benefits for reproduction (Buss, 2000a&b; Penke & Asendorpf, 2008). They have also studied behaviors in various animals that appear to be similar to human jealousy. Such research supports the view that jealousy functions to promote long-term mating bonds. All animals that form long-term bonds exhibit jealous-like behaviors; they behave in ways that seem designed to drive off, or in other ways discourage, any individuals that would lure away their mates (discussed in Chapter 3).

Explanations That Focus on Environmental Experiences, Knowledge, and Development

Learning Explanations Essentially all forms of human behavior and mental experience are modifiable by learning; that is, they can be influenced by prior experiences. Such experiences can affect our emotions, drives, perceptions, thoughts, skills, and habits. Most psychologists are in one way or another interested in the ways that learning can influence the types of behavior that they study. The psychological specialty that is most directly and exclusively concerned with explaining behavior in terms of learning is appropriately called ***learning psychology.*** For historical reasons (which will become clear in Chapter 4), this specialty is also often called *behavioral psychology*.

Learning psychologists might, for example, attempt to explain compulsive gambling in terms of patterns of rewards that the person has experienced in the past while gambling, or might attempt to explain a person's fears in terms of the person's previous experiences with the feared objects or situations. They might also conduct research, with animals or with people, to understand the most efficient ways to learn new skills (discussed in Chapter 4).

Differences among individuals in jealousy derive partly from genetic differences, but they also derive partly from differences in past experiences. Jealous reactions that prove to be effective in obtaining rewards—such as those that succeed in repelling competitors or attracting renewed affection from the mate—may increase in frequency with experience, and ineffective reactions may decrease. People and animals may also learn, through experience, what sorts of cues are potential signs of infidelity in their mates, and those cues may come to trigger jealous reactions. The intensity of sexual jealousy, the specific manner in which it is expressed, and the environmental cues that trigger it can all be influenced, in many ways, by learning. A learning psychologist might study any of those effects.

Cognitive Explanations The term *cognition* refers to information in the mind—that is, to information that is somehow stored and activated by the workings of the

> ---------------------**13**
>
> **How do learning and cognitive explanations differ? How might each be applied toward an understanding of jealousy?**

Walter Dawn / Photo Researchers, Inc.

Rat learning to press a lever To identify basic principles of learning, some learning psychologists study the processes by which animals learn simple responses for rewards. This thirsty rat receives a drop of water to drink each time it presses the lever.

brain. Such information includes thoughts, beliefs, and all forms of memories. Some information is innate to the human mind, as nativist philosophers pointed out, and other information is acquired through learning, as empiricist philosophers pointed out. Some information is conscious, in the sense that the person is aware of it and can describe it, and other information is unconscious but can still influence one's conscious experiences and behavior. One way to explain any behavioral action or mental experience is to relate it to the cognitions (items of mental information) that underlie that action or experience. The specialty focusing on this level of analysis is called *cognitive psychology.*

You can think of mental information as analogous to the operating rules (software) and data that are stored in a computer, which influence the way that the computer responds to new input. Cognitive psychologists are interested in specifying, as clearly as possible, the types of mental information that underlie and make possible the behaviors that they study. For instance, a cognitive psychologist who is interested in reasoning might attempt to understand the rules by which people manipulate information in their minds in order to solve particular classes of problems (discussed in Chapter 10). A cognitive psychologist who is interested in racial prejudice might attempt to specify the particular beliefs—including unconscious as well as conscious beliefs—that promote prejudiced behavior (discussed in Chapter 13). Cognitive psychologists are also interested in the basic processes by which learned information is stored and organized in the mind, which means that they are particularly interested in memory (discussed in Chapter 9).

In general, cognitive psychology differs from the psychology of learning in its focus on the mind. Learning psychologists typically attempt to relate learning experiences directly to behavioral changes and are relatively unconcerned with the mental processes that mediate such relationships. To a learning psychologist, experience in the environment leads to change in behavior. To a cognitive psychologist, experience in the environment leads to *change in knowledge or beliefs,* and that change leads to change in behavior.

A cognitive psychologist interested in jealousy would define jealousy first and foremost as a set of beliefs—beliefs about the behavior of one's mate and some third party, about the vulnerability of one's own relationship with the mate, and about the appropriateness or inappropriateness of possible ways to react. One way to study jealousy, from a cognitive perspective, is to ask people to recall episodes of it from their own lives and to describe the thoughts that went through their minds, the emotions they felt, and the actions they took. Such work reveals that a wide variety of thoughts can enter one's mind in the jealous state, which can lead to actions ranging from romantic expressions of love, to increased attention to potential sexual competitors, to murderous violence (Guerrero & others, 2005; Maner & Shackelford, 2007). Psychotherapists who use cognitive methods to treat cases of pathological jealousy try to help their clients change their thought patterns, so they will no longer misperceive every instance of attention that their mate pays to someone else as a threat to their relationship, and so they will focus on constructive rather than destructive ways of reacting to actual threats (Bishay & others, 1996).

14

How do social and cultural explanations differ? How might each be applied toward an understanding of jealousy?

Social Explanations We humans are, by nature, social animals. We need to cooperate and get along with others of our species in order to survive and reproduce. For this reason, our behavior is strongly influenced by our perceptions of others. We use others as models of how to behave, and we often strive, consciously or unconsciously, to behave in ways that will lead others to approve of us. One way to explain mental experiences and behavior, therefore, is to identify how they are influenced by other people or by one's beliefs about other people (discussed in Chapters 13 and 14). The specialty focusing on this level of explanation is called *social psychology.*

An often-quoted definition of social psychology (originally from Allport, 1968) is the following: "Social psychology is the attempt to understand and explain how the thought, feeling, and behavior of individuals are influenced by the actual, imagined, or implied presence of others." Social psychologists commonly attempt to explain behavior in terms of conformity to social norms, or obedience to authority, or living up to others' expectations. A popular term for all such influences is *social pressure.*

Social-psychological explanations are often phrased in terms of people's conscious or unconscious beliefs about the potential social consequences of acting in a particular way. This means that many social-psychological explanations are also cognitive explanations. Indeed, many modern social psychologists refer to their specialty as *social cognition.* A social psychologist interested in physical fitness, for example, might attempt to explain how people's willingness to exercise is influenced by their beliefs about the degree to which other people exercise and their beliefs about how others will react to them if they do or do not exercise.

A social psychologist interested in jealousy might focus on the norms and beliefs concerning romance, mating, and jealousy that surround and influence the jealous person. How do others react in similar situations? Are the beloved's flirtations with a third person within or outside the realm of what is considered acceptable by other dating or married couples? Would violent revenge be approved of or disapproved of by others who are important to the jealous person? Implicitly or explicitly, the answers to such questions influence the way the jealous person feels and behaves. An understanding of such influences constitutes a social-psychological explanation of the person's feelings and behavior.

Cultural Explanations We can predict some aspects of a person's behavior by knowing what culture that person grew up in. Cultures vary in language or dialect, in the values and attitudes they foster, and in the kinds of behaviors and emotions they encourage or discourage. Researchers have found consistent cultural differences even in the ways that people perceive and remember aspects of their physical environment (discussed in Chapter 10). The psychological specialty that explains mental experiences and behavior in terms of the culture in which the person developed is called ***cultural psychology.***

Cultural and social psychology are very closely related, but differ in emphasis. While social psychologists emphasize the immediate social influences that act on individuals, cultural psychologists strive to characterize entire cultures in terms of the typical ways that people within them feel, think, and act. While social psychologists use concepts such as conformity and obedience to explain an individual's behavior, cultural psychologists more often refer to the unique history, economy, and religious or philosophical traditions of a culture to explain the values, norms, and habits of its people. For example, a cultural psychologist might contend that the frontier history of North America, in which individuals and families often had to struggle on their own, with little established social support, helps explain why North Americans value independence and individuality so strongly.

Concerning jealousy, a cultural psychologist would point to significant cultural differences in romantic and sexual mores. Some cultures, for example, are more tolerant of extramarital affairs than are others, and this difference affects the degree and quality of jealousy that is experienced. In some cultures, a strong double standard exists by which women are condemned far more harshly than are men for sexual infidelity, and in those cultures violent revenge on the part of a jealous man toward his mate may be socially sanctioned (Bhugra, 1993; Vandello & Cohen, 2008). In other cultures, the same violence would dishonor the perpetrator and land him in jail. A full cultural analysis would include an account of the cultures' histories, which led to differences in the ways that infidelity is understood and treated.

Snapshots

Cartoon with permission from JasonLove.com.

"I don't care that you slept with him, Claire, but how dare you laugh at his jokes!"

15

What constitutes a developmental explanation? How can such an explanation be applied toward an understanding of jealousy?

◄ **Developmental Explanations** We can predict some aspects of a person's behavior by knowing his or her age. Four-year-olds behave differently from two-year-olds, and middle-aged adults differently from adolescents. The psychological specialty that documents and describes the typical age differences that occur in the ways that people feel, think, and act is called ***developmental psychology.*** Developmental psychologists may describe the sequence of changes that occur, from infancy to adulthood, for any given type of behavior or mental capacity. For example, developmental psychologists who study language have described a sequence of stages in speech production that goes from cooing to babbling, then to first recognizable words, to frequent one-word utterances, to two-word utterances, and so on, with each stage beginning, on average, at a certain age. At a superficial level, then, age can itself be an explanation: "She talks in such-and-such a way because she is 3 years old, and that is how most 3-year-olds talk."

Looking deeper, developmental psychologists are also interested in the processes that produce the age-related changes that they document. Those processes include physical maturation of the body (including the brain), instinctive behavioral tendencies that are genetically timed to emerge at particular ages, the accumulated effects of many learning experiences, and new pressures and opportunities provided by the social environment or the cultural milieu as one gets older. At this deeper level, then, developmental psychology is an approach that brings together the other levels of analysis. Neural, genetic, evolutionary, learning, cognitive, social, and cultural explanations might all be brought to bear on the task of explaining behavioral changes that occur with age. Developmental psychologists are particularly interested in understanding how experiences at any given stage of development can influence behavior at later stages.

A developmental analysis of jealousy might begin with a description of age-related changes in jealousy that correspond with age-related changes in social relationships. Infants become jealous when their mother or other primary caregiver devotes extended attention to someone else (Hart & Carrington, 2002). Children of middle-school age, especially girls, often become jealous when their same-sex "best friend" becomes best friends with someone else (Parker & others, 2005). These early forms of jealousy are similar in form and function to sexual jealousy, which typically emerges along with the first serious romantic attachment, in adolescence or young adulthood. Researchers have found evidence of continuity between early attachments to parents and friends and later attachments to romantic partners (discussed in Chapter 12). People who, in childhood, develop secure relationships with their parents and friends also tend, later on, to develop secure relationships with romantic partners, relatively untroubled by jealousy (Fraley, 2002; Guerrero, 1998).

A Comment on Psychological Specialties

Because of psychology's vast scope, research psychologists generally identify their work as belonging to specific subfields, or specialties. To some degree, as I have indicated in the foregoing discussion, different psychological research specialties correspond to different levels of analysis. This is most true of the eight specialties to which I have already referred: *behavioral neuroscience, behavioral genetics, evolutionary psychology, psychology of learning, cognitive psychology, social psychology, cultural psychology,* and *developmental psychology.*

16

What are some research specialties in psychology that are not defined primarily by the level of analysis employed?

◄ Other specialties, however, are defined more in terms of topics studied than level of analysis. For example, *sensory psychology* is the study of basic abilities to see, hear, touch, taste, and smell the environment; and *perceptual psychology* is the study of how people and animals make sense of, or interpret, the input they receive through their senses. Similarly, some psychologists identify their specialty as the *psychology of motivation* or the *psychology of emotion.* These specialists might use any or all of psychology's modes of explanation to understand particular phenomena related to the topics they study.

Two major specialties, which are closely related to each other, are devoted to the task of understanding individual differences among people. One of these is *personality psychology* (discussed in Chapter 15), which is concerned with normal differences in people's general ways of thinking, feeling, and behaving—referred to as personality traits. The other is *abnormal psychology* (discussed in Chapter 16), which is concerned with variations in psychological traits that are sufficiently extreme and disruptive to people's lives as to be classified as mental disorders. Personality psychologists and abnormal psychologists use various levels of analysis. Differences in the nervous system, in genes, in learning experiences, in beliefs, in social pressures, or in cultural milieu may all contribute to an understanding of differences in personality and in susceptibility to particular mental disorders.

Closely related to abnormal psychology is *clinical psychology* (discussed in Chapter 17), the specialty that is concerned with helping people who have mental disorders or less serious psychological problems. Most clinical psychologists are practitioners rather than researchers. They offer psychotherapy or drug treatments, or both, to help people cope with or overcome their disorders or problems. Clinical psychologists who conduct research are usually interested in identifying or developing better treatment methods.

In general, research specialties in psychology are not rigidly defined. They are simply convenient labels aimed at classifying, roughly, the different levels of analysis and topics of study that characterize the work of different research psychologists. Regardless of what they call themselves, good researchers often use several different levels of analysis in their research and may study a variety of topics that in some way relate to one another. My main reason for listing and briefly describing some of the specialties here has been to give you an overview of the broad scope of psychological science.

The Connections of Psychology to Other Scholarly Fields

Another way to characterize psychology is to picture its place in the spectrum of disciplines that form the departments of a typical college of arts and sciences. Figure 1.3 illustrates a scheme that I call (with tongue only partly in cheek) the

17
How does psychology link the three main divisions of academic studies?

FIGURE 1.3 Connections between psychology and other scholarly areas Psychology bridges the natural and social sciences, and it has strong connections to the humanities. In this sense, it lies in the center of the academic pursuits of the university.

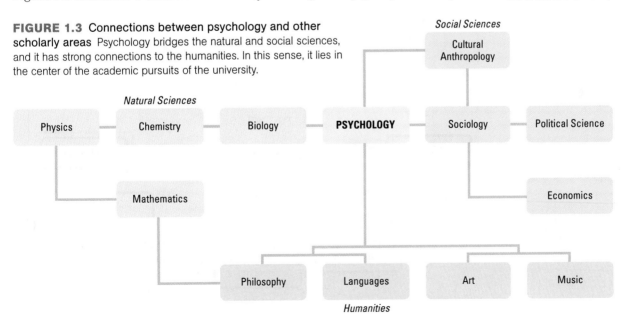

psychocentric theory of the university. The disciplines are divided roughly into three broad areas. One division is the natural sciences, including physics, chemistry, and biology, shown on the left side of the figure. The second division is the social sciences, including sociology, anthropology, political science, and economics, shown on the right side of the figure. The third division is the humanities—including languages, philosophy, art, and music—shown in the lower part of the figure. The humanities represent things that humans do. Humans, unlike other animals, talk to one another, develop philosophies, and create art and music.

Where does psychology fit into this scheme? Directly in the center, tied to all three of the broad divisions. On the natural science end, it is tied most directly to biology by way of behavioral neuroscience, behavioral genetics, and evolutionary psychology. On the social science end, it is tied most directly to sociology and anthropology by way of social and cultural psychology. In addition to bridging the natural and social sciences, psychology ties the whole spectrum of sciences to the humanities through its interest in how people produce and understand languages, philosophies, art, and music.

Many of you reading this book are planning to major in psychology, but many others are majoring in other subjects. No matter what you have chosen as your major field, you are likely to find meaningful connections between that field and psychology. Psychology has more connections to other subjects taught in the university than does any other single discipline (Gray, 2008).

Figure 1.4 shows an alternative, less subtle depiction of my psychocentric theory of the university. It's an exaggeration, of course, of the central importance of psychology, yet it represents some truths. Each one of the sunbeams between psychology and another subject represents a real, interdisciplinary subfield. Progressing clockwise around the sun, beginning with the connection to biology, we have *biopsychology, neurochemistry of behavior, cognitive psychology of logic* (connecting psychology to both math and philosophy), *psychology of religion, psychology of literature, psycholinguistics, psychology of art, psychology of music, cultural psychology, social psychology, political psychology,* and *psychoeconomics.* If you are majoring in a professional field, such as education, nursing (or health), or business management, you will again find major connections between that field

FIGURE 1.4 Psychocentric theory of the university

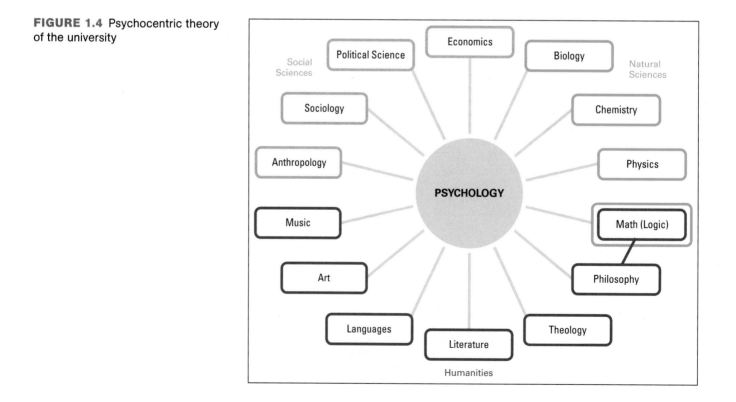

and psychology in *educational psychology, health psychology,* and *organizational psychology.* It should not be surprising that psychology has such meaningful connections to other disciplines. Psychology is the study of all that people do. No wonder it is very often chosen as a second major, or as a minor, by students who are majoring in other fields.

Psychology as a Profession

Psychology is not only an academic discipline but also a profession. The profession includes both academic psychologists, who are engaged in research and teaching, and practicing psychologists, who apply psychological knowledge and ideas in clinics, businesses, and other settings. The majority of professional psychologists in the United States hold doctoral degrees in psychology, and most of the rest hold master's degrees (Landrum & others, 2007). The main settings in which they work, and the kinds of services they perform in those settings, are:

- *Academic departments in universities and colleges* Academic psychologists are employed to conduct basic research, such as that which fills this book, and to teach psychology courses.
- *Clinical settings* Clinical and counseling psychologists work with clients who have psychological problems or disorders, in independent practice or in hospitals, mental health centers, clinics, and counseling or guidance centers.
- *Elementary and secondary schools* School psychologists administer psychological tests, supervise programs for children who have special needs, and may help teachers develop more effective classroom techniques.
- *Business and government* Psychologists are hired by businesses and government agencies for such varied purposes as conducting research, screening candidates for employment, helping to design more pleasant and efficient work environments, and counseling personnel who have work-related problems.

The decision to major in psychology as an undergraduate does not necessarily imply a choice of psychology as a career. Most students who major in psychology do so primarily because they find the subject fun to learn and think about. Most go on to careers in other fields—such as social work, law, education, and business—where they are quite likely to find their psychology background helpful (Carroll & others, 1992; Landrum & others, 2007). If you are considering psychology as a career, you might want to look at one or more of the books concerning careers in psychology that I have listed in the Further Reading section at the end of this chapter.

ARLO & JANIS® by Jimmy Johnson

SECTION REVIEW

Psychology is a broad, diverse field of research, and it is a profession.

Levels of Causal Analysis and Topics of Study in Psychology

➤ Three types of biological causal explanations are used in psychology—neural, genetic, and evolutionary explanations.

➤ Five other types of causal explanations in psychology are learning, cognitive, social, cultural, and developmental explanations.

➤ As demonstrated with jealousy, each level of analysis can be applied to any given type of behavior or mental experience.

➤ Some subfields in psychology are defined primarily by the level of analysis; others are defined more by the topics studied.

A Discipline Among Disciplines

➤ Broadly speaking, scholarly disciplines can be classified as belonging to natural sciences, social sciences, or humanities.

➤ Psychology has strong connections with each class of disciplines.

The Profession of Psychology

➤ The profession includes academic psychologists, who teach and do research, and practicing psychologists, who apply psychological knowledge and principles to real-world issues.

➤ Psychologists work in various settings—including universities, clinical settings, and businesses—and typically hold advanced degrees.

■ Thoughts About Using This Book and Its Special Features

This final section of this chapter normally would go in a preface; it's about how to study this book. I've put it here because I've found that people don't read prefaces, and I'd like you to read this. The suggestions here have proven to be helpful to thousands of previous students, and I want you to benefit from them.

Most of you reading this book are doing so because it was assigned to you as part of a college course. You are reading it not because you chose it, but because someone chose it for you. This creates a special difficulty.

◄ When you read nonfiction outside of a course, you usually do so because you have some question or questions in mind that you want to answer. You are curious about some issue, and you choose a book that seems to address it. In that case you read actively, constantly thinking about what you read to see if it helps answer your questions. But when a book is assigned to you for a course, the situation is different. You do not necessarily have particular questions in mind that you want to answer, and you may understand your job rather vaguely as that of "learning the material." This leads, often, to a passive and rather ineffective mode of reading, aimed more at memorizing than at thinking and understanding.

Our minds are not designed for memorizing what we don't understand or what we have not thought about actively. Our mental machinery evolved for the purpose of making sense of things, and we don't remember much of what doesn't make sense. So, when we read for the passive purpose of "learning" or "absorbing" the material, our minds often wander. We often find that we have read long passages—or, rather, that our eyes have moved across the lines of text—without our having any idea what we just read.

My sympathies are with you. I really want you to enjoy this book. I want you to read it actively, to question it, argue with it, and get excited by the ideas in it. Toward that end, I have done my best to present psychology as a set of ideas to think about, not as a set of facts to memorize. I have tried to give you enough information about each idea, enough of the evidence and logic supporting it, to enable you to have something to think about and

18

Why is it often more difficult to read a textbook for a course than to read nonfiction that you have chosen on your own?

argue with. Most of all, I do not want you to read this book as Truth with a capital T. Psychology is a science, and the essence of science is this: We do not accept anything on authority. It doesn't matter who says that something is or isn't true; what matters is the evidence and logic behind the statement. Each page of this book is offered for your consideration, not for your unquestioned acceptance.

Using the Focus Questions to Guide Your Study

In the introduction to this chapter, I pointed out the numbered *focus questions* that appear in the book's margins. I suggested a way to use these questions to guide both your initial reading and your review of the text. Here I'll elaborate on their use.

Each focus question is the main question that I am trying to answer in the portion of text that lies adjacent to and immediately below the question. You can make your reading of the text more interesting and active if you reflect on each focus question as you come to it, before reading the paragraphs aimed at answering it. One way to approach the question is to formulate a preliminary, possible answer based on what you already know or believe. You might also put the question into your own words, to make it *your* question rather than mine. This will prepare you to read the relevant portion of text with a clear purpose in mind—finding out how I answer the question, and how my answer compares to your preliminary thoughts about it.

> **19**
> **How can students use the focus questions in this textbook to make their reading more thought-provoking and effective?**

As an illustration, consider Focus Question 2, on page 3 of this chapter. This question consists of two parts: *What was Descartes's version of dualism? How did it help pave the way for a science of psychology?* When you first came to this question, you already had some good grounds for forming a preliminary answer. You had just read a definition of dualism in the previous paragraph, in which that term appeared in bold italics. You had read that dualism distinguishes between the body, which is physical and can be studied scientifically, and the soul, which is supernatural and cannot be studied scientifically. You may have also noticed that the section heading just above the focus question reads *Descartes's Version of Dualism: Focus on the Body,* and that the larger section heading above that (on page 2) reads, *The Idea of Physical Causation of Behavior.* So, in thinking about Focus Question 2, you might have said something like the following to yourself: "Okay, maybe Descartes's version of dualism placed greater emphasis on the physical body and less emphasis on the soul than did previous versions. Now, I wonder if that guess is correct. If it is correct, I wonder just how Descartes developed and supported this view. What attributes did he ascribe to the body that had previously been ascribed to the soul, and why?" Having said all this to yourself, you would be ready to read the adjacent portion of text with great understanding.

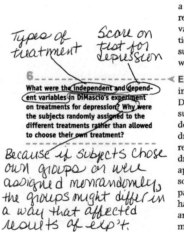

After reading the portion of text that is relevant to answering a given focus question, it is a good idea to stop and think about that question again and how you would answer it. You might jot down, next to the question, the gist of the answer that you would now give. If you aren't sure how to answer it, you might want to read that portion again. If you still aren't sure after that, you might want to mark that question as one to ask of your course instructor or study companions. Perhaps I didn't answer the question sufficiently clearly in the text, and perhaps a discussion with others will throw some light on it.

In later chapters, you will discover that many focus questions ask about the evidence for or against some idea. Be sure to think especially carefully about the answers you will read to those questions, and ask yourself whether or not the evidence seems convincing.

Example of a student's notes (see page 32) Don't be afraid to write your own notes in the margin of this textbook. Your note taking will help you think about what you are reading and will be useful for review.

Admittedly, this approach to study will slow down your initial reading of each chapter. At first, stopping to think about each focus question may seem awkward and annoying. But most students I have taught, using previous editions of this book, have told me on course surveys that the focus-question approach begins to seem natural with practice and that it improves their comprehension, enjoyment, and test performance. In the long run, for most students, it saves study time. Having understood and thought about the material the first time through, later study and review become relatively easy. Some students have even told me that they transfer this study skill to their reading of textbooks in other courses. In those books they do not find focus questions already written for them, but they use section headings and opening sentences to generate their own focus questions as they read. For more information about this study method, turn to page 327, in Chapter 9, where textbook reading is discussed in the context of a more general discussion of ways to improve memory.

I should add, however, that a few students—roughly 10 percent of those I have taught—find that they do not need the focus questions to read very actively, thoughtfully, and effectively. These are students who naturally form questions as they read. They don't have the problem of a drifting mind that most of us have when reading assigned material. If you are one of those, then you may happily choose to ignore the focus questions on your first reading and use them just for review after you have finished each major section.

Using the Headings and Section Reviews to See the Hierarchical Structure of Ideas

20

How can students use the section and subsection headings, and the section review charts, to preview and review each major idea or argument? Why is the hierarchical organization of these study tools useful?

Textbooks are always hierarchically organized. Each main heading refers to some major idea or argument, each subheading refers to a more limited idea that is part of the larger one, and each sub-subheading refers to a still more limited idea or observation that is part of the subheading's idea. In this book I have tried to compose all headings in such a way as to give you a pretty good idea of what each section, subsection, and sub-subsection is about. By turning pages and reading all the headings within a main section before you read that section, you can preview the material and give yourself a head start toward thinking about it. You will see the basic structure of the argument that you are about to read, which will help you make sense of it as you read. Just as importantly, it will help you generate your own set of questions to try to answer as you read.

At the end of each main section of this book you will find a *section review*, a chart that reflects the hierarchical organization of the ideas and observations described in that section. I already described (on p. 9) how to use these charts for review. Reviewing in this way allows you to reflect back on each observation and idea as it relates to the larger idea to which it pertains. It helps you to see the individual elements of the section not as separate nuggets to memorize but as integral parts of a larger argument, and that helps you to make sense of them and remember them. A common mistake in studying is to write out lists of key terms and definitions and then study only that list. That method causes the student to lose track of the larger arguments, which tie the various elements together and make them interesting and memorable. The section review charts offer you an alternative way to view the key ideas—a way that maintains their relationship to one another.

For example, the section review on page 24 of this chapter depicts the organization of my argument that three foundation ideas preceded scientific psychology historically and provided a conceptual base on which psychology could build. That chart should help you think about the individual concepts, such as *empiricism* and *nativism*, in relation to the argument and should discourage you from memorizing definitions out of context. Your main goal is not to memorize definitions of these terms but to think about how these philosophical ideas helped to provide a foundation for the emergence of a science of psychology.

Using the Book's Other Features

Numbered Figures As you read each chapter, pay attention to the *numbered figures*. Whenever the text refers you to a figure, take a few moments to study the figure and read the caption. Many figures are graphs of data that back up an idea described in the text. Others are photographs or drawings that are designed to help you understand a point that would be difficult to grasp from words alone.

21
What purposes are served, for students, by the numbered figures, the use of bold italics, the *Glossary*, the *Concluding Thoughts* sections, the reference citations, the *Further Reading* sections, and the *Subject Index* in this book?

Bold Italicized Terms and Glossary Another feature that runs through the text is the use of **bold italics** to highlight technical terms that are likely to be new to many students. I suggest that you not devote much effort, on your first reading, to learning term definitions. Rather, read with the aim of understanding and thinking about the main ideas and the lines of evidence for or against them. In that process you will learn most of the terms, in the context of the ideas, without explicitly trying to learn them. The bold italics will be more useful in your later review. While you are reviewing the focus questions, look also for each of the terms in bold italics and check your knowledge of its meaning. These terms are also defined in the *Glossary* at the back of the book. If an important term has been defined in an earlier chapter, it is sometimes, but not always, defined again when it reappears. If it is not defined, you can use the *Glossary* to find both the term's definition and the number of the page on which it was first used.

Concluding Thoughts Section Each chapter ends with a section called *Concluding Thoughts*. This is not a summary; rather, it provides some ideas and integrating themes that emerge from reflecting back on the chapter as a whole. It also suggests, in some cases, alternative ways for you to think about and review the whole chapter. This section is in a different format from the rest of the chapter, and there are no focus questions related to it; but that doesn't mean it is less important than the rest of the chapter. Some instructors, myself included, consider any new ideas or themes that emerge in the *Concluding Thoughts* section to be fair game for the test. In this first chapter, for example, you will find a discussion of the concept of mind in *Concluding Thoughts* that may be especially useful.

Reference Citations, Further Reading, and Subject Index A feature that this book shares with other books and articles on psychology is the use of *reference citations*. This first chapter has relatively few of them, but in most chapters you will find them on nearly every page. Each citation consists of the name of one or more researchers followed by a year. Sometimes both the name (or names) and the year are in parentheses, such as "(Jones & Smith, 2001)"; at other times, when the name or names are part of the sentence, only the year is in parentheses, such as "According to Alice Jones (2009). . . ." In either case, the year refers to the year of publication of an article or book, by the person or persons named, which describes more fully the idea or the research study being mentioned or discussed. The full reference to that article or book can be found in the *References* section at the back of the textbook, which is arranged alphabetically by authors' last names. At first you may find these citations disruptive to the flow of your reading, but you will soon learn to read right through them. Their purpose is to give credit to the people whose work or ideas are being described, and to give you the opportunity to look up, and read more about, any ideas or research findings that intrigue you. To entice you to read further, you will also find, at the very end of each chapter, in a section called *Further Reading*, brief reviews of several interesting books that pertain to topics that were discussed in that chapter.

Many students save their introductory psychology textbook and use it, after the course is over, as a reference to review topics that are relevant to other courses that they take. For them, the *Subject Index* at the back of the book, which lists topics alphabetically and indicates all the pages where each topic is discussed, is very useful. They also find the reference citations and *Further Readings* to be useful as sources for term papers, not just in psychology courses, but also in other social science courses, education courses, business courses, nursing courses, and some courses in such diverse subjects as biology, philosophy, and English. Those who decide to apply to graduate programs in psychology often use the book to help them prepare for the Graduate Record Examination in Psychology.

SECTION REVIEW

Using this book's special features can markedly increase your learning.

Focus Questions	Headings and Section Reviews	Other Features
➤ The focus questions in the margins are designed to help you read in an active, thoughtful way, which will help you understand and remember what you read.	➤ The book's hierarchically arranged headings can help you quickly preview a section and prepare an organized way of thinking about it.	➤ Exploring the numbered figures, checking your understanding of bold italicized terms, using the Glossary as needed, and considering the integrative discussions in Concluding Thoughts can also benefit your study.
➤ The focus questions are also very useful in reviewing and testing your knowledge after you have read a section or chapter.	➤ Section reviews can help you to check your understanding of content, visualize relationships among the ideas and facts discussed, and consolidate your learning.	➤ Reference citations, the Further Reading sections, and the Subject Index can help you access material of interest to you within and beyond the book.

Concluding Thoughts

In some cases, the *Concluding Thoughts* section at the end of a chapter is intended to help you organize your review of the chapter. In other cases, it makes explicit some idea that was implicit in the chapter or that emerges in reflecting back on the chapter as a whole. Here are two concluding thoughts, of the latter type, for the chapter you have just read.

1. Psychology as the study of normal behavior In the world outside of colleges and universities, psychology is often associated with the study of mental problems or disorders and how to help people overcome them. When people "go to see a psychologist," they are seeking help. But, as you have gleaned from this chapter, psychology as a research field is primarily aimed at understanding normal human ways of feeling, thinking, and behaving. From an intellectual point of view, the problem of how any entity normally works—whether it is an automobile, a computer, or a human being—is much more interesting than the problem of how it breaks down. Philosophers such as Descartes, Hobbes, and the British empiricists were fascinated by the workings of the normal human mind, and that is what fascinates most academic psychologists today. The normal mental experiences that we take for granted in our everyday lives—such as our ability to see the color red, or to remember anything, or to learn our native language—become intriguing mysteries when we stop to think about them. As you go through this book, I hope you will allow yourself to become fascinated by all the normal things that you and other human beings do. If your ultimate interest is clinical psychology, keep in mind that some knowledge of normal functioning is essential background for figuring out where a breakdown has occurred and how normality might be restored. After all, automobile mechanics and computer repair specialists need to understand the normal operations of the machines they fix.

2. The concept of the mind as a product of the brain After reading this chapter, you may be confused about the meaning of the term *mind*. Join the club. Even today, *mind* ranks as perhaps the most debated of all philosophical concepts. Psychologists use the term in two quite different ways. In one use, it refers to people's *conscious experiences*—to the sensations, perceptions, memories, thoughts, desires, and emotions that run through our conscious awareness such that we can describe them to ourselves and to others. This is the usage that generates the most debate in philosophy, because it is hard to imagine just what "consciousness" is or how it emerges from physical matter. This difficulty leads some philosophers even today to be dualists. In psychology we usually sidestep that philosophical mystery by defining consciousness as whatever it is that a person can tell us about his or her experiences. If a person can tell us about a memory, or about something that he or she is looking at, then we say that the person is conscious of that memory or that visual perception.

In its other use, *mind* refers to all of the *knowledge and operating rules* that are somehow built into or stored in the brain and that provide the foundation for organizing behavior and conscious experiences. By this definition, mind is analogous to the knowledge and rules that are programmed into a computer to organize its ability to calculate and perform all the operations we expect of it. In this usage, mind is not equated with consciousness. People are not aware of most of the inner knowledge and processes that organize their feelings, thoughts, and behavior, any more than a computer is aware of its software programs.

I have used the term *mind* in both of these ways in various parts of this book, but it should be clear from the context which meaning I am using at any given time. Many psychologists in the past, and a few even today, have argued that we should avoid the concept of mind entirely. They point out that by either definition, *mind* refers to something that we cannot see directly. What we observe is people's behavior, including their verbal reports of their thoughts and feelings. With modern techniques of monitoring the brain, we can also observe physical changes in the brain, but, again, that is not the same as observing the mind. According to some psychologists, therefore, we should define our science as the study of behavior, or as the study of the brain and behavior, and leave the unobservable mind out of it. Most psychologists, however, find the concept of mind to be very useful. We can *infer* characteristics of the mind by observing behavior, and then we can use those inferences to make predictions about further behavior. Gravity can't be seen directly, either—it is inferred by observing the behavior of physical entities; yet physicists find the concept of gravity to be very useful.

Further Reading

D. Brett King, Wayne Viney, & William Woody (2009). *A history of psychology: Ideas and context* (4th ed.). Boston: Pearson.

This is one of many good introductions to the history of psychology. Nearly half of it is devoted to psychological ideas developed before the founding of psychology as a formal discipline. Chapter 2, "Philosophical Issues," is especially useful in helping new students view psychology from a philosophical perspective.

Jeroen Jansz & Peter van Drunen (Eds.) (2004). *A social history of psychology.* Malden, MA: Blackwell.

While most histories of psychology focus on the ideas and discoveries of philosophers and scientists, this one focuses on larger developments in society as a whole that influenced and motivated psychological thought and research. It includes chapters on child rearing and education, madness and mental health, work and organizations, culture and ethnicity, and delinquency and law, as well as three more general chapters that describe relationships between psychology and social developments.

Eric Landrum, Stephen Davis, & Teresa Landrum (2007). *The psychology major: Career options and strategies for success* (3rd ed.). Upper Saddle River, NJ: Prentice-Hall.

If you are considering psychology as a major, this brief book can help you decide. If you have already chosen to major in psychology, it can help guide you through your years of study. It is packed with practical information and suggestions—about jobs and careers, how to conduct library research and write papers, how to find research and internship opportunities, and how to prepare for and apply for graduate study.

Tara L. Kuther (2003). *The Psychology Major's Handbook.* Belmont, CA: Wadsworth.

This helpful paperback provides information and ideas on many topics relevant to the psychology major, from the initial chapters *What is Psychology?* and *Is Psychology for You?* on through chapters offering study tips, advice for writing papers, and information about career choices and graduate school in psychology.

Tara L. Kuther & Robert D. Morgan (2007). *Careers in psychology: Opportunities in a changing world* (2nd ed.). Belmont, CA: Wadsworth.

This book describes a wide variety of careers in psychology, including careers in clinical and counseling psychology, school psychology, legal psychology, health psychology, sports psychology, industrial/organizational psychology, and various subdisciplines of academic research psychology.

Methods of Psychology

In Chapter 1, *psychology* was defined as the *science* of behavior and the mind. But what does it mean to say that psychology is a science? Science is the attempt to answer questions through the systematic collection and analysis of objective, publicly observable data (data that all observers can agree on). In psychology, the data are usually measures or descriptions of some form of behavior produced by humans or animals. Special problems exist in choosing what data to collect, collecting the data, and drawing conclusions from them. If we fail to deal with those problems carefully and intelligently, the answers we arrive at will not enlighten us, but mislead us.

This chapter is about scientific methods as applied to psychology. You will read sections on the research strategies psychologists use to answer questions, the statistical procedures they use to analyze data, the safeguards they employ to avoid biased results, and the protections they provide to human and animal research subjects. But first, to ease ourselves into the topic, here is a story about a horse—and a psychologist.

Lessons from Clever Hans

This story, a true one, took place in Germany near the beginning of the twentieth century. The horse was Clever Hans, famous throughout Europe for his ability to answer questions, and the psychologist was Oskar Pfungst. In a preface to the original account (Pfungst, 1911/1965), James Angell wrote, "Were it offered as fiction, it would take high rank as a work of imagination. Being in reality a sober fact, it verges on the miraculous." I tell the story here because of the lessons it teaches about scientific attitude and methods.

The Mystery

Hans's owner, a Mr. von Osten, was an eccentric retired schoolteacher and devoted horseman who had long believed that horses would prove to be as intelligent as people if only they were given a proper education. To test his theory, von Osten

Pfungst, O. (1965). *Clever horse: The horse of Mr. Von Osten.* New York: Holt, Rinehart & Winston.

Clever Hans at a mathematics lesson Mr. von Osten believed that his horse was intellectually gifted, and so did many other people until the psychologist Oskar Pfungst performed some simple experiments.

spent four years tutoring Hans in the manner employed in the most reputable German schools for children. Using flash cards, counting frames, and the like, he set about teaching his horse reading, arithmetic, history, and other scholarly disciplines. He always began with simple problems and worked toward more complex ones, and he rewarded Hans frequently with praise as well as carrots. Recognizing that horses lack the vocal apparatus needed for speech, von Osten taught Hans to spell out words using a code in which the letters of the alphabet were translated into hoof taps and to answer yes–no questions by tossing his head up and down for "yes" and back and forth for "no." After four years of this training, Hans was able to answer practically any question that was put to him in either spoken or written German, whether about geography, history, science, literature, mathematics, or current events. Remarkably, he could also answer questions put to him in other languages, even though he had never been trained in them.

Now you might think that von Osten was a charlatan, but he wasn't. He genuinely believed that his horse could read and understand a variety of languages, could perform mathematical calculations, and had acquired a vast store of knowledge. He never charged admission or sought other personal gain for displaying Hans, and he actively sought out scientists to study the animal's accomplishments. Indeed, many scientists, including some eminent zoologists and psychologists, came to the conclusion that von Osten's claims were true. The evidence that most convinced them was Hans's ability to answer questions even when von Osten was not present, a finding that seemed to rule out the possibility that the horse depended on secret signals from his master. Moreover, several circus trainers, who specialized in training animals to give the appearance of answering questions, studied Hans and could find no evidence of trickery.

The Solution

1

How did Clever Hans give the appearance of answering questions, and how did Oskar Pfungst unveil Hans's methods?

Hans's downfall finally came when the psychologist Oskar Pfungst performed a few simple experiments. Pfungst (1911/1965) theorized that Hans answered questions not through understanding them and knowing the answers but through responding to visual signals inadvertently produced by the questioner or other observers. Consistent with this theory, Pfungst found that the animal failed to answer questions when he was fitted with blinders so that he could not see anyone, and that even without blinders he could not answer questions unless at least one person in his sight knew the answer. With further study, Pfungst discovered just what the signals were.

Immediately after asking a question that demanded a hoof-tap answer, the questioner and other observers would naturally move their heads down just a bit to observe the horse's hoof. This, it turned out, was the signal for Hans to start tapping. To determine whether Hans would be correct or not, the questioner and other observers would then count the taps and, unintentionally, make another response as soon as the correct number had been reached. This response varied from person to person, but a common component was a slight upward movement of either the whole head or

Cues from the audience When members of the audience knew the answer to a question asked of Clever Hans, they inadvertently signaled the horse as to when to start and stop tapping, or which way to shake his head, through their own head movements.

some facial feature, such as the eyebrows. This, it turned out, was the signal for Hans to stop tapping. Hans's yes–no head-shake responses were also controlled by visual signals. Questioners and observers would unconsciously produce slight up-and-down head movements when they expected the horse to answer yes and slight back-and-forth head movements when they expected him to answer no, and Hans would shake his head accordingly.

All the signals that controlled Hans's responses were so subtle that even the most astute observers had failed to notice them until Pfungst pointed them out. And Pfungst himself reported that the signals occurred so naturally that, even after he had learned what they were, he had to make a conscious effort to prevent himself from sending them after asking a question. For 4 years, von Osten had believed that he was communicating scholarly information to Hans, when all he had really done was teach the horse to make a few simple responses to a few simple, though minute, gestures.

Facts, Theories, and Hypotheses

The story of Clever Hans illustrates the roles of facts, theories, and hypotheses in scientific research. A *fact*, also referred to as an *observation,* is an objective statement, usually based on direct observation, that reasonable observers agree is true. In psychology, facts are usually particular behaviors, or reliable patterns of behaviors, of persons or animals. When Hans was tested in the manner typically employed by von Osten, the horse's hoof taps or head shakes gave the appearance that he was answering questions correctly. That is a fact, which no one involved in the adventure disputed.

A *theory* is an idea, or a conceptual model, that is designed to explain existing facts and make predictions about new facts that might be discovered. Any prediction about new facts that is made from a theory is called a **hypothesis.** Nobody knows what facts (or perhaps delusions) led von Osten to develop his theory that horses have humanlike intelligence. However, once he conceived his theory, he used it to hypothesize that his horse, Hans, could learn to give correct answers to verbally stated problems and questions. The psychologist, Pfungst, had a quite different theory of equine intelligence: Horses don't think like humans and can't understand human language. In keeping with this theory, and to explain the fact that Hans seemed to answer questions correctly, Pfungst developed the more specific theory that the horse responded to visual cues produced by people who were present and knew the answers. This theory led Pfungst to hypothesize that Hans would not answer questions correctly if fitted with blinders or if asked questions to which nobody present knew the answer.

Facts lead to theories, which lead to hypotheses, which are tested with experiments or other research studies, which lead to new facts, which sometimes lead to new theories, which . . . . That is the cycle of science, whether we are speaking of psychology, biology, physics, or any other scientific endeavor.

2
How are facts, theories, and hypotheses related to one another in scientific research?

The Lessons

In addition to illustrating the roles of fact, theory, and hypothesis, the story contains three more specific lessons about scientific research:

3
How does the Clever Hans story illustrate (1) the value of skepticism, (2) the value of controlled experimentation, and (3) the need for researchers to avoid communicating their expectations to subjects?

1. *The value of skepticism.* People are fascinated by extraordinary claims and often act as though they want to believe them. This is as true today as it was in the time of Clever Hans. We have no trouble at all finding otherwise rational people who believe in astrology, psychokinesis, water divining, telepathy, or other occult phenomena, despite the fact that all these have consistently failed when subjected to controlled tests (Hines, 2003). Von Osten clearly wanted to believe that his horse could do amazing things, and to a lesser degree, the same may have been true of the scholars who had studied the horse before Pfungst. Pfungst learned the truth partly because he was highly skeptical of such claims. Instead of setting out to prove them correct, he set out to prove them wrong. His skepticism led him to look more carefully; to notice what others had missed; to think of an alternative, more mundane explanation; and to pit the mundane explanation against the astonishing one in controlled tests.

Skepticism should be applied not only to extraordinary theories that come from outside of science but also to the usually more sober theories produced by scientists themselves. The ideal scientist always tries to disprove theories, even those that are his or her own. The theories that scientists accept as correct, or most likely to be correct, are those that could potentially be disproved but have survived all attempts so far to disprove them.

2. *The value of careful observations under controlled conditions.* Pfungst solved the mystery of Clever Hans by identifying the conditions under which the horse could and could not respond correctly to questions. He tested Hans repeatedly, with and without blinders, and recorded the percentage of correct answers in each condition. The results were consistent with the theory that the animal relied on visual signals. Pfungst then pursued the theory further by carefully observing Hans's examiners to see what cues they might be sending. And when he had an idea what the cues might be, he performed further experiments, in which he deliberately produced or withheld the signals and recorded their effects on Hans's hoof-tapping and head-shaking responses. Careful observation under controlled conditions is a hallmark of the scientific method.

3. *The problem of observer-expectancy effects.* In studies of humans and other sentient animals the observers (the people conducting the research) may unintentionally communicate to subjects (the individuals being studied) their expectations about how the subjects "should" behave, and the subjects, intentionally or not, may respond by doing just what the researchers expect. The same is true in any situation in which one person administers a test to another. Have you ever taken an oral quiz and found that you could tell whether you were on the right track by noting the facial expression of your examiner? By tentatively trying various tracks, you may have finally hit on just the answer that your examiner wanted. Clever Hans's entire ability depended on his picking up such cues. We will discuss the general problem of expectancy effects later in this chapter (in the section on avoiding biases).

SECTION REVIEW

The case of the horse named Clever Hans illustrates a number of issues fundamental to scientific research.

Facts, Theories, and Hypotheses	The Importance of Skepticism	Observation and Control	Observer-Expectancy Effects
➤ Objective observations about behavior (facts) lead psychologists to create conceptual models or explanations (theories), which make specific, testable predictions (hypotheses). ➤ Pfungst drew testable hypotheses from his theory that Hans was guided by visual cues from onlookers.	➤ Skeptics seek to disprove claims. That is the logical foundation of scientific testing. ➤ A scientific theory becomes more believable as repeated, genuine attempts to disprove it fail. ➤ Pfungst's skepticism caused him to test rather than simply accept claims about Hans's abilities.	➤ To test hypotheses, scientists control the conditions in which they make observations, so as to rule out alternative explanations. ➤ Pfungst measured Hans's performance in conditions arranged specifically to test his hypothesis—with and without blinders, for example.	➤ Science is carried out by people who come to their research with certain expectations. ➤ In psychology, the subjects— the people and animals under study—may perceive the observer's expectations and behave accordingly. ➤ Cues from observers led Hans to give responses that many misinterpreted as signs of vast knowledge.

■ Types of Research Strategies

In their quest to understand the mind and behavior of humans and other animals, psychologists employ a variety of research strategies. Pfungst's strategy was to observe Clever Hans's behavior in controlled experiments. But not all research studies done by psychologists are experiments. A useful way to categorize the various research strategies used by psychologists is to think of them as varying along the following three dimensions (Hendricks & others, 1990):

1. The *research design,* of which there are three basic types—experiments, correlational studies, and descriptive studies.

2. The *setting* in which the study is conducted, of which there are two basic types—field and laboratory.

3. The *data-collection method,* of which there are two basic types—self-report and observation.

Each of these dimensions can vary independently from the others, resulting in any possible combination of design, setting, and data-collection method. Here I will first describe the three types of research designs and then, more briefly, the other two dimensions.

Research Designs

Experiments

An experiment is the most direct and conclusive approach to testing a hypothesis about a cause–effect relationship between two variables. A *variable* is simply anything that can vary. It might be a condition of the environment, such as temperature or amount of noise; or it might be a measure of behavior, such as a score on a test. In describing an experiment, the variable that is hypothesized to cause some effect on another variable is called the **independent variable,** and the variable that is hypothesized to be affected is called the **dependent variable.** The aim of any experiment is to learn whether and how the dependent variable is affected by (depends on) the independent variable. In psychology, dependent variables are usually measures of behavior, and independent variables are factors that are hypothesized to influence those measures.

More specifically, an **experiment** can be defined as a procedure in which a researcher systematically manipulates (varies) one or more independent variables and looks for changes in one or more dependent variables, *while keeping all other variables constant.* If all other variables are kept constant, and only the independent variable is changed, then the experimenter can reasonably conclude that any change observed in the dependent variable *is caused by* the change in the independent variable.

The people or animals that are studied in any research study are referred to as the *subjects* of the study. (Many psychologists today prefer to call them *participants* rather than subjects, because it seems more politically correct to do so, but that term is imprecise because it does not distinguish between those who are being studied and those who are doing the studying. So I will stick with *subjects.*) In some experiments, called *within-subject experiments,* each subject is tested in each of the different conditions of the independent variable. In other experiments, called *between-groups experiments*, there is a separate group of subjects for each different condition of the independent variable.

Example of a Within-Subject Experiment In most within-subject experiments, a number of subjects are each tested in each condition of the independent variable. But within-subject experiments can be conducted with just one subject. In Pfungst's experiments with Clever Hans, there was just one subject, Hans. In each experiment, Pfungst tested Hans repeatedly, under varying conditions of the independent variable.

4

How can an experiment prove the existence of a cause–effect relation between two variables?

5

What were the independent and dependent variables in Pfungst's experiment with Clever Hans?

In one experiment, to determine whether or not visual cues were critical to Hans's ability to respond correctly to questions, Pfungst tested the horse sometimes with blinders and sometimes without. In that experiment the independent variable was the presence or absence of blinders, and the dependent variable was the percentage of questions the horse answered correctly. The experiment could be described as a study of the effect of blinders (independent variable) on Hans's percentage of correct responses to questions (dependent variable). Pfungst took care to keep other variables, such as the difficulty of the questions and the setting in which the questions were asked, constant across the two test conditions. This experiment is a within-subject experiment, because the different conditions of the independent variable were applied to the same subject.

6------------------------------

What were the independent and dependent variables in DiMascio's experiment on treatments for depression? Why were the subjects randomly assigned to the different treatments rather than allowed to choose their own treatment?

◄ **Example of a Between-Groups Experiment** To illustrate a between-groups experiments, I'll use a classic experiment in clinical psychology conducted by Alberto DiMascio and his colleagues (1979). These researchers identified a group of patients suffering from major depression (defined in Chapter 16) and assigned them, by a deliberately random procedure, to different treatments. One group received both drug therapy and psychotherapy, a second received drug therapy alone, a third received psychotherapy alone, and a fourth received no scheduled treatment. The drug therapy consisted of daily doses of an antidepressant drug, and the psychotherapy consisted of weekly talk sessions with a psychiatrist that focused on the person's social relationships. After 16 weeks of treatment, the researchers rated each patient's degree of depression using a standard set of questions about mood and behavior. In this experiment, the independent variable was the kind of treatment given, and the dependent variable was the degree of depression after 16 weeks of treatment. This is a between-groups experiment, because the manipulations of the independent variable (that is, the different treatments used) were applied to different groups of subjects.

Notice that the researchers used a random method (a method relying only on chance) to assign the subjects to the treatment groups. *Random assignment* is regularly used in between-group experiments to ensure that the subjects are not assigned in a way that could bias the results. If DiMascio and his colleagues had allowed the subjects to choose their own treatment group, those who were most likely to improve even without treatment—maybe because they were more motivated to improve—might have disproportionately chosen one treatment condition over the others. In that case we would have no way to know whether the greater improvement of one group compared with the others derived from the treatment or from preexisting differences in the subjects. With random assignment, any differences among the groups that do not stem from the differing treatments must be the result of chance, and, as you will see later, researchers have statistical tools for taking chance into account in analyzing their data.

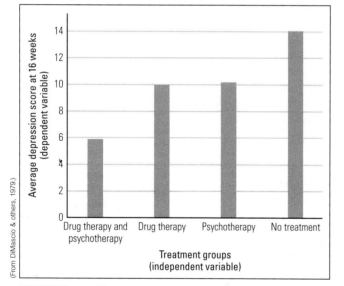

FIGURE 2.1 Effect of treatment condition on depression Subjects who received both drugs and psychotherapy were the least depressed at the end of the 16-week treatment period (according to the results of a standard interview procedure scored on a 17-point scale). In contrast, subjects who received no treatment were the most depressed.

(From DiMascio & others, 1979.)

The results of this experiment are shown in Figure 2.1. Following a common convention in graphing experimental results, which is used throughout this book, the figure depicts variation in the independent variable along the horizontal axis and variation in the dependent variable along the vertical axis. As you can see in the figure, those in the drug-plus-psychotherapy group were the least depressed after the 16-week period, and those in the no-treatment group were the most depressed. The results support the hypothesis that both drug therapy and psychotherapy help relieve depression, and that the two treatments together have a greater effect than either alone.

Correlational Studies

Often in psychology we cannot conduct experiments to answer the questions that we want to answer, because we cannot—for practical or ethical reasons—assign subjects to particular experimental conditions and control their experiences. Suppose, for example, that you are interested in the relationship between the disciplinary styles of parents and the psychological development of their children. Perhaps you entertain the theory that strict punishment is harmful, that it promotes aggressiveness or other unwanted characteristics. To test that theory with an experiment, you would have to manipulate the discipline variable and then measure some aspect of the children's behavior. You might consider randomly assigning some families to a strict punishment condition and others to other conditions. The parents would then have to raise their children in the manners you prescribe. But you know that you cannot control families that way; it's not practical, not legal, and not ethical. So, instead, you conduct a correlational study.

A *correlational study* can be defined as a study in which the researcher does not manipulate any variable, but observes or measures two or more already existing variables to find relationships between them. Correlational studies can identify relationships between variables, which allow us to make predictions about one variable based on knowledge of another; but such studies do not tell us in any direct way whether change in one variable is the cause of change in another.

▶ - - - - - - - - - - - - - - - - -7
What are the differences between a correlational study and an experiment, in procedure and in types of conclusions that can be drawn?

Example of a Correlational Study A classic example of a correlational study is Diana Baumrind's (1971) study of the relationship between parents' disciplinary styles and children's behavioral development. Instead of manipulating disciplinary styles, she observed and assessed differences in disciplinary styles that already existed between different sets of parents. Through questionnaires and home observations, Baumrind classified disciplinary styles into three categories: *authoritarian* (high exertion of parental power), *authoritative* (a kinder and more democratic style, but with the parents still clearly in charge), and *permissive* (parental laxity in the face of their children's disruptive behaviors). She also rated the children on various aspects of behavior, such as cooperation and friendliness, through observations in their nursery schools. The main finding (discussed more fully in Chapter 12) was that children of authoritative parents scored better on the measures of behavior than did children of authoritarian or permissive parents.

Why Cause and Effect Cannot Be Determined from a Correlational Study It is tempting to treat Baumrind's study as though it were an experiment and interpret the results in cause-effect terms. More specifically, it is tempting to think of the parents' disciplinary style as the independent variable and the children's behavior as the dependent variable and to conclude that differences in the former caused the differences in the latter. But because the study was not an experiment, we cannot justifiably come to that conclusion. The researcher did not control either variable, so we cannot be sure what was cause and what was effect. Maybe the differences in the parents' styles did cause the differences in the children's behavior, but other interpretations are possible. Here are some of these possibilities:

▶ - - - - - - - - - - - - - - - -8
How does an analysis of Baumrind's classic study of parental disciplinary styles illustrate the difficulty of trying to infer cause and effect from a correlation?

- Differences in children's behavior may cause differences in parents' disciplinary style, rather than the other way around. Some children may be better behaved than others for reasons quite separate from parental style, and parents with well-behaved children may simply glide into an authoritative mode of parenting, while those with more difficult children fall into one of the other two approaches as a way of coping.

- The causal relationship may go in both directions, with parents and children influencing each other's behavior. For example, children's disruptive behavior may promote authoritarian parenting, which may promote even more disruptive behavior.

What causes what? Although many correlational studies have found a relationship between the viewing of televised violence and the displaying of aggressive behavior, such studies cannot tell us whether television inspires the aggressive behavior or whether aggressive individuals are more likely than others to watch violent television programs.

© Mary Kate Denny/Photo Edit

- A third variable, not measured in Baumrind's study, may influence both parental style and children's behavior in such a way as to cause the observed correlation. For example, anything that makes families feel good about themselves (such as having good neighbors, good health, and an adequate income) might promote an authoritative style in parents and, quite independently, also lead children to behave well. Or maybe the causal variable has to do with the fact that children are genetically similar to their parents and therefore have similar personalities: The same genes that predispose parents to behave in a kind but firm manner may predispose children to behave well, and the same genes that predispose parents to be either highly punitive or neglectful may predispose children to misbehave.

If you understand and remain aware of this limitation of correlational studies, you will be not only a stronger psychology student, but a much shrewder consumer of media reports about research results. All too frequently, people—including even scientists who sometimes forget what they should know—use correlations to make unjustified claims of causal relationships on subjects including not only psychology, but health, economics, and more.

In some correlational studies, one causal hypothesis may be deemed to be more plausible than others, but that is a judgment based on logical thought about possible causal mechanisms or on evidence from other sources, not from the correlation itself (Rutter, 2007). For example, if I found a correlation between brain damage to a certain part of the brain, due to accidents, and the onset of a certain type of mental disorder immediately following the accident, I would probably be correct in inferring that the brain damage caused the mental disorder. That possibility seems far more plausible than any other possible explanation of the relationship between the two variables.

In Baumrind's study, one variable (parents' disciplinary style) was used to place subjects into separate groups, and then the groups were compared to see how they differed in the other variable (the children's behavior). Many correlational studies are analyzed in that way, and those are the ones most likely to be confused with experiments. In many other correlational studies, however, both variables are measured numerically and neither is used to assign subjects to groups. For example, a researcher might be interested in the correlation between the height of tenth grade boys (measured in centimeters or inches) and their popularity (measured by counting the number of classmates who list the boy as a friend). In such cases, the data are assessed by a statistic called the *correlation coefficient,* which will be discussed later (in the section on statistical methods).

Descriptive Studies

9 ⋯⋯⋯⋯⋯⋯⋯⋯⋗
How do descriptive studies differ, in method and purpose, from experiments and from correlational studies?
⋯⋯⋯⋯⋯⋯⋯⋯⋯

Sometimes the aim of research is to describe the behavior of an individual or set of individuals without assessing relationships between different variables. A study of this sort is called a ***descriptive study.*** Descriptive studies may or may not make use of numbers. As an example of one involving numbers, researchers might survey the members of a given community to determine the percentage who suffer from various mental disorders. This is a descriptive study if its aim is simply to describe the prevalence of each disorder without correlating the disorders to other characteristics of the community's members. As an example of a descriptive study not involving numbers, an animal behaviorist might observe the courtship behaviors of mallard ducks to describe in detail the sequence of movements that are involved.

Some descriptive studies are narrow in focus, concentrating on one specific aspect of behavior, and others are broad, aiming to learn as much as possible about the habits of a particular group of people or species of animal. One of the most extensive and heroic descriptive studies ever conducted is Jane Goodall's research on wild chimpanzees in Africa. She observed the apes' behavior over a period of 30 years and provided a wealth of information about every aspect of their lives (Goodall, 1986, 1988).

Research Settings

The second dimension of research strategy is the research setting, which can be either the laboratory or the field. A **_laboratory study_** is any research study in which the subjects are brought to a specially designated area that has been set up to facilitate the researcher's collection of data or control over environmental conditions. A **_field study_** is any research study conducted in a setting other than a laboratory. Field studies in psychology may be conducted in people's homes, at their workplaces, at shopping malls, or in any place that is part of the subjects' real environment.

Laboratory and field settings offer opposite sets of advantages and disadvantages. The laboratory allows the researcher to collect data under more uniform, controlled conditions than are possible in the field. However, the strangeness or artificiality of the laboratory may induce behaviors that obscure those that the researcher wants to study. A laboratory study of parent-child interactions, for example, may produce results that reflect not so much the subjects' normal ways of interacting as their reactions to a strange environment in which they know that they are being observed. To counteract such problems, some researchers combine laboratory and field studies. When, as often happens, the same conclusions emerge from tightly controlled laboratory studies and less controlled but more natural field studies, researchers can be reasonably confident that the conclusions are meaningful (Anderson & others, 1999).

As you might expect, experiments are most often conducted in the laboratory because greater control of variables is possible in that setting, and correlational and descriptive studies are more often conducted in the field. But these relationships between research design and setting are by no means inevitable. Experiments are sometimes performed in the field, and correlational and descriptive studies are sometimes carried out in the laboratory. For an example of a field experiment, read the caption to Figure 2.2.

> ──────────── **10**
> **What are the relative advantages and disadvantages of laboratory studies and field studies?**
> ────────────────

Many past visitors have removed petrified wood from the park, changing the natural state of the Petrified Forest.

Robert Cialdini

FIGURE 2.2 Sign used in a field experiment in Petrified Forest National Park Park visitors often see signs describing and depicting undesired behaviors. Psychologist Robert Cialdini (2003) wondered if such signs are effective in reducing the behaviors that they are designed to reduce. As a test, he varied, on different days, the signs that were placed along trails in Petrified Forest National Park, and he measured, by observation, the amount of theft of petrified wood that occurred. When this sign was used, visitors actually took more pieces of petrified wood than when there was no sign. An explanation of why this might have happened is offered in Chapter 14.

Data-Collection Methods

The third dimension of research is the data-collection method, of which there are two broad categories: self-report methods and observational methods.

Self-report methods are procedures in which people are asked to rate or describe their own behavior or mental state in some way. For example, in a study of generosity subjects might be asked to respond to questions pertaining to their own degree of generosity. This might be done through a written _questionnaire,_ in which people check off items on a printed list that apply to them, indicate the degree to which certain statements are true or not true of them, or write answers to brief essay questions about themselves. Or it might be done through an interview, in which people describe themselves orally in a dialogue with the interviewer. An

> ──────────── **11**
> **How do self-report methods, naturalistic observations, and tests differ from one another? What are some advantages and disadvantages of each?**
> ────────────────

interview may be tightly structured, with the interviewer asking questions according to a completely planned sequence, or it may be more loosely structured, with the interviewer following up on some of the subjects' responses with additional questions.

Observational methods include all procedures by which researchers observe and record the behavior of interest, rather than rely on subjects' self-reports. In one subcategory, ***naturalistic observation,*** the researcher avoids interfering with the subjects' behavior. For example, a researcher studying generosity might unobtrusively watch people passing by a charity booth outside of a grocery store to see who gives and who doesn't. In the other subcategory, ***tests,*** the researcher deliberately presents problems, tasks, or situations to which the subject responds. For example, to test generosity a researcher might allow subjects to win a certain amount of money in a game and then allow them to donate whatever amount of that they wish to other subjects or to some cause.

Observing without interfering An obstacle to naturalistic observation is that the researchers may inadvertently, by their mere presence, influence the behavior they are observing. To minimize the degree to which her presence would affect the behavior of the Efe people she was studying, Gilda Morelli (at left) spent many months living among the Efe in Africa. People go about their daily activities more naturally in the presence of someone who is familiar and has proved trustworthy than they do in the presence of a stranger.

None of these data-collection methods is in any absolute sense superior to another. Each has its purposes, advantages, and limitations. Questionnaires and interviews can provide information that researchers would not be able to obtain by watching subjects directly. However, the validity of such data is limited by the subjects' ability to observe and remember their own behaviors or moods and by their willingness to report those observations frankly, without distorting them to look good or to please the researcher. Naturalistic observations allow researchers to learn firsthand about their subjects' natural behaviors, but the practicality of such methods is limited by the great amount of time they take, the difficulty of observing ongoing behavior without interfering with it, and the difficulty of coding results in a form that can be used for statistical analysis. Tests are convenient and easily scored but are by nature artificial, and their relevance to everyday behavior is not always clear. What is the relationship between a person's giving in a laboratory test and that person's giving in real life? . . . or between a score on an IQ test and the ability to solve real-life problems? These are the kinds of question that psychologists must address whenever they wish to use test results to draw conclusions about behaviors outside of the testing situation.

SECTION REVIEW

Research strategies used by psychologists vary in their design, setting, and data-collection method.

Research Designs	Research Settings	Data-Collection Methods
➤ In an experiment (such as the experiment on treatments for depression), the researcher can test hypotheses about causation by manipulating the independent variable(s) and looking for corresponding differences in the dependent variable(s), while keeping all other variables constant.	➤ Laboratory settings allow researchers the greatest control over variables, but they may interfere with the behavior being studied, by virtue of being unfamiliar or artificial.	➤ Self-report methods require the people being studied to rate or describe themselves, usually in questionnaires or interviews.
➤ In a correlational study, a researcher measures two or more variables to see if there are systematic relationships among them. Such studies do not tell us about causation.	➤ Field studies, done in "real-life" settings, have the opposite advantages and disadvantages, offering less control but perhaps more natural behavior.	➤ Observational methods require the researcher to observe and record the subjects' behavior, through naturalistic observation or some form of test.
➤ Descriptive studies are designed only to characterize and record what is observed, not to test hypotheses about relationships among variables.		➤ Each data-collection method has advantages and disadvantages.

▓ Statistical Methods in Psychology

To make sense of the data collected in a research study, we must have some way of summarizing the data and some way to determine the likelihood that observed patterns in the data are (or are not) simply the results of chance. The statistical procedures used for these purposes can be divided into two categories: (1) **descriptive statistics,** which are used to summarize sets of data, and (2) **inferential statistics,** which help researchers decide how confident they can be in judging that the results observed are not due to chance. We shall look briefly here at some commonly used descriptive statistics and then at the rationale behind inferential statistics. A more detailed discussion of some of these procedures, with examples, can be found in the *Statistical Appendix* at the back of this book.

Descriptive Statistics

Describing a Set of Scores

Descriptive statistics include all numerical methods for summarizing a set of data. If our data were a set of check marks indicating who showed a particular behavior and who didn't, we might summarize the data by calculating the percentage who showed it. If our data were a set of numerical measurements (such as ratings from 1 to 10 on how generous they were), we might summarize them by calculating either the mean or the median. The **mean** is simply the arithmetic average, determined by adding the scores and dividing the sum by the number of scores. The **median** is the center score, determined by ranking the scores from highest to lowest and finding the score that has the same number of scores above it as below it. (The *Statistical Appendix* explains when the mean or the median is the more appropriate statistic.)

> ----------- **12**
> **How do the mean, median, and standard deviation help describe a set of numbers?**

TABLE 2.1	Two sets of data, with the same mean but different amounts of variability
Set A	**Set B**
7	2
7	4
8	8
11	9
12	14
12	16
13	17
Median = 11	Median = 9
Total = 70	Total = 70
Mean = 70/7 = 10	Mean = 70/7 = 10
Standard deviation = 2.39	Standard deviation = 5.42

For certain kinds of comparisons, researchers need to describe not only the central tendency (the mean or median) but also the variability of a set of numbers. **Variability** refers to the degree to which the numbers in the set differ from one another and from their mean. In Table 2.1 you can see two sets of numbers that have identical means but different variabilities. In set A, the scores cluster close to the mean (low variability); in set B, they differ widely from the mean (high variability). A common measure of variability is the **standard deviation,** which is calculated by a formula described in the *Statistical Appendix*. As illustrated in Table 2.1, the further most individual scores are from the mean, the greater is the standard deviation.

Describing a Correlation

Correlational studies, you recall, assess two or more variables to determine whether or not a nonrandom relationship exists between them. When both variables are measured numerically, the strength and direction of the relationship can be assessed by a statistic called the **correlation coefficient.**

13

How does a correlation coefficient describe the direction and strength of a correlation? How can correlations be depicted in scatter plots?

◄ Correlation coefficients are calculated by a formula (described in the *Statistical Appendix*) that produces a result ranging from +1.00 to −1.00. The sign (+ or −) indicates the direction of the correlation (positive or negative). In a *positive correlation,* an increase in one variable coincides with a tendency for the other variable to increase; in a *negative correlation,* an increase in one variable coincides with a tendency for the other variable to decrease. The absolute value of the correlation coefficient (the value with sign removed) indicates the *strength* of the correlation. To the degree that a correlation is strong (close to +1.00 or −1.00), you can predict the value of one variable by knowing the other.

As an example, consider a hypothetical research study conducted with 10 students in a college course, aimed at assessing the correlation between the students' most recent test score and each of four other variables: (1) the hours they spent studying for the test; (2) the score they got on the previous test; (3) their level of psychological depression, measured a day before the test; and (4) their height in centimeters. Suppose the data collected in the study are those depicted in the table at the left in Figure 2.3. Each row in the table shows the data for a different student, and the students are rank ordered in accordance with their scores on the test.

To visualize the relationship between the test score and any of the other four variables, the researcher might produce a *scatter plot,* in which each student's test score and that student's value for one of the other measurements are designated by a single point on the graph. The scatter plots relating test score to each of the other variables are shown at the right in Figure 2.3:

- Plot A illustrates the relation between test score and hours of study. Notice that each point represents both the test score and the hours of study for a single student. Thus, the point indicated by the red arrow denotes a student whose score is 85 and who spent 9 hours studying. By looking at the whole constellation of points, you can see that, in general, higher test scores correspond with more hours spent studying. This is what makes the correlation positive. But the correlation is far from perfect. It can be described as a *moderate positive correlation.* (The calculated correlation coefficient is +.51.)

- Plot B, which relates this test score to the score on the previous test, illustrates a *strong positive correlation.* Notice that in this plot the points fall very close to an

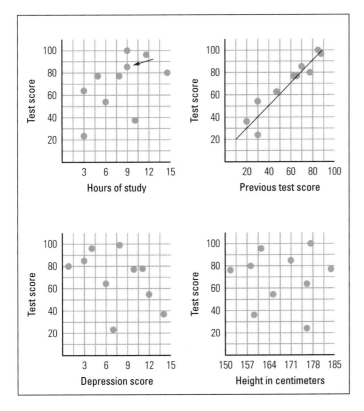

Student ranked by test score	Test score	Hrs of study	Prvs. Test Score	Depression	Height (cm)
1	100	9	85	8	177
2	97	11	88	4	160
3	85	9	70	3	171
4	80	14	79	1	158
5	78	8	62	10	184
6	78	5	65	11	152
7	62	3	44	6	176
8	54	6	30	12	165
9	38	10	20	14	159
10	22	3	30	7	176
Correlation with test score		+.51	+.93	−.43	−.04

FIGURE 2.3 Examples of correlations, using made-up data
The table above shows the most recent test score and four other measures for each of 10 students in a college course. At the bottom of each of the four right-hand columns is the correlation coefficient relating the data of that column to the test score. (The study is fictitious and the data were made up for illustrative purposes.) The four scatter plots at right depict, separately, the correlation between the test score and each of the four other measures. By comparing the plots, you can see the difference between weaker and stronger correlations and between positive and negative correlations.

upwardly slanted line. The closer the points are to forming a straight line, the stronger is the correlation between the two variables. In this study, score on the previous test is an excellent predictor of score on the new test. (The correlation coefficient is +.93.)

- Plot C, which shows the relation between test score and depression, illustrates a *moderate negative correlation*. Test score tends to decrease as depression increases. (The correlation coefficient here is −.43.)

- Plot D, which shows the relation between test score and height, illustrates uncorrelated data—a correlation coefficient close to or equal to 0. Knowing a person's height provides no help in predicting the person's test score. (The correlation coefficient here is −.04.)

Inferential Statistics

Any set of data collected in a research study contains some degree of variability that can be attributed to chance. That is the essential reason why inferential statistics are necessary. In the experiment comparing treatments for depression summarized back in Figure 2.1, the average depression scores obtained for the four groups reflect not just the effects of treatment but also random effects caused by uncontrollable variables. For example, more patients who were predisposed to improve could by chance have been assigned to one treatment group rather than to another. Or measurement error stemming from imperfections in the rating procedure could have contributed to differences in the depression scores. If the experiment were repeated several times, the results would be somewhat different each time because of such uncontrollable random variables. Given that results can vary as a result of chance, how confident can a researcher be in inferring a general conclusion from the study's data? Inferential statistics are ways of answering that question using the laws of probability.

14

Why is it necessary to perform inferential statistics before drawing conclusions from the data in a research study?

Statistical Significance

When two groups of subjects in an experiment have different mean scores, the difference might be meaningful, or it might be just the result of chance. Similarly, a nonzero correlation coefficient in a correlational study might indicate a meaningful relationship between two variables, or it might be just the result of chance. Inferential statistical methods, applied to either an experiment or a correlational study, are procedures for calculating the probability that the observed results could derive from chance alone.

15 ◄ What does it mean to say that a result from a research study is statistically significant at the 5 percent level?

◄ Using such methods, researchers calculate a statistic referred to as p, or the *level of significance*. When two means are being compared, p is the probability that a difference as great as or greater than that observed would occur by chance if, in the larger population, there were no difference between the two means. ("Larger population" here means the entire set of scores that would be obtained if the experiment were repeated an infinite number of times with all possible subjects.) In other words, in the case of comparing two means in an experiment, p is the probability that a difference as large as or larger than that observed would occur if the independent variable had no real effect on the scores. In the case of a correlational study, p is the probability that a correlation coefficient as large as or larger than that observed (in absolute value) would occur by chance if, in the larger population, the two variables were uncorrelated. By convention, results are usually labeled as **statistically significant** if the value of p is less than .05 (5 percent). To say that results are statistically significant is to say that the probability is acceptably small (generally less than 5 percent) that they could be caused by chance alone. All of the results of experiments and correlational studies discussed in this textbook are statistically significant at the .05 level or better.

The Components of a Test of Statistical Significance

16 ◄ How is statistical significance affected by the size of the effect, the number of subjects or observations, and the variability of the scores within each group?

◄ There is no need to present here the precise formulas used to calculate p values for various kinds of research studies, but it is worthwhile to think a bit about the elements that go into such calculations. They are:

1. *The size of the observed effect.* Other things being equal, a large effect is more significant than a small one. For example, the larger the difference found between the mean scores for one group compared to another in an experiment, or the larger the absolute value of the correlation coefficient in a correlational study, the more likely it is that the effect is statistically significant. A large effect is less likely to be caused just by chance than is a small one.

2. *The number of individual subjects or observations in the study.* Other things being equal, the more subjects or observations included in a research study, the more significant are the results. Large samples of data are less distorted by chance than are small samples. The larger the sample, the more accurately an observed mean, or an observed correlation coefficient, reflects the true mean, or correlation coefficient, of the population from which it was drawn. If the number of subjects or observations is huge, then even very small effects will be statistically significant.

3. *The variability of the data within each group.* This element applies to cases in which group means are compared to one another and an index of variability, such as the standard devi-ation, can be calculated for each group. Variability can be thought of as an index of the degree to which uncontrolled, chance factors influence the scores in a set of data. For example, in the experiment assessing treatments for depression, greater variability in the depression scores

"He's charged with expressing contempt for data-processing."

within each treatment group would indicate greater randomness attributable to chance. Other things being equal, the *less* the variability within each group, the more significant the results. If all of the scores within each group are close to the group mean, then even a small difference between the means of different groups may be significant.

In short, a large observed effect, a large number of observations, and a small degree of variability in scores within groups all reduce the likelihood that the effect is due to chance and increase the statistical significance of the results.

Statistical significance tells us that a result probably did not come about by chance, but it does not, by itself, tell us that the result has practical value. Don't confuse statistical significance with practical significance. If I were to test a new weight-loss drug in an experiment that compared 10,000 people taking the drug with a similar number not taking it, I might find a high degree of statistical significance even if the drug produced an average weight loss of only a few ounces (or only a few grams). In that case, most people would agree that, despite the high statistical significance, the drug has no practical significance in a weight-loss program.

SECTION REVIEW

Researchers use statistics to analyze and interpret the results of their studies.

Descriptive Statistics	Inferential Statistics
➤ Descriptive statistics help to summarize sets of data.	➤ Inferential statistics help us assess the likelihood that relationships observed are real and repeatable or due merely to chance.
➤ The central tendency of a set of data can be represented with the mean (the arithmetic average) or the median (the middle score).	➤ Statistically significant results are those in which the observed relationships are very unlikely to be merely the result of chance.
➤ The standard deviation is a measure of variability, the extent to which scores in a set of data differ from the mean.	➤ Researchers calculate a statistic called p, which must generally be .05 or lower (indicating a 5% or lower probability that the results are due to chance) before the results are considered to be statistically significant.
➤ Correlation coefficients represent the strength and direction of a relationship between two numerical variables.	➤ The calculation of a p value takes into account the size of the observed effect, the number of subjects or observations, and the variability of data within each group.

■ Minimizing Bias in Psychological Research

Good scientists strive to minimize both error and bias, especially the latter, in their research. ***Error,*** as a technical term, refers to random variability in results. We've already been talking about error, in the previous section, having to do with random influences that increase the variability of a set of data. Some degree of error is inevitable in psychological research, as a researcher can never precisely control all the extraneous variables that can influence a measure of behavior. The occurrence of error does not imply that the researcher has made a mistake. Individual differences among the research subjects and imperfections in the measure of behavior, for example, contribute inevitably to error. Because error is random, its consequences tend to disappear when averages are calculated, especially when the data set is large. Moreover, researchers can measure error precisely, by calculating the standard deviation, and can take it into account in their inferential statistics. Therefore, error is not a devastating problem in research. But bias *is* a devastating problem. ***Bias,*** as a technical term, refers to nonrandom (directed) effects caused by some factor or factors extraneous to the research hypothesis.

The difference between error and bias can be visualized by thinking of the difference between the sets of bullet holes produced by two men engaged in target practice. One is a novice. He hasn't learned to hold the gun steady, so it wavers

➤ — — — — — — — — — — — — — — — **17**
What is the difference between error and bias, and why is bias the more serious problem?

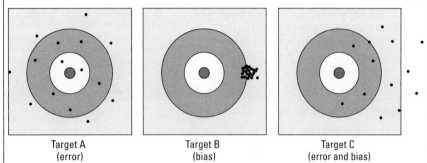

FIGURE 2.4 Error, bias, and both
The difference between error and bias in research is like the difference between the sets of bullet holes produced by a novice shooter (target A) and by a skilled marksman whose rifle sights are misaligned (target B).

randomly as he shoots. The bullets rarely hit the bull's-eye but scatter randomly around it (target A of Figure 2.4). His average shot, calculated as the average geometric location of his entire set of shots, is on or near the bull's-eye, even if few or none of his individual shots are on or near it. The distance between each bullet hole and the bull's-eye in this case exemplifies error. The other man is an experienced marksman, but the sights on his rifle are out of alignment. Because of that defect, all his bullets strike the target some distance to the right of the bull's-eye (target B). Those misses exemplify bias, and they are not correctable by averaging. No matter how many times the man shoots or how carefully he aims, the average location of the whole set of bullet holes will be off the bull's-eye. Of course, error and bias can occur together, as would happen if a novice shooter were given a defective rifle (target C). In that case, the holes would be widely scattered around a center that was some distance away from the bull's-eye.

Bias is a very serious problem in research because statistical techniques cannot identify it or correct for it. Whereas error only reduces the chance that researchers will find statistically significant results (by increasing the variability of the data), bias can lead researchers to the false conclusion that their hypothesis has been supported when, in fact, some factor irrelevant to the hypothesis has caused the observed results. Three types of bias are sampling biases, measurement biases, and expectancy biases.

Avoiding Biased Samples

One source of bias in research has to do with the way in which the individuals to be studied are selected or assigned to groups. If the members of a particular group are initially different, in some systematic way, from those of another group, or are different from the larger population that the researcher is interested in, then that group is a ***biased sample.*** Conducting research with a biased sample is like shooting a rifle whose sights are misaligned. No matter how large the sample, the results will be off target.

18

How can a nonrepresentative selection of research subjects introduce bias into (a) an experiment and (b) a descriptive study?

◄ Suppose that in the experiment on depression (Figure 2.1), the researchers had not randomly assigned the subjects to the different treatments but had allowed them to choose their own. In that case, biased samples could have resulted, because people's choices might have been based on preexisting differences among them. For example, those who felt most motivated to overcome their depression might have been particularly likely to choose the psychotherapy condition. Thus, any greater improvement by those in psychotherapy compared with the others might have resulted not from the psychotherapy but from the preexisting difference in motivation. When subjects are assigned randomly to groups, their individual differences are merely a source of error (and can be taken into account by inferential statistics); but when subjects are not assigned randomly, their differences can be a source of bias as well as error.

A sample is biased when it is not representative of the larger population that the researchers are trying to describe. A classic example of the effect of a biased sample in descriptive research is the *Literary Digest's* poll of U.S. voters in 1936, which led the *Digest* to announce that Alf Landon would beat Franklin D. Roosevelt in the presidential election that year by a margin of 2 to 1 (Huff, 1954). It turned out that the publication's conclusion could not have been more mistaken—Roosevelt won by a landslide. The *Digest* had conducted its poll by telephoning its subscribers. In 1936, in the midst of the Great Depression, people who could afford magazine subscriptions and telephones may indeed have favored Landon, but the great majority of voters, as the election showed, did not.

Avoiding Measurement Bias

Psychological researchers must give careful thought to their measures of behavior. A good measure is reliable and valid. Reliability has to do with measurement error, not bias. A measure is reliable to the degree that it yields similar results each time it is used with a particular subject under a particular set of conditions. Measuring height with a cloth measuring tape is not as reliable as measuring it with a metal measuring tape because the elasticity of the cloth causes the results to vary from one time to the next. A psychological test is not reliable if the scores are greatly affected, in a random manner, by the momentary whims of the research subjects. Because it is a source of error, low reliability decreases the chance of finding statistical significance in a research study.

Validity is an even more critical issue than reliability, because lack of validity can be a source of bias. A measurement procedure is valid if it measures or predicts what it is intended to measure or predict. A procedure may be reliable and yet not be valid. For example, assessing intelligence in adults by measuring thumb length is highly reliable (you would get nearly the same score for a given person each time) but almost certainly not valid (thumb length is almost assuredly unrelated to adult intelligence). This invalid measure exemplifies bias because it would produce false conclusions, such as the conclusion that tall people (who would have longer thumbs) are more intelligent than short people. If common sense tells us that a measurement procedure assesses the intended characteristic, we say the procedure has *face validity*. A test of ability to solve logical problems has face validity as a measure of intelligence, but thumb length does not.

A more certain way to gauge the validity of a measurement procedure is to correlate its scores with another, more direct index of the characteristic that we wish to measure or predict. In that case, the more direct index is called the *criterion,* and the validity is called *criterion validity*. Suppose, for example, that I defined intelligence as the quality of mind that allows a person to achieve greatness in any of various realms, including business, diplomacy, science, literature, and art. With this definition, I might use the actual achievement of such greatness as my criterion for intelligence. I might identify a group of people who have achieved such greatness and a group who, despite similar environmental opportunities, have not, and assess the degree to which they differ on various potential measures of intelligence. The more the two groups differ on any of the measures, the greater the correlation between that measure and my criterion for intelligence, and the more valid the test. As you can see from this example, the assessment of validity requires a clear definition of the characteristic to be measured or predicted. If your definition of intelligence differs from mine, you will choose a different criterion from mine for assessing the validity of possible intelligence tests.

As another illustration of how an invalid measure can bias a research study, think once more about the study of depression (Figure 2.1). Suppose that the interview procedure used in the study was not a valid measure of depression but actually measured subjects' desire to appear depressed or not. In that case, the results would still be statistically significant, but the researchers' conclusion (that treatment affects depression) would be mistaken. A more accurate conclusion would be that some treatments lead to a stronger desire to appear not depressed than do others.

19

What is the difference between the reliability and the validity of a measurement procedure? How can lack of validity contribute to bias?

"The drug has, however, proved more effective than traditional psychoanalysis."

20

How can the validity of a measurement procedure be assessed?

Avoiding Biases from Observers' and Subjects' Expectancies

Being human, researchers inevitably have wishes and expectations that can affect how they behave and what they observe when recording data. The resulting biases are called ***observer-expectancy effects.*** A researcher who desires or expects a subject to respond in a particular way may unintentionally communicate that expectation and thereby influence the subject's behavior. As you recall, Pfungst discovered that this sort of effect provided the entire basis for Clever Hans's apparent ability to answer questions. That episode occurred nearly a century ago, but the power of observer expectancies to delude us is as strong today as ever. A dramatic example concerns a technique designed to enable people with autism to communicate.

The Facilitated-Communication Debacle

21

How can the supposed phenomenon of facilitated communication by people with autism be explained as an observer-expectancy effect?

Autism is a congenital (present at birth) disorder of development, characterized by a deficit in the ability to form emotional bonds and to communicate with other people. Some people with autism fail almost completely to develop either spoken or written language. Some years ago, in the prestigious *Harvard Educational Review,* Douglas Biklen (1990) described an apparently remarkable discovery, made originally by Rosemary Crossley in Australia. The discovery was that people with severe autism, who had previously shown almost no language ability, could type meaningful statements with one finger on a keyboard. They could answer questions intelligently, describe their feelings, display humor, and write emotionally moving poetry by typing. To do this, however, a "facilitator" had to help by holding the typing hand and finger of the autistic person. According to Crossley and Biklen, the handholding was needed to calm the person, to keep the typing hand steady, and to prevent repeated typing of the same letter. (People with autism tend to repeat their actions.)

The community concerned with autism—including special educators and parents of autistic children—responded with great excitement to this apparent discovery. It is difficult emotionally to care for and work with people who don't communicate their thoughts and feelings; it takes enormous dedication. You can imagine the thrill that parents and teachers felt when their autistic children typed, for the first time, something like "I love you." The motivation to believe in this new method was enormous. Workshops were held to teach people to be facilitators, and thousands of teachers and parents learned the technique. By 1993, over $100 million a year was being spent by the U.S. educational system on equipment and personnel for facilitated communication (Levine & others, 1994).

Who is typing the message? In the technique of facilitated communication, a facilitator holds the hand of the disabled person in order to "help" that person type a message on a keyboard. Experiments have shown that when this technique is used with autistic individuals, it is the facilitator, not the autistic person, who composes the message and controls the typing, even though the facilitator is not conscious of doing so.

Yet, from the beginning, there were skeptics. The credulity of some was strained by the sudden appearance of literary skills and erudition in people who had never previously shown evidence that they could read, write, speak, or understand much of what others said. As an alternative theory, the skeptics proposed that the messages were not communications from the autistic persons but unconscious creations of the facilitators (Dillon, 1993; Levine & others, 1994). The skeptics suggested that hand movements, made unconsciously by the facilitator, guided the autistic person's finger to the keys. Consistent with this view, some skeptics noticed that the autistic persons often did not even look at the keyboard as they ostensibly did their typing, while the facilitators always looked. The issue soon became important for moral and legal reasons as well as educational and scientific ones. Some autistic children, working with facilitators, typed out messages that accused parents or other caregivers of sexually abusing them (Bligh & Kupperman, 1993; Heckler, 1994). Could facilitated messages be used by child-welfare authorities as a basis for taking a child from a parent?

Partly in response to ensuing court cases, many experiments were performed in the 1990s to test whether facilitated messages are creations of the autistic person or of the facilitator. In a typical experiment, pairs consisting of a facilitator and an autistic person, chosen because of their experience working together and their putative skill at the technique, were tested under two conditions. In one condition, the item of information that the autistic person was asked to communicate was also shown to the facilitator, and in the other condition it was not. For example, the autistic person might be shown a picture of a common object and asked to type the name of that object, under conditions in which the facilitator either saw the object or did not. The inevitable result was that many correct responses were typed in the first condition (in which the facilitator was shown what the autistic person was shown), but not in the second condition. When the facilitator did not know what the autistic person was shown, the number of correct responses was no more than what would be produced by random guessing (Jacobson & others, 1995; Mostert, 2001). Subsequent research revealed directly that, in fact, facilitators unconsciously control the other person's hand movements (Wegner & others, 2003). It does not feel to them that they are creating the messages and controlling the typing, even though they are.

The original observers of facilitated communication, who were also the original facilitators, were deluded by a powerful effect of their own expectations. To understand that effect, imagine that you are a facilitator who truly believes that the autistic person you are helping can type meaningful messages. At any given time during the facilitation, you have some idea in mind (perhaps unconsciously) of what the autistic person is trying to type and what letter should come next. Your expectation that a particular letter will be typed next leads you to feel that the autistic person's finger is moving toward that letter on the keyboard, so you experience yourself as merely "facilitating" that movement, when you are actually guiding it and creating it.

Avoiding Observer-Expectancy Effects in Typical Experiments

In the experiments testing the validity of facilitated communication, the influence of observer expectancy was the focus of study and was assessed by varying the observers' (in this case, the facilitators') knowledge about what was supposed to be communicated. In a more typical psychological experiment, the objective is not to study observer-expectancy effects, but to eliminate them in order to observe other effects without this form of bias.

Suppose you are conducting an experiment to test the hypothesis that subjects given treatment A will smile more than those given treatment B. Your expectation of more smiling by the former than the latter might cause you, unconsciously, to behave differently toward the two groups of subjects, in ways that could produce the results you expect. For example, you might unconsciously smile more yourself at the A subjects than at the B subjects, causing them to smile more in return. In that case, you would end up believing that treatment A caused the increased smiling, when in fact it was your own smiling that caused it.

In addition to influencing subjects' behavior, observers' expectations can influence observers' perceptions or judgments concerning that behavior. In the smiling experiment, for example, your expectation to see more smiles in one condition than in another might lead you to interpret ambiguous facial expressions as smiles in the one condition and as something else in the other.

The best way to prevent observer-expectancy effects is to keep the observer *blind*—that is, uninformed—about those aspects of the study's design that could lead him or her to form potentially biasing expectations. Thus, in a between-groups experiment, a blind observer would not be told which subjects received which treatment, so the observer would have no basis for expecting particular subjects to behave differently from other subjects. In our hypothetical experiment on smiling, you, as the blind observer, would not know who got which treatment, so you would have no basis for knowing which subjects "should" smile more or less than others. In DiMascio's study of treatments for depression (illustrated in Figure 2.1), the clinicians who evaluated the patients' depression at the end of the treatment period were blind to treatment condition. To keep them blind, patients were instructed not to say anything about their treatment during the evaluation interviews.

Avoiding Subject-Expectancy Effects

Subjects also have expectations. If different treatments in an experiment induce different expectations in subjects, then those expectations, rather than anything else about the treatments, may account for observed differences in how the subjects

> ----------------22
> **What are two ways by which an observer's expectations can bias results in a typical experiment? How does blind observation prevent such bias?**

> ----------------23
> **How can subjects' expectancies bias the results of an experiment? How does a double-blind procedure control both subjects' and observers' expectancies?**

respond. Effects of this sort are called **subject-expectancy effects.** For example, people who take a drug may subsequently behave or feel a certain way simply because they believe that the drug causes such a behavior or feeling. Similarly, subjects who receive psychotherapy may improve simply because they believe that psychotherapy will help them.

Ideally, to prevent bias from subject expectancy, subjects should be kept blind about the treatment they are receiving. Any experiment in which both the observer and the subjects are kept blind in this way is called a **double-blind experiment.** In double-blind drug experiments, for example, some subjects receive the drug while others receive a **placebo,** an inactive substance that looks like the drug, and neither the subjects nor the observers know who received the drug and who did not. Consequently, any observed difference between those who got the drug and those who did not must be due to the drug's chemical qualities, not to the subjects' or observers' expectancies.

Subjects cannot always be kept blind concerning their treatment. For instance, it is impossible to administer psychotherapy to people without their knowing it. As a partial control in some psychotherapy experiments, subjects in the nonpsychotherapy group are given a fake form of therapy designed to induce subject expectancies equivalent to those induced by actual psychotherapy. In DiMascio's depression experiment described earlier, subjects were not blind about their treatment. Those in the nondrug groups did not receive a placebo, and those in the nonpsychotherapy groups did not receive fake psychotherapy. The results depicted in Figure 2.1 might possibly, therefore, be placebo effects, that is, subject-expectancy effects caused by subjects' beliefs that the treatment would help them. Other experiments (discussed in Chapter 17) have shown that placebos can indeed reduce depression (Kirsch & others, 2002).

SECTION REVIEW

Bias—nonrandom effects caused by extraneous factors—must be avoided.

Biased Samples	Measurement Error and Bias	Expectancy Effects
➤ Unless subjects in a between-groups experiment are assigned to groups randomly, an observed difference in the dependent variable may be caused by systematic a priori differences between the groups rather than by the independent variable.	➤ A good measure is reliable—able to yield similar results with repeated use on the same subjects in the same conditions.	➤ A researcher's expectations about a study's results can influence those results. This is observer-expectancy bias.
	➤ An unreliable measure leads to error—random variability that makes it harder to establish statistical significance.	➤ Subjects' expectations as to how they should respond can also influence results. This is subject-expectancy bias.
➤ If the subjects in any type of study are not representative of the group to which the researcher wants to generalize, false conclusions may be drawn.	➤ A good measure is also valid—able to measure what it is intended to measure. Invalid measures are sources of bias.	➤ Such expectancy effects can occur without intention or even awareness.
	➤ A measure that seems valid on the basis of common sense has face validity. A measure that correlates significantly with another, more direct measure of the variable has criterion validity.	➤ In observer-blind studies, the observer is deliberately kept ignorant of information that could create expectancies. In double-blind studies, observers and subjects are kept ignorant of such information.

▌ Ethical Issues in Psychological Research

Psychologists must consider ethical as well as scientific issues in designing their studies. DiMascio and his colleagues could, from a scientific vantage point, have improved their study of treatments for depression by using a placebo in the nondrug conditions and a fake form of psychotherapy in the nonpsychotherapy conditions to reduce differences among the groups in subject expectancies. But the researchers felt that their subjects should know which form of treatment they were getting, so that they could make an informed decision about whether or not to participate and could understand any side effects that might arise as treatment progressed.

Research with Humans

In research with humans, ethical considerations revolve around three interrelated issues:

24
What are the ethical concerns pertaining to privacy, discomfort, deception, and animal welfare in psychological research? How do researchers strive to minimize problems related to these concerns?

1. *The person's right to privacy.* Common safeguards to protect privacy include obtaining informed consent from subjects before they take part, informing subjects that they do not have to share any information about themselves that they do not wish to share, and keeping reports and records in ways that ensure anonymity.

2. *The possibility of discomfort or harm.* If a planned research study involves some risk of discomfort or harm to subjects, researchers are obliged to determine whether the same question can be answered in a study that involves less risk. If the answer is no, a determination must be made that the risk is minimal and is outweighed by the human benefits of the study. In addition, in any research study, human subjects must be advised that they are free to quit at any time. (In reality, the great majority of psychological studies involve completely harmless procedures, such as reading rapidly flashed letters, memorizing lists of terms, or carrying on a discussion with other research participants.)

3. *The use of deception.* This is the most controversial ethical issue in human psychological research. In a minority of experiments, the independent variable involves a lie. Subjects may be falsely told or led to believe that something is happening, or is going to happen, so that the researcher can study the effects of that belief. Some psychologists are opposed to all use of deception. They argue that deception (a) is intrinsically unethical and (b) undermines the possibility of obtaining truly informed consent (Carroll & others, 1985). Others, however, justify some use of deception on the grounds that some psychological processes cannot be studied effectively without it. These psychologists contend, further, that research deception usually takes the form of benign "white lies," which are cleared up when the researcher informs the subjects of the true nature of the study after the session has ended (Benham, 2008). They also point out that informed consent can still be obtained by telling subjects about any realistic dangers they will face and by telling them that some details of the study must be withheld until the data have been collected.

Research with Animals

The use of nonhuman animals in research presents another area of ethical controversy. Most people agree that some procedures that would be unethical to use with humans can be used ethically with other animal species. One can breed animals in controlled ways, raise them in controlled environments, and surgically intervene in their physiology for research purposes. Basic biological mechanisms underlying animal behavior are similar to those underlying human behavior, so such research contributes to our understanding of humans as well as the species studied. Still, research on nonhuman animals can sometimes cause them to suffer, and any researcher who employs animals as subjects has an ethical obligation to balance the animals' suffering against the potential benefits of the research. Animals must be well cared for and not subjected to unnecessary deprivation or pain.

Some people question whether subjecting animals to pain or deprivation for research purposes is ever justifiable. But others, pointing to the enormous gains in knowledge and the reduction in human (and animal) suffering that have come from such research, have turned the ethical question around. In the words of one (Miller, 1986): "Is it morally justifiable to prolong human (and animal) suffering in order to reduce suffering by experimental animals?"

A rat with an electrode in its brain Experiments in behavioral neuroscience frequently involve operations on animal brains. For scientific as well as ethical reasons, conscientious researchers are scrupulous about minimizing discomfort to the animals. Discomfort can produce behaviors that interfere with those that the researcher wishes to study.

Joel Gordon

Formal Principles and Safeguards for Ethical Research

The American Psychological Association (2002) has established a set of ethical principles for psychological research, which researchers must follow if they are to publish their results in the research journals of that association. Moreover, in the United States, Canada, and many other countries, publicly funded research institutions are required by law to establish ethics review panels, whose task is to evaluate all proposed research studies that have any potential for ethical controversy. Such panels often turn down research proposals that once were regarded as quite acceptable. A few studies that are now considered classics and are cited in most general psychology textbooks, including this one, would not be approved today. As you read about the studies in the chapters that follow, questions of ethics may well occur to you from time to time. Such questions are always legitimate, as are those about the scientific merit of a study's design and the interpretation of its results. Psychology needs and usually welcomes people who raise those questions.

SECTION REVIEW

Psychologists must deal with ethical concerns in conducting research.

Human Subjects	Animal Subjects
➤ A human subject's right to privacy must be protected.	➤ Many procedures that would be unethical with humans—such as controlled breeding and surgical interventions—are performed with animals.
➤ The risk of discomfort or harm to human subjects must be minimal.	➤ The benefits of the knowledge gained from such research are the primary ethical justification for them, since common biological mechanisms often enable us to apply findings from animal studies to humans.
➤ Deceiving subjects about some aspect of a study is both common and controversial.	
➤ Routine measures to protect subjects include obtaining informed consent, letting subjects know they can quit at any time, ensuring anonymity in results, and debriefing subjects about deception after the study ends.	➤ Animals used in research must be well cared for, must not suffer unnecessary deprivation or pain, and must have their suffering balanced against the potential value of the knowledge gained.

Concluding Thoughts

As you review and think about the concepts in this chapter, you might think also about the following two questions.

1. How does science compare with everyday observation and thought? No sharp dividing line exists between science and the kinds of observation and thought that all of us use every day to learn about the world around us. In our everyday learning, we begin with the data of our senses and use those data to draw tentative conclusions (make inferences) about specific aspects of our world. For example, we might one day observe someone from town X acting politely and someone from town Y acting rudely and infer from those observations that people from X are more polite than people from Y. Most of us make such inferences all the time, often on scarcely more evidence than that. Science is simply the attempt to improve on our natural ways of learning by systematizing the data-collection procedures, controlling conditions to be more certain about which variables are having which effects, striving to eliminate sources of bias, deliberately thinking

of alternative explanations, and using statistical procedures to assess the degree of confidence we should have in our tentative conclusions.

As you review each of the main concepts discussed in the sections on research strategies, statistical methods, and sources of bias in this chapter, you might think about how that concept applies—somewhat less formally—to the distinctions between good and poor observation and thought in everyday life. We are observing and thinking poorly when we draw firm conclusions from too little evidence, or neglect to think about alternative explanations, or fail to see what is really there because of our biased expectations.

2. What is a science of psychology for? I remember, as a college freshman on my first visit home, expressing pride about an *A* that I had received in calculus. My mother, hearing me boast and having a knack for fostering humility and putting things into perspective, asked a simple question: "What is calculus for?"

I was floored. I could rattle off terms and equations about calculus, and I could solve the problems as they were given to me in the class, but I had no understanding at all of what calculus was for. Perhaps that is why, by a few months after the class had ended, I had completely forgotten the terms, the equations, and the way to solve them. So what is a science of psychology for?

Some people think of psychology purely in applied terms, as a means of solving human problems. These people are likely to appreciate the study on treatments for depression (illustrated in Figure 2.1) but are less likely to appreciate research motivated by simple curiosity rather than by pragmatic concerns. The issue of pragmatism occurs in other sciences as well. What good does it do us to know what the other side of the moon looks like?

For the most part, people go into psychological research, or any other research field, because they are curious or because they are thrilled by the prospect of being the first to uncover some mystery of nature, large or small. So psychology, like any other science, has two purposes: to solve practical problems and to satisfy the human quest for knowledge. It is hard to separate the two, however, because research done solely to satisfy curiosity very often reveals solutions to practical problems that at first seemed unrelated to the research. As you read the remaining chapters of this book, I hope you will allow yourself to become engaged by the questions for their own sake, regardless of whether you think they have practical applications. Each chapter contains mysteries—some solved, some not.

Further Reading

Randolph A. Smith & Stephen F. Davis (2007). *The psychologist as detective: An introduction to conducting research in psychology* (4th ed.). Upper Saddle River, NJ: Prentice-Hall.

By presenting the research psychologist as a detective, and by giving many examples of the solving of psychological mysteries, this book enlivens the often-dry stuff of research methodology. It deals with all aspects of the research process: forming hypotheses or questions, using the library, designing research studies, considering ethical issues, analyzing and graphing data, and writing reports.

Keith E. Stanovich (2007). *How to think straight about psychology* (8th ed.). Boston: Allyn & Bacon.

This fun-to-read book deals with popular misconceptions about psychological phenomena, the faulty uses of evidence and logic that lead to such misconceptions, and the processes through which enduring psychological knowledge has been developed. The author's goal, well achieved, is to help readers acquire the tools needed for critical thinking in psychology.

Darrell Huff (1954). *How to lie with statistics.* New York: Norton.

This witty paperback, filled with anecdotes and cartoons, has a serious message. It tells you how not to lie with statistics and how to spot lies when they occur. It is guaranteed to make you a more critical consumer of statistical information. Don't be put off by the publication date; the book is reprinted regularly and is widely available.

Terence Hines (2003). *Pseudoscience and the paranormal* (2nd ed.). Amherst, NY: Prometheus Books.

This is a book about the "evidence," faulty reasoning, and (in some cases) trickery that lead many people to believe in phenomena that violate our normal expectations of how the world works. Among the beliefs discussed are those concerning psychic readings, prophetic dreams, astrology, biorhythm theory, ESP, psychokinesis, UFOs, alien abductions, faith healing, psychic surgery, certain forms of pseudo-psychotherapy, facilitated communication, and water dowsing. Central to the book is the idea of an unfalsifiable theory, a theory or belief stated in such a way that it cannot be proved wrong. With such a theory, any evidence that would seem to contradict it is discounted.

John Ruscio (2006). *Critical thinking in psychology: Separating sense from nonsense* (2nd ed.). Belmont, CA: Thompson/Wadsworth.

This is a fascinating book about pop psychology's many myths, and about the social pressures, faulty reasoning, and pseudoscientific "evidence" that promote such myths. It is well designed to empower readers to think for themselves, to question the evidence, and to be especially skeptical of claims that defy common sense. In the final chapter, Ruscio summarizes his suggestions for critical thinking, including "beware of wishful thinking," "don't be misled by testimonials," "keep in touch with reality," "remember that correlation does not imply causation," "challenge conspiracy theories," and "take advantage of the power of statistical decision making."

PART 2

The Adaptiveness of Behavior

We are the products of our genes and our environments. Our genes have been shaped by millions of years of evolution, adapting us to the general conditions of human life on earth. Through this process, we have acquired, among other things, an immense capacity to learn. In this unit, Chapter 3 examines the role of genes and evolution in the production of the underlying mechanisms of behavior, and Chapter 4 deals with basic processes of learning, through which an individual's behavior is constantly modified to meet the unique conditions of that person's life.

Genetic and Evolutionary Foundations of Behavior

3

Have you ever stood before a chimpanzee enclosure at a zoo and watched for a while? If you haven't, I urge you to seize the next opportunity to do so. It is impossible, I think, to look for long without sensing strongly the animal's kinship to us. Its facial expressions, its curiosity, even its sense of humor, are so like ours that we intuitively see it as a hairy, long-armed cousin. Indeed, the chimpanzee *is* our cousin. It is—along with the bonobo, a chimp-like ape discussed later in this chapter—one of our two closest animal relatives. Geneticists have lined up the DNA molecules of chimpanzees against those of humans and found that they match at 98.8 percent of their individual base units (Cryanoski, 2002). In genetic material, you and I are just 1.2 percent different from a chimpanzee. Language and culture, and the knowledge these have given us, have in some ways separated us markedly from our cousins. But in our genes—and in our basic drives, emotions, perceptual processes, and ways of learning—we are kin not just to chimpanzees, but in varying degrees to all of the mammals, and in lesser degrees to other animals as well.

Nearly 150 years ago, in *The Origin of Species,* Charles Darwin (1859/1963) presented a theory of evolution that explains both the similarities and the differences among the animal species. According to Darwin, all species are to varying degrees similar to one another because of common ancestry, and all species are to some degree unique because natural selection has adapted each species to the unique aspects of the environment in which it lives and reproduces. Darwin presented massive amounts of evidence for his theory, and essentially everything that scientists have learned since, about our own and other species, is consistent with it.

This chapter is primarily about the application of evolutionary theory to the behavior of humans and other animals. It is also the first of a two-chapter sequence on the *adaptiveness of behavior*. Adaptation refers to modification to meet changed life circumstances. Evolution is the long-term adaptive process, spanning generations, that equips each species for life in its ever-changing natural habitat. The next chapter is on learning, a set of shorter-term adaptive processes that occur within the life span of each individual. The mechanisms that permit learning to occur are themselves products of evolution.

Darwin developed his theory of evolution without any knowledge of genes, but the theory is best understood today in the light of such knowledge. Therefore, the chapter begins with a discussion of basic genetic mechanisms and their implications for the inheritance of behavioral characteristics. With that as background, the rest of the chapter is concerned with the evolution of behavior and with ways in which we can learn about our own behavior by comparing it to that of our animal relatives. Among other things, we shall examine patterns of mating, aggression, and helping, in our species and in others, from an evolutionary perspective.

◼ Review of Basic Genetic Mechanisms

You have almost certainly studied the mechanisms of gene action and reproduction in a biology course at one time or another, so I will not go into detail on these processes here. But a brief review of them, focused on their implications for psychology, may be useful.

How Genes Affect Behavior

1

How can genes affect behavioral traits through their role in protein synthesis?

Sometimes, as a sort of shorthand (which I will use occasionally in this book), researchers speak of genes "for" particular behavioral traits. For example, they might speak of genes *for* singing ability, *for* aggression, or *for* cooperation. But genes never produce or control behavior directly. All the effects that genes have on behavior occur through their role in building and modifying the physical structures of the body. Those structures, interacting with the environment, produce behavior. Thus, a gene might influence singing ability by promoting the development of a brain system that analyzes sounds or by promoting certain physical aspects of the vocal cords. Similarly, a gene might affect aggressiveness by fostering the growth of brain systems that organize aggressive behavior in response to irritating stimuli. In a sense, all genes that contribute to the body's development are "for" behavior, since all parts of the body are involved in behavior. Especially relevant for behavior, however, are genes that contribute to the development of sensory systems, motor systems (muscles and other organs involved in movement), and, most especially, the nervous system (which includes the brain).

Genes Provide the Codes for Proteins

Genes affect the body's development through, and only through, their influence on the production of protein molecules. We are what we are, biologically speaking, because of our proteins. A class of proteins called *structural proteins* forms the structure of every cell of the body. Another, much larger class called *enzymes* controls the rate of every chemical reaction in every cell.

Physically, genes are components of extremely long molecules of a substance called DNA (deoxyribonucleic acid). These molecules exist in the egg and sperm cells that join to form a new individual, and they replicate themselves during each cell division in the course of the body's growth and development. A replica of your whole unique set of DNA molecules exists in the nucleus of each of your body's cells, where it serves to code for and regulate the production of protein molecules.

Each protein molecule consists of a long chain of smaller molecules called amino acids. A single protein molecule may contain anywhere from several hundred up to many thousand amino acids in its chain. There are a total of 20 distinct amino acids, which can be arranged in countless sequences to form different protein molecules. Some portions of the DNA in your cells serve as templates (that is, as molds or patterns) for producing another molecular substance called RNA (ribonucleic acid), which in turn serves as a template for producing protein molecules. One definition of the gene, which until quite recently was the most common definition, is that it is a segment of a DNA molecule that contains the code that dictates the particular sequence of amino acids for a single type of protein. With that definition, geneticists have determined that human beings (and also chimpanzees and mice) have about 30,000 genes (Tecott, 2003).

Recent molecular work has led many geneticists to change their definition of a gene, so that it includes portions of DNA that have other functions, not just the coding of protein molecules (Gerstein & others, 2007). We now know that most of the DNA in human cells does not code for proteins. Some of this non-coding DNA is called "junk DNA," because it is passed along from generation to generation without having any apparent effect at all on the body's development. But much of the non-coding DNA serves a vital role in regulating the activity of the coding DNA. Geneticists now distinguish between *coding genes,* which code for unique protein molecules, and *regulatory genes,* which work through various biological means to help activate or suppress specific coding genes and thereby influence the body's development. Recent research comparing human and chimpanzee DNA suggests that the biggest genetic differences between the two species lie in certain regulatory genes that affect the development of the brain (Prabhakar & others, 2006; Smith, 2006).

Genes Work Only Through Interaction with the Environment

At every level, from biochemical to behavioral, the effects of genes are entwined with the effects of the environment. *Environment,* as used in this context, refers to every aspect of an individual and his or her surroundings except the genes themselves. It includes the nourishing womb and maternal bloodstream before birth; the internal chemical environment of the individual; and all the events, objects, and other individuals encountered after birth. Foods—a part of the environment—supply genes with amino acids, which are needed to manufacture proteins. Environmental effects also help to turn genes "on" and "off," resulting in bodily changes that alter the individual's behavioral capacity. Such changes can occur in adulthood as well as earlier in development. For example, physical exercise modifies the chemical environment of muscle cells in a way that activates genes that promote further growth of the muscle. One's body and behavioral capacities result from a continuous, complex interplay between genes and environment (see Figure 3.1). In no sense is one more basic than the other.

> **2**
>
> What does it mean to say that genes can influence behavioral traits only through interaction with the environment? How, in general, are genes involved in long-term behavioral changes that derive from experience?

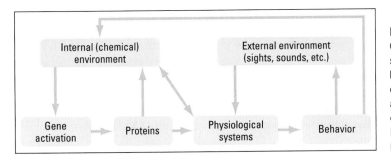

FIGURE 3.1 Route through which genes affect behavior Genes build proteins, which form or alter the body's physiological systems (including brain systems), which, in turn, produce behavior. Each step in this process involves interaction with the environment. Aspects of the internal environment control gene activation, and aspects of both the internal and the external environments act on physiological systems to control behavior. Behavior, in turn, can affect gene activation through direct and indirect effects on the internal environment.

Researchers have begun to learn about specific mechanisms through which experiences can activate genes and thereby alter the individual's brain and behavior. One well-studied example has to do with parental behavior in mice and rats. Adult mice and rats that have not given birth will normally avoid newborns of their species that are placed in their cage. However, if exposed to newborns continuously for several hours or more, they gradually begin to care for them. This change in behavior involves the environmental induction of gene activity (Brown & others, 1996; Numan, 2007). The sight, sound, or smell of newborns activates a particular gene. The activated gene produces a protein molecule that stimulates activity in a specific cluster of brain cells that are known to be crucial for the motivation and organization of such behaviors as retrieving young to a nest and hovering over them. The result is that a mouse or rat that previously did not take care of young is transformed into a mouse or rat that does.

There is good reason to believe that all sorts of prolonged behavioral effects that derive from experience, including those that we call "learning," involve the activation of genes (Johnston & Edwards, 2002). The experience activates genes, which produce proteins, which in turn alter the function of some of the neural circuits in the brain and thereby change the manner in which the individual behaves. More about this is discussed in Chapter 5.

Distinction Between Genotype and Phenotype

3.
How can the same genotype produce various phenotypes?

◀ Geneticists use the term *genotype* to refer to the set of genes that the individual inherits and the term *phenotype* to refer to the observable properties of the body and behavioral traits. The same genes can have different effects, depending on the environment and the mix of other genes. Two individuals with the same genotype can be quite different in phenotype as a result of differences in their environments. Genetically identical rats will differ phenotypically in their behavior toward infant rats if one has been previously exposed to infant rats and the other has not. Genetically identical human twins will differ in size if they have been exposed differently to growth-promoting factors in their environments (see Figure 3.2), and they will differ in behavior if they have been subjected to different learning experiences.

FIGURE 3.2 Identical twins These 13-year-old girls have the same genotype, but they obviously differ in at least one aspect of their phenotype. It is uncertain what caused this difference. It may have derived from their occupying different positions in the womb such that one received more early nutrition than the other, which activated genes promoting more growth.

Van Bucher/Photo Researchers

How Genes Are Passed Along in Sexual Reproduction

Genes not only provide the codes for building proteins; they also serve as the biological units of heredity. They are replicated and passed along from parents to offspring, and they are the cause of offsprings' resemblance to parents.

To understand how genes are passed along in sexual reproduction, it is useful to know something about their arrangement within cells. The genetic material (strands of DNA) exists in each cell in structures called *chromosomes,* which are usually dispersed throughout the cell nucleus and are not visible. Just prior to cell division, however, the chromosomes condense into compact forms that can be stained, viewed through a microscope, and photographed. The normal human cell has 23 pairs of chromosomes. Twenty-two of these are true pairs in both the male and the female, in the sense that each chromosome looks like its mate and contains similar genes (discussed later). The remaining pair is made up of the sex chromosomes. In the normal human male cell, that "pair" consists of a large chromosome labeled X and a small chromosome labeled Y (see Figure 3.3). Genetically, the only difference between the sexes is that females have two X chromosomes (XX—a true pair) rather than the XY of the male.

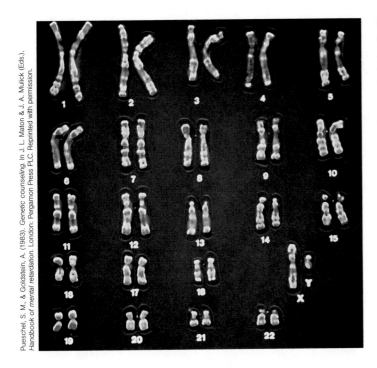

FIGURE 3.3 Chromosomes of a normal human male cell The 22 numbered pairs of chromosomes are the same in a normal female cell as they are in a normal male cell. The remaining two, labeled X and Y, are the sex chromosomes. The normal human female cell (not shown) has a second X chromosome instead of a Y.

The Production of Genetically Diverse Egg and Sperm Cells

When cells divide to produce new cells *other than* egg or sperm cells, they do so by a process called **mitosis.** In mitosis, each chromosome precisely replicates itself and then the cell divides, with one copy of each chromosome moving into each of the two cell nuclei thus formed. Because of the faithful copying of genetic material in mitosis, all your body's cells, except your egg or sperm cells, are genetically identical to one another. The differences among different cells in your body—such as muscle cells and skin cells—arise from the differential activation of their genes, not from different gene content.

When cells divide to produce egg or sperm cells, they do so by a different process, called **meiosis,** which results in cells that are not genetically alike (depicted in Figure 3.4). During meiosis, each chromosome replicates itself once, but then the cell divides twice. Before the first cell division, the chromosomes of each pair line up next to one another and exchange genetic material in a random manner. Although the

> 4
> **How does meiosis produce egg or sperm cells that are all genetically different from one another?**

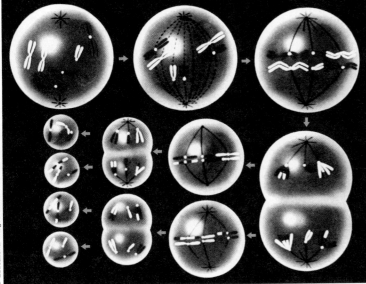

FIGURE 3.4 Schematic illustration of meiosis in sperm production This illustration is for a creature that has only three pairs of chromosomes rather than the 23 pairs that humans have. At the beginning (top left), each chromosome has already replicated itself and remains attached to its replica. The pairs of replicated chromosomes (one blue and one white in each pair in the diagram) then line up next to one another and exchange genetic material through a process called *crossing over.* The cell then divides twice, resulting in four sperm cells, each with just one member of each pair of chromosomes. Notice that each sperm cell is genetically different from the others, having a different mix of the original (blue and white) material from the parental pairs of chromosomes. The diagram greatly oversimplifies the effects of crossing over. In fact, each chromosome would cross over many times with its paired mate, resulting in a random mixing of genetic material. Meiosis in egg production is similar to that in sperm production, but only one of the two cells produced at each division survives.

chromosomes in each pair look the same, they do not contain precisely the same genes. The result of this random exchange of genetic material and of the subsequent cell divisions is that each egg or sperm cell produced is genetically different from any other egg or sperm cell and contains only half of the full number of chromosomes (one member of each of the 23 pairs).

The Genetic Diversity of Offspring

It may seem ironic that the very cells you use for "reproduction" are the only cells in your body that cannot, in theory, reproduce you. They are the only cells in your body that do not have all your genes. In sexual reproduction you are, of course, not really reproducing yourself. Rather, you are creating a genetically unique individual who has half of your genes and half of your partner's. When a sperm and an egg unite, the result is a single new cell, the **zygote,** which contains the full complement of 23 paired chromosomes. One member of each of these pairs comes from each parent. The zygote then grows, through mitosis, eventually to become a new person. Because each sperm or egg is different from any other sperm or egg (even from the same parent), each zygote is different from any other.

5
What is the advantage of producing genetically diverse offspring?

◀ The value of sex, as opposed to simple cloning (the asexual production of genetically identical offspring), apparently lies in the production of genetically diverse offspring. In a world where the environment keeps changing, genes have a better chance of surviving if they are rearranged at each generation in many different ways, to produce different kinds of bodies, than if they are all put into the same kind of body. This is an almost literal example of the old saying, "Don't put all your eggs in the same basket." By producing diverse offspring, parents are reducing the chance that all of their offspring will die as a result of some unforeseen change in the environment. In Chapter 15, you will see how this idea—that there is value in genetic diversity—may apply in the realm of human personality.

The only people who are genetically identical to each other are **identical twins.** They are formed when two bundles of cells separate from each other during the early mitotic divisions following the formation of a zygote. Because they originate from one zygote, identical twins are also known as *monozygotic twins.* **Fraternal twins,** or *dizygotic twins,* originate from two zygotes, each formed from different egg and sperm cells. Fraternal twins are no more or less similar to each other genetically than are any two non-twin siblings. In later chapters (especially Chapter 10), you will see how psychologists make use of twins in research aimed at understanding how much of the variability among people, in certain psychological traits, results from differences in their genes and how much results from differences in their environments.

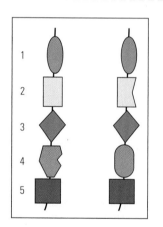

FIGURE 3.5 Schematic illustration of gene loci on a pair of chromosomes Successive genes are depicted here as beads on a string. This pair of chromosomes is *homozygous* at loci 1, 3, and 5 (the paired genes there are identical to each other) and *heterozygous* at loci 2 and 4 (the paired genes there are not identical to each other). Nonidentical genes that can occupy the same locus on a pair of chromosomes are referred to as alleles of each other. Thus the two genes at locus 2 are alleles, as are the two at locus 4.

Consequences of the Fact That Genes Come in Pairs

You have seen that genes exist on long DNA strands in chromosomes, rather like beads on a string, and that chromosomes come in pairs. The two genes that occupy the same **locus** (location) on a pair of chromosomes are sometimes identical to each other and sometimes not. When they are identical, the individual is said to be **homozygous** [home-oh-**zai**-gus] at that locus, and when they are not identical, the individual is said to be **heterozygous** [het-er-oh-**zai**-gus] at that locus (see Figure 3.5). Different genes that can occupy the same locus, and thus can potentially pair with each other, are referred to as **alleles.**

6
What is the difference between a dominant and a recessive gene (or allele)?

◀ For example, a gene for brown eyes and a gene for blue eyes in humans are alleles because they can occupy the same locus. If you are homozygous for brown eyes, you have two copies of a gene that manufactures an enzyme that makes your eyes brown. What if you were heterozygous for eye color, with one copy of the allele for brown eyes and one copy for blue eyes? In this case, you would have brown eyes, no different from the eye color you would have if you were homozygous for brown eyes. This effect is described by saying that the allele for brown eyes is *dominant* and the one for blue eyes is *recessive.* A **dominant** gene (or allele) is one that will produce its observable effects in either the homozygous or the heterozygous condition, and a **recessive** gene (or allele) is one that will produce its effects in the homozygous condition only. But not all pairs of alleles manifest dominance or recessiveness. Some pairs blend their effects. For example, if you cross red four-o'clocks (a kind of flower) with white four-o'clocks, the offspring will be pink, because neither the red nor the white allele is dominant over the other.

Mendelian Pattern of Heredity

The idea that the units of heredity come in pairs and that one member of a pair can be dominant over the other was developed in the mid-nineteenth century by an Austrian monk named Gregor Mendel. In a typical experiment, Mendel would start with two purebred strains of peas that differed in one or more easily observed traits. He could cross-pollinate them to observe the traits of the offspring, called the F_1 (first filial) generation. Then he would pollinate the F_1 peas with pollen from other F_1 peas to produce the F_2 (second filial) generation.

In one experiment, for example, Mendel cross-pollinated a strain of peas that regularly produced round seeds with a strain that regularly produced wrinkled seeds. His famous findings were that (a) all of the F_1 generation had round seeds and (b) three-fourths of the F_2 generation had round seeds and one-fourth had wrinkled seeds.

Mendel's findings make perfect sense if we assume that seed texture is controlled by a single pair of genes, with the allele for round dominant over that for wrinkled. To illustrate this, let us use the capital letter R to stand for the dominant, round-producing allele, and the small letter r for the recessive, wrinkle-producing allele. The purebred round strain is homozygous for the "round" allele (RR), and the purebred wrinkled strain is homozygous for the "wrinkled" allele (rr). (Purebred strains are homozygous for all traits.) Because one allele must come from each parent, the only possible result for the F_1 generation, produced by crossing the two purebred strains, is the heterozygous condition (Rr). This explains why all the F_1 peas in Mendel's experiment were round. At the next step, when Rr peas receive pollen from other Rr peas to produce the F_2 generation, four equally likely combinations can occur: (1) an R from each parent (RR), (2) an R from the female parent and an r from the male (Rr), (3) an r from the female parent and an R from the male (rR), and (4) an r from each parent (rr). (See Figure 3.6.) Since only one of these possible outcomes (rr) is wrinkled, the expectation is that one-fourth of the F_2 generation will be wrinkled and the other three-fourths, round. This is just what Mendel found.

Whenever a trait is inherited in a pattern like that observed by Mendel, we can assume that the trait results from variation in alleles at a single gene locus that interact in a dominant-recessive manner.

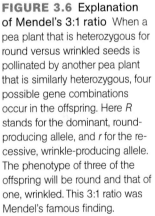

7

Why do three-fourths of the offspring of two heterozygous parents show the dominant trait and one-fourth show the recessive trait?

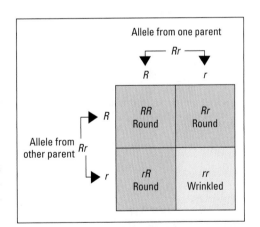

Allele from one parent

Allele from other parent

FIGURE 3.6 Explanation of Mendel's 3:1 ratio When a pea plant that is heterozygous for round versus wrinkled seeds is pollinated by another pea plant that is similarly heterozygous, four possible gene combinations occur in the offspring. Here R stands for the dominant, round-producing allele, and r for the recessive, wrinkle-producing allele. The phenotype of three of the offspring will be round and that of one, wrinkled. This 3:1 ratio was Mendel's famous finding.

SECTION REVIEW

Genes affect behavior by affecting the bodily structures involved in behavior.

Nature of Genetic Influence	Meiosis and Sexual Reproduction	Gene Pairing
➤ Through their influence on protein synthesis, genes affect bodily structures and behavior. ➤ Genes act in concert with the environment, not in isolation. For example, environmental cues can activate genes that make rats or mice nurturant to newborns.	➤ Meiosis results in egg and sperm cells that are genetically unique and contain only half the full number of chromosomes. ➤ Meiosis involves random assortment of paired genes. ➤ Genetic diversity produced by sexual reproduction promotes genes' survival by reducing the chance that all offspring will die.	➤ Paired genes, which occupy the same locus (location) on a pair of chromosomes, may be identical (homozygous) or different (heterozygous). Gene variations that can occupy the same locus are called alleles. ➤ Mendel's discovery of consistent ratios of traits in offspring of cross-pollinated strains of peas led to the gene concept and to the concepts of dominance and recessiveness.

■ Inheritance of Behavioral Traits

Variation in genes contributes to the variation in behavior that one sees in any animal species. Some behavioral characteristics are inherited in accordance with the same pattern that Mendel observed, indicative of control by a single pair of genes. Most behavioral characteristics, however, depend on many genes. In this section, we shall look first at two examples of single-gene traits and then at traits that are affected by many genes.

Examples of Single-Gene (Mendelian) Behavioral Traits

Mendelian Inheritance of Fearfulness in Dogs

8
- - - - - - - - - - - - - ◄

How did Scott and Fuller show that the difference in fearfulness between cocker spaniels and basenji hounds is controlled by a single gene locus, with the "fear" allele dominant over the "non-fear" allele?

- - - - - - - - - - - - - - -

One of the first demonstrations of single-gene control of a behavioral trait in dogs occurred nearly 50 years ago. In pioneering research on the role of genes in behavior, John Paul Scott and John Fuller (1965) studied the behavior of basenji hounds, cocker spaniels, and their mixed-breed offspring. Basenjis are timid dogs, showing fear of people until they have received much gentle handling. Cockers, in contrast, show little fear under normal rearing conditions. In a standard test with 5-week-old puppies, Scott and Fuller found that all the basenji puppies yelped and/or ran away when approached by a strange person, whereas only a few of the cocker puppies showed these reactions. When cockers and basenjis were crossbred (see Figure 3.7), the offspring (F_1 hybrids) were like basenjis in this test: All showed signs of fear when approached. Since this was as true of hybrids raised by cocker mothers as of those raised by basenji mothers, Scott and Fuller concluded that the effect stemmed from the hybrid dogs' genes and not from anything they learned from their mothers.

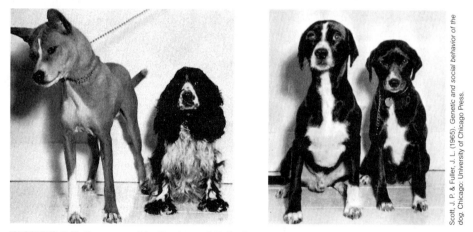

Scott, J. P. & Fuller, J. L. (1965). Genetic and social behavior of the dog. Chicago: University of Chicago Press.

FIGURE 3.7 Dogs used in Scott and Fuller's research At left are a male basenji and a female cocker spaniel; at right are two F_1 (first-generation) hybrids resulting from a basenji-cocker cross.

FIGURE 3.8 Explanation of Scott and Fuller's results of mating basenji-cocker hybrids with pure-bred cockers The finding that half the offspring were fearful and half were not makes sense if fearfulness results from a dominant allele (F) and lack of fearfulness results from a recessive allele (f). Because half the offspring receive F from their hybrid parent and all receive f from the purebred parent, half the offspring will be Ff (phenotypically fearful) and the other half, ff (not fearful).

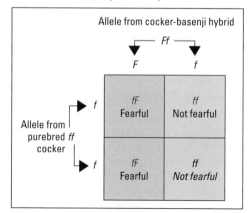

The fact that the F_1 hybrids were as fearful as the purebred basenjis suggested to Scott and Fuller that the difference in fearfulness between the two purebred strains might be controlled by a single gene locus, with the allele promoting fear dominant over that promoting confidence. If this were so, then mating F_1 hybrids with each other should produce a group of offspring (F_2 generation) in which three-fourths would show basenji-like fear and one-fourth would show cocker-like confidence—the same ratios that Mendel had found with seed texture in peas. Scott and Fuller did this experiment and, indeed, found ratios very close to those predicted. As additional evidence, they also mated F_1 hybrids with purebred cockers. About half the offspring of those backcrosses were basenji-like in fear, and the other half were cocker-like in confidence—just as can be expected if the "fear" allele is dominant over the "non-fear" allele (see Figure 3.8).

Be careful not to misinterpret this finding. It concerns a difference between two breeds of dogs in certain behavioral tests. It would not be reasonable to conclude that fear in all its various forms is controlled by a single gene. Many different genes must contribute to building the complex neural structure needed to experience fear and express it in behavior. Scott and Fuller's work demonstrates only that the difference between cocker spaniels and basenji hounds in a particular test of fear is controlled by a single gene. Recognize also that their studies do not diminish the role of environmental influences. Scott and Fuller could detect the effect of a specific gene pair because they raised all the dogs in similar environments. In other research, Scott (1963) showed that any puppy isolated from people for the first 4 months of life will be fearful of humans. Had Scott and Fuller isolated the cockers from all human contact and given the basenjis lots of kind handling before the behavioral test, they might well have found the cockers to be more fearful than the basenjis, despite the genetic predispositions toward the opposite behavior.

> ------ 9
Why would it be a mistake to conclude, from Scott and Fuller's work, that fear in dogs is caused just by one gene or that it is caused just by genes and not by the environment?

Mendelian Inheritance of a Specific Language Disorder

Most of the behaviorally relevant traits in humans that derive from alteration at a single gene locus are brain disorders, caused by relatively rare, mutant, malfunctioning genes that are passed from generation to generation.

> ------ 10
How did the pattern of inheritance of a disorder in language ability, in a particular family, show that the disorder is caused by a single dominant gene? Also, what other general ideas about genetic influences are illustrated by this example?

A particularly interesting example is a specific language impairment that has been studied extensively in three generations of one family, known as the KE family. The disorder, which is rare outside of the KE family, is characterized primarily by difficulty in articulating words, distinguishing speech sounds from other sounds, and learning grammatical rules (Gopnik, 1999; Vargha-Khadem & Liégeois, 2007). With much effort, people with this disorder learn to speak and understand language well enough to get along, but language never becomes natural to them. For example, they never develop the intuitive understanding of grammatical categories and rules that even normal 3-year-olds manifest. Brain scans of people with this disorder have revealed underdevelopment in several areas of the brain that are known to be critical for producing and understanding language (Vargha-Khadem & Liégeois, 2007).

The pattern of heredity of this disorder in the KE family is depicted in Figure 3.9. As you can see by examining the results for the third generation, when neither parent had the specific language impairment (SLI), no child had it, and when one

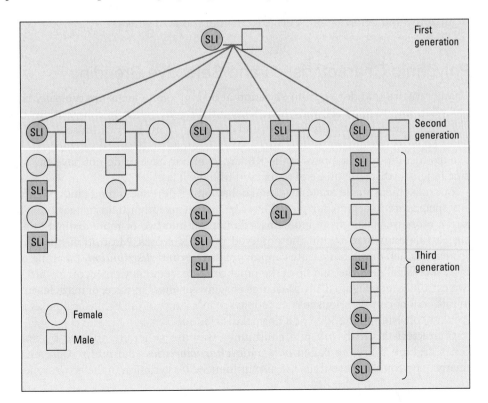

FIGURE 3.9 Inheritance of a specific language impairment This diagram shows the members of three generations of a family in which a specific language impairment (SLI) recurred. Circles depict females; squares, males; horizontal lines, marriage bonds; and slanted or vertical lines, lines of descent. "SLI" indicates presence of the disorder. Notice that approximately half (10 of 21) of the third-generation children who had one parent with the disorder also had the disorder. This pattern is consistent with the theory that the disorder is inherited through a single dominant gene. (Based on Gopnik & Crago, 1991.)

parent had it, about half of the offspring had it—just what you would expect if the impairment results from a single dominant gene. The logic behind this expectation is identical to that shown in Figure 3.8 for fearfulness in dogs. If one parent has one copy of the abnormal gene and the other parent lacks the abnormal gene, each offspring has a 50 percent chance of inheriting a copy of that gene. Because the abnormal gene is dominant, each person inheriting it is linguistically impaired.

Researchers have identified the specific gene that causes this language impairment in the KE family (Fisher, 2003). It is located on Chromosome 7, and in its normal (unimpaired) form it codes for a type of protein known as a *transcription factor.* Transcription factors are proteins that act on other genes to control the rate at which those genes produce their protein molecules. The normal version of this gene is responsible for activating a set of other genes that are involved in the development of various areas of the brain that are crucial for human language. The mutated (SLI) version of the gene fails to activate the other genes. Two copies of the normal gene are required to activate the other genes sufficiently for normal development of the language areas of the brain. Thus, the disorder appears in people who have one normal gene and one SLI gene.

The normal human version of this gene appears to be unique to humans. The chimpanzee version of the same gene is slightly different from that of the human version and produces a slightly different protein molecule (Marcus & Fisher, 2003). Apparently, modification of this particular gene was one of the evolutionary steps that enabled language to occur in humans and helped to distinguish us from chimpanzees and other apes.

I chose this particular example of a single-gene trait not just because it illustrates Mendelian inheritance in human behavior but also because it illustrates four other general ideas about genes:

- Genes can influence behavior by influencing the development of particular areas of the brain.

- A single gene can have multiple effects (in this case, the gene affects various aspects of linguistic ability by altering the brain in various locations).

- Some genes exert their effects by activating sets of other genes, thereby controlling the production of several or many different protein molecules.

- The evolution of human beings (and of other species) involves alterations in anatomy and behavior that derive from alterations in genes.

Polygenic Characteristics and Selective Breeding

11

How does the distribution of scores for a polygenic trait differ from that usually obtained for a single-gene trait?

◀ Characteristics that derive from variation at a single gene locus are typically *categorical* in nature. That is, they are characteristics that sharply differentiate one group from another. Peas are either round or wrinkled; mixed-breed basenji-cockers differ so sharply from one another in fearfulness that they can be categorized into two distinct groups; members of the KE family either have or do not have the specific language disorder (none of them "sort of have it").

But most measurable anatomical and behavioral differences among individuals of any species are in degree, not type. They are *continuous* rather than categorical. That is, the measures taken from individuals do not fall into two or more distinct groups but can lie anywhere within the observed range of scores. Most often, the set of scores obtained on such measures approximate a **normal distribution,** meaning that most scores fall near the middle of the range and the frequency tapers off toward the two extremes (see Figure 3.10). Measures of aggressiveness in mice, of maze learning in rats, and of conscientiousness in people are just a few of the behavioral measures that are consistently found to fit a normal distribution.

Characteristics that vary in a continuous way are generally affected by many genes and are therefore called **polygenic characteristics** (the prefix *poly-* means "many"). Of course, these traits are also influenced by variation in the environment,

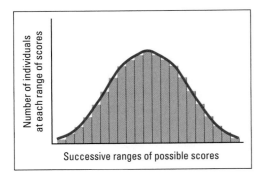

FIGURE 3.10 **Normal distribution** When many individuals are tested for a polygenic characteristic, the majority usually fall in the middle of the range of scores and the frequency tapers off toward zero at the extremes. Mathematically, this defines a normal curve. (For a more complete description, see the *Statistical Appendix* at the end of the book.)

so the variability observed in a graph such as Figure 3.10 results from a combination of genetic differences at many gene loci and environmental differences. In animals it is possible to study the role of genes in polygenic traits through the procedure of selective breeding.

Selective Breeding for Behavioral Characteristics in Animals

To the degree that individuals within a species differ in any measurable characteristic because of differences in their genes, that characteristic can be modified over successive generations through **selective breeding.** This procedure involves the mating of individuals that lie toward the same extreme on the measure in question. For single-gene characteristics the effects of selective breeding are immediate, but for polygenic characteristics the effects are gradual and cumulative over generations.

⟩ ─────── 12
How are the characteristics of animals shaped through selective breeding?

The basic procedure of selective breeding is by no means new. For thousands of years before a formal science of genetics existed, plant and animal breeders used selective breeding to produce new and better strains of every sort of domesticated species. Grains were bred for plumper seeds; cows, for docility and greater milk production; horses, along separate lines for working and racing; canaries, for their song; and dogs, along dozens of different lines for such varied purposes as following a trail, herding sheep (running around them instead of at them), and being gentle playmates for children. The procedure in every case was essentially the same: The members of each generation that best approximated the desired type were mated to produce the next generation, resulting in a continuous genetic molding toward the varieties we see today.

Under controlled laboratory conditions, researchers have used selective breeding to produce many behaviorally specialized strains of animals, usually for the purpose of understanding better the biological foundations of the behaviors in question. Fruit flies have been bred to move instinctively either toward or away from a source of light, mice to be either more or less inclined to fight, rats to either prefer or not prefer alcohol over water, and foxes to be either highly aggressive or extraordinarily docile and friendly toward humans (Crabbe & others, 1999a; Kukekova & others, 2008; Wimer & Wimer, 1985). That selective breeding can influence essentially any behavioral trait should come as no surprise. It follows logically from the fact that all behaviors depend on particular sensory, motor, and neural structures, all of which are built from proteins whose production depends on genes.

A fox bred for tameness Since 1959, researchers in Russia have been selectively breeding silver foxes for tameness. At each generation, only those foxes that show the least fear and aggression and the most affection to humans have been bred. The result, after more than 30 generations, is a breed of foxes that are as friendly to humans as are dogs (Kukekova & others, 2008; Trut, 1999).

Selective Breeding for Maze Learning: Tryon's Classic Research

The first long-term, systematic study of selective breeding in psychology was begun in the 1920s by Robert Tryon (1942), partly in reaction to the belief then held by some psychologists that individual differences in behavior are caused entirely by environmental differences, not at all by genetic differences. Tryon wanted to demonstrate that a type of behavior frequently studied by psychologists could be strongly influenced by variation in genes.

13
How did Tryon produce "maze bright" and "maze dull" strains of rats? How did he show that the difference was the result of genes, not rearing?

◀ Tryon began by testing a genetically diverse group of rats for their ability to learn a particular maze. Then he mated the males and females that had made the fewest errors in the maze to begin what he called the "maze bright" strain and those that had made the most errors to begin the "maze dull" strain. When the offspring of succeeding generations reached adulthood, he tested them in the same maze and mated the best-performing members of the bright strain, and the worst-performing members of the dull strain, to continue the two lines.

Some of his results are shown in Figure 3.11. As you can see, with each generation the two strains became increasingly distinct, until by the seventh there was almost no overlap between them. Almost all seventh-generation bright rats made fewer errors in the maze than even the best dull rats. To control for the possibility that the offspring were somehow learning to be bright or dull from their mothers, Tryon cross-fostered the rats so that some of the offspring from each strain were raised by mothers in the other strain. He found that rats in the bright strain were equally good in the maze, and those in the dull strain equally poor, regardless of which mothers raised them.

14
Why is the strain difference produced by Tryon not properly characterized in terms of "brightness" or "dullness"?

◀ Once a strain has been bred to show some behavioral characteristic, the question arises as to what other behavioral or physiological changes accompany it. Tryon referred to his two strains of rats as "bright" and "dull," but all he had measured was their performance in a particular type of maze. Performance in the maze no doubt

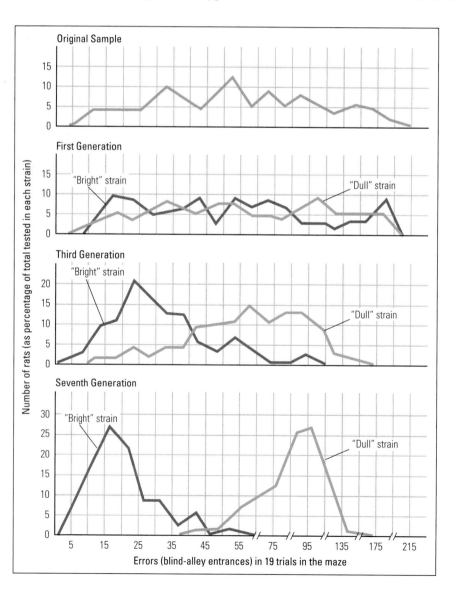

FIGURE 3.11 Selective breeding for "maze brightness" and "maze dullness" in rats The top graph shows, for the original parent stock, the distribution of rats according to the number of errors they made in the maze. Subsequent graphs show this distribution separately for the rats bred to be "bright" or "dull." With successive generations of selective breeding, an increasing percentage in the "bright" strain made few errors and an increasing percentage in the "dull" strain made many errors. (From Tryon, 1942.)

depended on many sensory, motor, motivational, and learning processes, and specific changes in any of them could in theory have mediated the effects that Tryon observed. In theory, Tryon's "dull" rats could simply have been those that had less acute vision, or were less interested in the variety of food used as a reward, or were more interested in exploring the maze's blind alleys.

In later studies, another researcher found that Tryon's "dull" rats were as good as the "bright" ones, and sometimes even better, at other learning tasks (Searle, 1949). We do not know what underlying abilities or dispositions changed in Tryon's two strains of rats to produce their difference in maze performance, but the change was apparently not one of general learning ability. This problem still occurs in modern behavioral genetics research, in which new strains of animals (usually mice) are created by adding, deleting, or modifying known genes using sophisticated genetic-engineering methods. The behavioral differences between two strains found in one laboratory often fail to occur in another laboratory, apparently because of subtle differences in the way the animals are housed or tested (Cabib & others, 2000; Crabbe & others, 1999b).

Polygenic Behavioral Characteristics in Humans

Most of the measures of human traits that interest psychologists—such as scores on personality tests—are continuous and normally distributed, and are affected by many genes as well as by environmental variables. Some psychologists are interested in the degree to which the differences in such scores, for a particular group of people, are the result of differences in their genes or differences in their environmental experiences. Of course, psychologists can't perform selective breeding studies with humans, but they have developed other methods to estimate that degree. Those methods involve comparing the average difference in test scores for people who are closely related to one another with that for people who are less closely related, using people who are chosen in such a way that the environments of the closely related people are no more similar to one another than are those of the less closely related people. Comparisons of identical twins with fraternal twins, and of biologically related siblings with adoptive siblings, have proven particularly useful. In Chapters 10, 15, and 16 you will read about such methods as they apply, respectively, to intelligence tests, personality tests, and predisposition to various mental disorders.

SECTION REVIEW

Hereditary effects on behavioral traits can involve just one gene, but usually involve many.

Single-Gene Traits	Polygenic Traits
➤ Single-gene traits (controlled by one pair of genes) are categorical (all or none) in nature.	➤ Polygenic traits (influenced by many gene pairs) are continuous (present in varying degrees) and often fit a normal distribution.
➤ Mendelian patterns of inheritance indicate single-gene control.	➤ Through selective breeding, a trait can be strengthened or weakened gradually over generations.
➤ Examples are breed differences in fearfulness in dogs and a language disorder in the KE family. General lessons concerning inheritance are illustrated with each example.	➤ An example is Tryon's breeding of rats for maze ability, which illustrates certain general lessons.

▪ Evolution by Natural Selection

Darwin's Insight: Selective Breeding Occurs in Nature

The idea that plants and animals can be modified by selective breeding was understood long before Darwin was born. In the first chapter of *The Origin of Species*, Darwin (1859/1963) referred to such human-controlled selective breeding as ***artificial***

➤ ---------------- **15**
What insight led Darwin to his theory of evolution? How is natural selection similar to and different from artificial selection?

selection, and he reminded readers of the enormously diverse varieties of plants and animals that had been produced through that procedure. He then pointed out—and this was his true, original insight—that breeding in nature is also selective and can also produce changes in living things over generations.

Selective breeding in nature, which Darwin labeled *natural selection,* is dictated not by the needs and whims of humans but by the obstacles to reproduction that are imposed by the natural environment. Those obstacles include predators, limited food supplies, extremes of temperature, difficulty in finding and attracting mates for sexual reproduction—anything that can cut life short or otherwise prevent an organism from producing offspring. Animals and plants that have characteristics that help them overcome such obstacles are, by definition, more likely to have offspring than those that lack these characteristics.

NON SEQUITUR by Wiley

Darwin's essential point was this: Individuals of a species vary in the number of offspring they produce. Some produce none, because they die early or fail to mate; others produce many. Any inherited trait that increases the number of offspring that an individual produces is automatically "selected for," as the trait is passed on to those offspring. Conversely, any inherited trait that decreases the number of one's offspring is automatically "selected against," appearing in fewer members of the next generation. Thus, as long as inheritable differences exist among individuals in an interbreeding population, and as long as some of those differences affect survival and reproduction, evolution will occur.

Genetic Diversity Provides the Fodder for Natural Selection

16

How are genes involved in evolution? What are the sources of genetic diversity on which natural selection acts?

Darwin knew nothing of genes. He realized that something, passed along through eggs and sperm, must provide the hereditary foundation for evolution, but he did not know what. Mendel's work, which was the first step toward our modern knowledge of genes, was unknown to most scientists until about 1900, well after Darwin had published his work. Today we know that genes are the units of heredity and that evolution entails changes, from generation to generation, in the frequencies of particular genes in an interbreeding population. Genes that improve an individual's ability to survive and reproduce in the existing environment increase from generation to generation, and genes that impede this ability decrease from generation to generation.

The genetic variability on which natural selection acts has two main sources: (1) the reshuffling of genes that occurs in sexual reproduction (already discussed) and (2) mutations.

Mutations are errors that occasionally and unpredictably occur during DNA replication, causing the "replica" to be not quite identical to the original. In the long run of evolution, mutation is the ultimate source of all genetic variation. As would be expected of any random change in a complex, organized structure, new mutations are more often harmful than helpful, and natural selection usually weeds them out. But occasionally a mutation is useful, producing a protein that affects the organism's development in a way that increases its ability to reproduce. Because of its effect on reproduction, the gene arising from such a mutation increases in frequency from generation to generation. At the level of the gene, that is evolution.

Prior to the modern understanding of genes, many people believed that changes in an individual that stem from practice or experience could be inherited and therefore provide a basis for evolution. For example, some argued that early giraffes, by frequently stretching their necks to reach leaves in trees, slightly elongated their necks in the course of their lives and that this change was passed on to their offspring, resulting, over many generations, in the long-necked giraffes we see today. That idea, referred to as the inheritance of acquired characteristics, is most often attributed to Jean-Baptiste de Lamarck (1744–1829), although many other evolutionists, both before and after Lamarck, held the same view (Futuyma, 1997). Even Darwin did not reject that idea, but he added to it the concepts of random variation and natural selection.

Now, however, we know that evolution is based entirely on genetic changes and that no amount of practice or experience can change one's genes in a way that affects the next generation. Random change in genes, followed by natural selection—not directed change stemming from individual experience—provides the basis for evolution.

Environmental Change Provides the Force for Natural Selection

Evolution is spurred by changes in the environment. If the environment were completely stable, organisms would adapt as fully as possible and change little or not at all thereafter. But the environment keeps changing. Climates change, sources of food change, predators change, and so on. When the conditions of life change, what was previously a useful characteristic may become harmful, and vice versa.

Darwin believed that evolution was a slow and steady process. But today we know that it can occur rapidly, slowly, or almost not at all, depending on the rate and nature of environmental change and on the degree to which genetic variability already exists in a population (Gould & Eldredge, 1993; Pagel & Meade, 2006). Environmental change spurs evolution not by causing the appropriate mutations to occur but by promoting natural selection. Some mutations that previously would not have been advantageous and would have gradually been weeded out by natural selection, are advantageous in the new environment, so they are passed along in increasing numbers from generation to generation. Evolution sometimes occurs so quickly that people can see it happen. In fact, scientists since Darwin's time have reported more than a hundred different examples of observed evolution (Endler, 1986; Weiner, 1994).

Some of the most well-documented examples of observed evolution come from the work of Peter and Rosemary Grant, who for more than 30 years studied a species of finch, the *medium ground finch,* on one of the Galápagos Islands, about 600 miles off the coast of Ecuador (Grant & Grant, 2008). The Grants found that the members of this species differ somewhat in the thickness of their beaks, that the variation is inheritable, and that environmental changes can result in rapid evolution toward either thicker or thinner beaks. In the 1970s, a severe drought lasting several years caused most of the finches to die because the plants that produce the seeds they eat failed to grow. The birds that survived and produced offspring were those that happened to have thicker, more powerful beaks—powerful enough to crack open the large, hard-shelled seeds that remained after the smaller seeds had been eaten (see Figure 3.12).

Two decades later, another species of ground finch, the *large ground finch,* established a breeding colony on the island and began competing with the medium ground finch for food. The intruders were much better adapted for eating the large, hard-shelled seeds than were the medium ground finches, but they were less well adapted for eating the small seeds. The result, for the medium ground finches, was depletion in the supply of large seeds but not of small seeds. Under this condition, the medium ground finches with thinner bills, better adapted for eating the small seeds, were more likely to survive and produce offspring than were those with thicker bills. Within a few generations under this new set of conditions,

▶ ‒ ‒ ‒ ‒ ‒ ‒ ‒ ‒ ‒ ‒ ‒ ‒ ‒ ‒ ‒ 17

How does change in the environment affect the direction and speed of evolution? How did a study of finches illustrate the role of environmental change in evolution?

Natural History Magazine

FIGURE 3.12 Rapid evolution
During years of drought, natural selection quickly produced the thicker beak, shown at right, in the medium ground finches studied by Peter and Rosemary Grant. During years of competition with a larger thick-billed species, natural selection quickly produced the thinner beak, shown at the left.

the average beak thickness of the medium ground finches declined considerably (Grant & Grant, 2006).

The evolution of simple or small changes, such as in skin pigmentation or in beak thickness, can occur in a few generations when selection conditions are strong, but more complex changes require much more time. The difference between, say, a chimpanzee brain and a human brain could not have come about in a few generations, as it must have involved many mutations, each of which would have promoted a slight selective advantage to the chimpanzee (in its environment) or to the human (in our environment). When evolutionists talk about "rapid" evolution of complex changes, they are usually talking about periods measured in hundreds of thousands of years (Gould & Eldredge, 1993).

Evolution Has No Foresight

18
- - - - - - - - - - - - - - - ◄
What are three mistaken beliefs about evolution, all related to the misconception that foresight is involved?
- - - - - - - - - - - - - - - - -

People sometimes mistakenly think of evolution as a mystical force working toward a predetermined end. One manifestation of this belief is the idea that evolution could produce changes for some future purpose, even though they are useless or harmful at the time that the change occurs. But evolution has no foresight. The finches studied by the Grants could not have evolved thicker beaks in anticipation of drought, or thinner ones in anticipation of thick-beaked competitors. Only genetic changes that increase survival and reproduction in the immediate environment can proliferate through natural selection.

Another manifestation of the belief in foresight is the idea that present-day organisms can be ranked according to the distance they have moved along a set evolutionary route, toward some planned end (Gee, 2002). For example, some may think of humans as the "most evolved" creatures, with chimpanzees next and amoebas way down on the list. But evolution has no set route or planned end. Humans, chimps, and amoebas have taken their different forms and behavioral characteristics because of chance events that led them to occupy different niches in the environment, where the selection criteria differed. The present-day amoeba is not an early step toward humans but rather a creature that is at least as well adapted to its environment as we are to ours. The amoeba has no more chance of evolving to become like us than we have of evolving to become like it.

A third manifestation of the belief in foresight is the idea that natural selection is a moral force, that its operation and its products are in some sense right or good. In everyday talk, people sometimes imply that whatever is natural (including natural selection) is good and that evil stems from society or human contrivances that go beyond nature. But nature is neither good nor bad, moral nor immoral. To say that natural selection led to such and such a characteristic does not lend any moral virtue to that characteristic. As you will see, fighting is as much a product of evolution as is cooperation, but that is no reason to consider them morally equivalent.

SECTION REVIEW

Natural selection is the driving force of evolutionary change.

How Natural Selection Works	Role of Environmental Change	Evolution Lacks Foresight
➤ To the degree that a trait enhances survival and reproduction, genes producing that trait are passed on to offspring. The result is that such genes become more frequent over generations.	➤ The rate and nature of environmental change affect the rate and course of evolution. Examples are the effects of drought and of competition from another species on the evolution of beak thickness in finches.	➤ Natural selection can only lead to changes that are immediately adaptive; it cannot anticipate future needs.
➤ Mutations and reshuffling of genes in sexual reproduction provide genetic diversity on which natural selection operates.	➤ Complex changes, requiring many mutations, require a long time to evolve.	➤ There is no preset pathway for evolution.
		➤ Natural selection is not a moral force.

■ Natural Selection as a Foundation for Functionalism

The mechanisms underlying behavior are products of natural selection, and, like all products of natural selection, they came about because they promoted survival and reproduction. Just as Tryon, through artificial selection, bred rats to be better at learning a particular maze, natural selection automatically breeds animals to be better at doing what they must to survive and reproduce in their natural environments. This idea provides a foundation for the psychological approach known as *functionalism*—the attempt to explain behavior in terms of what it accomplishes for the behaving individual.

The functionalist approach to explaining behavior is essentially the same as the functionalist approach to explaining anatomy: Why do giraffes have long necks? Why do humans lack fur? Why do male songbirds sing in the spring? Why do humans have such an irrepressible ability to learn language? The anatomist trying to answer the first two questions, and the behavioral researcher or psychologist trying to answer the latter two, would look for ways by which each trait helped ancestral members of the species to survive and reproduce.

19

How does an understanding of evolution provide a basis for functionalism in psychology?

Ultimate and Proximate Explanations of Behavior

Biologists and psychologists who think in evolutionary terms find it useful to distinguish between two kinds of explanations of behavior—ultimate and proximate:

20

How are ultimate explanations of behavior different from, but complementary to, proximate explanations?

- *Ultimate explanations* are functional explanations at the evolutionary level. In other words, they are statements of the role that the behavior plays in the animal's survival and reproduction. Viewed from the vantage point of the gene, they are statements of how the behavior helps the individual's genes make it into the next generation.

- *Proximate explanations* are explanations that deal not with function but with mechanism; they are statements of the immediate conditions, both inside and outside the animal, that bring on the behavior.

Illustration of the Complementarity of Ultimate and Proximate Explanations

As an illustration of these two modes of explanation, consider how they might be applied to the question of why male songbirds (of many species) sing in the spring. An *ultimate explanation* goes something like this (Koodsma & Byers, 1991): Over the course of evolution, songbirds have adapted to a mating system that takes place in the spring. The male's song serves to attract a female for mating and to warn other males to stay away from the singer's territory in order to avoid a fight. In the evolution of these birds, males whose genes promoted such singing produced more offspring (more copies of their genes) than did males whose genes failed to promote such singing.

A *proximate explanation,* in contrast, might go as follows (Ball & Hulse, 1998): The increased period of daylight in the spring triggers, through the birds' visual system, a physiological mechanism that leads to the increased production of the sex hormone testosterone, which in turn acts on certain areas of the brain (which we might call the "song areas"), promoting the drive to sing. Notice the complementary nature of these explanations. The ultimate explanation states the survival or reproductive value of the behavior, and the proximate explanation states the stimuli and physiological mechanisms through which the behavior occurs.

The Search for Ultimate Explanations in Human Psychology

All of the complex biological mechanisms underlying human behavior and experience—including the basic mechanisms of perception, learning, memory, thought, motivation, and emotion—are products of evolution by natural selection. They all

A redwing blackbird at home This male's singing warns other males of the species to stay away.

Anthony Mercieca/Photo Researchers, Inc.

came about because each small step in their evolution tended to promote the survival and reproduction of our ancestors. Thus, for any basic psychological characteristic that is part of human nature—for any basic drive or emotion, for example—it is legitimate to ask: How did this characteristic improve the survival and reproductive chances of our ancestors? How did it help our ancestors get their genes into the next generation?

The ultimate explanations of some human traits (especially those that we share with all other mammals) are relatively obvious. We have strong drives to breathe air, drink fluids, and consume foods because our bodies need these things to remain alive. We have strong drives to copulate, under certain conditions, because that is the means by which our genes get from one generation to the next. Individuals who lacked such drives are ancestors to nobody today; their genes died with them. The ultimate explanations of some other human traits, however, are not so obvious. It is not obvious, for example, why humans everywhere tend to sleep about eight hours each night (discussed in Chapter 6), or why humans everywhere under certain conditions experience the disturbing emotion of guilt (discussed in Chapter 14). In various places in this book, including in the last sections of this chapter, you will encounter examples of ultimate explanations that are not intuitively obvious but are supported by research evidence. As you will see, evidence for or against any particular ultimate explanation can come from detailed analysis of the behavior or trait in question, from cross-species comparisons, and sometimes from studies showing what happens when the behavior or trait is missing.

Limitations on Functionalist Thinking

21
What are four reasons for the existence of traits or behaviors that do not serve survival and reproductive functions?

◄ Before we go deeper into discussions of ultimate functions, it is useful to know something about the limitations of functionalist thinking. It is not the case that every detail of every trait serves a useful function, and some traits that were once functional may not be so today. Here are four reasons why a particular trait or behavior may not be functional.

Some Traits Are Vestigial

Some traits that evolved to serve the needs of our ancestors are no longer functional today, yet they remain. These remnants of our past are called ***vestigial characteristics.***

As an example, consider the grasp reflex by which newborn infants close their fingers tightly around objects in their hands. This reflex may well be useful today in the development of the infant's ability to hold and manipulate objects, but that does not explain why prematurely born infants grasp so strongly that they can support their own weight, why they grasp with their toes as well as their hands (see Figure 3.13), and why the best stimulus for eliciting the response is a clump of hair (Eibl-Eibesfeldt, 1975). These aspects of the reflex make more sense when we observe them in other primates. To survive, infant monkeys and apes cling tightly with hands and feet to their mother's fur while she swings in trees or goes about her other daily business. In the course of our evolution from ape-like ancestors, we lost our fur, so our infants can no linger cling to us in this way, but the reflex remains.

The concept of vestigial traits becomes especially relevant to psychologists when applied to our inherited drives, or motives. Because of culture, our habitats and lifestyles have changed dramatically in just a few centuries, a speck on the evolutionary time scale. Essentially all of our evolution as a species occurred in conditions that were quite different from those present today, and some of our inherited tendencies may be harmful, rather than helpful, in the habitat that we occupy today. An example is our great appetite for sugar. In the world

FIGURE 3.13 Premature infant clinging with hands and toes This ability may be a vestigial carryover from an earlier evolutionary time, when the infants of our ancestors clung to their parents' fur.

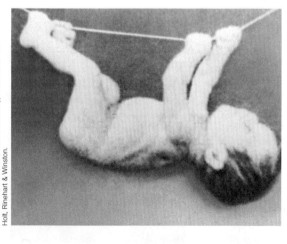

of our ancestors, sugar was a rare and valuable commodity. It existed primarily in fruits and provided energy needed for vigorous physical activity. But today sugar is readily available in most areas of the world, and life (for many of us) is less physically strenuous. Yet our preference for sugar persists as strong as ever, despite such negative consequences as tooth decay and obesity.

Some Traits Are Side Effects of Natural Selection for Other Traits

Useless changes can come about in evolution as by-products of natural selection for other, useful changes. A simple example, in humans, is the belly button (suggested by Buss & others, 1998). To the best of anyone's knowledge, the belly button serves no function related to survival or reproduction. It is simply a remnant left from the umbilical cord. The umbilical cord, of course, does serve a survival and reproductive function, that of conveying nutrients from the mother to the developing fetus. An anatomist from Mars who observed belly buttons on adult earthlings, but who never observed a fetus or the birth process, would be at a loss to explain why such a structure would have evolved.

It seems quite possible that some human psychological capacities, even some that are so general that we would consider them to be part of human nature, came about as side effects of the evolution of other capacities. It is reasonable to ask, for example, whether the universal human proclivities for art and music are direct effects of natural selection or side effects. Perhaps these proclivities served to attract mates during much of our evolutionary history (as they seem to today), and were therefore selected for directly, much as song was selected for in birds. It is also possible, however, that they emerged simply as by-products of selection for other proclivities, such as those for planning, constructing tools, and communicating through language. A third possibility, combining the first two, is that proclivities for art and music may have initially emerged as by-products and then been selected for because of their usefulness for attracting mates or other helpers. At present, we do not have evidence to support strongly any of these theories over the others.

Some Traits Result Simply from Chance

Some inheritable characteristics that result from just one or two mutations are inconsequential for survival and reproduction. Different races of people have somewhat differently shaped noses. Maybe that variation is caused by natural selection. Perhaps one shape worked best in one climate and another worked best in another climate, so natural selection molded the noses differently. But we can't automatically assume that. The different shapes might be a result of mutations that didn't matter and therefore were never weeded out by natural selection. Maybe the small group of people who migrated to a specific part of the world, and who were the ancestors of a particular racial group, just happened to carry along genes for a nose shape that was different from the average for the group they left. Such variation, due to chance alone without selection, is referred to as *genetic drift*.

Many years ago, researchers discovered that the incidence of schizophrenia (a serious mental disorder, discussed in Chapter 16) is three times greater among people living in northern Sweden, above the Arctic Circle, than among people in most other parts of the world (Huxley & others, 1964). There are at least three possible explanations of this observation: (a) Environmental conditions, such as the harsh climate or the isolation it produces, might tend to bring on schizophrenia in people who are prone to it. (b) Natural selection might have increased the frequency of schizophrenia-promoting genes among these people, perhaps because such genes help protect people from harmful effects of physical stressors such as cold climate. (This was the hypothesis suggested by Huxley and his colleagues.) (c) The Arctic population may have been founded by a small group of Swedish migrants who, just by chance, had a higher proportion of schizophrenia-promoting genes than the population at large. This last possibility (also mentioned by Huxley and his colleagues) would be an example of genetic drift. To this day, scientists do not know which of these theories is correct.

Evolved Mechanisms Cannot Deal Effectively with Every Situation

Our basic drives, emotions, and other behavioral tendencies came about in evolution because, on balance, they promoted survival and reproduction more often than they interfered with survival and reproduction. That does not mean, however, that every instance of activation of such a drive, emotion, or tendency serves survival or reproductive ends. In Chapter 14, I will present evidence that the emotion of guilt serves the ultimate function of helping us to preserve our relationships with people whose help we need for survival and reproduction. When we hurt someone on whom we depend, we feel guilty, which motivates us to make amends and patch up the relationship. That does not mean, however, that every manifestation of guilt in every person serves that function. Sometimes guilt can be crippling; sometimes our capacity for guilt is exploited by others for their ends at the expense of ours. The best that natural selection could do was to develop a guilt mechanism that is triggered by certain general conditions. It could not build a mechanism capable of distinguishing every possible condition from every other and triggering guilt only when it is useful, never when it is harmful. The same is true for all of our other evolved emotions and drives (and that is why we have psychotherapists).

SECTION REVIEW

The concept of natural selection provides a secure footing for functionalism.

The Functionalist Approach	Limitations of Functionalism
➤ Functionalism is an approach to psychology that focuses on the usefulness of a particular behavior to the individual engaging in it.	➤ Some traits are vestigial; they once served a function but no longer do.
➤ Ultimate explanations are functional explanations, stating the role that specific behaviors play in survival and reproduction.	➤ Some traits are side effects of other traits that arose through natural selection.
➤ Proximate explanations are complementary to ultimate explanations; they are concerned with mechanisms that bring about behavior.	➤ Some traits are products just of chance, not natural selection.
	➤ Even evolved mechanisms, such as that for guilt, are not useful in every situation in which they are active.

■ Natural Selection as a Foundation for Understanding Species-Typical Behaviors

Suppose you saw an animal that looked exactly like a dog, but it meowed, climbed trees, and ignored the mail carrier. Would you call it a dog or a cat? Clearly, we identify animals as much by their behavior as by their anatomy. Every species of animal has certain characteristic ways of behaving. These are commonly called *instincts,* but a more technical term for them is **species-typical behaviors.** Meowing, tree climbing, and acting aloof are species-typical behaviors of cats. Dam building is species-typical of beavers. Smiling, talking, and two-legged walking are species-typical of humans.

Species-Typical Behaviors in Humans

Species-typical behaviors are products of evolution, but that does not mean that they are necessarily rigid in form or uninfluenced by learning. To understand more fully the concept of species-typical behaviors, let us examine some examples in human beings.

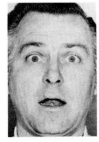 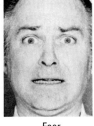  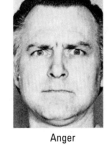 

| Surprise | Fear | Disgust | Anger | Happiness | Sadness |

Elkman, P. & Friesen, W. (1975). *Unmasking the face.* Englewood Cliffs, NJ: Prentice Hall.

FIGURE 3.14 **Six basic human emotional expressions** These expressions, taken from Ekman and Friesen's atlas of emotional expressions, were produced by a model who was asked to move specific facial muscles in specific ways. As you study each figure, try to describe the positions of the facial features for each expression. For example, surprise can be described as follows: The brows are pulled upward, producing horizontal wrinkles across the forehead; the eyes are opened wide, revealing white above the iris; and the lower jaw is dropped, with no tension around the mouth.

Human Emotional Expressions as Examples of Species-Typical Behaviors

Darwin noted that humans, like other animals, automatically communicate moods and behavioral intentions to one another through body postures, movements, and facial expressions. In his book *The Expression of the Emotions in Man and Animals,* Darwin (1872/1965) argued that specific facial expressions accompany specific emotional states in humans and that these expressions are universal, occurring in people throughout the world and even in people who were born blind and thus could not have learned them through observation.

In an extension of Darwin's pioneering work, Paul Ekman and Wallace Friesen (1975, 1982) developed an atlas that describes and depicts the exact facial-muscle movements that make up each of six basic emotional expressions in people: surprise, fear, disgust, anger, happiness, and sadness (see Figure 3.14). They then showed photographs of each expression to individuals in many different cultures, including members of a preliterate tribe in the highlands of New Guinea who had little previous contact with other cultures. They found that people in every culture described each depicted emotion in a way that was consistent with descriptions in the United States (Ekman, 1973; Ekman & others, 1987). In a reversal of this procedure, they also photographed members of the New Guinea tribe who had been asked to act out various emotions and showed the photographs to college students in the United States. The college students were quite accurate in labeling the emotions portrayed by the New Guineans.

In a further extension of Darwin's work, Irenäus Eibl-Eibesfeldt documented the cross-cultural universality of many nonverbal signals, including one that he labeled the *eyebrow flash,* a momentary raising of the eyebrows lasting about one-sixth of a second, usually accompanied by a smile and an upward nod of the head (see Figure 3.15). He observed this expression in every culture he studied—including those

> ▶ -----------------**22**
> **What evidence supports the idea that many human emotional expressions are examples of species-typical behaviors?**

FIGURE 3.15 **The eyebrow flash** This universal signal of greeting is shown in adjacent frames from films of (a) a French woman and (b) a Yanomami man (of the Brazil-Venezuela border).

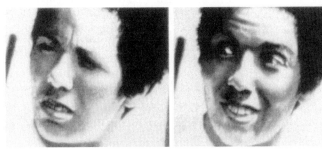

(a)

(b)

Eibl-Eibesfeldt, I. (1989). *Human ethology.* Hawthorne, NY: Walter de Gruyter, Inc.

in New Guinea, Samoa, and various parts of Africa, Asia, South America, and Europe— and concluded that it is a universal sign of greeting among friends (Eibl-Eibesfeldt, 1989). Raised eyebrows are also a component of the emotional expression of surprise (look at Figure 3.14 again), so the eyebrow flash with its accompanying smile might be interpreted as a nonverbal way of saying, "What a happy surprise to see you."

Eibl-Eibesfeldt (1975) also filmed children who were born blind, or both blind and deaf, and found that they manifest emotions in the same basic ways as sighted children do (see Figure 3.16). Such observations provide the most direct evidence that at least some human expressions do not have to be learned through observing them in others or hearing descriptions of them.

FIGURE 3.16 Some emotional expressions need not be learned through observation This young girl, manifesting joy, has been blind and deaf since birth.

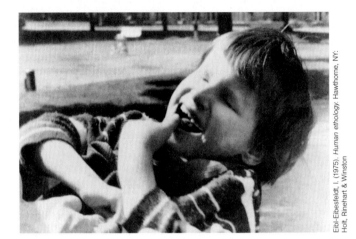

Eibl-Eibesfeldt, I. (1975). *Human ethology.* Hawthorne, NY: Holt, Rinehart & Winston

23

How do human emotional expressions illustrate the point that species-typical behaviors can be modified by learning?

Taking all the evidence together, there can be little doubt that we are biologically predisposed to express certain emotions in certain species-typical ways. It is also clear, however, that we can control and modify our emotional expressions and learn new ones. Even researchers who focus on universal expressions are quick to point out cross-cultural differences. For example, Eibl-Eibesfeldt (1975) found that despite its cross-cultural similarity in form and general meaning, large cultural differences exist in the use of the eyebrow flash. The Japanese, who are reserved in social expressions among adults, use it mainly when greeting young children, whereas Samoans, at the other extreme, greet nearly everyone in this way. More recently, researchers have shown that cultural dialects occur in the emotional expressions that Ekman and Friesen included in their atlas. In general, people can identify each emotion more easily and accurately when it is expressed by other members of their own culture than when it is expressed by members of a very different culture (Elfenbein & Amady, 2003; Elfenbein & others, 2007).

The Role of Learning in the Development of Species-Typical Behaviors

To say that a behavior is instinctive, or species-typical, is not to say that it is unaffected by learning. As I just pointed out, our basic emotional expressions are species-typical, but cultural differences among them are learned. The role of learning is even more obvious in two of our most characteristic species-specific behaviors—our manner of walking and our use of language.

24

How is the point that species-typical behaviors may depend on learning illustrated by the examples of two-legged walking and language in humans, and singing in white-crowned sparrows?

A scientist from Mars would almost certainly point to two-legged walking and use of a grammar-based language as among the defining behavioral characteristics of the human species. These characterize humans everywhere and clearly depend on inherited predispositions, yet their development also clearly depends on learning.

During the peak months of learning to walk (generally during the second year of life), infants spend an average of about 6 hours per day practicing balancing and walking and, on a typical day, take about 9,000 walking steps and travel the length of 29 football fields (Adolph & others, 2003). For the most part they are not trying to get to any particular place; they are just walking for the sake of walking. By the time they are proficient walkers, they have spent thousands of hours practicing, on their own initiative. During those same months, infants also, on their own initiative, intensely practice talking. With language, infants do not just learn the motor coordination needed to produce the sounds; they also, and more amazingly, learn the basic vocabulary and grammar of the language that they hear around them (to be discussed in Chapter 11). Two-legged walking and talking are species-typical behaviors in humans, but a human raised in an environment where either of these capacities was impossible to practice would not develop that capacity. Such an inhuman environment would not produce a normal human being.

Learning plays crucial roles in the development of species-specific behaviors in other animals as well. For example, white-crowned sparrows develop the ability to sing their species-typical song only if they are permitted to hear it during the first summer after hatching (Marler, 1970). Indeed, populations of the species living in different areas have somewhat different dialects, and young birds learn to sing the dialect that they hear (Nelson & others, 2004). Yet the range of possible songs that the birds can learn is limited by their biology. No matter what its environmental experiences, a white-crowned sparrow cannot learn to sing like a canary or like any species other than a white-crowned sparrow. In Chapter 4, you will encounter more examples of species-typical behaviors that require specific learning experiences to develop normally.

Biological Preparedness as the Basis for Species-Typical Behaviors

The difference between behaviors that we call instinctive, or species-typical, and those that we do not so label has to do with their degree of *biological preparedness.* Natural selection has equipped each species with anatomical structures, in the brain and elsewhere, that ensure that normal individuals of the species, who grow up in a normal environment for that species, will be physically able to perform their species-typical behaviors and will be motivated to learn what they must for adequate performance.

➤ ┄┄┄┄┄┄┄┄┄┄ **25**

How is the concept of biological preparedness related to that of species-typical behavior? How is biological preparedness illustrated with the examples of human walking and talking?

We humans clearly come into the world biologically prepared to learn to walk on two legs. Natural selection has provided us with anatomical features—such as strong hindlimbs with feet, weaker forelimbs without feet, an upwardly tilted pelvis, and a short, stiff neck—that combine to make it more convenient for us to walk upright than on all fours. Moreover, we are born with neural systems in the brain and spinal cord that enable us to move our legs correctly for coordinated two-legged walking and with neural structures that motivate us to practice this behavior at the appropriate stage in our development. Consider the difference between two-legged

(a) (b)

Biological preparedness Infants are born with a "stepping reflex," which shows that they have, inborn, the neural mechanisms for two-legged walking. Perfecting that behavior, however, requires extensive practice during the toddling stage, when the legs have become strong enough to support the child's weight.

walking in humans and in dogs. Dogs are capable of learning to walk on two legs, and much is made of that fact by circus trainers, but they are never very good at it. They do not have the appropriate muscular and skeletal systems to coordinate the behavior properly, and they have no natural impulse to walk in this manner. A dog, unlike a human child, will practice two-legged walking only if it receives immediate rewards, such as food, for doing so. Thus, two-legged walking is not a species-typical behavior in dogs.

The same is true for talking. Humans are born with anatomical structures, including a larynx and a flexible tongue, that can produce a wide range of sounds and with a brain that has special neural centers for understanding and producing language (discussed in Chapter 5). Infants begin talking at a certain stage even if they receive little encouragement from those around them. Chimpanzees can be taught to simulate some aspects of human language, just as dogs can be taught to walk on their hind legs, but they require lots of encouragement and are never very good at it (discussed in Chapter 11).

The Relative Nature of the Concept of Species-Typical Behavior

26

Why is the concept of species-typical behavior relative rather than absolute?

◄ Having characterized the concept of species-typical behavior in terms of biological preparedness, I must now add that the concept is relative rather than absolute. No behavior stems just from biological preparation; some sort of experience with the environment is always involved. Conversely, any behavior that an individual can produce—no matter how artificial it may seem or how much training is required— must make use of the individual's inherited biological capacities. The concept of species-typical behavior is useful as long as we accept it as relative and do not argue about whether one or another behavior really should or should not be called species-typical. *Big* and *little* are useful words in our vocabulary, but there is no point in arguing about whether a breadbox is properly called one or the other. Two-legged walking is more species-typical for humans than for dogs, as a breadbox is bigger than a matchbox.

The question to ask when we study a particular behavior is not, Is this a species-typical behavior? Rather, the meaningful questions are these:

- What are the environmental conditions needed for the full development of this behavior?

- What internal mechanisms are involved in producing this behavior?

- What consequences does this behavior have in the individual's daily life?

- In the course of evolution, why would the genes that make this behavior possible have been favored by natural selection?

These questions can be asked of any behavior, regardless of whether or not it is thought of as species-typical.

The Value of Cross-Species Comparisons of Species-Typical Behaviors

In psychology as well as biology, scientists have learned a lot about our species by comparing us to other animals. The basic rationales for learning about any one species by comparing it with others are found in the principle of evolution by natural selection.

Two Forms of Cross-Species Comparison: Homologies and Analogies

27

What is the difference between a homology and an analogy, and how can researchers tell whether a similarity between two species in some trait is one or the other?

◄ An understanding of evolution makes it clear that two conceptually different classes of similarities exist across species: homologies and analogies.

A **homology** is any similarity that exists because of the different species' common ancestry. All animals originated from a common ancestor, so it is not surprising that some homologies—such as those in the basic structure of DNA molecules and of certain enzymes—can be found between any two species. But the more closely related two species are, the more homologies they show.

An *analogy,* in contrast, is any similarity that stems not from common ancestry but from *convergent evolution.* Convergent evolution occurs when different species, because of some similarity in their habitats or lifestyles, independently evolve a common characteristic.

As an illustration, consider some comparisons among species that can fly. Flying has arisen separately in three taxonomic groups: birds, some insects (such as butterflies), and some mammals (bats). Similarities across these three groups in their flying motions, and in the anatomical structures that permit flight, are examples of analogies because they do not result from common ancestry (see Figure 3.17). However, similarities in flight and wings among species within any of these groups, such as between crows and sparrows, are likely to be homologies. The last common ancestor between a crow and a sparrow was itself a bird with wings, but the last common ancestor between a crow and a butterfly, or between a crow and a bat, did not have wings.

FIGURE 3.17 Analogous wings
Similarities in the wings and flying behavior of birds, bats, and butterflies are considered to be analogies, not homologies, because they arose independently in evolution.

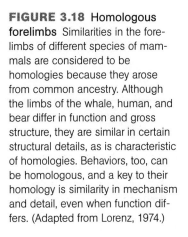

(a)   (b)   (c)

Aside from evidence based on knowledge about the degree of relatedness of the compared species, analogies and homologies can often be distinguished by the nature of the observed similarity (Lorenz, 1974). Analogies entail similarity in function and gross form, but not in detail and underlying mechanism. Thus, the wings of birds, bats, and butterflies are similar at the functional and gross anatomical level in that they provide broad, flappable surfaces that enable flight; but they are very different from one another in the details of their construction and in the neural and muscular mechanisms that control them. The difference in detail is great because they evolved independently, through different sets of genetic mutations. In contrast, because homologies arise from shared genes, they entail similarities in their underlying construction and physiological mechanisms, even when, because of divergent evolution, large differences have emerged in gross form or function (for example, see Figure 3.18).

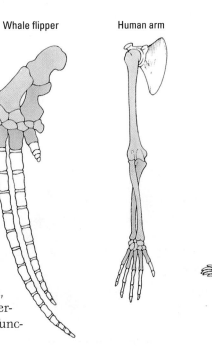

Whale flipper   Human arm   Bear leg

FIGURE 3.18 Homologous forelimbs Similarities in the forelimbs of different species of mammals are considered to be homologies because they arose from common ancestry. Although the limbs of the whale, human, and bear differ in function and gross structure, they are similar in certain structural details, as is characteristic of homologies. Behaviors, too, can be homologous, and a key to their homology is similarity in mechanism and detail, even when function differs. (Adapted from Lorenz, 1974.)

28
- - - - - - - - - - - - - - - - - ◀
How are homologies used for learning about (a) the physiological mechanisms and (b) the evolutionary pathways of species-typical traits?
- - - - - - - - - - - - - - - - -

FIGURE 3.19 Cells built by honeybees and bumblebees
Honeybees build hives with hexagonally shaped cells (a), which are the optimal shape for storing large amounts of honey and larvae using the least amount of precious wax. In order to understand how such behavior might have come about through small steps in natural selection, Darwin studied the homologous but simpler storage structures built by related bee species. The simplest, produced by bumblebees (b), consists simply of a cluster of spherical cells, which the bees easily build by sweeping their abdomens compass-like to carve out the spheres. Other species, more closely related to honeybees, build intermediate structures, with spherical cells that intersect and are patched up with flat wax walls at the places of intersection. From such observations, Darwin suggested that ancestors of modern honeybees built their hives in a way similar to that of modern bumblebees but, through evolution, began placing their cells ever closer together and more regularly spaced and patching up the intersections, resulting eventually in the hexagonal cells that honeybees build today.

The Value for Psychology of Studying Homologies

Homologies are useful for research on the physiological mechanisms of behavior (that is, research on how the brain and other biological structures operate to produce the behavior being studied). Because convergent evolution can produce similar behaviors that operate through different mechanisms, researchers who seek to understand the physiological mechanism of some behavior in humans through experiments on other species must study species in which the relevant behavior is homologous, not analogous, to that in humans. You will find many examples of such research in Chapters 4 through 8 of this book. Many basic mechanisms of learning, motivation (such as hunger), and sensation (such as vision) are homologous across all or at least most species of mammals, and we have learned much about these by studying them in mice, rats, cats, and other laboratory mammals.

Homologies are also useful for inferring the pathways along which species-typical behaviors evolved. By comparing the different forms of a particular species-typical behavior in closely related species, it is often possible to reconstruct how the more complex of these forms evolved through a series of steps from the simpler form. Darwin (1859/1963) himself used this method to figure out the evolutionary steps through which honeybees acquired their marvelous ability to construct complex hives consisting of wax combs of closely fitting hexagonal cells in which to store honey and larvae (see Figure 3.19).

Homologies as Clues to the Evolutionary Origins of Two Human Smiles

In research that is more directly relevant to psychology, Darwin also used homologies to understand the origins of species-typical emotional expressions in humans. At the London Zoo, he watched monkeys and apes and noted that a number of their expressions seemed to be homologous to human expressions, including the smile (Darwin, 1872/1965). Research following up on Darwin's work has suggested that people may produce two kinds of smiles, which may have separate evolutionary origins.

People smile in two quite different contexts: (1) when genuinely happy and (2) when wishing to show another person that they are favorably disposed toward that person. The latter situation need not entail happiness at all; in fact, people are especially likely to smile at others in potentially tense circumstances, apparently as a means of reducing the tension (Goldenthal & others, 1981). Darwin (1872/1965) pointed out that these two smiles are anatomically distinct. The happy smile involves not just the turning up of the corners of the lips but also the pulling in of the skin near the outside corners of the eyes. This creates the creases called crow's feet, which radiate from the eyes and seem to make them sparkle. The other smile, in contrast, typically involves the lips alone, without the eyes. This distinction has

(a)

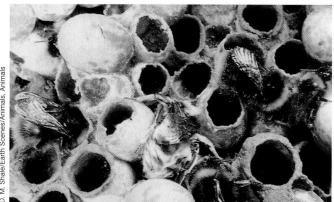

(b)

been confirmed in many studies with both adults and young children (Ekman, 1992; Sarra & Otta, 2001). In one study, for example, 10-month-old infants smiled with eyes and mouth when approached by their mother (presumably a happy situation) but smiled with mouth alone when approached by a stranger (a possibly tense situation) (Fox & Davidson, 1988).

Ekman (1992) considers the mouth-alone smile to be a derivative of the happy smile. He emphasizes its use in masking one's true feelings and calls it a "false smile." An alternative possibility, supported by research with monkeys and apes, is that the mouth-alone smile is a unique expression—let's call it the *greeting smile*—that arrived through a different evolutionary route from the happy smile (Redican, 1982).

Possible Origin of the Greeting Smile Non-human primates manifest two distinct smile-like displays. The one that seems most clearly to be homologous to the human greeting smile is the *silent bared-teeth display* (see Figure 3.20a). This facial expression involves contraction of the same facial muscles as are involved in the human greeting smile (Parr & others, 2007). If you have ever watched a cage of macaque monkeys at a zoo, you have almost certainly observed this display, a grimace usually shown by the more submissive of two monkeys as it glances nervously toward the more dominant. A direct stare in macaques (and other primates) is an aggressive signal, which precedes attack and can precipitate an attack by the other, and the silent bared-teeth display seems to have evolved as a means for a more submissive monkey to look at a more dominant one without provoking a fight. If it could be translated into words, it might be rendered as, "I'm looking at you but I'm not going to attack, so please don't attack me." In some monkey species, it is also used to promote affiliation after an aggressive encounter (Preuschoft & van Hooff, 1997).

J. A. van Hooff (1972, 1976) found that among chimpanzees this display takes on a new function, more similar to that of the human smile of greeting. Both the more submissive and the more dominant of two chimpanzees show the display upon meeting, and it usually precedes friendly interaction between them. From such observations, van Hooff proposed that the silent bared-teeth display originated in monkeys as a submissive gesture, but in the evolutionary line leading to chimpanzees and humans it evolved further into a general form of greeting. As used by the more submissive individual, it may retain its original meaning, "Please don't attack me," but as used by the more dominant, it may mean, "Rest assured, I won't attack," and as used by both it may mean, "Let's be friends."

Possible Origin of Laughter and the Happy Smile The other primate smile-like expression is the *relaxed open-mouth display*, or *play face* (see Figure 3.20b), which occurs mostly in young primates during playful fighting and chasing and is most clearly homologous to human laughter. It involves the same facial muscles as are involved in human laughter (Parr & others, 2007), and in chimpanzees it is often accompanied by a vocalized *ahh ahh ahh*, which sounds like a throaty human laugh. This display apparently originated as a means for young primates to signal to each other that their aggressive-like behavior is not to be taken seriously; nobody will really get hurt. Interestingly, in human children, laughter occurs during playful fighting and chasing more reliably than during any other form of play (Blurton-Jones, 1967), and even among us "sophisticated" adults, pie throwing, chase scenes, mock insults, and other forms of fake aggression are among the most reliable ways to elicit laughter. Thus, our laughter not only is similar in form to the relaxed open-mouth display of other primates but, at least in some cases, seems also to serve a similar function.

The smile of laughter is similar in form to the non-laughing happy smile, so the latter, too, may have its roots in the relaxed open-mouth display (Redican, 1982). There is, it seems to me, some poetry in the thought that the smile of happiness may have originated from a signal indicating that, although the world can be frightening and full of conflict, the aggression going on now is just in fun and we are safe.

29

How do studies of homologies between humans and other primates support the view that the human greeting smile and the human happy smile have separate evolutionary origins?

(a)

Tim Davis/Animals, Animals

(b)

Norman Tomalin/Bruce Coleman

FIGURE 3.20 Possible homologues to two types of human smiles The silent bared-teeth display (a) is believed to be homologous to the human greeting smile, and the relaxed open-mouth display (b) is believed to be homologous to the human laugh and happy smile. The animals in both photos are chimpanzees.

The Value for Psychology of Studying Analogies

30

How can analogies be used to make inferences about the ultimate functions of species-typical traits?

You have just seen examples of how homologies can be used to make inferences about the evolutionary origins of species-typical behaviors. Analogies, in contrast, are not useful for tracing evolutionary origins, but are useful for making inferences about the ultimate functions of species-typical behaviors. If different species have independently evolved a particular behavioral trait, then comparing the species may reveal commonalities of habitat and lifestyle that are clues to the ultimate function of that trait. You will see examples of this use of analogies in the remaining sections of this chapter, as applied to patterns of mating, patterns of aggression, and patterns of helping.

SECTION REVIEW

Species-typical behaviors have come to exist through natural selection.

Species-Typical Behaviors

➤ Commonly called instincts, species-typical behaviors are ways of behaving that characterize a species—such as cats meowing and humans walking upright.

➤ They may be influenced by learning or even require learning, as exemplified by cultural differences in the eyebrow flash, human language learning, and white-crowned sparrows' song development.

➤ They depend upon biological preparedness—i.e., upon having anatomical structures that permit and motivate the behavior.

Homologies and Analogies

➤ Homologies are similarities due to common ancestry. They are useful for studying underlying mechanisms and for tracing the evolutionary course of species-typical behaviors, exemplified by research on the greeting smile and happy smile in humans.

➤ Analogies are similarities due to convergent evolution (independent evolution of similar traits). They are useful for inferring ultimate functions.

off the mark.com   by Mark Parisi

offthemark.com

FEMALE GENETICISTS HAVE BEEN WORKING AROUND THE CLOCK SINCE THE DISCOVERY THAT **MALE** SEAHORSES GET PREGNANT

Mark Parisi: offthemark.com

■ Evolutionary Analyses of Mating Patterns

From an evolutionary perspective, no class of behavior is more important than mating. Mating is the means by which all sexually reproducing animals get their genes into the next generation. Mating is also interesting because it is the most basic form of social behavior. Sex is the foundation of society. Were it not necessary for female and male to come together to reproduce, members of a species could, in theory, go through life completely oblivious to one another.

Countless varieties of male-female arrangements for sexual reproduction have evolved in different species of animals. One way to classify them is according to the number of partners a male or female typically mates with over a given period of time, such as a breeding season. Four broad classes are generally recognized: **polygyny** [pah-**li**-ji-nee], in which one male mates with more than one female; **polyandry** [pah-lee-**an**-dree], in which one female mates with more than one male; **monogamy,** in which one male mates with one female; and **polygynandry** [pah-lee-**jin**-an-dree], in which members of a group consisting of more than one male and more than one female mate with one another (Rees & Harvey, 1991). (These terms are easy to remember if you know that *poly-* means "many"; *mono-,* "one"; *-gyn,* "female"; and *-andr,* "male." Thus, for example, polygynandry literally means "many females and males.") As illustrated in Figure 3.21, a feature of both polygyny and polyandry is that some individuals are necessarily deprived of a mating opportunity—a state of affairs associated with considerable conflict.

A Theory Relating Mating Patterns to Parental Investment

31

What is Trivers's theory of parental investment?

In a now-classic article, Robert Trivers (1972) outlined a theory relating courtship and mating patterns to sex differences in amount of **parental investment.** Parental investment can be defined roughly as the time, energy, and risk to survival that are

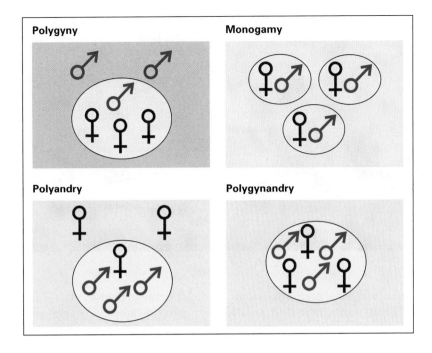

FIGURE 3.21 Four mating systems In a polygynous system (common in mammals), the unmated males are a threat to the mated male, and in a polyandrous system (present in some birds and fishes), the unmated females are a threat to the mated female. Threat is reduced by monogamy and polygynandry, because with those systems, most individuals find mates.

involved in producing, feeding, and otherwise caring for each offspring. More precisely, Trivers defined it as the loss, to the adult, of future reproductive capacity that results from the production and nurturance of any given offspring. Every offspring in a sexually reproducing species has two parents, one of each sex, but the amount of parental investment from the two is usually not equal. The essence of Trivers's theory is this: *In general, for species in which parental investment is unequal, the more parentally invested sex will be (a) more vigorously competed for than the other and (b) more discriminating than the other when choosing mates.*

To illustrate and elaborate on this theory—and to see how it is supported by cross-species comparisons focusing on analogies—let us apply it to each of the four general classes of mating patterns.

Polygyny Is Related to High Female and Low Male Parental Investment

Most species of mammals are polygynous, and Trivers's theory helps explain why. Mammalian reproductive physiology is such that the female necessarily invests a great deal in the offspring she bears. The young must first develop within her body and then must obtain nourishment from her in the form of milk. Because of the female's high investment, the number of offspring she can produce in a breeding season or a lifetime is limited. A female whose gestation and lactation periods are such that she can bear at most four young a year can produce no more than that regardless of the number of different males with which she mates.

Things are different for the male. His involvement with offspring is, at minimum, simply the production of sperm cells and the act of copulation. These require little time and energy, so his maximum reproductive potential is limited not by parental investment but by the number of fertile females with which he mates. A male that mates with 20 females, each of which can bear four young, can in theory produce 80 offspring a year. When the evolutionary advantage in mating with multiple partners is greater for males than for females, a pattern evolves in which males compete with one another to mate with as many females as they can.

Among mammals, males' competition for females often involves one-on-one battles, which the larger and stronger combatant most often wins. This leads to a selective advantage for increased size and strength in males, up to some maximum

> ------------------------------------32
>
> **Based on Trivers's theory of parental investment, why does high investment by the female lead to (a) polygyny, (b) large size of males, and (c) high selectivity in the female's choice of mate?**

Who's bigger and stronger? These male elephant seals are sizing each other up for possible battle over mating rights to the many females in the background. Because the larger combatant usually wins, male elephant seals have through natural selection become huge compared with females.

An aggressive female The spotted sandpiper is a polyandrous species. The female mates with several males and defends her territory from invading females. This female is stretching her wings in a threat display.

beyond which the size advantage in obtaining mates is outweighed by disadvantages, such as difficulty in finding sufficient food to support the large size. In general, the more polygynous a species, the greater is the average size difference between males and females. An extreme example is the elephant seal. Males of this species fight one another, sometimes to the death, for mating rights to groups averaging about 50 females, and the males outweigh females several-fold (Hoelzel & others, 1999). In the evolution of elephant seals, those males whose genes made them large, strong, and ferocious enough to defeat other males sent many copies of their genes on to the next generation, while their weaker or less aggressive opponents sent few or none.

For the same reason that the female mammal usually has less evolutionary incentive than the male to mate with many individuals, she has more incentive to be discriminating in her choice of mate (Trivers, 1972). Because she invests so much, risking her life and decreasing her future reproductive potential whenever she becomes pregnant, her genetic interests lie in producing offspring that will have the highest possible chance themselves to survive and reproduce. To the degree that the male affects the young, either through his genes or through other resources he provides, females would be expected to select males whose contribution will be most beneficial. In elephant seals, it is presumably to the female's evolutionary advantage to mate with the winner of battles. The male victor's genes increase the chance that the female's sons will win battles in the future and produce many young themselves.

Polyandry Is Related to High Male and Low Female Parental Investment

33 – – – – – – – – – – – – – – – ◀
What conditions promote the evolution of polyandry? How do sex differences within polyandrous species support Trivers's theory?

Polyandry is not the primary mating pattern for any species of mammal, but it is for some species of fishes and birds (Andersson, 2005). Polyandry is more likely to evolve in egg-laying species than in mammals, because a smaller proportion of an egg layer's reproductive cycle is tied to the female's body. Once the eggs are laid, they can be cared for by either parent, and, depending on other conditions, evolution can lead to greater male than female parental investment. Polyandry seems to come about in cases where the female can produce more eggs during a single breeding season than either she alone or she and one male can care for (Andersson, 2005). Her best strategy then becomes that of mating with multiple males and leaving each batch of fertilized eggs with the father, who becomes the main or sole caretaker.

Consistent with Trivers's theory, females of polyandrous species are the more active and aggressive courters, and they have evolved to be larger, stronger, and in some cases more brightly colored than the males (Berglund & Rosenqvist, 2001). An example is the spotted sandpiper, a common freshwater shorebird. A female spotted sandpiper can lay up to three clutches of eggs in rapid succession, each cared for by a different male that has mated with her (Oring, 1995). At the beginning of the breeding season, the females—which outweigh the males by about 20 percent and have somewhat more conspicuous spots—stake out territories where they actively court males and drive out other females.

Monogamy Is Related to Equivalent Male and Female Parental Investment

According to Trivers's theory, when the two sexes make approximately equal investments in their young, their degree of competition for mates will also be approximately equal, and monogamy will prevail. Equal parental investment is most likely to come about when conditions make it impossible for a single adult to raise the young but quite possible for two to raise them. Under these circumstances, if either parent leaves, the young fail to survive, so natural selection favors genes that lead parents to stay together and care for the young together. Because neither sex is much more likely than the other to fight over mates, there is little or no natural selection for sex differences in size and strength, and, in general, males and females of monogamous species are nearly identical in these characteristics.

Consistent with the view that monogamy arises from the need for more than one adult to care for offspring, over 90 percent of bird species are predominantly monogamous (Cézilly & Zayan, 2000; Lack, 1968). Among most species of birds, unlike most mammals, a single parent would usually not be able to raise the young. Birds must incubate and protect their eggs until they hatch, then must guard the hatchlings and fetch food for them until they can fly. One parent alone cannot simultaneously guard the nest and leave it to get food, but two together can. Among mammals, monogamy has arisen in some species that are like birds in the sense that their young must be given food other than milk, of a type that the male can provide. The best-known examples are certain carnivores, including foxes and coyotes (Malcolm, 1985). Young carnivores must be fed meat until they have acquired the necessary strength, agility, and skills to hunt on their own, and two parents are much better than one at accomplishing this task. Monogamy also occurs in several species of rodents, where the male may play a crucial role in protecting the young from predators while the mother forages (Sommer, 2000).

With modern DNA techniques to determine paternity, researchers have learned that *social monogamy* (the faithful pairing of female and male for raising young) does not necessarily imply *sexual monogamy* (fidelity in copulation between that female and male). Researchers commonly find that between 5 and 35 percent of offspring in socially monogamous birds are sired by a neighboring male rather than by the male at the nest (Birkhead & Moller, 1992); for one species, the superb fairy wren, that average is 75 percent (Mulder, 1994).

Why does such extra-mate copulation occur? From the female's evolutionary perspective, copulation with a male that is genetically superior to her own mate (as manifested in song and feathers) results in genetically superior young, and copulation with any additional male increases the chance that all her eggs will be fertilized by viable sperm (Zeh & Zeh, 2001). For the male, evolutionary advantage rests in driving neighboring males away from his own mate whenever possible and in copulating with neighboring females whenever possible. Genes that build brain mechanisms that promote such behaviors are passed along to more offspring than are genes that do not.

Polygynandry Is Related to Investment in the Group

Among the clearest examples of polygynandrous species are chimpanzees and bonobos, which happen to be our two closest animal relatives (see Figure 3.22 on the next page). Bonobos are similar in appearance to chimpanzees but are rarer

> ------------------------------------**34**
> **What conditions promote the evolution of monogamy? Why are sex differences in size and strength generally lacking in monogamous species?**

Natural History, November 1994, p. 60. Photo by C. Allan Morgan.

A not-so-faithful couple The superb fairy wren is socially but not sexually monogamous. The male (at the left) and the female stay together at the nest and raise the young together, but DNA testing has shown that about 75 percent of the offspring, on average, are sired by neighboring males.

> ------------------------------------**35**
> **For what evolutionary reasons might monogamously mated females and males sometimes copulate with partners other than their mates?**

> ------------------------------------**36**
> **What appear to be the evolutionary advantages of polygynandry for chimpanzees and bonobos, and in what ways is polygynandry more fully developed for the latter than the former?**

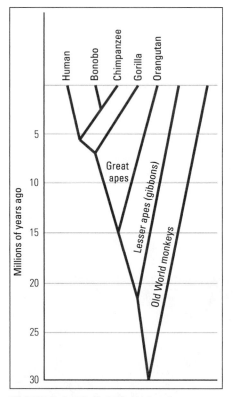

FIGURE 3.22 Relationship of humans to apes and Old World monkeys The ancestral line leading to humans split off from that leading to Old World monkeys 30 million years ago, and it split off from that leading to bonobos and chimpanzees about 6 million years ago. (Data from Corballis, 1999.)

Bonobo sex Bonobos seem to live by the motto, "Make love, not war." Research suggests that they are the most sexually active and the most peaceful of all primates. Here a male has mounted a female in a face-to-face position—a position long thought to be unique to humans. But bonobo sex occurs in all possible partner combinations (homosexual as well as heterosexual) and essentially all imaginable positions.

and have only recently been studied in the wild. The basic social structure of both species is the colony, which consists usually of two to three dozen adults of both sexes and their offspring. When the female is ovulating, she develops on her rump a prominent pink swelling, which she actively displays to advertise her condition. During the time of this swelling, which lasts about a week in chimps and 3 weeks in bonobos, she is likely to mate with most of the adult males of the colony, though she may actively choose to mate with some more often than with others, especially at the point in her cycle when she is most fertile (Goodall, 1986; Kano, 1992; Stumpf & Boesch, 2006).

Polygynandry has apparently evolved in these ape species because it permits a group of adult males and females to live together in relative harmony, without too much fighting over who mates with whom. A related advantage, from the female's perspective, is paternity confusion (Hrdy, 1981, 2000). Among many species of primates, males kill young that are not their own, and such behavior has been observed in chimpanzees when a female migrates into a colony bringing with her an infant that was sired elsewhere (Wrangham, 1993). Because almost any chimp or bonobo male in the colony could be the father of any infant born within the colony, each male's evolutionary interest lies not in attacking the young but in helping to protect and care for the group as a whole.

Polygynandry seems to be more fully developed in bonobos than in chimps. Male chimps sometimes use force to monopolize the sexual activity of a female throughout her ovulatory cycle or during the period of peak receptivity (Goodall, 1986; Wrangham, 1993), but this does not appear to occur among bonobos (Hohmann & Fruth, 2003; Wrangham, 1993). In fact, among bonobos sex appears to be more a reducer of aggression than a cause of it (Parish & de Waal, 2000; Wrangham, 1993). Unlike any other apes, female bonobos copulate at all times of their reproductive cycle, not just near the time of ovulation. In addition to their frequent heterosexual activity, bonobos of the same sex often rub their genitals together, and genital stimulation of all types occurs most often following conflict and in situations that could potentially elicit conflict, such as when a favorite food is discovered (Hohmann & Fruth, 2000; Parish, 1996). Field studies suggest that bonobos are the most peaceful of primates and that their frequent polygynandrous sexual activity helps keep them that way (de Waal, 2005; Kano, 1992).

What About Human Mating Patterns?

A Largely Monogamous, Partly Polygynous Species

When we apply the same criteria that are used to classify the mating systems of other species, we find that humans fall on the boundary between monogamy and polygyny (Dewsbury, 1988). In no culture are human beings as sexually promiscuous as are our closest ape relatives, the chimpanzees and bonobos. In every culture, people form long-term mating bonds, which are usually legitimized through some sort of culturally recognized marriage contract. Anthropologists have found that the great majority of non-Western cultures, where Western influence has not made polygyny illegal, practice a mixture of monogamy and polygyny (Marlowe, 2000; Murdock, 1981). In such cultures, a few men, who have sufficient wealth or status, have two or more wives, while the great majority of men have one wife and a few have none. Thus, even in cultures that permit and idealize polygyny, most marriages are monogamous.

37
What evidence suggests that humans evolved as a partly monogamous, partly polygynous species? How is this consistent with Trivers's parental investment theory?

Human children, more so than the young of any other primates, require an extended period of care before they can play full adult roles in activities such as food gathering. Cross-cultural research shows that in every culture mothers provide most of the direct physical care of children, but fathers contribute in various ways. In many cultures—especially in hunter-gatherer cultures—fathers share to some degree in the physical care of their offspring (Marlowe, 2000), and in nearly all cultures fathers provide indirect care in the form of food and other material provisions. In fact, in 77 percent of the cultures for which data are available, fathers provide more of the provisions for young than do mothers (Marlowe, 2000). Taking both direct and indirect care into account, we are a species in which fathers typically lag somewhat behind mothers, but not greatly behind them, in degree of parental investment. This, in line with Trivers's parental investment theory, is consistent with our being a primarily monogamous but moderately polygynous species.

The moderate size difference between men and women is also consistent with this conclusion (Dewsbury, 1988). The average size difference between males and females in humans is nowhere near that observed in highly polygynous species, such as elephant seals and gorillas, but is greater than that observed in monogamous species.

Roles of Emotions in Human Mating Systems

Our biological equipment that predisposes us for mating bonds includes brain mechanisms that promote the twin emotions of romantic love and sexual jealousy. These emotions are found in people of every culture that has been studied (Buss, 2000b; Fisher, 1992). People everywhere develop strong emotional ties to those toward whom they are sexually drawn. The predominant feeling is a need to be regularly near the other person. People also, everywhere, feel intensely jealous when "their" mates appear to be sexually drawn to others. While love tends to create mating bonds, jealousy tends to preserve such bonds by motivating each member of a mated pair to act in ways designed to prevent the other from having an affair with someone else.

38
From an evolutionary perspective, what are the functions of romantic love and sexual jealousy, and how is this supported by cross-species comparisons? How is sexual unfaithfulness explained?

Other animals that form long-term mating bonds show evidence of emotions that are functionally similar to human love and jealousy (e.g., Lazarus & others, 2004). In this sense, we are more like monogamous birds than we are like our closest ape relatives. The similarities between humans and birds in sexual love and jealousy are clearly analogies, not homologies (Lorenz, 1974). These evolved separately in humans and birds as means to create and preserve mating bonds that are sufficiently strong and durable to enable biparental care of offspring. Chimpanzees and bonobos (especially the latter) can engage in open, promiscuous sex with little emotional consequence, because they have not evolved strong emotions of sexual love and jealousy, but humans and monogamous birds cannot. The difference ultimately has to do with species differences in the need for care from both parents.

At the same time that love and jealousy tend to promote bonding, lust (another product of evolution) tends to motivate both men and women to engage surreptitiously in sex outside of such bonds. In this sense we are like those socially monogamous birds that are sexually unfaithful. A man who can inseminate women beyond his wife may send more copies of his genes into the next generation than a completely faithful man. A woman who has sex with men other than her husband may also benefit evolutionarily. Such escapades may (a) increase her chances of conception (serve as a hedge against the possibility that her husband's sperm are not viable or are genetically incompatible with her eggs); (b) increase the evolutionary fitness of her offspring (if she mates with a man whose genes are evolutionarily superior to those of her husband); and/or (c) result in provisions from more than one man (Hrdy, 2000). And so the human soap opera continues, much like that of the superb fairy wren, though not to such an extreme. Studies involving DNA testing, in cultures ranging from hunter-gatherer groups to modern Western societies, suggest that somewhere between 2 and 10 percent of children in socially monogamous families are sired by someone other than the mother's husband (Marlowe, 2000).

SECTION REVIEW

An evolutionary perspective offers functionalist explanations of mating patterns.

Relation of Mating Patterns to Parental Investment	Human Mating Patterns
➤ Trivers theorized that sex differences in parental investment (time, energy, risk involved in bearing and raising young) explain mating patterns and sex differences in size, aggressiveness, competition for mates, and selectivity in choosing mates.	➤ Parental investment is somewhat lower for fathers than for mothers, consistent with the human mix of monogamy and polygyny.
➤ Consistent with Trivers's theory, polygyny is associated with high female and low male parental investment; polyandry is associated with the opposite; monogamy is associated with approximately equal investment by the two sexes: and polygynandry, common to chimps and bonobos, seems to be associated with high investment in the group.	➤ Romantic love and jealousy help promote and preserve bonding of mates, permitting two-parent care of offspring.
	➤ Both sexual faithfulness and unfaithfulness can be evolutionarily adaptive, depending on conditions

---

■ Evolutionary Analyses of Hurting and Helping

Human beings, like other animals, are motivated both to hurt and to help one another in the struggle to survive and reproduce. From an evolutionary perspective, other members of one's species are competitors for food, mates, safe places to live, and other limited resources. Ultimately, such competition is the foundation of aggression. Yet, at the same time, others of one's kind are potential helpmates. Many life-promoting tasks can be accomplished better by two or more together than by one struggling alone. The human drama, like that of other social species, involves the balancing of competitiveness with the need for others' help. Let us look first at the grim topic of aggression and then end, more pleasantly, with cooperation.

Sex Differences in Aggression

Aggression, as the term is used here, refers to fighting and threats of fighting among members of the same species. Brain mechanisms that motivate and organize such behavior have evolved because they help animals acquire and retain resources needed to survive and reproduce. As you saw in the previous section, much animal aggression centers on mating. Polygynous males and polyandrous females fight for mates; monogamous males fight to prevent other males from copulating with their mates; and monogamous females fight to keep other females from leading their mates away (Slagsvold & others, 1999; Tobias & Seddon, 2000). Aggression can also serve to protect a feeding ground for oneself and one's offspring, to drive away individuals that may be a threat to one's young, and to elevate one's status within a social group. Much could be said from an evolutionary perspective about all aspects of aggression, but here I will focus just on sex differences in how aggression is manifested.

"If anyone calls, I'll be downstairs thumping my chest at the younger apes."

Why Male Primates Are Generally More Violent Than Female Primates

Among most species of mammals, and especially among primates, males are much more violently aggressive than are females. Female primates are not unaggressive, but their aggression is typically aimed directly toward obtaining resources and defending their young. When they have achieved their ends, they stop fighting. Male primates, in contrast, seem at times to go out of their way to pick fights, and they are far more likely to maim or kill their opponents than are females.

Most of the violence perpetrated by male primates has to do directly or indirectly with sex. Male monkeys and apes of many species have been observed to kill infants fathered by others, apparently as a means to get the females to stop lactating so they will ovulate again and become sexually active. Males also fight with one another, sometimes brutally, to gain access to a particular female or to raise their rank in the dominance hierarchy of the colony. High rank generally increases both their attractiveness to females and their ability to intimidate sexual rivals (Cowlishaw & Dunbar, 1991). Males are also often violent toward females; they use violence to force copulation or to prevent the female from copulating with other males. All of these behaviors have been observed in chimpanzees and many other primate species (Goodall, 1986; Smuts, 1992; Wittig & Boesch, 2003).

Evolution, remember, is not a moral force. It promotes those behaviors that tend to get one's genes passed on to the next generation. Female primates, because of their higher parental investment, don't need to fight to get the opposite sex interested in them. Moreover, aggression may have a higher cost for females than for males. The female at battle risks not just her life but also that of any fetus she is gestating or young she is nursing—the repositories of her genes. The male at battle risks just himself, and, in the cold calculus of evolution, his life isn't worth anything unless he can get a female to mate with him. Genes that promote mating, by whatever means, proliferate, and genes that fail to promote it vanish.

→ -**39**
How is male violence toward infants, toward other males, and toward females explained from an evolutionary perspective?
- -

Tough young males Male mammals of many species compete with one another for dominance. Much of their competition, however, involves threat and bluff rather than bloodshed, as illustrated by these two young mountain gorillas.

Male Violence in Humans

Humans are no exception to the usual primate rule. Cross-cultural studies show that everywhere men are more violent, more likely to maim or kill, than are women. In fact, in a survey of cross-cultural data on this issue, Martin Daly and Margo Wilson (1988) were unable to find any society in which the number of women who killed other women was even one-tenth as great as the number of men who killed other men. On average, in the data they examined, male-male killings outnumbered female-female killings by more than 30 to 1. One might construe a scenario through which such a difference in violence would be purely a product of learning in every culture, but the hypothesis that the difference resides at least partly in inherited sex differences seems more plausible.

According to Daly's and Wilson's analyses, the apparent motives underlying male violence and homicide are very much in accord with predictions from evolutionary theory. Among the leading motives for murder among men in every culture is sexual jealousy. In some cultures, men are expected to kill other men who have sex with their wives (Symons, 1979), and in others, such murders are common even though they are illegal (Daly & Wilson, 1988). Men also fight over status, which can affect their degree of success in mating (Daly & Wilson, 1990). One man insults another and then the two fight it out—with fists, knives, or guns. And men, like many male monkeys and apes, often use violence to control females. In the United States and Canada, between 25 and 30 percent of women are battered by their current or former mate at some time in their lives (Randall & Haskell, 1995; Williams & Hawkins, 1989). Analyses of domestic violence cases indicate that much of it has to do with the man's belief (often unfounded) that his partner has been or might become sexually unfaithful (Peters & others, 2002; Goetz, 2008).

How Female Bonobos Dominate Males

Bonobos appear to be an exception to the primate rule that males are the more violent sex. Bonobos, as you recall, are as closely related to us as are chimpanzees; and bonobos and chimpanzees are more closely related to each other than either species is to us (look back at Figure 3.22). Yet, in terms of their patterns of aggression, bonobos are quite different from chimpanzees. They are less aggressive than chimpanzees overall. In tense situations, which in chimpanzees would provoke fights, bonobos of both sexes tend to engage in bouts of rough-and-tumble play and/or sexual play, apparently as means of reducing the tension (Palagi & others, 2006). Moreover, to the degree that they are aggressive, female bonobos in group situations generally dominate males, despite the fact that the males are physically larger and stronger than the females (Kano, 1998; Parish & de Waal, 2000; White & Wood, 2007).

40

How have bonobo females countered the mammalian tendency for males to control females through violence?

◀ The females dominate because they form strong alliances and help one another in disputes with males (Parish & de Waal, 2000). A single female bonobo cannot defeat a male, but a group of three or more can easily do so. When a valued but limited source of food is found by a colony of bonobos, the females eat first. A male who attempts to violate that rule is beaten off by the females as a group. Even the most dominant male is subject to such attacks, which in some cases can be quite brutal. You might wonder why the males don't form alliances for counterattack. Nobody knows, but one possibility is that the males' self-interests, in their disputes with females, are too much at odds with one another to permit strong alliances. Consistent with that idea is the observation that male bonobos do fight with one another more than do female bonobos (White & Wood, 2007).

The tendency for female bonobos to form close alliances to control males seems to derive largely from their genetic makeup. It is seen among all bonobo groups that have been studied, both in the wild and in captivity. Human females, by contrast, don't universally form alliances to control males, yet such alliances are within human capacity. In a cross-cultural analysis, Barbara Smuts (1992) showed that men's violence toward women is lowest in those cultures and communities where women have strong alliances with one another and men have relatively weak alliances with one another. In those communities, women hear about and come to the aid of a woman who is being abused by a man, and, through humiliation or other means (usually not physical violence), teach the offending man a lesson. Other cross-cultural analyses reveal that women have relatively more control over economic resources in societies where alliances among women are strong than in societies where such alliances are weak (Yanca & Low, 2004).

Patterns of Helping

From an evolutionary perspective, **helping** can be defined as any behavior that increases the survival chance or reproductive capacity of another individual. Given this definition, it is useful to distinguish between two categories of helping: cooperation and altruism.

Cooperation occurs when an individual helps another while helping itself. This sort of helping happens all the time in the animal world and is easy to understand from an evolutionary perspective. It occurs when a mated pair of foxes work together to raise their young, a pack of wolves work together to kill an antelope, or a group of chimpanzees work together to chase off a predator or a rival group of chimpanzees. Most of the advantages of social living lie in cooperation. By working with others for common ends, each individual has a better chance of survival and reproduction than it would have alone. Whatever costs accrue are more than repaid by the benefits. Human beings everywhere live in social groups and derive the benefits of cooperation. Those who live as our ancestors did cooperate in hunting and gathering food, caring for children, building dwellings, defending against predators and human invaders, and, most human of all, in exchanging, through language, information that bears on all aspects of the struggle for survival.

Altruism, in contrast, occurs when an individual helps another while decreasing its own survival chance or reproductive capacity. This is less common than cooperation, but many animals do behave in ways that at least appear to be altruistic. For example, some animals, including female ground squirrels, emit a loud, distinctive call when they spot an approaching predator. The cry warns others of the predator's approach and, at the same time, tends to attract the predator's attention to the caller (Sherman, 1977). (See Figure 3.23.) The selfish response would be to remain quiet and hidden, or to move away quietly, rather than risk being detected by warning others. How can such behavior be explained from an evolutionary perspective? As Trivers (1971) pointed out long ago, any evolutionary account of apparent altruism must operate by showing that from a broader perspective, focusing on the propagation of one's genes, the behavior is not truly altruistic. Evolutionists have developed two broad theories to account for ostensible altruism in animals: the kin selection theory and the reciprocity theory.

The Kin Selection Theory of Altruism

The **kin selection theory** holds that behavior that seems to be altruistic came about through natural selection because it preferentially helps close relatives, who are genetically most similar to the helper (Hamilton, 1964). What actually survives over evolutionary time, of course, is not the individual but the individual's genes. Any gene that promotes the production and preservation of copies of itself can be a fit gene, from the vantage point of natural selection, even if it reduces the survival chances of a particular carrier of the gene.

Imagine a ground squirrel with a rare gene that promotes the behavior of calling out when a predator is near. The mathematics of inheritance are such that, on average, one-half of the offspring or siblings of the individual with this gene would be expected to have the same gene, as would one-fourth of the nieces or nephews and one-eighth of the cousins. Thus, if the altruist incurred a small risk (Δ) to its own life while increasing an offspring's or a sibling's chances of survival by more than 2Δ, a niece's or nephew's by more than 4Δ, or a cousin's by more than 8Δ, the gene would increase in the population from one generation to the next.

Many research studies have shown that animals do help kin more than non-kin. For example, ground squirrels living with kin are more likely to emit alarm calls than are those living with non-kin (Sherman, 1977). Chimpanzees and other primates are more likely to help kin than non-kin in all sorts of ways, including sharing food, providing assistance in fights, and helping take care of young (Goodall, 1986; Nishida, 1990). Consistent with the mathematics of genetic relatedness, macaque monkeys have been observed to help their brothers and sisters more readily than their cousins and their cousins more readily than more distant relatives (Silk, 2002). In these examples, the helpers can apparently distinguish kin from non-kin, and this ability allows them to direct help selectively to kin (Pfennig & Sherman, 1995; Silk, 2002). In theory, however, altruistic behavior can evolve through kin selection even without such discrimination. A tendency to help any member of one's species, indiscriminately, can evolve if the animal's usual living arrangements are such that, by chance alone, a sufficiently high percentage of help is directed toward kin.

Cross-cultural research shows that among humans the selective helping of kin more than non-kin is common everywhere (Essock-Vitale & McGuire, 1980). If a

FIGURE 3.23 An alarm-calling ground squirrel When they spot a predator, female ground squirrels often emit an alarm call, especially if they are living in a group of close kin. Males are less likely to live near close kin and do not show this response.

L. D. Klein/Photo Researchers

————————————41

How do the kin selection and reciprocity theories take the altruism out of "altruism"? What observations show that both theories apply to humans as well as to other animals?

mother dies or for other reasons is unable to care for a child, the child's grandmother, aunt, or other close relative is by far the most likely adopter (Kurland, 1979). Close kin are also most likely to share dwellings or land, hunt together, or form other collaborative arrangements. On the other side of the same coin, studies in Western culture indicate that genetic kin living in the same household are less often violent toward one another than are non-kin living in the same household (Daly & Wilson, 1988), and studies in other cultures have shown that villages in which most people are closely related have less internal friction than those in which people are less closely related (Chagnon, 1979). People report feeling emotionally closer to their kin than to their non-kin friends, even if they live farther away from the former than from the latter and see them less often (Neyer & Lang, 2003).

When leaders call for patriotic sacrifice or universal cooperation, they commonly employ kinship terms (Johnson, 1987). At times of war, political leaders ask citizens to fight for the "motherland" or "fatherland"; at other times, religious leaders and humanists strive to promote world peace by speaking of our "brothers and sisters" everywhere. The terms appeal to our instincts to be kind to relatives. Our imagination and intelligence allow us, at least sometimes, to extend our concept of kinship to all humanity.

The Reciprocity Theory of Apparent Altruism

The *reciprocity theory* provides an account of how acts of apparent altruism can arise even among non-kin. According to this theory, behaviors that seem to be altruistic are actually forms of long-term cooperation (Trivers, 1971). Computer simulations of evolution have shown that a genetically induced tendency to help non-kin can evolve if it is tempered by (a) an ability to remember which individuals have reciprocated such help in the past and (b) a tendency to refrain from helping again those who failed to reciprocate previous help (discussed in Chapter 14). Under these conditions, helping another is selfish because it increases the chance of receiving help from that other in the future.

Behavior fitting this pattern is found in various niches of the animal world. As one example, vampire bats frequently share food with unrelated members of their species that have shared food with them in the past (Wilkinson, 1988). As another example, bonobo females that establish friendship coalitions and are so very effective in helping one another are often unrelated to one another, having immigrated from different natal colonies (Kano, 1992; Parish & de Waal, 2000). The help each gives the others, in such acts as chasing off offending males, is reciprocated at another time.

Helpful little demons Vampire bats are gregarious mammals that demonstrate reciprocal altruism. After gorging itself on a blood meal, a bat will share some of what it has ingested with another bat, usually one that has fed it in the past.

The greatest reciprocal helpers of all, by far, are human beings. People in every culture feel a strong drive to return help that is given to them (Gouldner, 1960; Hill, 2002). Humans, more than any other species, can keep track of help given, remember it over a long period of time, and think of a wide variety of ways of reciprocating. Moreover, to ensure reciprocity, people everywhere have a highly developed sense of fairness and behave in ways that punish those who fail to fulfill their parts in reciprocal relationships (Fehr & Fischbacher, 2003). Certain human emotions seem to be well designed, by natural selection, to promote reciprocity. We feel gratitude (a sense of wanting to give) toward those who help us, pride when we return such help, guilt when we fail to return help, and anger when someone fails repeatedly to return help that we have given (discussed more fully in Chapter 14). Humans also help others, including others who may never be able to reciprocate, in order to develop a good reputation in the community at large, and those with a good reputation are valued and helped by the community (Fehr & Fischbacher, 2003).

Final Words of Caution: Two Fallacies to Avoid

Before closing this chapter it would be worthwhile to reiterate and expand on two points that I have already made: (1) Natural selection is not a moral force, and (2) our genes do not control our behavior in ways that are independent of the environment.

These statements contradict two fallacious ideas that often creep into the evolutionary thinking of people who don't fully understand natural selection and the nature of genetic influences.

The Naturalistic Fallacy

The **naturalistic fallacy** is the equation of "natural" with "moral" or "right." If natural selection favors sexual promiscuity, then promiscuity is right. If male mammals in nature dominate females through force, then aggressive dominance of women by men is right. If natural selection promotes self-interested struggle among individuals, then selfishness is right. Such equations are logically indefensible, because nature itself is neither moral nor immoral except as judged so by us. Morality is a product of the human mind. We have acquired, in our evolution, the capacity to think in moral terms, and we can use that capacity to develop moral philosophies that go in many possible directions, including those that favor real altruism and constrain individual self-interest for the good of the larger community.

42

Why is the equation of "natural" with "right" considered a fallacy? How did that fallacy figure into the philosophy of Herbert Spencer?

The term *naturalistic fallacy* was coined by the British philosopher G. E. Moore (1903) as part of an argument against the views of another British philosopher, Herbert Spencer (1879). A contemporary of Darwin, Spencer considered himself a strong believer in Darwin's theory, and his goal was to apply it to the spheres of social philosophy and ethics. Unlike Darwin, Spencer seemed to imply in his writings that natural selection is guided by a moral force. He distinguished between "more evolved" and "less evolved" behaviors in nature and suggested that "more evolved" means more moral. Although Spencer wrote of cooperation as highly evolved and virtuous, his philosophy leaned more toward the virtues of individualism and competition. Spencer's writings were especially popular in the United States, where they were championed by such industrialists as John D. Rockefeller and Andrew Carnegie (Rachels, 1990).

It was Spencer, not Darwin, who popularized the phrase "survival of the fittest"; and some of the so-called *social Darwinists,* who were inspired by Spencer, used that phrase to justify even the most ruthless extremes of capitalism. In their view, the fittest were those who rose to the top in unchecked capitalism, and the unfit were those who fell into poverty or starvation.

Darwin himself was not seduced by the naturalistic fallacy. He was repulsed by much of what he saw in nature and marveled at the human ability to rise, sometimes, above it. He conscientiously avoided phrases such as "more evolved" that would imply that evolution is a moral force, and he felt frustrated by his inability to stop others from assuming that it is. In a letter to a friend, shortly after publication of *The Origin of Species,* he wrote wryly, "I have noted in a Manchester newspaper a rather good squib, showing that I have proved 'might is right' and therefore Napoleon is right and every cheating tradesman is also right" (Rachels, 1990).

The Deterministic Fallacy

The second general error, called the **deterministic fallacy,** is the assumption that genetic influences on our behavior take the form of genetic control of our behavior, which we can do nothing about (short of modifying our genes). The mistake here is assuming or implying that genes influence behavior directly, rather than through the indirect means of working with the environment to build or modify biological structures that then, in interplay with the environment, produce behavior. Some popular books on human evolution have exhibited the deterministic fallacy by implying that one or another form of behavior—such as fighting for territories—is unavoidable because it is controlled by our genes. That implication is unreasonable even when applied to non-human animals. Territorial birds, for example, defend territories only when the environmental conditions are ripe for them to do so. We humans can control our environment and thereby control ourselves. We can either enhance or reduce the environmental ingredients needed for a particular behavioral tendency to develop and manifest itself.

43

Why is it a mistake to believe that characteristics that are influenced by genes cannot be changed except by modifying genes?

We also can and regularly do, through conscious self-control and well-learned social habits, behave in ways that are contrary to biases built into our biology. One might even argue that our capacity for self-control is the essence of our humanity. In our evolution, we acquired that ability in a greater dose than seems apparent in any other species, perhaps because of its role in permitting us to live in complex social groups. Our capacity for self-control is part of our biological heritage, and it liberates us to some degree—but by no means completely—from that heritage.

Our great capacity for knowledge, including knowledge of our own biological nature, can also be a liberating force. Most evolutionary psychologists contend that an understanding of human nature, far from implying fatalism, can be a step toward human betterment. For example, in her evolutionary analysis of men's violence against women, Smuts (1992) wrote:

> Although an evolutionary analysis assumes that male aggression against women reflects selection pressures operating during our species' evolutionary history, it in no way implies that male domination of women is genetically determined, or that frequent male aggression toward women is an immutable feature of human nature. In some societies male aggressive coercion of women is very rare, and even in societies with frequent male aggression toward women, some men do not show these behaviors. Thus, the challenge is to identify the situational factors that predispose members of a particular society toward or away from the use of sexual aggression. I argue that an evolutionary framework can be very useful in this regard.

As you review all of the human species-typical behaviors and tendencies discussed in this chapter, you might consider how each depends on environmental conditions and is modifiable by changes in those conditions.

SECTION REVIEW

An evolutionary perspective offers functionalist explanations of aggression and helping.

Male Violence	Helping	Common Fallacies
➤ Male primates, including men, are generally more violent than are females of their species.	➤ Helping (promoting another's survival or reproduction) takes two forms—cooperation and altruism.	➤ The naturalistic fallacy, indulged in by Social Darwinists, is the equation of what is natural with what is right.
➤ Most aggression and violence in male primates relate directly or indirectly to sex. Genes that promote violence are passed to offspring to the degree that they increase mating.	➤ Cooperation (helping others while also helping oneself, as in the case of wolves hunting together) is easy to understand evolutionarily.	➤ The deterministic fallacy is the belief that genes control behavior in ways that cannot be altered by environmental experiences or conscious decisions.
➤ Among bonobos, female alliances counter male violence.	➤ Apparent acts of altruism (helping others at a net cost to oneself) make evolutionary sense if explained by the kin selection or reciprocity theories.	

Concluding Thoughts

1. The indirect nature of genetic influences on behavior Genes are simply DNA molecules that provide the code for building the body's proteins. Variation in genes across species provides the basis for species-typical behaviors, and variation in genes among members of a species is one source of individual differences in behavior within a species. But genes never produce behaviors directly. Genes always work in conjunction with the environment, and so their effects depend on environmental conditions. Neither genes nor environment "determines" our behavior. Our behavior results from an interplay between the environment in which we live and our bodies' biological mechanisms, which themselves were built through an interplay between genes and environment.

2. The unconscious nature of ultimate functions Sigmund Freud (discussed in Chapters 15 and 17) is famous for his claim that we are often unconscious of the real reasons for our actions. On that point, at least, modern evolutionary psychologists and Freud agree. Our species-typical drives and behavioral tendencies evolved to promote functions related to survival and reproduction, but we rarely think of those functions, and we are often completely ignorant of them.

Toddlers toddle and play with words because it is "fun" to do so, without any thought about the value of such play in learning to walk and talk. We all smile, instinctively or because it seems like the right thing to do, when we are happy or when we meet someone, without thinking about the functions that smiling might serve. When we fall in love, we are far more likely to attribute that feeling to the sweet, charming, and irresistible nature of the beloved person than to anything having to do with the value of bonding for producing and raising children. When we feel jealous because of attention another is paying to our beloved, we think angry thoughts about betrayal and unfaithfulness, not about the role of jealousy in preserving monogamy. When we help a person in need, we do it out of felt sympathy and compassion; we do not coldly, consciously calculate the costs and long-term benefits to ourselves.

The reasons we give ourselves for what we do are an aspect of the *proximate causation* of our behavior. We are often no more aware of the *ultimate functions* of our actions than the cabbage fly is of why it is irresistibly drawn to the cabbage plant as the only proper place to lay its eggs.

3. Evolution as an integrative theme in psychology The evolutionary perspective provides the broadest view that we can take in psychology. It is concerned with the origins and ultimate functions of all aspects of human nature (and the nature of other animals). It is a perspective that can be applied to the whole vast range of topics with which psychology is concerned. All of the complex biological mechanisms that underlie our psychological nature came about because they helped our ancestors to survive and reproduce. We can expect, therefore, that all of our basic motivational and emotional mechanisms are biased toward generating behaviors that promote survival and reproduction; and we can expect that our sensory, perceptual, memory, and reasoning mechanisms are biased toward picking up and using information essential to those purposes. We are not general learning or thinking machines that indiscriminately analyze all information available; we are biological survival machines designed to use information selectively to achieve our ends. As you go through the rest of this book, crossing the whole range of psychology, you will see this idea applied in every chapter.

Further Reading

Charles Darwin (1859; reprinted 1963). *The origin of species.* New York: Washington Square Press.

Darwin was an engaging writer as well as a brilliant thinker. Why not read at least part of this book, which revolutionized the intellectual world? The most relevant chapter for psychologists is Chapter 8, *Instinct,* which includes Darwin's research on hive building in bees and many other insights about the behavior of wild and domesticated animals.

David Sloan Wilson (2007). *Evolution for everyone: How Darwin's theory can change the way we think about our lives.* New York: Delecorte Press.

Wilson is a brilliant biologist, a broad-ranging philosopher, a great storyteller, and a self-described optimist. His goal in this book is to show how all of us—as individuals and collectively—can benefit by understanding evolutionary theory and applying it in our everyday thinking. Wilson shows how evolutionary theory sheds insight on topics ranging from species of beetles to Abraham Lincoln to organized religions. A theme throughout is that evolution involves a constant balance between the characteristics we know as "good" and those we know as "evil." Understanding evolution can be a first step toward fostering the former and defeating the later.

Elizabeth Marshall Thomas (2006). *The old way: A story of the first people.* New York: Farrar, Straus, Giroux.

During most of our evolutionary history, our species lived as hunter-gatherers. Therefore, many of our instinctive tendencies make most sense in the context of the hunter-gatherers' ways of living. Elizabeth Marshall Thomas was among the pioneers to study a hunter-gatherer group in Africa, at a time when that group had almost no previous exposure to modern ways. In this fascinating book, Thomas describes the ingenious means by which these playful and democratic people kept peace among themselves and pursued their survival needs.

Jane Goodall (1988). *In the shadow of man* (rev. ed.). Boston: Houghton Mifflin.

Goodall's study of wild chimpanzees, which began in 1960, ranks as one of the most courageous and scientifically valuable studies of animal behavior ever undertaken. This book, first published in 1971, is an exciting account of her early struggle to locate and study the animals and of her early findings about their behavior. For a more complete and scientific account of her research, I recommend Goodall's 1986 book, *The Chimpanzees of Gombe.*

Frans de Waal (2005). *Our inner ape.* New York: Riverhead Books.

De Waal is a leading expert on both chimpanzees and bonobos. Here, in delightfully folksy and often humorous prose, he contrasts the two species and discusses the many ways that we resemble both of these close cousins of ours. De Waal helps us see, in chimps and bonobos, our own compassion, kindness, sexiness, meanness, violence, and political intrigue. Another excellent, quite different book by De Waal is *Bonobo: The forgotten ape* (1997, University of California Press), which includes dozens of full-color, full-page photographs of these apes, famous for their make-love-not-war style of life.

Dorothy Cheney & Robert Seyfarth (2007). *Baboon metaphysics: The evolution of a social mind.* Chicago: University of Chicago Press.

In 1838, twenty-one years before publication of *The Origin of Species,* Darwin wrote this note to himself: "He who understands baboon would do more towards metaphysics than Locke." This book, I think, proves Darwin's note to be right. Cheney and Seyfarth have spent many years carefully observing chacma baboons at a game reserve in Botswana, and here they provide a fascinating, thoughtful, often exciting account of these highly social primates. Read here of their competitions, murders, coalitions, friendships, cooperation, empathy, communication, and intelligence as they strive in their social groups to survive and reproduce.

Basic Processes of Learning

To survive, animals must adapt to their environments. Evolution by natural selection, discussed in Chapter 3, is the long-term adaptive process that equips each species for life within a certain range of environmental conditions. But the environment is never constant; it changes from place to place and from time to time, even during short periods of an individual's life. To be efficient in finding foods, finding mates, avoiding predators, and carrying out the other necessities of survival and reproduction, animals must adapt to the ever-changing conditions of the specific environments in which they live. In other words, they must learn.

The term *learning* is used in various ways by different psychologists to refer to a wide variety of phenomena. For our purposes, however, we can define it broadly as *any process through which experience at one time can alter an individual's behavior at a future time.* *Experience* in this definition refers to any effects of the environment that are mediated by the individual's sensory systems (vision, hearing, touch, and so on). *Behavior at a future time* refers to any subsequent behavior that is not part of the individual's immediate response to the sensory stimulation during the learning experience. If I make a clicking sound just before flashing a bright light into your eyes, your immediate response to the click or to the light (such as blinking) does not exemplify learning. Your increased tendency to blink to the click alone, the next time I present that sound, however, does exemplify learning.

Most of psychology is in one way or another concerned with the effects of experience on subsequent behavior. For examples, social psychologists try to explain people's beliefs and social behaviors in terms of their past experiences, clinical psychologists try to explain people's emotional problems in such terms, and cognitive psychologists try to understand the basic mental processes that are involved in people's ability to learn. Thus, most chapters in this book, or in any other introduction to psychology, are in one way or another about learning.

Note that this chapter is in the part of the book that links human psychology to the psychology of animals in general. From an evolutionary perspective, learning is a quite ancient set of abilities. All animals that have any kind of nervous system have acquired, through natural selection, some abilities to learn. We humans are in some ways unique but in many ways similar to other species in our basic mechanisms of learning. You will read more about our unique learning abilities—such as our ability to learn a grammar-based language—later in this book. Our present focus is on mechanisms of learning that characterize mammals (and other vertebrates) in general, including humans. We start with discussions of two very general varieties of learning, referred to respectively as classical conditioning and operant conditioning. Then we'll turn to discussions of the roles of play, exploration, and observation in learning; and finally we will look at some very specialized forms of learning, such as learning what foods are good or bad to eat.

■ Classical Conditioning I: Fundamentals

1
- - - - - - - - - - - - - - - - - - - ◀
What is a reflex, and how can it change through habituation?
- - - - - - - - - - - - - - - - - -

Classical conditioning is a learning process that creates new reflexes. A ***reflex*** is a simple, relatively automatic, stimulus-response sequence mediated by the nervous system. If your knee is tapped with a rubber mallet as you sit on an examining table, your lower leg will jerk forward. If a bright light is flashed in your eyes, you will blink. If lemon juice is squirted into your mouth, you will salivate. If a loud alarm suddenly clangs, your muscles will tighten. In each of these examples, a particular well-defined event in the environment, a ***stimulus,*** results in a particular well-defined behavior, a ***response.*** The tap on the knee, the flash of light, the squirt of lemon juice, and the sudden alarm are stimuli (note that *stimuli* is the plural form of *stimulus*). The leg jerk, the eye blink, the salivation, and the muscle tightening are responses.

To be considered a reflex, the response to a stimulus must be mediated by the nervous system. Messages carried by nerves from the eyes, ears, skin, or other sensory organs enter the spinal cord or brain and act there to produce messages in nerves running outward to muscles and glands. If something hits you and you fall down as a result of the direct force of the impact, that is not a reflex. If something hits you and your muscles respond in a way that tends to keep you from falling down, that *is* a reflex. Because reflexes are mediated by the nervous system, they can be modified by experience.

One simple effect of experience on reflexes is ***habituation,*** defined as a decline in the magnitude of a reflexive response when the stimulus is repeated several times in succession. Not all reflexes undergo habituation. One that does is the startle response to a sudden loud sound. You might jump the first time the sound occurs, but each time the sound is repeated you respond less reflexively, and soon you show no visible response at all. Habituation is one of the simplest forms of learning. It does not produce a new stimulus-response sequence but only weakens an already existing one. Classical conditioning, in contrast, is a form of reflex learning that does produce a new stimulus-response sequence. It was first described and most extensively studied by a Russian physiologist, Ivan Pavlov.

Pavlov's Initial Discovery of Classical Conditioning

Ivan Petrovich Pavlov (1849–1936) was the personification of the dedicated scientist. By the time of his most famous research on classical conditioning, he was in his fifties and had already earned a Nobel prize for studies of the reflexes involved in digestion. His research so engulfed his life that he is said to have hardly noticed such events as the Bolshevik Revolution of 1917, which radically transformed his country. One former co-worker (Gantt, in 1975, as quoted by Hothersall, 1995) recalled Pavlov's angry scolding of an assistant who arrived 10 minutes late to start an experiment: "But Professor," exclaimed the assistant, "there's a revolution going on, with shooting in the streets." To which Pavlov replied, "What the _____ difference does that make when you've work to do in the laboratory? Next time there's a revolution, get up earlier!"

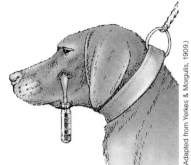

(Adapted from Yerkes & Morgulis, 1909.)

FIGURE 4.1 Pavlov's method for measuring salivation One of the dog's salivary ducts is surgically connected to a glass tube. In his early experiments, Pavlov learned that dogs produce different salivary secretions in response to different foods. Later he found that the dogs could be conditioned to produce these secretions in response to stimuli that reliably precede food.

Pavlov's initial discovery of what we now call classical conditioning emerged from his earlier studies of digestive reflexes in dogs. Using permanently implanted tubes to collect salivary and stomach juices from dogs (see Figure 4.1), he and his team of researchers found, for example, that a dog salivates differently when different kinds of food are placed in its mouth. Juicy meat triggers a very thick saliva; dry bread, a wetter saliva; and acidic fluids, a wetter one yet. In a fine-grained analysis, these represent three different reflexes, with three different stimuli eliciting measurably different salivary secretions.

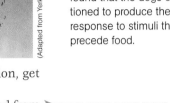

> **2**
> **How did Pavlov discover the conditioned reflex?**

In the course of these studies, Pavlov encountered a problem. Dogs that had been given food on previous occasions in Pavlov's experiments would salivate before they received any food. Apparently, signals that regularly preceded food, such as the sight of the food or the sound associated with its delivery, alerted the dogs to the upcoming stimulation and caused them to salivate. At first Pavlov was content to treat this simply as a source of experimental error. He called it "psychic secretion," implying that it was outside the physiologist's realm of study, and he attempted to eliminate it by developing ways to introduce the food into the dog's mouth without any warning. But then it occurred to Pavlov that this might well be a phenomenon that could be studied physiologically. Rather than call it psychic secretion, perhaps he could consider it a reflex and analyze it objectively, just as he had analyzed the reflexive salivary response to food in the mouth. This insight led Pavlov (1927/1960) to his first experiments on conditioned reflexes.

The Procedure and Generality of Classical Conditioning

To study such reflexes, Pavlov deliberately controlled the signals that preceded food. In one experiment he sounded a bell just before placing food in the dog's mouth. After several such pairings of a bell with food, the dog would salivate in response to the bell sound alone; no food was necessary.

> **3**
> **After his initial discovery, how did Pavlov systematize the process of conditioning, and what names did he give to the relevant stimuli and responses?**

Pavlov referred to this new reflex as a ***conditioned reflex*** because it depends on the unique *conditions* present in the dog's previous experience—the pairing of the bell sound with the food-in-mouth stimulus. He referred to the stimulus in a conditioned reflex (the bell sound, in this case) as a ***conditioned stimulus,*** and he referred to the response to that stimulus (salivation) as a ***conditioned response.***

Likewise, he referred to the original reflex, which did not require learning, as an ***unconditioned reflex,*** and referred to its stimulus (food placed in the mouth) and response (salivation) as an ***unconditioned stimulus*** and ***unconditioned response,*** respectively.

For a diagram of Pavlov's basic procedure and an opportunity to review all of these terms, see Figure 4.2 on the next page. The procedure is today called ***classical conditioning,*** or sometimes *Pavlovian conditioning.*

Pavlov (1927/1960) was impressed in these studies by the similarity between the dog's salivary response to a conditioned stimulus and its response to the unconditioned stimulus. A sound that had been paired with meat elicited a thick saliva, similar

FIGURE 4.2 Classical-conditioning procedure A neutral stimulus initially does not elicit a response. After it is paired for several trials with an unconditioned stimulus, however, it becomes a conditioned stimulus and does elicit a response.

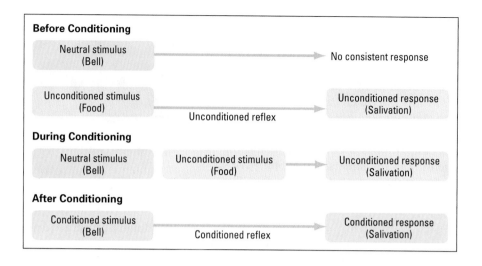

Before Conditioning

Neutral stimulus (Bell) ———————→ No consistent response

Unconditioned stimulus (Food) ———————→ Unconditioned response (Salivation)
Unconditioned reflex

During Conditioning

Neutral stimulus (Bell)   Unconditioned stimulus (Food) ———→ Unconditioned response (Salivation)

After Conditioning

Conditioned stimulus (Bell) ———————→ Conditioned response (Salivation)
Conditioned reflex

to that elicited by meat; and a sound that had been paired with bread elicited a thinner, wetter saliva, similar to that elicited by bread. In other experiments, Pavlov and his colleagues varied the stimulus used as the conditioned stimulus. They concluded that, essentially, any environmental event that the animal could detect could become a conditioned stimulus for salivation. Sounds produced by bells, buzzers, or tuning forks were highly effective and used most often because they were the easiest to control. But Pavlov's group also produced conditioned responses to visual stimuli, such as a black square; to olfactory stimuli, such as the odor of camphor; and to tactile (touch) stimuli, such as pressure applied to a spot on the animal's skin. In each case, the stimulus initially did not elicit the salivary response, but it did so after having been paired with food a number of times.

Of course, classical conditioning is not limited to salivary responses. Researchers have demonstrated this in hundreds of laboratory experiments, and you have experienced countless examples of such conditioning in your everyday life. The sound of a dentist's drill may elicit a conditioned cringing response because of its previous pairing with pain. The mere smell of coffee may help wake you up because of its previous pairing with coffee's stimulating effect. The sight of the toilet when you enter a bathroom to comb your hair may elicit a previously unfelt urge to urinate due to previous pairings of that sight with that urge. If you once had an automobile accident at a curve in the road on a wet day, each new encounter with such a curve

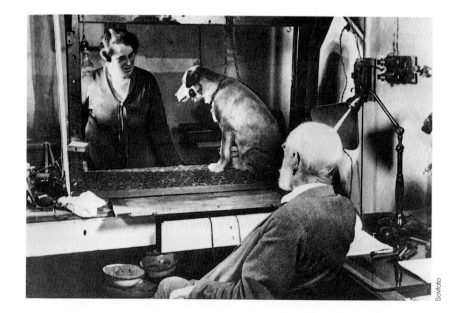

Pavlov conducting an experiment To conduct his pioneering research on conditioning, Pavlov developed a means to control the presentation of stimuli, such as the sound of a bell and the presentation of food, and to measure the dog's reflexive salivary response.

Sovfoto

on such a day may elicit a conditioned tensing of muscles. If you go through a day recording instances of conditioned responses, you will find that the list quickly becomes quite long.

Extinction of Conditioned Reflexes, and Recovery from Extinction

One question that interested Pavlov had to do with the permanence of a conditioned reflex. Once a dog has learned to salivate to the sound of a bell, does this reflex continue to occur if the bell is sounded for many trials *without* the unconditioned food-in-mouth stimulus? Pavlov's group found that without food, the bell elicited less and less salivation on each trial and eventually none at all, a phenomenon that they labeled ***extinction.*** But they also found that extinction does not return the animal fully to the unconditioned state. The mere passage of time following extinction can partially renew the conditioned reflex, a phenomenon now known as ***spontaneous recovery*** (see Figure 4.3). Moreover, a single pairing of the conditioned stimulus with the unconditioned stimulus can fully renew the conditioned reflex, which can be extinguished again only by another series of trials in which the conditioned stimulus is presented without the unconditioned stimulus.

On the basis of such findings, Pavlov (1927/1960) concluded that the conditioned reflex is not truly lost during extinction, but is somehow inhibited, and that it can be disinhibited by such means as the passage of time or the recurrence of the unconditioned stimulus. This conclusion has been validated in many experiments since Pavlov's time (Bouton & others, 2006). In research with conditioned eye-blink reflexes in rabbits, researchers have shown that conditioning and extinction involve different sets of neurons (nerve cells) in the brain (Medina & others, 2002). Neurons involved in the conditioning of this response excite other neurons that promote eye blinking. Neurons involved in extinction inhibit those same eye-blink neurons, thereby counteracting but not abolishing the conditioned neural response, just as Pavlov would have predicted.

Generalization and Discrimination in Classical Conditioning

Pavlov and his colleagues found that, after conditioning, animals would show the conditioned response not just to the original conditioned stimulus but also to new stimuli that resembled that stimulus. This phenomenon is called ***generalization.*** They found, further, that the magnitude of the response to the new stimulus depended on the degree of similarity between the new stimulus and the original conditioned stimulus. Thus, a dog conditioned to salivate to a 1,000-hertz (cycles-per-second) tone also salivated to tones of other frequencies, but the further the tone was in frequency from the original conditioned stimulus, the less the dog salivated to it (Pavlov, 1927/1960).

Generalization between two stimuli can be abolished if the response to one is reinforced while the response to the other is extinguished, a procedure called ***discrimination training.*** As an example of this procedure, Pavlov's group used a dog whose conditioning to the sight of a black square had generalized to a gray square. After a series of trials in which presentations of the gray square were never followed by food and presentations of the black square were always followed by food, the dog stopped salivating to the gray square but continued to salivate to the black one. The researchers continued this procedure with ever-darker shades of gray, until they eventually conditioned the dog to discriminate a black square from a gray one that was so nearly black that a human observer had difficulty telling them apart (Pavlov, 1927/1960).

Classical conditioning coupled with discrimination training provides an excellent tool for studying an animal's sensory capacities. A dog cannot tell you what it can or cannot hear, but you can find out by doing a conditioning experiment. If an animal can be conditioned to respond to a stimulus, we know that it can sense the

◢ - - - - - - - - - - - - - - - - 4

How can a conditioned reflex be extinguished? What evidence led Pavlov and others to conclude that extinction does not return the animal to its original, untrained state?

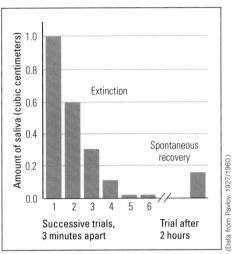

FIGURE 4.3 Extinction and spontaneous recovery of conditioned salivation The conditioned stimulus in this case was the sight of meat powder, presented repeatedly out of the animal's reach at 3-minute intervals. Extinction was complete by the fifth and sixth presentations, but when 2 hours were allowed to elapse before the seventh presentation, the reflex was partially renewed.

◢ - - - - - - - - - - - - - - - - 5

How can generalization in classical conditioning be abolished through discrimination training? How can discrimination training be used to assess an animal's sensory capacities?

stimulus; and if an animal can be trained to respond to one stimulus and not respond to another, we know that it can sense the difference between the two. Pavlov's team conditioned dogs to salivate to tones so high-pitched as to be inaudible to humans and to discriminate between pitches less than one-eighth of a note apart (Pavlov, 1927/1960).

Generalization as an Index of Subjective Similarity

6 ┄┄┄┄┄┄┄┄┄┄┄┄┄┄◀
How have researchers shown that the meaning of a stimulus, not just its physical characteristics, can provide a basis for generalization in classical conditioning?
┄┄┄┄┄┄┄┄┄┄┄┄┄┄┄

In experiments with human subjects, researchers following Pavlov discovered that generalization occurs not just when two stimuli are physically similar to one another but also when they are similar in their subjective meaning to the person.

In one experiment, for example, Gregory Razran (1939) used college students as subjects, printed words as conditioned stimuli, and injected a squirt of lemon juice into the mouth as the unconditioned stimulus. By pairing each word with lemon juice, Razran conditioned students to salivate to the words *style, urn, freeze,* and *surf.* He then tested the students to see if the conditioned response would generalize to other words that had never been paired with lemon juice. Of most interest, he found that the students salivated more to the words *fashion, vase, chill,* and *wave* than to the words *stile, earn, frieze,* and *serf.* That is, the conditioned response generalized more to printed words that resembled the original conditioned stimuli in meaning than to those that resembled the originals in physical appearance or sound. Thus, the true conditioned stimuli in this case were not the physical sights or sounds of the words but the subjects' interpretations of them.

An even more dramatic demonstration of stimulus generalization based on word meaning comes from the work of a Soviet psychologist (Volkova, 1953). A Russian schoolboy was conditioned to salivate to the Russian word for good and, by discrimination training, not to salivate to the word for bad. When the discrimination was well established, the boy was found to salivate copiously to such statements as *The Soviet army was victorious* and not at all to statements such as *The pupil was rude to the teacher.* In other words, those statements that the boy interpreted as good elicited salivation, and those that he interpreted as bad did not. A child who had a different set of conceptions of what is good or bad might have shown the opposite pattern of salivation. Thus, although classical conditioning is a very primitive phenomenon, it can be applied even toward understanding such uniquely human characteristics as a person's attitudes about particular, verbally described events.

SECTION REVIEW

Classical conditioning is the process involved in learning a new reflex.

Conditioning Procedure	Extinction	Generalization and Discrimination
➤ In classical conditioning, one begins with an unconditioned reflex (e.g., food ⟶ salivation).	➤ If a conditioned stimulus is repeatedly presented without the unconditioned stimulus, the conditioned reflex stops occurring.	➤ Generalization occurs when a stimulus similar to the conditioned stimulus also elicits the conditioned response.
➤ During conditioning, a neutral stimulus (e.g., bell sound) is presented just before the unconditioned stimulus (e.g., food).	➤ The conditioned reflex is not unlearned in extinction; it is merely suppressed, as shown by spontaneous recovery, etc.	➤ Discrimination (reduced generalization) results from repeatedly presenting the unconditioned stimulus followed by the conditioned stimulus and the similar stimulus followed by nothing.
➤ After sufficient pairings, the neutral stimulus becomes a conditioned stimulus which by itself elicits a conditioned response. This is the conditioned reflex (e.g., bell sound ⟶ salivation).	➤ Conditioning and extinction apparently involve different sets of neurons, one promoting the conditioned response, the other inhibiting it.	➤ Discrimination training is useful in studying sensory abilities and concept formation in animals.
		➤ Word meaning can provide a basis for generalization in humans.

▨ Classical Conditioning II: Beyond the Fundamentals

Having surveyed some of the basics of classical conditioning, let's now examine the process a little more deeply. What is actually learned in classical conditioning? What are some examples of conditioning that show its relevance to practical issues in psychology? Before considering these questions, it would be useful for you to know a little bit about an early school of thought in psychology referred to as behaviorism.

Relevance of Pavlov's Work to the Emergence of Behaviorism

Early in the twentieth century, psychologists in North America were struggling to develop scientific methods appropriate for psychology. Some of these psychologists, who referred to their school of thought as **behaviorism,** argued that their science should avoid terms that refer to mental entities, such as thoughts, emotions, motives, and so on, because such entities cannot be directly observed. They believed that psychology should focus on the relationship between observable events in the environment (stimuli) and observable behavioral reactions to those events (responses).

> ⟍ ─ ─ ─ ─ ─ ─ ─ ─ ─ ─ ─ ─ ─ ─ ─ ┐
>
> **What were the characteristics of early, North American behaviorism? Why were Pavlov's findings on conditioning particularly appealing to behaviorists?**

The principal founder of behaviorism, John B. Watson (1913), put it this way: "In a system of psychology completely worked out, given the response the stimuli can be predicted, and given the stimuli the response can be predicted." In Watson's view, all of behavior is, in essence, reflex-like in nature. Neither Watson nor subsequent behaviorists denied the existence of mental processes, but they believed that these are too obscure to be studied scientifically, and they argued that behavior could be understood and described without reference to mental processes.

In addition to developing objective, stimulus-response descriptions of behavior, the early behaviorists established learning as their main explanatory concept. They maintained that a person's behavior at any given time is determined by that person's past experiences with the environment. Watson and the other early behaviorists were much inspired by Pavlov's work on conditioning. In contrast to the empiricist philosophers (discussed in Chapter 1), who talked about learning in terms of unseen associations occurring in the mind, Pavlov seemed to provide an objective, stimulus-response way of studying and understanding learning. If all behavior is essentially reflexive, and if most behavior is learned, and if conditioning is the process by which reflexes are learned, then conditioning would appear to be psychology's most basic explanatory concept. In one of his early books, Watson (1924) attempted to describe even complex examples of human learning in terms of what we now call classical conditioning.

What Is Learned in Classical Conditioning?

We now return to the question raised earlier: What, really, is learned in classical conditioning? Watson's (1924) and other early behaviorists' answer to that question was simply that a new stimulus-response connection is learned. From their perspective, Pavlov's conditioned dog salivated to the bell sounding because of a direct, learned connection between that sound and salivation. This *stimulus-response (S-R)* theory of classical conditioning is diagrammed in the top part of Figure 4.4 on the next page. Pavlov himself, however, had a different theory.

PAVLOV'S CAT

www.harrybliss.com

FIGURE 4.4 Comparison of S-R and S-S theories of classical conditioning According to the S-R theory, conditioning produces a direct bond between the conditioned stimulus and the response. According to the S-S theory, conditioning produces a bond between the conditioned stimulus and a mental representation of the unconditioned stimulus, which, in turn, produces the response. Support for the S-S theory comes from experiments showing that weakening the unconditioned reflex (through habituation), after conditioning, also weakens the conditioned reflex.

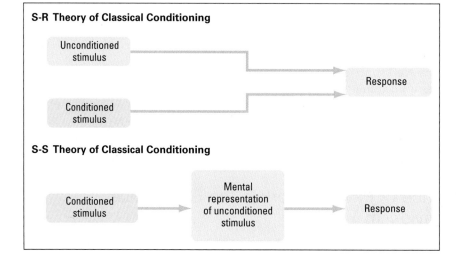

8

How did Pavlov's S-S theory of classical conditioning differ from Watson's S-R theory? How does an experiment involving habituation of the unconditioned stimulus support the S-S theory?

Evidence That Stimulus-Stimulus Associations Are Learned

Pavlov (1927/1960) believed that the animal does not learn a direct stimulus-response connection but, rather, learns a connection between two stimuli, the conditioned stimulus and the unconditioned stimulus. Because the bell and food have been paired in past experience, a neural bond is formed between their representations in the brain, such that the sound of the bell now activates the part of the brain that was formerly activated by food, and that, in turn, elicits salivation. Using mental rather than neural terms, we could say that the dog salivates to the bell because the bell sound elicits in the dog a mental representation of food (bell ⟶ mental representation of food ⟶ salivation). This *stimulus-stimulus (S-S)* theory of classical conditioning is illustrated in the bottom part of Figure 4.4.

The S-S theory did not appeal to Watson and his followers because it posited the existence of an unobserved event in the animal's mind, the mental representation of the original unconditioned stimulus. However, contrary to the early behaviorists' claims, reference to unseen events can be very useful in science if they lead to clear-cut predictions about events that can be seen. Gravity cannot be seen, yet theories of gravity can be developed and tested with experiments on falling objects. The S-S and S-R theories make different predictions about how animals will behave under certain conditions, so it is possible to test the theories with experiments. Many such experiments have by now been conducted, and the weight of the evidence favors the S-S theory for most examples of conditioning in mammals and birds (Anderson, 2000).

As an illustration, consider a classic experiment conducted by Robert Rescorla (1973) using rats as subjects, a loud sound as the unconditioned stimulus, and a signal light as the conditioned stimulus. The loud sound elicited freezing (a fear response in which the rat stands motionless) as an unconditioned response. By pairing the signal light with the loud sound, Rescorla conditioned rats to freeze when the signal light came on. Now, the question was: Did the rats freeze in response to the signal light because of a direct, learned connection between the light and freezing, in accordance with the S-R theory (light ⟶ freezing)? Or did they freeze because of a learned connection between the light and the loud sound, in accordance with the S-S theory (light ⟶ mental representation of loud sound ⟶ freezing)?

To answer the question, Rescorla habituated the response to the loud sound in half of the conditioned rats. That is, he presented the loud sound many times without the signal light until the rats no longer froze in response to it. Then he again tested the rats with the signal light. Would the rats that no longer froze in response to the loud sound continue to freeze in response to the light? The S-R and S-S theories make different predictions. According to the S-R theory, the habituated rats should continue, as much as before, to freeze in response to the light because conditioning would have produced a direct connection between the light and freezing. But according to the S-S theory, the habituated rats should not freeze in response to the light because conditioning would have produced a connection between the light and a representation of the loud sound, which itself no longer elicits freezing. Rescorla's results supported the S-S theory. Habituation to the sound greatly reduced the degree to which the rats froze in response to the light.

Classical Conditioning Interpreted as Learned Expectancy

The S-S theory of classical conditioning, by its nature, is more *cognitive* than the S-R theory. As explained in Chapter 1, the term *cognition* refers to knowledge, or information, held in the mind. Cognitive theories are theories in which hypothesized, unobserved entities within the mind are used to explain and predict behavior, contrary to the dictates of behaviorism. The S-S theory is cognitive because it holds that the observed stimulus-response relation is mediated by an inner, mental representation of the original unconditioned stimulus. Cognitive theorists have argued that this mental representation may be best understood as an *expectation* of the unconditioned stimulus. According to this view, Pavlov's dog learned to expect food when it heard the bell.

The *expectancy theory* helps make sense of the observation that a conditioned response is often quite different from the unconditioned response. Consider again a dog being conditioned to a sounding bell that precedes food. In response to food, the dog not only salivates but also chews (if it is solid food) and swallows. Salivation becomes conditioned to the bell, but chewing and swallowing usually do not. Moreover, the bell comes to elicit not only salivation but also responses that do not usually occur in response to the food-in-mouth stimulus—such as tail wagging, food begging, and looking in the direction of the usual source of food (Jenkins & others, 1978). According to the expectancy theory, all these responses, including salivation, occur not because they were previously elicited by the unconditioned stimulus but because they are the dog's responses to the expectation of food:

bell ⟶ expectation of food ⟶ tail wagging, food begging, salivation, etc.

Rescorla (1988) summed up his cognitive view of classical conditioning as follows: "[Classical] conditioning is not a stupid process by which the organism willynilly forms associations between any two stimuli that happen to co-occur. Rather, the organism is best seen as an information seeker using logical and perceptual relations among events, along with its own preconceptions, to form a sophisticated representation of its world." By this, Rescorla does not mean that animals spend time consciously deliberating about these relationships. Rather, he means that animals have built-in neural mechanisms that automatically make the appropriate calculations.

Conditioning Depends on the Predictive Value of the Conditioned Stimulus

Support for the expectancy theory of classical conditioning comes from research showing that conditioning occurs only, or at least mainly, when the new stimulus provides information that truly helps the animal predict the arrival of the unconditioned stimulus. Here are three classes of such findings:

1. *The conditioned stimulus must precede the unconditioned stimulus.* Classical conditioning is most effective if the onset of the conditioned stimulus comes immediately before the unconditioned stimulus. Conditioning commonly doesn't occur at all if the conditioned stimulus comes either simultaneously with or just after the unconditioned stimulus (Lieberman, 2000). (See Figure 4.5a and b on the next page.) This observation makes sense if the animal is seeking predictive information; a stimulus that does not precede the unconditioned stimulus

> **9**
>
> **How does the cognitive construct of expectancy help explain the ways in which conditioned responses differ from unconditioned responses?**

Mark Sherman/Bruce Coleman

Learned expectancy There is nothing inscrutable about this young tiger cat. The sound of the can being attached to the opener permits her to predict the arrival of food. Her response is not identical to her response to food itself, but one of rapt attention.

> **10**
>
> **What are three conditions in which the pairing of a new stimulus with an unconditioned stimulus does not result in classical conditioning? How do these observations support the idea that classical conditioning is a process of learning to predict the onset of the unconditioned stimulus?**

FIGURE 4.5 Patterns of stimulus presentation in which conditioning does or does not occur The top time line illustrates a pattern of stimulus presentation in which conditioning occurs. The three lower time lines illustrate patterns in which poor or no conditioning occurs even though the potential conditioned stimulus (blue) and unconditioned stimulus (red) are often paired. Strong conditioning occurs when the potential conditioned stimulus is a reliable and nonredundant predictor of the unconditioned stimulus.

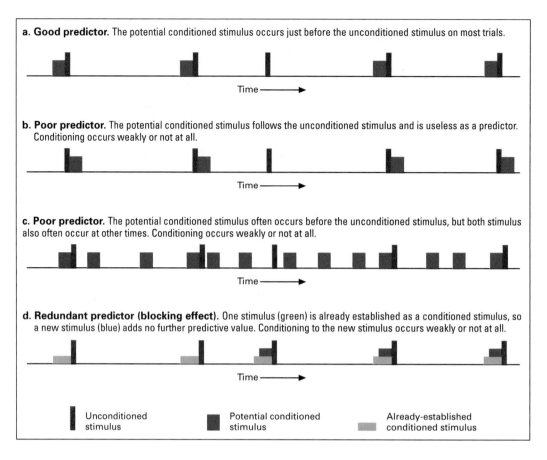

a. Good predictor. The potential conditioned stimulus occurs just before the unconditioned stimulus on most trials.

Time ⟶

b. Poor predictor. The potential conditioned stimulus follows the unconditioned stimulus and is useless as a predictor. Conditioning occurs weakly or not at all.

Time ⟶

c. Poor predictor. The potential conditioned stimulus often occurs before the unconditioned stimulus, but both stimulus also often occur at other times. Conditioning occurs weakly or not at all.

Time ⟶

d. Redundant predictor (blocking effect). One stimulus (green) is already established as a conditioned stimulus, so a new stimulus (blue) adds no further predictive value. Conditioning to the new stimulus occurs weakly or not at all.

Time ⟶

| Unconditioned stimulus | Potential conditioned stimulus | Already-established conditioned stimulus |

is useless as a predictor, and thus is ignored by the animal. Trying to achieve conditioning by placing the conditioned stimulus after the unconditioned stimulus is like trying to reduce traffic accidents by placing "Dangerous Curve" signs after the curves in the road rather than before them.

2. *The conditioned stimulus must signal heightened probability of occurrence of the unconditioned stimulus.* Conditioning depends not just on the total number of pairings of the conditioned stimulus and unconditioned stimulus, but also on the number of times that either stimulus occurs without being paired with the other. As the number of pairings increases, conditioning is strengthened; but as the number of stimulus occurrences without pairing increases, conditioning is weakened. (Rescorla, 1988; Rescorla & Wagner, 1972). (See Figure 4.5c.) The animal's behavior suggests that in some way its nervous system computes two probabilities—the probability that the unconditioned stimulus will immediately follow any given occurrence of the conditioned stimulus and the probability that the unconditioned stimulus will occur at other times—and accepts the conditioned stimulus as a predictor only if the first probability is greater than the second.

If dangerous curves in the road are no more likely to occur right after "Dangerous Curve" signs than they are to occur in the absence of such signs, the signs would be useless to us as predictors of curves, and we would be well advised to ignore them and try to predict curves using other means. This would be true no matter how many times, in our driving experience, we happened to come across such a sign right before an actual curve. Rats in conditioning experiments behave as if they have that insight.

3. *Conditioning is ineffective when the animal already has a good predictor.* If one conditioned stimulus already reliably precedes an unconditioned stimulus, a new stimulus, presented simultaneously with the original conditioned stimulus,

generally does not become a conditioned stimulus. Even after many such pairings the new stimulus fails to elicit the conditioned response if it is presented alone. This failure of conditioning is called the *blocking effect*; the already-conditioned stimulus *blocks* conditioning to the new stimulus that has been paired with it (Kamin, 1969). (See Figure 4.5d.) A cognitive interpretation of this is that the animal has already solved the problem of predicting the unconditioned stimulus and has no reason to look for a new predictor. In line with this interpretation, blocking does not occur if the new stimulus combined with the original stimulus is followed by an unconditioned stimulus that is larger in magnitude, or in some other way different from, the original unconditioned stimulus (Bradfield & McNally, 2008). In this case, the new stimulus does add new information, and the animal becomes conditioned to respond to it.

Cognitive psychologists often emphasize that their use of terms such as *expectation* and *prediction* does not imply anything mystical. The terms describe the type of information that underlies the animal's behavior but say nothing about the physical form of that information, which presumably results from computations automatically made by neurons in the brain. Some psychologists develop computer models to explain how such computations might be made.

Conditioned Fear, Hunger, and Sexual Arousal

From a functional, evolutionary perspective, classical conditioning is a process by which individuals learn to prepare themselves, reflexively, for biologically significant events that are about to happen. A conditioned stimulus preceding a painful or startling event can elicit fear and bodily reactions that help brace the individual for that event; a conditioned stimulus preceding delivery of food can elicit hunger and bodily responses that help prepare the gastrointestinal tract for food; and a conditioned stimulus preceding an opportunity for sex can elicit high sex drive and bodily responses that help prepare the body for copulation. Here I'll elaborate just a bit on these ideas.

Watson's Classic Demonstration of Fear Conditioning

John B. Watson was the first psychologist to show that the emotion of fear can be conditioned in human beings. Consistent with his behavioral perspective, Watson (1924) defined fear not as a feeling but as a set of observable responses: "a catching of the breath, a stiffening of the whole body, a turning away of the body from the source of stimulation, a running or crawling from it." On the basis of this definition, Watson found two unconditioned stimuli for fear in human infants—sudden loud sound and sudden loss of support (as when a baby slips out of an adult's hands). Other stimuli, he argued, come to elicit fear as a result of conditioning.

In a classic demonstration, Watson and Rosalie Rayner (1920) conditioned an 11-month-old baby named Albert to fear laboratory rats. At first, Albert played happily with a rat that was placed in front of him. To condition the fear, the experimenters struck a steel bar with a hammer to produce a loud sound just after the rat was placed in front of Albert. After two such pairings Albert exhibited moderate fear in response to the rat alone, and after four more pairings he responded with strong fear to the rat alone. Thus, in the terminology of classical conditioning, the rat had become a conditioned stimulus for fear through being paired with a loud sound, which was an unconditioned stimulus for fear. In subsequent tests, Watson and Rayner showed that Albert's conditioned fear generalized to other furry objects, such as a rabbit (see Figure 4.6 on the next page).

You might (quite appropriately) wonder about the ethics of this experiment. The experiment most likely would not be approved by a modern ethics review committee

11

How did Watson demonstrate that the emotion of fear can be conditioned?

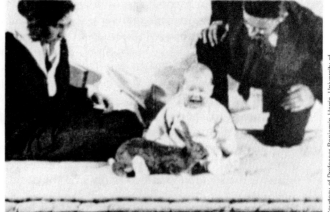

FIGURE 4.6 Little Albert with Watson, Rayner, and furry animals
Prior to the conditioning experience, 11-month-old Albert played happily with a live laboratory rat (left). After he was conditioned to respond fearfully to the rat, he also cried at the sight of other furry objects, including a rabbit, thereby exhibiting generalization (right).

and would not be allowed today. In fairness to Watson, however, there is no reason to believe that Albert's experience in this demonstration was any more frightening than are the countless startling events that everyone experiences in the normal course of growing up. Moreover, Watson was far more interested in how to eliminate unwanted fears than in how to produce them. In Chapter 17, you will see how Watson's research and ideas helped lead to clinical methods for extinguishing irrational fears through exposing the person to the fear-producing stimuli at gradually increasing magnitudes in a safe, relaxing context.

Conditioning young humans to love beer The unconditioned stimulus is the happy, sexually suggestive scene. The conditioned stimulus is the Budweiser label.

Fear, of course, is not the only emotional response that can be conditioned through Pavlovian procedures. When beer, cigarette, and car advertisers pair their products with scenes of beautiful people having wonderful times, they are trying to get you to drool with anticipated pleasure, like Pavlov's dogs, whenever you see their products.

Conditioned Hunger

12

How can the appetizer effect and sudden cravings for specific foods be explained in terms of classical conditioning?

◄ A signal that reliably precedes food becomes a conditioned stimulus not just for salivation, but for a set of responses that help prepare the body for food. These responses include the secretion of digestive juices into the stomach and the secretion of certain hormones into the bloodstream (Woods & others, 2000). Through means discussed in Chapter 6, these reflexive responses induce a state of hunger. Thus, we find in humans the well-known appetizer effect. The taste of a small morsel of food, the smell of food, a dinner bell, a clock indicating that it is dinnertime, or any other signal that reliably precedes a meal can rather quickly cause us to feel much hungrier than we were feeling just before the signal. Other animals, too, begin to act as if they are hungry, as indicated by their food-seeking behavior, when subjected to stimuli that have preceded food in the past (Pavlov, 1927/1960).

In cases where a conditioned stimulus always precedes a specific kind of food, the conditioned hunger that occurs may be specific for that food. For example, in one series of experiments, rats who were made hungry through food deprivation underwent conditioning in which a tone always preceded the delivery of a certain kind of food. Later, when they were not food-deprived, they would seek out and eat that same kind of food, but not other foods, when the tone sounded (Petrovich & Gallagher, 2007). The rats behaved as if the tone elicited a sudden craving for the specific food with which it had previously been paired when they were hungry. Such findings help us understand why those golden arches of McDonald's, spotted on road signs, can cause a sudden craving for precisely the kinds of foods that we have previously eaten at McDonald's. Purveyors of fast foods aren't throwing away their money when they plaster the environment with specific symbols that are associated over and over again with their specific foods.

Conditioned Sexual Arousal

A number of experiments have demonstrated that sexual arousal can be conditioned in human subjects (Both & others, 2008; Hoffman, 2007; Plaud & Martini, 1999). Typically, a previously neutral stimulus is used as the conditioned stimulus (a slide showing a jar of pennies was used in one experiment) and an erotic, sexually arousing film clip or sexually arousing vibration applied mechanically to the genitals is used as the unconditioned stimulus. Sexual arousal is measured in men by a strain gauge that indicates erection of the penis and in women by a device that responds to increased blood flow to the vagina. In such experiments, a stimulus that initially does not elicit arousal comes to elicit it after several pairings with the unconditioned stimulus.

Experiments on sexual conditioning in nonhuman animals have generally used males as subjects and either the sight of a sexually receptive female or physical access to such a female as the unconditioned stimulus. The usual result is that a signal that reliably precedes the presentation of the female becomes a conditioned stimulus for a set of responses that help prepare the male for courtship and mating (Domjan, 2003; Pfaus & others, 2001). Experiments have shown that such conditioning is biologically adaptive in the most direct sense of the term—it increases the number of offspring the animal produces.

In one experiment with blue gourami fish, males were conditioned, over several trials, to predict the arrival of a female when a signal light came on (Hollis & others, 1997). After conditioning, these fish responded to the signal by shifting rapidly from their normal aggressive mode of behavior to a courtship mode. When they were allowed access to a female after the signal, the conditioned males were much more successful in courtship than were the unconditioned males, primarily because the latter typically attacked the female before trying to court her. The biological payoff was that the conditioned males fathered many more offspring in these tests than did the unconditioned males.

In a similar experiment with domesticated quail, those male birds who received a conditioned stimulus prior to opportunity to copulate with a hen fathered many more offspring than did those who were presented with a hen without forewarning (Matthews & others, 2007). In this case, the improved fertilization rate apparently resulted from an increase in the number of sperm cells released by the male birds during ejaculation. The conditioned stimulus apparently mobilized the sperm-release mechanism prior to the presentation of the hen, so that more sperm were available at the time of copulation.

> ------------------13
> **How has sexual arousal been conditioned in humans and other animals? What is the evidence, from experiments with nonhuman animals, that such conditioning promotes success in reproduction?**

Conditioned Drug Reactions

As you have just seen, bodily reactions associated with natural emotions and drives can be conditioned. In their early experiments, Pavlov's group showed that bodily reactions to drugs can also be conditioned. In one demonstration with a dog, they paired a tone with injection of a drug that elicited restlessness and vomiting. After repeated parings the dog began to exhibit those responses to the tone alone (Pavlov, 1927/1960). Since then, many experiments have shown that drug reactions can be conditioned. Researchers have found, for example, that for habitual coffee drinkers the mere smell and taste of coffee can produce increased alertness, apparently because of the previous pairings of that smell and taste with the effects of caffeine (Flaten & Blumenthal, 1999).

Conditioned Compensatory Reactions to Drugs

14

Why is the conditioned response to a drug-related stimulus often the opposite of the direct effect of the drug?

Many drugs produce two effects: a direct effect followed by a compensatory reaction that counteracts the direct effect and tends to restore the normal bodily state. In such cases it is often found (for reasons to be explained shortly) that only the compensatory reaction becomes conditioned. As a result, a stimulus that reliably precedes delivery of the drug produces a conditioned response that is opposite to the drug's direct effect. An example of such a drug is morphine. A direct effect of morphine is reduction in sensitivity to pain, but this is counteracted by reflexive responses in the body that tend to restore normal pain sensitivity. When rats are repeatedly injected with morphine in a distinctive environment, that environment becomes a conditioned stimulus for the counteractive response. When the rats are subsequently placed in that environment without morphine, the conditioned reaction occurs in the absence of the direct effect of the drug. The result is that the rats become temporarily hypersensitive to pain (Hinson & others, 1986).

The explanation of such effects rests on the fact that only responses that occur in a reflexive manner, involving the central nervous system (spinal cord and brain), can be conditioned (Siegel, 1999). The direct effects of some drugs are not reflexes, and therefore cannot be conditioned, but the counteractive effects are reflexes. As an analogy, consider what would happen if a bell sound (conditioned stimulus) reliably preceded a shove from the front (unconditioned stimulus). The shove would tend to push you backward, but you would counter that with a reflexive movement forward. Only the reflexive movement forward would be conditioned, so if the bell were sounded without the shove, you might fall on your face—a reaction opposite to the direct (nonreflexive) effect of the shove. The body protects itself with counteractive reflexes to all sorts of interventions (such as shoves and drugs) that disrupt its normal functioning. The conditioning of such reflexes is normally useful because it allows the counteraction to begin even before the potentially harmful stimulus strikes.

Conditioned Reactions as Causes of Drug Tolerance

15

How does classical conditioning contribute to the development of drug tolerance? Why is it dangerous for a drug addict to take his or her usual drug dose in an unusual environment?

A powerful conditioned stimulus for a heroin addict The stimuli associated with drug preparation become strong conditioned stimuli for bodily responses that are opposite to the direct effect of the drug. Such responses help protect the body from the drug's harmful effects, but they also produce intense drug craving and contribute to relapse in people who have gone through a period of drug withdrawal.

Shepard Siegel and his colleagues in Canada have shown that the phenomenon of drug tolerance depends at least partly on conditioning. **Drug tolerance** refers to the decline in physiological and behavioral effects that occur with some drugs when they are taken repeatedly. Because of tolerance, people who regularly take a drug have to increase their doses over time to continue to achieve the original effects. To some degree, tolerance is a result of long-term buildup of physiological systems in the body that help to counteract the drug's effects (Poulos & Cappell, 1991). However, it is also to some degree the result of conditioning. Because of conditioning, stimuli that normally precede drug intake cause the conditioned compensatory reaction to begin before the drug is actually taken, and that reaction counteracts the direct effect of the drug. For example, a conditioned increase in heart rate would counteract the effect of a drug whose direct effect is to slow the heart.

Siegel and his colleagues have found that many cases of "overdose" in heroin addicts are actually cases in which addicts took their usual drug doses in unusual environments (Siegel, 1984; Siegel & Ramos, 2002). When an addict takes a drug in the usual drug-taking environment, cues in that environment produce a conditioned compensatory reaction that allows the addict's body to tolerate a large dose of the drug. If the addict takes the same amount of the drug in a novel environment, where the conditioned cues aren't present, the full impact of the drug kicks in before a counteractive reaction begins, and the result is severe illness or death. Consistent with this interpretation, rats that had received many morphine injections in a specific highly distinctive cage were much more likely to survive a high dose of the drug if it was given to them in that same cage than if it was given in a different setting (Siegel, 1976; 2005). Similar effects have been shown in animal experiments using alcohol (Melchior, 1990) and various other drugs (Goudie, 1990).

© Uwe Schmid/Corbis

Conditioned Reactions as Causes of Drug Relapse After Withdrawal

Another drug phenomenon that is at least partly explained by conditioned compensatory reactions is that of relapse by addicts who have undergone periods of drug withdrawal (Siegel, 1999). Addicts commonly withdraw from drugs during a stay at a treatment center that is quite unlike their home environment. After some period of drug-free existence at the center, they no longer experience withdrawal symptoms or feel a craving for the drug. However, when they return to their own homes and neighborhoods, they are once again surrounded by many cues that, for them, are associated with drug use. These cues elicit compensatory drug reactions, which feel like withdrawal symptoms and elicit a strongly felt need for the drug—a felt need that is all too often irresistible.

In an effort to prevent such relapse, some drug treatment programs attempt to extinguish the effects of conditioning by repeatedly presenting addicts with stimuli associated with drug intake without the drug itself. Such programs have met with only partial success, however (Siegel & Ramos, 2002). It is impossible to identify and present, for each addict, all of the cues that, in his or her home environment, have become conditioned stimuli for compensatory drug reactions. Moreover, as you recall, effects of extinction can be quickly undone. Even one exposure to the unconditioned stimulus (the drug, in this case) can renew the conditioned responses to cues associated with it.

An addict's best hope for overcoming a long-term addiction may be to move permanently, if possible, to an entirely new environment. During the Vietnam War, many American soldiers became addicted to heroin in Vietnam. When they returned home, a surprisingly large number overcame their addiction immediately and never took heroin again (Robins & others, 1975). According to Siegel's analysis, this observation makes sense in view of the fact that they had left behind the cues that had become triggers for drug compensatory reactions and returned to an environment that contained none or few of those cues (Siegel, 1999).

> **16**
> How does classical conditioning help explain drug relapse after an addict returns home from a treatment center?

SECTION REVIEW

Classical conditioning enables prediction of and preparation for unconditioned stimuli.

What Is Learned?	Conditioned Emotion and Motivation	Conditioned Drug Reactions
➤ According to the S-R theory, supported by early behaviorists, a link between the conditioned stimulus and response is learned. ➤ According to the S-S theory, an association between the conditioned and unconditioned stimulus is learned. ➤ The S-S theory implies expectancy and is supported by Rescorla's experiment. ➤ Consistent with the expectancy idea, conditioning occurs best when the conditioned stimulus is a reliable predictor of the unconditioned stimulus.	➤ Examples are the conditioning of fear (in little Albert), the conditioning of hunger (the appetizer effect), and the conditioning of sexual arousal. ➤ In general, conditioned stimuli trigger responses that help prepare the individual for a biologically significant event.	➤ With some drugs, repeated pairing with a conditioned stimulus causes that stimulus to elicit the same type of response as the drug. ➤ With some other drugs, the conditioned stimulus elicits a response that is opposite to the drug response. Such conditioned compensatory reactions contribute to drug tolerance and drug relapse.

◼ Operant Conditioning I: Fundamentals

We are pulled as well as pushed by events in our environment. That is, we do not just respond *to* stimuli, we also respond *for* stimuli. That is, we behave in ways that are designed to *obtain* certain stimuli, or changes in our environment. My dog rubs against the door to be let out. I flip a switch to illuminate a room, press keys on my computer to produce words on a screen, and say "Please pass the potatoes" to get potatoes. Most of my day seems to consist of behaviors of this sort, and I expect that most of my dog's day would, too, if there were more things that he could control. Surely, if Pavlov's dogs had had some way to control the delivery of food into their mouths, they would have done more than salivate; they would have pushed a lever, bitten open a bag, or done whatever was required to get the food.

Such actions are called ***operant responses,*** because they operate on the world to produce some effect. They are also called *instrumental responses,* because they function like instruments, or tools, to bring about some change in the environment. The process by which people or other animals learn to make operant responses is called ***operant conditioning,*** or *instrumental conditioning.* Operant conditioning can be defined as a learning process by which the effect, or consequence, of a response influences the future rate of production of that response. In general, operant responses that produce effects that are favorable to the animal increase in rate, and those that produce effects that are unfavorable to the animal decrease in rate.

From the Law of Effect to Operant Conditioning: From Thorndike to Skinner

Although the labels "operant" and "instrumental" were not coined until the 1930s, this learning process was studied well before that time, most notably by E. L. Thorndike.

Thorndike's Puzzle-Box Procedure

17
How did Thorndike train cats to escape from a puzzle box? How did this research contribute to Thorndike's formulation of the law of effect?

At about the same time that Pavlov began his research on conditioning, a young American student of psychology, Edward Lee Thorndike (1898), published a report on his own learning experiments with various animals, including cats. Thorndike's training method was quite different from Pavlov's, and so was his description of the learning process. His apparatus was a puzzle box—a small cage that could be opened from inside by some relatively simple act, such as pulling a loop or pressing a lever (see Figure 4.7).

In one experiment, Thorndike deprived cats of food long enough to make them hungry and then placed them inside the cage, one at a time, with food just outside it. When first placed inside, a cat would engage in many actions—such as clawing at the bars or pushing at the ceiling—in an apparent attempt to escape from the cage and get at the food. Finally, apparently by accident, the cat would pull the loop or push the lever that opened the door to freedom and food. Thorndike repeated this procedure many times with each cat. He found that in early trials the animals made many

Edward Lee Thorndike After earning his Ph.D. in psychology with his puzzle-box experiments, Thorndike became a professor of educational psychology at Columbia University. Perhaps partly because of his early animal research on learning, he maintained throughout his career that intelligence is a collection of separate learned skills, not a unitary characteristic of the person.

FIGURE 4.7 One of Thorndike's puzzle boxes Thorndike was a great psychologist, not a great carpenter! Shown here is a photograph of one of his actual puzzle boxes. A cat placed inside could open this box by pulling down on the loop hanging from the ceiling, which would pull up the bolt and allow the door to fall forward.

useless movements before happening on the one that re-leased the latch, but, on average, they escaped somewhat more quickly with each successive trial. After about 20 to 30 trials, most cats would trip the latch to freedom and food almost as soon as they were shut in (see Figure 4.8).

An observer who joined Thorndike on trial 31 might have been quite impressed by the animal's intelligence; but, as Thorndike himself suggested, an observer who had sat through the earlier trials might have been more im-pressed by the creature's stupidity. In any event, Thorndike came to view learning as a trial-and-error process, through which an individual gradually becomes more likely to make responses that produce beneficial effects.

Thorndike's Law of Effect

Thorndike's basic training procedure differed fundamentally from Pavlov's. Pavlov produced learning by controlling the relationship between two stimuli in the ani-mal's environment, so that the animal learned to use one stimulus to predict the occurrence of the other. Thorndike, in contrast, produced learning by altering the consequence of some aspect of the animal's behavior. Thorndike's cats, unlike Pavlov's dogs, had some control over their environment. They could do more than merely predict when food would come; they could gain access to it through their own efforts.

Partly on the basis of his puzzle-box experiments, Thorndike (1898) formulated the ***law of effect,*** which can be stated briefly as follows: *Responses that produce a sat-isfying effect in a particular situation become more likely to occur again in that situation, and responses that produce a discomforting effect become less likely to occur again in that situation.* In Thorndike's puzzle-box experiments, the *situation* presumably consisted of all the sights, sounds, smells, internal feelings, and so on that were experienced by the hungry animal in the box. None of them elicited the latch-release response in reflex-like fashion; rather, taken as a whole, they set the occasion for many possible responses to occur, only one of which would release the latch. Once the latch was released, the satisfying effect, including freedom from the box and access to food, caused that response to strengthen; so the next time the cat was in the same situa-tion, the probability of that response's recurrence was increased (see Figure 4.9).

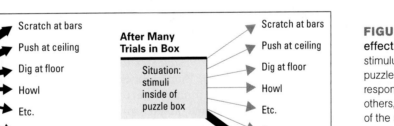

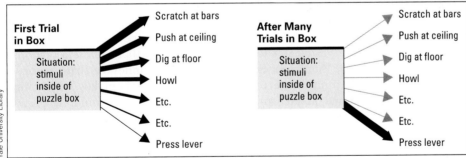

FIGURE 4.8 Typical learning curve for a cat in Thorndike's puzzle box As illustrated here for a single cat, Thorndike found that cats usually took less time to escape from the box on successive trials, although a great deal of variability occurred from trial to trial.

(Adapted from Thorndike, 1898.)

Yale University Library

FIGURE 4.9 Thorndike's law of effect According to Thorndike, the stimulus situation (being inside the puzzle box) initially elicits many responses, some more strongly than others, but the satisfying consequence of the successful response (pressing the lever) causes that response to be more strongly elicited on successive trials.

Skinner's Method of Studying and Describing Operant Conditioning

The psychologist who did the most to extend and popularize the law of effect for more than half a century was Burrhus Fredric Skinner. Like Watson, Skinner was a confirmed behaviorist. He believed that principles of learning are the most funda-mental principles in psychology, and he wanted to study and describe learning in ways that do not entail references to mental events. Unlike Watson, however, he did not consider the stimulus-response reflex to be the fundamental unit of all of behav-ior. Thorndike's work provided Skinner with a model of how nonreflexive behaviors could be altered through learning.

18

How did Skinner's method for studying learning differ from Thorndike's, and why did he prefer the term reinforcement to Thorndike's satisfaction?

FIGURE 4.10 B. F. Skinner and his operant-conditioning chamber
To study operant behavior in rats and other animals, Skinner invented an apparatus widely known as the Skinner box. When the rat shown here presses the lever, it activates an electrical relay system that causes the delivery of a food pellet into a cup next to the lever. Each lever press can be automatically recorded to produce a cumulative record, such as that shown in Figure 4.11.

Nina Leen/LIFE Magazine © Time Warner, Inc.

FIGURE 4.11 Typical cumulative response curve for a rat learning to press a lever in a Skinner box This graph is called a cumulative response curve because the height of the curve at any point indicates the total (cumulative) number of responses that the rat has made up to that time. The graph is automatically produced, while the rat is responding, by a recording machine outside the Skinner box. A pen moves horizontally across a roll of paper at a constant rate, and each lever press made by the rat produces a slight vertical movement of the pen. Thus, the degree to which the curve slopes upward is a measure of the animal's response rate. Note that early in learning the response rate was very low and then gradually increased to a fast, steady rate.

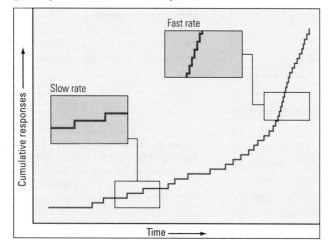

As a graduate student at Harvard University around 1930, Skinner developed an apparatus for studying animals' learning that was considerably more efficient than Thorndike's puzzle boxes. His device, commonly called a "Skinner box," is a cage with a lever or another mechanism in it that the animal can operate to produce some effect, such as delivery of a pellet of food or a drop of water (see Figure 4.10). The advantage of Skinner's apparatus is that the animal, after completing a response and experiencing its effect, is still in the box and free to respond again. With Thorndike's puzzle boxes and similar apparatuses such as mazes, the animal has to be put back into the starting place at the end of each trial. With Skinner's apparatus, the animal is simply placed in the cage and left there until the end of the session. Throughout the session, there are no constraints on when the animal may or may not respond. Responses (such as lever presses) can easily be counted automatically, and the learning process can be depicted as changes in the rate of responses (see Figure 4.11). Because each pellet of food or drop of water is very small, the hungry or thirsty animal makes many responses before becoming satiated.

Skinner developed not only a more efficient apparatus for studying such learning but also a new vocabulary for talking about it. It was he who coined the terms *operant response* to refer to any behavioral act that has some effect on the environment and *operant conditioning* to refer to the process by which the effect of an operant response changes the likelihood of the response's recurrence. Thus, in a typical experiment with a Skinner box, pressing the lever is an operant response, and the increased rate of lever pressing that occurs when the response is followed by a pellet of food exemplifies operant conditioning. Applying the same terms to Thorndike's experiments, the movement that opens the latch is an operant response, and the increase from trial to trial in the speed with which that movement is made exemplifies operant conditioning.

Skinner (1938) proposed the term **reinforcer,** as a replacement for such words as *satisfaction* and *reward,* to refer to a stimulus change that follows a response and increases the subsequent frequency of that response. Skinner preferred this term because it makes no assumptions about anything happening in the mind; it merely refers to the effect that the presentation of the stimulus has on the animal's subsequent behavior. Thus, in a typical Skinner-box experiment, the delivery of a pellet of food or drop of water following a lever-press response is a reinforcer. In Thorndike's experiment, escape from the cage and access to the food outside it were reinforcers. Some stimuli, such as food for a food-deprived animal or water for a water-deprived one, are naturally reinforcing. Other stimuli have reinforcing value only because of previous learning, and Skinner referred to these as *conditioned reinforcers.* An example of a conditioned reinforcer for humans is money. Once a person learns what money can buy, he or she will learn to behave in ways that yield more of it.

Operant Conditioning Without Awareness

To Skinner and his followers, operant conditioning is not simply one kind of learning to be studied; it represents an entire approach to psychology. In his many books and articles, Skinner argued that essentially all the things we do, from the moment we arise in the morning to the moment we fall asleep at night, can be understood as operant responses that occur because of their past reinforcement. In some cases we are clearly aware of the relationship between our responses and reinforcers, as when we place money in a vending machine for a candy bar or study to obtain a good grade on a test. In other cases we may not be aware of the relationship, yet it exists and, according to Skinner (1953, 1966), is the real reason for our behavior. Skinner argued that awareness—which refers to a mental phenomenon—is not a useful construct for explaining behavior. We can never be sure what a person is aware of, but we can see directly the relationship between responses and reinforcers and use that to predict what a person will learn to do.

An illustration of conditioning without awareness is found in an experiment conducted many years ago, in which adults listened to music over which static was occasionally superimposed (Hefferline & others, 1959). Unbeknownst to the subjects, they could turn off the static by making an imperceptibly small twitch of the left thumb. Some subjects (the completely uninformed group) were told that the experiment had to do with the effect of music on body tension; they were told nothing about the static or how it could be turned off. Others (the partly informed group) were told that static would sometimes come on, that they could turn it off with a specific response, and that their task was to discover that response.

The result was that all subjects in both groups learned to make the thumb-twitch response, thereby keeping the static off for increasingly long periods. But, when questioned afterward, none were aware that they had controlled the static with thumb twitches. Subjects in the uninformed group said that they had noticed the static decline over the session but were unaware that they had caused the decline. Most in the partly informed group said that they had not discovered how to control the static. Only one participant believed that he had discovered the effective response, and he claimed that it involved "subtle rowing movements with both hands, infinitesimal wriggles of both ankles, a slight displacement of the jaw to the left, breathing out, and then waiting"! While he was consciously making this superstitious response, he was unconsciously learning to make the thumb twitch.

If you think about it, the results of this experiment should not come as a great surprise. We constantly learn finely tuned muscle movements as we develop skill at playing the violin, riding a bicycle, hammering nails, or any other activity. The probable reinforcers are, respectively, the improved sound from the violin, the steadier movement on the bicycle, and the straight downward movement of the nail we are pounding; but often we do not know just what we are doing differently to produce these good effects. Our knowledge is often similar to that of the neophyte carpenter who said, after an hour's practice at hammering, "The nails you're giving me now don't bend as easily as the ones you were giving me before."

> **19**
> What is some evidence that people can be conditioned to make an operant response without awareness of the conditioning process? How is this relevant for understanding the acquisition of motor skills?

Principles of Reinforcement

Skinner and his followers identified and studied many behavioral phenomena associated with operant conditioning, including the ones described in this section.

Shaping of New Operant Responses

Suppose you put a rat in a Skinner box, and it never presses the lever; or you place a cat in a puzzle box, and it never pulls the loop; or you want to train your dog to jump through a hoop, but it never makes that leap. In operant conditioning, the reinforcer comes after the subject produces the desired response. But if the desired response never occurs, it can never be reinforced. The solution to this problem is a technique

> **20**
> How can operant conditioning be used to get an animal to do something that it currently doesn't do?

An effect of operant shaping Through the process of rewarding gradual approximations to the desired behavior, animals can be trained to do things that they would never do without such training.

ROSLAN RAHMAN/AFP/Getty Images

called *shaping,* in which successively closer approximations to the desired response are reinforced until the desired response finally occurs and can be reinforced.

Imagine that you want to shape a lever-press response in a rat whose initial rate of lever pressing is zero. To begin, you might present the reinforcer (such as a pellet of food) whenever the rat goes anywhere near the lever. As a result, the rat will soon be spending most of its time near the lever and occasionally will touch it. When that happens, you might provide the reinforcer only when the rat touches the lever, which will increase the rate of touching. Some touches will be more vigorous than others and produce the desired lever movement; when that has happened a few times, you can stop reinforcing any other response; your animal's lever pressing has now been shaped.

Animal trainers regularly use this technique in teaching domestic or circus animals to perform new tricks or tasks (Pryor, 1985), and we all tend to use it, more or less deliberately and not always skillfully, when we teach new skills to other people. For example, when teaching a novice to play tennis, we tend at first to offer praise for any swing of the racket that propels the ball in the right general direction, but as improvement occurs, we begin to bestow our praise only on closer and closer approximations of an ideal swing.

Extinction of Operantly Conditioned Responses

21
In what ways is extinction in operant conditioning similar to extinction in classical conditioning?

An operantly conditioned response declines in rate and eventually disappears if it no longer results in a reinforcer. Rats stop pressing levers if no food pellets appear, cats stop scratching at doors if nobody responds by letting them out, and people stop smiling at those who don't smile back. The absence of reinforcement of the response and the consequent decline in response rate are both referred to as *extinction.* Extinction in operant conditioning is analogous to extinction in classical conditioning. Just as in classical conditioning, extinction in operant conditioning is not true "unlearning" of the response. Passage of time following extinction can lead to spontaneous recovery of responding, and a single reinforced response following extinction can lead the individual to respond again at a rapid rate.

Schedules of Partial Reinforcement

In many cases, in the real world as well as in laboratory experiments, a particular response only sometimes produces a reinforcer. This is referred to as *partial reinforcement,* to distinguish it on the one hand from *continuous reinforcement,* where the response is always reinforced, and on the other hand from *extinction,* where the response is never reinforced. In initial training, continuous reinforcement is most efficient, but once trained, an animal will continue to perform for partial reinforcement. Skinner and other operant researchers have described the following four basic types of partial-reinforcement schedules:

- In a ***fixed-ratio schedule*** a reinforcer occurs after every *n*th response, where *n* is some whole number greater than 1. For example, in a *fixed-ratio 5 schedule* every fifth response is reinforced.

- A ***variable-ratio schedule*** is like a fixed-ratio schedule except that the number of responses required before reinforcement varies unpredictably around some average. For example, in a *variable-ratio 5 schedule* reinforcement might come after 7 responses on one trial, after 3 on another, and so on, in random manner, but the average number of responses required for reinforcement would be 5.

- In a ***fixed-interval schedule*** a fixed period of time must elapse between one reinforced response and the next. Any response occurring before that time elapses is not reinforced. For example, in a *fixed-interval 30-second schedule* the first response that occurs at least 30 seconds after the last reinforcer is reinforced.

- A ***variable-interval schedule*** is like a fixed-interval schedule except that the period that must elapse before a response will be reinforced varies unpredictably around some average. For example, in a *variable-interval 30-second schedule* the average period required before the next response will be reinforced is 30 seconds.

22

How do the four types of partial-reinforcement schedules differ from one another, and why do responses generally occur faster to ratio schedules than to interval schedules?

The different schedules produce different response rates, in ways that make sense if we assume that the person or animal is striving to maximize the number of reinforcers and minimize the number of unreinforced responses. Ratio schedules (whether fixed or variable) produce reinforcers at a rate that is directly proportional to the rate of responding, so, not surprisingly, such schedules typically induce rapid responding. With interval schedules, in contrast, the maximum number of reinforcers available is set by the clock, and such schedules result, not surprisingly, in relatively low response rates that depend on the length of the fixed or average interval.

Behavior that has been reinforced on a variable-ratio or variable-interval schedule is often very difficult to extinguish. If a rat is trained to press a lever only on continuous reinforcement and then is shifted to extinction conditions, the rat will typically make a few bursts of lever-press responses and then quit. But if the rat has been shifted gradually from continuous reinforcement to an ever-stingier variable schedule and then finally to extinction, it will often make hundreds of unreinforced responses before quitting. Rats and humans who have been reinforced on stingy variable schedules have experienced reinforcement after long, unpredictable periods of no reinforcement, so they have learned (for better or worse) to be persistent.

23

How do variable-ratio and variable-interval schedules produce behavior that is highly resistant to extinction?

Skinner (1953) and others (Rachlin, 1990) have used this phenomenon to explain why gamblers often persist at the slot machine or dice game even after long periods of losing: They are hooked by the variable-ratio schedule of payoff that characterizes nearly every gambling device or game. From a cognitive perspective, we could say that the gambler keeps playing because of his or her knowledge that the very next bet or throw of the dice might be the one that pays off.

Partial reinforcement in daily life
Winning at slot machines occurs on a variable-ratio schedule, which produces a rapid and steady style of play. Success at reaching a previously busy telephone number occurs on a variable-interval schedule, which results in a slow and steady rate of redialing.

Jeff Greenberg/Alamy

UpperCut Images/Alamy

Distinction Between Positive and Negative Reinforcement

24

How does negative reinforcement differ from positive reinforcement?

In Skinner's terminology, **reinforcement** refers to any process that increases the likelihood that a particular response will occur. Reinforcement can be positive or negative. **Positive reinforcement** occurs when the *arrival* of some stimulus following a response makes the response more likely to recur. The stimulus in this case is called a **positive reinforcer.** Food pellets, money, words of praise, and anything else that organisms will work to obtain can be used as positive reinforcers. **Negative reinforcement,** in contrast, occurs when the *removal* of some stimulus following a response makes the response more likely to recur. The stimulus in this case is called a **negative reinforcer.** Electric shocks, loud noises, unpleasant company, scoldings, and everything else that organisms will work to get away from can be used as negative reinforcers. The one example of negative reinforcement discussed so far was the experiment in which a thumb-twitch response was reinforced by the temporary removal of unpleasant static.

Notice that *positive* and *negative* here do not refer to the direction of change in the response rate; that increases in either case. Rather, the terms indicate whether the reinforcing stimulus appears (positive) or disappears (negative) as a result of the operant response.

Distinction Between Reinforcement and Punishment

25

How does punishment differ from reinforcement, and how do the two kinds of punishment parallel the two kinds of reinforcement?

In Skinner's terminology, **punishment** is the opposite of reinforcement. It is the process through which the consequence of a response *decreases* the likelihood that the response will recur. As with reinforcement, punishment can be positive or negative. In **positive punishment,** the arrival of a stimulus, such as electric shock for a rat or scolding for a person, decreases the likelihood that the response will occur again. In **negative punishment,** the removal of a stimulus, such as taking food away from a hungry rat or money away from a person, decreases the likelihood that the response will occur again. Both types of punishment can be distinguished from extinction, which, you recall, is the decline in a previously reinforced response when it no longer produces any effect.

To picture the distinction between positive and negative punishment, and to see their relation to positive and negative reinforcement, look at Figure 4.12. The terms are easy to remember if you recall that *positive* and *negative* always refer to the arrival or removal of a stimulus and that *reinforcement* and *punishment* always refer to an increase or decrease in the likelihood that the response will recur.

The figure also makes it clear that the same stimuli that can serve as positive reinforcers when presented can serve as negative punishers when removed, and the same stimuli that can serve as positive punishers when presented can serve as negative reinforcers when removed. It is easy to think of the former as "desired" stimuli and the latter as "undesired," but Skinner avoided such mentalistic terms. He argued that the only way to tell whether a stimulus is desired or undesired is by observing its reinforcing or punishing effects, so the mentalistic terms add nothing to our understanding. For instance, an adult who scolds a child for misbehaving may think that the scolding is an undesired stimulus that will punish the behavior, but, in fact, it may be a desired stimulus to the child who seeks attention. To Skinner, the proof is in the pudding. If scolding causes the undesired behavior to become less frequent, then scolding is acting as a positive punisher; if scolding causes the behavior to become more frequent, it is acting as a positive reinforcer.

FIGURE 4.12 Two types of reinforcement and two types of punishment Reinforcement (whether positive or negative) increases the response rate, and punishment (whether positive or negative) decreases the response rate. The terms positive and negative refer to whether the reinforcing stimulus arrives or is removed when the response is made.

| | | **Response rate** | |
		Increases	Decreases
Response causes stimulus to be	**Presented**	Positive reinforcement (Lever press→food pellet)	Positive punishment (Lever press→shock)
	Removed	Negative reinforcement (Lever press→turns off shock)	Negative punishment (Lever press→removes food)

Operant conditioning reflects the impact of an action's consequences on its recurrence.

Work of Thorndike and Skinner	Variations in Availability of Reinforcement	Reinforcement vs. Punishment
➤ An operant response is an action that produces an effect.	➤ Shaping occurs when successive approximations to the desired response are reinforced.	➤ Reinforcement increases response rate; punishment decreases response rate.
➤ Thorndike's puzzle box experiments led him to postulate the law of effect.	➤ Extinction is the decline in response rate that occurs when an operant response is no longer reinforced.	➤ Reinforcement can be either positive (e.g., praise is given) or negative (e.g., pain goes away).
➤ Skinner developed an efficient way to study operant conditioning. He defined reinforcer as a stimulus change that follows an operant response and increases the frequency of that response.	➤ Partial reinforcement can occur on various schedules of reinforcement. The type of schedule affects the response rate and resistance to extinction.	➤ Punishment can be either positive (e.g., a reprimand is given) or negative (e.g., computer privileges are taken away).
➤ Operant conditioning can occur without awareness.		

■ Operant Conditioning II: What Is Learned?

What does an animal learn in operant conditioning? It does not just learn to make a response more frequently. It learns something about the conditions in which the response will be rewarded and about the nature of the reward.

Learning When a Response Will Be Rewarded

A rat trained in a Skinner box has learned to make a lever-press response in a particular context, which includes being inside the Skinner box. The rat does not go foolishly about making the lever-pressing movement in its home cage or in other places where the response has never been reinforced. In his original formulation of the law of effect, Thorndike (1898) emphasized the importance of the *situation* in which the animal is trained, saying, "Of several responses made to the same situation, those which are accompanied or closely followed by satisfaction to the animal will, other things being equal, be more firmly connected with the situation, so that when it recurs, they will be more likely to recur." The set of stimuli inside a puzzle box or a Skinner box is an example of what Thorndike meant by a situation (look back at Figure 4.9). Only in the presence of those stimuli is the response reinforced; therefore, the response becomes likely to occur when those stimuli are present.

Discrimination Training in Operant Conditioning

Through *discrimination training,* an animal can be conditioned to make an operant response to a stimulus more specific than the entire inside of a Skinner box. Discrimination training in operant conditioning is analogous to discrimination training in classical conditioning. The essence of the procedure is to reinforce the animal's response when a specific stimulus is present and to extinguish the response when the stimulus is absent. Thus, to train a rat to respond to a tone by pressing a lever, a trainer would alternate between reinforcement periods with the tone on (during which the animal gets food pellets for responding) and extinction periods with the tone off. After considerable training of this sort, the rat will begin pressing the lever as soon as the tone comes on and stop as soon as it goes off. The tone in this example is called a ***discriminative stimulus.***

A discriminative stimulus can be thought of as a cue signaling the availability of a reinforcer; it is present when a particular response will be reinforced and absent

26

How can an animal be trained to produce an operant response only when a specific cue is present?

"Oh, not bad. The light comes on, I press the bar, they write me a check. How about you?"

otherwise. A discriminative stimulus in operant conditioning is similar to a conditioned stimulus in classical conditioning in that it promotes a particular response as a result of the subject's previous experience, but it does so in a different way. It *sets the occasion* for responding, rather than reflexively eliciting the response.

Operant discrimination training, like the analogous procedure in classical conditioning, can be used to study the sensory abilities of animals and human infants, who cannot describe their sensations in words. In one experiment, for example, researchers trained 1-day-old human babies to turn their heads in one direction, using a sip of sugar water as the reinforcer, whenever a tone was sounded, and in the other direction whenever a buzzer was sounded (Siqueland & Lipsitt, 1966). Thus, the babies learned to make two different responses to two different discriminative stimuli. This demonstrated, among other things, that the newborns could hear the difference between the two sounds. (More is said about such experiments in Chapter 11.) Operant discrimination training can also be used to study animals' understanding of concepts.

Discrimination and Generalization as Indices of Concept Understanding

In classical conditioning, as you may recall, animals that have learned to respond to a conditioned stimulus will respond also to new stimuli that they perceive as similar to the original conditioned stimulus, a phenomenon referred to as *generalization*. Generalization also occurs in operant conditioning. After operant discrimination training, animals will respond to new stimuli that they perceive as similar to the discriminative stimulus. Such generalization can be used to test an animal's understanding of a concept.

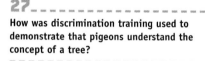

27 ───────────────────────
How was discrimination training used to demonstrate that pigeons understand the concept of a tree?

◄ Consider an experiment conducted by Richard Herrnstein (1979), who operantly conditioned pigeons to peck a key for grain, using slides depicting natural scenes as discriminative stimuli. Herrnstein divided the slides into two categories—those that had at least one tree or portion of a tree somewhere in the scene and those that didn't. The pigeons received grain (on a variable-ratio schedule of reinforcement) for pecking the key whenever a "tree" slide was shown and nothing when a "no tree" slide was shown. In the first phase, 80 slides were presented each day, 40 of which contained trees and 40 of which didn't. By the end of 5 days of such training—that is, after five presentations of all 80 slides—all the birds were successfully discriminating between the two categories of slides, pecking when the slide contained a tree and not pecking otherwise.

It's a flower
Researchers have developed various means to test animals' ability to categorize complex objects. In the experiment illustrated here, Edward Wasserman (1995) trained pigeons to peck a different one of four keys depending on whether the slide shown was of a car, cat, chair, or flower. The birds proved to be quite accurate at classifying objects that they had never seen before.

Now, the question is: What did Herrnstein's pigeons learn? Did they learn each slide as a separate stimulus, unrelated to the others, or did they learn a rule for categorizing the slides? Such a rule might be stated by a person as follows: "Respond whenever a slide includes a tree or part of a tree, and don't respond otherwise." To determine whether the pigeons had acquired such a rule, Herrnstein tested them with new slides, which they had never seen before, under conditions in which no grain was given. He found that the pigeons immediately pecked at a much higher rate when a new slide contained a tree than when it did not. In fact, the pigeons were as accurate with new slides as they were with slides that had been used during training. The birds apparently based their responses on a **concept** of trees (Herrnstein, 1990). A concept, as the term is used here, can be defined as a rule for categorizing stimuli into groups. The pigeons' tree concept, in this case, must have guided their decision to peck or not to peck.

American Scientist

How might one describe the pigeons' tree concept? That question is not easily answered. It is not the case, for example, that the pigeons simply learned to peck at slides that included a patch of green. Many of the "no tree" slides had green grass, and some of the tree slides were of fall or winter scenes in New England, where the trees had red and yellow leaves or none at all (see Figure 4.13). In some slides, only a small portion of a tree was apparent or the tree was in the distant background. So the method by which the pigeons distinguished tree slides from others cannot be easily stated in stimulus terms, although ultimately it must have been based on the birds' analysis of the stimulus material. Similar experiments have shown that pigeons can acquire concepts pertaining to such objects as cars, chairs, the difference between male and female human faces, and even abstract symbols (Cook & Smith, 2006; Loidolt & others, 2003; Wasserman, 1995). The point is that, even for pigeons—and certainly for humans—sophisticated analysis of the stimulus information occurs before the stimulus is used to guide behavior.

[Michael Thompson/Comstock]

[Naoki Okamoto/Stock Market]

FIGURE 4.13 Tree pictures similar to those used to study concepts in pigeons Pigeons that had been trained to peck whenever a slide contained a tree, or part of a tree, pecked when they saw slides such as these and refrained from pecking when they saw slides that did not include a tree.

Learning to Expect a Certain Reward

As they did for classical conditioning, some early behaviorists (for example, Guthrie, 1952) supported a stimulus-response (S-R) theory of operant conditioning. According to this theory, operant conditioning entails the strengthening of a bond between the reinforced response and stimuli that are present just before the response is made (the discriminative stimuli). Thus, for a rat learning to press a lever in a Skinner box, the learned connection could be described as: *stimuli inside Skinner box* ⟶ *lever press*. If a more specific discriminative stimulus such as a tone is used, it could be described as: *tone* ⟶ *lever press*. According to this view, the reinforcer (such as a pellet of food) is involved in learning only insofar as it helps stamp in the connection between the discriminative stimuli and the response.

Other theorists, however, taking a more cognitive perspective, have argued, with evidence, that during operant conditioning the animal learns more than the S-R relationship. The animal also learns the S-S relationship between the discriminative stimuli and the reinforcing stimulus (Mowrer, 1960) and the R-S relationship between the response and the reinforcing stimulus (Mackintosh & Dickinson, 1979). In other words, a rat in a Skinner box learns that the discriminative stimuli within the box signal that food is available there (S-S relationship) and that pressing the lever will make the food appear (R-S relationship). In an early cognitive theory, Edward Tolman (1959) described operant conditioning as the learning of relationships between means and ends. The animal learns to expect that a particular response, made at the appropriate time (when the discriminative stimuli are present), will produce a certain consequence.

Evidence That Animals Learn Means-End Expectancies

A *means-end expectancy* is the animal's knowledge or expectation that a particular response, in a particular situation, will have a particular effect. Thus, according to Tolman, if a rat is regularly reinforced with a specific kind of food for pressing a lever when a tone is on, the rat acquires the expectation that pressing the lever when the tone is on will produce that food. According to this view, the tone does not directly elicit a lever-press response, as the S-R theory would hold; rather, the tone activates the animal's expectation that pressing the lever will bring a certain food. The lever

28

How do cognitive theories of operant conditioning differ from the S-R theory?

[Sidney Harris]

"What it comes down to is you have to find out what reaction thy're looking for, and you give them that reaction."

29

How can the view that operant conditioning involves means-end knowledge be experimentally tested? What were the results of one such test?

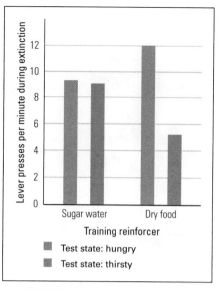

FIGURE 4.14 Evidence that rats learn what reinforcer a response produces Rats that were trained to press a lever for sugar water when hungry continued to press the lever at as high a rate (with no reinforcer given) when they were thirsty as when they were hungry (two left-hand bars). In contrast, rats that were trained to press a lever for dry food when they were hungry pressed the lever much less often (with no reinforcer given) when they were thirsty than when they were hungry (two right-hand bars). These results indicate that the rats expected the response to a certain reinforcer and knew whether it would satisfy both thirst and hunger or only hunger. (Adapted from Dickinson & Dawson, 1987.)

30
How are reward contrast effects explained from a cognitive perspective?

is understood as the means to a certain end. The animal may or may not press the lever, depending on its current interest in the food. Thus, in Tolman's view, the rat's behavior is best understood in terms of this sequence:

tone ⟶ expectation that lever press will now bring a certain kind of food ⟶ decision to press lever or not, depending on whether the food is desired

In support of this cognitive view, animals that have learned an operant response have been found to behave in ways that are consistent with the premise that they have learned a means-end relationship (Belleine & Dickinson, 2006; Dickinson & Balleine, 2000). For example, in one experiment, some hungry rats were trained to press a lever for sugar water, and others were trained to press a lever for dry food pellets as a reinforcer (Dickinson & Dawson, 1987). Later, all the rats were tested under extinction conditions (no reinforcer given) after having been deprived of either food or water. The interesting result was that when tested in the new drive state (thirst), those that had been reinforced with sugar water (which would satisfy thirst as well as hunger) pressed at a high rate, and those that had been reinforced with dry pellets (which would not satisfy thirst) pressed at a low rate (see Figure 4.14). The most direct way to explain this difference is to assume that the rats had acquired knowledge of the kind of reinforcer they would receive for pressing the lever and were able to use that knowledge to decide whether or not the reinforcer would satisfy their current drive state.

Evidence That Animals Keep Track of the Relative Value of Rewards

Further evidence that animals learn to expect a certain reward for making a certain response is found in the existence of *reward contrast effects,* which involve shifts in the response rate when the value of the reward changes (Flaherty, 1996). Suppose that one group of rats is trained to press a lever for a highly valued reward (such as tasty food) and another group is trained to press for a less valued reward (food that doesn't taste so good). As you might predict, rats in the first group would typically respond at a faster rate than those in the second. So far, this is consistent with S-R theory. Presumably, the S-R connection built by the strong reinforcer is stronger than that built by the weak reinforcer, resulting in faster responses from the first group.

Now suppose that the rats receiving the strong reinforcer are suddenly shifted to the weak one. According to the S-R model, they should continue, at least for a while, to respond at a higher rate than the other rats, because of the stronger S-R connection built during the first phase of the experiment. But, actually, the opposite happens: Rats that are shifted from a strong to a weak reinforcer show a sharp drop in their response rate, to a slower rate than that of rats that had been in the weak-reinforcer condition all along. This illustrates the **negative contrast effect.** Conversely, rats that are shifted from a weak to a strong reinforcer show an increase in their response rate, to a higher rate than that of rats that had been in the strong-reinforcer condition all along. This illustrates the **positive contrast** effect.

◄ Not surprisingly, reward contrast effects also occur for people. If you have been getting $1 per page for typing term papers, you will probably be delighted to discover that your pay is now $2 per page, and you may type with renewed vigor; but if you have been getting $4 per page, that same discovery (that you are now getting only $2) may lead you to quit. Clearly, our experience of reward value is relative to what we are used to receiving.

From a cognitive perspective, these contrast effects—in rats as in humans—are explained by assuming that the individual (a) has learned to expect a certain reward and (b) is able to compare the actual reward with the expected one. If the comparison is favorable, the animal increases its response rate; if unfavorable, the animal decreases its rate. The animal is constantly out to do better, and if a particular response leads to less reinforcement than it did before, the animal might do better by spending less time at it and more time looking for reinforcers elsewhere. In fact, animals that have experienced a downshift in reward size do engage in increased exploration, as if looking for the larger reward (Pecoraro & others, 1999).

When Rewards Backfire: The Overjustification Effect in Humans

In human beings, rewards have a variety of effects, either positive or negative, depending on the conditions in which they are used and the meanings that they engender in those who receive them.

Consider an experiment conducted with nursery-school children (Lepper & Greene, 1978). Children in one group were rewarded with attractive "Good Player" certificates for drawing with felt-tipped pens. This had the immediate effect of leading them to spend more time at this activity than did children in the other group (who were not rewarded). Later, however, when certificates were no longer given, the previously rewarded children showed a sharp drop in their use of the pens—to a level well below that of children in the unrewarded group. So, the long-term effect of the period of reward was to decrease the children's use of felt-tipped pens.

Many subsequent experiments, with people of various ages, have produced similar results. The drop in performance following a period of reward is particularly likely to occur when the task is something that is initially enjoyed for its own sake and the reward is given in such a manner that it seems to be designed deliberately to motivate the participants to engage in the task (Lepper & Henderlong, 2000). This decline is called the *overjustification effect,* because the reward presumably provides an unneeded extra justification for engaging in the behavior. The result, according to the usual cognitive interpretation, is that the person comes to regard the task as something that one does for an external reward rather than for its own sake—that is, as work rather than play. When they come to regard the task as work, they stop doing it when they no longer receive a payoff for it, even though they would have otherwise continued to do it for fun.

Such findings suggests that some rewards used in schools may have negative long-term effects. For example, rewarding children for reading might cause them to think of reading as work rather than fun, which would lead them to read less on their own. The broader point is that one must take into account the cognitive consequences of rewards in predicting their long-term effects, especially when dealing with human beings.

31
Why might a period of reward lead to a subsequent decline in response rate when the reward is no longer available?

When does play become work? Athletic games can be great fun for children, but when the focus is on winning trophies and pleasing parents and coaches, what was previously play can become work.

SECTION REVIEW

Operant conditioning entails learning about conditions and consequences.

Learning When to Respond

➤ If reinforcement is available only when a specific stimulus is present, that stimulus becomes a discriminative stimulus. Subjects learn to respond only when it is present.

➤ Learners generalize to stimuli that they perceive as similar to the discriminative stimulus, but can be trained to discriminate.

➤ Discrimination training has been used to study perception in infants and concepts in pigeons.

Learning What to Expect

➤ According to the cognitive view, subjects in operant conditioning learn a means-end relationship, i.e., that a certain response has a certain effect. This view is supported by an experiment in which the motivational state of rats was varied between training and testing.

➤ Means-end learning helps to explain reward contrast effects and overjustification effects. In these cases, expectations about reward influence the rate of operant responding.

◼ Activities Designed for Learning: Play, Exploration, and Observation

Classical and operant conditioning have long been popular research topics in psychology, partly because they truly are ubiquitous learning processes and partly because they are relatively easy to study in the laboratory. By tightly controlling an animal's environment and motivational state, a researcher can, more or less at will, induce predictable changes in the animal's behavior. Indeed, the very word *conditioning* implies an active researcher (or trainer) and a passive animal. The researcher *conditions* the animal. The idea that learning is imposed by external conditions rather than controlled by the learner accords closely with the philosophy of early behaviorism.

In nature, however, animals (especially mammals) are active learners. They move about in ways that are well designed for learning. Through *play* young animals learn how to control their own behavior in effective ways. Through *exploration* animals of all ages keep track of significant changes in their environment. In addition, at least some animals acquire useful information through *observing* the behavior of others of their kind. Play, exploration, and observation are instinctive behavioral tendencies, or drives, that came about through natural selection precisely because they promote learning. Unlike operant conditioning as studied in laboratories, these activities occur most fully when the animal is free of any strong, immediate need state, such as hunger or thirst, and is free to move about at will.

Play: How the Young Learn How

Play is behavior that serves no immediately useful purpose. It is behavior engaged in apparently for its own sake. The demeanor of the playing animal, just like that of a playing child, is often high-spirited and bouncing, which suggests that the animal is having fun. Play is clearly instinctive. The young of all mammals spend considerable portions of their time playing. Nobody has to teach them to play; they just do it.

Why do young mammals play? It is not enough to say that they play because play is *fun*. That answer only begs us to ask, "Why are young mammals constructed in such a manner that they enjoy playing?" Natural selection does not create instincts or pleasures that serve no purpose. So, what is the purpose of play?

Play clearly has some costs. It uses energy, which must be made up for in additional food, and it is sometimes directly dangerous. Young chimpanzees playfully chasing one another in trees sometimes fall and hurt themselves; goat kids frolicking on cliffs have been observed to slip and fall to their deaths; young fur seal pups are more likely to be snatched and eaten by predatory sea lions when they are at play than when they are at rest; and the play of cheetah cubs sometimes spoils their mothers' attempts to stalk and capture game (Bjorklund & Pellegrini, 2002; Byers, 1998; Caro, 1995). The value of play must outweigh such costs, or natural selection would have weeded it out. What is that value?

Jonathan And Angela / Getty Images

Young predators at play These lion cubs are playfully practicing maneuvers that will serve them well as they grow older.

32

What is Groos's theory about the evolutionary function of animals' play, and what are five lines of evidence supporting that theory?

Groos's Theory: Play is Practice of Species-Typical Skills

The first theorist to write about play from an evolutionary perspective was the German philosopher and naturalist Karl Groos. In a book entitled *The Play of Animals*, published in 1898, Groos argued that the primary purpose of play is to provide a means for young animals to practice their instincts, or, to use the term I introduced in Chapter 3, their species-typical behaviors. Groos was strongly influenced by the writings of Charles Darwin and had a sophisticated, modern understanding of instincts. He recognized that animals, especially mammals, must to varying degrees *learn* to use their instincts. Young mammals come into the world with biological drives and tendencies (instincts) to behave in certain ways, but to be effective such behaviors must be practiced and refined. Play, according to Groos, provides that practice. This theory, even today, is the most widely accepted explanation of play among people who study it in animals.

Evidence for Groos's Theory

Much of what we know about play in animals makes sense in the light of Groos's theory and thereby provides evidence supporting that theory. Here are five categories of such evidence:

- *Young animals play more than do adults of their species.* Among the most obvious evidence for Groos's practice theory is the simple fact that young animals, of all species that play, are much more playful than their elders. Young animals have more to learn than do adults of their species, so the fact that they are motivated to play more is no coincidence according to the practice theory.

- *Species of animals that have the most to learn play the most.* Another accurate prediction of Groos's practice theory is that those animal species that have the most to learn play the most (Power, 2000). Young mammals play more than do the young of any other animal class, and mammals, more than any other class, depend on learning in order to survive. Among mammals, primates (monkeys and apes) are the most flexible and adaptable order, and the most dependent on learning; they are also the most playful of all animal orders. Among primates, human beings, chimpanzees, and bonobos (introduced in Chapter 3) are the most flexible and adaptable species, and they appear to be the most playful of all species. Also among mammals, those in the carnivore order (which includes the dog-like and cat-like species) are more playful than herbivores, which is consistent with the observation that success in hunting requires more practice than does success in grazing.

- *Young animals play most at those skills that they most need to learn.* To a considerable degree it is possible to predict the activities that a young animal will play at by knowing what skills it must develop to survive and thrive. Young carnivores play at chasing, stalking, and pouncing—skills they will need in obtaining food (Schaller, 1972). Young herbivores do not play at grazing; that skill is easy to develop and can be practiced through serious grazing, so play is not needed. But young herbivores do play at fleeing and dodging, skills they need for evading predators (Fontaine, 1994). The young of almost all mammals play at fighting. Among most species of mammals, young males playfight more than do young females (Meaney & others, 1985), and this corresponds with the fact that among most mammals fighting is a more essential adult skill for males than it is for females (for reasons discussed in Chapter 3). At least among some species of primates, young females, but not young males, engage in playful care of infants (Goodall, 1986; Lancaster, 1971).

- *Play involves much repetition.* To practice something is to do it over and over again; and repetition is one of the hallmarks of play. Think of the difference between a cat seriously preying on a mouse and a cat *playing* at preying on a mouse. The *preying* cat pounces once, in its most efficient manner; it then kills the mouse and either eats it or takes it to its den. The *playing* cat, in contrast, lets the mouse go after catching it, so it can stalk and pounce again—and again, and again, until the poor mouse dies of fright and exhaustion. Similarly, bear cubs playing chase games repeatedly chase one another, taking turns being the pursued and the pursuer, like children playing tag. And monkeys, playing at swinging from branch to branch in a tree, sometimes swing repeatedly between the same two branches (Symons, 1978). The repetition is not stereotyped; each repetition may be a little different from the previous one. It is as if the young animal is trying out, each time, a different way of preying, chasing, or swinging.

- *Play is challenging.* In play, young animals seem deliberately to put themselves into situations that challenge their abilities. In playfighting, whether among rats or monkeys, the stronger of the two will allow the weaker one to pin it, and then will struggle to get out of the pinned position. In playful leaping and running, the young of many species seem to make deliberately awkward motions, from which they then have to recover skillfully to void a fall (Spinka & others, 2001). When young monkeys practice swinging from branch to branch, they commonly choose branches that are at such a distance that they often can't make it, but low enough that a fall doesn't hurt. Mountain goat kids that can already run well on flat ground tend to concentrate their playful running on steep slopes, where running is more difficult (Byers, 1977).

Applying the Theory to Humans

In a second book, entitled *The Play of Man* (1901), Groos extended his theory of play to human beings. Groos recognized basic differences between humans and other mammals. We humans have at least as many instincts as other mammals have, but our instincts are even less rigid, more modifiable by experience, enabling us to adapt to a wider range of environmental niches, than is true of other mammals. Moreover, we are the only truly cultural species. *Culture,* by definition, is the set of learned skills, knowledge, beliefs, and values that characterize a group of interconnected individuals and are passed along from generation to generation. To do well as human beings we must learn not just the skills that are common to the whole species, but also those that are unique to the specific culture in which we are developing.

So, according to Groos, in the evolution of our species the basic mammalian drive to play was elaborated upon, by natural selection, to include a heavy component of imitation. We are motivated to play not just at those activities (such as two-legged walking and running) that people everywhere do in pretty much the same way, but also to play at the very specific activities that we see are crucial to success in the particular culture in which we are growing up. Children in a hunting culture play at hunting, using and elaborating upon the particular methods of hunting that they see among their elders. Children in our present-day culture play at writing and computers. In the evolution of human beings, those individuals who were born with a genetic tendency to pay attention to and play at the human activities around them, especially those activities that are difficult yet crucial to success, were more likely to survive and reproduce than those born without such a tendency.

I will have more to say about human play in Chapter 12. There I will argue that play not only helps children learn physical skills, but also helps them learn to control their emotions and to get along well with other people.

Exploration: How Animals Learn What and Where

33

How does exploration differ from play in its evolutionary function?

◄ Play is not the only drive that came about in evolution to promote active learning. The other great one is curiosity, or the drive to explore. Groos (1898) considered exploration to be a category of play, but most students of play and exploration now consider the two to be distinct (Power, 2000). Learning can be divided at least roughly into two broad categories—learning *to do* (skill learning) and learning *about* (information learning). Play evolved to serve the former and exploration evolved to serve the latter.

Exploration is a more primitive and widespread category of behavior than is play. Animals whose activities are rather rigidly controlled by their genetic makeup, so that they don't have much to learn in the *to do* category, must nevertheless learn *about* their environment. They must learn where food, shelter, mates, and other necessities for life and reproduction are located. Fish don't play, at least not in any way that is reliably identified as such by researchers, but they do regularly approach and explore novel objects (Wilson & others, 1993). Even insects explore to find food and other necessities of life, although they do so in rather inflexible ways (Gordon, 1995). Mammals of all species, regardless of age, explore novel environments and objects with which they are confronted.

The Nature of Mammalian Exploration

Exploration, unlike play, is often mixed with a degree of fear. Exploration is elicited by novel stimuli, and novel stimuli often induce fear until they are fully explored. In fact, one purpose of exploration, in animals and people, is to determine whether or not an unfamiliar object or place is safe.

Explorers are often caught in a balance between curiosity, which drives them toward the unfamiliar terrain or novel object, and fear, which drives them away. A rat placed in a novel test arena with various objects in it will first cower in a corner. Then it will take a few steps out from the corner, along a wall, and dash back. Then it will venture a bit farther along the wall before dashing back again. Gradually, the rat will get bolder. It will eventually approach and explore—by smell, sight, and touch—the entire arena and all the objects within it. Once the rat is thoroughly familiar with the arena, it will reduce its movement but will continue periodically to tour the arena as if looking to see if anything has changed—a behavior referred to as *patrolling*. During its patrolling, the animal periodically rears up on its hind legs to get a better view. If a new object has been placed in the arena, the rat will attend to that rather than to old objects and will explore it at first gingerly and then more boldly (Inglis & others, 2001; Renner & Seltzer, 1991). Similar behaviors have been described in many other species of mammals.

Some of the earliest research on exploration came from studies of rats in mazes. Researchers learned that rats' movements through mazes are governed not just by their drive for the food in the goal box, but also by their drive to explore all of the maze's alleys (Dember & Fowler, 1958; Winfield & Dennis, 1934). Rats that have already learned the most direct route to the goal will often persist in exploring roundabout routes and dead-end alleys. Rats that are prevented from entering a particular alley, by a block placed at its entrance, will typically explore that alley first as soon as the block is removed. Not surprisingly, the hungrier a rat is (that is, the longer it has been deprived of food), the more directly it will run to the food-containing goal box, and the less hungry it is, the more time it will spend exploring the other alleys in a maze. But even very hungry rats will often spend some time exploring (Inglis & others, 2001).

──────────▶──34
How do rats explore a novel environment? How did Tolman and subsequent researchers show that rats learn useful information in their exploration?
──────────────

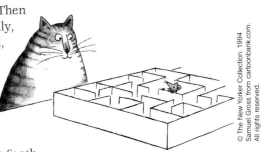

"Well you don't look like an experimental psychologist to me."

A curious monkey Sometimes naturalists find that the animals they study are as curious about them and their equipment as they (the naturalists) are about the animals. Here a squirrel monkey explores a camera.

Evidence That Animals Acquire Useful Information Through Exploration

In a now classic experiment, Edward Tolman and C. H. Honzik (1930) showed that rats can learn about the pathways in a maze even if no food or other such reward is provided for doing so. These researchers tested three groups of rats in a complex maze under different reward conditions. Group 1 received one trial per day in the maze with no food or other reward in the goal box. As expected, this group showed little improvement from day to day in the time they took to reach the goal box (the goal box contained no "goal" for them). Group 2 received one trial per day with food in the goal box. As expected, this group improved considerably from day to day in their rate of movement to the goal box. The most interesting group was group 3. Rats in this group received one trial per day with no reward for 10 days, like group 1, but, beginning on the 11th day, they received one trial per day with a food reward, like group 2. These rats improved dramatically between days 11 and 12. On day 11, they were no better than the other unrewarded group (group 1), but on day 12, after just one experience with the reward, they were as fast at reaching the goal box as the rats that had been rewarded all along (see Figure 4.15 on the next page).

FIGURE 4.15 Latent learning of a maze Each rat received one trial per day in the maze, with or without a food reward in the goal box. The group that received its first reward on day 11 performed as well on day 12 (and thereafter) as the group that had received a reward every day. From this, Tolman and Honzik concluded that the rats had learned the spatial layout of the maze even without a reward, but the rats did not use that knowledge until the changed conditions made it worthwhile for them to do so.

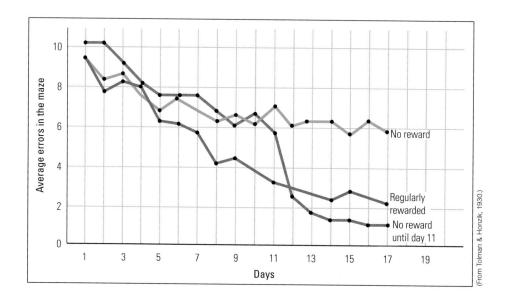

(From Tolman & Honzik, 1930.)

On the basis of this and other experiments, Tolman (1948) argued that rewards affect what animals *do* more than what they *learn*. Animals learn the locations of distinctive places in their environment through exploration, whether or not they have ever found rewards there, but they do not run directly to those places unless they have found rewards there. Tolman used the term **latent learning** to refer to learning that is not immediately demonstrated in the animal's behavior. In the experiment just described, the rats in group 3 learned the spatial layout of the maze in the first 10 trials, but that learning remained latent, not manifested in their behavior, until the addition of a reward gave the rats a reason to run straight to the goal box.

Latent learning has been demonstrated in many experiments since Tolman's time. Through exploration, without rewards, rats learn the layouts of mazes and then are able to take the shortest route to a reward when a reward is introduced (Roberts & others, 2007). Animals also learn about potential hiding places through exploration (Leonard & McNaughton, 1990). In one set of experiments, rats that had an opportunity to explore a novel arena that contained one or more hiding places ran much more quickly to a hiding place, when they were deliberately frightened in a later test, than did rats that had not previously explored the arena (Renner, 1988). There is also evidence, from experiments with mice, that animals that explore the most are the same animals that learn the most in a wide variety of tests of learning (Matzel & others, 2006).

In nature it is likely that most learning about the environment is latent. Animals learn about many aspects of their surroundings through exploration, but only an unpredictable portion of that knowledge becomes useful at a later time and affects the animal's behavior.

Observation: Learning by Watching Others

The objects of most intense exploration, for most people, are other people. By watching other people we learn an enormous amount about people, about how to do things, and about the human significance of the rest of our environment. Learning by watching others is referred to by psychologists as **observational learning.**

Through observation we learn about the unique characteristics of others, so we can judge how to get along with them and know who is likely to help us or hurt us in a given situation. When we are in a new social environment we look frequently to others to learn what sorts of behaviors are normal or expected in that setting—so when in Rome we can do as the Romans do. We also look frequently to others to see what they are looking at and how they are responding to what they are looking at. In that way we learn some of what they already know about the surrounding environment. To learn a new skill—whether it's a new dance step, driving a car, or surgery—we usually begin by observing the actions of a person who has already mastered the skill. Thank goodness for that; imagine what the world would be like if people learned driving and surgery only by trial and error.

The roles of observational learning in child development and in adult social behavior are discussed extensively in later chapters of this book (especially Chapters 11 through 14). Here, in this brief section, our focus is on some elementary aspects of such learning, which we share or partly share with other species.

Learning How By Watching Skilled Performers

Many experiments have shown that animals can learn or partially learn how to perform a new task by watching others do it. Kittens learned more quickly to press a lever for food if they had seen their mother do so than if they had not (Chesler, 1969). Dogs were better at moving around a barrier to get food if they had seen another dog or human being do it first than if they hadn't (Pongrácz & others, 2008). Mice who had observed a well-trained mouse make a sequence of two movements to get a food pellet learned that sequence of movements more readily than those who hadn't (Carlier & Jamon, 2006).

It is tempting to interpret such results as evidence that mammals in general are able to learn by imitating the actions of others of their kind. But, if you think about it, you realize that imitation is cognitively complex. To *imitate,* an animal must observe, remember, and reproduce the specific pattern of movements that were produced by the model. To reproduce the movements, the learner must map the observed actions onto its own movement control system. Many researchers argue, with evidence, that real imitation does not occur in mammals other than primates, and that observational learning by nonprimates involves simpler means, including stimulus enhancement and goal enhancement (Byrne & Russon, 1988; Zentall, 2003, 2006).

Stimulus enhancement refers to an increase in the salience or attractiveness of the object that the observed individual is acting upon. *Goal enhancement* refers to an increased drive to obtain rewards similar to what the observed individual is receiving. Thus, a kitten that sees its mother pressing a lever for food pellets may become attracted to the lever (stimulus enhancement) and motivated to eat food pellets (goal enhancement). In this case, stimulus enhancement increases the likelihood that the kitten will press the lever, goal enhancement increases the reward value of the pellets, and the two combined help the kitten learn very quickly to press the lever for pellets. By this account, the kitten is not imitating the movements of its mother but is going to the lever because that was made salient, pushing it more or less accidentally, and then eating the pellets because they too were made salient.

Careful studies have led to the conclusion that at least some nonhuman primates are capable of true imitation. The most convincing studies have been with chimpanzees. In laboratory experiments, chimps have been found to observe both human and chimpanzee "tutors" closely to learn new, sometimes complex sequences of actions to obtain rewards (Hirata & Morimura, 2000; Whiten, 1998). In one experiment, different groups of chimps observed different chimp models use different movements to obtain food from a certain apparatus. The result was that chimps in each group learned to obtain food using the unique action that their model had used (Hopper & others, 2007). This is good evidence that they had learned not just about the reward and relevant stimuli, but had also attended to and mimicked the model's movements.

Recently, neuroscientists have discovered that the brains of human beings and of at least some nonhuman primates contain organized systems of neurons (nerve cells) that seem to be well designed to make imitation easy and natural (Iacoboni & Dapretto, 2006; Jaffe, 2007). The neurons are referred to as **mirror neurons** because they are believed to help us behave in ways that mirror (mimic) what we see. Within this system, the same neurons that become active when the individual makes a particular motion also become active when the individual sees another individual make that motion. For example, the same neurons that are exercised when making an overhand serve in tennis are also exercised when watching someone else make an

> **35**
> **How does observation of skilled performers facilitate the learning of new operant tasks by animals? How does imitation differ from stimulus enhancement and goal enhancement? What evidence suggests that primates (especially chimpanzees), but not other mammals, are capable of imitation?**

overhand serve. In terms of its effect on these neurons, observing is like doing; thus, observing an action may alter the neurons and allow for new learning through the same means that occur when performing the action.

Cultural Transmission in Chimpanzees

We humans are the supremely cultural animal. *Culture,* as I said before, refers to the beliefs and traditions that are passed along from generation to generation. Because of culture we do not have to reinvent the wheel, or how to grow crops, or how to build houses; we merely improve on what our ancestors invented. Observational learning appears to be a prerequisite for human culture. The skills and rituals acquired by each generation are passed on to the next not so much because the older generation deliberately trains the younger (though that is part of it) but more because members of the younger generation intently observe their elders to learn to behave as they do.

36

What is the evidence that chimpanzees transmit cultural traditions from generation to generation?

◄ The species that comes second to us in exhibition of culture—though a far distant second—is, not surprisingly, the chimpanzee. Wild chimpanzees living in different groups, geographically isolated from one another, have different cultural traditions, which pass from generation to generation. Researchers studying wild chimpanzees at seven different field stations have identified at least 39 different behaviors, ranging from tool design to mating displays, that are distinct to specific groups and that seem to arise from cultural tradition rather than from constraints imposed by the environment (Whiten & others, 1999).

For example, chimpanzees in some colonies crack hard-shelled nuts by placing a nut on a carefully selected rock and hitting it with another carefully selected rock (see Figure 4.16; Mercader & others, 2002). The young in these colonies learn this skill by observing their elders and practicing elements of it over a period of several months (Inoue-Nakamura & Matsuzawa, 1997). In other colonies, however, chimpanzees have never been observed to crack nuts, even though plenty of nuts and stones are available. Apparently, in those colonies the discovery that nuts can be cracked was never made, so it could not be passed along. Research conducted with chimpanzees living in a wildlife sanctuary has shown that the introduction of one nut-cracking chimp can lead quickly to spread of that skill throughout the colony (Marshall-Pescini & Whiten, 2008).

FIGURE 4.16 A not completely attentive observer Chimpanzees learn through observation to crack nuts with rocks. The infant hanging overhead is too young to work seriously at nut cracking but may be learning something about it through watching the older master.

Tetsuro Matsuzawa, Primate Institute, Kyoto University. From Matsuzawa, T. (1994). Field experiments on use of stone tools in the wild. In R. Wrangham, F. de Waal, and P. Heltne (Eds.), *Chimpanzee cultures* (pp. 351–370). Cambridge, MA: Harvard University Press.

Gaze Following as an Aid in Learning from Others

When we are attending to another person our eyes move, automatically, reflexively, in the same direction that his or her eyes move, so we look at the same object at which he or she is looking. This reflexive action, called **gaze following,** helps us understand what the other person is thinking about and, in conversations, helps us to know what he or she is talking about (Richardson & others, 2007). When a person says, "Oh, that is beautiful," our gaze following helps us figure out what *that* refers to.

Gaze following has been most extensively studied in young children. Beginning in the latter half of their first year of life, human infants reflexively tend to look at whatever their caregiver is looking at (Brooks & Meltzoff, 2002; Woodward, 2003). Such gaze following ensures that the infants pay attention to the same objects and events in their environment that their elders attend to, which may be the most important things to learn about for survival in their culture. It also, no doubt, helps infants learn language. If you are an infant and hear your mother say some new word—maybe *goat*—for the first time, you have a chance of learning what that word refers to if you are looking at the same object that she is looking at. Consistent with this idea, researchers have found that babies who show the most reliable gaze following learn language faster than those who exhibit less gaze following (Brooks & Meltzoff, 2008).

No other animal gaze follows to the extent that we humans do. In fact, the unique coloring of our eyes may be a special human adaptation that came about through natural selection to enable us to follow each others' gazes and thereby understand each other better (Tomasello, 2007). The relatively dark circular iris of the human eye is sharply set off by the bright white of the rest of the visible portion of the eyeball, the sclera, which makes it easy for others to see where we are looking (see Figure 4.17). Other primates, including chimpanzees and bonobos, have dark sclera, which do not contrast with the iris, so it is not possible to see which way their eyes have shifted (look back at the nut-cracking chimpanzee in Figure 4.16). Research has shown that chimpanzees and bonobos do engage in some gaze following and are able to learn through that means, but their gaze following is less automatic than humans' and depends entirely on observations of the model's head, not on shifts of the eyes within their sockets (Okamoto-Barth & others, 2007; Tomonaga, 2007).

Of course, one disadvantage of our white scleras is that it is hard for us to deceive others about where we are looking. For that, we need sunglasses. People wearing sunglasses seem a little frightening to us, partly because we don't know where they are looking, which reduces our ability to guess what they are thinking. Presumably, in the course of our evolution, the advantages of cuing others into our thoughts outweighed the advantages of deception.

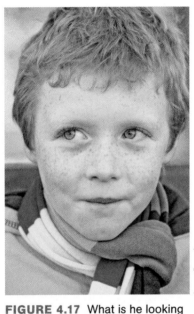

37

How might gaze following help us learn from other people? What characteristic of human eyes makes gaze following easier for us than for other primates?

FIGURE 4.17 What is he looking at? When people look at faces like this, even in photographs, they reflexively shift their own eyes in the direction at which the observed eyes are looking. Because of the white sclera, it is easy to see where human eyes are pointed. Contrast this to the obscuring coloration of the sclera of other primates, such as chimpanzees (in Figure 4.16).

SECTION REVIEW

In the natural environment, learning is promoted by play, exploration, and observation.

Play	Exploration	Observational Learning
➤ In line with a theory originated by Karl Groos, young mammals appear to play in ways that help them to develop crucial survival skills. Play is most frequent in those species that have the most to learn.	➤ Exploration is more primitive than play, occurring in many more species and at all ages. It promotes learning about the environment.	➤ Stimulus enhancement and goal enhancement are simpler forms of observational learning than is imitation. Mirror neurons may facilitate imitation in primates.
➤ Human children play not just at skills that are crucial to people everywhere, but also at those unique skills that are crucial to the society in which they develop.	➤ Curiosity motivates exploration of novel objects and places, but is balanced by fear.	➤ Cultural differences among chimpanzee groups apparently result from imitative ability.
	➤ Latent learning experiments show that exploration alone, without external reward, produces useful knowledge.	➤ Reflexive gaze following helps humans learn from one another.

◼ Specialized Learning Abilities: Filling the Blanks in Species-Typical Behavior Patterns

Thus far we have been examining learning processes and activities that are quite general in the sense that they operate in a wide variety of contexts. Animals can learn many different things through classical conditioning, operant conditioning, play, exploration, and observation. But natural selection has also endowed animals with specialized learning abilities that have quite limited domains of operation. These may be best thought of as adjuncts to particular instinctive, species-typical behavior patterns. Each such learning ability helps to mesh some aspect of the animal's instinctive behavior with particular variable characteristics of the animal's environment.

In Chapter 3, I cited the white-crowned sparrow's learning of its father's song as an example of specialized learning. That ability does not stem from a general capacity of sparrows to imitate. Instead, it results from a special learning mechanism that is specific to song learning and narrow in scope. It allows the bird to learn any given white-crown sparrow song dialect, but does not allow the bird to learn the song of another bird species. In Chapter 11, I'll present evidence that human language is acquired through unique, specialized learning abilities, somewhat analogous to the sparrow's song-learning ability, which causes all human languages to resemble one another in basic ways. Now, however, we shall look at special learning abilities related to food preferences and then, more briefly, at a few other examples of specialized learning mechanisms.

Special Abilities for Learning What to Eat

For some animals, learning what to eat is a relatively minor problem. Koalas, for instance, eat only the leaves of eucalyptus trees. Through natural selection, koalas evolved a food-identifying mechanism that tells them that eucalyptus leaves are food and everything else is not. That simplifies their food choice, but if eucalyptuses vanish, so will koalas. Other animals are more flexible in their diets. Most flexible of all are omnivorous creatures, such as rats and humans, which treat almost all organic matter as potential food and must *learn* what is safe to eat. Such animals have evolved special mechanisms for learning to identify healthful foods and to avoid potential poisons.

Food-Aversion Learning: How It Differs from Typical Classical Conditioning

If rats become ill after eating a novel-tasting food, they subsequently avoid that food. In experiments demonstrating this, researchers induce illness by adding a toxic substance to the food or by administering a drug or a high dose of x-rays to the animals after they have eaten (Garcia & others, 1972). Similarly, people who by chance get sick after eating an unusual food often develop a long-term aversion to the food (Bernstein, 1991; Logue, 1988). For years as a child, I hated the taste and smell of a particular breakfast cereal, because once, a few hours after I ate it, I happened to develop a bad case of stomach flu. I knew, intellectually, that the cereal wasn't the cause of my illness, but that didn't help. The learning mechanism kicked in automatically and made me detest that cereal.

38
- ◄ Some psychologists choose to describe such cases of food-aversion learning in
What are two ways in which food-aversion learning differs from typical examples of classical conditioning? How do these differences make sense in terms of the function of such learning?
terms of classical conditioning. In that description, the feeling of illness or nausea induced by the x-ray treatment or drug is the unconditioned stimulus for a reaction of aversion or revulsion, and the taste and smell of the food become conditioned stimuli for that reaction. But John Garcia, the researcher who pioneered the study of food-aversion learning, argues that such learning is quite different from standard cases of classical conditioning (Garcia & others, 1989).

One special characteristic of food-aversion learning has to do with the optimal delay between the conditioned and unconditioned stimuli. In typical cases of classical conditioning, such as the salivary reflex studied by Pavlov, conditioning occurs only when the unconditioned stimulus follows immediately (within a few seconds) after the conditioned stimulus. But food-aversion learning has been demonstrated even when the x-rays were administered as much as 24 hours after the animals had eaten the food (Etscorn & Stephens, 1973). In fact, food-aversion learning fails to occur if the gap between tasting the food and the induction of illness is less than a few minutes (Schafe & others, 1995).

Another special characteristic has to do with the sorts of stimuli that can serve as conditioned stimuli for such learning. In typical cases of classical conditioning, almost any kind of detectable stimulus can serve, but in food-aversion learning the stimulus must be a distinctive taste or smell (and taste generally works better than smell). Rats that become ill after eating a particular food subsequently avoid any food that tastes or smells like what they had eaten, even if it looks different, but they do not avoid a food that looks like what they had eaten if it tastes and smells different (Garcia & others, 1968, 1989).

These distinguishing characteristics of food-aversion learning make excellent sense when considered in the light of the function that such learning serves in the natural environment. In general, poisons and spoiled foods do not make an individual ill immediately, but only after many minutes or several hours. Moreover, it is the chemical quality of a food, detectable in its taste and smell, not the visual quality, that affects health. For example, a food that has begun to rot and makes an animal sick may look quite like one that has not begun to rot, but its taste and smell are quite different. Thus, to be effective, a learning mechanism for food aversion must tolerate long delays and be tuned especially to those sensory qualities that correspond with the food's chemistry.

Food-Preference Learning

The other side of the coin of learning to avoid harmful foods is learning to choose foods that satisfy a specific nutritional requirement. Just as rats can learn to associate the taste of a food with subsequent illness and thereafter avoid that food, they can also associate a taste with a subsequent improvement in health and thereafter prefer that food.

A number of experiments have shown that when rats are deprived of a mineral (such as calcium) or a vitamin that is essential for health, they will learn to prefer the flavor of a new food that contains that mineral or vitamin (Rozin & Schull, 1988; Tordoff, 2002). In one series of experiments, researchers deprived rats of thiamine (one of the B vitamins, essential for health) for a period of time and then offered them a choice of foods, only one of which contained thiamine (Overmann, 1976; Rozin & Kalat, 1971). Each food had a distinct flavor, and thiamine—which itself has no flavor— was added to a different food for different rats. The result was that, within a few days of experience with the foods, most rats strongly preferred the thiamine-containing food.

How did the rats "figure out" which food contained the thiamine? Close inspection of their eating patterns suggests a possible answer (Rozin & Kalat, 1971). When first presented with the choices, a rat usually ate just one or two of the foods. Then, typically after several hours, the rat would switch to a different food or two. Such behavior—eating just one or two foods at a time—seems ideally suited for isolating particular foods that lead to an increase or a decrease in health. If the rat had sampled all the foods at once, it would have had no basis for knowing which one had affected its health.

We don't know if our species has a similar ability to learn which foods have a vitamin or mineral that we need, as no controlled experiments have been conducted to find out. It would not be ethical to deprive people of necessary nutrients for the sake of such research. However, there is evidence that people, as well as rats, learn

John Garcia In the 1960s, Garcia discovered that food-avoidance learning violates certain principles of conditioning that had been accepted by mainstream psychologists as general laws of learning. He pursued this work despite the "better judgment" of his thesis advisers and even though the editor of a leading psychology journal refused to publish his early findings on the grounds that they could not be true. Garcia was a stubborn, charismatic, Spanish American son of migrant workers. One historian of psychology (Bolles, 1993) notes that Garcia was fond of saying "*Viva yo,*" which translates literally into "Long live me" but actually means something like "To hell with you guys."

39
How might rats learn which food contains a needed vitamin or mineral?

40
How has flavor-preference learning been demonstrated in humans?

to prefer a food that is high in calories (Brunstrom, 2005). This learning mechanism, which was no doubt valuable both to our evolutionary ancestors and to some people today, may have an unfortunate effect on those of us who are overweight and surrounded by wide choices of foods.

In the typical human flavor-preference learning experiment, college students are presented each day with one of two differently flavored foods, which is either laced with a high-calorie substance or not so laced. Initially the two foods are rated as equally pleasant (or unpleasant) in taste, but, over the course of days, the students' average rating of the high-calorie food goes up, while their rating of the low-calorie food stays the same or declines (Brunstrum, 2005; Brunstrom & Mitchell, 2006). Apparently some delayed satisfying effect of the calories causes the students to develop a preference for the high-calorie version. This may be no news to people trying to lose weight, who are already convinced that all of human nature is stacked against them.

Learning from Others What to Eat

41
How do rats and people learn food preferences by attending to others of their kind?

◄ In addition to learning from their own experiences with foods, rats learn what to eat from one another. Newly weaned wild rats generally limit their diets to foods that older rats in the colony regularly eat. Through this means, they can avoid even tasting a food that older animals have learned is poisonous (Galef & Clark, 1971) and can choose, from the beginning, a nutritious food that older animals have learned to prefer (Beck & Galef, 1989). Similar results have been found with kittens (Wyrwicka, 1996). Even in adulthood, rats are strongly influenced by one another's food choices. Bennett Galef (1990, 2002) has found that rats in a colony sniff near the mouth of a rat that has recently eaten and then show a strong preference for the food they had smelled on the demonstrator rat's breath. Through this and other means, adult rats introduced into a new colony acquire the colony's food preferences. The tendency to eat what others of one's kind have been eating has been demonstrated in many other species of animals as well (Galef & Giraldeau, 2001).

We humans, presumably, don't learn food preferences by smelling one another's breath, but we are certainly influenced by our observations of what those around us eat. In one experiment, children between 1 and 4 years old were more willing to taste a new food if they saw an adult eat it first than if they had never seen anyone eat it (Harper & Sanders, 1975). Other research suggests that children are most open to new foods from about 1 to 2 years of age, which is when they are most likely to be closely watched and fed by adults, and are least willing to try new foods between about 4 and 8 years of age, a time when they have greater freedom of movement and are not so closely watched but have not yet learned to distinguish foods from poisons (Cashdan, 1994). From this point of view, the finicky eating of 4-to-8-year-olds is an evolutionary adaptation that reduces the chance of eating something poisonous.

Observational learning has its limits Children acquire the food preferences of their culture by observing their elders, but sometimes it takes a while.

Summary of Rules for Learning What to Eat

Suppose that you were a wise teacher of young omnivorous animals and wanted to equip your charges with a few rules for food selection that could be applied no matter what food was available. Two that you would probably come up with are these: (1) When possible, eat what your elders eat. Such food is probably safe, as evidenced by the fact that your elders have most likely been eating it for some time and are still alive. (2) When you eat a new food, remember its taste and smell. If the food is followed within a few hours by feelings of improved health, continue choosing foods of that taste and smell, but if you feel sick, avoid such foods.

42

In sum, what has natural selection imparted to young omnivores about food selection?

Notice that these rules do not specify what to eat, but specify *how to learn* what to eat. The first rule describes a specific variety of observational learning, and the second describes a specific, efficient variety of associative learning. As you have just seen, rats do in fact behave in accordance with these rules, and humans may also. Of course, we assume that these rules have been imparted not by a wise teacher of young omnivores but by natural selection, which has shaped the brain to operate automatically in accordance with the rules.

Other Examples of Special Learning Abilities

Food selection is by no means the only domain in which special learning abilities have apparently come about through evolution. Here are some other well-studied examples.

Innate Biases in Fear-Related Learning

Do you remember the demonstration by Watson and Rayner (1920), in which a young child was conditioned to fear a white rat by pairing it with a loud noise? Several years later, Elsie Bregman (1934), a graduate student working with Thorndike, tried to repeat that demonstration with one important modification. Instead of using a rat as the conditioned stimulus, she used various inanimate objects, including wooden blocks and pieces of cloth. Despite numerous attempts, with 15 different infants as subjects, she found no evidence of conditioning. What are we to make of this apparent discrepancy? One possibility, suggested by Martin Seligman (1971), is that people are biologically predisposed to acquire fears of situations and objects, such as rats and snakes, that posed a threat to our evolutionary ancestors and are less disposed to acquire fears of other situations and objects.

43

What is some evidence that people and monkeys are biologically predisposed to learn to fear some things more easily than other things?

More recently, Susan Mineka and her colleagues (1984) showed that rhesus monkeys are not afraid of snakes when first exposed to them but easily learn to fear them. In one experiment, monkeys raised in the laboratory did not react fearfully to snakes until they saw a monkey that had been raised in the wild do so. After that, they showed strong fear reactions themselves when a snake was present (see Figure 4.18). In subsequent experiments, Michael Cook and Mineka (1989, 1990) used splicing to produce films in which a monkey was shown reacting fearfully in the presence of various objects, including toy snakes, flowers, and a toy rabbit. Through observing the films, monkeys that previously feared none of these objects developed a fear of toy snakes (and real snakes) but not of flowers or toy rabbits.

From an evolutionary perspective, this learning bias makes a good deal of sense. In some regions where macaques live there are dangerous snakes, but in other regions all of the snakes are harmless. In places where snakes are harmless, an inflexible instinctive fear of them would be maladaptive. Thus, the learning mechanism may have evolved because it allows monkeys living in areas where snakes are dangerous to learn quickly to fear and avoid them, while it allows monkeys living elsewhere to go about their business relatively oblivious to snakes. We humans also vary greatly in the degree to which we fear snakes. Research suggests that we learn to fear snakes and other objects that posed threats to our evolutionary ancestors—such as spiders, rats, and angry faces—more readily than we learn to fear equally

FIGURE 4.18 A biologically prepared learned reaction Monkeys that have never been harmed by snakes nevertheless learn quickly to fear them through watching the fearful reactions of other monkeys.

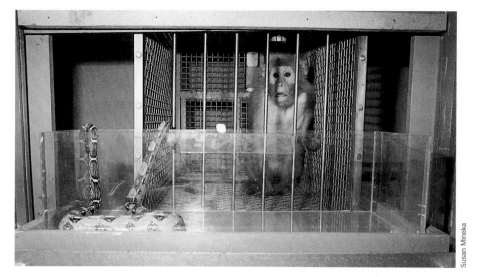

Susan Mineka

dangerous objects that were not present in our early evolutionary history, such as electrical outlets, sharp knives, and automobiles (Mineka & Öhman, 2002; Seligman, 1971).

Imprinting in Precocial Birds: Learning to Identify One's Mother

44

What aspects of a young fowl's ability to follow its mother depend on learning, and how is that learning guided by inborn biases?

Some of the earliest evidence for specialized learning abilities came from studies of young precocial birds. Precocial birds are those species—such as chickens, geese, and ducks—in which the young can walk almost as soon as they hatch. Because they can walk, they can get separated from their mother. To avoid that, they have acquired, through natural selection, an efficient means to determine who their mother is and a drive to remain near her. The means by which they learn to recognize their mother was discovered by Douglas Spalding near the end of the nineteenth century.

Spalding (1873/1954) observed that newly hatched chicks that were deprived of their mother, and that happened to see him (Spalding) walk by shortly after they were hatched, would follow him as if he were their mother. They continued to follow him for weeks thereafter, and once attached in this way they would not switch to following a real mother hen. Some 60 years later, Konrad Lorenz (1935/1970) made the same discovery with newly hatched goslings. Lorenz labeled the phenomenon *imprinting,* a term that emphasizes the very sudden and apparently irreversible nature of the learning process involved. It's as if the learning is immediately and indelibly stamped in.

One interesting feature of imprinting is the rather restricted *critical period* during which it can occur. Spalding (1873/1954) found that if chicks were prevented from seeing any moving object during the first 5 days after hatching and then he walked past them, they did not follow. Instead, they showed "great terror" and ran away. In more detailed studies, Eckhard Hess (1958, 1972) found that the optimal time for imprinting mallard ducklings is within the first 18 hours after hatching.

Although early studies suggested that young birds could be imprinted on humans or other moving objects as easily as on their mothers, later studies proved otherwise. Given a choice between a female of their species and some other object, newly hatched birds invariably choose to follow the former. Experiments with chicks indicate that this initial preference centers on visual features of the head. Newly hatched chicks will follow a box with a chicken head attached to it as readily as they will a complete stuffed chicken and more readily than any object without a chicken head (Johnson & Horn, 1988). The experience of following the object brings the imprinting mechanism into play, and this mechanism causes the chicks to be attracted

Konrad Lorenz and followers
Lorenz conducted research on imprinting and many other aspects of behavior in ducks and geese. These geese, which were hatched by Lorenz in an incubator, followed him everywhere, as if he were their mother.

THE FAR SIDE

When imprinting studies go awry . . .

thereafter to all the features of the moving object (Bateson, 2000). Under normal conditions, of course, the moving object is their mother, so imprinting leads them to distinguish their mother from any other hen.

In sum, we have here a learning process for which the timing (the critical period), the stimulus features (characteristics typical of a mother bird of the species), and the behavioral response (following) are all genetically prepared in ways that promote its specific adaptive function—staying near the mother.

Specialized Place-Learning Abilities

Many animals have specialized abilities for learning and remembering specific locations that have biological significance to them. As one example, Clark's nutcrackers (a species of bird inhabiting the southwestern United States) bury food in literally thousands of different sites, to which they return during the winter when the food is needed (Gould-Beierle & Kamil, 1999). Experiments have shown that the birds' abilities to find each location depend on their memories of visual landmarks, such as stones, near the site (Kamil & Balda, 1985; Shettleworth, 1983). In other experiments, various bird species that hide seeds have been found to remember spatial locations better than do species that don't hide seeds and to have an enlargement of an area of the brain, called the hippocampus, that is crucial for spatial memory (Papini, 2002; Shettleworth & Westwood, 2002).

A quite different example of specialized place learning is the ability of Pacific salmon to return to their hatching grounds. Salmon that hatch in small streams in the northwestern United States migrate into the Pacific Ocean, where they swim around for 5 years or more, carrying a precise memory of the unique smell of the water in which they hatched. Then, when they are ready to spawn, they use their sense of smell to find their way back to the same stream from which they had come (Hasler & Larsen, 1955; Navitt & others, 1994) .

So, in certain very specific ways, species of birds and fish appear to be "smarter" than chimpanzees or people. The more we understand about animal behavior, the more it becomes apparent that intelligence is a relative concept. To make the concept meaningful, we have to ask, "Intelligent at what?" Animals appear extraordinarily intelligent when we observe them in nature dealing with the kinds of learning tasks and problems for which they have been biologically equipped by natural selection. The same animals appear relatively stupid when we observe them on early trials in artificial test apparatuses, such as Thorndike's puzzle boxes or Skinner's operant conditioning chambers. The intelligence of animals comes not from a general ability to reason but from specialized learning abilities that have evolved over thousands of generations in the wild. This will be an interesting point to keep in mind when reading about human intelligence in Chapters 10 and 11.

45
What special place-learning abilities have been found in (a) birds that hide food and (b) Pacific salmon? How do all examples of specialized learning mechanisms influence thought about the concept of intelligence?

A seed-hiding bird Clark's nutcrackers, like many bird species, hide seeds in many different sites for the winter. Their ability to remember each hiding place is an example of a specialized learning ability.

Might it be that we, too, have not one general intelligence but various specialized intelligences that evolved to solve different kinds of problems faced by our evolutionary ancestors?

SECTION REVIEW

Specialized learning abilities have evolved related to species-typical behaviors.

Choosing Food	Objects of Fear	Imprinting on Mother	Place Memory
➤ Rats and people avoid foods that they had eaten some minutes or hours before becoming ill. Such food-avoidance learning differs in significant ways from general classical conditioning. ➤ Rats, and possibly humans, can learn to prefer foods associated with health improvement or nutritional gain. ➤ Observation of what others eat influences food choice, differently in rats and people.	➤ We (and other species) are innately biased to learn to fear objects or situations that were threatening in the species' evolutionary past. ➤ In experiments, monkeys learned to fear real and toy snakes, but not flowers or toy rabbits, by observing others' fearful reactions.	➤ Ducklings and goslings follow the first moving object they see within a critical period, and continue to follow it. ➤ Certain characteristics of imprinting help to ensure that, under normal conditions, the young of these species will learn to identify and follow their own mothers.	➤ Birds that hide food in many locations have special abilities to remember where. ➤ Pacific salmon return to streams where they hatched years before, using memory of the stream's smell.

Concluding Thoughts

In reviewing this or any chapter it is useful to think not just about the relationships among ideas within each major section, but also about the relationships among ideas across sections. One way to do that, for the present chapter, is to think about the three different perspectives on learning that are referred to at various places in the chapter: the *behavioral, cognitive,* and *evolutionary* perspectives. A perspective is a point of view, a framework, a set of ground rules and assumptions that scientists bring to the topic studied. The perspective helps determine the kinds of questions asked, the kinds of evidence regarded as important, the kinds of studies conducted, and the vocabulary used to describe the observations. Here are some thoughts about each of the perspectives referred to in this chapter:

1. The behavioral perspective Behaviorists such as Watson and Skinner held strongly to two assumptions: (1) the assumption that behavior is shaped by the environment and (2) the assumption that all aspects of behavior, including learning, are best described in terms of observable stimuli and responses, without reference to unseen mental events. These assumptions led behaviorists to focus heavily on classical and operant conditioning. Conditioning, from the behaviorists' viewpoint, is something that is done to the animal (or person) by the environment. The environmental conditions that produce learning, in these cases, can be described in terms of relationships among stimuli in the environment or between responses and stimuli (including reinforcing stimuli), and learning can be quantified in terms of immediate changes in behavior (increased frequency of conditioned responses). Borrowing from Pavlov's terms for describing classical conditioning, and adding a parallel set of terms for operant conditioning, behaviorists brought to psychology a rich, objective vocabulary for talking about learning and many learning-related phenomena. That vocabulary is still very much a part of psychology today.

2. The cognitive perspective Among the pioneers of this perspective were psychologists, such as Tolman, who began as behaviorists but found that approach too limiting. They argued that you can go only so far in understanding learning (or anything else in psychology) without talking about mental processes. For example, you can establish the principle of stimulus generalization in classical and operant conditioning, but you can't predict the degree to which an individual will generalize from one stimulus to another unless you understand something about the individual's mental concepts. Depending on concepts, a person or animal can perceive two stimuli as similar even if they aren't physically similar. Using such cognitive constructs as expectancies, predictions, and means-end relationships, cognitive psychologists have helped solve the problem of what is learned in classical and operant conditioning. In addition, they have expanded the realm of learning research to include learning that stems from exploration and observation, which does not always manifest itself immediately in the animal's behavior. To be scientifically useful, however, cognitive constructs must make testable predictions about observable behavior, and most cognitive research involves such tests.

3. The evolutionary perspective This is the perspective that most clearly unites the two chapters on adaptation—the preceding one on evolution and the present one on learning. While behaviorism and cognitivism have roots in philosophy, which has traditionally tried to understand human behavior and the human mind in terms of general principles that have wide applicability (such as principles of mental associations and the law of effect), the evolutionary perspective grew out of biology, which recognizes the diversity of life processes. The view that learning mechanisms are products of natural selection implies that they should be specially designed to solve biologically significant problems pertaining to survival and reproduction. In this chapter the evolutionary perspective manifested itself most clearly in research having to do with the value of conditioning in helping animals to predict biologically significant events (such as foods, dangers, and opportunities for sex); the role of play in motivating animals to practice life-sustaining skills; the special human adaptations for observational learning; and the specialized, domain-specific learning mechanisms (such as for food preferences, fear learning, imprinting on the mother, and place learning) that are unique to certain species.

Further Reading

B. F. Skinner (1978). *Reflections on behaviorism and society.* Englewood Cliffs, NJ: Prentice-Hall.

Skinner—who wanted to be a novelist before he went into psychology—is always fun to read, and there is no better way to begin than with this collection of essays. The titles include "Human Behavior and Democracy," "Why I Am Not a Cognitive Psychologist," "The Free and Happy Student," "The Force of Coincidence," and "Freedom and Dignity Revisited." You will find here Skinner's basic philosophy about psychology and his suggestions for using behavioral learning principles to improve society.

Stephen Ray Flora (2004). *The power of reinforcement.* Albany: State University of New York Press.

Flora, in the tradition of Skinner, is an unabashed advocate for the deliberate use of positive reinforcement (rewards) to improve people's behavior. In this clearly written, well-argued work, Flora advocates the intelligent use of reinforcement in parenting, educational settings, correctional institutions, and health-improvement programs. He presents the case against what he sees as harmful "myths" about reinforcement—that it is "rat psychology," that it undermines intrinsic motivation and creativity, and that it runs counter to people's experience of freedom and self-worth.

John D. Baldwin & Janice I. Baldwin (2001). *Behavior principles in everyday life* (4th ed.). Upper Saddle River, NJ: Prentice-Hall.

This is an easy-to-read introduction to the principles of classical conditioning, operant conditioning, and observational learning, with examples taken from everyday human existence. Readers will discover many ways by which their own behavior is influenced by conditioned stimuli and reinforcers, and may learn how to use learning principles to modify their own behavior in desired ways.

Mark E. Bouton (2007). *Learning and behavior: A contemporary synthesis.* Sunderland, MA: Sinauer Associates.

Bouton is a leading researcher on classical conditioning, and this is a well-written textbook on basic principles of learning, dealing especially with classical and operant conditioning. Bouton does a good job of presenting basic research finding in a context of history, big psychological ideas, biological relevance, and practical application that helps to stimulate the reader's thinking and motivate further reading.

Robert C. Bolles & Michael Beecher (Eds.) (1988). *Evolution and learning.* Hillsdale, NJ: Erlbaum.

This collection of essays, each by one or more specialists in the subject, shows how the traditions of laboratory research on learning and naturalistic studies of animals in the wild have merged and begun to provide rich detail about species-typical learning processes. The book begins with historical chapters about the relationship of learning theory to evolutionary theory, then turns to studies of learning in such biologically important domains as feeding, defending against predators, and sexual behavior. The book is a bit out of date, but is still, I think, the best work available on the integration of evolutionary theory and research on learning.

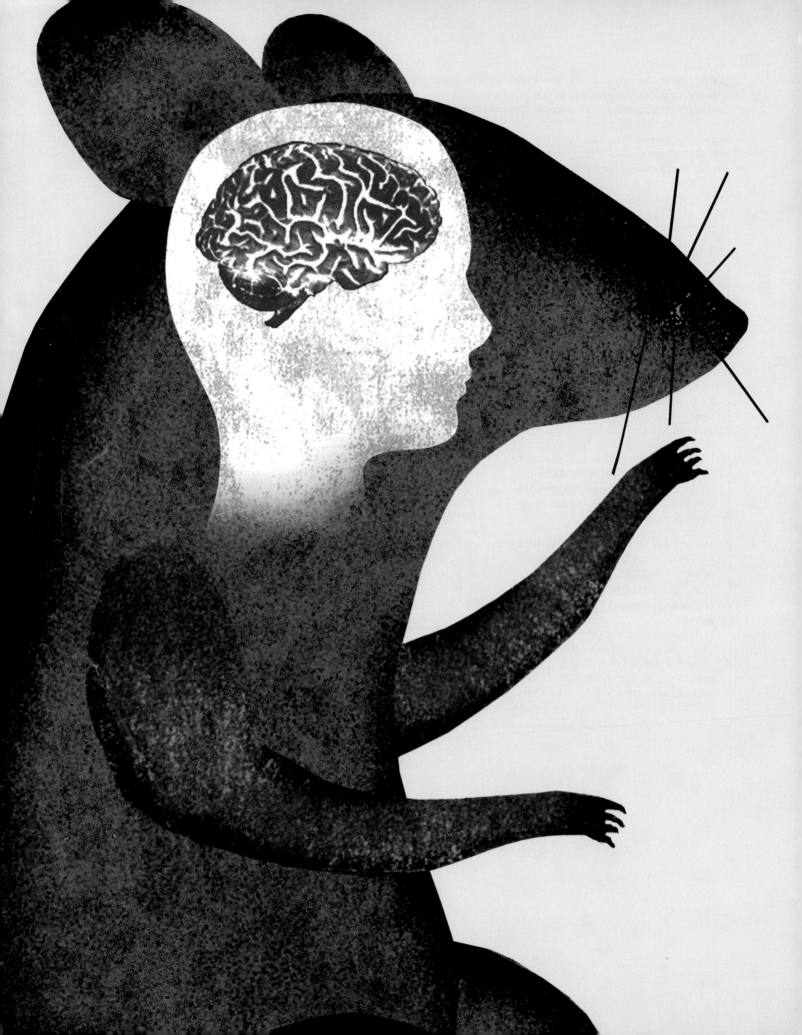

PART 3

Physiological Mechanisms of Behavior

Behavior is a product of the body's machinery, especially the nervous system. The nervous system receives information about the body's internal and external environments, integrates that information, and controls the body's movements. In this unit, Chapter 5 examines the structure of the nervous system and its principles of operation, including its role in learning, and Chapter 6 is concerned with the neural and hormonal mechanisms underlying motivation and emotion.

The Neural Control of Behavior

5

A human brain is, I must admit, somewhat disappointing in appearance. It is about the size and shape of a cantaloupe, but more gnarled. To the eye it seems relatively dormant, even when viewed in a living person. Aristotle and many other ancient Greeks—who were among the first to try to figure out what the various parts of the body are for—were not much impressed by the brain. Noticing that the blood vessels leading into it are larger than those entering other organs, they suggested that the brain's main function was to cool the blood. They were much more impressed by the heart, an obviously dynamic organ, and proposed that the heart and blood are the source of feelings, thoughts, and all else that we today call "psychological."

Not all of the ancients agreed with the heart theory of psychology, however. One who didn't was the Greek physician Hippocrates, whose observations of the effects of head injuries on people's thoughts and actions led him to focus on the brain. In the fourth century B.C., Hippocrates (1923) wrote: "From the brain, and from the brain only, arise our pleasures, joys, laughter and jests, as well as our sorrows, pains, griefs and tears. Through it, in particular, we think, see, hear. . . . Eyes, ears, tongue, hands and feet act in accordance with the discernment of the brain."

Hippocrates was right, of course, and that is why nearly every introductory psychology text, from William James's (1890/1950) classic on, contains a chapter about the nervous system, especially the brain. As psychologists and neuroscientists learn more about the brain, the nervous-system chapter becomes ever more meaningfully connected to the rest of the book, and material on the brain spills ever more copiously out of that chapter into others. In a real sense, psychology is the study of what the nervous system does; indeed, psychology focuses on the most complex aspects of what the nervous system does.

Every chapter of this book is at least indirectly about the nervous system, and this chapter is directly about it. The chapter begins with discussions concerning the basic units of the nervous system—individual neurons—and how they communicate with one another. Then it moves to discussions of each of the larger structures of the nervous system, focusing on their roles in controlling behavior. The final sections deal, respectively, with brain processes involved in learning and with ways by which drugs and hormones can alter the brain. These discussions all provide background for many discussions of brain processes that you will come across in later chapters.

■ Neurons: Cells That Create the Mind

The brain may look inactive to the naked eye, but at a microscopic level it is the most dynamic organ of the body. It makes up about 2 percent of an average person's body weight, but consumes about 20 percent of the person's metabolic energy (Magistretti,

© Tom Swick

"The body is made up of millions and millions of crumbs."

2008). It is by far the most complex and compact computing machine in the known universe. The human brain contains roughly 100 *billion* nerve cells, or **neurons,** and roughly 100 *trillion* points of communication, or synapses, between neurons. These are all more-or-less constantly active, and their collective activity monitors our internal and external environments, creates all of our mental experiences, and controls all of our behavior.

The seeming magic of the nervous system—its abilities to analyze sensory data, create mental experiences, and control movements in adaptive ways—lies not in the individual neurons, but in the organization of their multitudes. Yet each neuron is itself a complex decision-making machine. Each neuron receives information from multiple sources, integrates that information, and sends its response out to many other neurons or, in some cases, to muscle cells or glands. In this section we examine the structure and functions of individual neurons as a prelude to examining the larger structures and functions of the nervous system as a whole.

Three Basic Varieties of Neurons, and Structures Common to Them

The overall layout of the human nervous system is sketched in Figure 5.1. The *brain* and *spinal cord* (which extends from the brain down through the bones of the spinal column) make up the **central nervous system.** Extensions from the central nervous system, called *nerves,* make up the **peripheral nervous system.**

Don't confuse the terms *neuron* and *nerve.* A neuron, as just defined, is a single cell of the nervous system. A **nerve** is a bundle of many neurons—or, more precisely, a bundle consisting of the axons (defined below) of many neurons—within the peripheral nervous system. Nerves connect the central nervous system to the body's sensory organs, muscles, and glands. Note also that despite their names, the central and peripheral nervous systems are not two separate systems, but are parts of an integrated whole.

1 - ◄ Neurons come in a wide variety of shapes and sizes and serve countless specific

What are three types of neurons, and what is the function of each?

functions, but at the broadest level of analysis, they can be grouped into three categories according to their functions and their locations in the overall layout of the nervous system (see Figure 5.2): (1) **Sensory neurons,** bundled together to form

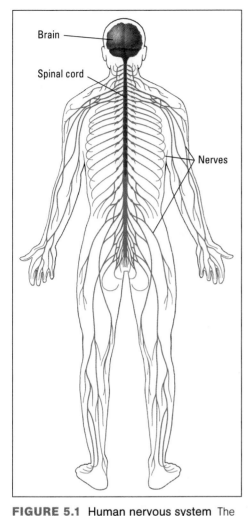

FIGURE 5.1 Human nervous system The central nervous system consists of the brain and the spinal cord, which runs through the bones of the spinal column down the center of the back. The peripheral nervous system consists of the entire set of nerves, which connect the brain and spinal cord to the sensory organs, muscles, and glands.

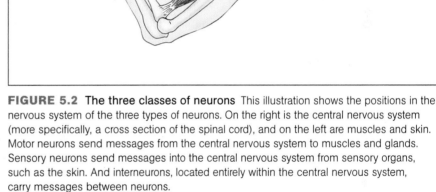

FIGURE 5.2 The three classes of neurons This illustration shows the positions in the nervous system of the three types of neurons. On the right is the central nervous system (more specifically, a cross section of the spinal cord), and on the left are muscles and skin. Motor neurons send messages from the central nervous system to muscles and glands. Sensory neurons send messages into the central nervous system from sensory organs, such as the skin. And interneurons, located entirely within the central nervous system, carry messages between neurons.

nerves, carry information from sensory organs (including the eyes, ears, nose, tongue, and skin) into the central nervous system. (2) **Motor neurons,** also bundled into nerves, carry messages out from the central nervous system to operate muscles and glands. (3) **Interneurons** exist entirely within the central nervous system and carry messages from one set of neurons to another. Interneurons collect, organize, and integrate messages from various sources. They vastly outnumber the other two types. The human nervous system contains a few million sensory and motor neurons and roughly 100 *billion* interneurons. Our interneurons make sense of the input that comes from sensory neurons, generate all our mental experiences, and initiate and coordinate all our behavioral actions through their connections to motor neurons.

Although neurons vary tremendously in shape and size, most contain the same basic parts. The parts, listed below, are labeled for all three types of neurons in Figure 5.2 and illustrated more fully for a motor neuron in Figure 5.3 on the next page.

● The **cell body** is the widest part of the neuron. It contains the cell nucleus and other basic machinery common to all bodily cells.

2

What are the main parts common to all or most neurons, and what is the function of each part?

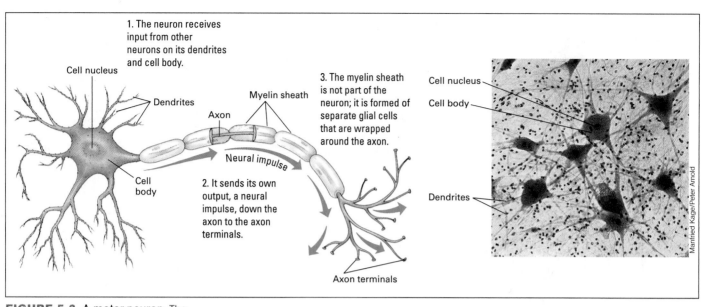

1. The neuron receives input from other neurons on its dendrites and cell body.

Cell nucleus

Dendrites

Axon

Myelin sheath

3. The myelin sheath is not part of the neuron; it is formed of separate glial cells that are wrapped around the axon.

Neural impulse

Cell body

2. It sends its own output, a neural impulse, down the axon to the axon terminals.

Axon terminals

Cell nucleus

Cell body

Dendrites

Manfried Kage/Peter Arnold

FIGURE 5.3 A motor neuron The parts common to many neurons can be seen in this diagram of a motor neuron. The neuron receives input from other neurons on its dendrites and cell body and sends its own output down the axon to the axon terminals. The myelin sheath is not part of the neuron; it is formed of separate cells that are wrapped tightly around the axon.

- *Dendrites* are thin, tubelike extensions that branch extensively and function to receive input to the neuron. In motor neurons and interneurons, the dendrites extend directly off the cell body and generally branch extensively near the cell body, forming bushlike structures. These structures increase the surface area of the cell and thereby allow for receipt of signals from many other neurons. In sensory neurons, dendrites extend from one end of the axon, rather than directly from the cell body. They extend into a sensory organ and respond to sensory signals, such as sound waves in the ear or touch on the skin (shown for skin in Figure 5.2).

- The *axon* is another thin, tubelike extension from the cell body. Its function is to carry messages to other neurons or, in the case of motor neurons, to muscle cells. Although microscopically thin, some axons are extremely long. You have axons of sensory neurons extending all the way from your big toe into your spinal cord and then up to the base of your brain—a distance of 5 feet or more. Most axons form many branches some distance away from the cell body, and each branch ends with a small swelling called an *axon terminal.* Axon terminals are designed to release chemical transmitter molecules onto other neurons or, in the case of motor neurons, onto muscle cells or glandular cells. The axons of some neurons are surrounded by a casing called a *myelin sheath,* formed from special nonneural cells that are wrapped tightly around the axon. As will be described later, this sheath helps to speed up the movement of neural impulses along the axon.

How Neurons Send Messages Down Their Axons

Neurons exert their influence on other neurons and muscle cells by firing off all-or-none impulses, called *action potentials.* In motor neurons and interneurons, action potentials are triggered at the junction between the cell body and the axon, and they travel rapidly down the axon to the axon terminals. In sensory neurons they are triggered at the dendritic end of the axon (shown in Figure 5.2) and travel through or past the cell body to the axon terminals. Action potentials are described as "all or none" because they either occur or don't occur; that is, they don't partially occur or occur in different sizes or gradations. Each action potential produced by a given neuron is the same strength as any other action potential produced by that neuron, and each action potential retains its full strength all the way down the axon.

Although each action potential is all or none, a neuron can convey varying degrees of intensity in its message by varying its rate of producing action potentials.

A given neuron might fire off action potentials at a rate anywhere from zero per second to as high as 1,000 per second. By varying its rate of action potentials, a neuron varies the strength of its effect on other neurons or muscle cells.

The Resting Neuron Has a Constant Electrical Charge Across Its Membrane

To understand how action potentials travel down the axon, you have to know something about the functioning of the **cell membrane** that encloses each neuron. The membrane is a porous "skin" that permits certain chemicals to flow into and out of the cell, while blocking others. Think of the neuron as a tube, the walls of which are the cell membrane. The tube is filled with a solution of water and dissolved chemicals called *intracellular fluid* and is bathed on the outside by another solution of water and dissolved chemicals called *extracellular fluid*.

Among the various chemicals dissolved in the intracellular and extracellular fluids are some that have electrical charges. These include *soluble protein molecules* (A^-), which have negative charges and exist only in the intracellular fluid; *potassium ions* (K^+), which are more concentrated in the intracellular than the extracellular fluid; and *sodium ions* (Na^+) and *chloride ions* (Cl^-), which are more concentrated in the extracellular than the intracellular fluid. For the reason described in Figure 5.4, more negatively charged particles exist inside the cell than outside. This imbalance results in an electrical charge across the membrane, with the inside typically about −70 millivolts (a millivolt [mV] is one-thousandth of a volt) relative to the outside. This charge across the membrane of an inactive neuron is called its **resting potential.** Just as the charge between the negative and positive poles of a battery is the source of electrical energy in a flashlight, so the resting potential is the source of electrical energy that makes an action potential possible.

3

How does the resting potential arise from the distribution of ions across the cell membrane?

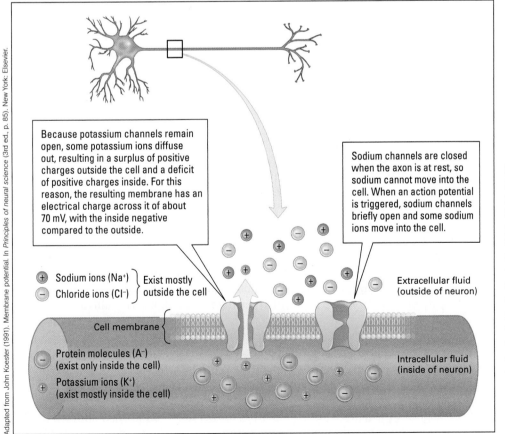

Because potassium channels remain open, some potassium ions diffuse out, resulting in a surplus of positive charges outside the cell and a deficit of positive charges inside. For this reason, the resulting membrane has an electrical charge across it of about 70 mV, with the inside negative compared to the outside.

Sodium channels are closed when the axon is at rest, so sodium cannot move into the cell. When an action potential is triggered, sodium channels briefly open and some sodium ions move into the cell.

(+) Sodium ions (Na^+) ⎤ Exist mostly
(−) Chloride ions (Cl^-) ⎦ outside the cell

Extracellular fluid (outside of neuron)

Cell membrane {

Intracellular fluid (inside of neuron)

(−) Protein molecules (A^-) (exist only inside the cell)

(+) Potassium ions (K^+) (exist mostly inside the cell)

FIGURE 5.4 The resting potential Illustrated here is a portion of a neuron's cell membrane with dissolved ions on each side. Negatively charged protein molecules (A^-) exist only inside the cell. Potassium ions (K^+) exist mostly inside the cell. Sodium ions (Na^+) and chloride ions (Cl^-) exist mostly outside the cell. Because channels in the membrane that are permeable to potassium remain open, some potassium ions diffuse out, resulting in a surplus of positive charges outside the cell and a deficit of positive charges inside. For this reason, the resting membrane has an electrical charge across it of about 70 mV, with the inside negative compared to the outside.

The Action Potential Derives from a Brief Change in Membrane Permeability

4

How do the two phases of the action potential (depolarization and repolarization) result from the successive opening and closing of two kinds of channels in the cell membrane?

The action potential is a wave of change in the electrical charge across the axon membrane, which moves rapidly from one end of the axon to the other. Figure 5.5 depicts an electrical recording of the action potential, over time, at a given location on the axon.

The action potential is initiated by a change in the structure of the cell membrane at one end of the axon: Thousands of tiny channels that permit sodium ions to pass through open up (look again at Figure 5.4). Two forces tend to drive sodium ions into the cell when the channels are open: (1) a concentration force, which occurs simply because more sodium ions exist outside the cell than inside; and (2) an electrical force, which occurs because like charges repel each other, so the positive electrical environment outside the cell pushes the positive sodium ions inward. As a result of these two forces, enough sodium moves inward to cause the electrical charge across the membrane to reverse itself and become momentarily positive inside relative to outside. This sudden shift constitutes the *depolarization phase* of the action potential (the rising part of the wave shown in Figure 5.5).

As soon as depolarization occurs, the channels that permitted sodium to pass through close, but channels that permit potassium to pass through remain open. Because potassium ions are more concentrated inside the cell than outside, and because they are repelled by the temporarily positive environment inside the cell, they are pushed outward. In this process, enough positively charged potassium ions move out of the cell to reestablish the original resting potential. This constitutes the *repolarization* phase of the action potential. As shown in Figure 5.5, the entire action potential, from depolarization to repolarization, takes about one millisecond (one-thousandth of a second) to occur at any given point on the axon.

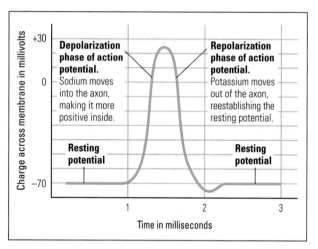

FIGURE 5.5 Electrical change during an action potential This graph depicts the change, with time, in the electrical charge across a given point on the axon membrane as an action potential passes through that point.

With each action potential, a small amount of sodium enters the cell and a small amount of potassium leaves it. To maintain the original balance of these ions across the membrane, each portion of the membrane contains a chemical mechanism, referred to as the *sodium-potassium pump,* that continuously moves sodium out of the cell and potassium into it.

The Action Potential Regenerates Itself from Point to Point Along the Axon

Action potentials are triggered at one end of an axon by influences that tend to reduce the electrical charge across the membrane. In sensory neurons these influences derive from sensory stimuli acting on the dendrites; in motor neurons and interneurons they derive from effects of other neurons that act eventually on the axon at its junction with the cell body.

The axon's membrane is constructed in such a way that depolarization (reduction in charge across the membrane) to some critical value causes the sodium channels to open, thereby triggering an action potential. This critical value (for example, −65 millivolts inside, compared with a resting potential of −70 millivolts inside) is referred to as the cell's *threshold.* Once an action potential occurs at one location on the axon, it depolarizes the area of the axon just ahead of where it is occurring, thus triggering the sodium channels to open there. In this way the action potential keeps renewing itself and moves continuously along the axon. When an axon branches, the action potential follows each branch and thus reaches each of the possibly thousands of axon terminals.

5

How is an axon's conduction speed related to its diameter and to the presence or absence of a myelin sheath?

The speed at which an action potential moves down an axon is affected by the axon's diameter. Large-diameter axons present less resistance to the spread of electric currents and therefore conduct action potentials faster than thin ones. Another feature that speeds up the rate of conduction in many axons is the presence of a myelin sheath (look back at Figure 5.3). The cells that form the sheath insulate the axon's membrane, so ions can move through it only at spaces (nodes) between adjacent cells. Each action potential skips down the axon, from one node to the next, faster than it could move as a continuous wave.

The thickest and most thoroughly myelinated axons in the nervous system can conduct action potentials at a velocity of about 100 meters per second. Thus, it takes about one-hundredth of a second for an action potential to run along that kind of axon from the central nervous system to a muscle about 1 meter away (a toe or finger muscle, for example). Very thin axons without myelin sheaths, in contrast, may conduct at rates as slow as 1 or 2 meters per second. When you poke your finger with a pin, you feel the pressure of the pin before you feel the pain. That is partly because the sensory neurons for pressure are large and myelinated, while those for pain are thin and mostly unmyelinated.

How Neurons Are Influenced by Other Neurons: Synaptic Transmission

Neurons generate action potentials at rates that are influenced by all the information that is sent to them from other neurons. The cell body and dendrites of a typical motor neuron or interneuron are blanketed by tens of thousands of axon terminals, which come from the branching axons of hundreds or thousands of different neurons (see Figure 5.6). The junction between each axon terminal and the cell body or dendrite of the receiving neuron is referred to as a **synapse.** When an action potential reaches an axon terminal, it causes the terminal to release packets of a chemical substance, called a **neurotransmitter,** or *transmitter,* which alters the receiving neuron in ways that influence its production of action potentials.

Synapses can be categorized into two basic types, *fast* and *slow.* The classic, most fully studied synapses are the fast type. We shall look at them first.

Fast Synapses Quickly Excite or Inhibit Postsynaptic Neurons

The most fully studied and best-understood fast synapses are those that exist between axon terminals and muscle cells or between axon terminals and the dendrites of other neurons (see Figure 5.7 on the next page). The axon terminal is separated from the membrane of the cell that it influences by a very narrow gap, the *synaptic cleft.* The membrane of the axon terminal that abuts the cleft is the *presynaptic membrane,* and that of the cell on the other side of the cleft is the *postsynaptic membrane.* Within the axon terminal are hundreds of tiny globelike *vesicles,* each of which contains several thousand molecules of a chemical neurotransmitter.

When an action potential reaches an axon terminal, it causes some of the vesicles to spill their neurotransmitter molecules into the cleft. The molecules then diffuse through the fluid in the cleft, and some become attached to special receptors on the postsynaptic membrane. Each molecule of transmitter can be thought of as a key, and each receptor can be thought of as a lock. A molecule key entering a receptor lock opens a gate in the channel, allowing ions to pass through. If the postsynaptic cell is a muscle cell, this flow of ions triggers a biochemical process that causes the cell to contract. If the postsynaptic cell is a neuron, the result is a change in the polarization of that neuron, but the direction of change depends on whether the synapse is excitatory or inhibitory (Byrne, 2003).

At an **excitatory synapse** (as shown in Figure 5.7 on page 144), the transmitter opens sodium (Na^+) channels in the postsynaptic membrane. The movement of the positively charged sodium ions into the cell causes a slight *depolarization* of the receiving neuron (the neuron becomes less negative inside), which tends to increase the rate of action potentials triggered in that neuron. At an **inhibitory synapse,** the transmitter opens either chloride (Cl^-) channels or potassium (K^+) channels. The movement of negatively charged chloride ions into the cell or of positively charged potassium ions out of the cell causes a slight *hyperpolarization* of the receiving

FIGURE 5.6 Axon terminals This electron micrograph shows the terminals of many axons forming synapses on a portion of the cell body of a single neuron. Synaptic vesicles, filled with neurotransmitter molecules, reside within the button-like swelling of each axon terminal. In the central nervous system, the cell bodies and dendrites of motor neurons and some interneurons are covered with tens of thousands of such terminals.

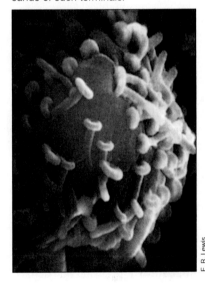

E. R. Lewis

> ──────────────────────6

How do neurotransmitters at excitatory and inhibitory fast synapses affect the rate at which action potentials are produced in the postsynaptic neuron?

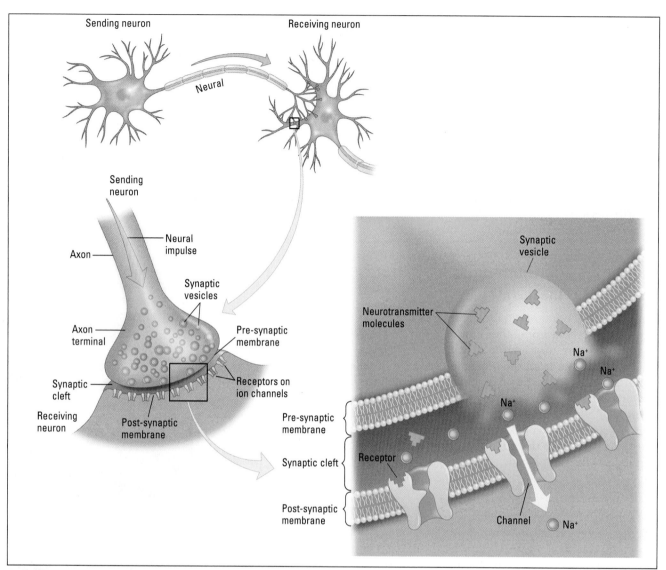

FIGURE 5.7 Transmission across the synapse When an action potential reaches an axon terminal, it causes some of the synaptic vesicles to spill their transmitter molecules into the synaptic cleft. Some of the molecules diffuse across the cleft and bind at special receptors on the postsynaptic membrane, where they open channels that permit ions to flow through the membrane. At an excitatory synapse (as in this example), channels permeable to sodium ions (Na+) open, allowing an influx of positive charges into the receiving neuron. At an inhibitory synapse, channels permeable to chloride ions (Cl−) open, allowing an influx of negative charges.

neuron (the neuron becomes even more negative inside than it was before), which tends to decrease the rate of action potentials triggered in that neuron.

All the chemical substances that have been identified as fast synaptic transmitters are small molecules (containing fewer than 10 carbon atoms) that can diffuse quickly across a synaptic gap. Many of them fall into the chemical class called *amino acids,* which are also the basic building blocks of protein molecules. The amino acid *glutamate* is the transmitter at most of the brain's excitatory fast synapses, and the amino acid *GABA* (*gamma-aminobutyric acid*) is the transmitter at most of the brain's inhibitory fast synapses (Greengard, 2001).

Postsynaptic Neurons Integrate Their Excitatory and Inhibitory Inputs

At any given moment, a single neuron may receive input at dozens, hundreds, or even thousands of its fast synapses. Some of these synapses are excitatory and some inhibitory (see Figure 5.8). At each excitatory synapse the transmitter causes a slight depolarization, and at each inhibitory synapse the transmitter causes a slight hyperpolarization. These effects spread passively through the dendrites and cell body, combining to have an integrated effect on the electrical charge across the membrane of the axon at its junction with the cell body.

Recall that whenever the axon membrane is depolarized below the critical value, action potentials are triggered. The greater the degree of depolarization below that

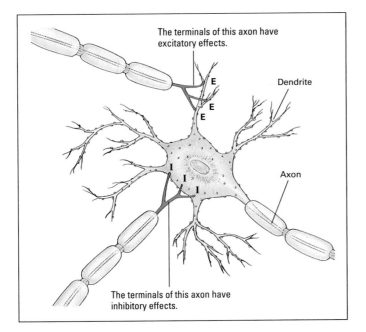

FIGURE 5.8 Excitatory and inhibitory synapses Neurons in the central nervous system receive many synaptic connections from other neurons, some excitatory and some inhibitory. All synapses from any single neuron are either excitatory or inhibitory.

The terminals of this axon have excitatory effects.

Dendrite

Axon

The terminals of this axon have inhibitory effects.

value, the greater the number of action potentials per second. Thus, the rate of action potentials in the postsynaptic neuron's axon depends on the net effect of the depolarizing and hyperpolarizing influences from excitatory and inhibitory synapses.

Slow Synapses Alter Postsynaptic Neurons in Prolonged Ways

At slow synapses, presynaptic neurons exert a wide variety of long-term effects on postsynaptic neurons. Instead of directly opening ion channels for brief periods (a few milliseconds), slow neurotransmitters trigger sequences of biochemical events in postsynaptic neurons that take time to develop and can alter the neuron's functioning for periods ranging from several hundred milliseconds up to hours, weeks, or longer (Greengard, 2001).

Within the central nervous system are dozens, and maybe hundreds, of different types of slow-acting synapses, which differ in their effects. At some synapses, slow-acting transmitters (like fast-acting transmitters) open ion channels and thereby produce either depolarization or hyperpolarization of the postsynaptic membrane, but they do this in an indirect way that lasts much longer than does the effect of a fast-acting transmitter. At other synapses, slow-acting transmitters cause changes in the postsynaptic neuron that do not directly alter its electrical charge, but rather alter the way the neuron responds to fast-acting transmitters. For instance, a slow-acting transmitter might stimulate the growth of new receptors on the postsynaptic membrane, which make the postsynaptic cell more responsive to the effects of one or another fast-acting transmitter. Transmitters that alter the cell in long-lasting ways such as this are sometimes referred to as *neuromodulators.* They work by modulating the postsynaptic neuron's response to other transmitters.

Researchers still have much to learn about the functions and mechanisms of neuromodulators and other slow-acting transmitters. New discoveries in this area are of great interest to psychologists, because slow-acting transmitters are responsible for changes in a person's psychological state (discussed in Chapter 6). Through their actions in various parts of the brain, slow-acting transmitters produce states of sleep, arousal, motivation (such as hunger or sexual drive), and emotion (such as fear, anger, or joy). Slow-acting transmitters also trigger the more-or-less permanent changes in neurons that provide the neural foundation for learning (discussed later in this chapter).

The nervous system contains many more types of slow-acting than fast-acting transmitter substances. Researchers have identified over 100 different substances

How does slow synaptic transmission differ from fast transmission, and what kinds of functions are served by slow transmission?

that appear to act as slow-acting transmitters (Deutch & Roth, 2008). Many of these substances fall into a chemical class referred to as *neuropeptides*. These are relatively large molecules consisting of chains of amino acids. One subset of neuropeptide transmitters, called *endorphins*, can reduce the experience of pain through their modulating effects on pain neurons in the spinal cord and brain (discussed in Chapter 7). Another chemical class of transmitters that work primarily (if not entirely) through slow-acting means consists of the *biogenic amines*, which include *dopamine, norepinephrine,* and *serotonin* (Greengard, 2001). As discussed in Chapter 6, these are particularly involved in producing states of sleep, arousal, motivation, and emotion.

SECTION REVIEW

Neurons—individual nerve cells—"fire" electrochemically and communicate at synapses.

Basic Neural Anatomy	Basic Functioning of the Neuron	Synapses
➤ Interneurons exist entirely within the central nervous system (brain and spinal cord) and carry message from one set of neurons to another.	➤ The resting potential is an electrical imbalance that exists across the neural cell membrane when the neuron is not firing; the inside of the cell is negative relative to the outside.	➤ Neurotransmitter molecules released from an axon terminal cross the synaptic cleft to affect another neuron or a muscle cell.
➤ Sensory neurons carry information from sensory organs into the central nervous system and motor neurons carry messages out from the central nervous system to operate muscles and glands.	➤ An action potential involves a very brief reversal of polarization across the cell membrane, followed by a return to the resting state. These changes sweep down the axon at a speed relative to the axon's diameter.	➤ Fast synapses have brief, immediate effects—either excitatory or inhibitory—on the postsynaptic neuron.
➤ A typical neuron has a cell body, dendrites (which receive input to the neuron), and an axon (which carries the neuron's output).	➤ Action potentials are all-or-none; they do not vary in strength in a given neuron. A neuron's rate of action potentials does vary, however.	➤ Slow synapses, of which there are many varieties, produce sustained effects, including effects that underlie drives and moods.

■ Methods of Mapping the Brain's Behavioral Functions

With its billions of neurons and trillions of synapses, the brain is a daunting subject of study. It would be hopeless, with present technology, to try to work out all of the details of its wiring, as one might with a human-made machine such as a radio or a computer. Fortunately, though, for those of us who want to understand as much as we can of it, patterns exist in the brain's trillions of connections.

Neurons in the central nervous system are organized into nuclei and tracts. A **nucleus** is a cluster of cell bodies in the central nervous system (not to be confused with the cell nucleus, which exists within each cell), and a **tract** is a bundle of axons that course together from one nucleus to another (see Figure 5.9). A tract in the central nervous system is analogous to a nerve in the peripheral nervous system. Tracts are referred to collectively as *white matter*, because the myelin sheaths around axons make tracts appear relatively white; nuclei, which are darker, are referred to collectively as *gray matter*.

In general, neurons whose cell bodies occupy the same nucleus and whose axons run in the same tract have identical or similar functions, and groups of nuclei located near one another have functions that are closely related to one another. Because of this pattern of organization, we can speak of the general functions of relatively large anatomical structures within the brain.

FIGURE 5.9 Diagram of a **nucleus and tract** A nucleus is a cluster (usually thousands or millions) of cell bodies of neurons, and a tract is a group of axons that run parallel with one another.

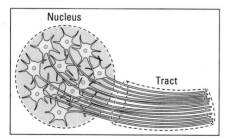

Nucleus

Tract

Methods Used for Studying the Human Brain

Psychologists and other neuroscientists have developed a number of methods of identifying the functions of specific brain areas. The methods fall into three general categories: (1) observing behavioral deficits that occur when a part of the brain is destroyed or is temporarily inactivated; (2) observing behavioral effects of artificially stimulating specific parts of the brain; and (3) recording changes in neural activity that occur in specific parts of the brain when a person or animal is engaged in a particular mental or behavioral task. What follows are brief descriptions of the most common methods used within each of these three categories. We'll look first at methods used in studying the brains of humans and then, in the next section, at more intrusive methods used in studying the brains of nonhuman animals.

Observing Effects of Localized Brain Damage

At the height of his career, the Russian composer V. G. Shebalin suffered a stroke (a rupturing of blood vessels in the brain) that damaged a portion of his left cerebral cortex (the highest outermost part of the brain). From then on, he had great difficulty expressing himself in words or understanding what others were saying, but he continued to create great music. His Fifth Symphony, composed after his stroke, was described by the composer Dmitri Shostakovich as "a brilliant work, filled with highest emotions, optimistic and full of life" (Gardner, 1974).

As illustrated by this case, brain damage often leaves a person deficient in some areas of mental functioning yet fully capable, or nearly so, in others. By studying many people who have damage in the same general area of the brain, psychologists can draw reasonable inferences about the behavioral and mental functions of that area. The logic here is that if some abilities are missing and other abilities remain when a part of the brain is missing, then that brain part must contribute in some essential way to the missing abilities but not to those that remain. As you will discover later in this chapter and elsewhere in the book, much has been learned about the human brain through systematic studies of people who have suffered brain damage.

Observing Effects of Magnetic Interference with Normal Brain Activity

A relatively new procedure for localizing functions in the human brain is ***transcranial magnetic stimulation,*** or **TMS** (Pascual-Leone & Walsh, 2003). A pulse of electricity sent through a small copper coil induces a magnetic field around the coil. If the coil is held just above a person's scalp, the magnetic field passes through the scalp and skull and induces an electric current in the neurons immediately below the coil. Repetitive pulses cause a temporary loss in the neurons' abilities to fire normally. The effect is comparable to that of producing a small area of damage to the brain, but the effect is temporary and reversible. For instance, if the coil is held over an area of the brain that is crucial for fluent speech, the person becomes unable to speak fluently while the current is on but then resumes fluent speech soon after the current is turned off. Because the magnetic field affects only that part of the brain that lies immediately below the skull, TMS can be used for mapping the functions only of the outermost yet largest part of the brain, the cerebral cortex.

A good example of the research use of TMS is found in recent work by Sara Torriero and her colleagues in Italy (2007). These researchers were interested in the neural foundations of observational learning (learning from watching others). In one of their experiments, human subjects observed others solve a problem in which they had to press a series of squares in a specified order. Different groups of subjects received TMS over different parts of the brain just prior to the observation. The result was that those who received the TMS directly over a portion of the brain called the *dorsolateral prefrontal cortex* failed

▶ - 8

How do researchers identify functions of areas of the human brain through (a) studying the effects of brain damage, (b) using a magnetic field to interrupt normal brain activity, (c) recording electrical activity that passes through the skull and scalp, and (d) creating images that depict patterns of blood flow?

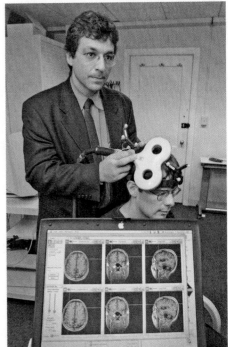

Transcortical magnetic stimulation (TSM) The electrical coil placed over the subject's skull induces a magnetic field. Repetitive pulses of the magnetic field inhibit the activity of underlying neurons. Single brief pulses activate neurons. The researcher here is Alvaro Pascual-Leone, who is one of the pioneers of the research use of TSM.

© Journal-Courier/Clayton Stalter/The Image Works

to benefit from the observation. It took them as long to learn the observed sequence, by trial and error, as it took them to learn a new sequence that they had never observed, even though the stimulation did not interfere with their vision. This study now constitutes part of the evidence that a system of *mirror neurons* (introduced in Chapter 4) exists in this part of the cerebral cortex, which is crucial for translating observed actions into self-produced actions.

Although TMS is usually used to study the effects of temporary *inactivation* of an area of the brain, it can also be used to study the effects of temporary *activation* of a brain area. A single pulse of current can cause the sets of neurons just below the coil to send a burst of action potentials through their axons. When the coil is held over an area of the brain responsible for controlling the body's muscle movements, the result is a brief muscle twitch somewhere in the body—such as in the thumb of one hand. In this way, TMS can be used to produce a map showing the functional connections between specific areas within movement-control portions of the cerebral cortex and the muscles controlled by those areas.

Recording Brain Activity Electrically, Through the Scalp

The constant activity of the brain's billions of neurons produces continuous electrical "chatter," which to some degree penetrates the overlying skull and scalp. By placing electrodes on a person's scalp, researchers can detect and amplify these signals. The resulting record of brain activity is referred to as an **electroencephalogram** [ee-**lec**-trow-en -**sef**-uh-low-gram] (abbreviated **EEG**). As discussed in Chapter 6, patterns in the EEG can be used as an index of whether a person is highly aroused, or relaxed, or asleep, and can be used to identify various stages of sleep.

With modern computer technology, it is possible to record and analyze brain activity simultaneously from many electrodes, each at a different location on the scalp, to see how brain activity varies from place to place as well as from instant to instant (see Figure 5.10). In some of these studies, subjects are asked to respond to stimuli

FIGURE 5.10

Electroencephalography The brain waves depicted on the screen reflect the electrical activity of neurons existing below each of the areas of the scalp where electrodes have been placed.

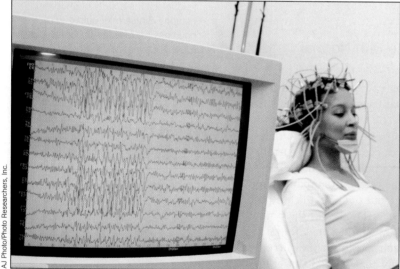

AJ Photo/Photo Researchers, Inc.

that are presented to them as their brain activity is being recorded. For instance, a person might be presented with sets of letters flashed on a screen and instructed to push a button if and only if the letters spell out an English word. The brief change in the EEG record immediately following the stimulus is referred to as an *event-related potential*, or *ERP*. By testing the person repeatedly in such a task and averaging the EEG records obtained, it is possible to produce an average ERP for each electrode location. Comparison of the average ERPs recorded at different scalp locations reveals the pattern of activity in the brain as the person detects and responds to the stimulus. For the task just described, areas of the brain that are involved in seeing the letters would respond first, and areas that are involved in reading and making judgments would respond a split second later.

Viewing Brain Activity with Imaging Methods Sensitive to Blood Flow

Some methods for localizing brain activity rely on the fact that increased neural activity in any area of the brain is accompanied by increased blood flow to that area. Like other bodily tissues, the brain is permeated by tiny blood vessels. When a portion of the brain becomes more active, blood vessels there immediately enlarge, so more blood enters that portion. The blood carries oxygen and glucose, which are the sources of energy required to sustain the increased neural activity. Using technically complex methods, researchers can create three-dimensional pictures, referred to as *neuroimages,* that depict the relative amount of blood flowing through each part of the brain. The assumption, now well validated, is that increased blood flow reflects increased neural activity (Logothetis, 2008).

The first of these neuroimaging methods (developed in the 1970s) was ***positron emission tomography*** [tah -**mah**-graf-ee], or ***PET.*** This method involves injecting a radioactive substance into the blood (in an amount that is not dangerous to the subject) and measuring the radioactivity that is emitted from each portion of the brain. Another method (first used extensively in the 1990s) is ***functional magnetic resonance imaging,*** or ***fMRI.*** This method involves the creation of a magnetic field around a person's head, which causes hemoglobin molecules that are carrying oxygen in the blood to give off radio waves of a certain frequency, which can be detected and used to assess the amount of blood in each part of the brain. With either method, the person's head must be surrounded by a set of sensors, and with fMRI also by magnetic coils (see Figure 5.11). However, the person can communicate with the experimenter through a microphone and can respond to visual stimuli presented on a screen inside the scanning device. With either PET or fMRI, a computer is used to generate a three-dimensional image of the brain that depicts variations in amount of blood flow as variations in color.

Unlike the EEG, both PET and fMRI can depict activity anywhere in the brain, not just on the surface near the skull. These methods also produce a more fine-grained picture of the spatial locations of activity than is possible with EEG. Today fMRI is used much more often than PET, partly because it shows better spatial resolution.

At any given time, the brain is doing many things, and all portions of it are always active to some degree. To determine, with either PET or fMRI, which brain areas are most directly involved in a particular task, researchers need to employ an appropriate control condition. By subtracting the amount of activity measured in each brain area in the control condition (when the person is not performing the specific task) from the amount measured in the same areas in the experimental condition (when the person is performing the task), the researcher can determine which areas show the greatest increase in activity during the task. (For an example of such an experiment, and to see sample PET images, look ahead to Figure 5.28 on p. 171.)

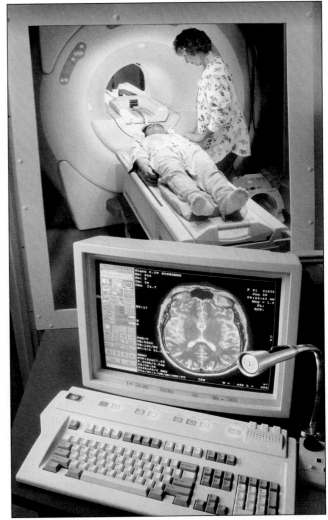

© Lester Lefkowitz/Corbis

FIGURE 5.11 Functional magnetic resonance imaging (fMRI) When the subject is in the scanner, the researchers will be able to communicate with him using an intercom and visual projection system. The image of the brain depicts, with colors of the rainbow, the amount of blood flow in each part of the brain, which indicates the amount of neural activity in each part.

Methods Used for Studying the Brains of Nonhuman Animals

With nonhuman animals, researchers can localize brain functions using methods that are more intrusive than those used with humans. They can destroy, stimulate, or record neural activity in small, well-localized areas anywhere in the brain in order to assess the behavioral functions of those areas.

Observing Effects of Deliberately Placed Brain Lesions

Areas of damage (referred to as lesions) can be produced in the brains of rats or other laboratory animals by either electrical or chemical means. To produce a lesion electrically, a thin wire electrode, insulated everywhere except at its tip, is surgically inserted into the brain with the help of a *stereotaxic instrument* (see Figure 5.12 on the next page), and enough current is sent through the electrode to destroy the

9

How do researchers damage, stimulate, and record from neurons in specific areas of animal brains to learn about the functions of those brain areas?

FIGURE 5.12 Method for making lesions in or stimulating a rat's brain A stereotaxic instrument (left) is used to insert an electrode into a precise location in the anesthetized (unconscious) animal's brain (right). To produce a lesion, an electric current that is strong enough to destroy neurons near the tip is sent through the electrode, and then the electrode is removed. To prepare the animal for electrical brain stimulation, the electrode is cemented in place so that it can be stimulated through wire leads during behavioral tests after the animal has recovered from surgery.

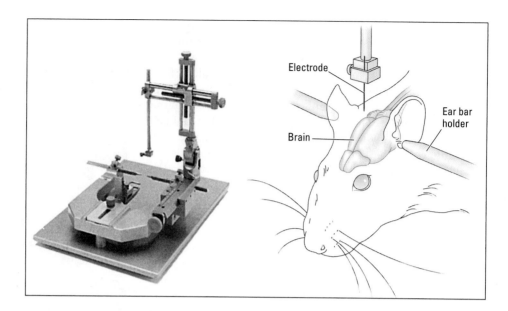

neurons adjacent to its tip. To produce a lesion chemically, a tiny tube called a *cannula* is inserted into the brain, again using a stereotaxic instrument, and a small amount of a chemical is injected through the cannula, destroying neurons whose cell bodies are located near the cannula's tip. The lesions produced by such means can be as small as one-fourth of a millimeter in diameter. By varying the precise location of the damage in different groups of animals, and then comparing the groups in behavioral tests, researchers can identify precise areas of the brain that are crucial for specific types of behaviors.

In most such studies, the lesions are made in deep, primitive areas of the brain, areas whose functions are similar for all mammals, including humans. Such studies have helped researchers identify specific brain nuclei that are crucial for basic motivational and emotional states, such as hunger, sexual drive, and fear (all discussed in Chapter 6).

Effects of Stimulating Specific Areas of the Brain

Stimulation of specific brain areas can also be accomplished either electrically or chemically. To stimulate neurons electrically, a wire electrode is lowered into the brain using the same surgical method as that used to produce a lesion. The electrode is then cemented in place (as shown in Figure 5.12) and can be activated at any time after surgery, through a wire connection or by radio waves. The electrical current used for stimulation is much weaker than that used for producing a lesion; it is strong enough to induce action potentials in, but not destroy, neurons near the electrode tip. To stimulate neurons chemically, a cannula is permanently implanted in the brain, and shortly before behavioral testing a tiny amount of a neurotransmitter substance or other chemical known to activate neurons is injected through it.

Electrical or chemical stimulation in certain deep areas of the brain can cause an animal to exhibit drive states or emotional states that last only as long as the period of stimulation (discussed in Chapter 6). For instance, stimulation in one area causes a previously sated animal to eat, and stimulation in another area causes a previously calm animal to behave as if frightened, as long as the stimulation continues.

Electrical Recording from Single Neurons

Electrodes can be used not just to destroy or stimulate specific brain areas, but also to record neural activity in specific areas as the animal engages in some behavioral task. Extremely thin microelectrodes, with very fine points that can penetrate into the cell bodies of single neurons, can be permanently implanted in the brain. In some experiments many such electrodes are inserted at once, each able to record the activity of a different single neuron.

Experiments using this technique have revealed some remarkable correlations between an animal's behavior and the rate of action potentials produced by individual neurons. For example, certain neurons in one area of the brain (the hippocampus, introduced later in the chapter) fire rapidly when, and only when, the animal (usually a rat) faces in a specific direction within the environment in which it is tested (Best & others, 2001; Moser & others, 2008). If the entire test environment (such as an enclosed box with a maze in it) is rotated, the preferred orientations of these neurons rotate too. Thus, a cell that originally fired whenever the animal faced north will fire whenever the animal faces south after the apparatus is turned 180 degrees. Apparently, these neurons, called *place cells,* help animals keep track of the direction they are facing within familiar environments. If the area of the brain in which these cells are located is destroyed, animals lose their ability to find their way through mazes or to locate objects easily in environments that they have explored.

SECTION REVIEW

A number of techniques are used to map the brain's behavioral functions.

Some Fundamentals	Human Studies	Animal Studies
➤ Neurons in a given nucleus and tract have the same or similar functions, and groups of neighboring nuclei generally have closely related functions. ➤ To study a brain area's function, we can observe behavioral effects of inactivating or artificially stimulating that area, or we can measure it's neural activity during behavioral tasks.	➤ One method is to study of the effects of existing localized brain damage. ➤ A noninvasive technique, TMS temporarily disrupts or briefly triggers activity in specific cortical areas by means of a magnetic field. ➤ An EEG records gross electrical activity in areas of the brain just beneath the skull from electrodes placed on the scalp. ➤ PET and fMRI produce images that depict changes in neural activity in each area of the brain by measuring changes in blood flow.	➤ Precisely placed lesions in the brain can be created electrically or chemically to see how damage affects behavior. ➤ Electrical or chemical stimulation of a specific brain area can help to reveal its functions. ➤ Microelectrodes permit the recording of electrical activity in single neurons under varying conditions.

▉ Functional Organization of the Nervous System

So far in this chapter we have examined the basic workings of individual neurons and have overviewed the main methods for learning about the functions of large groups of neurons in the brain. Now it is time to tour the whole nervous system. We shall look into each of its major divisions with an eye toward understanding its role in the broad task of governing the person's behavior.

As we proceed, it will be helpful to keep in mind that the nervous system is hierarchically organized. Indeed, it contains two distinct but interacting hierarchies. One, the *sensory-perceptual hierarchy,* is involved in data processing. It receives sensory data about a person's internal and external environment, and it analyzes those data to make decisions about the person's bodily needs and about threats and opportunities in the outside world. The flow of information in this hierarchy is primarily from bottom (sensory receptors) to top (perceptual centers in the brain). The other hierarchy, the *motor-control hierarchy,* is involved in control of movement. The flow of information here is primarily from top to bottom. At the top of this hierarchy are executive centers that make decisions about the activities that the person as a whole should engage in, and at lower levels are centers that translate those decisions into specific patterns of muscle movement.

Most of the large anatomical divisions of the nervous system are involved in both hierarchies, so we shall examine both at once. We'll pay most attention here, though, to the motor hierarchy; the sensory-perceptual system is discussed in detail in Chapters 7 and 8. Let's start at the bottom and work our way upward. The bottom parts of the hierarchy are evolutionarily the most primitive and are most directly tied to the muscles and the sensory organs.

Peripheral Nerves: The Nervous System's Interface with the World

The peripheral nervous system, as you may recall, consists of the entire set of nerves, which connect the central nervous system to the body's sensory organs, muscles, and glands (look back at Figure 5.1). Nerves are divided into two classes that correspond to the portion of the central nervous system from which they protrude. **Cranial nerves** project directly from the brain. **Spinal nerves** project from the spinal cord. Like most other structures in the body, nerves exist in pairs; there is a right and a left member in each pair. Humans have 12 pairs of cranial nerves and 31 pairs of spinal nerves. With their many branches, these nerves extend to all portions of the body.

Three pairs of cranial nerves contain only sensory neurons and five pairs contain only motor neurons; the remaining four pairs of cranial nerves and all 31 pairs of spinal nerves contain both sensory and motor neurons. The total number of sensory and motor neurons combined is "only" about five or six million, a tiny fraction of the roughly 100 billion neurons of the nervous system as a whole (the rest are all interneurons). Yet these neurons are crucially important. Without them, the rest of the nervous system would be useless, because it would have no way of receiving sensory input or controlling the person's actions.

Sensory Neurons Provide Data Needed for Governing Behavior

As noted earlier, sensory neurons are activated, at their dendritic ends, by the effects of sensory stimuli (such as light in the eye, chemicals on the tongue or in the nose, sound waves in the ear, or pressure on the skin). They send their action potentials all the way into the central nervous system by way of their very long axons. The rates and patterns of action potentials in sensory neurons are the data that perceptual areas of the central nervous system use to figure out the state of the external and internal environment. Without such input, the central nervous system would have no information on which to base its behavior-controlling decisions.

Sensory input from the specialized sensory organs of the head—the eyes, ears, nose, and tongue—enters the brain by way of cranial nerves. Sensory input that comes from the rest of the body—from the skin, muscles, tendons, and various internal organs—enters the central nervous system by way of all of the spinal nerves and some of the cranial nerves. The sensations conveyed by these inputs, which include touch and pain, are referred to collectively as **somatosensation.** *Soma* means "body," and *somatosensation* is the set of sensations that derive from the whole body as opposed to those that come just from the special sensory organs of the head. (A full discussion of the processes of sensation and perception is found in Chapters 7 and 8.)

Motor Neurons Are the "Final Common Path" for Control of Behavior

Motor neurons, as noted earlier, have their cell bodies in the central nervous system and send their long axons out, by way of cranial or spinal nerves, to terminate on muscles or glands. Ultimately, all of the behavioral decisions of the nervous system are translated into patterns of action potentials in the axons of motor neurons, and those patterns determine our behavior. In the words of the pioneering neurophysiologist Charles Sherrington (1906), motor neurons are the "final common

FIGURE 5.13 Artificial limb controlled by rewired nerves Claudia Mitchell lost her left arm in a motorcycle accident. Bravely, she agreed to be a test case for a pioneering new kind of surgery. Surgeons reconnected the nerves that used to go to her arm and hand to muscles in her chest. After that she could make different muscles in her chest twitch by thinking about moving her missing arm or fingers. The next step was to use the signals from those muscle twitches, amplified and analyzed by a tiny computer, to operate her new artificial arm and fingers. The result is that she can move the artificial arm and fingers in a wide variety of useful ways, just by thinking about doing so. For example, if she wills herself to reach out and grasp an object with her left hand, the artificial limb obeys her will, just as her biological limb did before it was lost (Kiuken, 2007).

path" of the nervous system. Through them, and only through them, can the nervous system control behavior. All of the brain's calculations—including those that we experience consciously as perceptions, thoughts, emotions, desires, and intentions—would be useless if they could not act on muscles and glands. The 100 billion neurons of the central nervous system are all involved, ultimately, in controlling the 2 or 3 million motor neurons, which in turn control behavior. For a wonderful example of how knowledge of motor neurons has been put to medical use, see Figure 5.13 and its caption.

The Motor System Includes Skeletal and Autonomic Divisions

Motor neurons act on two broad classes of structures. One class consists of the *skeletal muscles,* the muscles that are attached to bones and produce externally observable movements of the body when contracted. The other class consists of the visceral muscles and glands. Visceral muscles are muscles that are not attached to bones and do not move the skeleton when they contract. They form the walls of such structures as the heart, arteries, stomach, and intestines. Glands are structures that produce secretions, such as the salivary glands and sweat glands. Neurons that act on skeletal muscles make up the **skeletal** portion of the peripheral motor system. Those that act on visceral muscles and glands make up the **autonomic** portion.

Whereas skeletal motor neurons initiate activity in the skeletal muscles, autonomic motor neurons typically *modulate* (modify) rather than initiate activity in the visceral muscles. Skeletal muscles are completely inactive in the absence of neural input, but visceral muscles have built-in, nonneural mechanisms for generating activity. The heart continues to beat and the muscular walls of such structures as the intestines and arteries continue to contract in response to local influences, even if all the nerves to these organs are destroyed. Most visceral muscles and glands receive two sets of neurons, which produce opposite effects and come from two anatomically distinct divisions of the autonomic system: *sympathetic* and *parasympathetic* (see Figure 5.14).

The **sympathetic division** responds especially to stressful stimulation and helps prepare the body for possible "fight or flight." Among its effects are (a) increased heart rate and blood pressure, (b) the release of

> **10**
> **How do the autonomic and skeletal motor systems differ from one another in function? How do the sympathetic and parasympathetic divisions of the autonomic system differ from one another in function?**

FIGURE 5.14 Divisions of the motor portion of the peripheral nervous system The motor portion of the peripheral nervous system consists of the skeletal and autonomic systems, and the autonomic system consists of the sympathetic and parasympathetic systems.

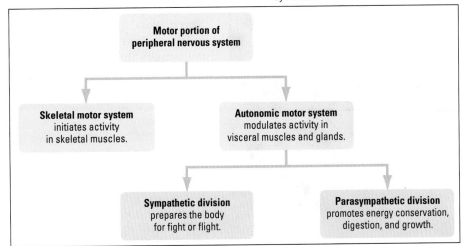

Motor portion of
peripheral nervous system

Skeletal motor system
initiates activity
in skeletal muscles.

Autonomic motor system
modulates activity in
visceral muscles and glands.

Sympathetic division
prepares the body
for fight or flight.

Parasympathetic division
promotes energy conservation,
digestion, and growth.

energy molecules (sugars and fats) from storage deposits to permit high energy expenditure, (c) increased blood flow to the skeletal muscles (to help prepare them for action), and (d) inhibition of digestive processes (which helps explain why a heated argument at the dinner table can lead to a stomachache). Conversely, the ***parasympathetic division*** serves regenerative, growth-promoting, and energy-conserving functions through effects that include the opposites of those just listed for the sympathetic division. If you are relaxed while reading this book, your parasympathetic activity probably predominates over your sympathetic, so your heart is beating at a slow, normal rate and your digestion is working fine. If you are cramming for a test that is coming up in an hour or so, the opposite may be true.

The Spinal Cord: A Conduit and an Organizer of Simple Behaviors

The spinal cord (depicted in Figure 5.1, on p. 139) connects the spinal nerves to the brain. It also organizes some simple reflexes and rhythmic movements.

11
What are three categories of functions of the spinal cord?

The Spinal Cord Contains Pathways to and from the Brain

The spinal cord contains *ascending tracts,* which carry somatosensory information brought in by the spinal nerves up to the brain, and *descending tracts,* which carry motor control commands down from the brain to be transmitted out by spinal nerves to muscles. A person whose spinal cord is completely severed will be completely paralyzed and lacking in sensation in those parts of the body that are innervated by nerves that come from below the place of injury. The closer the place of injury is to the head, the greater the number of spinal nerves that are cut off from the brain and the greater the extent of paralysis and insensitivity. Thus, if the spinal cord is cut through just below the brain, paralysis and insensitivity will include the arms, trunk, and legs; but if the cut is farther down, only the legs may be paralyzed.

The Spinal Cord Organizes Simple Reflexes

Some reflexive behaviors do not require the brain; they are organized by the spinal cord alone. Such reflexes are most clearly demonstrated in animals whose spinal cords have been surgically separated from the brain. (Experiments of this sort may seem cruel, but the knowledge gained from them has been extremely valuable in helping people who have spinal cord injuries.) Animals that have had this operation—referred to as *spinal animals*—still have both a brain and a spinal cord, but these structures no longer communicate with each other.

If the paw of a spinal cat is pricked with a pin, the animal does not hiss or show facial signs of pain, as a normal cat would, because the stimulus input cannot reach the pain and vocalization centers of the brain. The cat cannot feel sensations from below the neck because feeling is mediated by the brain. Nevertheless, the animal's paw quickly withdraws from the pin. This reflex is called the *flexion reflex* because it involves contraction of the flexor muscles— the muscles that bend the limb at each joint, causing it to be pulled inward (flexed) toward the body. The adaptive advantage of the flexion reflex is obvious: It quickly and automatically moves the limb away from potentially damaging stimuli. In the intact, normal cat, this reflex occurs quickly, even before the cat shows evidence of feeling pain. It occurs quickly precisely because it occurs at the level of the spinal cord and does not require that messages be sent up to the brain for further processing and then be sent back down again.

New hope for spinal cord regeneration Researchers are making progress in learning how to use stem cells to generate damaged spinal cord pathways. This young woman, who became partially paralyzed as a result of an automobile accident, has been treated with stem cells from her own olfactory mucosa.

Alex Wong/Getty Images

The Spinal Cord Contains Pattern Generators for Locomotion

If you have ever witnessed a freshly decapitated chicken flapping its wings and running around the barnyard, you know that the spinal cord is capable of generating sustained, organized movements that are not immediate responses to stimuli. The spinal cord contains networks of neurons that stimulate one another in a cyclic manner and thereby produce bursts of action potentials that wax and wane in a regular, repeating rhythm (Kiehn, 2006). These networks, called **pattern generators,** activate motor neurons in the spinal cord in such a way as to produce the rhythmic sequence of muscle movements that results in walking, running, flying (in birds), or swimming (in fish). In some animals (but not in humans), the pattern generators become active when released from the brain's inhibitory control over them, which accounts for the wing flapping and running motions of the headless chicken. Normally, in intact animals, pattern generators are controlled by neurons descending from the brain. They can be either inhibited, producing a motionless animal, or activated to varying degrees, producing varying rates of locomotion.

Subcortical Structures of the Brain

We now leave the spinal cord and enter the brain itself. The lower, more primitive parts of the brain are referred to as *subcortical* structures because of their position beneath the cerebral cortex, the topmost part of the brain. Working our way upward from the bottom, we begin our tour of the brain with the brainstem.

The Brainstem Organizes Instinctive Behavior Patterns

As it enters the head, the spinal cord enlarges and becomes the **brainstem.** The parts of the brainstem, beginning closest to the spinal cord and going upward toward the top of the head, are the **medulla, pons,** and **midbrain** (see Figure 5.15). The brainstem is functionally and anatomically quite similar to the spinal cord, but is more elaborate. The spinal cord is the site of entry of spinal nerves, and the brainstem is the site of entry of most (10 of the 12 pairs) of the cranial nerves. Both the spinal cord and the brainstem contain ascending (sensory) and descending (motor) tracts that communicate between nerves and higher parts of the brain. Also like the spinal cord, the brainstem has some neural centers that organize reflexes and certain instinctive behavior patterns.

> **————————12**
> **How is the brainstem similar to and different from the spinal cord? What role does the brainstem play in the control of behavior?**

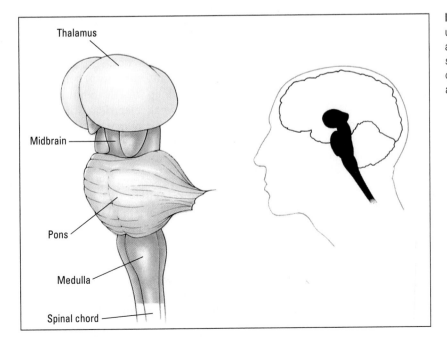

FIGURE 5.15 Brainstem and thalamus This figure makes clear why the medulla, pons, and midbrain are collectively called the *brainstem.* They form a stem-like continuation from the spinal cord, to which other brain structures are connected. The thalamus is attached to the top of the brainstem.

Thalamus

Midbrain

Pons

Medulla

Spinal chord

The medulla and pons organize reflexes that are more complex and sustained than spinal reflexes. They include *postural reflexes,* which help an animal maintain balance while standing or moving, and certain so-called *vital reflexes,* such as those that regulate breathing rate and heart rate in response to input signaling the body's metabolic needs. The midbrain contains neural centers that help govern most of an animal's species-typical movement patterns, such as those involved in eating, drinking, attacking, or copulating (Klemm, 1990). Also in the midbrain are neurons that act on pattern generators in the spinal cord to increase or decrease the speed of locomotion (Pearson & Gordon, 2000).

An animal (such as a cat) whose central nervous system is cut completely through just above the brainstem, referred to as a *brainstem animal,* is a fascinating creature to watch. It can produce most of the instinctive behaviors that a normal animal can produce (Klemm, 1990; Schmidt, 1986). It can walk, run, jump, climb, groom itself, attack, produce copulatory movements, chew, swallow, and so on. Unlike a normal animal, however, it makes these responses only when provoked by immediate stimuli; it does not behave in either a spontaneous or a goal-directed manner. If placed on a pole, for example, the animal automatically climbs, but it does not itself *choose* to climb a pole that has food at the top or avoid one that does not. The animal behaves like a machine that responds to certain triggers rather than like an intelligent, decision-making mammal. Such behavior indicates that the midbrain and the structures below it contain neural systems that organize instinctive patterns of movement but do not contain neural systems that permit deliberate decisions to move or refrain from moving in accordance with the animal's long-term interests or needs.

The Thalamus Is a Relay Station for Sensory, Motor, and Arousal Pathways

13

What are the main functions of the thalamus?

Directly atop the brainstem is the ***thalamus*** [**thal**-uh-muss] (see Figure 5.15). This structure, seated squarely in the middle of the brain, is most conveniently thought of as a relay station that connects various parts of the brain with one another. Most of the sensory tracts that ascend through the brainstem terminate in special nuclei in the thalamus; those nuclei, in turn, send their output to specific areas in the cerebral cortex (discussed in Chapter 7). The thalamus also has nuclei that relay messages from higher parts of the brain to movement-control centers in the brainstem.

In addition to relaying specific sensory and motor signals, the thalamus also plays a role in the arousal of the brain as a whole. Arousal pathways in the midbrain converge in the center of the thalamus and then project diffusely to all areas of the cerebral cortex. The arousal function of the thalamus was nicely exemplified recently when medical researchers were able to awaken a patient who, because of a brain injury, had spent the previous 6 years in a minimally conscious state (Schiff & others, 2007). The researchers implanted electrodes deep into the central nuclei of the patient's thalamus. In response to prolonged weak electrical stimulation through those electrodes, the patient would open his eyes, respond to simple requests, recognize and respond to family members, chew and swallow food placed in his mouth, and could begin a course of physical therapy that had previously been impossible.

The Cerebellum and the Basal Ganglia Help to Coordinate Skilled Movements

14

What are the functional similarities and differences between the cerebellum and the basal ganglia?

We move now to two portions of the brain that are anatomically distinct but closely related in function—the cerebellum and the basal ganglia (see Figure 5.16). *Cerebellum* means "little brain" in Latin, and the ***cerebellum*** [sair-uh-**bell**-um] indeed looks something like a smaller version of the rest of the brain, riding piggyback on the rear of the brainstem. The ***basal ganglia*** [**bay**-sul **gang**-glee-uh] are a set of interconnected structures lying on each side of the thalamus. Damage to either the

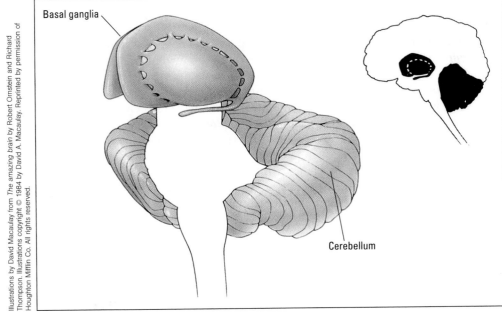

Basal ganglia

Cerebellum

FIGURE 5.16 Cerebellum and basal ganglia These two structures are critically involved in the initiation and coordination of movement.

cerebellum or the basal ganglia can greatly interfere with a person's ability to produce learned, skilled, well-coordinated movements.

Damage to the cerebellum is especially associated with loss in ability to behave in ways that require rapid, well-timed sequences of muscle movements, such as pitching a baseball, leaping over a hurdle, playing a musical instrument, or typing a series of words at a computer (Houk & Mugnaini, 2003). In contrast, damage to the basal ganglia is especially associated with loss of ability to coordinate slower, deliberate movements, such as reaching out to pick up an object (Packard & Knowlton, 2002).

Both structures are specialized to use sensory information to guide movements, but they apparently use that information in different ways. The basal ganglia appear to use sensory information primarily in a *feedback* manner. In other words, sensory input pertaining to an ongoing movement (such as the sight of how the hand is moving) feeds back into the basal ganglia and is used to adjust the movement as it progresses. The cerebellum, in contrast, uses sensory information primarily in a *feed-forward* manner (Ohyama & others, 2003). That is, it uses sensory information to program the appropriate force and timing of a movement before the movement is initiated. That is why the cerebellum is especially crucial for movements that occur too rapidly to be modified once they are in progress.

These characterizations are useful, but they do not describe the full range of functions of these large brain structures. People with damage in either the cerebellum or the basal ganglia can show a wide range of motor deficits, depending on the precise location of damage. Moreover, neuroimaging studies (using PET and fMRI) show that portions of the cerebellum, basal ganglia, and certain motor-planning areas of the cerebral cortex become active not just when people are producing movements but also when they are imagining themselves producing movements (Houk & Mugnaini, 2003). Perhaps when divers, gymnasts, or pianists "visualize" their performance before they act, what they are doing, partly, is warming up specific neurons in these motor areas, thereby setting up the neural programs that will eventuate in their best performance.

The cerebellum in action The cerebellum is involved in well-coordinated, precisely timed movements, which occur too fast to be controlled by sensory feedback.

The Limbic System and the Hypothalamus Play Essential Roles in Motivation and Emotion

15

Why is the limbic system so named, and what functions does it perform?

◄ The term limbic comes from the Latin word *limbus,* meaning "border." The *limbic system* can be thought of as the border dividing the evolutionarily older parts of the brain, below it, from the newest part (the cerebral cortex), above it. The limbic system consists of several distinct structures that interconnect with one another in a circuit wrapped around the thalamus and basal ganglia (see Figure 5.17). Some of these structures—including especially the *amygdala* [uh-**mig**-duh-luh]—are involved in the regulation of basic drives and emotions (discussed in Chapter 6). But the limbic system also plays other roles. One of its most prominent structures, the *hippocampus* [hip-oh-**camp**-us], is crucial for keeping track of spatial location (the direction-sensitive place cells, noted earlier in the chapter, are located there) and for encoding certain kinds of memories (discussed in Chapter 9).

FIGURE 5.17 Limbic system and hypothalamus The most conspicuous structures of the limbic system are the hippocampus and the amygdala, which have strong connections to the hypothalamus. The pituitary gland is strongly tied to the hypothalamus and is controlled by it.

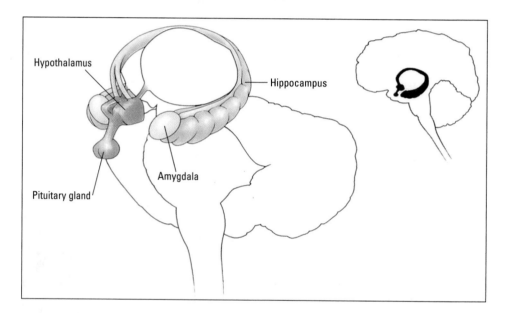

The limbic system is believed to have evolved originally as a system for the sophisticated analysis of olfactory input (Thompson, 1985), and its connections with the nose remain strong. This may help explain the special influence that smells—such as the aroma of good food or perfume, or the stench of vomit, or the scent of freshly mown grass—can have on drives, emotions, and memories. But the limbic system also receives input from all the other sensory organs. In addition, it is intimately connected to the basal ganglia, and that connection is believed to help translate emotions and drives into actions.

16

What are three ways by which the hypothalamus controls the body's internal environment?

◄ The *hypothalamus* [**hype**-oh-**thal**-uh-muss] is a small but vitally important structure. Its name derives from its position directly underneath the thalamus (*hypo* in this case means "underneath"). The hypothalamus is not technically part of the limbic system, but is intimately connected to all the structures of that system (see Figure 5.17). Its primary task is to help regulate the internal environment of the body. This it accomplishes by (a) influencing the activity of the autonomic nervous system, (b) controlling the release of certain hormones (to be described later), and (c) affecting certain drive states, such as hunger and thirst. In addition, through its connections with the limbic system, the hypothalamus helps regulate emotional states, such as fear and anger. You will read in Chapter 6 about the role of the hypothalamus in drives and emotions.

If I had to give up a cubic millimeter (a tiny speck) of tissue from some part of my brain, the last place I would want it taken from is the hypothalamus. Depending on just which part was taken, I could be left without one or more of my basic drives, without a normal cycle of sleep and wakefulness, or without the ability to regulate my rate of metabolism.

The Cerebral Cortex

We now move up to the anatomically outermost and evolutionarily newest part of the brain, the ***cerebral cortex.*** *Cerebrum* is the Latin word for "brain," and the term now generally refers to all parts of the brain other than the brainstem and cerebellum. *Cortex* is the Latin word for "bark," and in anatomical usage it refers to the outside layer of any structure. So, the cerebral cortex is the outside layer of the major portion of the brain. It is by far the largest part of the human brain, accounting for approximately 80 percent of its total volume (Kolb & Whishaw, 2009). Its surface area is much greater than it appears because it folds inward in many places. If the cortex were unfolded and spread out as a single sheet, it would be only 2 to 3 millimeters thick and would occupy a surface area equivalent to a square that is half a meter long on each side (Kolb & Whishaw, 2009).

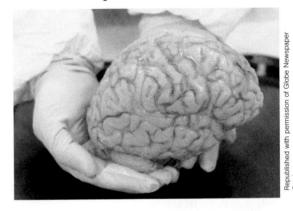

A human brain Only about one-third of the surface area of the brain's cortex is visible from the outside. The remaining two-thirds is hidden in the folds.

Republished with permission of Globe Newspaper Co., Inc.

The entire folded cerebral cortex is divided into left and right *hemispheres,* and each hemisphere is further divided into four lobes, or segments, demarcated at least partly by rather prominent inwardly folding creases, referred to as *fissures.* The lobes, whose positions you can see in Figure 5.18, are, from back to front, the ***occipital*** [ock-**sip**-it-ul], ***temporal*** [**temp**-or-ul], ***parietal*** [pah-**rye**-ut-ul], and ***frontal*** lobes.

The Cortex Includes Sensory, Motor, and Association Areas

Researchers who study the functions of the cortex divide it into three categories of functional regions, or areas. One category consists of the ***primary sensory areas,*** which receive signals from sensory nerves and tracts by way of relay nuclei in the thalamus. As shown in Figure 5.18, primary sensory areas include the visual area in the occipital lobe, the auditory area in the temporal lobe, and the somatosensory area in the parietal lobe. A second category is the ***primary motor area,*** which sends axons down to motor neurons in the brainstem and spinal cord. As shown in Figure 5.18, this area occupies the rear portion of the frontal lobe, directly in front of the somatosensory area. The third category consists of all the remaining parts of the cortex, which are called ***association areas.*** These areas receive input from the sensory areas and lower parts of the brain and are involved in the complex processes that we call perception, thought, and decision

17

What are the four lobes of the cortex, and what are three functional categories of areas that exist within these lobes?

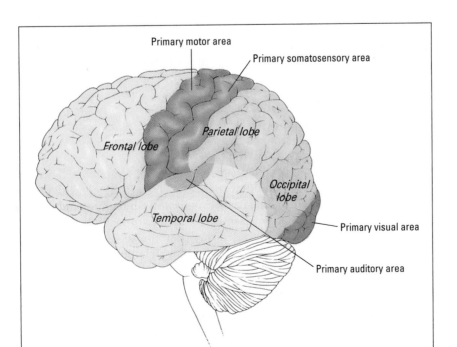

Primary motor area

Primary somatosensory area

Parietal lobe

Frontal lobe

Occipital lobe

Temporal lobe

Primary visual area

Primary auditory area

FIGURE 5.18 Cerebral cortex This figure shows the four lobes of the cortex, as well as the locations of the primary motor area and the primary sensory areas for vision, hearing, and somatosensation.

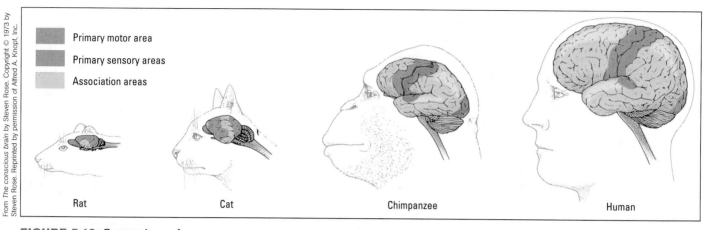

Primary motor area

Primary sensory areas

Association areas

Rat   Cat   Chimpanzee   Human

FIGURE 5.19 Comparison of the brains of four mammals All the brains contain the same structures, but in the chimpanzee and human, proportionately much more cortical space is devoted to association areas than in the rat and cat.

making. As shown in Figure 5.19, the amount of association cortex, relative to the other two categories, increases dramatically as one goes from simpler mammals, such as the rat and the cat, to more complex ones, such as the chimpanzee and the human.

The Primary Sensory and Motor Areas Are Topographically Organized

18

What does it mean to say that cortical sensory and motor areas in the cortex are topographically organized?

The primary sensory and motor areas of the cortex are organized in such a way that adjacent neurons receive signals from or send signals to adjacent portions of the sensory or muscular tissue to which they are ultimately connected. This fact is referred to as the *principle of topographic organization*. For example, neurons that are near one another in the visual cortex receive signals from receptor cells that are near one another in the retina of the eye. Similarly, neurons that are near one another in the somatosensory cortex receive signals from adjacent areas of the skin, and neurons that are near one another in the primary motor cortex send signals to adjacent sets of muscle fibers. It is possible to map onto the somatosensory cortex the parts of the body from which each portion of somatosensory cortex receives its signals, and onto the motor cortex the part of the body to which each portion of motor cortex sends its signals.

The resulting maps, depicted in Figure 5.20, show a distorted view of the human body. This is because the amount of cortex devoted to each part of the body corresponds not to the size of the body part but to the degree of sensitivity of that part (in the case of the sensory map) or the fineness of its movements (in the case of the motor map). As you can see, huge areas of the human primary motor cortex are devoted to control of the fingers and vocal apparatus, where fine control is needed. In other animals, other body parts have greater representation, depending on the range and delicacy of their movements. In a cat, for example, large portions of the somatosensory and primary motor areas of the cortex are devoted to the whiskers, and in a spider monkey—a creature that uses its tail as a fifth arm and hand—large areas are devoted to the tail (Walker, 1973).

19

What is some evidence that the primary motor cortex comes relatively late in the chain of command preceding an action and that its function is to refine the more delicate parts of the action?

The primary motor cortex is part of the chain of command in controlling movements, but it is not at the top of that chain and is not involved in all types of movements. It receives input from the basal ganglia and cerebellum and is specialized to fine-tune the signals going to small muscles, such as those of the fingers and tongue, which must operate in a finely graded way (Lemon, 2008).

Experiments conducted many years ago, in which monkeys made well-controlled hand movements to obtain food rewards, revealed that each movement was preceded first by a burst of activity in the basal ganglia and then by a burst in the primary motor cortex (Evarts, 1979; Kornhuber, 1974). This is part of the evidence that the primary motor cortex generally comes later than the basal ganglia and the cerebellum in the chain of command. In other experiments, monkeys whose primary

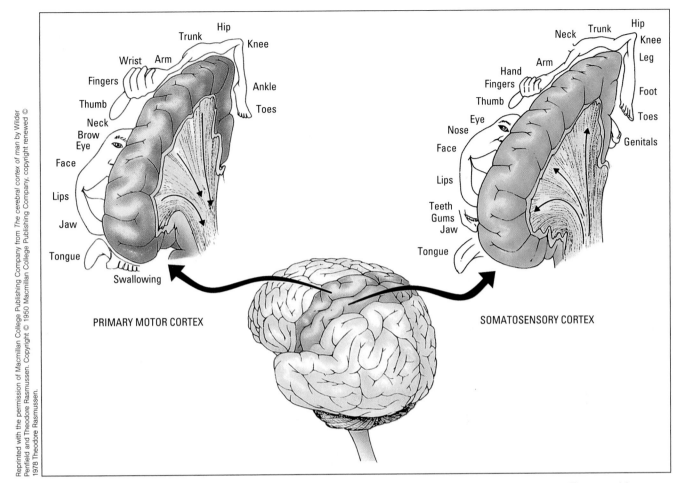

PRIMARY MOTOR CORTEX

SOMATOSENSORY CORTEX

FIGURE 5.20 Topographic organization of the somatosensory and primary motor areas
Proportionately more cortical tissue is devoted to the more sensitive and delicately controlled body parts than to other parts.

motor cortex had been entirely destroyed behaved normally in most respects but were unable to make delicate hand movements, such as those needed to lift a small piece of food out of a narrow hole (Passingham & others, 1983). More recently, researchers have found that electrical stimulation of the motor cortex produces not just muscle twitches, but also well-organized movements. For example, stimulating the hand area of the motor cortex in a monkey can result in a well-coordinated grasping response, or pushing response, depending on just where the stimulus is applied (Graziano, 2006).

Premotor Areas Help Organize Specific Patterns of Movement

Directly in front of the primary motor area lie a set of other cortical areas devoted to motor control, referred to collectively as ***premotor areas*** (see Figure 5.21 on the next page). These areas set up neural programs for producing organized movements or patterns of movements. To choose what program to set up, they use information sent to them from anterior (forward) portions of the frontal lobe that are involved in overall behavioral planning. To execute an action program they send information out to the cerebellum, basal ganglia, and motor cortex, which refine the program further before sending messages down toward the muscles.

Like the cerebellum and basal ganglia, premotor areas become active during the mental rehearsal of coordinated movements as well as during the actual production of such movements (Cisek & Kalaska, 2004). Medical researchers have begun to exploit this fact in order to learn about the mental capacities and potential for recovery of severely brain-injured patients who are in a so-called "vegetative state." Patients in such a state show evidence of sleep-wake cycles but are unable to speak or move in a deliberate fashion. Until recently, there was no way to know if they were conscious

20

What is the role of the premotor areas in the control of behavior? How has activity there been used to assess consciousness in brain-damaged patients?

and could hear and understand what people said to them. Recently, researchers in the United Kingdom began testing the consciousness of vegetative patients by assessing premotor neural activity, with fMRI neuroimaging, while asking them to imagine specific movements—such as swinging a tennis racket or kicking a soccer ball (Owen & Coleman, 2008). In early tests they identified two patients (out of 17 tested) who, repeatedly, in response to such instructions, exhibited patterns of neural activity in premotor regions that were indistinguishable from those produced by people with intact brains who were given the same instructions. The results showed clearly that those two patients could understand the instructions and were able to imagine the specified movement.

Prefrontal Association Areas Create General Plans for Action

21

What is the role of the prefrontal cortex in the control of behavior?

The portion of the cerebral cortex that has expanded the most in human beings compared to other animals is the ***prefrontal cortex,*** consisting of the entire frontal lobe anterior to (in front of) the premotor areas (see Figure 5.21). This part of the brain is involved in all sorts of planning, both short-term and long-term. Portions of the prefrontal cortex concerned with short-term planning use perceptual information sent in from posterior association areas to decide on a course of action and send information to premotor areas to execute the action.

To review the general flow of information in the cortex involved in the control of movement, notice the arrows in Figure 5.21. Association areas in the rear parts of the cortex, especially in the parietal and temporal lobes, analyze information that comes to them from sensory areas. These areas, in turn, send output to prefrontal association areas, which also receive information about the internal environment through strong connections with the limbic system. Combining all this information, the prefrontal areas set up general plans for action that can be put into effect through connections to the premotor cortex and through downward links to the basal ganglia and cerebellum.

Consistent with this model of cortical control, damage in the prefrontal lobe does not, as a rule, reduce one's ability to extract information from the environment, but does reduce one's ability to use that information effectively to control behavior. Depending on the location and extent of the injury, such damage can destroy either short-range planning, such as working out the series of movements needed to solve a particular puzzle, or long-range planning, such as organizing one's day, week, or life (Kolb & Whishaw, 2009).

FIGURE 5.21 Control of movement by the cerebral cortex
The prefrontal cortex integrates information received from other association areas and makes a general plan for action. The premotor areas convert this plan into neural programs for movement, which are then executed through connections to the cerebellum, basal ganglia, and primary motor cortex.

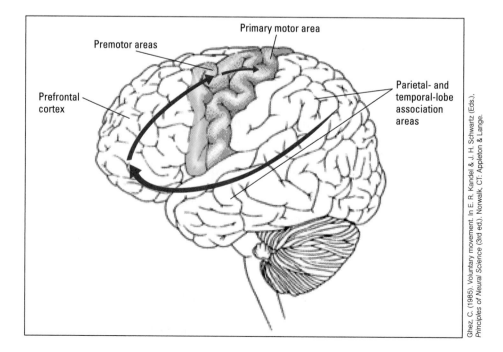

Ghez, C. (1985). Voluntary movement. In E. R. Kandel & J. H. Schwartz (Eds.), *Principles of Neural Science* (3rd ed.). Norwalk, CT: Appleton & Lange.

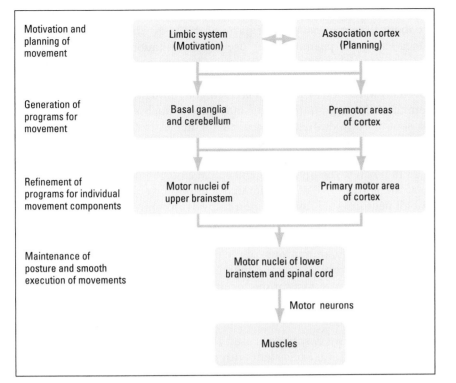

FIGURE 5.22 Hierarchy of motor control
This figure summarizes the broad functions of various structures of the nervous system in the control of movement. The structures shown higher up are involved in the more global aspects of an action, and those shown farther down are involved in the finer details of carrying it out. Notice that both subcortical and cortical structures exist at each of the top three levels of the hierarchy. Although this portrayal does not show all the known pathways, it provides a useful way to think about the neural flow of information from the planning of an action to its execution. (Based partly on information in Ghez & Krakauer, 2000, and Schmidt, 1986.)

Hierarchical Organization in the Control of Movement: A Summary

We have ascended the nervous system, from bottom to top, and glimpsed the functions of each of its divisions in the overall task of controlling behavior. The parts, as I said at the outset, work together in a hierarchical manner. To review the movement-control functions of the various parts and to visualize their hierarchical organization, look at Figure 5.22. Structures are organized there according to their general roles in controlling movement, not according to their anatomical positions. The highest structures are involved in motivation and planning, and the lower structures are involved in refining and executing the plans, turning them into action. Notice that both subcortical and cortical structures (shown, respectively, on the left and right sides of the diagram) are involved at each of the top three levels in the hierarchy.

To illustrate the hierarchy further, imagine what might occur in the nervous system of a person who has not eaten in a while and sees some peanuts. At the top of the hierarchy, the limbic system (which most directly monitors the internal state of the body) senses that food is needed and sends a message of "hunger" to cortical association areas with which it is connected. These areas, which share the top of the hierarchy with the limbic system, analyze information coming to them from the visual cortex and determine that some peanuts lie in a bowl across the room. Other information is also considered by the association areas, including memories about the taste of peanuts, about how to eat them, and about the propriety of eating them in this room at this time. Such information, integrated by prefrontal association areas, leads to a decision to cross the room, pick up some peanuts, and eat them.

At the second level, the basal ganglia, cerebellum, and premotor cortex receive the program of planned

▶— — — — — — — — — — — —**22**

How are the movement-control functions of the nervous system summarized as a hierarchical, top-down flow of information? How is the hierarchy illustrated by an imaginative tour through the nervous system of a person who decides to eat some peanuts?

"The prefrontal cortex is involved in higher mental functioning, like using a can opener and remembering to feed you."

action from the limbic system and prefrontal cortex. They also receive somatosensory input about the exact position of parts of the body and visual input about the exact location of the peanuts. They use this information to refine the motor program—that is, to work out the specific timing and patterning of the movements to be made.

At the third level, the motor program is conveyed through two pathways for further refinement. The program for larger movements, such as walking toward the peanuts, is sent directly down to a set of motor nuclei in the upper part of the brainstem. The program for delicate movements, such as those needed for removing the peanuts from their shells, is conveyed to the motor cortex, which, in turn, sends its output down to the brainstem and spinal cord.

Finally, at the fourth level of the hierarchy, in the lower brainstem and spinal cord, are motor neurons—the final common pathway in control of behavior. Skeletal motor neurons send their messages out to the skeletal muscles of the body to trigger all the movements needed to reach the peanuts, pick them up, and put them in the mouth. Autonomic motor neurons (of the parasympathetic division) send their messages out to the salivary glands and muscular walls of the gastrointestinal system to prepare the digestive tract for the receipt of peanuts.

A Word of Caution

The hierarchical model just described is useful as a first approach to understanding the nervous system, and it is consistent with the kinds of behavioral deficits that occur when different parts of the nervous system are damaged. However, there is a possible danger in this portrayal: It can seduce us into believing that we know more than we actually do know.

23
What is the difference between knowing where a brain function occurs and knowing how it occurs?

◄ Specifically, the knowledge that certain parts of the brain are essential for certain aspects of behavioral control can be mistaken for knowledge about how those processes are accomplished. But the discovery of "where" does not explain "how." In illustrating the hierarchy, I spoke of "decisions" made in prefrontal areas of the cortex and of programs for action developed and refined by other brain areas. What do such statements mean? They mean only that individuals who suffer damage in one part of the brain lose the ability to make reasonable choices for action, and that those who suffer damage in another part retain the ability to make reasonable choices but lose the ability to carry them out in a coordinated manner. Such statements don't address the far more difficult question of how the association cortex makes decisions or how various other structures develop and refine programs for action.

SECTION REVIEW

Divisions of the nervous system are organized hierarchically to control behavior.

Peripheral Nervous System	Spinal Cord	Subcortical Structures	Cerebral Cortex
➤ This division consists of spinal and cranial nerves and their various branches, which contain sensory and motor neurons. ➤ Motor neurons include skeletal motor neurons, which contract skeletal muscles, and sympathetic and parasympathetic autonomic motor neurons, which act in opposing ways on internal organs.	➤ The spinal cord acts as a conduit, carrying somatosensory information to the brain and motor commands from the brain. ➤ It also organizes spinal reflexes and contains pattern generators that produce rhythmic movement sequences, such as walking.	➤ The brainstem is similar to the spinal cord but more elaborate. ➤ The thalamus is a major sensory and motor relay station. ➤ The cerebellum and basal ganglia are crucial for the production of coordinated actions. ➤ The hypothalamus and limbic system are critically involved in motivation and emotion as well as other functions.	➤ The cortex is divided into two hemispheres, each with four lobes. ➤ Cortical areas include primary sensory and primary motor areas, which are organized topographically, and association areas, which are crucial for thought. ➤ Prefrontal and premotor association areas plan and establish neural programs for actions.

Asymmetry of Higher Functions of the Cerebral Cortex

Nearly every part of the brain exists in duplicate. We have a right and a left member of each anatomical portion of the brainstem, thalamus, cerebellum, and so on. The part of the brain in which the right-left division is most evident, however, is the cerebral cortex. Each half of the cortex folds inward where it would abut the other half, forming a deep, fore-to-aft midline fissure that divides the cortex into distinct right and left hemispheres. The two hemispheres are connected, however, by a massive bundle of axons called the ***corpus callosum*** [cuh-**loh**-sum], which is located below that fissure (see Figure 5.23).

The two hemispheres are quite symmetrical in their primary sensory and motor functions. Each does the same job, but for a different half of the body. Most of the neural paths between the primary sensory and motor areas of the cortex and the parts of the body to which they connect are crossed, or *contralateral*. Thus, sensory neurons that arise from the skin on the right side of the body send their signals to the somatosensory area of the left hemisphere, and vice versa. Similarly, neurons in the primary motor area of the left hemisphere send their signals to muscles on the right side of the body, and vice versa. Such symmetry breaks down, however, in the association areas.

The most obvious distinction between the two cortical hemispheres in humans is that large areas in the left are specialized for language and comparable areas in the right are specialized for nonverbal, visuospatial analysis of information. The earliest evidence of this difference came from observing people who had suffered strokes or other injuries that affected just one hemisphere. In general, damage to the left hemisphere results in deficits in using and comprehending language, and damage to the right results in deficits in such tasks as recognizing faces, reading maps, and drawing geometric shapes, all of which depend on perceiving spatial relationships.

24

In what ways are the two hemispheres of the cerebral cortex symmetrical, and in what ways are they asymmetrical?

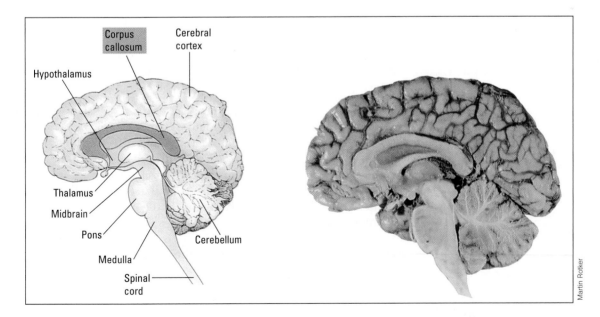

Martin Rotker

FIGURE 5.23 Corpus callosum The corpus callosum is a huge bundle of axons that connects the right and left hemispheres of the cerebral cortex. You can see it here in an inside view of the right hemisphere of a human brain that has been cut in half. This photograph and the matched diagram also give you an inside view of other brain structures.

Effects of Surgical Separation of the Hemispheres: Split Brain, Split Mind

Dramatic further evidence of the separate abilities of the two hemispheres appeared in the 1960s, when Michael Gazzaniga and his colleagues began to study people who, as a last-resort treatment for epilepsy, had undergone an operation in which the two hemispheres were separated by cutting the corpus callosum.

Early, more casual observations had revealed no remarkable deficits in people who had undergone this operation. The operation was generally successful in reducing or eliminating epileptic seizures, and, after a period of recovery, there is usually no drop in measured IQ, in ability to carry on conversations, or even in ability to coordinate the two sides of the body in skilled tasks. But Gazzaniga (1967, 1998) showed that under special test conditions, in which information is provided to just one hemisphere or the other, these people behave as though they have two separate minds with different abilities.

25
_____◀

How is it possible to test each hemisphere separately in people whose corpus callosum has been cut? How do such tests confirm that the left hemisphere controls speech and the right hemisphere has superior spatial ability?

How Each Hemisphere Can Be Tested Separately After the Split-Brain Operation

Split-brain studies take advantage of the crossed sensory and motor connections between the brain and peripheral parts of the body. Recall that each hemisphere most directly controls movement in, and receives somatosensory information from, the opposite half of the body. In addition, as illustrated in Figure 5.24, connections from the eyes to the brain are such that input from the right visual field (the right-hand half of a person's field of view) goes first to the left hemisphere and input from the left visual field goes first to the right hemisphere. In the normal brain, all information that goes to either hemisphere subsequently travels to the other through the corpus callosum. But the split-brain operation destroys those connections. Therefore, with the testing apparatus shown in Figure 5.25 and with split-brain patients as subjects, it is possible to (a) send visual information to just one hemisphere by presenting the stimulus in only the opposite half of the visual field, (b) send tactile (touch) information to just one hemisphere by having the subject feel an object with the opposite hand, and (c) test the knowledge of just one hemisphere by having the subject respond with the hand opposite to that hemisphere.

Split-Brain Evidence for Left-Hemisphere Language and Right-Hemisphere Spatial Ability

In a typical experiment, Gazzaniga flashed pictures of common objects to either the right or the left visual field of a split-brain patient. When a picture was flashed in the right field (projecting to the left hemisphere), the patient described it as well as someone with an intact brain would; but when a picture was flashed in the left field (projecting to the right hemisphere), the patient either claimed to see nothing or made a random guess. Then Gazzaniga asked the same person to reach under a barrier with one hand or the other and identify, by touch, the object that had been flashed. The fascinating result was that the person could reliably identify with the left hand (but not with the right) the same object that he or she had just vocally denied having seen (Gazzaniga, 1967). For example, if the object flashed to the right

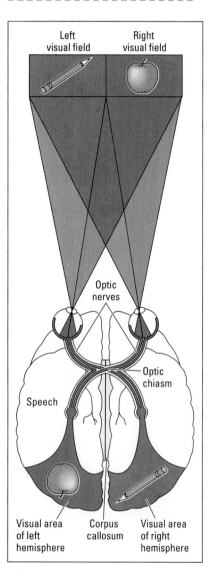

FIGURE 5.24 Neural pathways from the eyes to the right and left hemispheres of the cortex Neurons of the optic nerves either cross or don't cross at the optic chiasm. The pattern of crossing is such that neurons on the right side of either retina, which receive input from the left visual field, go to the right hemisphere of the brain, and vice versa.

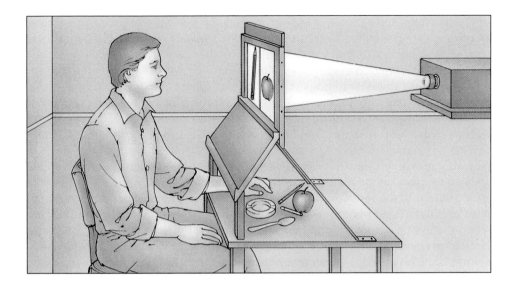

FIGURE 5.25 Testing apparatus for split-brain subjects With this apparatus, it is possible to flash a stimulus in either visual field (or in both at once) and to ask the person to identify objects by touch with either hand. With the image of a pencil flashed in his left visual field, this split-brain subject will be able to identify the pencil by touch with his left hand. Vocally, however, he will report having seen an apple on the screen, as that was flashed in his right visual field, which projects to his left, speaking hemisphere. (Adapted from Gazzaniga, 1967.)

hemisphere was a pencil, the subject's left hand picked out the pencil from a set of objects even while the subject's voice was continuing to say that nothing had been flashed. Such findings are consistent with the conclusion that only the left hemisphere can generate speech and that neither hemisphere has direct access to what the other one knows.

Research of this sort also revealed large individual differences among split-brain patients in the degree to which the right hemisphere can comprehend speech. Some show essentially no right-hemisphere comprehension. They cannot participate in experiments such as that just described, because their right hemispheres don't understand such instructions as "Pick up the object that you saw on the screen." Some have reasonably good right-hemisphere comprehension, although their right hemisphere is still unable to generate speech; and a few show a reversal, with the right hemisphere superior to the left in language comprehension and production. Other tests, on people whose corpus callosum has not been cut, have shown that about 4 percent of right-handed individuals and 15 percent of left-handed individuals have their speech centers located in the right hemisphere rather than the left (Rasmussen & Milner, 1977).

Other experiments with split-brain patients revealed that although the right hemisphere is unable to generate speech, it is much better than the left in solving visuospatial problems. When asked to arrange puzzle pieces to match a particular design or to copy three-dimensional pictures, each subject performed far better with the left hand (controlled by the right hemisphere) than with the right hand (controlled by the left hemisphere), even though all of the subjects were right-handed (see Figure 5.26). In more recent experiments, split-brain patients were asked to judge small differences between visual stimuli presented as pairs to either hemisphere. The results showed that the left hemisphere is as good as the right in judging nonspatial differences, such as differences in brightness or in color, but not as good as the right in judging spatial differences, such as differences in size or in the slant of two lines (Corballis, 2003).

How Split-Brain Patients Cope as Well as They Do

How do people who have had the split-brain operation get along in the world as well as they do? What keeps their two hemispheres from going off in opposite directions and creating continuous conflict between the two halves of the body? In some instances, especially shortly after the surgery, conflict does occur. One man described a situation in which, while he was dressing

FIGURE 5.26 Evidence for right-hemisphere superiority in spatial representation Although the split-brain patient who produced these drawings was right-handed, he could copy geometric figures much better with his left hand (controlled by his right hemisphere) than with his right hand.

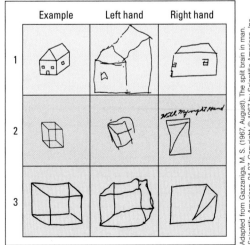

in the morning, his right hand was trying to pull his pants on while his left hand was trying to pull them back off (Gazzaniga, 1970); apparently, his right hemisphere wanted to go back to bed. But such conflicts are rare, and when they do occur, the left hemisphere (right hand) usually wins.

The patient's ability to coordinate the two hemispheres probably involves several mechanisms. First, only the cerebral cortex and some parts of the limbic system are divided when the corpus callosum is cut. Motor centers that control movements of the larger muscles, such as those of the legs and arms (but not the fingers) lie in the lower, undivided parts, and some sensory information also passes from one hemisphere to the other by way of those lower routes (Reuter-Lorenz & Miller, 1998). The intact connections also apparently allow each hemisphere to inhibit the motor output of the other, so the more competent hemisphere can take control of any given task (Reuter-Lorenz & Miller, 1998). In addition, under normal conditions, when the eyes can move around and things can be felt with both hands, the two hemispheres can receive the same or similar information through their separate channels. Finally, each hemisphere apparently learns to communicate indirectly with the other by observing and responding to the behavior that the other produces, a process that Gazzaniga (1967) labeled *cross-cuing*. For example, the right hemisphere may perceive something unpleasant and precipitate a frown, and the left may feel the frown and say, "I'm displeased."

Split-Brain Insight into Consciousness: The Left-Hemisphere Interpreter

26

How do studies of split-brain patients tend to confirm and extend an idea about the nature of consciousness that was developed long ago by Sigmund Freud?

One of the most fascinating findings from studies of split-brain patients is that they rarely express surprise or confusion concerning the seemingly contradictory actions that their two hemispheres generate. When asked to explain some behavior triggered by the right hemisphere, the person (speaking from the left hemisphere) usually generates quickly and confidently a seemingly logical (but often false) explanation.

For instance, in one experiment a split-brain patient was presented simultaneously with a picture of a chicken claw shown to the left hemisphere and a picture of a snow scene shown to the right hemisphere (Gazzaniga, 2000). Then he was shown (in a way that could be seen by both hemispheres) a set of pictured objects and was asked to point with both hands to the one most closely related to what he had seen on the screen. He immediately pointed with his right hand to the chicken (clearly related to the chicken claw) and with his left hand to the snow shovel (clearly related to the snow scene). When asked why he was pointing to these two objects, his left, speaking hemisphere responded, "Oh, that's simple. The chicken claw goes with the chicken, and you need a shovel to clean out the chicken shed." He seemed completely satisfied by this explanation. In other experiments, Gazzaniga and his colleagues found that they could induce states of annoyance or of pleasure in split-brain patients by flashing annoying or pleasant scenes to their right hemispheres. When asked to explain their feelings, the patients always came up with plausible (but clearly false) answers. For example, they might comment on some aspect of the experimental equipment—or of the experimenter's behavior—that was either annoying them or pleasing them.

Such observations have led Gazzaniga (2000) to posit that one of the natural functions of the left hemisphere is to interpret, or try to make logical sense of, everything that the person does. You might think of this *left-hemisphere interpreter* as analogous to the public relations department of a business or government. Its role is to tell stories, both to the self and to others, designed to make sense of the seemingly contradictory and irrational things that the person does. The idea of such an interpreter in the human brain or mind is by no means new. It was the centerpiece of a theory of consciousness proposed by Sigmund Freud (1912/1932) nearly 100 years ago (discussed in Chapter 15). According to Freud, we do things because unconscious decision-making processes in our mind make us do them.

But one part of our mind observes what we do and tells a running story about it; that story constitutes our conscious understanding of our actions and the reasons for them. The split-brain studies indicate that the neural mechanism for generating such stories is located in the left hemisphere and is intimately connected with the brain areas that generate speech.

Language Areas of the Left Hemisphere

Perhaps the most distinctively human behavioral ability is that of producing and understanding a complex, grammar-based language (discussed in more detail in Chapter 11). Much of the left hemisphere of the human cortex is devoted in one way or another to language. Damage anywhere within large portions of the left hemisphere disrupts language ability, and the nature of the disruption depends on just where the destruction occurs.

Any loss of language ability resulting from brain damage is called **aphasia** [uh -**fay**-zyuh]. Aphasias have been classified into a number of types, depending on the specific nature and degree of loss (Dronkers & others, 2000). The best-known and most fully studied of these are two that were first described by nineteenth-century neurologists—one by Paul Broca and the other by Carl Wernicke.

Effects of Damage to Broca's Area

Broca (1861/1965) observed that people who had brain damage that included an area of the left frontal lobe now called *Broca's* [**broke**-uh's] *area*, just anterior to the primary motor area (see Figure 5.27), suffered from a type of aphasia in which speech becomes labored and *telegraphic*, meaning that the minimum number of words are used to convey the message. The speech consists mostly of nouns and verbs, and a sentence is rarely more than three or four words long. If you ask a person with this disorder what he or she did today, the answer might be, "Buy bread store." This disorder is now called **Broca's aphasia** or, more descriptively, *nonfluent aphasia*. The lack of fluency in Broca's aphasia suggests that neurons in Broca's area are crucial for setting up the motor programs that are involved in fluent speech production. This conclusion is also consistent with the observation that Broca's area lies very near to the region of the primary motor cortex that controls movements of the tongue and other speech muscles.

Research since Broca's time indicates that people with damage to Broca's area also have difficulty understanding language. They understand most of what they hear, but often fail to understand grammatically complex sentences. They become confused, for example, by sentences in which the agent and object of an action are reversed from the usual word order and the meaning cannot be inferred from the individual word meanings alone (Grodzinsky, 2000; Zurif, 1990). Thus, they easily understand *The boy pushed the girl* (a simple, active sentence) or *The apple was eaten by the boy* (which can be understood just from word meanings, because apples don't eat boys), but *The girl was pushed by the boy* leaves them unsure as to who pushed whom. Research suggests that people with an intact Broca's area understand that last sentence by transforming it mentally into its simpler, active equivalent—*The*

-----------------------27

What are the differences between Broca's and Wernicke's aphasias in (a) language production, (b) language comprehension, and (c) areas of the brain damaged?

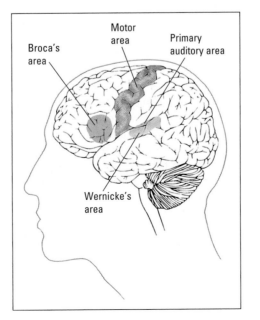

FIGURE 5.27 Left-hemisphere language areas Damage to Broca's area leads to a loss of the ability to generate fluid, grammatically complete sentences but not to a loss of the ability to supply the words needed to convey the main content of the sentence. Damage to Wernicke's area has the opposite effect on speech production and greatly impairs speech comprehension.

The preserved brain of Broca's patient In 1861, a man who had great difficulty speaking after suffering a stroke and who identified himself merely as "Tan" checked into a hospital and was examined by Paul Broca. After Tan's death, Broca examined his brain and found the massive damage, shown here, to the region of the left hemisphere now called "Broca's area."

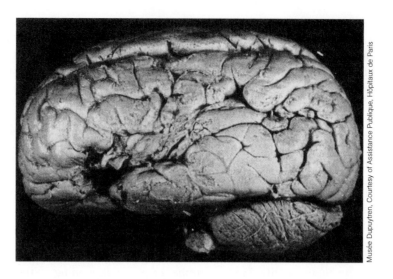

Musée Dupuytren, Courtesy of Assistance Publique, Hôpitaux de Paris

boy pushed the girl. People lacking Broca's area apparently fail to produce such transformations.

In sum, studies of people with damage to Broca's area suggest that neurons in and around this area are crucial for at least two seemingly distinct language functions: (1) articulating words and sentences in a fluent manner and (2) transforming grammatically complex sentences that are heard into simpler ones in order to extract the meaning.

Effects of Damage to Wernicke's Area

Wernicke (1874/1977) observed that people who had damage to a certain area of the left temporal lobe, now called *Wernicke's* [**wur**-nick-ee's] *area* (see Figure 5.27), suffered from a type of aphasia quite different from that described by Broca. These patients, unlike Broca's aphasics, had difficulty understanding the meanings of words that they heard and also had difficulty finding the appropriate words to express the meanings that they wanted to convey.

The speech of patients with damage in Wernicke's area is almost the opposite of that of Broca's aphasics. It is rich in the little words that serve primarily to form the grammatical structure of a sentence—the articles (*a, the*), prepositions (such as *of, on*), and conjunctions (*and, but*). However, it is markedly deficient in the nouns, verbs, and adjectives that give a sentence its meaning. One such patient, asked to describe the contents of a simple picture, said: "Nothing the keesereez the, these are davereez and these and this one and these are living. This one's right in and these are . . . uh . . . and that's nothing, that's nothing" (Schwartz, 1987). The inability to come up with the correct names of objects and actions leads to a heavy use of pronouns and nonsense words as substitutes. The speech retains its fluency and grammatical structure but loses its meaning.

This disorder is now called **Wernicke's aphasia,** or, more descriptively, *fluent aphasia.* Theories to explain it generally center on the idea that neurons in and near Wernicke's area are crucially involved in translating the sounds of words into their meanings and in locating, through connections to other cortical association areas, the words needed to express intended meanings (Dronkers & others, 2000). The location of this area near to the primary auditory area (see Figure 5.27 on page 169) is consistent with the role of translating sounds into meaningful words (Geschwind, 1972).

Identifying Language Areas Through Neuroimaging

With PET or fMRI it is possible to determine which areas of the brain become more active when a person engages in a language-related task. Such studies tend in some ways to confirm the theories about the functions of Broca's and Wernicke's areas that were derived from studies of people with brain damage and in other ways to challenge those theories.

One of the earliest and most often cited of such studies was conducted by Steven Petersen and his colleagues (1989). These researchers used PET to image the brains of people as they carried out four types of language-related tasks that varied stepwise in level of complexity. At the first level (simplest task), the subjects simply gazed at a spot marked by crosshairs in the center of a video screen. At the second level, they continued to gaze at the crosshairs while they either saw (superimposed on the crosshairs) or heard (through earphones) a series of common English nouns. The third level was just like the second, except that now they were asked to speak aloud each word that they saw or heard. The fourth level was like the third, except that instead of simply repeating each noun, they were asked to think of and say aloud a verb that represented an action appropriate to the noun (for example, in response to *hammer,* they might say "pound").

➤ - - - - - - - - - - - - - - - - - -28
How was PET used to identify brain areas involved in word perception and production?

In order to identify the brain areas brought into play by each type of task, the researchers computed, for each small area of the brain, the difference between the average amount of activity during that task and the average amount during the task that ranked one level below that task. The results are depicted in Figure 5.28 and can be summarized as follows:

• Viewing or hearing words, without having to act on them in any way, resulted (as expected) in high activity in the relevant sensory areas—visual areas of the occipital lobe for viewing and auditory areas of the temporal lobe for hearing.

• Repeating aloud words that were seen or heard resulted in high activity in areas of the primary motor cortex that are involved in control of the vocal apparatus.

• Generating appropriate verbs in response to seen or heard nouns resulted in high activity in an area of the frontal lobe that encompassed Broca's area and in a portion of the temporal lobe somewhat behind Wernicke's area.

Notice that these results are not completely consistent with the theories about Broca's and Wernicke's areas developed from the brain-damage studies. Those theories would predict that Broca's area should be involved in speaking words that have just been seen or heard as well as in speaking words that are mentally generated, and that Wernicke's area, rather than the spot behind it, should be involved in generating words with the appropriate meaning. Neuroimaging studies are leading to new theories that implicate many cortical regions, not just Broca's and Wernicke's areas, in language comprehension and production (Bookheimer, 2002; Grodzinsky & Friederici, 2006).

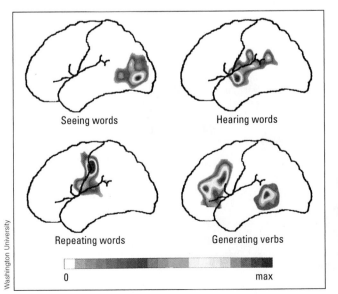

Seeing words

Hearing words

Repeating words

Generating verbs

0   max

Washington University

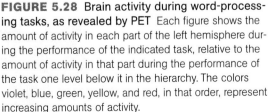

FIGURE 5.28 Brain activity during word-processing tasks, as revealed by PET Each figure shows the amount of activity in each part of the left hemisphere during the performance of the indicated task, relative to the amount of activity in that part during the performance of the task one level below it in the hierarchy. The colors violet, blue, green, yellow, and red, in that order, represent increasing amounts of activity.

The right and left hemispheres are specialized for different higher functions.

Split-Brain Studies

➤ Split-brain patients enable researchers to study the functioning of each hemisphere independent of the other.

➤ Results indicate that only the left hemisphere produces language in most people, while the right hemisphere is superior in visuospatial tasks.

➤ Split-brain studies also suggest that the verbal left hemisphere interprets a person's own behavior, making "sense" of it even when the two hemispheres produce contradictory actions.

Language and the Left Hemisphere

➤ Much of the left hemisphere is devoted to language use.

➤ Aphasia is any language deficit due to brain damage. Deficits observed in Broca's and Wernicke's aphasia are used to infer functions of the corresponding brain areas.

➤ Results of neuroimaging studies are only partly consistent with aphasia research and have led to more extensive mapping of language areas in the brain.

■ Effects of Experience on the Brain

People sometimes speak of the "wiring" of the nervous system, or even of its "hardwiring." This metaphor is useful for some purposes, but it has its limits. The nervous system is not hardwired like a computer or other human-made device. Neurons are soft, pliable, living cells. They can change their sizes, shapes, excitabilities, and patterns of connections in ways that help adapt their possessors to life's ever-changing circumstances. Every day you grow millions of new synapses and lose millions of others, and at least some of that change depends on the unique experiences you had that day.

If You Use It, It Will Grow

Like muscles, regions of the brain tend to grow when used and to atrophy when not used. Here is some of the evidence for that statement.

Effects of Deprived and Enriched Environments on the Brain

29

What brain changes have been observed in rats and mice caged in enriched environments?

Early evidence that experience can change the structure of the brain arose from experiments, conducted in the 1960s and later, in which rats were housed in either enriched or deprived environments (Greenough & Black, 1992; Rosenzweig & others, 1972). The enriched environments were large cages in which rats lived with others and had many objects to explore. ("Enriched" is a relative term. These environments were enriched compared to the typical barren cages of laboratory rats

A playground for mice In mice, as well as in other mammals, experience in an enriched environment enhances growth in the brain

James Aronovsky

but not compared to, say, a garbage dump, where wild rats might live.) The deprived environments were small cages in which each rat lived alone and had no objects except food and a water bottle. After weeks in these environments, the brains of the two groups showed many differences. The brains of the enriched group had thicker cerebral cortexes, larger cortical neurons, more acetylcholine (a prominent neurotransmitter in the cortex), more synapses per neuron, and thicker, more fully developed synapses than did those of the deprived group. These changes occurred even when rats were not placed in the differing environments until well into adulthood. Correlated with these brain differences were marked increases in learning ability in the enriched-environment animals compared to their deprived-environment counterparts.

The researchers who performed these early experiments assumed that the brain growth they observed must derive solely from modifications of existing neurons and possibly the addition of new glial cells (the nonneural cells in the brain that provide structural and nutritional support to neurons). It was believed then that the mammalian brain is incapable of producing new neurons after birth. In the late 1990s, however, researchers using new techniques found ample evidence that new neurons are constantly being generated in the brain, including the adult human brain (Kempermann & Gage, 1999).

Generation of new neurons is most apparent in the hippocampus, a structure known to be involved in learning and memory. New hippocampal neurons are generated more rapidly in rats and mice housed in enriched environments than in those housed in deprived environments (Brown & others, 2003; Prickaerts & others, 2004). These new neurons develop functional synapses with already-existing neurons in the hippocampus and appear to contribute significantly to the animals' capacities for learning and memory (Ge & others, 2007; Toni & others, 2007). Other research shows that many areas of the brain, not just the hippocampus, generate new neurons in response to brain injury (Ming & Song, 2005). These new neurons may well play a role in the gradual recovery of behavioral functions that can occur after brain injury.

Restructuring of the Cortex During Skill Development

As an animal or person develops skill at a task, ever more neurons in the brain are recruited into the performance of that skill. In one of the first clear demonstrations of this phenomenon, Gregg Recanzone and his colleagues (1992) trained monkeys to discriminate between subtly different rates of vibration applied to a particular patch of skin on one finger. The monkeys received banana pellets for making a certain response each time the vibration rate increased even slightly above 20 cycles per second. Other, "untrained" monkeys received the same vibrations to the skin but were not required to discriminate among them for a food reward. Subsequently, the researchers mapped the somatosensory area of the cortex of all the monkeys by touching points on the skin with a thin probe while recording the activity of cortical neurons. They found that in the trained monkeys the area of the cortex that received input from the "trained" spot of skin was, on average, two to three times larger than the equivalent area in untrained monkeys. Apparently, the brain reorganization resulted not from the skin stimulation per se but from the monkeys' use of that stimulation to guide their behavior.

Subsequently, researchers have found comparable brain changes in visual or auditory sensory areas when animals are trained to discriminate among subtly different sights or sounds (Bakin & others, 1996; Zohary & others, 1994). Research using PET and fMRI neuroimaging has shown that effects like these occur for people, too (Pascual-Leone & others, 2005). In one such study with stringed-instrument players (six violinists, two cellists, and a guitarist), unusually large areas of the somatosensory cortex responded to stimulation of the fingers of the left hand—the same fingers that the musicians had used for years in fingering the strings of their instruments (Elbert & others, 1995).

30

What evidence shows that practice at a skill alters neural connections so that more neurons become devoted to that skill?

Restructuring the cerebral cortex
Whenever people learn new skills, regardless of age, neurons in the cerebral cortex form new long-lasting connections, so that more neurons are recruited into performance of the skill.

Some of the most dramatic evidence of the brain's ability to restructure itself comes from studies of blind people. In sighted people, the whole occipital lobe of the cortex is used for analyzing visual input. Neuroimaging studies have shown that in blind people the occipital lobe becomes devoted to various other purposes, which help them to compensate for their blindness. For example, regions of the occipital lobe that in sighted people are involved in the visual analysis of three-dimensional space become devoted, in the blind, to the task of identifying the locations from which sounds are coming (Gougoux & others, 2005; Weeks & others, 200). In Braille readers, large parts of the occipital cortex become devoted to the task of analyzing the tactile input from the fingers in the finally graded way needed to read Braille (Pasqual-Leone & others, 2005). Blind people also commonly develop superior verbal memory to compensate for their inability to look up information easily or to find objects by looking. In one fMRI study, blind and sighted people were given lists of nouns to memorize as their brains were scanned (Amedi & others, 2003). The blind subjects showed marked activation of portions of the occipital cortex during this task, which did not occur in the sighted people, and they also showed superior memory. Moreover, those blind subjects who scored best on the memory test showed the most activity in the occipital cortex.

Alvaro Pascual-Leone and his colleagues (2005) found that at least some of these brain changes began to occur in sighted people who had been blindfolded for just five days. When the blindfolds were removed, the changes quickly reversed themselves.

Spatial Learning and Growth of the Hippocampus

31

What evidence, with birds and with humans, indicates that spatial learning can result in growth in the hippocampus?

As described in Chapter 4, some bird species hide seeds in multiple locations and retrieve them in the winter, and these birds generally have larger hippocampi than do related species that do not hide seeds. Researchers working with one of these species, the mountain chickadee, have shown that enlargement of the hippocampus depends at least partly on experience (Clayton, 2001). When caged chickadees are allowed to hide and retrieve seeds, their hippocampi grow, and when they are then prevented from hiding and retrieving seeds for a period of time, their hippocampi shrink again. The hippocampus is involved in many forms of memory, especially memory for spatial locations.

A study of London cabbies suggests that extensive spatial learning can increase hippocampal size in humans, too. Cab drivers in big cities develop remarkable spatial abilities, and this is especially true of London cab drivers, who, to get a license, must go through prolonged training and pass a test of their ability to find the shortest route between any two locations in that large city. Brain scans revealed that the posterior (rear) part of the hippocampus (the part most involved in spatial memory) is significantly larger in London cab drivers than in otherwise similar people who do not drive cabs (Maguire & others, 2000). They also revealed a significant positive correlation between years of cab-driving experience and growth in the hippocampus: In general, the longer a man had been driving a cab, the larger was his posterior hippocampus.

Strengthening of Synapses as a Foundation for Learning

Learning undoubtedly involves many types of changes in the brain. But at the cellular level the type of change that has been most clearly linked to learning is the strengthening of synaptic connections between already existing neurons.

The Hebbian Synapse: Neurons That Fire Together Wire Together

Many years ago, the Canadian psychologist Donald Hebb (1949) theorized that some synapses in the brain have the property of growing stronger (more effective) whenever the postsynaptic neuron fires immediately after the presynaptic neuron fires (see Figure 5.29). Through this means, Hebb suggested, neurons could acquire the capacity to respond to input that they previously didn't respond to. This could provide a basis for classical conditioning and other forms of learning. In the 1970s, Timothy Bliss and Terge Lømo (1973) discovered a phenomenon called **long-term potentiation,** or **LTP,** which strongly supports Hebb's theory.

32

How has the discovery of long-term potentiation tended to confirm Hebb's theory about synaptic strengthening?

In the laboratory, LTP is produced by artificially stimulating, with a burst of electrical pulses, a bundle of neurons entering a particular region of an animal's brain. This results in the strengthening of the synapses that those neurons form with postsynaptic neurons, so that subsequent weak stimulation of the same bundle elicits a stronger response in the postsynaptic neurons than it would have before. This potentiation (strengthening) is *long term:* It lasts for hours or even months, depending on the conditions. Subsequent research has shown that, at least in some brain areas, LTP works in the following manner.

Imagine a weak synapse between neuron A and neuron C (depicted in Figure 5.29). When neuron A becomes active, some of the neurotransmitter molecules it releases become bound to conventional, fast-acting receptors on the postsynaptic membrane, where they produce a depolarization that is too slight to play a significant role in triggering action potentials. Other transmitter molecules at the same synapse, however, become bound temporarily to special LTP-inducing receptors on the postsynaptic membrane. If neuron C then fires an action potential (due to input from other neurons, such as B in Figure 5.29), the combination of that firing and the presence of transmitter molecules in the LTP-inducing receptors triggers a series of biochemical events that strengthen the synapse (Bi & Poo, 2001; Byrne, 2008). The presynaptic terminal becomes larger, able to release more transmitter substance than it could before, and the postsynaptic membrane develops more conventional receptor sites than it had before.

As a result of such changes, firing in neuron A produces more depolarization in neuron C than it did before and therefore plays a greater role in triggering action potentials in that cell than it did before. Sets of neurons that behave like this have been found in many parts of the mammalian brain, including various areas of the cerebral cortex, the hippocampus, the cerebellum, and the amygdala—all of which are known to be involved in various kinds of learning (Byrne, 2008).

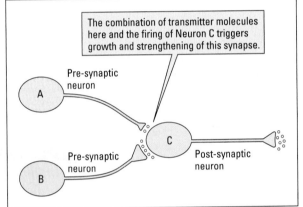

The combination of transmitter molecules here and the firing of Neuron C triggers growth and strengthening of this synapse.

Pre-synaptic neuron

A

Pre-synaptic neuron

B

C

Post-synaptic neuron

FIGURE 5.29 **A Hebbian synapse** The synapse between neuron A and neuron C is initially weak, so A is ineffective in stimulating C. However, if C fires (because of the firing of neuron B) immediately after neurotransmitter molecules have been released from A onto C, the synapse between A and C will grow stronger. If this happens a sufficient number of times, the synapse may become sufficiently strong that A will be able to trigger action in C even when B is inactive. This type of synapse is called *Hebbian* because its existence was first postulated by Donald Hebb. Recent research into the phenomenon of long-term potentiation confirms the existence of such synapses.

Evidence That Long-Term Potentiation Is a Basis for Learning

Evidence that LTP is actually involved in learning comes from many experiments showing that interference with the brain's normal capacity for such potentiation interferes with the animal's ability to learn (Byrne, 2008). In one experiment with mice, for example, a drug that prevents LTP was injected into a portion of the amygdala that is known to be crucial for fear learning. After this treatment, the researchers tried, through classical conditioning, to train the mice to fear a tone that was paired with an electric shock. (As you may recall from Chapter 4, classical conditioning occurs when a neutral stimulus, which does not initially elicit a response, is paired with an unconditioned stimulus, which does elicit a response. After a sufficient number of pairings, the neutral stimulus, now called a conditioned stimulus, elicits a response even in the absence of the unconditioned stimulus.) The LTP-inhibited mice failed to learn such fear. They responded to the shock as did normal mice, but, unlike normal mice, they did not subsequently show fear responses to the tone (Maren, 1999).

33

What evidence shows that long-term potentiation is involved in learning?

Given such evidence that LTP is essential for learning, what would happen if the capacity for LTP were increased above the normal level? Joe Tsien (2000) and his colleagues found a way to answer that question. The postsynaptic receptors that are involved in initiating LTP come in two forms—a strong form, which is highly effective in triggering LTP, and a weak, less effective form. Through genetic engineering, Tsien and his colleagues produced a strain of mice—which they named "Doogie," after the boy genius of the old television show, *Doogie Howser, M.D.*—that had many more of the strong receptors and fewer of the weak ones than do normal mice. As predicted, brain neurons in the Doogie mice showed more LTP in response to electrical stimulation than did those in the normal, unaltered mice. Remarkably, but just as predicted, the Doogie mice also showed better memory than the unaltered mice in a series of three widely different tests: maze learning, classical conditioning of a fear response, and object recognition (see Figure 5.30). In each case, the altered mice behaved similarly to the unaltered mice during the learning experience but showed significantly better memory when tested a day or more later (Tang & others, 1999; Tsien, 2000). More recently, Tsien and his colleagues showed that such genetic modification can also prevent the decline in memory that normally occurs in aged mice (Cao & others, 2007).

The results of these experiments raise many questions that have not yet been answered. Will similar results be found with other animals and other forms of learning? Could memory in people be improved through methods that increase LTP? If a simple genetic change can improve memory by increasing LTP, then why hasn't evolution already produced that change through natural selection? Perhaps LTP beyond a certain level, or even memory beyond a certain level, is maladaptive in the conditions of everyday life.

FIGURE 5.30 A genetically altered "smart" mouse being tested for object recognition Mice, like other mammals, explore new objects more than familiar ones. In this test, each mouse was exposed to two objects: one that it had explored in a previous 5-minute session and one that was new. Mice that were genetically altered to produce enhanced LTP explored the new object (in this case, the one on the right) more than the old one even when several days had elapsed since the initial session. In contrast, unaltered mice explored the new object more than the old one only when a shorter period of time had elapsed. These results indicate that the altered mice remembered the original object for a longer period of time than did the unaltered mice. (Photograph from Tsien, 2000.)

Peter Murphy

SECTION REVIEW

The brain physically changes in response to experience.

Growth and Reorganization	Long-Term Potentiation (LTP)
➤ Rats in enriched environments develop thicker cortexes with larger neurons and more and stronger synaptic interconnections. They also generate new neurons at a faster rate.	➤ LTP strengthens synaptic connections in ways that mediate learning.
➤ Skill learning causes larger portions of the brain to become involved in performing that particular skill.	➤ In line with Hebb's theory, the coordinated firing of a presynaptic and postsynaptic neuron strengthens the synaptic connections of the first onto the second.
➤ The hippocampus, an area critical to spatial memory, grows as a result of spatial learning (as demonstrated in London taxi drivers).	➤ LTP involves enlargement of axon terminals and generation of new receptor sites on postsynaptic membranes.

■ How Hormones and Drugs Interact with the Nervous System

When the ancient Greeks argued that the heart is the seat of thought, feeling, and behavioral control, they were not without reasons. Like the brain, the heart has long protrusions (blood vessels, in this case) that connect it with other parts of the body. Blood vessels are easier to see than nerves, and because they can be found in all the sense organs and muscles, as well as in other tissues, early theorists believed that blood vessels were the conduits of sensory and motor messages. Today we know that the circulatory system does indeed play a vital communicative role in the body, though not the one envisioned by the ancients. A slower messenger system than the nervous system, it carries chemicals that affect both physical growth and behavior. Among these chemicals are hormones, which are secreted naturally into the bloodstream, and drugs, which may enter the bloodstream artificially through various routes.

Hormones

Hormones are chemical messengers that are secreted into the blood. They are carried by the blood to all parts of the body, where they act on specific *target tissues*. Dozens of hormones have been identified. The classic hormones—the first to be identified and the best understood—are secreted by special hormone-producing glands called *endocrine glands* (see Figure 5.31). But many other hormones are secreted by organs that are not usually classed as endocrine glands, such as the stomach, intestines, kidneys, and brain.

Comparison of Hormones and Neurotransmitters

Hormones and neurotransmitters appear to have a common origin in evolution 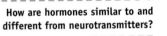 (Snyder, 1985). The earliest multicellular animals evolved a system of chemical messengers that allowed cells to communicate and coordinate their actions, enabling the animal to behave as a unit. As organisms grew more complex, the chemical communication system differentiated along two distinct routes. One route involved the nervous system and was designed for rapid, specific, point-to-point communication. Here the primitive chemical messengers evolved into neurotransmitters. The other route involved the circulatory system and was designed for relatively slow, diffuse, widespread communication. Here the primitive chemical messengers evolved into hormones.

34

How are hormones similar to and different from neurotransmitters?

The main difference between a hormone and a neurotransmitter is the distance that each must travel from its site of release, through fluid, to its site of action. Neurotransmitter molecules released from an axon terminal must diffuse across the synaptic cleft—a distance of about 20 nanometers (20 billionths of a meter)—in order to affect the postsynaptic cell. In contrast, hormone molecules often must travel through the entire circulatory system before they bind to their target cells and exert their effects.

One line of evidence for a common origin of hormones and neurotransmitters lies in their chemical similarity. In fact, some hormones are chemically identical to some neurotransmitters. The chemical *norepinephrine,* for example, is a hormone when secreted into the blood by the adrenal gland (shown in Figure 5.31) but is a neurotransmitter when released by sympathetic motor neurons of the autonomic nervous system on visceral

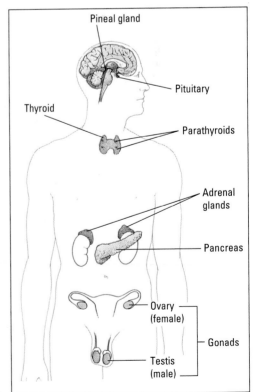

FIGURE 5.31 Endocrine glands These are some of the glands that secrete hormones into the bloodstream. The pituitary, which is controlled by the brain, secretes hormones that, in turn, control the production of hormones by the thyroid, adrenals, and ovaries or testes.

FIGURE 5.32 Four modes of chemical communication between cells The primitive mode (a) of intercellular chemical communication evolved to form three more complex modes of such communication. These are a neural mode (b), in which chemicals from a neuron diffuse across a small synaptic gap to their target cell (another neuron or muscle cell); a neurohormonal mode (c), in which chemicals from neurons enter the bloodstream and are carried to target cells; and a hormonal mode (d), in which chemicals from an endocrine gland enter the bloodstream and are carried to target cells. (Based on a figure in Snyder, 1985.)

muscles and glands. It is also a neurotransmitter in certain pathways in the brain. In each of these roles, norepinephrine helps arouse and alert the body. As a hormone and a sympathetic transmitter, it has effects such as increasing the heart rate and diverting more blood to the skeletal muscles. As a transmitter in the brain, it helps produce a state that we experience psychologically as high arousal or alertness.

Other evidence for a common origin of hormones and neurotransmitters lies in the existence of ***neurohormones.*** Like neurotransmitters, these chemicals are produced by neurons and released from axon terminals in response to action potentials. But they are classed as hormones because they are released not into a synaptic cleft but into a bed of capillaries (tiny blood vessels), where they are absorbed into the bloodstream. As you will see, some neurohormones promote the secretion of other hormones, and in that way they provide a means by which the nervous system controls the activity of the endocrine system. To compare the four modes of chemical communication just discussed, see Figure 5.32.

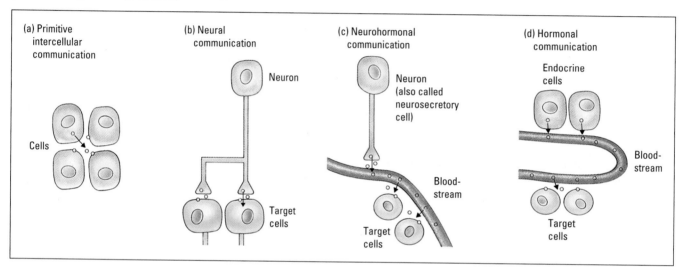

How Hormones Affect Behavior

Hormones influence behavior in many ways. They affect the growth of peripheral bodily structures, including muscles and bones, and in that way influence behavioral capacity. Hormones also affect metabolic processes throughout the body and thereby influence the amount of energy that is available for action. Of greatest interest to psychologists is the fact that hormones also act in the brain in ways that influence drives and moods (discussed in Chapter 6).

35
What are some examples of long-term and short-term effects of hormones?

◀ Some effects of hormones are long-term or irreversible, and some of these occur before birth. For example, almost all the anatomical differences between newborn boys and girls are caused by the hormone testosterone, which is produced by the male fetus but not by the female fetus. These anatomical differences are evident in the brain as well as in the genitals, and the brain differences provide one basis for sex differences in behavior throughout life (discussed in Chapter 6). At puberty, the increased production of sex hormones—especially testosterone in the male and estrogen in the female—stimulates a new set of growth processes that further differentiate males and females anatomically and thereby influence their behavior.

The short-term effects of hormones range in duration from a few minutes to many days. In response to stressful stimulation, for example, the adrenal cortex (the external layer of the adrenal gland) secretes various hormones, including cortisol, which are sometimes referred to as "stress hormones." These hormones produce a variety of effects throughout the body that help the animal in a stressful situation. For example, they release sugar and fat molecules into the blood to supply extra energy for possible "fight or flight," and they suppress inflammation caused by wounds. These hormones are also taken up by neurons in certain parts of the brain and apparently act there to help the animal adapt behaviorally to the stressful situation (McEwen, 1989).

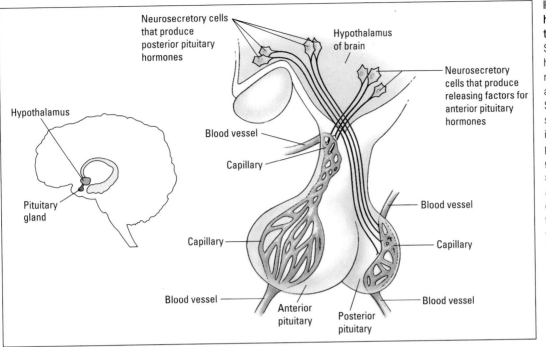

FIGURE 5.33 How the hypothalamus controls pituitary hormones
Specialized neurons in the hypothalamus, called neurosecretory cells, control the activity of the pituitary gland. Some neuro-secretory cells secrete hormones directly into capillaries in the posterior pituitary, where they enter the general bloodstream. Others secrete hormones called *releasing factors* into a special capillary system that carries them to the anterior pituitary, where they stimulate the release of hormones manufactured there.

How Hormones Are Controlled by the Brain

The pituitary, which sits at the base of the brain, is sometimes called the master endocrine gland because it produces hormones that, in turn, stimulate the production of other hormones in other glands, including the adrenal cortex and the gonads (ovaries in the female and testes in the male). But we might more accurately say that the *brain* is the master endocrine gland, because through neurohormones it controls the pituitary.

To visualize the intimate relationship between the brain and the pituitary, look at Figure 5.33. The rear part of the pituitary, the *posterior lobe,* is in fact a part of the brain. The posterior lobe consists mainly of modified neurons, referred to as *neurosecretory cells,* which extend down from the hypothalamus. When these neurosecretory cells are activated, by brain neurons that lie above them, they release their neurohormones into a bed of capillaries. Once these hormones enter the capillaries, they are transported into the rest of the circulatory system to affect various parts of the body.

The remainder of the pituitary, the *anterior lobe,* is not part of the brain (no neurons descend into it) but is intimately connected to the brain by a specialized set of capillaries, as shown in Figure 5.33. Neurosecretory cells in the brain's hypothalamus produce *releasing factors,* neurohormones that are secreted into the special capillary system and are carried to the anterior pituitary, where they stimulate the anterior pituitary cells to synthesize and release hormones into capillaries that carry the hormones into the general bloodstream. Different releasing factors, produced by different sets of neurosecretory cells in the hypothalamus, act selectively to stimulate the production of different anterior pituitary hormones.

Consider the sequence of hormonal events, triggered by the brain, that is diagrammed in Figure 5.34 on the next page: (1) A shadowy figure is seen at night, and the brain interprets it as fearsome. (2) The association cortex sends a neural message to the viewer's hypothalamus that causes it to secrete *corticotropin-releasing factor.* (3) The specialized capillary system transports this releasing factor to the anterior pituitary, where it stimulates the release of another hormone, *corticotropin,* into the bloodstream. (4) From the bloodstream, corticotropin enters the adrenal cortex, where it causes the release of adrenal cortical hormones, including cortisol. (5) These adrenal hormones are carried throughout the body to help prepare it for a possible emergency. At the same time, many other brain-controlled effects are also occurring to deal with the possible emergency suggested by the sight of the

36

How does the brain control the release of hormones from the two lobes of the pituitary and thereby control the release of other hormones as well?

FIGURE 5.34 Brain-pituitary-adrenal response to a fearful stimulus This is one example of a brain-mediated hormonal response to sensory stimulation.

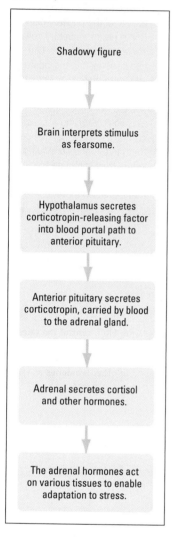

shadowy figure. They range from the activation of the sympathetic portion of the autonomic nervous system to the development of a plan to escape.

Drugs

The main difference between a hormone and a drug is that the former is produced in the body and the latter is introduced from the outside. Like hormones, drugs are carried by the blood and taken up in target tissues in various parts of the body.

How Drugs Get into the Brain

To be carried to potential sites of action, a drug first must get into an individual's bloodstream. Sometimes drugs are introduced directly into the blood by intravenous (into-a-vein) injection, but more commonly they are administered by routes that bring them into contact with capillaries, where they are gradually absorbed into the blood. Drugs are absorbed by capillaries in the intestines if taken orally, by capillaries in the lungs if taken by inhalation, by capillaries in the rectum if taken by rectal suppository, and by capillaries under the skin or in the muscles if taken by subcutaneous or intramuscular injection. The preferred route of administration depends largely on the properties of the drug and the desired time course of action. A drug that is destroyed by digestive juices in the stomach, for example, cannot be taken orally. A drug that is injected intravenously will act more quickly than one that is administered by any other route.

If a drug is going to act in the brain, it must pass from the blood into the extracellular fluid that surrounds neurons in the brain. The walls of capillaries in the brain are much less porous than those in other tissues and are tightly surrounded by the fatty membranes of various nonneural cells. The tight capillary walls and the other cells surrounding them form the ***blood-brain barrier,*** which helps protect the brain from poisons (Banarjee & Bhat, 2007). To act in the brain, a drug (or hormone) must be able to pass through this barrier. In general, fat-soluble substances pass through easily, and non-fat-soluble substances may or may not pass through, depending on other characteristics of their chemistry. Alcohol, for example, is a drug that readily enters the brain because it is highly soluble in fat.

How Drugs Can Alter Synaptic Transmission

Many different drugs are used in psychiatry and neurology to alter a person's mood or behavioral capacities. Nearly all such drugs work by enhancing or blocking synaptic transmission somewhere in the nervous system. In normal synaptic transmission, neurotransmitter molecules are released from the presynaptic neuron, diffuse across the narrow synaptic cleft, and then bind to the membrane of the postsynaptic cell and alter its activity. (To review this process, look back at Figure 5.7, on p. 144.) The means by which drugs can influence activity at a synapse fall into at least three categories:

37

What are three general ways in which drugs can alter activity at a synapse?

1. They can act on the presynaptic neuron to either promote or inhibit the release of the transmitter, thereby affecting the amount of transmitter that enters the cleft.

2. They can act within the cleft to either promote or inhibit the processes that normally terminate the action of the transmitter once it has been released, either prolonging or shortening the amount of time that the transmitter remains in the cleft and exerts its effects.

3. They can act directly on postsynaptic receptors, either producing the same effect as the transmitter or blocking the transmitter from producing its normal effect.

Of these three categories, the postsynaptic effects are best understood. To visualize how such effects occur, recall the comparison of neurotransmitter molecules to keys and postsynaptic receptors to locks (and look at Figure 5.35). A drug molecule that diffuses into a synapse may act as a substitute key, producing the same effect as the transmitter would, or it may act as a misshapen key, filling the keyhole without

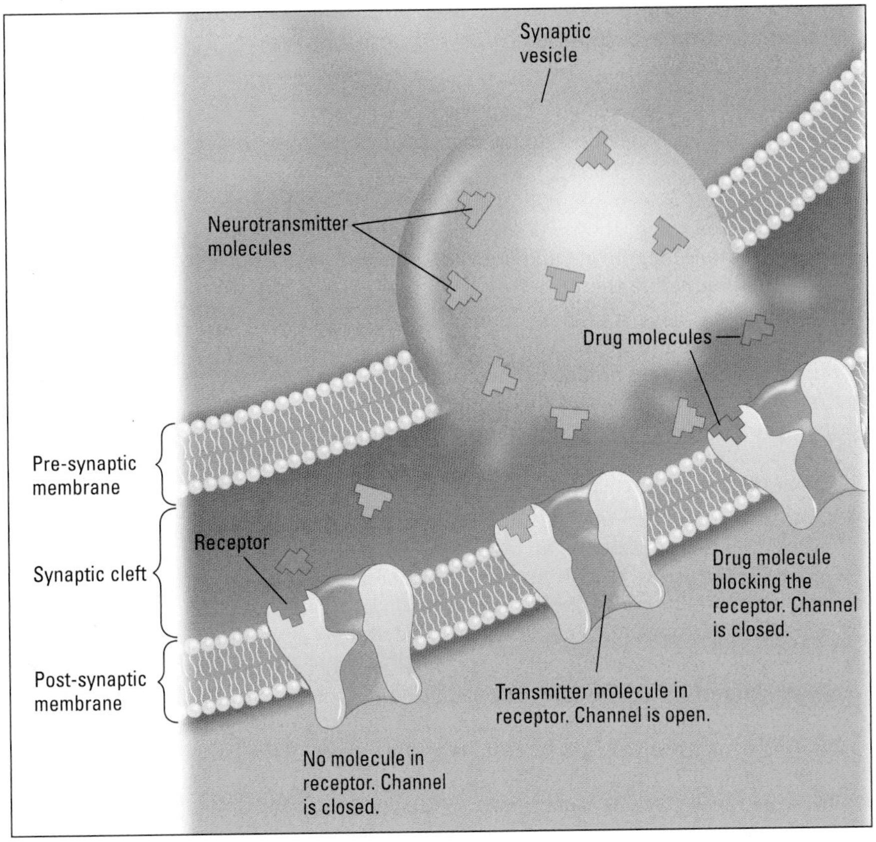

FIGURE 5.35 Lock-and-key view of drug effects in a synapse Each receptor on the membrane of the postsynaptic cell can be thought of as a keyhole, and each neurotransmitter molecule as a key that fits into it and opens the lock, causing the ion channel in the cell membrane to open. A drug molecule can serve as a substitute key and produce the same effect as the neurotransmitter, or it can serve as a misshapen key (as shown here) that occupies the keyhole without activating the lock and thus prevents the neurotransmitter from acting.

Synaptic vesicle

Neurotransmitter molecules

Drug molecules

Pre-synaptic membrane

Receptor

Synaptic cleft

Post-synaptic membrane

Drug molecule blocking the receptor. Channel is closed.

Transmitter molecule in receptor. Channel is open.

No molecule in receptor. Channel is closed.

turning the lock, thereby preventing the transmitter from having its normal effect. Many different types of neurotransmitters exist in the nervous system, and a particular drug may alter the activity of just one or several of them. Thus, drugs can be more or less specific, affecting either a small or a large class of synapses, and hence can be more or less specific in the effects they have on behavior.

How Drugs Act at Different Levels of the Behavior-Control Hierarchy

One way to imagine the many kinds of effects that drugs can have on behavior is to think of them in relation to the hierarchy of behavioral control depicted in Figure 5.22 (on p. 163). Drugs that act at a particular level of the hierarchy have behavioral effects that are consistent with the functions of that level, as described in the figure.

Curare is an example of a drug that acts at the lowest level, at synapses between motor neurons and skeletal muscle cells. This poison, long used by certain South American Indians on the tips of their arrows for hunting, paralyzes the animal that is hit. Curare paralyzes by blocking the postsynaptic receptors for acetylcholine, which is the transmitter released by skeletal motor neurons onto muscle cells. Because the muscle cells can no longer respond to acetylcholine, they can no longer contract, so the animal is unable to move. Acetylcholine is also a transmitter at many places within the central nervous system, but curare does not act in those places because it cannot pass the blood-brain barrier.

A drug that acts somewhat higher up in the movement-control hierarchy is *L-dopa,* which is used to treat Parkinson's disease. Parkinson's disease is caused by the degeneration of certain neurons whose axons originate in the brainstem and terminate in the basal ganglia. The disease is characterized by muscle tremors and severe difficulty in initiating and coordinating movements. These symptoms are manifested when the degenerating neurons fail to release a sufficient quantity of the neurotransmitter dopamine onto neurons in the basal ganglia. It might seem logical to treat these symptoms by introducing additional dopamine into the body, but dopamine cannot cross the blood-brain barrier. However, L-dopa, a precursor in the synthesis of dopamine, can cross the barrier. Once in the brain, L-dopa is converted to dopamine.

Drugs that work at the highest levels of the behavior-control hierarchy are called *psychoactive drugs,* because they influence processes that we think of as psychological. These are drugs that alter mood or level of arousal or alter one's thoughts and perceptions. Table 5.1 on the next page shows one way of categorizing psychoactive drugs and what is known about the mechanism of action of some of them, including such everyday examples as caffeine, nicotine, and alcohol. Chapter 17 describes some of the clinical uses of psychoactive drugs in the treatment of severe anxiety, depression, and other mental disorders.

> **38**
> How can the effects of curare, L-dopa, and psychoactive drugs be interpreted in terms of the hierarchical model of behavioral control?

TABLE 5.1 Some categories of psychoactive drugs

1. Behavioral stimulants and antidepressants

Drugs that increase alertness and activity level and elevate mood, including:

- *Amphetamines and cocaine* Often abused because of the psychological "high" they produce, these drugs increase the release of norepinephrine and dopamine into synapses and prolong their action there.

- *Clinical antidepressants* These counteract depression but do not produce the sleeplessness or euphoria that amphetamines and cocaine produce. One class, the *monoamine oxidase inhibitors,* increases the synaptic activity of monoamine neurotransmitters (serotonin, norepinephrine, and dopamine) by inhibiting the enzyme that breaks them down (discussed in Chapters 16 and 17).

- *Caffeine* Found in coffee, tea, and cocoa beans, this drug promotes arousal partly by activating the peripheral sympathetic nervous system. In the brain, it increases neural activity by inhibiting the postsynaptic action of adenosine, which functions as an inhibitory neuromodulator.

- *Nicotine* Found in tobacco, this drug increases activity in many neurons in the brain by acting on some of the same postsynaptic receptor sites as does the neurotransmitter acetylcholine (through the substitute-key mechanism). In this way, it also activates portions of the peripheral sympathetic nervous system, causing, as one effect, increased heart rate.

2. Tranquilizers and central-nervous-system depressants

Drugs that counteract anxiety and/or decrease alertness and activity level, including:

- *Benzodiazepines* Prescribed to counteract anxiety, these drugs (including diazepam, sold as Valium) act on postsynaptic receptors to make them more responsive to GABA, which is an inhibitory transmitter. Increased responsiveness to GABA causes a decrease in neural activity in those parts of the brain where it is present.

- *Alcohol and barbiturates* These often-abused drugs depress neural activity throughout the brain by a variety of means that are not well understood. Low doses may produce relief from anxiety, and higher doses produce sedation, sleep, unconsciousness, coma, and death, in that order. Their antianxiety effects are believed to work in the same way as those of benzodiazepines.

3. Opiates

These include *opium,* a crude extract from the opium plant; *morphine,* the most active ingredient in opium; *codeine,* an extract from opium that is chemically similar to morphine but less active; and *heroin,* which is synthesized by chemical modification of morphine. All are potent pain reducers and can cause feelings of euphoria. They produce at least some of their effects by activating neurons that normally respond to *endorphins,* a class of slow-acting transmitters that are part of the body's natural system for relieving pain (discussed in Chapter 7).

4. Antipsychotic drugs

These are prescribed mostly to treat schizophrenia. The so-called "typical" antipsychotic drugs (including chlorpromazine and haloperidol) are believed to work primarily by decreasing activity at synapses where dopamine is the transmitter. Newer, "atypical" antipsychotic drugs appear to work by a variety of other means (discussed in Chapter 17).

5. Hallucinogenic drugs

These induce hallucinations and other sensory distortions. Some, such as *mescaline* and *psilocybin,* exist naturally in plants and have a long history of use among various peoples, including Native Americans, in religious rites. Others, such as *LSD* (lysergic acid diethylamide), are synthetic compounds. Most are structurally similar to neurotransmitters, and they are believed to act either by mimicking or blocking transmitters that they resemble. Both LSD and psilocybin resemble the transmitter serotonin.

Source: Compiled largely from McKim, W. A. (2007) *Drugs and behavior: An introduction to behavioral pharmacology* (6th ed.) Upper Saddle River, NJ: Prentice-Hall.

SECTION REVIEW

Hormones and drugs in the bloodstream can affect the nervous system and thus behavior.

Hormones

➤ Hormones are chemical messengers secreted into the bloodstream. They are chemically similar (sometimes identical) to neurotransmitters but travel farther and exert their effects on many different target tissues.

➤ Hormones can influence behavior by affecting bodily growth, metabolism, and brain activity, including brain activity responsible for drives and moods.

➤ Hormonal effects can be long term or even permanent, as in the case of prenatal testosterone's effects on brain development. They can also be short term, as in the case of stress hormones' effects in preparing for an emergency.

➤ The pituitary gland controls hormone production by other glands, but is itself controlled by the brain.

Drugs

➤ Drugs can be introduced into the bloodstream in several ways. To act directly on the brain, they must pass through the blood-brain barrier.

➤ Drugs influence behavior largely by influencing synaptic transmission. They may stimulate neurotransmitter release, mimic neurotransmitter effects, or block receptors.

➤ Drugs can affect different levels of the behavior-control hierarchy. Curare works at the bottom level, L-dopa works at a middle level, and psychoactive drugs such as alcohol work at the top.

Concluding Thoughts

Hippocrates was right: The brain is the organ of the mind. The mind is a set of processes (feeling, thinking, initiating action, and so on) carried out by physical activities in the brain. The brain, of course, does not work in isolation from the rest of the body or the environment. It needs input from sensory nerves, is affected by chemicals carried in the blood, and acts through motor nerves and (to a lesser degree) hormones. Yet the brain is the center of all that we call the mind: It contains the mechanisms needed to analyze all inputs and organize all outputs.

In reviewing this chapter, so full of terms and details, you may find it useful to keep the following broad points in mind:

1. The value of a functionalist perspective As you review the structures described in this chapter—ranging from the little ones, such as *synaptic vesicles* and *neurohormones,* to the big ones, such as the *cerebellum* and *autonomic nervous system*—ask yourself, for each: What is it for? That is, what role does it play in the workings of the larger machine that is the human being? How is it related to other parts of the machine, and how can variations in it affect human behavior? The structures are a lot easier to remember, and certainly more interesting, if you think of them in terms of their roles in a larger system rather than as isolated entities.

2. Uses of the hierarchical model The hierarchical model described in this chapter (summarized in Figure 5.22 on page 163) provides a way to organize thinking about the nervous system. It is a useful memory scheme because it allows us to see each part in relation to the whole. It summarizes, in a very general way, the effects of damage to different parts of the nervous system. It also summarizes, again in a general way, the effects of drugs that act in different parts of the nervous system. As you review the discussion of the central nervous system, and the later discussion of drugs, tie the bits and pieces together into the hierarchical model.

3. Brain science in relation to the rest of psychology As more is learned about the brain, knowledge about it becomes relevant to broader areas of psychology. In later chapters, you will read about the brain in relation to psychology's attempt to understand basic processes of motivation, sensation, memory, and thought. Still later, you will read of brain-based theories of mental disorders and of drugs that are believed to alleviate specific mental disorders through their interactions with neurotransmitters. Your review of this chapter will be more effective if you try to anticipate the ways that each topic discussed here might be relevant later. Ask yourself: Why might a *psychologist* want to know about this structure or process? You may be surprised at how often you come up with a good answer.

Further Reading

Allan Siegel & Hredy Sapru (2007). *Essential neuroscience.* Baltimore: Lippincott Williams & Wilkins

This is an excellent source for students who would like to go further in learning about the nervous system or some portion of it. Although it is designed for medical students, it is written in such a clear manner that a motivated undergraduate student would have no difficulty understanding it and learning from it. The illustrations are exceptionally clear. You are not likely to want to read this cover-to-cover, but it is a great resource if you want to find out more about any particular part of the nervous system.

Daniel Wegner (2002). *The illusion of conscious will.* Cambridge, MA: MIT Press.

An underlying assumption of the chapter you have just read is that events in our nervous system make us do what we do. Where, then, does free will come in? Wegner's thesis in this enjoyable book is that the experience of willing a movement is not the cause of a movement, but derives from brain activity that occurs milliseconds *after* the

nervous system has begun to produce the movement. Wegner explores the function of this feeling and presents examples of situations in which our actual movements are not the same as those that we consciously feel that we have willed.

Norman Doidge (2007). *The brain that changes itself.* New York: Viking.

This is a fun-to-read book about the plasticity of the human brain. It describes case histories of brain-damaged patients who made remarkable recoveries. It is also about the science behind those recoveries and about some of the scientists who have pioneered the study of the brain's plasticity—people such as Alvaro Pacual-Leone, whose work I mentioned in this chapter. You can read here about a woman who gets along quite well with only half a brain, about people who have recovered from strokes and other serious brain injuries through deliberate brain exercises, and about brain-stimulating programs that seem to help children with learning disabilities overcome those disabilities.

Steven Johnson (2005). *Mind wide open: Your brain and the neuroscience of everyday life.* New York: Scribner.

Steven Johnson is a popular writer, not a psychologist or neuroscientist, and this is as nontechnical a book about the brain and mind as you are likely to find. Johnson's quest is to come to grips with certain aspects of his own emotions, thoughts, and actions, and to do so he interviews brain scientists, submits himself to various brain tests and biofeedback procedures, and writes philosophically and humorously about his experiences. It is a fun yet thought-provoking entryway into the world of the brain, for the person who has just begun to think about it.

William McKim (2007). *Drugs and behavior: An introduction to behavioral pharmacology* (6th ed.). Upper Saddle River, NJ: Prentice-Hall.

Each major class of drugs that alters mood or behavior is discussed here in a separate chapter. McKim describes clearly not just the behavioral effects and physiological mechanisms of each drug but also the drug's role in human history and culture.

Mechanisms of Motivation and Emotion

6

The kaleidoscope that makes a day or a year of mental life has both fast-moving and slow-moving components. Sensations, perceptions, thoughts, and muscle movements flit through our consciousness and behavior at speeds measured in milliseconds. But slower changes, measurable in minutes or hours, modulate and help direct these rapid changes. These slower-changing components of the mind are referred to as *behavioral states*; they include variations in motivation, emotion, and level of arousal.

Are you hungry right now, or angry or sleepy? Even as you attempt to study this chapter, your mental state affects your capacity to pay attention, and it may direct your attention to some things over others. If you are hungry, your thoughts of food may capture most of your attention. If you are sleepy, your reaction even to the most interesting ideas in the chapter might be "oh hmmmm . . . zzzzzz." Clearly, your mental state affects your momentary thoughts and actions. But what affects your mental state? What exactly makes you hungry, angry, or sleepy? This question links psychology tightly to the study of the brain and its interactions with the body's internal environment as well as the external environment.

This chapter is about the physiological underpinnings of motivation and emotion. You will read first about the general concept of motivation from a physiological perspective, then about reward mechanisms in the brain, and then about hunger, the sexual drive, sleep, dreams, and emotionality—in that order. Social and cultural influences on motivation and emotion, which are only touched on here, are discussed more fully in later chapters (especially Chapters 12 and 14).

■ General Principles of Motivation

To *motivate,* in the most general sense of the term, is to set in motion. In psychology, the term **motivation** is often used to refer to the entire constellation of factors, some inside the organism and some outside, that cause an individual to behave in a particular way at a particular time. Motivation defined this way is a very broad concept, almost as broad as all of psychology. Every chapter in this book deals with one or another facet of motivation. Genes, learning, physiological variables, perceptual and thought processes, developmental variables, social experiences, and personality characteristics can all play a part in motivation.

Motivation The predatory drive of this cat is activated by the goldfish—the incentive.

1 ─────────────────

How do drives and incentives (a) complement one another and (b) influence one another in their contributions to motivation?

A more precise label for the specific topic of our present discussion is **motivational state** or **drive.** These terms are used interchangeably to denote an internal condition that orients an individual toward a specific category of goals and that can change over time in a reversible way (the drive can increase and then decrease). Different drives direct a person toward different goals. *Hunger* orients one toward food, sex toward sexual gratification, curiosity toward novel stimuli, and so on.

Drives in psychology are generally thought of as hypothetical constructs. The psychologist does not observe a state of hunger, thirst, or curiosity inside the animal but infers the existence of that state from the animal's behavior. An animal is said to be hungry if it behaves in ways that bring it closer to food, to be sexually motivated if it behaves in ways that bring it into contact with a sexual partner, and to be curious if it seeks out and explores new environments. To say that the drive varies over time is to say that the animal will work harder, or accept more discomfort, to attain the goal at some times than at others. The assumption is that something inside the animal changes, causing it to behave differently, at different times in the same environment.

◀ But the inside interacts constantly with the outside. Motivated behavior is directed toward *incentives,* the sought-after objects or ends that exist in the external environment. Incentives are also called *reinforcers* (the term used in Chapter 4), *rewards,* or *goals.* The motivational state that leads you to stand in line at the cafeteria is presumably hunger, but the incentive for doing so is the hamburger you intend to purchase. Drives and incentives complement one another in the control of behavior; if one is weak, the other must be strong to motivate the goal-directed action. Thus, if you know that the cafeteria's hamburger tastes like cardboard (weak incentive), you are likely to wait in line for it only if your hunger drive is strong; but if the cafeteria serves a really great hamburger (strong incentive), you are likely to wait even if your hunger drive is weak.

Drives and incentives not only complement each other but also influence each other's strength. A strong drive can enhance the attractiveness (incentive value) of a particular object: If you are very hungry, even a hamburger that tastes like cardboard might seem quite attractive. Conversely, a strong incentive can strengthen a drive: The savory aroma of a broiling hamburger wafting your way as you wait in line might increase your hunger drive, which might in turn induce you to eat something that previously wouldn't have interested you if, by the time you get to the grill, all the hamburgers are gone.

Varieties of Drives

In general, drives motivate us toward goals that promote our survival and reproduction. Some drives promote survival by helping us maintain the internal bodily conditions that are essential for life.

Drives That Help Preserve Homeostasis

In a now classic book entitled *The Wisdom of the Body* (1932/1963), the physiologist Walter B. Cannon described simply and elegantly the requirements of the tissues of the human body. For life to be sustained, certain substances and characteristics within the body must be kept within a restricted range, going neither above nor below certain levels. These include body temperature, oxygen, minerals, water, and energy-producing food molecules. Physiological processes, such as digestion and respiration, must continually work toward achieving what Cannon termed **homeostasis,** the constancy of internal conditions that the body must actively maintain. Most relevant for psychology, Cannon pointed out that maintenance of homeostasis involves the organism's outward behavior as well as its internal processes. To stay alive, individuals must find and consume foods, salts, and water and must maintain their body temperature through such means as finding shelter. Cannon theorized that the basic physiological underpinning for some drives is a loss of homeostasis, which acts on the nervous system to induce behavior designed to correct the imbalance.

➤ ─ ─ ─ ─ ─ ─ ─ ─ ─ ─ ─ ─ ─ **2**

How is the concept of homeostasis related to that of drive? How is this relationship demonstrated in the case of a little boy who craved salt?

Photo Edit

Ahh, homeostasis When the body's water level is reduced as a result of prolonged exertion, nothing is more satisfying than replenishing it. Thirst is a typical example of a regulatory drive.

Following Cannon, psychologists and physiologists performed experiments showing that animals indeed do behave in accordance with the needs of their bodily tissues. For example, if the caloric (energy) content of its food is increased or decreased, an animal will compensate by eating less or more of it, keeping the daily intake of calories relatively constant. As another example, removal of the adrenal glands causes an animal to lose too much salt in its urine (because one of the adrenal hormones is essential for conserving salt). This loss of salt dramatically increases the animal's drive to seek out and eat extra salt, which keeps the animal alive as long as salt is available (Stricker, 1973).

The force of homeostasis in human behavior was dramatically and poignantly illustrated by the clinical case of a boy, referred to as D. W., who when 1 year old developed a great craving for salt (Wilkins & Richter, 1940). His favorite foods were salted crackers, pretzels, potato chips, olives, and pickles; he would also take salt directly from the shaker. When salt was denied him, he would cry until his parents gave in, and when he learned to speak, salt was one of his first and favorite words. D. W. survived until the age of 3½, when he was hospitalized for other symptoms and placed on a standard hospital diet. The hospital staff would not yield to his demands for salt, and he died within a few days. An autopsy revealed that his adrenal glands were deficient; only then did D. W.'s doctors realize that his salt craving came from physiological need. His strong drive for salt and his ability to manipulate his parents into supplying it, even though they were unaware that he needed it, had kept D. W. alive for more than 2 years after the onset of the adrenal deficiency—powerful evidence for "the wisdom of the body."

Limitations of Homeostasis: Regulatory and Nonregulatory Drives

Homeostasis is a useful concept for understanding hunger, thirst, and the drives for salt, oxygen, and an appropriate body temperature, but not for understanding many other drives. Consider sex, for example. People are highly motivated to engage in sex, and sex serves an obvious evolutionary function, but there is no tissue need for it. No vital bodily substance is affected by engaging in sexual behavior; nobody

➤ ─ ─ ─ ─ ─ ─ ─ ─ ─ ─ ─ ─ ─ **3**

What is the distinction between regulatory and nonregulatory drives, and how can mammalian drives be classified into five categories based on function?

can die from lack of sex (despite what an overly amorous someone may have told you). Psychologists therefore find it useful to distinguish between two general classes of drives—regulatory and nonregulatory. A **regulatory drive** is one, like hunger, that helps preserve homeostasis, and a **nonregulatory drive** is one, like sex, that serves some other purpose.

A Functional Classification of Mammalian Drives

One way to think about the whole set of drives that we share with other mammals is to categorize them in accordance with their evolutionary functions—their roles in promoting survival and reproduction. From an evolutionary perspective, it is useful to distinguish among the following five categories of mammalian drives:

1. *Regulatory drives.* As already noted, these are drives that promote survival by helping to maintain the body's homeostasis. Hunger and thirst are prime examples.

2. *Safety drives.* These are drives that motivate an animal to avoid, escape, or fend off dangers such as precipices, predators, or enemies. The most obvious safety drive is fear, which motivates individuals to flee from danger. Another is anger, which is manifested when fight (or threatening to fight) rather than flight is needed to ensure one's safety. I will argue later in this chapter that sleep is also a safety drive. It evolved at least partly as a means of keeping animals tucked quietly away during that part of each 24-hour day when they would be most in danger if they were moving around.

3. *Reproductive drives.* The most obvious of these are the sexual drive and the drive to care for young once they are born. When they are at a peak, these drives can be extraordinarily powerful. Animals (including people) will risk their lives to mate and to protect their offspring. As discussed in Chapter 3, sexual jealousy, including the anger associated with it, also serves the function of reproduction to the degree that it promotes the fidelity of one's sexual partner.

4. *Social drives.* Most mammals, and especially humans, require the cooperation of others to survive. The social drives include the drives for friendship and for acceptance and approval by the social groups of which one is a part. In humans, these drives can be as powerful as the regulatory, safety, and reproductive drives. People will risk their lives for friendship and for social approval. The social drives figure prominently in the discussions that run through Chapters 12, 13, and 14 of this book.

5. *Educative drives.* These consist primarily of the drives to play and to explore (curiosity). As discussed in Chapter 4, the young of nearly all mammals practice life-sustaining skills through play, and mammals of all ages acquire useful information about their environment by exploring novel objects and territories. When other drives are not too pressing, the drives for play and exploration come to the fore.

Human Drives That Seem Not to Promote Survival or Reproduction

4
What are two possible explanations of the universal human drives for art, music, and literature?

◄ Not all of human motivation is easily understood in terms of survival and reproduction. For instance, humans everywhere like to produce and experience art, music, and literature (including oral stories and poetry). What motivates these activities? Have we evolved special aesthetic drives? If so, what adaptive functions prompted the natural selection of such drives?

At present, these questions are much debated and there is no firm answer. My own view is that the pursuits of art, music, and literature are natural extensions of our drives for play and exploration. These pursuits can exercise perceptual and motor skills, imagination, and creative thinking in ways that may be useful in future real-life situations and can also provide us with ideas for governing our own lives. Like other playful and exploratory activities, these pursuits help our minds to grow during periods when there are no more pressing survival needs that must be fulfilled.

A somewhat different (but not incompatible) view, presented by Steven Pinker (1997), is that art, music, and literature appeal to us not because we have special drives for them but because they tap into many of our already existing drives and proclivities, which evolved for other purposes. For example, in describing the appeal of fiction, Pinker (1997, p. 539) writes: "When we are absorbed in a book or movie, we get to see breathtaking landscapes, hobnob with important people, fall in love with ravishing men and women, protect loved ones, attain impossible goals, and defeat wicked enemies." In this example, a book or movie appeals to our drives for sex, love, social esteem, parenting, achievement, and aggression. To suggest that art, music, and literature may be vicarious means of satisfying other drives rather than drives in and of themselves is not to diminish them. These pursuits enrich our lives immensely; they extend us beyond evolution's narrow dictates of mere survival and reproduction.

Of course, some things that people become motivated for are truly harmful. Drug addictions and compulsive gambling are artificial drives, created by human inventions, which can ruin people's lives. How these tap artificially into our natural drive mechanisms is a topic to which we shall return soon.

Early art We have no idea whether or not the person who produced this drawing—about 18,000 years ago in one of the Lascaux Caves, in France—had a concept of art or a word for it. To the modern eye, however, this is a work of art. It may represent a universal human proclivity.

Serge de Sazo/Photo Researchers

Drives as States of the Brain

I said that drives are normally considered to be hypothetical entities, inferred from observed behavior. Yet, essentially all psychologists would agree that drives are products of physical processes within the body, particularly within the brain. In theory, at least, every drive that we experience corresponds with some state of the brain.

According to the ***central-state theory of drives,*** which will guide much of the discussion in this chapter, different drives correspond to neural activity in different sets of neurons in the brain. A set of neurons in which activity constitutes a drive is called a ***central drive system.*** Although the central drive systems for different drives must be at least partly different from one another, they may have overlapping components. For example, because hunger and sex are different drives, the neural circuits for them cannot be identical. If they were, hunger and sex would always occur in tandem, the drives would always rise and fall together. However, those circuits may share components that produce behavioral effects common to both drives, such as increased alertness.

What characteristics must a set of neurons have to serve as a central drive system? First, it must receive and integrate the various signals that can raise or lower the drive state. For hunger, these signals include chemicals in the blood, the presence or absence of food in the stomach, and the sight and smell of food in the environment. Second, a central drive system must act on all the neural processes that would be involved in carrying out the motivated behavior. It must direct perceptual mechanisms toward stimuli related to the goal, cognitive mechanisms toward working out strategies to achieve the goal, and motor mechanisms toward producing the appropriate movements. Look back at Figure 5.22 (p. 163), which depicts a hierarchical model of the control of action, with mechanisms involved in motivation and planning at the top. The central drive systems are part of that top level of the hierarchy. To affect behavior (for example, to cause a hungry person to cross a room for some peanuts), they must influence the activity of motor systems at lower levels of the hierarchy.

5

In theory, what characteristics must a set of neurons have to function as a central drive system? What characteristics of the hypothalamus seem to suit it to be a hub of such systems?

FIGURE 6.1 Location of the **hypothalamus** The hypothalamus is ideally situated to serve as a hub for central drive systems. It has strong connections to the brainstem below, the limbic system and cerebral cortex above, and the endocrine system (by way of its tie to the pituitary gland).

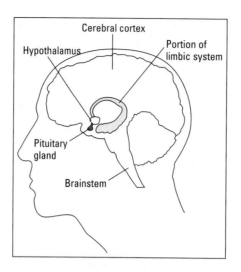

Researchers have sound reasons to believe that the hypothalamus is the hub of many central drive systems. Anatomically, this brain structure is ideally located to play such a role (see Figure 6.1). It is centered at the base of the brain, just above the brainstem, and is strongly interconnected with higher areas of the brain. It also has direct connections to nerves that carry input from, and autonomic motor output to, the body's internal organs. It has many capillaries and is more sensitive to hormones and other substances carried by the blood than are other brain areas. Finally, through its connections to the pituitary gland, it controls the release of many hormones (as described in Chapter 5). Thus, the hypothalamus has all the inputs and outputs that central drive systems would be expected to have. And, as you will see later in the chapter, small disruptions in particular parts of the hypothalamus can have dramatic effects on an animal's drives.

SECTION REVIEW

Drives are reversible internal conditions that orient individuals toward specific types of goals.

Varieties of Drives

➤ Regulatory drives (e.g., hunger) promote homeostasis, while nonregulatory drives (e.g., sex) serve other purposes.

➤ Mammalian drives can be classified by function into regulatory, safety, reproductive, social, and educative categories.

➤ Humans everywhere also exhibit aesthetic drives; the evolutionary functions of these are not obvious.

Drives as States of the Brain

➤ According to the central-state drive theory, different drives correspond to neural activity in different but overlapping central drive systems in the brain.

➤ The hypothalamus is ideally located to be a hub of central drive systems.

■ Reward Mechanisms of the Brain

As I noted in the previous section, motivated behavior involves the pursuit of *rewards* (also known as incentives, goals, or reinforcers). Let us now look more closely at the concept of reward and at research into how rewards act on the brain to promote and reinforce the behaviors that led to them.

Three Components of Reward: Liking, Wanting, and Reinforcement

6
What are three interrelated components of the concept of reward?

◄ Psychologically, the term *reward* has three interrelated but in some ways separable meanings. A reward is something that we *like*, something that we *want*, and something that serves as a *reinforcer* in learning (Berridge & Kringelbach, 2008).

Liking refers to the subjective feeling of pleasure, or satisfaction, that occurs when one receives a reward. We know this feeling from our own experience. We experience pleasure from good food when we are hungry, from water when we are thirsty, from drifting off to sleep when we are tired, and from sexual activity when we are sexually motivated. We also experience pleasure from pay, praise, the company of good friends, play, music, discoveries made through exploration, and our own assessment of a job well done. Most of the things we seek in life bring us pleasure when we obtain them. We have no way to know for sure that other mammals also experience pleasure from the rewards they receive, but their behavior certainly suggests that they do (see Figure 6.2).

Wanting refers to the desire to obtain a reward. This is the component of reward that links most clearly to the concept of motivation. To want something is to be motivated to get it. Whereas pleasure occurs when a reward is received, wanting occurs before it is received. Wanting is typically measured by assessing the amount of effort an individual will exert, or the amount of pain the individual will bear, in order to obtain the reward. Usually objects that are wanted are also liked, but, as you will see later, it is possible to separate the two.

Reinforcement refers to the effects that rewards have in promoting learning. As discussed in Chapter 4 (in the section on operant conditioning), animals and people learn to attend to stimuli that signal the availability of rewards, and they learn to make responses that bring rewards in the presence of those stimuli. Somehow, through its effects on the brain, a reward helps to stamp in, or *reinforce,* the memory of stimuli and actions that occurred just before the reward was received. Such learning helps the individual to become more effective in finding and procuring the same type of reward in the future.

Studies of the brain to which we now turn have provided some clues to the mechanisms of each of these three components of reward.

FIGURE 6.2 Liking Many species of mammals show a similar facial reaction to tasty foods. The reaction includes a tongue protrusion, which looks as if the individual were lapping up the last bits of the food. This expression has been used as an objective index of "liking" in research involving food rewards in laboratory rats. (Berridge & Robinson, 2003.)

Identification of Reward Neurons in the Brain

The study of brain mechanisms of reward was initiated in the 1950s, when James Olds and Peter Milner made a remarkable discovery. These researchers observed, by accident at first, that when rats received electrical stimulation through thin wires implanted in certain brain areas, they behaved as if they were trying to get more of that stimulation. For example, if a rat happened to receive the stimulation while exploring a particular corner of the cage, the animal would return repeatedly to that corner. To see if such brain stimulation would serve as a reinforcer for learning, Olds and Milner tested rats in an apparatus in which they could electrically stimulate their own brains by pressing a lever (see Figure 6.3). With electrodes placed in certain brain areas, rats learned very quickly to press the lever and continued to press at high rates, sometimes for many hours without stopping (Olds & Milner, 1954).

7

How did Olds and Milner identify reward pathways in the brain?

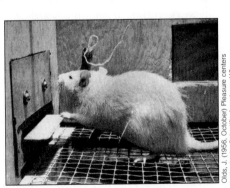

FIGURE 6.3 Lever pressing for electrical stimulation to the brain Each time this rat presses the lever, it receives a brief pulse of electrical current through an electrode implanted in its brain. Some of Olds's rats continued to press the lever for 24 hours without rest, as often as 5000 times per hour. (From Olds, 1956.)

Subsequent research showed that rats and other animals will work hardest and longest to stimulate a tract in the brain called the ***medial forebrain bundle.*** The neurons of this tract that are most crucial for this rewarding effect have their cell bodies in nuclei in the midbrain and synaptic terminals in a large nucleus in the basal ganglia called the ***nucleus accumbens*** [uh-**cum**-bens] (see Figure 6.4 on the next page). The nucleus accumbens itself has connections to large areas of the limbic system and the cerebral cortex, and it is now understood to be a crucial center for the behavioral effects of rewards, in humans as well as in other mammals.

When Olds and Milner inserted electrodes into the medial forebrain bundle, they were tapping artificially but very effectively into the brain's natural reward

8

What is some evidence that the medial forebrain bundle and nucleus accumbens are essential pathways for the effects of a wide variety of rewards?

FIGURE 6.4 A reward pathway in the brain The medial forebrain bundle is a neural tract consisting of neurons whose cell bodies are in nuclei in the midbrain and whose synaptic terminals are in the nucleus accumbens of the basal ganglia. Rats will quickly learn to press a lever to electrically stimulate the medial forebrain bundle or the nucleus accumbens.

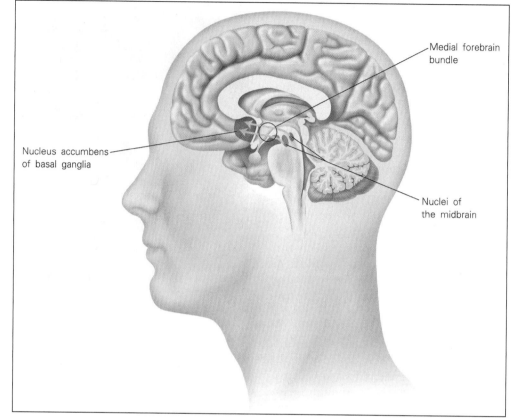

system. Subsequent research, involving the recording of activity in the brain, has shown that the medial forebrain bundle and the nucleus accumbens become active in all sorts of situations in which an individual receives a reward, whether the reward is food, opportunity to copulate, novel objects to explore, or (in humans) a prize received for winning a game (Breiter & others, 2001; Damsma & others, 1992; Fiorello & others, 2003). Moreover, damage to either of these brain structures destroys all sorts of motivated behaviors (Koop & others, 2008; Grossman, 1979). Without a functioning medial forebrain bundle or nucleus accumbens, animals will not work to find or obtain rewards and will die unless they are provided with food and water through a stomach tube.

Separating the "Liking" and "Wanting" Systems

9

What is some evidence that different neurotransmitters in the nucleus accumbens are involved in the "wanting" and "liking" components of reward?

Many of the neurons of the medial forebrain bundle that terminate in the nucleus accumbens release **dopamine** [**dope**-uh-mean] as their neurotransmitter. This release appears to be essential for the "wanting" component of reward, but not for the "liking" component. Animals that have been well trained to press a lever for some reward, such as food, show a release of dopamine into the nucleus accumbens just before they begin to press the lever, but not after they receive the reward (Phillips & others, 2003). This pattern is consistent with the idea that dopamine helps motivate the animal to obtain the reward (promotes "wanting") but is not essential for the pleasure received from obtaining the reward. Other research shows that the larger the expected reward, the greater the degree of dopamine release in the nucleus accumbens (Roesch & others, 2007).

More direct evidence that dopamine is involved in "wanting" but not "liking" comes from studies in which rats are treated with drugs that block the effect of dopamine in the nucleus accumbens. These animals continue to consume foods, copulate with sexual partners, and explore novel stimuli that are immediately present. They also continue to exhibit the facial "liking" expression (shown in Figure 6.2) when they taste a sugar solution. However, they do not continue to seek out or work for rewards that are not immediately present (Berridge & Robinson, 2003; López & Ettenberg, 2002; Zhang & others, 2003). Their behavior suggests that they continue to enjoy the consumption of rewards but are no longer concerned with (no longer behave as if they want) rewards that are absent. Conversely, drugs that increase the activity of dopamine in the nucleus accumbens increase the rate at which rats and other animals will work for food, but do not increase the facial "liking" response to sucrose or the animal's consumption of food that is immediately available (Berridge & Robinson, 2003).

If dopamine is responsible for the "wanting" component of reward, what is responsible for the "liking" component? Some of the neurons of the medial forebrain bundle that terminate in the nucleus accumbens release not dopamine but a different transmitter, one that is in the **endorphin** [en-**dorf**-in] family. The term endorphin is short for endogenous morphine-like substance. (Endogenous means "created within the body.") Endorphins are chemicals created within the body that have effects similar to those of morphine and other opiate drugs such as opium and heroin. As discussed in Chapter 7, endorphins are best known for their role in inhibiting the sense of pain. A number of experiments suggest, however, that endorphins released into the nucleus accumbens are also crucial for the immediate pleasure experienced when rewards are received or consumed. Injections, into the nucleus accumbens, of drugs that activate endorphin receptors increase the facial "liking" reaction to sucrose (Smith & Berridge, 2007) and also increase the amount of immediately present food that an animal will eat (Zhang & Kelley, 2000). In humans, drugs that decrease the effectiveness of endorphins have been reported to decrease people's perceived enjoyment of food and other rewards (Yeomans & Gray, 1996).

Role of Dopamine in Reinforcement for Learning

The learning component of reward is closely related to the "wanting" component. Animals learn that certain cues signal the availability of a reward, and those cues prompt the animal to search for or work for the reward, which is the behavioral indicator of "wanting." The release of dopamine into the nucleus accumbens appears to be crucial not just for motivating animals to work for rewards, but also for their ability to learn to use cues to predict when and where rewards are available. One line of evidence for this is the observation that dopamine release promotes long-term potentiation (LTP) of neural connections within the nucleus accumbens (Reynolds & others, 2001). As discussed in Chapter 5, LTP is believed to be part of the cellular basis for learning throughout the brain.

Other evidence comes from studies in which the amount of dopamine released into the nucleus accumbens is directly measured as animals anticipate and receive rewards (Day & others, 2007; Schultz, 1998). If food is occasionally, at unpredictable times, presented to a hungry monkey or rat, a burst of dopamine is released into the nucleus accumbens each time food is presented. If the situation is then changed so that a signal light comes on a few seconds prior to each presentation of food, the animal soon learns to anticipate food each time the light comes on. In this new situation, after several trials, a burst of dopamine release occurs when the light comes on, but not when food is presented. The animal eats and apparently enjoys the food, but no dopamine release accompanies that behavior.

This pattern of dopamine release is consistent with the idea that dopamine is involved in new learning (Schultz, 1998). When a reward is unexpected, dopamine release immediately after the reward helps to reinforce an association between the reward and any stimulus or response that happened to precede it. When the cues and responses leading to a reward have already been well learned, however, there is no need for further reinforcement of that learning, and dopamine release in response to the reward (the food) ceases. Dopamine release now occurs in response to the signal preceding reward (the light), because now the animal's interest lies in learning how to predict when the signal will appear or how to make it appear.

> ⟩— — — — — — — — — — — — — **10**
>
> **What evidence suggests that dopamine is crucial to the capacity of rewardsto to to promote new learning—that is, to serve as reinforcers?**

11

How does an understanding of the brain's reward system help us to understand drug addiction and compulsive gambling?

◄ Drug Addiction: Hijacking the Brain's Reward System

When Olds and Milner delivered electrical impulses into the medial forebrain bundle in rats, they were short-circuiting the rats' natural reward systems. When people take drugs such as cocaine, amphetamine, heroin, or opium they are doing essentially that same thing with their own brains. All these drugs, and other often-abused drugs as well, exert their euphoric and habit-producing effects through action on the brain's reward pathways (Koop & others, 2008). In various ways, these drugs mimic or promote the effects of dopamine and endorphins in the nucleus accumbens.

Wanting without liking After repeated use, a drug such as cocaine or heroin continues to promote dopamine release in the brain, and thus to reinforce "wanting," but the drug may no longer promote endorphin release, so the "liking" response no longer occurs.

Rats fitted with mechanisms for pumping drugs into their bloodstreams will self-administer cocaine and other such drugs, and become addicted, but will stop self-administering the drugs if the nucleus accumbens is destroyed or chemically blocked (Wise, 1996). Rats will work as hard to administer tiny amounts of cocaine or amphetamine through a cannula (tiny tube) directly into the nucleus accumbens as they will to administer much larger amounts into the bloodstream (Hoebel & others, 1983; Wood & Emmett-Oglesby, 1989). These findings are consistent with other evidence that the nucleus accumbens is a key area where drugs act to produce their addictive effects.

Our understanding of the brain's reward mechanisms gives us a clue as to why such drugs are addictive. Not only do they produce an immediate sense of euphoria, but even more significant for the problem of addiction, they strongly activate the dopamine-receiving neurons in the nucleus accumbens that are responsible for promoting reward-based learning. Normal rewards, such as food, activate these neurons only when the reward is unexpected; but cocaine and other addictive drugs, through their direct chemical effects, activate these neurons every time the drug is taken. The result may be a sort of super learning (Hyman & others, 2006). With each dose of the drug, the dopamine response acts to reinforce, once again, associations between any cues that are present in the environment and the feelings and behaviors of wanting and taking the drug. The result is the buildup of an extraordinarily strong craving and habit, which are triggered whenever cues that have been present during past drug-taking are present.

It has often been observed that drug addicts gradually lose their "liking" of the drug (experience less pleasure) over time, even while their "wanting" of the drug increases (Kelley & Berridge, 2002). The loss in liking occurs, presumably, because of drug-induced changes in the brain that reduce the endorphin-mediated pleasure response. However, because the dopamine response is not reduced, the learned drug craving and habit continue to grow stronger with each dose (Kelley & Berridge, 2002; Nestler & Malenka, 2004). The craving itself, rather than any expected pleasure, becomes the main reason for taking the drug. Drug taking becomes a compulsion rather than something that one freely chooses to do for pleasure. (Another reason why drug addicts continue to take drugs, having to do with conditioned counteractive responses, is discussed in Chapter 4.)

A Brain-Based Theory of Compulsive Gambling

In North America somewhere between 1 and 2 percent of adults suffer from a compulsive, pathological drive to gamble (Grant & others, 2004), a drive that persists even though it may leave the person and his or her family in financial ruins. Compulsive gambling is in some ways similar to drug addiction (Holden, 2001). Gamblers claim to feel a euphoric high when they are gaming and winning, and to experience withdrawal symptoms—such as sweating, restlessness, and sleeplessness—when they try to abstain. Every cue in the environment that has been previously associated with gambling elicits in them a strong, often irresistible urge to gamble. Our understanding of the brain's reward mechanisms gives us some clues about the origins of this compulsion.

Brain imaging studies (using the fMRI technique, discussed in Chapter 5) with healthy human subjects have revealed that games of chance, with monetary rewards, are powerful activators of the nucleus accumbens and other structures known to be part of the brain's reward system (Breiter & others, 2001; Knutsen & others, 2001). Because the payoff is never predictable, every instance of payoff results in a new burst of dopamine release in the nucleus accumbens, no matter how many times the person plays. Thus, gambling, like drug taking, overrides the brain's dopamine-conserving mechanism—the mechanism that shuts off the dopamine response once the reward has become predictable.

Consciously, the person may know that the game pays off in a way that is unpredictable and uninfluenced by anything that he or she does, but the brain's primitive reward system nevertheless behaves as if it is constantly trying to learn how to predict and produce the reward. The repeated reinforcement, by dopamine, of associations between payoffs and the cues and behaviors that precede each payoff results in the buildup of an abnormally strong habit.

People who, for genetic reasons, have high levels of dopamine receptors in their brains have an unusually high susceptibility to compulsive gambling (Sabbatini da Silva Lobo & others, 2007). The same is true for people who, because of Parkinson's disease or other disorders, are taking drugs that increase the potency of dopamine transmission in the brain (Giladi & others, 2007; Quickfall & Suchowersky, 2007). These findings are consistent with the theory that compulsive gambling is reinforced by the dopamine response to unpredicted rewards.

JOEL RYAN/PA Photos/Landov

Internet gambling Whether done on the Internet or at an actual casino, gambling can become compulsive. Because wins are essentially random and unpredictable, each win may result in a new burst of dopamine release, which helps to create the compulsion.

SECTION REVIEW

Brain reward systems mediate three aspects of reward: wanting, liking, & reinforcement.

Neurochemistry of Reward

➤ The medial forebrain bundle and nucleus accumbens contain essential pathways of the brain's reward system. Animals will work for electrical stimulation in these areas.

➤ The release of dopamine into the nucleus accumbens is associated with wanting; the release of endorphins into this area is associated with liking.

➤ The release of dopamine into the nucleus accumbens is also crucial to reinforcement; it promotes learning how to predict and obtain a given reward.

Drug Addiction and Compulsive Gambling

➤ Addictive drugs cause dopamine release into the nucleus accumbens each time they are taken, which may cause super-reinforcement of cues and actions associated with obtaining the drug; hence addiction.

➤ Because of the unpredictability of rewards in gambling, each reward may stimulate release of dopamine into the nucleus accumbens, resulting in super-reinforcement of cues and actions associated with gambling.

■ Hunger: An Example of a Regulatory Drive

It is no accident that eating is one of life's great pleasures. Throughout our evolutionary history, the difficulty of finding adequate food was one of the major barriers, if not the major barrier, to survival. As a result, natural selection built into us (and other animals) powerful, robust hunger mechanisms that lead us to search for food, to eat when food is available, and to experience pleasure when we eat. Natural selection also built into us satiety mechanisms, which tend to keep us from overeating and becoming obese. But the satiety mechanisms are not as robust as the hunger mechanisms. In our evolutionary history, food scarcity was a much bigger problem than overabundance. Far more people died of starvation than of obesity, and this is still true in many parts of the world today. Things are different, however, for those of us who live in postindustrial parts of today's world. For us (and especially for those of us in North America), obesity has become a major health problem. In what follows, we will examine some of the mechanisms that control appetite and then look at the modern problem of obesity.

Neural and Hormonal Control of Appetite

12

What is meant by feedback control, and how does the arcuate nucleus of the hypothalamus serve as a control center for appetite?

The purpose of hunger and satiety is to regulate the amount of food materials in the body at an appropriate level for survival and well being. Any regulatory system, whether manmade or organic, makes use of *feedback control*. The substance or quality being regulated feeds back upon the controlling device and inhibits the production of more of that substance or quality when an appropriate level is reached. A home thermostat, which controls the operation of the heating system, is a good example. The thermostat is sensitive to temperature. When the temperature is low, a switch closes in the thermostat, which turns on the furnace, which provides heat. When the temperature rises above the set level, the switch opens and the furnace turns off. Thus heat, produced by the furnace, feeds back onto the thermostat to shut off the source of heat when enough of it is present.

The mammalian brain regulates food intake in a manner that is a bit like the operation of a home thermostat, but far more complicated. Sets of neurons in the brain's hypothalamus raise or lower the animal's drive to eat, and these neurons are themselves regulated by the body's deficit or surfeit of food materials. We might think of these neurons as the brain's "food-o-stat." When food materials are relatively low in the body, the food-o-stat cranks appetite up, which motivates the animal to consume more food. When food materials are plentiful in the body, various indicators of that plenitude feed back upon the food-o-stat and turn appetite off, or at least down a bit.

A Nucleus in the Hypothalamus Serves as an Appetite-Control Center

The neurons that comprise the food-o-stat exist in several closely interconnected portions of the hypothalamus, but are most concentrated in the ***arcuate*** [**arc**-you-ut] ***nucleus,*** which lies in the center of the lowest portion of the hypothalamus, very close to the pituitary gland (Berthoud & Morrison, 2008). This tiny brain area has been described as the "master control center" for appetite and weight regulation (Marx, 2003). It contains two classes of neurons that have opposite effects on appetite. One class, the appetite-stimulating neurons, connect to various parts of the brain and promote all the effects that are associated with increased hunger, including craving for food, increased attention to food-related cues, increased exploration in search of food, and heightened enjoyment of the taste of food. The other class, the appetite-suppressing neurons, have effects on various parts of the brain that are opposite to those of the appetite-stimulating neurons.

Both of these classes of arcuate neurons exert their effects on other brain areas through the release of slow-acting neurotransmitters. Unlike fast transmitters, slow transmitters (discussed in Chapter 5) have the capacity to alter neural activity for long periods of time—in this case for periods ranging from minutes to several hours. One of the neurotransmitters released by appetite-stimulating neurons is ***neuropeptide Y,*** which is the most potent appetite stimulator yet discovered. When injected into any of various regions in the hypothalamus, this chemical causes a previously sated animal to eat voraciously (Stanley & Gillard, 1994). The neurons of the arcuate nucleus are themselves acted upon by many different inputs that, in one way or another, reflect the need or lack of need for food.

Many Internal Signals Contribute to Short-Term Regulation of Appetite

Eating a large meal produces a number of physiological changes in the body. Among these are slightly elevated body temperature (resulting from a heightened rate of metabolism), increased blood level of glucose (a simple sugar molecule derived from the breakdown of carbohydrate foods), distention of the stomach and intestines (resulting from food inside those structures), and the release of certain hormones produced by endocrine cells in the stomach and intestines. There is evidence that all these changes can act either directly or indirectly on neurons in the arcuate nucleus and nearby areas of the hypothalamus to activate hunger-suppressing neurons and inhibit hunger-stimulating neurons (Berthoud & Morrison, 2008; Korner & Leibel, 2003). When all these effects are operating properly, the result is a decline in appetite for several hours following ingestion of a meal.

"What if these guys in white coats who bring us food are, like, studying us and we're part of some kind of big experiment?"

One appetite-suppressing hormone that has received considerable attention is *peptide YY$_{3-36}$* (abbreviated **PYY**), which is produced by special endocrine cells in the large intestine. Food entering the intestines after a meal stimulates secretion of PYY into the bloodstream. In humans, blood levels of the hormone begin to increase 15 minutes after a meal is eaten, peak at about 60 minutes, and remain elevated for as long as 6 hours after a large meal (Batterham & others, 2003). Research with rodents shows that one of the target tissues of PYY is the arcuate nucleus, where the hormone excites appetite-suppressing neurons and inhibits appetite-stimulating neurons (Marx, 2003).

In both rats and humans, injection of extra PYY into the bloodstream reduces total food consumed over the next several hours (Gardiner & others, 2008). In one double-blind experiment with humans, PYY injection reduced the amount of food eaten at a buffet luncheon, by both lean and obese human volunteers, by an average of about 30 percent, and also reduced reported level of appetite in both groups (Batterham & others, 2003). The same researchers also found that lean subjects had higher baseline levels of naturally produced PYY than did obese subjects, and exhibited a much greater increase in PYY following a meal (see Figure 6.5). This result suggests that insufficient PYY production may be a contributing cause of obesity. As you can well imagine, pharmaceutical companies are currently investigating the possibility that PYY, or some modified form of it, might be developed and marketed as a weight-control drug.

> **13**
> What is the evidence that the hormone PYY helps reduce appetite after a meal and that underproduction of PYY may contribute to obesity?

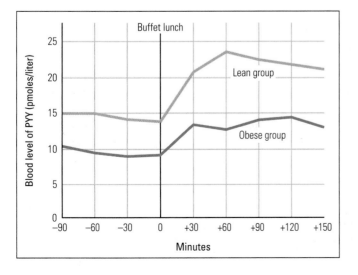

FIGURE 6.5 Blood levels of the hormone PYY in obese and lean human subjects Blood levels of PYY were found to be lower in obese subjects than in lean subjects. After eating a meal, lean subjects showed a much larger increase in PYY than did obese subjects. Researchers believe that this difference may be a cause of obesity, as PYY acts on the brain to suppress appetite. (From Batterham & others, 2003.)

Leptin Contributes to the Long-Term Control of Appetite and Body Weight

14

How does the hormone leptin contribute to weight regulation, and why isn't leptin a good anti-obesity drug?

In the short term, eating provides an immediate supply of building blocks (such as amino acids) and energy molecules (such as glucose) needed to grow, repair, and fuel the body. Over the long term, eating more than is immediately needed adds to the amount of fat that is stored in special fat cells in various tissues of the body. Fat stores provide an extra source of energy that the body can call upon when food is not available in the environment. Too much fat, however, impedes movement and puts stress on all the body's organs. Not surprisingly, the hunger mechanism, when it is working optimally, is sensitive not just to the short-term indicators of amount of food recently eaten but also to the amount of fat stored in the body.

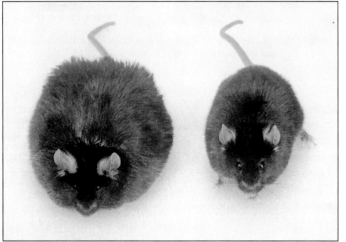

John Sholtis/AP

FIGURE 6.6 Lacking leptin
The mouse on the left, which lacks the gene needed to synthesize the weight-regulating hormone leptin, greatly outweighs the genetically normal mouse. Without leptin, the animal overeats and becomes obese.

Fat cells in mice, humans, and other mammals secrete a hormone, called *leptin*, at a rate that is directly proportional to the amount of fat that is in the cells (Woods & others, 2000). Leptin is taken up into the brain and acts on neurons in the arcuate nucleus and other parts of the hypothalamus to reduce appetite. Animals that lack either the gene needed to produce leptin or the gene needed to produce the receptor sites for leptin in the hypothalamus become extraordinarily obese (see Figure 6.6) (Friedman, 1997). Some people—though very few—lack the gene needed to produce leptin. Such individuals are extremely obese, but they reduce their eating, lose weight rapidly, and keep it off, when given daily injections of leptin (Farooqi & others, 2002).

When the hunger-suppressing effect of leptin was discovered in the 1990s, there was much excitement about the possibility that injections of this hormone could help many people lose weight. Subsequent research, however, proved otherwise. The great majority of overweight people are not lacking in leptin. Their fat cells constantly produce very high levels of the hormone. Research shows that hunger is reduced by increased leptin up to a certain level, but most overweight people already have blood concentrations of leptin well above that level, and additional leptin has no effect (Marx, 2003). Other research suggests that many obese people feel chronically hungry not because they lack leptin but because their brains are relatively insensitive to the hormone (Berthoud & Morrison, 2008; Friedman, 2003). A drug that helped restore leptin sensitivity might help them lose weight, but so far no such drug is in sight.

Roles of Sensory Stimuli in Control of Appetite

15

How do conditioned stimuli and the availability of many foods, with different flavors, contribute to appetite and obesity?

As you well know, hunger is provoked not just by events inside us but also by sensory stimuli in the environment. Even if you were not initially hungry, the sight or smell of good food might make you hungry. This effect of the environment makes good sense from an evolutionary perspective. For most of our history as a species, food was not always available. Evolution led us and other animals to be opportunists with regard to food; our hunger increases when food is available so that we don't pass up opportunities to eat when eating is possible.

Through classical conditioning (discussed in Chapter 4), any cues that have previously signaled opportunity to eat—such as the sight or smell of good food, the sound of a dinner bell, or the sight of a clock showing it is dinner time—can bring on a sudden surge of appetite. Such conditioning is reflected not just in reports of increased hunger but also in the occurrence of reflexive physiological responses, such as the secretion of saliva and digestive juices, that help to prepare the body for food and add further to the sense of hunger (Woods & others, 2000).

Once a person begins to eat, the taste of the food can influence the reduction or prolongation of appetite during a meal. People and laboratory animals who eat one type of food until they are satiated experience renewed appetite when a different food, with a different taste, is placed before them. This phenomenon is referred to as ***sensory-specific satiety,*** and many experiments show that it is mediated primarily by the sense of taste (Raynor & Epstein, 2001). When people eat one food at a meal, their rating of the taste pleasantness of that food declines relative to their rating of the taste pleasantness of other foods. This effect begins immediately after eating the food and lasts typically for several hours. Experiments with animals show that the sight and smell of a new food can result in renewed activity in appetite-stimulating neurons in the hypothalamus after the animal has been sated on a different food (Rolls & others, 1986). Laboratory animals that can regularly choose from a variety of different-tasting foods eat more, and become fatter, than do animals that have only one food choice, even if the nutritional content of various foods is identical (Raynor & Epstein, 2001). People, too, eat more when there are more food choices (Raynor & Epstein, 2001; Temple & others, 2008).

Problems of Obesity

Human evolution occurred almost entirely in environments where food choices were far fewer, and far lower in fat and sugar, than are the foods available to people in modern cultures. Natural selection built into us excellent mechanisms to defend against weight loss in times of scarcity, but rather poor mechanisms to defend against obesity in times of plenty. Obesity is a cultural disease of our time and place.

To assess obesity, the World Health Organization uses a measure called the *body mass index,* or *BMI,* defined as body weight in kilograms divided by the square of the person's height in meters. A BMI of 25 or more is considered overweight, and one of 30 or more is considered obese. Thus a person who is 1.7 meters (5 feet 7 inches) tall and weighs 73 kilograms (161 pounds) is deemed overweight (BMI $= 73/1.7^2 = 25.3$), and a person of that same height who weighs 88 kilograms (194 pounds) is considered obese (BMI $= 88/1.7^2 = 30.4$).

By these criteria, according to a survey taken in 2003–2004, 66 percent of adults in the United States were overweight, and half of those who were overweight were obese (Ogden & others, 2006). Comparison of these findings with those of studies done earlier (for example, Hill & others, 2003) reveal that the rate of obesity has risen rapidly over the past few decades. Obesity is also rising rapidly in many other parts of the world. As obesity rises, so does the rate of diseases that are secondary to it, including Type 2 diabetes, coronary heart disease, stroke, and certain types of cancers (Marx, 2003). In the United States, obesity is rapidly overtaking smoking as the major underlying cause of death (Marx, 2003). The immediate causes of this obesity epidemic are clear: People consume more calories and exercise less than they used to.

Overriding the satiety mechanism People on a cruise typically gain weight, partly because of the large variety of food that is served. These people may become satiated with one type of food but still have an appetite for others.

Effects of Genes and Culture on Body Weight

Within the United States, or any other Western culture, the determination of who does or does not become obese depends very much on genes and relatively little on the specific home environment (Barsh & others, 2000). The weights of adopted children correlate much more strongly with the weights of their biological parents than with those of their adoptive parents; identical twins usually have very similar weights even if raised in different homes; and pairs of biological siblings raised in different homes are, on average, nearly as similar to each other in weight as are pairs raised in the same home (Grilo & Pogue-Geile, 1991; Stunkard & others, 1986). This does not mean that body weight is little influenced by the environment. It simply means that the environmental conditions that promote obesity are fairly constant within Western cultures, so differences in weight have mostly to do

16

What is the evidence that within a culture, differences in body weight result mostly from differences in genes, but across cultures, environment plays a large role?

John Annerino

FIGURE 6.7 Effect of culture on body weight If the only Pima Indians you ever saw were those living in Mexico and following traditional Pima practices (like these photographed at a holy festival), you might conclude that they are genetically predisposed to be slender. Obesity is almost nonexistent among the Mexican Pima. However, their close relatives living across the border in the United States are often obese. That difference lies not in genes but in the choices of foods available.

17 – – – – – – – – – – – – – – – –

On the basis of the reports of successful dieters and the advice of appetite researchers, what can people do to maintain a lower weight?

– – – – – – – – – – – – – – – –

with genetic differences in how individuals respond to those conditions.

Across cultures, environmental differences can have a large effect on body weight. As one example, obesity is very common among Pima Indians living in Arizona but is essentially absent among their genetic relatives living in Mexico (see Figure 6.7). The Mexican Pimas subsist mainly on grains and vegetables; their culture does not include the high-calorie foods available to the American Pimas (Gibbs, 1996). The genes that promote obesity in our culture apparently do so by increasing the person's attraction to high-calorie foods, by decreasing one or another of the feedback effects that high food intake or fat level has on the hunger mechanisms in the hypothalamus, and by decreasing the body's ability to burn up excess calories quickly (Barsh & others, 2000; Friedman, 2003). Where high-calorie foods are unavailable, the same genes generally don't lead to obesity.

Problems of Dieting

Weight gained is often very difficult to lose. Decreased food intake not only activates the hunger mechanisms in the brain but can also produce a decline in basal metabolism (the rate at which calories are burned while the individual is at rest), so food is converted more efficiently to fat (Keesey & Corbett, 1984; Leibel & others, 1995). In one extreme case, a woman managed to reduce her weight from 312 pounds to a still-obese but much healthier 192 pounds through diet. For at least 18 months after that she maintained her new weight, without losing any more, by eating a total of 1000 to 1200 calories a day—less than half of what most women would have to eat to maintain that weight (Rodin & others, 1989).

◀ Despite the odds, some people do lose significant amounts of weight and avoid regaining it. A study of approximately 3,000 highly successful dieters, who had lost an average of over 60 pounds per person and had kept it off for an average of 5 years at the time of the study, revealed that they succeeded primarily by avoiding high-fat foods and by greatly increasing their exercise (Butler, 2004; Wing & Hill, 2004). Many other studies, too, have shown that a combination of exercise and dieting is far more effective in producing long-term weigh loss than is dieting alone (Cudjoe & others, 2007). Regular exercise not only burns up calories immediately but also builds muscle, which, even when resting, burns calories at a higher rate than do other body tissues (Van Itallie & Kissileff, 1990).

Researchers who study appetite and metabolism often have some sensible advice for people who want to lose weight. Here is a summary of what I have gleaned from their work:

- Don't try to lose weight rapidly. Don't go on a diet that you can't stay on for the rest of your life. Weight rapidly lost through starvation dieting is rapidly regained when the diet ends.

- Instead of reducing food intake to a level that leaves you hungry, shift the foods you eat away from high-calorie fats and sweets and toward gut-filling but low-calorie vegetables, fruits, and complex carbohydrates (whole-grain breads and cereals).

- Make the sensory-specific satiety effect work for you instead of against you. Provide yourself, over time, with a luscious variety of vegetables and fruits and very few choices of high-calorie meats and dairy products; and omit the pastries, soda pop, potato chips, and French fries entirely.

- Eat each meal slowly, so as to enjoy it and to provide time for the food's satiety-producing effects to develop. If you still feel hungry after eating what you initially planned to eat, wait at least 15 minutes before deciding whether or not to eat more. By that time you may no longer feel hungry. It takes about 15 minutes for PYY and other satiety-producing consequences of a meal to begin to exert their effects on the brain's arcuate nucleus.

- If you have a sedentary job or are a student, develop some pleasurable hobbies that involve muscle-building exercise for at least a few hours a week. (I for one can't stand jogging and get quickly bored with weight lifting, but I love bicycling, kayaking, and cross-country skiing.) And when you need to get from one place to another, use your muscles rather than an automobile or an elevator to convey you whenever you can.

Through such changes in habits, many people can lose a significant amount of weight and keep it off for a lifetime, without feeling deprived at all.

SECTION REVIEW

Hunger is a regulatory drive controlled by neural, hormonal, and sensory factors.

Control Mechanisms of Hunger	Obesity
➤ The arcuate nucleus of the hypothalamus is a feedback-based appetite control center, with both appetite-stimulating and appetite-suppressing neurons.	➤ Within a culture, genetic differences are the primary determinants of who becomes obese, but across cultures, environmental differences play a substantial role.
➤ Eating a large meal causes physiological changes, including the release of PYY, that influence the arcuate nucleus and nearby areas to reduce hunger.	➤ Decreasing food intake activates hunger mechanisms in the brain and can reduce basal metabolism, making weight loss harder.
➤ Leptin, a hormone produced by fat cells, helps to regulate body weight by acting on the hypothalamus to reduce appetite.	➤ Certain techniques help at least some people lose substantial amounts of weight and keep it off.
➤ Sensory stimuli also affect appetite, as illustrated by sensory-specific satiety and by the appetite-boosting power of learned cues that signal the availability of food.	

■ Sex: An Example of a Nonregulatory Drive

Just as hunger is the most thoroughly studied regulatory drive, sex is the most thoroughly studied nonregulatory drive. As with hunger, much of the basic research on the physiological basis of the sex drive has been conducted with laboratory animals.

There are limits, of course, in the degree to which we can understand hunger, sex, or any drive in humans by studying it in other animals. Human culture, intellect, sensibility, and capacity for conscious self-control affect our behavior in ways that cannot be studied in laboratory animals. People don't just eat; they *dine,* which connotes all sorts of social, cognitive, and aesthetic influences. And people don't just copulate; they fall in love, compose romantic sonnets, gaze into each other's eyes over candlelit dinners, swear by the moon to be faithful, have affairs, suffer guilt, and engage in long, intimate discussions with their beloved. Keep in mind, as you read on, that our concern here is with the basic physiological mechanisms that we humans share, more or less, with other mammals, not the whole range of issues concerning human sexuality. (Sex is discussed more from a social and cultural perspective in Chapter 12.)

Even when dealing with the copulatory act itself, humans differ quite sharply from rats and other laboratory animals. Among nonhuman mammals, including most other primates, copulation occurs in a stereotyped way, with one set of postures

18

Why is caution advised in extrapolating from laboratory animals to humans in the study of drives, especially the sex drive?

Barnett, S. A. (1975). *The study of rat behavior* (rev. ed.). Chicago: University of Chicago Press.

FIGURE 6.8 Copulation in rats
Rats, like most other nonhuman mammals, have a stereotyped (unvarying) pattern of copulation, with clearly different postures for the female and the male.

and movements for the female and a different set for the male (see Figure 6.8). Among humans, by contrast, the variety of ways to copulate is limited only by imagination. As you will discover when you read further, humans differ from other species also in the hormonal regulation of the sexual drive, especially in females.

In the discussion of hunger, I pointed out that the drive state depends on external conditions—such as the sight and smell of good food—as well as on the internal state of the body. Perceptions and thoughts concerning the external environment are even more obviously crucial to the sexual drive. The attributes and apparent willingness of a potential sexual partner, the perception of safety or danger associated with the behavior, the presence or absence of conditioned stimuli associated with past sexual experiences (discussed in Chapter 4), concerns about the long-term consequences, and so on and so on, all greatly affect the degree to which a person feels sexually motivated at any given moment. In this discussion, though, my focus is on the longer-term effects of hormones on sexual drive. The hormonal regulation of sexual drive differs by sex, so I'll discuss such regulation separately for males and females.

Hormonal Influences on Male Sex Drive

Testosterone Maintains the Capacity for Male Sex Drive

19
What is some evidence that testosterone is needed to maintain the male's sex drive and that, at least in some species, it does so by direct action in the hypothalamus?

In male mammals, the most crucial hormone for the maintenance of the sexual drive is *testosterone*, produced by the testes. Castration (removal of the testes, and hence of the main supply of testosterone) causes a marked decline in the sex drive—not all at once, but gradually (Feder, 1984). It takes days to occur in rats, weeks in dogs, sometimes months in monkeys. But the injection of testosterone into the bloodstream of castrated animals gradually but eventually fully restores their drive.

The sex drive can also be restored in castrated male animals by implanting a tiny crystal of testosterone into an area of the hypothalamus called the *medial preoptic area* (see Figure 6.9) (Davidson, 1980). Neurons in this area contain many receptor sites for testosterone, and small lesions there abolish sexual behavior in male rats (Meisel & Sachs, 1994). Apparently, the medial preoptic area of the hypothalamus is a crucial part of the central drive system for sex in male rats and other male animals that have been studied, and testosterone acts there in a rather prolonged way to enable neural activity to occur and sustain the drive.

Testosterone is also crucial for maintaining the sex drive in human males. Men castrated in an accident or for medical reasons almost always experience a decline (though often not a complete loss) in sex drive and behavior, and testosterone injections restore their drive, usually fully (Money & Ehrhardt, 1972). In other studies, testosterone injections administered to noncastrated men whose testes were producing unusually low amounts of the hormone sharply increased their reported sexual drive and behavior (Davidson & others, 1979; Reyes-Vallejo & others, 2007). At least for many men, the effects of such treatment have more to do with drive than with sexual capability. Low-testosterone men are generally capable of the mechanics of sexual behavior, including erection and ejaculation, but have relatively little desire for it until injected with testosterone (Davidson & Myers, 1988).

FIGURE 6.9 Hypothalamic areas where hormones activate sexual behavior In rats, testosterone promotes male sexual behavior by activating neurons in the medial preoptic area of the hypothalamus, and estrogen promotes female sexual behavior by activating neurons in the ventromedial area of the hypothalamus.

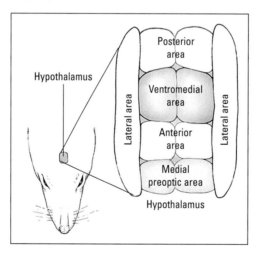

Posterior area

Hypothalamus

Ventromedial area

Lateral area

Lateral area

Anterior area

Medial preoptic area

Hypothalamus

Causes and Possible Consequences of Increased Testosterone Secretion

Many experiments have shown that the amount of testosterone that men secrete into their blood is affected by psychological conditions. In general, conditions that would seem to promote self-confidence tend to increase a man's production of testosterone. For example, winning a game, even a sedentary game like chess, commonly results in increased blood levels of testosterone in men, detectable within minutes of the victory (Archer, 2006). Pleasant social encounters with women may also increase testosterone production in men (Roney & others, 2007).

Nobody knows for sure what purposes such temporary increases in testosterone might serve. As I just noted, the effect of testosterone on male sexual drive appears to be a long-term effect; there is no evidence that sexual drive waxes and wanes in accordance with the immediate current level of testosterone. Perhaps, however, the integrated effect of many such bursts of testosterone, over time, could help to maintain a man's long-term capacity for sexual drive. Each burst may have some prolonged growth-promoting effect on neural systems in the brain that are involved in sexual motivation. It is also possible that testosterone has other effects on behavior that take less time to develop. Neurons in many areas of the brain have special receptors for testosterone, so the hormone could potentially influence many types of behaviors.

There is some reason to believe that fluctuating levels of testosterone may affect a man's aggressive and competitive tendencies more than sexual drive per se. On average, men with naturally high testosterone levels are more aggressive and more interested in competition and status than are men with lower levels; and there is some (though mixed) evidence that injections of testosterone can increase indexes of aggressiveness and competitiveness in men (reviewed by Archer, 2006). Moreover, in one experiment, men who showed increased levels of testosterone after *losing* a game were more likely to want a rematch than were men who showed the more typical decline in testosterone after losing (Mehta & Josephs, 2006). High status and dominance is one route by which men attract women, so an effect of testosterone on competition and status seeking could be an indirect means toward increased sexual behavior.

20

What kinds of experiences have been shown to increase testosterone production in men? What effects might such increased testosterone have on a man's subsequent behavior?

Hormonal Influences on Female Sex Drive

After puberty, a female's ovaries begin to secrete the female hormones *estrogen* and *progesterone* in a cyclic pattern over time, producing the cycle of physiological changes referred to as the *menstrual cycle* in humans and the *estrous cycle* in most other mammals. In both humans and nonhumans, this cycle controls ovulation (the release of one or more eggs so that pregnancy can occur). This cycle of hormones also influences sexual drive.

Effects of the Estrous Cycle in Nonhuman Mammals

In most mammals, female sexual drive and behavior are tightly controlled by the estrous cycle. The female will seek out opportunities for mating, and will copulate, only at that time in the cycle when she is ovulating and hence capable of becoming pregnant. Removal of the ovaries completely abolishes sexual behavior in most nonhuman female mammals, and injection of hormones can fully restore it. For some species an injection of estrogen alone is most effective, and for others (including rats) a sequence of estrogen followed 2 or 3 days later by progesterone is most effective, a sequence that mimics the natural change of hormones during the estrous cycle.

At least in rats, the *ventromedial area of the hypothalamus* (see Figure 6.9) plays a role in sexual behavior in the female analogous to that of the preoptic area in the male. Insertion of small amounts of estrogen and progesterone directly into

21

What evidence indicates that ovarian hormones act directly on the brain to activate the sexual drive in female rats? How do female primates differ from female rats concerning the regulation of sexual drive?

"My ideal man is kind, sensitive, intelligent, six-two, a hundred-eighty pounds, and made of solid milk chocolate."

Patrick Hardin

22

What is the evidence that women's sexual drive depends more on androgens than on ovarian hormones? What evidence suggests, nevertheless, that female sexual drive does increase during the time of ovulation?

---

this area brings on sexual behavior in rats whose ovaries have been removed, and lesions in this area abolish sexual behavior in otherwise intact females (Blaustein, 2008; Pleim & Barfield, 1988; Schwartz-Giblin & others, 1989). Apparently the cyclic variation in ovarian hormones acts on the ventromedial area to cause the cyclic waxing and waning of sexual drive.

Many species of monkeys and apes, unlike most nonprimate females, can and sometimes do copulate with males at times in their cycle when they are not fertile, though they are much more likely to seek out and initiate sexual contact with a male when they are fertile (Pawlowksi, 1999; Wallen, 2001). In at least some species of primates, including rhesus monkeys, sexual drive during nonfertile times depends not on ovarian hormones but on testosterone and other androgens. The term **androgen** refers to a category of hormones, including testosterone, which are produced by the testes in male animals and are normally thought of as "male hormones." These hormones are also produced at lower levels by the adrenal glands, in females as well as in males.

Effects of the Menstrual Cycle in Women

◀ Human females exhibit still greater liberation of sexual behavior from cyclic hormonal control than do other primates. Women can experience a high or low sex drive at any time in their hormone cycle. Apparently, in women, hormonal activation of the drive has been taken over largely by adrenal androgens. In clinical studies, women whose ovaries have been removed generally do not report a decline in sexual drive, but women whose adrenals have been removed generally do report such a decline; and long-term treatment with testosterone reliably increases sexual desire and satisfaction in women who previously reported low or no sex drive (de Paula & others, 2007; Guay, 2001; Sherwin & Gelfand, 1987).

We know almost nothing about the brain mechanisms of sexual drive in human beings. A fascinating possibility is that, in humans, the sexual drive mechanism that evolved to serve only for males in nonprimate mammals serves for both sexes in humans. Over the course of evolution, from our primate ancestors to modern humans, the value of extending sexual behavior beyond simply the needs of reproduction may have led to a decline, for females, in the role of the estrogen-ventromedial-hypothalamamic system and an expansion the role of the androgen-preoptic-hypothalamic system. I look forward to research on brain mechanisms that would test that hypothesis. Consistent with the hypothesis that men and women may share common mechanisms for sexual drive and behavior is evidence that the two sexes manifest similar patterns of physiological changes during sexual arousal and describe their subjective feelings during such arousal in similar ways (Masters & others, 1992; Vance & Wagner, 1976).

Although women are relatively liberated sexually from the ovarian cycle, there is evidence that the cycle still does influence their sexual drive to some degree. A number of studies, using various measures, indicate that women are significantly more motivated sexually at the time in their cycle when they are fertile than at other times. The studies have shown that, on average, women during the fertile phase dress more provocatively, speak in more appealing tones of voice, are relatively more drawn to men with highly masculine features, feel themselves to be more sexually attractive and sexually motivated, and initiate sex more frequently than at other times of their menstrual cycle (Adams & others, 1978; Gangestad & others, 2004; Pipitone & Gallup, 2008; Schwarz & Hassebrauck, 2008).

A useful distinction here is that between arousability and proceptivity (Diamond, 2006). **Arousability** refers to the capacity to become sexually aroused in response to appropriate stimuli (the right partner, the right music, the romantic talk, the gentle touches, and so on), and **proceptivity** refers to the person's motivation to seek out and initiate sexual activity, even when sexually arousing stimuli are not already present. The data suggest that arousability remains relatively constant for women over the course of the menstrual cycle, but proceptivity increases during the fertile period. The increased proceptivity might result from the rise of estrogen and/or progesterone during the fertile period, but it could also result from the rise of adrenal androgens. Researchers have found that secretion of adrenal androgens, especially testosterone, increases markedly during the fertile stage of the menstrual cycle (Salonia & others, 2008).

Sexual Differentiation and Determinants of Sexual Orientation

Sex hormones influence sexual drive and behavior through two different kinds of effects on the brain: activating and differentiating. **Activating effects** are the kinds of effects that we have been discussing so far. They occur around the time of puberty and after, when hormones work on already-developed brain structures to prime, or *activate*, sexual drive. **Differentiating effects,** in contrast, occur before and (in some species) immediately after birth and cause the brain to develop in a male or female direction. They are responsible for the biological *differences* between males and females in sexual drive and orientation. We turn now to a discussion of the role of hormones in differentiating males and females sexually, and to the general issue of causes of human differences in sexual orientation.

Brain-Differentiating Effects of the Early Presence or Absence of Testosterone

As noted in Chapter 3, the only initial difference between the two sexes, in all mammals, is that females have two X chromosomes and males have a small Y chromosome in place of the second X. A specific gene on the Y chromosome causes the growth of testes (the male gonads) from structures that would otherwise develop into ovaries (the female gonads) (Page & others, 1987). Before birth the testes begin to produce testosterone, which acts on the brain and other bodily structures of the fetus to steer development in the male direction. The rudimentary genitals of the fetus develop into male structures (including the penis and scrotum) if testosterone is present, and they develop into female structures (including the clitoris and vagina) if testosterone is absent. Early testosterone also promotes the development of brain pathways involved in the male sex drive and inhibits the development of brain pathways involved in the female sex drive (Gorski, 1996; Simerly, 2002). For an example of one such effect, see Figure 6.10.

In order to produce these brain-differentiating effects, testosterone must act within a critical period in the animal's development. In rats, this period runs from a few days before birth to a day or so after birth. In many other species, including humans, the critical period ends before birth. The critical period for testosterone's effect on the brain is later than that for its effect on the genitals—a fact that can have some interesting consequences. Because of this difference in timing of critical period, manipulation of hormones at the appropriate time can produce animals

━ ━ ━ ━ ━ ━ ━ ━ ━ ━ ━ ━ ━ 23

What are some effects of the presence or absence of testosterone before birth on development of the genitals, the brain, and behavior? What has been learned from studies of girls and women born with congenital adrenal hyperplasia?

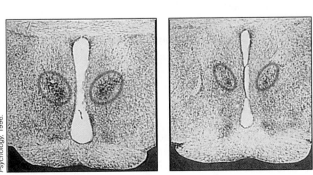

FIGURE 6.10 A sex difference in the rat's hypothalamus Shown here is a cross section of the medial preoptic area of the hypothalamus of a male rat (left) and a female rat (right). The dark spots represent cell bodies of neurons, and the dense cluster of them represents the sexual dimorphic nucleus (marked by red circles). The nucleus receives its name from the fact that it is clearly different in the two sexes; it is about 5 times larger, on average, in the male than in the female (Gorski & others, 1980). The difference is due entirely to the presence or absence of testosterone early in the rat's development. Early treatment with testosterone in females and early deprivation of testosterone in males can reverse this sex difference. The nucleus is believed to be part of the neural circuitry controlling male sexual drive and behavior. (DeJonge & others, 1989.)

Rosenzweig, Leithman, & Breedlov. *Biological Psychology,* 1996.

that have the genitals of one sex but the brain structures and behavior of the other sex (Feder, 1984; Ward, 1992).

The capacity for testosterone to at least partly masculinize the brain in human females is well demonstrated by cases of girls born with *congenital adrenal hyperplasia (CAH)*, a rare genetic disorder in which the adrenal glands of the developing fetus produce an overabundance of androgens, including testosterone. Girls born with CAH have partially masculinized genitals. At birth or shortly after, hormone treatments are begun to terminate the overproduction of androgens, and surgery is used to feminize the genitals. The girls are raised by their parents as normal girls, but many studies have shown that in various ways they exhibit masculine characteristics. As children, they play more actively and aggressively than do most girls, and they typically prefer to play with boys and with boys' toys (Pasterski & others, 2007). As adults, they are statistically more likely than other women to be homosexual or bisexual or to report that they are uncomfortable with heterosexual behavior (Hines & others, 2004). These effects seem clearly to be caused by the prenatal androgens and not by any difference in how they were treated during their development.

Perhaps you are wondering why a male hormone, not a female hormone, plays the key role in early sexual differentiation in mammals, including humans. The answer is that the female hormones (progesterone and estrogen) are produced by pregnant females at high levels and get into the tissues of all fetuses, of both sexes. If female hormones promoted growth of female structures during fetal development, all mammalian infants would be feminized. In birds and reptiles—which develop in eggs outside the mother's body—early sexual differentiation is determined by the presence or absence of estrogen, not testosterone (Adkins-Regan, 1981).

Effects of Genes and Prenatal Environment on Sexual Orientation

Using various criteria and survey methods, researchers estimate that 2 to 5 percent of men, and 1 to 2 percent of women, are exclusively homosexual in orientation (Rahman & Wilson, 2003). A possibly larger percentage, even harder to estimate precisely, are bisexual (attracted to members of both sexes), and bisexuality appears to be more common in women than in men (Diamond, 2006; Rahman & Wilson, 2003). Most people, whether homosexual or heterosexual, experience their sexual orientation as a deep-seated, fundamental part of their being, something they discover about themselves as they are growing up, not something that they have a choice about (Bell & others, 1981; Herdt & Boxer, 1993; Rahman & Wilson, 2003).

Genetic differences among individuals play a significant role in determining sexual orientation, but not the sole role. Several research studies reveal that roughly 50 percent of the genetically identical twin brothers and sisters of homosexual men and women are also homosexual, compared with about 15 percent of the same-sex nonidentical twins or nontwin siblings of homosexual men and women (Hyde, 2005; Rahman & Wilson, 2003). If homosexuality were completely determined by genes, then 100% of the identical twin brothers and sisters of homosexuals would be homosexual.

Other studies suggest that sexual orientation might be affected by a variety of prenatal environmental factors—ranging from prenatal stress to certain medications taken by the mother during pregnancy—that alter the amount of testosterone or other androgen available to the fetus's brain during a critical period in development (Ellis & Cole-Harding, 2001; Ellis & Hellberg, 2005). Such work suggests that a high level of androgen action during the critical period may promote the development of brain mechanisms that predispose sexual attraction toward women and not toward men and that a relative lack of androgen during the same period may promote the opposite.

The single most consistent, non-genetic influence on sexual orientation discovered to date is the *fraternal birth-order effect* on male homosexuality (Blanchard, 2008). The more older brothers a man has, the greater is the likelihood of his being homosexual. The effect is quite strong. One large study revealed that, on average, a couple's

24

What is the evidence that genes and prenatal environment can influence sexual orientation in humans? What is the effect of fraternal birth order on male sexual orientation, and how might it be explained in terms of the prenatal environment?

first son has a 2.0 percent chance of being homosexual and that this percentage increases to about 2.6 percent for a second son, 3.4 percent for a third son, 4.6 percent for a fourth son, and 6.0 percent for a fifth son (Blanchard, 2001). In contrast, the number of older sisters a man has plays no role in the likelihood of his being homosexual, and there is no birth-order effect on homosexuality in women. Another study revealed that, for boys adopted in infancy, homosexuality increased with the number of older *biological* brothers, not with the number of older adoptive brothers. In other words, the crucial factor in increasing the likelihood of homosexuality was the number of prior male offspring their biological mothers had produced, not the number of older boys in the family in which they were raised (Bogaert, 2006). This result strongly suggests that the effect derives from the prenatal environment.

The most fully developed current hypothesis is that the effect results from a change in the prenatal environment that is induced by previously born sons (Blanchard, 2001; 2008). Genes on the Y chromosome of a male fetus produce certain proteins that may help androgens to masculinize regions of the fetus's brain. These proteins are foreign to the mother's body, so if they get into her bloodstream they may induce an immune reaction in her. With successive sons, the immune reaction could generate a sufficient supply of antibodies in the mother's bloodstream to inactivate one or more of those proteins within a developing fetus and thereby reduce the masculinizing effect of androgens in a portion of the fetus's brain. At present, this explanation lies in the realm of reasonable speculation; there is no direct evidence supporting or refuting the hypothesis.

Gay marriage The idea that homosexual couples should be allowed to enjoy the benefits and take on the responsibilities of marriage is still politically controversial. The fact that the controversy is even occurring, however, illustrates that the culture has taken strides toward accepting homosexuality as a normal human condition.

Possible Effects of Experiences, after Birth, on Sexual Orientation

There was a time, more than three or four decades ago, when most psychologists and psychiatrists believed that homosexuality results primarily from experiences that young people have growing up. Various theories about such environmental causes were proposed, but subsequent interviews and surveys of thousands of homosexuals and heterosexuals failed to support them (Bell & others, 1981; Dawood & others, 2000; Rahman & Wilson, 2003). Such studies revealed little or no evidence that style of parenting, absence of the father or mother, early seduction or rape by someone of the same or opposite sex, or degree of opportunity for one or another type of sexual experience in adolescence contributes significantly to the development of sexual orientation.

However, recent research has revived the idea that experiences in life can affect sexual orientation, especially for women. Women, in general, appear to be more flexible in their sexual orientation than men. One line of evidence for this comes from direct physiological measures of sexual arousal in response to erotic films (Chivers & others, 2005). Such measures show that most women, whether they are self-declared homosexuals or heterosexuals, can become sexually aroused by erotic films of *either* men or women engaged in sexual acts. In contrast, men are much more categorical in their arousal: Homosexual men typically respond only to men and heterosexual men typically respond only to women.

Lisa Diamond (2006) has argued that because women are capable of sexual arousal to either men or women, they are more capable than are men of switching their sexual orientation at any time in life. Extensive interviews of women, by Diamond and others, seem to bear this out. Women are more likely than men to report that their sexual orientation is a choice, and they are more likely than men to change their sexual orientation in response to events that occur in their lives. For example, some women become homosexual as a result of falling in love with a particular woman. They are not so much attracted to women in general as to one particular woman. Some others (whom Diamond refers to as "political lesbians") adopt a lesbian identity and behavior because they have become involved with a social group that values lesbianism.

> ---------------- **25**
>
> **What evidence suggests that sexual orientation may more often be influenced by postnatal experience and personal choice for women than for men?**

Such interviews also suggest, however, that some homosexual women are less flexible in their sexual orientation than are others. The distinction seems to fall roughly along the line of the popular culture's distinction between "butch" and "femme" lesbians (Diamond, 2006; James, 2005). The former tend to be more masculine in appearance, more sexually assertive, and more firmly homosexual than the latter. These may generally be women whose brains have been partly masculinized prenatally. The women that Diamond finds are most likely to change their sexual orientation as a result of life experiences are most often those in the "femme" category.

Nothing about human behavior is simple. We are complex creatures. All of our behavior, including our sexual behavior, is determined by many factors, only some of which we have begun to fathom. Beware of any theory of human sexual orientation, or of anything else in psychology, that tries to explain everything in terms of just one simple cause or another.

SECTION REVIEW

Sex is a nonregulatory drive powerfully influenced by hormones.

Male Sex Drive	Female Sex Drive	Sexual Orientation
➤ Testosterone maintains male sex drive over the long term. In rats, at least, this occurs by action on the preoptic area of the hypothalamus.	➤ In most nonhuman female mammals, ovarian hormones promote sexual drive at the time of fertility, apparently through action on the ventromedial hypothalamus.	➤ In mammals, prenatal androgens masculinize and defeminize the developing brain. This effect may explain some characteristics of girls and women born with CAH.
➤ Confidence-boosting events cause increased testosterone secretion in men, which may increase their tendency toward competitiveness or aggression.	➤ In women and some other female primates, adrenal androgens promote sexual receptivity throughout the ovarian cycle. But sexual proceptivity appears to increase at the time of fertility, perhaps because of increased androgen production at that time.	➤ Genes influence sexual orientation in both men and women, as does the prenatal environment.
		➤ The fraternal birth order effect on male homosexuality may be mediated by the prenatal environment.
		➤ Women appear to be more flexible than men in sexual orientation.

■ The Sleep Drive

Sleepiness is clearly a drive. A sleepy person is motivated to go to sleep and will expend effort to reach a safe and comfortable place to do so. Achieving this goal and drifting off to sleep provides a sense of pleasure analogous to that which comes from eating when hungry or copulating when sexually motivated.

Sleepiness operates in some ways like a regulatory drive. As with hunger, thirst, or other regulatory drives, the longer one goes without satisfying the sleep drive, the stronger the drive becomes. But, unlike other regulatory drives, it is not clear what the sleep drive regulates, except sleep itself. Also, sleepiness is controlled not just by amount of sleep deprivation but also by a biological clock that keeps time within the 24-hour day-night cycle. Regardless of how much sleep one has had recently, sleepiness tends to increase at night and decrease during daytime hours.

The discussion in this section focuses on three questions: (1) What is sleep? (2) What are the functions of sleep? (3) What brain mechanisms control sleepiness and arousal?

Description of Sleep as a Physiological and Behavioral State

Sleep is a condition of relative unresponsiveness to the environment. Because people show little overt behavior and cannot answer questions when they are asleep, scientists who study this state must focus on physiological and subtle behavioral changes.

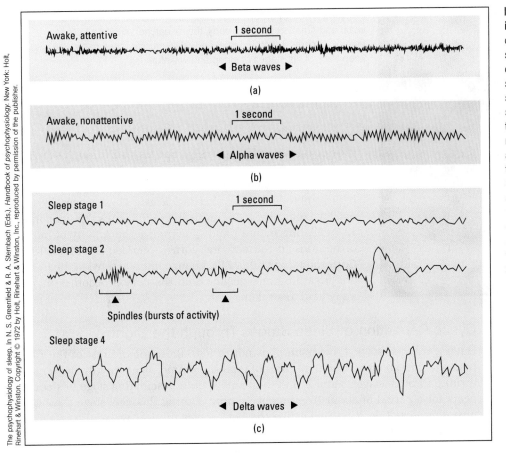

FIGURE 6.11 EEG waves of waking and sleep stages In general, as one goes from an alert to a relaxed state, and then to ever-deeper stages of sleep, the EEG waves become slower in frequency (fewer waves per second) and higher in amplitude (as shown by their greater vertical extent in the EEG record). The brief bursts of rapid waves called sleep spindles that appear in stage 2 are the most distinctive markers of the onset of sleep. Sleep stage 3 is not shown here; it is arbitrarily defined as the period when 10 to 50 percent of the EEG consists of delta waves. REM sleep, also not shown, is characterized by beta waves that look like those of the awake, attentive state. (From Snyder & Scott, 1972.)

The most valuable index of sleep is based on the electroencephalogram (abbreviated EEG). As discussed in Chapter 5, the EEG is an amplified recording of the electrical activity of the brain that is picked up by electrodes pasted to the person's skull. The electrical signals can be stored and analyzed by a computer and can also be used to move pens up and down on a continuously moving roll of paper, producing records like those shown in Figure 6.11. The EEG recording is a gross index of the electrical activity of the brain, representing a sort of average of the activity of billions of neurons, with the greatest weight given to those lying closest to the recording site.

EEG Waves Accompanying Wakefulness and Stages of Sleep

When a person is relaxed but awake, with eyes closed and not thinking of anything in particular, the EEG typically consists of large, regular waves called *alpha waves*, which occur at a frequency of about 8 to 13 cycles per second (see Figure 6.11b). These relatively slow waves stem from a synchronized pulsing of neurons in the thalamus and cerebral cortex that occurs in the absence of focused mental activity or emotional excitement. When a person concentrates on an external stimulus, or tries to solve a problem, or becomes excited, the EEG pattern changes to low-amplitude, fast, irregular waves called *beta waves* (see Figure 6.11a). The low amplitude of these waves indicates that neurons are firing in an unsynchronized manner, such that their contributions to the EEG tend to cancel one another out. Whereas alpha waves are analogous to the large, regular waves that occur on a pond undisturbed by anything but a steady wind, beta waves are more akin to the effect of a million pebbles tossed suddenly onto the surface of the pond. The crests of the ripples created by some pebbles would cancel out the troughs created by others, resulting in a chaotic, high-frequency, low-amplitude pattern of ripples.

When a person falls asleep, the EEG goes through a fairly regular sequence of changes, which are used by researchers to divide sleep into four stages, using the criteria described in the caption to Figure 6.11. Stage 1 is a brief transition stage, when

26

How does a person's EEG change as the person goes from alert to relaxed to various stages of sleep?

Keeping track of sleep With electrodes attached to the man's scalp and other areas of his body, the researcher monitors EEG, eye movements, breathing rate, and other muscle movements to keep track of his stages of sleep and wakefulness.

the person is first falling asleep, and stages 2 through 4 are successively deeper stages of true sleep. As sleep deepens, an increased percentage of the EEG is devoted to slow, irregular, high-amplitude waves called *delta waves*. These waves, like others, are controlled by neurons in the thalamus that respond in an oscillating manner and synchronize the activity of billions of neurons in the cerebral cortex (Steriade & others, 1993). Corresponding to this EEG change, muscle tension, heart rate, and breathing rate decline, and the person becomes increasingly hard to awaken.

Cyclic Repetition of Sleep Stages Through the Night

27

How do REM and non-REM sleep differ, and how do they cycle through the night?

Having reached stage 4, a person does not remain there for the rest of the night. Instead, after about 80 to 100 minutes of total sleep time, sleep rapidly lightens, returning through stages 3 and 2, and then a new, quite fascinating stage of sleep appears for a period of about 10 minutes or more. During this new stage the EEG is unsynchronized, looking much like the beta waves of alert wakefulness. On the basis of the EEG alone, one might think that the person had awakened, but direct observation shows that the person is sound asleep, and the record of muscle tension shows that the muscles are more relaxed than at any other sleep stage. Yet, consistent with the unsynchronized EEG, other indices of high arousal are apparent: Breathing and heart rate become more rapid and less regular; penile erection occurs in males (even in infants and young boys); twitching movements occur in the small muscles of the fingers and face; and, most indicative of all, the eyes move rapidly back and forth and up and down under the closed eyelids. These eye movements, which can be recorded electrically along with the EEG, give this stage of sleep its name, *rapid-eye-movement sleep,* abbreviated **REM sleep.** As you may have guessed, it is during REM sleep that most dreams occur. REM sleep is also sometimes called *emergent stage 1,* because, even though it is different from the original stage 1, it marks the onset of a new sleep cycle. Stages 2, 3, and 4 are referred to collectively as **non-REM sleep.**

In a typical night's sleep, a person goes through four or five sleep cycles, each involving gradual descent into deeper stages of non-REM sleep, followed by a rapid lightening of non-REM sleep, followed by REM sleep (Hobson, 1995). Each complete cycle takes about 90 minutes. As depicted in Figure 6.12, the deepest non-REM sleep

FIGURE 6.12 The cycle of sleep stages through a night People usually go through four or five sleep cycles per night, each ending with a period of REM sleep. With successive cycles, the depth of slow-wave sleep becomes less and the amount of time spent in REM sleep increases. (From Snyder, F., & Scott, J., 1972.)

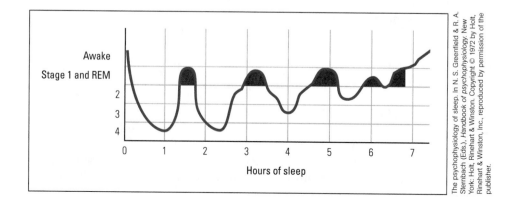

occurs in the first cycle or two. With each successive cycle, less time is spent in the deeper stages of non-REM sleep (stages 3 and 4), and more time is spent in light non-REM sleep (stage 2) and REM sleep.

Dreams and Other Mental Activity During Sleep

When people are awakened during REM sleep, they usually (in about 90 percent of cases) report a mental experience that researchers call a *true dream* (Foulkes, 1985). Such a dream is experienced as if it were a real event rather than something merely imagined or thought about. The dreamer has the feeling of actually seeing or in other ways sensing various objects and people and of actually moving and behaving in the dream environment. Moreover, a true dream usually involves a progression of such experiences, woven into a somewhat coherent though often bizarre story. The more time the sleeper spends in REM sleep before awakening, the longer and more elaborate is the reported dream. Studies show that essentially everyone dreams several times a night. Those who believe that they rarely dream, or who can recall only fragments of dreams upon normal awakening in the morning, describe vivid, detailed dreams if awakened during REM periods.

Analyses of the contents of hundreds of reported dreams reveal a number of generalities about them (Domhoff, 2003; Valli & others, 2008). Most dreams are about people, objects, and activities that are well known and meaningful to the dreamer, but very few dreams are repetitions of events that actually happened in the dreamer's daytime experience. Most dreams involve emotions, especially negative emotions. Dreams involving fear, worry, or embarrassment are more common than joyous dreams. Among college students, dreams of being lost, of being late for an examination, and of being inappropriately dressed (or undressed) in public are common.

People who are awakened during non-REM sleep report some sort of mental activity just before awakening roughly half the time (Foulkes, 1985; Hobson, 1995). Such reports are sometimes of true dreams, but more often they are of *sleep thought,* which lacks the vivid sensory and motor hallucinations of true dreams and is more akin to daytime thinking. Often the subject of sleep thought is some problem that had been of concern during the day. For example, a student who had been cramming for a math exam might report working on a calculus problem while sleeping. A major difference between sleep thought and daytime thought is that the former is usually ineffective.

> **28**
>
> **What are some general characteristics of dreams that people describe when aroused from REM sleep, and how do these differ from the "sleep thought" that people more often describe when aroused from non-REM sleep?**

Although the sleeper may feel that he or she is solving a calculus problem, questions upon awakening indicate that no real progress was made (Hobson, 1987).

During sleep a person is less responsive to events in the environment than when awake, but not completely unresponsive. The eyes are closed, but all of the other sensory channels remain open. In one study using fMRI, people's brains were observed to respond to various sounds when they were asleep in much the same way as they did when they were awake (Portas & others, 2000). Both when asleep and when awake, the sound of the person's own name had effects on emotional centers in the limbic system that did not occur in response to sounds that were less meaningful to the person. The fact that a parent can sleep through a thunderstorm but become aroused by the whimpering of his or her child in the next room is further evidence that sounds are sorted out to some degree by meaning in the sleeping person's brain.

One characteristic of all mental activity during sleep is that it is quickly forgotten. Dreams, sleep thoughts, and sensory experiences during sleep are lost unless the person wakes up during them and thinks about them while awake. This is fortunate. Such forgetting prevents us from carrying around thousands of bizarre and confusing memories or of mixing up real events with dreamed ones.

Theories About the Functions of Sleep

Why must we sleep? Countless children have asked that question to protest being put to bed, and many scientists have asked it, too. Sleep must have come about in the course of evolution to serve some function or functions related to survival and reproduction; otherwise it would not be such a universal and compelling drive. Several theories have been proposed to explain the evolution of the sleep drive. The theories are not incompatible with one another, and they all appear to have some degree of validity.

The Preservation and Protection Theory

The *preservation and protection theory* of sleep derives primarily from comparison of sleep patterns across different species of animals. It posits that sleep came about in evolution to preserve energy and protect individuals during that portion of each 24-hour day when there is relatively little value and considerable danger in moving about. An animal needs only a certain number of hours per day to do the things that are necessary or useful for survival, and the rest of the time, according to this theory, it is better off asleep—quiet, hidden, and protected from predators and other possible dangers (Meddis, 1977).

29
What evidence supports the preservation and protection theory of sleep?

◄ Support for this theory comes from evidence that variations in sleep time among different species do not correspond with differences in physical exertion while awake but do correspond with feeding habits and ways of achieving safety (Allison & Cicchetti, 1976; Lima & others, 2005). At one extreme, large grazing animals such as bison and horses average only 2 or 3 hours of sleep per 24-hour day. Because of their large size and because they eat grass and other vegetation, which are extremely low in calories, they must spend most of their time eating, and therefore they have little time to sleep. Moreover, because of their size and the fact that they cannot burrow or climb trees, such animals are not adept at finding safe places in which to sleep. Thus, they are safer awake.

Even among animals that are roughly the same size as each other, grazing animals sleep less than do meat-eaters. Sheep and goats, for example, sleep only 4 or 5 hours per 24 hours, while lions and tigers sleep 14 to 16 hours (Campbell & Tobler, 1984). Sheep and goats must spend more time eating than lions and tigers, and, because they are more preyed upon, the former are at much greater risk when asleep than are the latter. At the extreme in sleep time are opossums and bats, which average about 20 hours of sleep each 24-hour day. These two species need little time to obtain food (such as high-calorie insects or grubs), and they are adapted to hide in out-of-the-way places. According to the preservation and protection theory, they sleep so much because they have no need to be awake for long and are protected from predators while asleep.

In addition to explaining differences in total amount of sleep, the preservation and protection theory also explains differences in the time of day at which different species sleep. Animals that rely heavily on vision generally forage during the day and sleep at night. Conversely, animals such as mice and rats that rely more on other senses, and are preyed upon by animals that use vision, generally sleep during the day and forage at night. The theory also offers an explanation for the fact that infants in most species of mammals sleep much more than adults. Infants who are being cared for by adults do not need to spend time foraging, and sleep protects them from wandering away into danger. Their sleep also gives their caregivers an opportunity to rest or attend to other needs.

It is interesting to speculate, in this vein, about the evolutionary conditions behind the 8-hour nighttime sleep pattern that characterizes adult humans throughout the world. Humans are highly visual creatures who need light to find food and do other things necessary for survival. At night it may have been best for us, during most of our evolution, to be tucked away asleep in a cave or other hiding place, so as not to be tempted to walk about and risk falling over a cliff or being attacked by a nocturnal predator. Only during the past few centuries—an insignificant speck of evolutionary time—have lights and other contrivances of civilization made the night relatively safe for us. According to this line of thinking, our pattern of sleep might be in part a vestigial trait, a carryover from a period when the night was a time of great danger. To the degree that nighttime is still more dangerous than daytime, our pattern of sleep may continue to serve an adaptive function.

Kenneth M. Highfill/Photo Researchers

Asleep and protected According to the preservation and protection theory, a major function of sleep is to keep animals quiet and hidden during that portion of the day or night when it would be most dangerous and least profitable for them to be moving about.

The Body-Restoration Theory

The body-restoration theory of sleep function is the theory that most people intuitively believe. It is the theory that your parents probably repeated to you as their reason for sending you to bed at a certain hour. According to this view, the body wears out during the day and sleep is necessary to put it back in shape.

Scientific support for this theory includes the observation that sleep is a time of rest and recuperation. The muscles are relaxed, metabolic rate is down, and growth hormone, which promotes body repair, is secreted at a much higher rate than during wakefulness (Douglas, 2002; Siegel, 2003). Also consistent with the restoration theory is the observation that prolonged, complete sleep deprivation in rats results in breakdown of various bodily tissues, leading, within about 3 weeks, to death (Everson, 1993; Everson & others, 1989).

The theory also offers an explanation for the general tendency of small mammals to sleep longer than large ones. Small mammals need to maintain a higher overall level of metabolism than do large mammals because they lose body heat more rapidly, and higher metabolism leads to greater wear and tear on bodily tissues (Siegel, 2005). However, contrary to this theory, research with birds has failed to show any correlation across species between sleep time and metabolic rate, but has shown a strong correlation between sleep time and risk of predation, which tends to support the preservation and protection theory discussed previously; birds that are most protected from predators while asleep, sleep longest regardless of their body size or metabolic rate (Roth & others, 2006). The theory also does not explain the large differences in sleep time between grazing animals and meat-eating animals that have similar body sizes and metabolic rates. Nor does it explain the

➤ - - - - - - - - - - - - - - - - - -**30**

What evidence supports the body-restoration theory of sleep, and what are some limitations of the theory?

failure of researchers to find consistent positive correlations, either across species or within species, between the amount of time an animal sleeps and the average amount of energy it expends through vigorous activity during the day.

The fact that all vertebrate animals sleep at least an hour or two out of every 24 hours, regardless of the degree to which they are at risk while sleeping, suggests that some amount of sleep is needed for body repair. But the body-restoration theory does not provide a satisfactory explanation of the large differences among species in sleep time, and it offers no explanation for the fact that some animals sleep during the day while others sleep at night. (Chapter 9 discusses an additional apparent function of sleep that involves growth process, that of consolidating new long-term memories into neural circuits in the brain.)

The Brain-Maintenance Theory of REM Sleep

If sleep in itself serves purposes of energy conservation, protection from danger, and bodily restoration, then what is the function of REM sleep? Why is restful non-REM sleep interrupted regularly by these periods of increased brain activity and energy expenditure? This question has generated much debate and research.

31

What evidence supports the theories that REM sleep promotes the maintenance of brain circuits?

◀ One longstanding theory is that REM sleep provides regular exercise to groups of neurons in the brain (Hobson, 1988). Synapses can degenerate if they go too long without being active (Edelman, 1987), so neural activity during REM sleep may help preserve important circuits. One line of evidence for this theory is that the longer a person or animal sleeps, the greater is the proportion of sleep time spent in REM sleep. With longer sleep periods there may be more need to interrupt non-REM sleep with exercise.

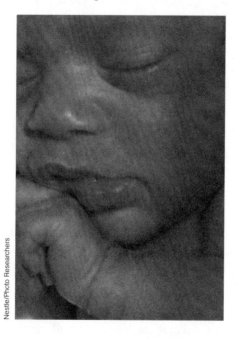

Nestle/Photo Researchers

Sweet dreams? We have no idea whether human fetuses, such as this one of 7 months, experience dream sensations or not, but we do know that they spend most of their time in REM sleep.

The theory also helps explain why REM sleep occurs to a much greater degree in fetuses and infants than in adults, regardless of species (see Figure 6.13). In fact, the peak of REM sleep in humans occurs in 30-day-old fetuses, which spend almost 24 hours a day in this state. Perhaps as their brains are developing in the relative isolation of the womb, they need to exercise sensory and motor pathways, and REM sleep is their means for doing that (Hobson, 1988). In the fetus, REM sleep is accompanied by body movements such as kicking and twisting, which are apparently triggered by the bursts of activity in motor areas of the brain, so muscles as well as brain circuits are exercised. By the time of birth a neural inhibitory system matures, which inactivates most motor neurons during REM sleep and thus prevents most movements that would otherwise occur. However, the motor neurons to the eyes and to various internal structures, such as the heart, remain uninhibited, so eye movements and increased heart rate persist as observable effects of the brain's activity.

Do Dreams Have Functions?

As just noted, there is good reason to think that REM sleep serves useful functions, but nobody knows if the dreams that accompany such sleep also serve useful functions. One theory, founded on the observation that dreams so often involve fearful content and negative emotions, is that dreams somehow provide a means of

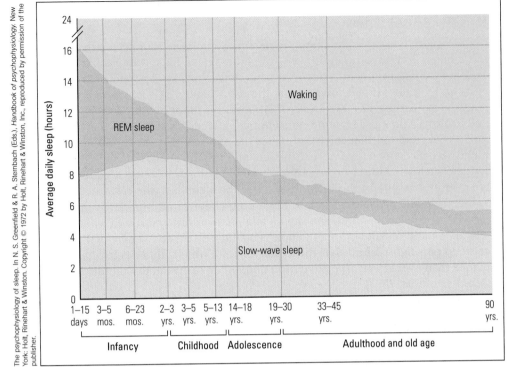

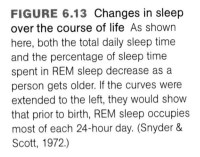

FIGURE 6.13 Changes in sleep over the course of life As shown here, both the total daily sleep time and the percentage of sleep time spent in REM sleep decrease as a person gets older. If the curves were extended to the left, they would show that prior to birth, REM sleep occupies most of each 24-hour day. (Snyder & Scott, 1972.)

rehearsing and resolving threatening experiences that either have happened or could happen in the person's real life (Valli & others, 2008).

Other sleep researchers, however, have suggested that dreams may not serve any life-promoting functions, but may simply be side effects of the physiological changes that occur during REM sleep (Antrobus, 2000; Hobson, 2002, 2004). Neurons in visual and motor areas of the brain become active during REM sleep, and hallucinations of sights and movements may be an inevitable consequence of such activity. Neurons involved in memory retrieval and emotions also become active, and these may bring familiar images and strong emotional feelings into the sleeping person's mind. In research done many years ago, electrical stimulation in portions of the cerebral cortex produced dreamlike hallucinations in people who were awake (Penfield & Perot, 1963). A similar phenomenon may well occur in REM sleep. In addition to producing hallucinations, the brain continues in REM sleep to engage in some degree of thought, just as it does in non-REM sleep. But now the thought becomes wrapped up in trying to make sense of the hallucinations. The result is the weaving of a story connecting one hallucination to the next—hence, the dream. Because of reduced mental capacity during sleep, the story is less logical than one the awake brain would develop, but it still contains some degree of logic.

Sometimes the side-effect theory just described is interpreted as an argument against the psychoanalytic view that dream analysis can be useful for understanding a person's mind. But that interpretation seems unjustified. Even if dreams are triggered by random events in the brain, the actual images, emotions, and story lines that constitute the dream are not random. They certainly contain elements based on the dreamer's experience, and because they occur at a time of reduced mental capacity, ideas or feelings that are normally suppressed by higher mental processes could emerge and perhaps be useful in psychoanalysis (Reiser, 1991). In fact, in one experiment, people were more likely to dream about a particular person if they were asked to suppress thoughts about that person just before going to sleep than if they were asked to think actively about that person just before going to sleep (Wegner & others, 2004). This finding is at least consistent with the idea that dream analysis might reveal ideas and concerns that a person is actively suppressing during the day.

➤- - - - - - - - - - - - - - -**32**

How might dreams be explained as inevitable consequences of the state of the brain during REM sleep?

Individual Variation in the Sleep Drive, and Effects of Failure to Satisfy That Drive

33
How does insomnia differ from nonsomnia? What negative consequences occur when people fail to satisfy their sleep drive?

◄The sleep drive varies from person to person. Some need more sleep than the typical 8 hours a night to function well, and others need less (Douglas, 2002). At the extreme are rare people, referred to as *nonsomniacs,* who sleep much less than most of us and yet do not feel tired during the day. A study of such people conducted many years ago by Ray Meddis (1977) found that they were generally vigorous and healthy. The most extreme nonsomniac in Meddis's sample was a 70-year-old nurse who reported that for most of her life she had slept about 50 minutes per night. She was very active during the day and usually spent the night in quiet activities, such as reading or painting. To verify her nonsomnia, Meddis observed her continuously for a prolonged period in the sleep lab. She slept not at all the first 3 days and nights in the lab, remaining cheerful and talkative throughout. Finally, on the fourth night, she slept a total of 99 minutes and awoke feeling fully rested. A more recent study, of people who did well on an average of 3 to 6 hours of sleep per night, found that these people were unusually energetic and scored higher than average, in a positive direction, on an "Attitude to Life" questionnaire (Monk & others, 2001).

The fact that nonsomnia is compatible with physical and psychological health adds to the evidence that only a relatively small amount of sleep is needed for body repair and growth of new synapses in the brain. Yet, most of us do need roughly 8 hours of sleep to function well. We need that sleep because we have a sleep drive that overwhelms our mind and makes us tired, miserable, and relatively ineffective at mental tasks when we fail to meet it. The drive for that much sleep may have evolved for reasons other than body repair and brain growth, but that doesn't mean we can ignore it. It is important to distinguish nonsomnia, which is very rare, from *insomnia,* which is relatively common. An insomniac is someone who has a normal drive for sleep but who, for some reason (such as worry), has great difficulty sleeping at night. Unlike a nonsomniac, an insomniac feels tired during the day as a result of not sleeping. And so do most people who voluntarily reduce their sleep.

Many laboratory studies have been conducted in which people with normal sleep drives voluntarily stay awake for periods of 3 or 4 days or even longer. After about 72 hours awake, some people begin to experience symptoms such as distorted perceptions and extreme irritability (Borbély, 1986). Sleepiness waxes and wanes during such studies, in accordance with the inner clock that controls it. People find it much harder to stay awake during the late night and early morning hours than they do during the rest of the 24-hour day, even after several days of sleep deprivation. In such experiments, scores on tests of vigilance, judgment, and creative thinking also wax and wane in a 24-hour cycle, keeping pace with sleepiness (Horne, 1979, 1988; Jennings & others, 2003). Scores on such tests decline when sleepiness rises, apparently because sleepy people have difficulty attending to the task and because their performance is often interrupted by brief moments of falling asleep, from which they arouse themselves. In general, stimulants such as caffeine, which counteract

"Sleep disorders in cats." Mother Goose & Grimm, Mike Peters. From Boston Globe, Tues., June 27, 2006.

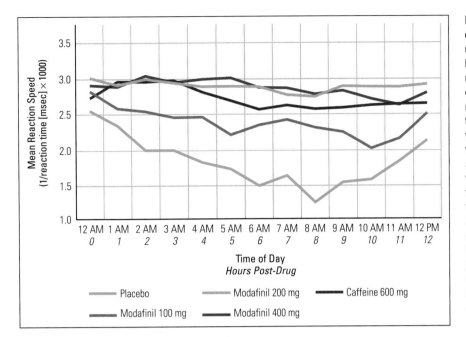

FIGURE 6.14 Decline and rise in vigilance during sleep deprivation In this experiment, university students were kept awake for 42 hours before the start of testing. Just before testing, some received a strong dose of caffeine, others received one of three doses of another stimulant drug, modafinil, and still others received a placebo. In the test of vigilance, conducted every hour, the subjects watched a time display on a computer screen and were instructed to press a button as quickly as possible each time it began to increment. The measure was response speed (the reciprocal of response time). As shown in the graph, in the placebo group vigilance declined steadily from midnight to 8 a.m. and then began to increase. This is consistent with other evidence that the circadian rhythm of sleepiness and wakefulness continues even after long periods of sleep deprivation. There was no such decline in the groups receiving caffeine or in those receiving high doses of modafinil. (From Wesensten & others, 2002.)

sleepiness, also remove the negative effects of sleep deprivation on the performance of such tasks. For an example of data showing the effects both of sleepiness and of stimulants on a test of vigilance, see Figure 6.14 (Wesensten & others, 2002).

In the real world outside of the laboratory, sleepiness—with its accompanying decline in attention and judgment—is dangerous. Many accidents in the workplace result from it, and sleepiness rivals drunkenness as a leading cause of traffic fatalities (Horne & Reyner, 1995, 2001).

Brain Mechanisms Controlling Sleep

In the early years of sleep research, some researchers believed that sleep is the natural state that the brain slips into when not aroused by external stimulation, so they saw no need to posit the existence of special sleep-inducing mechanisms. But such a view is inconsistent with the observation that sometimes sleepiness overwhelms us even when external stimulation is high, while at other times we can't sleep no matter how quiet, dark, and nonstimulating the environment may be. We now know that sleepiness, like other drives, is actively promoted by neural mechanisms located in the hypothalamus and in brain areas closely connected to the hypothalamus.

Rhythm-Generating Neurons in the Hypothalamus Control the Daily Cycle of Sleepiness

In all animals, as I noted earlier, the sleep drive waxes and wanes in a cyclic manner over the 24-hour day. This cycle of sleepiness and wakefulness continues, in laboratory animals and human volunteers, even after many days in an artificial "time-free environment"—an environment where there are no regular changes in lighting or other cues that could indicate the time of day. In such an environment, the cycle is typically a few minutes longer or shorter than 24 hours, and it varies from individual to individual, but it is remarkably constant within a given individual (Lavie, 2001; Takahashi & Zatz, 1982).

The technical term for any repetitive biological change that continues at close to a 24-hour cycle in the absence of external cues is ***circadian*** [sir-**kade**-ee-un] ***rhythm.*** The term comes from the Latin words *circa*, meaning "about," and *dies*, meaning "day." The clock that controls the circadian rhythm of sleep in all mammals is located in a specific nucleus of the hypothalamus called the

34

What is some evidence that the sleep drive is affected by an internal clock, located in the hypothalamus, that can operate even without external time cues?

suprachiasmatic [**soup**-ra-**kai**-az-**mat**-ick] *nucleus.* If this nucleus is damaged, animals lose their regular sleep-wake rhythms and sleep at rather random times over the 24-hour day, and the same is true of human patients (Cohen & Albers, 1991). This nucleus contains rhythm-generating neurons, which gradually increase and decrease their rate of action potentials over a cycle of approximately 24 hours, even when surgically isolated from other parts of the brain (Herzog, 2008).

In addition to controlling sleepiness, the suprachiasmatic nucleus also controls a daily rhythm of body temperature (which normally declines in the evening and increases in the morning) and of certain hormones. The hormone that is most directly locked to the circadian clock, and is often used by researchers as an index of the clock's timing, is *melatonin.* This hormone, produce by the pineal gland, begins to be secreted into the bloodstream in the evening, typically about two hours before a person is ready to fall asleep, and is secreted at relatively high levels until approximately the time when the person is ready to awaken naturally in the morning (Dumont & Beaulieu, 2007).

Input from the Eyes Synchronizes the Hypothalamic Clock to the Light-Dark Cycle

35

What is some evidence that the internal clock is continuously reset by daily changes in light? Through what pathway does that resetting occur?

◄ Under normal conditions, the circadian clock is synchronized with the 24-hour day by the regular waxing and waning of daylight, so rhythms occur in periods of exactly (rather than approximately) 24 hours. Experiments with animals show that the cycle can be lengthened or shortened, by as much as a couple of hours either way, by artificially changing the period of light and dark. Other experiments, with humans as well as nonhuman animals, show that the cycle can be reset through exposure to bright fluorescent lights (Czeisler & others, 1989; 1990).

In general, bright light in the morning and/or dim light or darkness in the evening advances the cycle, so that the person becomes sleepy earlier in the evening. In contrast, bright light in the evening and/or avoidance of light in the morning has the opposite effect. It delays the cycle, so that sleepiness occurs later at night. A series of several days of such changed conditions can alter the cycle significantly (Dumont & Beaulieu, 2007).

This knowledge about the effects of light has been put to practical use. In one clinical experiment, for example, people with *sleep-onset insomnia,* inability to fall asleep until very late at night or the wee hours of the morning, were cured or at least partly cured of their insomnia by morning treatments with bright light. After a week of such exposure, the subjects showed an earlier peak of melatonin than before, earlier sleep onset, and an increase of nearly an hour's more sleep per night, on average, than before treatment. This improvement lasted throughout a 3-week follow-up period after the treatment had ended (Lack & others, 2008). Other research suggests that a tendency to avoid morning light and to use relatively bright lights at home in the evening may be a cause of sleep-onset insomnia in many people today (Dumont & Beauliu, 2007). If you suffer from this problem, you might shift your own cycle to an earlier sleep time by spending some time every morning in sunlight and dimming your room lights in the evening.

Brain researchers have found that changes in lighting influence the rhythm-generating neurons by way of a neural tract that runs from the retinas of the eyes to the suprachiasmatic nucleus. These neurons differ from those that are involved in vision, and they derive from light receptors in the retina that differ from the receptors (rods and cones, discussed in Chapter 7) that are essential for vision (Van Gelder, 2008).

Resetting the circadian clock
Steven Lockley and his colleagues have found that blue light works better than white light in resetting the circadian clock that times the onset of sleepiness. Timed exposures to such light can help shift workers and world travelers adapt their sleep schedules to the requirements of their work or travel.

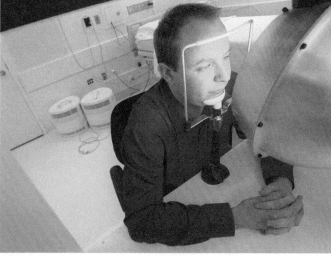

Kris Snibbe/Harvard University News Office

Other Neurons in the Hypothalamus Promote Sleepiness and Wakefulness

In addition to the suprachiasmatic nucleus, researchers have identified two other neural centers in the hypothalamus that are involved in sleep and wakefulness. One of these is a sleep-activating center located in the *ventromedial preoptic nucleus,* which lies in front of the suprachiasmatic nucleus (Saper & others, 2001). Electrical stimulation in this area can cause a previously alert animal to fall asleep, and lesions there can result in permanent sleeplessness, eventuating in death in rats. In humans, a rare viral infection that destroys neurons in this nucleus greatly reduces sleepiness and average daily sleep time (Saper & others, 2001). This nucleus receives neural connections from the suprachiasmatic nucleus, and its neurons are also responsive to certain chemical changes in the body that are believed to reflect the body's need for sleep. Neurons from this nucleus connect to almost all parts of the brain and release the inhibitory neurotransmitter GABA. The resulting dampening of neural activity throughout the brain is believed to bring on the state of sleepiness and, subsequently, sleep itself.

The other crucial hypothalamic center is a wake-activating set of neurons located in portions of the lateral and posterior hypothalamus (side and rear part of the hypothalamus). These neurons send their axons to many other parts of the brain, including certain arousal centers in the brainstem, where they release *orexins,* which are two recently discovered peptide neurotransmitters that have excitatory effects (Sakurai, 2007). People who for genetic reasons lack the ability to produce a normal amount of orexins suffer from a disease called *narcolepsy,* which is characterized by a tendency to fall suddenly asleep at unpredictable times during the day. Orexins, through their actions in various parts of the brain, enable a person to maintain a long-lasting state of alertness. The orexin-producing neurons of the hypothalamus are activated by many sources of input, including input from emotion centers in the limbic system (Sakurai, 2007). Presumably, these connections are at least partly responsible for the alertness and inability to sleep that accompanies emotional states.

In sum, your likelihood of feeling sleepy or alert at any given time depends, apparently, on the balance of neural activity in these two opposing centers of the hypothalamus. The suprachiasmatic nucleus influences both of these centers through direct and indirect connections, so sleepiness and alertness generally follow the circadian rhythm. But other inputs, such as those reflecting the length of time you have gone without sleep, or those reflecting a threat and a need to stay awake, can override the circadian input and cause sleepiness during the day or wakefulness at night. As was the case with hunger, the sleep drive is affected by many different factors, all of which are integrated by centers in the hypothalamus.

> ◄ --------------------------------- **36**
>
> **How are sleepiness and arousal controlled by two sets of neurons in the hypothalamus? How are these neurons influenced by the circadian clock and by emotion-producing centers in the brain?**

SECTION REVIEW

There is a drive for sleep, a state involving relative unresponsiveness to the environment.

Basic Characteristics	Functions of Sleep	Brain Mechanisms
➤ Researchers use EEG records to divide sleep into stages, with stage 4 being deepest.	➤ The preservation and protection theory asserts that sleep is needed to conserve energy and increase safety. It is supported by cross-species comparisons of amount and timing of sleep.	➤ The suprachiasmatic nucleus in the hypothalamus acts as an internal clock for sleepiness and wakefulness.
➤ A sleeper progresses through the sleep stages, from light to deep and rapidly back to light, in approximately 90-minute cycles.	➤ The body-restoration theory contends that the body needs sleep to recover from wear and tear. It is supported by sleep-deprivation studies in animals.	➤ Light synchronizes the internal clock with the light-dark cycle.
➤ REM (rapid-eye-movement) sleep occurs at the transition between one sleep cycle and the next.	➤ REM sleep may function to maintain brain circuits and consolidate new learning.	➤ Sleep-promoting and arousal-promoting sets of neurons exist in the hypothalamus. They receive inputs from the suprachiasmatic nucleus and emotion areas of the limbic system and send outputs to most parts of the brain.
➤ Most true dreams occur in REM sleep, and sleep thought occurs in non-REM sleep.	➤ Different people need different amounts of sleep. Sleep deprivation reduces performance, especially on tests of vigilance.	

▮ Foundations for Understanding Emotions

Enough sleep; wake up and face the challenges of the day. Midterm exams are just around the corner, your family is after you to get your life in order, your lover has just left you for another, and a hungry tiger is crouched behind you. Are you awake now? All these events have something in common: All (if you believe them) have the potential to elicit strong emotions.

Emotion, like *motivation,* is a concept that applies to almost all of psychology. Much, if not all, of our thought and behavior is tinged with emotion. My goal in this section is to introduce to you some ideas about the underlying processes and mechanisms of emotion. You will find much more about particular emotions in other chapters.

The Nature and Value of Emotions

Emotion is a concept that has been difficult for psychologists to pin down and define in an agreed-upon way. According to one estimate, psychologists have generated at least 90 different definitions of emotion (Plutchik, 2001). My own preferred definition is one that closely resembles the way the term is used in everyday life: An **emotion** is a subjective feeling that is mentally directed toward some object. This brief definition requires some elaboration, however.

Emotions Are Feelings Directed Toward Objects

37
According to the definitions used here, how does *emotion* differ from *affect* and from *mood*?

◄An emotion, as just defined, has two components: feeling and object. The *object* of an emotion may be a person, thing, or event, real or imagined, but that object is always something that is in some way meaningful to the one who experiences the emotion. The feeling and the object are inextricably entwined in the emotional experience; the object is perceived as the cause of the emotion. The person *loves* John because John is so *loveable, hates* war because war is *detestable, fears* snakes because snakes are *frightening,* and *grieves* the loss of a friend because that loss is *grievous.* In these examples, John, war, snakes, and loss of friend are the objects of emotions. In some emotions—specifically, *pride, shame, guilt,* and *embarrassment* (all discussed in Chapter 14)—one's self or one's own behavior is the object. These are called *self-conscious emotions.*

The *feeling* associated with emotion, independent of the object, is referred to by some psychologists as **affect** [**aph**-ect]. Such feelings can vary along two dimensions. One dimension has to do with the degree of pleasantness or unpleasantness of the feeling, and the other has to do with the degree of mental and physical arousal. Figure 6.15 shows one way of describing and depicting various affects. Notice that by moving upward or downward on the circle, one goes toward increasing or decreasing arousal; by moving rightward or leftward, one goes toward increasing degrees of pleasure or displeasure. The terms in the figure describe not emotions, but feelings devoid of objects. An emotion depends on the object as well as the feeling. Thus, a feeling of pleasure may be experienced as the emotion of *pride* when the object is oneself and as the emotion of *love* when the object is someone else.

Delight and its object An emotion is a subjective feeling directed toward an object that is experienced as the cause of the feeling.

Emotional feelings are not always attached to objects. Sometimes an emotional feeling is experienced as free-floating rather than directed at a particular object, and in that case, if it lasts for a sufficiently long period, it is referred to as a **mood.** Moods can last for hours, days, or even longer and can color all aspects of one's thought and behavior. In some cases, everyday language provides different terms for moods and emotions that have similar underlying feelings. A feeling of being tense, jittery, and unhappy may be labeled as *anxiety* when it is a free-floating mood but as *fear* when it is an emotion associated with an object such as a snake or an upcoming examination. A feeling of being sad and upset may be labeled *depression* when it is free-floating and as *grief* when it is associated with a specific loss.

Radius Images/Alamy

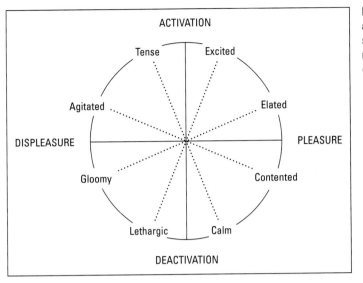

FIGURE 6.15 **Affects** Basic affects are shown here arranged in a circle in which the vertical dimension represents degree of perceived arousal and the horizontal dimension represents degree of pleasure or displeasure. (Adapted from Russell, 2003.)

There Is No Agreed-upon Way to Classify Emotions

How many different emotions are there? The answer to that is quite arbitrary; it depends on how finely graded a taxonomy (system of classification) we wish to create. Fear, for example, might be understood as one emotion or as a cluster of emotions that all have some things in common. One's fear of snakes, fear of death, and fear of others' judgments, for example, may be experienced as qualitatively different from one another.

Some psychologists have attempted to identify a set of primary emotions by analyzing the emotion labels that are common to a language or to several languages. In English several hundred different words are used as labels for emotions, but many of them are synonyms or near synonyms. By asking people to rate pairs of common emotion labels for the degree of similarity between the emotions they describe, psychologists have found that the labels can be clustered into a relatively small number of groups. Using this method, Robert Plutchik (2003) identified what he considers to be eight primary emotions, which can be arranged as four pairs of opposites: *joy* versus *sorrow, anger* versus *fear, acceptance* versus *disgust*, and *surprise* versus *expectancy*. According to Plutchik's model (depicted and described more fully in Figure 6.16), these

- **38**
Through what strategy did Plutchik arrive at his model of eight primary emotions? Why is this model not universally accepted?
- -

FIGURE 6.16 **A model of primary emotions** Robert Plutchik has proposed that the spectrum of all emotions can be represented by a cone with eight sectors. The vertical dimension of the cone represents emotional intensity. The eight sectors represent eight primary emotions, arranged such that similar emotions are next to one another and opposite emotions are on opposite sides of the cone. In the exploded view of the cone, with the sectors laid out flat, the emotion labels in the spaces between sectors represent mixtures of the adjacent two primary emotions. (This model of emotions may appear similar to the model of affects shown in Figure 6.15, but it was developed from a different set of observations and premises; the two models are not directly comparable.) (From Plutchik, 2001.)

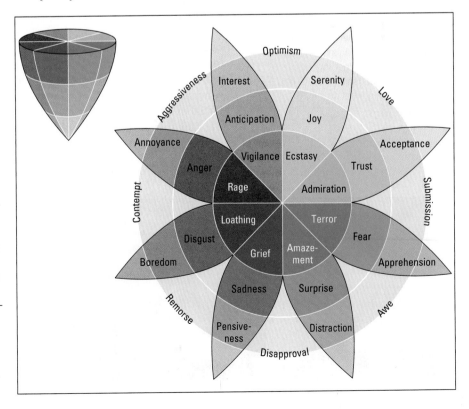

primary emotions can mix with one another in any number of ways to produce an essentially infinite variety of different emotional experiences, just as a small set of primary colors can mix to create virtually all the colors the human eye can see.

Plutchik's model is elegant and useful, but by no means universally accepted. Other psychologists, using similar means, have generated different sets of basic emotions. Still others have argued that emotional experiences are so subjective and variable, and emotional descriptions are so much influenced by culture and language, that any attempt to arrive at a universally agreed-upon list of basic emotions is futile (Russell, 2003). One view is that emotions do not, at a biological level, come in discrete categories, but come in an infinite set of varieties that are best described in terms of their position in a multidimensional universe of physiological changes and subjective feelings (Barrett, 2006; Fontaine & others, 2007).

Emotions Serve Adaptive Functions

39
How can emotions promote adaptive ends through their motivating and communicative effects?

Emotions must have come about through natural selection because of their adaptive value. This line of thinking draws attention to the motivating qualities of emotions. Implicit in the positive-negative dimension of emotional feelings is the idea that emotions motivate us to approach objects that can help us, and to avoid or repel objects that hinder us, in our efforts to survive and reproduce. When passionately in love, we behave in all sorts of ways, including ways that under other conditions would seem foolish, to get close to our beloved, a potential partner in reproduction. When fearful, we run away, or freeze, or try to look inconspicuous, or in other ways attempt to avoid the dangerous predator or enemy. When angry, we puff ourselves up, threaten, and sometimes even fight, in order to repulse or change the behavior of one who tries to harm us or who stands in the way of what we want or need. Strong emotions of all sorts focus our attention narrowly on the object of the emotion and lead us to ignore, for a time, other events and drives that would distract us from that object.

Emotions also promote our survival and reproduction through their capacity to communicate our intentions and needs to others. Our expressions of love may signal to our beloved that we will be faithful mates. Our expressions of fear may signal submission to our human attackers and thereby prevent a fight, or they may draw friends to our aid. Mere hints of anger in our demeanor may, all by themselves, convince the objects of our anger to change their ways in desired directions. As discussed in Chapter 3, many emotions are automatically and unconsciously expressed on the face in ways that are universal. Such expressions most likely came about through natural selection primarily because of their communicative value.

Facial expressions of at least some emotions may serve more than communicative value; they may be part of the body's way of dealing with the emotion-arousing situation. The expression of fear, for example, involves a widening of the eyes and an opening of the nasal passages, which increases the field of vision and increases sensitivity to odors (see Figure 6.17a). In a fear-provoking environment, such increased sensitivity to sights and smells may have been useful to our evolutionary ancestors, and may still be useful, as a means of detecting potential threats (Susskind, 2008). Conversely, in the emotion of disgust—which involves a rejection of some object in the environment—the field of vision and the nasal passages narrow, cutting off the offending sight or odor (see Figure 6.17b).

Anger serves valuable functions Sometimes the person we are most angry at is also the person we care most about. This woman's anger is a clear signal to her partner that something in their relationship is out of balance and needs correction.

(a)

(b)

FIGURE 6.17 Emotional Expressions May Influence Sensory Processing In the expression of *fear* (a), the eyes and nostrils are wide open, which may facilitate vision and smell. In the expression of *disgust* (b), the eyes and nostrils are partly shut, which may serve to cut off vision and smell.

Effects of Bodily Responses on Emotional Feelings

Most emotional states are accompanied by peripheral changes in the body. By *peripheral* changes, I mean all changes in the body outside of the central nervous system. These include changes in heart rate, blood pressure, diversion of blood from one set of tissues to another, activation of certain glands, tension in particular muscles, and facial expression of the emotion. The changes, overall, are adaptive because of their communicative function or their role in helping prepare the body for possible action.

Common sense and everyday language tell us that these peripheral changes are caused by our emotions. We say: "My heart pounds and I tremble because I am afraid"; "My face is flushed and my teeth are clenched because I am angry"; "Tears well up in my eyes and a lump forms in my throat because I feel grief." Over a hundred years ago, in his classic textbook, *The Principles of Psychology,* William James (1890/1950) turned common sense upside down and suggested that bodily reactions precede the emotions and cause them, rather than the reverse.

James's Peripheral Feedback Theory of Emotion

James's evidence for his theory of emotion came not from experiments but from introspection. Looking inward at his own emotions, James concluded that his emotional feelings were really sensations stemming from bodily changes. Thus, his feeling of fear was his feeling of a quickened heart, shallow breathing, gooseflesh, and trembling limbs. Similarly, his feeling of anger was his feeling of a flushed face, dilated nostrils, and clenched teeth. James believed that he could identify a different constellation of bodily changes for each emotion, and that if he could not feel these changes he would not feel the emotion.

◄------------------------40

What is James's theory of emotion? What evidence did James supply for the theory, and what modern evidence is consistent with the theory?

The essence of James's theory is that the bodily reaction to an emotion-provoking stimulus is automatic, occurring without conscious thought or feeling, and that the assessment of one's emotional state comes later and is based on the perception of the bodily state. In an unexpected encounter with a bear, the brain instantly, at some unconscious level, judges the bear to be dangerous and precipitates a bodily change that helps prepare the person for flight. There is no time, in an emergency, for conscious reflection. The body reacts immediately. Then, later on, when the danger is over or at least reduced, the person may sense his beating heart and trembling knees and conclude that he is or was frightened. The contrast between James's theory and the common-sense theory that he was arguing against is illustrated in the top two portions of Figure 6.18.

FIGURE 6.18 Three theories of emotion
Each theory proposes a different set of causal relationships among perception of the stimulus, bodily arousal, and emotional feeling. According to the common-sense theory (so labeled by James), the emotional feeling precedes and causes the bodily arousal. James's theory reverses that relationship, and Schachter's theory holds that the intensity of the emotional feeling depends on the bodily response, but the type of emotion experienced (such as fear, anger, or love) depends on the person's cognitive assessment of the external stimulus or situation.

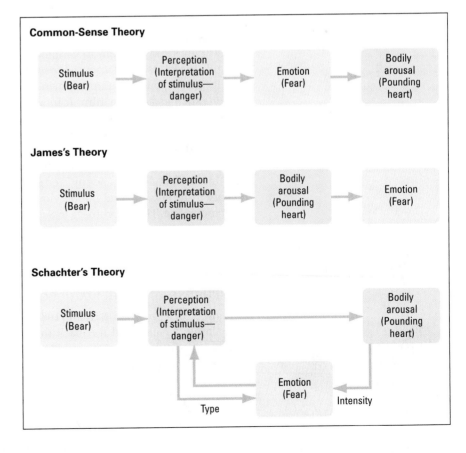

A considerable amount of evidence today tends to support James's theory. People throughout the world describe their emotions in terms of bodily changes and are quite consistent in the kinds of changes they associate with each emotion (Cacioppo & others, 1992; Rime & others, 1990). Researchers have also found that people who are particularly good at detecting changes in their own internal condition, such as changes in their heart rate, are more likely than others to detect and report emotional states in themselves (Critchely & others, 2004; Wiens & others, 2000). Moreover, brain imaging studies have shown that a certain portion of the somatosensory area of the cerebral cortex, which becomes active when a person is sensing his or her own bodily state, also becomes active when a person is consciously assessing his or her own emotional state (Critchely & others, 2004; Damasio, 2001).

Schachter's Cognition-Plus-Feedback Theory

41

How does Schachter's theory differ from James's? How did Schachter support his theory with experiments?

In the 1960s, Stanley Schachter developed a theory of emotion that can be understood as a variation of James's theory. According to Schachter, the feeling of an emotion depends not just on sensory feedback pertaining to the body's response but also on the person's perceptions and thoughts (cognitions) about the environmental event that presumably evoked that response. More specifically, he proposed that perception and thought about the environment influence the *type* of emotion felt, and that sensory feedback about the degree of bodily arousal influences the *intensity* of the emotion felt (see the bottom portion of Figure 6.18). Thus, if you see a bear, your perception that it is dangerous leads you to interpret your emotion as fear, and your perception of the degree to which your heart is pounding and your knees are trembling determines the amount of fear you experience. Schachter also proposed that the intensity of the emotional feeling influences the interpretation of the stimulus. Thus, if your bodily arousal was already high, perhaps from drinking too much coffee, that arousal would contribute to your emotional intensity and might lead you to perceive the bear as more dangerous than you would otherwise perceive it to be.

In experiments testing his theory, Schachter (1971) injected people with either epinephrine (a hormone also known as adrenaline, which raises heart rate and produces other effects associated with high arousal) or a placebo (an inactive substance) and then exposed them to various emotion-eliciting conditions. He found that epinephrine by itself did not produce any particular emotion (the subjects just said they felt jumpy), but when epinephrine was combined with an emotion-inducing situation, such as a horror film, it increased the intensity of the subject's emotion. As predicted by his theory, the kind of emotion subjects felt depended on the external situation, but the intensity was heightened by epinephrine. The epinephrine-injected subjects manifested and reported more anger when insulted, more fear when watching a frightening film, and more hilarity when watching a slapstick comedy than did placebo-injected subjects. This emotion-enhancing effect occurred only if the subjects had not previously been informed of the physiological effects of epinephrine. Thus, according to Schachter, high physiological arousal increases emotion only when people believe that the arousal is caused by the external situation. Schachter's theory fits well with the modern idea that emotions are defined not just by feelings but also by the perceived objects of those feelings.

Influence of Facial Feedback on Emotional Experience

Some years ago, Paul Ekman (1984) proposed a theory of emotions that is similar to James's peripheral feedback theory but focuses particularly on the role of the face. As discussed in Chapter 3, Ekman and his colleagues found that different basic emotions are associated with different facial expressions. Those expressions are produced rapidly and automatically (though they can be inhibited). According to Ekman, sensory feedback from facial expressions contributes both to emotional feelings and to the production of the full-body reactions that accompany emotions.

"Just once I would like to laugh or to frown."

FIGURE 6.19 Forcing a smile In Soussignan's (2002) experiment testing the facial feedback theory of emotion, some subjects were asked to hold a pencil between their teeth in a manner that led to their lips being pulled back and their cheeks raised, similar to a full-faced smile, and others were asked to hold a pencil between their lips, which prevented smiling.

If you form your face into a smile, will you feel happier? A Pollyannaish suggestion, perhaps, but research indicates that there may be some truth to it. In one experiment, for example, some subjects were each asked to hold a pencil tightly between their teeth, which forced their faces into smiling expressions, and others were asked to hold a pencil between their lips in a manner that did not produce smiles (see Figure 6.19), as they watched films of happy or funny scenes (Soussignan, 2002). The result was that the former reported more enjoyment of the films than did the latter. In other experiments, subjects have been asked to contract certain facial muscles—in ways (unbeknownst to the subject) designed to mimic the facial expressions of fear, anger, sorrow, or happiness. The results, generally, are that people who hold their faces in these ways subsequently report experiencing more of the specific emotion that their faces were mimicking—whether or not they were aware that they were mimicking a particular emotion (e.g. Flack, 2006).

Ekman and his colleagues (1983) found that induced facial expressions not only can alter self-reports of emotion but also can produce physiological responses throughout the body that are consistent with the induced expression. In one experiment, these researchers asked subjects to move specific facial muscles in ways designed to mimic each of six basic emotional expressions (see Figure 6.20). For comparison, they asked other subjects to experience each emotion by mentally reliving an event in which that emotion had been strong. As the subjects held the facial expressions or imagined the emotional events, various indices of their physiological arousal were recorded. The main finding was that different patterns of arousal accompanied different emotions, but the pattern for a given emotion was the same whether the person had been asked to relive that emotion or simply to move certain facial muscles (see Figure 6.21). For instance, anger, whether it was relived or mimicked by facial molding, was accompanied by increases in skin temperature that did not occur for the other emotions (consistent with evidence that blood tends to flow into the skin during anger). As another example, both anger and fear—in both the mimicking and the reliving conditions—increased the subjects' heart rates more than did any other

◄ - - - - - - - - - - - - - - - - -**42**

What is some evidence supporting Ekman's theory that a person's facial response influences the person's feeling of an emotion and also influences the person's bodily responses to the emotional situation?

(a)   (b)   (c)

FIGURE 6.20 Inducing an expression of fear Shown here are frames from a videotape of a man following the instructions used by Ekman and his colleagues (1983) to induce an expression of fear: (a) "Raise your brows and pull them together," (b) "now raise your upper eyelids," and (c) "now stretch your lips horizontally, back toward your ears." Other instructions were used to induce other emotional expressions, producing the results shown in Figure 6.21.

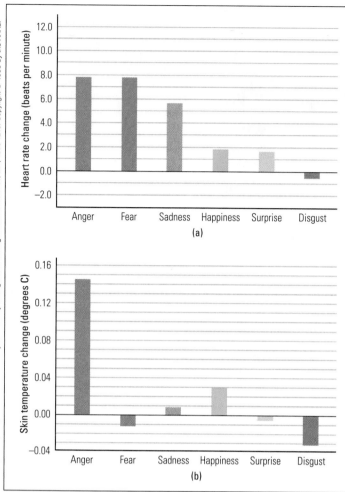

FIGURE 6.21 **Effect of induced emotional expressions on heart rate and skin temperature** Ekman and his colleagues (1983) found that (a) heart rate increased most when the induced facial expression was of anger, fear, or sadness and (b) skin temperature increased most when the induced expression was of anger. Although not shown here, the same pattern of effects also occurred when subjects were asked to relive specific emotional experiences through imagination.

emotion. Researchers subsequently replicated these findings with a wide variety of people, including people in non-Western cultures (Levenson, 1992; Levenson & others, 1992).

Brain Mechanisms of Emotion

Thus far, I have focused on emotional feelings and peripheral bodily changes and have said little about the role of the brain in emotions. But of course the brain is the center both for producing the bodily changes and for experiencing emotional feelings. Research on the brain's emotional systems has focused particularly on two structures: the amygdala and the prefrontal portion of the cerebral cortex.

The Amygdala Assesses the Emotional Significance of Stimuli

In James's classic example (diagrammed in Figure 6.18, page 223), a person sees a bear and reacts in a manner that the person subsequently interprets as fear. What causes the initial reaction? James assumed that somehow the brain can quickly and unconsciously assess the significance of stimuli and can generate appropriate bodily reactions. We now know that a crucial structure for this capacity of the brain is the amygdala.

43
- - - - - - - - - - - - - - - - -
What is some evidence that the amygdala initiates emotional reactions to stimuli and that this effect can occur even without conscious awareness of the emotion-eliciting stimuli?
- - - - - - - - - - - - - - - - -

◀ The *amygdala* [uh-**mig**-duh-luh], a cluster of nuclei buried underneath the cerebral cortex, in the temporal lobe, is part of the limbic system (introduced in Chapter 5). This structure appears to be, among other things, the brain's early warning system. It receives stimulus input from all of the body's sensory systems; performs continuous, rapid assessments of that input; and alerts the rest of the brain and body if it judges that some sort of whole-body or behavioral reaction may be called for.

The amygdala receives sensory input by way of two routes: a very rapid *subcortical* route and a somewhat slower *cortical* route (diagrammed in Figure 6.22 for the sense of vision). Through the former, it analyzes incoming information even before that information has been processed by sensory areas of the cerebral cortex. Through the latter, it analyzes, in more detail, information that has been processed by the cerebral cortex. The amygdala sends its output to many other brain structures. Through those outputs it alerts the rest of the brain to pay attention to the stimulus of concern and it generates such bodily reactions as increased heart rate and muscle tension (Davis, 1992).

In a set of classic experiments with monkeys, removal of the amygdala along with nearby portions of the temporal lobe of the cerebral cortex on both sides of the brain produced a dramatic set of changes in behavior described as *psychic blindness* (Klüver & Bucy, 1937; Weiskrantz, 1956). The monkeys could still see objects and could move in a coordinated fashion, but they seemed indifferent to the psychological significance of objects. They no longer responded fearfully to objects that had previously frightened them or aggressively to objects that had previously angered them. They also failed to distinguish in the usual ways between foods and nonfoods or between appropriate and inappropriate objects for sexual attention.

People who have suffered even partial damage to the amygdala exhibit striking losses in fear and anger, even though they don't show the other symptoms of psychic blindness (Allman & Brothers, 1994; Berridge, 2003). For instance, one woman with such damage failed to react emotionally, or even to show much concern, when she and her husband were mugged (Bruce & Young, 1998). In experiments, people with damage to the amygdala generally fail to respond emotionally to stimuli—such as pictures of frightening or disgusting scenes—that regularly elicit emotional responses and feelings in brain-intact people (Berntson & others, 2007; Helmuth, 2003). Moreover, in brain-imaging studies with brain-intact people, increased neural activity in the amygdala correlates strongly with increases in fear, anger, or dis-

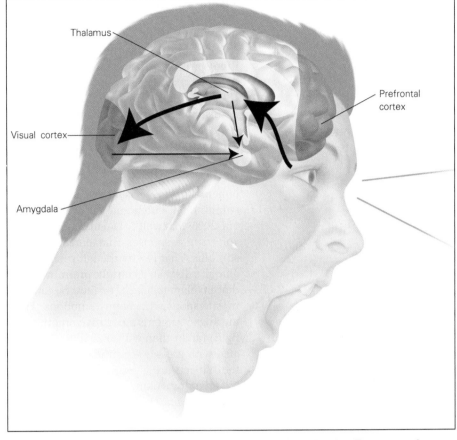

gust (Hamann & others, 2002; Whalen, 1998). The amygdala may also be activated, but less so, by stimuli that induce positive emotions. In one brain-imaging study with men, the left amygdala (but not the right) became active in response to a variety of appealing pictures, including depictions of attractive seminude women and of appetizing foods (Hamann & others, 2002).

Researchers have found that people react emotionally even to stimuli—such as angry words or faces—that are flashed on a screen too rapidly for conscious perception (Öhmann, 1999; Ruys & Stapel, 2008). This effect most likely occurs by way of the subcortical sensory input to the amygdala. Joseph LeDoux and his colleagues found that rats with lesions destroying the entire visual and auditory cortex, but not the amygdala, continued to respond emotionally to sights and sounds that had previously been paired with electric shock, but rats with lesions destroying the amygdala did not (LeDoux, 1996; LeDoux & others, 1989). Similarly, people who have damage to the visual cortex have been shown to respond emotionally to visual stimuli that they could not consciously see (Anders & others, 2004). Sensory areas of the cortex are essential for conscious perception of stimuli, but not for unconscious emotional responses to them. The fact that emotional responses can be generated by subcortical pathways to the amygdala helps explain why our emotions are often irrational and so difficult to control through conscious reasoning.

FIGURE 6.22 Two routes from the eyes to the amygdala Most visual input goes from relay nuclei in the thalamus to the visual area of the cerebral cortex, and from there to other areas of the brain, including the amygdala. However, some visual input goes directly from the thalamus to the amygdala, bypassing the cerebral cortex. The direct input from the thalamus to the amygdala may be responsible for fast, unconscious emotional responses to visual stimuli.

The Prefrontal Cortex Is Essential for Conscious Experience of Emotion

While the amygdala is essential for unconscious emotional responses, the **prefrontal cortex**—that is, the foremost portion of the frontal lobe of the cerebral cortex (see Figure 6.22)—is essential for the full conscious experience of emotions and the ability to act in deliberate, planned ways based on those feelings. One line of evidence for this comes from observations many years ago of people who were subjected to prefrontal lobotomy—an operation that disconnects the prefrontal area from the rest of the brain and was, before the development of drug treatments,

44

What is some evidence that the prefrontal cortex is involved in the conscious feeling of emotions, and that the right and left prefrontal cortices are differentially involved with different types of emotional responses?

a relatively common treatment for severe mental disorders. The operation usually relieved people of their crippling emotional feelings, but it also left them unable to plan and organize their lives effectively (Valenstein, 1986). The prefrontal cortex receives input from the amygdala and from the somatosensory cortex, and such input provides it with information about the amygdala's assessment of the stimulus and the body's state of arousal.

A good deal of research suggests that, to some degree at least, the two cortical hemispheres are involved in processing different emotions. Much research using EEG or fMRI has shown greater neural activity in the right prefrontal cortex when experiencing negative emotions (especially fear and disgust), and greater activity in the left prefrontal cortex when experiencing positive emotions (Haller & others, 1998; Davidson & others, 2003). Recent studies, however, suggest that this laterality of neural activity has more to do with neural preparation to respond to the emotional stimuli than with actual experience of the emotional feeling (Harmon-Jones & others, 2006; Maxwell & Davidson, 2007). The left prefrontal cortex seems to be most involved in responses that entail *withdrawal*, or moving away from the emotional stimulus. That is why the left prefrontal cortex is most responsive in the emotions of fear and disgust. The right prefrontal cortex seems to be most involved in responses that involve *approach*, or moving toward the emotional stimulus, which is why it is most responsive in happy emotions. The most telling data come from studies involving anger. Anger is a negative emotion, but it tends to evoke approach (to confront or fight) rather than withdrawal. Researchers have found that anger is generally associated with greater activation of the right prefrontal cortex than the left, especially if the subjects are given instructions that lead them to visualize possible responses to the anger-provoking stimulus (Harmon-Jones & others, 2006).

Such research on the brain and emotions illustrates nicely the increasing conjoining of psychological theories with knowledge of physiological mechanisms. Conscious and unconscious assessments of differing emotion-provoking stimuli, and anticipated responses to those stimuli, differ not just in the realm of subjective experience but also in the brain pathways that underlie those assessments and response preparations.

SECTION REVIEW

Emotions are subjective feelings directed toward specific objects.

Nature of Emotion	Peripheral Feedback	Brain Mechanisms
➤ An *emotion* is a feeling that is tied subjectively to an object of that feeling, as exemplified by anger at someone who insulted you.	➤ James argued that peripheral bodily reactions precede and cause emotions.	➤ The amygdala rapidly evaluates sensory information for its significance to survival or well-being and triggers bodily responses.
➤ The feeling aspect of emotion, called *affect*, can vary in degree of arousal and degree of pleasantness or unpleasantness.	➤ Schachter proposed that peripheral feedback affects emotional intensity, but perceptions and thoughts determine the type of emotion.	➤ The prefrontal cortex is crucial for conscious emotional experience and deliberate action based on it.
➤ Psychologists have theories, but no consensus, about how to classify emotions.	➤ Ekman suggested that feedback from facial muscles can induce feelings and bodily reactions indicative of emotion.	➤ The right and left prefrontal cortices are relatively specialized for emotional responses involving, respectively, withdrawal and approach.
➤ Emotions have adaptive value, motivating us and communicating our intentions and needs to others.	➤ Evidence was presented supporting all three of these ideas.	

Concluding Thoughts

As you review the mechanisms of reward, hunger, sex, sleep, and emotions described in this chapter, you might find the following two points useful in organizing some of your thoughts.

1. The attempt to relate behavioral states to physiological states Hunger, sexual drive, sleepiness, and emotions are examples of *behavioral states*—sustained but reversible changes in the way a person or animal behaves in a given environment. In this chapter you read many examples of research aimed at finding relationships between behavioral states and *physiological states*. The general goals of such work are to identify the changes in the brain that provide the foundations for behavioral states and to identify the various neural and chemical inputs that control those changes. These goals are both fascinating and difficult to achieve because the machine being studied is so extraordinarily complex (not to mention alive and mortal). As you think about each type of behavioral state discussed in this chapter, ask yourself: What changes in the brain correspond to this state, and how are these changes regulated through means that tend to promote the individual's survival?

2. Two categories of methods in the physiological study of states Like the rest of the book, this chapter is about methods and evidence, not just findings. As you review the specific methods described in the chapter, you will find that they fall into two broad categories. One category involves *intervention* in ongoing physiological processes to see what happens to the behaviorally measured state. What happens to a drive or emotion if a particular part of the brain is destroyed or stimulated, or if the activity of a particular hormone or neurotransmitter is increased or decreased in some way? As you review the chapter, notice how often such methods were mentioned.

Intervention is a powerful way to identify causal relationships between physiology and behavior. But most intervention procedures are harmful or at least risky to the subject, so they are used primarily in studies of animals other than humans. The intervention approach is approximated, however, in studies of people whose natural physiology has been disrupted through accident or disease. Several studies of that sort were described in the chapter.

The other category involves the *measurement* of physiological processes and the *correlation* of the measures with changes in behavioral state. What natural changes in brain activity (measured by EEG or by brain imaging methods) or in hormonal secretions, heart rate, or other physiological variables accompany specific changes in behavioral state? Most measurement procedures are safe and can be used with humans. Notice, as you review the chapter, how often this correlational method was used in the human studies described. This method helps identify reliable relationships but does not, by itself, inform us about cause and effect. The observation that brain waves slow down during sleep, or that skin temperature rises during anger, or that the amygdala is active during fear, tells us about correlations but not necessarily about cause and effect. To test cause-effect hypotheses, researchers seek to manipulate the physiological system and measure the effect on behavior. That is why intervention experiments with nonhuman animals often go hand-in-hand with correlational studies in humans to get at the full story.

Further Reading

Alexandra W. Logue (2004). *The psychology of eating and drinking* (3rd ed.). New York: Brunner-Routledge.

This is an interesting introduction to the variables, both inside and outside the body, that affect hunger, thirst, and the ways they are expressed in behavior. The book also discusses major eating and drinking disorders.

Joann Rodgers (2001). *Sex: A natural history*. New York: Holt.

This engaging 500-page book, written for nonspecialists, deals with almost every aspect of sex that one can imagine: meiosis, gametes, the physiology and psychology of orgasms, differences between males and females, determinants of sexual orientation, brain mechanisms, species differences, cultural influences, alternative sex, physical and psychological underpinnings of attraction, and foundations for long-term mating attachments. Rodgers is a science writer, not a scientist, but she prepared well by reading much of the research literature and interviewing many of the leading researchers concerned with various aspects of sexual drive and behavior.

Jim Horne (2006). *Sleepfaring: A journey through the science of sleep*. Oxford: Oxford University Press.

This well-written, simple account of current knowledge of sleep, by a leading sleep researcher, includes chapters on animal sleep, brain control of sleep, measures and stages of sleep, effects of sleep deprivation (including an account of Randy Gardner's record-setting performance of 11 straight days without sleep), dreams, and sleep problems. Horne argues that many people worry more than necessary about lack of sleep; most people, he says, do fine with less sleep than they think they need.

Nadine Käthe Monem (Ed.) (2007). *Sleeping and dreaming*. London: Black Dog Publishing.

This 175-page book presents brief summaries of some of the major scientific findings regarding sleeping and dreaming. But the book's real joy comes from its lavish illustrations and many quotations, culled from works of art and literature having to do with sleep and dreams. The book was originally developed to accompany a museum exhibit on sleeping and dreaming at the Deutsches Hygiene-Museum, in Dresden.

Robert Plutchik (2003). *Emotions and life: Perspectives from psychology, biology, and evolution*. Washington, DC: American Psychological Association.

This is a well-written, up-to-date introductory textbook on emotion by a long-time leading researcher into that topic. Plutchik contends that emotions are part and parcel of nearly all of the behavior of human and nonhuman animals, and that they help to guide behavior in adaptive ways. From this perspective, he discusses the major theories of emotions, his own model of primary emotions, the role of emotions in human thought, the evolution of emotions, the measurement of emotions, the development of emotions in children, brain mechanisms of emotions, and emotional disorders.

PART 4

Sensation and Perception

Our senses are the conduits that connect our brains and minds to the rest of the world. Nothing is more fundamental to psychology than an understanding of the senses. All of our perceptions, all that we learn, all of our memories and thoughts, derive from our senses. How does our nervous system respond to and interpret the patterns of energy in the physical world in ways that provide us with useful information? In Chapter 7 we apply this question to smell, taste, pain, and hearing; and in Chapter 8 we apply it to vision.

Smell, Taste, Pain, Hearing, and Psychophysics

What would your mental life be like if you had no senses? What if, from birth, you could not see, hear, touch, taste, smell, or in any other way sense the world around you? You would not be able to react to anything, because reaction requires sensory input. You would not be able to learn anything, because learning begins with sensory input. Would you be able to think? What could you think about with no knowledge gained from the senses? Philosophers, from Aristotle on, have pondered these questions and have usually concluded that without sensation there would be no mental life. It is no wonder that the study of the senses has always been a fundamental part of the science of psychology.

Sensory systems have evolved in all animals for the purpose of guiding their behavior. To survive and reproduce, animals must respond to objects and events in the world in which they live. They must move toward food and mates, for example, and away from predators and precipices. Sensory systems did not evolve to provide full, objective accounts of the world's physical properties. Rather, they evolved to provide the specific kinds of information that the animal needs in order to survive and reproduce. To understand an animal's sensory systems is to understand its way of life. For instance, frogs' eyes contain "bug detectors," neurons that respond only to small, moving dark spots and that trigger tongue movements in the spot's direction; they also contain color detectors that are ideally tuned to distinguish the hue of the pond from that of the grass and lily pads (Muntz, 1964). Many species of migrating birds have a magnetic sense, sensitive to the earth's magnetic field, that allows the birds to fly in the correct direction even on cloudy nights, when visual cues are not available (Hughes, 1999). Bats, which fly at night, have tiny, almost useless eyes but huge ears. They emit ultrasonic beeps and hear the echoes, which they use to detect objects (such as edible insects) and barriers as they navigate in complete darkness (Griffin, 1986).

This chapter and the next one are about sensation and perception. Roughly speaking, *sensation* refers to the basic processes by which sensory organs and the nervous system respond to stimuli in the environment and to the elementary psychological experiences that result from those processes (such as our experience of the bitterness of a taste, loudness of a sound, or redness of a sight). *Perception,* in contrast, refers to the more complex organizing of sensory information within the brain and to the meaningful interpretations extracted from it (such as "This is strong coffee," "My alarm clock is ringing," or "That object is an apple"). Thus, the study of perception is more closely tied to the study of thought and memory than is the study of sensation. The distinction is fuzzy, however, because the organizing of stimulus information in ways useful for extracting meaning actually begins during the earliest steps of taking that information in.

This chapter begins with a brief overview of basic processes involved in sensation. It continues with sections on smell, taste, pain, and hearing, and it concludes with a discussion of psychophysics, which is an approach to finding and describing reliable relationships between physical stimuli and sensory experiences of those stimuli. The next chapter deals exclusively with vision, which is by far the most thoroughly studied of the senses.

❚ Overview of Sensory Processes

1
- ◁ Most broadly, the process of sensation can be diagrammed as follows:

How can the process of sensation be described as a chain of three different kinds of events?
- - - - - - - - - - - - - - - - - - -

$$\text{physical stimulus} \longrightarrow \text{physiological response} \longrightarrow \text{sensory experience}$$

We have here three classes of events, each of which is entirely different from the others: (1) The *physical stimulus* is the matter or energy of the physical world that impinges on sense organs; (2) the *physiological response* is the pattern of chemical and electrical activity that occurs in sense organs, nerves, and the brain as a result of the stimulus; and (3) the *sensory experience* is the subjective, psychological sensation or perception—the taste, sound, or sight, for instance—experienced by the individual whose sense organs have been stimulated. The sensory experience generally tells us something about the physical stimulus, but it is a very different thing from the physical stimulus. We encounter molecules of caffeine on our tongue and we experience a bitter taste. The bitterness is not a chemical property of the caffeine molecules; it exists only in our sensory experience triggered by the molecules. Electromagnetic energy of a certain wavelength enters our eyes and we experience the color red. The redness is not a property of the electromagnetic energy, but exists only in our sensory experience.

Sensory psychologists are interested in identifying lawful relationships among the three just-described classes of events. Here, before discussing particular senses separately, let's consider some general principles that apply to all sensory systems.

Each Sensory System Has Distinct Receptors and Neural Pathways

Ever since Aristotle, people have spoken of the *five senses,* identifying them as smell, taste, touch, hearing, and vision. Actually, humans have more than five senses, and any attempt to tally them up to an exact number is arbitrary, because what one person thinks of as one sense may be thought of as two or more by another. For example, our skin is sensitive not just to touch but also to temperature

TABLE 7.1 Stimuli, receptors, and the pathways to the brain for various senses

Sense	Stimulus	Receptors	Pathway to the brain
Smell	Molecules dissolved in fluid on mucous membranes in the nose	Sensitive ends of olfactory neurons in the olfactory epithelium in the nose	Olfactory nerve (1st cranial nerve)
Taste	Molecules disolved in fluid on the tongue	Taste cells in taste buds on the tongue	Portions of facial, glossopharyngeal, and vagus nerves (7th, 9th, and 10th cranial nerves)
Touch	Pressure on the skin	Sensitive ends of touch neurons in skin	Trigeminal nerve (5th cranial nerve) for touch above the neck; spinal nerves for touch elsewhere
Pain	Wide variety of potentially harmful stimuli	Sensitive ends of pain neurons in skin and other tissues	Trigeminal nerve (5th cranial nerve) for pain above the neck; spinal nerves for pain elsewhere
Hearing	Sound waves	Pressure-sensitive hair cells in cochlea of inner ear	Auditory nerve (8th cranial nerve)
Vision	Light waves	Light-sensitive rods and cones in retina of eye	Optic nerve (2nd cranial nerve)

and pain, neither of which is included in Aristotle's five. Other senses omitted by Aristotle have to do with body position and the body's internal environment. We have a sense of balance, mediated by a mechanism in the inner ear, and a sense of limb position and movement, mediated by receptors in muscles and joints. Each sense has distinct sensory receptors and neural pathways to and within the brain.

Sensory receptors are specialized structures that respond to physical stimuli by producing electrical changes that can initiate neural impulses in sensory neurons. **Sensory neurons** (described and illustrated in Chapter 5) are specialized neurons that carry information from sensory receptors into the central nervous system. For some senses the receptors are simply the sensitive ends of sensory neurons; for others they are separate cells that form synapses upon sensory neurons. For some senses the receptors all exist in a specific, localized sensory organ, such as the ear, eye, or nose; for others they exist in a wide variety of locations. Pain receptors, for example, exist not just throughout the skin but also in muscles, tendons, joints, and many other places. The stimuli, receptors, and peripheral nerves involved in the most thoroughly studied senses are listed in Table 7.1.

Regardless of whether they come from one location or many, the neurons for any given sense lead to pathways in the central nervous system that are unique to that sense. These pathways send their messages to many different parts of the brain, including specific **sensory areas** of the cerebral cortex— including areas devoted to vision, hearing, and touch, for example (see Figure 7.1). Although brain structures below the cortex can organize unconscious behavioral reactions to sensory stimuli, conscious sensory experiences depend on activity within the cerebral cortex.

Every sensation that you experience consciously is a product, ultimately, of some pattern of activity within a sensory area of your cerebral cortex. You see light because light receptors in your eyes are connected to visual areas of your cortex, and you hear sound because sound receptors in your ears are connected to auditory areas

FIGURE 7.1 Primary sensory areas of the cerebral cortex Shown here are the locations of the primary cortical areas for vision, hearing, somatosensation (which includes touch, temperature sensitivity, and pain), taste, and smell. The primary taste area lies in a portion of the cerebral cortex called the *insula*, which is buried in the fold between the parietal and temporal lobes. The primary olfactory area lies in a portion of cerebral cortex called the *piriform cortex*, which wraps underneath the temporal lobe. Secondary sensory processing areas generally lie near the primary areas.

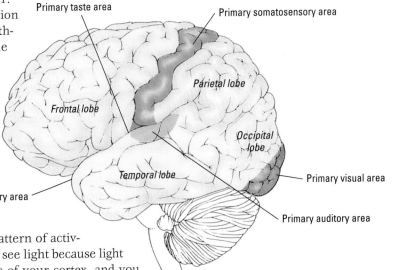

of your cortex. If we could somehow rewire those connections, sending your optic nerves to your auditory brain areas and your auditory nerves to your visual brain areas, you would hear light and see sound. When you bump the back of your head, you may "see stars," because the bump artificially activates neurons in visual areas of your brain.

Sensory Receptors Generate Action Potentials Through a Process of Transduction

2
───────────────────────────◄
In general, how do physical stimuli produce action potentials in sensory neurons?
────────────────────────

The process by which a receptor cell produces an electrical change in response to physical stimulation is called **transduction.** It is the process by which receptors in the eye respond to light, receptors in the ear respond to sound, receptors on the tongue respond to chemicals dissolved there, and so on. Although the details of transduction are different for each sense, basic similarities exist across the senses. In every case, the membrane of the receptor cell becomes more permeable to certain electrically charged particles, such as sodium or potassium ions, when the appropriate type of stimulus energy acts on the receptor cell. These charged particles then flow through the membrane, either from outside the cell to inside or vice versa, and change the electrical charge across the membrane. This electrical change is called the **receptor potential,** and it is analogous to the postsynaptic potential produced on neurons by the action of synaptic transmitters (described in Chapter 5). Receptor potentials in turn trigger events that lead to the production of action potentials (also described in Chapter 5) in the axons of sensory neurons.

Sensory Systems Preserve Information About Stimulus Quantity and Quality

For senses to be useful, they must preserve—in the patterns of neural activity they produce—relevant information about the physical stimuli to which they are responding. That preservation of information is referred to as **sensory coding.**

Every form of energy can vary along at least two dimensions—a quantitative dimension and a qualitative one. The *quantitative variation* has to do with the amount or intensity of energy. A sound or light can be weak or strong; molecules stimulating taste or smell can be dilute or highly concentrated. The *qualitative variation* has to do with the precise kind of energy. Lights of different wavelengths (which we perceive as different colors) are considered to be qualitatively different, as are sounds of different frequencies (which we perceive as different pitches), as are different chemicals (which we perceive as different smells or tastes). For each of our senses, transduction occurs in such a way that information about the quantity and quality of the stimulus is preserved in the pattern of action potentials sent to the brain.

3
───────────────────────────◄
In general, how do sensory systems code information about the amount and kind of stimulus energy?
────────────────────────

Coding of stimulus *quantity* results from the fact that stronger stimuli produce larger receptor potentials, which in turn produce faster rates of action potentials in sensory neurons. The brain interprets a fast rate of action potentials as a strong stimulus and a slow rate as a weak stimulus.

In contrast, the coding of stimulus *quality* occurs because qualitatively different stimuli optimally activate different sets of neurons. Different receptors within any given sensory tissue are tuned to respond best to somewhat different forms of energy. In the eye, for example, three different kinds of receptor cells, each most sensitive to a different range of wavelengths of light, provide the basis for color vision. In the ear, different receptors are most sensitive to different sound frequencies. And in the nose and mouth, different receptors are most sensitive to different kinds of molecules. Thus, in general, qualitative variations are coded as different ratios of activity in sensory neurons coming from different sets of receptors. For an illustration of how quantitative and qualitative information about a stimulus can be independently coded for the sense of taste, see Figure 7.2. The same principle applies to other senses, as you will discover later in this chapter.

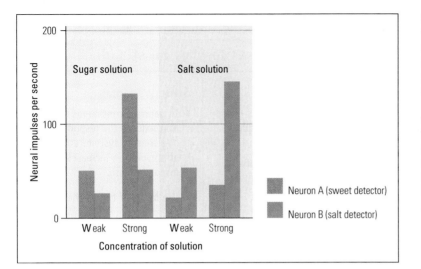

FIGURE 7.2 Quantitative and qualitative coding of taste Shown here are the rates of action potentials in two different taste sensory neurons when a weak or strong solution of sugar or salt is placed on the tongue. Each neuron responds at a faster rate to a strong solution of a given substance than to a weak one (quantitative coding); but neuron A always responds at a faster rate than neuron B when the stimulus is sugar, and the reverse is true when the stimulus is salt (qualitative coding). This illustrates the general principle that sensory quantity is coded in the overall rate of action potentials in sensory neurons and sensory quality is coded in the ratio of activity across different sets of neurons. (Data are hypothetical, but are based on such findings as those of Nowlis & Frank, 1977.)

Sensory Systems Respond to Changes More Than to Steady States

Our senses are designed to alert us to changes in our sensory environment and to be relatively oblivious to steady states. When you first put on your wristwatch, you feel the pressure on your skin, but later you don't. When you first enter a well-lit room from the dark, the room seems very bright, but later not so bright. When you first wade into a lake, the water may seem terribly cold, but later only slightly cool. When you first enter a chemistry lab, the odor may seem overwhelming, but later you hardly notice it. The change in sensitivity that occurs when a given set of sensory receptors and neurons is either strongly stimulated or relatively unstimulated for a length of time is called ***sensory adaptation.*** In general, when the amount of stimulation of a sensory system increases for a period of time, the sensory system adapts by becoming less sensitive than it was before; and when the amount of stimulation decreases, the sensory system adapts by becoming more sensitive than it was before.

In many cases, sensory adaptation is mediated by the receptor cells themselves. If a stimulus remains for a period of time, the receptor potential and rate of action potentials are at first great, but over time they become much reduced, resulting in reduced sensation. In other cases, however, adaptation is mediated at least partly by changes further inward in the central nervous system. You can prove this yourself for the sense of smell (Matlin & Foley, 1997). If you place an odorous substance (such as an open bottle of nail-polish remover or cologne) on a desk in front of you, with one nostril plugged, you will adapt to it within about 5 minutes (it won't smell as strong). Then, if you unplug that nostril and quickly plug the other, you will find that you are still partly (but not completely) adapted to the odor, even though it is now acting on receptors in the other nostril, different from those that it was acting on before. Thus, adaptation for smell must result in part from changes in neurons in the brain that receive input from both nostrils.

> **4**
> **What is the value of sensory adaptation? How can you demonstrate that adaptation can occur in neurons in the brain, not just in receptors?**

Sabine Weiss/Photo Researchers

It's a nice place to work, but I wouldn't want to visit Can you imagine the pungent smell you would experience if you walked into this cave full of Roquefort cheese? Yet, as suggested by this worker's equable expression, one adapts after a while. In general, our senses are designed to register changes in the environment, not steady states.

▦ Smell

Smell and taste are called chemical senses, because the stimuli for them are chemical molecules. The chemical senses are first and foremost systems for warning and attracting. They play on our drives and emotions more than on our intellects. Think of the effects produced by a valentine gift of chocolates, perfume, or fresh roses; by the aroma and taste of your favorite meal; or by the stench of feces or rotting meat.

Although the human sense of smell is much less sensitive than that of many other animals, it is still remarkably sensitive and useful. We can smell smoke at concentrations well below that needed to trigger even the most sensitive of household smoke detectors. We can distinguish among roughly 10,000 different chemicals by smell (Axel, 1995). Blind people regularly identify individuals by their unique odors, and sighted people can do that too when they try. And smell contributes greatly to what we call "flavor" in foods.

Anatomy and Physiology of Smell

Great progress has been made within the past 10 years or so in understanding the sense of smell.

Transduction and Coding for the Sense of Smell

5

How do transduction, qualitative coding, and quantitative coding occur for the sense of smell?

The basic layout of the olfactory (smell) system is illustrated in Figure 7.3. The stimuli for smell are molecules that evaporate into the air, are taken with air into the nasal cavity, and then become dissolved in the mucous fluid covering the olfactory epithelium, the sensory tissue for smell, which lines the top of the nasal cavity. The olfactory epithelium contains the sensitive terminals of roughly 6 million olfactory sensory neurons (Doty, 2001). Each terminal contains many olfactory receptor sites, which are large protein molecules woven into the cell membrane that are capable of binding molecules of specific odorants (odorous substances). The binding of a molecule to a receptor site changes the structure of the cell membrane, which results in an electrical change that tends to trigger action potentials in the neuron's axon. The greater the number of binding sites activated by odorous molecules, the greater the rate of action potentials triggered in the axon.

The olfactory nerve contains roughly 350 different types of sensory neurons, each of which is characterized by a distinctly shaped binding site on its terminals within the olfactory epithelium (Wilson & Mainen, 2006). Any given type of binding site can bind more than one odorant, but any given odorant binds more readily to some

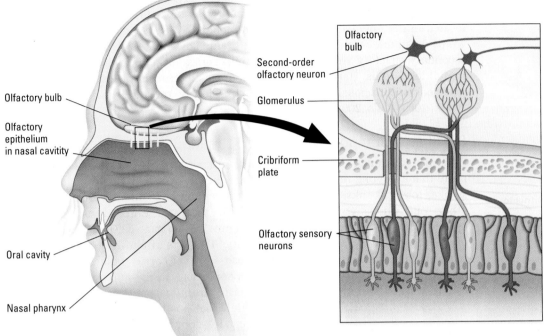

FIGURE 7.3 The anatomy of smell Molecules of odorants enter the nose through the nostrils, become dissolved in the mucous fluid covering the olfactory epithelium, and bind to receptor sites on the sensitive tips of olfactory sensory neurons, where they initiate action potentials. The sensory neurons send their axons through the cribriform plate (a small bone shelf) to form synapses on second-order olfactory neurons in the glomeruli of the olfactory bulb, directly above the nasal cavity. As illustrated in the right-hand diagram by the use of color, each glomerulus receives input from only one type of olfactory sensory neuron (defined by its type of receptor sites). Only two types of such neurons are shown here (depicted as yellow and blue), of the roughly 400 types that exist in the human olfactory system.

types than to others. Thus, each type of olfactory neuron differs from the other types in its degree of sensitivity to particular odorants.

The axons of the olfactory sensory neurons pass through a thin, porous bone into the *olfactory bulb* of the brain, where they form synapses upon other neurons in structures called *glomeruli* [glom-**air**-you-lee] (see Figure 7.3). The pattern of these connections is remarkably orderly. Each glomerulus in the olfactory bulb receives input from several thousand olfactory sensory neurons, but all these neurons are of the same type. For each of the 350 different types of olfactory sensory neurons, there is a different receiving glomerulus (or a set of two or three such glomeruli) in the olfactory bulb (Wilson & Mainen, 2006).

From this work, researchers have inferred the process by which qualitative and quantitative coding occurs for the sense of smell. Each odorant that we can distinguish is apparently characterized by its ability to produce a unique pattern of activity across the 350 different types of olfactory neurons and their corresponding glomeruli in the olfactory bulb. Thus, odorant A might trigger much activity in one set of glomeruli, a moderate amount in another set, and very little in others. The greater the amount of odorant A, the greater would be the total amount of activity triggered in each of the glomeruli that it affects, but the ratio of activity across glomeruli would remain relatively constant. Thus, the ratio indicates the type of odorant (quality of the smell), while the total amount of activity indicates the amount of odorant (quantity, or intensity of the smell).

Olfactory Brain Areas Beyond the Olfactory Bulb

The glomeruli in the olfactory bulb send output to various other parts of the brain. Most of this output goes to structures in the limbic system and the hypothalamus, which (as discussed in Chapters 5 and 6) are involved in basic drives and emotions. These connections, presumably, help to account for the strong and often unconscious effects that smell can have on our motivational and emotional states. The connections from the olfactory bulb to the limbic system are so strong, in fact, that the limbic system was at one time referred to as the *rhinencephalon*, which literally means "nose brain." Output from the olfactory bulbs also goes to various portions of the cerebral cortex. The primary olfactory cortex, called the *piriform cortex,* is located in the underside of the temporal lobe (shown in Figure 7.1, on page 233) wraps down underneath the rest of the brain. This area in turn sends output to a secondary olfactory area in the *orbitofrontal cortex,* located on the underside of the frontal lobe (Rolls, 2004). These cortical areas are crucial for the ability to experience odors consciously and identify consciously the differences among them (Buck, 2000; Rolls, 2004).

Smell as a Component of Flavor: The Mouth-to-Nose Connection

6 ─ ─ ─ ─ ─ ─ ─ ─ ─ ─ ─ ─ ◄
How do we smell foods that are already in our mouths, and what evidence indicates that smell contributes greatly to flavor?

Odorants can reach the olfactory epithelium through two different routes. The route that everyone recognizes is through the nostrils, which allows you to smell smoke, roses, skunks, and other odor sources that are outside your mouth. The other route allows you to smell substances that have entered your mouth. An opening (the nasal pharynx, shown in Figure 7.3, on page 237) connects the back of the mouth cavity with the nasal cavity. The acts of chewing and swallowing push air from the mouth up into the nose—air that carries volatile molecules of whatever you are eating. What most people call taste—and what is properly called *flavor*—consists not just of true taste (from taste receptors in the mouth) but also of smell that has been triggered through this mouth-to-nose, back-door route. Remarkably, you experience this sensation as coming from the mouth, where the food exists, and as indistinguishable from taste, even though it actually comes from the olfactory epithelium (Shepherd, 2006).

If you pinch your nostrils shut, you cut off both routes to the olfactory epithelium. If air can't flow out through the nostrils, it can't stream into the nasal cavity from the mouth. Experiments have shown repeatedly that people's abilities to identify foods and drinks by flavor decline markedly when their nostrils are shut. You can easily demonstrate the role of smell in your own ability to identify flavors, using jellybeans as stimuli (suggested by Schiffman, 1996). With eyes closed, chew one jellybean at a time and try to identify its flavor. You will probably find this task to be relatively easy as long as you keep your nostrils open. Then try the same task with your nostrils pinched shut. You will most likely find that now all the jellybeans taste the same; all you can taste is the sugar. The differences that allow you to distinguish among cherry, grape, orange, and licorice depend on smell. Smell and taste inputs converge in a certain portion of the orbitofrontal cortex, and this area appears to be critical for the psychological experience of flavor (Rolls, 2004).

An excellent bouquet This professional wine taster samples the wine's scent through both his nose and his mouth. Through the mouth, odorant molecules reach the nasal cavity by way of a connection called the nasal pharynx. Much of what we think of as taste is actually smell.

Tim O'Hara/Corbis

Differences Among People in Olfactory Sensitivity

7 ─ ─ ─ ─ ─ ─ ─ ─ ─ ─ ─ ─ ◄
How do sex, age, genetic differences, and experience affect sensitivity to smells?

Big differences exist among individuals in general olfactory sensitivity. Women are, on average, more sensitive to odors than are men (Doty, 2001), and many women become especially sensitive to odors during pregnancy (Nordin & others, 2004). In both sexes, sensitivity to odors declines with age. By age 65 roughly 11 percent of women and 25 percent of men have serious olfactory impairment, and by age 85 those numbers are 60 percent and 70 percent (Murphy & others, 2002). Many elderly people complain of loss in ability to taste foods, but tests typically show that their real loss is not taste but smell (Bartoshuk & Beauchamp, 1994). The most dangerous effect of such impairment is the inability to smell smoke or toxic gases in the air. A high proportion of people who die from asphyxiation are elderly people who have lost much or all of their olfactory ability.

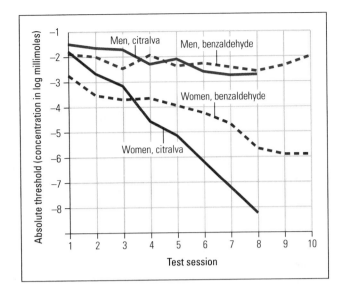

FIGURE 7.4 A sex difference in olfactory ability When women and men were tested in repeated sessions for their ability to smell weak concentrations of benzaldehyde (an almond-cherry smell) and citralva (an orange-lemon smell), the women but not the men showed dramatic improvement. By the eighth session, the women's absolute threshold for citralva was more than five log units less than that of the men. In other words, the women were smelling this substance at concentrations less than one hundred-thousandth of the minimal concentration that the men could smell. (Data from Dalton & others, 2002.)

Many people with otherwise normal olfactory ability are completely unable to smell particular chemicals that other people can smell easily. In fact, at least 75 different chemicals have been identified that most people can smell but some cannot (Pierce & others, 2004). These differences are at least partly the result of genetic differences that affect the production of specific olfactory receptors on olfactory neurons. The most fully studied example concerns ability to smell the chemical substance *androstenone*, which is a derivative of testosterone. This chemical is found in human sweat, more so in males than in females, and big differences exist among individuals of both sexes in their ability to smell it. Researchers have found, in different people, three different variants of the gene that codes for the receptor protein for androstenone. People with the most common variant of the gene find androstenone's odor to be strong and putrid; those with the second most common variant find it to be relatively weak and pleasant ("sweet and fruity"); and those with the least common variant cannot smell the chemical at all (Keller & others, 2007).

Sensitivity to specific odors is also very much affected by experience. With repeated tests, people can learn to distinguish the odors of slightly different chemicals, which initially smelled identical to them (Li & others, 2008), and can learn to detect specific odors at a much lower concentration than they could initially (Boulkroune & others, 2007). In some cases, such effects of experience have been found for both sexes, but in others it has been found to occur only in women. In one series of experiments, Pamela Dalton and her colleagues (2002) tested women and men repeatedly, with certain odorous chemicals, to determine their absolute thresholds (the minimal concentrations of the chemical that they could smell). As shown in Figure 7.4 (above), the women, but not the men, exhibited dramatic increases in sensitivity (declines in absolute thresholds) with repeated testing. In further experiments, the researchers found the increased sensitivity only for women who were in their reproductive years; it did not occur for prepubescent girls or postmenopausal women. Such findings are consistent with theories that olfaction serves one or more special functions related to reproduction in women, such as choosing mates, avoiding toxins during pregnancy, or bonding with infants.

Discriminating Among Individuals by Smell

As dog owners well know, dogs greet and recognize others of their kind (and sometimes of our kind too) by smell. We humans living in a somewhat odor-phobic culture may not often admit it or even be aware of it, but we too can identify individuals of our species by smell. In a typical experiment, one set of subjects wear initially clean T-shirts for a day without washing or using deodorants or perfumes,

------------------------------------- **8**

What is the evidence (a) that people can identify other individuals by smell; (b) that mothers can identify the scents of their infants very soon after birth; and (c) that infants quickly learn to identify their mother's scent?

----

and then other subjects are asked to identify by smell alone which shirt had been worn by whom. Such experiments have revealed that parents can tell which of their children wore the shirt, children can tell which of their siblings wore it, and people generally can distinguish between the odors of two strangers (Porter, 1991; Wallace, 1977).

Role of Smell in Mother-Infant Bonding

Among some mammals, notably goats and sheep, odor recognition is a crucial part of the bond between mother and young (Kendrick & others, 1992). Might smell also play a role in human mother-infant bonding?

In one study conducted in a hospital maternity ward, 90 percent of mothers who had been exposed to their newborn babies for just 10 to 60 minutes after birth were able to identify by smell alone which of several undershirts had been worn by their own babies (Kaitz & others, 1987). In another study, breast-fed babies as young as 6 days old turned their heads reliably toward cotton pads that their own mothers had worn against their breasts, when given a choice between that and identical-looking pads that had been worn by other lactating women (Macfarlane, 1975). In still another study, babies who were exposed to a particular unusual odor (not that of their mothers) within the first hour after birth turned reliably toward that odor when given a choice between it and another unusual odor 6 days later (Varendi & others, 2002). All such evidence suggests that odor figures into the complex of stimuli that are involved in the attachment between human infants and their mothers. Unlike the case for goats and sheep, however, odor is certainly not essential for such attachment.

B. Daemmrich/The Image Bank

A sweet aroma Every human being has a unique, identifiable odor.

9 —————————————————————

From an evolutionary perspective, why might mice prefer to mate with others that smell most different from themselves? What evidence suggests that the same might be true of humans?

Possible Role of Smell in Choosing a Genetically Compatible Mate

In mice, odor has been shown to play a role in mating choices. Mice, like dogs and humans, can identify other individuals of their species by smell, and, remarkably, they prefer to mate with opposite-sex mice whose odor is *most different* from their own (Potts & others, 1991; Yamazaki & others, 1988). Why this preference? Researchers have found that the individual differences in odor that determine these mating preferences result from a set of about 50 highly variable genes (genes with many different alleles) referred to collectively as the *major histocompatibility complex (MHC)* (Yamazaki & others, 1994). These same genes also determine the precise nature of the cells used by the immune system to reject foreign substances and kill disease-producing bacteria and viruses. Thus, by choosing mates that smell most different from themselves, mice choose mates that (a) are not likely to be close relatives of themselves and (b) will add much new genetic variation to the mix of disease-fighting cells that develop in the offspring. As explained in Chapter 3, such genetic variety increases the chance that the offspring will survive.

The MHC also exists in human beings and contributes greatly to individual differences in odor (Brennan & Zufall, 2006). The advantages of mating with someone who has a very different MHC presumably exist in humans as much as in mice. Do humans, to any degree at all, prefer sexual mates who smell most different from themselves and differ most in MHC? At present, the answer to that is not known, but some research suggests that it might be yes (Penn, 2002). In one series of experiments, Claus Wedekind and his colleagues (1995, 1997) asked young men and women to rate the "pleasantness" (and in one study the "sexiness") of the odors of T-shirts that had been worn by young adults of the opposite sex. All the subjects were assessed biochemically for differences in their MHCs. The result was that any given donor's odor was, on average, rated as more pleasant by raters who differed from that person in MHC than by raters who were similar to that person in MHC.

There is some evidence that MHC differences can affect actual sexual behavior in humans. In one study, romantically involved young couples were tested for the degree of MHC difference between them and were asked to respond to a confidential questionnaire about their sexual desires and activities. The significant findings pertained to the women's sexual desires for their partners. On average, the more different her partner's MHC was from hers, the greater was the woman's interest in having sex with him and the less likely she was to have sex with someone outside of the relationship (Garver-Apgar & others, 2006). In this study, the men's sexual desires were unrelated to the MHC differences. It is possible that this sex difference exists because, for women, the biological costs of producing children are much greater than are those for men, so selectivity for compatible genes is more important for women than for men. Other studies on effects of MHC differences on choices of sexual partners have produced mixed results, with some showing effects and others not (Penn, 2002).

"Would you like to try a more manly scent?"

Smell as a Mode of Communication: Do Humans Produce Pheromones?

A ***pheromone*** [**fair**-uh-**moan**] is a chemical substance that is released by an animal and acts on other members of its species to promote some specific behavioral or physiological response. The most dramatic examples occur in insects. For instance, sexually receptive female cabbage moths secrete a pheromone that attracts male cabbage moths from as far as several miles away (Lerner & others, 1990). Most species of mammals also produce pheromones, which serve such functions as sexual attraction, territorial marking, and regulation of hormone production (Hughes, 1999; Wyatt, 2009). Most species of mammals have in their nasal cavities a structure called the *vomeronasal* [voh-**mair**-oh-**nay**-zul] *organ,* which contains receptor cells specialized for responding to pheromones. Whereas the main olfactory epithelium is designed to distinguish somewhat imprecisely among many thousands of different odorants, the vomeronasal organ appears to be designed for very precise recognition of, and exquisite sensitivity to, a small number of specific substances— the species' pheromones (Buck, 2000).

Do humans communicate by pheromones? We do have the structures that would make such communication possible. Like other mammals, we have specialized glands in the skin that secrete odorous substances. Such glands are especially concentrated in areas of the body where our species has retained hair—such as in the axillary region (armpits) and genital region (see Figure 7.5). One theory is that the

➤ ------------------------- **10**

What anatomical characteristics of our species are consistent with the possibility that we produce and respond to pheromones? What observations and reasoning suggest that we do not produce sex-attractant pheromones?

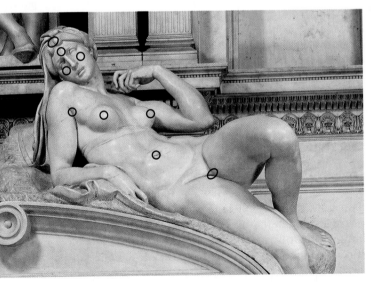

Scala/Art Resource

FIGURE 7.5 Locations of maximal scent production by humans In humans, specialized scent-producing glands (apocrine glands) are concentrated most highly in the axillary region (underarms) and also exist in high concentrations in the genital area, the area around the nipples, the navel area, on the top of the head, and on the forehead and cheeks (Stoddart, 1990), as shown by the added circles. (The statue here is Michelangelo's Aurora, from the tomb of Lorenzo de Medici, in Florence.)

function of hair in these locations is to retain the secretions and provide a large surface area from which they can evaporate, so as to increase their effectiveness as odorants (Stoddart, 1990). Some substances secreted by these glands, such as androstenone, are steroid molecules that resemble substances known to serve as pheromones in other mammals. We also have at least a rudimentary vomeronasal organ, but the evidence to date is inconclusive as to whether it functions in our species or is entirely vestigial (Brennan & Zufall, 2006).

Motivated partly by the perfume and cologne industry, most human pheromone research has centered on whether or not we produce sex-attractant pheromones. In many experiments, men and women have been exposed to various secretions taken from the other sex and have rated the attractiveness of the odor or changes in their own mood. To date, despite the often lurid claims in ads, such experiments have failed to yield convincing evidence that such pheromones exist (Brennan & Zufall, 2006; Hays, 2003). Certainly some people find some of the odorous substances secreted by other people to be pleasant, but individual differences are great, and no specific human secretion has been found to be consistently attractive to members of the opposite sex. Perhaps that should not be surprising. Sex-attractant pheromones are valuable for animals that mate only at certain times of the year or only when the female is ovulating, as a means of synchronizing the sex drives of males and females to maximize the chance of conception. As discussed in Chapter 6, humans have taken a different evolutionary route, such that sexual drive and behavior are not tied to a season, cycle, or variable physiological state. For that reason, perhaps, there is little or no need for us to advertise by scent our readiness to mate.

SECTION REVIEW

Smell, one of two human chemical senses, serves functions of warning and attraction.

Basic Facts of Smell	Telling People Apart by Their Smell	Communicating via Smell
➤ Roughly 350 different types of sensory neurons exist in olfactory nerves. The receptive ends of each type are most responsive to particular types of odorant molecules that reach the olfactory epithelium in the nose.	➤ Humans can identify individuals by smell alone.	➤ For many animal species, including most mammals, pheromones serve as chemical messengers between individuals.
➤ These different types of neurons are connected in an orderly way to corresponding parts of the olfactory bulb. Their differential responsiveness allows us to distinguish one scent from another.	➤ Mothers and their infants quickly learn to recognize the other's smell, a fact that may contribute to bonding.	➤ Though the evidence is mixed regarding the possibility of human pheromones, we do not need or appear to have sex-attractant pheromones.
➤ Odorants that enter the nose through a connection from the mouth contribute to the flavor of foods, experienced as taste.	➤ Odor allows mice (and perhaps humans) to choose mates that will enhance genetic variety in their offspring.	
➤ Olfactory sensitivity is generally greater in women than in men, and it declines with age. Sensitivity to specific chemicals varies as a result of both genes and experience.		

■ Taste

Some insects have taste receptors on their feet, which allow them to taste what they are walking on. Fish have taste receptors not just in their mouths but all over their bodies (Hara, 1994). They can taste their prey before they see it, and they use taste to help them track it down. For us and other mammals, taste has a more limited but still valuable function. Our taste receptors exist only in our mouths, and their function is to help us decide whether a particular substance is good or bad to eat.

Anatomy and Physiology of Taste

The receptors for taste are found on specialized *taste receptor cells,* not directly on the sensory neurons (unlike the case for smell). These cells exist in spherical structures called taste buds. Each bud contains between 50 and 100 receptor cells, arranged something like segments in an orange (see Figure 7.6). Most people have between 2,000 and 10,000 taste buds, about two-thirds of which are on the tongue and the rest of which are on the roof of the mouth and in the opening of the throat (Herness & Gilbertson, 1999). People who have more taste buds are typically more sensitive to tastes—especially to bitter tastes—than are people who have fewer taste buds (Bartoshuk & Beachamp, 1994).

> ------------------------- **11**
> **How, in general, does transduction occur in taste?**

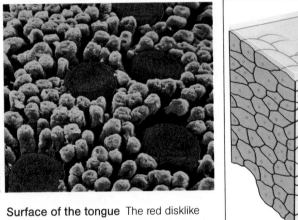

Surface of the tongue The red disklike structures are fungiform papillae. Most taste buds are located within the walls of these papillae with their sensitive ends oriented toward the surrounding saliva-filled trough. The magnification is about 100X.

Omikron/Photo Researchers

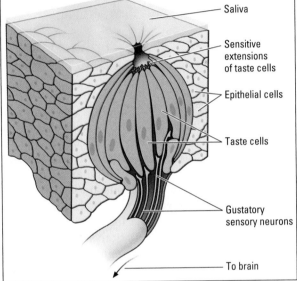

Saliva

Sensitive extensions of taste cells

Epithelial cells

Taste cells

Gustatory sensory neurons

To brain

FIGURE 7.6 A taste bud
Taste buds are found in the surface tissue (epithelium) of the tongue and elsewhere in the mouth. Each one contains 50 or more taste receptor cells. From the tip of each cell, hairlike extensions make contact with the fluid lining the epithelial tissue. These extensions contain binding sites and channels where substances to be tasted exert their effects. The receptor cells produce action potentials in response to such input and, in turn, induce action potentials in taste sensory neurons through synaptic transmission (Herness & Gilbertson, 1999).

To be tasted, a chemical substance must first dissolve in saliva and come into contact with the sensitive ends of appropriate taste receptor cells, where it triggers electrical changes that result in action potentials, first in the taste receptor cells and then, by synaptic transmission, in sensory neurons that run to the brain (see Figure 7.6). The specifics of the transduction mechanism vary from one type of taste receptor cell to another.

Five Primary Tastes, Five Types of Receptor Cells

For many years Western scientists believed that in humans (and other mammals) taste receptor cells were of just four types—*sweet, salty, sour,* and *bitter*—each named after the taste sensation that results when that type is activated. Every taste, it was believed, could be understood as a combination of those four primary tastes. Japanese scientists, in contrast, generally spoke of five primary tastes—the four just mentioned plus *umami,* which, loosely translated, means "savory" or "delicious" (Kurihara & Kashiwayanagi, 1998). Umami, they held, is a unique taste, unmatched by any combination of the other primary tastes, and is a major contributor to the taste of many natural foods, especially those that are high in protein, such as meats, fish, and cheese. Umami is also the taste produced by monosodium glutamate (MSG), an amino acid frequently used as a flavor enhancer in Asian cuisine. Taste researchers have recently identified distinct receptor cells and brain areas responsive to MSG, and now even Western taste specialists generally write of five rather than four primary tastes and types of taste receptor cells (Chandrashekar & others, 2006; Shadan, 2009).

> ------------------------- **12**
> **What are the five primary tastes, and how, in general, does transduction occur in taste receptor cells?**

Hmm, umami The savory umami taste of Chinese food is often enhanced by monosodium glutamate. Umami is believed to be one of the five primary tastes.

Taste Areas in the Brain

Taste sensory neurons have strong connections (via several way stations) to the limbic system and cerebral cortex. The connections to the primary taste area of the cortex (located largely in the *insula,* which is buried in the central fissure that separates the temporal and parietal lobes) are arranged in such a way that different sets of neurons are selectively responsive to each of the five basic categories of taste stimuli (Kobayashi, 2006; Rolls, 2004). People with extensive damage to this area lose their conscious experience of taste (Pritchard, 1991), and artificial stimulation here produces experiences of taste in the absence of any stimuli on the tongue (Penfield & Faulk, 1955). The primary taste area in turn sends connections to several other areas of the cortex, including the orbitofrontal cortex, where, as mentioned in the section on smell, neural connections for taste and smell intermingle and enable us to experience the mixed taste-smell sensation called flavor.

An Evolutionary Account of Taste Quality

13

From an evolutionary perspective, (a) what is the function of each of the primary tastes, (b) why do so many chemically diverse substances taste bitter, and (c) why does bitter sensation increase in women at pregnancy?

The purpose of taste is to motivate us to eat some substances and avoid eating others. Generally speaking, salty (at low to moderate intensity), sweet, and umami are pleasant tastes, which, in the course of evolution, became attached to substances that are good for us, or at least were good for our evolutionary ancestors, given their nutritional needs and the environment in which they had to meet those needs. A certain amount of salt intake is needed to maintain a proper salt balance in bodily fluids. Sugars, in fruits and other natural foodstuffs, were a valuable source of energy to our evolutionary ancestors. Protein (the main natural source of umami flavor) is essential for building and restoring tissues. Our ability to taste and enjoy salt, sugars, and proteins is part of the mechanism that helps ensure that we consume adequate amounts of these nutrients.

Still speaking generally, sour and bitter are unpleasant experiences, which natural selection has attached to certain substances that are bad for us. Bacterial decay produces acidic compounds. Since decaying substances can cause disease when eaten, natural selection produced a taste system that experiences most acids as unpleasant (sour). Many plants (hemlock is a famous example) and some animals (notably some species of caterpillars), as part of their own evolution, have concentrated toxic substances into their tissues—substances that can harm or kill animals that eat them. As a consequence, our ancestors evolved a taste system that experiences most of those toxic substances as unpleasant (bitter).

Evolution of the Ability to Taste Toxic Substances as Bitter

To pursue this evolutionary line of thinking, let's consider further the relationship between bitter taste and poisons. A wide variety of chemical substances all taste bitter to us, even though they may be very different chemically from one another, because each is able to bind to one or another of the approximately 25 different types of receptor sites located on bitter receptor cells (Behrens & others, 2007). The receptor sites are specialized protein molecules that bind certain molecules that come into contact with them. The binding of any substance to these sites triggers a chemical change in the cell. This chemical change results in action potentials in the sensory neurons and, ultimately, activity in areas of the brain that produce the bitter sensation.

From an evolutionary perspective it is no accident that there are so many different types of receptor sites on bitter receptor cells and that most of the chemicals they bind are either poisonous to us or chemically similar to poisons. Imagine an early species of animal that ate plants, some of which contain substance A, a poison that kills by interfering with the animal's respiratory system. Any mutations affecting the taste system of an individual of this species in such a way as to make it dislike the taste of A would promote that individual's survival and reproduction, so those new A-rejecting genes would multiply from generation to generation.

Individuals having the new genes would experience substance A as having a negative, bitter taste and would avoid it; but they would continue to eat plants that contain another poison, substance B, which kills animals by paralyzing the muscular system. Because B is an entirely different compound from A, it does not attach to the A receptors on the taste cells that trigger bitterness, so the animals have no sensory grounds for avoiding it. Now imagine a single mutation, which results in a new variety of receptor protein on the surface of bitter taste cells, a protein that can bind molecules of B. The animal with this mutation would experience the same bitter sensation upon eating leaves containing B as it experiences when eating leaves containing A, and it would avoid both of them. It would be more likely to survive and send progeny into the next generation than would other members of the species, and many of those progeny would inherit the new gene.

Extending this scenario, you can imagine how natural selection might have produced modern mammals that have bitter taste cells containing many different types of receptor proteins, able collectively to bind molecules of most toxic substances found in plants and other potential foods. We can't go back and prove with certainty that this is how the present state of affairs relating to bitterness came about, but this account helps make sense of the facts of bitter taste.

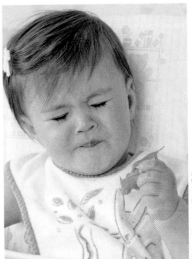

Yuck, bitter This response may protect children from eating poisonous substances. The mammalian taste system evolved to sense many poisons as bitter. Among humans, young children are especially sensitive to, and rejecting of, bitter taste.

Possible Explanation of Sex and Age Differences in Bitter Sensitivity

Although avoidance of bitter-tasting foods is generally adaptive, too much avoidance of them is not. Plants protect themselves from being eaten not just by producing truly poisonous substances, but also by producing nonpoisonous substances that are sufficiently similar to poisons that they bind to bitter taste receptors and produce bitter taste. Individuals that avoided all bitter tastes would lose the nutritional value of plants that taste bitter but are safe to eat. Through observation and experience, people and other plant-eating animals can learn to eat and enjoy bitter foods that have no toxins or low levels of toxins.

Among humans, women are generally more sensitive to bitter taste than are men, and women become still more sensitive to it during the first 3 months of pregnancy (Duffy & Bartoshuk, 1996; Nordin & others, 2004). A possible reason is found in evidence that human fetuses are highly subject to damage by poisons, especially during the first 3 months of their development (Profet, 1992). With the stakes being survival of offspring, the value of avoiding even mild toxins increases. Young children also appear to be highly sensitive to bitter tastes (Cowart, 1981), which may help explain why it is so difficult to get them to eat nutritious but bitter-tasting greens, such as spinach or Brussels sprouts. Children's extra sensitivity to bitterness may help protect them from eating poisonous materials during their early development, before they have learned what is safe to eat and what is not.

SECTION REVIEW

Taste is a chemical sense that helps us decide what is good or bad to eat.

Basic Facts of Taste	Evolution and Taste Quality
➤ Human taste receptors are specialized cells contained in taste buds on the tongue and other parts of the mouth and throat.	➤ Through evolution, we have generally come to experience beneficial nutrients as pleasant in taste (sweet, salty, or umami) and harmful substances as unpleasant (sour or bitter).
➤ Five types of taste receptors have been identified, which correspond to five primary tastes—sweet, salty, sour, bitter, and umami.	➤ Bitter receptor cells evolved to respond to many chemically varied substances that are poisonous or chemically similar to poisons.
➤ Taste receptors can trigger neural impulses in taste sensory neurons, which send input to the primary taste area in the frontal lobe and to other parts of the brain.	➤ Natural selection may explain why children and women, especially pregnant women, are particularly sensitive to bitter tastes.

14

In what ways is pain a "body" sense, an emotion, and a drive? How does observation of people born without pain sensitivity illustrate pain's value?

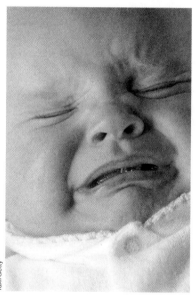

Taxi/Getty

FIGURE 7.7 The face of pain
People everywhere, including newborn infants, express pain in a similar way. The full expression includes a lowered brow, closed or partly closed eyes, tightened eyelids, raised cheeks, wrinkled nose, and raised upper lip (Williams, 2002).

◼ Pain

Pain is one of the somatosenses (introduced in Chapter 5). That is, like touch, temperature sensitivity, and proprioception (the sense of body position), pain is a sense that can originate from multiple places throughout the body rather than just from specialized sensory organs in the head. (Recall that *soma* means "body.") Pain receptors exist over the whole surface of the skin and in many other bodily tissues.

Pain is a "body" sense in another way, too. When you see, hear, smell, taste, or touch something, you experience the sensation as coming from outside yourself (from the thing you are seeing, hearing, smelling, tasting, or touching); but when you feel pain, you experience it as coming from your own body. If you cut yourself with a knife, your feeling of pain is a sense not of the knife (which you experience with vision and touch) but of your own injured bodily state. Pain is not only a sense but also an emotion and a drive. As an emotion, strong pain overwhelms a person's conscious mind, making it hard to think about anything except the pain; and, like many other emotions, pain has its own well-recognized facial expression (see Figure 7.7) (Williams, 2002). As a drive, pain motivates a person both to reduce the pain and to avoid future behaviors like the one that produced it (such as careless handling of knives). In psychology, pain is by far the most thoroughly studied of the somatosenses. That, no doubt, is largely due to the dramatic ways that pain can affect, and be affected by, a person's other psychological experiences.

The evolutionary value of pain—its role in promoting survival—is dramatically illustrated in those rare, unlucky people who are born with a genetic disorder that makes them insensitive to it (Brand & Yancey, 1993; Cox & others, 2006). They can experience all other sensations—including touch, warmth, cold, tickle, and pressure on the skin—and they can report increasing intensities of those sensations, but pain, with its warning and motivating qualities, is missing. Children with this disorder are not motivated to remove their hands from hot stoves, or to refrain from chewing on their tongues as they eat, or to change their body positions (as most of us do from minute to minute) to relieve the strain on muscles and joints. Even if they are constantly watched throughout childhood, and even if they learn intellectually to avoid certain activities, people with this disorder usually die young from the tissue deterioration and infections that result from their wounds.

Neural Pathways for Pain

Anatomically, pain is closely related to the other somatosenses, such as touch and temperature sensitivity. For all these senses, the receptor cells are the sensory neurons themselves. These neurons have receptive endings in the skin and long axons that enter the central nervous system. Pain neurons are thinner than other

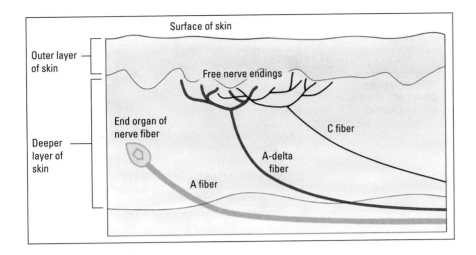

FIGURE 7.8 Pain receptors in the skin The pain receptors are the sensitive endings of sensory neurons, called free nerve endings. The slower second wave of pain is carried by the very thin C fibers, and the faster first wave is carried by the thicker A-delta fibers. The sense of touch is carried by still thicker (and faster) A fibers, whose endings are not "free" but, rather, are surrounded by a capsule, or end organ, that modifies the pressure stimulus.

neurons from the skin, and their sensitive terminals, called *free nerve endings,* are not encased in special capsules, or end organs, as are the endings of touch and temperature receptors (see Figure 7.8). Free nerve endings can be found in all body tissues from which pain is sensed (Lynn & Perl, 1996)—not just the skin but also the pulp of the teeth (from which comes the dreaded toothache), muscles (giving us the pain of cramps and muscle aches), membranes around bones and joints (from which people my age experience the pain of arthritis), and various visceral organs (giving us stomachaches and other inner pains).

Sensory Neurons for Two Waves of Pain

Pain sensory neurons are of two general types—very thin, unmyelinated, slow-conducting neurons called *C fibers* and slightly thicker, myelinated, faster-conducting neurons called *A-delta fibers* (again see Figure 7.8). Some A-delta fibers are specialized to respond to strong pressure (such as from a pinprick), while others are specialized to respond to extremes of temperature (hot or cold). C fibers respond to all sorts of stimuli that produce pain, including strong pressure, intense heat or cold, and chemicals that produce pain when applied to the skin (Basbaum & Jessell, 2000). When your skin is pricked or burned, you feel two separate waves of pain: a sharp, highly localized *first pain,* followed (1 or 2 seconds later) by a dull, burning, more diffuse, longer-lasting *second pain.* The first is mediated by A-delta fibers, and the second by the slower C fibers (Basbaum & Jessell, 2000). The C fibers also respond in a more prolonged way to a variety of chemicals that are released by damaged or infected cells, accounting for the persistent pain that accompanies burns, wounds, and infections.

Pain neurons enter the spinal cord (via a spinal nerve) or the brainstem (via a cranial nerve) and terminate there on interneurons. Some of these interneurons promote reflexive responses—such as the automatic withdrawal of the hand from a hot stove—independent of conscious experience. Others send their axons to the thalamus, in the center of the brain, which, in turn, sends output to portions of the brain that are involved in the conscious experience of pain.

> ────────── **15**
> **What is the anatomical basis for a distinction between first and second pain?**
> ──────────

Brain Areas for Three Components of Pain Experience

Pain as a psychological experience can be divided meaningfully into three different components, each of which depends most critically on a different portion of the brain (see Figure 7.9):

1. The *sensory* component of pain depends largely on the somatosensory cortex, the area of the parietal lobe that receives input for touch and temperature as well as pain (for its location, look back at Figure 7.1, on page 233). This area appears to be crucial for the ability to perceive pain as a sensation, to describe its intensity and qualities (as sharp or dull, for example), and to locate it in a particular portion of the body.

> ────────── **16**
> **What are three different components of pain experience, and what evidence links these to three different portions of the brain?**
> ──────────

FIGURE 7.9 Brain areas involved in three components of pain experience Pain input from tracts through the spinal cord and midbrain is relayed by one portion of the thalamus to the somatosensory cortex and by another portion to the insular cortex and certain portions of the limbic system. These areas, in turn, send output to the prefrontal cortex. These different areas account for three relatively distinct components of pain experience, described in the figure. (Based on information reviewed by Price, 2000.)

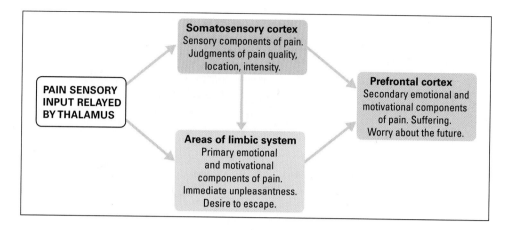

2. The immediately experienced *primary emotional and motivational* component of pain depends on portions of the limbic system referred to as the cingulate cortex and the insular cortex, which lie buried in the folds of the brain's frontal lobe. People with damage to these brain regions experience a condition called *asymbolia for pain* (Foltz & White, 1968; Price, 2000). They can perceive a painful stimulus and describe it as such, identify the location of the pain, describe its qualities, and rate its intensity; but they do not feel a normal desire to escape the pain. The pain doesn't bother them.

3. A third component of pain, in humans, is the more cognitively based *secondary emotional and motivational* component—the suffering that derives from the person's worrying about the future or about the meaning of the pain. The brain area that is crucial for this troubled state lies in the prefrontal lobe, the frontmost portion of the cerebral cortex, which is involved in all aspects of planning and concern for the future (as noted in Chapter 5). People with damage here feel and respond to the immediate threat and unpleasantness of pain, but they do not worry about it, just as they do not worry about or make plans based on other experiences (Price, 2000).

The experience of pain, with all three of the above components, does not always originate from stimulation of pain receptors. This fact is all too well known by many people who have had a limb amputated. Such people often feel as if the missing limb were still present and full of pain. Such phantom-limb pain can persist even if all the nerves from the limb's stump have been destroyed and even if the pain pathways entering the brain from the spinal cord have been destroyed (Flor & others, 2006; Melzack, 1992). Apparently, in such cases the brain's mechanism for experiencing pain and assigning that experience to a particular body location can be activated without sensory input from that part of the body. In fact, the *lack* of sensory input might trigger phantom-limb pain by removing a source of inhibition to the pain mechanisms of the brain.

The Modulation of Pain

The experience of pain depends not just on the physical stimulus or its damaging effects but also on other conditions that exist at the time the stimulus or damage occurs. The same degree of wound may at one time feel excruciatingly painful and at another time be barely detected. Over 40 years ago, Ronald Melzack and Patrick Wall (1965, 1996) proposed a **gate-control theory** of pain, aimed at explaining such variability. In essence, the theory holds that the experience of pain depends on the degree to which input from pain sensory neurons can pass through a neural "gate" and reach higher pain centers in the brain. Conditions can increase or decrease pain by opening or closing the gate. Much research has confirmed this general theory and has added many details to it.

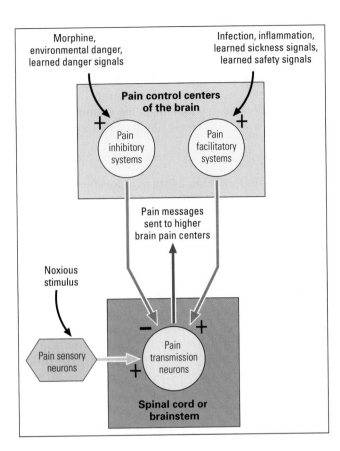

FIGURE 7.10 Gate control of pain Pain transmission neurons in the spinal cord or brainstem, which receive input from pain sensory neurons coming from the body, can be made more or less excitable by descending connections from the brain. In the figure, + indicates excitatory connections and − indicates inhibitory connections. The excitatory and inhibiting effects on the pain transmission neurons constitute the metaphorical "gate" in the gate-control theory of pain. (Modified from Watkins & Maier, 2000, p. 31.)

The major gate, where pain input is most strongly enhanced or inhibited, is at the first way station in the pain pathway in the central nervous system. Pain sensory neurons enter either the spinal cord (by way of a spinal nerve) or the brainstem (by way of a cranial nerve) and terminate there on second-order pain neurons that send signals upward, to higher brain areas that enable the experience of pain. The responsiveness of these second-order neurons to pain input is controlled, in part, by pain-enhancing and pain-inhibiting neurons that extend their axons down from higher portions of the brain. The effects of these descending neurons, in the spinal cord and brainstem, is metaphorically referred to as the "gate" for pain. Pain-enhancing neurons tend to open the gate, and pain-inhibiting neurons tend to close it, as illustrated in Figure 7.10 (above). The intensity of pain sensation experienced depends on the stimulus and on the balance of forces tending to open or close the gate (discussed in the following paragraphs).

Try falling down and scraping your knee. Then you can talk to me about pain.

Mechanisms of Pain Enhancement

As your own experience may have shown you, illness often increases pain sensitivity all over the body, especially if high fever is involved. This effect may have evolved to motivate ill individuals to rest rather than move around, in order to conserve energy needed to fight the disease (Kluger, 1991). Although the details are not fully understood, this illness-induced effect is believed to occur through an action of the immune system on pain-enhancing neurons in the brain (again, see Figure 7.10) (Watkins & Maier, 2000; Watkins & others, 2007).

Pain sensitivity can also be increased in specific locations of the body as a result of injury at those locations. This heightened sensitivity occurs partly because of changes in the free nerve endings of C fibers and A-delta fibers that are induced by chemicals released from damaged cells (Basbaum & Jessell, 2000). The sensitized

17

How does illness produce a general increase in pain sensitivity, and how does injury produce a localized increase in pain sensitivity?

sensory neurons respond to much weaker stimuli than they would have before the injury. In addition, second-order pain neurons in the spinal cord and brainstem become sensitized by intense activation, such that they become more responsive to subsequent input for periods ranging from minutes to weeks (Ji & others, 2003; Woolf & Salter, 2000). The result is that even light touch to a recently burned or wounded area of skin can be intensely painful. Such pain-enhancing systems presumably evolved as a means of motivating individuals to protect damaged areas of their bodies.

Neural and Chemical Mechanisms of Pain Reduction

18

How can pain input be inhibited at its entry into the central nervous system, and how might endorphins be involved in this process?

A major neural center for pain inhibition exists in a portion of the midbrain called the *periaqueductal gray* (abbreviated *PAG*). Neurons in this area send their axons down into the lower brainstem and spinal cord to inhibit pain input there, as illustrated in Figure 7.10. Electrical stimulation of the PAG has a powerful analgesic (pain-reducing) effect—so powerful, in fact, that abdominal surgery can be performed without drugs in animals that are receiving such stimulation (Mason, 2001; Reynolds, 1969). Electrical stimulation of this area has also, in humans, successfully reduced or abolished chronic pain that could not be relieved by other means (Hosobuchi & others, 1979; Perlmutter & Mink, 2006).

Morphine and other *opiate drugs* (derivatives of opium) exert their well-known analgesic effects partly through direct action in the PAG. Morphine that passes into the brain is taken up at special binding sites on neurons in the PAG, where it increases neural activity and thereby reduces pain (Basbaum & Fields, 1984). Morphine binding sites are also found on neurons in the spinal cord, and injection of a tiny amount of morphine directly into the spinal cord can greatly reduce or eliminate pain in the part of the body that sends its sensory neurons into that spinal cord area (Basbaum & Jessell, 2000).

Of course, the pain-inhibiting system did not evolve to respond specifically to morphine or other foreign substances. Its basic function is to mediate the body's own capacity to reduce pain. The body produces a variety of chemicals that act like morphine and are collectively referred to as **endorphins.** As was noted in Chapter 6, the term *endorphin* is short for *endogenous morphine-like substance* (*endogenous* means "created within the body"). Some endorphins are produced in the brain or spinal cord and serve as neurotransmitters or neuromodulators to alter the activity or excitability of neurons to which they bind. Others are secreted from the pituitary and adrenal glands as hormones, which enter the bloodstream and have a variety of effects both peripherally and in the central nervous system (Henry, 1986). Endorphins are believed to inhibit pain by acting both in the PAG and at the places (illustrated in Figure 7.10) where pain-carrying neurons enter the spinal cord and lower brainstem.

Stress-Induced Analgesia

During his search for the source of the Nile River, the famous explorer David Livingston was attacked by a lion. He survived the incident and later wrote that although the lion shook him "as a terrier does a rat" and crushed his shoulder, he had felt "no sense of pain nor feeling of terror, though quite conscious of all that was happening" (Livingston, 1857). Other people have had similar experiences. For example, soldiers severely wounded in battle often do not notice their wounds until the battle is over. We are apparently endowed with a mechanism that prevents us from feeling pain at times when, for survival purposes, it is best to ignore our wounds. A person or nonhuman animal faced with a predator or similar threat cannot afford to nurse a wound or favor it by limping; all the body's resources must be used to fight or flee. The decreased pain sensitivity that accompanies highly stressful situations is referred to as **stress-induced analgesia.**

19

What is some evidence that stress-induced analgesia is at least partly mediated by endorphins?

Many experiments have shown that stress-induced analgesia depends partly, if not entirely, on the release of endorphins. In one experiment, rats that were subjected to a series of electric shocks to their feet (the source of stress) became relatively insensitive to pain for several minutes afterward, as indicated by their lack of response to normally painful heat applied to their tails (Lewis & others, 1980).

Rats treated with a drug that blocks the action of endorphins did not show this stress-induced analgesia, indicating that the effect must have been mediated by endorphins. In similar experiments, the mere presence of a cat (Lichtman & Fanselow, 1990) produced analgesia in rats; the presence of biting flies produced analgesia in mice (Kavaliers & others, 1999); a stressful math test produced analgesia in students (Bandura & others, 1988); and films depicting combat produced analgesia in veterans who had experienced the trauma of war (Pitman & others, 1990). In all of these cases injection of a drug that blocks the actions of endorphins prevented the analgesic effect from occurring.

Endorphins are also secreted during periods of prolonged, strenuous physical exertion, such as long-distance running, and may account for the pain reduction and euphoric "runner's high" that many people enjoy during and after such exertion. In one experiment both the reduced pain and the sense of euphoria failed to occur in runners who had been treated with an endorphin-blocking drug (Janal & others, 1984).

Belief-Induced Analgesia

In humans, dramatic reduction in pain can also, at times, be produced by the power of belief or faith. Some religious groups engage in practices that most of us would regard as torture, yet the participants appear to feel no pain. One group in India, for example, practices a hook-hanging ritual. A man who has been chosen to represent the power of the gods is secured to a rope by two steel hooks that pierce the skin and muscles on his back. He hangs from this rope, swinging back and forth, while he blesses the children and the crops of the village. He feels honored to have been chosen and apparently feels little or no pain (Melzack & Wall, 1996).

> **20**
> **What is some evidence that pain can be reduced by belief?**

A less dramatic example, in cultures where faith is more often placed in science and medicine, is the *placebo effect* on pain. In many cases a pill or injection that contains no active substance (the placebo) can reduce pain in a person who believes that the drug is a painkiller. A number of experiments have shown that placebo-induced pain reduction depends partly, and in some cases entirely, on the secretion of endorphins (Price & others, 2008). In one of the first such experiments, people who had undergone a tooth extraction reported less pain if given a placebo than if not, and this placebo effect did not occur in subjects who were treated with an endorphin-blocking drug (Levine & others, 1979). Other experiments have shown that various cognitive techniques for relieving pain, such as meditating on the idea that the pain is disconnected from the rest of the body, also work at least partly through endorphins (Bandura & others, 1987). Might the man hanging from hooks in India also be secreting large quantities of endorphins? Nobody knows for sure, but most pain researchers would bet that he is.

SECTION REVIEW

Pain is an emotion and drive as well as a somatosense.

Basic Facts of Pain

➤ Pain receptors are free nerve endings of pain sensory neurons, located in many parts of the body.

➤ C fibers and A-delta fibers, two types of pain sensory neurons, mediate two different waves of pain.

➤ The experience of pain has three identifiable components—sensory, primary emotional and motivational, and secondary emotional and motivational—each relying on different areas of the brain.

Pain Modulation

➤ The gate-control theory maintains that the degree of pain felt depends on how much input from pain neurons passes through a neural "gate" to higher areas of the brain.

➤ The enhanced pain sensitivity that accompanies illness or injury helps protect the body from further harm.

➤ The PAG and endorphins provide the body with a means of pain inhibition.

➤ Endorphins play a part in stress-induced and belief-induced analgesia.

An auditory animal Bats, which navigate and hunt by sonar, have large, mobile outer ears. This is especially true of some species, such as *Macrotus californicus*, pictured here.

Hearing

Among mammals, the greatest listeners are the bats. In complete darkness, and even if blinded, bats can flit around obstacles such as tree branches and capture insects that themselves are flying in erratic patterns to escape. Bats navigate and hunt by sonar, that is, by reflected sound waves. They send out high-pitched chirps, above the frequency range that we can hear, and analyze the echoes in a way that allows them to *hear* the scene in front of them. From echoes, they can hear such characteristics as the size, shape, position, direction of movement, and texture of a target insect (Feng & Ratnam, 2000).

Hearing may not be as well developed or as essential for us as it is for bats, but it is still enormously effective and useful. It allows us to detect and respond to potentially life-threatening or life-enhancing events that occur in the dark, or behind our backs, or anywhere out of view. We use it to identify animals and such natural events as upcoming storms. And, perhaps most important, it is the primary sensory modality of human language. We learn from each other through our ears.

Sound and Its Transduction by the Ear

If a tree falls in the forest and no one is there to hear it, does it make a sound? This old riddle plays on the fact that the term *sound* refers both to a type of physical stimulus and to the sensation produced by that stimulus.

Sound as a Physical Stimulus

As a physical stimulus, sound is the vibration of air or some other medium produced by an object such as a tuning fork, one's vocal cords, or a falling tree. The vibration moves outward from the sound source in a manner that can be described as a wave (see Figure 7.11). The height of the wave indicates the total pressure exerted by the molecules of air (or another medium) as they move back and forth, which is referred to as the sound's ***amplitude,*** or intensity, and corresponds to what we hear as the

FIGURE 7.11 Characteristics of sound The oscillating tuning fork (a) causes air molecules to vibrate in a manner that can be represented as a wave of pressure. Each wave contains an area in which the air molecules are more compressed (the dark regions in the upper diagram) and an area in which they are less compressed (the light regions) than normal. The peak pressure (the highest compression) of each wave defines the amplitude of the sound, and the number of waves that pass a given point per second defines the frequency. The higher the amplitude, the louder the sound; and the higher the frequency, the higher the pitch (b). All the wave drawings in this figure are sine waves, indicative of pure tones. (Adapted from Klinke, 1986.)

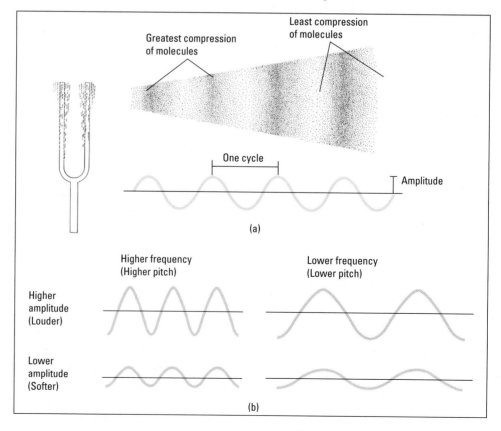

TABLE 7.2 Sound-pressure amplitudes of various sounds, and conversion to decibels*

Example	P (in sound-pressure units)	Log P	Decibels
Softest detectable sound	1	0	0
Soft whisper	10	1	20
Quiet neighborhood	100	2	40
Average conversation	1,000	3	60
Loud music from a radio	10,000	4	80
Heavy automobile traffic	100,000	5	100
Very loud thunder	1,000,000	6	120
Jet airplane taking off	10,000,000	7	140
Loudest rock band on record	100,000,000	8	160
Spacecraft launch (from 150 ft.)	1,000,000,000	9	180

*One sound-pressure unit (P) is defined as 2×10^{-5} newtons/square meter (Klinke, 1986). When measured in sound-pressure units, the amplitude range of human hearing is enormous. A reason for converting to logarithmic units is to produce a smaller range of numbers. The logarithm (log) of a number is the power to which 10 must be raised to produce that number. For example, the log of 10,000 is 4, because $10^4 = 10,000$. A decibel (dB) is defined as $20 \log P$. Thus, 4 log units = 80 dB.

Sources: Lindsay, P. H., & Norman, D. A. (1977). *Human information processing,* 2nd ed. (p. 161). New York: Academic Press; Matlin, M. W., & Foley, H. J. (1997). *Sensation and perception,* 4th ed. (p. 281). Boston: Allyn and Bacon.

sound's **loudness.** Sound amplitude is usually measured in logarithmic units of pressure called *decibels* (abbreviated *dB*). (See Table 7.2, which further defines decibels and contains the decibel ratings for a number of common sounds.)

In addition to varying in amplitude, sound waves vary in **frequency,** which we hear as the sound's **pitch.** The frequency of a sound is the rate at which the molecules of air or another medium move back and forth. Frequency is measured in *hertz* (abbreviated *Hz*), which is the number of complete waves (or cycles) per second generated by the sound source. Sounds that are audible to humans have frequencies ranging from about 20 to 20,000 Hz. To give you an idea of the relationship between frequency and pitch, the dominant (most audible) frequency of the lowest note on a piano is about 27 Hz, that of middle C is about 262 Hz, and that of the highest piano note is about 4186 Hz (Matlin & Foley, 1997). The simplest kind of sound is a pure tone, which is a constant-frequency sound wave that can be described mathematically as a sine wave (depicted in Figure 7.11). Pure tones, which are useful in auditory experiments, can be produced in the laboratory, but they rarely if ever occur in other contexts. Natural sources of sound, including even musical instruments and tuning forks, vibrate at several frequencies at once and thus produce more complex waves than that shown in Figure 7.11. The pitch that we attribute to a natural sound depends on its dominant (largest-amplitude) frequency.

How the Ear Works

Hearing originated, in the course of evolution, from the sense of touch. Touch is sensitivity to pressure on the skin, and hearing is sensitivity to pressure on a special sensory tissue in the ear. In some animals, such as moths, sound is sensed through modified touch receptors located on flexible patches of skin that vibrate in response to sound waves. In humans and other mammals the special patches of skin for hearing have migrated to a location inside the head, and special organs, the ears, have developed to magnify the pressure exerted by sound waves as they are transported inward. A diagram of the human ear is shown in Figure 7.12 (on the next page). To review its structures and their functions, we will begin from the outside and work inward.

The **outer ear** consists of the *pinna,* which is the flap of skin and cartilage forming the visible portion of the ear, and the *auditory canal,* which is the opening into

> ─────────── 21
> **What are the functions of the outer ear, middle ear, and inner ear?**

FIGURE 7.12 Parts of the human ear Sound waves (vibrations of air) that enter the auditory canal cause the eardrum to vibrate, which causes the ossicles (the hammer, anvil, and stirrup bones) to vibrate, which causes the oval window to vibrate, setting up waves of motion in the fluid inside the cochlea. The semicircular canals are involved in the sense of balance, not hearing.

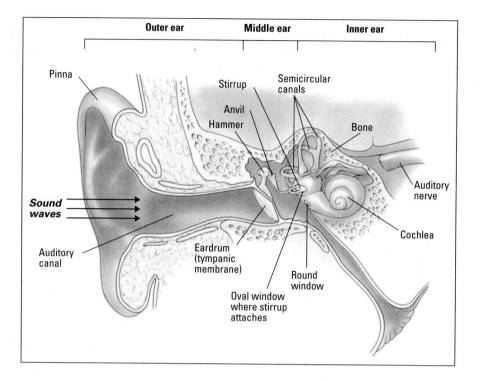

the head that ends at the eardrum. The whole outer ear can be thought of as a funnel for receiving sound waves and transporting them inward. The vibration of air outside the head (the physical sound) causes air in the auditory canal to vibrate, which, in turn, causes the eardrum to vibrate.

The **middle ear** is an air-filled cavity, separated from the outer ear by the eardrum (technically called the *tympanic membrane*). The middle ear's main structures are three tiny bones collectively called *ossicles* (and individually called the *hammer, anvil,* and *stirrup,* because of their respective shapes), which are linked to the eardrum at one end and to another membrane called the *oval window* at the other end. When sound causes the eardrum to vibrate, the ossicles vibrate and push against the oval window. Because the oval window has only about one-thirtieth the area of the tympanic membrane, the pressure (force per unit area) that is funneled to it by the ossicles is about 30 times greater than the pressure on the eardrum. Thus, the main function of the middle ear is to increase the amount of pressure that sound waves exert upon the inner ear so that transduction can occur.

The oval window separates the middle ear from the **inner ear,** which consists primarily of the **cochlea,** a coiled structure where transduction takes place. As depicted in the uncoiled view in Figure 7.13, the cochlea contains a fluid-filled *outer duct,* which begins at the oval window, runs to the tip of the cochlea, and then runs back again to end at another membrane, the *round window.* Sandwiched between the outgoing and incoming portions of the outer duct is another fluid-filled tube, the *inner duct.* Forming the floor of the inner duct is the **basilar membrane,** on which are located the receptor cells for hearing, called **hair cells.** There are four rows of hair cells (three outer rows and one inner row), each row running the length of the basilar membrane. Tiny hairs (called *cilia*) protrude from each hair cell into the inner duct and abut against another membrane, called the *tectorial membrane.* At the other end from its hairs, each hair cell forms synapses with several *auditory neurons,* whose axons form the *auditory nerve* (eighth cranial nerve), which runs to the brain.

22

How does transduction occur in the inner ear?

The process of transduction in the cochlea can be summarized as follows: The sound-induced vibration of the ossicles against the oval window initiates vibration in the fluid in the outer duct of the cochlea, which produces an up-and-down waving motion of the basilar membrane, which is very flexible. The tectorial membrane, which runs parallel to the basilar membrane, is less flexible and does not

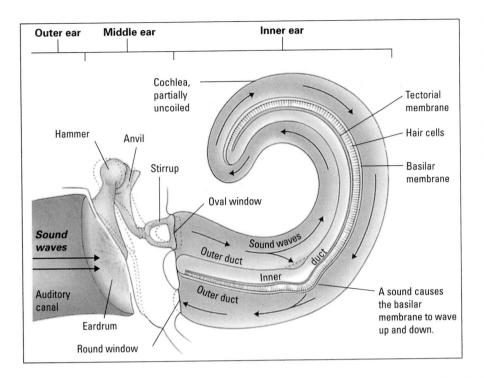

FIGURE 7.13 Transduction mechanism in the inner ear This diagram depicts a longitudinal section of the cochlea (partially uncoiled), showing the outer and inner ducts. Sound waves in the fluid of the outer duct cause the basilar membrane to wave up and down. When the basilar membrane moves upward, its hairs bend against the tectorial membrane, initiating receptor potentials in the hair cells.

move when the basilar membrane moves. The hairs of the hair cells are sandwiched between the basilar membrane and the tectorial membrane, so they bend each time the basilar membrane moves toward the tectorial membrane. This bending causes tiny channels to open up in the hair cell's membrane, which leads to a change in the electrical charge across the membrane (the receptor potential) (Corey, 2007). This in turn causes each hair cell to release neurotransmitter molecules at its synapses upon auditory neurons, thereby increasing the rate of action potentials in those neurons (Hudspeth, 2000b).

Deafness and Hearing Aids

With this knowledge of the ear it is possible to understand the physiological bases for deafness. One form of deafness, called *conduction deafness,* occurs when the ossicles of the middle ear become rigid and cannot carry sounds inward from the tympanic membrane to the cochlea. People with conduction deafness can hear vibrations that reach the cochlea by routes other than the middle ear. A *conventional hearing aid* is helpful for such people, because it mag-nifies the sound pressure sufficiently for vibrations to be conducted by other bones of the face into the cochlea.

23

How do two kinds of deafness differ in their physiological bases and in possible treatment?

The other form of deafness is *sen-sorineural deafness,* which results from damage to the hair cells of the cochlea or damage to the auditory neurons. Damage to hair cells is particularly likely to occur among people who are regularly exposed to loud sounds (see Figure 7.14 on page 256). Indeed, some experts on human hearing are concerned that the regular use of portable mp3 players, which can play music at sound pressure levels of more than 100 decibels through their stock earbuds, may cause partial deafness in many young people today as they grow older (*Nature Neuroscience* editorial, 2007).

© Michael Newman/Photo Edit

External portions of a cochlear implant A microphone hooked around the boy's ear picks up sound waves and sends signals down, through a cable connection, to an auditory processor attached to a belt around his waist. The auditory processor converts the signals into electrical pulses, suit-able for stimulating the cochlea, and sends those pulses up the cable to a transmitter fastened to the boy's head above and behind his ear. The trans-mitter sends the pulses through the skin to a receiver implanted in his skull, and from there the pulses are sent by thin wire electrodes to stimulate appro-priate sets of auditory neurons in the cochlea of the inner ear.

FIGURE 7.14 Warning: Noise can be dangerous These electron micrographs show hair cells on the basilar membrane of a guinea pig (a) before and (b) after exposure to 24 hours of sound at an intensity comparable to a rock concert. The tiny hairs are disarranged on some cells and completely destroyed on others. Notice also that the hair cells exist in four rows—three outer rows and one inner row.

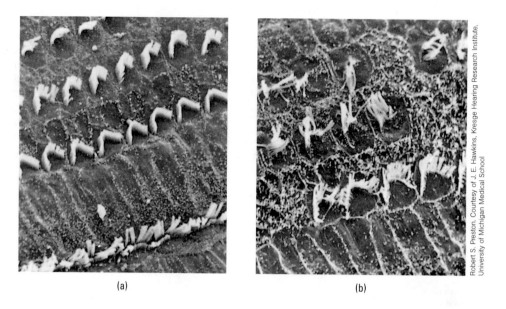

(a)   (b)

Congenital deafness (deafness present at birth) may involve damage to either the hair cells or the auditory neurons.

People with complete sensorineural deafness are not helped by a conventional hearing aid but can in many cases be helped by a newer form of hearing aid called a *cochlear implant*. This device performs the transduction task normally done by the ear's hair cells (though not nearly as well). It transforms sounds into electrical impulses and sends the impulses through thin wires permanently implanted into the cochlea, where they stimulate the terminals of auditory neurons directly. It can be used when deafness has resulted from the destruction of hair cells, but not when the auditory nerve has been destroyed. The best cochlear implants today permit sufficient sound resolution to enable deaf children to acquire vocal language at a nearly normal rate (Ertmer, 2007; Svirsky & others, 2000). They also allow adults who became deaf after learning language to regain much of their ability to understand speech (Gifford & others, 2008).

Pitch Perception

The first step in perceiving pitch is that receptor cells on the basilar membrane must respond differently to different sound frequencies. How does that occur? The first real breakthrough in answering that question came in the 1920s, with the work of Georg von Békésy, which eventuated in a Nobel Prize.

The Traveling Wave as a Basis for Frequency Coding

24

How does the basilar membrane of the inner ear operate to ensure that different neurons are maximally stimulated by sounds of different frequencies?

In order to study frequency coding, Békésy developed a way to observe directly the action of the basilar membrane. He discovered that sound waves entering the cochlea set up traveling waves on the basilar membrane, which move from the proximal end (closest to the oval window) toward the distal end (farthest away from the oval window), like a bedsheet when someone shakes it at one end. As each wave moves, it increases in amplitude up to a certain maximum and then rapidly dissipates. Of most importance, Békésy found that the position on the membrane at which the waves reach their peak amplitude depends on the frequency of the tone. High frequencies produce waves that travel only a short distance, peaking near the proximal end, not far from the oval window. Low frequencies produce waves that travel farther, peaking near the distal end, nearer to the round window. For an illustration of the effects that different tones and complex sounds have on the basilar membrane, see Figure 7.15.

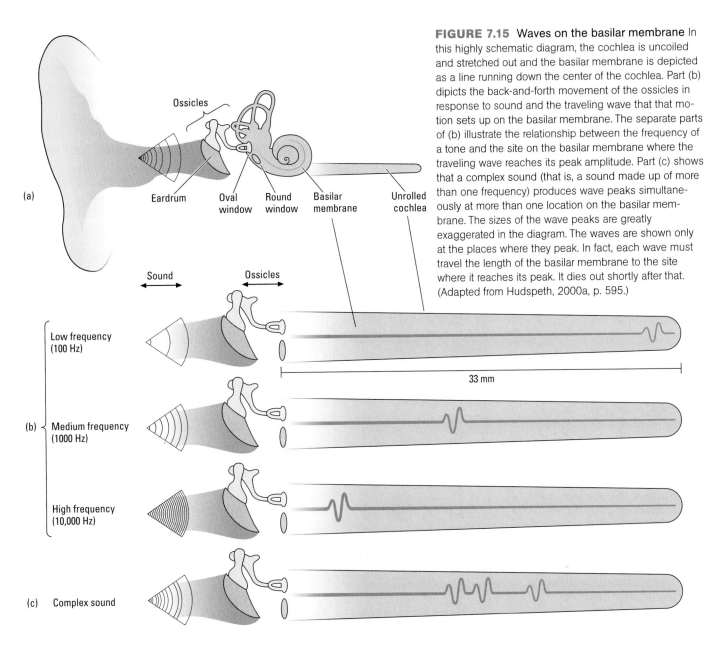

FIGURE 7.15 Waves on the basilar membrane In this highly schematic diagram, the cochlea is uncoiled and stretched out and the basilar membrane is depicted as a line running down the center of the cochlea. Part (b) dipicts the back-and-forth movement of the ossicles in response to sound and the traveling wave that that motion sets up on the basilar membrane. The separate parts of (b) illustrate the relationship between the frequency of a tone and the site on the basilar membrane where the traveling wave reaches its peak amplitude. Part (c) shows that a complex sound (that is, a sound made up of more than one frequency) produces wave peaks simultaneously at more than one location on the basilar membrane. The sizes of the wave peaks are greatly exaggerated in the diagram. The waves are shown only at the places where they peak. In fact, each wave must travel the length of the basilar membrane to the site where it reaches its peak. It dies out shortly after that. (Adapted from Hudspeth, 2000a, p. 595.)

From this observation, Békésy hypothesized that (a) rapid firing in neurons that come from the proximal end of the membrane, accompanied by little or no firing in neurons coming from more distal parts, is interpreted by the brain as a high-pitched sound and (b) rapid firing in neurons coming from a more distal portion of the membrane is interpreted as a lower-pitched sound.

Subsequent research has confirmed the general validity of Békésy's hypothesis and has shown that the waves on the intact, living basilar membrane are in fact much more sharply defined than those that Békésy had observed. There is now good evidence that the primary receptor cells for hearing are the inner row of hair cells and that the outer three rows serve mostly a different function. They have the capacity to stiffen when activated, and they do so in a manner that amplifies and sharpens the traveling wave (Géléoc & Holt, 2003).

Two Sensory Consequences of the Traveling-Wave Mechanism

The manner by which the basilar membrane responds to differing frequencies helps us make sense of a number of auditory phenomena. One such phenomenon is *asymmetry in auditory masking*, which is especially noticeable in music production.

> **25**
>
> **How does the traveling-wave theory explain (a) an asymmetry in auditory masking and (b) the pattern of hearing loss that occurs as we get older?**

Auditory masking refers to the ability of one sound to mask (prevent the hearing of) another sound. Auditory masking is asymmetrical in that low-frequency sounds mask high-frequency sounds much more effectively than the reverse (Scharf, 1964). A bassoon can easily drown out a piccolo, but a piccolo cannot easily drown out a bassoon. To see how this can be explained in terms of the waves the two instruments produce on the basilar membrane, look at Figure 7.16. The wave produced by a low-frequency bassoon note encompasses the entire portion of the basilar membrane that is encompassed by the piccolo note (and more). Thus, if the bassoon note is of sufficient amplitude, it can interfere with the effect of the piccolo note; but the piccolo note, even at great amplitude, cannot interfere with the effect that the bassoon note has on the more distal part of the membrane, because the wave produced by the piccolo note never travels that far down the membrane.

Another effect of the traveling-wave mechanism concerns the pattern of hearing loss that occurs as we get older. We lose our sensitivity to high frequencies to a much greater degree than to low frequencies. Thus, young children can hear frequencies as high as 30,000 Hz, and young adults can hear frequencies as high as 20,000 Hz, but a typical 60-year-old cannot hear frequencies above about 15,000 Hz. This decline is greatest for people who live or work in noisy environments and is caused by the wearing out of hair cells with repeated use (Kryter, 1985). But why should cells responsible for coding high frequencies wear out faster than those for coding low frequencies? The most likely answer is that the cells coding high frequencies are acted upon by all sounds (as shown in Figure 7.16), while those coding low frequencies are acted upon only by low-frequency sounds.

FIGURE 7.16 Why a low-frequency tone masks a high-frequency tone better than the reverse (a) When a low-frequency tone (such as that from a bassoon) and a high-frequency tone (such as that from a piccolo) are played simultaneously, the bassoon can mask the piccolo because the bassoon's action on the basilar membrane encompasses the entire portion on which the piccolo acts. (b) But the piccolo cannot mask the bassoon because, even when played at high amplitude, the piccolo does not affect the distal part of the membrane to which the bassoon's waves extend. (Adapted from Scharf, 1964.)

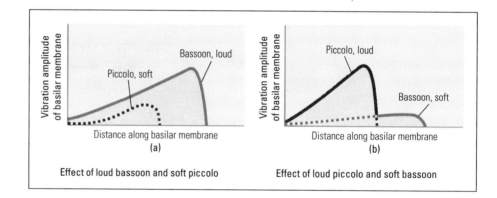

Another Code for Frequency

26
How does the timing of action potentials code sound frequency? How do cochlear implants produce perception of pitch?

Although the traveling-wave theory of frequency coding has been well validated, it is not the whole story. For frequencies below about 4,000 Hz (which include most of the frequencies in human speech), perceived pitch depends not just on which part of the basilar membrane is maximally active but also on the timing of that activity (Moore, 1997). The electrical activity triggered in sets of auditory neurons tends to be locked in phase with sound waves, such that a separate burst of action potentials occurs each time a sound wave peaks. The frequency at which such bursts occur contributes to the perception of pitch.

Consistent with what is known about normal auditory coding, modern cochlear implants use both place and timing to produce pitch perception (Dorman & Wilson, 2004). These devices break a sound signal into several (typically six) different frequency ranges and send electrical pulses from each frequency range through a thin wire to a different portion of the basilar membrane. Pitch perception is best when the electrical signal sent to a given locus of the membrane is pulsed at a frequency similar to that of the sound wave that would normally act at that location.

Further Pitch Processing in the Brain

Auditory sensory neurons send their output to nuclei in the brainstem, which in turn send axons upward, ultimately to the primary auditory area of the cerebral cortex, located in each temporal lobe (look back at Figure 7.1, on p. 233). Neurons in the primary auditory cortex are **tonotopically** organized. That is, each neuron there is maximally responsive to sounds of a particular frequency, and the neurons are systematically arranged such that high-frequency tones activate neurons at one end of this cortical area and low-frequency tones activate neurons at the other end. Ultimately, the pitch or set of pitches we hear depends largely on which neurons in the auditory cortex are most active.

27

How is tone frequency represented in the primary auditory cortex? What evidence suggests a close relationship between musical pitch perception and visual space perception?

As is true of other sensory areas in the cortex (discussed in Chapter 5), the response characteristics of neurons in the primary auditory cortex are very much influenced by experience. When experimental animals are trained to use a particular tone frequency as a cue guiding their behavior, the number of auditory cortical neurons that respond to that frequency greatly increases (Bakin & others, 1996) Heredity determines the general form of the tonotopic map, but experience determines the specific amount of cortex that is devoted to any particular range of frequencies. A great deal of research, with humans as well as with laboratory animals, shows that the brain's response to sound frequencies, and to other aspects of sound as well, is very much affected by previous auditory experience. For example, musicians' brains respond more strongly to the sounds of the instruments they play than to the sounds of other instruments (Kraus & Banai, 2007).

Our capacity to distinguish pitch depends not just upon the primary auditory cortex, but also upon activity in an area of the parietal lobe of the cortex called the *intraparietal sulcus,* which receives input from the primary auditory cortex. This part of the brain is involved in both music perception and visual space perception. In one research study, people who described themselves as "tone deaf" and performed poorly on a test of ability to distinguish among different musical notes also performed poorly on a visual-spatial test that required them to mentally rotate pictured objects in order to match them to pictures of the same objects from other viewpoints (Douglas & Bilkey, 2007). Perhaps it is no coincidence that we (and also people who speak other languages) describe pitch in spatial terms—"high" and "low." Our brain may, in some way, interpret a high note as *high* and a low note as *low,* using part of the same neural system as is used to perceive three-dimensional space.

Making Sense of Sounds

Think of the subtlety and complexity of our auditory perception. With no cues but sound, we can locate a sound source within about 5 to 10 degrees of its true direction (Hudspeth, 2000a). At a party we can distinguish and listen to one person's voice in a noisy environment that includes many other voices and a band in the background. To comprehend speech, we hear the tiny difference between *plot* and *blot,* while ignoring the much larger differences between two different voices that speak either of those words. All sounds set up patterns of waves on our basilar membranes, and from those seemingly chaotic patterns our nervous system extracts all the information needed for auditory perception.

Locating Sounds

The ability to detect the direction of a sound source contributes greatly to the usefulness of hearing. When startled by an unexpected rustling, we reflexively turn toward it to see what might be causing the disturbance. Even newborn infants do this (Muir & Field, 1979), indicating that the ability to localize a sound does not require learning. Such localization is also a key component of our ability to keep one sound distinct from others in a noisy environment. People can attend to one voice and ignore another much more easily if the two voices come from different locations in the room than if they come from the same location (Feng & Ratnam, 2000).

28
How does the difference between the two ears in their distance from a sound source contribute our ability to locate that source?

◄ Sound localization depends at least partly, and maybe mostly, on the time at which each sound wave reaches one ear compared to the other. A wave of sound coming from straight ahead reaches the two ears simultaneously, but a wave from the right or the left reaches one ear slightly before the other (see Figure 7.17). A sound wave that is just slightly to the left of straight ahead reaches the left ear a few microseconds

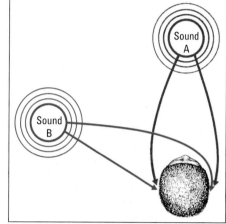

FIGURE 7.17 Locating a sound
Sound waves coming from the left (sound B) reach the left ear sooner than the right ear. The converse would be true of sound waves coming from the right. Neurons receiving input from the two ears are sensitive to this difference, which provides a code for sound localization. Without moving the head, it is difficult to distinguish a sound in front of the head from one that is at the same angle in back of the head, but a head rotation quickly resolves that problem.

(millionths of a second) before it reaches the right ear, and a sound wave that is 90 degrees to the left reaches the left ear about 700 microseconds before it reaches the right ear. Many auditory neurons in the brainstem receive input from both ears. Some of these neurons respond most to waves that reach both ears at once; others respond most to waves that reach one ear some microseconds—ranging from just a few on up to about 700—before, or after, reaching the other ear. These neurons, presumably, are part of the brain's mechanism for perceiving the direction from which a sound is coming (Recanzone & Sutter, 2008; Thompson & others, 2006).

Analyzing Patterns of Auditory Input

In the real world (outside of the laboratory), sounds never come in the form of pure tones. The sounds we hear, and from which we extract meaning, consist of highly complex patterns of waveforms. How is it that you identify the sweet word *psychology* regardless of whether it is spoken in a high-pitched or low-pitched voice, or spoken softly or loudly? You identify the word not from the absolute amplitude or frequency of the sound waves, but from certain patterns of change in these that occur over time as the word is spoken.

Beyond the primary auditory area are cortical areas for analyzing such patterns (Lombar & Malhotra, 2008; Poremba & others, 2003). For example, some neurons in areas near the primary auditory area respond only to certain combinations of frequencies, others only to rising or falling pitches, others only to brief clicks or bursts of sound, and still others only to sound sources that are moving in a particular direction (Baumgart & others, 1999; Phillips, 1989). In macaque monkeys, some cortical neurons respond selectively to particular macaque calls (Rauschecker & others, 1995). In the end, activity in some combination of neurons in your cerebral cortex must provide the basis for each of your auditory experiences, but researchers are only beginning to learn how that is accomplished.

Phonemic Restoration: An Auditory Illusion

In certain situations our auditory system provides us with the perception of sounds that are not really present as physical stimuli. A well-documented example is the sensory illusion of *phonemic restoration*. **Phonemes** are the individual vowel and consonant sounds that make up words (discussed further in Chapter 11), and phonemic restoration is an illusion in which people hear phonemes that have been deleted from words or sentences as if they were still there. The perceptual experience is that of really *hearing* the missing sound, not that of inferring what sound must be there.

29
Under what conditions does our auditory system fill in a missing sound? What might be the value of such an illusion?

◄ Richard Warren (1970) first demonstrated this illusion in an experiment in which he removed an *s* sound and spliced in a coughing sound of equal duration in the following tape-recorded sentence at the place marked by an asterisk: *The state governors met with their respective legi*latures convening in the capital city.* People listening to the doctored tape could hear the cough, but it did not seem to coincide with any specific portion of the sentence or block out any sound in the sentence. Even when they listened repeatedly, with instructions to determine what sound was missing, subjects were unable to detect that any sound was missing. After they were told which sound was missing, they still claimed to hear that sound each time they listened to the tape. In other experiments, thousands of practice trials failed to improve people's abilities to judge which phoneme was missing (Samuel, 1991). Not surprisingly, phonemic restoration has been found to be much more reliable for words that are very much expected to occur in the sentence than for words that are less expected (Sivonen & others, 2006).

Which sound is heard in phonemic restoration depends on the surrounding phonemes and the meaningful words and phrases they produce. The restored sound is always one that turns a partial word into a whole word that is consistent in meaning with the rest of the sentence. Most remarkably, even words that occur *after* the missing phoneme can influence which phoneme is heard. For example, people heard the stimulus sound *eel (again, the asterisk represents a cough-like sound) as *peel, heel,* or *wheel,* depending on whether it occurred in the phrase *The *eel was on the orange, The *eel was on the shoe,* or *The *eel was on the axle* (Warren, 1984). The illusory phoneme was heard as occurring at its proper place, in the second word of the sentence, even though it depended on the words that followed it.

One way to make sense of this phenomenon is to assume that much of our perceptual experience of hearing derives from a brief auditory sensory memory, which lasts for a matter of seconds and is modifiable. The later words generate a momentary false memory of hearing, earlier, a phoneme that wasn't actually present, and that memory is indistinguishable in type from memories of phonemes that actually did occur. Such brief, compelling memories and their role in perceptual experiences are discussed more fully in Chapter 9. Illusory restoration has also been demonstrated in music perception. People hear a missing note, in a familiar tune, as if it were present (DeWitt & Samuel, 1990).

A limiting factor in these illusions is that the gap in the sentence or tune must be filled with noise; it can't be a silent gap. In everyday life the sounds we listen to are often masked by bits of noise, never by bits of silence, so perhaps illusory sound restorations are an evolutionary adaptation by which our auditory system allows us to hear meaningful sound sequences in a relatively uninterrupted stream. When a burst of noise masks a phoneme or a note, our auditory system automatically, after the fact, in auditory memory, replaces that burst with the auditory experience that, according to our previous experience, belongs there. Auditory restoration nicely exemplifies the general principle that our perceptual systems often modify sensory input in ways that help to make sense of that input. You will find more examples and much more discussion of that principle in Chapter 8, which deals with vision.

SECTION REVIEW

Hearing allows us to glean information from patterns of vibrations carried by air.

Basic Facts of Hearing	Pitch Perception	Making Sense of Sounds
➤ Physically, sound is the vibration of air or another medium caused by a vibrating object. A sound wave's amplitude is related to its perceived loudness and its frequency is related to its perceived pitch.	➤ Sounds set up traveling waves on the basilar membrane, which peak at different positions depending on frequency. This allows frequency to be coded.	➤ Brain neurons that compare the arrival time of sound waves at our two ears enable us locate a sound's source.
➤ The outer ear funnels sound inward, the middle ear amplifies it, and the inner ear transduces and codes it.	➤ The traveling-wave theory helps to explain the asymmetry of auditory masking and the typical pattern of age-related hearing loss.	➤ Most sounds are complex waveforms requiring analysis in cortical areas beyond the primary auditory area.
➤ Conduction deafness is due to middle ear rigidity; sensorineural deafness is due to inner ear or auditory nerve damage.	➤ For frequencies below 4000 Hz, the timing of action potentials also codes sound frequency.	➤ The phonemic restoration effect illustrates the idea that context and meaning influence sensory experience.
	➤ The primary auditory cortex is tonotopically organized. The pitch we hear depends on which cortical neurons become most active.	

■ Psychophysics

Psychophysics is the study of relationships between physical characteristics of stimuli and the sensory experiences produced by those stimuli. (You can remember the term by recalling that *psychophysics* relates *psycho*logical sensory experiences to *physic*al characteristics of stimuli.) Sensory experience is typically assessed by asking subjects to make some judgment about each stimulus, such as whether it is present or absent or whether it is the same as or different from another stimulus. Many experiments already alluded to in this chapter were psychophysical, including those assessing people's abilities to detect or identify particular substances by taste or smell and those relating the frequency of a tone to its perceived pitch.

This section describes some psychophysical methods and findings related to (a) the detection of weak stimuli, (b) the detection of small changes in stimuli, and (c) the attempt to develop a general law relating the physical intensity of a stimulus to the intensity of the sensory experience it produces.

As you will see, psychophysics is more mathematical than most other areas of psychology. That is one of the reasons why some psychologists find it exciting. Psychophysics is the perfect cup of tea for those psychologists who like a degree of precision in their science, are drawn by the elegance of mathematics, and are fascinated by the idea that certain psychological phenomena can be described meaningfully with algebraic equations. Historically, research in psychophysics by such scientists as Ernst Weber and Gustav Fechner, in the nineteenth century, played a vital role in the founding of psychology as a science, and many of the specific questions they raised are still topics of research and debate today.

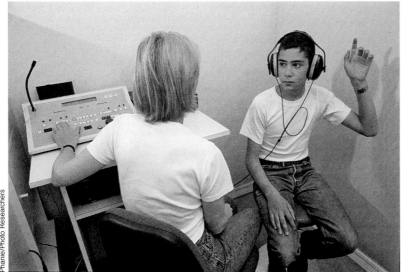

Finding the absolute threshold In a hearing test, faint sounds of varying frequencies and amplitudes are presented to one ear at a time. To find the absolute threshold for a given frequency, for a given ear, the sound is presented at decreasing amplitudes until the person cannot detect it, and at increasing amplitudes until the person can detect it.

The Absolute Threshold Is a Measure of Sensitivity

Psychophysicists refer to the faintest detectable stimulus of any given type as the ***absolute threshold*** for that type of stimulus. For example, the weakest intensity of a particular tone (say, middle C on the piano) that you can hear is your absolute threshold for that tone, and the weakest solution of sodium chloride (table salt) that you can taste is your absolute threshold for sodium chloride. Absolute thresholds vary from person to person and are used clinically as measures of a person's sensitivity to specific types of stimuli. You may well have undergone a test of your absolute threshold for various sound frequencies as a clinical test of your hearing. In general, for most senses, absolute thresholds are higher (meaning that sensitivity is lower) for older adults than for younger adults. Some research applications of absolute thresholds were mentioned earlier in this chapter. For example, Figure 7.4 (page 239) shows differences between men and women in absolute thresholds for detecting certain odors.

The Difference Threshold Depends on the Magnitude of the Original Stimulus

Another measure of sensitivity is the ***difference threshold,*** defined as the minimal difference in magnitude (or intensity) between two stimuli that is required for the person to detect them as different. Another name for the difference threshold is the ***just-noticeable difference,*** abbreviated ***jnd*** (by convention, small letters are used for this abbreviation).

In the early nineteenth century, the German physicist Ernst Weber (1834) conducted a systematic study of just-noticeable differences. Weber asked: What is the relationship between the jnd and the magnitude of the original stimulus? Is the jnd the same for a given type of stimulus regardless of the magnitude of the original stimulus, or does it vary in some systematic way with that magnitude?

In one series of experiments, Weber applied this question to people's abilities to judge differences between weights. On each trial he asked the subjects to pick up each of two weights (the "original" weight and a comparison weight), one at a time, and to judge which was heavier. Weber found that the jnd varied in direct proportion to the original weight. Specifically, he found that for any original weight that he used (within a certain range), the jnd was approximately 1/30 of that weight (Gescheider, 1976). Thus, a typical subject could just barely detect the difference between a 15-gram and a 15.5-gram weight or between a 90-gram and a 93-gram weight. In the first case the jnd was 0.5 gram, and in the second it was 3 grams, but in both cases it was 1/30 of the original weight (which was always the lower of the two weights being compared).

In other experiments, Weber studied people's abilities to discriminate between the lengths of two lines, one presented after the other, and again he found a constant proportionality between the original stimulus and the difference threshold. For this task, however, the constant fraction was 1/100 rather than 1/30. Thus, a typical subject could just barely detect the difference between a 100- and a 101-millimeter line or between a 1,000- and a 1,010-millimeter line.

On the basis of these and similar experiments, Weber formulated a general law, now called **Weber's law,** stating that *the jnd for stimulus magnitude is a constant proportion of the magnitude of the original stimulus.* The law can be abbreviated as

$$\text{jnd} = kM$$

in which M is the magnitude or intensity of the stimulus used as the original stimulus and k is a proportionality constant referred to as the *Weber fraction,* which is different for different sensory tasks (1/30 for weight judgment and 1/100 for length judgment in the examples just cited). Since Weber's time, researchers have confirmed Weber's law for many different types of stimuli, including sounds, sights, tastes, and smells. The law holds up rather well over a wide portion of the possible range of intensities or magnitudes for most types of stimuli, but not at the very low (near the absolute threshold) and very high ends of the range.

Sensory Magnitude Is Lawfully Related to Stimulus Magnitude

When a physical stimulus increases, our sensory experience of it also increases. When a sodium chloride solution becomes more concentrated, we taste its saltiness as stronger; when a sound increases in amplitude, we hear it as louder; when a light becomes more intense, we see it as brighter; and so on. Is it possible to specify in a mathematical equation the relationship between the magnitude of a stimulus and the magnitude of the sensory experience it produces? Such an equation was proposed by Gustav Fechner in the middle of the nineteenth century and was tested experimentally and modified by S. S. Stevens a century later.

Fechner's Logarithmic Law Fechner (1860/1966), in Germany, used Weber's law to derive a mathematical relationship between stimulus magnitude and sensory magnitude. The jnd is measured in physical units (such as grams or sound-pressure units), yet it reflects a sensory phenomenon, the just-noticeable difference between two sensations. Therefore, Fechner reasoned, the jnd could serve as a unit for relating physical and sensory magnitudes. His crucial assumptions were (a) that every jnd along a sensory dimension is equivalent to every other jnd along that dimension in the amount it adds to the sensory magnitude and (b) that jnd's can be added together. In other words, he assumed that a sound that is 100 jnd's above threshold would sound twice as loud as one that is 50 jnd's above threshold, or one-tenth as loud as one that is 1000 jnd's above threshold.

30

How did Weber derive a law from data on just-noticeable differences? How can Weber's law be used to predict the degree to which two stimuli must differ for a person to tell them apart?

31

What reasoning led Fechner to propose that sensory magnitude is proportional to the logarithm of the stimulus magnitude? If a physical stimulus keeps doubling in magnitude, how will the sensory magnitude change, according to Fechner?

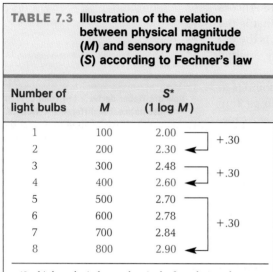

Number of light bulbs	M	S* (1 log M)
1	100	2.00
2	200	2.30
3	300	2.48
4	400	2.60
5	500	2.70
6	600	2.78
7	700	2.84
8	800	2.90

TABLE 7.3 Illustration of the relation between physical magnitude (M) and sensory magnitude (S) according to Fechner's law

*In this hypothetical example, c in the formula S = c log M is 1. A change in c would change the values of S but would not change the fact that each doubling of M adds a constant increment to S, which is the point that the table is designed to illustrate.

Fechner assumed that jnd's are subjectively equal, but he knew from Weber's work that they are not physically equal. As you just learned, the jnd is directly proportional to the magnitude of the original stimulus. Thus, Fechner assumed that the amount of physical change needed to create a constant sensory change is directly proportional to the magnitude of the stimulus, and he showed mathematically that this can be expressed as a logarithmic relationship. (If you wish to see how he could prove this, turn to page A-9 of the Statistical Appendix at the back of the book.) Thus, Fechner derived what he believed to be a general psychophysical law, now called **Fechner's law,** stating that the magnitude of the sensory experience of a stimulus is directly proportional to the logarithm of the physical magnitude of the stimulus. This law can be abbreviated as

$$S = c \log M$$

where S is the magnitude of the sensory experience, c is a proportionality constant, and M is the magnitude of the physical stimulus.

To gain a sense of the meaning of Fechner's law (if you are a bit foggy on logarithms), look at Table 7.3, which shows hypothetical data that are consistent with the law. Imagine a person judging the brightness of a room's illumination with one light bulb on, then two bulbs, then three bulbs, and so on. Although each successive bulb adds a constant amount (100 units) to the physical intensity (M) of the room's illumination, each bulb adds a progressively smaller amount to the perceived brightness (S). Thus, in the example, the second bulb adds 0.30 unit to the brightness, the third adds another 0.18 unit, the fourth adds 0.12, and so on. Notice too that every time the physical intensity (M) doubles, the sensed brightness (S) increases by a constant amount (0.30 unit in the example). Stated differently, as the physical scale increases geometrically, the sensory scale increases arithmetically. That is the essence of a logarithmic relationship. Consequently, a huge intensity range on the physical scale is condensed to a much smaller and more manageable range on the psychological scale. Imagine what our sensory experiences would be like if our perceptions of brightness or loudness were directly proportional to the physical intensities of lights or sounds. We would hear thunder as a thousand times louder than a normal conversation, and we would hear loud rock bands as a thousand times louder than thunder (refer back to Table 7.2, on page 253).

Stevens's Power Law Although Fechner believed his law was valid on theoretical grounds, he did not believe it could be tested experimentally. He wrote (in 1860), "A real measure of sensation would demand that we be able to call a given sensation twice, thrice, or so-and-so as many times as intense as another—but who would say such a thing?" (quoted in Stevens, 1975). The belief that people could not report the magnitudes of their sensations in a consistent way went relatively unchallenged until the early 1950s, when S. S. Stevens, a Harvard psychophysicist, began a series of experiments in which he asked people to do exactly that.

32

How did Stevens test Fechner's law, and what did he find? How does Stevens's law differ from Fechner's?

◄ Stevens's technique, called the *method of magnitude estimation,* involved asking subjects to assign numbers to the magnitudes of their sensations. For example, he would present a standard stimulus and call that a 10, then present a comparison stimulus and ask the subject to assign it a number that best approximated its sensory magnitude compared with that of the standard. Thus, a sensation that appeared to the subject to be twice that of the standard would be a 20, one that seemed half that of the standard would be a 5, and so on. Stevens found that people had little difficulty carrying out these instructions and that their responses were remarkably consistent for any given set of stimuli.

If Fechner's law were correct, Stevens should have found that his subjects' magnitude estimates were directly proportional to the logarithms of the stimulus intensities he used. He found, however, that the logarithmic relationship was only roughly accurate for most senses and quite inaccurate for some senses. For every sense, according to Stevens, the results could be described better by a different mathematical relationship—a power relationship. On this basis, Stevens proposed an alternative to Fechner's logarithmic law. According to **Stevens's power law,** *the magnitude of a sensation is directly proportional to the magnitude of the physical stimulus raised by a constant power.* The law can be abbreviated as

$$S = cM^p$$

where *S* is the reported magnitude of the sensory experience, *M* is the physical magnitude of the stimulus, *p* is the power (or exponent) to which *M* must be raised (which differs from one sensory dimension to another), and *c* is a constant whose value depends on the size of the measurement units used.

Stevens and his colleagues performed dozens of experiments, involving magnitude estimates for many different kinds of stimuli, and they almost always found that the results could be quite well represented by a power equation. For each kind of stimulus, they could determine a unique exponent (*p*) to which the physical magnitude had to be raised to approximate the experienced magnitude. Table 7.4 shows the exponents that they compiled for several different kinds of stimuli. For most tasks the exponent is less than 1, but for one task shown in the table (estimating the length of a line) it is exactly 1, and for another (estimating the pain of an electric shock) it is greater than 1.

In cases where *p* is less than 1, equal physical changes produce smaller sensory changes at the high end of the scale than at the low end, as was also true with Fechner's logarithmic law. When *p* is greater than 1, however, the opposite relationship holds. Thus, adding a certain amount of electric shock to a relatively strong shock produces a greater increase in pain than does adding the same amount to a relatively weak shock. Finally, when *p* is equal to 1, equal physical changes produce the same amount of sensory change regardless of whether one is starting with a strong or a weak stimulus. All these relationships are graphically portrayed in Figure 7.18.

TABLE 7.4 Power-law exponents for various stimuli

Type of stimulus	Measured exponent (p)*
Brightness of a spot of light in the dark	0.33
Loudness of a 3000-cps tone	0.67
Smell of heptane	0.60
Taste of saccharine	0.80
Length of a line	1.00
Pain of an electric shock on the fingers	3.50

*The exponent (*p*) is the power to which the stimulus magnitude must be raised to approximate the sensory magnitude.

Source: From Stevens, S. S. (1975). *Psychophysics: Introduction to its perceptual, neural, and social prospects* (p. 13). New York: Wiley.

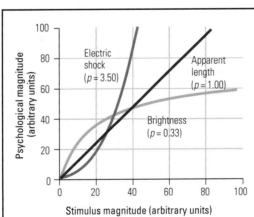

FIGURE 7.18 Power law illustrated for three sensory dimensions This shows how subjects' estimates of sensory magnitude increased as the stimulus magnitude increased, separately for the pain of an electric shock, the length of a line, and the brightness of a spot of light. Notice that the curvature is upward or downward depending on whether the exponent, p, is greater or less than 1. (Adapted from Stevens, 1962.)

Why a Power Law?

Why do our senses obey a power law for so many different kinds of stimuli? Is it just coincidence, or is there some advantage that would lead each sense, in the course of evolution, to operate in accordance with a power law? Stevens (1975) thought a good deal about that question, and the answer he suggested was essentially the following:

> Our world of stimuli is constantly changing. As we move closer to or farther from the sources of stimulation, or as day turns to dusk, the overall intensity of the energy reaching us from specific objects in the environment changes greatly. If we are to recognize the same scenes, sounds, and smells under such varying conditions, then we must extract those features of each stimulus constellation that remain constant. One such constancy is the ratio of the magnitudes of the stimulus elements with respect to each other.

As you move toward or away from a sound source, the ratio of the amplitudes of the various tones in the sound remains relatively constant, even though the overall amplitude increases or decreases greatly. Similarly, the ratio of light reflected from

33

Why is it advantageous that our senses operate according to a power law rather than a logarithmic law?

Value of the power law Because of the power law relating the physical intensity of light to its perceived brightness, the ratios in brightness among different elements of this scene remain constant as the overall illumination changes, from daylight to dusk.

Todd Gipstein/National Geographic/Getty

a darker compared with a lighter portion of a visual scene remains nearly constant as the overall intensity fades at dusk. A power law, and only a power law, preserves constant sensory ratios as the overall intensity waxes or wanes. (You can find a proof of this statement on page A-10 of the Statistical Appendix at the back of the book.) For example, in the case of the power function for brightness, with an exponent of 0.33, every eightfold change in light intensity results in a twofold change in apparent brightness, no matter where on the intensity continuum we start. Thus, if the light illuminating a scene decreases in physical intensity to one-eighth of what it was before, each part of the scene will appear half as bright as before, and the ratios of brightnesses among the parts will remain what they were before. The elegant feature of the power law, with p less than 1, is that it compresses large physical changes down to smaller sensory changes, as does the logarithmic law; but, unlike the logarithmic law, it does this while preserving the constancy of stimulus ratios.

SECTION REVIEW

Psychophysics relates sensations to physical characteristics of stimuli.

Sensory Thresholds	Sensory Magnitude Related to Physical Magnitude
➤ A person's absolute threshold for a specific type of stimulus is the lowest detectable intensity of the stimulus. ➤ The smallest difference in intensity of a given type of stimulus that a person can detect is a difference threshold, or jnd. ➤ According to Weber's law, the jnd is a constant proportion of the magnitude of the original stimulus.	➤ Fechner's law, derived from Weber's, holds that the magnitude of the sensory experience of a stimulus is directly proportional to the logarithm of the stimulus's physical magnitude. For example, a ound's perceived loudness is proportional to the logarithm of the sound's physical intensity. ➤ Using the method of magnitude estimation, Stevens found evidence for an alternative to Fechner's law: The magnitude of a sensation is directly proportional to the magnitude of the physical stimulus raised to a constant power. ➤ A power relationship between sensory and physical magnitudes may have evolved because it maintains constant ratios among the sensory magnitudes produced by different stimuli in the face of changes that affect both (or all) of the stimuli equally. For example, because of the power law, the ratio of the perceived loudness of sound A to sound B remains constant as one moves away from or closer to the two sound sources.

Concluding Thoughts

To review this chapter, you would do well to focus on major themes. Even details are easier to remember if tied to larger themes, or arguments, than if seen as isolated facts. Here are two themes that ran through the chapter and may help you to organize your review:

1. The mechanisms of transduction and coding All sensory systems respond to physical stimuli by producing action potentials (the process of transduction), and all sensory systems do

this in such a way as to preserve useful information about the stimulus (coding). For each sense discussed in this chapter—smell, taste, pain, and hearing—you might think about each of the following questions pertaining to transduction and coding: (a) To what type of physical stimulus does this sense respond, and what is the range of stimuli to which it responds? (b) How is the sensory organ designed for receiving (and possibly concentrating or amplifying) the stimulus? (c) What are the receptors for the stimulus, and how do they respond in such a way as to generate action potentials in sensory neurons? (d) How does the transduction process code the different qualities of stimuli to which the sensory system responds? (e) How do neural mechanisms in the central nervous system alter or reorganize the input, and for what purposes? The chapter does not answer all these questions (especially not the last) completely for each sense, but the questions provide a good framework for organizing and thinking about the information that is provided.

2. The survival functions of sensory processes Our sensory systems, like all the basic mechanisms underlying our behavior, evolved through natural selection because they promoted our ancestors' survival and reproduction. They are not unbiased recorders of physical energies but biological tools designed to pick out from the sea of energy around us the information that is potentially most useful. We are sensitive to some kinds of energies and not others, and, within the kinds to which we are sensitive, our senses extract and enhance some relationships and not others.

Here are some examples, described in the chapter, of how sensory processes can be understood in terms of their survival advantages: (a) Sensory adaptation (the decline in sensitivity to prolonged, constant stimuli) helps us to ignore stimuli that remain unchanged and to notice changes. (b) Attraction to the smell of individuals who differ in MHC may help to create genetic diversity. (c) Smell and taste work together to produce flavors that are experienced as pleasant or unpleasant, in ways that are generally consistent with what is good for us or bad for us (or for our evolutionary ancestors) to eat. The association of bitter taste with poisons is an example. (d) Pain is a sensory system for warning us when our actions are damaging our tissues and for motivating us to avoid such actions. Evolved mechanisms increase pain sensitivity at times of illness, when it is best to rest, and decrease pain sensitivity at times of threat, when strenuous action without favoring one's wounds may be necessary. (e) The phonemic-restoration illusion helps us to hear speech in a continuous, meaningful flow and to ignore extraneous noises and interruptions. (f) The fact that our senses obey a power law in converting stimulus magnitude to sensory magnitude may have come about because the power law preserves the constancy of ratios, helping us recognize a pattern in sound or light as the same pattern even when its overall intensity increases or decreases.

Further Reading

Howard C. Hughes (1999). *Sensory exotica: A world beyond human experience.* Cambridge, MA: MIT Press.

The fit between an animal's senses and its habitat and behavior becomes most apparent when we look at animals whose sensory world is very different from our own. This fascinating, well-researched book examines sonar in bats and dolphins, magnetic-field sensitivity in migrating birds, sun compasses in bees and ants, electroreception in fishes, and pheromone communication in insects and mammals.

Avery Gilbert (2008). *What the Nose Knows: The Science of Scent in Everyday Life.* New York: Crown.

Avery is a professional sniffer as well as an olfactory scientist. This light but well-documented book will raise any reader's esteem for human olfactory ability. According to Avery, the main difference between people who appreciate and don't appreciate their smell world is one of attention to it. Most of us have the ability to smell our world far more than we do. The book includes such topics as drug sniffing (by humans as well as dogs), the role of scent in flavor, attempts to odorize movies, and the role of odor in evoking memories.

Scott Fishman, with Lisa Berger (2000). *The war on pain.* Dublin, Ireland: Newleaf.

In this relatively brief, nontechnical book, Fishman, a physician specializing in the treatment of pain, shares poignant stories of people's suffering and his efforts to relieve it. Along the way, he discusses the many causes of pain and the many weapons in the arsenal against it, ranging from acupuncture and behavior therapy to drugs and surgery. The epilogue is about making peace with pain in cases where it can't be defeated.

Tiffany Field (2003). *Touch.* Cambridge, MA: MIT Press.

In this fascinating book, based on her own research and that of others, Field describes the psychological functions of the sense of touch. Of greatest interest is research on the medical benefits of touch and massage, including growth-promoting effects of touch in infants.

Daniel J. Levitin (2006). *This is your brain on music: The science of a human obsession.* New York: Dutton.

This delightful book, about the neuroscience and psychology of music, is written by a former musical performer and producer turned neuroscientist. It deals with questions of how our brains process musical sounds, how such sounds act upon emotional mechanisms in our brains, and the reasons for individual differences in musical preferences. In the final chapter, Levitin argues that music played an important evolutionary role in attracting mates and in binding people together into cooperate groups.

S. S. Stevens (1975). *Psychophysics: Introduction to its perceptual, neural, and social prospects.* New York: Wiley.

A brilliant description of the research leading to the power law (which relates sensory magnitude to stimulus magnitude) and the implications of that law, this slender classic is quite readable by the beginning student who is not intimidated by exponents or algebraic equations. Stevens also shows how the power law applies to magnitude judgments other than those about sensations, such as judgments about the seriousness of crimes. Despite its date, this book is still highly relevant to modern psychology.

The Psychology of Vision

We are visual creatures. Our eyes are our primary gateway for perceiving and understanding the physical world in which we survive. We say "I see" to mean "I understand," and when we doubt some claim, we say "I'd have to see it to believe it." Our visual system provides us with such rich, clear, solid-looking, and generally useful perceptions of the physical world that it is easy for us to forget that the physical world and our sight of it are not one and the same thing.

In reality, our visual perceptions are subjective, psychological experiences, which our brains create almost instantly, and continuously as long as our eyes are open, from clues that lie in the patterns of light reflected off objects. The machinery that underlies our ability to produce such perceptions is incredibly complex. Brain scientists have estimated that somewhere between 25 and 40 percent of the human brain is devoted exclusively or primarily to the analysis of input from the eyes (Gross, 1998; Sereno & others, 1995). It is no wonder that vision is the sense to which psychologists have paid by far the greatest attention.

Vision begins with activity in the eyes, and that is where this chapter begins. From there we go on to examine our abilities to perceive colors, patterns, objects, and depth in three-dimensional space.

■ How the Eye Works

Life on earth evolved in a world illuminated by the sun during the day and by starlight and the moon's reflected sunlight at night. Most forms of earthly life are sensitive in one way or another to that light (Land & Furnald, 1992). Even single-celled organisms contain chemicals that respond to light and alter the organism's activity in survival-promoting ways. In many species of multicellular animals, specialized light-detecting cells called ***photoreceptors*** evolved and became connected to the animal's nervous system. Earthworms, for example, have photoreceptors distributed throughout their skin. Stimulation of these cells by light causes the worm to wriggle back down into the earth, where it finds safety, moisture, and food.

1

Through what steps might sophisticated eyes like ours have evolved from primitive beginnings?

◀ Cross-species comparisons, based on homologies (discussed in Chapter 3), suggest that the modern vertebrate eye came about through the following evolutionary steps, or something like them (Gregory, 1996; Lamb & others, 2007): In some early ancestor to vertebrate animals, photoreceptors became concentrated into groups, forming light-detecting organs, or eye spots, just under the skin. These organs may have initially served to enable circadian rhythms—the cyclic biological changes that accompany the day-night light-dark cycle (discussed in Chapter 6). With time, however, they may have taken on the additional function of responding to shadows, which could be useful in detecting predators. With further natural selection, the skin covering the eye spots became transparent, allowing in both more light and clearer shadows. The spots then gradually moved inward, into fluid-filled pits underneath the transparent skin, which would reduce glare and enable the animal to detect the direction from which changes in illumination were coming. Subsequent evolution led to the thickening of one of the membranes covering each eye spot to form a crude lens, which at first may have served merely to magnify the light reaching the photoreceptors. With further evolutionary refinement, the lens became capable of projecting an image onto the lining of photoreceptors. Through such gradual steps, coupled with appropriate changes in the nervous system, the primitive ability to detect shifts in lightness and darkness evolved into the ability to see the shapes of things and eventually into the marvelously complex and precise visual ability that this the subject of this chapter.

Functional Organization of the Eye

The main parts of the human eye are shown in Figure 8.1. The photoreceptors lie in the *retina,* a membrane lining the rear interior of the eyeball. The eyeball is filled with a clear gelatinous substance through which light easily passes. The structures at the front of the eye are devices for focusing light reflected from objects in such a way as to form images on the retina.

Structures at the Front of the Eye Focus Images on the Retina

2

How do the cornea, iris, and lens help to form images on the retina?

◀ The front of the eyeball is covered by the *cornea,* a transparent tissue that, because of its convex (outward) curvature, helps focus the light that passes through it. Immediately behind the cornea is the pigmented, doughnut-shaped *iris,* which provides the color (usually brown or blue) of the eye. The iris is opaque, so the only light that can enter the interior of the eye is that which passes through the *pupil,* the black-appearing center in the iris, which is simply a hole through which light can pass into the eyeball. Muscle fibers in the iris enable it to increase or decrease the diameter of the pupil to allow more or less light to enter.

Behind the iris is the *lens,* which adds to the focusing process begun by the cornea. Unlike the cornea, the lens is adjustable; it becomes more spherical when focusing

FIGURE 8.1 Cross section of the eye, depicting the retinal image The light rays that diverge from any given point on the surface of an object are brought back together (focused) at a distinct point on the retina to create an image of the object on the retina. This drawing shows light rays diverging and being brought together for just two points on the leaf, but the same process is occurring for light rays coming from every point.

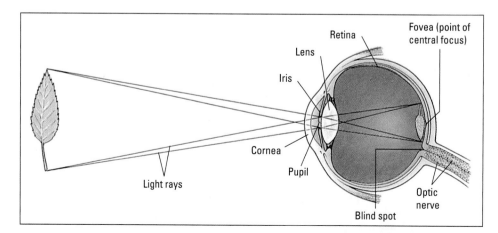

on objects close to the eye and flatter when focusing on those farther away. Light rays diverge as they move toward the eye from any given point on a visual object. The focusing properties of the cornea and lens bring the light rays back together at a particular point on the retina, thereby forming an image of the object on the retina. The image is upside down (as shown in Figure 8.1), but that does not matter, since its only purpose is to trigger patterns of activity in neurons running to the brain. The brain is wired to the retina in such a way that input from lower on the retina is interpreted as up, and input from higher on the retina is interpreted as down.

Transduction Occurs in the Retina

As noted in Chapter 7, the process by which a stimulus from the environment generates electrical changes in neurons is called *transduction*. In vision, transduction is the function of the photoreceptor cells. In each eye millions of photoreceptor cells are arranged, mosaic-like, in one thin layer of the multilayered retina. These cells are of

3

How are cones and rods distributed on the retina, and how do they respond to light?

two types: ***cones,*** which permit sharply focused color vision in bright light, and ***rods,*** which permit vision in dim light. They are so named because of their shapes (see Figure 8.2). Cones are most concentrated in the ***fovea,*** the pinhead-size area of the retina that is in the most direct line of sight (look again at Figure 8.1), which is specialized for high visual *acuity* (the ability to distinguish tiny details). The concentration of cones decreases sharply with increasing

Omikron / Photo Researchers

FIGURE 8.2 Rods and cones This electron micrograph shows that the photoreceptors are aptly named: Rods (stained blue) are rod-shaped; cones (stained blue-green) taper at the ends. Rods are responsible for vision in dim light, and cones for vision in bright light.

distance from the fovea. Rods, in contrast, exist everywhere in the retina except in the fovea and are most concentrated in a ring about 20 degrees away from the fovea (see Figure 8.3). Each human retina contains about 6 million cones and 120 million rods (Wade & Swanston, 1991).

The outer segment of each photoreceptor contains a *photochemical*—a chemical that reacts to light. The rods' photochemical is called ***rhodopsin*** [roh-**dop**-sin]. When hit by light, rhodopsin molecules undergo a structural change that triggers a series of chemical reactions in the rod's membrane, which in turn causes a change in the electrical charge across the membrane (Schnapf & Baylor, 1987). The transduction process for cones is similar to that for rods, but (for reasons discussed in the section on color vision) three varieties of cones exist, and each contains a different photochemical. The electrical changes in rods and cones cause electrical responses in other cells in the retina, which lead to the production of action potentials (neural impulses) in neurons that form the ***optic nerve,*** which runs from the back of the

FIGURE 8.3 Distribution of cones and rods in the retina Cones are most concentrated in the fovea. Rods are absent from the fovea and most concentrated in a ring 20 degrees away from it. No receptors at all exist in the blind spot.

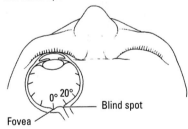

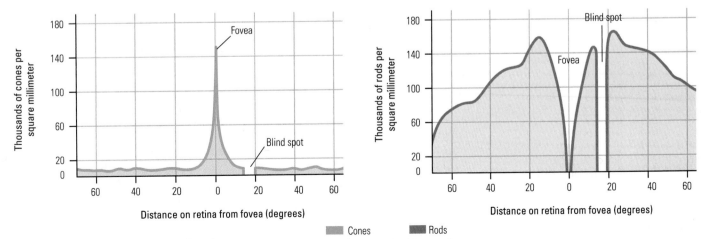

FIGURE 8.4 Demonstration of the blind spot Close your left eye and focus on the X with your right eye. Start with the page a little more than a foot from your eye and move it gradually closer, still focusing on the X. At about 10 inches, the bird will disappear. At that location, the image of the bird falls on the blind spot of the retina, shown in Figure 8.3. Yet you will probably still see the bars of the cage running across the area where the bird was located, and the background color may fill the space previously occupied by the bird. The bars and color are perceptually filled in by your visual system.

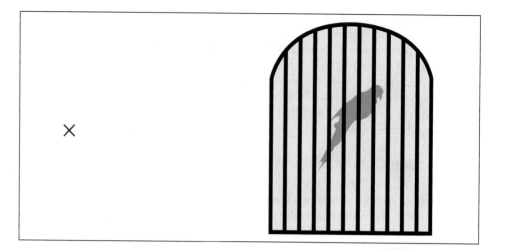

eye to the brain. At the place on the retina where the axons of these neurons converge to form the optic nerve there is a **blind spot,** due to the absence of receptor cells (shown in Figure 8.3). We normally do not notice the blind spot, but you can demonstrate its existence by following the instructions in Figure 8.4.

Differences Between Cone Vision and Rod Vision

4
How do cone vision and rod vision differ?

Cones and rods provide the starting points for what can be thought of as two separate but interacting visual systems within the human eye. **Cone vision,** also called *photopic vision* or bright-light vision, is specialized for high acuity (the ability to see fine detail) and for color perception. **Rod vision,** also called *scotopic vision* or dim-light vision, is specialized for sensitivity (the ability to see in very dim light). Rod vision lacks acuity and the capacity to distinguish colors, but, according to calculations from laboratory studies, it is sensitive enough to allow a person on a clear night to detect a single candle flame from 30 miles away if no other lights are present (Galanter, 1962). Cone vision came about, through natural selection, to allow us to see fine details during daylight, and rod vision came about to allow us to see at least the vague outlines of objects at night.

In very dim light, too dim to activate cones, you see only with rod vision; you can make out the general shapes of objects but not their details and colors. In such light you can see dim objects best when you don't look directly at them—because, as noted before, the fovea (the part of the retina in the direct line of sight) contains no rods. If you find yourself in the country on a starry but moonless night, away from all artificial lights, try to stare at the dimmest star that you can see. It will disappear when you look straight at it, but reappear when you look just a little off to one side. You can see it best when looking 20 degrees away, because this angle allows the light from the star to strike the part of the retina where rods are most concentrated.

Roles of Rods and Cones in Dark Adaptation and Light Adaptation

One of the many problems that our visual system has to solve is that of adjusting to the enormous range of light intensities that occur over the course of a day. A white object in sunlight at noon reflects roughly 100 million times as much light as the same object reflects on a starlit but moonless night (Riggs, 1965), yet we can see the object in either condition.

5
What is the chemical basis for dark adaptation and light adaptation? Why do we see mostly with cones in bright light and with rods in dim light?

As you know from experience, it takes time for your vision to adapt to sudden large changes in illumination. The gradual increase in sensitivity that occurs after you enter a darkened room or turn off the lights is called **dark adaptation,** and the more rapid decrease in sensitivity that occurs after you turn on a bright lamp or step out into sunlight is called **light adaptation.** The iris contributes to these adaptive processes by dilating (widening) the pupil in dim light and constricting it in

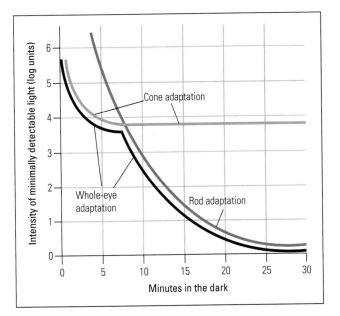

FIGURE 8.5 Dark-adaptation curves
The black curve depicts the minimal intensity of a spot of light that a person with normal vision can see after varying periods in the dark after having been in bright light. The lower the curve, the greater the sensitivity to light. For the first 7 minutes or so, the cones are more sensitive than the rods, but after that the rods are more sensitive. The two-part nature of the curve can be understood by comparing it to the dark-adaptation curve obtained for a person who has only rods (the blue curve) and to that obtained if the light is presented in such a way that it strikes just the fovea, where only cones exist (the green curve).

bright light. A fully dilated pupil allows in about 16 times as much light as a fully constricted pupil (Matlin & Foley, 1997). Temporary changes in the sensitivity of visual neurons that receive input from the receptor cells also contribute (Dunn & others, 2007). However, the major contribution to dark and light adaptation comes from the different sensitivities of rods and cones.

Rhodopsin, the rod photochemical, is much more sensitive to light than are the cone photochemicals (Kefalov & others, 2003). Bright light causes rhodopsin to break down into two inactive substances, making the rods nonfunctional. In sunlight, therefore, you see entirely with your cones, and even in a typical artificially lit room you see mostly with your cones. When you first step from bright light into a dark room, you may see nothing, because your rods are still inactive and there isn't enough light to activate your cones. With time in the dark, however, rhodopsin regenerates, your rods regain their sensitivity, and you gradually see more and more. It takes about 25 minutes for rhodopsin to regenerate fully. If you then step out of the dark room into sunlight, you are at first blinded by the dazzling light, because your highly sensitive rods are responding maximally and indiscriminately. Within about 5 minutes, however, the rhodopsin breaks down and you begin to see normally, with your less sensitive cones. The cone photochemicals also break down somewhat in bright light and regenerate in dim light and thereby contribute to light and dark adaptation, but this change is smaller than that which occurs in rods (see Figure 8.5).

Neural Convergence as a Basis for Differences Between Rod and Cone Vision

The superiority of rods over cones in detecting dim light stems not just from the greater sensitivity of rhodopsin but also from a difference in the neural wiring that connects these receptor cells to the brain. This same difference in wiring also helps explain cone vision's superior acuity.

Both rods and cones form synapses on short neurons called *bipolar cells,* which in turn form synapses on longer neurons called *ganglion cells,* whose axons leave the eye at the blind spot to form the optic nerve. As depicted schematically in Figure 8.6 (on page 274), there is a great deal of *convergence* in the connections from rods to bipolar cells to ganglion cells. Many rods synapse on each bipolar cell, and many bipolar cells synapse on each ganglion cell. Such convergence increases the sensitivity of rod vision in dim light by adding together the output of many rods to generate activity in the ganglion cells. The principle here is similar to that of a funnel, which can collect raindrops from over a relatively wide area and channel them into a single steady stream.

6

How does the pattern of neural connections within the retina help account for the greater sensitivity and reduced acuity of rod vision compared with cone vision?

FIGURE 8.6 Difference between rods and cones in neural convergence This schematic diagram illustrates the fact that there is much more neural convergence between rods and ganglion cells than between cones and ganglion cells in the retina. In the actual human retina, the convergence for rods is much greater than shown here. On average, about 1,000 rods converge onto any given ganglion cell in the periphery of the retina (Masland, 2001).

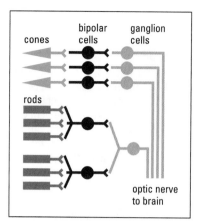

While it increases sensitivity, neural convergence necessarily decreases acuity. Because of convergence, two nearby spots of light striking a peripheral portion of the retina, where rods predominate, will activate the same ganglion cell, with the result that they will be seen as one blurry spot rather than two distinct spots. To be seen as distinct, two spots must activate different ganglion cells, whose axons carry separate messages to the brain. Again, the analogy to a funnel is helpful. Just as two raindrops lose their distinctiveness when they are channeled together by the funnel, two spots in a visual stimulus striking the retina lose their distinctiveness when their neural effects are channeled together by convergence.

In the fovea, where all the receptor cells are cones, there is little or no convergence (Masland, 2001). The result is reduced sensitivity to dim light, because there is no funneling of activity, but high acuity, because each small spot of visual stimulation activates a separate pathway to the brain (again see Figure 8.6).

SECTION REVIEW

The sophisticated human eye focuses light to form images on photoreceptors in the retina.

Basic Structures and Functions of the Eye

➤ The cornea and the adjustable lens focus incoming light onto the retina at the back of the eye's interior.

➤ Light energy is then transduced by two types of photoreceptor cells in the retina—rods and cones—that contain photochemicals that react to light with structural changes.

➤ These changes can lead to further chemical and electrical changes, ultimately triggering action potentials in neurons that form the optic nerve.

Cone and Rod Vision

➤ While cones provide color vision, high visual acuity, and ability to see in bright illumination, rods provide the sensitivity that allows vision in dim illumination.

➤ The rate and degree of dark adaptation and light adaptation are different for rods and cones. A result is that we see only with rods in very dim light and only with cones in bright light.

➤ Greater neural convergence helps to explain the greater sensitivity and lower acuity of rod vision compared to cone vision.

■ Seeing Colors

Many animals—including humans, other primates, birds, bees, and most fishes and reptiles—that depend greatly on vision to identify objects have evolved color vision, which helps to make objects stand out vividly from their backgrounds. The colors that we and other animals see in objects depend on the wavelengths of the light that is reflected from those objects.

How Color Varies with the Physical Stimulus

7
How can light be described physically, and what is the relationship of its wavelength to its perceived color?

Light is a form of electromagnetic energy, and like all such energy it can be described as both particles and waves. The particles, or individual packets of light, are called *photons*, and as they travel through space they pulsate in a wavelike way. Light travels at a constant speed (186,000 miles per second), and the distance that photons travel between the beginning of one pulse and the beginning of the next defines the wavelength of the light. The wavelengths of light visible to humans range

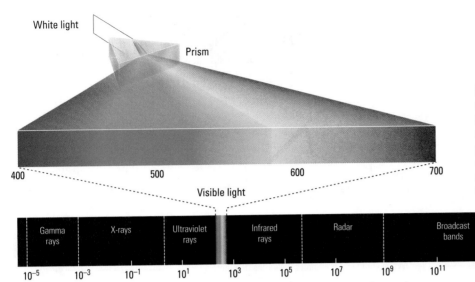

FIGURE 8.7 The electromagnetic spectrum Light is the visible portion of the electromagnetic spectrum. White light, separated according to wavelength with a prism, produces the spectrum of visible colors, extending from violet and blue at the short-wavelength end to red at the long-wavelength end.

from about 400 to 700 nm (1 nm, or nanometer, is a billionth of a meter). Shorter waves of electromagnetic energy, below our visible range, include ultraviolet rays, x-rays, and gamma rays; longer waves, above our visible range, include infrared rays, radar rays, and radio waves.

White light, such as that from the sun, contains all visible wavelengths combined (plus some of the nonvisible wavelengths). When the wavelengths in white light are separated—by shining the light through a prism, for example—the visual effect is an array of colors like that of a rainbow, because different wavelengths are seen as different colors. Progressing from the shortest to the longest wavelengths of visible light, we see the familiar rainbow spectrum, from violet through shades of blue, blue-green, green, green-yellow, yellow, orange, and red, in that order (see Figure 8.7).

Objects vary in the wavelengths of light that they reflect because they have on their surfaces different *pigments*, chemicals that absorb some wavelengths and thereby prevent them from being reflected. A pigment that absorbs short and medium waves, for example, appears red, because only long (red-appearing) waves are reflected. Similarly, a pigment that allows only short waves to be reflected appears violet or blue, and one that allows only medium waves to be reflected appears green or yellow. A surface that reflects all wavelengths about equally appears white, gray, or black, depending on whether the relative amount of each wavelength reflected is, respectively, high (none absorbed), moderate (some absorbed), or low (all absorbed).

8

How do pigments affect the perceived color of an object in white light? How does the mixing of pigments affect color by subtracting from the light that is reflected to the eye?

Subtractive Color Mixing

Because pigments create the perception of color by *subtracting* (absorbing) some of the light waves that would otherwise be reflected to the eye, the mixing of pigments is called **subtractive color mixing.** As illustrated in Figure 8.8, if a blue pigment, which absorbs long waves, is mixed with a yellow pigment, which absorbs short waves, only medium-length waves will be reflected, and the mixture will be seen as green. When you were a child playing with watercolors, you probably proved the basic facts of subtractive color mixing many times. You may remember being disappointed when you mixed all the paints together and produced something pretty close to black rather than the brilliant reddish-yellowish-greenish-blue that you had hoped for. In that experiment you subtracted essentially all the wavelengths by combining all the pigments, leaving essentially none to be reflected.

FIGURE 8.8
Subtractive color mixing In this example, the blue pigment (a) absorbs most of the light that has wavelengths above 550 nm, and the yellow pigment (c) absorbs most of the light that has wavelengths below 500 nm. When the two pigments are mixed (b), the only light that is not strongly absorbed is that with wavelengths between 500 and 550 nm. This is the light that will be reflected, causing the mixture to appear green.

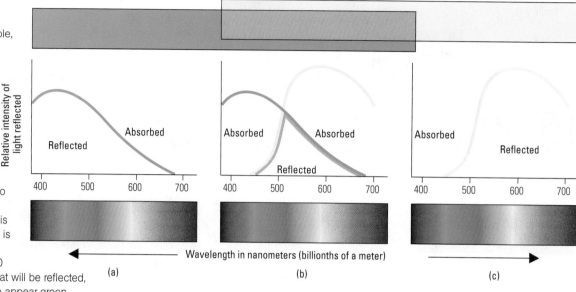

Relative intensity of light reflected

Reflected   Absorbed

Absorbed   Absorbed

Reflected

Absorbed   Reflected

Wavelength in nanometers (billionths of a meter)

(a)   (b)   (c)

Two Psychological Laws of Additive Color Mixing

9

How does additive color mixing differ from subtractive color mixing? What are the two laws of additive color mixing, and how is each illustrated in the standard chromaticity diagram?

The opposite of subtractive color mixing is ***additive color mixing,*** which occurs when colored lights rather than pigments are mixed. Additive color mixing can be demonstrated by shining two or more beams of light of different wavelengths at the same spot on a white screen; the screen then reflects them back mixed together (see Figure 8.9, below). By the early eighteenth century, scientists had discovered that additive color mixing follows two quite surprising laws—the three-primaries law and the law of complementarity—neither of which could be predicted from anything that one could know about the physics of light. These early researchers realized that these laws of color mixing are laws of psychology, not physics.

According to the ***three-primaries law,*** three different wavelengths of light (called *primaries*) can be used to match any color that the eye can see if they are mixed in the appropriate proportions. The primaries can be any three wavelengths as long as one is taken from the long-wave end of the spectrum (red), one from the short-wave end (blue or violet), and one from the middle (green or green-yellow). According to the ***law of complementarity,*** pairs of wavelengths can be found that, when added together, produce the visual sensation of white. The wavelengths of light in such a pair are referred to as complements of each other.

FIGURE 8.9 Additive color mixing
Additive color mixing occurs when lights of different wavelengths are mixed by shining them together on a surface that reflects all wavelengths. By varying the intensity of the three lights shown here, it is possible to produce essentially all the colors that the eye can see.

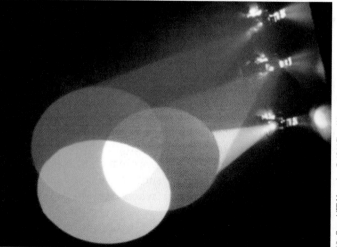

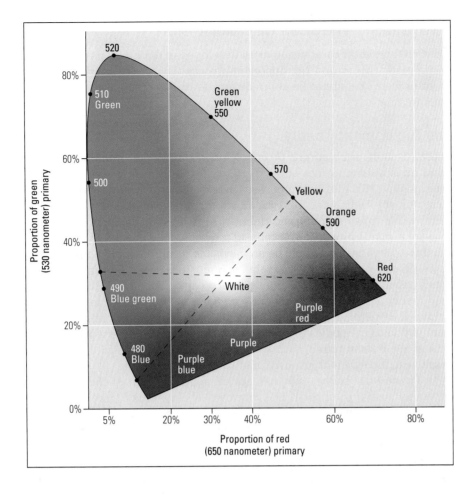

FIGURE 8.10 The standard chromaticity diagram All the facts of additive color mixing—related to both the three-primaries law and the law of complementarity—are summarized in this diagram. The three primaries here are lights of 460 nm (blue), 530 nm (green), and 650 nm (red). The proportions of red and green primaries that must be added to the blue primary to match any given color on the diagram are shown, respectively, on the horizontal and vertical axes. The proportion of blue can be calculated by subtracting the other two proportions from 100 percent. For example, if you wish to match the blue-green produced by a 490-nm light, the figure indicates that your mixture must contain about 5 percent red primary, 30 percent green primary, and 65 percent blue primary (100% − 5% − 30% = 65%). As another example, the figure shows that the best white is produced by approximately equal (33.3 percent) proportions of the three primaries.

The chromaticity diagram can also be used to find all possible pairs of complementary colors. Two colors are complementary if their additive mixture produces white. In the diagram, the possible colors produced by mixing any two wavelengths lie along the straight line connecting the points representing the two wavelengths on the diagram. Thus, the two ends of any straight line passing through the white center of the diagram represent complementary colors. Two such lines are drawn on the figure for purposes of illustration. Notice that wavelengths in the red-to-orange part of the spectrum have their complements in the green-to-blue-green part, and that wavelengths in the yellow part of the spectrum have their complements in the blue part.

All the facts associated with the two laws of additive color mixing are taken into account in the *standard chromaticity diagram*, shown in Figure 8.10. The colors along the curved edge of the diagram are produced by single wavelengths and are called *saturated* colors. As you move from any point near the edge toward the white center, the color comes more and more to resemble white; that is, it becomes increasingly *unsaturated* (white is regarded as fully unsaturated). For example, as you go along the line from the 620-nm point on the edge to the center, you go from red (produced by light with a wavelength of 620 nm) to progressively whiter shades of pink (unsaturated red) to white. (Because of the limitations of color printing, Figure 8.10 does not show the gradualness of this change in saturation, but you can imagine it.) The figure's caption describes how the diagram can be used to determine (a) the color that will result from mixing the three standard primaries in any given proportion and (b) which pairs of wavelengths are complements of each other.

It is rather exciting to realize that the facts of color mixing portrayed by the chromaticity diagram are facts of *psychology*, not physics. The wavelengths of the three primaries do *not* become physically blended into one wavelength when added together to match the color produced by a fourth wavelength. A machine that detects wavelengths has no difficulty distinguishing, say, a 550-nm light from the mixture of three primaries that would exactly match its greenish-yellow color. Similarly, when two complementary wavelengths are mixed to produce the sensation of white, they do not physically produce white light (which contains all the wavelengths). Instead, such color matches, in which physically distinct stimuli look identical, occur because of processes in the eye and the brain. Indeed, the matches just described provided the insight that led to two theories of how the eye and brain produce color vision.

Two Classic Theories of Color Vision

The two theories of color vision, both developed in the nineteenth century, are the trichromatic theory and the opponent-process theory. For many years these two theories were thought to be contradictory to one another, but we now know that both are true.

The Trichromatic Theory

10
How does the trichromatic theory explain the three-primaries law? How was the theory validated by the discovery of three cone types?

◄ According to the **_trichromatic theory,_** color vision emerges from the combined activity of three different types of receptors, each most sensitive to a different range of wavelengths. This idea was proposed first (in 1802) by Thomas Young and later by Hermann von Helmholtz (1852) as an attempt to explain the three-primaries law of additive color mixing. Young and Helmholtz reasoned that if every color we see is the result of a unique proportion, or ratio, of activity among three types of receptors, then the three-primaries law would be an inevitable result: It would be possible to match any visible color by varying the relative intensities of three primary lights, each of which acts maximally on a different type of receptor. Young and Helmholtz developed their theory purely from behavioral data on the perceptual effects of color mixing, at a time when nothing was known about photoreceptors in the retina. We now know from physiological studies that their theory was correct. Three types of cones indeed exist in the human retina, each with a different photochemical that makes it most sensitive to the light within a particular band of wavelengths.

In Figure 8.11 (below), you can see an approximation of the actual sensitivity curves for each type of cone. The cones are labeled "blue," "green," and "red," after the color that is experienced when that type of cone is much more active than the other types. Notice that any given wavelength of light produces a unique ratio of activity in the three types of cones. For example, a 550-nm light, which is seen as greenish-yellow, produces a slightly larger response in "red" cones than in "green" cones and a very low response in "blue" cones. That same ratio of response in the three cone types could be produced by shining into the eye a mixture of red, green, and blue primaries, with the first two much more intense than the last. The result would be a perceptual experience of greenish-yellow indistinguishable from that produced by the 550-nm light.

Exceptions to Trichromatic Vision

11
Why does vision in some people obey a two-primaries law rather than the three-primaries law, and why are these people not good at picking cherries? How does the color vision of most nonprimate mammals, and that of most birds, differ from that of most humans?

◄ Some people, referred to as _dichromats_, have only two, not three, types of cone photochemicals. These people, as you might expect, obey a two-primaries law of color mixing rather than the three-primaries law. For them, any color that they can see

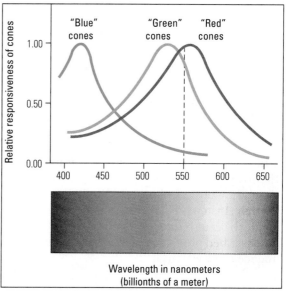

FIGURE 8.11 **How the three types of cones respond to different wavelengths of light** Any given wavelength produces a unique ratio of activity in the three cone types, and that ratio provides the initial code that permits us to see different wavelengths as different colors. For example, a 550-nm light, which is seen as greenish-yellow, produces a slightly larger response in "red" cones than in "green" cones and very little response in "blue" cones. Any combination of lights that would produce that same ratio of responses would be seen as greenish-yellow. (For precise data, see Bowmaker & Dartnall, 1980, or Merbs & Nathans, 1992.)

can be matched by varying the proportion of just two different wavelengths of light. The most common forms of dichromia involve the absence of the normal photochemical for either the "red" or the "green" cones (usually the latter) due to a defect in the gene that produces that photochemical (Neitz & others, 1996). Because the defective gene is recessive and the genes for both the "red" and the "green" photochemicals are located on the X chromosome, this trait appears much more often in men than in women. Men (as discussed in Chapter 3) have only one X chromosome, inherited from the mother, so a single defective gene on that chromosome can produce color blindness. Women have

The value of color vision Our sensitivity to the wavelength of reflected light helps us to distinguish objects of interest from their background.

two X chromosomes, one inherited from each parent, and are color-blind only if the defective gene exists on both of them.

Approximately 5 percent of men and 0.25 percent of women lack either the "red" or "green" cone photochemical and are *red-green color-blind*, meaning that they have difficulty distinguishing colors ranging from green to the red end of the spectrum (Masland, 2001). If you look again at Figure 8.11, you will see why this is so. The normal ability to distinguish colors in this range (from about 500 to 700 nm) is mediated almost entirely by differential activity in the "red" and "green" cones, because "blue" cones are quite inactive in this range. If either the "red" or the "green" cone photochemical is missing, then the person has no or little physiological basis for distinguishing one wavelength from another in this range. Many people who have red-green color blindness don't know it and may wonder why certain perceptual tasks that are hard for them are easy for others. One man's red-green color blindness was not discovered until he told his family how much he admired the perceptual skill of cherry pickers: "After all," he said, "the only thing that tells 'em it's a cherry is . . . that it's round and the leaves aren't. I just don't see how they find 'em in those trees!" (Coren & Ward, 1989).

Most nonprimate mammals, including dogs and cats, have just two types of cones, corresponding to our "blue" and "green" cones, and have the same difficulty discriminating among colors at the long-wavelength end of the spectrum as do people who are red-green color blind (Solomon & Lennie, 2007). Most birds, in contrast, have four types of cones (Dalton, 2004). Birds rely heavily on vision to guide their flight and to locate food, and they have evolved color vision that is better than ours. In addition to "red," "green," and "blue" cones, they have a fourth set of cones that are maximally sensitive to wavelengths in the ultraviolet range (shorter than 400 nm), which we cannot see (see Figure 8.12).

FIGURE 8.12 Ultraviolet mouths These starling nestlings' gaping beaks and mouths would appear black to us, but, as shown in this UV photograph, they reflect ultraviolet light intensely. They are ideally designed to attract the attention of the mother starling without attracting that of mammalian predators who cannot see ultraviolet light. (From Dalton, 2004, p. 596.)

The Opponent-Process Theory

The trichromatic theory explains the three-primaries law and certain types of color blindness well, but it does not explain the law of complementarity—how certain pairs of wavelengths produce the experience of white. To explain that, Ewald Hering, another nineteenth-century scientist, developed the **opponent-process theory.** Hering was most impressed by the observation that complementary colors (blue and yellow, or green and red) seem to swallow each other up, erasing each other's color, when added together. For example, if you begin with blue light and gradually add more of its complement (yellow), the result is not "bluish-yellow" but an ever-paler (more unsaturated) blue, which finally becomes white. To explain such observations, Hering (1878/1964) proposed that color perception is mediated by physiological units (which we now call neurons) that can be either excited or inhibited, depending on the wavelength of light, and that complementary wavelengths have opposite effects (that is, they activate "opposing processes") on these opponent-process units.

◄ More specifically, Hering's proposal (in modern language) was that the ability to see blues and yellows is mediated by blue-yellow opponent neurons, which are excited by wavelengths in the blue part of the spectrum and inhibited by those in the yellow part, or vice versa. Similarly, he proposed that the ability to see greens and reds is mediated by green-red opponent neurons, which are excited by wavelengths in the green part of the spectrum and inhibited by those in the red part, or vice versa. In addition, he proposed that the ability to distinguish bright from dim light, independent of wavelength, is mediated by a third set of neurons (brightness detectors), which are excited by lights of any wavelength. This theory nicely accounts for the facts of complementary colors. A mixture of wavelengths from the blue and yellow parts of the spectrum, or from the green and red parts, appears white (colorless but bright) because the two sets of wavelengths cancel each other out in their effects on color detectors but act in concert to excite brightness detectors.

Color Afterimages Explained by the Opponent-Process Theory

The opponent-process theory also accounts wonderfully for another psychological phenomenon, the *complementarity of afterimages*. For a demonstration of this phenomenon, follow the instructions in the first paragraph of the caption of Figure 8.13. You will see that the colors in the afterimage are the complements of those in the original: What was green becomes red; what was yellow becomes blue; and what was black becomes white. How does the opponent-process theory explain this phenomenon? Consider the example of green becoming red in the afterimage. The neurons in the retina that respond most strongly to the green-appearing (middle-wavelength) light as you stare at the picture become fatigued. Therefore, when you shift your eyes to the white paper (which reflects all wavelengths), those neurons don't respond as strongly as they normally would, but other neurons, including those that respond to red-appearing (long-wavelength) light, do respond strongly. Thus, opponent-process neurons that are normally excited by red-appearing light and inhibited by green-appearing light in that part of the retina become excited, resulting in the perception

12

How does the opponent-process theory explain (a) the law of complementarity in color mixing and (b) the complementarity of afterimages?

FIGURE 8.13 Complementarity of afterimages Stare at the dot in the middle of the flag for at least half a minute. Then look at the dot on the white space beside the flag. What do you see?

To demonstrate that this effect involves a change within the retina, or at least somewhere early in the visual system before the input from the two eyes converges, repeat the demonstration but this time keep one eye closed as you stare at the middle of the flag. Then look at the dot in the white space first with one eye and then with the other. What happens?

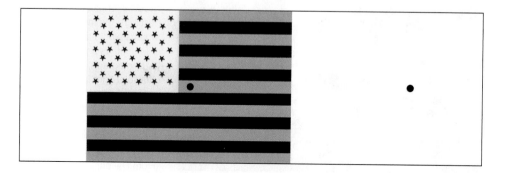

of red. To convince yourself that this adaptive process occurs early in the visual pathway, before the inputs from the two eyes converge, follow the instructions in the second paragraph of the caption of Figure 8.13.

A Physiological Reconciliation of the Two Theories

For many years the trichromatic and opponent-process theories were thought to be contradictory, but in the 1950s and 1960s research showed that both theories are fundamentally correct (De Valois & others, 1966; Hurvich & Jameson, 1957). The retina indeed contains three types of cones, consistent with Young and Helmholtz's trichromatic theory. But the cones feed into ganglion cells (the neurons of the optic nerve) in a pattern that translates the trichromatic code into an opponent-process code, conforming to Hering's theory. Some ganglion cells behave in a red-green opponent manner: They are excited by input from "red" cones and inhibited by input from "green" cones, or vice versa. Others behave in a blue-yellow opponent manner: They are excited by input from "blue" cones and inhibited by input from both "green" and "red" cones (which, in combination, respond best to yellow light), or vice versa. To see how connections from the three cone types could produce such opponent-process cells, look at Figure 8.14. Neurons in the cerebral cortex that are most directly involved in color perception maintain these opponent-process characteristics (Dacey, 2000; Solomon & Lennie, 2007).

The research and theories on color vision just presented are a wonderful early illustration of the value of combining behavioral and physiological research. The trichromatic and opponent-process theories were developed, in the nineteenth century, from behavioral evidence having to do with the perceptual effects of additive color mixing, before anything was known about the physiology of receptors and neurons. Later, both theories were confirmed physiologically, and today neuroscientists and psychologists are working out the finer details of the theories.

13

How has the opponent-process theory been validated in studies of the activity of neurons that receive input from cones?

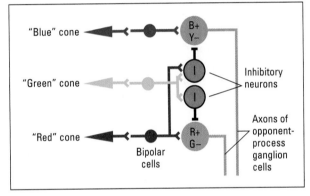

FIGURE 8.14 Reconciliation of the trichromatic and opponent-process theories Shown here is a schematic diagram illustrating how connections from the three types of cones can result in opponent-process cells—cells that are excited by blue and inhibited by yellow (BY-) and cells that are excited by red and inhibited by green (RG-). Excitatory neural connections are shown as Y-shaped axonal endings, and inhibitory connections are shown as straight lines perpendicular to the axon. The cells marked "I" are inhibitory intermediary neurons. As an exercise, try constructing diagrams that would produce B-Y and R-G opponent neurons.

SECTION REVIEW

The experience of color results from the visual system's response to wavelengths of light.

Wavelength and Color

➤ We experience different wavelengths of light as different colors.

➤ Objects appear colored because their pigments absorb some wavelengths from white light and reflect others.

➤ Mixing pigments is called subtractive color mixing because each pigment removes the wavelengths it absorbs.

➤ Additive color mixing involves mixing lights of different wavelengths. It is characterized by the three-primaries law and the law of complementarity.

Trichromatic Theory of Color Vision

➤ This theory, derived from the three-primaries law, holds that we have three types of receptors, each most responsive to a particular range of wavelengths.

➤ The theory was confirmed by the discovery that the retina has three types of cones, each with a different curve of sensitivity to visible wavelengths.

Opponent-Process Theory of Color Vision

➤ This theory, derived from the law of complementarity, holds that physiological units involved in color vision are affected in opposite ways (excited or inhibited) by complementary wavelengths.

➤ The theory explains the complementarity of afterimages.

➤ The theory was confirmed by the discovery of visual neurons that behave just as the theory predicted.

■ Seeing Forms and Patterns

The purpose of human vision is not to detect the simple presence or absence of light or different wavelengths, but to identify meaningful objects and actions. As I look at the top of my desk, my retinas are struck by a continuous field of light, varying from point to point in intensity and wavelength. But I see the scene neither as a continuous field nor as a collection of points. Instead, I see objects: a computer, a pencil, a stapler, and a pile of books. Each object stands out sharply from its background. My visual system has sorted all the points and gradations that are present in the reflected light into useful renditions of the objects on my desk. It has provided me with all the information I need to reach out and touch, or pick up, whichever object I want to use next. How does my visual system accomplish this remarkable feat?

Vision researchers generally conceive of object perception as a type of unconscious problem solving, in which sensory information provides clues that are analyzed using information that is already stored in the person's head. In this section and the next, we shall concerned with how our visual system organizes such clues in ways that allow us to see forms, patterns, and objects.

Enhancement of Contours

14

What is the value of the visual system's ability to exaggerate contrast at contours, and how can that ability be demonstrated? How is contrast enhancement explained by lateral inhibition?

◄ Objects are defined principally by their *contours*, that is, by their edges or borders. Contours give objects their distinctive shapes. The contours of the pencil on my desk, for example, consist of two long, parallel edges, which are connected at one end by the curved edge of the pencil's eraser and at the other end by the two converging edges of the pencil's sharpened point. That outline, by itself, would allow me to distinguish the pencil from other objects on my desk. Visually, contours are sudden changes in brightness or color that separate objects from their backgrounds.

Exaggeration of Contrast at Contours

As an aid in detecting objects, our visual system has evolved in such a way that it exaggerates the amount of physical change that occurs across contours. To experience that effect, look at Figure 8.15. Each stripe is physically uniform in its lightness (that is, in the actual amount of light it reflects), but our perception of it is not uniform. Each stripe appears to be lighter near its boundary with a darker stripe, and darker near its boundary with a lighter stripe, than it is in the middle. Compare the perceived lightness just above arrow 1 with that just above arrow 2, for example. The graph above the stripes shows how the actual lightness and the perceived lightness change across the set of stripes. The exaggeration of contrast that our visual system imposes on these stripes helps us to see each one as distinct from its neighbors.

Lateral Inhibition as a Mechanism for Enhancing Contours

Neuroscientists have discovered that enhancement of contrast, such as that illustrated in Figure 8.15, occurs through a process of *lateral inhibition*. Some neurons in the retina and in visual areas of the brain have inhibitory connections with their neighboring neurons. The result is that activity in any given neuron declines when its neighboring neurons are active, by an amount that is proportional to the degree of activity in those neighbors.

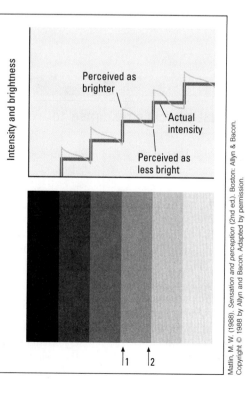

FIGURE 8.15
Enhancement of contrast Each solid gray stripe appears lighter near its boundary with a darker stripe and darker near its boundary with a lighter stripe. This effect is believed to result from lateral inhibition among neighboring neurons in the visual system. (Adapted from Matlin & Foley, 1997.)

Matlin, M. W. (1988). *Sensation and perception* (2nd ed.). Boston: Allyn & Bacon. Copyright © 1988 by Allyn and Bacon. Adapted by permission.

To understand how lateral inhibition can enhance contrast at edges, imagine a person looking at the two patches of gray shown in Figure 8.16. Neighboring portions of this stimulus activate neighboring neurons in the visual system, and neighboring neurons tend to inhibit one another. For simplicity, imagine four non-neighboring neurons—A, B, C, and D—which are excited, respectively, by light coming from the circular spots labeled A, B, C, and D in the figure. In this example, neuron A, which is excited by a spot in the middle of the lighter patch, will be less active than neuron B, which is excited by a spot in the lighter patch near its border with the darker patch. Both neurons receive the same amount of excitatory input, but neuron A is completely surrounded by very active neighbors, while neuron B is only partly surrounded by very active neighbors. Some of B's neighbors are receiving input from the darker patch and are therefore less active than A's neighbors. As a result, neuron B receives less inhibitory input than does neuron A and is more active.

Similar logic, applied to the neurons responding to light reflected from the darker patch, shows that neuron D, next to the contour, will be less active than neuron C. Both neurons receive the same (relatively small) amount of excitatory input, but neuron D receives more inhibitory input because some of its neighbors are stimulated by the lighter patch and are therefore very active. The result of all this, compounded over the thousands of neurons that receive input from these gray patches, is an exaggeration of the contrast at the border. The light patch appears lighter near its border with the dark patch than elsewhere, and the dark patch appears darker near its border with the light patch than elsewhere.

The Detection and Integration of Stimulus Features

Any object that we see can be thought of as consisting of a set of elementary stimulus features. The features may include the various straight and curved lines that form the object's contours, the brightness and color of the light that the object reflects, and the object's movement or lack of movement with respect to the background. Somehow our visual system registers all these features and brings them together to form one unified perception of the object. A major objective of brain research on vision, for the past 60 years or so, has been to understand how the brain detects and integrates the elementary stimulus features of objects.

Feature Detection in the Visual Cortex

The primary method that researchers have used to learn how the brain registers stimulus features has been to record the activity of individual neurons in visual areas of the brain, in laboratory animals, while directing visual stimuli into the animals' eyes. As depicted in Figure 8.17, ganglion cells of the optic nerve run to the thalamus, in the middle of the brain, and synapse there on other neurons that carry their output to the **primary visual area** of the cerebral cortex (introduced also in Chapter 5, Figure 5.18). Within the primary visual area, millions of neurons are involved in analyzing the sensory input. Researchers have inserted thin electrodes into individual neurons in this area of the cortex, in animals, in order to record the neurons' rates of action potentials as various visual stimuli are presented. In a typical experiment the animal—usually a cat or a monkey—is anesthetized, so it is unconscious, but its eyes are kept open and the neural connections from the eyes to the relevant brain neurons are intact.

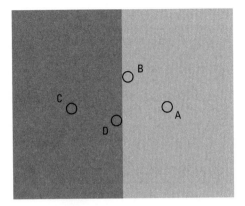

FIGURE 8.16 Neural explanation of contrast enhancement In this figure, spots A, B, C, and D represent areas of the visual stimulus that activate neurons A, B, C, and D, respectively, in the visual system. As explained in the text, because of lateral inhibition, neuron B in this example will be more active than neuron A, and neuron D will be less active than neuron C. Such differences in neural activity, over all of the neurons that receive input from this stimulus, account for contrast enhancement at edges.

FIGURE 8.17 Pathway from the eyes to the primary visual cortex Neurons in the optic nerves come together at the optic chiasm at the base of the brain and form the optic tracts, which run to nuclei in the thalamus, where they synapse on neurons that run to the primary visual area of the cerebral cortex.

Visual area of the thalamus

Optic nerve

Optic chiasm

Optic tract

Retina

Primary visual area of cortex

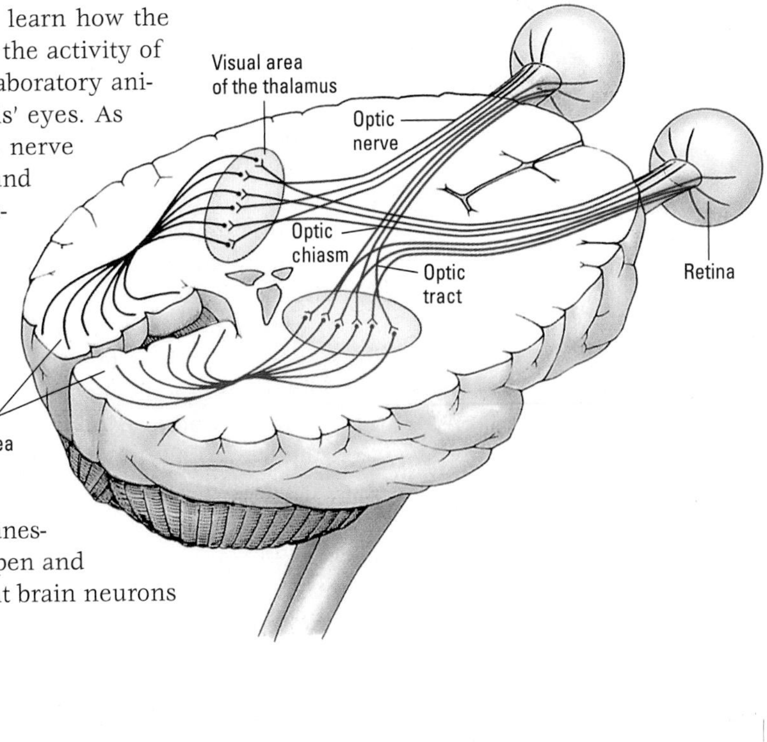

15

What sorts of stimulus features influence the activity of neurons in the primary visual cortex?

◄ In a classic series of experiments of this sort, David Hubel and Torsten Wiesel (1962, 1979) recorded the activity of individual neurons in the primary visual cortex of cats while the cats' eyes were stimulated by simple black-and-white patterns of various shapes, sizes, and orientations. They found that different neurons responded preferentially to different patterns. For example, some neurons responded best (most strongly) to stimuli that contained a straight contour separating a black patch from a white patch. Hubel and Wiesel referred to these neurons as *edge detectors*. Other neurons responded best to a narrow white bar against a black background, or to a narrow black bar against a white background. The researchers referred to these as *bar detectors*. Hubel and Wiesel found, moreover, that any given edge or bar detector responded best to a particular orientation of the edge or bar. Some responded best when it was oriented vertically, others responded best when it was oriented horizontally, and still others responded best when it was slanted at a specific angle.

Subsequent research showed that neurons in the primary visual cortex are sensitive not just to the orientation of visual stimuli, but also to other visual features, including color and rate of movement. Thus, one neuron might respond best to a yellow bar on a blue background, tilted 15 degrees clockwise and moving slowly from left to right. Recording from visual cortical areas just outside of the primary area, researchers identified individual neurons that are most sensitive to contours that are more complex than those described for the primary visual area. For example, they found neurons that responded most strongly to arcs or circles of a specific radius and other neurons that responded most strongly to angles of a specific number of degrees (Anzai & others, 2007; Hegdé & Van Essen, 2003). Taken as a whole, the neurons of the primary visual cortex and nearby areas seem to keep track of all the bits and pieces of visual information that would be available in a scene. Because of their sensitivity to the elementary features of a scene, these neurons are often referred to as **feature detectors.**

Treisman's Two-Stage Feature-Integration Theory of Perception

16

What is the difference between parallel processing and serial processing? What role does each play in Treisman's feature-integration theory of perception?

◄ Some years ago, Anne Treisman (1986, 1998) developed a theory of visual perception that she called a *feature-integration theory*. She developed the theory partly from neurophysiological evidence concerning feature detectors, but mostly from behavioral evidence concerning the speed with which people can perceive various stimuli. The theory begins with the assertion that any perceived stimulus, even a simple one such as the X shown in Figure 8.18 (on page 285), consists of a number of distinct *primitive sensory features*, such as its color and the slant of its individual lines. To perceive the stimulus as a unified entity, the perceptual system must detect these individual features and integrate them into a whole. The essence of Treisman's theory is that the detection and integration occur sequentially, in two fundamentally different steps or stages of information processing.

The first stage in Treisman's theory is the *detection of features*, which occurs instantaneously and involves **parallel processing.** Parallel processing means that this step operates simultaneously on all parts of the stimulus array. That is, according to Treisman, our visual system picks up at once all the primitive features of all the objects whose light rays strike our retinas. Even if we are paying attention just to the X in Figure 8.18, our visual system picks up at the same time the primitive features of the V in that figure and of all other stimuli in our field of view.

The second stage is the *integration of features*, which requires more time and leads eventually to our perception of whole, spatially organized patterns and objects. This step involves **serial processing,** which occurs sequentially, at one spatial location at a time, rather than simultaneously over the entire array. When looking at Figure 8.18, we can integrate the features of the X and then, an instant later, the features of the V, but we cannot integrate the two sets of features simultaneously.

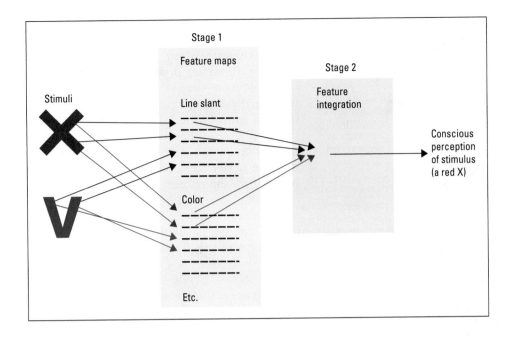

FIGURE 8.18 Treisman's theory of feature detection and integration During stage 1 of visual processing, in Treisman's theory, the primitive features of all stimuli that reach the eyes are registered automatically and simultaneously—that is, in parallel. In this example, all the features of both the X and the V are registered simultaneously in the appropriate feature-mapping areas of the brain. Integration of features occurs at stage 2, during which information is processed serially, from one localized area of the visual field at a time. In this example, only the information from one stimulus, the X, is being processed. An instant later, stage 2 might operate on the V, but it cannot operate on the X and V at the same time.

Research Support for Treisman's Theory

To understand some of the evidence on which Treisman based her theory, look at the array of stimuli in Figure 8.19a. Notice that no effort is needed to find the single slanted line. You don't have to scan the whole array in serial fashion to find it; it just "pops out" at you. According to Treisman, this is because line slant is one of the primitive features that are processed automatically through parallel processing. Now look at Figure 8.19b and find the single slanted green line among the vertical green lines and slanted red lines. In this case the target does not pop out; you have to scan through the array in serial fashion to find it (though you can still find it quite quickly).

In controlled experiments, Treisman and Stephen Gormican (1988) measured the time it took for people to locate specific target stimuli in arrays like those of Figure 8.19 but with varying numbers of *distractors* (defined as the nontarget stimuli). As long as the target differed from all the distractors in one or more of Treisman's list of primitive features—such as slant, curvature, color, brightness, and movement—subjects detected it equally quickly no matter how many distractors were present.

─────────────────── **17**

How do pop-out phenomena and mistakes in joining features provide evidence for Treisman's theory?

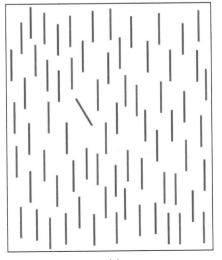

(a)   (b)

FIGURE 8.19 Stimuli that pop out or do not pop out These stimulus arrays are similar to those used by Treisman and Gormican (1988). In (a) the target stimulus (slanted green line) differs from the distractor stimuli in a primitive feature; it is the only slanted line in the array. Here the target pops out at you; you notice it immediately even if you aren't looking for it. In (b) the target stimulus (slanted green line) does not differ from the distractors in a primitive feature; its greenness is matched by some distractors and its slant is matched by other distractors. Rather, this target is distinct in the way its features are conjoined. It is the only line that is both green and slanted. This target does not pop out at you; you have to look for it to notice it.

Alvey & Towers Picture Library/Alamy

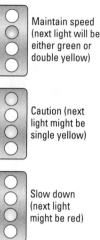

Maintain speed (next light will be either green or double yellow)

Caution (next light might be single yellow)

Slow down (next light might be red)

Stop

FIGURE 8.20 Conjoined features make detection harder Shown here are the light signals used along railroad tracks in the United Kingdom to tell drivers how to proceed. The "slow down" signal is critical, because if a driver misses it there will be insufficient time to come to a full stop when the "stop" signal becomes visible. According to Treisman's theory, however, this signal should be the most difficult to detect, because it is the only signal that is distinguished from the others by a conjoining of two elementary features (color and number) rather than by a single feature. To identify the "slow down" signal as distinct from the others, you have to see that there is only one light *and* that it is yellow. In contrast, the green and red signals are uniquely defined by color alone (no other signal is green or red), and the double-yellow signal is uniquely defined by number alone (no other signal involves illumination of two lights). In an experiment, John Groeger and his colleagues (2005) showed that, indeed, research subjects who had practice identifying the signals were significantly slower at identifying the single-yellow ("slow down") signal than any of the others. According to Groeger, a redesign of the UK railroad signal system could save lives, as accidents do sometimes occur because train drivers misperceive the single-yellow signal.

This lack of effect of the number of distractors on detection time is indicative of parallel processing. In contrast, when the target did not differ from the distractors in any single visual feature, but differed only in its conjoining of two or more features that were present in different sets of distractors, as in Figure 8.19b, the amount of time required to locate the target increased in direct proportion to the number of distractors. This increase in detection time is indicative of serial processing—the necessity to attend to each item (or to small groups of items) separately until the target is found. Identification of a single unique feature can be accomplished with parallel processing (stage 1 in Treisman's model), but identification of a unique conjoining of two or more features requires serial processing (stage 2 in Triesman's model).

Treisman also found that subjects who saw simple stimuli flashed briefly on a screen easily identified which primitive features were present but sometimes misperceived which features went together, a phenomenon called *illusory conjunctions*. For example, when shown a straight red line and a green curved one, all subjects knew that they had seen a straight line and a curved line, and a red color and a green color, but some were mistaken about which color belonged to which line. Such findings led Treisman to conclude that stage 1 (parallel processing) registers features independently of their spatial location and that different features that coincide in space (such as the color and curvature of a given line) are joined perceptually only at stage 2 (serial processing), which requires separate attention to each spatial location. In Triesman's theory, stage 2 operates by assigning primitive features to specific spatial locations and then weaving the features together in patterns that reflect their locations.

Not all research findings are consistent with Treisman's theory. Some researchers have argued, with evidence, that the registration and integration of visual features are not as separate as Treisman proposed (Mordkoff & Halterman, 2008; Roelfsema, 2006). However, to date, no well-accepted newer theory has emerged to replace Treisman's. Moreover, researchers continue to find new examples of perceptual phenomenon that fit with predictions from Treisman's theory. For one such example, which could have serious practical consequences, read the caption to Figure 8.20.

Gestalt Principles of Perceptual Grouping

In the early twentieth century, long before Treisman had developed her model of feature integration, adherents to the school of thought known as **Gestalt psychology** had argued that we automatically perceive whole, organized patterns and objects. *Gestalt* is a German word that can be translated roughly as "organized shape" or "whole form." The premise of the Gestaltists—including Max Wertheimer, Kurt Koffka, and Wolfgang Köhler—was that the mind must be understood in terms of organized wholes, not elementary parts. A favorite saying of theirs was, "The whole is different from the sum of its parts." A melody is not the sum of the individual notes, a painting is not the sum of the individual dots of paint, an idea is not the sum of its elementary concepts. In each of these examples, something new emerges from the arrangement of the parts, just as meaning emerges when words are arranged to form a sentence. From the Gestalt point of view, the attempt by psychologists to understand perception by focusing on elementary features was like trying to explain the beauty of the *Mona Lisa* by carefully weighing the amount of paint used to produce each part of the masterpiece.

Most early Gestalt research was in the area of visual perception. In many laboratory demonstrations, Gestalt psychologists showed that in conscious experience whole objects and scenes take precedence over parts. For example, when looking at a chair, people perceive and recognize the chair as a whole before noticing its arms, legs, and other components. Treisman and other modern perceptual psychologists would not disagree with this point. In our conscious experience we do typically perceive wholes before we perceive parts; the building up of the wholes from the parts occurs through unconscious mental processes. They would also agree that the whole is different from the sum of its parts, because the whole is defined by the way the parts are *organized*, not just by the parts themselves.

Built-in Rules for Organizing Stimulus Elements into Wholes

The Gestaltists proposed that the nervous system is innately predisposed to respond to patterns in the stimulus world according to certain rules or principles of grouping. These principles include the following (Koffka, 1935; Wertheimer, 1923/1938).

18
What are some principles of grouping proposed by Gestalt psychologists, and how does each help explain our ability to see whole objects?

1. ***Proximity*** We tend to see stimulus elements that are near each other as parts of the same object and those that are separated as parts of different objects. This helps us organize a large set of elements into a smaller set of objects. In Figure 8.21a, because of proximity, we see 3 clusters of dots rather than 13 individual dots.

2. ***Similarity*** We tend to see stimulus elements that physically resemble each other as parts of the same object, and those that do not resemble each other as parts of different objects. For example, as illustrated in Figure 8.21b, this helps us distinguish between two adjacent or overlapping objects on the basis of a change in their texture elements. (Texture elements are repeated visual features or patterns that cover the surface of a given object.)

3. ***Closure*** We tend to see forms as completely enclosed by a border and to ignore gaps in the border. This helps us perceive complete objects even when they are partially occluded by other objects. For example, in Figure 8.21c we automatically assume that the boundary of the circle is complete, continuing behind the square.

4. ***Good continuation*** When lines intersect, we tend to group the line segments in such a way as to form continuous lines with minimal change in direction. This helps us decide which lines belong to which object when two or more objects overlap. In Figure 8.21d, for example, we see two smooth lines, *ab* and *cd*, rather than four shorter lines or two sharply bent lines such as *ac* or *bd*.

5. ***Common movement*** When stimulus elements move in the same direction and at the same rate, we tend to see them as part of a single object. This helps us distinguish a moving object (such as a camouflaged animal) from the background. If the dots marked by arrows in Figure 8.21e were all moving as a group, you would see them as a single object.

6. ***Good form*** The perceptual system strives to produce percepts that are elegant—simple, uncluttered, symmetrical, regular, and predictable (Chater, 1996; Koffka, 1935). This rather unspecific principle encompasses the other principles listed above but also includes other ways by which the perceptual system organizes stimuli into their simplest (most easily explained) arrangement. For example, in Figure 8.21f, the left-hand figure, because of its symmetry, is more likely than the middle figure to be seen as a single object. The middle figure, because of its lack of symmetry, is more likely to be seen as two objects, as shown to its right.

FIGURE 8.21 Gestalt principles of grouping These drawings illustrate the six Gestalt principles that are described in the text.

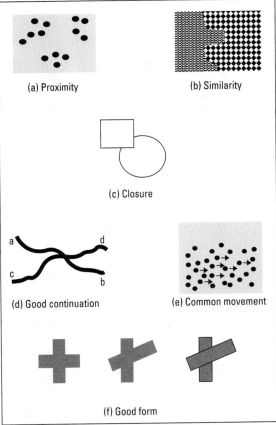

(a) Proximity

(b) Similarity

(c) Closure

(d) Good continuation

(e) Common movement

(f) Good form

Principle of similarity When we look at a scene such as this one, we automatically group together portions that contain similar stimulus elements. The similarity may be in color, brightness, texture, or orientation of contours.

Figure and Ground

In addition to proposing the six principles of grouping just listed, the Gestaltists (particularly Rubin, 1915/1958) called attention to our automatic tendency to divide any visual scene into *figure* (the object that attracts attention) and *ground* (the background). As an example, see Figure 8.22. The illustration could, in theory, be described as two unfamiliar figures, one white and one black, whose borders happen to coincide, but you almost certainly do not see it that way. Most people automatically see it as just one white figure against a black background. The division into figure and ground is not arbitrary, but is directed by certain stimulus characteristics. In Figure 8.22, the most important characteristic is probably *circumscription*: Other things being equal, we tend to see the circumscribing form (the one that surrounds the other) as the ground and the circumscribed form as the figure.

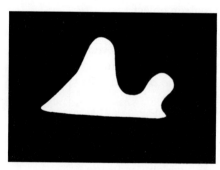

FIGURE 8.22 Figure and ground Because the white form is completely surrounded by the black form, we tend to see the white form as the figure and the black form as the ground.

◀ The figure-ground relationship is not always completely determined by characteristics of the stimulus. With some effort, you can reverse your perception of figure and ground in Figure 8.22 by imagining that the illustration is a black square with an oddly shaped hole cut out of it, sitting on a white background. When cues in the scene are sparse or ambiguous, the mind may vacillate in its choice of which shape to see as figure and which as ground. This is illustrated by the **reversible figure** in Figure 8.23, where at any given moment you may see either a white vase against a dark ground or two dark profiles against a white ground. In line with the Gestalt figure-ground principle, the same part of the figure cannot simultaneously be both figure and ground, and thus at any instant you may see either the vase or the faces, but not both.

19 ---------

How do reversible figures illustrate the visual system's strong tendency to separate figure and ground, even in the absence of sufficient cues for deciding which is which?

FIGURE 8.23 Reversible figure Because it lacks strong cues as to which is figure and which is ground, this image—developed by the Danish Gestalt psychologist Edgar Rubin—may be seen either as a white vase against a dark ground or as two dark profiles against a white ground. If you stare at it, your perception may alternate between the two.

Stefano Scala/Tips Images

Evidence That Wholes Can Affect the Perception of Parts

When you look at a visual scene, the elementary stimulus features certainly affect your perception of the whole, but the converse is also true: The whole affects your perception of the features. Without your conscious awareness, and at a speed measurable in milliseconds, your visual system uses the sensory input from a scene to draw inferences about what is actually present—a process referred to as **unconscious inference.** Once your visual system has hit upon a particular solution to the problem of what is there, it may actually create or distort features in ways that are consistent with that inference. Examples of such creations and distortions are illusory contours and illusory lightness differences.

Illusory Contours

Look at Figure 8.24. You probably see a solid white triangle sitting atop some other objects. The contour of the white triangle appears to continue across the white space between the other objects. This is not simply a misperception caused by a fleeting glance. The longer you look at the whole stimulus, the more convinced you may become that the contour (border) between the white triangle and the white background is really there; the triangle seems *whiter* than the background. But if you try to see the contour isolated from the rest of the stimulus, by covering the black portions with your fingers or pieces of paper, you will find that the contour isn't really there. The white triangle and its border are illusions.

────────────────────── **20**

How do illusory contours illustrate the idea that the whole influences the perception of parts? How are illusory contours explained in terms of unconscious inference?
──────────────────────

The white triangle, with its illusory contour, apparently emerges from the brain's attempt to make sense of the sensory input (Parks & Rock, 1990). The most elegant interpretation of the figure—consistent with the Gestalt principle of good form and with expectations drawn from everyday experience—is to assume that it contains a white triangle lying atop a black triangular frame and three black disks. That is certainly simpler and more likely than the alternative possibility—three disks with wedges removed from them and three unconnected black angles, all oriented with their openings aimed at a common center. According to this unconscious-inference explanation, the perceptual system uses the initial stimulus input to infer that a white triangle must be present (because that makes the most sense), and then it *creates* the white triangle, by influencing contour-detection processes in the brain in such a way as to produce a border where one does not physically exist in the stimulus.

Illusory contours cannot be explained in simple stimulus terms, having to do, for example, with the amount of actual lined-up contour existing in the figure. Many experiments have shown that people are more likely to see illusory contours in cases where they are needed to make sense of the figure than in cases where they are not, even when the amount of actual dark-light border is constant (Hoffman, 1998; Gillam & Chan, 2002). For an example, look at Figure 8.25. Most people see an illusory contour, outlining a white square, more clearly in pattern b than in pattern a, even though the actual black-white borders at the corners of the imagined white square are identical in the two figures. The unconscious-inference explanation of this is that the white square is more needed in b than in a to make sense of the stimulus input. The arrangement of four black angular objects in a is more likely to occur in everyday experience than is the arrangement of four disks with wedges cut out in b.

FIGURE 8.24 Illusory contour In response to this stimulus, the perceptual system creates a white triangle, the borders of which appear to continue across the white page, such that the triangle seems whiter than the white page.

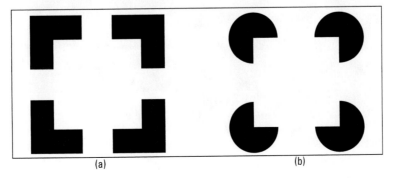

(a) (b)

FIGURE 8.25 Which pattern shows the clearer illusory contour? Most people see an illusory contour (outlining a white square) more clearly in pattern (b) than in pattern (a), a finding that is consistent with the unconscious-inference explanation of pattern perception. (Based on Hoffman, 1998, p. 58.)

Illusory Lightness Differences

In Figure 8.26, most people see the small gray square on the left as lighter than the one on the right. In reality, the two squares are identical in lightness: They are exactly the same shade of gray. A common explanation of this illusion is similar to that discussed earlier for contour enhancement. The right-hand square may appear darker because the neurons that respond to it are inhibited by nearby neurons, which are strongly stimulated by the greater amount of light surrounding the square. The left-hand square may appear lighter because its dark surround produces relatively little lateral inhibition.

21 ‒ ‒ ‒ ‒ ‒ ‒ ‒ ‒ ‒ ‒ ‒ ‒ ‒ ‒ ‒ ‒ ‒ ◄ However, not everyone agrees that such lightness illusions can be explained by simple lateral inhibition. Dale Purves and his colleagues (2004) have argued that more complex processes, involving unconscious inference, must be involved. These researchers suggest that the illusion depicted in Figure 8.26 may derive from the brain's unconscious inference that the left-hand portion of the figure is in a shadow, or for some other reason is receiving less light than is the

What is some evidence that illusory lightness differences cannot be fully explained by lateral inhibition? How can such differences be explained in terms of unconscious inference?

right-hand portion. In order to compensate for the reduced light, the brain may respond in a way that lightens the appearance of any object in the left-hand portion. This explanation is supported by the observation that the contrast effect is even stronger in realistic scenes and photographs where it is obvious that one object is in a shadow and another is not, as illustrated in Figure 8.27. Notice that the "illusion" in Figure 8.27 gives us a more accurate understanding of the

FIGURE 8.26 A lightness illusion The small gray square on the left looks lighter than that on the right, but the two squares are actually identical in lightness. The lateral-inhibition theory of this illusion has been challenged by evidence such as that illustrated in Figures 8.27 and 8.28.

objects in question (tiles A and B) than we would obtain if our visual system recorded the physical properties of the reflected light without taking the whole scene into account.

The strongest support for unconscious-inference explanations of lightness illusions comes from examples that run directly counter to what would be expected from simple lateral inhibition. In Figure 8.28 (on page 291), the gray patches on the left appear to be lighter than those on the right, when, in reality, all of the gray

FIGURE 8.27 Lightness contrast in a real scene In this photograph (from Purves & others, 2002) tile A looks white and tile B looks dark gray. In reality, the light reflected from the two tiles is an identical shade of gray. You can prove this to yourself by cutting two small holes in a sheet of paper, the appropriate distance apart, and positioning them over the tiles to compare them without seeing the rest of the picture. In this example the perception that tile A is lighter than tile B gives us useful, real-world information. In reality, tile A is white and tile B is dark gray. They reflect the same amount of light only because tile A is in a shadow and tile B is in bright light. Our visual system takes the shadow and the bright light into account and adjusts the perceived lightness of the tiles appropriately.

Courtesy of Daniel Purves, MD, and R. Beau Lotto, MD

patches are physically identical to one another. This illusion cannot be explained in any straightforward way by lateral inhibition. The patches on the left are actually surrounded by more white and less black than are those on the right, so the lateral-inhibition theory would predict that those on the left should appear darker, not lighter, than those on the right. The illusion must result from some more complex analysis of the scene. One possible explanation, in terms of unconscious inference, is that the visual system interprets the left-hand patches to be parts of a vertical stripe painted down the rails of a fence (or something like a fence) and interprets the right-hand patches to be visible portions of a post that stands behind the fence. Given this interpretation, the relevant background for the painted stripe is the set of black rails, and the relevant background for the post is the white space behind the fence. To make the stripe and the post stand out more clearly from their respective backgrounds, the visual system lightens the stripe and darkens the post.

FIGURE 8.28 Lightness contrast that can't be explained by lateral inhibition The gray patches on the left appear lighter than the physically identical patches on the right. This illusion is the opposite of what one would expect from lateral inhibition.

Unconscious Inference Involves Top-Down Control Within the Brain

When psychologists explain perceptual phenomena in terms of unconscious inference, they do not mean to imply that these phenomena result from anything other than neural processes in the brain. All reasoning, unconscious or conscious, is a product of neural activity. Unconscious-inference theories imply that the phenomena in question result from neural activity in higher brain areas, which are able to bring together the pieces of sensory information and make complex calculations concerning them.

Neuroscientists have learned that the connections between the primary visual area and higher visual areas in the brain are not one-way. The higher areas receive essential input from the primary visual area, but they also feed back to that area and influence neural activity there. Thus, complex calculations made in perceptual portions of the temporal, parietal, and frontal lobes (discussed later) can feed back to the primary visual area in the occipital lobe and influence the activity of feature detectors there. Researchers have found, for example, that visual stimuli that produce illusory contours activate edge-detector neurons, in the primary visual cortex, that are receiving input from precisely that part of the stimulus where the illusory contour is seen (Albert, 2007; Lee, 2002). In this case, the activity of the edge detector is not the direct result of input from the optic nerve to the edge detector, but, rather, is the result of descending connections from higher visual centers that have determined that there *should* be an edge at that location.

Brain scientists and perceptual psychologists refer to control that comes from higher up in the brain as **top-down control,** and they refer to control that comes more directly from the sensory input as **bottom-up control.** Perception always involves interplay between bottom-up and top-down control in the brain. Bottom-up processes bring in the sensory information that is actually present in the stimulus. Top-down processes bring to bear the results of calculations based on that sensory information plus other information, such as that derived from previous experience and from the larger context in which the stimulus appears. Remember, all these calculations are being conducted by a calculating machine—the human brain—that is vastly more complex and powerful than any nonbiological computer that humans have developed.

22

How is unconscious inference described as top-down control within the brain? What is the difference between top-down and bottom-up control?

A central purpose of the human visual system is to identify objects.

Contour Enhancement	Integration of Features	Gestalt Principles	Top-Down Processes
➤ An object's shape is defined by its contour, the edge between it and its background. ➤ Lateral inhibition among sensory neurons heightens the perceived contrast in lightness at contours. This helps us see objects' shapes.	➤ Neurons in the primary visual cortex and nearby areas are maximally responsive to specific visual features—such as particular line orientations, movements, and colors. ➤ Behavioral evidence suggests that features are detected through rapid parallel processing and then are integrated spatially through serial processing.	➤ Gestalt psychologists asserted that whole objects are not merely the sums of their parts and that wholes take precedence in conscious perception. ➤ The Gestalt principles of grouping describe rules by which we automatically organize stimulus elements into wholes. ➤ We also automatically separate figure from ground.	➤ Wholes influence our perception of parts through unconscious inference, as illustrated by illusory contours and illusory lightness differences. ➤ The effects of unconscious inference occur through top-down control mechanisms in the brain.

■ Recognizing Objects

To recognize an object is to categorize it: "It's a bird, it's a plane, it's Superman!" To recognize an object visually, we must form a visual perception of it that we can match to our stored definition, or understanding, of the appropriate object category. We normally do this so naturally and easily that we fail to think of the extraordinary complexity of the task. Computer scientists have, to date, been unable to develop artificial visual systems that come anywhere close to our ability to recognize objects.

In a famous essay entitled "The Man Who Mistook His Wife for a Hat," the neurologist Oliver Sacks (1970) described the plight of one of his patients, who, as a result of brain damage caused by a stroke, could no longer recognize objects by sight. He could still see colors, textures, lines, and shapes; he could describe in exquisite detail the shapes he saw; and he could recognize objects using other senses, such as touch and smell. But the step that normally leads so naturally from seeing shapes to seeing familiar, recognizable objects was completely missing in him.

When Sacks showed the man a rose and asked him to identify it, the man responded by trying to figure out, aloud, what it was from the shapes and colors he saw: "About six inches in length," he said. "A convoluted red form with a linear green attachment. It lacks the simple symmetry of the Platonic solids, although it may have a higher symmetry of its own. . . ." After several minutes of such erudite discourse about the object's parts, the man finally guessed, uncertainly, that it might be some kind of flower. Then Sacks asked him to smell it. "Beautiful!" he exclaimed. "An early rose. What a heavenly smell!" He could tell a rose by smell but not by sight, even though he could see and describe each of its parts in terms of geometry and color.

Perceptual researchers don't know how the normal brain sees and identifies a rose or any other object so easily, but many are working on that problem. Here I will describe some of that work and some ideas that have emerged from it.

Piecing Together the Parts to See the Whole

Logically, for us to see and recognize an object such as a rose, the brain must somehow pick up, from the optic nerves' input, the relevant features of the object and integrate those features into a perceptual whole, which can be matched with stored representations of familiar object categories. Some years ago, Irving Biederman developed the *recognition-by-components theory* of object perception. The theory did not specify *how* the brain does what it does, but did specify *what* the brain must do in order to recognize objects. Although developed more than 20 ago, the theory still underlies much research on object recognition (Peissig & Tarr, 2007).

Biederman's Recognition-by-Components Theory

A basic problem in object perception lies in the fact that the image an object projects onto our retinas varies greatly depending on the object's orientation with respect to our line of sight. An airplane, for example, projects very different images depending on whether we view it from the side, top, or front (see Figure 8.29); yet, in every case we recognize it as an airplane. Biederman's recognition-by-components theory is an attempt to explain how we see an object as the same object regardless of its orientation.

According to the theory, to recognize an object our visual system first organizes the stimulus information into a set of basic, three-dimensional components, which Biederman referred to as *geons*, and then it uses the arrangement of those components to recognize the object. An airplane, no matter how it is positioned relative to our eyes, always consists of the same set of geons, arranged in the same manner with respect to one another. If we can see the geons and their arrangement, then, according to Biederman, we have the information necessary for identifying the object.

On the basis of fundamental properties of three-dimensional geometry, Biederman proposed that there are 36 different geons, some of which are illustrated in Figure 8.30 (on page 294). By smoothing the edges and ignoring the details, according to Biederman, we can depict any object as a small subset of such geons organized

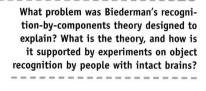

23

What problem was Biederman's recognition-by-components theory designed to explain? What is the theory, and how is it supported by experiments on object recognition by people with intact brains?

FIGURE 8.29 **It's a plane no matter how you look at it** Theories of object perception must account for the fact that we can see an object as the same object, even though its outline is very different depending on the orientation from which we view it.

FIGURE 8.30 Some geons From principles of geometry, Biederman developed a list of 36 simple, three-dimensional forms, which he labeled "geons," six of which are shown here. He suggests that geons provide the basic perceptual components of more complex forms.

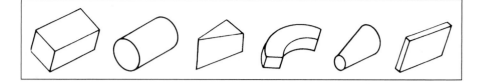

in a certain way. You may already be familiar with this general idea from experience with learn-to-draw books that recommend sketching any object as a set of three-dimensional geometric shapes before fleshing it out with details. To see an object, according to Biederman, the visual system first integrates the elementary stimulus features in such a way as to detect the geons, then integrates the geons in such a way as to identify the object. These integrative processes occur unconsciously. We consciously perceive the object, seemingly immediately and effortlessly, blissfully unaware of the complex mental calculations that permit us to do so.

You might think of Biederman's geons as analogous to letters of the alphabet. Just as a finite number of letters can be arranged in different ways to form an infinite number of words, a finite number of geons can be arranged in different ways to form an infinite number of objects. When you read words, your brain must unconsciously identify the letters and their arrangement for you to identify each word. When you "read" the world of visual objects, your brain must unconsciously identify the geons and their arrangement for you to identify each object.

Some of Biederman's evidence for the theory comes from studies showing that object recognition by normal, brain-intact people depends on their ability to detect at least some of the object's geons and their arrangement. In one series of experiments, Biederman (1987) asked people to identify objects in pictures that were flashed briefly on a screen. He found that the speed and accuracy of recognizing any given object depended very much on the intactness and arrangement of an object's geons and very little on other aspects of the stimulus, such as the amount of detail occurring within the geons or the exterior outline of the object as a whole. Figure 8.31 shows some of the stimuli that Biederman used. The airplane in Figure 8.31a was recognized as an airplane even when some of its geons were removed, thereby changing its overall outline, as long as the geons still present were intact and properly arranged. The various objects in Figure 8.31b were recognized when the lines were degraded in ways that preserved the recognizability of individual

FIGURE 8.31 Support for Biederman's recognition-by-components theory Part (a) shows an airplane consisting of nine, four, or two components (geons). Even with just a few components present, it is recognizable. Part (b) shows a set of line drawings of objects degraded in two different ways. The degradation in the middle column preserves the connections between adjacent components, and that in the right-hand column does not. When subjects saw the degraded figures alone, they recognized those in the middle column but not those in the right-hand column.

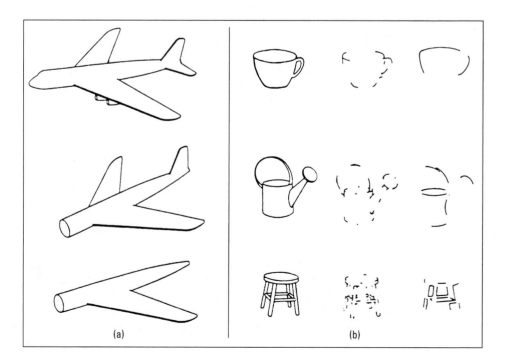

(a)   (b)

geons and their connections to one another (middle column), but not when the same amount of line degradation occurred in ways that obscured the geons and their connections (right-hand column).

Evidence from People Who Suffer from Visual Agnosias

Further support for Biederman's theory comes from observations of people who, after a stroke or other source of brain damage, can still see but can no longer make sense of what they see, a condition called *visual agnosia.* It's interesting to note that the term *agnosia* was coined in the late nineteenth century by Sigmund Freud, who then was a young, little-known neurologist (Goodale & Milner, 2004). Freud derived the term from the Greek words *a*, meaning not, and *gnosia*, meaning knowledge. People with visual agnosia can see, but they do not know what they are seeing.

▷ - - - - - - - - - - - - - - - - - - - **24**

How is the recognition-by-components theory supported by the existence of two types of visual deficits caused by brain damage?

Visual agnosias have been classified into a number of general types (Farah, 1989; Milner & Goodale, 1995), of which two are most relevant here. People with *visual form agnosia* can see that something is present and can identify some of its elements, such as its color and brightness, but cannot perceive its shape. They are unable to describe or draw the outlines of objects or patterns that they are shown (see Figure 8.32). In contrast, people with *visual object agnosia* can describe and draw the shapes of objects that they are shown, but still cannot identify the objects. For instance, when shown an apple and asked to draw it, such a person might produce a drawing that you and I would recognize as an apple, but would still be unable to say what it was. This is the kind of agnosia that characterized Oliver Saks's patient, who could see and describe all the parts of a rose but could not identify it as a rose until he smelled it. Another patient with visual object agnosia described a bicycle that he was shown as a pole and two circles, but he could not identify it as a bicycle or guess what purpose it serves (Hécaen & Albert, 1978).

The existence of these two types of agnosia, as distinct disorders, is consistent with Biederman's recognition-by-components theory and thereby lends support to the theory. The theory posits that recognition of an object occurs through the following sequence:

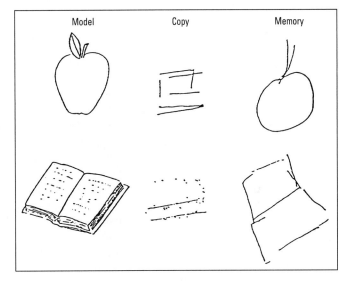

FIGURE 8.32 Drawings made by a person with visual form agnosia The patient D. F. was unable to recognize the drawings on the left. When she was asked to try to copy them, she produced drawings (middle column) that bore no resemblance to the originals. When asked to draw an apple and a book from memory, however, she succeeded (right-hand column). Later, when she was shown the drawings she had produced from memory, she had no idea what they represented. (From Milner & Goodale, 1995, p. 127.)

$$\text{pick-up of sensory features} \longrightarrow \text{detection of geons} \longrightarrow \text{recognition of object}$$

The two arrows represent two different steps of integration. People with visual form agnosia are unable to carry out the step indicated by the first arrow. They can see elementary sensory features but can't integrate them into larger shapes (geons). People with visual object agnosia, in contrast, can carry out the first step but not the second. They can see the three-dimensional components of objects but can't integrate them to identify the objects.

Two Streams of Visual Processing in the Brain

In recent years researchers have found out a great deal about the neural mechanisms that are involved in higher-order visual processing. The primary visual cortex, which occupies the rearmost part of the occipital lobe, sends its output to (and receives feedback from) many other visual-processing areas, which occupy the rest of the occipital lobe and extend forward into much of the temporal and parietal lobes. The visual areas beyond the primary area exist in two relatively distinct cortical pathways, or "streams," which serve different functions (Konen & Kasner, 2008). As shown in Figure 8.33, one stream runs into the lower portion of the temporal lobe and the other runs upward into the parietal lobe.

▷ - - - - - - - - - - - - - - - - - - - **25**

What are the anatomical and functional distinctions between two different visual pathways in the cerebral cortex?

FIGURE 8.33 The "what" and "where-and-how" visual pathways Neurons in the primary visual area send output into two relatively distinct streams for further visual processing. The "what" pathway, into the lower temporal lobe, is specialized for perceiving shapes and identifying objects. The "where-and-how" pathway, into the parietal lobe, is specialized for perceiving spatial relationships and for guiding actions.

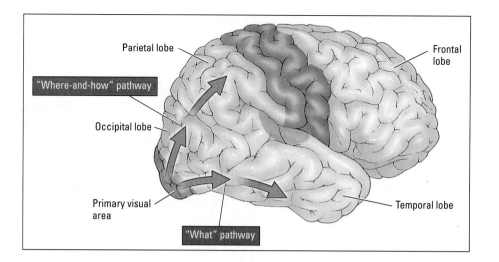

The lower, temporal stream, often referred to as the *"what" pathway,* is specialized for identifying objects. Damage in this stream, on both sides of the brain, can result in the types of visual agnosias that we have just been discussing, in which people cannot tell what they are looking at. Experiments involving single-cell recording in monkeys and fMRI in humans have shown that neurons in this pathway typically respond best to complex geometric shapes and to whole objects, in ways that are quite consistent with the recognition-by-components theory (Grill-Spector & Sayres, 2008; Yamane & others, 2008).

The upper, parietal stream is commonly referred to as the *"where" pathway,* because it is specialized for maintaining a map of three-dimensional space and localizing objects within that space. More recently, researchers have found that this pathway is also crucial for the use of visual information to guide a person's movements (Goodale, 2007). Neurons in this pathway are concerned not just with *where* the object is located, but also with *how* the person must move in order to pick up the object, or move around it, or interact with it in some other way. For this reason, I use the label "where-and-how," rather than just "where," to refer to the parietal pathway. (Look again at Figure 8.33.)

Effects of Damage in the "What" Pathway

26
What abilities are preserved in people with damage to the "what" pathway but lost in people with damage to the "where-and-how" pathway?

People with damage in specific portions of the "what" pathway on both sides of the brain generally suffer from deficits in ability to make conscious sense of what they see, depending on just where the damage is. The examples of visual agnosias that I already described resulted from damage in this pathway. An interesting further observation concerning such patients is that they retain the ability to reach accurately for objects and act on them in coordinated ways, guided by vision, even if they can't consciously see the objects.

A dramatic example is the case of a woman known as D. F., the same person whose drawings are reproduced in Figure 8.32, who has been extensively studied by Melvyn Goodale (2007) and his colleagues. This woman suffers from very severe visual form agnosia, stemming from carbon monoxide poisoning that destroyed portions of the "what" pathway close to the primary visual area on both sides of her brain. Despite her complete inability to perceive consciously the shapes of objects, D. F. responds to objects in ways that take into account shape as well as size, position, and movement. When she walks, she moves around obstacles with ease. She is good at catching objects that are thrown to her, even though she can't consciously see the object coming toward her. When asked to pick up a novel object placed in front of her, she moves her hand in just the correct way to grasp the object efficiently.

In one experiment, D. F. was shown an upright disk with a slot cut through it (Goodale & Milner, 2004). She claimed to be unable to see the orientation of the slot and, indeed, when she was asked to hold a card at the same angle as the slot, her accuracy (over several trials with the slot at varying orientations) was no better than chance. But when she was asked to slip the card into the slot as if mailing a letter, she did so quickly and accurately on every trial, holding the card at just the right orientation before it reached the slot. She could not use conscious perception to guide her hand, but her hand moved correctly when she wasn't trying to use conscious perception to guide it. Apparently the "where-and-how" pathway, which was intact in this woman, is capable of calculating the sizes and shapes of objects, as well as their places, but does not make that information available to the conscious mind.

Effects of Damage in the "Where-and-How" Pathway

Damage in the "where-and-how" pathway—in the upper parts of the occipital and parietal lobes of the cortex—interferes most strongly with people's abilities to use vision to guide their actions. People with damage here have relatively little or no difficulty identifying objects that they see, and often they can describe verbally where the object is located, but they have great difficulty using visual input to co-ordinate their movements. They lose much of their ability to follow moving objects with their eyes or hands, to move around obstacles, or to reach out and pick objects up in an efficient manner (Goodale & Milner, 2004; Schindler & others, 2004). Even though they can consciously see and describe an object verbally and report its general location, they reach for it gropingly, much as a blind person does. They frequently miss the object by a few inches, then move their hand around until they touch it (see Figure 8.34). Only when they have touched the object do they begin to close their fingers around it to pick it up.

FIGURE 8.34 Efficient and inefficient reaching for an object People with damage to the "what" pathway reach for an object in the efficient manner depicted in (a), even though they can't consciously see the object's shape. In contrast, people with damage to the "where-and-how" pathway reach in the inefficient, groping manner depicted in (b), even though they can consciously see the object's shape.

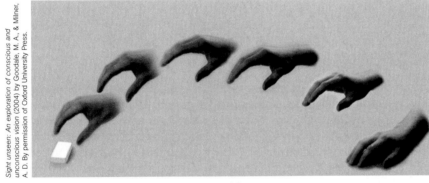

Sight unseen: An exploration of conscious and unconscious vision (2004) by Goodale, M. A., & Milner, A. D. By permission of Oxford University Press.

(a)

(b)

Complementary Functions of the Two Visual Pathways in the Intact Brain

The two just-described visual pathways apparently evolved to serve different but complementary functions. The "what" pathway provides most of our conscious vision. It provides the input that allows us to see and identify objects consciously, to talk about those objects, to make conscious plans concerning them, and to form conscious memories of them. In contrast, the "where-and-how" pathway provides the input that is needed for the automatic, rapid, and largely unconscious visual control of our movements with respect to objects. This pathway is able to register the shape of an object to the degree that shape is necessary for effectively reaching for and picking up the object, but it does not register shape in a manner that enters consciousness.

Think for a moment about the unconscious roles that vision plays in your movements. As you follow a moving object with your eyes, your eye movements are constantly guided by visual input. As you walk through a world of objects, you automatically use visual input to stay on your path and avoid bumping into things. You can demonstrate the unconscious operation of your "where-and-how" pathway

27

In sum, what are the distinct functions of the "what" and "where-and-how" visual pathways?

with a simple exercise. If you focus your eyes at a specific point and someone places an object in your peripheral vision, far enough away from your direct line of sight that you can just barely see that something is there but can't make out its size and shape, you can, without moving your eyes, reach out and grab that object, accurately and without fumbling (Goodale & Murphy, 1997). As you do this, you make hand movements that are well attuned to the object's size and shape, even though you can't consciously see that size and shape. The visual pathway that guides your hand has enough information about the size and shape of the object, as well as its location, to allow you to reach for it effectively, but that information does not enter your consciousness.

SECTION REVIEW

To identify an object, we must perceive it well enough to match it to a stored representation.

Recognition by Components	Two Streams of Visual Processing
➤ Objects can be understood visually as sets of geons (basic three-dimensional shapes) arranged in specific ways.	➤ Visual processing beyond the primary visual cortex in the occipital lobe takes place along two independent streams (pathways)—a "what" stream leading into the temporal lobe, and a "where-and-how" stream leading into the parietal lobe.
➤ Biederman's theory holds that the visual system integrates features to detect geons and integrates geons to identify objects.	
➤ The theory is supported by recognition experiments with normal subjects and through observations of people with visual form agnosia and visual object agnosia.	➤ Bilateral damage to parts of the "what" stream impairs conscious object recognition but preserves the ability to use vision to direct physical actions with respect to objects, such as grasping or moving around objects. Bilateral damage to the "where-and-how" stream has the opposite effect.

■ Seeing in Three Dimensions

One of the great early puzzles of vision, about which philosophers speculated for centuries, was that of depth perception. We automatically, effortlessly, see the world in three dimensions. Objects occupy and move in space that includes not only a vertical (up-down) and a horizontal (right-left) dimension but also a dimension of depth, or distance from our eyes. Our retinas and the images that are projected on them are two-dimensional. It is relatively easy to understand how our retinas might record the vertical and horizontal dimensions of our visual world, but how do they record the third dimension, that of depth?

28
How did Helmholtz describe perception as a problem-solving process?

◄ A major step toward answering this question was the publication of a treatise on vision, in the mid-nineteenth century, by Hermann von Helmholtz (1867/1962), the same German physiologist who developed the trichromatic theory of color vision.

Hermann von Helmholtz Considered by many to be the greatest of all nineteenth-century physiologists, Helmholtz was also a pioneer of what we now call cognitive psychology. His unconscious-inference theory of perception posits that the mind constructs, through unconscious calculations, meaningful percepts from cues picked up by the senses.

The Granger Collection

He argued that seeing is an active mental process. The light focused onto our retinas is not the scene we see but is simply a source of hints about the scene. Our brain infers the characteristics and positions of objects from cues in the reflected light, and those inferences are our perceptions. Helmholtz pointed out that the steps in this inferential process can be expressed mathematically, in equations relating information in the reflected light to conclusions about the positions, sizes, and shapes of objects in the visual scene. We are not conscious of these calculations and inferences; our brain works them out quickly and automatically, without our awareness.

Helmholtz was the first scientist to use the term *unconscious inference* to describe visual perception. Earlier in the chapter you read about unconscious inferences that affect the perception of an object's contours and lightness. Now, in the more direct tradition of Helmholtz, let us examine how unconscious inferences may underlie our ability to perceive the depths and sizes of objects.

Cues for Depth Perception

Depth perception works best when you use both eyes. You can prove that with a simple demonstration. Pick up two pencils and hold them in front of you, one in each hand, with their points toward each other. Close one eye and move the pencils toward each other to make the points touch at their tips. Chances are, you will miss by a little bit on your first attempt, and your subsequent adjustments will have something of a trial-and-error quality. Now repeat the task with both eyes open. Is it easier? Do you find that now you can see more clearly which adjustments to make to bring the points together and that you no longer need trial and error? You can see depth reasonably well with one eye alone, but you can see it better with both eyes together.

Binocular Cues for Depth

Two types of cues contribute to the binocular (two-eye) advantage. The less important is *eye convergence*, the inward turning of the eyes that occurs when you look at an object that is close to you. The closer an object is, the more the two eyes must converge in order to focus on it. To experience eye convergence consciously, try focusing both eyes on your finger as you move it slowly from arm lengths to a few inches in front of your nose. In theory, the perceptual system could judge the distance of an object from the degree to which the eyes converge when looking at it. In practice, however, researchers have found that eye convergence is a poor distance cue even for objects close to the eyes and a useless one for objects more than a few feet away (Arditi, 1986; Hochberg, 1971).

The other, far more important cue requiring two eyes is **binocular disparity,** which refers to the slightly different (disparate) views that the two eyes have of the same object or scene. Because the eyes are a few centimeters apart, they view any given object from slightly different angles. To see how the degree of binocular disparity varies depending on an object's distance from your eyes, hold your index finger about a foot in front of your eyes with a wall in the background. Look at your finger with just your right eye open, then with just your left eye open, alternately back and forth. As you alternate between the two eyes, your finger appears to jump back and forth with respect to the background wall. That is because each eye views the finger from a different angle. Now move your finger farther away (out to full arm's length), and notice that your view of it jumps a smaller distance with respect to the wall as you again alternate between right-eye and left-eye views. The farther your finger is from your eyes, the smaller is the difference in the angle between each eye and the finger; the two lines of sight become increasingly parallel.

Thus, the degree of disparity between the two eyes' views can serve as a cue to judge an object's distance from the eyes: The less the disparity, the greater the distance. In normal, binocular vision your brain fuses the two eyes' views to give a

29
How does binocular disparity serve as a cue for depth?

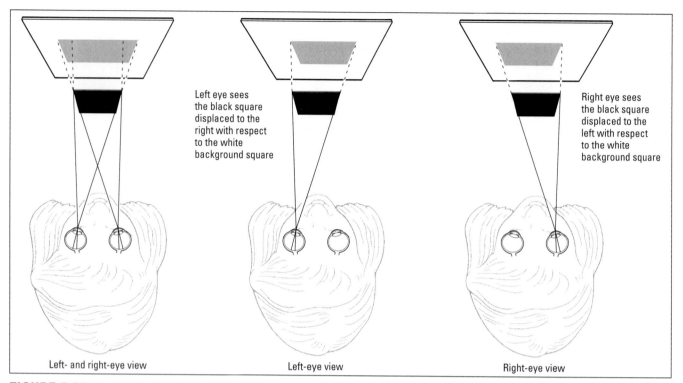

Left eye sees the black square displaced to the right with respect to the white background square

Right eye sees the black square displaced to the left with respect to the white background square

Left- and right-eye view   Left-eye view   Right-eye view

FIGURE 8.35 Demonstration of **binocular disparity** The two eyes see somewhat different views of the relationship between the closer figure and the more distant figure. The disparity (degree of difference) between the two views is proportional to the distance between the two objects, and that information is used by the perceptual system to perceive the depth between them.

30

How do stereoscopes provide an illusion of depth?

perception of depth. Helmholtz (1867/1962) showed mathematically how the difference in two objects' distance from the eyes can be calculated from differences in the degree of binocular disparity. More recently, researchers have found that neurons in an area of the visual cortex close to the primary visual area respond best to stimuli that are presented to both eyes at slightly disparate locations on the retina (Thomas & others, 2002). These neurons appear to be ideally designed to permit depth perception. For another demonstration of binocular disparity, see Figure 8.35.

Illusions of Depth Created by Binocular Disparity

The ability to see depth from binocular disparity—an ability called stereopsis—was first demonstrated in the early nineteenth century by Charles Wheatstone (described by Helmholtz, 1867/1962). Wheatstone wondered what would happen if he drew two slightly different pictures of the same object or scene, one as seen by the left eye and one as seen by the right, and then viewed them simultaneously, each with the appropriate eye. To permit such viewing, he invented a device called a *stereoscope*. The effect was dramatic. When viewed through the stereoscope, the two pictures were fused perceptually into a single image containing depth.

Stereoscopes became a great fad in the late nineteenth century. People could see scenes such as Buckingham Palace or the Grand Canyon in full depth by plac-

An old-fashioned stereoscope The two photos on the card are from slightly different perspectives. The stereoscope presents each photo to a different eye, and the visual system fuses the two into a single three-dimensional image.

ing cards that contained two photographs of the same scene, shot simultaneously from slightly different angles, into their stereoscope. (The Viewmaster, a well-known child's toy, is a modern example of a stereoscope.) Three-dimensional motion pictures and comic books employ the same general principle. In the simplest versions, each frame of the film or comic strip contains an overlapping pair of similar images, each in a different color, one slightly displaced from the other, and the viewer wears colored glasses that allow

Leonard Lessin/Peter Arnold Inc.

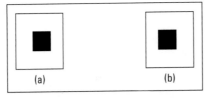

FIGURE 8.36 A depth illusion created by binocular disparity The two patterns are constructed to appear as they would to the left and right eye, respectively, if the dark square were actually a certain distance in front of the white square (like that shown in Figure 8.35). In order to experience the three-dimensional effect, hold the book about a foot in front of your eyes and let your eyes drift in an unfocused way until you see double images of everything. You will see four renditions of the white frame with a darker square center—two renditions of (a) and two of (b). When all four of these images are clear, converge or diverge your eyes a little in order to get the right-hand image of (a) to sit right atop the left-hand image of (b). You have fused your left-eye view of (a) and your right-eye view of (b) into a single image, which now appears to be three-dimensional: The dark square seems to float in space in front of the white square.

only one image to enter each eye. You can demonstrate stereopsis without any special viewer by looking at the two patterns in Figure 8.36 in the manner described in the caption.

Monocular Cues for Depth

Although depth perception is most vivid with two eyes, it is by no means absent with one. People who have just one functioning eye can drive cars, shoot basketballs, and reach out and pick objects up without fumbling around.

Motion Parallax Perhaps the most valuable monocular (one-eye) cue for depth is *motion parallax,* which refers to the changed view one has of a scene or object when one's head moves sideways. To demonstrate motion parallax, hold your finger up in front of your face and view it with one eye as you rock your head back and forth. As your head moves, you gain different views of the finger, and you see it being displaced back and forth with respect to the wall in the background. If you now move your finger farther away from your eye, the same head movement produces a less changed view. Thus, the degree of change in either eye's view at one moment compared with the next, as the head moves in space, can serve as a cue for assessing the object's distance from the eyes: The smaller the change, the greater the distance.

As you can infer from this demonstration, motion parallax is very similar to binocular disparity. In fact, binocular disparity is sometimes called *binocular parallax.* The word *parallax* refers to the apparent change in an object or scene that occurs when it is viewed from a new vantage point. In motion parallax the changed vantage point comes from the movement of the head, and in binocular parallax (or disparity) it comes from the separation of the two eyes.

Pictorial Cues Motion parallax depends on the geometry of true three-dimensionality and cannot be used to depict depth in two-dimensional pictures. All the remaining monocular depth cues, however, can provide a sense of depth in pictures as well as in the real three-dimensional world, and thus they are called ***pictorial cues for depth.*** You can identify some of these by examining Figure 8.37 and considering all the reasons why you see some objects in the scene as standing in the foreground and others as more distant. The pictorial cues include the following.

1. *Occlusion* The trees occlude (cut off from view) part of the mountains, which indicates that the trees are closer to us than are the mountains. Near objects occlude more distant ones.

2. *Relative image size for familiar objects* The image of the woman (both in the picture and on the viewer's retina) is taller than that of the mountains. Because we know that people are not taller than mountains, we take the woman's larger image as a sign that she must be closer to us than are the mountains.

31

How does motion parallax serve as a cue for depth, and how is it similar to binocular disparity?

32

What are some cues for depth that exist in pictures as well as in the actual, three-dimensional world?

FIGURE 8.37 Pictorial cues for depth Depth cues in this picture include occlusion, relative image size for familiar objects, linear perspective, texture gradient, position relative to the horizon, and differential lighting of surfaces.

3. *Linear perspective* The rows of plants converge (come closer together) as they go from the bottom toward the mountains, indicating that objects toward the mountains are farther away. Parallel lines appear to converge as they become more distant.

4. *Texture gradient* Texture elements in the picture—specifically, the individual dots of color representing the flowers—are smaller and more densely packed near the trees and mountains than they are at the bottom of the picture. In general, a gradual decrease in the size and spacing of texture elements indicates depth.

5. *Position relative to the horizon* The trees are closer to the horizon than is the woman, indicating that they are farther away. In outdoor scenes, objects nearer the horizon are usually farther away than those that are displaced from the horizon in either direction (either below it or above it). If there were clouds in this picture, those seen just above the edge where the earth and sky meet (close to the horizon) would be seen as farther away than those seen farther up in the picture (farther from the horizon).

6. *Differential lighting of surfaces* In real three-dimensional scenes the amount of light reflected from different surfaces varies as a function of their orientation with respect to the sun or other source of light. The fact that the sides of the rows of lavender are darker than the tops leads us to see the rows as three-dimensional rather than flat. We see the brightest parts of the plants as their tops, closest to us (as we look down on them); and we see the darker parts as their sides, shaded by the tops, and farther from us. For an even more dramatic demonstration of an effect of lighting, see Figure 8.38 and follow the directions in its caption.

FIGURE 8.38 Depth perception created by light and shade Because we automatically assume that the light is coming from above, we see the smaller disruptions on the surface here as bumps and the larger ones as pits. Turn the picture upside down and see what happens. (The bumps and pits reverse.)

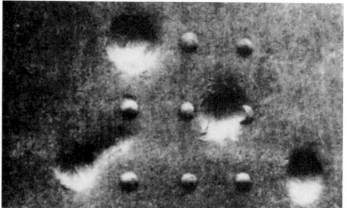

The Role of Depth Cues in Size Perception

The ability to judge the size of an object is intimately tied to the ability to judge its distance. As Figure 8.39 illustrates, the size of the retinal image of an object is inversely proportional to the object's distance from the retina. Thus, if an object is moved twice as far away, it produces a retinal image half the height and width of the one it produced before. You don't see the object as smaller, though; just farther away.

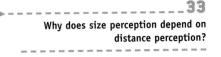
Why does size perception depend on distance perception?

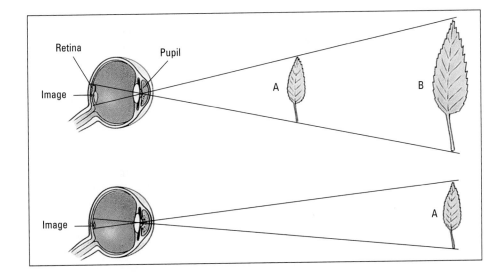

FIGURE 8.39 Relationship of retinal-image size to object size and distance If, as in the upper sketch, object B is twice as tall and wide as object A and also twice as far from the eye, the retinal images that the two objects produce will be the same size. If, as in the lower sketch, object A is moved twice its former distance from the eye, the retinal image produced will be half its former height and width.

The ability to see an object as unchanged in size, despite change in the image size as it moves farther away or closer, is called *size constancy.* For familiar objects, such as a pencil or a car, previous knowledge of the object's usual size may contribute to size constancy. But size constancy also occurs for unfamiliar objects if cues for distance are available, and even familiar objects can appear to be drastically altered in size if misleading distance cues are present (for an example, see Figure 8.40).

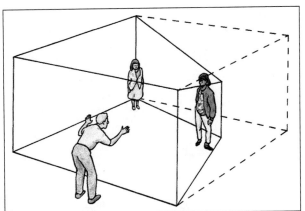

FIGURE 8.40 A size-distance illusion We know that these young women must be approximately the same size, so what explains this illusion? The room they are standing in is distorted. The back wall and both windows are actually trapezoidal in shape, and the wall is slanted so that its left-hand edge is actually twice as tall and twice as far away from the viewer as its right-hand edge (see drawing at right). When we view this scene through a peephole (or the camera's eye), we automatically assume that the walls and window are normal, that the occupants are the same distance away, and therefore that their size is different. This distorted room is called an Ames room, after Adelbert Ames, who built the first one.

34

How might the unconscious assessment of depth provide a basis for the Ponzo, Müller-Lyer, and moon illusions?

Unconscious Depth Processing as a Basis for Size Illusions

It is not difficult to produce drawings in which two identical lines or objects appear to be different in size. Two classic examples are the ***Ponzo illusion*** (first described by Mario Ponzo in 1913) and the ***Müller-Lyer illusion*** (first described by F. C. Müller-Lyer in the mid-nineteenth century), both illustrated in Figure 8.41. In each illusion two horizontal bars appear to be different in length; but if you measure them, you will discover that they are in fact identical.

Several decades ago, Richard Gregory (1968) offered a *depth-processing theory* to account for these and various other size illusions. This theory—consistent with everything said so far about the relation between size and distance—maintains that one object in each illusion appears larger than the other because of distance cues that, at some early stage of perceptual processing, lead it to be judged as farther away. If one object is judged to be farther away than the other but the two produce the same-size retinal image, then the object judged as farther away will be judged as larger. This theory applies most readily to the Ponzo illusion, in which the two converging lines provide the depth cue of linear perspective, causing (according to the theory) the upper bar to be judged as farther away and hence larger than the lower one. The photograph in Figure 8.42 makes this point clear.

The application of the depth-processing theory to the Müller-Lyer illusion is a bit more subtle. The assumption here is that people register the figures as three-dimensional objects, something like sawhorses viewed from above. The object with wings extending outward (top drawing in Figure 8.41b) resembles an upside-down sawhorse, with legs toward the viewer, and the one with inward wings (bottom drawing) resembles a right-side-up sawhorse, with its horizontal bar closer to the observer. If real sawhorses were viewed this way, the horizontal bar of the upside-down one would be farther from the observer than that of the right-side-up one, and if it produced the same-size retinal image, it would in fact be longer (see Figure 8.43).

The depth-processing theory seems to offer an elegant explanation of the Ponzo and Müller-Lyer illusions, but perhaps you have already thought of an objection to it. Most people claim to see the Müller-Lyer figures not as three-dimensional objects but as flat, arrowlike objects, yet they experience the illusion. Even with the Ponzo illusion, many people do not notice depth in the picture; they do not see the top bar

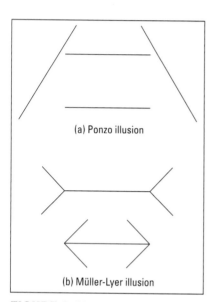

FIGURE 8.41 The Ponzo and Müller-Lyer illusions In both (a) and (b), the top horizontal bar looks longer than the bottom one, although they are actually the same length.

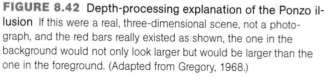

FIGURE 8.42 Depth-processing explanation of the Ponzo illusion If this were a real, three-dimensional scene, not a photograph, and the red bars really existed as shown, the one in the background would not only look larger but would be larger than the one in the foreground. (Adapted from Gregory, 1968.)

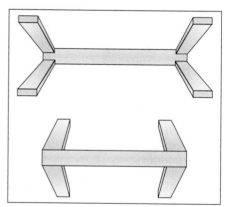

FIGURE 8.43 Depth-processing explanation of the Müller-Lyer illusion Compare these sawhorses with the Müller-Lyer drawings in Figure 8.41b. If these were real sawhorses, viewed from above in the three-dimensional world, the upside-down one would be longer than the right-side-up one.

as being farther away than the bottom one, yet they see the illusion. Researchers who support the depth-processing theory of these illusions are well aware of this objection, but it does not lead them to abandon the theory. They remind the dissenters, as did Helmholtz, that the mental processes leading to perceptions are unconscious. The cues to depth in the Müller-Lyer and Ponzo figures may be too weak, or too ambiguous, to lead to a conscious perception of depth, yet they may still lead to an unconscious assessment of depth. That unconscious assessment may enter into the mental calculation that leads to a conscious perception of size differences.

The Moon Illusion

The **moon illusion** has provoked debate since ancient Greek and Roman times. You have probably noticed that the moon looks huge when it is near the earth's horizon, just above the trees or buildings in the distance, but looks much smaller when it is closer to the zenith (directly overhead). This difference is truly an illusion. Objectively, the moon is the same size, and the same distance from us, whether it is at the horizon or the zenith. If you view the horizon moon through a peephole, so that you see it in isolation from other objects such as trees and buildings, the illusion disappears and the moon looks no larger than it does at the zenith.

A depth-processing account of this illusion was first proposed by the Greek astronomer Ptolemy in the second century, was revived by Helmholtz (1867/1962) in the nineteenth century, and has been supported in modern times through research conducted by Lloyd Kaufman and his colleagues (Kaufman & others, 2007; Kaufman & Rock, 1962). The account can be summarized as follows: Our visual system did not evolve to judge such huge distances as that from the earth to the moon, so we automatically assess its distance in relation to more familiar earthly objects. Most objects that we see near the earth's horizon are farther away than objects that we see farther from the horizon (as noted earlier, in the discussion of pictorial cues for depth). For example, birds or clouds seen near the horizon are usually farther away than are those seen higher up, closer to the zenith. Thus, our perceptual system assumes that the moon is farther away at the horizon than at the zenith, even though in reality it is the same distance away from us in either position. As in the case of the Ponzo and Müller-Lyer illusions, when two objects produce the same-size retinal image and are judged to be different distances away, the one that is judged to be farther away is seen as larger than the other.

Even today, the main objection to this explanation of the moon illusion is that people do not consciously see the horizon moon as farther away than the zenith moon (Hershenson, 1989, 2003). When people see the large-appearing horizon moon and are asked whether it seems farther away or closer than usual, they usually say closer. Again, however, as with the Ponzo and Müller-Lyer illusions, Kaufman and Irving Rock (1989) contend that we must distinguish between unconscious and conscious assessments. From their perspective, the sequence of perceptual assessments about the horizon moon might be described as follows: (1) Unconscious processes judge that the moon is farther away than usual (because objects near the horizon are usually farthest away). (2) Unconscious processes judge that the moon is larger than usual (because if it is farther away but produces the same-size retinal image, it must be larger), and this judgment enters consciousness. (3) If asked to judge distance, most people say that the horizon moon looks closer (because they know that the moon doesn't really change size, so its large apparent size must be due to closeness). This explanation has been referred to as the *farther-larger-nearer theory* (Ross & Plug, 2002).

Paul Souders/The Image Bank/Getty

The moon illusion The moon at the horizon sometimes looks huge, much bigger than it ever looks when it is higher up in the sky. This is an unaltered photo; the moon really looked this big.

Not all perceptual psychologists agree with the depth-processing account of the moon illusion, or with that of the Ponzo or Müller-Lyer illusions, but that account seems to be supported by more evidence and logic than any other explanations that have been offered to date (Hershenson, 1989; Kaufman & Kaufman, 2000; Ross & Plug, 2002).

It is perhaps fitting that we end this chapter, now, on a tentative note. Although perceptual psychologists have made great strides since the days of Ptolemy, we are still a long way from a full account of the calculations that our brains make to infer the sizes, distances, and shapes of all the objects in our field of view.

SECTION REVIEW

We see three-dimensionally—that is, with depth—though the retina is two-dimensional.

Depth-Perception Cues

➤ Our visual system uses various cues to infer the depth (distance) of objects or parts of objects.

➤ Binocular disparity is a major depth cue that derives from the fact that the two eyes, because of their different spatial positions, receive somewhat different images of an object.

➤ Another depth cue, motion parallax, is similar to binocular disparity but can occur with just one eye. It makes use of the different images of an object that either eye receives as the head moves right or left.

➤ Pictorial depth cues, such as linear perspective, do not depend on actual three-dimensionality. They allow us to infer depth even in two-dimensional pictures.

Size Perception

➤ The size of an object's retinal image is inversely proportional to its distance from the viewer, so size perception depends on depth perception.

➤ Size constancy is the ability to perceive an object as the same size when its retinal image size varies as a result of changes in its distance.

➤ The Ponzo, Müller-Lyer, and moon size illusions may derive at least partly from unconscious inferences about depth. If two objects create identical retinal images, the one that is unconsciously judged to be farther away will be seen as larger.

Concluding Thoughts

As you review this chapter, you may find it useful to think about the following three themes.

1. The survival functions of vision Our visual system, like all the basic mechanisms underlying behavior, evolved through natural selection to promote our ancestors' survival and reproduction. Our visual system is not an unbiased recorder of physical patterns of light. Rather, it is a biological tool designed to pick out the information in patterns of light that is potentially most useful. As you review, think about the survival advantage of each of the following: (a) the processes of light and dark adaptation, (b) the distinctions between cone vision and rod vision, (c) color vision, (d) the enhancement of contrast at borders, (e) feature detection by neurons, (f) Treisman's postulated two stages of feature pickup and integration, (g) the complementary roles of parallel and serial processing, (h) the Gestalt laws of perceptual grouping and of figure and ground, (i) illusory contours, (j) illusory lightness differences, (k) Biederman's idea of geons serving as a basic alphabet of perception, (l) the distinction between the "what" and "where-and-how" visual pathways, (m) the multiple cues that allow us to assess depth, and (n) the role of depth cues in perception of size. In most cases the "illusions" that our visual system produces are useful in helping us to recognize and interact effectively with objects in the real world in which we live.

2. The interaction of bottom-up and top-down processes in vision The neural processes that bring sensory information into the brain and move it along to higher centers of analysis are referred to as bottom-up processes Those that bring information down from higher centers to contribute to the analysis occurring at lower centers are referred to as top-down processes. Bottom-up processes discussed in this chapter include (a) the coding of variations in light by rods and cones; (b) the organization of that information to register elementary sensory features such as color, lightness, contour orientations, and degree of binocular disparity; and (c), in Treisman's theory, the integration of sensory features that occupy a given spatial location. Top-down processes are assumed to be involved whenever the perception of the whole, or expectations generated by the context, are brought to bear in the analysis of the sensory information. The phenomena discussed in this chapter that are assumed to involve top-down control include illusory contours, illusory lightness differences that cannot be explained by lateral inhibition, and size judgments that are based on unconscious assessments of depth.

3. The integration of behavioral and neurophysiological discoveries Herman Helmholtz realized long ago that all our perceptions result somehow from the interaction between physical properties of the external world and physiological processes occurring in our sensory organs and brain. His trichromatic theory of color vision is an example of his attempts to explain perceptual phenomena—in this case, the three-primaries law of color mixing—in physiological terms. In recent times, great strides have been made in carrying out the general program of research pioneered by Helmholtz.

Examples of modern explanations of perceptual phenomena, discussed in this chapter, that are in the direct tradition of Helmholtz include (a) the explanation of differences between bright-light vision and dim-light vision in terms of differences between cones and rods in their photochemicals and their degree of neural convergence; (b) the explanations of the two laws of additive color mixing in terms of three varieties of cones and the pattern of neural wiring of those cones to opponent-process neurons; (c) the explanation of contour enhancement in terms of lateral inhibition; (d) the explanation of rapid stimulus feature detection in terms of the properties of individual neurons in the primary visual cortex; (e) the explanation of distinctions between conscious visual perception and unconscious use of visual input to guide movement in terms of two separate pathways of visual processing; (f) the explanation of the role of components in object perception in terms of processes occurring in the "what" pathway of visual processing; and (g) the explanation of binocular disparity as a depth cue in terms of neurons that receive input from slightly different locations on the retinas of the two eyes.

Further Reading

Simon Ings (2008). *A natural history of seeing: The art and science of vision.* New York: Norton.

Ings is a science writer and novelist, not a vision scientist, but he did his homework well. This is a fun and sometimes funny, intelligent presentation of much about the physics and psychology of vision. Ings's topics include the evolution of vision, the chemistry of vision, and color vision. In one chapter he discusses the close relationship between vision and thought, and wonders to what degree we might consider thought to be an extension of vision. Reading this book will get you thinking at least as much about the unsolved mysteries of sight as about the facts we know.

Dale Purves & R. Beau Lotto (2003). *Why we see what we do: An empirical theory of vision.* Sunderland, MA: Sinauer.

This book is concerned with the relation between physical patterns of light and the percepts that our visual system generates in response to those patterns. It is filled with illusions—of lightness, color, depth, and motion—that are not readily explained in terms of bottom-up neural wiring or straightforward logical calculations. According to the authors' empirical theory, evolution and learning have shaped the visual system such that it can match any given pattern of reflected light, probabilistically, with some percept that, in the past, has been most useful when a similar pattern was present. The book, clearly written and beautifully illustrated, challenges much conventional thinking about vision.

Melvyn Goodale & A. David Milner (2004). *Sight unseen: An exploration of conscious and unconscious vision.* Oxford: Oxford University Press.

In this brief, well-written, well-illustrated book, Goodale and Milner develop, for nonspecialists, their thesis that the brain contains two rather distinct visual-processing systems, one for conscious visual perception and one for immediate, unconscious guidance of action. Included is a full account of the visual abilities and deficits of D. F., the patient who suffers from visual form agnosia but can nevertheless act on objects in ways that take form into account.

Helen E. Ross & Cornelis Plug (2002). *The mystery of the moon illusion: Exploring size perception.* Oxford: Oxford University Press.

This book discusses the many theories and lines of evidence concerning the moon illusion that have been presented since ancient times. Considerable evidence emerges supporting the farther-larger-nearer theory described in this chapter, but the authors conclude that other factors probably contribute to the illusion as well. The book reveals some of the methodological problems associated with research on size perception.

Roger Shepard (1990). *Mind sights.* New York: Freeman.

This is a book of playful drawings by a distinguished perceptual psychologist who is also a talented artist and humorist. The drawings use size illusions, figure-ground ambiguities, and other visual tricks to present jokes and puns. The author's commentary on his drawings explains what the various tricks tell us about perception.

The Human Intellect

The effectiveness of our behavior depends on knowledge we have stored as memory. It also depends on our ability to call up and combine the portions of that knowledge that are useful for the task at hand. How do we store and organize our memories? How do we recall memories when we need them? How do we manipulate knowledge in our minds in order to reason and solve problems? What causes individual differences in problem-solving ability? These big questions concern us in Chapter 9, on memory and consciousness, and Chapter 10, on intelligence and reasoning.

Memory and Consciousness

Repeatedly, while working on this book, I have lamented my seeming lack of memory. I can't remember who did that experiment. I forgot to bring home the articles I need for this section. Now, where did I put my laptop?

Like digestion, memory is one of those abilities that we tend to take for granted except when it fails us. Usually we are more aware of forgetting than of remembering. But if we stop to think about it, we realize that our remembering is far more impressive than our forgetting. Every waking moment is full of memories. Every thought, every learned response, every act of recognition is based on memory. We use memory not just to think about the past but also to make sense of the present and plan for the future. It can reasonably be argued that memory is the mind.

Memory, clearly, is intimately tied to learning. Memory is often thought of as the change within an individual, brought on by learning, that can influence the individual's future behavior: Learning → memory → effect on future behavior. **Chapter 4** of this book examines basic learning processes that occur in other animals as well as humans. Consistent with its behavioral theme, the focus there is on the relationship between observable aspects of the learning experience (the training conditions) and subsequent behavior, with little concern for the inner change—memory—that mediates that relationship. The present chapter, in contrast, is primarily about that inner change, and it deals with types of learning and memory that may be unique to human beings. Our main focus here is on the conscious human mind.

Consciousness is one of those words that different philosophers and psychologists use in different ways and about which they often debate. For practical purposes, many psychologists define consciousness simply as the experiencing of one's own mental events in such a manner that one can report on them to others (Baars & Franklin, 2003). The practical value of this definition, which is the one that I use throughout this book, is that it provides an objective criterion for identifying conscious experiences. If you tell me, correctly, that a picture I show you has a bluebird in it, then I assume that you consciously see the bluebird. If, sometime later, you say, "a bluebird," when I ask you what was in the picture, then I assume you have consciously recalled the bluebird. Defined this way, *consciousness* and *awareness* are synonyms.

The chapter begins with a general model of memory that psychologists have long used as a framework for talking and thinking about the human mind. It then discusses issues of attention, mental imagery, the formation and recall of long-term memories, and the idea that the human mind is composed of several different but interacting memory systems that have distinct neural bases.

■ Overview: An Information-Processing Model of the Mind

As I noted in **Chapter 1,** cognitive psychologists commonly look at the mind (or brain) as a processor of information, analogous to a computer. Information is brought into the mind by way of the sensory systems, and then it can be manipulated in various ways, placed into long-term storage, and retrieved when needed to solve a problem. **Memory,** broadly defined from this perspective, refers to all of the information in a person's mind and to the mind's capacity to store and retrieve that information. Memory is too large and multifaceted a topic to be studied or talked about all in one piece. Progress has been made in understanding memory by breaking it into components that can be described and studied separately. But any such breakdown implies a theory about memory—a theory that memory consists of the proposed components, that these can be studied relatively separately from one another, and that an understanding of the components contributes to an understanding of the whole.

1 -
In cognitive psychology, what is meant by a model of the mind? What are the main components of the so-called modal model of the mind?
- - - - - - - - - - - - - - - - - - - -

In cognitive psychology, theories are commonly called *models* and are often summarized visually with diagrams that use boxes to represent the mind's components and arrows to represent the movement of information from one component to another. In interpreting such a model, it is crucial to keep in mind that the boxes and arrows are metaphors. They represent at an abstract level the operations through which the mind modifies, stores, and uses the input it receives from the senses. Each component in the model is considered to be a center for a particular set of such operations. The boxes do not imply that we know just *where* in the brain the mental operations occur and the arrows do not imply that we know, at a nuts-and-bolts neural level, anything about *how* the operations occur. Cognitive psychologists test their models by using them to develop specific hypotheses about people's performance on particular tasks. A model is considered to be successful if the predictions about behavior prove to be accurate and unsuccessful if the predictions prove to be inaccurate.

The model that guides much of the discussion in this chapter (depicted in Figure 9.1) has been so influential, for so long, that it has come to be called the **modal model of the mind,** where *modal* means "standard." Versions of this model were first proposed in the 1960s (by Waugh & Norman, 1965, and Atkinson & Shiffrin, 1968), and ever since it has served as a general framework for thinking and talking about the mind. As you

FIGURE 9.1 The modal model of the mind This model has long served as a framework for thinking about the human mind, and we will use it for that purpose throughout the chapter.

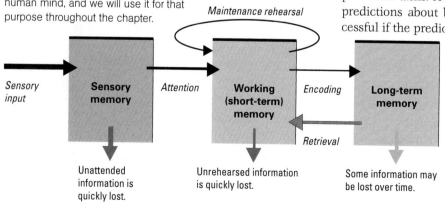

use this model throughout this chapter, keep in mind that it is only a model. It is simply a way of trying to make sense of the data from many behavioral studies. Like any model, it can place blinders on thought and research if taken literally rather than as a metaphor.

The model portrays the mind as containing three types of **memory stores**—sensory memory, working (or short-term) memory, and long-term memory—conceived of metaphorically as places (boxes in the diagram) where information is held and operated on. Each store type is characterized by its *function* (the role it plays in the overall workings of the mind), its *capacity* (the amount of information it can hold at any given instant), and its *duration* (the length of time it can hold an item of information). In addition to the stores, the model specifies a set of **control processes,** including *attention, rehearsal, encoding,* and *retrieval,* which govern the processing of information within stores and the movement of information from one store to another. As a prelude to the more detailed later discussions, here is a brief description of the three stores and the control processes.

Why don't we see this way? If you're wondering why multiple sensory-memory representations of a scene don't overlap and distort your view of the world, the answer is that each new image from instant to instant overrides the sensory memory of the previous image.

Sensory Memory: The Brief Prolongation of Sensory Experience

When lightning flashes on a dark night, you can still see the flash and the objects it illuminated for a split second beyond its actual duration. Somewhat similarly, when a companion says, "You're not listening to me," you can still hear those words, and a few words of the previous sentence, for a brief time after they are spoken. Thus, you can answer (falsely), "I was listening. You said . . ."—and then you can repeat your annoyed companion's last few words even though, in truth, you weren't listening when the words were uttered. These observations demonstrate that some trace of sensory input stays in your information-processing system for a brief period—less than 1 second for sights and up to several seconds for sounds—even when you are not paying attention to the input. This trace and the ability to hold it are called **sensory memory.**

A separate sensory-memory store is believed to exist for each sensory system (vision, hearing, touch, smell, and taste), but only those for vision and hearing have been studied extensively. Each sensory store is presumed to hold, very briefly, all the sensory input that enters that sensory system, whether or not the person is paying attention to that input. The function of the store, presumably, is to hold on to sensory information, in its original sensory form, long enough for it to be analyzed by unconscious mental processes and for a decision to be made about whether or not to bring that information into the next store, that of working memory. Most of the information in our sensory stores does not enter into our consciousness. We become conscious only of those items that are transformed, by the selective process of *attention,* into working memory.

> **2**
> **What is the function of sensory memory?**

Working Memory: Conscious Perception and Thought

According to the modal model, information in the sensory store that is attended to moves into the next compartment, which is called **working memory** (the central compartment in Figure 9.1). This is conceived of as the major workplace of the mind. It is, among other things, the seat of conscious thought—the place where all conscious perceiving, feeling, comparing, computing, and reasoning take place. An older and still often-used alternative name for this memory compartment is **short-term memory,** a term that calls attention to the relatively fleeting nature of information in this store; each item fades quickly, and is lost within seconds when it is no longer actively attended to or thought about.

> **3**
> **What are the basic functions of working memory, and how is this memory store equated with consciousness? In what way is working memory like the central processing unit of a computer?**

The passing moment
The flow of thought through working memory is not unlike the flow of scenery past the window of a moving train.

Lee Foster/Bruce Coleman, Inc.

As depicted by the arrows in Figure 9.1, information can enter working memory from both the sensory-memory store (representing the present environment) and the long-term-memory store (representing knowledge gained from previous experiences). In this sense, working memory is analogous to the central processing unit of a computer. Information can be transmitted into the computer's central processing unit from a keyboard (comparable to input from the mind's sensory store), or it can be entered from the computer's hard drive (comparable to input from the mind's long-term store). The real work of the computer—computation and manipulation of the information—occurs within its central processing unit.

The sensory store and long-term store both contribute to the continuous flow of conscious thought that constitutes the content of working memory. *Flow* is an apt metaphor here. The momentary capacity of working memory is very small: only a few items of information can be perceived or thought about at once. Yet the total amount of information that moves through working memory over a period of minutes or hours can be enormous, just as a huge amount of water can flow through a narrow channel over time.

Long-Term Memory: The Mind's Library of Information

4

In the modal model, what is the function of long-term memory, and how is this memory store different from working memory?

Once an item has passed from sensory memory into working memory, it may or may not then be encoded into **long-term memory** (again, see Figure 9.1 on page 310). Long-term memory corresponds most closely to most people's everyday notion of memory. It is the stored representation of all that a person knows. As such, its capacity must be enormous. Long-term memory contains the information that enables us to recognize or recall the taste of an almond, the sound of a banjo, the face of a grade-school friend, the names of the foods eaten at supper last night, the words of a favorite sonnet, and the spelling of the word *sonnet*. We are not conscious of the items of information in our long-term store except when they have been activated and moved into working memory. According to the model, the items lie dormant, or relatively so, like books on a library shelf or digital patterns on a computer disk, until they are called into working memory and put to use.

In the modal model, long-term memory and working memory are sharply differentiated. Long-term memory is passive (a repository of information), and working memory is active (a place where information is thought about). Long-term memory is of long duration (some of its items last a lifetime), and working memory is of short duration (items disappear within seconds when no longer thought about). Long-term memory has essentially unlimited capacity (all your long-lasting knowledge is in it), and working memory has limited capacity (only those items of information that you are currently thinking about are in it).

Control Processes: The Mind's Information Transportation Systems

5

In the modal model, what are the functions of attention, encoding, and retrieval?

According to the modal model, the movement of information from one memory store to another is regulated by the control processes of *attention*, *encoding*, and *retrieval*, all indicated in Figure 9.1 by arrows between the boxes.

Attention, as the term is used here, is the process that controls the flow of information from the sensory store into working memory. Because the capacity of sensory memory is large and that of working memory is small, attention must restrict the flow of information from the first into the second.

Encoding is the process that controls movement from working memory into the long-term store. When you deliberately memorize a poem or a list of names, you are consciously encoding it into long-term memory. Most encoding, however, is not deliberate; rather, it occurs incidentally, as a side effect of the special interest that you devote to certain items of information. If you become interested in, and think about, ideas in this book you will, as a side effect, encode many of those ideas and the new terms relating to them into long-term memory.

Retrieval is the process that controls the flow of information from the long-term store into working memory. Retrieval is what we commonly call *remembering* or *recalling*. Like attention and encoding, retrieval can be either deliberate or automatic. Sometimes we actively search our long-term store for a particular piece of information. More often, however, information seems to flow automatically into the working store from the long-term store. One image or thought in working memory seems to call forth the next in a stream that is sometimes logical, sometimes fanciful.

Now, having previewed the memory stores and processes represented in the model, let's examine them in more detail, beginning with sensory memory and attention.

Control processes at play The man who best controls his control processes of attention, encoding, and retrieval is likely to win this game—unless, of course, he was dealt a lousy hand.

Yann Layma/Tony Stone

SECTION REVIEW

The modal model posits three memory stores and various control processes.

Sensory Memory	Working Memory	Long-Term Memory	Control Processes
➤ A separate sensory store for each sensory system (vision, hearing, etc.) holds brief traces of all information registered by that system. ➤ Unconscious processes may operate on these traces to determine which information to pass on to working memory.	➤ This store is where conscious mental work takes place on information brought in from sensory memory and long-term memory. ➤ It is also called short-term memory because information in it that is no longer attended to quickly disappears.	➤ This is the repository of all that a person knows. ➤ Information here is dormant, being actively processed only when it is brought into working memory.	➤ Attention brings information from sensory memory into working memory. ➤ Encoding brings information from working memory into long-term memory. ➤ Retrieval brings information from long-term memory into working memory.

▉ Sensory Memory and Attention: The Portal to Consciousness

Imagine one of our prehistoric hunting-and-gathering ancestors foraging for certain nutritious roots. Most of her conscious attention is devoted to perceiving and analyzing visual stimuli in the soil that tell her where the roots might be. At the same time, however, at some level of her mind, she must monitor many other sensory stimuli. The slight crackling of a twig in the distance could signal an approaching tiger. The stirring of the infant on her back could indicate that the baby needs comforting before it begins to cry and attract predators. A subtle darkening of the sky could foretell a dangerous storm. On the positive side, a visual clue in the foliage, unrelated to stimuli she is focusing on, could indicate that an even more nutritious form of vegetation exists nearby.

Natural selection endowed us with mechanisms of attention that can meet two competing needs. One need is to focus mental resources on the task at hand and not be distracted by irrelevant stimuli. The other, opposing need is to monitor stimuli that are irrelevant to the task at hand and to shift attention immediately to anything

6

What two competing needs are met by our attentional system? How do the concepts of preattentive processing and top-down control of the attentive gate pertain to these two needs?

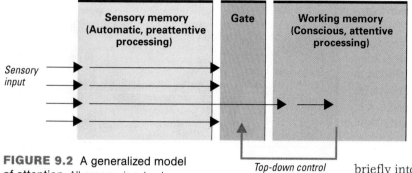

FIGURE 9.2 A generalized model of attention All sensory input enters the sensory memory store, where it is processed preattentively. Then some of it is selected to pass through the gate into conscious, working memory. The arrow going from working memory to the gate indicates top-down control of the selection criteria.

that signals some danger or benefit that outweighs that task. Cognitive psychologists have been much concerned with the question of how our mind manages these two competing needs.

Figure 9.2 depicts a very general model, in which attention is portrayed as a gate standing between sensory memory and working memory. According to this model, all information that is picked up by the senses enters briefly into sensory memory and is analyzed to determine its relevance to the ongoing task and its potential significance for the person's survival or well-being. That analysis occurs at an unconscious level and is referred to as **preattentive processing.** Logically, such processing must involve some comparison of the sensory input to information already stored in working memory or long-term memory. Without such comparison, there would be no basis for distinguishing what is relevant or significant from what is not. The portions of the brain that are involved in preattentive processing must somehow operate on the attention gate to help determine what items of information will be allowed to pass into the limited-capacity, conscious, working-memory compartment at any given moment. In Figure 9.2, that top-down control is depicted by the arrow running from the working-memory compartment to the gate. The degree and type of preattentive processing that occurs, and the nature of the top-down control of the gate, are matters of much speculation and debate (Knudsen, 2007; Pashler, 1998).

With this general model in mind, let's now consider some research findings that bear on the two competing problems that the attention system must solve: focusing attention narrowly on the task at hand and monitoring all stimuli for their potential significance.

The Ability to Focus Attention and Ignore the Irrelevant

7
How have researchers shown that people very effectively screen out irrelevant sounds and sights when focusing on difficult perceptual tasks?

We are generally very good—in fact, surprisingly good—at attending to a relevant train of stimuli and ignoring stimuli that are irrelevant to the task we are performing. Here is some evidence for that.

Selective Listening

The pioneering research on attention, beginning in the 1940s and 1950s, centered on the so-called *cocktail-party phenomenon*, the ability to listen to and understand one person's voice while disregarding other, equally loud or even louder voices nearby. In the laboratory this ability is usually studied by playing recordings of two spoken messages at once and asking the subject to shadow one message—that is, to repeat immediately each of its words as they are heard—and ignore the other message. The experiments showed that people perform well at this as long as there is some physical difference between the two voices, such as in their general pitch levels or in the locations in the room from which they are coming (Hawkins & Presson, 1986; Haykin & Chen, 2005). When asked immediately after the shadowing task about the unattended voice, the subjects could usually report whether it was a woman's voice or a man's but were usually unaware of any of the message's meaning or even whether the speaker switched to a foreign language partway through the session (Cherry, 1953; Cherry & Taylor, 1954).

Selective Viewing

On the face of it, selective viewing seems to be a simpler task than selective listening; we can control what we see just by moving our eyes, whereas we have no easy control over what we hear. But we can also attend selectively to different, nearby parts of a visual scene without moving our eyes, as demonstrated in a classic experiment by Irvin Rock and Daniel Gutman (1981). These researchers presented, in rapid succession, a series of slides to viewers whose eyes were fixed on a spot at the center of the screen. Each slide contained two overlapping forms, one green and one red (see Figure 9.3), and subjects were given a task that required them to attend to just one color. Most of the forms were nonsense shapes, but some were shaped like a familiar object, such as a house or a tree. After viewing the sequence, subjects were tested for their ability to recognize which forms had been shown. The result was that they recognized most of the forms that had been presented in the attended color but performed only at chance level on those that had been presented in the unattended color, regardless of whether the form was nonsensical or familiar.

The most dramatic evidence of selective viewing comes from experiments in which subjects who are intent on a difficult visual task fail to see large, easily recognized objects directly in their line of sight. In one such experiment (Simons & Chabris, 1999), college students watched a 75-second video in which three black-shirted players tossed a basketball among themselves, and three white-shirted players tossed another basketball among themselves, while all six moved randomly around in the same small playing area. Each subject's task was to count the number of passes made by one of the two groups of players while ignoring the other group. Midway through the video, a woman dressed in a gorilla costume walked directly into the center of the two groups of players, faced the camera, thumped her chest, and then, several seconds later, continued walking across the screen and out of view (see Figure 9.4). Remarkably, when questioned immediately after the video, 50 percent of the subjects claimed they had not seen the gorilla. When these subjects were shown the video again, without having to count passes, they expressed amazement—with such exclamations as, "I missed *that*?!"—when the gorilla came on screen.

Stage magicians and pickpockets have long made practical use of this phenomenon of *inattentional blindness* (Macknik & others, 2008). The skilled magician dramatically releases a dove with his right hand, while his left hand slips some new object into his hat. Nobody notices what his left hand is doing, even though it is in their field of view, because their attention is on the right hand and the dove. The skilled pickpocket creates a distraction with one hand while deftly removing your wallet with the other.

FIGURE 9.3 Overlapping forms used in an experiment on attention To assess the degree to which vision can be selective, Rock and Gutman (1981) directed subjects to attend to either just the red or just the green shape in slides such as this and then tested their recognition of both shapes in each slide.

FIGURE 9.4 The unseen gorilla Subjects who were asked to count the number of times one group of players threw the basketball failed to see the gorilla. (From Simons & Chabris, 1999.)

The Ability to Shift Attention to Significant Stimuli

There are limits to inattentional blindness. If our hunter-gatherer ancestors frequently missed real gorillas, or lions or tigers, because of their absorption in other tasks, our species would have become extinct long ago. Similarly, neither you nor I would be alive today if we didn't shift our attention to unexpected dangers while crossing the street. We are good at screening out irrelevant stimuli when we need to focus intently on a task, but we are also good (although far from perfect) at shifting our attention to stimuli that signal danger or benefit or are otherwise significant to us.

Our ability to shift attention appears to depend, in part, on our capacity to listen or look backward in time and "hear" or "see" stimuli that were recorded a moment earlier in sensory memory. A major function of sensory memory, apparently, is to hold on to fleeting, unattended stimuli long enough to allow us to turn our attention to them and bring them into consciousness if they prove to be significant (Lachter & others, 2004). Here is some evidence for that idea.

8 _ _ _ _ _ _ _ _ _ _ _ _ _ _ _ _ _ _
According to the theory described here, how does sensory memory permit us to hear or see, retroactively, what we were not paying attention to? How have experimenters measured the duration of auditory and visual sensory memory?
_ _ _ _ _ _ _ _ _ _ _ _ _ _ _ _ _ _ _

Shifting Attention to Meaningful Information in Auditory Sensory Memory

Auditory sensory memory is also called **echoic memory,** and the brief memory trace for a specific sound is called the *echo*. Researchers have found that the echo fades over a period of seconds and vanishes within at most 10 seconds (Cowan & others, 2000; Gomes & others, 1999).

In a typical experiment on echoic memory, subjects are asked to focus their attention on a particular task, such as reading a prose passage that they will be tested on, and to ignore spoken words that are presented as they work. Occasionally, however, their work on the task is interrupted by a signal, and when that occurs they are to repeat the spoken words (usually digit names, such as "seven, two, nine, four") that were most recently presented. Sometimes the signal comes immediately after the last word in the spoken list, and sometimes it comes after a delay of several seconds. The typical result is that subjects can repeat accurately the last few words from the spoken list if the signal follows immediately after the last word of the list, but performance drops off as the delay is increased, and it vanishes at about 8 to 10 seconds (Cowan & others, 2000). The subjective experience of people in such experiments is that they are only vaguely aware of the spoken words as they attend to their assigned task, but when the signal occurs, they can shift their attention back in time and "hear" the last few words as if the sounds were still physically present.

In experiments such as this, it is the experimenter's signal that alerts the subjects to shift attention. In other cases, however, the shift occurs because of the subject's unconscious, preattentive processing of the unattended stimuli. In the original experiments on selective listening, in which people shadowed one voice and ignored another, subjects typically showed no conscious memory for any of the ideas or words spoken by the unattended voice. However, if their own names appeared in the unattended voice, they noticed and reported that about one third of the time (Moray, 1959). How were they able to hear their own names when they had heard nothing earlier in that voice? Presumably all the words spoken by the unattended voice entered into sensory memory and were to some degree processed preattentively for meaning. Since one's own name has special meaning, preattentive processing alerted the attention mechanism, and the person could then "hear" his or her own name because it was still stored in sensory memory.

Shifting Attention to Meaningful Information in Visual Sensory Memory

Visual sensory memory is also called **iconic memory,** and the brief memory trace for a specific visual stimulus is called the *icon*. The first psychologist to suggest the existence of iconic memory was George Sperling (1960). In experiments on visual perception, Sperling found that when slides containing rows of letters were flashed for one twentieth of a second, people could read the letters, as if they were still physically present, for up to one third of a second after the slide was turned off. For instance, if a slide was flashed containing three rows of letters and then a signal came on that told the subjects to read the third row, subjects could do that if the signal occurred within a third of a second after the slide was flashed (see Figure 9.5). Such findings led Sperling to propose that a memory store must hold visually presented information, in essentially its original sensory form, for about a third of a second beyond the termination of the physical stimulus.

A number of experiments have shown that people who are attending to one set of visual stimuli and successfully ignoring another set notice stimuli in the ignored set that have special meaning to them. For example, if the task is to identify names of types of animals in sets of words and to ignore pictures, people are more likely to notice a picture of an animal than other pictures (Koivisto & Revonsuo, 2007). Similarly, people commonly notice their own name in a set of stimuli that they are supposed to ignore (Frings, 2006; Mack & others, 2002). In such cases, preattentive processes apparently analyze the picture or name, recognize it as significant, and shift the person's attention to it while it is still available in sensory memory.

```
X N Q
B W G
Z L D
```

FIGURE 9.5 Sample of slide used to demonstrate iconic memory When slides like this were flashed for a twentieth of a second, followed by a pointer indicating which row to read, subjects could still read the letters in that row because of iconic memory.

Effect of Practice on Attentional Capacity

The gate between sensory memory and working memory is narrow: Only a few items of information can cross through it at any given instant. If an array of visual stimuli—such as digits or simple shapes—is flashed quickly on a screen, and then a bright patterned stimulus (called a *masking stimulus*) is immediately flashed so as to erase the iconic memory for the original array, most people can identify only about three of the stimuli in the original array. In the past, some psychologists regarded this limitation to be an unalterable property of the nervous system, but others argued that the capacity to attend to several items at once can be increased with practice (Neisser, 1976). The best evidence that this capacity can indeed be improved comes from research on the effects of videogame playing.

In a series of experiments, C. Shawn Green and Daphne Bavelier (2003, 2006) compared the visual attentional capacity of young men who regularly played action videogames with those who never or rarely played such games. On every measure, the videogame players greatly outperformed the other group. In one test, for example, the videogame players correctly identified an average of 4.9 items in a briefly flashed array, compared to an average of 3.3 for the non-videogame players. In another test, in which target stimuli appeared in random places amid distracting stimuli on the video screen, videogame players correctly located twice as many target stimuli as did the non-players. The same researchers also showed that non-players improved dramatically on all measures of visual attention if they went through a training program in which they played an action videogame (such as "Medal of Honor") that required them to track known enemies while watching constantly for new enemies or other dangers.

In another set of experiments, Jing Feng and his colleagues (2007) found that men generally outperformed women on tests of ability to locate target stimuli quickly amid distracting stimuli, but that this sex difference disappeared when both men and women went through 10 hours of training on an action videogame. The women improved more than did the men as a result of the training, with the result that there was no significant sex difference on the attention tests after the training.

Tim Hawley/Photographer's Choice/Getty

> **9**
>
> **What is the effect of action-videogame playing on attentional capacity?**

Learning to split attention Action videogames require players to notice target stimuli that can appear at any time while they are attending to other stimuli. Researchers have found that playing such games increases people's ability to attend to many stimuli at once.

Unconscious, Automatic Processing of Stimulus Input

The modal model, as depicted in Figure 9.1 (p. 310), is a useful beginning point for thinking about the mind, but it is far from complete. Perhaps its greatest deficiency is its failure to account for unconscious effects of sensory input. In the model, sensory information can influence behavior and consciousness only if it is attended to and enters the conscious working-memory compartment; otherwise, it is simply lost from the system. In fact, however, there is much evidence that sensory input can alter behavior and conscious thought without itself becoming conscious to the person. One means by which it can do this is called *priming*.

Unconscious Priming of Mental Concepts

Priming can be defined as the activation, by sensory input, of information that is already stored in long-term memory. The activated information then becomes more available to the person, altering the person's perception or chain of thought. The activation is not experienced consciously, yet it influences consciousness. Most relevant for our present discussion, there is good evidence that such activation can occur even when the priming stimulus is not consciously perceived.

One of the earliest demonstrations of unconscious priming was an experiment in which researchers showed students either of the two visual stimuli depicted in Figure 9.6 (Eagle & others, 1966). The left-hand stimulus contains the outline of a duck, formed by the tree trunk and its branches. The researchers found that subjects

> **10**
>
> **What is some evidence that concepts stored in long-term memory can be primed by stimuli that are not consciously perceived?**

FIGURE 9.6 Tree with and without a duck Subjects who briefly saw the stimulus on the left did not consciously see the duck but were subsequently more likely to draw a scene having to do with ducks than were those who saw the stimulus on the right. (From Eagle & others, 1966.)

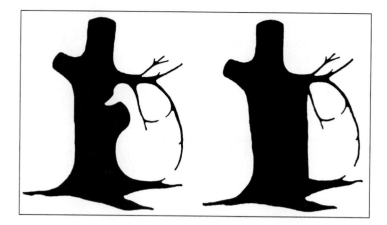

who were shown the duck-containing stimulus, in three 1-second flashes on a screen, did not consciously notice the duck. Yet when all subjects were subsequently asked to draw a nature scene, those who had been shown the duck-containing stimulus were significantly more likely to draw a scene containing a duck or a duck-related object (such as a pond) than were the other subjects.

Another early example involves a selective-listening procedure (MacKay, 1973). Subjects wore headphones that presented different messages to each ear and were instructed to shadow (repeat) what they heard in one ear and ignore what was presented to the other ear. The shadowed message included sentences, such as *They threw stones at the bank*, that contained words with two possible meanings. At the same time, the other ear was presented with a word that resolved the ambiguity (*river* or *money* in this example). After the shadowing task, the subjects were asked to choose from a pair of sentences the one that was most like the shadowed sentence. In the example just cited, the choice was between *They threw stones at the savings and loan association* and *They threw stones toward the side of the river*. Although the subjects could not report the non-shadowed word, they usually chose the sentence that was consistent with the meaning of that word. Thus, the unattended word influenced their interpretation of the shadowed message, even though they were unaware of having heard that word.

In everyday life, priming provides a means by which contextual information that we are not attending to can help us make sense of information that we are attending to. I might not consciously notice a slight frown on the face of a person I am listening to, yet that frown might prime my concept of sadness and cause me to experience more clearly the sadness in what he is saying. As you will discover later in the chapter, priming also helps us retrieve memories from our long-term store at times when those memories are most useful.

Automatic, Obligatory Processing of Stimuli

11
How is the concept of automatic, unconscious processing of stimuli used to help explain (a) people's ability to do more than one task at once, and (b) the Stroop interference effect?

◀ A wonderful adaptive characteristic of the mind is its capacity to perform routine tasks automatically, which frees its limited, effortful, conscious working memory for more creative purposes or for dealing with emergencies. Such automatization depends at least partly on the mind's ability to process relevant stimuli preattentively, unconsciously, and to use the results of that processing to guide behavior. When you were first learning to drive, for example, you probably had to devote most of your attention to such perceptual tasks as monitoring the car right ahead of you, watching for red traffic signals, and attending to your actions on the steering wheel, brake, and accelerator. With time, however, these tasks became automatic, allowing you to devote ever more attention to other tasks, such as carrying on a conversation or looking for a particular street sign.

Another example of a skill at which most of us are experts is reading. When you look at a common printed word, you read it automatically, without any conscious effort. You unconsciously, preattentively, use the word's individual letters to make sense of the word. Because of that, when you read a book you can devote essentially all of your attention to the meaningful words and ideas in the book and essentially no attention to the task of recognizing the individual letters that make up the words. In fact, researchers have found that, in some conditions at least, reading is not only automatic but obligatory (impossible to suppress). In certain situations, people can't refrain from reading words that are in front of their open eyes, even if they try.

An often-cited demonstration of the obligatory nature of reading is the **Stroop interference effect,** named after J. Ridley Stroop (1935), who was the first to describe it. Stroop presented words or shapes printed in colored ink to subjects and asked them to name the ink color of each as rapidly as possible. In some cases each word was the name of the color in which it was printed (for example, the word *red* printed in red ink); in others it was the name of a different color (for example, the word *blue* printed in red ink); and in still others it was not a color name. Stroop found that subjects were slowest at naming the ink colors for words that named a color different from the ink color. To experience this effect yourself, follow the instructions in the caption of Figure 9.7.

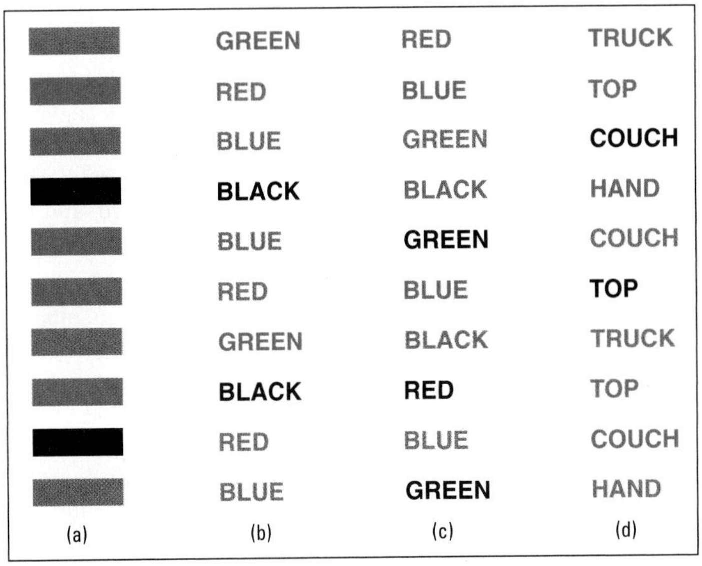

A variety of specific explanations of the Stroop effect have been offered (Luo, 1999; Melara & Algom, 2003), but all agree that it depends on people's inability to prevent themselves from reading the color words. Apparently, the preattentive processes involved in reading are so automatic that we cannot consciously stop them from occurring when we are looking at a word. We find it impossible not to read a color name that we are looking at, and that interferes with our ability to think of and say quickly the ink color name when the two are different.

(a)	(b)	(c)	(d)
▬	GREEN	RED	TRUCK
▬	RED	BLUE	TOP
▬	BLUE	GREEN	**COUCH**
▬	**BLACK**	BLACK	HAND
▬	BLUE	**GREEN**	COUCH
▬	RED	BLUE	**TOP**
▬	GREEN	BLACK	TRUCK
▬	**BLACK**	**RED**	TOP
▬	RED	BLUE	COUCH
▬	BLUE	**GREEN**	HAND

FIGURE 9.7 The Stroop interference effect Time yourself (or a friend) on each of the following tasks: (1) Name the colors in each box in column (a). (2) Name the ink colors used to print the words in columns (b), (c), and (d), timing each column separately. Column (c) will take the longest, because the color words interfere with naming the ink colors—that is the Stroop interference effect. Column (d) may also take somewhat longer than either (a) or (b), because the non-color words interfere somewhat with naming the ink colors. Column (b) should be quickest, because there the words facilitate naming the ink colors.

Brain Mechanisms of Preattentive Processing and Attention

For many years psychologists were content to develop hypothetical models about mental compartments and processes, based on behavioral evidence, without much concern about what was physically happening in the brain. In recent years, with the advent of fMRI and other new methods for studying the intact brain, that has changed. Many studies have been conducted to see how the brain responds during preattentive processing of stimuli, during attentive processing of stimuli, and at moments when shifts in attention occur. Much is still to be learned, but so far three general conclusions have emerged from such research:

1. *Stimuli that are not attended to nevertheless activate sensory and perceptual areas of the brain.* Sensory stimuli activate specific sensory and perceptual areas of the cerebral cortex whether or not the person consciously notices those stimuli. Such activation is especially apparent in the primary sensory areas, but it also occurs, to some degree, in areas farther forward in the cortex that are involved in the analysis of stimuli for their meaning. For instance, in several fMRI studies, words that were flashed on a screen too quickly to be consciously seen activated neurons in portions of the occipital, parietal, and frontal cortex that are known, from other studies, to be involved in reading (Dehaene & others, 2001, 2004). Apparently, the unconscious, preattentive analysis of stimuli for meaning involves many of the same brain mechanisms that are involved in the analysis of consciously perceived stimuli.

2. *Attention magnifies the activity that task-relevant stimuli produce in sensory and perceptual areas of the brain, and it diminishes the activity that task-irrelevant stimuli produce.* Attention, at the neural level, seems to be a process that temporarily

12

What three general conclusions have emerged from studies of brain mechanisms of preattentive processing and attention?

sensitizes the relevant neurons in sensory and perceptual areas of the brain, increasing their responsiveness to the stimuli that they are designed to analyze, while having the opposite effect on neurons whose responses are irrelevant to the task (Reynolds, 2008; Treue, 2001). For example, in a task that requires attention to dots moving upward and inattention to dots moving downward, those neurons in the visual system that respond to upward motion become more responsive, and those neurons that respond to downward motion become less responsive, than they normally are (Yantis, 2008).

3. *Neural mechanisms in anterior (forward) portions of the cortex are responsible for control of attention.* Many research studies have shown that areas in the frontal lobe and in anterior portions of the temporal and parietal lobes become active at moments when shifts in attention occur (Ruff & others, 2007; Shipp, 2004). Other studies have shown that the prefrontal cortex (the most anterior portion of the frontal lobe) is especially active during tasks, such as the Stroop task, that require intense concentration on relevant stimuli and screening out of irrelevant stimuli (van Veen & Carter, 2006). Such findings suggest that these anterior regions control attention by acting, top-down, on sensory and perceptual areas farther back in the cerebral cortex.

Attention, whatever else it is, appears to be a state of the brain in which neural resources are shifted, such that more resources are devoted to analyzing certain selected stimuli and fewer resources are devoted to analyzing other stimuli that are picked up by the senses. Apparently, the more neural activity a stimulus produces, the more likely it is that we will experience that stimulus consciously.

SECTION REVIEW

Attention is the means by which information enters consciousness.

Focused Attention	Shifting Attention	Preattentive Processing	Brain Mechanisms
➤ Selective listening and viewing studies show that we can effectively focus attention, screening out irrelevant stimuli. ➤ In general, we are aware of the physical qualities, but not the meaning, of stimuli that we do not attend to.	➤ We unconsciously monitor unattended stimuli, in sensory memory, so that we can shift our attention if something significant turns up. ➤ Such monitoring includes preattentive processing for meaning. ➤ Practice can enhance the capacity to attend to several items of information at once.	➤ Through preattentive processing, unattended sensory information can affect conscious thought and behavior. ➤ For example, in unconscious priming, stimuli that are not consciously perceived can activate information in long-term memory, which can influence conscious thought. ➤ Preattentive processing is automatic and in some cases obligatory, as exemplified by the Stroop interference effect.	➤ Preattentive and conscious processing of stimuli for meaning involve many of the same brain areas. ➤ However, attention causes greater activation of the relevant sensory and perceptual areas. ➤ Areas of the cerebral cortex anterior to (forward of) sensory and perceptual areas control shifts in attention.

◼ Working Memory: The Active, Conscious Mind

As defined earlier in the chapter, working memory, or short-term memory, is the center of conscious perception and thought. This is the part of the mind that thinks, makes decisions, and controls such processes as attention and retrieval of information from long-term memory.

By far the most influential psychological model of working memory to date is that developed by Alan Baddeley (1986, 2006), which divides working memory into a number of separate but interacting components. The components include a *phonological loop,* responsible for holding verbal information; a *visuospatial sketch-pad,* responsible for holding visual and spatial information; and a *central executive,* responsible for coordinating the mind's activities and for bringing new information into working memory from the sensory and long-term stores. We have already discussed one function of the central executive, attention, and will discuss some of its other functions later in this chapter and in **Chapter 10.** Here we'll focus on the phonological loop and the visuospatial sketchpad.

Verbal Working Memory: The Phonological Loop

As a test of one aspect of your own working memory, read the digits at the end of this sentence and then close your eyes and try to keep them in mind for a minute or so: 2 3 8 0 4 9 7. What did you do to keep them in mind? If you are like most people, you repeated the digit names over and over to yourself in the order you read them: *two three eight zero four nine seven.* Some IQ tests (discussed in **Chapter 10**) include a measure of digit span, the number of digits that the person can keep in mind for a brief period and report back accurately. Most people have a digit span of about seven digits. More generally, the number of pronounceable items—such as digits, other words, or nonsense syllables—that a person can keep in mind and report back accurately after a brief delay is called the *span of short-term memory.* According to Baddeley's model, it might better be called the *span of the phonological loop of working memory.* The phonological loop is the part of working memory that holds on to verbal information by subvocally repeating it.

Research has shown that the span of short-term memory, measured this way, depends on how rapidly the person can pronounce the items to be remembered (Baddeley, 1986). Generally, people can keep in working memory about as much verbal material as they can state aloud in 2 seconds (Baddeley & others, 1975). Unrehearsed items fade quickly; some of them begin to disappear within about 2 seconds or slightly longer. People who can speak rapidly have larger spans than people who cannot speak so rapidly. The span for single-syllable words is greater than that for multiple-syllable words. Try repeating from memory the following seven-word list, with eyes closed, immediately after reading it: *disentangle appropriation gossamer anti-intellectual preventative foreclosure documentation.* Was that list harder than the list of digits?

Any manipulation that interferes with a person's ability to articulate the words to be remembered interferes with verbal short-term memory (Baddeley, 2003). Try to hold seven digits in mind while repeating over and over, out loud, the word *the.* You probably can't do it; the act of saying *the* interferes with your ability to articulate to yourself the digit names.

Keeping a list of memory items in the phonological loop is a bit like a circus performer's keeping a set of plates spinning on the ends of sticks. As the number of plates increases, the performer must work more frantically to get back to each and renew its spinning before it falls. Performers who can move quickly can spin more plates than performers who move slowly. Larger plates take longer to set in motion than smaller ones, so the performer can't spin as many large plates as small ones. If the performer attempts to do at the same time another task that involves his or her arms and hands—such as building a tower of cups and saucers—the number of plates he or she can spin decreases.

"To find out if you're someone who could benefit from our Memory Improvement Seminar, press 15973622258309521706110137."

© 2005 by RandyGlasbergen

------13

What is some evidence that people keep information in the phonological loop through subvocal repetition?

Richard T. Nowitz/Corbis

An analogy to the phonological loop of working memory Holding several items of information in the phonological loop is a bit like spinning several plates on the ends of sticks. Just as you have to go back to each plate and renew its spin before it falls, you have to go back to each item in the phonological loop and repeat it before it vanishes from working memory.

Of course, in everyday life we don't normally use our phonological loop to keep nonsensical lists in mind, any more than we use our hands to keep plates spinning. Rather, we use it for useful work. We say words silently to ourselves, and we bring ideas together in the form of words, as we reminisce about our experiences, solve problems, make plans, or in other ways engage in verbal thought (discussed in **Chapter 10**). We don't just hold material in working memory; we stream material through it, in an often-logical fashion.

Visual Working Memory: The Visuospatial Sketchpad

14

How do we use the visuospatial sketchpad to make judgments about spatial relationships?

We think not only with words but also with mental pictures. We are especially likely to think in pictures when concerned with the spatial layout of things. I can never remember which way is west when I am facing south unless I picture myself standing on a map of North America looking toward South America. Then I can "see" immediately that the West Coast is on my right. Similarly (but at a slightly higher level of thought), Albert Einstein claimed that the concept of relativity came to him through visualizing what would happen if he chased a beam of light and caught up to it (Kosslyn & Koenig, 1992).

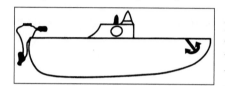

FIGURE 9.8 Sample stimulus used in a mental-imagery experiment Subjects saw line drawings such as this, and later, when answering questions based on their memory of a drawing, showed reaction times suggesting that they were scanning a mental image. (From Kosslyn, 1980.)

If you rotate the second letter of the alphabet 180 degrees clockwise, do you get a *p* or a *q*? Who had a bigger nose, your fifth-grade teacher or your sixth-grade teacher? Examine the boat in Figure 9.8 for a few seconds; then turn to page 324 and answer the question posed there in the margin near the top. If you are like most people, you probably answered each of these questions by creating and examining a visual image. According to Baddeley's model, you held that image on the visuospatial sketchpad of your working memory, where you examined and possibly manipulated the image to answer the question.

15

How did Kosslyn demonstrate a similarity between examining a visual image and looking?

No cognitive psychologist would say that a visual image really is, physically, a picture in the mind; but examining such an image is in some ways like examining a picture. In a classic study demonstrating that, Stephen Kosslyn (1973) showed people drawings, including the one in Figure 9.8, and later asked them to visualize each drawing from memory. He asked them to focus, in their memory, on either the left or the right end of the drawing and then, as quickly as possible, to indicate (by pushing one of two buttons) whether or not a particular named component was present in the drawing. For example, referring to the boat drawing, he would say "motor" or "porthole" or "anchor" while the person was focusing at either the left or the right end of the boat in memory. He found that the farther away the named object was from the place of focus, the longer it took subjects to push the correct button. These time lags suggested that the subjects had to scan across the mental image to find the named component before they could respond, just as they would if they were looking at an actual picture. Kosslyn took the lags as evidence that mental images indeed are organized spatially, like pictures. Other studies have revealed that when people form a mental image of a picture that they had looked at previously, they physically move their eyes in much the same ways that they did when they were originally looking at the picture (Laeng & Teodorescu, 2002).

Testing the Limits of Working Memory: Dual-Task Performance

People are much better at doing two mental tasks at once if one task involves the phonological loop and the other involves the visuospatial sketchpad than they are if both tasks involve the same working-memory component. You can easily rotate a *b* in your mind, to see what it looks like upside down, while repeating a set of digit names; but you cannot easily do so while trying to visualize those same digits as mental pictures.

Simulated driving while talking on hands-free cell phone In their simulated-driving experiments, Strayer and Drews (2007) found that talking on a cell phone created more driving errors, regardless of whether or not the phone was hands-free.

In one set of experiments, subjects were required to perform two challenging working-memory tasks at the same time (Cocchini & others, 2002). One task was to keep a series of digits in mind and repeat them later. The other was to keep a visual pattern of randomly arranged black-and-white checkerboard-like squares in mind and reproduce it later. The result was that neither task interfered with the other. Subjects made about the same number of errors on each task when they performed the two simultaneously as they did when they performed each one separately. In contrast, the addition of a second verbal task to the digit-span task, or of a second visual task to the pattern-memory task, sharply increased the number of errors. From such findings, Baddeley (2003) has concluded that the phonological loop and the visuospatial sketchpad are two separate components of working memory rather than two aspects of the same component. As long as one task is verbal and the other is visual, we can operate, more or less, as if we have two minds working together in parallel.

> **16**
>
> **How have dual-task experiments demonstrated that verbal and visual working memory can operate independently of each other? Why, even so, is it dangerous to talk on a cell phone while driving?**

In everyday life, however, few tasks are purely visual or purely verbal. Consider, for example, the dual tasks of driving a car and conversing on a cell phone. Driving is largely a visual task, but not entirely so. You need to read road signs (which is both visual and verbal), and you may need to think verbally about such issues as where you are supposed to turn and how to operate a particular piece of the car's equipment. Conversely, engaging in a phone conversation is largely a verbal task, but not entirely so. Any conversation is likely to call up visual images. For instance, if your conversational partner asks you how she can recognize a particular person, you are likely to form a visual image of that person in order to describe him. It is not surprising, therefore, that research indicates that phone conversations while driving contribute heavily to the rate of traffic accidents.

In a correlational study involving only drivers who sometimes used their cell phones while driving, the accident rate during phone use was four times that for the same group when they did not use their phones (Redelmeier & Tibshirani, 1997). In a simulated-driving experiment in the laboratory, conversing on a phone doubled the number of driving errors made (Strayer & Johnston, 2001). In both of these studies, the disruptive effect on driving was as great for hands-free phones as for hand-held phones.

"Man talking on cell phone walking over cliff (with evolutionary progression behind him)."

The interference is a mental one, involving competing uses of working memory, not a motor one, involving competing uses of the hands. Subsequent simulated-driving experiments showed that drivers whose minds were occupied with phone conversations frequently missed road signs because of inattentional blindness, the same reason that people in the basketball pass-counting experiment (discussed on p. 315) missed the gorilla (Strayer & Drews, 2007). Conversations with passengers did not have the deleterious effects that cell phone conversations had. Passengers, unlike phone partners, experience the driving conditions that the driver experiences, so the conversation becomes synchronized with the driving; when the driving gets difficult, the conversation temporarily stops.

Brain Areas Involved in Working Memory

17

How has brain research supported Baddeley's model of the phonological loop and the visuospatial sketchpad?

◀ Brain research supports the idea that holding information in the phonological loop of working memory involves an internalized process that is similar to actually speaking words and listening to the spoken words. In neuroimaging studies, people who are asked to hold a list of words in working memory manifest extra neural activity in portions of the left hemisphere that are known to be involved in speaking and in listening to words (Buchsbaum & D'Esposito, 2008; Paulesu & others, 1993). Moreover, brain damage that interferes with either the ability to articulate words or the ability to understand words that are heard reduces a person's ability to hold words in working memory (Wilson, 2001).

Brain research also supports the idea that holding visual information in the visuospatial sketchpad involves mental processes akin to looking and seeing (Jonides & others, 2005; Wilson, 2001). As was discussed in **Chapter 8** (and depicted in Figure 8.33), visual areas of the brain are divisible into two pathways. The "what" pathway is involved in recognizing patterns and objects. The "where-and-how" pathway is involved in perceiving spatial locations of objects and controlling a person's movements in relation to those objects. People who have deficits in visual perception resulting from damage to either of these pathways have comparable deficits in visual working memory (Baddeley, 2003).

Answer this question from your memory of the boat in Figure 9.8: Is the anchor closer to the front of the boat or to the center of the boat?

For example, after suffering damage in the "what" pathway of his cortex, one man lost much of his ability to see the shapes of objects even though he could still see the relative locations of objects in a scene (Farah, 1989a). In memory tests for information that he would have learned before the accident, he performed poorly on such shape-dependent questions as "Does a bear have a long tail or a short tail?" and "What does a cocker spaniel's ear look like?" Just as he was unable to see shapes in objects before his eyes, he was unable to "see" them in images recalled from memory. Yet he had no difficulty answering questions about the relative locations of objects. He could describe accurately, from memory, the layout of the furniture in his living room or the arrangement of buildings along a familiar street. Another man, with damage in the "where-and-how" pathway, showed just the opposite pattern of working-memory deficits: He could describe from memory the shapes of objects but not their locations (Farah, 1989a).

18

What general roles are played by the prefrontal cortex in working memory?

◀ In addition to involving verbal or visual areas of the cortex, working-memory tasks also involve the prefrontal cortex, the anterior portion of each frontal lobe. In neuroimaging studies, increased activity in the prefrontal cortex occurs whenever a person is deliberately holding either verbal or visual information in mind (Nee & others, 2008). In one study, neural activity in the prefrontal cortex was significantly greater in trials in which the person successfully kept the information in mind than in unsuccessful trials (Sakai & others, 2002). The prefrontal cortex appears to be the neural hub of the central executive portion of working memory (Huey & others, 2006). It is the part of the brain that somehow organizes the efforts of the other portions of the brain and keeps them focused on the task. People with damage in the prefrontal cortex suffer from an inability to organize their behavior in meaningful, goal-directed ways, apparently because they cannot focus on a plan or call forth information in the right sequence to complete a task (Kimberg & others, 1997).

Working memory is the seat of conscious mental activity.

Verbal and Visual Components	Dual-Task Performance	Brain Areas Involved
➤ The phonological loop maintains verbal information through subvocal repetition and permits verbal thought.	➤ We can perform two tasks simultaneously, without interference, if one involves only the phonological loop and the other only the visuospatial sketchpad.	➤ Neuroimaging shows that mental rehearsal of words involves activity in the same brain areas as speaking and listening to words.
➤ The visuospatial sketchpad permits us to hold and process mental images. There are similarities between the way the mind deals with mental images and the way it deals with external visual stimuli—for example, in the use of spatial relationships.	➤ However, real-life tasks (e.g., driving or talking on a cell phone) generally involve both verbal and visual processing, so doing both at once leads to mental interference.	➤ The "what" and "where-and-how" pathways are involved in mental imagery in ways that correspond to their roles in visual perception.
➤ Without active processing, information is quickly lost from working memory.		➤ The prefrontal cortex serves as the neural hub for the central executive, which is a third component of working memory (responsible for regulating and coordinating the mind's activities).

■ Encoding Information into Long-Term Memory

As you read a book, or attend to a conversation, or admire scenery, some of the sensory information that reaches your conscious mind enters your long-term-memory store, allowing you to recall it later. Why does some but not all of the information that reaches working memory get encoded into the long-term store?

As was discussed in the previous section, verbal information can be maintained in working memory simply by repeating it over and over. This is not, however, a good way to encode information into long-term memory. People who participate in a digit-span test, holding a list of digits in mind by reciting them over and over, rarely remember the digits even a minute after the test is over.

Everyday life also has many examples of the failure of repetition to promote long-term memory. Long ago a psychologist named Edmund Sanford (1917/1982) illustrated this point by describing his own poor memory of four short prayers that he had read aloud thousands of times over a 25-year period as part of his daily religious practice. He found, when he tested himself, that he could recite, on average, no more than three or four successive words of each prayer from memory before having to look at the printed text for prompting. I myself have looked up certain telephone numbers dozens of times and held them in working memory long enough to dial them, without ever encoding them into long-term memory. Yet I remember some other numbers that I have looked up only once or twice. The ones I remember are the ones I thought about in some way that helped me encode them into long-term memory.

Cognitive psychologists today distinguish between two kinds of rehearsal. *Maintenance rehearsal* is the process by which a person holds information in working memory for a period of time, and *encoding rehearsal* is the process by which a person encodes information into the long-term store. The activities that are effective for maintenance are not necessarily effective for encoding. Research suggests that some of the most effective activities for encoding involve elaboration, organization, and visualization.

Thinking through the lines It is not exactly clear how performers commit long passages to memory, but, as suggested by the thoughtful expression on opera star Marilyn Horne's face, they apparently do much more than repeat the passages over and over.

Robert McElroy/Woodfin Camp & Associates

Elaboration Promotes Encoding

Most of what we learn and remember in our everyday lives does not come from consciously trying to memorize. Rather, we remember things that capture our interest and stimulate our thought. The more deeply we think about something, the more likely we are to remember it later. To think deeply about an item is to do more than simply repeat it; it is to tie that item to a structure of information that already exists in long-term memory. Psychologists who study this process call it **elaboration,** or *elaborative rehearsal*. The immediate goal of elaboration is not to memorize but to understand, yet attempting to understand is perhaps the most effective of all ways to encode information into long-term memory.

Memory techniques centering on elaborative rehearsal capitalize on the human tendency to remember things that conform to some sort of logic, even if the logic is fictional. There is no obvious logic to the fact that stone formations hanging down in a cave are called *stalactites* while those pointing up are called *stalagmites*. But you can invent a logic: A stalactite has a *c* in it, so it grows from the *c*eiling; a stalagmite has a *g*, so it grows from the *g*round. Memory of a person's name can be improved by thinking of a logical relation between the name and some characteristic of the person. Thus, you might remember Mr. Longfellow's name by noting that he is tall and thin or, if he is actually short and stout, by recalling that he is definitely not a long fellow. I suspect that my students easily remember my name by relating it to the color of my hair.

19‒ ‒ ‒ ‒ ‒ ‒ ‒ ‒ ‒ ‒ ‒ ‒ ‒ ‒ ‒ ‒ ◀

What is some evidence, from the laboratory and from the classroom, that the more deeply a person thinks about an item of information, the more likely it is to be encoded into long-term memory?

‒ ‒ ‒ ‒ ‒ ‒ ‒ ‒ ‒ ‒ ‒ ‒ ‒ ‒ ‒ ‒ ‒ ‒ ‒ ‒

Laboratory Evidence for the Value of Elaboration

In a classic experiment demonstrating the value of elaboration, Fergus Craik and Endel Tulving (1975) showed subjects a long series of printed words, one at a time, and for each word asked a question that required a different form of thought about the word. In some cases, the question was simply about the printing of the word ("Is it in capital letters?"). In other cases, the question asked about the word's sound ("Does it rhyme with *train?*"). In still others, the question referred to the word's meaning ("Would it fit in the sentence, *The girl placed the ___ on the table?*"). As you can see by looking at Figure 9.9, subjects remembered many more words when they had been asked questions that focused on meaning than they did in the other conditions.

Many subsequent experiments have confirmed the idea that thinking about meaning promotes long-term memory. In one experiment, for example, the best memory for a list of objects occurred in the group of subjects who were asked to think about how each object might help them to survive if they were stranded in the grasslands of a foreign country (Nairne & others, 2008). In another experiment, on memory for lines from a play, the best memory was shown by those who were asked to study the lines in the manner that professional actors study their lines— by thinking about the meanings that each line is meant to convey and how best to convey those meanings in reading the lines (Noice & Noice, 2006). In both of these experiments, those given the thought instructions performed better on a subsequent test of memory than did those who were asked to memorize the words or lines deliberately. This was despite the fact that the thought groups, unlike the memorize groups, did not know that the experiment was concerned with memory and that they would be tested later.

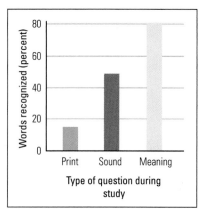

FIGURE 9.9 Superior memory resulting from meaningful elaboration Subjects were shown a long sequence of words and, for each, were asked questions that required them to focus on the way the word was printed, how it sounded, or what it meant. The type of question dramatically affected the subjects' later ability to recognize words as ones that had appeared in the sequence. (Adapted from Craik & Tulving, 1975.)

The Value of Elaboration for School Learning

In a study of fifth graders, John Bransford and his colleagues (1982) found that students who received high marks in school were far more likely to use elaborative rehearsal than were those who received lower marks. The researchers gave the children written passages to study for a later test and asked them to explain what they did as they studied each passage. For example, one passage described two different kinds of boomerangs, a returning kind and a non-returning kind, each used for different purposes. Academically successful students often reported that they rehearsed the material by asking themselves questions about it. They might wonder what a non-returning boomerang looks like or why it is called a boomerang if it doesn't return, and this caused them to think deeply about what a boomerang really is and about the information in the passage. Less successful students, in contrast, usually studied the passages simply by rereading them.

Bransford's study was correlational in nature, so it does not prove that elaborative study caused better test performance; it shows only that the two tended to go together. But other research suggests that elaborative study can improve students' grades. In one long-standing program aimed at helping students perform better in college, students are taught to write down questions about every textbook section that they read as they read it and about the lecture notes they take as they take them. The process of generating these questions and trying to answer them presumably deepens students' thought about the ideas and facts that they are reading about or hearing and thereby improves both understanding and memory. In a series of field experiments, students who were taught these techniques subsequently achieved higher grades in their college courses than did otherwise comparable students who received either subject-matter tutoring or no special help (Heiman, 1987).

Such findings are compatible with the following advice for studying this or any other textbook:

- Don't passively highlight or copy passages as you read, for later rereading. Focus on the ideas, not the author's exact words.

- Constantly ask yourself questions such as these: Do I understand the idea that the author is trying to convey here? Do I agree with it? Is it relevant to my own life experiences? Has the author given evidence supporting it? Does the evidence seem reasonable? How is this idea relevant to the larger issues of the chapter? (In this textbook, the numbered focus questions that appear in the margins give you a start on this task.)

- As you ask such questions, jot down notes in the margins that bear on your answers, such as "This idea seems similar to . . . ," or "I don't understand what he means by . . . ."

Through this active process, you will encode the material in a far richer and more lasting way than you could accomplish by simple rereading. You will also, in the process, generate questions that you might want to ask other students or your instructor.

Organization Promotes Encoding

As a memory strategy, organization is closely tied to elaboration. Organizing items to be remembered is itself a means of elaboration; you must think about the items, not just repeat them, in order to organize them. Moreover, organization can improve memory by revealing or creating links among items that would otherwise be perceived as separate.

Chunking

One way to increase memory efficiency is to group adjacent items that are at first perceived as separate, thus making them a single item. This procedure, known as **chunking**, decreases the number of items to be remembered and increases the amount of information in each item (Miller, 1956). As a simple illustration, if you had to memorize the series *M D P H D R S V P C E O I H O P,* your task would be made easier if you saw the series not as a string of 16 independent letters but as a set of five common abbreviations—M.D., Ph.D., RSVP, CEO, and IHOP. You could make your task still easier if you then chunked these five abbreviations into one sentence: "The M.D. and Ph.D. RSVPed to the CEO of IHOP." In developing such a story, you would not only be chunking but also elaborating—making the information more meaningful by adding some new information of your own.

Beginning music students find it easier to remember the notes on the lines of the treble clef as one sentence, "*Every Good Boy Does Fine,*" than as the senseless string of letters *E G B D F.* Similarly, physiology students can recall the seven physiological systems (skeletal, circulatory, respiratory, digestive, muscular, nervous, and reproductive) by matching their first letters to the consonants in SACRED MANOR. Both devices involve chunking. In the first example, the five notes are

> **20**
>
> How can chunking be used to increase the amount of information that can be maintained in short-term memory or encoded into long-term memory?

chunked into one meaningful sentence, and in the second the seven systems are chunked into two meaningful words. By reducing the number of separate items, and by attaching more meaning to each item, chunking provides an advantage both for maintaining information in working memory and for encoding it into long-term memory.

The Role of Chunking in Expert Memory

21

How does chunking figure into experts' excellent memories for information that is within their realm of expertise?

◀ We are all much better at forming long-term memories for information that is within rather than outside our realm of expertise. For example, master chess players can look for just a few seconds at a chess game in progress and form a long-term memory of the locations of all the pieces on the board (de Groot, 1965). Similarly, football coaches have excellent memories for diagrams of football plays (Garland & Barry, 1991), architects have excellent memories for floor plans (Atkin, 1980), and physicians have excellent memories for information gained in diagnostic interviews of patients (Coughlin & Patel, 1987).

As a step toward explaining the expertise advantage in memory, K. Ander Ericsson and his colleagues have posited the existence of a special kind of long-term memory, called *long-term working memory* (Ericsson & Delaney, 1999; Ericsson & Kintsch, 1995). They conceive of this as memory for the interrelated set of items (such as a patient's case history or the pieces on a chess board) that is crucial for solving the problem or completing the task at hand. Such memories are encoded into long-term storage in a manner that makes the entire structure of information easily accessible to working memory, at least until the problem is solved or the task is finished. Such memories allow a physician to puzzle over a particular patient's symptoms as she drives home from work or a chess master to mull over the possibilities inherent in a particular set of chess positions while he is away from the game. Such memories are not lost as a result of interruptions, as short-term working memories are, so they allow the person to go back to a previous task after time spent on another task (Oulasvirta & Saariluoma, 2006).

Chunking plays a major role in the formation of long-term working memories. In order to form such a memory of, say, a particular arrangement of pieces on a chess board, a person must already have in long-term storage a great deal of well-established information about possible and likely ways that such items might be arranged. This knowledge provides a foundation for the efficient chunking of new items of information. Chess games normally progress in certain logical ways, so logical relationships exist among the pieces, which experts can chunk together and remember as familiar formations rather than as separate pieces. If the chess pieces are arranged randomly rather than in ways that could occur in a real game, masters are no better, or little better, than novices at remembering their locations (Gobet & others, 2001; see Figure 9.10). Experts in other realms also lose their memory advantage when information is presented randomly rather than being grouped in ways that make sense to them (Vicente & Wang, 1998; Weber & Brewer, 2003).

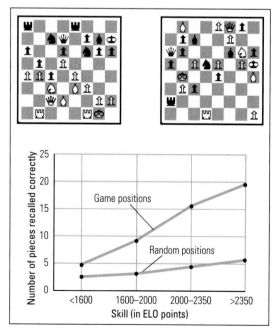

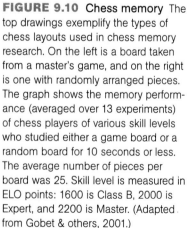

FIGURE 9.10 Chess memory The top drawings exemplify the types of chess layouts used in chess memory research. On the left is a board taken from a master's game, and on the right is one with randomly arranged pieces. The graph shows the memory performance (averaged over 13 experiments) of chess players of various skill levels who studied either a game board or a random board for 10 seconds or less. The average number of pieces per board was 25. Skill level is measured in ELO points: 1600 is Class B, 2000 is Expert, and 2200 is Master. (Adapted from Gobet & others, 2001.)

The Value of Hierarchical Organization

The most useful format for organizing some kinds of information is the hierarchy. In a hierarchy, related items are clustered together to form categories, related categories are clustered to form larger (higher-order) categories, and so on.

22
What is a hierarchical organization, and how can such an organization facilitate encoding into long-term memory?

In an experiment demonstrating the advantage of hierarchical organization for long-term memory, Andrea Halpern (1986) gave subjects a chart listing 54 well-known song titles to be memorized. In some cases the chart was organized in a hierarchical manner, with songs arranged according to meaningful categories and subcategories. In other cases a similar chart was used but organized randomly, with no systematic relation among categories, subcategories, and song titles. When tested later for their memory of the song titles, subjects who had studied the organized chart recalled accurately many more titles than did those who had studied the disorganized chart. During the test the former group of subjects would first recall a category name and then the songs that had been listed under that name.

As was pointed out in **Chapter 1,** the information in this textbook (like that in nearly all textbooks) is hierarchically arranged: Each main heading refers to a set of related ideas, and each subheading refers to a smaller subset of ideas within the larger set. An efficient way to summarize the information in almost any textbook chapter is to sketch it out in a manner that preserves the author's hierarchical organization. As an illustration, a hierarchical sketch of the section you are now reading appears in Figure 9.11. Notice that the top node indicates in key words the theme of the section, the nodes subordinate to it indicate the main ideas pertaining to that theme, and the comments under them indicate the examples or evidence provided for each idea. You could summarize the whole chapter with six such sketches, one for each of the chapter's main sections. Such a summary would be a far more efficient aid in helping you commit the information to memory for a test than would a string of terms and names that does not preserve the connections of ideas to each other or of ideas to evidence. The section reviews of this textbook also preserve the hierarchical organization of ideas and evidence within each section (as discussed in **Chapter 1**).

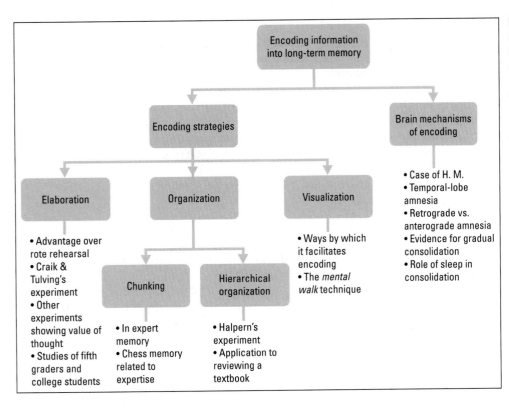

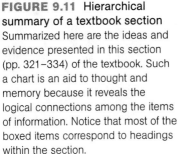

FIGURE 9.11 Hierarchical summary of a textbook section Summarized here are the ideas and evidence presented in this section (pp. 321–334) of the textbook. Such a chart is an aid to thought and memory because it reveals the logical connections among the items of information. Notice that most of the boxed items correspond to headings within the section.

Visualization Promotes Encoding

Our discussion of encoding so far has centered mostly on memory for verbal information. But we can also encode pictures or visual scenes into long-term memory, apparently in a non-verbal form, which can be recalled later into the visuospatial sketchpad of working memory. Visual and verbal memories interact and supplement one another in our everyday experience. If you asked me to describe my living room, I would summon a pictorial memory of that room and then find the words to describe it.

A good deal of research suggests that people can improve their memory for verbally presented information if they encode that information visually as well as verbally. One study, for example, demonstrated that memory for information in news stories improves if relevant pictures accompany the stories (Prabu, 1998). Lacking pictures, people can improve their memory for verbally presented information by constructing visual images to represent that information (Paivio, 1986).

◄ Visualization may improve memory through several different means. It may provide a distinct visual memory trace to supplement the verbal memory trace, thereby increasing the chance that the memory will be recalled in the future (Paivio, 1986). It may also provide an efficient way to chunk several verbally presented ideas together. For example, a verbal description of a person you haven't met may contain many separate items of information that you can combine into a single visual image. In addition, visual imagery may improve memory by linking newly learned information to information that is already well encoded in long-term memory. An example of that is found in a memory technique called the *mental walk*, used by nearly all contestants in the annual World Memory Championships when they are asked to memorize, in order, the names of a long list of objects (Maguire & others, 2003). As they hear the list of objects, they imagine themselves taking a walk along a familiar route and leaving each object next to a familiar landmark on the route. Then, during recall, they mentally walk the route again, inspect each landmark, and "see" each item that they had previously deposited there.

23

Through what means might visualization help improve memory for verbally presented information?

Courtesy of Behavioral Neuroscience Lab/MIT

H. M. Henry Molaison, known as H. M., has been famous to psychology researchers and students for half a century. His lack of ability to form new long-term memories after surgery for epilepsy led to new insights about the distinctions among different memory types. Molaison died in 2008.

Brain Mechanisms of Long-Term-Memory Encoding

Imagine what life would be like if, as a result of an operation, you became unable to form new explicit (conscious) long-term memories. At any given moment you would be fully aware of your environment and able to think about it, but you would have no idea how you arrived at that moment. You would live first in one moment, then in another, then in another, with no memory of the previous moments. If you made a plan for the future—even the future of just a few minutes ahead—you would forget the plan forever the instant you stopped thinking of it. Your life would be like that of Henry Molaison—known in the psychological literature as H. M.—who indeed did lose his ability to form new explicit long-term memories.

The Case of H. M.: A Man Unable to Encode New Long-Term Memories

In 1953, at age 27, H. M. underwent surgery as treatment for severe epilepsy. A portion of the temporal lobe of the cortex and underlying parts of the limbic system on each side of his brain were removed. The surgery was effective against the epilepsy, but it left him unable to encode new explicit long-term memories. Between the time of his surgery and his death, in 2008, H. M. participated in hundreds of memory experiments. He is almost certainly the most fully studied person in the history of psychology and neurology.

24

How does the case of H. M. support the idea of a sharp distinction between working memory and long-term memory?

◄ Throughout his life, H. M. could remember events that occurred well before the operation. His long-term-memory store was full of knowledge acquired largely in the 1930s and 1940s. He could converse, read, solve problems, and keep new information in mind as long as his attention remained focused on it. He had an excellent vocabulary and was a skilled solver of crossword puzzles (Scotko & others, 2008).

But the minute his attention was distracted, he would lose the information he had just been thinking about, and he would be unable to recall it later. To hold information in mind for a period of time, H. M. sometimes used elaborate memory schemes. In one test, for example, he successfully kept the number 584 in mind for 15 minutes, and when asked how he did this, he replied: "It's easy. You just remember 8. You see, 5, 8, 4 add to 17. You remember 8; subtract from 17 and it leaves 9. Divide 9 by half and you get 5 and 4, and there you are—584. Easy." Yet a few minutes later, after his attention had shifted to something else, he could not remember the number or the memory scheme he had used, or even that he had been given a number to remember (Milner, 1970).

H. M.'s memory impairment made it impossible for him to live independently. He had to be accompanied wherever he went and needed constant reminders of what he was doing (Hilts, 1995). He was aware of his memory deficit and once described it in the following way (Milner, 1970): "Right now, I'm wondering, have I done or said anything amiss? You see, at this moment everything looks clear to me, but what happened just before? That's what worries me. It's like waking from a dream. I just don't remember." As you'll see later in the chapter, the case of H. M. also provides evidence that different kinds of memories are encoded in different ways. H. M. could not form new conscious memories, but he could form certain kinds of unconscious memories.

Involvement of Temporal-Lobe Structures and Prefrontal Cortex in Encoding

There have been many other studies of people who have a memory loss like H. M.'s, though usually not as complete, after strokes or other sources of brain damage. The disorder is called *temporal-lobe amnesia,* and the areas of destruction most strongly correlated with it are the *hippocampus* (the limbic-system structure buried within the temporal lobe, depicted in Figure 9.12, and introduced in **Chapter 5**) and cortical and subcortical structures closely connected to the hippocampus in both halves of the brain (Gold & Squire, 2006; Squire, 1992).

Neuroimaging studies complement the evidence from brain-damage research. When people with intact brains are presented with new information to memorize, they manifest increased activity in the hippocampus and adjacent parts of the temporal lobe, and the degree of that increase correlates positively with the likelihood that they will recall the information successfully in a later test (Otten & others, 2001; Reber & others, 2002). Apparently, activity in the hippocampus is essential for the formation of at least some types of long-term memories.

> **25**
> **What evidence indicates that the hippocampus and temporal-lobe structures near it are involved in encoding explicit long-term memories?**

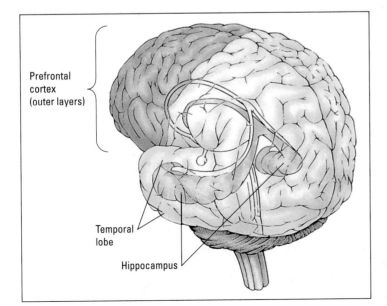

FIGURE 9.12 Brain areas involved in temporal-lobe amnesia The hippocampus, buried within the temporal lobe, is critically involved in long-term memory encoding. The most severe form of amnesia occurs when this structure and some of the surrounding areas of the temporal lobe are destroyed on both sides of the brain. As discussed later in the chapter, the prefrontal cortex is also involved in long-term memory encoding.

Prefrontal cortex (outer layers)

Temporal lobe

Hippocampus

Retrograde Amnesia and Evidence for Gradual Consolidation of Long-Term Memories

The term *amnesia* refers to any loss of long-term memory, usually resulting from some sort of physical disruption or injury to the brain. The most dramatic type of amnesia observed in H. M. and other temporal-lobe patients is **anterograde** [an-**teer**-oh-**grade**] amnesia, the loss of capacity to form long-term memories of events that occur after the injury. However, these patients also show a considerable degree of **retrograde amnesia,** loss of memories of events that occurred before the injury.

◄ Retrograde amnesia is generally time-graded; it is greatest for memories acquired just before the injury and least for those acquired long before (Wixted, 2004, 2005). H. M., for example, lost all his memories of events that occurred within several days of his surgery, some of his memories of events that occurred within a few years of his surgery, and essentially none of his memories of events that occurred in his childhood, many years before the surgery (Eichenbaum, 2001). Such time-graded retrograde amnesia is also seen in people who have suffered a severe blow to the head or have had a series of electroshock treatments—a procedure (discussed in **Chapter 17**) in which the brain is subjected to a jolt of electricity as a treatment for severe depression.

The time-graded nature of retrograde amnesia suggests that long-term memories are encoded in the brain in at least two forms—a labile, easily disrupted form and a stable, not easily disrupted form. Long-term memories appear to be encoded first in the labile form. Then, gradually over time, they apparently are either re-encoded in the stable form or lost (forgotten). The process by which the labile memory form is converted into the stable form is referred to as **consolidation.**

A prominent theory today is that the labile form of long-term memory involves neural connections in the hippocampus and that the stable form involves neural connections in various parts of the cerebral cortex, without dependence on the hippocampus (Eichenbaum, 2001; Medina & others, 2008). This theory is supported by the time-graded retrograde amnesia observed after loss of the hippocampus, and it is also supported by neuroimaging research with people who have intact brains and normal memories. When people recall memories that were acquired relatively recently, neural activity in the hippocampus increases; but when they recall memories that were first acquired many years earlier, increased activity occurs in parts of the cerebral cortex but not in the hippocampus (Haist & others, 2001).

Role of Retrieval in Memory Consolidation and Modification

Nobody knows just how memory consolidation occurs, though it apparently involves modification of existing synaptic connections and growth of new synaptic connections in the brain (discussed in **Chapter 5**). It is also not clear why some memories appear to consolidate relatively quickly (within days) and others much more slowly (over years) or why many memories are forgotten within minutes, hours, or days and never become consolidated. There is, however, evidence that memories that are recalled and used repeatedly, over relatively long time periods, are the ones most likely to be consolidated into a form that resists disruptions (Altmann & Gray, 2002).

Recent research, mostly with animals, suggests that every time a memory is recalled and put to use, the neural trace for that memory enters temporarily into a new labile stage—that is, a stage when it can be modified (Lee, 2008; Tronson & Taylor, 2007). Depending on what happens when the memory is recalled, that memory may be strengthened, or weakened, or changed by the addition of some new content to it. From this point of view, long-term memories are not static, like words on a page, but are dynamic entities, changing in some ways every time they are used.

◄ From a functional point of view, the modifiability of memories during retrieval makes sense. There is no need to clutter up my permanent collection of memories with information such as where I parked my bicycle this morning—information that I will not need after the end of the day. It is better to reserve that memory space for information that might always be useful. Cues that my brain might use to consolidate

---

26 ‒ ‒ ‒ ‒ ‒ ‒ ‒ ‒ ‒ ‒ ‒ ‒ ‒ ‒ ‒

What evidence supports the theory that long-term memories first exist in a labile (unstable), temporal-lobe-dependent state and then, if not lost, are gradually consolidated into a more stable form that doesn't depend on temporal-lobe structures?

---

27 ‒ ‒ ‒ ‒ ‒ ‒ ‒ ‒ ‒ ‒ ‒ ‒ ‒ ‒ ‒

What might be the value of the increased modifiability of long-term memories that occurs during retrieval?

memories into a very long-lasting form include the frequency and time-course of my retrieving them. At the end of today, when I go to my bicycle, I will retrieve for the last time the information about where I parked this morning. There may even be something about my mental attitude in retrieving it that signals my memory system that I won't need this memory again, so it can fade. I will, however, continue for a long time to retrieve memories of more enduring value, such as information about what my bicycle looks like, so those memories are likely to consolidate into forms that resist disruption and are not dependent on my hippocampus. Moreover, each time that I retrieve my memory of what my bicycle looks like, in the presence of my bicycle, that memory may be updated to include any modifications in the bike's appearance. Researchers are only barely beginning to learn about the kinds of cues that the long-term memory system uses strengthen, weaken, or modify memories in useful ways.

Role of Sleep in Memory Consolidation

Have you ever found that your memory for, and maybe even your understanding of, some newly learned information was better after a period of sleep than it was before? Many recent experiments have shown that sleep, shortly after learning, helps to consolidate newly acquired memories, making them more easily retrievable and less susceptible to disruption than they were before the sleep (Rasch & Born, 2008; Stickgold, 2005). A similar period of wakefulness does not have this effect. The effect seems to occur no matter what time of day the sleep occurs, as long as it occurs within a few hours after the learning experience. Some of these experiments used paired-associate tasks, in which subjects were presented with pairs of words and then were tested for their ability to recall the second member of each pair after seeing just the first member (e.g., Backhaus & others, 2008). But improved memory after sleep has been shown with many other tasks as well.

> **28**
> **What is some evidence that sleep promotes the durability and quality of long-term memories?**

For paired-associate tasks and other tasks involving conscious recall, the type of sleep that seems most valuable is slow-wave, non-REM sleep (Rasch & Born, 2008). The improved learning correlates positively with the amount of slow-wave sleep, not the amount of REM sleep. (The sleep stages are discussed in **Chapter 6.**) There is also evidence that the hippocampus becomes activated at various times during slow-wave sleep. One prominent theory is that the hippocampal activity represents activation of the memory trace, which allows consolidation of the memory into a new, more stable form.

Sleep may improve not just the durability of new memories, but also their quality, in a manner that helps to achieve new insights. In one experiment demonstrating this, Ullrich Wagner and his colleagues (2004) trained people to solve a certain type of mathematical problem by following a series of seven steps. Unbeknownst to the subjects, the problems could also be solved by a simpler method, involving just two steps. In the experiment, the subjects were given a small amount of training on the task and then, eight hours later, were tested with a long series of the same type of problem to see how quickly they could solve them. Some subjects were trained in the morning and then tested in the evening, after no sleep; others were trained in the evening and tested in the morning after a night's sleep; and still others were trained in the evening but kept awake during the night before testing in the morning. For comparison, two other groups received their training and testing all in one block, occurring either in the morning after sleep or in the evening after a period awake.

The results of the study are shown in Figure 9.13. As you can see, the subjects who had a period of sleep between training and testing

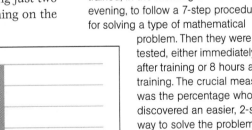

FIGURE 9.13 Sleep after training improved insight Subjects were trained, in the morning or in the evening, to follow a 7-step procedure for solving a type of mathematical problem. Then they were tested, either immediately after training or 8 hours after training. The crucial measure was the percentage who discovered an easier, 2-step way to solve the problem (achieved "insight"). As the graph shows, the 8-hour interval increased insight only if subjects slept during that period. An 8-hour interval spent awake, whether it was during the day or during the night, did not increase insight. (Graph modified from Wagner & others, 2004.)

were more than twice as likely to discover the simpler way of solving the problem than were any of the other subjects. Notice that the improvement is not simply the result of sleep, but is the result of sleep occurring after initial training. Those who were both trained and tested in the morning, after sleep, did not do any better than any of the other groups. The experiment suggests that there is some validity to the adage that the best thing to do if you have a problem to solve is to "sleep on it," but only if you have first spent some time working on the problem.

SECTION REVIEW

For later recall, information must be encoded into long-term memory.

Thoughtful Means of Encoding

➤ Elaboration involves actively extending one's understanding of something, thereby connecting it with information already in long-term memory. Its effectiveness has been demonstrated in field research (e.g., of school learning) as well as in the laboratory.

➤ Chunking facilitates encoding by grouping separate items into one higher-level unit (e.g., SACRED MANOR). Experts use previously learned chunks to create long-term working memories in areas of their expertise.

➤ Organizing information into a logical hierarchy facilitates encoding and retrieval.

➤ Visualizing verbally presented information may improve memory by creating an additional memory trace, by chunking separate items together into one image, and by forming links to information already in long-term memory.

Mechanisms of Encoding and Consolidation

➤ People with temporal-lobe amnesia, such as H. M., lack abilities to form new long-term memories.

➤ Studies of such brain damage and neuroimaging studies suggest that temporal-lobe structures (especially the hippocampus) and the prefrontal cortex are critically involved in encoding.

➤ The time-graded nature of retrograde amnesia suggests that long-term memories exist first in a labile form, becoming gradually more stable through consolidation.

➤ Frequent recall of memories can promote both their modification and their consolidation.

➤ Sleep shortly after learning helps to consolidate memories and in some cases may reorganize memories in ways that promote new insights.

■ Retrieving Information from Long-Term Memory

Once we encode an item into long-term memory, we may or may not be able to find it there when we need it. Why are we sometimes unable to remember a name or fact that we "know" that we know? Why do we at other times remember a name or fact that we thought we had long since forgotten? Why, in some cases, do we remember an event differently each time we retell it, or remember an event that didn't really happen as if it did? These are some of the questions that cognitive psychologists have addressed in research and theories concerning the retrieval of information from long-term memory.

Mental Associations and Memory Retrieval Cues

The World Wide Web contains literally billions of pages of textual information, sitting in hundreds of thousands of servers throughout the world. All that information would be useless to you and me were it not for search engines, such as Google, that can rapidly scan the pages and find what we are looking for. The long-term-memory store of your or my brain likewise contains vast quantities of information (though not as much as the World Wide Web), which is useful only to the degree that we can call it forth at the moment we need it.

Retrieval of specific items from any information-storage system depends on how the stored information is organized. Books in a library are organized by topic, making it easier for us to find all there is about, say, the Civil War or flower gardening. Words in a dictionary are organized alphabetically, so we can find them on the basis of their spelling. Web pages on the Internet contain links to other pages that deal with related issues, and efficient search engines take advantage of those links to rank pages in the order of their relevance to the search terms that we have typed in. In the human mind, long-term memories are stored not in isolation, but in networks in which each item is linked to many others through connections referred to as **associations,** somewhat analogous to the links among pages in the World Wide Web (Griffiths & others, 2007). When any one memory is activated by an appropriate stimulus or thought, other memories associated with it become temporarily activated, or *primed*, to become more easily retrievable. A stimulus or thought that primes a particular memory is referred to as a **retrieval cue** for that memory.

The evidence for these ideas about memory organization and retrieval comes not from knowledge of how memories are stored physically in the brain, but from behavioral studies.

Mental Associations as Foundations for Retrieval

Speculation about mental associations goes back at least to the time of Aristotle. Aristotle considered two concepts to be associated if the thought of one tends to evoke (call forth from long-term memory) the thought of the other, and he proposed several principles of association, the most central of which are contiguity and similarity.

According to Aristotle's principle of **association by contiguity,** some concepts are associated because they have occurred together (contiguously) in the person's previous experience. Thus, *napkin* and *plate* might be associated in your mind because you have frequently seen napkins and plates together. When you see the face of someone you know, his or her name leaps to your mind (or at least often does) because you have often experienced that face and that name together in the past. The contiguity principle also accounts for our ability to bring quickly to mind the various properties of an object when we hear its name. If I hear *apple*, I can immediately think *red, round, sweet, tart, grows on trees, good in pies* because I have experienced all those properties of apples contiguously with apples themselves and with the word *apple*.

According to the principle of **association by similarity,** items that share one or more properties in common are linked in memory whether or not they were ever experienced together. Your thought *apple* might evoke the thought *rose*, because both are red, even if you have never seen an apple and a rose together.

In his great introductory psychology textbook, written more than a century ago, Willliam James (1890/1950) pointed out that association by similarity can be understood as a derivative of the more primitive and fundamental principle of association by contiguity. Contiguity allows us to think of the properties of any given object and then allows us to think of other objects that have those same properties, leading to associations by similarity. Thus, my thought *apple* leads to my thought *red* (because of contiguity), and my thought *red* leads to my thought *rose* (again because of contiguity), with the result that my thought *apple* leads to *rose* (similarity). James suggested that the ability to separate mentally the various properties of objects and events from their concrete referents, and to use those properties to link objects and events that were never experienced contiguously, represents a basic difference between the human mind and that of other animals. "Thoughts [in dogs] will not be found to call up their similars, but only their habitual successors," he wrote. "Sunsets will not suggest heroes' deaths, but supper-time. This is why man is the only metaphysical animal."

Network Models of Memory Organization

Continuing the tradition begun by Aristotle, many cognitive psychologists today depict the mind's storehouse of knowledge as a vast network of mental concepts linked by associations. Figure 9.14 (on page 336) illustrates such a model. Allan Collins and

29

What do the principles of association by contiguity and association by similarity say about retrieval from long-term memory? According to James, how does the second principle depend on the first?

30

What sorts of experimental results was Collins and Loftus's spreading-activation model designed to explain? How does the model expand on the idea that mental associations provide a basis for memory and thought?

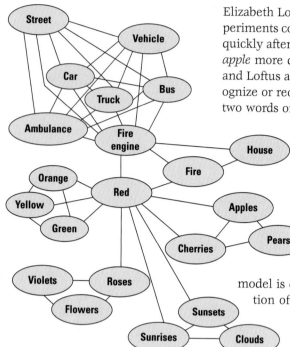

FIGURE 9.14 A network model of memory organization This diagram depicts schematically some of the links, or associations, among a tiny fraction of the thousands of different concepts that are stored in a typical person's long-term memory. (From Collins & Loftus, 1975.)

Elizabeth Loftus (1975) developed this specific diagram to explain the results of experiments concerned with people's abilities to recognize or recall specific words very quickly after exposure to other words. For example, a person can recognize the word *apple* more quickly if the previous word was *pear* or *red* than if it was *bus*. Collins and Loftus assumed that the degree to which one word speeds up the ability to recognize or recall another reflects the strength of the mental association between the two words or concepts. Similar experiments have shown that many types of memory items—including memories for famous people—can be organized in networks based on strengths of association among them (Stone & Valentine, 2007).

In Figure 9.14, the strength of association between any two concepts is represented by the length of the path between them; the shorter the path, the stronger the association. Notice how the diagram incorporates the idea that common properties of objects often provide a basis for their link in memory. *Roses, cherries, apples, sunsets*, and *fire engines* are all linked to the concept *red*, and through that common tie they are all linked to one another. The model is called a *spreading-activation model* because it proposes that the activation of any one concept initiates a spread of activity to nearby concepts in the network, which primes those concepts so they become temporarily more retrievable than they were before. The spreading activity declines with distance, so concepts that are closely linked with the active concept receive more priming than those that are more distantly linked. Such models are convenient ways to depict the results of many memory experiments, and they help us to visualize the patterns of associations that make up the mind.

Modern brain theories posit that memories for concepts, such as those depicted in Figure 9.14, are stored in overlapping neural circuits in the cerebral cortex (Fuster, 2006; Patterson & others, 2007). Some of the neurons that are part of the circuit for one concept are part of the circuit for other concepts as well. The more overlap there is between the circuits for two concepts, the more closely they are associated in the person's mind. According to these theories, priming occurs because the activation of the circuit for one concept literally does activate part of the circuit for another, making that whole circuit more easily activated than it was before.

Why Elaborative Rehearsal Creates Easily Retrievable Memories

31

How might elaborative encoding facilitate retrieval? How is this idea supported by an experiment in which subjects were tested for their memory of a long list of nouns they had been shown?

How you place new information into your network of associations has a big effect on your subsequent ability to retrieve it. This brings us back to the role of elaborative rehearsal in memorization, discussed earlier. The more mental associations you create in learning a new item of information, the more ways will be available for you to retrieve it later.

Suppose you are learning for the first time that the capital of Vermont is Montpelier. You might notice, as you encode this new fact, that the syllable *mont* appears in both the capital name and the state name, and you might then think about the fact that *mont* is French for mountain, that Vermont is known as the Green Mountain state, and that many of the early settlers were French. More imaginatively, you might notice that *Montpelier* sounds like *mount peeler* and you might think of a strong wind peeling the snow off one of Vermont's mountains. Through such observations and thoughts you are setting up many possible retrieval cues for remembering, later, that the capital of Vermont is Montpelier. The last syllable of *Vermont*, or the thought of Vermont's mountains, or of French settlers, or of wind, or of snow, or of anything that can be peeled, could prime the name Montpelier in your memory store.

In an experiment that demonstrated the value of retrieval cues generated by elaborative encoding, Timo Mäntylä (1986) presented 500 nouns one by one in a single very long session. He did not ask the subjects to memorize the nouns but asked them to write down either one or three words that they regarded as properties of the object named by each noun. For example, for the word *barn* a subject might write *large, wooden, red*. He then surprised the subjects with a test of their ability to recall all 500 nouns. As cues, he gave them either their own self-generated properties or those generated by a different subject in the same experiment. Subjects who received three self-generated properties for each word were able to recall correctly more than 90 percent of the 500 nouns. When only one property was available or when the properties had been generated by someone else, recall was much poorer (see Figure 9.15).

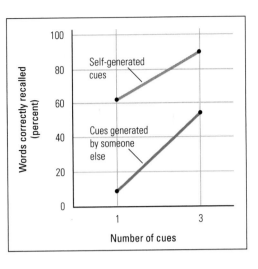

FIGURE 9.15 Value of self-generated retrieval cues Subjects generated either one or three single-word properties related to each of 500 nouns. Later they were tested for their ability to recall each noun, using either their own self-generated properties or another subject's self-generated properties as retrieval cues. (Data from Mäntylä, 1986.)

Contextual Stimuli as Retrieval Cues

The environmental context that we find ourselves in at any given moment provides retrieval cues that prime our memories for our past experiences in that context. Such priming is generally adaptive, because our past experiences in a given context are often relevant to our future experiences in that context. Sitting behind the steering wheel of an automobile primes my memories relevant to driving, the sight and smell of a gymnasium prime my memories of basketball rules and strategies, and standing at a podium primes my memories of lecture techniques that were helpful in the past.

Many experiments have shown that people who are given facts or word lists to memorize in a particular context do better at recalling that information if tested in that same context than if tested in a different context (Smith & Vela, 2001). The context might be a particular room, or it might be a single very noticeable stimulus that seems to be incidental to the learning task. In one series of experiments, for example, people who studied a list of words in a room that smelled of chocolate or cinnamon/apple or mothballs performed better on a recall test if that same smell was present than they did if a different smell, or no smell, was present (Schab, 1990). Other experiments have shown that even instructions to imagine the context that was present during learning can facilitate recall (Smith & Vela, 2001).

32

How is the effect of context on memory adaptive? What is some evidence that retrieval is best when the retrieval context is similar to the encoding context?

Memory Construction as a Source of Distortion

Remembering is not just a process of retrieving traces that were laid down during the original encoding. The brain is not a tape recorder, video camera, or CD burner that records information at high fidelity; and remembering is not a matter of finding the right cassette or disk and playing it back. Instead, remembering is an active, inferential process guided by a person's general knowledge and intuitions about the world and by cues in the present environment. When you hear a story or experience an event, your mind encodes into long-term memory only some parts of the available information. Later, when you try to recount the story or event, you retrieve the encoded fragments and fill in the gaps through your logic and knowledge, which tell you what must have happened even if you can't quite remember it. With repeated retelling, it becomes harder to distinguish what was present in the original encoding from what was added later. Thus, memory of the story or experience is not a simple readout of the original information but a *construction* built and

33

What does it mean to say that memories are constructed?

rebuilt from various sources. Our ability to construct the past is adaptive because it allows us to make logical and useful sense of our incompletely encoded experiences. But the process can also lead to distortions.

Effects of Preexisting Beliefs: Fitting Memories to Schemas and Scripts

One of the first psychologists to call attention to the role of people's general knowledge or beliefs in their more specific memories was the British psychologist Frederick Bartlett. Bartlett (1932) used the term **schema** to refer to one's generalized mental representation, or concept, of any given class of objects, scenes, or events. He used the term especially in relation to concepts that may vary from culture to culture and that involve spatial or temporal relationships among the individual units of the object, scene, or event. For example, in our culture today people might share a relatively common schema of a living room, perhaps including a couch, an easy chair, and a rocking chair, all oriented around a television set, with a coffee table in front of the couch. When we enter a new living room, we recognize it as a living room and assess its unique features by comparing it with our already-existing schema. Schemas that involve the organization of events in time, rather than of objects in space, are commonly called **scripts** by today's cognitive psychologists (Schank & Abelson, 1977). The typical children's birthday party is a good example: There are games, followed by the presentation of the cake, the singing of "Happy Birthday," the blowing out of the candles, the eating of the cake, the opening of the presents, and then more games.

According to Bartlett and the results of many studies since his time, schemas do not just help us recognize and label the objects, scenes, and events that we encounter in daily life; they also affect the way we remember them later. We tend to remember any particular living room or birthday party as being more like the standard living room or birthday party than it really was. That is because we fill gaps in our memories for specific scenes and events with information drawn from our more general schemas and scripts.

34 ─ ─ ─ ─ ─ ─ ─ ─ ─ ─ ─ ─ ─ ─ ◄ In a classic demonstration of the effect of general knowledge on memory for the

How did Bartlett demonstrate that culture-specific schemas affect the way that people remember a story?

specific, Bartlett (1932) asked British university students to listen to a Native American story entitled "The War of the Ghosts" and later asked them to retell the story from memory. He found that the story often changed in the retelling, and he found certain consistencies in those changes. Details not essential to the plot tended to drop

Following the script Years from now, this boy may construct a memory of his seventh-birthday party largely from his knowledge of the typical birthday-party script.

out, and those that were essential were often exaggerated. Also, points in the story that were consistent with Native American beliefs but not with the students' own beliefs were often changed to be more consistent with the latter. For example, the protagonist's obligation to certain spirits—a key component of the original story—tended to be transposed into an obligation to his parents. The changes were not deliberate; the students were trying to retell the story accurately, but they inevitably used their own ways of understanding things—their own schemas—to fill the gaps in their memory.

False Eyewitness Memories: Effects of Suggestion

Memory construction is affected not just by preexisting schemas but also by events that occur after the event being remembered was encoded. Such constructions assume more than academic importance in courtrooms or psychotherapists' offices, where they can have serious consequences.

Perhaps the most egregious of false memories are those that send innocent persons to prison or, sometimes, to death. In the 1990s, when DNA testing began to identify dozens of people who had been convicted of serious crimes they did not commit, the U.S. Attorney General's office ordered a study to discover the causes of those injustices. That study, and similar studies since then, concluded that the great majority of those convictions came about because of highly confident eyewitness identifications (Wells & others, 2002, 2006). In many cases the eyewitness was not confident early in the investigative process, but became so over time. An example is the case of Larry Mayes, who spent 21 years in prison for a rape he did not commit (Loftus, 2004). The victim failed to pick Mayes in two initial police lineups, but then became confident that he was the rapist after police helped her "recover" her memory of him through hypnosis. By the time of trial, the face of Larry Mayes was clearly embedded in her mind and she was certain he was the rapist.

Hypnosis is a state of high suggestibility; psychologists have shown repeatedly that false memories can be created relatively easily through suggestions or encouragement made in that state (Lynn & others, 1997; Steblay & Bothwell, 1994). People who hold steadfastly to truly bizarre memories—such as having been abducted by aliens from another planet—often first recalled or became confident about those memories when questioned under hypnosis by investigators who believe in such phenomena (Newman & Baumeister, 1996). Many experiments—some involving simulated crimes—have shown that memories can also be altered or created through suggestions and encouragement without hypnosis (Spinney, 2008). In one study, simply saying, "Good job, you are a good witness," dramatically increased witnesses' confidence in their memories of who committed the simulated crime, whether or not the memories were true (Wells & Bradfield, 1999). Other studies have shown that leading questions can alter people's memories not just of who was involved in an incident, but also of what happened.

In a classic experiment, Elizabeth Loftus and J. C. Palmer (1974) had adults view a film depicting a traffic accident. Later, the researchers asked some of the subjects how fast the cars were going when they *hit* each other, and they asked others how fast the cars were going when they *smashed into* each other. The question with the word *smashed* elicited estimates of faster speed than did the question with the word *hit*. Moreover, when the subjects returned a week later and were asked to remember the film and say whether there was any broken glass in the accident, those who had heard the word *smashed* were more likely to say they saw broken glass (though actually there was none in the film) than were those who had heard the word *hit*. In subsequent studies,

➤ - - - - - - - - - - - - - - - - - - - **35**

What is some evidence that eyewitnesses' memories, even when very confidently expressed, are not always reliable? What is some evidence that suggestions made after the event can influence eyewitnesses' memories?

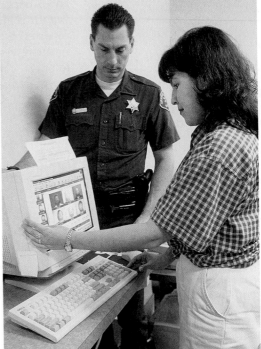

Trying not to influence her memory
This woman's judgment as to whether any of these men committed the crime that she witnessed could be affected by facial expressions of approval or disapproval from the officer standing before her. He may be trying to remain expressionless, but, ideally, he should not be in the room with her at all.

Spencer Grant/Photo Edit

Loftus and others showed that such memory distortion is especially likely if the misinformation is introduced in just the manner that a clever but biased detective or cross-examiner is likely to introduce it—repeatedly but subtly, in the context of recounting aspects of the event that really did occur (Loftus, 1992; Zaragoza & Mitchell, 1996).

False Memories of Childhood Experiences: Effects of Suggestion and Imagination

If an adult in psychotherapy begins to recall instances of having been abused in childhood, does the memory necessarily reflect the truth, or might it have been constructed from ideas implanted by a well-intentioned but misguided therapist? In the 1980s, a number of high-profile court cases centered on this question. Some people were suing their parents for past, horrible abuses discovered in therapy, and some parents were suing therapists for implanting false memories in their offspring. The cases led to a spate of psychological research showing that techniques of suggestion, encouragement, and imagination indeed can create false memories of childhood experiences.

◄ In one such study, Elizabeth Loftus and Jacqueline Pickrell (1995) led adults to believe that at age 5 they had been lost in a certain shopping mall and had been helped and comforted there by an elderly woman—an experience that in fact had never happened, according to the subjects' parents and other close relatives who served as informants. Yet 25 percent of the subjects maintained—both at initial questioning and in follow-up interviews 1 and 2 weeks later—that they could remember the event. Some even elaborated upon it with details beyond those supplied by the researchers.

Subsequent studies showed that false-memory construction can be abetted by imagination. In one experiment, researchers told each subject (falsely) that according to the subject's parents, a particular embarrassing incident had occurred in his or her childhood (Hyman & Pentland, 1996). The made-up incident was one in which the subject, at age 5, had been running around at a wedding reception and had knocked over the punch bowl, spilling punch on the bride's parents. Subjects in the *imagination condition* were asked, in two successive sessions, to form vivid mental images of this event to help them remember it, and others, in the *control condition*, were asked just to think about the event as a way of remembering it. The result was that mental imagery sharply increased reported memory (see Figure 9.16). In an interview conducted after the second imagery session, 38 percent of the subjects in the imagery condition, compared to only 12 percent in the control condition, claimed that they could remember the punch-spilling incident.

Other experiments have shown that imagery alone, even without misleading suggestions from the researcher, can create false memories. In one, adults were simply asked to imagine a certain painful medical procedure—a procedure that in fact is never performed—and then, later, were asked to try to remember whether or not that procedure had ever been done to them in their childhood. The result was that over 20 percent of those in the imagination condition, compared to about 5 percent in the control condition, said that they could remember enduring that procedure (Mazoni & Memon, 2003).

36 – – – – – – – – – – – – – – – – – –
How have false memories for childhood experiences been implanted in experiments, and what evidence indicates that imagination can facilitate false-memory construction?
– – – – – – – – – – – – – – – – – – – –

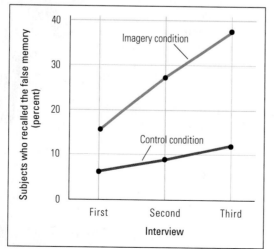

FIGURE 9.16 Effect of imagery on development of a false memory Adult subjects were told (falsely) about an incident that happened in their childhood. They were asked to try to remember it either by thinking about it (control condition) or by vividly imagining what might have happened (imagery condition). This procedure was repeated the next day, and the subjects' memories were again assessed in a third session, 2 days after the first. The graph shows the percentage of subjects in each condition, at each interview, who claimed to remember the incident. (Based on data in Hyman & Pentland, 1996.)

Such research should not lead us to conclude that all our childhood memories are false constructions. The research does, however, suggest strongly that childhood memories are even more subject to distortion by suggestion and imagination than are memories acquired later in life.

Source Confusion and Social Pressure as Causes of False-Memory Construction

According to some theorists, a basic cause of most if not all cases of false-memory construction is *source confusion* (Lindsay, 2008). We acquire information from various sources—including firsthand experiences, stories we have heard, and scenes we have imagined—and our minds reorganize the information in ways that may be meaningful but that obscure the ties between each item and its original source. Events that are conceptually linked but came from different sources may become confounded in memory. The memory of the actual traffic accident witnessed becomes confounded with the memory of what the cross-examiner implied about the accident. The memory of an actual event in childhood becomes confounded with a story heard from others or with an imagined scene constructed by free association in a psychotherapy session.

Social pressure also, no doubt, figures into many cases of false memory (Loftus, 1997). In most of the experiments just described, subjects were in one way or another led to believe that they should remember the suggested events. Similar pressure occurs in crime investigations, where the investigator acts as if any normal person should remember the incident's details. And it sometimes occurs in psychotherapists' offices, where a misguided therapist conveys the message that certain kinds of incidents, such as childhood abuse, must have happened and that the patient's task is to remember those incidents (McNally, 2003; Pendergrast, 1995). A person who feels pressured, even gently so, to come up with a memory is more likely than an unpressured person to identify a vague, possible memory as an actual memory; and the more often the memory is repeated, and the more praise the person receives for recalling it, the more confident the person becomes that the memory is true. The opposite is probably true also: a person who feels pressured by family members or an abuser to believe that certain memories are figments of his or her imagination may come to doubt memories that are accurate.

> ──────────── ─37
> **How might source confusion and social pressure contribute to false-memory construction?**

SECTION REVIEW

To use information held in long-term memory, we must be able to retrieve it.

Mental Associations and Retrieval

➤ Mental associations are links among items of information in long-term memory, which provide a basis for retrieval.

➤ The principles of contiguity and similarity underlie the formation of mental associations. The second of these two principles is a derivative of the first.

➤ Network models describe long-term memory as a vast web of associations that vary in strength. Activation can spread along associative pathways in a way that enables memory retrieval and thought.

➤ Elaborative rehearsal affects the number and meaningfulness of associations to new information and thereby its retrievability.

➤ The environmental context of learning can provide useful retrieval cues resulting from associations created at the time of encoding.

Memory Construction and Distortion

➤ Memories are not passive, complete records like photographs or sound recordings; instead, they are constructed and reconstructed.

➤ Schemas and scripts, which represent our general knowledge and beliefs, can affect memory construction at both encoding and retrieval, assisting memory but also sometimes distorting it.

➤ Leading questions, suggestions (especially those made under hypnosis), imagination, source confusion, and social pressures can distort memories or create false ones by influencing the constructive process of memory.

■ Multiple Memory Systems: Beyond the Modal Model

Most of the research and ideas about memory described thus far have fit at least moderately well into the framework of the modal model. The model has helped differentiate active (working) memory from dormant (long-term) memory and has provided a basis for defining the processes of attention, encoding, and retrieval. But the model does not account for the entire range of phenomena that can reasonably be classified as memory.

38 ----------------------------------
What types of memories are not accounted for by the modal model?

◄ Look again at the diagram of the modal model in Figure 9.1 (p. 310). Its central feature is the box labeled "Working memory," which is equated with conscious perception and thought. According to the model, new information can be encoded into long-term memory only if it is first perceived consciously in working memory, and information in long-term memory can influence behavior only if it is called back into working memory. Thus the model does not account for memories that can affect behavior without becoming conscious.

Distinctions Among Explicit- and Implicit-Memory Systems

39 ----------------------------------
What are the differences between explicit and implicit memory, and how is each memory type assessed? In what sense are implicit memories more context-dependent than explicit memories?

◄ *Explicit memory* is the type of memory that can be brought into a person's consciousness. It provides the content of conscious thought, and it is highly flexible. Explicit memories can be called to mind even in settings quite different from those in which they were acquired, and they can be combined with other explicit memories for purposes of reflection, problem solving, and planning. Such memory is called *explicit* because it is assessed through explicit tests—tests in which the person is asked to report directly (explicitly) what he or she remembers about a particular entity or event. It is also called *declarative memory* because the remembered information can be declared (stated in words).

Implicit memory, in contrast, is the type of memory that does not enter into the contents of consciousness. It consists of all the unconscious means through which previous experiences can influence a person's actions and thoughts. Such memory is called *implicit* because it is assessed through implicit tests—tests in which the memory is not reported directly but is inferred from behavioral responses. I would test your memory for balancing on a bicycle not by asking you how to do it but by asking you *to* do it. Your good performance on the bicycle would imply to me that you know how to balance on it. Because people do not report in words the relevant information, implicit memory is also called *nondeclarative memory*. Implicit memories are much more closely tied to the contexts in which they were acquired than are explicit memories. Whereas explicit memories can be called forth voluntarily outside of their original context, implicit memories exert their effects automatically in the context of the specific stimuli, tasks, or problems to which they pertain.

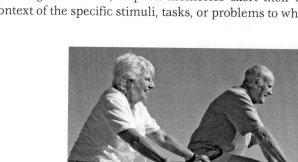

Procedural memory The learned skill of balancing on a bicycle is retained as implicit procedural memory. You can't say just how you do it, but you don't forget it.

© pixland/Corbis

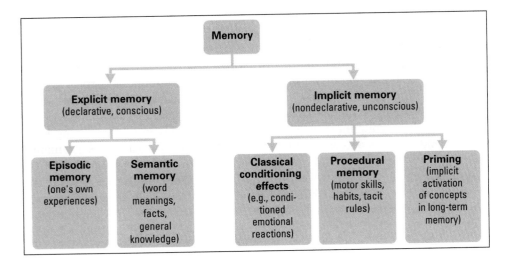

FIGURE 9.17 Types of long-term memory Explicit- and implicit-memory systems follow different rules and involve different neural systems in the brain. The explicit and implicit categories can be further subdivided into narrower memory categories that may also involve different neural systems. (Based on Tulving, 1985, and Squire & others, 1993.)

In addition to distinguishing between explicit and implicit memories, cognitive psychologists also distinguish among subclasses of each type, along the lines depicted in Figure 9.17.

Varieties of Explicit Memory: Episodic and Semantic

As shown in Figure 9.17, explicit memory is divisible into two subclasses. ***Episodic memory*** is explicit memory of one's own past experiences. Your memory of what you did and how you felt on your 16th birthday, or of what you ate for dinner last night, or of any other specific episode in your life, is episodic memory. Episodic memories always have a personal quality. An integral part of your episodic memory of an event is your memory of yourself experiencing that event—as participant, witness, or learner. The experiments on constructed memories in the previous section all had to do with episodic memories.

Semantic memory, by contrast, is explicit memory that is not tied mentally to a particular past experience. It includes knowledge of word meanings (which is one definition of semantics) plus the myriad facts, ideas, and schemas that constitute one's general understanding of the world. It also includes knowledge of oneself that is not mentally tied to the re-experiencing of a particular episode in one's life. Your memories that apples are red, that penguins are birds, that you were born on such-an-such a date, and that psychology is the most fascinating of all academic subjects are examples of semantic memory. Of course, all such information had to have been acquired through past experiences in your life, but your memory of the information does not depend on remembering those experiences. To remember your birth date, or that penguins are birds, you do not have to remember anything about the circumstances in which you learned that fact.

Recalling an item from semantic memory is a bit like looking for information in an encyclopedia. To find an item that doesn't come easily to mind, you probe your mind with terms or concepts that have meaningful associations to that item. The network model of knowledge organization that you saw in Figure 9.14 (p. 336) has to do with the organization of semantic memory.

40

How do the two subclasses of explicit memory differ from one another?

Arlo & Janis comic strip.

Here is a test question: *What is classical conditioning?* After answering the question, think about *how* you answered it. Did you think back to your experience of reading about classical conditioning in **Chapter 4** of this book, or to your experience of hearing your professor define classical conditioning, and try to reconstruct the definition from your memory of that experience? Or did you just *know* the answer, without having to reflect on any particular past experience? If the first is the case, then your memory of the definition of classical conditioning is an episodic memory (or at least partly so); if the second is the case, it is a semantic memory. In general, episodic memories are more fleeting, less stable, than semantic memories. Over time, we forget most of our memories of our specific past experiences, but the general knowledge that we extract from those experiences often stays with us. In the comic strip on this page, Gene's recall of the renting of the movie is episodic memory, while Arlo's knowledge of what is best for Gene is semantic memory.

Varieties of Implicit Memory

41

What are some examples of procedural memory, and why are such memories classed as implicit?

◄ Implicit memory can also be divided into subclasses, as depicted in the right-hand portion of Figure 9.17 on page 343. One subclass consists of the memories resulting from classical conditioning—the internal changes that lead a person or animal to respond to conditioned stimuli (discussed in **Chapter 4**). A second subclass is a broad one referred to as **procedural memory,** which includes motor skills, habits, and unconsciously learned (tacit) rules. With practice you improve at a skill such as riding a bicycle, hammering nails, or weaving a rug. The improvement is retained (remembered) from one practice session to the next, even though you are unaware of the changes in muscle movements that make the difference. (An operant-conditioning account of such improvement is discussed in **Chapter 4.)** You can even learn to make decisions based on complex rules without ever becoming aware of the rules (Greenwald, 1992), and that phenomenon, too, exemplifies procedural memory.

Some experiments demonstrating rule-based procedural memories use what are called *artificial grammars* (Frensch & Rünger, 2003; Reber, 1989). The grammars consist of sets of rules specifying which letters may or may not follow certain other letters in strings that are several letters long. For example, one rule might be that an *X* at the beginning of a string must be followed by either another *X* or a *V*, and another rule might be that a *J* anywhere in the middle of a string must be followed by a *B*, *K*, or *T*. Subjects are not told the rules. Instead, they are shown examples of grammatical and non-grammatical strings, labeled as such, and then are asked to categorize new examples as grammatical or not, on the basis of their "gut feelings." The subjects typically do not learn any of the rules explicitly—they cannot state the rules—yet they learn to make correct categorizations at a rate significantly better than chance. The memories that guide their correct choices are implicit.

42

Why is priming considered to be implicit memory? What function does priming play in a person's everyday thought?

◄ A third variety of implicit memory is priming (Tulving, 2000). *Priming* was defined earlier in this chapter (on p. 318) as the activation, by sensory input, of information that is already stored in long-term memory. This activation is not experienced consciously, yet it influences subsequent conscious perception and thought and thus provides a link between implicit and explicit memory. Priming helps keep our stream of thought running along consistent, logical lines. When we see or think about an object, event, or idea, those elements of our semantic memory that are relevant to that perception or thought become activated (primed) for a period of time, so they are more easily retrievable into conscious, working memory. Priming is classed as implicit memory because it occurs independently of the person's conscious memory for the priming stimulus. As noted in the discussion of attention, priming can even occur when the priming stimulus is presented in such a way that it is never consciously perceived.

Neuropsychological Evidence for Separate Memory Systems

Further evidence for multiple, distinct memory systems comes from studies of people who have impaired memory resulting from brain damage. Brain damage can destroy one kind of memory while leaving another kind intact.

Implicit Memory Remains Intact in Temporal-Lobe Amnesia

Earlier in the chapter you read of the severe memory deficits of H. M. and other patients with temporal-lobe amnesia. Those deficits had to do entirely with explicit memory. Such patients generally behave normally on all sorts of implicit-memory tests. If classically conditioned to blink their eyes in response to a conditioned stimulus, they show the conditioned response as strongly in subsequent tests as do non-amnesic subjects (Daum & others, 1989). If given practice with a new motor skill, such as tracing a pattern that can be seen only in its mirror image, they show normal improvement from session to session and retain the effects of previous learning even if months elapse between one session and the next (see Figure 9.18; Gabrieli & others, 1993; Milner, 1965). Similarly, they can learn and retain artificial grammars and tacit rules for grouping objects into categories (Knowlton & others, 1992; Poldrack & Foerde, 2008), and they show as much activation of long-term semantic memories in response to priming stimuli as do normal subjects (Gabrieli, 1998; Levy & others, 2004).

43

What is the evidence that the hippocampus and nearby temporal-lobe structures are not essential for forming or using implicit memories?

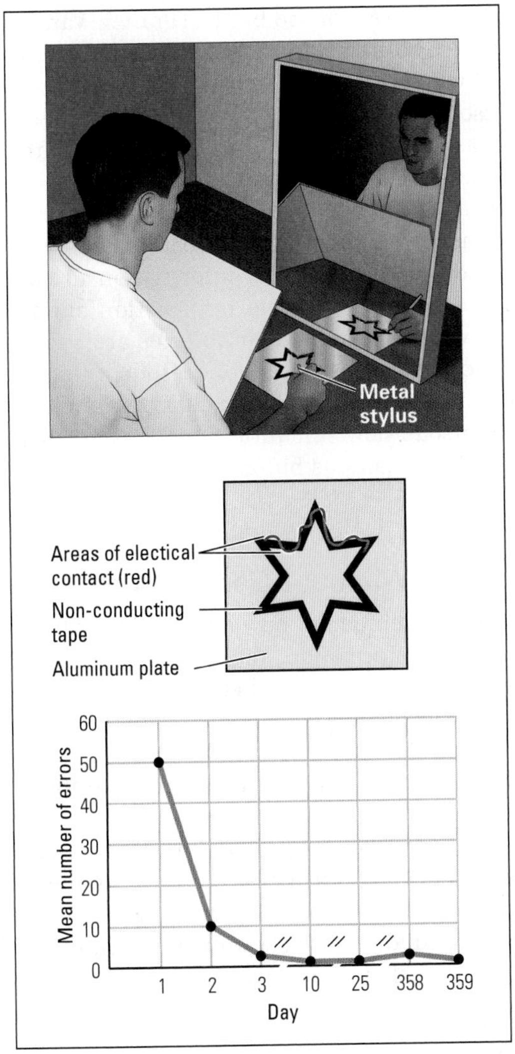

Metal stylus

Areas of electical contact (red)

Non-conducting tape

Aluminum plate

FIGURE 9.18 Implicit memory without explicit memory As shown in the graph, the temporal-lobe-amnesic patient H. M. improved from session to session in a mirror-tracing task, even though at each session he could not remember having performed the task before. The task was to trace a star under conditions in which the star and hand could be seen only in a mirror, so that movements had to be made oppositely from the way in which they appeared. An error was counted whenever the stylus moved off the star's outline. The data points on the graph represent the average number of errors per trial for the seven trials that occurred in each session. Sessions occurred on three successive days and then after delays of 1 week, 15 days, and nearly a year. (Graph adapted from Gabrieli & others, 1993.)

In all these examples the implicit memory is manifested even when the amnesic subjects cannot consciously remember anything at all about the learning experience. In one experiment, a severely amnesic patient learned to program a computer over a series of sessions. At each session his programming ability was better than it was in the previous session, even though he had no explicit memory of ever having programmed a computer before (Glisky & others, 1986).

Semantic Memory Without Episodic Memory in Some Amnesic Patients

The most severe cases of temporal-lobe amnesia entail loss of both episodic- and semantic-memory encoding. H. M. not only failed to remember anything about his own experiences that occurred after his surgery (in 1953) but also failed to remember almost all factual information that he had experienced after that date (Corkin, 2002). He could not name new world leaders or entertainers, and if asked to draw a car or a radio from memory, he would draw a 1940s or early 1950s version (Milner, 1984). But patients with less severe forms of amnesia typically manifest a greater deficit in episodic memory than in semantic memory (Bayley & others, 2008; Tulving, 2002).

◄ The most extreme differentiation between episodic and semantic memory is found in patients who suffer from a rare disorder called *developmental amnesia*. These people have bilateral damage to the hippocampus, but not to structures surrounding it, caused by temporary loss of blood flow to the brain at the time of birth or in early childhood. The hippocampus is more susceptible to permanent damage caused by lack of oxygen than is the rest of the brain. Faraneh Vargha-Khadem and her colleagues (1997, 2002; Gardiner & others, 2008) have identified and studied several young people who suffer from this disorder. All these individuals have severe deficits of episodic memory. If asked what happened a few hours ago or yesterday or at their last birthday party, they can recount little or nothing. Yet, despite this, they developed speech, reading, vocabulary, and other verbal capacities within the normal range. They all attended mainstream schools and learned and remembered facts well enough to perform passably on school tests. When they were presented with new factual information in controlled studies, they later remembered a good deal of that information but did not remember the episodic experience of learning it. Their abilities are consistent with other evidence that the hippocampus is essential for episodic-memory encoding but not for semantic-memory encoding (Eichenbaum, 2003). Amnesiacs such as H. M., who lose the ability to encode new semantic as well as episodic memories, have damage not just to the hippocampus but also to other portions of the temporal lobes.

44 — — — — — — — — — — — — —
What is some evidence that semantic memory can occur in the absence of episodic memory and that the hippocampus is more important for the latter than the former?
— — — — — — — — — — — —

Other Evidence of Semantic Memory Without Episodic Memory

It may at first seem surprising that people can remember new information without remembering the experience of learning that information. Yet, with a little poking around in your own semantic store, you will find many facts that you yourself know but can't relate to any episodes in your life (though it probably took you longer to forget the episodes than amnesic patients would take). I know that kumquats are a kind of fruit, but I can't recall any instance in my life of ever seeing, reading about, or hearing of kumquats.

Older people are especially familiar with the phenomenon of knowing without knowing how they know. In old age, the capacity to form new episodic memories generally declines more rapidly than does the capacity to form new semantic memories (Johnson & others, 1993). Young children also show excellent semantic memory and poor episodic memory. During their first 4 years of life, children acquire an enormous amount of semantic information—including word meanings and facts about their world—that will stay with them throughout their lives. But children under 4 are relatively poor at recalling specific episodes in their lives, and none of us in adulthood can recall much about our own childhood prior to about age 4 (Eacott, 1999). Apparently the human ability for episodic-memory encoding develops more slowly and unravels more quickly than that for semantic-memory encoding.

The relatively poor episodic memory at both ends of the life span may be related to prefrontal cortical functioning (Li & others, 2005; Wheeler & others, 1997). The prefrontal cortex develops more slowly in childhood and tends to suffer more damage in old age than does the rest of the brain. People with prefrontal cortical damage typically experience a much greater loss in episodic-memory encoding than in semantic-memory encoding (Wheeler, 2000). This brain area, which is much larger in humans than in other species and is crucial for planning and complex thought, may be essential for our sense of ourselves, including our sense of our own past experiences. We are not only a conscious species but also a self-conscious species. We—unlike any other animal, or at least much more so than any other animal—reminisce about our past, think about our position in the present, and project ourselves into the future as we make plans and contemplate their consequences. Such abilities are intimately tied to our capacity to form episodic memories (Schacter & others, 2007). This evolutionarily recent addition to the mammalian cognitive machinery is apparently more fragile—more destructible by aging and injuries—than is the more ancient semantic-memory system or the still more ancient implicit-memory system (Tulving, 2002; Wheeler & others, 1997).

> ⟶ ------------------------------- **45**
> **How might the relative lack of episodic memory in early childhood and old age be explained? How does episodic memory seem to distinguish us from other species?**

PEANUTS

SECTION REVIEW

Our brain has various memory systems, some not accounted for by the modal model.

Explicit and Implicit Memory

➤ Information in explicit (declarative) memory can be brought into consciousness, while that in implicit (nondeclarative) memory cannot, though it can influence thought and behavior.

➤ Explicit memory includes two subclasses: episodic memory, which is memory of particular past experiences, and semantic memory, which is one's store of general knowledge and beliefs.

➤ Subclasses of implicit memory include the learning that arises from classical conditioning, procedural memories (e.g., how to play a guitar chord), and priming. These are not described by the modal model.

Neuropsychological Evidence

➤ People with temporal-lobe amnesia exhibit normal capacities to form and use all sorts of implicit memories.

➤ People with temporal-lobe amnesia typically show greater loss of episodic memory than of semantic memory, probably because of episodic memory's greater reliance on the hippocampus.

➤ Children under 4 and the elderly generally exhibit poorer episodic memory than semantic memory, which may be related to immaturity of or damage in the prefrontal cortex.

Concluding Thoughts

Memory is the central topic of cognitive psychology. It is relevant to all aspects of both conscious and unconscious mental activity. To help yourself organize, elaborate upon, and thereby encode into long-term memory the ideas in this chapter, you may find useful the following general thoughts.

1. The modal model as a functional representation of the mind Throughout this chapter, the modal model served as the organizing structure for thinking about memory and the mind. You read of three memory stores, of control processes related to the stores, and of research aimed at characterizing the stores and processes. Your review and thoughts about all this will be most effective, I think, if you adopt a functionalist perspective. From that perspective, each store and process represents not a different part (or structure) of the mind but a different job that the mind performs in its overall task of acquiring and using information. As you review each mental component and process, think first of its main function—how it contributes to normal, everyday thought and behavior—and then think about how its special characteristics help it serve that function.

You might apply such elaborative reasoning to (a) sensory memory and differences between iconic and echoic memory; (b) the process of attention, including roles played by the unconscious, automatic processing of unattended stimuli; (c) working memory and differences between the phonological loop and the visuospatial sketchpad; (d) means of encoding information into long-term memory, including elaboration, organization, and visualization as encoding strategies; (e) the selective consolidation of long-term memories into a more stable form; (f) the role of retrieval cues in retrieving information from long-term memory; (g) the roles of general knowledge and inferences in constructing memories of past experiences; and (h) distinctions between semantic and episodic forms of long-term explicit memories.

2. Unconscious supports for conscious thought and behavior Long ago, Sigmund Freud (1933/1964) drew an analogy between the human mind and an iceberg. Consciousness, he suggested, is the small visible tip of the mind, which is supported by massive unconscious portions of the mind that are invisible, submerged under the ocean's surface. Although Freud's view of the functions of the unconscious mind (discussed in Chapter 15) was different from that presented here, the analogy remains apt. We are conscious only of the perceptions and thoughts that course through our limited-capacity working memory. We are unconscious of all the preattentive analysis of information and of the top-down control of selective attention that help determine which stimuli make it into working memory. We are also unconscious at any given time of the vast store of information we have in long-term memory and of the priming processes that

determine which portions of that store will, at that moment, be most available for retrieval into consciousness. And we are unconscious of the vast set of procedural memories and effects of conditioning that allow us to carry out routine tasks and respond adaptively to stimuli without conscious attention. As you review the chapter, think about all the ways in which unconscious information and processes support that small part of your mental activity that enters your consciousness.

3. The mind as a product of the brain In cognitive psychology the term *mind* refers to the entire set of processes—unconscious as well as conscious—by which information is acquired and used within a person to organize and direct the person's behavior. The mind is entirely a product of the brain. In recent times, cognitive psychology has merged increasingly with neuropsychology into what is now often called *cognitive neuropsychology*. Neuroimaging methods allow psychologists to identify which parts of the brain become most active as people engage in specific mental tasks. Such findings complement the results of more traditional neuropsychological studies of deficits in people who have suffered damage to specific portions of the brain.

Of course, there is a big difference between knowing *where* in the brain a particular task is accomplished and knowing *how* it is accomplished. At this point we are far from knowing how neural activity in the brain provides the basis for memories, thoughts, and decisions. The brain may be a computer, but it is vastly more complex than any non-biological computer that has yet been built. At this point the mapping of mental tasks onto brain areas is useful primarily as an adjunct to behavioral evidence in helping us to categorize mental tasks. The contention that two mental tasks are fundamentally different from one another can be supported by evidence that they involve different areas of the brain.

One way to review the results of the neuroimaging and brain-damage studies presented in this chapter is to think about how each helps to validate the distinctions among the different memory systems and processes described in the chapter. Stated differently, what evidence concerning the brain was presented to support the ideas that (a) attention involves top-down processes that magnify the neural analysis of attended stimuli; (b) verbal working memory and visuospatial working memory are distinct from each other; (c) verbal working memory is like talking and listening; (d) using visual memories to answer questions about *what* and *where* is like looking at an actual object or scene to answer those questions; (e) long-term memory is distinct from working memory; (f) long-term memory exists in more and less stable forms; (g) explicit memory is distinct from implicit memory; and (h) episodic memory is at least partly distinct from semantic memory.

Further Reading

Larry R. Squire & Eric R. Kandel (2009). *Memory: From mind to molecules, 2nd ed.* Greenwood Village, Colorado: Roberts & Company.

Larry Squire is a leader in the cognitive neuroscience of memory, and Eric Kandel is a Nobel laureate known especially for his research on the neural and molecular basis of memory in invertebrates. In *Memory*, a beautifully illustrated 250-page book, they combine their two realms of expertise to present the general reader with a story about the nature and neuronal basis of implicit- and explicit-memory systems. The story is as coherent as the data reasonably allow.

Gillian Cohen & Martin A. Conway (2008). *Memory in the real world, 3rd ed.* New York: Psychology Press.

This is a scholarly book, with each chapter written by a different expert or set of experts. Yet it is written clearly enough that a typical first-year undergraduate psychology major could enjoy it. As the title implies, the book deals with the kinds of memory problems that we all face in our daily lives. It deals, in separate chapters, with memories for past experiences, faces and names, intentions, places and routes, general knowledge, stories, and thoughts and dreams. There are also chapters on changes in memory across the life span, consciousness, and dysfunctions of memory. Gillian Cohen collaborated with the authors of most of the chapters, so the book has more coherence than do most books with multiple authors.

Philip J. Hilts (1995). *Memory's ghost: The strange tale of Mr. M. and the nature of memory.* New York: Simon & Schuster.

This is a literary essay on the role of memory in human existence, and it is also the biography of a man who has no autobiography of adult life. It is the story of H. M., who at age 27 (42 years before Hilts's book) lost his ability to form new explicit, long-term memories. We learn here something of what it is like to live in a disconnected series of eyeblinks, where the past is but a few seconds long.

Richard J. McNally (2003). *Remembering trauma.* Cambridge, MA: Harvard University Press.

Ever since Freud, some psychiatrists and psychologists have contended that people often repress traumatic memories, suffer from the unconscious effects of the memories, and recover in part by discovering the repressed memories in psychotherapy. In this book, McNally, a clinical psychologist and memory researcher, examines the clinical and laboratory evidence pertaining to this view and finds little support for it. The book reviews evidence concerning the poor formation of episodic memories in early childhood, the power of suggestion to distort and create memories, and the inability of real trauma survivors to forget their experiences.

Reasoning and Intelligence

Compared with other species, we are not the most graceful, nor the strongest, nor the swiftest, nor the fiercest, nor the gentlest, nor the most long-lived, nor the most resistant to the poisons accumulating in our atmosphere. We do, however, fancy ourselves to be the most intelligent of animals; and, at least by our own definitions of intelligence, our fancy is apparently correct. We are the animal that knows and reasons; that classifies and names the other animals; that tries to understand all things, including ourselves. We are also the animal that tells one another what we know, with the effect that each generation of our species starts off with more knowledge, if not more wisdom, than the previous one.

In the last chapter I equated the mind with memory, defining memory broadly as all the information we store, whether for long periods or only fleetingly, and all the mechanisms we have for manipulating that information. But what is the purpose of memory, thus defined? From an evolutionary perspective, there is no value in reminiscence for its own sake. What's past is past; we can't do anything about it. We can, however, influence our future. The evolutionary functions of memory—indeed, the functions of the mind—are to understand our present situation, recognize and solve problems posed by that situation, anticipate the future, and make plans that will help us prepare for and in some ways alter that future for our own (or our genes') well-being. Our memory of the past is useful to the degree that it helps us understand and deal adaptively with the present and the future. The processes by which we use our memories in these adaptive ways are referred to as *reasoning,* and our general capacity to reason is referred to as *intelligence*. Reasoning and intelligence are the topics of this chapter.

How People Reason I: Analogies and Induction

To a very large extent, we reason by using our memories of previous experiences to make sense of present experiences or to plan for the future. To do so, we must perceive the similarities among various events that we have experienced. Even our most basic ability to categorize experiences and form mental concepts depends on our ability to perceive such similarities.

When you see dark clouds gathering and hear distant thunder, you know from similar past experiences that rain is likely, so you take precautions against getting wet. If I were to show you a new invention that rolls along the ground on wheels, you would probably assume, from past experiences with other objects that move on wheels, that it is designed to convey things or people from place to place. Can you imagine any plan, any judgment, any thought that is not founded in some way on your ability to perceive similarities among different objects, events, or situations? My bet is that you can't.

Most of our everyday use of similarities to guide our thinking comes so easily and naturally that it doesn't seem like reasoning. In some cases, however, useful similarities are not so easily identified. As William James (1890) pointed out long ago, the ability to see similarities where others don't notice them is what, more than anything else, distinguishes excellent reasoners from the rest of us. Two kinds of reasoning that depend quite explicitly on identifying similarities are *analogical reasoning* and, closely related to it, *inductive reasoning*. These are the topics of this section.

Analogies as Foundations for Reasoning

In the most general sense of the term, an *analogy* is any perceived similarity between otherwise different objects, actions, events, or situations (Hofstadter, 2001). Psychologists, however, generally use the term more narrowly to refer to certain types of similarities and not to others. In this more restricted sense, an ***analogy*** refers to a similarity in behavior, function, or relationship between entities or situations that are in other respects, such as in their physical makeup, quite different from each other (Gentner & Kurtz, 2006).

By this more narrow and more common definition, we would not say that two baseball gloves are analogous to one another, because they are too obviously similar and are even called by the same name. But we might say that a baseball glove is analogous to a butterfly net. The analogy here lies in the fact that both are used for capturing some category of objects (baseballs or butterflies) and both have a somewhat funnel-like shape that is useful for carrying out their function. If you saw some brand-new object that is easily maneuverable and has a roughly funnel-like shape, you might guess, by drawing an analogy to either a baseball glove or a butterfly net, that it is used for capturing something.

Use of Analogies in Scientific Reasoning

1 ◄

What is some evidence concerning the usefulness of analogies in scientific reasoning?

Scientists often attempt to understand and explain natural phenomena by thinking of analogies to other phenomena that are better understood. As I pointed out in **Chapter 3,** Charles Darwin came up with the concept of natural selection as the mechanism of evolution partly because he saw the analogy between the selective breeding of plants and animals by humans and the selective breeding that occurs in nature. Since the former type of selective breeding could modify plants and animals over generations, it made sense to Darwin that the latter type could too. Johannes Kepler developed his theory of the role of gravity in planetary motion by drawing analogies between gravity and light, both of which can act over long distances but have decreasing effects as distance becomes greater (Gentner & Markman, 1997). Neuroscientists have made progress in understanding some aspects of the brain through analogies to such human-made devices as computers.

Analogies are often mothers of invention The Wright brothers succeeded in developing the first functional airplane (left-hand photo) because of many analogies they perceived to both large soaring birds (such as eagles) and bicycles (they were bicycle mechanics by profession) (Johnson-Laird, 2006). Bringing together many of the attributes of birds and bikes, they built a plane that was light and highly maneuverable, had a broad wingspan, and could be easily tilted to facilitate turns and counter buffeting winds. Their competitors, who failed, had instead been focusing on building heavy planes with powerful engines, based more on analogies to automobiles than to birds and bikes.

In an analysis of discussions held at weekly laboratory meetings in many different biology labs, Kevin Dunbar (1999, 2001) discovered that biologists use analogies regularly to help them make sense of new findings and to generate new hypotheses. In a typical one-hour meeting, scientists generated anywhere from 2 to 14 different analogies as they discussed their work. Most of the analogies were to other biological findings, but some were to phenomena completely outside the realm of biology.

To see if nonscientists would generate and use analogies to reason about physical systems, Dedre Gentner and Donald Gentner (1983) tested high school and college students with little training in physical sciences on their understanding of electrical circuits. As they tried to answer questions having to do with the movement of electricity through wires, some students thought of analogies to water moving through pipes and others thought of analogies to crowds of people or cars moving through tunnels or along roads.

Those who used plumbing analogies were best at answering questions about the effects of adding extra batteries to the circuit. They thought of batteries as being like pumps or like raised reservoirs, which add to the water pressure, and this helped them answer the battery questions correctly. Those thinking about traffic or crowd movement usually did not think of a good analogy to batteries, but did often think of an excellent analogy to resistors. They thought of resistors as being like gates or turnstiles, which restrict the number of cars or people that can pass through at any given time, and this analogy helped them to answer correctly questions about the effects of adding extra resistors to the circuit. Thus, the plumbing analogy was best for thinking about batteries and voltage (a measure of electrical force), but the traffic or crowd analogy was best for thinking about resistors and amperage (a measure of the amount of electricity moving through the circuit).

Traffic resistor The George Washington Bridge, which connects New Jersey and New York, restricts the flow of traffic into the city in a manner analogous to the way a resistor in an electrical circuit restricts the flow of electrons. In a research study, subjects who thought of such analogies performed better in answering questions about electrical circuits than did those who failed to think of them.

Use of Analogies in Judicial and Political Reasoning and Persuasion

2

How are analogies useful in judicial and political reasoning? What distinguishes a useful analogy from a misleading one?

Lawyers, politicians, and ordinary people frequently use analogies to convince others of some claim or course of action they support. The following example is taken from a novel (Bugliosi, 1978, cited by Halpern, 1996), but it certainly could occur in real life. At the end of a trial involving much circumstantial evidence, the defense attorney, in his summation to the jury, said that evidence is like a chain: it is only as strong as its weakest link. If one piece of evidence is weak, the chain breaks and the jurors should not convict the accused. The prosecutor then stood up and told the jurors that evidence is not like a chain, but is like a rope made of many separate strands twisted together. The strength of the rope is equal to the sum of that of the individual strands. Even if some of the weaker strands break, the strong ones still hold the rope together. The prosecutor had the more convincing analogy and won the case.

Researchers have found that university students are good at generating analogies to defend political viewpoints. In one study, in Canada, some students were asked to defend the position that the Canadian government should eliminate deficit spending even if that would require a sharp reduction in such social programs as health care and support for the needy, and other students were asked to defend the opposite position (Blanchette & Dunbar, 2000). Students arguing on either side developed many potentially convincing analogies. Not surprisingly, many of the analogies were from the closely related realm of personal finances—comparing the national debt to one's personal debt, or comparing a reduction in social programs to a failure to invest one's personal money for future gain. But many other analogies were taken from more distant realms. For instance, failure to eliminate the debt was compared to failure to treat a cancer, which grows exponentially over time and becomes uncontrollable if not treated early; and failure to provide care for the needy was compared to a farmer's failure to care for crops that have been planted, which ruins the harvest.

The next time you become involved in, or listen to, a political discussion, tune your ears to the analogies presented and, for each, ask yourself whether it helps to clarify the issue or misleads. You may be surprised at how regularly and easily analogies slip into conversations; they are a fundamental component of human thought and persuasion. We reason about new or complicated issues largely by comparing them to more familiar or less complicated issues, where the answer seems clearer. Such reasoning is useful to the degree that the structural relationships in the analogy hold true; it is misleading to the degree that those relationships don't hold true. Good reasoners are those who are good at seeing the structural relationships between one kind of event and another.

Analogy Problems Are Used in Tests of Reasoning Ability

3

How do the Miller Analogy Test and Raven's Progressive Matrices test assess a person's ability to perceive analogies?

Tests of reasoning ability commonly use analogy problems. The Miller Analogy Test, for example, is made up entirely of analogy problems. This test is commonly required of people applying for graduate study and for certain kinds of jobs. Many correlational studies show that a person's score on this test is a reasonably good predictor of how well he or she will perform in graduate study or in a job that requires one to take new information into account and solve complex problems (Kuncel & Hezlett, 2007; Kuncel & others, 2004). Two examples of the types of problems in the Miller Analogy Test are the following:

1. PLANE is to AIR as BOAT is to (a) submarine, (b) water, (c) oxygen, (d) pilot.

2. SOON is to NEVER as NEAR is to (a) close, (b) far, (c) nowhere, (d) seldom.

To answer such questions correctly, you must see a relationship between the first two concepts and then apply it to form a second pair of concepts that are related to each other in the same way as the first pair. The relationship between PLANE and AIR is that the first *moves through* the second, so the correct pairing with BOAT is WATER. The second problem is a little more difficult. Someone might mistakenly think of SOON and NEVER as opposites and might therefore pair NEAR with its opposite, FAR. But *never* is not the opposite of *soon*; it is, instead, the negation of the entire dimension that *soon* lies on (the dimension of time extending from now into the future). Therefore, the correct answer is NOWHERE, which is the negation of the dimension that *close* lies on (the dimension of space extending outward from where you are now). If you answered the second problem correctly, you might not have consciously thought it through in terms like those I just presented; you may have just intuitively seen the correct answer. But your intuition must have been based, unconsciously if not consciously, on your deep knowledge of the concepts referred to in the problem and your understanding of the relationships among those concepts.

Another mental test that makes exclusive use of analogy problems is Raven's Progressive Matrices test, which is often used by psychologists as a measure of fluid intelligence, a concept discussed later in this chapter. In this test, the items are visual patterns rather than words, so knowledge of word meanings is not essential. Figure 10.1 illustrates a typical Raven's problem. The task is to examine the three patterns in each of the top two rows to figure out the rule that relates the first two patterns in each row to the third pattern. The rows are analogous to one another in that the same rule applies to each, even though the substance of the patterns is different from row to row. Once the rule is figured out, the problem is solved by applying that rule to the bottom row. In the example shown in Figure 10.1, the rule for each row is that the first pattern is superimposed onto the second pattern to produce the third pattern. Applying that rule to the third row shows that the correct solution to this problem, chosen from the eight pattern choices at the bottom, is number 8.

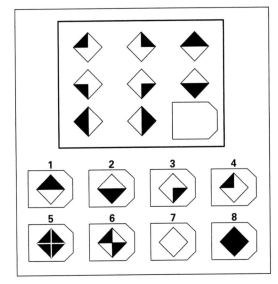

FIGURE 10.1 Sample Raven's problem This problem (from Carpenter & others, 1990, p. 409) is similar to the problems in Raven's Progressive Matrices test. The task is to infer the rule describing how the pattern changes within each of the first two rows and then to apply that rule to the third row to arrive at the correct solution. The solution is one of the eight choices at the bottom.

Inductive Reasoning and Some Biases in It

Inductive reasoning, or *induction*, is the attempt to infer some new principle or proposition from observations or facts that serve as clues. Induction is also called *hypothesis construction* because the inferred proposition is at best an educated guess, not a logical necessity. Scientists engage in inductive reasoning all the time as they try to infer rules of nature from their observations of specific events in the world. Psychologists reason inductively when they make guesses about the workings of the human mind on the basis of observations of many instances of human behavior under varied conditions. Detectives reason inductively when they piece together bits of evidence to make inferences as to who might have committed a crime. In everyday life we all use inductive reasoning regularly to make sense of our experiences or predict new ones. When I look outside in the morning, see that the ground is wet, and say, "It probably rained last night," I am basing that guess on inductive reasoning. My past observations of relationships between rain and wet ground have led me to induce the general rule that wet ground usually (though not always) implies rain.

All the examples of reasoning by use of analogies, discussed earlier, are also examples of inductive reasoning. In fact, in general, inductive reasoning is reasoning that is founded on perceived analogies or other similarities. The evidence from which one induces a conclusion is, ultimately, a set of past experiences that are in some way similar to one another or to the experience one is trying to explain or predict.

In general, we are very good at inductive reasoning, certainly far better at it than is any other species of animal (Gentner, 2003). However, most psychologists who study inductive reasoning have focused not on our successes but on our mistakes, and such research has led to the identification of several systematic biases in our reasoning. Knowledge of such biases is useful to psychologists for understanding the cognitive processes that are involved in reasoning and to all of us who would like to reason more effectively.

> **4**
>
> **What is inductive reasoning, and why is it also called hypothesis construction? Why is reasoning by analogy inductive?**

SPEED BUMP   **Dave Coverly**

The Availability Bias

5

What kinds of false inferences are likely to result from the availability bias?

The **availability bias** is perhaps the most obvious and least surprising bias in inductive reasoning. When we reason, we tend to rely too strongly on information that is readily *available* to us and to ignore information that is less available. When students were asked whether the letter *d* is more likely to occur in the first position or the third position of a word, most people said the first (Tversky & Kahneman, 1973). In reality, *d* is more likely to be in the third position; but, of course, people find it much harder to think of words with *d* in the third position than to think of words that begin with *d*. That is an example of the availability bias.

As another example, when asked to estimate the percentage of people who die from various causes, most people overestimate causes that have recently been emphasized in the media, such as terrorism, murders, and airplane accidents, and underestimate less-publicized but much more frequent causes, such as heart disease and traffic accidents (Brase, 2003). The heavily publicized causes are more available to conscious recall than are the less-publicized causes.

The availability bias can have serious negative consequences when it occurs in a doctor's office. In a book on how doctors think, Jerome Groopman (2007) pointed out that many cases of misdiagnosis are the result of the availability bias. For example, a doctor who has just treated several cases of particular disease, or for some other reason has been thinking about that disease, may be predisposed to perceive that disease in a new patient who has some of the expected symptoms. If the doctor then fails to ask the questions that would rule out other diseases that produce those same symptoms, the result may be misdiagnosis and mistreatment.

The Confirmation Bias

Textbooks on scientific method (and this book, in **Chapter 2**) explain that scientists should design studies aimed at disconfirming their currently held hypotheses. In principle, one can never prove absolutely that a hypothesis is correct, but one can prove absolutely that it is incorrect. The most creditable hypotheses are those that survive the strongest attempts to disprove them. Nevertheless, research indicates that people's natural tendency is to try to confirm rather than disconfirm their current hypotheses (Lewicka, 1998).

6

What are two different ways by which researchers have demonstrated the confirmation bias?

In an early demonstration of this **confirmation bias,** Peter Wason (1960) engaged subjects in a game in which the aim was to discover the experimenter's rule for sequencing numbers. On the first trial the experimenter presented a sequence of three numbers, such as *6 8 10*, and asked the subject to guess the rule. Then, on each subsequent trial, the subject's task was to test the rule by proposing a new sequence of three numbers to which the experimenter would respond *yes* or *no*, depending on whether or not the sequence fit the rule. Wason found that subjects overwhelmingly chose to generate sequences consistent with, rather than inconsistent with, their current hypotheses and quickly became confident that their hypotheses were correct, even when they were not. For example, after hypothesizing that the rule was *even numbers increasing by twos*, a person would, on several trials, propose sequences consistent with that rule—such as *2 4 6* or *14 16 18*—and, after getting a *yes* on each trial, announce confidently that his or her initial hypothesis was correct. Such persons never discovered that the experimenter's actual rule was *any increasing sequence of numbers.*

In contrast, the few people who discovered the experimenter's rule proposed, on at least some of their trials, sequences that contradicted their current hypothesis. A successful subject who initially guessed that the rule was *even numbers increasing by twos* might, for example, offer the counterexample *5 7 9*. The experimenter's *yes* to that would prove the initial hypothesis wrong. Then the subject might hypothesize that the rule was any sequence of numbers increasing by twos and test that with a counterexample, such as *4 7 10*. Eventually, the subject might hypothesize that the rule was any increasing sequence of numbers and, after testing that with counterexamples, such as *5 6 4*, and consistently eliciting *no* as the response, announce confidence in that hypothesis.

Reasoning that matters Doctors use inductive reasoning to diagnose medical problems on the basis of evidence that they gain from interviewing patients about their symptoms. The availability bias and confirmation bias can sometimes result in false diagnoses.

In other experiments demonstrating a confirmation bias, subjects were asked to interview another person to discover something about that individual's personality (Skov & Sherman, 1986; Snyder, 1981). In a typical experiment, some were asked to assess the hypothesis that the person is an *extravert* (socially outgoing), and others were asked to assess the hypothesis that the person is an *introvert* (socially withdrawn). The main finding was that subjects usually asked questions for which a *yes* answer would be consistent with the hypothesis they were testing. Given the extravert hypothesis, they tended to ask such questions as "Do you like to meet new people?" And given the introvert hypothesis, they tended to ask such questions as "Are you shy about meeting new people?" This bias, coupled with the natural tendency of interviewees to respond to all such questions in the affirmative, gave most subjects confidence in the initial hypothesis, regardless of which hypothesis that was or whom they had interviewed.

Groopman (2007) points out that the confirmation bias can couple with the availability bias in producing misdiagnoses in a doctor's office. A doctor who has jumped to a particular hypothesis as to what disease a patient has may then ask questions and look for evidence that tends to confirm that diagnosis while overlooking evidence that would tend to disconfirm it. Groopman suggests that medical training should include a course in inductive reasoning that would make new doctors aware of such biases. Awareness, he thinks, would lead to fewer diagnostic errors. A good diagnostician will test his or her initial hypothesis by searching for evidence *against* that hypothesis.

The Predictable-World Bias

We are so strongly predisposed to find order in our world that we are inclined to "see" or anticipate order even where it doesn't exist. Superstitions often arise because people fail to realize that coincidences are often just coincidences. Some great event happens to a man when he is wearing his green shirt and suddenly that becomes his "lucky" shirt.

The ***predictable-world bias*** is most obvious in games of pure chance. Gamblers throwing dice or betting at roulette wheels often begin to think that they see reliable patterns in the results. This happens even to people who consciously "know" that the results are purely random. Part of the seductive force of gambling is the feeling that you can guess correctly at a better-than-chance level or that you can

What is your lucky number? The predictable-world bias may operate consciously or unconsciously to lead gamblers, in games of pure chance, to believe that they have some control over the outcome. Some might bet their "lucky numbers," for example, in the belief that those numbers will come up more often than other numbers. This ad exploits people's vulnerability to a pre-dictable-world bias by suggesting that they have a better chance of winning by "playing now" than by playing later.

Tim Boyle / Getty Images

7

How does a die-tossing game demonstrate the predictable-world bias?

control the odds. In some games such a belief can lead people to perform *worse* than they should by chance. Here's an example.

◄ Imagine playing a game with a 6-sided die that has 4 red sides and 2 green sides. You are asked to guess, on each trial, whether the die will come up red or green. You will get a dollar every time you are correct. By chance, over the long run, the die is going to come up red on four sixths, or two thirds, of the trials and green on the remaining one third of trials. Each throw of the die is independent of every other throw. No matter what occurred on the previous throw, or the previous 10 throws, the probability that the next throw will come up red is two chances in three. That is the nature of chance. Thus, the best strategy is to guess red on every trial. By taking that strategy you will, over the long run, win on about two thirds of the trials. That strategy is called *maximizing*.

But most people who are asked to play such a game do not maximize (Stanovich & West, 2003, 2008). Instead, they play according to a strategy referred to as *matching*; they vary their guesses over trials in a way that matches the probability that red and green will show. Thus, in the game just described, they guess red on roughly two thirds of the trials and green on the other one third. They know that, over the long run, about two thirds of the throws will be red and one third green, and they behave as if they can predict which ones will be red and which ones will be green. But in reality they can't predict that, so the result is that they win less money over the long run than they would if they had simply guessed red on every trial.

Depending on how you look at it, you could say that the typical player in such a game is either too smart or not smart enough for his own good. Rats, in analogous situations—where they are rewarded more often for pressing a red bar than for pressing a green one—quickly learn to press the red one all the time when given a choice. Presumably, their maximizing derives from the fact that they are not smart enough to try to figure out a pattern; they just behave in accordance with what has worked best for them. Very bright people, those with the highest IQ scores, also typically maximize in these situations, but for a different reason (Stanovich & West, 2003, 2008): They do so because they understand that there is no pattern, so the best bet always is going to be red.

The predictable-world bias, really, is a tendency to engage in inductive reasoning even in situations where such reasoning is pointless because the relationship in question is completely random. Not surprisingly, researchers have found that compulsive gamblers are especially prone to this bias (Toplak & others, 2007). They act as if they can beat the odds, despite all evidence to the contrary and even if they consciously know that they cannot.

Outside of gambling situations, a tendency to err on the side of believing in order rather than randomness may well be adaptive. It may prompt us to seek order and make successful predictions where order exists, and that advantage may outweigh the corresponding disadvantage of developing some superstitions or mistaken beliefs. There's no big loss in the man's wearing his lucky green shirt every day, as long as he takes it off to wash it now and then.

We reason largely by perceiving similarities between new events and familiar ones.

Analogies as a Basis for Reasoning

➤ Analogies are similarities in behavior, functions, or relationships in otherwise different entities or situations.

➤ Scientists and also nonscientists often use analogies to make sense of observations and generate new hypotheses.

➤ Analogies are commonly used in legal and political persuasion.

➤ The Miller Analogies Test and Raven's Progressive Matrices measure an individual's ability to see and apply analogies.

Inductive Reasoning

➤ In inductive reasoning, or hypothesis construction, a new principle or proposition is inferred on the basis of specific observations or facts. We are generally good at inductive reasoning, but are susceptible to certain biases.

➤ The availability bias is our tendency to give too much weight to information that comes more easily to mind than does other relevant information.

➤ The confirmation bias leads us to try to confirm rather than disconfirm our current hypothesis. Logically, a hypothesis cannot be proven, only disproven.

➤ The predictable-world bias leads us to arrive at predictions through induction even when events are actually random.

■ How People Reason II: Deduction and Insight

Deductive reasoning, or *deduction,* is the attempt to derive logically the consequences that must be true if certain premises are accepted as true. Whereas inductive reasoning is reasoned guesswork, deductive reasoning (when done correctly) is logical proof, assuming that the premises really are true. In everyday life we reason deductively to derive the logical implications of statements that we hear. If you tell me that everyone in your family is over 6 feet tall, then, assuming I believe you, I know, by deduction, that everyone in your family is also over 5 feet tall. If you studied plane geometry, then you engaged in deductive reasoning that is more complex than most everyday examples as you tried to prove or disprove various correlates based on axioms that were given to you. In fact, all of mathematics is deduction. One starts, in mathematics, with certain givens and deduces the consequences.

Table 10.1 presents deductive problems that are typical of the types of problems used by psychologists who study such reasoning. Before looking at the answers, try solving each problem. The first is a *series problem,* which requires you to organize items into a series on the basis of a set of comparison statements and then arrive at a conclusion that was not contained in any single statement. The second is

8

How does deductive reasoning differ from inductive reasoning? How is it illustrated by series problems and syllogisms?

TABLE 10.1 Deductive-reasoning problems

Series problem	Syllogism	
John is taller than Henry.	All chefs are violinists (major premise).	*Answers:*
John is shorter than Mary.	Mary is a chef (minor premise). Is Mary a violinist?	indeterminate, no.)
Mary is shorter than Billy.	*Alternative forms, based on different minor premises:*	indeterminate, (Alternative forms:
Is Billy shorter than Henry?	Mary is a violinist. Is she a chef?	*Syllogism: yes.* *Series problem:* no.
	Mary is not a chef. Is she a violinist?	
	Mary is not a violinist. Is she a chef?	

a *syllogism*, which presents a major premise, or proposition, and a minor premise that you must combine mentally to see if a particular conclusion is true, false, or indeterminate (cannot be determined from the premises). Did you get the correct answer to each problem? If you did, you deduced correctly.

The Concrete Nature of Deductive Reasoning

There was a time when many psychologists believed that deductive reasoning is, at root, a logical process best understood in mathematical terms. For example, the highly influential Swiss developmental psychologist Jean Piaget (whose work is discussed in **Chapter 11**) believed that people who are roughly 13 years of age or older reason deductively by applying abstract logical principles, which can be expressed mathematically (Inhelder & Piaget, 1958). According to that view, problems are solved by a sort of mental algebra, in which the specific contents of the problem are mapped onto the *x*s and *y*s of logical equations, the equations are solved, and the answers are delivered.

Today relatively few psychologists accept the "abstract logic" or (to use Piaget's term) "formal operational" view of deductive reasoning (Evans, 2005). One reason for rejecting that view is that study after study, with people all over the world, including highly educated people in universities, has revealed that we are much better at solving problems put to us in concrete terms than problems put to us in terms of *x*s and *y*s or other abstract symbols. Research has repeatedly shown that our natural inclination is to solve deductive problems by reflecting on our real-world knowledge, not by thinking about laws of logic. With training, people can learn laws of logic, but even those who learn them well rarely apply them to the problems of daily life.

Bias to Attend to the Content of Deductive Problems Rather than to the Logic

9

How has it been shown that our strong tendency to rely on real-world knowledge can overwhelm our deductive-reasoning ability?

If people used formal logic to solve syllogisms, then it should not matter whether the statements in the problem are consistent with everyday experience, violate everyday experience, or are nonsensical. All that should matter is the formal structure of the problem. But numerous experiments show that the content does matter. Consider, for example, the following two syllogisms. In each, you are instructed to use logic alone, not your knowledge of the real world. In each, you are to assume that the first two propositions are valid and you are to judge whether or not the conclusion follows logically from those propositions.

1. All living things need water.
Roses need water.
Therefore, roses are living things.

2. All insects need oxygen.
Mice need oxygen.
Therefore, mice are insects.

Structurally, these two problems are identical. In each case, the conclusion is not valid. It does not necessarily follow, from the first two premises of the first problem, that roses are living things, or, from the first two premises of the second problem, that mice are insects. The correct conclusion for both of these syllogisms is "indeterminate." According to the premises, roses may be living things but they don't have to be, and mice may be insects but they don't have to be. The premises do not say that all things that need water are living, or that all things that need oxygen are insects.

When university students were given these problems, only about 30 percent got the first problem correct, but nearly all of them got the second problem correct (Stanovich, 2003). Even though the students understood that these are logic problems, not questions about real-world facts, they apparently could not resist being influenced by their knowledge of the real world. Their knowledge that roses are living things led them to believe that the conclusion to the first problem is logically valid, and their knowledge that mice are not insects led them to believe that the conclusion to the second problem is logically not valid. When the same type of problem is put to students using nonsense terms—such as "All schniezels need quisics"—an intermediate number, typically around 70 percent, get it correct (Stanovich, 2003). In that case, the content neither helps nor hinders.

The bias to use knowledge rather than formal logic in answering deductive reasoning questions can be construed as a bias to think inductively rather than deductively. Our natural tendency is to reason by comparing the current information with our previous experience, and, outside the mathematics classroom or psychology experiment on logic, that tendency generally serves us well. Part of the skill in solving problems that contradict our knowledge gained from past experience lies in our ability or willingness to suppress that knowledge.

Use of Diagrams and Mental Models to Solve Deductive Problems

A major difficulty in solving any complex deductive reasoning problem is that of representing all the problem information in a way that allows you to see all the relationships implied by that information. When you solved the series problem in Table 10.1 (on page 359), you may—either on paper or in your head—have made little stick figures to represent the relative heights of each of the four individuals—a longer stick for John than for Henry, a longer one yet for Mary, and a still longer one for Billy. Then all you had to do was examine the drawing or mental model and see that the stick for Billy is longer than that for Henry.

10

How are diagrams and mental models used to solve deductive problems? Specifically, how are Euler circles used to solve syllogisms?

People who are well trained in deductive reasoning make much use of diagrams. In one study, Ph.D. mathematicians were asked to reason aloud as they solved complex mathematical problems (Stylianou, 2002). All the mathematicians drew diagrams as part of the reasoning process. Typically, they would draw an initial diagram to represent the information given in the problem, perform some calculations, draw another diagram to represent the result of those calculations, perform some more calculations, draw another diagram, and so on, until they reached a solution. With diagrams, reasoners depict the problem information in a way that allows them to "see" the solution, or to visualize the next steps toward solution. A diagram on paper, rather than one held mentally, has the added advantage of freeing the mind for further thought about the problem.

Most people who can solve syllogisms easily, regardless of content, have mastered a little trick that allows them to turn any syllogistic premise into a picture. One version of this trick involves *Euler circles*, named after Leonard Euler, who used them in teaching logic to a German princess (Johnson-Laird, 1983). As an illustration of this method, Figure 10.2 shows how Euler circles can be used to represent the major premise of the syllogism presented in Table 10.1, "All chefs are violinists." The set of all chefs is represented by a circle, and the set of all violinists is represented by another circle. Since all chefs are violinists, the circle representing chefs falls entirely within the circle representing violinists. The problem information does not say whether or not all violinists are chefs, so there are two possible ways to represent the world of chefs within the world of violinists. The left-hand diagram depicts the possibility that some violinists are not chefs, and the right-hand diagram depicts the possibility that chefs and violinists are identical sets. Now, having drawn the two logically possible diagrams, it is easy to inspect them to answer all four questions posed by the syllogism in Table 10.1. For example, the question, "If Mary is a violinist, is she a chef?" must be judged as indeterminate. The left-hand diagram shows that it is possible for Mary to be in the violinist circle without being in the chef circle, but it is also possible for her to be in both circles.

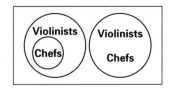

FIGURE 10.2 Euler circles Here the proposition "All chefs are violinists" is represented by Euler circles. Two diagrams are necessary to include both the possibility that some violinists are not chefs (left-hand diagram) and the possibility that all violinists are chefs (right-hand diagram).

Phillip Johnson-Laird (1985, 2006) contends that people who solve deductive reasoning problems without formal training and without pencil and paper typically do so by constructing mental models. To construct a good model, the reasoner must understand the premises and find a way to represent that information mentally in an easily accessible form. Once the information is well represented in a model, the reasoner can examine the model to find the answer to the problem.

Although Johnson-Laird does not claim that mental models must take the form of visual images, the easiest such models to understand are those that do. The most efficient mental models might be mental versions of diagrams comparable to Euler circles. According to Johnson-Laird, however, the models most people construct are more closely linked to the actual content of the problem than are Euler circles. For instance, a person reasoning about the chefs and violinists syllogism might imagine a group of people in a room, some of whom are wearing chefs' hats and holding violins, some of whom are holding violins but aren't wearing chefs' hats, and some of whom have neither violins nor chefs' hats. If the image includes all the possibilities allowed by the first premise and no other possibilities, then the reasoner can inspect that image to answer all the syllogism's questions.

11 – – – – – – – – – – – – – – – – – – –
What is some evidence for the mental-model theory of deductive reasoning and for the idea that such models often involve visual imagery?
– – – – – – – – – – – – – – – – – – –

◀ Research support for Johnson-Laird's mental model theory of deduction comes from a variety of sources. As is predicted by the theory, the difficulty that people have with deductive problems correlates positively with the number and complexity of the models that are required to represent all the information in the premises (Johnson-Laird & others, 1994, 2000). Consistent with the idea that people solve such problems by constructing mental models and holding them in working memory (the conscious mind), researchers have found that people who have large working memory spans (as measured by the standard tests of working memory described in **Chapter 9** and later in this chapter) are better at solving syllogisms requiring more than one model than are those who have smaller working memory spans (Oberauer & others, 2006).

Consistent with the idea that the models often take the form of visual images, researchers have found that performance on syllogisms correlates more strongly with visuospatial ability than with verbal ability, as measured by standard intelligence tests (Frandsen & Holder, 1969; Guyote & Sternberg, 1981). Also, neuroimaging studies reveal that areas of the brain that are involved in visuospatial reasoning become active during deductive reasoning, especially if the problem requires construction of a complex mental model or more than one model (Fangmeier & others, 2006; Goel, 2007).

Elements of Insight: How People Solve Problems Creatively

Sometimes a problem will stymie us for hours, or days, and then suddenly, "Aha!"—we see the solution. What causes such flashes of insight? What do we do to bring them about? What might we do to achieve such insights more quickly and regularly? To address these questions, psychologists have studied people's performance on *insight problems,* problems that are specially designed to be unsolvable until one looks at them in a way that is different from the usual way. Insight problems often entail a mix of inductive and deductive reasoning. Sometimes the crucial insight involves perceiving some similarity or analogy that one didn't perceive before, and sometimes it involves a new understanding of the problem's propositions or of the steps that could or could not lead to a solution.

Two Examples of Insight Problems

One problem that psychologists have used in insight experiments is the *mutilated-checkerboard problem* (Robertson, 2001). Subjects are presented with a standard checkerboard that has had two of its squares, at opposite corners of the board, removed or blocked off, as shown in Figure 10.3. They are also given 31 dominos, each of which is just the right size to fit over two adjacent squares of the checkerboard.

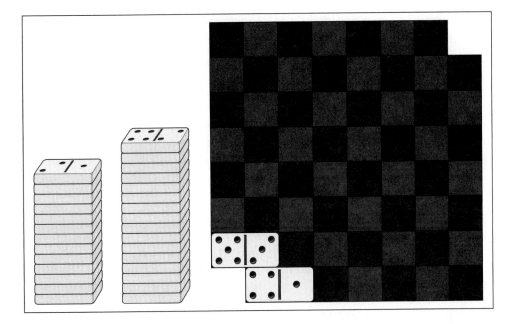

FIGURE 10.3 The mutilated-checkerboard problem Is it possible to fully cover all 62 squares of this incomplete checkerboard with 31 dominos?

Their task is to answer correctly the following question and to explain their answer: *Is it possible or impossible to set the 31 dominos on the board in such a way that they fully cover all 62 of the remaining squares of the checkerboard?*

Another classic insight problem is the *candle problem*. Subjects are given a candle, a book of matches, and a box of tacks and are asked to attach the candle to a bulletin board in such a way that the candle can be lit and will burn properly (see Figure 10.4). They are allowed to use no objects other than those they have been given.

Before reading the next section, spend a few minutes trying to solve each of these problems. As you work on each, pay attention to your own thought processes. If you solved either problem, how did you do it? What thoughts led you to insight? If you did not solve either problem, join the crowd. Relatively few people solve them without hints or clues of some kind. That is especially true of the mutilated-checkerboard problem. We'll come to the solutions shortly.

FIGURE 10.4 The candle problem
Using only the objects shown here, attach the candle to the bulletin board in such a way that the candle can be lit and will burn properly.

Breaking Out of a Mental Set: Broadening One's Scope of Perception and Thought

Insight problems are difficult, in general, because their solution depends on abandoning a well-established habit of perception or thought, referred to as a ***mental set,*** and then viewing the problem in a different way.

12
How is the concept of a mental set illustrated by the mutilated-checkerboard problem and the candle problem?

◀ Almost everyone presented with the mutilated-checkerboard problem sees it, at first, as a problem that can be solved by trial and error (Kaplan & Simon, 1990; Robertson, 2001). By trying all possible ways of arranging the 31 dominos over the checkerboard, with each domino covering two squares, it should be possible to find out if at least one arrangement will cover all the squares. Indeed, that is a reasonable route to solving the problem—for a computer, but not for a person. Craig Kaplan and Herbert Simon (1990) wrote a computer program to solve the problem by the trial-and-error method. The program solved the problem correctly, but had to make a total of 758,148 domino placements to do so. By eliminating, through mathematical means, those that are redundant with one another, it is possible to reduce the number of required domino placements to several thousand, but that is still far more than most people have time or patience for. (Some people, however, are more patient than others. Kaplan and Simon reported that a chemical engineering graduate student spent 18 hours trying to solve the problem through a combination of trial and error and mathematical formulas before giving up.)

So far, every person who has solved the mutilated-checkerboard problem and offered a convincing explanation for the solution, without writing a computer program, has done so by abandoning the trial-and-error approach. The problem is difficult partly because people fail to see that trial-and-error won't work, so they take a long time to give up that mental set. It is not obvious to most people that to solve it that way, they would have to run through thousands of different arrangements of the dominos and keep track of all of those arrangements so as not to repeat themselves.

ALICE, I'VE NOTICED A DISTURBING PATTERN. YOUR SOLUTIONS TO PROBLEMS ARE ALWAYS THE THINGS YOU TRY LAST.

The candle problem is difficult because people see the objects that they are given in too narrow a way. They see the tacks and matches as potentially useful, and they try to find ways of tacking the candle to the board, or using a match to melt wax to stick the candle to the board in such a way that it tilts out from the board so it can be lit. None of those methods work. Most subjects fail to see that the box that the tacks are in could help them solve the problem. Their mental set is to see that as just a container for the tacks, not as something that can be used to help solve the problem. Karl Duncker (1945), who invented the candle problem and performed the first experiments with it, referred to this type of mental set as *functional fixedness,* the failure to see an object as having a function other than its usual one.

Research in which subjects describe their thoughts aloud as they try to solve such problems shows that the first step to insight, generally, is to realize that the method they are trying is not likely to work and that a new method must be found. This realization leads people to reexamine the objects of the problem more broadly, to notice aspects of those objects that they didn't notice before, to think more broadly about possible ways of solving the problem, and in some cases to say, "Aha!" At this point, before reading the next section, you might try again to solve the mutilated-checkerboard problem and the candle problem if you haven't already solved them.

Discovering a Solution

13
How can deliberate attempts to look at the problem materials differently lead to solution of the mutilated-checkerboard and candle problems?

◀ Deliberate attention to aspects of the problem and materials that were not noticed before can lead to the sudden perception of a solution. Transcripts from the think-aloud study with the mutilated-checkerboard task revealed thought sequences something like the following for those who solved the problem (modified, for clarity, from Kaplan & Simon, 1990):

Hmmm. . . . Okay, each domino can fit over two squares. And no matter which way a domino is placed it always fits over one black square and one red one. A single domino can never cover two squares of the same color. Maybe that's important. I need to think about color. . . . Oh! The two squares that are removed from the board are both red. That means there are two more black squares to be covered than red ones. . . . That's it! No matter how you place the dominoes, you will always cover exactly the same number of black squares as red squares, because each domino covers one square of each color. Since the board has two more black squares than red ones, no matter how you place the dominoes there will be two black squares that are left uncovered! So, the answer to the question is *no: It is not possible to cover all the squares.*

Kaplan and Simon (1990) concluded the report of their study of the mutilated-checkerboard problem by saying, "[Good problem solvers] are good noticers." Those few who solved the problem quickly, with no or few hints, were those who noticed, early on, things about the problem to which others paid no attention. In an experiment, Kaplan and Simon (1990) showed that they could make the problem easier by making the relevant clues more obvious. Instead of using a standard checkerboard, they used, for one condition, a board in which the squares were labeled "bread" and "butter" in the alternating pattern shown in Figure 10.5. Because of the unusualness of this board, subjects paid more attention to the bread and butter pattern than to the black and red pattern on a standard board, and this led them to solve the problem more quickly. Each domino covers one bread and one butter, but there are two more breads to cover than butters, so there will always be two breads that can't be covered.

bread	butter	bread	butter	bread	butter	bread	
butter	bread	butter	bread	butter	bread	butter	bread
bread	butter	bread	butter	bread	butter	bread	butter
butter	bread	butter	bread	butter	bread	butter	bread
bread	butter	bread	butter	bread	butter	bread	butter
butter	bread	butter	bread	butter	bread	butter	bread
bread	butter	bread	butter	bread	butter	bread	butter
	bread	butter	bread	butter	bread	butter	bread

FIGURE 10.5 Variation of mutilated checkerboard The mutilated-checkerboard problem becomes easier if this bread-and-butter board is substituted for the standard checkerboard. Why?

With the candle problem, people might overcome functional fixedness by trying a different way of thinking about the problem. Instead of thinking, "How can I solve the problem with the materials I have?" they might step mentally back a bit and think, "What would I need to solve this problem?" The latter question might lead them to think, "I need something like a shelf, which can be tacked to the bulletin board." This might then lead them to look again at the materials to see if there is anything that could serve as a shelf, and—Aha!—They see that the tack box will make an adequate shelf if the tacks are removed. They remove the tacks, tack the box to the bulletin board so it forms a shelf, melt some wax onto the shelf, and stick the candle to it. By thinking about the problem differently, they were able to see the analogy between the tack box and a shelf, and that solved the problem. Researchers have shown that the candle problem becomes easier if the tacks are placed next to the box rather than in it (Adamson, 1952). Seeing the tack box empty makes it more obvious to subjects that it could be used for something other than holding tacks.

Unconscious Mental Processes May Lead to Insight

A good deal of research suggests that the mental capacities required for solving insight problems are different from those required for deductive reasoning. For example, one study showed that people's ability to solve insight problems, but not their ability to solve syllogisms, correlated positively with their *creativity,* measured by their ability to think of clever titles for jokes (Niu & others, 2007). Another study found that working memory capacity, which correlates positively with the ability to solve deductive reasoning problems, did not correlate at all with the ability to achieve insight in insight problems (Ash & Wiley, 2006). Researchers have also found that people commonly solve insight problems best if they take some time off from the problem, do something else, and then come back to it (Sio & Ormerod, 2009). The time off is referred to as an *incubation period.* The assumption is that during incubation the person is unconsciously reorganizing the material related to the problem while consciously doing and thinking about other things. Incubation appears to facilitate insight, not deduction. Deduction requires conscious attention to the problem.

All such observations suggest that unconscious mental processes, which do not involve working memory, are more important for solving insight problems than for

> **14**
>
> What evidence suggests that solving insight problems is qualitatively different from deductive reasoning? How might mental priming be involved in achieving insight?

solving deductive reasoning problems. One way to think about how the brain can reach insight through unconscious means involves the notion of priming.

As discussed in **Chapter 9,** *priming* refers to the activation of a mental concept to a level that does not reach the level of consciousness, but that nevertheless makes that concept more available for forming connections to other concepts. During an incubation period, all of the elementary concepts related to an unsolved problem may remain primed, even though the person is not consciously thinking about them. As the person goes about other activities and thinks about other things, some of those primed concepts may form new associations, and, eventually, some new association may create a solution. For example, a person who has failed to solve the candle problem may, during an incubation period, come into contact with a small shelf, which may create an association to the primed concept of the tack box. Either immediately or sometime later (when the person returns to thinking about the problem), that new association may cause the solution to leap into the person's conscious mind—"Aha! A tack box can be a shelf!"

The Value of a Happy, Playful Frame of Mind

◀ **15**

What evidence suggests that happiness or playfulness helps to solve insight problems? According to the "broaden-and-build" theory, how do positive emotions differ from negative emotions in their effects on perception and thought?

In a classic series of experiments, Alice Isen and her colleagues showed that people are better at solving insight problems if they are made to feel happy than if they are in a serious or somber mood (Isen, 2001). In one experiment, for example, college students who had just watched a comedy film were far more successful in solving the candle problem than were those who had seen either a serious film or no film (Isen & others, 1987). In another experiment, physicians were quicker to arrive at the correct diagnosis of a liver disease, based on evidence provided by the experimenter, if they had first been given a bag of candy (Estrada & others, 1997). Those who had received the candy reasoned more flexibly, took into account all the evidence more readily, and were less likely to get stuck on false leads than those who had not received candy. Other experiments have shown that a happy mood improves people's performance on various tests of creativity and on the ability to see whole patterns, rather than just the parts, in tests of visual perception (Fredrickson, 2003).

From the results of such research, Barbara Fredrickson (2001, 2006) has developed what she calls the *broaden-and-build theory* of positive emotions. Negative emotions, such as fear and anger, tend to narrow one's focus of perception and thought. Those emotions lead people to focus only on the specific emotion-evoking objects and to think only of routine, well-learned ways of responding. As pointed out in **Chapter 6,** such narrowing may be adaptive. A moment of emergency is not the right time to test creative new ideas; it is a time for action that has proven effective in the past. In contrast, according to Fredrickson, positive emotions—such as joy and interest—broaden one's scope of perception and thought and increase creativity. Positive emotions are felt when there is no imminent danger and one's immediate biological needs are relatively well satisfied. That, according to Fredrickson, is the time to think creatively and to come up with new ideas and ways of dealing with the world. From an evolutionary perspective, the building of ideas and knowledge during periods of safety and happiness is adaptive; those ideas may prove useful in satisfying future needs or preventing future emergencies.

My own interpretation (discussed more fully in **Chapters 4, 11, and 12**) is that it is not so much happiness per se, but the feeling of playfulness, that is conducive to learning and creativity (Gray & Chanoff, 1984). I suspect that the comedy films and bags of candy used by Isen and her colleagues put their subjects not just in a happy frame of mind, but in a playful one. Play is a time when people regularly view objects and information in new ways. In play, a tack box can easily be something other than a box for tacks. In play, one is open to considering all the information available, not just that which would seem at first glance to be most useful. A good problem solver may be one who combines the creative spirit of play with a serious search for a solution that really works.

Deduction and insight contribute to problem-solving ability.

Concrete Nature of Deductive Reasoning

➤ Deduction is the derivation of conclusions that must be true if the premises are true. Syllogisms are classic examples of deductive-reasoning problems.

➤ Older theories suggested that we reason by applying formal logic to the abstract structure of such problems, irrespective of specific content. Newer theories recognize that we are biased toward using content knowledge even when we are told not to.

➤ Our deductive reasoning is also concrete in that we tend to construct diagrams or mental models to represent problem information and then examine them to "see" the solution.

Insight

➤ The mutilated-checkerboard problem and the candle problem have been used to study insight, where sudden solutions come from seeing things in a new way.

➤ Insight often derives from abandoning a mental set (a habitual way of perceiving or thinking).

➤ Paying attention to aspects of the problem and materials that might otherwise be overlooked can lead to insight.

➤ Insight may also be facilitated by an incubation period, during which unconscious priming may prompt a solution. It may also be facilitated by a happy or playful frame of mind, which broadens the scope of perception and thought.

■ Effects of Culture and Language on Thought

Most studies of reasoning have been conducted in Western cultures, usually with university students as subjects. Thus, the studies may tell us more about how schooled Westerners think than about how human beings in general think. Researchers who have compared reasoning across cultures have found some interesting differences.

Some Cross-Cultural Differences in Perception and Reasoning

Responses of Unschooled Non-Westerners to Western-Style Logic Questions

Some psychologists have given standard tests of reasoning, prepared originally for Westerners, to people in non-Western cultures. A general conclusion from such research is that the way people approach such tests—their understanding of what is expected of them—is culturally dependent. Non-Westerners, who haven't attended Western-style schools, often find it absurd or presumptuous to respond to questions outside their realm of concrete experiences (Cole & Means, 1981; Scribner, 1977). Thus, the logic question, "If John is taller than Carl, and Carl is taller than Henry, is John taller than Henry?" is likely to elicit the polite response, "I'm sorry, but I have never met these men." Yet the same person has no difficulty solving similar logic problems that present themselves in the course of everyday experience.

Researchers have also found that non-Westerners are more likely than Westerners to answer logic questions in practical, functional terms rather than in terms of abstract properties (Hamill, 1990). To solve classification problems, for example, Westerners generally consider it smarter to sort things by taxonomic category than by function, but people in other cultures do not. A taxonomic category, here, is a set of things that are similar in some property or characteristic, and a functional group is a set of things that are often found together, in the real world, because of their functional relationships to one another. For instance, consider this problem: Which of the following objects does not belong with the others: ax, log, shovel, saw? The correct answer, in the eyes of Western cognitive psychologists, is *log*, because

16

How do unschooled members of non-Western cultures typically perform on classification problems? Why might we conclude that differences in classification are based more on preference than on ability?

it is the only object that is not a tool. But when the Russian psychologist Alexander Luria (1971) presented this problem to unschooled Uzbekh peasants, they consistently chose *shovel* and explained their choice in functional terms: "Look, the saw and the ax, what could you do with them if you didn't have a log? And the shovel? You just don't need that here." It would be hard to argue that such reasoning is any less valid than the reasoning a Westerner might give for putting all the tools together and throwing out the log.

This difference in reasoning may be one of preference more than of ability. Michael Cole and his colleagues (1971) described an attempt to test a group of Kpelle people in Nigeria for their ability to sort pictures of common objects into taxonomic groups. No matter what instructions they were given, the Kpelle persisted in sorting the pictures by function until, in frustration, the researchers asked them to sort the way stupid people do. Then they sorted by taxonomy!

An East–West Difference: Focus on Wholes Versus Parts

Richard Nisbett and his colleagues have documented a number of differences in the perception and reasoning of people in East Asian cultures, particularly in Japan and China, compared to that of people in Western cultures, particularly in North America (Masuda & Nisbett, 2006; Nisbett & others, 2001). According to these researchers, East Asians perceive and reason more holistically and less analytically than do Westerners. In perceptual tests, East Asians tend to focus on and remember the whole scene and the interrelationships among its objects, whereas Westerners tend to focus on and remember the more prominent individual objects of the scene as separate entities, abstracted from their background.

17 _____

How have researchers documented a general difference between Westerners and East Asians in perception and memory? How might this difference affect reasoning?

In one experiment, Japanese students at Kyoto University and American students at the University of Michigan viewed animated underwater scenes such as that depicted in Figure 10.6 (Masuda & Nisbett, 2001). Each scene included one or more large, active fish, which to the Western eye tended to dominate the scene, but also included many other objects. After each scene, the students were asked to describe fully what they had seen. The Japanese, on average, gave much more complete descriptions than did the Americans. Whereas the Americans often described just the large fish, the Japanese described also the smaller and less active creatures, the water plants, the flow of current, the bubbles rising, and other aspects of the scene.

The Japanese were also much more likely than the Americans to recall the relationships among various elements of the scene. For instance, they would speak

FIGURE 10.6 Sample scene viewed differently by Japanese and American students This is a still from one of the animated scenes used by Masuda and Nisbett (2001) to study cultural differences in perception and memory. While American students generally attended to and remembered the large "focal fish," the Japanese students generally attended to and remembered the whole scene.

Taka Masuda, Ph.D.

of the large fish as swimming against the water's current, or of the frog as swimming underneath one of the water plants. Subsequently, the students were shown pictures of large fish and were asked to identify which ones they had seen in the animated scenes. Some of the fish were depicted against the same background that had existed in the original scene and some were depicted against novel backgrounds. The Japanese were better at recognizing the fish when the background was the same as the original than when it was different, whereas the Americans' ability to recognize them was unaffected by the background. Apparently the Japanese had encoded the fish as integrated parts of the whole scene, while the Americans had encoded them as entities distinct from their background.

East Asians' attention to background, context, and interrelationships apparently helps them to reason differently in some ways from the way Westerners do (Nisbett & Masuda, 2007; Nisbett & others, 2001). For instance, when asked to describe why an animal or a person behaved in a certain way, East Asians more often than Americans talk about contextual forces that provoked or enabled the behavior. Americans, in contrast, more often talk about internal attributes of the behaving individual, such as motivation or personality. Thus, in explaining a person's success in life, East Asians might talk about the supportive family, the excellent education, the inherited wealth, or other fortunate circumstances that made such success possible, while Americans are relatively more likely to talk about the person's brilliant mind or capacity for hard work. (This East–West difference is discussed more fully in **Chapter 13.**)

Nobody knows for sure why these differences in perception and reasoning between Westerners and East Asians came about. The difference certainly is not the result of genetic differences. The offspring of East Asians who have emigrated to North America begin to perceive and think more like other Americans than like East Asians within a generation or two (Nisbett & others, 2001). Nisbett and his colleagues suggest that the roots of the difference are in ancient philosophies that underlie the two cultures. Western ways of thinking have been much influenced, historically, by ancient Greek philosophy, which emphasizes the separate, independent nature of individual entities, including individual people. East Asian ways of thinking have been much influenced by ancient Asian philosophies, such as Confucianism, which emphasize the balance, harmony, and wholeness of nature and of human society.

The Words of One's Language Can Affect One's Thinking

As you worked to solve the sample problems earlier in this chapter, you undoubtedly called forth information from long-term memory that you had originally learned through language. You may also have uttered words to yourself, subvocally, as part of your work on the problem.

We proudly conceive of ourselves as the thinking animal; but if beings from outer space were to contrast our species with other earthly creatures, they might well call us the linguistic animal. Other species can learn and use what they have learned to solve problems (discussed in **Chapter 4**), and they share with us a highly developed capacity for nonverbal communication (discussed in **Chapter 3**). But no other species has the well-developed, flexible, abstract, symbol-based mode of communication that we call *language*, which permits the conveyance of an infinite variety of facts and ideas.

Language allows us to tell one another not just about the here and now but also about the past, future, far away, and hypothetical. We are effective problem solvers largely because we know so much, and we know so much because we learn not only from our own experiences but also from others' reports. As the philosopher Daniel Dennett (1994) put it, "Comparing our brains with bird brains or dolphin brains is almost beside the point, because our brains are in effect joined together into a single cognitive system that dwarfs all others. They are joined by an innovation that has invaded our brain and no others: language."

Language not only is a vehicle of communication that allows us to learn from one another but also is a vehicle of thought. To some degree, perhaps a great degree, we think with words. As the Russian psychologist Lev Vygotsky (1934/1962) pointed out, young children often speak words out loud as they think to themselves, but with time they learn to speak the words subvocally and then to use words purely mentally, in abbreviated forms that may no longer be recognized as words. Such thought, which uses symbols that were acquired originally in the form of words, is called *verbal thought*. **Chapter 11** explains more about the nature of human language, its development in children, and its role in the development of thought. Right now our focus is on the idea that one's particular language and linguistic habits can affect the way one thinks about particular classes of problems.

18
What reasoning lies behind the idea of linguistic relativity?

◀ If language is a basis for thought, then people who speak different languages might think differently because of their different languages. This idea is most often attributed to the American linguists Edward Sapir and Benjamin Whorf. Sapir (1941/1964) and Whorf (1956) both argued that language affects many of the ways that we perceive, remember, and think about the world. Whorf coined the term **linguistic relativity** to refer to all such effects. Today most psychologists dispute the strongest forms of the linguistic relativity theory, which hold that even our most basic perceptions, such as our perceptions of color, depend on language. But nobody disputes the general idea that language affects some of the ways we think. Here I will describe three well-studied examples of such effects.

19
What is the difference between an egocentric and an absolute frame of reference? How is the use of these frames of reference dependent on language?

◀## Effect of Spatial Terms on Spatial Reasoning

We who speak English or other European languages regularly represent space in terms of an *egocentric frame of reference*—that is, a frame of reference that puts ourselves at the center. When looking at the objects on the table depicted in Figure 10.7, from the vantage point of the viewer shown at the left, we would say that the triangle is right of the circle, the square is left of the circle, and the oval is behind the circle. If we walked around to the other side of the table, all this would change: Then we would say that the triangle is left, the square is right, and the oval is in front. Because we have and regularly use the terms "right" and "left" to describe locations, people growing up in our culture learn to think of locations in terms of the egocentric frame of reference.

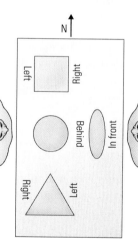

FIGURE 10.7 Egocentric and absolute spatial relationships When viewed from opposite sides of the table, the egocentric spatial relationships of these objects change, but the absolute spatial relationships do not.

Some languages do not have words for egocentric locations. People who speak those languages regularly use an *absolute frame of reference*, even when talking about things nearby. An absolute frame is one that does not depend on point of view; it is a frame that is based on the cardinal directions, what we call north, south, east, and west. When people who speak those languages look at the table depicted in Figure 10.7, they say, in effect, that the square is north of the circle, the triangle is south of the circle, and the oval is east of the circle. When they move from one side of the table to another, they do not have to change the words they use to describe the objects' positions. Because of this way of speaking, they are constantly keyed in to thinking of positions and directions in relation to the earth's coordinates, not in relation to their own momentary point of view. Reliance on the absolute frame of reference seems to have come about most often in the languages of people who make their living by hunting or fishing and must travel over broad, often unfamiliar, territories, either on land or sea, without getting lost (Levinson, 2003).

20
Why might we conclude that people who lack egocentric spatial terms develop much better absolute spatial abilities and think differently about space than do people who have such terms?

◀ Steven Levinson (1997, 2003) spent much time living with a group of Australian Aboriginal speakers of Guugu Yimithirr, which has no words for egocentric referencing. They would tell him such things as, "There is a big ant just north of your west foot" or "John is standing northeast of George and southwest of Henry." Even when they told stories or described their dreams, they would refer to the positions of objects and directions of movements in cardinal terms. By questioning them as

Stephen Levinson of the Max-Planck Institute

A head for directions Australian speakers of Guugu Yimithirr, such as the man shown here, constantly monitor the movements and relative positions of objects in their environment in terms of an absolute frame of reference—that is, in terms of the earth's coordinates. Their language forces them to do so, as they have no words for an egocentric frame of reference.

they went about their activities, Levinson discovered that they were always aware of the compass directions. Even when they were driven by car, along winding roads, at night, they could tell him correctly, without hesitation, which way was north, any time he asked. They could also point directly to their home, from wherever they were, any time he asked. Levinson himself would have to check his compass and map to see if they were correct.

Levinson describes one case in which several Guugu Yimithirr speakers were driven 250 kilometers (155 miles) to the south from their home village to discuss land-rights issues with other Aboriginal groups. The meeting took place in a room without windows, in a building reached through a parking garage. Weeks later, without forewarning, Levinson asked each of them about the meeting room and hotel rooms they had stayed in. He found that all of them could tell him immediately the layout of the main furnishings of these rooms in terms of cardinal positions, such as, "The speaker's podium was near the middle of the southeast wall."

Levinson suggests that these people learn, beginning early in childhood, to pay attention to cues concerning cardinal direction because their language forces them to. If they did not attend to such cues, they would have no way to describe later, either to others or to themselves in verbal thought, the positions and directions of things they had experienced. Their attention to directional cues becomes so automatic that they are not very articulate in describing just which cues they use. Levinson suggests that they automatically use such cues as the positions of the sun and stars, the lichen or other plant life growing on the sides of the trunks of certain trees, the directions of the prevailing winds in particular seasons, and, when unable to use other cues, their own ability to keep track of the turns they have made as they move about.

People who speak languages that lack egocentric spatial terms not only are far better at knowing where they are at any given time than are those who speak European languages, but they also respond differently in certain nonverbal tests of spatial reasoning. In one experiment, for example, a group of Tzeltal speakers was compared with a group of Dutch speakers in a test using the setup depicted in Figure 10.8 on page 372 (Majid & others, 2004). Tzeltal is a Mexican Mayan language that, like Guugu Yimithirr, lacks egocentric spatial terms. Each subject was first shown a sample card that contained a small green circle and a large yellow circle. Then the subject turned around, 180 degrees, and looked at a table that had four test cards, all identical to the original sample but oriented in different ways. When asked to choose the card that was most similar to the one they had seen on the other table, most of the Tzeltal speakers chose the card that was oriented identically to the original card in cardinal direction

FIGURE 10.8 Test of egocentric versus absolute spatial reasoning
After viewing the card on Table 1, the subject was asked to turn around and pick the card on Table 2 that is most similar to that on Table 1. Which would you have picked? Most Tzeltal speakers chose that which was identical to the original in its absolute spatial orientation, and most Dutch speakers chose that which was identical in egocentric orientation. (Adapted from Levinson, 2003, Figure 4.13, p. 160.)

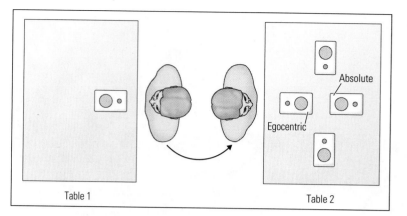

(the "absolute" choice in Figure 10.8) and nearly all the Dutch speakers chose the card that was oriented in the same direction relative to their own bodies as the original card (the "egocentric" choice in the figure).

According to Levinson and his colleagues, results such as these suggest strongly that language affects the way people think about space, not just the way they talk about it (Levinson, 2003; Majid & others, 2004). People who speak English, Dutch, or other languages that have egocentric spatial terms tend to think of space as it relates to themselves; people who speak Guugu Yimithirr, Tzeltal, or other languages that lack egocentric spatial terms tend always to think of space as it relates to the earth's coordinates.

Effect of Number Words on Math Ability

The languages of many hunter-gatherer groups contain very few number words. For instance, the language of the Piraha of Brazil has only three number words, which, translated to English, are *one, two,* and *more than two.* The Piraha do not count. In one experiment, tribe members were shown sets of nuts containing from one to nine nuts. Then the researcher placed the nuts in a can and drew them out one by one while asking, as each nut was removed, if any nuts were left in the can. Most of the tribe members were correct for one, two, or three nuts, but were incorrect for larger sets (Gordon, 2004). If the Piraha wanted to keep exact counts of things or to think mathematically, they would have to start by inventing or learning number words.

A more subtle linguistic effect on numerical reasoning may lie in the comparison of people who speak English or certain other European languages with those who speak Asian languages such as Chinese, Japanese, and Korean. Asian children greatly outperform American and European children in mathematics at every stage of their schooling. Usually that effect is attributed to differences in how mathematics is taught, but some researchers have argued that the difference may stem at least partly from a difference in language (Miller & others, 1995; Miura & Okamoto, 2003).

21

How might the number words of Asian languages help children learn the base-10 number system more easily than American and European children? What evidence suggests that they do learn the base-10 system earlier?

In English and other European languages the number words do not precisely mirror the base-10 number system that is used in all of arithmetic, but they do so in Chinese, Japanese, and Korean. While we count *one, two, . . ., nine, ten, eleven, twelve, thirteen, . . ., twenty, twenty-one, . . .,* the speakers of the Asian languages count (if their words were translated literally into English) *one, two, . . ., nine, ten, ten one, ten two, ten three, . . ., two-tens, two-tens one, ...* The words *eleven* and *twelve* give the English-speaking child no clue at all that the number system is based on groups of 10, whereas *ten one* and *ten two* make that fact abundantly clear to the Asian child. Even many English-speaking adults do not know that *teen* means "ten" (Fuson & Kwon, 1992), and children do not automatically think of *twenty* as "two tens." Because the Asian words make the base-10 system transparent, Asian children might develop an implicit grasp of that system and thereby gain an advantage in learning arithmetic.

Consider children learning to add two-digit numbers—say, 34 plus 12. English-speaking children pronounce the problem (aloud or to themselves) as "*thirty-four* plus *twelve*," and the words give no hint as to how to solve it. Chinese-speaking children, however, pronounce the problem (in effect) as "*three-tens four* plus *ten two*," and the words themselves point to the solution. In the two numbers together, there are four tens (*three tens* plus *one ten*) and six ones (*four* plus *two*), so the total is *four-tens six* (forty-six). From the perspective of Johnson-Laird's mental-model theory of reasoning, discussed earlier in the chapter, we might say that the words *three-tens four* and *ten two* lead directly to mental models that keep the tens and ones separate, whereas the words *thirty-four* and *twelve* do not.

Consistent with this view, a number of experiments have shown that children who speak Asian languages have a much better implicit understanding of the base-10 system, even before they begin formal mathematics training, than do children who speak European languages. In one experiment, for example, 6-year-olds in the United States and in France and Sweden (where number words contain irregularities comparable to those in English) were compared with 6-year-olds in China, Japan, and Korea on a task that directly assessed their use of the base-10 system (Miura & others, 1994). All the children had recently begun first grade and had received no formal training in mathematics beyond simple counting. Each was presented with a set of white and purple blocks and was told that the white blocks represented units (ones) and the purple blocks represented tens. The experimenter explained, "Ten of these white blocks are the same as one purple block," and set out ten whites next to a purple to emphasize the equivalence.

Each child was then asked to lay out sets of blocks to represent specific numbers—11, 13, 28, 30, and 42. The results were striking. The Asian children made their task easier by using the purple blocks correctly in over 80 percent of the trials, but the American and European children did so in only about 10 percent. While the typical Asian child set out four purples and two whites to represent 42, the typical American or European child laboriously counted out 42 whites. When they were subsequently asked to think of a different method to represent the numbers, most of the American and European children attempted to use the purple blocks, but made mistakes in about half the trials.

"*Big deal, an A in math. That would be a D in any other country.*"

Sexism and the Generic *Man*

My final example of an effect of language on thought has to do with a revolutionary change that began to occur in English usage in the 1970s. Most of you reading this book are too young to have experienced this change firsthand, but your professor may have struggled with it at some time in his or her career. The revolution was a deliberate movement to rid English of constructions that tended to characterize males as more typically human than females. One such construction was use of the word *man* to stand for both human beings in general (the generic *man*) and human males in particular. Many reformers argued that because these two concepts had the same label, they became fused into the same schema in people's minds, leading people to think, automatically, of males as more typical examples of human beings than are females. Historically, the use of the same word to stand both for human males and for human beings in general was no accident. Historically, and still among many people today, men have been considered quite explicitly to be the primary humans and women have been considered to be secondary.

To test the degree to which *man*, used in the generic sense, elicited a mental perception of humans in general versus human males in particular, Joseph Schneider and Sally Hacker (1973) performed an experiment involving hypothetical titles for chapters of a sociology textbook. One set of titles used the generic man construction, which was still common in textbooks of that time: *Social Man, Urban Man, Economic Man,* and so on. Another set avoided that construction, with titles such as *Society, Urban Life,* and *Economic Behavior.* The researchers gave one set of titles to one group of students and the other set to a similar group and asked each student to find pictures from newspapers and magazines that would be suitable for illustrating each chapter.

> 22
> **What logic and evidence suggest that the linguistic tradition of using the word *man* to refer to human beings in general was worth changing?**

Time **catches up** In recognition of the widely accepted cultural change in language, *Time* magazine changed its annual designation of "man of the year" to "person of the year," beginning in 2000.

The result was that about 65 percent of the pictures brought back by students in the *man* group depicted males only (the rest contained either both genders or females only), compared with about 50 percent male-only pictures brought back by the other group. These percentages were about the same for female and male students. From this, the researchers argued that the two meanings of *man* were in fact not distinct in people's minds. The students in this experiment knew consciously that *man* as used in those titles meant human beings in general, but their behavior suggested an unconscious mental compromise between that meaning and the male-only meaning.

Subsequent studies produced comparable results, not just for *man* but also for the use of *he* to refer to a person of unspecified gender (Harrison, 1975; Khorsroshahi, 1989; MacKay, 1980). Such research suggests that it was worth the effort for people of my generation to alter some of our ingrained ways of speaking and writing, which were considered proper when we were students.

SECTION REVIEW

Culture and language can affect perception, memory, and reasoning.

Cross-Cultural Differences in Perception and Reasoning	Effects of Language
➤ Unschooled non-Westerners do not deal with Western-style logic problems in the same way that Westerners do; they take a more concrete, practical, and functional approach.	➤ The term *linguistic relativity* refers to differences in perceiving, remembering, and thinking that result from differences in language.
➤ Compared with Westerners, people from East Asian cultures perceive more holistically—that is, in a more contextual, integrated, and relational way. This focus on wholes as opposed to parts can affect memory and reasoning.	➤ Speakers of languages that use an absolute rather than an egocentric frame of reference think differently about spatial relations and are more able to discern and remember the absolute positions of objects.
	➤ Compared to European languages, Asian languages use number words that more directly reflect the base-10 number system and apparently make it easier to learn that system.
	➤ The generic use of words such as "man" and "he" leads to interpretations slanted toward male examples.

▌ The Practice and Theory of Intelligence Testing

People differ from one another in many ways. Some are stronger, some are braver, some are more sociable, some are more dependable, some are kinder, and some are more mentally adept than others. It is that last difference that concerns us here.

The variable capacity that underlies individual differences in reasoning, solving problems, and acquiring new knowledge is referred to as ***intelligence.***

Psychologists have long been interested in measuring intelligence. Much of that interest derives from practical concerns. The first applied psychologists—practitioners who try to solve real-world problems using insights from psychology—were intelligence testers. School systems wanted intelligence tests to determine who could profit most from education; employers wanted them to help decide whom to hire for jobs that require mental ability; armies wanted them to help decide how to assign recruits to ranks and tasks. Intelligence tests have long served all these functions. But psychologists have also been interested in intelligence testing for theoretical, scientific reasons. By correlating individual differences in intelligence test scores with other characteristics of people and their experiences, psychologists have aimed to understand the biological and experiential factors that contribute to intelligence.

A Brief History of Intelligence Testing

Let's begin historically. Modern ideas and controversies about intelligence and its measurement have their roots in the very different ideas of Sir Francis Galton (1822–1911), in England, and Alfred Binet (1857–1911), in France.

Francis Galton's Tests of Mental Quickness and Sensory Acuity

Galton was a wide-ranging scholar and scientist who happened to be a half-cousin of Charles Darwin. He admired Darwin's work and was interested in extending it into the realm of human mental abilities. In 1869, he published a book entitled *Hereditary Genius*, in which he argued that the capacity for high intellectual achievement is inborn and passed along biologically in family lines. In line with this idea, he defined intelligence as the biological capacity for intellectual achievement, and he initiated a research program to measure it. He hoped to show that intelligence, as he defined it, lies in certain basic characteristics of the nervous system, which manifest themselves as mental quickness and sensory acuity—the speed and accuracy with which people can detect and respond to environmental stimuli. To pursue this idea, he devised various measures of basic motor and sensory abilities, such as the ability to react quickly to a signal or to detect slight differences between two sounds, lengths, or weights.

To assess the relationship among the various measures that he devised, Galton invented a statistical method that was later refined by Karl Pearson (1920) to produce the correlational method still used today (discussed in **Chapter 2**). To his disappointment, using this mathematical tool, Galton found only weak correlations among his various measures of reaction time and sensory abilities (Fancher, 1985). They did not seem to be measuring a unitary underlying biological capacity.

Research by other psychologists using Galton's measures proved even more disappointing. For example, an analysis of scores collected from 300 students at Columbia University and Barnard College showed no significant correlation between either reaction time or sensory acuity and academic grades (Wissler, 1901). Because Galton's measures seemed to be only weakly related to one another and unrelated to academic achievement, most researchers in the field of intelligence lost interest in them (Fancher, 1985). As you will see later, however, in recent times some psychologists have revived Galton's approach, using more refined measures of mental quickness, and have found significant correlations between such measures and other indices of intellectual ability.

Alfred Binet's Tests of School-Related Abilities

Modern intelligence tests have their ancestry not in Galton's measures of sensory acuity and reaction time, but in a test called the *Binet-Simon [Bin-**ay**-See-**mahn**] Intelligence Scale,* which was developed in France in 1905 by Alfred Binet (1857–1911) and his assistant Theophile Simon. Binet's view of intelligence was quite different from Galton's. He disputed Galton's claim that intelligence is closely related to sensory acuity, citing as one bit of evidence the example of Helen Keller, who had

23
According to Galton, what was the biological foundation of intelligence? How did Galton attempt to measure intelligence, and how did his measures prove to be disappointing?

24
How did Binet's view of intelligence and approach to measuring it differ from Galton's? What was the purpose of Binet and Simon's intelligence test, and how did they develop the test?

Alfred Binet and subject Before he was asked by the French Ministry of Education to develop a measure of intelligence, Binet experimented with various tests of motor and sensory capacities in children, using methods similar to those pioneered by Galton. The apprehensive expression on this boy's face reminds us that part of doing well on any ability test is overcoming the fear that stems from the novelty of the test situation.

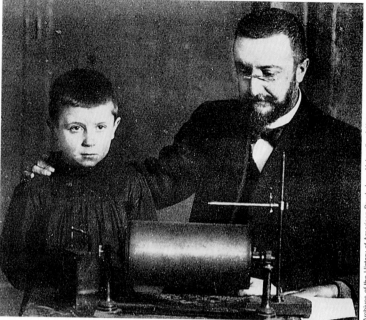

Archives of the History of American Psychology, University of Akron

been blind and deaf since her early childhood but was universally regarded as highly intelligent (Binet & Simon, 1916/1973). Binet believed that intelligence is best understood as a collection of various higher-order mental abilities that are only loosely related to one another (Binet & Henri, 1896). He also differed from Galton on the heredity question, arguing that intelligence is nurtured through interaction with the environment and that the proper goal of schooling is to increase intelligence. In fact, the major purpose of Binet and Simon's test—developed at the request of the French Ministry of Education—was to identify children who were not profiting as much as they should from their schooling so that they might be given special attention.

Binet and Simon's test was oriented explicitly toward the skills required for schoolwork. It included questions and problems designed to test memory, vocabulary, common knowledge, use of numbers, understanding of time, and ability to combine ideas. To create the test, problems were pretested with schoolchildren of various ages, and the results were compared with teachers' ratings of each child's classroom performance (Binet & Simon, 1916/1973). Items were kept in the test only if more of the high-rated than low-rated children answered them correctly; otherwise, they were dropped. Binet was aware of the circularity of this process: His test was intended to measure intelligence better than existing measures did, but to develop it, he had to compare results with an existing measure (teachers' ratings). Yet, once developed, the test would presumably have advantages over teachers' ratings. Among other things, it would allow for comparison of children who had had different teachers or no formal schooling at all.

By 1908, the Binet-Simon test was widely used in French schools. Not long after that, English translations of the test appeared, and testing caught on in England and North America even more rapidly than it did in France.

Modern Intelligence Tests Patterned After Binet's

25
What sorts of subtests make up modern IQ tests, such as the Wechsler tests, and how is IQ determined?

The first intelligence test commonly used in North America was the *Stanford-Binet Scale,* a modification of Binet and Simon's test that was developed in 1916 at Stanford University. The Stanford-Binet Scale has been revised over the years and is still used, but the most common individually administered intelligence tests today are variations of a test that was developed by David Wechsler in the 1930s and was modeled after Binet's. The descendants of Wechsler's tests that are most widely used today are the Wechsler Adult Intelligence Scale, Third Edition (WAIS-III), and the Wechsler Intelligence Scale for Children, Fourth Edition (WISC-IV).

TABLE 10.2 Subtests of the Wechsler Adult Intelligence Scale, Third Edition

Verbal subtests	Performance subtests
Vocabulary Words to be defined.	*Block Design* Blocks are to be arranged to match specific designs.
Similarities On each trial, the person must say how two objects or concepts are alike.	*Picture Completion* The person identifies the missing elements in each picture.
Information Questions about generally well-known people, places, events, and objects.	*Picture Arrangement* Cartoon drawings are to be arranged in sequence to tell a logical story.
Comprehension Questions tapping knowledge of practical information and ability to organize that information.	*Object Assembly* Puzzle pieces are put together to form a picture.
Digit Span String of orally presented digits must be repeated verbatim (and, in a second phase, in reverse order).	*Matrix Reasoning* Geometric shapes that change according to some rule are presented in an incomplete grid. From a set of choices, the person selects the shape that best completes the grid.
Letter-Number Sequencing Letters and numbers are presented in random order and the person must repeat the numbers in ascending order followed by the letters in alphabetical order.	*Digit-Symbol Coding* The person translates a series of single-digit numbers into symbols as quickly as possible, using a code that is provided.
Arithmetic Arithmetic problems to be solved mentally.	*Symbol Search* On each trial a target set and a search set of symbols are presented. The person says as quickly as possible whether or not a target symbol appears in the search set.

Sources: Compiled from information in A. S. Kaufman & E. O. Lichtenberger (1999), *Essentials of WAIS-III Assessment*. New York: Wiley.

Table 10.2 summarizes the various subtests of the WAIS-III. As indicated there, the subtests are grouped into two categories. The *verbal subtests* assess vocabulary, ability to explain how similar concepts are similar, general knowledge and general understanding of the social and physical world, verbal short-term (working) memory span, ability to organize verbal information quickly, and arithmetic ability. The *performance subtests* are designed to depend much less than the verbal subtests on verbal skills and already-acquired knowledge. These tests assess the abilities to match visual designs, to arrange pictures in a way that tells a story, to put puzzle pieces together to form a complete picture, to solve matrix reasoning problems (similar to the problem shown in Figure 10.1 on p. 355), to transform digits according to the rules of a code, and to spot target symbols quickly in arrays of visual symbols. The *full-scale* score is based on the sum of the scores of all the verbal and performance subtests.

The scoring system for every modern intelligence test uses results obtained from large samples of individuals who have already taken the test. These results are used as normative data to translate each individual's raw score on an intelligence test into an **IQ** (*intelligence quotient*) score. A person whose performance is exactly average for the comparison group is assigned an IQ score of 100. People whose performance is above or below average receive scores above or below 100, assigned in such a way that the overall distribution of scores fits the bell-shaped form known as a normal distribution, depicted in Figure 10.9. (For a more precise

Second-grader taking the WISC IQ test In one of the subtests of the Wechsler Intelligence Scale for Children (WISC), the child must arrange blocks to match specific designs.

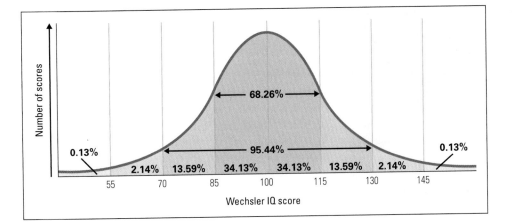

FIGURE 10.9 Standardized scoring of Wechsler IQ tests The scoring system for Wechsler IQ tests is based on the assumption that intelligence is distributed in the population according to a normal distribution (represented by the bell-shaped curve). Thus raw scores on the test are converted into IQ scores in such a way as to produce a normal distribution. Notice that with this system about 68 percent of IQ scores are between 85 and 115 and about 95 percent are between 70 and 130.

description of normal distributions and the method for standardizing test scores, see the Statistical Appendix at the end of the book.) For children, the comparison group for determining IQ is always a set of children who are the same age as the child being scored.

The Validity of Intelligence Tests as Predictors of Achievement

26

How have psychologists assessed the validity of IQ tests? What are the general results of such assessments?

A test is *valid* if it measures what it is intended to measure (as discussed in **Chapter 2**). If intelligence tests measure intellectual ability, then IQ scores should correlate with other indices of a person's intellectual ability. For the most part, researchers have assessed IQ validity in terms of the tests' abilities to predict success in school and careers. Not surprisingly—given that most modern intelligence tests are direct or indirect descendants of Binet's, which was explicitly designed to measure school abilities—IQ scores do correlate moderately well with grades in school; the correlation coefficients in various studies range from 0.3 to 0.7 (Brody, 1992; Jensen, 1980).

How well do IQ scores predict achievement outside of school? Many studies have shown that people with higher IQ scores are much more likely than those with lower scores to gain employment in intellectually demanding occupations such as medicine, law, science, and business management. This is true even if the comparison is just among people who were raised in the same or similar families, originating from the same socioeconomic background (Schmidt & Hunter, 2004). Still, the conclusions one can draw from such studies are limited by the fact that intellectually demanding jobs generally require high educational attainment. Thus, in theory, the relation between IQ and employment could be secondary to the fact that people with high IQs perform better in school.

A better index of the relation between IQ and career success comes from research correlating IQ with on-the-job performance as measured by supervisors' ratings, colleagues' ratings, or direct observations. Many such studies have been conducted, and they regularly show moderate positive correlations (Schmidt & Hunter, 2004). Not surprisingly, the strength of the correlations depends on the type of job. For jobs that require relatively little judgment and reasoning—such as assembly-line work—the average correlation is about 0.2; for jobs that require a great deal of judgment and reasoning—such as scientist, accountant, and shop manager—the correlation is typically about 0.5 to 0.6 (Schmidt & Hunter, 2004). For jobs in the high mental complexity category, IQ tests are better predictors of performance than any other measures that have been developed, including measures aimed at testing specific knowledge and skills related to the job (Gottsfredson, 2002; Schmidt & Hunter, 2004).

In addition to predicting school and work performance, IQ scores predict longevity (Deary, 2008). A study in Scotland, for example, revealed that people who scored high on an IQ test that was given to all 11-year-olds in the nation were significantly more likely to still be alive at age 76 than were those who scored lower on the test (Deary, 2008; Deary & Der, 2005). This was true even for people who were similar in education and socioeconomic status. The numbers were such that a 15-point difference in IQ was associated with a 21 percent difference in survival rate. At least one reason for longer survival, apparently, is better self-care. In that study as well as others, IQ scores were found to correlate positively with physical fitness and healthy diets and negatively with alcoholism, smoking, obesity, and traffic accidents (Gottfredson & Deary, 2004).

A common use of intelligence testing The scores that these French army recruits achieve on this IQ test will help determine the tasks and positions they are assigned to for their compulsory national service.

The Concept of General Intelligence and Attempts to Explain It

Historically, concern with the practical uses of intelligence tests for placement in school and jobs has always been paralleled by theories and research aimed at characterizing and explaining intelligence. What is the rationale for conceiving of "intelligence" as a unitary, measurable entity? How broadly, or narrowly, should intelligence be defined? Can variations in intelligence be related to properties of the nervous system? What is the evolutionary function of intelligence? These questions are still subject to heated debate. What I tell here, very briefly, is the most common story, the one told most often by those who are most centrally concerned with these questions.

"Do you have 'Intelligence for Idiots'?"

General Intelligence (*g*) as the Common Factor Measured by Diverse Mental Tests

In the early 20th century, the British psychologist and mathematician Charles Spearman (1927) conducted many research studies in which he gave dozens of different mental tests to people—all of whom were members of the same broad cultural group—and found that the scores always correlated positively with one another if his sample was large enough. That is, people who scored high on any one test also, on average, tended to score high on all other tests. Scores on tests of simple short-term memory span correlated positively with scores on tests of vocabulary, which correlated positively with scores on tests of visual pattern completion, which correlated positively with scores on tests of general knowledge, and so on. Most of the correlations were of moderate strength, typically in the range of 0.3 to 0.6.

> **27**
>
> What was Spearman's concept of general intelligence, or *g*? Why did Spearman think that *g* is best measured with a battery of tests rather than with any single test?

From this observation—coupled with a mathematical procedure that he invented, called *factor analysis* (discussed in **Chapter 15**), for analyzing patterns of correlations—Spearman concluded that some common factor is measured, more or less well, by every mental test. Spearman labeled that factor **g**, for **general intelligence.** To Spearman and to the many researchers still following in his footsteps, general intelligence is the underlying ability that contributes to a person's performance on all mental tests.

To Spearman and his followers, every mental test is partly a measure of *g* and partly a measure of some more specific ability that is unique to that test. From this point of view, the best measures of *g* are derived from averaging the scores on many diverse mental tests. That is exactly the logic that lies behind the use of many very different subtests, in standard intelligence tests such as the WAIS-III, to determine the full-scale IQ score (look back at Table 10.2 on p. 377).

The Distinction Between Fluid Intelligence and Crystallized Intelligence

Raymond Cattell was a student and research associate of Spearman's in England until he moved to the United States in 1937. He devoted most of his subsequent long career to developing a theory of personality (described in **Chapter 15**), but he also developed a new theory of intelligence, which he considered to be a modification of Spearman's theory. Cattell (1943, 1971) agreed with Spearman that scores on mental tests reflect a combination of general intelligence and a specific factor that varies from test to test, but he contended that general intelligence itself is not one factor but two. More specifically, he proposed that Spearman's *g* is divisible into two separate *g*'s. He called one of them *fluid intelligence*, abbreviated g_f, and the other crystallized intelligence, abbreviated g_c.

28

What evidence led Cattell to distinguish between fluid intelligence and crystallized intelligence?

◄ **Fluid intelligence,** as defined by Cattell (1971), is the ability to perceive relationships among stimuli independently of previous specific practice or instruction concerning those relationships. It is best measured by tests in which people identify similarities or lawful differences between stimulus items that they have never previously experienced or between items so common that everyone in the tested population would have experienced them. An example of the first type is *Raven's Progressive Matrices* test, discussed earlier and illustrated in Figure 10.1 (on p. 355). Examples of the second type are verbal analogy problems constructed only from common words, which essentially all speakers of the language would know—such as the two problems presented back on page 354.

A verbal analogy problem that would *not* be a good measure of fluid intelligence is the following (modified from Herrnstein & Murray, 1994):

RUNNER is to MARATHON as OARSMAN is to (a) boat, (b) regatta, (c) fleet, or (d) tournament.

Solving this problem is limited not just by ability to perceive relationships but also by knowledge of uncommon words (especially *regatta*), which reflects crystallized intelligence.

Crystallized intelligence, according to Cattell (1971), is mental ability derived directly from previous experience. It is best assessed in tests of knowledge, such as knowledge of word meanings (*What is a regatta?*), cultural practices (*Do forks go to the right or left of plates in a proper table setting?*), and how particular tools or instruments work (*How does a mercury-filled thermometer work?*). Although people may differ in the domains of their knowledge (one person may know a lot of words but little about tools, for example), Cattell considered crystallized intelligence to be a component of general intelligence. One's accumulated knowledge can be applied broadly to solve a wide variety of problems.

Like Spearman, Cattell based his theory largely on the factor analysis of scores on many different mental tests. Cattell's analysis showed him that mental tests tend to fall into two clusters: those that seem to depend mostly on raw reasoning ability and those that seem to depend mostly on previously learned information. Test scores within each cluster correlate more strongly with one another than with scores in the other cluster (as illustration, see Figure 10.10). In addition, Cattell (1971) found that measures of fluid and crystallized intelligence change differently with age. Fluid ability typically peaks at about age 20 to 25 and declines gradually after that, while crystallized ability typically continues to increase until about age 50 or even later.

Many research studies have corroborated Cattell's conclusions about the differences between fluid and crystallized intelligence in their variation with age. Figure 10.11 (on page 381) shows the combined results from many such studies for four mental tests (Salthouse, 2004). As you can see in the figure, vocabulary (ability to identify synonyms) increases steadily until the mid-50s and then levels off or decreases slightly. In contrast, ability to solve Raven's matrix problems decreases steadily throughout adulthood. The figure also shows that word span (a measure of working memory capacity) and mental speed decline in a manner that is essentially identical to the decline in scores on Raven's Progressive Matrices.

FIGURE 10.10 Hypothetical correlations among test scores, suggestive of two underlying intelligences Each coefficient in the matrix is the correlation between the two tests indicated by its row and column. Thus, 0.35 is the correlation between test 1 and test 2. All the correlations are positive. Notice, however, that the correlations among tests 1, 3, and 5 (in gold) and among tests 2, 4, and 6 (in purple) are higher than any of the other correlations. This pattern of correlations suggests that the tests measure two different but somewhat overlapping abilities. Tests 1, 3, and 5 are the best measures of one ability, and tests 2, 4, and 6 are the best measures of the other. This result could be taken as support for Cattell's theory if the items in one cluster of tests seem to measure raw reasoning (fluid intelligence) and those in the other seem to measure learned information (crystallized intelligence).

Tests	2	3	4	5	6
1	0.35	0.62	0.40	0.59	0.45
2	–	0.41	0.55	0.39	0.64
3	–	–	0.28	0.63	0.30
4	–	–	–	0.34	0.60
5	–	–	–	–	0.38

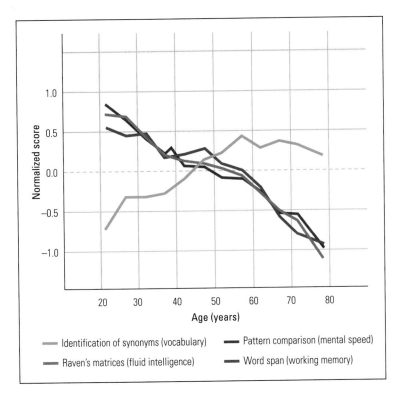

FIGURE 10.11 Average scores on four mental tests as a function of age The scores on each test are normalized (by the method described in the Appendix at the back of this book) such that 0 is the average for all subjects combined. A score of +1 or more would place a person in the top 84 percent of all subjects tested, and a score of −1 or less would place one in the bottom 16 percent. (Adapted from Salthouse, 2004, Figure 1, p. 141.)

The evidence from the analysis of correlation patterns, and the differing effects of age, led Cattell to argue that fluid and crystallized intelligences are distinct from each other. He did not, however, think that they are entirely independent. He noted that within any given age group crystallized- and fluid-intelligence scores correlate positively. This, he suggested, is because people with higher fluid intelligence learn and remember more from their experiences than do people with lower fluid intelligence. In that sense, he claimed, crystallized intelligence depends on fluid intelligence. Researchers indeed have found significant correlations between measures of fluid intelligence and at least some measures of verbal learning ability (Tamez & others, 2008).

Mental Speed as a Possible Basis for *g*

As noted earlier, Galton had hoped to characterize intelligence in terms of basic properties of the nervous system, measurable in simple behavioral tests such as speed of reacting to stimuli. In recent times, researchers have revived this quest, using more sophisticated measures and measuring devices, and have found positive correlations between a number of simple reaction-time measures and scores on conventional IQ tests (Sheppard & Vernon, 2008).

One such measure is *inspection time*—the minimal time that subjects need to look at or listen to a pair of stimuli to detect the difference between them. In one common test of inspection time, two parallel lines, one of which is 1.4 times as long as the other, are flashed on a screen and subjects must say which line is longer. The duration of the stimulus varies from trial to trial, and inspection time is the shortest duration at which a subject can respond correctly at some level significantly above chance. Studies correlating fast inspection time with IQ scores have typically revealed correlation coefficients of about 0.3 for measures of fluid intelligence and about 0.2 for measures of crystallized intelligence (Sheppard & Vernon, 2008). The correlations are about as strong when untimed IQ tests are used as when timed tests are used (Vernon & Kantor, 1986), so they do not simply result from the fact that the subtests of some standard IQ tests require quick reaction.

How might mental speed contribute to general intelligence? One view is that it does so by contributing to the capacity of working memory.

29
What findings have revived Galton's idea of mental quickness as a basis for general intelligence?

Working-Memory Capacity as a Possible Basis for *g*

According to the standard information-processing model of the mind (the *modal model*, described at length in **Chapter 9**), working memory is the center of conscious thought (look back at Figure 9.1, on p. 310). Information enters working memory from the environment (through the senses) and from one's long-term-memory store (through the act of retrieval). To solve a problem on an intelligence test, according to this model, you must bring the appropriate information from the senses and from long-term memory into the working-memory store and combine the information in an appropriate way to come up with a solution. But working memory can hold only a limited amount of information at any given time. While it is the center of conscious thought, it is also a bottleneck that limits the amount of information you can bring together to solve a problem. Information fades quickly from working memory when it is not being acted upon, so the faster you can process information, the more items you can maintain in working memory at any given time, to make a mental calculation or arrive at a reasoned decision. This, according to some psychologists, is why mental speed correlates positively with fluid intelligence (Miller & Vernon, 1992).

Consistent with the idea that mental speed contributes to fluid intelligence by increasing the capacity of working memory, researchers have found that measures of fluid intelligence correlate even more strongly with measures of working memory than with measures of mental speed. The former average about 0.5 and the latter about 0.3 (Schweizer, 2007; Sheppard & Vernon, 2008). Also consistent with this idea are the comparatively high correlations found between measures of mental speed and working memory (Miller & Vernon, 1992). The pattern of correlations fits with the idea that fast mental speed helps to create high-capacity working memory, which helps to create high fluid intelligence.

Working-memory capacity is measured in two quite different ways. One type of measure is referred to as *digit span* or *word span*, the number of single-digit numbers or unrelated words that a person can hold in mind and report back accurately after hearing the list just once (discussed in **Chapter 9**). That type of measure, as noted in Table 10.2 (on page 377), is one of the subtests of the Wechsler IQ tests. The other type of measure of working memory, more commonly used in recent research, is more complicated and is exemplified by a test called the *three-back test*. In this test, the person is presented visually with words or letters in a steady stream and must indicate, on each trial, whether the current stimulus does or does not match the stimulus that had been shown three items earlier. Tests of this type require a rather high degree of mental gymnastics. The person must keep ever-changing previous items in mind while reading new ones, remember how far back each previous item occurred, and make the appropriate item comparisons. Scores on tests of this type generally correlate more strongly with standard measures of fluid intelligence than do digit-span or word-span tests (Conway & others, 2003; Engle, 2002).

Mental Self-Government as a Possible Basis for g

One leading intelligence researcher, Robert Sternberg (1986), has described intelligence as "mental self-government." By this he means that people who perform well on intelligence tests are those who can control their mental resources in a way that allows for efficiency in problem solving. In a similar vein, other researchers have equated intelligence with the mind's *central executive*, conceived of as the set of mental processes that deals with overall goals and strategies and that coordinates all the rest of the mind's activities.

As was noted in **Chapter 9,** the central executive is considered to be the supervisory component of working memory—the component that decides what information to attend to or to recall from long-term memory and that keeps the mind as a whole focused on the task at hand. The three-back test of working memory, and other tests like it, are considered to be at least partly tests of central executive function

(Engle, 2002). To perform well, one must remain focused, avoid distraction, and distinguish between relevant and irrelevant information. These skills also seem to be involved in most if not all IQ tests and subtests, especially those that tap fluid intelligence more than crystallized intelligence. Some psychologists, in fact, consider fluid intelligence and central executive function to be essentially the same concept (Gray & others, 2003; Kane & Engle, 2002).

Central executive processes are involved not just in rapid, moment-to-moment judgments, but also in judgments having to do with overall problem-solving strategy. Sternberg (1985) found that people who performed well on logical-reasoning problems spent relatively more time encoding the problem (thinking about the meaning of each statement in it), and relatively less time on subsequent steps, than did people who performed poorly. This is not a particularly surprising result. Understanding the problem fully is key to solving almost any problem. I have observed that students often make mistakes, on tests of all sorts, because they fail to read the questions carefully enough to know exactly what is being asked before trying to answer them. According to Sternberg, deciding how much time to devote to each step of a problem is part of mental self-government. Through practice in solving problems, people can improve their ability to make such judgments and, in doing so, can raise their intelligence.

General Intelligence as an Evolutionary Adaptation for Novelty

Sometimes general intelligence is equated with a general ability to cope adaptively with one's environment (Snyderman & Rothman, 1987). In the opinion of most intelligence researchers, however, that is much too broad a definition. Cockroaches cope very well with their environment but perform poorly on IQ tests. All basic human capacities, like the basic capacities of any other species, came about through natural selection because they helped individuals adapt to the prevailing conditions of life. For example, human emotionality and sociability are valuable, evolved characteristics that help us survive in our social environments (as discussed in **Chapters 6 and 12–15**). People vary in measures of social and emotional competence, and these measures generally do not correlate reliably with measures of either fluid or crystallized intelligence (Kanazawa, 2004). You can be intellectually brilliant but emotionally and socially incompetent, or vice versa.

> **32**
> What reasoning suggests that general intelligence is an adaptation for dealing with evolutionarily novel problems?

Kennan Ward/Corbis

Two intelligent species
Chimpanzees and, to a much greater degree, human beings have the capacity to solve novel problems—problems that were not regularly posed by the environment in which the species evolved. Some theorists consider this capacity to be the essence of intelligence.

From an evolutionary perspective, it is reasonable to assume that general intelligence evolved in humans as a means of solving problems that are evolutionarily novel (Kanazawa, 2004). People, more than other creatures, are capable of dealing effectively with a wide range of environmental conditions, including conditions that were never regularly faced by our evolutionary ancestors. Our capacity to see analogies, to reason inductively, to deduce the logical consequences of statements, to achieve creative insights, and to predict and plan for future events all help us to cope with the novelties of life and to find ways to survive in conditions for which we are not in other ways biologically well prepared. The same intelligence that allowed hunter-gatherers to find new way of hunting game or processing roots to make them edible allows us to figure out how to operate computers

---

SECTION REVIEW

Efforts to characterize and measure intelligence have both practical and theoretical goals.

History and Validity of Intelligence Testing

➤ Galton proposed that intelligence reflects the biological capacity for mental quickness and sensory acuity.

➤ Binet regarded intelligence as a loose set of higher-order mental abilities that can be increased by schooling. His tests used school-related questions and problems.

➤ Most modern intelligence tests are rooted in Binet's approach and use a variety of verbal and nonverbal subtests.

➤ IQ scores correlate moderately well with school grades and job performance. Such correlations are commonly used as indices of IQ validity.

Nature of General Intelligence

➤ Spearman proposed that general intelligence, or g, is a single factor that contributes to all types of mental performance.

➤ Cattell argued that g consists of two factors—fluid and crystallized intelligence.

➤ Modern measures of mental quickness correlate significantly with IQ. Mental quickness may contribute to intelligence through effects on working-memory capacity.

➤ Sternberg proposed that the efficiency of mental self-government accounts for individual differences in intelligence.

➤ General intelligence may have been selected for in human evolution because it helps us deal with novel problems.

▮ Genetic and Environmental Contributions to Intelligence

Galton's research on intelligence, over a century ago, marked the beginning of what is often called the *nature–nurture debate,* which in various guises has continued throughout psychology's history. *Nature* here refers to a person's genetic inheritance, and *nurture* refers to the entire set of environmental conditions to which the person is exposed. In essence, the question of the debate is this: *Are psychological differences among people primarily the result of differences in their genes (nature) or in their environments (nurture)?* The psychological differences that have been most often subjected to this debate are differences in personality (discussed in **Chapter 15**), in susceptibility to mental disorders (discussed in **Chapter 16**), and, especially, in intelligence as measured by IQ. As you will discover, the answer to the nature–nurture question concerning IQ is, *it depends.* It depends on just whose IQs you are comparing.

Like parents, like child Eminent people often pass on more than genes to their offspring. Anthropologist Richard Leakey, shown here discussing a fossil with his father, has benefited from the genes and the wisdom of both of his eminent parents—anthropologists Louis and Mary Leakey.

AP/Wide World Photos

Contributions to IQ Differences Within a Cultural Group

A common misunderstanding is that the nature–nurture question has to do with the degree to which a particular trait, in an individual, results from genes or environment. Some might ask, for example, "Does a person's intelligence result more from genes or from environment?" But if you think about that question, you will realize it is absurd. With no genes there would be no person and hence no intelligence, and with no environment there would also be no person and no intelligence. Given that genes and environment are both essential for any trait to develop, it would be absurd to think that one contributes more than the other to the trait. But it is not absurd to ask whether *differences* in a trait among individuals result more from *differences* in their genes or in their environments.

A useful analogy (suggested by Hebb, 1958a) concerns the contribution of length and width to the areas of rectangles. It is absurd to ask whether the area of any given rectangle results more from its length or its width, because both dimensions are essential to the area. If you shrink either to zero, there is no rectangle and no area. But it is not absurd to ask whether the differences in area among a given set of rectangles result more from differences in their length or in their width. As illustrated in Figure 10.12, the answer could be length or it could be width, depending on the specific set of rectangles asked about.

33
What is the difference between the absurd form of the nature–nurture question and the reasonable form? Why is one absurd and the other reasonable?

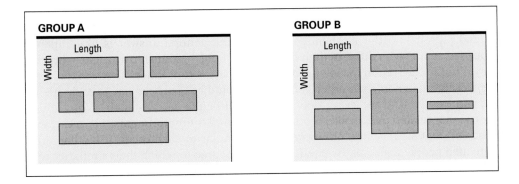

FIGURE 10.12 A geometric analogy to heritability It is senseless to say that a given rectangle's area results more from its length than from its width, or vice versa. However, differences among rectangles in area can result primarily or entirely from differences in length (as shown in group A) or in width (as shown in group B). Similarly, one can imagine one group of people in which IQ variation results mostly from their differing genes and another group in which it results mostly from their differing environments.

Similarly, when we ask whether differences in intelligence derive primarily from differences in genes or in environment, the answer might be genes for one set of people and environment for another. Logic tells us, for example, that IQ differences are likely to result more from environmental differences if the people we are studying live in very diverse environments than if they live in similar environments. If you were raised in a typical middle-class home and I were raised in a closet, the difference between us in IQ would certainly be attributable mostly to differences in our environments; but if we were both raised in typical middle-class environments, then whatever difference exists between us in IQ might well result mostly from differences in our genes.

The Concept of Heritability

The central concept in any modern scientific discussion of the nature–nurture question is **heritability**. Heritability is the degree to which variation in a particular trait, within a particular population of individuals, stems from genetic differences as opposed to environmental differences. Heritability is often quantified by a statistic called the **heritability coefficient**, abbreviated h^2. This coefficient is technically defined as the proportion of the variance of a trait, in a given population, that derives from genetic variation. As a formula, it can be written:

34
How is heritability defined? Why would we expect heritability to be higher in a population that shares a similar environment than in an environmentally diverse population?

$$h^2 = \frac{V_g}{V_T} = \frac{V_g}{(V_g + V_e)}$$

"I don't know anything about the bell curve, but I say heredity is everything."

The denominator, V_T, or *total variance,* is simply a measure of the degree to which the individuals being studied differ from one another in the characteristic that was measured. If the scores tend to be similar to one another, variance is low; if the scores differ greatly from one another, variance is high. It can be calculated directly from the set of scores obtained from the individuals in the group. (The formula for variance can be found at the end of the book, in the Statistical Appendix.) The numerator, V_g, or *variance resulting from genetic differences,* in contrast, cannot be calculated directly but must be estimated by comparing sets of individuals who differ in known ways in their degree of genetic relationship to one another (by methods to be explained soon). The right-hand extension of the equation simply represents the fact that the total variance is equal to the variance resulting from genetic differences (V_g) plus the variance resulting from environmental differences (V_e).

Examination of the formula shows that the heritability coefficient can, in theory, vary from 0.00 to 1.00. A coefficient of 0.00 means that none of the observed variance in the characteristic results from genetic differences ($V_g = 0$); all of it results from environmental differences. A coefficient of 1.00 means that all the variance results from genetic differences; none of it results from environmental differences ($V_e = 0$). A coefficient of 0.40 means that 40 percent of the variance results from genetic differences and the remaining 60 percent results from environmental differences.

The Value of Studying Twins to Separate Genetic and Environmental Influences

How might one estimate heritability, given that there is no direct way to measure V_g and plug it into the heritability formula? The general answer is to compare groups of people who differ in their degree of genetic relationship to see how much they differ in the trait in question. To the degree that a trait is heritable, people who are closely related to each other genetically should be more similar to each other than are people who are less closely related. A difficulty with using this logic, however, is that related people also typically share similar environments. Thus, the observation that siblings are, on average, more similar to each other in IQ than are unrelated people does not, by itself, tell us the degree to which their similarity results from similarities in their genes or in their environment.

35

What is the logic of comparing identical and fraternal twins to study the heritability of traits? What difference is observed between identical and fraternal twins in IQ correlation, and how does that difference change as the pairs of twins get older?

◀ In an attempt to separate the contributions of genes and environment to IQ differences, behavior geneticists often compare pairs of individuals who differ from other pairs in their degree of genetic relatedness and were either raised in the same home or were adopted at an early age into different homes. Twins are especially valuable subjects in such studies, because some pairs of twins are genetically identical and other pairs (fraternal twins) are, like non-twin siblings, only 50 percent genetically related (as explained in **Chapter 3**). A common way to estimate the heritability of IQ is to compare the correlation in IQ scores of identical twins with that of fraternal twins.

As explained in **Chapter 2,** correlation coefficients can run from 0.00 to either plus or minus 1.00. A correlation of 0.00 in this case would mean that the IQs of twins are no more alike, on average, than are those of any two people chosen at random from the population being studied; at the other extreme, a correlation of 1.00 would mean that the twins in each pair have identical IQs. In Figure 10.13, the IQ correlations between twins raised in the same home are shown, separately, for identical and fraternal twins in various age groups.

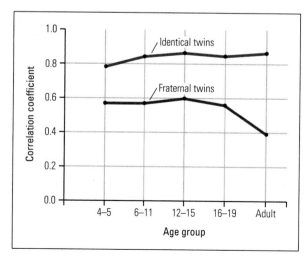

FIGURE 10.13 IQ correlations between twin pairs who were raised together The correlation in IQ between pairs of identical twins remains high throughout their lives. That between pairs of fraternal twins declines as they enter adulthood and go their separate ways. The data are averages for all studies published prior to 1993. (McGue & others, 1993, p. 63.)

As you can see in the figure, in each age group the correlation coefficient is considerably greater for identical twins than for fraternal twins, indicating that genes play a relatively large role. The difference between the two classes of twins is especially great for adults, because of a drop in the correlation that occurs during adulthood for fraternal twins but not for identical twins. When fraternal twins leave home and go their separate ways, they become more different from each other in IQ than they were before, but when identical twins leave home, their IQs remain as similar as ever (an observation to which we shall return soon).

IQ Heritability Assessed from Studies of Twins

Correlation coefficients are not the same as heritability coefficients, but they can be used to estimate heritability coefficients. One common method is simply to subtract the correlation for fraternal twins from that for identical twins and multiply the difference by 2 (Plomin & others, 1990). The precise logic behind this method involves more mathematical detail than most readers would desire, but you can get a sense of that logic without the mathematics. The assumption is that the environment is equally similar for the two categories of twins, so the difference between the two in IQ correlation must stem from the difference in their degree of genetic relatedness; that is, the difference must reflect heritability. Because fraternal twins are themselves 50 percent genetically related, the difference between the two correlation coefficients is assumed to reflect only half the difference that would be observed if the comparison were between identical twins and completely unrelated individuals. Therefore, the difference is doubled to arrive at an estimate of the heritability coefficient.

If we apply this formula to the data in the figure, we arrive at a heritability coefficient of 0.46 for the 12-to-15 age group [$(0.83 - 0.60) \times 2 = 0.46$] and 0.86 for the adults [$(0.83 - 0.40) \times 2 = 0.86$]. In other words, according to these calculations, about half of the IQ variance in the teenagers and younger children results from genetic variance, but over 80 percent of the IQ variance in the adults results from genetic variance. Apparently (for reasons discussed later) the environment plays a greater role in IQ variation among younger people than it does among adults.

Another way to assess heritability of IQ is to locate pairs of identical twins who were adopted at an early age into separate homes and determine their IQ correlation. On the assumption that the environments of raised-apart identical twins are no more similar to each other than are the environments of any two members of the study population chosen at random, the correlation coefficient for raised-apart identical twins is itself an estimate of the heritability coefficient (Loehlin & others, 1988). The average coefficient determined from many such studies is 0.73 (McGue & others, 1993). So, using this method, the estimated heritability for IQ is 0.73. Most of the twin pairs in those studies were adults, but a few were adolescents, and no attempt was made to determine the coefficient separately for different age groups.

Every procedure for assessing heritability involves assumptions that may not be entirely true, so any heritability coefficient should be taken as only a rough estimate. But the studies suggest, overall, that genetic differences account for roughly 30 to 50 percent of the IQ variance among children and for considerably more than 50 percent of the IQ variance among adults in the populations that were studied (Davis & others, 2008; McGue & others, 1993).

Contrary to what might be expected, studies that have assessed fluid and crystallized intelligence separately indicate that the two are about equally heritable (Horn, 1985). Apparently, within the populations that have been studied, genetic differences influence the amount of factual knowledge that people have learned just as much as they influence people's ability to think quickly or to see relationships in novel stimuli. It is not hard to think of many ways by which genetic differences could have such an effect. Genes can influence curiosity, reading ability, long-term memory, or any of countless other traits that influence the acquisition and recall of facts.

36

How can IQ heritability be estimated using the correlation coefficients for the IQs of identical and fraternal twins raised together? Using this method, what is the evidence that IQ heritability is greater for adults than for children?

37

How can IQ heritability be estimated by studying identical twins who were adopted into different homes?

Identical twins learning together
Whether they are raised together or apart, identical twins tend to exhibit similar mental abilities. Genetic dispositions to enjoy certain classes of activities may promote similarity in their development.

Myrleen Ferguson Cate/PhotoEdit, Inc.

The Short-Lived Influence of the Family in Which One Is Raised

It seems reasonable to expect that the IQs of children raised in the same family would be more similar than average not just because of shared genes but also because of shared environments. After all, children in the same family are exposed to the same parents, the same neighborhoods, the same schools, and the same learning opportunities at home. But is this expectation correct?

38
What is the evidence that the effect of a shared family environment on IQ correlations is lost in adulthood? How might this loss be explained?

The most direct way to assess the degree to which a shared family environment leads to similarity in IQ is to study pairs of adoptive siblings who are genetically unrelated but are raised together. Assuming that such pairs are genetically no more similar to each other than any two random people from the study population, any correlation greater than 0 in their IQs must stem from their shared environment. Several such studies have been done, and the results tell a remarkably consistent story. As long as the unrelated siblings are still children, their IQs do correlate positively with each other; but the correlation is lost completely by the time they reach adulthood.

Taking all such studies together, the average IQ correlation for genetically unrelated children living in the same family is 0.25, and the average for genetically unrelated adults who had been raised in the same family is −0.01, or essentially 0 (McGue & others, 1993). Other studies have shown that the IQ correlations for other categories of children raised in the same family also decline as the children enter adulthood, but the greater the degree of genetic relationship, the smaller the decline (Plomin & Daniels, 1987). You saw that effect in Figure 10.13 (on page 386), where the IQ correlation for fraternal twins declined at adulthood while that for identical twins did not. Apparently, families have a moderately strong early influence on children's IQ, but the effect fades as the children become adults.

The transient nature of the effect of the family on IQ is perhaps the most surprising result that has emerged from studies of IQ correlations. Before such studies were done, many if not most psychologists believed that even subtle differences in the early environments of children would give some an advantage in intellectual development that would last a lifetime. But the research has shown quite conclusively that the advantage or disadvantage that comes from being raised in a particular home, within the range of homes the studies sampled, disappears by early adulthood.

One way to explain this finding is to assume that as children grow into adulthood, they increasingly choose their own environments, and their genetic differences influence the kinds of environments they choose (Dunn & Plomin, 1990; Scarr & McCartney, 1983). Those who are genetically similar, and therefore more similar in interests and temperament, may choose more similar environments than do those who are genetically different, and so they remain more similar in intelligence. If you think of intelligence as analogous to muscle strength, which can wax and wane depending on exercise, then you can understand why an adult's IQ may be more influenced by his or her adult environment than by his or her past, childhood environment.

Seeking his own path This young man's mental development may have been considerably influenced up until now by his parents and the home they provided. From now on, however, that influence will be reduced. His own dispositions will play a greater role in determining what he learns and how his mind develops. This may help explain why the heritability coefficients for IQ are greater for adults than for children.

Effects of Personality and Life Experiences on Intelligence

39
What evidence suggests that intellectual involvement can increase a person's fluid intelligence over time?

Intelligence is maintained and strengthened through active, intellectual engagement with the world. Not surprisingly, people who score high on a personality test designed to measure openness to experience have, on average, higher IQs than do those who score lower on that personality measure (Ackerman & Heggestad, 1997; Gignac & others, 2004). Openness to experience includes the characteristics of curiosity, independence of mind, and broad interests (discussed in **Chapter 15**).

Presumably, people who have these characteristics choose intellectually engaging styles of life, and that choice tends to raise their intelligence. Openness appears to correlate at least as strongly with measures of fluid intelligence as with measures of crystallized intelligence. Intellectual engagement apparently does not just increase one's store of knowledge, but also increases one's capacity for mental gymnastics.

More direct evidence that activities can alter intelligence is found in a long-term study, conducted by Melvin Kohn and Carmi Schooler, of the effects of men's occupations on their intellectual development. Kohn and Schooler periodically tested a large sample of men, throughout their careers, with a test of *intellectual flexibility*. The test included a number of subtests that are quite similar to those found on standard IQ tests, and it was later shown to correlate strongly with fluid intelligence as measured by standard IQ tests (Schooler, 2001).

The most general finding was that the men's intellectual flexibility tended to change when their job demands changed. When they were in jobs that required them to handle a great deal of information and make complex decisions, their intellectual flexibility increased over time. When they were in routine jobs that depended more on brawn and/or tolerance of drudgery, their intellectual flexibility decreased over time. In subsequent research, done with both men and women, Schooler and his colleagues found that engagement in intellectually challenging leisure-time activities, even without career change, can also increase intellectual flexibility (Schooler, 2007; Schooler & Mulatu, 2001). These effects—both of occupation and of leisure-time activities—were greater for older adults (age 58 and older) than for younger adults (Schooler, 2001, 2007).

Here, again, the analogy between mental strength and physical strength seems to hold. Young people can maintain relatively strong muscles without much exercise, but as we get older our muscles begin to atrophy unless we increase their use. The same, apparently, is true for brain power.

Use it and keep it Elderly people who have careers or interests that keep them intellectually active retain their full intelligence longer than those who retire to a non-intellectual life. Shown here is business professor Russell Ackoff who, in his 90s, is still a popular lecturer, prolific author, and creative thinker. One of his most recent books, co-authored with Daniel Greenberg, calls for innovations in education designed to make learning more self-directed and joyful.

Origins of IQ Differences Between Cultural Groups

The conclusions about the high heritability of IQ discussed so far in this chapter were properly qualified by the phrase "for the population that was studied." In almost all cases that population was white, North American or European, and in the upper two thirds of the socioeconomic scale (Stoolmiller, 1999). Heritability coefficients are always limited to the population that was studied. The more uniform the environment of that population, the smaller is the proportion of IQ variance that stems from environmental variation and the greater is the heritability coefficient (look back at the formula on p. 385). If heritability studies included people occupying the entire range of human environments rather than just a slice of that range, the resultant heritability coefficients would be smaller than those presented earlier.

Comparisons of racial or cultural groups routinely reveal average differences in IQ. The difference that has attracted the most attention, and on which we will focus here, is that between blacks and whites in the United States: Blacks, on average, score about 12 points lower than whites on standard IQ tests (Dickens & Flynn, 2006). The question is why. Some people who have heard of the heritability studies that you have just read about assume that those studies can be applied to understand the black–white difference. They assume that if IQ is highly heritable within a group, then any IQ difference between two groups must also be largely the result of genetic differences. But that assumption is false.

Why Within-Group Heritability Coefficients Can't Be Applied to Between-Group Differences

40------------------------

Why can't heritability coefficients found within groups be used to infer the source of differences between groups?

◄ The heritability of a trait within a group, in fact, tells us nothing about differences between groups. To understand why, consider the example illustrated in Figure 10.14. Imagine two wheat fields, each planted from the same package of genetically diverse wheat seeds. Imagine further that the soil fertility is relatively constant within each field but quite different between the two—one has richer topsoil than the other. Within either field, differences in the sizes of individual plants would be the result primarily of genetic differences in the seeds, yet the average difference between the two fields would almost certainly be due entirely to the difference in the environment (the richness of the soil).

FIGURE 10.14 Why high within-group heritability tells us nothing about group differences In this example the same genetically diverse mix of wheat seeds was planted in two fields. Within each field the environment is quite uniform (same thickness of topsoil), so the differences in plant size are mostly the result of differences in genes (high heritability). However, the difference between the two fields in average plant size in this case cannot result from genes, because genetic differences would cancel out in the averages; it must result from differences in the environment.

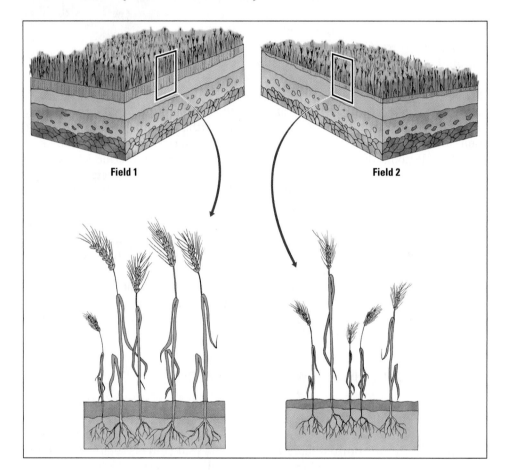

Field 1   Field 2

To take another example, height in people is more than 90 percent heritable when measured for a given cultural group, yet group differences in height can be found that are clearly the result of the environment (Ceci, 1996). In the 1950s, for example, researchers found that men of full Japanese ancestry born in California were nearly 3 inches taller, on average, than Japanese men born in Japan (Greulich, 1957). That difference almost certainly resulted from differences in diet between the two groups during their childhoods.

Evidence that Black–White IQ Differences Are Cultural in Origin

In the examples just given, we could be quite certain that the group differences were environmental in origin because there was reason to believe that the members of the two groups (of wheat plants and of Japanese men) did not differ genetically, on average. In contrast, many people automatically think of differences between the so-called black and white "races" as racial differences, and they automatically assume that racial means "genetic."

In the United States and many other countries, however, blacks and whites are not truly distinct races in a biological sense but, rather, are different cultural groups. We generally classify people as "black" who have any detectable black African ancestry, no matter how small a proportion it is. Thus, a person who is half English, one-fourth French, and one-fourth African is called "black," whereas that person's cousin, who is half English, one-fourth French, and one-fourth Polish, is called "white." While some average genetic differences exist between the two groups—which show up in skin pigmentation, for example—the amount of genetic variation *within* each group is far greater than the average difference *between* them.

Researchers who have attempted to separate the effect of black African ancestry from the effect of the social designation "black" have consistently failed to find evidence that genetic ancestry plays a role in the black–white IQ difference. In the first such study, Paul Witty and Martin Jenkins (1935) attempted to determine if high-IQ black children have more European and less African ancestry than blacks who have lower IQs. They identified a sample of black children in Chicago who had IQs in the superior range (125 or better) and then interviewed their parents to see if they had more European ancestry than the average black person. The results were negative: The proportion of European ancestry in the high-IQ black children was neither more nor less than that in the black population at large. (The highest IQ of all in that study, incidentally, was a whopping 200 scored by a girl with 100 percent black African ancestry.) Later, other researchers have performed similar studies, using biochemical methods to determine the degree of black African and other ancestry (Loehlin & others, 1973; Scarr & Carter-Saltzman, 1983). Like Witty and Jenkins, they found no relationship between ancestry and IQ, and they concluded that the *social* designation of black or white, not biological ancestry, is most likely the critical variable in determining the black–white IQ difference.

> **— 41**
> **What evidence suggests that the average IQ difference between black and white Americans derives from the environment, not genes?**

Different Types of Minority Status Can Have Different Effects on IQ

How might the social designation of black or white affect IQ? Nobody knows for sure, but John Ogbu (1986; Ogbu & Stern, 2001) suggested an interesting line of thought about it. On the basis of cross-cultural research, Ogbu distinguished between *voluntary minorities* and *involuntary* or *castelike minorities*. Voluntary minorities are groups, such as Italian Americans and Chinese Americans, who emigrated in hopes of bettering themselves, who typically see themselves as well-off compared with those they left behind, and who see themselves as on their way up, regardless of how the dominant majority may see them. Involuntary minorities are groups, such as African Americans and Native Americans, who became minorities through being conquered, colonized, or enslaved. They are people who for long periods were, and in many ways still are, treated as if they are a separate, inferior class. According to research summarized by Ogbu, involuntary minorities everywhere perform more poorly in school, and score an average of 10 to 15 points lower on IQ tests than the dominant majority.

> **— 42**
> **What evidence suggests that the status of being an involuntary minority may be particularly detrimental to IQ development?**

Particularly informative, in Ogbu's work, is the comparison of the Buraku outcasts of Japan with blacks of the United States. The Buraku, who are a purely cultural class, not racially distinct from other Japanese, were emancipated from official outcast status by a royal edict in 1871, just 8 years after blacks in the United States were emancipated from slavery; yet both groups, to this day, often occupy menial

Chris Duffey

John Uzo Ogbu Ogbu was born to nonliterate farmers in a village in Nigeria, but emigrated as a young man to the United States and eventually became a renowned professor of anthropology at the University of California, Berkeley. Some of his ideas about intelligence are exemplified by his own experience. He was a voluntary minority in the United States, not an involuntary minority. Ogbu once wrote of himself, "My intelligence changed when I moved from a village in Nigeria to a major U.S. university" (Ogbu & Stern, 2001). Ogbu died of a heart attack in 2003 at age 64.

positions and are implicitly, if not explicitly, perceived as inferior by many members of the dominant majority. (Implicit prejudice is discussed extensively in **Chapter 13.**) The gap in school achievement and IQ between the Buraku and the majority group in Japan is about the same as that between blacks and whites in the United States—but the gap disappears when Buraku move to the United States. Most people in the United States do not know the difference between Buraku and other Japanese, and the two groups of immigrants are treated the same and perform equally well in school and on IQ tests. According to Ogbu, it is the sense that one is an outcast, and that standard routes to achievement are cut off, that oppresses caste-like minorities and depresses their scholastic achievements and IQs.

A Buraku protest The Buraku of Japan are descendants of people who worked as tanners and butchers, jobs that were traditionally believed to be unclean and worthy only of lowly people. Although they are no longer legally categorized as outcasts, they continue to be discriminated against. Like outcast groups elsewhere, they perform more poorly in school and have lower average IQ scores than other citizens of their nation. However, when they emigrate to America, where most people do not know their caste status, the IQ difference between them and other Japanese Americans vanishes. Here a group of Buraku activists protest the continuing discrimination.

Tom Wagner/SABA

The Historical Increase in IQ

43 - - - - - - - - - - - - - - - - - - ◄
How does history provide further evidence that IQ is highly susceptible to cultural influence? On which measures has IQ increased the most?

Perhaps the most dramatic evidence of cultural influence on intelligence is the improved performance on intelligence tests that has been observed worldwide over the years since they were invented. As you know, IQ tests are literally graded on a curve, with the average score for the population at any given time in history assigned a value of 100. But the average score keeps rising, indicating that the tests become easier for each successive generation, so researchers periodically modify the scoring system and increase the difficulty of the questions.

James Flynn (1987, 2007) has compiled data on norm adjustments for many different countries, from the dawn of IQ testing to the present, and has found that the increase in IQ has occurred at a rather steady rate of about 9 to 15 points every 30 years, depending on the type of test. It has occurred for people of all races and ethnicities and has occurred in countries as varied as the United States, Belgium, Argentina, and Kenya (Daley & others, 2003; Flynn, 2003). The greatest increases, interestingly, are in the tests geared toward fluid intelligence, such as Raven's Progressive Matrices—the very tests that were originally conceived of as least affected by cultural experience and most indicative of raw reasoning ability.

As an example, Figure 10.15 (on page 393) illustrates the gains in IQ scores that would have occurred in the United States between 1948 and 2002 if the tests and scoring system had not been periodically adjusted. The graph depicts data for various subtests of a standard IQ test (the WISC), for the full-scale IQ score, and for

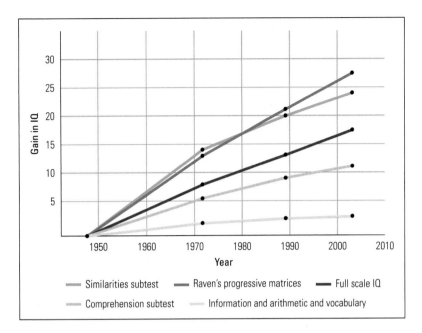

FIGURE 10.15 Examples of gains in intelligence-test scores Shown here are IQ gains from 1948 to 2002, in the United States, as measured by Raven's Progressive Matrices, by the Wechsler Intelligence Scale for Children (Full Scale), and by several subtests of the Wechsler Intelligence Scale for Children. (For brief descriptions of the subtests, see Table 10.2 on p. 377.) These are the gains that would have occurred if the tests were not made more difficult and the scoring systems were not adjusted at each test revision. (Adapted from Flynn, 2007, p. 8.)

Raven's Progressive Matrices. Notice that the biggest gains are for Raven's Matrices and the Similarities subtest of the WISC, both of which are deemed to be excellent measures of fluid intelligence. (In the Similarities subtest, the person is presented on each trial with the names of two common objects or events, such as *mouse* and *crow*, and has to say what is similar about them; a correct answer might be that they are both animals.)

What accounts for these massive gains in IQ from one generation to the next? Flynn (1999, 2003) has argued against the idea that increased or improved schooling has much to do with it. He points out that the tests that are most reflective of school learning—such as the Arithmetic, Information, and Vocabulary subtests of Wechsler's IQ tests—have shown the least improvement. To understand the gains in measures of fluid intelligence, according to Flynn, we have to set aside the notion that these tests measure something that is stable and timeless. Rather, they measure certain habits of thought, which are very much exercised in modern cultures but were not so much exercised in times past.

In today's world—partly because of television, computers, and other such technology—we are constantly being presented with new ideas, new information, new problems to solve. Fluid IQ tests require us to answer questions or solve problems on the spot, based upon information that we have just been given. In today's world, that is something that we do all the time, so we have become good at it.

Even television, so often disparaged as intellectually stifling, may promote the kind of thinking that leads to good performance on fluid IQ tests. As Steven Johnson (2005) has demonstrated with quantitative analyses, television programs have, over time, grown immensely in complexity and pace. Programs that have been popular relatively recently—such as *Hill Street Blues*, *The Sopranos*, and *24*—require viewers to keep many subplots and different characters in mind, and to shift mental set frequently, as the action jumps quickly from one time and place to another and the dialogue often provides only hints about what is going on. Compare that, say, to *I Love Lucy*, of the 1950s. Moreover, as I pointed out in **Chapter 9,** fast-paced videogames exercise attention and working memory capacity, which are the aspects of mind that contribute most to measures of fluid intelligence. We aren't necessarily any better than our grandparents were at solving real-world problems, but we are definitely better at the gamelike problems that make up the fluid components of IQ tests.

44

How might the historical increase in fluid intelligence scores be explained?

We must be careful in how we ask and how we try to answer nature–nurture questions.

IQ Differences Within a Cultural Group

➤ The reasonable version of the nature–nurture question asks whether genetic or environmental variation contributes more to observed IQ variation within a population.

➤ Heritability is the extent to which variation in a trait (e.g., IQ), within a particular population, derives from genetic differences among the individuals.

➤ Twin studies have shown that, within a population, genetic variation accounts for about half of IQ variance in children and for more than that in adults.

➤ Effects of the shared family environment (aspects of the environment shared by children growing up in the same home) on IQ are temporary; they disappear in adulthood.

➤ There is evidence that a person's job or leisure activities can alter his or her fluid intelligence.

IQ Differences Between Cultural Groups

➤ Heritability coefficients for IQ *within* groups cannot be legitimately used to explain the source of average IQ differences *between* groups (e.g., racial or cultural groups).

➤ The average black–white IQ difference found in the United States is related to the social designation of black or white rather than to the degree of African or European ancestry.

➤ Involuntary minority status is particularly likely to reduce a group's IQ.

➤ The large historical gains in IQ—perhaps resulting from changes in technology—also demonstrate the influence of cultural factors.

Concluding Thoughts

One way to organize your review of this chapter would be to think about its content in relation to each of the following four themes:

1. The concrete nature of human reasoning Mathematics, which is formal reasoning, plays a relatively small role in the everyday reasoning of most of us. Normally we reason by comparing the current problem situation with memories that seem relevant to that situation. You might keep this idea in mind, as a unifying theme, as you review the discussions of (a) reasoning by analogy; (b) biases in inductive reasoning; (c) the content bias and use of mental models in deductive reasoning; and (d) the role of mental sets, and overcoming mental sets, in solving insight problems.

2. Cultural and other environmental influences on reasoning Consistent with the idea that people reason concretely is the idea that people whose experiences are quite different from each other are likely to develop different reasoning abilities. In this chapter you read about (a) cross-cultural differences in responses to classification problems; (b) East–West differences in holistic versus analytic perception and thought; (c) evidence that scores on IQ tests vary across cultures and have been increasing over time as a result of cultural changes; and (d) evidence that a person's IQ can increase or decrease over time, depending on the work environment. You have also read of evidence that the words of a person's language, acquired from cultural experience, can influence spatial reasoning, mathematical reasoning, and one's concept of gender.

3. Concepts of intelligence are rooted in correlational research Research on intelligence makes heavy use of correlational methods. If two tests or measures correlate positively with each other—that is, if people who tend to score high (or low) on one also tend to score high (or low) on the other—then they can to some degree be considered to be measures of the same underlying characteristic, though it may not be clear just what that characteristic is. As you review the section on intelligence testing, note how patterns of correlations have been used to support (a) the concept of general intelligence; (b) the claim that intelligence tests are valid predictors of academic and employment success; (c) the distinction between fluid and crystallized intelligence; and (d) the ideas that variations in mental speed, working memory, and central executive processes may contribute to variations in intelligence.

4. Limitation of the concept of heritability Heritability is a valuable concept because it brings clarity to the long-standing nature–nurture debate. It is important, however, to understand exactly what heritability means and the limitations of the concept. Heritability does not tell us about the relative roles of genes and environment in the development of a trait within an individual, but only about their relative roles in contributing to the variability of the trait within a population. If you understand the formula for heritability, you should be able to explain (a) why heritability for a trait might be different for one population than for another; (b) why heritability decreases when the environmental diversity of the population increases; (c) why heritability of a trait can be greater for adults than for children; and (d) why high heritability within a culture at a particular time is compatible with strong environmental effects across cultures and over historical time.

Further Reading

Philip N. Johnson-Laird (2006). *How we reason.* Oxford, UK: Oxford University Press.

This is a sophisticated but clearly written and enjoyable book by a leading researcher on the psychology of reasoning. In this book Johnson-Laird expands on his mental-models view of reasoning and shows how we reason well and how we sometimes reason poorly. In the category of reasoning well, I particularly enjoyed Chapter 25, in which Johnson-Laird explains how intelligent use of analogies allowed the Wright brothers to create the first workable airplane.

Jerome Groopman (2007). *How doctors think.* Boston: Houghton Mifflin.

Groopman is a prominent physician and a highly skilled writer. In this book he brings psychological knowledge about reasoning to bear in an analysis of how doctors make diagnoses and other medical decisions. Being human, doctors are subject to the same reasoning biases as all of us are, and Groopman shows how those biases can lead to serious errors. The case stories are fascinating; and the lessons may help you know how to present information to your doctor in ways that will reduce the possibility of mistaken diagnoses.

Stephen C. Levinson (2003). *Space in language and cognition: Explorations in cognitive diversity.* Cambridge, UK: Cambridge University Press.

To read this book is to introduce yourself to cross-cultural psychology at its best. The book describes, in very readable detail, the methods and results of Levinson's research on spatial reasoning among Guugu Yimithirr speakers in Australia and Tzeltal speakers in Mexico. The work combines the observational and cultural-immersion methods of anthropology with controlled psychological experiments, all aimed at developing a rather full understanding of how these people, who lack egocentric spatial terms, understand space and use spatial concepts in their daily lives.

Richard E. Nisbett (2009). *Intelligence and how to get it.* New York: Norton.

Nisbett is a leading social psychologist who has devoted much of his career to understanding how intelligence is influenced by the social and cultural environment. In this book for the general reader, he clearly describes such influences, including the influences of schooling and of cultural differences, particularly the differences between Asian and Western cultures.

James R. Flynn (2007). *What is intelligence? Beyond the Flynn effect.* Cambridge, UK: Cambridge University Press.

While other intelligence researchers were immersed in the complexities of factor-analyzing yet more batteries of mental tests, Flynn noticed something that should have been obvious to everyone but wasn't: IQs had been rising steeply with every generation. Why? What does that fact tell us about the IQ construct? How can it be that by today's standards most of our great-grandparents would have been classified as retarded? What, really, is intelligence? If it is that which is measured by IQ tests, perhaps it is not so important after all; our great-grandparents did quite well, despite their dreadful performances on Raven's Matrices. This is a thoughtful and clearly written book by a psychologist who has that rare quality, common sense.

Steven Johnson (2005). *Everything bad for you is good for you: How today's popular culture is actually making us smarter.* New York: Riverhead Books.

This is a light, entertaining book that contains some profound thoughts about the experiences that improve our minds. Johnson will make you feel less guilty about whiling away hours playing videogames or watching popular television programs. If these activities are stretching your working memory, they may well be making you smarter. Johnson's most valuable contribution is a qualitative analysis of the mental complexity of modern videogames and many modern television series. I especially enjoyed his entertaining turnabout on the conventional and stuffy argument that reading is mentally superior to television watching.

PART 6

Growth of the Mind and Person

One way to understand any complex entity, whether it's a building under construction or a person growing, is to watch it develop over time. This is the approach taken by developmental psychologists, who study the changes through which human behavior becomes increasingly complex and sophisticated from infancy to adulthood. In this unit, on developmental psychology, Chapter 11 is about the development of thought and language, and Chapter 12 is about the development of social relationships and the roles they play in promoting other aspects of development.

The Development of Thought and Language

When I first saw my newborn son, my words did not match my thought. I said something like, "Oh, he's beautiful," but my thought was, "My goodness, will he turn into a real human being?" Of course, I knew intellectually that he already was a human being, but at the moment he looked more like a cross between that and a garden slug.

Over the next weeks, months, and years the little slug's mother and I watched in amazement as he grew not only to look increasingly human but also to do the things that humans everywhere do. He began to smile in response to our smiles; he began eventually to walk upright on two legs and to talk, sometimes incessantly; and, true to his species' name (*Homo sapiens,* where *sapiens* means "wise"), he manifested from early on an insatiable curiosity and soon developed a remarkable store of knowledge and theories about his world.

This chapter is about the millions of new human beings who enter the world every year. More specifically, it is the first of two chapters concerned with ***developmental psychology,*** the study of changes that occur in people's abilities and dispositions as they grow older. Some developmental psychologists study changes that occur in adulthood (as you will discover in **Chapter 12**), but most study changes that occur in infancy and childhood. They do so not only because they find infants and children fascinating and worthy of understanding for their own sake, but also because they see in infants and children the origins of adult abilities. Human thought and language in particular are extraordinarily complex, and developmental psychologists have learned a great deal about them by watching them grow in infants and children.

The chapter begins by examining how infants learn about the physical world. Then it turns to some theories and research concerning the development of reasoning, including reasoning about people's minds as well as about physical objects. Finally, it discusses the acquisition of language. A theme throughout is that children's own exploratory and playful activities are prime forces for children's mental development. Through play and exploration, in a responsive social environment, children acquire the abilities and knowledge that enable them to survive and thrive in the world into which they are born.

■ How Infants Learn About the Physical World

Infancy, roughly the first 18 to 24 months after birth, is the time of most rapid developmental change, change that lays the foundation for further development. How do infants learn about the physical world around them? What do they know, early on, about that world?

The Infant as Explorer

Infants' sensory systems all function at birth (although one sense, vision, is still quite immature). On the day they are born, infants will turn toward sounds, turn toward anything that touches their faces, turn away from unpleasant odors, suck a nipple more readily for a sweet liquid than for a sour one, and orient their eyes toward high-contrast or moving visual stimuli (Maurer & Maurer, 1988). Within a short time after birth, they not only respond to stimuli but do so selectively, in ways that seem well designed for learning.

Infants Look Selectively at Novel Objects

1

How do infants reveal, in their behavior, that they are actively exploring their environments with their eyes and that they remember what they have seen?

Hundreds of experiments have shown that babies gaze longer at new stimuli than at familiar ones. When shown a pattern, they look at it intently at first and then, over the course of minutes, look at it less and less—a phenomenon referred to as *habituation.* This decline in attention does not stem from general fatigue; if a new pattern is substituted for the old one, infants immediately increase their looking time. Similarly, if shown the new and old patterns at the same time, they look more at the new one than the old one. This preference for novelty makes sense if we assume that infants are actively trying to learn about their world. They look at new stimuli because they have more to learn from them than from old stimuli, which they have already explored.

Infants' preference to look at novel stimuli is so reliable that developmental psychologists use it to assess infants' abilities to perceive and remember. Babies who look significantly longer at a new stimulus than at one they have already seen must perceive the difference between the two and must, at some level, remember having seen the old one before. In one such experiment, infants as young as 1 day old perceived the difference between two checkerboards with different-sized squares and remembered that difference over the seconds that separated one trial from the next (Friedman, 1972). This was shown by the fact that they looked longer at the checkerboard that they had not seen before when they were given a choice. Later, you will read about research in which infants' selective looking is used to assess their knowledge and expectations about the physical world.

Infants Seek to Control Their Environments

2

How does infants' behavior reveal that they are motivated to control their environments and are emotionally involved in retaining control?

Within a few weeks after birth, infants begin to show a special interest in aspects of the environment that they can control. In one experiment, 2-month-olds smiled and attended much more to a mobile that moved in response to their own bodily movement than to a motor-driven mobile that they could not control (Watson, 1972).

In another experiment, 4-month-olds learned quickly to make a particular movement to turn on a small array of lights but lost interest and responded only occasionally after they became good at this task. When the conditions were changed so that a different movement was needed to turn on the lights, the infants regained interest and made another burst of responses (Papousek, 1969). Their renewed interest must have been generated by the new relationship between a response and the lights, because the lights themselves were unchanged. Apparently, the babies were interested not so much in the lights per se as in their ability to control them.

In still another experiment, infants as young as 2 months old, who had learned to turn on a video and sound recording of the *Sesame Street* theme song by pulling strings tied to their wrists, showed facial expressions of anger when the device was disconnected so that they could no longer control it (Lewis & others, 1990). In subsequent, similar experiments, 4- and 5-month-old babies showed facial expressions of both anger and sadness at losing control of their ability to turn on the recording, even when the recording still came on as often as before but under the control of the experimenter rather than themselves (Sullivan & Lewis, 2003). Apparently, it was the loss of control, not the loss of opportunities to see and hear the recording, that upset them. The desire to control our environment seems to be a facet of human nature that exists in every phase of development, and its function seems obvious: We, more than any other species, survive by controlling our environment.

In control Researchers have found that babies take more delight in objects they can control than in objects they can't control. The same jingly sound would hold little interest for the infant if she could not control it herself.

Infants Explore Increasingly with Hands and Eyes Together

During their first 3 or 4 months of life, babies, like puppies and other young mammals, put practically anything that they can reach into their mouths. They mouth objects in ways that seem designed to test the objects' properties. With time, however, they gradually give up their puppy ways and explore increasingly in the more uniquely human way, with hands and eyes together, rather than with mouths (Rochat, 1989).

By 5 or 6 months, babies regularly manipulate and explore objects in the sophisticated manner that researchers label *examining* (Ruff, 1986). They hold an object in front of their eyes, turn it from side to side, pass it from one hand to the other, rub it, squeeze it, and in various other ways act as if they are deliberately testing its properties. Such actions decline dramatically as the infant becomes familiar with a given object but return in full force when a new object, differing in shape or texture, is substituted for the old one (Ruff, 1986, 1989). As evidence that examining involves focused mental activity, researchers have found that babies are more difficult to distract, with bright visual stimuli, when they are examining an object than at other times (Oakes & Tellinghuisen, 1994).

Infants vary their examining in ways consistent with an object's properties. They preferentially *look at* colorfully patterned objects, *feel* objects that have varied textures, *shake* objects that make a sound when shaken, *squeeze* objects that are pliable, and *pound* with objects that are hard (Bourgeois & others, 2005; Lockman & McHale, 1989). Other experiments have shown that infants do, indeed, learn about objects' properties through such examination. In one experiment, 9-month-olds explored toys that produced interesting non-obvious effects when manipulated in certain ways, including a can that wailed when tilted and a doll that separated into two parts when pulled. The infants soon learned to produce each toy's unique effect, and when given a new toy that was similar (but not identical) to the one they had just explored, they immediately tried to produce the previously experienced effect. If the new toy differed in its basic structure from the original one, they did not try to produce the effect but explored the toy afresh, as if intent on discovering its unique properties (Baldwin & others, 1993).

Infants do not have to be taught to examine objects. They do it in every culture, whenever objects are in their reach, whether or not such behavior is encouraged. Roger Bakeman and his colleagues (1990) studied the exploratory behavior of infants among the !Kung San, a hunting-and-gathering group

- - - - - - - - - - - - - - - - - - - **3**

What is the evidence that infants' examining of objects (a) helps them learn about objects' unique properties and (b) occurs whether or not adults encourage it?

A small scientist By 5 to 6 months of age, infants learn about the properties of objects by manipulating them with their hands while watching intently to observe the effects.

of people in Botswana, Africa, who have been relatively uninfluenced by industrialized cultures. (The !K in !Kung stands for a clicklike sound that is different from the pronunciation of our K.) !Kung adults do not make toys for infants or deliberately provide them with objects for play. Yet !Kung babies examine objects that happen to be within their reach—such as stones, twigs, food items, and cooking utensils—in the same manner as do babies in industrialized cultures; and, as in industrialized cultures, their examining increases markedly in frequency and intensity between about 4 and 6 months of age. The adults do not encourage such behavior because they see no reason to, yet they recognize its value and do not discourage it. Their view of child development seems to be well summarized by one of their folk expressions, which can be translated roughly as "Children teach themselves" (Bakeman & others, 1990).

Infants Use Social Cues to Guide Their Exploration

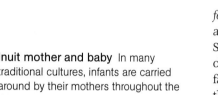

4 ◄ What are three ways by which infants, beginning before 12 months of age, use their observations of adults' behavior to guide their own explorations?

Although babies act upon and explore their environments independently of adult encouragement, they often use cues from adults to guide such actions. By 6 months of age, babies often mimic adults' actions on objects. In one experiment, 6-month-olds frequently rolled a ball if they had recently seen their mother roll it, and they frequently pounded with a ball if they had seen their mother do that (Hofsten & Siddiqui, 1993).

Beginning in the latter half of their first year of life, babies regularly exhibit *gaze following* (introduced in **Chapter 4**)—that is, they watch the eyes of a nearby person and move their own eyes to look at what that person is looking at (Woodward, 2003). Such behavior really does depend on attention to the eyes; if the adult's eyes are closed or covered, the baby does not look preferentially in the direction the adult is facing (Brooks & Meltzoff, 2002). Gaze following ensures that infants will attend to those objects and events that are of greatest interest to their elders, which may be the most important things to attend to and learn about for survival within their culture. It also helps to promote language development. If the adult is naming an object, it is useful to the child to know what object the adult is looking at and naming. Researchers have found that babies who show the most reliable gaze following learn language faster than those who exhibit less gaze following (Brooks & Meltzoff, 2008).

Inuit mother and baby In many traditional cultures, infants are carried around by their mothers throughout the day, and they learn about the world by seeing it from their mother's vantage point. This baby can't see where her mother's eyes are looking, but she can see what her mother is doing.

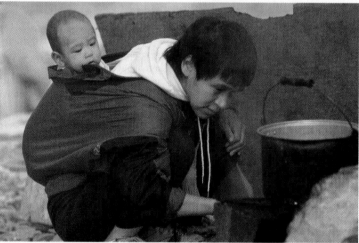

Momatiuk Eastcott/The Image Works

By the time they can crawl or walk freely on their own (toward the end of their first year), infants engage in what is called **social referencing**—they look at their caregivers' emotional expressions for clues about the possible danger of their own actions (Walden, 1991). In an experiment with 12-month-olds, not one crawled over a slight visual cliff (an apparent 30-centimeter drop-off under a solid glass surface) if the mother showed a facial expression of fear, but most crawled over it if her expression was one of joy or interest (Sorce & others, 1985). In another experiment, 12-month-olds avoided a new toy if the mother showed a facial expression of disgust toward it, but they played readily with it otherwise (Hornik & others, 1987).

Infants' Knowledge of Core Physical Principles

You and I share certain assumptions about the nature of physical reality. We assume, for example, that objects continue to exist even when they disappear from view; that two solid objects cannot occupy the same space at the same time; and that if an object moves from one place to another, it must do so along a continuous path. Such assumptions constitute *core principles* of our knowledge of the physical world (Spelke, 2000). We expect these principles always to be true, and when they seem to be violated, we usually assume that our senses have been somehow deceived, not that the principles have really been overturned.

At what age do people begin to make these core assumptions about physical reality? This question has spurred much research in developmental psychology, partly because of its intrinsic interest and partly because of its relevance to a centuries-long philosophical debate. Empiricist philosophers, such as John Locke (1690/1975) and George Berkeley (1710/1820), argued that each person gradually acquires an understanding of core principles through sensory experience and general learning ability. In contrast, nativist philosophers, such as René Descartes (1649/1985) and Immanuel Kant (1781/1965), argued that knowledge of at least some core principles is inborn. According to the nativists, such principles are so central to human perception and thought that they must in some way be known from the beginning, in order for useful learning to occur. Without certain initial assumptions about the nature of physical reality, infants would have no way to interpret their sensory experiences and, therefore, no way to learn from them. (This idea is discussed more fully in **Chapter 1**.) Psychological research has not settled the question about the origin of knowledge of core principles, but it has shown that such knowledge is manifested in the patterns of infants' exploration beginning at a very young age.

> ----- 5
How did empiricist and nativist philosophers explain the origin of a person's knowledge of core physical principles?

Peek-a-boo The results of selective-looking experiments suggest that babies even much younger than this one know that objects continue to exist when out of view. Nevertheless, they take delight in having that understanding confirmed, especially when the object is a familiar, friendly person.

© Laura Dwight / Corbis

Infants Reveal Core Knowledge in Selective-Looking Experiments

Just as babies look longer at novel objects than at familiar ones, they also look longer at unexpected events than at expected ones. Researchers have capitalized on this with many experiments that have used selective looking to assess what infants expect to happen in specific conditions (Baillargeon, 2004, 2008).

----- 6
What is the violation-of-expectancy method for studying infants' knowledge of physical principles? With this method, what have researchers discovered about the knowledge of 2- to 4-month-olds?

A classic example of such a *violation-of-expectancy experiment* is illustrated in Figure 11.1. First, in the habituation phase, the baby is repeatedly shown a physical event until he or she is bored with it, as indexed by reduced time spent looking at it. In the example shown in the figure, that event is the back-and-forth movement of a hinged screen over a 180-degree arc. Then, in the test phase, the infant is shown one of two variations of the original event. One variation, the *impossible event,* is an illusion, arranged with mirrors or other trickery, that appears to violate one or more core physical principles. In the example, this event is one in which an object placed behind the rotating screen fails to prevent the screen from rotating all the way back. It is as if the object magically disappears each time the screen rotates back and then magically reappears each time the screen rotates forward. The other event, the *possible event,* does not violate any physical principle. In the example, this event is one in which the rotating screen stops in each rotation at the place where it would bump into the object behind it.

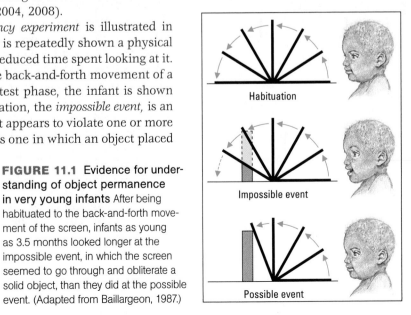

FIGURE 11.1 Evidence for understanding of object permanence in very young infants After being habituated to the back-and-forth movement of the screen, infants as young as 3.5 months looked longer at the impossible event, in which the screen seemed to go through and obliterate a solid object, than they did at the possible event. (Adapted from Baillargeon, 1987.)

Habituation

Impossible event

Possible event

Notice that the two test events are designed so that, on purely sensory grounds, the possible event differs more from the original habituation event than does the impossible one. Thus, if infants respond simply on the basis of sensory novelty, they should look longest at the possible event. But if they respond from knowledge of physical principles, they should look longest at the impossible event, because that differs most from what they would expect to happen. In fact, using the setup shown in Figure 11.1, Renée Baillargeon (1987) found that infants as young as 3.5 months old looked longer at the impossible event than at the possible event. This result is strong evidence that even such young infants understand, in some way, that solid objects do not normally pass through and temporarily obliterate other solid objects.

Similar experiments have demonstrated infants' knowledge of other core principles. For instance, babies as young as 2.5 to 3 months expect an object to appear behind the screen where it was originally placed, not behind a different screen (Baillargeon, 2004); expect a rolling ball to stop at a solid barrier rather than pass through it (Spelke & others, 1992); and expect a stationary ball to remain stationary unless pushed by another object (Spelke & others, 1994). Of course, young infants do not manifest entirely the same expectations about the physical world that adults do. Core principles may be present early on, but nuances related to them are acquired with age and experience (Baillargeon, 2008). For example, Baillargeon (1994, 1998) and her colleagues found that 4-month-olds expected a box to fall to the ground when it was released in midair but did not expect it to fall when it was set on the edge of a shelf with most of its weight hanging off the shelf. Only by 6 to 7 months did babies show evidence that they expected the unbalanced box to fall.

Infants Reveal Less Knowledge in Search Tasks than in Selective-Looking Tasks

◄ 7 — — — — — — — — — — — — — — — — —

How did Jean Piaget test infants' understanding of object permanence? What might explain the discrepancy between Piaget's results and the results of selective-looking experiments?

— — — — — — — — — — — — — — — —

The findings supporting infants' early knowledge of core principles surprised many developmental psychologists. Previous research, using a different procedure, had suggested that infants under about 5 months of age lack even the most basic understanding of **object permanence,** the principle that objects continue to exist when out of view. The pioneer of that research was the famous Swiss developmental psychologist Jean Piaget (1936/1963), who tested infants' understanding by having them search for hidden objects. In the simplest of his tests, the *simple hiding problem,* an attractive toy is shown to a baby and then is placed under a napkin as the baby watches. Babies younger than about 5 months typically follow the toy with their eyes as it disappears under the napkin but do not reach for it once it is there and almost immediately seem to lose interest in it. Piaget and his successors interpreted this result as evidence that babies this age completely lack the concept of object permanence.

Between about 6 and 9 months of age, most infants solve the simple hiding problem but fail the *changed-hiding-place problem,* also developed by Piaget (Wishart & Bower, 1984). In the first phase of this test, the toy is hidden under one napkin for a series of trials, and the baby retrieves it each time. Then, in the crucial phase, the toy is hidden under another napkin, right next to the first. Despite having watched the object disappear under the new napkin, the baby reaches toward the original napkin. Piaget concluded that at this age the emerging understanding of object permanence is still very fragile; when pitted against a learned motor habit (reaching toward the original hiding place), the habit wins out. Only by about 10 to 12 months do most infants solve this problem.

Why do infants younger than 5 months, who appear to understand object permanence in selective-looking experiments, fail even the simplest of Piaget's tests of object permanence? Nobody knows for sure, but a number of researchers have suggested that the difficulty in Piaget's tests has to do with the ability to plan the correct arm and hand movement to obtain the hidden object (Baillargeon, 1998; Keen, 2003). In order to retrieve a hidden object, the baby not only must know where the object is but also must be able to use that knowledge to guide his or her reaching movement. Babies under 5 months of age have no difficulty reaching for objects that are in full view, but may be unable to use mental images of hidden objects to guide their reaching. Consistent with this interpretation, researchers have found that infants as young as 3 to 4 months old who fail to reach for a hidden object nevertheless *look* at the location where the object was hidden, even after a moment's distraction (Ruffman & others, 2005).

Myrleen Ferguson Cate/PhotoEdit

Self-produced locomotion promotes cognitive development
When babies are able to move around on their own—through crawling or walking with the aid of a walker, such as that shown here—they gain new perspectives on their world and make rapid gains in their ability to solve Piagetian search problems. (Caution: Walkers can be dangerous; pediatricians advise against their use except in very safe places, with no ledges or stairs.)

Dramatic improvement in infants' search abilities occurs shortly after they learn to crawl or in other ways move about on their own (Campos & others, 2000). In one experiment, 8-month-olds were tested in a series of search tasks, including a version of Piaget's classic changed-hiding-place problem (Kermoian & Campos, 1988). One group had learned to crawl at least 9 weeks before the tests; a second group had not learned to crawl but had at least 9 weeks of experience moving around in walkers at home; and a third group had neither learned to crawl nor been provided with walkers. Approximately 75 percent of the babies in the first two groups succeeded on the changed-hiding-place problem, compared with only 13 percent of those in the third group. Self-produced locomotion allows infants to view stationary objects from varying perspectives, and it requires them to coordinate their vision with their muscular movements in new ways, to avoid bumping into objects. Such experiences may well help them learn to plan all sorts of effective movements, including those involved in retrieving hidden objects.

> **8**
> **What evidence suggests that self-produced locomotion promotes rapid development of infants' search abilities?**

SECTION REVIEW

Infants actively explore their physical world and know some of its core principles.

Exploring the World Around Them

➤ Infants prefer novel stimuli, as demonstrated by the fact that they look longer at them. This reliable tendency is used to study infant perception and memory.

➤ Infants exhibit a strong drive to control their environment; they become upset when control is taken away.

➤ By 5 or 6 months, independent of adult encouragement, infants examine objects with their hands and eyes, focusing on the objects' unique properties.

➤ From 6 to 12 months of age, infants use their observations of adults to guide their own exploration. They mimic adults' actions, look where adults are looking, and use adults' emotional expressions to identify danger or safety.

Knowledge of Core Physical Principles

➤ Infants' knowledge of core physical principles is revealed by the fact that they look longer at physically impossible events than at physically possible events. Such research indicates that infants as young as 2.5 to 4 months old know some core principles.

➤ Search tasks that involve manual reaching (such as Piaget's simple hiding problem) appear to show later development of even the rudimentary concept of object permanence, perhaps because such tasks require the infant to form a plan to obtain the hidden object.

➤ Experience with self-produced locomotion, either by crawling or by using a walker, promotes the ability to solve manual search problems.

■ Three Theories of Children's Mental Development

As children grow from infancy toward adulthood, their thinking becomes ever more logical, ever more effective in solving problems. How can these changes be characterized, and what are the processes through which they develop? Here we shall address these questions from three theoretical perspectives. The first is Piaget's theory, which focuses on the child's actions on the physical world as a driving force for cognitive development. The second is Lev Vygotsky's sociocultural theory, which focuses on the child's interactions with other people as a driving force. The third is the information-processing perspective, which accounts for mental development in terms of maturational changes in basic components of the child's mind.

Piaget's Theory: Role of the Child's Own Actions in Mental Growth

In his long career at the University of Geneva (from the 1920s until his death in 1980), Piaget wrote more than 50 books and hundreds of articles on children's reasoning. His goal was to understand how the adult mind, particularly its capacity for objective reasoning, develops from the child's more primitive abilities. His primary methods were those of observation, testing, and questioning. From his observations of children's conversations and play, he would extract clues about their understanding. He would also present children with specific tasks to solve and question them about their reasons for the solutions they offered. From this work, Piaget developed an elaborate, comprehensive theory of cognitive development.

Piaget's fundamental idea was that mental development derives from the child's own actions on the physical environment. According to Piaget, children are constantly, in their play and exploration, striving to figure out what they can do with the various objects that exist in their world. By acting on objects, children develop mental representations, called **schemes,** which are mental blueprints for actions.

Piaget's term *scheme* is related to but not identical in meaning to the term *schema,* used by other psychologists. A *schema,* as noted in **Chapter 9,** is a mental representation that brings together all that one knows about the typical appearance and properties of some category of objects, scenes, or events. In contrast, a *scheme,* to Piaget, refers more specifically to a mental representation of a bodily movement or of something that a person can *do* with an object or category of objects. The earliest schemes, according to Piaget, are closely tied to specific objects and are called forth only by an object's immediate presence. Thus a young infant might have a sucking scheme most applicable to nipples, a grasping and shaking scheme most applicable to rattles, and a smiling scheme most applicable to human faces. As children grow older, they develop new, more sophisticated, more abstract schemes that are less closely tied to the immediate environment or to actual physical actions. They become schemes for mental actions.

Schemes Develop Through Assimilation and Accommodation

9 - ◀
In Piaget's theory, how do schemes develop through assimilation and accommodation?

Piaget conceived of the growth of schemes as involving two complementary processes: assimilation and accommodation.

Assimilation is the process by which new experiences are incorporated into existing schemes. Piaget was a biologist by training, and he considered the assimilation of experiences to be analogous to the assimilation of food. Two people may eat the same type of food, but the food will be assimilated into the tissues differently, depending on the inner structures involved in digestion and building the body. Moreover, just as nondigestible foods will not result in body growth, new experiences that are too different from existing schemes to be mentally digested will not result in mental growth. A calculator given to an infant will not contribute to the child's arithmetic skills, because the infant has no calculating scheme into which to assimilate the calculator's functions. Instead, the infant will probably assimilate the calculator into his or her already well-developed sucking scheme or banging scheme.

Few new stimuli perfectly fit an existing scheme. Assimilation usually requires that existing schemes expand or change somewhat to accommodate the new object or event. Appropriately, Piaget referred to this process as **accommodation.** In Piaget's theory, the mind and its schemes are not like a brick wall, which just grows bigger as each new brick (unit of knowledge) is added; they are more like a spider's web, which changes its entire shape somewhat as each new thread is added. The web accommodates to the thread while the thread is assimilated into the web. The addition of new information to the mind changes somewhat the structure of schemes that are already present.

Jean Piaget Because of his interest in the influence of the environment on children's cognitive development, Piaget preferred to observe children in natural settings. Here he is shown during a visit to a nursery school.

Anderson/Monkmeyer Press

Children Behave Like Little Scientists

In Piaget's view infants and children at play behave like little scientists. Their exploratory play—in which they manipulate objects in all sorts of ways to see what happens—can be thought of as experimentation. They are most strongly motivated to explore those objects and situations that they partly but do not fully understand. Stated differently, in Piaget's terms, they are most drawn to experiences that can be *assimilated* into existing schemes but not too easily, so that *accommodation* is required. This natural tendency leads children to direct their playful activities in ways that maximize their mental growth.

Consider, for example, an infant who already has a scheme for stacking objects, which includes the notion that an object placed on top of another will remain on top. One day this infant happens to place an object above an open container and, instead of remaining on top, the object falls into the container. This observation is intriguing to the infant, because it seems to violate his stacking scheme. As a result, the infant may spend lots of time dropping various objects into various containers. Such exploration eventually leads the infant to modify (accommodate) his stacking scheme to include the notion that if one object is hollow and open-topped, a smaller object placed over its top it will fall inside. At the same time, other schemes that include the notion that two objects cannot occupy the same place at the same time may also undergo accommodation.

As another illustration of the little scientist concept, consider an experiment performed by Laura Schulz and Elizabeth Bonawitz (2007). These researchers presented preschool children (ages 4 to 5), one at a time, with a box that had two levers sticking out of it. Pressing one lever caused a toy duck to pop up through a slit on top of the box, and pressing the other lever caused a puppet made of drinking straws to pop up. The box was demonstrated to different children in two different ways. In one demonstration condition, each lever was pressed separately, so the child could see the effect that each lever produced when pressed. In the other condition, the two levers were always pressed simultaneously, so the child could not know which lever controlled which object. After the demonstration, each child was allowed to play with the two-lever box or with a different toy.

The result was that children who had only seen the two levers operated simultaneously chose to play much more with the demonstrated box than with the new toy, while the opposite was true for the other children. The logical interpretation is this: The children who could see, from the demonstration, what each lever did were no longer much interested in the box because they had little more to learn from it. In contrast, those who had only seen the two levers pressed simultaneously wanted to play with the box so they could try each lever separately and discover whether it moved the duck, or the puppet, or both. Consistent with Piaget's theory, the children's play was oriented toward discovery, not toward repetition of already known effects.

➤ ----------------- 10
How is Piaget's "little scientist" view of children's behavior illustrated by the example of an infant playing with containers and by an experiment with preschool children allowed to play with a two-lever toy?

Bruce Plotkin / The Image Works

Accommodation This 11-month-old may be accommodating her "stacking scheme" to assimilate the experience of one block fitting inside another. From such experiences, a new "fits inside" scheme may develop.

Reversible Actions (Operations) Promote Development

11

In Piaget's theory, what is the special value of operations?

As children grow beyond infancy, according to Piaget, the types of actions most conducive to their mental development are those called **operations,** defined as *reversible actions*—actions whose effects can be undone by other actions. Rolling a ball of clay into a sausage shape is an operation because it can be reversed by rolling the clay back into a ball. Turning a light on by pushing a switch up is an operation because it can be reversed by pushing the switch back down. Young children perform countless operations as they explore their environments, and in doing so, they gradually develop *operational schemes*—mental blueprints that allow them to think about the reversibility of their actions.

Understanding the reversibility of actions provides a foundation for understanding basic physical principles. The child who knows that a clay ball can be rolled into a sausage shape and then back into a ball of the same size as it was before has the basis for knowing that the amount of clay must remain the same as the clay changes shape—the principle of *conservation of substance*. The child who can imagine that pushing a light switch back down will restore the whole physical setup to its previous state has the basis for understanding the principle of cause and effect, at least as applied to the switch and the light.

Four Types of Schemes; Four Stages of Development

Piaget conceived of four types of schemes, which represent increasingly sophisticated ways of understanding the physical environment. His research convinced him that the four types develop successively, in stages roughly correlated with the child's age.

12

In Piaget's theory, what are the four stages and the ages roughly associated with each? How are the child's capacities and limitations at each stage related to the kind of scheme that is most prominent? How does the child's behavior at each stage promote advancement to the next stage?

The Sensorimotor Stage The most primitive schemes in Piaget's theory are **sensorimotor schemes,** which provide a foundation for acting on objects that are present but not for thinking about objects that are absent. During the sensorimotor stage (from birth to roughly 2 years of age), thought and overt physical action are one and the same. The major task in this stage is to develop classes of schemes specific for different categories of objects. Objects the child explores become assimilated into schemes for sucking, shaking, banging, squeezing, twisting, dropping, and so on, depending on the objects' properties. Eventually the schemes develop in such a way that the child can use them as mental symbols to represent particular objects and classes of objects in their absence, and then they are no longer sensorimotor schemes.

The Preoperational Stage *Preoperational schemes* emerge from sensorimotor schemes and enable the child to think beyond the here and now. Children in the preoperational stage (roughly from age 2 to 7) have a well-developed ability to symbolize objects and events that are absent, and in their play they delight in exercising that ability (Piaget, 1962). Put a saucepan into the hands of a preschooler and it is magically transformed into a ray gun or a guitar—the saucepan becomes a symbol in the child's play. The schemes at this stage are called preoperational because, although they can represent absent objects, they do not permit the child to think about the reversible consequences of actions.

According to Piaget, understanding at the preoperational stage is based on appearances rather than principles. If you roll a ball of clay into a sausage shape and ask the child if the shape now contains more than, less than, or the same amount of clay as before, the child will respond in accordance with how the clay looks. Noting that the sausage is longer than the ball was, one preoperational child might say that the sausage has more clay than the ball had. Another child, noting that the sausage is thinner than the ball, might say that the sausage has less clay. (For another test of operational thinking, see Figure 11.2 on page 407.)

Hazel Hankin

The Concrete-Operational Stage Although (or perhaps because) preoperational children have not yet internalized an understanding of operations, they continually produce operations as they explore their environment. As they push, pull, squeeze, mix, and so on, they gradually develop ***concrete-operational schemes*** and eventually enter the *concrete-operational stage* (roughly from age 7 to 12). These schemes permit a child to think about the reversible consequences of actions and thereby provide the basis for understanding physical principles such as conservation of substance and cause and effect (Piaget, 1927).

A concrete-operational child who has had experience with clay will correctly state that the sausage has the same amount of clay as the ball from which it was rolled because it can be rolled back into that ball. A concrete-operational child who has had experience with bicycles will correctly say that the chain is crucial to the bicycle's movement but the fender is not, because the child can picture the reversible consequences of removing each and knows that the pedals can move the wheels only if there is a physical connection between the two.

FIGURE 11.2 A test of conservation of substance Sarah, here age five and three quarters, does not pass Piaget's test of conservation of substance, which is consistent with her being in the preoperational stage. She knows that the two short glasses contain the same amount of milk, and she carefully watches the milk being poured into the tall glass, yet she points to the tall glass when asked, "Which has more?" She uses perception rather than logic to answer the question.

The earliest schemes for operations are referred to as *concrete* because they are still tied closely to the child's actual experiences in the world. The child might have schemes, for example, for the conservation of clay rolled into various shapes and of fluids poured from one container to another but still lack an understanding of conservation of substance as a general principle that applies regardless of the type of substance.

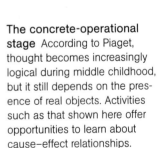
Bernard Boutrit / Woodfin Camp & Associates, Inc.

The concrete-operational stage According to Piaget, thought becomes increasingly logical during middle childhood, but it still depends on the presence of real objects. Activities such as that shown here offer opportunities to learn about cause–effect relationships.

The Formal-Operational Stage During the concrete-operational stage, the child begins to notice certain similarities about the operations that can be performed on different entities. For instance, the child who understands that that the amount of clay remains the same no matter what shape it is molded into, and that amount of water remains the same no matter what the shape of the glass it is poured into, may begin to understand the principle of conservation of substance as a general principle, applicable to all substances. In this way, according to Piaget, the child develops ***formal-operational schemes,*** which represent abstract principles that apply to a wide variety of objects, substances, or situations. When such schemes characterize a significant portion of a person's thinking, the person is said to be in the *formal-operational stage* (which begins roughly at the onset of adolescence and continues throughout adulthood). Formal-operational schemes permit a person to think theoretically and apply principles even to actions that cannot actually be performed (Inhelder & Piaget, 1958).

You cannot really unbeat an egg, but with an appropriate formal-operational scheme you can understand the theoretical principle that an egg can be unbeaten and restored to its original form. Thus, you can answer correctly a conservation question about a beaten egg as well as about a rolled-out piece of clay: Is the amount of egg more, less, or the same after it is beaten compared with before? Formal-operational thinkers can extend principles into hypothetical realms that neither they nor anyone else has actually experienced. While the concrete-operational reasoner is limited to empirical (fact-based) science and arithmetic, the formal-operational reasoner is capable of theoretical (principle-based) science and formal mathematics.

Criticism of Piaget's Theory of Stages

Historically, Piaget's theory played a valuable role in motivating developmental psychologists to focus more closely than they had before on children's actions and on the ways that those actions promote mental growth. The concepts of assimilation and accommodation and the idea that operations contribute significantly to cognitive development are still much valued by many developmental psychologists. Especially valued is the general idea that children actively build their own minds through their exploration of the world around them.

The most frequent criticisms of Piaget's theory today center on his concept of developmental stages (Kohler, 2008). Piaget himself acknowledged that the transitions from stage to stage are gradual, not abrupt. His own research convinced him that each new type of scheme develops slowly, over the course of years, and that a child at any given point in development might use a more advanced type of scheme for one class of problems while still using a more primitive type for other problems. Subsequent research, however, has led many developmental psychologists to reject the whole concept that people think in fundamentally different ways at different ages.

13

Why is Piaget's theory of stages of mental development doubted by many developmental psychologists today?

◄ Much research suggests that Piaget underestimated the mental abilities of infants and young children and overestimated those of adolescents and adults. Earlier in this chapter you read about violation-of-expectation experiments showing that infants as young as 3 months expect objects to continue to exist when out of view, contrary to Piaget's assertion that infants in the sensorimotor stage cannot think of absent objects. Children as young as 4 or 5 years can pass at least some tests of concrete-operational reasoning if the problems are presented clearly, without distracting information, and with words that the child understands (McGarrigle & Donaldson, 1975; Siegler & Svetina, 2006). At the other end of the developmental scale, research with adults (discussed in **Chapter 10**) challenges the distinction between concrete-operational and formal-operational thought. Such research suggests that people who are good at solving abstract problems usually do so by thinking of analogies to more familiar problems or by turning the problem statement into a familiar visual image, thereby converting a formal task into a concrete one.

In light of such studies, it seems reasonable to suggest that all of us, throughout the great bulk of our childhood and throughout adulthood, are what Piaget would call concrete-operational thinkers. Our thought advances more because of our gradually increasing stores of knowledge and ability to manipulate that knowledge efficiently than because of fundamental revolutions in our ways of thinking.

Vygotsky's Theory: Role of the Sociocultural Environment in Mental Growth

14

How does Vygotsky's perspective on cognitive development differ from Piaget's?

◄ Children do not develop in a social vacuum. They develop in a sociocultural milieu in which they interact constantly with other people and with products of their cultural history. The person most often credited with originating the sociocultural perspective on cognitive development is Lev Vygotsky, a Russian scholar who died in 1934 at age 38, after devoting just 10 years to formal research and writing in psychology.

Vygotsky (1934/1962) agreed with Piaget that the main force for development is the child's active interaction with the environment, but he disagreed with Piaget's conception of the relevant environment. Whereas Piaget emphasized the child's interaction with the physical environment, Vygotsky emphasized the child's interaction with the social environment. In Vygotsky's view, cognitive development is largely a matter of internalizing the symbols, knowledge, ideas, and modes of reasoning that have evolved over the course of history and constitute the culture into which the child is born.

The distinction between Vygotsky's and Piaget's perspectives can be illustrated by applying those perspectives to a story, told by Piaget (1970), about how a mathematician friend of his had, as a child, become fascinated by mathematics:

> When he was a small child, he was counting pebbles one day; he lined them up in a row, counted them from left to right, and got to ten. Then, just for fun, he counted them from right to left to see what number he would get, and was astonished that he got ten again. He put the pebbles in a circle and counted them, and once again there were ten. And no matter how he put the pebbles down, when he counted them, the number came to ten. He discovered there what is known in mathematics as commutativity—that is, the sum is independent of the order.

The story is prototypically Piagetian. The child, through acting on physical objects (pebbles), discovers and is exhilarated by a core principle of mathematics (commutativity). As Piaget goes on to explain, "The knowledge that this future mathematician discovered that day was drawn, then, not from the physical properties of the pebbles, but from the actions that he carried out on the pebbles."

How might Vygotsky have reacted to this story? It was told long after Vygotsky had died, but I imagine him saying: "Where did that young boy learn to count in the first place? Of all the things he might do with pebbles, why did he decide that counting them was worthwhile? The answer lies in the boy's social environment. He was growing up in a culture where number words are in the air and people value counting. He may have discovered with pebbles that day the principle of commutativity, but his social environment had prepared him to make that discovery."

Lev Vygotsky A leader of Russian psychology during the early days of the Soviet Union, Vygotsky developed a theory of human development that emphasized the roles of culture and social interaction.

The Role of Language in Mental Development

While Piaget (1970) considered language to be more or less a side effect of the child's development of thought and not essential to it, Vygotsky (1934/1962) argued that language is the foundation not only for children's acquisition of information and ideas from other people, but also for their own higher thought. According to Vygotsky, children first learn words as means of communicating with others but then begin to use them also as symbols for their own thinking. This leads to *verbal thought*, which, according to Vygotsky, is more powerful than a child's earlier, non-verbal forms of thought. Words are symbols developed over countless generations of human language use. By internalizing language and using it for thought, children acquire a far richer set of symbols than they could possibly invent on their own.

_15

In Vygotsky's view, how does the acquisition of language lead to a higher form of thought?

The words of a language not only provide the building blocks for verbal thought but also direct such thought in ways that reflect the culture's activities and values. For example, cultures in which counting is important have developed an efficient set of number words. Children growing up in those cultures begin to recite number words sequentially even before they understand their meaning; and through that ritual act they eventually learn the meaning.

As another example, consider the word *because*. Both Vygotsky (1934/1962) and Piaget (1927) noted that children begin to use this word (or rather its Russian or French equivalent) before they fully understand its meaning. Children younger than 6 or 7 years commonly reverse cause and effect, saying such things as "Billy fell off the porch because he broke his arm." To Piaget, the word is incidental to cognitive development; its correct or incorrect usage only reflects the child's level of understanding. But to Vygotsky, the word is critical. Using the word in a communicative social context induces the child to think about its meaning, which leads the child toward a more advanced understanding of cause-effect relationships. *Because* becomes not just a tool for communication but also a tool for private thought.

16
According to Vygotsky, what is the function of children's noncommunicative, private speech? What evidence supports Vygotsky's view?

Elizabeth Crews

Thinking with lips and fingers
According to Vygotsky, young children talk to themselves as a means of solving problems. With time and experience, such talk becomes internalized in the form of verbal thought.

17
According to Vygotsky, how are a child's abilities stretched and improved through collaboration with other people?

In the zone This boy may not be quite ready to repair his bicycle himself, but he can with a little help and advice from his dad. Vygotsky pointed out that skill development often occurs best when children collaborate with more skilled others to do things that are within the child's *zone of proximal development*.

© Ariel Skelley / Corbis

Children's Private Speech: A Transition Toward Verbal Thought

In support of his view that language is critical to thought, Vygotsky (1934/1962) noted that children about 4 to 6 years old often talk aloud in a noncommunicative manner. A 4-year-old drawing a picture of a horse might say, for example, "Horses have long necks. I'll make it long." Vygotsky (1934/1962) interpreted such speech as a transition stage in the development of verbal thought. At around age 4 children discover that they can use words not just to communicate to others but also as part of planning, to direct their own behavior. By talking to themselves as they work on a task, they can maintain their focus on the task and solve problems related to it. Out-loud private speech generally declines beginning at around age 7 and is replaced increasingly by *inner speech* (Vygotsky's term), or *verbal thought*. With experience, inner speech becomes increasingly abbreviated, and in older children and adults the words are usually not pronounced even to the self but are purely mental symbols.

Consistent with Vygotsky's view, researchers have since found that young children manifest more out-loud private speech when working on difficult problems than when working on easy ones (Berk, 1994; Winsler & others, 2003) and solve problems better when asked to think aloud than when asked to work silently (Kendler, 1972; Kohlberg & others, 1968). In another study, first- and second-graders who manifested the most muttering and lip movement while solving arithmetic problems showed the greatest improvement in their arithmetic ability over the course of a year (Bivens & Berk, 1990).

The Role of Collaboration and Dialogue in Mental Development

Vygotsky's fundamental idea is that development occurs first at the social level and then at the individual level. People learn to converse with words (a social activity) before they learn to think with words (a private activity). People also learn how to solve problems in collaboration with more competent others before they can solve the same kinds of problems alone. Vygotsky (1935/1978) coined the term **zone of proximal development** to refer to the realm of activities that a child can do in collaboration with more competent others but cannot yet do alone. According to Vygotsky, children's development is promoted most efficiently through their behavior within their zones of proximal development.

In research at an alternative, age-mixed school, Jay Feldman and I found many examples of collaboration between adolescents and younger children that nicely illustrate Vygotsky's concept of a zone of proximal development (Gray & Feldman, 2004). In one case, for example, a teenage boy helped a 5-year-old girl find her lost shoes by asking her to think of all the places she had been that day and all the places where she had already looked. Through such suggestions, the teenager added structure to the little girl's thinking, which allowed her to think and search more systematically than she would have been able to do on her own. Such collaboration not only enabled the child to find her shoes but also probably promoted her mental development by suggesting questions that she might ask herself to guide future searches for missing objects.

From a Vygotskian perspective, critical thinking—in adults as well as children-derives largely from the social, collaborative activity of dialogue. In actual dialogue, one person states an idea and another responds with a question or comment that challenges or extends the idea. In the back-and-forth exchange, the original statement is clarified, revised, used as the foundation for building a larger argument, or rejected as absurd. From many such experiences we develop the capacity for internal self-dialogue, so that we (or what may seem like voices within us that represent our friends and critics) question and extend our own private thoughts and ideas and in that way improve them or throw them out. Consistent with Vygotsky's view, researchers have found that students who engage in covert dialogues with authors as they read, or who explain ideas they are studying or logic problems they are working on to other people, real or imagined, acquire a more complete understanding of what they are reading or studying than do students who do not engage in such activities (Chi & others, 1989, 1994; Heiman, 1987; Mercer & Littleton, 2007).

The Child as Apprentice

While Piaget's child can be characterized as a little scientist performing experiments on the world and discovering its nature, Vygotsky's child can be characterized as an apprentice (Rogoff, 1990). Children are born into a social world in which people routinely engage in activities that are important to the culture. Children are attracted to those activities and seek to participate. At first their roles are small, but they grow as the children gain skill and understanding. From this view, cognitive development is a progression not so much from simple tasks to more complex ones as from small roles to larger roles in the activities of the social world. Barbara Rogoff (1990, 1993) has documented many ways by which children in various cultures involve themselves in family and community activities and learn from those activities.

One prediction of the apprenticeship analogy is that people who grow up in different cultures will acquire different cognitive abilities. A child surrounded by people who drive cars, use computers, and read books will not learn the same mental skills as a child surrounded by people who hunt game, weave blankets, and tell stories far into the night. The apprenticeship analogy also reminds us that logic itself is not the goal of mental development; the goal is to function effectively as an adult in one's society. To achieve that goal, children must learn to get along with other people and to perform economically valuable tasks. In our society, such tasks may involve for some people the kind of mathematical and scientific reasoning that Piaget labeled formal operational; but in another society, they may not.

> **18**
> How does Vygotsky's "apprentice" view of the child contrast with Piaget's "scientist" view?

An Information-Processing Perspective on Mental Development

As you have just seen, developmental psychologists in the tradition of Piaget and Vygosky attempt to understand how children's interactions with their physical or social environment increase their knowledge and lead to new ways of thinking about the world around them. In contrast, developmental psychologists who adopt the *information-processing perspective* attempt to explain children's mental development in terms of operational changes in basic components of their mental machinery.

The information-processing approach to cognition, as described in **Chapter 9,** begins with the assumption that the mind is a system, analogous to a computer, for analyzing information from the environment. According to the standard information-processing model (see Figure 9.1 on p. 310), the mind's machinery includes attention mechanisms for bringing information in, working memory for actively manipulating (or thinking about) information, and long-term memory for passively holding information so that it can be used in the future. As children grow, from birth to adulthood, their brains continue to mature in various ways, resulting in changes in their abilities to attend to, remember, and use information gleaned through their senses.

> **19**
> What is the information-processing perspective on cognitive development, and how does it differ from Piaget's and Vygotsky's perspectives?

Development of Long-Term Memory Systems: Episodic Memory Comes Last

In **Chapter 9** I described the distinction between explicit and implicit long-term memory systems. *Explicit memories* are those that people can consciously think about and report to others. When we ask people to say what they know or remember

> **20**
> At what ages, and in what contexts, do researchers first see evidence of (a) implicit memory, (b) explicit semantic memory, and (c) explicit episodic memory in young children?

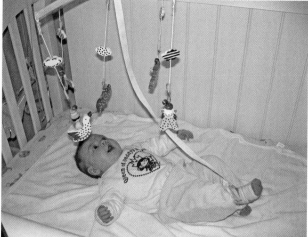

Courtesy of Dr. Carolyn Rovee-Collier

FIGURE 11.3 A test of infants' implicit procedural memories The infant, as young as 2 months of age, learns to operate the mobile by kicking one leg (a). During the test, on another day, the mobile is again presented, but now the ribbon is connected to another hook, so the infant can't control the mobile (b). The infant's immediate kicking in this condition is a sign of long-term memory for how to control the mobile.

about something, we are testing their explicit memory. We have no certain way to assess children's explicit memories until they have learned to talk. *Implicit memories,* in contrast, are memories that affect behavior even though the person is unable to report them. They include procedural memories, such as how to pound with a hammer or ride a bicycle, and effects of classical and operant conditioning, which are demonstrated in nonverbal behavior.

Even very young infants show, in their behavior, that they can form implicit memories. A newborn who looks at a new stimulus more than at an old one demonstrates implicit memory for the old stimulus. A 2-month-old who learns to kick with one leg to move a mobile and who then, a day later, kicks again as soon as the mobile appears, demonstrates implicit memory of how to operate the mobile (see Figure 11.3). Carolyn Rovee-Collier and her colleagues found that 2-month-olds, who received just a few minutes' experience with moving a mobile by kicking, remembered the response as much as 4 months later if given occasional reminders (in which they saw the mobile but did not have a chance to operate it) (Rovee-Collier & Cuevas, 2009).

I also described in **Chapter 9** the distinction between two categories of explicit memories—semantic and episodic. *Semantic memories* are explicit memories for facts, beliefs, and word meanings. The first clear evidence of semantic memory occurs when babies, at the age of about 10 or 12 months, begin to name objects in their environments correctly: *Mama, blankee, ball. Episodic memories* are explicit memories of one's own previous experiences. To demonstrate episodic memory, a person must be able to mentally re-live some past experience and then describe that experience. This ability develops relatively slowly. Typically by about 20 to 24 months of age, children begin to make comments about things that happened to them earlier in the day or on a previous day, but such comments are infrequent and fragmentary (Nelson & Fivush, 2004). Only by about 3 or 4 years of age do children begin to answer reliably at least some questions about their past experiences.

21

Through what developmental steps do young children develop the capacity to form episodic memories?

Research suggests that young children must develop the ability to encode their experiences into words before they can form episodic memories of those experiences (Nelson & Fivush, 2004; Richardson & Hayne, 2007). At about age 3 children begin, with some reliability, to talk about their experiences as they experience them. Such talk seems to help them make sense of what they are doing, as I noted earlier (in the discussion of Vygotsky's theory), and it may also be essential to the formation of episodic memories. At first such talk depends on the existence of an older conversation partner who can help the child organize the experience in a coherent way and find the appropriate words for it. In one study, researchers recorded the conversations of mothers and their 3-year-old children at visits to a natural history museum and then, a week later, asked the children to recall what they had seen at the museum (Tessler & Nelson, 1994). The result was that the children correctly recalled only those items that had been commented on jointly by both the mother and child in conversation. Items that had been commented on just by the mother or just by the child were not recalled.

Many other research studies have shown that the ability to form detailed, long-lasting episodic memories increases gradually throughout the years of childhood and reaches a plateau in late adolescence or young adulthood (Ofen & others, 2007; Piolino & others, 2007). This improvement is accompanied by continued maturation of the brain, particularly in the prefrontal lobes (Ofen & others, 2007). As noted at the end of **Chapter 9,** connections between the prefrontal lobes and other portions of the brain seem to be crucial to the formation and recall of episodic memories.

The sequence in the development of memory systems—from implicit to semantic to episodic—makes sense in terms of children's developmental needs. From birth on, infants need to form implicit memories in order to recognize familiar people and objects and respond appropriately to stimuli in their environment. Beginning in late infancy (around a year old), an excellent semantic memory system is essential for learning language, acquiring a large vocabulary, and learning and remembering many facts. Finally, as children gradually become more independent, beginning at around age 4, they need to be able to think about their own actions and the consequences of those actions. Such thought, which is essential for planning, requires that they be able to recall past experiences (episodic memories) and think verbally about those experiences in order to anticipate the consequences of future actions.

Forming episodic memories To form long-term episodic memories, young children must encode their experiences verbally. Such encoding is facilitated by adults who share the experience and, through conversation, help the child to find words for what he or she sees.

Development of Working Memory and Faster Speed of Processing

In the standard model of the mind, *working memory* is the center of conscious thought and the place where information—from the environment and from explicit long-term memory—is combined and manipulated to solve problems. As discussed in **Chapters 9 and 10,** the working-memory system is limited in the amount of information it can hold and use at any given time, and this limit constrains a person's problem-solving ability.

> ---------------------22
> **How do working-memory capacity and speed of processing change with age during childhood and early adolescence? How might working-memory capacity depend on speed of processing?**

Many experiments, using many different sorts of measures, have shown that the amount of either verbal or visual information that a person can hold in working memory at any given time increases steadily throughout childhood and reaches adult levels at about age 15. For instance, the number of digits or random single-syllable words that a person can hold in mind and repeat, after hearing them just once, increases from about three at age 4 to about seven at age 15 (Gathercole & others, 2004). These increases are accompanied by improved performance on standard tests of fluid intelligence (Kail, 2007; Swanson, 2008).

Closely correlated with increased working-memory capacity, and possibly a cause of it, is increased *speed of processing*—the speed at which elementary information-processing tasks can be carried out. Speed of processing is usually assessed with reaction-time tests that require a very simple judgment, such as whether two letters or shapes flashed on a screen are the same or different or whether an arrowhead is pointing right or left. Such tests consistently reveal age-related improvement in speed up to about 15 years of age (Kail, 1993, 2007; Wassenberg & others, 2008; see Figure 11.4). As was discussed in **Chapter 10,** faster processing speed permits faster mental movement from one item of information to another, which improves one's ability to keep track of (and thereby hold) a number of different items in working memory at once. Faster processing speed may result at least partly from the physical maturation of the brain that occurs throughout childhood, independent of specific experiences. Consistent with that view, 9- and 10-year-old boys who were judged as

FIGURE 11.4 Reaction time for simple tasks decreases with age Children and adolescents were tested for their speed on six different tests, including a test of elementary reaction time (releasing a button in response to a signal) and a test of picture matching (judging whether two pictures are identical or not). Each person's average time for the six tests was converted by dividing it by the average time achieved by young adults, and the results were then averaged for each age group. Note that a decline in reaction time implies an increase in speed. (Data from Kail, 1993.)

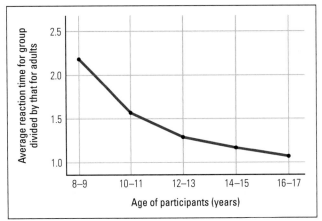

physically mature for their age—on the basis of their height as a percentage of their predicted adult height—exhibited significantly faster reaction times than did boys of the same age who were judged as physically less mature (Eaton & Ritchot, 1995).

SECTION REVIEW

Three complementary perspectives help us understand children's mental growth.

Piaget: The Child as Little Scientist	**Vygotsky: The Child as Apprentice**	**The Information-Processing Perspective**
➤ Piaget believed that cognitive development occurs through the child's actions on the physical environment, which promote the development of schemes—mental blueprints for actions.	➤ Vygotsky considered the child's interaction with the social and cultural environment to be the key to cognitive development, leading to internalization of symbols, ideas, and ways of thinking.	➤ Children exhibit implicit long-term memory from early infancy on, but we cannot assess their explicit memory capacity until they have sufficient language skills.
➤ Piaget held that mental growth involves assimilation (fitting new experiences into existing schemes) and accommodation (modifying those schemes to fit with new experiences).	➤ Vygotsky saw language as crucial to mental development, with words serving not only as a means of communication but also as the building blocks of verbal thought. Private, noncommunicative speech provides evidence of this.	➤ Semantic long-term memory is evident as soon as children begin to use words, at about 10 to 12 months. It underlies, among other things, the growth of vocabulary.
➤ Operational schemes—schemes for reversible actions—are particularly important to cognitive development, according to Piaget.		➤ Episodic long-term memory apparently requires that the child encode personal experiences verbally, which begins to happen with some regularity at about age 3.
➤ Piaget described four successive stages of cognitive development (sensorimotor, preoperational, concrete-operational, and formal-operational), each employing an increasingly sophisticated type of scheme.	➤ Through dialogue and collaboration with more competent others, children acquire skills socially before being able to perform them individually. Such learning takes place within the child's zone of proximal development.	➤ Working-memory capacity increases as the child grows older, up to about age 15. A parallel increase in processing speed may provide the basis for this increase in capacity.

▤ Children's Understanding of Minds

To develop as fully functional humans, we must learn not just about the physical world but also about the social world around us. Most of us—adults and children alike—spend more time trying to understand other people than trying to understand inanimate objects, and we apply entirely different explanatory concepts to the two endeavors. In our explanatory frameworks, billiard balls move because they are hit by other balls or cue sticks, but people move because they want to get somewhere. We are all psychologists in our everyday lives, continually trying to account for people's behavior in terms of their minds. We attribute emotions, motives, feelings, desires, goals, perceptions, and beliefs to people, and we use those attributes to explain their actions.

David Premack (1990) has suggested that beginning at a very early age, humans automatically divide the world into two classes of entities—those that move on their own and those that don't—and attribute psychological properties to the former but not the latter. When 3- to 5-year-olds saw videos of balls moving like billiard balls, only in response to physical impacts, they described the movements in purely physical terms; but when they saw videos of balls moving and changing direction on their own, they immediately regarded the balls as representing people or animals and described the movements in mental terms (Premack, 1990). A child described one sequence of movements as one ball trying to help another ball get out of a hole.

Even Very Young Children Explain Behavior in Mental Terms

23
- - - - - - - - - - - - - - - - ◀ By the time children have learned language sufficiently to offer verbal explanations—

What do children under 3 years old understand about other people's minds?
- - - - - - - - - - - - - - - -
that is, by about 2 to 3 years of age—they already explain people's behavior in terms of mental constructs, especially in terms of perceptions, emotions, and desires

(Hickling & Wellman, 2001; Lillard & Flavell, 1990). They expect others to respond to objects that they (the others) can see but not to objects that they cannot see. They describe a crying person as sad. They say that a person filling a glass with water is thirsty and wants a drink. In one experiment, 2-year-olds demonstrated an understanding that another person's desires could be different from their own. Having learned that a particular adult preferred broccoli to crackers as a snack, they gave that adult broccoli, even though their own preference was for crackers (Repacholi & Gopnik, 1997).

In another experiment, researchers showed that even 12-month-olds can display a remarkable understanding of what is in another person's mind (Tomasello & Haberl, 2003). In that experiment, each infant played with two adults and three new toys, one toy at a time. One of the two adults left the room while one of the three toys was being played with and therefore did not see or play with that toy. Then, at the end of the play session, all three toys were brought into the room on a tray and the adult who had missed playing with one of them looked in the direction of the three toys and said, "Wow! Cool! Can you give it to me?" In response, the majority of infants gave the adult the toy that that adult had not played with before, not one of the two toys with which the adult was already familiar. To perform in this way, the infants must have known which toy was new to the adult, even though it wasn't new to them, and must also have known that people are more excited by new things than by familiar ones.

Delay in Understanding Beliefs, Especially False Beliefs

You and I explain people's behavior not just in terms of their perceptions, emotions, and desires but also in terms of their *beliefs,* and we know that beliefs can be mistaken. For example, if we see a man carrying an umbrella on a sunny day, we might explain that he must have believed it was going to rain that day. Three-year-olds, however, rarely offer explanations in terms of beliefs (Colonnesi & others, 2008; Saxe & others, 2004), and tests indicate that they do not clearly understand that beliefs can differ from reality (Wellman & others, 2001).

A typical test of false-belief understanding is the following (illustrated in Figure 11.5). The child is told a story, which is also acted out with puppets for clarity, in which Maxi puts his candy bar in a blue cupboard. Then Maxi leaves the room and his mother comes in, finds the candy bar, and moves it into the red cupboard. Then Maxi re-enters the room to get his candy bar and the child is asked: "In which cupboard will Maxi look first?" Most 4-year-olds answer, just as you or I would, "In the blue cupboard," but most 3-year-olds insist that he'll look in the red cupboard (Wellman & others, 2001). The problem isn't poor memory, because the 3-year-olds in these experiments have no difficulty reporting accurately on all the factual details of the story when questioned. Rather, they seem not to understand that someone can believe something that isn't true.

Three-year-olds' denials of false belief apply even to their own false beliefs. In one experiment, 3-year-olds were shown a crayon box and asked to say what they believed was inside (Atance & O'Neill, 2004). They all said, "Crayons." Then the children (who were tested individually) were told that they could get some paper to draw on with the crayons if they wanted to. When the children returned with drawing paper, the box was opened and it proved to have candles inside rather than crayons. When asked what they thought the box had in it when they first saw it, most said, "Candles." When asked why they had gotten the paper if they thought the box contained candles, most had no cogent explanation.

Perhaps the concept of false belief is particularly difficult to grasp because of its inherent contradiction. False beliefs are both false and true at the same time. They are false in reality but true in the minds of the believers. In this way they differ from the products of make-believe.

> **24**
> What evidence suggests that an understanding that people can hold false beliefs usually does not develop prior to age 4? Why might false beliefs be particularly difficult for young children to understand?

FIGURE 11.5 A test of ability to understand false belief In this test, which is usually presented with the help of puppets that act out the sequence, most children under age 4 say that Maxi will look in the red cupboard.

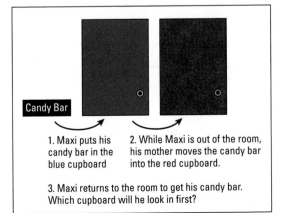

1. Maxi puts his candy bar in the blue cupboard

2. While Maxi is out of the room, his mother moves the candy bar into the red cupboard.

3. Maxi returns to the room to get his candy bar. Which cupboard will he look in first?

25

What logic and evidence suggest that engagement in pretend play, especially in role-play with other children, may help children acquire an understanding of false beliefs?

Make-Believe as a Precursor to the Belief–Reality Distinction

Three-year-olds may have difficulty understanding false beliefs, but they have no difficulty understanding pretense. Toddlers who are 2 and 3 years old, as well as older children, engage in an enormous amount of pretend play, and researchers have found that even 1.5-year-old infants differentiate between make-believe and reality (Leslie, 1994; Rakoczy, 2008). An 18-month-old who turns a cup filled with imaginary water over a doll and says, "Oh oh, dolly all wet," knows that the doll isn't really wet.

Alan Leslie (1987, 1994) has suggested that children's understanding of false beliefs emerges from their earlier understanding of pretense. Pretense is similar to false belief. Both, by definition, are mental conceptions that depart from reality. The only difference between the two is that pretenders know that their conception doesn't match reality, whereas believers think that theirs does. Three-year-olds, who fail false-belief tests, such as the test in which a crayon box actually holds candles, do not fail analogous tests in which they are asked to report what either they or another person had *pretended* was in the box before it was opened (Lillard & Flavell, 1992; Woolley, 1995).

Children everywhere engage in pretend play, whether or not they are encouraged to do so (Carlson & others, 1998). Piaget (1962) regarded such play as an expression and exercise of the child's ability to symbolize objects in their absence, but many developmental psychologists today ascribe even further significance to it. Leslie (1991) suggests that the brain mechanisms that enable and motivate pretend play came about in evolution because such play provides a foundation for understanding non-literal mental states, including false beliefs. A child who understands that pretense differs from reality has the foundation for understanding that people's beliefs (including the child's own beliefs) can differ from reality and that people can fool others by manipulating their beliefs.

Evidence for the view that pretend play promotes false-belief understanding comes from research showing strong correlations between the two. Children who have engaged in lots of pretend role-play with other children pass false-belief tests at a higher rate than do children who have engaged in less (Jenkins & Astington, 1996). Other research has shown that children who have child-age siblings at home, especially older siblings, pass false-belief tests at a much higher rate than do same-age children who lack such siblings (McAlister & Peterson, 2007; Ruffman & others, 1998; see Figure 11.6). Children with siblings engage in much more role-play than do those without siblings, because their siblings are always-present potential playmates (Youngblade & Dunn, 1995). Social role-play (role-play with another child) may be more valuable for development of false-belief understanding than is solo role-play, because in social role-play children must respond appropriately to the pretend statements of the other child, not just to their own pretend statements: *I'm your mommy and you must obey me*, or *Bang, you're dead*. They get used to the idea that other people can hold concepts in their heads that do not reflect reality.

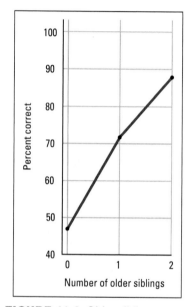

FIGURE 11.6 Older siblings promote false-belief understanding
Three–and 4-year-old children with older siblings succeeded on a standard test of understanding of false belief at a much higher rate than did those who had no older siblings. (Adapted from Ruffman & colleagues, 1998, p. 164.)

A fine lady buying eggs and milk
These 3-year-olds may not understand false beliefs but they certainly understand pretense. Pretend play helps children acquire the belief–reality distinction and also helps them learn to reason hypothetically.

Make-Believe May Also Promote Hypothetical Reasoning

Pretend play may provide a foundation not just for false-belief understanding but also for all sorts of logical reasoning that involves premises not anchored in physical reality. Consider this syllogism: *All cats bark. Muffins is a cat. Does Muffins bark?* Children under about 10 years old usually answer "no," and their explanations show that they either can't or won't accept the initial premise. Yet in a series of experiments, 4-year-olds, and to a lesser extent even 2-year-olds, succeeded on syllogisms like this when they were presented in a playful voice and in words that made it clear that the world being described is a pretend world different from the world in which we live (Dias & Harris, 1988; Richards & Sanderson, 1999).

➤ **26** How have researchers shown that pretend play can help very young children solve syllogisms that are based on counterfactual premises?

Children apparently have, early in their development, two separate modes of thinking: a fictional mode and a reality mode. Young children can apparently think quite well in either mode, but they do not at first combine the two. Advancement in thinking may entail, in part, the bringing together of these two modes for specific types of problems. Understanding false beliefs may be an early and universal result of such conjoining, and deductive reasoning from hypothetical premises may be a later, more culture-dependent result.

Autism: A Disorder in Understanding Minds

Suppose you were oblivious to the minds of other people. You would not feel self-conscious or embarrassed in others' presence, because you would have no understanding of, or concern for, their thoughts about you. You would not ask others about their thoughts or inform them of yours, because you would have no reason to. You would not look where others look, attend to their words, or in any way try to fathom their perceptions and beliefs. People would serve the same function to you as inanimate objects or machines. You might try to get a bigger person's attention to help you get a cookie from the top shelf in the kitchen, but that person's attention would have no value to you in and of itself.

If you had these characteristics, you would almost certainly be diagnosed as having *autism,* a congenital (present at birth) disorder that in some cases is genetic in origin and in others may stem from prenatal damage to the brain (Rodier, 2000). The major diagnostic features of autism are severe deficits in social interaction, severe deficits in acquiring language, a tendency toward repetitive actions, and a narrow focus of interest (American Psychiatric Association, 2000). Among the earliest signs of autism in infants are failure to engage in prolonged eye contact, failure to synchronize emotional expressions with those of another person, and failure to follow another person's gaze (Baron-Cohen, 1995; Mundy & others, 1990). The deficit in language seems to be secondary to the lack of interest in communication. Unlike children who fail to learn language because of deafness, autistic children rarely use gestures as an alternative form of communication, and when they do, it is almost always for instrumental purposes (for example, to get someone to help them reach a cookie). Those who learn language at all learn it late, almost invariably with the help of deliberate teaching, and their language always contains peculiarities that seem to reflect a lack of sensitivity to other people's minds and perspectives.

➤ **27** How does research on people with autism support the premise that the understanding of minds and the understanding of physical objects are fundamentally different abilities?

As you might expect, people with autism perform poorly on false-belief tests and on tests of ability to either deceive or detect deception (Tager-Flusberg, 2007; Yirmiya & others, 1996). In one experiment (Leslie & Thaiss, 1992), relatively high-functioning autistic children and adolescents, whose ages averaged 12 years and whose verbal abilities were equivalent to those of normal 6-year-olds, were compared with normal 4-year-olds on two false-belief tests and two "false-picture" tests. The false-belief tests were versions of the changed-location and container tests described previously, and the false-picture tests were constructed to be analogous to those but to assess the understanding that a photograph, rather than a belief, might misrepresent reality. In one false-picture test, for example, the child saw a photograph being taken of an object at one location. Then the object was moved to a new location, and the child was asked where the object would be in the photograph when it was developed. The results of the experiment are shown in Figure 11.7. As you can see, the autistic individuals performed much worse than the normal 4-year-olds on the false-belief tests but much better than they did on the false-picture tests. This experiment not only demonstrates the specificity of the intellectual impairment in autism but also suggests that the human capacity to understand mental representations (beliefs) is distinct from the capacity to understand physical representations (pictures).

28

How does research on autism support the idea that an understanding of false beliefs may derive, in part, from prior engagement in pretend play?

◄ In line with Leslie's theory that make-believe play is a developmental precursor to understanding false beliefs and other nonliteral mental representations, autistic children have consistently been found to lack such play (Mastrangelo, 2009; Wulff, 1985). Autistic children explore the real physical properties of objects, as do normal children, but they do not make one object stand for another or pretend that an object has properties different from those it actually has. In contrast, children with developmental disorders such as Down syndrome, including those who have less understanding of the physical world than autistic children, do engage in pretend play (Hill & McCune-Nicolich, 1981) and eventually develop a much better understanding of false beliefs and deception than do autistic children (Baron-Cohen & others, 1985; Yirmiya & others, 1996).

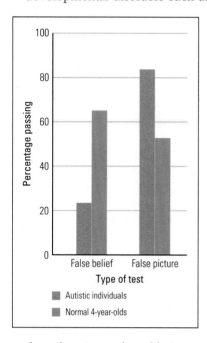

FIGURE 11.7 Performance of autistic individuals and normal 4-year-olds on false-belief and false-picture tests As shown here, autistic individuals were much more likely to understand that a picture could misrepresent current reality than to understand that a person's belief could misrepresent current reality. In contrast, normal 4-year-olds performed better on the false-belief tests than on the false-picture tests. (Data from Leslie & Thaiss, 1992).

A few people, with milder forms of autism or a related disorder called *Asperger's syndrome,* can perform well in school and employment, but even they have difficulty understanding false beliefs and other nonliteral mental states. In describing one such person, who had earned a Ph.D. and developed a successful career in agricultural science, Oliver Sacks (1995) wrote: "In her ingenuousness and gullibility, Temple [Grandin] was at first a target for all sorts of tricks and exploitations; this sort of innocence or guilelessness arising not from moral virtue but from failure to understand dissembling and pretense." In her autobiography, Grandin (2006) describes herself as a literal thinker, concerned with facts more than theories and unable to appreciate most poetry and fiction. She explains that she can get along reasonably well in society not because she has any intuitive understanding of people's hidden thoughts and intentions but because she has carefully studied the surface forms of people's behavior, can mimic those forms, and can use them with moderate success to predict people's actions. She describes herself in this endeavor as "an anthropologist on Mars."

SECTION REVIEW

Children begin quite early to understand not only physical reality but also the mind.

Using Mental Constructs

➤ Young children seem to automatically ascribe psychological characteristics to objects that move on their own.

➤ Well before the age of 3, children use such mental constructs as perception, emotion, and desire to explain people's behavior.

➤ The understanding that beliefs can be false—that is, not congruent with reality—takes longer to develop, appearing at about age 4.

Make-Believe

➤ Children everywhere engage in make-believe play; even toddlers distinguish between reality and pretense.

➤ Make-believe play, especially role-play, may provide a foundation for the later understanding of false beliefs.

➤ Make-believe may also help children to develop the ability to reason on the basis of hypothetical or counterfactual premises.

Autism

➤ People with autism lack motivation and skills for making connections with other people.

➤ Autistic children typically do not engage spontaneously in make-believe play, do not develop false-belief understanding, and think literally rather than hypothetically.

The Nature of Language and Children's Early Linguistic Abilities

Of all the things that people can do, none seems more complex than understanding and speaking a language. Thousands of words and countless subtle grammatical rules for modifying and combining words must be learned. Yet nearly all people master their native language during childhood; in fact, most are quite competent with language by the time they are 3 or 4 years old. How can children too young to tie their shoes or to understand that 2 plus 2 equals 4 succeed at such a complex task? Most developmentalists agree that language learning requires innate mechanisms that predispose children to it, coupled with an environment that provides adequate models and opportunity to practice. In this section, we will first consider briefly the question of what language is and then chart the normal course of its development. Then, in the next section, we will explore the innate and environmental requirements for language development.

Some Universal Characteristics of Human Language

Just what is it that children learn when they learn a language? Linguists estimate that at least 3,000 separate languages exist in the world today, all distinct enough that the speakers of one cannot understand those of another (Grimes, 2000). Yet these languages are all so fundamentally similar to one another that we can speak of *human language* in the singular (Pinker & Bloom, 1992).

All Languages Use Symbols (Morphemes) That Are Arbitrary and Discrete

Every language has a vocabulary consisting of a set of symbols, entities that represent other entities. The symbols in a language are called **morphemes,** defined as the smallest meaningful units of a language—that is, the smallest units that stand for objects, events, ideas, characteristics, or relationships. In all languages except the sign languages used by the deaf, morphemes take the form of pronounceable sounds. Most morphemes are words, but others are prefixes or suffixes used in consistent ways to modify words. Thus, in English, *dog* is both a word and a morpheme, *-s* is a morpheme but not a word, and *dogs* is a word consisting of two morphemes (*dog* and

> **29**
> What are the universal characteristics of morphemes? How do morphemes differ from nonverbal signals?

-s). The word *antidisestablishmentarianism* contains six morphemes (*anti-dis-establish-ment-arian-ism*), each of which has a separate entry in an English dictionary.

In any language, we can distinguish two general classes of morphemes. One class, **content morphemes,** includes nouns, verbs, adjectives, and adverbs—the morphemes that carry the main meaning of a sentence. The other class, **grammatical morphemes,** includes (in English) articles (*a, an, the*), conjunctions (such as *and, but*), prepositions (such as *in, of*), and some prefixes and suffixes (such as *re-, -ed*). These serve primarily to fill out the grammatical structure of the sentence, although they also contribute to meaning.

Morphemes in any language are both arbitrary and discrete. A morpheme is *arbitrary* in that no similarity need exist between its physical structure and that of

AP Photo/Ng Han Guan

The flexibility of language Any human language—unlike nonverbal forms of communication—can be used to express an infinite number of different ideas and observations. Moreover, any idea or observation that can be expressed in one language can be translated into any other language, although in some cases new words may have to be invented and defined to facilitate the translation.

the object or concept for which it stands. Nothing about the English morpheme *dog,* or the French morpheme *chien,* naturally links it to the four-legged, barking creature it represents. Because morphemes are arbitrary, new ones can be invented whenever needed to stand for newly discovered objects or ideas or to express newly important shades of meaning. This characteristic gives language great flexibility. A morpheme is *discrete* in that it cannot be changed in a graded way to express gradations in meaning. For example, you cannot say that one thing is bigger than another by changing the morpheme *big.* Rather, you must add a new morpheme to it (such as *-er*) or replace it with a different morpheme (such as *huge*).

In contrast, nonverbal signals, used by other animals as well as by humans (discussed in **Chapter 3**), are neither arbitrary nor discrete. Nonverbal signals typically develop from and bear physical resemblance to such actions as fighting or fleeing, and the signals communicate intentions to engage in the actions that they resemble. Moreover, nonverbal signals can be presented in a graded manner. One expresses more surprise, anger, or whatever nonverbally by presenting the signal more vigorously or with greater amplitude. In everyday speech, you might communicate that one thing is bigger than another by saying, "This one is big but that one is *big,*" but the vocal emphasis placed on the second big is a nonverbal addition. In speech, we commonly mix nonverbal with verbal communication to get a point across (which is one reason why speaking is easier than writing).

All Languages Are Hierarchically Structured in a Similar Way

30

How can any sentence, in any language, be described as a four-level hierarchy? How can rules of grammar be described in relation to that hierarchy?

In addition to commonalities in their symbol systems, all languages share a particular hierarchical structure of units (see Figure 11.8). The top level (largest unit) is the sentence, which can be broken down into phrases, which can be broken down into words or morphemes, which can be broken down into elementary vowel and consonant sounds called **phonemes.** The power of this four-level organization is that the relatively few phonemes (anywhere from 15 to 80 occur in any given language) can be arranged in different ways to produce an enormous number of possible words, which themselves can be arranged in different ways to produce a limitless number of possible phrases and sentences.

Every language has rules—collectively referred to as the **grammar** of the language—that specify permissible ways to arrange units at one level to produce the next higher level in the hierarchy. Grammar includes rules of *phonology,* which specify how phonemes can be arranged to produce morphemes; rules of *morphology,* which specify how morphemes can be combined to form words; and rules of **syntax,** which specify how words can be arranged to produce phrases and sentences. These rules differ from language to language, but every language has them, and similarities exist across languages in the fundamental nature of the rules (Pinker & Bloom, 1992; Pinker & Jackendoff, 2005).

FIGURE 11.8 The hierarchical structure of language These four levels of organization characterize every spoken language.

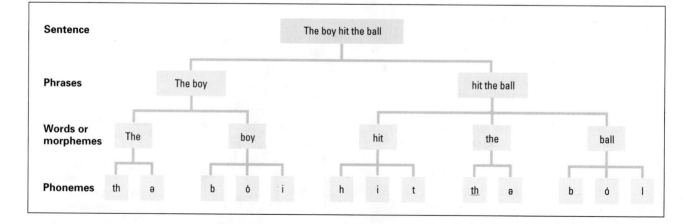

Grammatical Rules Are Usually Learned Implicitly, Not Explicitly

People often think of grammar as something they learned (or tried to learn) in elementary school (which used to be called *grammar* school, perhaps for that very reason). But grammar is learned implicitly, without conscious effort, long before formal schooling. The fact that 4-year-olds can carry on meaningful conversations with adults, producing and understanding new and unique sentences, indicates that by age 4 children have already acquired much of the essential grammar of their native language. Four-year-olds can't name or describe the rules of grammar (nor can most adults), yet they use them every day. Indeed, even professional linguists have yet to describe the full grammar of any of the world's languages (Jackendoff, 2003). Grammatical rules in this sense are like the rules that underlie the sequence and timing of specific muscle movements in walking or running; both sets of rules are generally encoded in implicit rather than explicit memory. We generally can't state them, but we use them when we walk, run, or carry on a conversation.

31
What does it mean to say that knowledge of grammar is usually implicit rather than explicit?

People's implicit knowledge of grammar is demonstrated in their ability to distinguish acceptable from unacceptable sentences. Nearly every English speaker can identify *The mouse crawled under the barn* as a grammatical sentence and *The crawled barn mouse the under* as nongrammatical, although few can explain exactly why. The ability to distinguish grammatical from nongrammatical sentences is not based simply on meaning. As the linguist Noam Chomsky (1957) pointed out, English speakers recognize *Colorless green ideas sleep furiously* as grammatically correct but absurd.

The Course of Language Development

Early Perception of Speech Sounds

Infants seem to treat speech as something special as soon as they are born and maybe even before. In experiments in which newborns, just 1 to 4 days old, could produce sounds by sucking on a nipple, the babies sucked more vigorously to produce the sound of a human voice than to produce any other sounds that were tested (Butterfield & Siperstein, 1974; Vouloumanos & Werker, 2007). In other experiments, babies as young as 2 hours old who had not heard their mother speak since their birth chose their own mother's voice over that of another woman (DeCasper & Fifer, 1980; Querleu & others, 1984). The mother's voice is audible in the womb, and during the last few weeks before birth her voice has a quieting effect on the fetus, as indexed by reduced muscle movements (Hepper & others, 1993).

32
What is the evidence that humans pay special attention to speech from birth on, perhaps even from before birth?

The ability of very young infants to hear the differences among speech phonemes has been demonstrated in many experiments. One technique is to allow an infant to suck on a pacifier that is wired to trigger the playing of a particular sound each time a sucking response occurs. When the baby becomes bored with a sound, as indicated by a reduced rate of sucking, the sound is changed (maybe from *pa* to *ba*). Typically, the rate of sucking increases immediately thereafter, which indicates that the infant hears the new sound as different from the previous one. Another method, which can be used with infants 5 months old and older, involves rewarding the baby with an interesting sight for turning his or her head when the sound changes. This method is illustrated and described further in Figure 11.9 (on page 422).

33
How have researchers shown that very young infants can distinguish between subtly different speech sounds? How do infants' abilities to distinguish among such speech sounds change during the second half-year of their lives? What is the value of these changes?

The results of such experiments suggest that babies younger than 6 months old hear the difference between any two sounds that are classed as different phonemes in any of the world's languages. At about 6 months of age, however, two kinds of changes begin to occur in their ability to discriminate between similar speech sounds: They become *better* at discriminating between sounds that represent different phonemes in their native language, and they become *worse* at discriminating

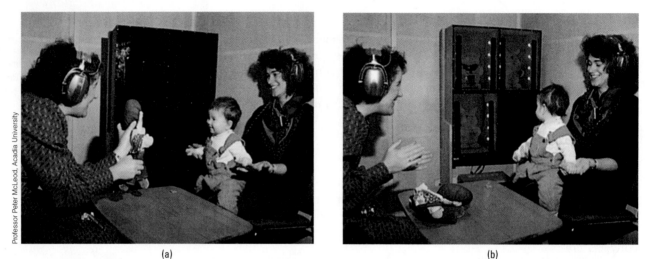

(a)   (b)

FIGURE 11.9 Test of an infant's ability to detect changes in a speech sound The baby attends to a toy held by the researcher while a speech sound is played repetitively through a loudspeaker. Occasionally the speech sound changes (perhaps from *pa* to *ba*), and shortly after each such change an attractive toy to the baby's right is lit up and begins to move. The baby soon learns to look to the right each time the sound changes, and this response serves as an index that the baby distinguishes the new sound from the old one. The mother and researcher wear headphones that prevent them from hearing the critical sound and inadvertently cuing the infant to turn. (From Werker & Tees, 1992.)

between sounds that are classed as the same phoneme in their native language (Kuhl & others, 2008). For example, infants growing up in English-speaking cultures gradually become better than they were before at distinguishing between the English /l/ and /r/, which are distinct phonemes in English but not in Japanese, and they gradually *lose* the ability to distinguish among the subtly different /t/ sounds that constitute different phonemes in Hindi but not in English (Kuhl & others, 2008; Werker & Tees, 1999). In contrast, Japanese infants gradually lose the ability to distinguish among /l/ and /r/, and Indian infants in Hindi-speaking homes become better at distinguishing among the /t/ sounds relevant to their language.

These changes—which are believed to occur at the neural level in auditory portions of the brain—are apparently helpful in acquiring language. Children who, by 7.5 months of age, show the greatest increase in ability to hear sound differences that are relevant to their language and the greatest decline in ability to hear sound differences that are not relevant to their language subsequently, over the next two years, learn words more rapidly than do other children (Kuhl & others, 2005, 2008).

Cooing and Babbling

34 - - - - - - - - - - - - - - - - - - ◀

What is the distinction between cooing and babbling? What are the reasons for thinking that these vocalizations are precursors to language production?

Beginning at birth, infants can cry and produce various other vocal signs of distress, but at about 2 months they begin to produce a new, more speechlike category of sounds called *cooing,* which consists of repeated drawn-out vowels (*oooh-oooh, eeeh-eeeh*). At about 6 months, cooing changes gradually to *babbling,* which consists of repeated consonant-and-vowel sounds such as *paa-paa-paa* or *tooda-tooda* (Masataka, 2003). Cooing and babbling occur most often when the infant is happy. They seem to be forms of vocal play that have evolved to help the infant exercise and refine the complex muscle movements needed to produce coherent speech.

Coos and the earliest babbles do not depend on the infant's hearing spoken sounds. Deaf infants coo and begin to babble at about the same age and in the same manner as hearing infants (Lenneberg, 1969), and early babbles are as likely to contain foreign-language sounds as native-language sounds (Locke, 1983). By 8 months of age, however, hearing infants begin to babble in ways that mimic the rhythm and pitch patterns of the language they hear around them; the babbling of a French baby becomes recognizably French, and that of a British baby becomes recognizably British (de Boysson-Bardies, 1999). Beginning at about 10 months of age, hearing infants produce babbled sounds that increasingly resemble syllables and words of their native language (de Boysson-Bardies, 1999; Locke, 1983). Also at this age,

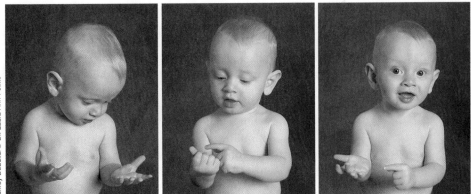

Manual babbling Deaf or hearing infants whose deaf parents communicate by sign language go through a stage of babbling with their hands. Their babbling gestures resemble the signs of the language but do not yet express meaning.

deaf infants who are exposed to a sign language begin to babble with their hands—repeating over and over hand movements that are similar in form and rhythm to those of the language they see around them (Petitto & others, 2001). Eventually, recognizable words appear in the hearing infant's vocal babbling and the deaf infant's manual babbling.

Word Comprehension Precedes Word Production

During the babbling phase of life, before the first production of recognizable words, infants begin to show evidence that they understand some words and phrases that they hear regularly. In one experiment, 6-month-olds were shown side-by-side videos of their parents. When they heard the word "Mommy" or "Daddy," they looked reliably more at the video of the named parent than at the unnamed parent (Tincoff & Juscyk, 1999). Other experiments have revealed that 9-month-olds can respond to a number of common words by looking at the appropriate object when it is named (Balaban & Waxman, 1997) and can follow simple verbal commands, such as "Get the ball" (Benedict, 1979). By the time that they say their first word, at about 11 months of age, infants may already know the meaning of dozens of words (Swingley, 2008).

> **35**
> **What is the evidence that babies begin to understand words well before they begin to speak?**

Naming and Rapid Vocabulary Development

Babies' first words, typically at about 10 to 12 months of age, are most often produced in a playful spirit. The child at first uses words to point things out, or simply to name them for fun, not generally to ask for them (Bloom & Lahey, 1978). For instance, my son used the word *ba* joyfully to name his bottle, after he received it, weeks before he began using it to ask for his bottle when he wanted it.

New words come slowly at first, but then, typically at about 15 to 20 months of age, the rate begins to accelerate. Between the ages of 2 and 17 years, the typical person learns about 60,000 words, an average of about 11 new words per day (Bloom, 2001). Relatively few of these are explicitly taught; most often, the child must infer the meaning of a new word from the context in which others use it. How do young children, early in the language-learning process, draw these inferences?

Most of the earliest words learned, in any language culture, are nouns that refer to categories of objects in the child's environment (Golinkoff & others, 1994). Young children's tendency to look at whatever an older person is looking at (discussed earlier) no doubt helps them identify objects that the older person is referring to when speaking. Infants are especially likely to follow an adult's gaze when the adult is labeling an object in the environment (Baldwin, 2000). Researchers have found that those infants who show the most reliable gaze following, when tested at 10 and 11 months of age, show the greatest gains in vocabulary over the next several months (Brooks & Meltzoff, 2008).

> **36**
> **How do young children make the link between new words that they hear and appropriate referents in their environments?**

First words Naming objects is an important step in the mastery of language. It is also a source of great delight to infants and their caregivers. Here 1-year-old Genevieve uses her favorite word, *light*.

In addition, young children seem to have a number of cognitive biases, or built-in assumptions, that help them narrow down the likely referent to a new word they hear (Golinkoff & others, 1994; Regier, 2003). One of these is a strong tendency to link new words with objects for which they do not already know a name. Other things being equal, young children assume that a new word is not a synonym for a word they already know but a label for something whose name they don't know. In one experiment, 3- and 4-year-olds were presented with toy animals that they could name (a pig, a sheep, and a cow) plus one that they could not name (a tapir). When they heard the novel word *gombe* in the presence of these objects, all the children applied it to the novel animal (Clark, 1987). Other research indicates that toddlers begin to manifest this bias at about the same time—in their second year of life—at which their rate of vocabulary learning begins to increase rapidly (Mervis & Bertrand, 1994). Although the bias leads to some mistakes, it is apparently more helpful than harmful to their acquisition of words.

By the time they can understand multiword sentences, young children are able to use their tacit knowledge of grammar to help them infer the meaning of new words, including verbs and other parts of speech as well as nouns (Bernal & others, 2007; Fisher, 2000). Thus if they are shown a videotaped scene and told, "The duck and bunny are biffing," 2-year-olds—who understand *duck* and *bunny* and know implicitly that words ending in *-ing* refer to actions—infer that *biffing* means whatever the duck and bunny are both doing (Naigles, 1990). If told, instead, "The duck is biffing the bunny," they infer that *biffing* means whatever the duck is doing to the bunny. As another example, 2-year-olds who heard "Mommy feeds the ferret" inferred that a ferret is an animal, not an inanimate object (Goodman & others, 1998).

Extending Words to Fit Appropriate Categories

37

How do infants "decide" whether a new name that they hear is a proper noun or a common noun?

In addition to linking a new word to its immediate referent, children must learn how to extend it to new referents. Common nouns such as *ball* refer to categories of objects, and a full understanding is demonstrated when a child applies the word to all members of the category and not to non-members. Researchers have found that young children, including even infants as young as 12 months, behave as though they assume that a newly heard label applies not just to the specific object that has been labeled but also to other objects that are perceptually like the original one (Golinkoff & others, 1995; Waxman & Markow, 1995). That is, infants are biased toward assuming that labels are common nouns, not proper nouns. The bias leads to some mistakes, as when a child refers to all men as *Daddy,* but is useful overall because the vast majority of nouns to be learned are common nouns.

By the time they are 2 years old, children can use the grammatical context of a sentence to discern whether a name for an object is a proper noun or a common noun. In one experiment, 24-month-old children were shown a stuffed animal and were told either "This is *a* ZAV" or "This is ZAV." Those in the first group subsequently applied the label to other stuffed animals that looked like the original one, and those in the second group did not (Hall & others, 2001).

38

What are two reasons why children might overextend common nouns that they have learned?

Children sometimes overextend common nouns, using them more broadly than adult usage would allow. On the basis of an analysis of a large collection of examples, Eve Clark (1973) proposed that overextension results when a child implicitly defines a new word in terms of just one or a few of the prominent features of the original referent object. Thus a child who hears *ball* in association with a specific ball might take the object's most prominent feature—its roundness—as the defining characteristic and subsequently refer to all round objects, including oranges and full moons, as balls. In other cases, overextensions may not represent errors at all but simply derive from children's attempts to communicate about objects that they have not yet learned to name (Clark, 1995). A toddler who says, "Look doggie," while pointing to a cat, may in essence be saying, "Look at that thing that is something like a doggie."

Ohh, Kermit When young children overextend common nouns and proper nouns to apply to objects beyond the appropriate category, they may not always be making mistakes. A child who sees an alpine marmot for the first time and says, "Ohh, Kermit," may really be saying, "Ohh, there is an animal that looks like Kermit the Frog from *Sesame Street*." The drive to speak and communicate is so strong that, lacking the appropriate word, children will come up with the closest approximation they know.

The same child, when asked which animals in a set of pictures are dogs, may pick the actual dogs and not the cats (Thomson & Chapman, 1977).

Children also sometimes *underextend* words, applying them to more narrowly defined categories than do adults. In fact, some research suggests that underextension is more common than overextension (MacWhinney, 1998). But underextensions do not result in errors in children's spontaneous speech, so they are difficult to detect and have been little studied.

The remarkable fact, however, is not that children make errors in their extensions but that they usually extend new words appropriately (Bloom, 2001). Somehow they figure out quickly the categories that are referred to by the words they hear adults and older children using.

Using Grammatical Rules

All children go through a relatively prolonged period during which each of their utterances is only one word long. When they do begin to put words together, typically at about 18 to 24 months of age, they at first use content words almost exclusively, especially nouns and verbs, and usually arrange them in the grammatically correct sequence for simple, active sentences (Brown, 1973). For an English-speaking child, this means that subjects are placed before verbs, and verbs before objects. A child at the two-word stage will say "Billy kick" to mean that Billy is kicking something, and "Kick Billy" to mean that someone is kicking Billy.

When children acquire a new grammatical rule, such as adding *-ed* to the end of a verb to create the past tense, they almost invariably overgeneralize it at first (Kuczaj, 1977; Marcus & others, 1992). The 3-year-old who says "kicked," "played," and "laughed" also says "goed," "thinked," and "swimmed." Similarly, children who have just learned to add *-s* to pluralize nouns will talk about many *mouses, sheeps,* and *childs.* This overgeneralization confirms that children really know the rule. If they followed the rule only when adults did, their usage might be attributed to simple imitation. As further evidence suggesting that their grammar is based on rules, young children have been shown to use the rules with made-up words that they had never heard before, as illustrated in Figure 11.10.

Children are not taught the rules of grammar explicitly; nobody sits a 2-year-old down and tries to explain how to create infinitives, possessives, or past-tense verbs. Some parents correct their children's grammar, but even this is rare (Brown & Hanlon, 1970), and long-term experiments in preschools have shown that deliberate programs of correcting grammar have little

─────────────39

How do children demonstrate knowledge of grammatical rules in their early speech? How do some of their "mistakes" in grammar confirm that they know the rule and are not just mimicking?

This is a wug.

FIGURE 11.10 One wug and two _____ ? With this test, Jean Berko found that children who had just begun to use the rule of forming plurals by adding *-s* would use the rule correctly even for words they had never heard before. (From Berko, 1958.)

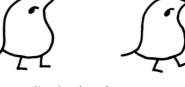

Now there is another one.
There are two of them.
There are two _____.

effect on rule acquisition (de Villiers & de Villiers, 1979). Through their own devices, children actively (and mostly unconsciously) infer grammatical rules from examples of rule-based language spoken around them and to them.

SECTION REVIEW

Children rapidly acquire the complex tools of language, beginning in infancy.

Linguistic Universals

➤ All languages include a set of symbols called morphemes, which are a language's smallest meaningful units; morphemes are arbitrary and discrete.

➤ All languages are hierarchically structured, with sentences at the top of the hierarchy and phonemes (elementary vowel and consonant sounds) at the bottom.

➤ Every language has a grammar—a set of rules that specify the permissible ways to combine units at one level of the hierarchy to create a unit at the next higher level.

➤ A person's knowledge of the grammar of his or her language is generally more implicit than explicit.

The Course of Language Development

➤ Babies under 6 months can apparently distinguish any two phonemes of any language. After that, they become even better at hearing sound differences that represent different phonemes in their native language but worse at distinguishing between sounds that represent the same phoneme in their native language.

➤ Infants coo and later babble as a form of vocal play that helps to prepare the vocal apparatus for speech. By 8 months, their babbling starts to mimic their native language.

➤ The first recognizable words appear at about 10 to 12 months; vocabulary growth accelerates soon after and continues for years, aided by innate biases and knowledge of grammar, though children sometimes over- or under-extend words.

➤ Children first combine words at about 18 to 24 months, demonstrating knowledge of word-order rules. Knowledge of other grammatical rules is demonstrated in overgeneralizations of them (such as saying *deers* or *goed*).

■ Internal and External Supports for Language Development

How is it that children can learn language so early, with so little apparent conscious effort and without deliberate training? There is no doubt that humans enter the world equipped in many ways for language. We are born with (a) anatomical structures in the throat (the larynx and pharynx) that enable us to produce a broader range of sounds than any other mammal can produce (Lieberman, 2007); (b) brain areas specialized for language (including Broca's and Wernicke's areas, discussed in **Chapter 5**); (c) a preference for listening to speech and an ability to distinguish among the basic speech sounds of any language; and (d) mechanisms that cause us to exercise our vocal capacities through a period of cooing and babbling. There is also no doubt that most of us are born into a social world that provides rich opportunities for learning language. We are surrounded by language from birth on, and when we begin to use it, we achieve many rewards through this extraordinarily effective form of communication.

The Idea of Special Inborn Mechanisms for Language Learning

Chomsky's Concept of an Innate Language-Learning Device

40

How did Noam Chomsky link the study of grammar to psychology? What did he mean by a language-acquisition device?

The linguist Noam Chomsky, more than anyone else, was responsible for drawing psychologists' attention to the topic of language. In his highly influential book *Syntactic Structures* (1957), Chomsky characterized grammatical rules as fundamental properties of the human mind. In contrast to an earlier view, held by some psychologists, that sentences are generated in chainlike fashion, with one word triggering the next in a sequence, Chomsky emphasized the hierarchical structure of sentences. He argued convincingly that a person must have some meaningful representation of the whole sentence in mind before uttering it and then must apply grammatical rules to that representation in order to fill out the lower levels of the hierarchy (phrases, morphemes, and phonemes) to produce the utterance.

Chomsky (1957, 1965, 1968) conceived of grammatical rules as aspects of the human mind that link spoken sentences ultimately (through one or more intermediary stages) to the mind's system for representing meanings. Although specific grammatical rules vary from one language to another, they are all, according to Chomsky, based on certain fundamental principles, referred to as *universal grammar,* that are innate properties of the human mind. These properties account for the universal characteristics of language (discussed earlier) and for other, more subtle language universals (Pinker, 1994). To refer to the entire set of innate mental mechanisms that enable a child to acquire language quickly and efficiently, Chomsky coined the term **language-acquisition device,** or **LAD.** The LAD includes the inborn foundations for universal grammar plus the entire set of inborn mechanisms that guide children's learning of the unique rules of their culture's language. Support for the concept of an innate LAD comes partly from observations of language-learning deficits in people who have suffered damage to particular brain areas (discussed in **Chapter 5**) or who have a particular genetic disorder (specific language impairment, discussed in **Chapter 3**).

Noam Chomsky In his book *Syntactic Structures*, Chomsky called attention to the idea that producing a verbal statement is a creative act guided by implicit mental rules. This work and the revolution in psycholinguistics that it inspired have enriched research and theory in cognitive psychology.

Children's Invention of Grammar

Further support for the LAD concept comes from evidence that young children invent grammar when it is lacking in the speech around them. Here are two examples of such evidence.

Children's Role in Development of Creole Languages New languages occasionally arise when people from many different language cultures simultaneously colonize an area and begin to communicate with one another. These first-generation colonists communicate through a primitive, grammarless collection of words taken from their various native languages—a communication system referred to as a *pidgin language.* Subsequently, the pidgin develops into a true language, with a full range of grammatical rules, at which point it is called a **creole language.** Derek Bickerton (1984) studied creole languages from around the world and found that at least some of them were developed into full languages within one generation by the children of the original colonists. Apparently, the children imposed grammatical rules on the pidgin they heard and used those rules consistently in their own speech—powerful evidence, in Bickerton's view, that children's minds are innately predisposed to grammar.

Deaf Children's Invention of a Grammatical Sign Language Bickerton's evidence of children's role in creating new languages was necessarily indirect, as he was studying languages that emerged many years ago. More recently, Ann Senghas and her colleagues have documented directly the emergence of a new sign language among deaf children in Nicaragua (Senghas & Coppola, 2001; Senghas & others, 2004). Prior to 1977, deaf Nicaraguans had little opportunity to meet other deaf people. There was no deaf community or common sign language, and the deaf were typically treated as though they were retarded. In 1977 the first Nicaraguan school for the deaf was founded, so deaf children for the first time came into extended contact with one another. On the basis of outmoded ideas, the school did not at first teach any sign language but, instead, attempted to teach the deaf to speak and lip-read the nation's vocal language (Spanish), an approach that rarely succeeds. Despite the official policy, the students began to communicate with one another using hand signs.

At first their signing system was a manual pidgin, an unstructured and variable amalgam of the signs and gestures that the individuals had been using at home. But over the course of a few

41

How have studies of creole languages and studies of deaf children in Nicaragua supported the idea that children invent grammar in the absence of a preexisting grammatical language?

Creating a language When deaf children in Nicaragua were brought together for the first time, in a school community, they gradually created a new sign language. The youngest children contributed most to the grammatical structure of the language.

years the signs became increasingly regularized and efficient, and a system of grammar emerged. All this occurred naturally, with no formal teaching, simply through the students' desires to communicate with one another. Of most significance for our discussion, the new grammar was produced not by the oldest, wisest members of the community but by the youngest. In fact, those who were more than about 10 years old when the deaf community was formed not only failed to contribute to the development of a grammar but learned little of the one that did develop. The sign language invented by the children has since become the official sign language of Nicaragua. It is a true language, comparable to American Sign Language, in which the morphemes are elementary hand movements and grammatical rules stipulate how the morphemes can be combined and sequenced into larger units.

Children's improvement of grammar may be viewed by us as a creative act, but it is almost certainly not experienced as that by the children themselves. Children tacitly assume that language has grammar, so they unconsciously read grammar into language even where it doesn't exist. Just as children learning English overgeneralize grammatical rules when they say things like *goed* and *mouses,* and thereby temporarily make English grammar more consistent and elegant than it really is, children exposed to a pidgin language or to an early version of the Nicaraguan sign language may accept the slightest random hint of a grammatical rule as a true rule and begin to use it as such. In the case of a newly emerging language—unlike the case of a long-established language such as English—the children's rules are incorporated into the language and are learned by the next generation.

Critical Period for Learning the Grammar of One's First Language

42

What evidence supports the view that grammar is learned more readily in early childhood than later in life?

The LAD apparently functions much more effectively during the first 10 years of childhood than later in life. Children who are deprived of the opportunity to hear and interact with a language during their first 10 years have great difficulty learning language later on, and never master the grammar of the language they learn. That is one of the lessons learned from observations of deaf children who were not exposed to a true language until adolescence or late in childhood (Mayberry & others, 2002; Senghas & others, 2004). Much more rarely, a hearing person is discovered who was deprived of language throughout childhood, and in every such case that has been documented, the person was subsequently unable to learn language fully (Curtiss, 1989).

The most thoroughly studied language-deprived hearing person is a woman known as Genie. She was rescued in 1970, at age 13, from the inhuman conditions in which her deranged, domineering father and partly blind and submissive mother had raised her (Curtiss, 1977; Rymer, 1993). From shortly after birth until her rescue, Genie had been locked in a tiny bedroom and exposed to almost no speech. At the time of her rescue she understood a few words but could not string words together and had learned no grammar. She was then placed in a foster home where she was exposed to English much as infants normally are and received tutorial help. In this environment, she eventually acquired a large vocabulary and learned to produce meaningful, intelligent statements; but even after 7 years of language practice, at age 20, her grammar lagged far behind other indices of her intelligence (Curtiss, 1977). A typical sentence she produced was "I hear music ice cream truck," and she often misunderstood sentences whose meaning depended on grammar. Over subsequent years of adulthood, her grammar showed little improvement (Rymer, 1993).

Learning within the critical period is much less important for second-language learning than for first-language learning. People who learned their first language within the critical period can learn a second language reasonably well at any time in life, although not quite as well as they could have if they had learned it earlier. Those who learn a second language after the age of about 10 or 11 almost always speak with an accent and generally do not acquire the grammar of the language as fully or easily as do those who learn the language at a younger age (Au & others, 2002; Johnson & Newport, 1989).

The Language-Acquisition Support System

Children come into the world predisposed to acquire language, but they do not acquire it in a social vacuum. Neither Genie nor any other child has ever invented language alone. Normal language development requires not just the LAD but also the **LASS**—the *language-acquisition support system*—provided by the social world into which the baby is born (Bruner, 1983).

43

How do parents in our culture modify
their speech to infants?

In our culture and most others, adults regularly simplify their speech to infants and young children in ways that might help the children learn words and some aspects of grammar. They enunciate more clearly than when speaking to adults, use a more musical tone of voice with greater pitch variation, use short sentences that focus on the here and now, repeat and emphasize salient words, and use gestures to help convey meaning (Snow, 1984; Soderstrom, 2007). A 6-month-old playing with a ball might be told, "Oh, you have a *ball*. A nice *ball*. What a pretty *ball*." Such speech is often referred to as *motherese* (although it is not just mothers who speak this way to babies). Researchers have found that such speech does help infants to distinguish individual words and to make connections between words and their referents (Soderstrom, 2007; Thiessen & others, 2005). Adults also frequently treat infants' early vocalizations as if they were verbal statements. For instance, a mother or father might respond to the baby's *ba-ba-ga-goo-goo* with, "Oh, yes, very interesting!" Such responsiveness can lead to back-and-forth, conversation-like exchanges between infant and adult.

Taking account of the listener Most people automatically simplify their speech when talking to infants and young children. Even young children addressing younger children deliberately slow their rate of speech, choose simple words and grammatical structures, and gesture broadly.

Parents' Speech to Infants Affects Language Acquisition

A number of research studies have shown positive correlations between the degree to which mothers speak to their infants, using appropriately simplified language, and the rate at which the infants develop language (e.g., Furrow & others, 1979; Tamis-LeMonda & others, 2001). A problem with such studies, however, is that the observed correlations might derive more from genetic similarities between mothers and their children than from differences in the language environments that the mothers provide. Genetically verbal mothers may produce genetically verbal children.

44

What evidence suggests that differences
in the language environments provided
by parents can affect the rates at which
infants acquire language?

Better evidence for an effect of mothers' influence on language development comes from a study involving infants who were adopted at birth (Hardy-Brown & others, 1981). In that study, adopted infants' rates of language development correlated more strongly with their biological mothers' verbal abilities than with their adoptive mothers' verbal abilities, but the linguistic environments provided by the adoptive mothers also played a significant role. In particular, infants whose adoptive mothers often responded verbally to their early vocalizations developed language more rapidly than did those whose adoptive mothers were less responsive. Further evidence comes from a series of studies in which parents were trained to engage frequently in back-and-forth verbal play with their infants, from age 3 months to 15 months (Fowler & others, 2006). Those children developed language considerably sooner than did children in otherwise comparable families without such training. Apparently, parents' verbal responsiveness to infants' vocalizations plays a significant role in the rate of language acquisition.

Cross-Cultural Differences in the LASS

Cross-cultural research shows that children all over the world acquire language at roughly similar rates, despite wide variations in the degree and manner of adults' verbal interactions with infants (Ochs & Schieffelin, 1995). For example, the Kalikuli people of the New Guinea rain forest believe that there is no reason to speak to babies who cannot yet speak themselves. These babies hear no motherese, and little speech of any kind is directed toward them. However, unlike infants in our culture,

45

What light has been shed on the LASS
by cross-cultural research?

they go everywhere with their mothers and constantly overhear the speech not only of their mothers but of other adults and children around them. This rich exposure to others' conversations may compensate for the lack of speech directed to them. Apparently, large variations can occur in the LASS without impairing infants' abilities to learn language.

Language Learning by Non-Human Apes

46

What has motivated researchers to study the abilities of non-human animals to learn human languages? Why did the Gardners try to teach their chimp, Washoe, a sign language rather than spoken English?

◄ To what degree does language depend on special, inborn, language-learning mechanisms that are unique to humans, and to what degree does it depend on more general learning abilities that we share with other animals? That question has motivated much research on the abilities of non-human animals to learn human-like languages.

Our closest relatives, chimpanzees and bonobos (discussed in **Chapter 3**), have brains that are structurally quite similar to ours. Although neither species communicates in its natural environment with anything like the symbol-based, grammar-based system we call human language, both species are highly gregarious and have complex systems of nonverbal communication (Pollick & de Waal, 2007). What would happen if you took such a creature out of its natural community and raised it in a human environment, exposing it to language in the same rich way that human children normally are exposed? Even dogs raised in our homes learn to make some use of our language. My golden retriever gets excited whenever she hears *outside* or *leash* in the conversation around her, and some dogs have learned to respond appropriately to as many as 200 different verbal commands (Kaminski & others, 2004). What might a chimpanzee or bonobo learn if it were raised in a world of humans attempting to communicate with it through language?

In an attempt to find out, Allen and Beatrix Gardner (1978, 1989) began in 1966 to raise a young female chimp named Washoe in the constant presence of people who directed language toward her as well as toward one another. Because the Gardners hoped that Washoe would learn to produce as well as understand language, they and Washoe's other caretakers used a modified version of American Sign Language rather than a vocal language. Chimpanzees lack the vocal apparatus needed to produce the sounds of human speech, but they have flexible fingers capable of producing manual signs. Washoe's success in acquiring some of the elements of language inspired many subsequent ape-language projects. Researchers have since studied language learning in a number of other chimpanzees, several bonobos, a gorilla, and an orangutan (Miles, 1983; Patterson & Linden, 1981; Savage-Rumbaugh & Fields, 2000).

Fetch the cuddly This border collie, Rico, has been trained to fetch at least 200 different objects by name. When presented with a new name, which he hasn't heard before, he will pick the one new object, not an object that he has already been taught to fetch (Kaminski & others, 2004). Here he fetches a Pokémon cuddly.

The Accomplishments of Kanzi

47

What LASS was supplied for the bonobo Kanzi? What are Kanzi's linguistic accomplishments?

◄ The most linguistically accomplished ape to date is a bonobo named Kanzi, whose learning has been nurtured and documented for many years by Sue Savage-Rumbaugh and her associates. Before working with Kanzi, Savage-Rumbaugh had been using operant conditioning to teach chimpanzees to communicate through an invented language in which the words are geometric figures, called *lexigrams*, that are arranged on a keyboard (see Figure 11.11 on page 431). In 1981, Savage-Rumbaugh was, with little success, training Kanzi's mother in the lexigram system when she noticed that young Kanzi, who had been allowed to run free in the laboratory, was learning to use some of the lexigrams correctly just by watching, even though he wasn't being rewarded. This inspired Savage-Rumbaugh to try a different method with Kanzi: immersion in a language culture rather than systematic training.

Kanzi was continuously free, but not forced, to communicate, using a stationary keyboard in the lab and a portable one outdoors. Kanzi's caregivers used both spoken English and lexigrams to communicate with him, and they responded to Kanzi's lexigrams and gestures as parents might to the communicative attempts of their children. Their task was not to teach Kanzi language, but to communicate with him as best they could as they and he went about their daily activities, just as they might with a human child. My inference from the reports and films on Kanzi is that he received even more linguistic attention and heard even more motherese than does a typical human child.

Kanzi has learned to use roughly 200 lexigrams appropriately, and his behavior indicates that he does not simply use them to get rewards (Lyn, 2007; Savage-Rumbaugh & others, 1986, 1993). For example, he used the lexigram for *apple* after he already had an apple. He also often announces his intentions before acting. For example, before taking a trip to his tree house, he pressed the lexigram for *tree house*. In addition, he often combines lexigrams with nonverbal gestures in order to get across more complex ideas than would be possible with the limited set of lexigrams on his board. For example, to get caretaker A to chase caretaker B, he pressed the lexigram for *chase* and then pushed A's hand in the direction of B.

Even more impressive than Kanzi's use of lexigrams is his understanding of spoken English. His behavior suggests that he knows the meanings of at least 500 English words (Savage-Rumbaugh & Fields, 2000). When Kanzi was 8 years old, he was tested for his ability to carry out spoken requests that he had never heard before, such as "Put the egg in the noodles" and "Hammer the ball." The requests were made by a caretaker who stayed out of view so that nonverbal cues could not guide Kanzi's behavior. Kanzi carried out most of the requests successfully, performing at a rate comparable to that of a 2.5-year-old human girl who was given the same requests (Savage-Rumbaugh & others, 1993). Kanzi also responded appropriately to requests whose meaning depended on word order, such as "Make the doggie bite the snake" and "Make the snake bite the doggie" (using a toy dog and toy snake as props).

Kanzi is not unique in the ape world. Savage-Rumbaugh and her colleagues have more recently raised another bonobo and a chimpanzee in a manner similar to that of Kanzi, and both animals exhibit language abilities that approach those of Kanzi (Greenfield & Lyn, 2007; Savage-Rumbaugh & Fields, 2000).

FIGURE 11.11 Kanzi using the lexigram keyboard Each symbol on the keyboard is a word. When Kanzi, the bonobo, depresses a key, the symbol is illuminated both on the keyboard and on a larger screen that his caretakers can see. Kanzi also had a portable keyboard that he carried with him as he roamed a forested area with his caretakers. This photo was taken when Kanzi was still quite young, early during his language learning.

Courtesy of Sue Savage-Rumbaugh/Yerkes Language Research Center

Tentative Conclusions from the Ape-Language Studies

Has Kanzi or any other ape learned human language? Some scholars argue about that as if it were a meaningful question, but it isn't. The answer depends entirely on how one chooses to define human language. A more sensible question is this: What aspects of human language have non-human apes been able to acquire, and what aspects, at least so far, seem beyond them? Taking all the studies together, apes appear to be relatively adept at acquiring a vocabulary, and systematic tests suggest that they can use signs and lexigrams as true symbols, standing for referents, and not merely as operant responses to obtain rewards (Lyn, 2007; Sevcik & Savage-Rumbaugh, 1994). Moreover, Kanzi can apparently use word order to decipher the meanings of some simple multiword sentences. However, on the basis of the published research, there is little or no evidence that any ape to date has acquired or invented a rule for distinguishing plural from singular nouns, for marking the tense of verbs, or for marking any words by grammatical class. Apparently, the brain mechanism that makes grammar so easy and natural for human children came about in our evolution sometime after we split off from the line leading to chimpanzees and bonobos.

To me, the most interesting general conclusion from the ape-language research has to do with the conditions that optimize learning. Attempts at deliberate, focused training, involving rewards for correct language usage, have generally failed (for

48
What conclusions may be tentatively drawn from the ape-language studies?

example, Terrace, 1985). In those cases the animals learned to produce word-like gestures as ways to get rewards rather than truly as symbols to label their experiences. Success has occurred when the focus was on communication rather than training. It has occurred when the researchers entered the ape's world for long periods and brought the ape into their world, using words and sentences along the way (Shanker & King, 2002). This is similar to the conditions in which most human children learn language. The function of language is communication, and a major prerequisite for acquiring language is a desire to communicate.

SECTION REVIEW

Inborn mechanisms and the social context jointly support children's acquisition of language.

Innate Mechanisms for Language Acquisition	External Support for Language Acquisition	Language Learning by Apes
➤ Chomsky hypothesized the existence of an innate language-acquisition device (LAD), consisting of a universal grammar and mechanisms that guide native-language learning.	➤ The social context provides children with a language-acquisition support system (LASS).	➤ Washoe, a chimpanzee, successfully learned some American Sign Language, inspiring other ape-language studies.
➤ The reality of the LAD is supported by children's imposition of grammatical rules to create creole languages and, in Nicaragua, a sign language.	➤ Caregivers generally assist language acquisition by speaking "motherese" and by being responsive to early linguistic efforts.	➤ Kanzi, a bonobo that has learned to use lexigrams and gestures to express meaning, understands at least 500 English words and can use word order to interpret meaning.
➤ The LAD appears to function most effectively in the first 10 years of life. Children deprived of sufficient exposure to language during that period do not fully learn language later.	➤ Children acquire language at roughly the same rate everywhere, despite wide cross-cultural variation in the LASS.	➤ Successful efforts like those involving Washoe and Kanzi used immersion in an environment rich with linguistic communication, not systematic training by operant conditioning.
		➤ Apes are much better at acquiring vocabulary than grammar.

Concluding Thoughts

Thinking and talking are—to use a term introduced in **Chapter 3**—*species-typical* activities of humans. We are biologically predisposed for thought and language, just as we are predisposed to smile and walk on two legs. The human brain has been specialized for these activities in the course of evolution; people everywhere, in every culture, think and talk in ways that are recognizably human and distinguishable from the activities of any other species. Yet, despite their universality, these abilities must develop anew in each human being.

1. Why thought and language must develop Why aren't these species-typical abilities fully present at birth? An immediate answer is that birth occurs in humans at a relatively early stage in the body's growth. The brain, including the pathways required for thought and language, continues to mature after birth. A more profound answer, however, lies in the ultimate functions of thought and language.

Thought serves to make sense of the environment so that we can navigate safely through it and use parts of it to promote our survival and reproduction. We can survive in a wide range of conditions because we can think of ways to modify them to suit

our needs. To do so, we must consider not just the universals of every environment, such as the fact that unsupported objects fall to the earth, but also the particulars of our specific environment, such as the foods that are available and the tools that are needed. Similarly, to communicate effectively in our particular cultural group, we must acquire the specific linguistic elements (the words and grammar) that have emerged in our group's history and represent concepts that are crucial to survival in that group. That is, to be effective, thought and language must be fine-tuned to the unique physical and social environment in which each individual must survive, and such adjustment can be accomplished only when thought and language develop in that environment.

2. Innate foundations for development Evolution could not endow human beings with the specific knowledge and skills needed to survive in every human environment, but it could and did endow the species with a solid foundation for acquiring them. This theme, of innate foundations for development, can help you tie together many of the ideas and research findings that are described in this chapter. As you review, consider the following questions: What inborn assumptions may help each new person make sense of his or her physical, social, and linguistic worlds? What universal aspects of babies' and children's explorations and play may help them learn about the particulars of their native environments and languages?

The findings and ideas to which you can relate these questions include (a) infants' preferences for novelty, their mode of examining objects, their drive to control their environment, and their knowledge of core physical principles; (b) Piaget's ideas about the roles of action, assimilation, and accommodation in development, and other researchers' theories about domain-specific development; (c) young children's understanding of other people's minds, their delayed understanding of false beliefs, the possible role of make-believe in acquiring that understanding, and the absence of such understanding in autistic children; (d) the roles of early attention to language, of vocal play, and of inborn biases and drives affecting vocabulary and grammar acquisition; and (e) Chomsky's concept of a language-acquisition device and other researchers' studies of children who invented language.

3. Social supports for development The innate tendencies and drives that promote development are useless without a responsive environment. Babies need solid surfaces against which to exercise their muscles in order to learn to walk, objects to explore in order to learn about the physical world, and people to listen to and with whom to exercise their linguistic play in order to learn to talk. Young children may, as Piaget contended, choose what to assimilate from the smorgasbord of information around them, but adults help provide the smorgasbord.

As you review the chapter, consider the specific ways in which the child uses and is influenced by the social environment. In particular, consider (a) infants' employment of mimicry, gaze following, and social referencing to guide their explorations; (b) Vygotsky's theory of the roles of language, dialogue, and cooperative action in the development of thought; and (c) the role of the language-acquisition support system in language development. In the next chapter, on the development of social relationships, you will read much more about ways in which variation in the social environment can influence development.

Further Reading

Tiffany Field (2007). *The amazing infant* (2007). Malden, MA: Blackwell.

Field is a leading researcher on infant development, whose most valuable contributions have been concerned with the role of touch in infants' emotional and physical growth. This highly readable book presents fascinating basic information about infant cognitive, linguistic, social, and emotional development—and about research methods for studying infants—that is useful for new parents as well as for students.

Robert S. Siegler & Martha W. Alibali (2005). *Children's thinking, 4th ed.* Upper Saddle River, NJ: Prentice Hall.

This is a well-written midlevel paperback textbook on cognitive development primarily from an information-processing perspective. Three early chapters are devoted to three theories of development—Piaget's theory, information-processing theory, and sociocultural theory. These are followed by chapters on the development of perception, language, memory, concepts, social cognition, problem solving, and academic skills.

Jean Piaget (1929). *The child's conception of the world.* London: Routledge & Kegan Paul.

Many of Piaget's books are difficult to read, but this one, written early in his career, is an exception. In the introduction, he spells out his method of learning about children's understanding through interviewing them. The book is about children's thoughts on such issues as where the names of things come from, where rain comes from, and what it means to think. The book provides a historical foundation not just for Piaget's subsequent work but for the whole subfield of psychology concerned with cognitive development.

Lev S. Vygotsky (1934; reprinted 1962). *Thought and language* (E. Haufmann & G. Vaker, Eds. and Trans.). Cambridge, MA: MIT Press.

This book was first published in the Soviet Union in 1934, shortly after Vygotsky's death from tuberculosis at age 38, but was not translated into English until 1962. It is a fascinating collection of papers in which Vygotsky sets forth his theory that the internalization of language is critical to the development of human thought.

Steven Pinker (1994). *The language instinct.* New York: Morrow.

Pinker is not only a leading expert on language but a gifted user of it. In delightfully clear and humorous prose, he elaborates on essentially all the ideas about language and its development that are touched on in this chapter, plus much more. Have you ever wondered why baseball announcers say the batter "flied out" the last time up, rather than "flew out"? Pinker answers this and dozens of other questions about language.

Philip Lieberman (2006). *Toward an evolutionary biology of language.* Cambridge, MA: Harvard University Press.

Lieberman brings together research on the nature of human language, the communicative capacities of other animals, the anatomical bases for human speech, the archeology of that anatomy, and the genetics of human language to present an authoritative, fascinating account of how our species acquired its most distinctive ability—language.

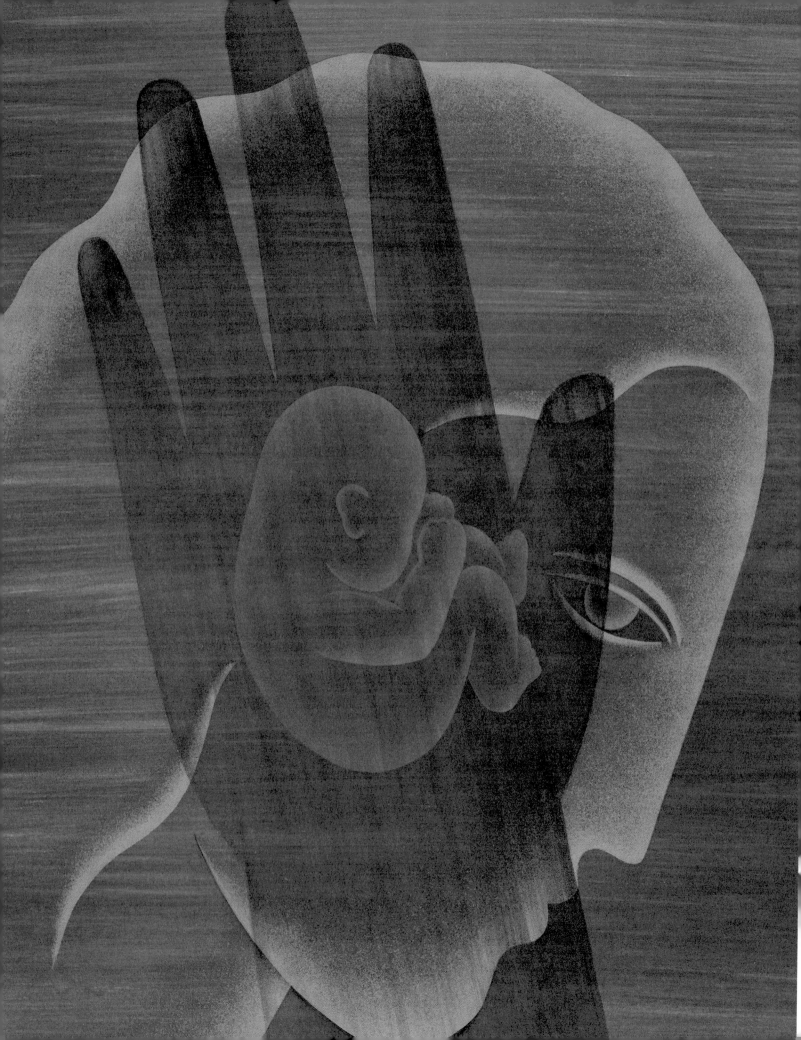

Social Development

12

The natural human environment is a social environment. We are adapted to survive with the help of others. Natural selection has endowed us with brain mechanisms that enable us to make the kinds of connections with other people—at each stage in our lives—that are essential to our survival and reproduction.

Over the span of our lives we are involved continuously in interpersonal relationships that sustain, enhance, and give meaning to our existence. As *infants* we depend physically and emotionally on adult caregivers. As *children* we learn to get along with others and to abide by the rules and norms of society. As *adolescents* we begin to explore romantic relationships and, in other ways, seek niches in the adult world. As *adults* we assume responsibility for the care and support of others and contribute, through work, to the broader society.

Social development refers to the changing nature of our relationships with others over the course of life. What characterizes our ties to other people at each phase of life? How do those relationships promote our survival and influence our subsequent development? How variable is social development from culture to culture and between males and females? These are some of the principal questions of this chapter, which begins with infancy and then proceeds, section by section, through childhood, adolescence, and adulthood.

Infancy: Using Caregivers as a Base for Growth

In the mid-20th century, the psychoanalytically oriented child psychologist Erik Erikson (1963) developed an elaborate theory of social development. The theory posited that each stage of life is associated with a particular problem or set of problems to be resolved through interactions with other people. It also posited that the way the person resolves each problem influences the way he or she approaches subsequent life stages. In infancy, according to Erikson, the primary problem is that of developing a sense of *trust*—that is, a secure sense that other people, or certain other people, can be relied upon for care and help.

Other theorists, too, have focused on the infant's need for care and on the psychological consequences of the manner in which care is provided. One such theorist was John Bowlby, a British child psychologist who, in the mid-20th century, brought an evolutionary perspective to bear on the issue of early child development. Bowlby (1958, 1982) contended that the emotional bond between human infant and adult caregiver—especially the mother—is promoted by a set of instinctive tendencies in both partners. These include the infant's crying to signal discomfort, the adult's distress and urge to help on hearing the crying, the infant's smiling and cooing when comforted, and the adult's pleasure at receiving those signals.

Human infants are completely dependent on caregivers for survival, but, consistent with Bowlby's theory, they are not passively dependent. They enter the world biologically prepared to learn who their caregivers are and to elicit from them the help they need. By the time they are born, babies already prefer the voices of their own mothers over other voices (discussed in **Chapter 11**), and shortly thereafter they also prefer the smell and sight of their own mothers (Bushnell & others, 1989; Macfarlane, 1975). Newborns signal distress through fussing or crying. By the time they are 3 months old, they express clearly and effectively their interest, joy, sadness, and anger through their facial expressions, and they respond differentially to such expressions in others (Izard & others, 1995; Lavelli & Fogel, 2005).

Through such actions, infants help build emotional bonds between themselves and those on whom they most directly depend, and then they use those caregivers as a base from which to explore the world. In the 1950s, Bowlby began to use the term *attachment* to refer to such emotional bonds, and since then the study of infants' attachment to caregivers has become a major branch of developmental psychology.

Attachment to Caregivers

At about the same time that Bowlby was beginning to write about attachment, Harry Harlow initiated a systematic program of research on attachment with rhesus monkeys. Harlow controlled the monkeys' living conditions experimentally to learn about the developmental consequences of raising infants in isolation from their mothers and other monkeys. Most relevant to our present theme are experiments in which Harlow raised infant monkeys with inanimate surrogate (substitute) mothers.

Harlow's Monkeys Raised with Surrogate Mothers

1 ╌╌╌╌╌╌╌╌╌╌╌╌╌╌╌╌╌╌╌╌◀ In one experiment, Harlow (1959) raised infant monkeys individually in isolated
What was Harlow's procedure for studying attachment in infant monkeys, and what did he find? cages, each containing two surrogate mothers—one made of bare wire and the other covered with soft terry cloth (see Figure 12.1). The infants could feed themselves by sucking milk from a nipple that was affixed either to the wire surrogate or

FIGURE 12.1 Harlow's motherless monkeys Harlow raised infant monkeys with two surrogate (substitute) mothers, one wire and one cloth. The monkey shown here received its nourishment from a bottle attached to the wire surrogate but went to the cloth surrogate for comfort, affection, and reassurance.

Courtesy of University of Wisconsin Primate Lab, Madison, WI

Monkmeyer Press

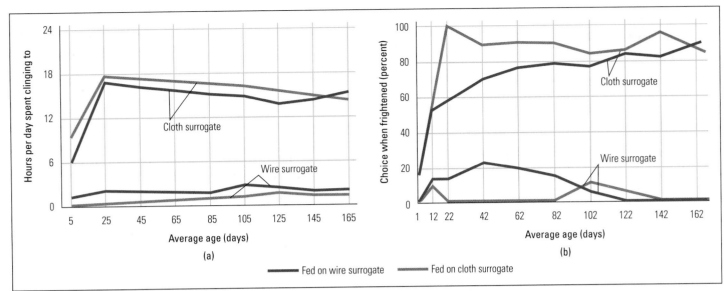

(a)

(b)

— Fed on wire surrogate   —— Fed on cloth surrogate

FIGURE 12.2 Evidence of infant monkeys' preference for the cloth surrogate These graphs show (a) the average number of hours that Harlow's monkeys spent on each of the surrogate mothers and (b) the percentage of time that they ran to each when they were frightened by a strange object. Notice that the preference for the cloth surrogate was as strong for the monkeys that were fed on the wire surrogate as for those fed on the cloth surrogate. (Adapted from Harlow, 1959.)

to the cloth surrogate. Harlow's purpose was to determine if the infants would become attached to either of these surrogate mothers as they would to a real mother; he also wanted to know which characteristic—the milk-providing nipple or the soft cloth exterior—was most effective in inducing attachment.

Harlow's main finding was that regardless of which surrogate contained the nutritive nipple, all the infant monkeys treated the cloth-covered surrogate, not the wire one, as a mother. They clung to it for much of the day and ran to it when frightened by a strange object (see Figure 12.2). They also were braver in exploring an unfamiliar room when the cloth surrogate was present than when it was absent, and they pressed a lever repeatedly to look at it through a window in preference to other objects. This work demonstrated the role of contact comfort in the development of attachment bonds, and it helped to revolutionize psychologists' thinking about infants' needs. Provision of adequate nutrition and other physical necessities is not enough; infants also need close contact with comforting caregivers.

The Form and Functions of Human Infants' Attachment

Bowlby (1958, 1982) observed attachment behaviors in young humans, from 8 months to 3 years of age, that were similar to those that Harlow observed with monkeys. He found that children showed distress when their mothers (the objects of their attachment) left them, especially in an unfamiliar environment; showed pleasure when reunited with their mothers; showed distress when approached by a stranger unless reassured or comforted by their mothers; and were more likely to explore an unfamiliar environment when in the presence of their mothers than when alone. Many research studies have since verified these general conclusions (Crittenden & Claussen, 2003).

Bowlby contended that attachment is a universal human phenomenon with a biological foundation that derives from natural selection. Infants are potentially in danger when out of sight of caregivers, especially in a novel environment. During our evolutionary history, infants who scrambled after their mothers and successfully protested their mothers' departure, and who avoided unfamiliar objects when their mothers were absent, were more likely to survive to adulthood and pass on their genes than were those who were indifferent to their mothers' presence or absence. Evidence that similar behaviors occur in all human cultures (Kagan, 1976; Konner, 2002) and in other species of mammals (Kraemer, 1992) supports Bowlby's evolutionary interpretation.

> 2
> **According to Bowlby, what infant behaviors indicate strong attachment, and why would they have come about in natural selection?**

3 ────────────────────

From an evolutionary perspective, why does attachment strengthen at about 6 to 8 months of age?

────────────────────

◄ Also consistent with the evolutionary explanation is the observation that attachment begins to strengthen at about the age (6 to 8 months) when infants begin to move around on their own. A crawling or walking infant—who for good evolutionary reasons is intent on exploring the environment—can get into more danger than an immobile one. For safety's sake, exploration must be balanced by a drive to stay near the protective caregiver. As was noted in **Chapter 11,** infants who can crawl or walk exhibit much *social referencing;* that is, they look to their caregivers for cues about danger or safety as they explore. To feel most secure in a novel situation, infants require not just the presence of their attachment object but also that person's emotional availability and expressions of reassurance. Infants who cannot see their mother's face typically move around her until they can (Carr & others, 1975), and infants who are approached by a stranger relax more if their mother smiles cheerfully at the stranger than if she doesn't (Broccia & Campos, 1989).

The Strange-Situation Measure of Attachment Quality

4 ────────────────────

How does the strange-situation test assess the security of attachment?

────────────────────

◄ In order to assess attachment systematically, Mary Ainsworth—who originally worked with Bowlby—developed the ***strange-situation test.*** In this test the infant and mother (or another caregiver to whom the infant is attached) are brought into an unfamiliar room with toys. The infant remains in the room while the mother and an unfamiliar adult move out of and into it according to a prescribed sequence. The infant is sometimes with just the mother, sometimes with just the stranger, and sometimes alone.

Infants in this test are classed as *securely attached* if they explore the room and toys confidently when their mother is present, become upset and explore less when their mother is absent (whether or not the stranger is present), and show pleasure when the mother returns (see Figure 12.3). Other response patterns are taken to indicate one or another form of insecure attachment. An infant who avoids the mother and seems to act coldly toward her is said to have an *avoidant attachment,* and an infant who does not avoid the mother but continues to cry and fret despite her attempts to comfort is said to have an *anxious attachment.* By these criteria, Ainsworth and other researchers have found that about 70 percent of middle-class North American infants in their second year of life are securely attached to their mothers, about 20 percent are avoidant, and about 10 percent are anxious (Ainsworth & others, 1978; Waters & others, 2000).

Like most measures of psychological attributes, the strange-situation test has limitations. The test assesses fear-induced aspects of attachment but fails to capture the harmonious caregiver–child interactions that typically occur in less stressful situations (Field, 1996). Moreover, the test is designed to assess the infant's reactions to the caregiver in a mildly fearful situation, but for some infants, because of innate temperament or past experience, the situation may be either too stressful or insufficiently stressful to induce the appropriate responses.

FIGURE 12.3 The strange-situation test In this test of attachment, the mother (or other person to whom the infant is attached) moves into and out of an unfamiliar room, leaving the infant either with a stranger or alone. Here we see one infant, Brian, at different stages in the test: In (a) he plays confidently when his mother is present, in (b) he cries when she leaves, and in (c) he is comforted when she returns. Brian's behavior indicates that he is securely attached to his mother.

(a)

(b)

(c)

Sensitive Care Correlates with Secure Attachment and Positive Later Adjustment

Ainsworth hypothesized that infants would become securely attached to mothers who provide regular contact comfort, respond promptly and helpfully to the infant's signals of distress, and interact with the infant in an emotionally synchronous manner (see Figure 12.4)—a constellation of behaviors referred to today as *sensitive care*. Consistent with that hypothesis, Ainsworth, and other researchers subsequently, found significant positive correlations between ratings of the mother's sensitive care and security of the infant's attachment to the mother (Ainsworth, 1979; Posada & others, 2004; Seifer & others, 1996). In most such studies, the mother's style of parenting was assessed through home visits early in infancy and attachment was assessed with the strange-situation test several months later, after the baby could move about on its own.

▶ ------------------- **5**

What evidence suggests that sensitive parenting correlates with secure attachment and subsequent emotional and social development? How did Ainsworth interpret the correlations, and how else might they be interpreted?

Ainsworth (1989) also postulated that secure attachment would lead to positive effects later on in life. This view was very much in line with that of Bowlby (1973), who postulated that infants develop an internal "working model," or cognitive representation, of their first attachment relationship and that this model affects their subsequent relationships throughout life. It was also consistent with Erikson's (1963) theory that secure attachment in infancy results in a general sense of trust of other people and oneself, which permits the infant to enter subsequent stages of life in a confident, growth-promoting manner. Consistent with such views, children judged to be securely attached in infancy have been found, on average, to be more confident, better at solving problems, emotionally healthier, and more sociable later in childhood than those who had been found to be insecurely attached (Ainsworth, 1989; Raikes & Thompson, 2008; Schneider & others, 2001).

FIGURE 12.4 Interactional synchrony Interactions such as this during the first 3 months of life correlate with secure attachment measured several months later.

As you well know by now, however, we must be cautious about inferring causal relationships from correlations. Ainsworth's theory was that sensitive parenting causes secure attachment, which causes positive subsequent emotional and social development; but the correlations could be explained in other ways. For example, some children might for genetic reasons be more cheerful than others, and maybe that temperament leads them to (a) show the "secure" pattern in the strange-situation test, (b) succeed in eliciting sensitive care from their mothers, and (c) get along well with all sorts of people later in childhood. By that theory, all the correlations among sensitive parenting, attachment, and positive social adjustment might be driven by differences in children's temperaments rather than by differences in parental sensitivity. To test most directly the theory that sensitive parenting causes the good effects, one would have to conduct an experiment: get some mothers to behave in a more sensitive manner toward their children than other mothers do, and then assess their children's behavior later on. A number of such studies have been conducted—to which we now turn.

Effects of Improving Parental Care Through Training

The first experimental evidence for a causal relationship between sensitive parenting and secure attachment came from an experiment conducted in the Netherlands by Dymphna van den Boom (1994). Van den Boom focused on mothers with temperamentally irritable babies—babies who by disposition are unusually fussy, easily angered, and difficult to comfort. She had previously observed that mothers of such babies tended to withdraw emotionally from them, which seemed to set off a spiral of decline in the mother–infant relationship (van den Boom, 1991). For her experiment, she recruited 100 mother–infant pairs, in each of which the infant had been judged by a standard test of temperament to be highly irritable. Half the mothers, randomly chosen, participated in a 3-month training program, beginning when their infants were 6 months old, designed to help and encourage the mothers to perceive and respond appropriately to their babies' signals, especially signals of distress. When the infants were 12 months old, all of them were tested with their mothers in the strange-situation test. The result was that 62 percent of the infants

▶ ------------------- **6**

What experimental evidence supports the theory that sensitive care promotes secure attachment?

with trained mothers showed secure attachment and only 22 percent of the other infants did.

More recently, a number of other maternal-training experiments have shown similar results (Bakermans-Kranenburg & others, 2003). One study, for example, was conducted with depressed mothers, who typically fail to respond appropriately to their infants' signals. Depressed mothers who received training exhibited more sensitive care than did those who did not receive training, and their infants showed more secure attachment and better socioemotional functioning than did those whose mothers did not receive training (van Doesum & others, 2008). Other experiments have shown that parental training for foster parents can result in more sensitive parenting, more secure attachment, reduced physiological evidence of distress in the child, and fewer reported problem behaviors in the child (Dozier & others, 2006; Fisher & others, 2006).

Some Children Are More Susceptible to Parental Effects than Are Others

7

What evidence suggests that some infants are relatively invulnerable to negative effects of insensitive parenting?

Several studies have suggested that the relationship between parental care and infants' attachment depends, at least partly, on the genetic makeup of the child (Bakermans-Kranenburg & van Ijzendoorn, 2007; Belsky & others, 2007). The most dramatic such effect revealed to date comes from an experiment involving infants who differ in a certain gene that is involved in the manner by which the brain uses the neurotransmitter serotonin.

The gene at issue (called the 5-HTLLPR gene) comes in two forms (or *alleles*, as defined in **Chapter 3**), a short (*s*) form and a long (*l*) form. The *l* allele results in greater uptake of serotonin into brain neurons than does the *s* allele. Previous research had shown that children who are homozygous for the *l* allele (in other words, have *l* on both paired chromosomes, as discussed in **Chapter 3**) are less affected by negative environmental experiences than are other children. For example, they are less likely to become depressed or highly fearful as a result of living in abusive homes (Kaufman & others, 2004, 2006). In the study of attachment, parents were assessed for their level of sensitive care when their infants were 7 months old, and then the infants' attachment behavior was assessed using the strange-situation test when the infants were 15 months old (Barry & others, 2008). A genetic test revealed that 28 of the 88 infants had the *ll* genotype and the rest had either *ss* or *sl*.

The results of the study are shown in Figure 12.5. Attachment security increased significantly and rather sharply with increased maternal sensitivity for the *ss/sl* group but was not significantly affected by maternal sensitivity for the *ll* group. The *ll* infants showed highly secure attachment regardless of the level of maternal sensitivity. Currently much new research centers on this and other relationships between parenting and children's genetic makeup. It will be interesting to see how such work turns out.

FIGURE 12.5 Interaction between genes and environment Security of attachments to their mothers was positively correlated with the sensitivity of maternal care for most infants, but not for those with the *ll* genotype, who showed secure attachment regardless of quality of care. Attachment security was scored numerically, based on each infant's behavior in the strange situation, and the scores were standardized, such that 0 is the average overall of the infants combined. (Standardized scores are explained in Statistical Appendix.) The upward slope for the *ss/sl* infants is statistically significant; the slight downward slope for the *ll* infants is not significant. (Adapted from Barry & others, 2008.)

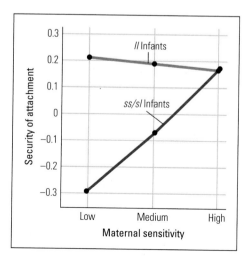

High-Quality Day Care Also Correlates with Positive Adjustment

Most studies of attachment have focused on infants' relationships with mothers, because mothers usually are the primary caregivers to infants. But research has shown that infants can also develop secure attachments with fathers, grandparents, older siblings, and day-care providers (Cox & others, 1992; Goossens & van Ijzendoorn, 1990). During the decades after Bowlby and Ainsworth developed their theories, the use of day-care providers increased dramatically. Currently in the United States, roughly 80 percent of preschool children are in some form of day care, usually with caregivers who are not relatives, for an average of 40 hours per week (Marshall, 2004). Concern about the developmental effects of such care has led to many research studies aimed at correlating variations of day care with children's subsequent behavioral development.

By permission of Dave Coverly and Creators Syndicate, Inc.

8

What have researchers found about possible developmental effects of day care?

The results, taken as a whole, suggest that high-quality day care correlates with positive development just as high-quality home care does (Marshall, 2004; NICHD, 2006). High-quality day care is generally defined as that in which children are with the same familiar caregivers each day; the caregivers are warm, sensitive, responsive, and happy; and developmentally appropriate, interesting activities are available to the children. The higher the quality of day care during infancy and toddlerhood, by these measures, the better is the social and academic adjustment of children in their early school years (Hrdy, 2005; Marshall, 2004). Researchers have also found that day care generally does not interfere with the abilities of infants and toddlers to maintain secure attachments with their mothers and fathers, and that parental attachments are better predictors of positive subsequent adjustment than are attachments with day-care providers, regardless of the amount of time spent in day care (Marshall, 2004).

Cross-Cultural Differences in Infant Care

Beliefs and practices regarding infant care vary considerably from culture to culture. Our Western, Euro-American culture is in many ways less indulgent of infants' desires than are other cultures. Are such differences in care associated with any differences in infant social behavior and subsequent development?

Sleeping Arrangements

Our Western culture (especially that of the United States) is unusual in the expectation that infants and young children should sleep alone. A survey of 90 other cultures revealed that, in every one, infants and toddlers normally slept in the same room as the mother or another closely related adult, usually in the same bed (Barry & Paxson, 1971). Young chimpanzees, bonobos, and gorillas—our closest nonhuman relatives—sleep in direct contact with their mothers during their first few years of life (Mosko & others, 1993; de Waal, 1997).

Interviews with Mayan mothers in rural Guatemala and middle-class mothers in the United States revealed that differing beliefs and values support the differing sleeping practices (Morelli & others, 1992). The Mayan mothers, who all slept with their infants and toddlers, emphasized the comforting value of physical closeness. When told that young children in the United States often sleep alone, in their own rooms, they expressed dismay and pity at what seemed to them a heartless practice. In contrast, the U.S. mothers, none of whom slept regularly with their youngsters, expressed concern that to do so would establish a hard-to-break habit, would foster dependence, and might even be physically dangerous because the infant could be smothered. (Concerning this last point, there is, indeed, evidence that sleeping with infants can in rare cases cause accidental smothering (Mesich, 2005; Scheers & others, 2003). Parents who wish to consider this practice are advised to

9

How do adults in different cultures explain their practice of sleeping or not sleeping with their young children? What evidence suggests that co-sleeping may be beneficial?

Security In Western cultures, babies and young children are commonly required to sleep alone. As a consequence, they often develop a strong attachment to a blanket, teddy bear, or other soft inanimate object that they sleep with.

10

How might our culture's typical sleeping arrangements explain infants' attachments to "security blankets"?

review that evidence and take precautions against smothering, such as not using too soft a bed and never sleeping with an infant if intoxicated.) Moreover, the U.S. mothers saw bedtime as a time for intimate relations with their husbands, whereas the Mayan mothers saw it as a time for family togetherness. Not surprisingly, the task of putting young children to bed was much easier for the Mayan mothers than for the U.S. mothers, who commonly engaged in elaborate bedtime rituals.

Some researchers who began with the view that sleeping with parents is likely to be developmentally harmful—a view held not long ago by most pediatricians in the United States (Lozoff & others, 1984)—have concluded just the opposite. In one study, conducted in Spain, adult women who had slept with their parents up to the age of 4 or 5 years showed somewhat healthier, more mature personalities (higher "ego strength") on a standard paper-and-pencil test of personality than did otherwise-comparable women who had slept alone during infancy and early childhood (Crawford, 1994). In another study, conducted with U.S. military families in which the father was often away, children who had been diagnosed with behavioral or psychological problems were significantly less likely than other children to have slept regularly with their mothers (Forbes & Weiss, 1992). In still another study, conducted in the United States, children who had slept regularly with their parents during their first few years were reported to be more self-reliant and to have better relationships with playmates than was the case for children who had usually slept alone (Keller & Goldberg, 2004). Again, of course, these are correlational studies, so we don't know for sure what is cause and what is effect.

◄ One intriguing consequence of requiring infants and toddlers to sleep alone, apparently, is a high rate of attachment to inanimate objects—the "security blanket" or the special doll or teddy bear. Several studies, some across cultures and some comparing different families within the same culture, have shown that infants who sleep alone are much more likely to develop such attachments than are those who sleep with or in the presence of an adult (Ahluvalia & Schaefer, 1994; Honig & Townes, 1976; Wolf & Lozoff, 1989). Perhaps, to relieve their fear at night, infants who sleep alone—much like Harlow's monkeys—attach themselves to the softest, most comforting mother substitute available. Unlike Harlow's monkeys, of course, the human infants are in contact with their mothers and other caregivers during the day, so the attachment to the inanimate object is in addition to other attachments.

Caregiving in Hunter-Gatherer Societies

During the great bulk of our species' history, our ancestors lived in small groups, made up mostly of close relatives, who survived by gathering and hunting food cooperatively in the forest or savanna. The biological underpinnings of infants' and caregivers' behaviors evolved in the context of that way of life. Partly for that reason, an examination of infant care in the few hunter-gatherer cultures that have survived into recent times is of special interest.

11

What observations suggest that hunter-gatherers are highly indulgent toward infants? What parenting styles distinguish the !Kung, Efe, and Aka?

◄ Melvin Konner (1976, 2002, 2005) studied the !Kung San people, who live in Africa's Kalahari Desert. He observed that !Kung infants spend most of their time during their first year in direct contact with their mothers' bodies. At night the mother sleeps with the infant, and during the day she carries the infant in a sling at her side. The sling is arranged in such a way that the infant has constant access to the mother's breast and can nurse at will—which, according to Konner, occurs on average every 15 minutes. The infant's position also enables the infant to see what the mother sees and in that way to be involved in her activities. When not being held by the mother, the infant is passed around among others, who cuddle, fondle, kiss, and enjoy the baby. According to Konner, the !Kung never leave an infant to cry alone, and usually they detect the distress and begin to comfort the infant before crying even begins.

Studies of other hunter-gatherer cultures have shown a similarly high degree of indulgence toward infants (Lamb & Hewlett, 2005), but the people who provide the care can vary. Among the Efe (**Eff**-ay)-who gather and hunt in the Ituri forest of central Africa-infants are in physical contact with their mothers for only about half the day (Ivey Henry & others, 2005; Morelli & Tronick, 1991). During the rest of the day they are in direct contact with other caregivers, including siblings, aunts, and unrelated women. Efe infants nurse at will, not just from their mothers but also from other lactating women in the group. However, at about 8 to 12 months of age—the age at which research in many cultures has shown that attachment strengthens—Efe infants begin to show increased preference for their own mothers. They are less readily comforted by other people and will often reject the breast of another woman and seek the mother's.

In no culture yet studied is the average father nearly as involved as the average mother in direct care of infants and young children; but, in general, paternal involvement appears to be greater in hunter-gatherer cultures than in agricultural or industrial cultures (Hewlett, 1988). The record on this score seems to be held by the Aka of central Africa, a hunter-gatherer group closely related to the Efe (Hewlett, 1988). Aka fathers have been observed to hold their infants an average of 20 percent of the time during daylight hours and to get up with them frequently at night. Among the Aka, the whole family—mother, father, infant, and other young children—sleep together in the same bed.

An Efe girl and her infant brother In hunter-gatherer cultures, infants are in direct physical contact with a caregiver almost constantly. Efe infants spend about half of each day with their mothers and the rest of the day with other members of the group.

Courtesy of Gilda Morelli

Issues of Indulgence, Dependence, and Interdependence

Books on infant care in our culture (for example, Spock & Rothenberg, 1985) commonly advise that indulgent parenting—including sleeping with infants and offering immediate comfort whenever they cry—can lead infants to become ever more demanding and prevent them from learning to cope with life's frustrations. Konner (1976, 2002), however, contends that such indulgence among the !Kung does not produce overly demanding and dependent children. Indeed, by all reports, !Kung children are extraordinarily cooperative and brave. In a cross-cultural test, !Kung children older than 4 years explored more and sought their mothers less in a novel environment than did their British counterparts (Blurton-Jones & Konner, 1973).

Some researchers speculate that high indulgence of infants' desires, coupled with a complete integration of infants and children into the community's social life, in non-Western societies may foster long-lasting emotional bonds that are stronger than those developed by our Western practices (Rogoff, 2003; Tronick & others, 1992). The result is apparently not dependence, in the sense of fear when alone or inability to function autonomously, but *interdependence*, in the sense of strong loyalties or feelings of obligation to a particular set of people. In cultures such as the !Kung San and the Efe, where people depend economically throughout their lives on the cooperative efforts of their relatives and other members of their group, such bonds may be more important to each person's well-being than they are in our mobile society, where the people with whom we interact change as we go from home to school to work, or when we move from one part of the country to another.

In our culture, where nuclear families live in relative isolation from one another, most parents cannot indulge their infants to the degree seen in many other cultures. !Kung mothers are constantly in contact with their young infants, but they are also constantly surrounded by other adults who provide social stimulation and emotional and material support (Konner, 1976). A survey of infant care in 55 cultures in various parts of the world revealed a direct correlation between the degree of indulgence and the number of adults who live communally with the infant (Whiting, 1971). Indulgence is greatest for infants who live in large extended families or close-knit village groups, and least for those who live just with one or both parents.

12
What evidence suggests that indulgence of infants' desires does not spoil them?

13
How might indulgence of infants be related to interdependence and to living in extended families?

Infants develop emotional attachment bonds with the caregivers on whom they depend.

Attachment to Caregivers

➤ Harlow found that infant monkeys became attached to a cloth surrogate mother but not to a wire one, even if the latter provided milk. They turned to the cloth "mother" for contact comfort and explored the environment more fully in its presence.

➤ Bowlby found that human infants also exhibit attachment behaviors. Such behaviors, which help protect the baby from danger, intensify when the baby can move around on its own.

➤ Secure attachment of infants to caregivers, measured by the strange-situation test, correlates with the caregiver's responsive, emotionally sensitive care. Parent-training experiments indicate that sensitive care promotes secure attachment.

➤ Some infants, who have a particular genotype, appear to develop secure attachment regardless of the sensitivity or insensitivity of care.

➤ Secure attachment to caregivers and high-quality day care are both correlated with positive behaviors later in life (e.g., greater sociability).

Infant Care in Different Cultures

➤ Co-sleeping with infants and young children, which is the norm in most cultures but unusual in North America, appears to be associated with positive social and emotional development.

➤ Hunter-gatherer societies such as the !Kung treat infants with extraordinary indulgence, keeping them in nearly constant physical contact, permitting nursing at will, and responding quickly to signs of distress.

➤ The indulgent approach taken by hunter-gatherers appears to produce a strong sense of interdependence and group loyalty, not demanding or overly dependent individuals.

■ Childhood I: Continuing Interactions with Caregivers

As children grow from infancy into toddlerhood and beyond, they become increasingly mobile and capable of a wide variety of actions in their physical and social worlds. In his life-span theory of social development, Erikson (1963) divided the years from age 1 to 12 into three successive stages, concerned, respectively, with the development of *autonomy* (self-control), *initiative* (willingness to initiate actions), and *industry* (competence in completing tasks). These characteristics are all closely related to one another; they have to do with the child's ability to control his or her own actions.

As Erikson pointed out, however, children's actions frequently bring them into conflict with caregivers and others around them. According to Erikson, caregivers' responses to children's actions, and the ways by which caregivers and children resolve their conflicts, influence children's social development. On the positive side, children may develop the ability to behave appropriately, with confidence, in ways that are satisfying both to themselves and to others. On the negative side, children may develop feelings of shame, doubt, and inferiority that interfere with autonomy, initiative, and industry. The psychologically healthy, moral person, in Erikson's theory, is one who responds appropriately to others' needs without sacrificing his or her own sense of self-control.

In the years since Erikson developed his theory, much research has been conducted on child–caregiver interactions and the possible effects these have on children's development. Much of this research has to do, broadly, with the development of morality. This section, then, is about ways by which children develop morally through their interactions with caregivers.

Behavioral and Emotional Foundations for Morality

Long ago, philosophers who thought about children's social development tended to view young children as akin to either wild animals that must be tamed or lumps of clay that must be shaped into socially acceptable humans. Most present-day developmental psychologists, in contrast, consider children to be the primary movers of their own development, with caregivers and others in their environments serving as the substrate with which they work. Of course, that substrate is important. Without feedback from others or good models of acceptable social behavior, children would be hard put to create acceptable social selves. Here we shall examine some instinctive tendencies of children that seem to have been designed, by natural selection, to promote children's development as social, moral individuals.

The Young Child's Natural Tendency to Give and Help

Giving appears to be a human instinct, much like smiling and babbling. Near the end of their first year of life, infants routinely, without any special encouragement, begin to give objects to their caregivers and to delight in games of give-and-take, in which the child and caregiver pass an object back and forth to each other. In a series of experiments conducted in the United States, nearly every one of more than 100 infants, aged 12 to 18 months, spontaneously gave toys to an adult during brief sessions in a laboratory room (Hay & Murray, 1982; Rheingold & others, 1976). They gave not just to their mothers or fathers but also to unfamiliar researchers, and they gave new toys as frequently as familiar ones. They gave when an adult requested a toy by holding a hand out with palm up (the universal begging posture), and they gave when no requests were made. Infants in a !Kung hunter-gatherer community were likewise observed to give objects regularly, beginning near the end of their first year of life (Bakeman & others, 1990).

In our culture, young children's enjoyment of giving is known to most parents but is not much commented on. Books on childcare, for example, rarely mention it, and very few psychologists have studied it. In contrast, the !Kung treat a child's early acts of giving as a crucial developmental milestone, much as we treat a child's first words. The sharing of food and supplies often marks the difference between life and death for these hunting-and-gathering people, and the culture as a whole ascribes great value to its system of giving and receiving, referred to as *hxoro*. Grandmothers are especially charged with the task of initiating infants into *hxoro* by encouraging their giving and by guiding the infants' hands in the giving of beads to relatives (Bakeman & others, 1990; Wiessner, 1982). Whether or not such training increases the !Kung's tendency to give is unknown, but it surely must help alert young !Kung to the special significance of such behavior in their culture.

In addition to liking to give, young children enjoy helping with adult tasks. In one study, children between 18 and 30 months old were frequently observed joining their mothers, without being asked, in such household tasks as making the bed, setting the table, and folding laundry (Rheingold, 1982). Not surprisingly, the older children helped more often, and more effectively, than the younger ones.

One might argue that young children's early giving and helping are largely self-centered rather than other-centered, motivated more by the child's own needs and wishes than by the child's perception of others' needs and wishes. But the very fact that such actions seem to stem from the child's own wishes is evidence that our species has evolved prosocial (socially beneficial) drives, which motivate us—with no feeling of sacrifice—to involve ourselves in positive ways with other people. Giving and helping become increasingly other-focused as they become linked to another apparently innate capacity in the child, that of *empathy*, the capacity to perceive and feel the emotions that another person is feeling.

The Early Emergence of Empathy and Empathic Comforting

Newborn babies, as young as 2 or 3 days old, reflexively cry and show other signs of distress in response to another baby's crying. Martin Hoffman (2000, 2007) has suggested that this instinctive tendency to feel discomfort in response to another's expressed discomfort is a foundation for the development of empathy. Over time,

© Elizabeth Crews/The Image Works

Giving is natural Infants and young children all over the world delight in games of give and take with adults or older children. Sharing appears to be an aspect of human nature that begins to be exercised as soon as the child's capacity for motor coordination makes it possible.

➤ ────────── 14

What evidence suggests that young children naturally enjoy giving? How do the !Kung use that enjoyment for moral training?

➤ ────────── 15

According to Hoffman, how does empathy develop during infancy and early toddlerhood?

Martin Hoffman and grandchild
Hoffman has documented that even infants respond empathically to others' emotional feelings. That capacity, he argues, lies at the root of moral development. As children become linguistically competent, parents can help them develop morally by drawing attention to the effects that their actions have on others' feelings.

© E. Ann Kaplan

the response gradually becomes less reflexive and more accompanied by thought. By about 6 months of age, babies may no longer cry immediately in response to another's crying, but rather turn toward the distressed individual, look sad, and whimper.

Until about 15 months of age, the child's distress when others are distressed is best referred to as *egocentric* empathy (Hoffman, 2007). The distressed child seeks comfort for himself or herself rather than for the other distressed person. At about 15 months, however, children begin to respond to another's discomfort by attempting to comfort that person, and by 2 years of age they begin to succeed at such comforting (Hoffman, 2000; Knafo & others, 2008). For example, Hoffman described a case in which 2-year-old David first attempted to comfort his crying friend by giving him his (David's) own teddy bear. When that didn't work, David ran to the next room and returned with his friend's teddy bear and gave it to him. The friend hugged the bear and immediately stopped crying. To behave in such an effective manner, the child must not only feel bad about another's discomfort, but must also understand enough about the other person's mind to know what will provide comfort. Another example of empathic comforting is illustrated in Figure 12.6.

In their relationships with caregivers, young children are most often on the receiving end of acts of giving, helping, and comforting. They therefore have ample opportunity not only to witness such behaviors but also to feel their pleasurable and comforting consequences. Correlational studies indicate, not surprisingly, that children who have received the most sensitive care, and who are most securely attached to their caregivers, also demonstrate the most giving and comforting to others (Bretherton & others, 1997; Kiang & others, 2004).

FIGURE 12.6 A toddler's empathic concern In this sequence, a 21-month-old (a) notices and (b) examines his mother's simulated expression of sadness; (c) tries to cheer her with a puppet; (d) expresses concern; (e) asks the researcher to come to help; and (f) gives his mother a hug while uttering consoling sounds and statements. (From Zahn-Waxler & Radke-Yarrow, 1990, pp. 116–117.)

Carolyn Zahn-Waxler

(a)

(b)

(c)

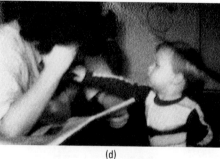

(d)

(e)

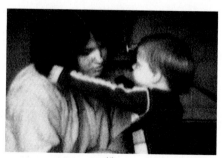

(f)

Guilt as a Force for Moral Development

Of course, young children are not always giving, helpful, and caring, no matter how sensitively they are treated. Very often they are disruptive, selfish, and even hurtful to others around them. Toddlers under the age of about 2 years often look to caregivers for guidance about what is appropriate, but between their second and third birthdays—the period known to many parents as the "terrible twos"—they become increasingly willful and ready to challenge authority. At this stage a goal of good parenting is to correct the child's disruptive or hurtful behaviors without damaging the child's positive sense of autonomy and initiative. A developmental event that tempers the 2-year-old's behavior and can serve as a powerful force for moral development is the gradual emergence of the capacity for *guilt*.

Until relatively recently, most developmental psychologists tended to think of guilt primarily in negative terms. For instance, Erikson (1963) considered guilt to be a harmful outcome of interactions between toddlers and guilt-inducing caregivers. Some forms of guilt certainly are harmful, as when children feel guilty about events that they cannot control (Donenberg, 1998) or about every attempt to exert their will. But guilt about one's own hurtful actions, which one can control, may be crucial to healthy social development. Hoffman (1982, 1998) distinguishes between *empathy-based guilt,* which is constructive, and *anxiety-based guilt,* which can be harmful. He suggests that empathy-based guilt emerges from the capacity for empathy coupled with the child's growing understanding of the relationship between his or her own actions and others' feelings. A child who can sense another's hurt, and who knows that the hurt came from his or her actions, can feel discomforting guilt. Guilt helps curb aggression and selfishness and promotes acts of kindness and helping.

Consistent with Hoffman's theory, a number of studies have shown that expressions of guilt by young children, when they break something or hurt someone, are *positively* correlated with sensitive parenting and secure attachment to parents (Kochanska & others, 2002). According to Hoffman (2000), sensitive parents can draw on their child's capacity for guilt to help the child become a moral person.

> ----- **16**
> **How might the capacity for empathy-based guilt serve as a force for moral development in young children?**

Parents' Styles of Discipline

Discipline refers to the methods by which parents and other caregivers attempt to stop or correct their children's misbehavior. Of course, parents do not just discipline their children; they also play with them, converse with them, interpret the world to them, and serve as models through their own behavior. Nevertheless, a relatively high percentage of the interactions between parents and young children are disciplinary in nature, and most of the controversy about what constitutes good or bad parenting has to do with styles of discipline.

Hoffman's Theory About the Role of Discipline in Moral Development

Hoffman (1983, 2000) categorizes disciplinary techniques into three classes. The first—which he favors—is *induction,* a form of verbal reasoning in which the parent induces the child to think about the harmful consequences of the child's actions, from the point of view of the person who is hurt. Induction draws on the child's capacity for empathy and empathy-based guilt. For example, a parent may say to a young child, "When you hit Billy, it hurts him and makes him cry," or to a somewhat older child, "When you tease Susan and call her names, it makes her feel that nobody likes her." Such statements demonstrate respect for the child's desire to act responsibly. The child who then stops hitting or teasing can attribute the change in behavior to his or her own moral standards: "I don't want to hurt anyone." According to Hoffman, induction helps the child develop a set of personal moral standards that can promote good behavior even when no authority figure is watching.

The second category of disciplinary style in Hoffman's taxonomy is *power assertion*—the use of physical force, punishment, or (less often) rewards or bribes

> ----- **17**
> **What are Hoffman's three categories of discipline, and why does he favor the category called induction?**

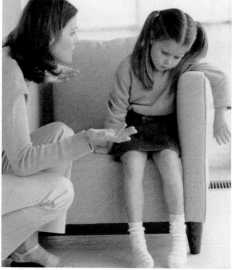

Induction In the discipline technique of induction, the parent explains to the child how her actions have hurt another person. The technique draws on the child's capacity to empathize with the hurt person and to feel empathy-based guilt.

to control a child's behavior. The third is *love withdrawal,* which occurs when parents, often unwittingly, express disapproval of the child, rather than just of the child's specific action. Love withdrawal may take the form of verbal statements, such as "You are worthless," or nonverbal actions, such as coldly ignoring the child.

Like many other psychologists, Hoffman points to the harmful effects of power assertion and love withdrawal. He argues that power assertion focuses attention on the punishments and rewards rather than on reasons why an action is wrong or right. A child so disciplined may continue the undesirable behavior when there is little chance of being caught and may behave well only when someone is sure to notice and provide a reward. Moreover, both punishment and love withdrawal elicit negative emotions in the child (anger in the case of punishment, anxiety in the case of love withdrawal), which interfere with the child's ability to experience empathy for the person who was hurt and to grow morally from that experience. Anger and anxiety can also weaken the parent–child relationship and promote further misbehavior.

Hoffman acknowledges that sometimes a degree of power assertion may be necessary to stop a child from engaging in a seriously wrong or dangerous action; in that case, according to Hoffman, the additional use of induction can blunt the potentially harmful effects of the power assertion. The child who understands that he has been forcibly removed from the playground because he has been hurting another child, not because his parent hates him, has grounds for thinking morally.

Correlations Between Disciplinary Styles and Children's Behavior

Many research studies have shown correlations between parenting styles and children's behavior that are consistent with Hoffman's theory (Eisenberg, 2000). The best-known, pioneering study of this sort was conducted many years ago by Diana Baumrind (1967, 1971), before Hoffman had developed his theory.

18 ━━━━━━━━━━━━━━━━◀ Baumrind assessed the behavior of young children by observing them at nursery schools and in their homes, and she assessed parents' behaviors toward their children through interviews and home observations. On the basis of the latter assessments, she classed parents into three groups:

What three parental discipline styles did Baumrind identify? How do her findings support Hoffman's theory?

- *Authoritarian* parents strongly value obedience for its own sake and use a high degree of power assertion to control their children.

- *Authoritative* parents are less concerned with obedience for its own sake and more concerned that their children learn and abide by basic principles of right and wrong. In Hoffman's terms, they prefer inductive discipline but couple it with power assertion when they feel it is needed.

- *Permissive* parents are most tolerant of their children's disruptive actions and least likely to discipline them at all. The responses they do show to their children's misbehavior seem to be manifestations of their own frustration more than reasoned attempts at correction.

Consistent with what one would expect from Hoffman's theory, Baumrind found that children of authoritative parents exhibited the most positive qualities. They were friendlier, happier, more cooperative, and less likely to disrupt others' activities than were children of either authoritarian or permissive parents. In a follow-up study of the same children, the advantages for those with authoritative parents were still present at age 9 (Baumrind, 1986).

Other researchers have also found correlations consistent with Hoffman's theory. In one series of studies, 4-year-olds whose mothers used much power assertion were less likely to comply with rules when they thought they could not be seen, and exhibited less guilt when they broke a toy lent to them by the experimenter, compared to 4-year-olds whose mothers used less power assertion and more induction (Kochanska & others, 2002, 2008).

"What do I think is an appropriate punishment? I think an appropriate punishment would be to make me live with my guilt."

The Cause–Effect Problem in Relating Discipline to Children's Behavior

As always, we must be cautious in drawing causal inferences from correlational research. It is tempting to conclude from studies such as Baumrind's that the positive parenting style caused the good behavior of the offspring, but the opposite causal relationship may be just as plausible. Some children are temperamentally, for genetic reasons, less cooperative and more disruptive than others, and that behavior may elicit harsh, power-assertive discipline and reduced warmth from parents. Several studies have shown that children with different innate temperaments do, indeed, elicit different disciplinary styles from their parents (Jaffee & others, 2004; O'Connor & others, 1998).

The best evidence that disciplinary styles influence children's development comes from experiments that modify, through training, the styles of one group of parents and then compare their offspring to those of otherwise similar parents who did not receive such training. In one such experiment, divorced mothers of 6- to 8-year-old sons were assigned either to a training condition, in which they were taught how to use firm but kind methods of discipline, or to a comparison condition, in which no such training was given. Assessments a year later showed that the sons whose mothers had undergone training had better relationships with their mothers, rated themselves as happier, and were rated by their teachers as friendlier and more cooperative than was the case for the sons of the comparison mothers (Forgatch & DeGarmo, 1999). Further assessment, three years later, revealed significantly less delinquent behavior by sons of the trained mothers compared to those of the untrained mothers.

> **19**
> How have experiments supported the idea that parents' disciplinary styles influence children's development?

SECTION REVIEW

The child's inborn drives and emotions, and interactions with caregivers, promote social development.

The Beginnings of Morality

➤ Young children have an inborn predisposition to give; they give objects spontaneously to others beginning near the end of their first year.

➤ The development of empathy during the second year causes children, increasingly, to base actions of giving, helping, and comforting on an understanding of and concern for others' needs and feelings.

➤ Empathy-based guilt, which emerges as children connect their own actions with others' pain or sorrow, provides a foundation for moral development.

Styles of Discipline

➤ Hoffman contends that the style of parental discipline referred to as induction is most conducive to the child's moral development.

➤ Baumrind found that children of parents with an authoritative disciplinary style were happier, friendlier, and more cooperative than children of parents with either authoritarian or permissive styles.

➤ Though Baumrind's study was correlational, experimental research also supports Baumrind's and Hoffman's ideas about effective disciplinary styles.

■ Childhood II: Roles of Play and Gender in Development

Parents play important roles in children's social development, but so do peers. Indeed, if developmental psychology were an endeavor pursued by children rather than by adults, I suspect that research would focus more than it currently does on children's relationships with one another and less on their relationships with adults. Parents and other caregivers provide a base from which children grow, but peers are the targets toward which children are oriented and about which they often have the most conscious concerns. A mother and father want their daughter to wear a certain pair of shoes, but the neighborhood children think the shoes are "geeky" and a different style is "cool." Which shoes will the girl want to wear? From an evolutionary perspective, children's strong orientation toward peers—that is, toward members of their own generation—makes sense. After all, it is the peer group, not the parental group, that will provide the child's most direct future collaborators in life-sustaining work and reproduction.

Across cultures and over the span of history, a child's social world is and has been a world largely of other children. In most cultures for which data are available, children beyond the age of 4 or 5 years spend more of their daytime hours with other children than with adults (Konner, 1975; Whiting & Edwards, 1988). What are they doing together? Mostly they are playing. In every culture that has been studied, children play when they have the opportunity, and their play takes certain universal forms (Pellegrini & Bjorklund, 2004; Power, 2000; Schwartzman, 1978). It is also true that in every culture that has been studied, children tend to segregate themselves by sex when they play: Boys play mostly with boys, and girls play mostly with girls (Maccoby, 1998, 2002; Whiting & Edwards, 1988). Through playing with others of their own sex, children develop the gender-specific skills and attitudes of their culture.

Developmental Functions of Play

Play Is a Vehicle for Acquiring Skills

20
What are some universal forms of human play, and what developmental functions do they seem to serve?

◀ **Chapter 4** presents evidence that play evolved in mammals as a means to ensure that the young of the species will practice and become expert at skills that are necessary for their long-term survival and reproduction. Young mammals play at fleeing, chasing, fighting, stalking, and nurturing. The play of young humans is often like that of other young mammals and appears to serve many of

Tag, you're it Children, like all young mammals, enjoy chase games. Such play promotes physical development and skill in escaping from predators and enemies.

the same functions. Children all over the world play chase games, which promote physical stamina, agility, and the development of strategies to avoid getting caught. Play nurturing, often with dolls or other infant substitutes rather than real infants, and play fighting are also universal, and everywhere the former is more prevalent among girls and the latter is more prevalent among boys (Eibl-Eibesfeldt, 1989).

Other universal forms of human play are specific to our species and help children develop human-specific skills (Power, 2000). Children everywhere become good at making things with their hands through constructive play (play at making things), become skilled with language through word play, and exercise their imaginations and planning abilities through social fantasy play. In cultures where children can observe directly the sustenance activities of adults, children focus much of their play on those activities (Gray, 2009; Kamei, 2005). For instance, young boys in hunter-gatherer cultures spend enormous amounts of time at play hunting, such as shooting at butterflies with bows and arrows, and develop great skill in the process.

21
How do observations of two Mexican villages illustrate the role of play in the transmission of cultural skills and values from one generation to the next? How might play promote cultural advancement?

◀ In a study of two Mexican villages, Douglas Fry (1992) showed how children's play reflects and may help transmit a culture's values and skills. The two villages were alike in many ways, and the similarity was reflected in aspects of the children's play. In both communities, for example, boys made toy plows with sticks and used them to furrow the earth as their fathers worked at real plowing in the fields, and girls made pretend tortillas, mimicking their mothers. In one respect, however, the two communities differed markedly.

For generations in La Paz the people had prided themselves on their peaceful-ness and nonviolence, but the same was not true in San Andrés (the villages' names are pseudonyms). Often in San Andrés, but rarely in La Paz, children saw their parents fight physically, heard of fights or even murders among men stemming from sexual jealousy, and themselves were victims of beatings administered by their parents. In his systematic study of the everyday activities of 3- to 8-year-olds, Fry observed that the San Andrés children engaged in about twice as much serious fighting, and about three times as much play fighting, as the La Paz children. When fighting is common in a culture, fighting will apparently be understood intuitively by children as a skill to be practiced not just in anger but also in play, for fun.

Children's play can help create and advance culture as well as reflect it. When the computer revolution began in North America, children, who usually had no use for computers other than play, were in many families the first to become adept with the new technology. They taught their parents how to use computers. Some of the same children—as young adults, but still in the spirit of play—invented new and better computers and computer programs. Many years ago the Dutch cultural historian Johan Huizinga (1944/1970) wrote a book contending that much, if not most, of what we call "high culture"—including art, literature, philosophy, and legal systems—arose originally in the spirit of play where play was extended from childhood into adulthood.

Play as a Vehicle for Learning About Rules and Acquiring Self-Control

In addition to practicing species-typical and culturally valued skills, children may, through play, acquire more advanced understandings of rules and social roles and greater self-control. Both Jean Piaget and Lev Vygotsky—the famous developmental psychologists introduced in **Chapter 11**—developed theories along these lines.

In his book *The Moral Judgment of the Child*, Piaget (1932/1965) argued that un-supervised play with peers is crucial to moral development. He observed that adults use their superior power to settle children's disputes, but when adults are not present, children argue out their disagreements and acquire a new understand-ing of rules based on reason rather than authority. They learn, for example, that rules of games such as marbles are not immutable but are human contrivances de-signed to make the game more interesting and fair and can be changed if everyone agrees. By extension, this helps them understand that the same is true of the social conventions and laws that govern life in democratic societies. Consistent with Piaget's theory, Ann Kruger (1992) found that children showed greater advances in moral reasoning when they discussed social dilemmas with their peers than when they discussed the same dilemmas with their parents. With peers, children engaged actively and thought-fully in the discussions, which led to a higher level of moral reasoning; with parents they were far more passive and less thoughtful.

In an essay on the value of play, Vygotsky (1933/1978) theorized that children learn through play how to control their own impulses and to abide by socially agreed-upon rules and roles—an ability that is crucial to social life. He pointed out that, contrary to common belief, play is not free and spontaneous but is always governed by rules that define the range of permissible actions for each participant. In real life, young children behave spontaneously—they cry when they are hurt, laugh when they are happy, and express their immediate desires. But in play they must suppress their spontaneous urges and behave in ways prescribed by the rules of the game or the role they have agreed to play. Consider, for example,

> -------------------------------**22**
> **What ideas did Piaget and Vygotsky present concerning the value of play in social development? What evidence supports their ideas?**

Let's pretend In sociodramatic play, children plan out situations and abide by the rules and roles they invent.

Laura Dwight

A helping hand In age-mixed play, older children enable younger children to do things that they would not be able to do alone. As a result, younger children acquire new physical and intellectual skills and older children acquire nurturing skills. Age-mixed play is also more frequently gender-mixed than is same-age play.

children playing a game of "house," in which one child is the mommy, another is the baby, and another is the dog. To play this game, each child must keep in mind a conscious conception of how a mommy, a baby, or a dog behaves, and must govern his or her actions in accordance with that conception.

Play, then, according to Vygotsky, has this paradoxical quality: Children freely enter into it, but in doing so they give up some of their freedom. In Vygotsky's view, play in humans evolved at least partly as a means of practicing self-discipline of the sort that is needed to follow social conventions and rules.

Consistent with Vygotsky's view, researchers have found that young children put great effort into planning and enforcing rules in their social fantasy play (Furth, 1996; Garvey, 1990). Children who break the rules—who act like themselves rather than the roles they have agreed to play—are sharply reminded by the others of what they are supposed to do: "Dogs don't sit at the table; you have to get under the table." Also in line with Vygotsky's view, researchers have found positive correlations between the amount of social fantasy play that children engage in and subsequent ratings of their social competence and self-control (Connolly & Doyle, 1984; Elias & Berk, 2002).

The Special Value of Age-Mixed Play

In age-graded school settings, such as recess, children play almost entirely with others who are about the same age as themselves. But in neighborhood settings in our culture, and even more so in cultures that don't have age-graded schools (Whiting & Edwards, 1988), children often play in groups with age spans of several years. Indeed, as Konner (1975) has pointed out, the biological underpinnings of human play must have evolved under conditions in which age-mixed play predominated. Hunter-gatherer communities are small and births within them are widely spaced, so a given child rarely has more than one or two potential playmates who are within a year of his or her own age.

23 - - - - - - - - - - - - - - - - - - ◁ Psychologists have paid relatively little attention to age-mixed play, but the work

What features of age-mixed play may make it particularly valuable to children's development?

that has been done suggests that such play is often qualitatively different from play among age mates. One difference is that it is less competitive; there is less concern about who is best (Feldman, 1997; Feldman & Gray, 1999). An 11-year-old has nothing to gain by proving himself or herself stronger, smarter, or more skilled than a 7-year-old, and the 7-year-old has no chance of proving the reverse. Konner (1972) noted that age-mixed rough-and-tumble play among the !Kung children whom he observed might better be called "gentle-and-tumble," because an implicit rule is that participants must control their movements so that they do not hurt a younger child.

I have studied age-mixed play at an alternative school in the United States, where children from age 4 to 18 intermingle freely. At this school, age mixing appears to be a primary vehicle of education (D. Greenberg, 1992). Young children acquire more advanced interests and skills by observing and interacting with older children, and older children develop skills at nurturing and consolidate some of their own knowledge by helping younger children. We observed this happening in a wide variety of forms of play, including rough-and-tumble, sports of various types, board games, computer play, constructive play (such as play with blocks or with art materials), and fantasy play (Gray & Feldman, 2004). In each of these contexts, to make the game more fun, older children helped younger children understand rules and strategies. Studies of play among siblings who differ by several years in age have yielded similar findings (Brody, 2004).

Unfortunately, our age-graded system of schooling, coupled with the decline in neighborhood play that has occurred in recent times, deprives many children in our culture of a powerful natural source of education—the opportunity to interact closely, over prolonged periods, with other children who are substantially older or younger than themselves.

Gender Differences in Social Development

Life is not the same for girls and boys. That is true not just in our culture but in every culture that has been studied (Maccoby, 1998; Whiting & Edwards, 1988). To some degree, the differences are biological in origin, mediated by hormones (Else-Quest & others, 2006; also see **Chapter 6**). But, as the anthropologist Margaret Mead (1935) noted long ago, the differences also vary from culture to culture and over time within a given culture in ways that cannot be explained by biology alone.

The words *sex* and *gender* are in some contexts used as synonyms, but in typical psychological usage *sex* refers to the clear-cut biological basis for categorizing people as male or female, while *gender* refers to the entire set of differences attributed to males and females, which can vary across cultures (Deaux, 1985). You were born one sex or the other, but from the moment of birth—from the moment that someone announced, "It's a girl!" or "It's a boy!"—you also had a gender. Immediately, in the minds of all who heard the announcement, you were tied through a web of mental associations to all kinds of "girlish" or "boyish" traits, activities, and material belongings. Biological sex differences combined with cultural models and expectations produce the gender differences observed in any given culture.

My tough little boy Researchers have found that fathers generally play more vigorously with their infant sons than with their infant daughters.

Gender Differences in Interactions with Caregivers

Even in early infancy, boys and girls, on average, behave somewhat differently from each other. Newborn boys are more irritable and less responsive to caregivers' voices and faces than are newborn girls (Hittelman & Dickes, 1979; Osofsky & O'Connell, 1977). By 6 months of age, boys squirm more and show more facial expressions of anger than do girls when confined in an infant seat, and girls show more facial expressions of interest and less fussing than do boys when interacting with their mothers (Weinberg & others, 1999). By 13 to 15 months of age, girls are more likely than are boys to comply with their mothers' requests (Kochanska & others, 1998). By 17 months, boys show significantly more physical aggression than do girls (Baillargeon & others, 2007).

Parents and other caregivers behave differently toward girls and boys, beginning at birth. They are, on average, more gentle with girls than with boys; they are more likely to talk to girls and to jostle boys (Maccoby, 1998). Such differences in treatment may in part reflect caregivers' sensitivity and responsiveness to actual differences in the behaviors and preferences of the infant girls and boys, but it also reflects adult expectations that are independent of the infants' behaviors and preferences. In one study, mothers interacted more closely with, talked in a more conversational manner to, and gave fewer direct commands to their infant daughters than to their infant sons, even though the researchers could find no differences in the infants' behavior (Clearfield & Nelson, 2006). In another study, mothers were asked to hold a 6-month-old female infant, who in some cases was dressed as a girl and introduced as Beth, and in other cases was dressed as a boy and introduced as Adam. The mothers talked to Beth more than to Adam, and gave Adam more direct gazes unaccompanied by talk (Culp & others, 1983).

Other research suggests that, regardless of the child's age, adults offer help and comfort more often to girls than to boys and more often expect boys to solve problems on their own. In one experiment, college students were quicker to call for help for a crying infant if they thought it was a girl than if they thought it was a boy (Hron-Stewart, 1988). In another study, mothers of 2-year-old daughters helped their toddlers in problem-solving tasks more than did mothers of 2-year-old sons (Hron-Stewart, 1988). Theorists have speculated that the relatively warmer treatment of girls and greater expectations of self-reliance for boys may lead girls to become more affectionate and sociable and boys to become more self-reliant than they otherwise would (Dweck & others, 1978; MacDonald, 1992).

Adults' assumptions about the different interests and abilities of girls and boys may play a role in the types of careers that the two sexes eventually choose. In particular, parents and teachers often express the belief that math and science are harder and

24

What are some of the ways that girls and boys are treated differently by adults in our culture, and how might such treatment promote different developmental consequences?

FIGURE 12.7 More explanations to boys than to girls At a science museum, parents were much more likely to explain the mechanisms or principles of interactive exhibits to sons than to daughters, regardless of age. (Adapted from Crowley & others, 2001.)

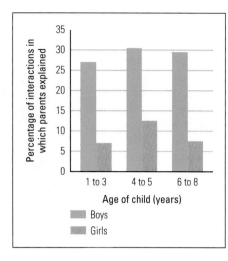

less interesting for girls than for boys. A number of studies suggest that such different expectations influence the way that adults talk about science and math to boys and girls, even when measures of children's abilities and self-reported interests show no such differences (Lindberg & others, 2008; Tenenbaum & Leaper, 2003).

In one study, parents and their young children were observed at interactive exhibits at a science museum (Crowley & others, 2001). The main finding was that parents, both fathers and mothers, were far more likely to explain something about the workings of the exhibits, or the underlying principles being demonstrated, to their sons than to their daughters. This occurred regardless of the age of the child (see Figure 12.7) and despite the fact that the researchers could find no evidence, from analyzing the children's behavior and questions, that the sons were more interested in the exhibits or in the principles being demonstrated than were the daughters. Perhaps such differential treatment helps explain why many more men than women choose careers in the physical sciences.

Gender Identity and its Effects on Children's Behavior

25

How do children mold themselves according to their understanding of gender differences?

Children's gender development may be influenced by adults' differential treatment, but children also actively mold themselves to behave according to their culture's gender conceptions. By the age of 4 or 5, most children have learned quite clearly their culture's stereotypes of male and female roles (Martin & Ruble, 2004; Williams & Best, 1990) and recognize that they themselves are one gender or the other and always will be, an understanding referred to as ***gender identity*** (Kohlberg, 1966). Once they have this understanding, children in all cultures seem to become concerned about projecting themselves as clearly male or female. They attend more closely to people of their own gender and model their behavior accordingly, often in ways that exaggerate the male–female differences they see. When required to carry out a chore that they regard as gender-inappropriate, they often do so in a style that clearly distinguishes them from the other gender. For example, in a culture where fetching water is considered women's work, young boys who are asked to fetch water carry it in a very different manner from that employed by women and girls (Whiting & Edwards, 1988).

From a biological perspective, gender is not an arbitrary concept but is linked to sex, which is linked to reproduction. A tendency toward gender identity may well have evolved as an active assertion of one's sex as well as a means of acquiring culture-specific gender roles. By acting "girlish" and "boyish," girls and boys clearly announce that they are on their way to becoming sexually viable women and men. Researchers have found that young children often create or overgeneralize gender differences (Martin & Ruble, 2004). For example, when preschoolers were told that a particular boy liked a certain sofa and a particular girl liked a certain table, they generalized this to assume that all boys would like the sofa and all girls would like the table (Bauer & Coyne, 1997). Children's active imposition of gender roles upon their world has been likened to their active imposition of grammatical rules upon the language that they hear (Martin & others, 2002).

Children's Self-Imposed Gender Segregation

26

What function might children's self-segregation by gender serve? In our culture, why might boys avoid playing with girls more than the reverse?

In all cultures that have been studied, boys and girls play primarily with others of their own sex (Maccoby, 1998; Pellegrini & others, 2007), and, at least in our culture, such segregation is more common in activities structured by children themselves than in activities structured by adults (Berk & Lewis, 1977; Maccoby, 1990). Even 3-year-olds have been observed to prefer same-sex playmates to opposite-sex playmates (Maccoby & Jacklin, 1987), but the peak of gender segregation, observed in many different settings and cultures, occurs in the age range of 8 to 11 years (Gray & Feldman, 1997; Hartup, 1983; Whiting & Edwards, 1988). In their separate playgroups, boys practice what they perceive to be the masculine activities of their culture, and girls practice what they perceive to be the feminine activities of their culture.

In some settings, children reinforce gender segregation by ridiculing those who cross gender lines, but this ridicule is not symmetrical. Boys who play with girls are much more likely to be teased and taunted by both gender groups than are girls who play with boys (Petitpas & Champagne, 2000; Thorne, 1993). Indeed, girls who prefer to play with boys are often referred to with approval as "tomboys" and retain their popularity with both sexes. Boys who prefer to play with girls are not treated so benignly. Terms like "sissy" or "pansy" are never spoken with approval. Adults, too, express much more concern about boys who play with girls or adopt girlish traits than they do about girls who play with boys or adopt boyish traits (Martin, 1990). Perhaps the difference reflects the culture's overall view that male roles are superior to female roles, which might also help explain why, over the past several decades, many women in our culture have moved into roles that were once regarded as exclusively masculine, while relatively fewer men have moved into roles traditionally considered feminine.

Richard Hutchings/PhotoEdit

Sex-segregated play Even in preschool, girls tend to play with girls and boys with boys. The little girl looking at the truck might want to join the two boys, but she will probably stay with the girls.

Gender Differences in Styles of Play

Girls and boys tend to play differently as well as separately, and the differences are in some ways consistent from culture to culture (Rose & Rudolph, 2006; Whiting & Edwards, 1988). Some social scientists consider boys' and girls' peer groups to be so distinct that they constitute separate subcultures, each with its own values, directing its members along different developmental lines (Maccoby, 1998, 2002; Maltz & Borker, 1982).

The *world of boys* has been characterized as consisting of relatively large, hierarchically organized groups in which individuals or coalitions attempt to prove their superiority through competitive games, teasing, and boasting. A prototypical boys' game is king of the hill, the goal of which is to stand on top and push everyone else down. The *world of girls* has been characterized as consisting of smaller, more intimate groups, in

27

In what ways can girls' and boys' peer groups be thought of as separate subcultures? Why might differences in boys' and girls' play be greater in age-segregated settings than in age-mixed settings?

A lack of symmetry We are much more accepting of the little girl who dresses and acts like a boy (left-hand photo) than we are of the little boy who dresses and acts like a girl. Why?

which cooperative forms of play predominate and competition, although not absent, is more subtle. A prototypical girls' game is jump rope, the goal of which is to keep the action going as long as possible through the coordinated activities of the rope twirlers and the jumper.

The "two-worlds" concept may exaggerate somewhat the typical differences in the social experiences of boys and girls. Most research supporting the concept has been conducted in age-segregated settings, such as school playgrounds and summer camps. At home and in neighborhoods children often play in age-mixed groups. As noted earlier, age-mixed play generally centers less on winning and losing than does same-age play, so age mixing reduces the difference in competitiveness between boys' and girls' play. Moreover, several studies indicate that boys and girls play together more often in age-mixed groups than in age-segregated groups (Ellis & others, 1981; Gray & Feldman, 1997).

Whether or not they play together, boys and girls are certainly interested in each other. On school playgrounds, for example, the separate boys' and girls' groups interact frequently, usually in teasing ways (Thorne, 1993). That interest begins to peak, and interactions between the sexes take on a new dimension, as children enter adolescence.

SECTION REVIEW

The child's development is influenced by play with other children and by gender.

Developing Through Play

➤ Children everywhere play in ways that promote the development of skills needed for their survival. These include culture-specific skills, acquired by observing adults.

➤ Piaget contended that children learn about rules and become better moral reasoners through play, and Vygotsky contended that children develop self-control through play. Contemporary research supports these ideas.

➤ Age-mixed play appears to be less competitive and more conducive to teaching, learning, and development of nurturing skills than is play among age mates.

Gender and Social Development

➤ Adults treat girls and boys differently beginning at birth, at least partly on the basis of socially grounded beliefs about gender. This may help to create or widen some gender differences.

➤ Once gender identity is established, by age 4 or 5, children attend to and mimic the culturally appropriate behaviors for their gender. They also exaggerate gender stereotypes and play increasingly with same-sex peers.

➤ Boys' and girls' groups are in some ways different subcultures. Boys tend to play competitively, in relatively large, hierarchical groups. Girls play more cooperatively, in smaller, more intimate groups. These differences may be muted in age-mixed play.

▮ Adolescence: Breaking Out of the Cocoon

28

Why does adolescence last longer today in our culture than in times past or in some other cultures?

Adolescence is the transition period from childhood to adulthood. It begins with the first signs of puberty (the physical changes leading to reproductive capacity), and it ends when the person is viewed by himself or herself, and by others, as a full member of the adult community. Defined this way, adolescence in our culture begins earlier and ends later than it did in times past or still does in many other cultures. ◄ The physical changes of puberty include a growth spurt in height, as well as changes in sexual organs and body shape toward their adult forms. In North America today the average age at which the growth spurt begins is about 10 in girls and 12 in boys (Eveleth & Tanner, 1990). In contrast, 125 years ago in North America it began an average of 4 years later in both sexes, and it still begins about 4 years later in many pre-industrial cultures (Eveleth & Tanner, 1990). Likewise, menarche—a girl's first menstruation—typically occurs between ages 12 and 13 in North America today but occurred most often between ages 16 and 17 in the 19th century and still occurs at that age or later in hunter-gatherer groups and some other pre-industrial cultures (Worthman, 1999; Zacharias & Wurtman, 1969). The early onset of puberty in industrialized cultures is believed to stem primarily from more food intake and less disease.

Acceptance by self and others into adulthood—the end of adolescence—comes gradually in our culture and has no clear-cut markers. In traditional societies, where adult roles are clearly defined and are learned through the child's direct involvement in the adult world, the transition to adulthood may coincide with one or another of the physical changes near the end of puberty and be officially marked by rites of passage or other celebrations. But our culture lacks such rites, and our laws dole out adult privileges and responsibilities inconsistently over a wide age span. In most states of the United States, young people are first allowed to drive a car at 16, enlist in the military at 17, vote at 18, and purchase alcohol at 21. The legal age for marriage varies from 13 to 21, depending on state of residence, sex, and whether parental permission has been granted. More important, the age at which people actually begin careers or families, often seen as marks of entry into adulthood, varies greatly. The average age for first marriage is currently about 28 in the United States and many other industrialized countries. If you prefer to define adolescence as the teenage years, as many people do, you can think of this section as about adolescence and youth, with *youth* defined as a variable period after about age 20 that precedes one's settling into routines of career or family.

In Erikson's life-span theory, adolescence is the stage of *identity crisis,* the goal of which is to give up one's childhood identity and establish a new identity—including a sense of purpose, a career orientation, and a set of values—appropriate for entry into adulthood (Erikson, 1968). Many developmental psychologists today disagree with Erikson's specific definition of identity and with his idea that the search for identity necessarily involves a "crisis," but nearly all agree that adolescence is a period in which young people either consciously or unconsciously act in ways designed to move themselves from childhood toward adulthood. With an eye on how they affect adolescents' emerging self-identities, we shall look here at adolescents' breaking away from parents, forming closer relationships with peers, risk taking, delinquency, bravery, morality, and sexual explorations.

Shifting from Parents to Peers for Intimacy and Guidance

Breaking Away from Parental Control

"I said, 'Have a nice day,' to my teenage daughter as she left the house, and she responded, 'Will you *please* stop telling me what to do!'" That joke, long popular among parents of adolescents, could be matched by the following story, told by an adolescent: "Yesterday, I tried to really communicate with my mother. I told her how important it is that she trust me and not try to govern everything I do. She responded, 'Oh, sweetie, I'm so glad we have the kind of relationship in which you can be honest and tell me how you really feel. Now, please, if you are going out, wear your warmest coat and be back by 10:30.'"

Adolescence is often characterized as a time of rebellion against parents, but it rarely involves out-and-out rejection. Surveys taken at various times and places over the past several decades have shown that most adolescents admire their parents, accept their parents' religious and political convictions, and claim to be more or less at peace with them (Offer & Schonert-Reichl, 1992; Steinberg, 2001). The typical rebellion, if one occurs at all, is aimed specifically at some of the immediate controls that parents hold over the child's behavior. At the same time that adolescents are asking to be treated more like adults, parents may fear new dangers that can accompany this period of life—such as those associated with sex, alcohol, drugs,

29

What is the typical nature of the so-called adolescent rebellion against parents?

and automobiles—and try to tighten controls instead of loosening them. So adolescence is often marked by conflicts centering on parental authority.

For both sons and daughters, increased conflict with parents is linked more closely to the physical changes of puberty than to chronological age (Steinberg, 1989). If puberty comes earlier or later than is typical, so does the increase in conflict. Such conflict is usually more intense in the early teenage years than later (Steinberg, 2001); by age 16 or so, most teenagers have achieved the balance of independence and dependence they are seeking.

Establishing Closer Relationships with Peers

30

How do young people's friendships change during their teenage years?

As adolescents gain more independence from their parents, they look increasingly to their peers for emotional support. In one study, for example, fourth graders indicated that their parents were their most frequent providers of emotional support, seventh graders indicated that they received almost equal support from their parents and friends, and tenth graders indicated that they received most of their emotional support from friends (Furman & Buhrmester, 1992). When asked to describe the meaning of friendships, adolescents of both genders talk about the sharing of thoughts, feelings, and secrets, whereas younger children are more likely to talk about playing together and sharing material things (Berndt, 1992; Damon & Hart, 1992).

Conforming to Peers

31

What evidence suggests that peer pressure can have negative and positive effects? What difference in attitude about peer pressure is reported to exist in China compared to the United States?

As children approach and enter their teenage years, they become even more concerned than they were before about looking and behaving like their peers. Self-report measures indicate that young people's tendency to conform peaks in the years from about age 10 to 14 and then declines gradually after that (Steinberg & Monahan, 2007). The early teenage years are, quite understandably, the years when parents worry most about possible negative effects of peer pressure. Indeed, teenagers who belong to the same friendship groups are more similar to one another with regard to such risky behaviors as smoking, drinking, drug use, and sexual promiscuity than are teenagers who belong to different groups (Steinberg, 2008a). Such similarity is at least partly the result of selection rather than conformity; people tend to choose friends who have interests and behaviors similar to their own. Still, a number of research studies have shown that, over time, friends become more similar to one another in frequency of risky or unhealthful behaviors than they were originally (Curran & others, 1997; Jaccard & others, 2005).

Western parents and researchers tend to emphasize the negative influences of peers, but adolescents themselves, when questioned, often describe positive peer pressures, such as encouragement to avoid unhealthful behaviors and engage in healthful ones (Steinberg, 2008a). On the basis of extensive studies in China, Xinyin Chen and his colleagues (2003) report that peer pressure is viewed there, by parents and educators as well as by adolescents, much more as a positive force than as a negative one. In China, according to Chen, young people as well as adults place high value on academic achievement, and adolescent peer groups do homework together and encourage one another to excel in school. In the United States, in contrast, peer encouragement for academic achievement is relatively rare (Steinberg, 1996).

Good friends During adolescence, friends become increasingly important as confidants and sources of emotional support.

© Bob Daemmrich/Photo Edit

Increased Rates of Recklessness and Delinquency

On a statistical basis, throughout the world, people are much more likely to engage in disruptive or dangerous actions during adolescence than at other times in life. In Western cultures, rates of theft, assault, murder, reckless driving, unprotected sex, illicit drug use, and general disturbing of the peace all peak between the ages of 15 and 25 (Archer, 2004; Arnett, 1995, 2000). The adolescent peak in recklessness and delinquency is particularly sharp in males, as exemplified in the graphs in Figure 12.8, below.

What causes the increased recklessness and delinquency? Some psychologists have tried to address this question by attempting to discern the underlying cognitive, motivational, or brain characteristics of adolescents that differentiate them from adults. Adolescents have been described as having a *myth of invulnerability*— that is, a false sense that they are protected from the mishaps and diseases that can happen to other people (Elkind, 1978). They have also been described as *sensation seekers*, who enjoy the adrenaline rush associated with risky behavior; as having heightened *irritability* or *aggressiveness*, which leads them to be easily provoked; and as has having *immature inhibitory control centers* in the prefrontal lobes of their brains (Arnett, 1992, 1995; Bradley & Wildman, 2002; Martin & others, 2004; Steinberg, 2008b). Reasonable evidence has been compiled for all of these ideas, but such concepts leave one wondering why adolescents have such seemingly maladaptive characteristics, which can lead to their deaths. Why would natural selection not have weeded out such traits?

"Young man, go to your room and stay there until your cerebral cortex matures"

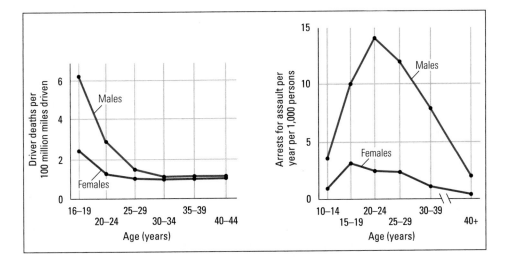

FIGURE 12.8 Evidence of heightened recklessness and aggressiveness in adolescence and youth The top graph is based on an analysis of traffic fatalities in the United States in 1970 by Wilson and Daly (1985, p. 69). The high rate of death for young drivers is probably due to inexperience as well as recklessness, but inexperience can't explain why the rate is so much higher for young men than for young women. The bottom graph, from Campbell (1995, p. 100), shows the rate of arrests for assault in 1989 in the United States, as reported by the U.S. Department of Justice.

Explanations That Focus on Adolescents' Segregation from Adults

One line of explanation focuses on aspects of adolescence that are relatively unique to modern, Western cultures. In this view, adolescent recklessness is largely an aberration of modern times, not a product of natural selection. Terrie Moffitt (1993), for example, suggests that the high rate of delinquency is a pathological side effect of the early onset of puberty and delayed acceptance into legitimate adult society. She cites evidence that the adolescent peak in violence and crime is greater in modern cultures than in traditional cultures, where puberty usually comes later and young people are more fully integrated into adult activities. According to Moffitt, young people past puberty, who are biologically adults, are motivated to enter the adult world in whatever ways are available to them. Sex, alcohol, and crime are understood as adult

‣ - - - - - - - - - - - - - - - 32

What are two theories about how adolescents' segregation from adults might contribute to their recklessness and delinquency?

activities. Crime, in particular, is taken seriously by adults and brings adolescents into the adult world of lawyers, courtrooms, and probation officers. Crime can also bring money and material goods that confer adultlike status.

Moffitt's theory makes considerable sense, but it does not account well for risky adolescent activities that are decidedly not adultlike. Adults do not "surf" on the tops of fast-moving trains or drive around wildly in stolen cars and deliberately crash them, as adolescents in various cities have been observed to do (Arnett, 1995).

In a theory that is in some ways the opposite of Moffitt's, Judith Harris (1995, 1998) suggests that adolescents engage in risky and delinquent activities not to join the adult world but to set themselves apart from it. Just as they dress differently from adults, they also act differently. According to Harris, their concern is not with acceptance by adults but with acceptance by their own peers—the next generation of adults. Harris agrees with Moffitt that our culture's segregation of adolescents from adult society contributes to adolescents' risky and sometimes delinquent behavior, but she disagrees about the mechanism. To Moffitt, such segregation reduces the chance that adolescents can find safe, legitimate ways to behave as adults; to Harris it does so by producing adolescent subcultures whose values are relatively unaffected by those of adults. Moffitt's and Harris's theories may each contain part of the truth. Perhaps adolescents seek adultlike status while, at the same time, identifying with the behaviors and values of their adolescent subculture.

An Evolutionary Explanation of the "Young-Male Syndrome"

Neither Moffitt nor Harris addresses the question of why risky and delinquent activities are so much more readily pursued by young males than by young females or why they occur, at least to some degree, in cultures that do not segregate adolescents from adults. Even in hunter-gatherer communities, young males take risks that appear foolish to their elders and die at disproportionate rates from such mishaps as falling from trees that they have climbed too rapidly (Hewlett, 1988). To address such issues, Margo Wilson and Martin Daly (1985; Daly & Wilson, 1990) have discussed what they call "the young-male syndrome" from an evolutionary perspective, focusing on the potential value of such behavior for reproduction.

33 –
How have Wilson and Daly explained the recklessness and delinquency of adolescent males in evolutionary terms?
– – – – – – – – – – – – – – – – – – – –

◄ As discussed in **Chapter 3,** among mammals in general, the number of potential offspring a male can produce is more variable than the number a female can produce and is more closely tied to status. In our species' history, males who took risks to achieve higher status among their peers may well have produced more offspring, on average, than those who didn't, so genes promoting that tendency may have been passed along. This view gains credibility from studies in which young women report that they indeed are sexually attracted to men who succeed in risky, adventurous actions, even if such actions serve no social good (Kelly & Dunbar, 2001; Kruger & others, 2003). In hunter-gatherer times, willingness to take personal risks in hunting and defense of the tribe and family may well have been an especially valuable male trait. According to Wilson and Daly, train surfing, wild driving, careless tree climbing, and seemingly senseless acts of violence are best understood as ways in which young men gain status by demonstrating their fearlessness and valor.

Pure recklessness Risk taking reaches a peak in adolescence and young adulthood, especially among males.

In support of their thesis, Wilson and Daly point to evidence that a high proportion of violence among young men is triggered by signs of disrespect or challenges to status. One young man insults another, and the other responds by punching, knifing, or shooting him. Such actions are more likely to occur if other young men are present than if they aren't. No intelligent person whose primary goal was murder would choose to kill in front of witnesses, but young men who commit murder commonly do so in front of witnesses. Young men also drive more recklessly when another young person is in the car than when they drive alone, while young women's driving appears to be unaffected by the presence or absence of passengers (Jackson & Gray, 1976).

Of course, not all young males are reckless or violent, but that does not contradict Wilson and Daly's thesis. Those who see safer paths to high status—such as through college, inherited wealth, or prestigious jobs—have less need to risk their lives for prestige and are less likely to do so.

Females also exhibit a peak in violence during adolescence and youth, although it is a much smaller peak than men's (look back at Figure 12.8). Anne Campbell (1995, 2002) has argued that when young women do fight physically, they, like young men, do so for reasons that can be understood from an evolutionary perspective. According to Campbell's evidence, young women fight most often in response to gossip or insults about their alleged sexual activities, which could tarnish their standing with men, and in instances when one woman appears to be trying to attract another's boyfriend.

An Expanded Moral Vision and Moral Sense of Self

Adolescence seems to bring out both the worst and the best in people. Adolescents can be foolhardy and violent, but they can also be heroic and work valiantly toward making the world better. Adolescence is, among other things, a period of rapid growth in the sophistication of moral reasoning and a time in which many people develop moral self-images that guide their actions.

Advancement on Kohlberg's Scale of Moral Reasoning

Over the past 45 years or so, most research on moral development has been based on a theory and methods developed originally by Lawrence Kohlberg. Kohlberg assessed moral reasoning by posing hypothetical dilemmas to people—primarily to adolescents—and asking them how they believed the protagonist should act and why. In one dilemma, for example, a man must decide whether or not to steal a certain drug under conditions in which that theft is the only way to save his wife's life. To evaluate the level of moral reasoning, Kohlberg was concerned not with whether people answered yes or no to such dilemmas but with the reasons they gave to justify their answers. Drawing partly on his research findings and partly on concepts gleaned from the writings of moral philosophers, Kohlberg (1984) proposed that moral reasoning develops through a series of stages, which are outlined in Table 12.1.

> **34**
> How did Kohlberg assess moral reasoning? How can his stages be described as the successive broadening of one's social perspective? How does research using Kohlberg's system help explain adolescent idealism?

TABLE 12.1 Kohlberg's stages of moral reasoning

The quotations in each stage description exemplify how a person at that stage might justify a man's decision to steal an expensive drug that is needed to save his wife's life.

Stage 1: Obedience and punishment orientation

Reasoners in this stage focus on direct consequences to themselves. An action is bad if it will result in punishment, good if it will result in reward. "If he lets his wife die, he will get in trouble."

Stage 2: Self-interested exchanges

Reasoners here understand that different people have different self-interests, which sometimes come into conflict. To get what you want, you have to make a bargain, giving up something in return. "It won't bother him much to serve a little jail term if he still has his wife when he gets out."

Stage 3: Interpersonal accord and conformity

Reasoners here try to live up to the expectations of others who are important to them. An action is good if it will improve a person's relationships with significant others, bad if it will harm those relationships. "His family will think he's an inhuman husband if he doesn't save his wife."

Stage 4: Law-and-order morality

Reasoners here argue that to maintain social order, each person should resist personal pressures and feel duty-bound to follow the laws and conventions of the larger society. "It's a husband's duty to save his wife. When he married her he vowed to protect her."

Stage 5: Human-rights and social-welfare morality

Reasoners here balance their respect for laws with ethical principles that transcend specific laws. Laws that fail to promote the general welfare or that violate ethical principles can be changed, reinterpreted, or in some cases flouted. "The law isn't really set up for these circumstances. Saving a life is more important than following this law."

Note: The quotations are based on examples in Kohlberg (1984) and Rest (1986). A sixth stage, which emphasized universal ethical principles almost to the exclusion of other considerations, has been dropped in current versions, because of failure to find people who reason in accordance with it.

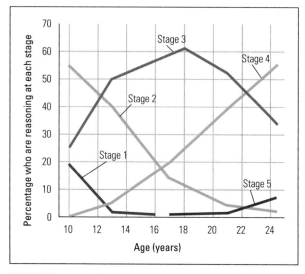

FIGURE 12.9 Changes in moral reasoning from age 10 to 24 This graph, based on a longitudinal study of males from a relatively high socioeconomic background, shows the percentage of subjects at each age who were reasoning at each of Kohlberg's stages. Notice the sharp decline of Stages 1 and 2 reasoning during early adolescence, the rise and fall of Stage 3 reasoning, and the consistent increase of Stage 4 reasoning during adolescence and young adulthood. Little Stage 5 reasoning was found, but it, too, increased with age. (Adapted from Colby & others, 1983.)

35
What ideas about moral development have been derived from studying morally committed adolescents?

As you study the table on page 461, notice the logic underlying Kohlberg's theory of moral reasoning. Each successive stage takes into account a broader portion of the social world than does the previous one. The sequence begins with thought of oneself alone (Stage 1) and then progresses to encompass other individuals directly involved in the action (Stage 2), others who will hear about and evaluate the action (Stage 3), society at large (Stage 4), and, finally, universal principles that concern all of humankind (Stage 5).

According to Kohlberg, the stages represent a true developmental progression in the sense that, to reach any given stage, a person must first pass through the preceding ones. Thinking within one stage and discovering the limitations of that way of thinking provide the impetus for progression to the next. Kohlberg did not claim that everyone goes through the entire sequence; in fact, his research suggested that few people go beyond Stage 4, and many stop at Stage 2 or Stage 3. Nor did he link his stages to specific ages; but he did contend that adolescence and young adulthood are the times when advancement to the higher stages is most likely to occur. Figure 12.9 illustrates the results of one long-term study that supports Kohlberg's claim about the rapid advancement of moral reasoning during adolescence.

Kohlberg's theory is about moral reasoning, which is not the same thing as moral action. Kohlberg recognized that one can be a high-powered moral philosopher without being a moral person, and vice versa, yet he argued that the ability to think abstractly about moral issues does help account for the idealism and moral commitment of youth. In line with this contention, several research studies found that adolescents who exhibited the highest levels of moral reasoning were also the most likely to help others, to volunteer to work for social causes, or to refrain from taking part in actions that harm other people (Haan & others, 1968; Kuther & Higgins-D'Alessandro, 2000; Muhlberger, 2000).

Developing a Moral Image of Oneself

Another way to study moral development is to identify individuals who have distinguished themselves through moral actions and then to try to understand how their experiences and thoughts contributed to their moral commitment. Daniel Hart and his colleagues (1995) took this approach in a study of 15 exceptionally morally committed young people residing in low-income, inner-city neighborhoods in Camden, New Jersey. They had resisted the temptations of crime, drugs, and violence around them and were volunteering large amounts of time to improving their community

Brave youth Rebellions are often spearheaded by young people who combine moral principles with relative fearlessness. Shown here is a young Chinese protester following clashes with military forces during the 1989 pro-democracy demonstrations in Beijing's Tiananmen Square.

and the lives of those within it. Extensive interviews revealed that these adolescents were motivated not by a selfless sense of duty or abstract principles of right and wrong, as Kohlberg's theory might predict, but, rather, by their intense personal investment in doing the right thing. Being moral and setting good examples for others were core aspects of their self-images, so their community services were acts of self-assertion, not of self-denial. It felt good to them to help, and it would hurt them not to.

Some of these young people developed their moral self-images in reaction to specific acts of violence they saw in their neighborhoods. For instance, one 17-year-old African American youth became committed to civic action and personal morality after his older sister was murdered. He developed the view that young people saw too many bad examples, and he became determined to be a good example himself.

Perhaps the most common influence for all these people, however, was the presence of at least one adult, usually a parent, who exemplified moral virtue and had a warm relationship with the adolescent. Other studies of morally committed people, of various ages and from a variety of backgrounds, have likewise revealed the value of good parental models (Colby & Damon, 1995; Snyder & Omoto, 1992; White & Matawie, 2004). Young people may reject the specific controls that their parents attempt to exert over them, yet may guide their own actions by the values and virtues they perceive in their parents.

Sexual Explorations

Adolescence is first and foremost the time of sexual blooming. Pubertal hormones act on the body to make it reproductively functional and on the brain to heighten greatly the level of sexual desire (discussed in **Chapter 6**). Girls and boys who previously watched and teased each other from the safety of their same-sex groups become motivated to move closer together, to get to know each other, to touch in ways that aren't just teasing. The new thoughts and actions associated with all these changes can bring on fear, exhilaration, dread, pride, shame, and bewilderment—sometimes all at once.

In their early dating, teenagers who have grown more or less separately in the "world of boys" and the "world of girls" come together and learn how to communicate with one another. For boys it may be a matter of learning how to pay closer attention to another's needs and to speak in a more accommodating, less assertive manner. For girls it may often be a matter of learning to be more assertive. One study found that 10th graders' discussions with their romantic partner were more difficult than their discussions either with a close same-sex friend or with their own mother (Furman & Shomaker, 2008). More negativity was expressed and there was more failure in communication. Yet, when asked, teenagers commonly regard their romantic relationship as their closest relationship and their most important source of emotional support (Collins & others, 2009). Longitudinal studies indicate, not surprisingly, that success in developing emotional intimacy in early romantic relationships is highly predictive of eventual success in marriage (Karney & others, 2007).

Gay pride and social change For those whose sexual orientation is not the culture's ideal, the sexual awakening of adolescence can be especially difficult. Increasingly, support groups have been established by and for members of the gay and lesbian community, which offer opportunities for education, empowerment, comfort, and opportunities to work for social change that reduces the stigma of homosexuality.

© Jim West/The Image Works

Problems Associated with Emerging Sexuality

As a culture, we glorify sex and present highly sexual images of teenagers in advertisements and movies; yet, at the same time, we typically disapprove of sex among the real teenagers of everyday life. Teenage sex is associated in the public mind with delinquency, and, indeed, the youngest teenagers to have sexual intercourse are often those most involved in delinquent or antisocial activities (Capaldi & others, 1996). Earliest intercourse usually occurs surreptitiously, often without benefit of adult advice, and often without a condom or other protection against pregnancy and sexually transmitted diseases.

In the United States in recent times, roughly 8 percent of teenage females aged 15 to 19 became pregnant in any given year (Guttmacher Institute, 2004). About half of these pregnancies were terminated by abortion, and most of the rest resulted in births. Most teenage pregnancies occurred outside of marriage, often to mothers who were not in a position to care for their babies adequately. The good news is that the rate of teenage pregnancy has fallen, from a peak of about 12 percent reached in the late 1980s, and it may be declining further still. The decline apparently stems primarily from a sharp increase in teenagers' use of condoms and other birth control methods, which itself appears to be a result of increased sex education in schools and parents' greater willingness to discuss sex openly with their children and teenagers (Abma & others, 2004).

36

What correlations have been observed between sex education and rates of teenage pregnancy?

The United States, however, still lags behind the rest of the industrialized world in sex education and in use of birth control by teenagers, and still has the highest teenage pregnancy rate of any industrialized nation. Such countries as Germany, France, and the Netherlands have teenage pregnancy rates that are less than one-fourth the rate in the United States (Abma & others, 2004), despite the fact that their rates of teenage sexual activity are equivalent to that in the United States.

Another long-standing problem arises from the persistent double standard regarding sexuality for girls and boys, which probably stems from biological as well as cultural influences. Not just in our culture, but apparently everywhere, boys are more often encouraged in their sexual adventures, and more likely to feel proud of them, than are girls (Gordon & Gilgun, 1987; Michael & others, 1994). Boys, more often than girls, say that they are eager to have sex for the sheer pleasure of it, and girls, more often than boys, equate sex with love or say that they would have intercourse only with someone they would marry. One index of this difference is depicted in Figure 12.10, which shows results of a survey conducted in the United States in 2002 (Abma & others, 2004). Far more young women than young men reported that they did not want their first sexual intercourse to happen at the time that it did happen. A separate analysis showed that the younger a teenage female was when she had her first intercourse, the less likely she was to have wanted it to happen.

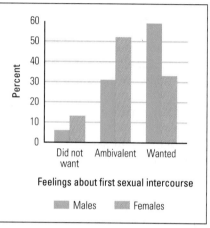

FIGURE 12.10 A difference in desire This graph shows differences in the degree to which young males and females wanted their first sexual intercourse to happen when it did happen, according to their own reports. (Adapted from Abma & others, 2004.)

37 How might the double standard regarding boys' and girls' sexuality contribute to the incidence of date rape?

One consequence of the sex difference in sexual eagerness is the high frequency of date rape. In a survey taken some years ago, 6 percent of incoming college women said that they had been raped during their high school or junior high years, and an additional 33 percent said that they had experienced at least one serious form of sexual victimization short of full rape (Himelein & others, 1994). Other research suggests that rates of rape of non-college-bound young women are even higher (Rickert & others, 2004). To some degree, such events may be attributable to social pressure experienced by young men to have sexual intercourse. They may also have heard from peers, and from society at large, that a woman's resistance is a natural part of the process, or even that women secretly want to be forced to have sex—a notion belied by studies showing that all forms of sexual coercion are extremely negative, and often traumatic, experiences for the victim (Gordon & Gilgun, 1987).

Evolutionary Explanation of Sex Differences in Sexual Eagerness

38 How can the sex difference in desire for uncommitted sex be explained in evolutionary terms?

In culture after culture, young men are more eager than young women to have sexual intercourse without a long-term commitment (Buss, 1994, 1995; Schmitt, 2003). Why? The standard evolutionary explanation is founded on the theory of parental investment, developed by Robert Trivers (1972) to account for sex differences in courtship and mating in all animal species. According to the theory (discussed more fully in **Chapter 3**), the sex that pays the greater cost in bearing and rearing young will—in any species—be the more discriminating sex in choosing when and with whom to copulate, and the sex that pays the lesser cost will be the more aggressive in seeking copulation with multiple partners.

The theory can be applied to humans in a straightforward way. Sexual intercourse can cause pregnancy in women but not in men, so a woman's interest frequently lies in reserving intercourse until she can afford to be pregnant and has found a mate who will help her and their potential offspring over the long haul. In contrast, a man loses little and may gain much—in the amoral economics of natural selection—through uncommitted sexual intercourse with many women. Some of those women may succeed in raising his children, sending copies of his genes into the next generation, at great cost to themselves and no cost to him. Thus natural selection may well have produced an instinctive tendency for women to be more sexually restrained than men.

How Teenage Sexuality May Depend on Conditions of Rearing

A key word in the last sentence of the preceding paragraph is *tendency*. Great variation on the dimension of sexual restraint versus promiscuity exists within each sex, both across cultures and within any given culture (Belsky & others, 1991; Small, 1993). As in any game of strategy, the most effective approach that either men or women can take in courtship and sex depends very much on the strategy taken by the other sex. In communities where women successfully avoid and shun men who seek to behave promiscuously, promiscuity proves fruitless for men and the alternative strategy of fidelity works best. Conversely, in communities where men rarely stay around to help raise their offspring, a woman who waits for "Mr. Right" may wait forever. Cross-cultural studies have shown that promiscuity prevails among both men and women in cultures where men devote little care to young, and sexual restraint prevails in cultures where men devote much care (Barber, 2003; Draper & Harpending, 1988; Marlowe, 2003).

Some researchers have theorized that natural selection may have predisposed humans to be sensitive to cues in childhood that predict whether one or the other sexual strategy will be more successful. One such cue may be the presence or absence of a caring father at home. According to a theory originated by Patricia Draper and Henry Harpending (1982), the presence of a caring father leads girls to grow up assuming that men are potentially trustworthy providers and leads boys to grow up assuming that they themselves will be such providers; these beliefs promote sexual restraint and the seeking of long-term commitments in both sexes. If a caring father is not present, according to the theory, girls grow up assuming that men are untrustworthy "cads" rather than "dads," and that assumption leads them to flaunt their sexuality to extract what they can from men in short-term relationships; and boys grow up assuming that long-term commitments to mates and care of children are not their responsibilities, and that assumption leads them to go from one sexual conquest to another. These assumptions may not be verbally expressed or even conscious, but are revealed in behavior.

In support of their theory, Draper and Harpending (1982, 1988) presented evidence that even within a given culture and social class, adolescents raised by a mother alone are generally more promiscuous than those raised by a mother and father together. In one early study, teenage girls who were members of the same community playground group and were similar to one another in socioeconomic class were observed for their degrees of flirtatiousness, both with boys on the playground and with an adult male interviewer. Girls who were raised by a mother alone—after divorce early in the girl's childhood—were, on average, much more flirtatious than girls who still had a father at home (Hetherington, 1972). Other, more recent studies have revealed that girls raised by a mother alone are much more likely to become sexually active in their early teenage years and to become pregnant as teenagers than are girls raised by a mother and father (Ellis, 2004; Ellis & others, 2003). The results of two studies, conducted in the United States and New Zealand, are depicted in Figure 12.11 (Ellis & others, 2003).

Researchers have also found that girls raised in father-absent homes tend to go through puberty earlier than do those raised in homes where a father is present (Belsky, 2007; Ellis, 2004). This difference has even been shown within families, in a study comparing the age of menarche for full sisters (Tither & Ellis, 2008). In

─ 39

How can sexual restraint and promiscuity, in both sexes, be explained as adaptations to different life conditions? What evidence suggests that the presence or absence of a father at home, during childhood, may tip the balance toward one strategy or the other?

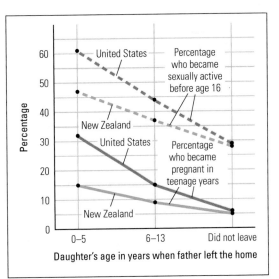

FIGURE 12.11 Effect of fathers' absence on daughters' rates of early sexual activity and teenage pregnancy These data came from two large-scale studies, one in the United States and one in New Zealand. The rates of early sexual activity and teenage pregnancy were statistically adjusted to factor out possible confounding variables, including race, socioeconomic class, the mother's age at first birth, family life stress, parental discipline style, degree of parental monitoring, and neighborhood dangers. (Adapted from Ellis & others, 2003.)

A matter of time and place

Victorians were probably somewhat less concerned with propriety and contemporary Western couples are probably somewhat more ambivalent about sexual freedom than these illustrations suggest. Nevertheless, permissible sexual behavior varies greatly from culture to culture. Across cultures, sexual promiscuity correlates positively with a high divorce rate and a low rate of paternal support of children.

cases where the father left the family, the younger sisters—the ones who were still young children when the father left—reached menarche at an earlier age than did the older sisters. Since the sisters in each pair had the same mother and father, this consistent difference must have been the result of a difference in experience, not a difference in genes. Early puberty may be part of the mechanism through which experiences at home affect the onset of sexual activity.

Draper and Harpending's theory is still controversial, though an increasing amount of evidence supports it (Belsky, 2007). Regardless of whether or not the theory eventually proves to be true, it nicely illustrates the attempt of many contemporary psychologists to understand the life course in terms of alternative strategies that are at least partly prepared by evolution but are brought selectively to the fore by life experience.

SECTION REVIEW

Adolescence is a period of breaking away and developing an adult identity.

Shifting from Parents to Peers	Recklessness and Delinquency	The Moral Self	Sexual Explorations
➤ Adolescent conflict with parents generally centers on the desire for greater independence from parental control.	➤ Risky and delinquent behaviors are more frequent in adolescence than in other life stages.	➤ In Kohlberg's theory, moral reasoning develops in stages, progressing in breadth of social perspective. Rapid advancement in moral reasoning often occurs in adolescence.	➤ Across cultures, rates of teenage pregnancy are inversely related to the availability of sex education and contraceptives.
➤ Increasingly, adolescents turn to one another rather than to their parents for emotional support.	➤ Segregation from adults may promote delinquency by depriving adolescents of positive adult ways to behave or by creating an adolescent subculture divorced from adult values.	➤ A study of morally committed adolescents suggests that their moral actions were rooted in their self-images as moral persons who set good examples for others.	➤ Sex differences in eagerness to have sex can be explained in terms of differences in parental investment.
➤ Peer pressure can have positive as well as negative influences.	➤ Risky and delinquent behavior is especially common in young males. It may serve to enhance status, ultimately as part of competition to attract females.		➤ An evolution-based theory, supported by correlational research, suggests that the presence or absence of a father at home may affect the sexual strategy—restraint or promiscuity—chosen by offspring.

▮ Adulthood: Finding Satisfaction in Love and Work

In his life-span theory, Erikson (1963) proposed that establishing intimate, caring relationships and finding fulfillment in work are the main tasks of early and middle adulthood. In this respect he was following the lead of Sigmund Freud (1935/1960), who defined emotional maturity as the capacity to love and to work. Some psychologists believe that adult development follows a predictable sequence of crises or problems to be resolved (Erikson, 1963; Levinson, 1986), while others contend that the course of adulthood in our modern culture is extraordinarily variable and unpredictable (Neugarten, 1979, 1984). But in essentially every psychological theory of adult development, caring and working are the two threads that weave the fabric of adulthood.

Love

We are a romantic species. In every culture for which data are available, people describe themselves as falling in love (Fisher, 2004; Jankowiak & Fischer, 1991). We are also a marrying species. In every culture, adults of child-producing age enter into long-term unions sanctioned by law or social custom, in which the two members implicitly or explicitly promise to care for each other and the offspring they produce (Fisher, 1992; Rodseth & others, 1991), although cultures vary greatly in the degree to which people abide by those promises. Love and marriage do not necessarily go together, but they often do, and in most cultures their combination is considered ideal. In some cultures people fall in love and then get married; in others they get married—through an arrangement made by the couple's parents—and then, if fate works as hoped for, fall in love. Researchers have attempted to understand the underlying psychological elements of romantic love and to learn why some marriages are happy and others are not.

Romantic Love Viewed as Adult Attachment

Romantic love is similar in form, and perhaps in underlying mechanism, to the attachment that infants develop with their parents (Diamond, 2004; Hazan & Shaver, 1994). Close physical contact, caressing, and gazing into each other's eyes are crucial to the early formation of both types of relationships, and cooing and baby talk are common. A sense of fusion with the other reigns when all is well, and a feeling of exclusivity—that the other person could not be replaced by anyone else—prevails. The partners feel most secure and confident when they are together and may show physiological evidence of distress when separated (Feeney & Kirkpatrick, 1996).

The emotional bond is not simply a by-product of shared pleasures. In long-married couples it may exist even when the two have few interests in common. Sometimes the bond reveals its full intensity only after separation or divorce or the death of one partner. Common experiences in such cases are intense anxiety, depression, and feelings of loneliness or emptiness that are not relieved even by highly supportive friends and an active social life (Stroebe & others, 1996; Weiss, 1975).

As with infants' attachments with their caregivers, the attachments that adults form with romantic partners can be classed as *secure* (characterized by comfort), *anxious* (characterized by excessive worry about love or lack of it from the partner), or *avoidant* (characterized by little expression of intimacy or by ambivalence about commitment). Studies using questionnaires and interviews have revealed continuity between people's descriptions of their adult romantic attachments and their recollections of their childhood relationships with their parents (Fraley, 2002; Mikulincer & Shaver, 2007). People who recall their relationships with parents as warm and secure typically describe their romantic relationships in similar terms, and those who recall anxieties and ambiguities in their relationships with parents tend to describe analogous anxieties and ambiguities in their romances. Such continuity could stem from a number of possible causes, including a tendency for adult experiences to color the person's memories of childhood. Most attachment researchers, however, interpret it as support for a theory developed by Bowlby (1982), who suggested that people form mental models of close relationships based on their early experiences with their primary caregivers and then carry those models into their adult relationships (Fraley & Brumbaugh, 2004).

40

How is romantic love like infant attachment? What evidence suggests continuity in attachment quality between infancy and adulthood?

Ingredients of Marital Success

In the sanitized version of the fairy tale (but not in the Grimm brothers' original), love allows the frog prince and the child princess to transform each other into perfect human adults who marry and live happily ever after. Reality is not like that. Roughly half of new marriages in North America are predicted to end in divorce (Bramlett & Mosher, 2002), and even among couples who don't divorce, many are unhappy in marriage. Why do some marriages work while others fail?

In interviews and on questionnaires, happily married partners consistently say that they like each other; they think of themselves not just as husband and wife but also as best friends and confidants (Buehlman & others, 1992; Lauer & Lauer, 1985). They use the term *we* more than *I* as they describe their activities, and they tend to value their interdependence more than their independence. They also talk about their individual commitment to the marriage, their willingness to go more than halfway to carry the relationship through difficult times.

Happily married couples apparently argue as often as unhappily married couples do, but they argue more constructively (Gottman, 1994; Gottman & Krokoff, 1989). They genuinely listen to each other, focus on solving the problem rather than "winning" or proving the other wrong, show respect rather than contempt for each other's views, refrain from bringing up past hurts or grievances that are irrelevant to the current issue, and intersperse their arguments with positive comments and humor to reduce the tension. Disagreement or stress tends to draw them together, in an effort to resolve the problem and to comfort each other, rather than to drive them apart (Murray & others, 2003).

In happy marriages, both partners are sensitive to the unstated feelings and needs of the other (Gottman, 1998; Mirgain & Cordova, 2007). In contrast, in unhappy marriages, there is often a lack of symmetry in this regard; the wife perceives and responds to the husband's unspoken needs, but the husband does not perceive and respond to hers (Gottman, 1994, 1998). Perhaps this helps explain why, in unhappy marriages, the wife typically feels more unhappy and manifests more physiological distress than does her partner (Gottman, 1994; Levenson & others, 1993). Such observations bring to mind the differing styles of interaction and communication shown by girls and boys in their separate play groups. Researchers have found that in all sorts of relationships, not just marriages, women are on average better than men at attending to and understanding others' unspoken emotions and needs (Thomas & Fletcher, 2003). Success in marriage may often depend on the husband's willingness and ability to acquire some of the intimacy skills that he practiced less, as a child, than did his wife.

41

What are some characteristics of happily married couples? Why might marital happiness depend even more on the husband's capacity to adjust than on the wife's?

Employment

Work, of course, is first and foremost a means of making a living, but it is more than that. It occupies an enormous portion of adult life. Work can be tedious and mindnumbing or exciting and mind-building. At its best, work is for adults what play is for children. It brings them into social contact with their peers outside the family, poses interesting problems to solve and challenges to meet, promotes development of physical and intellectual skills, and is fun.

The Value of Occupational Self-Direction

In surveys of workers, people most often say they enjoy their work if it is (a) complex rather than simple, (b) varied rather than routine, and (c) not closely supervised by someone else (Galinsky & others, 1993; Kohn, 1980). Sociologist Melvin Kohn refers to this much-desired constellation of job characteristics as *occupational self-direction*. A job high in occupational self-direction is one in which the worker makes many choices and decisions throughout the workday. Research suggests that jobs of this sort, despite their high demands, are for most people less stressful—as measured by effects on workers' mental and physical health—than are jobs in which workers make few choices and are closely supervised (Spector, 2002). Research also suggests that such jobs promote certain positive personality changes.

In a massive, long-term study, conducted in both the United States and Poland, Kohn and his colleague Kazimierz Slomczynski found that workers who moved into jobs that were high in self-direction, from jobs that were low in that quality, changed psychologically in certain ways, relative to other workers (Kohn & Slomczynski, 1990). Over their time in the job, they became more intellectually flexible, not just at work but in their approaches to all areas of life. They began to value self-direction more than they had before, in others as well as in themselves. They became less authoritarian and more democratic in their approaches to child rearing; that is, they became less concerned with obedience for its own sake and more concerned with their children's abilities to make decisions. Kohn and Slomczynski also tested the children. They found that the children of workers in jobs with high self-direction were more self-directed and less conforming than children of workers whose jobs entailed less self-direction. Thus the job apparently affected the psychology not just of the workers but also of the workers' children.

42

What evidence suggests that the type of job one has can alter one's way of thinking and style of parenting, and can influence the development of one's children?

All these effects occurred regardless of the salary level or prestige level of the job. In general, blue-collar jobs were not as high in self-direction as white-collar jobs, but when they were as high, they had the same effects. Kohn and Slomczynski contend that the effects they observed on parenting may be adaptive for people whose social class determines the kinds of jobs available to them. In settings where people must make a living by obeying others, it may be sensible to raise children to obey and not question. In settings where people's living depends on their own decision making, it makes more sense to raise children to question authority and think independently.

Occupational self-direction
Self-employed people, and others who make most of their own decisions throughout a typical workday, learn to think independently and question authority, and they tend to raise their children to do the same. They are also far more likely to enjoy their work than are people who work under the thumb of a micromanaging boss.

Balancing Out-of-Home and At-Home Work

Women, more often than men, hold two jobs—one outside the home and the other inside. Although men today spend much more time at housework and child care than they did in decades past, the average man is still less involved in these tasks than the average woman (Barnett & Hyde, 2001; Deutsch, 2001). Moreover, in dual-career families, women typically feel more conflict between the demands of family and those of work than do men (Bagger & others, 2008; McElwain & others, 2005).

43

What difference has been found between husbands' and wives' enjoyment of out-of-home and at-home work? How did the researchers explain that difference?

◀ Despite the traditional stereotype of who "belongs" where—or maybe because of it—some research suggests that wives enjoy their out-of-home work more than their at-home work, while the opposite is true for husbands. Reed Larson and his colleagues (1994) asked 55 working-class and middle-class married parents of school-age children to wear pagers as they went about their daily activities. The pagers beeped at random times during the daytime and evening hours, and at each beep the person filled out a form to describe his or her activity and emotional state just prior to the beep. Over the whole set of reports, wives and husbands did not differ in their self-rated happiness, but wives rated themselves happier at work than at home and husbands rated themselves happier at home than at work. These results held even when the specific type of activity reported at work or at home was the same for the two. When men did laundry or vacuumed at home, they said they enjoyed it; when women did the same, they more often said they were bored or angry. Why this difference?

The men's greater enjoyment of housework could stem simply from the fact that they did it less than their wives, but that explanation doesn't hold for the women's greater enjoyment of out-of-home work. Even the wives who worked away from home for as many hours as their husbands did, at comparable jobs, enjoyed that work more than their husbands did. Larson and his colleagues suggest that both differences derived from the men's and women's differing perceptions of their choices and obligations. Men enjoyed housework because they didn't really consider it their responsibility; they did it by choice and as a gallant means of "helping out." Women did housework because they felt that they had to; if they didn't do it, nobody else would, and visitors might assume that a dirty house was the woman's fault. Conversely, the men had a greater sense of obligation, and reduced sense of choice, concerning their out-of-home work. They felt that it was their duty to support their family in this way. Although the wives did not experience more actual on-the-job choice in Kohn's sense of occupational self-direction than their husbands did, they apparently had a stronger global belief that their out-of-home work was optional.

As Larson and his colleagues point out, the results do match a certain traditional stereotype: Men "slave" at work and come home to relax, and women "slave" at home and go out to relax. What's interesting is that the very same activity can be slaving for one and relaxing for the other, depending apparently on the feeling of obligation or choice.

Growing Old

According to current projections of life expectancy, and taking into account the greater longevity of college graduates compared with the rest of the population, the majority of you who are reading this book will live past your 80th birthday. How will you change as you grow beyond middle adulthood into old age?

Some young people fear old age. There is no denying that aging entails loss. We lose gradually our youthful looks and some of our physical strength, agility, sensory acuity, mental quickness, and memory. We lose some of our social roles (especially those related to employment) and some of our authority (as people take us less seriously). We lose loved ones who die before we do, and, of course, with the passing of each year we lose a year from our own life span.

Yet, if you ask the elderly, old age is not as bad as it seems to the young. In one study, the ratings that younger adults gave for their expected life satisfaction in late adulthood were much lower than the actual life-satisfaction scores obtained from people who had reached old age (Borges & Dutton, 1976). Research studies, using a variety of methods, have revealed that elderly people, on average, report greater current enjoyment of life than do middle-aged people, and middle-aged people report greater enjoyment than do young adults (Mroczek, 2001; Sheldon & Kasser, 2001). This finding has been called the "paradox of aging": Objectively, life looks worse in old age—there are more pains and losses—but subjectively, it feels better. As we age, our priorities and expectations change to match realities, and along with losses there are gains. We become in some ways wiser, mellower, and more able to enjoy the present moment.

"What's the Succession of power if anything happens to Grandma?"

© Patrick Hardin

A Shift Toward Focus on the Present and the Positive

Laura Carstensen (1992; Carstensen & Mikels, 2005) has developed a theory of aging—called the *socioemotional selectivity theory*—which helps explain why elderly people commonly maintain or increase their satisfaction with life despite losses. According to Carstensen, as people grow older—or, more precisely, as they see that they have fewer years left—they become gradually more concerned with enjoying the present and less concerned with activities that function primarily to prepare for the future. Young people are motivated to explore new pathways and meet new people, despite the disruptions and fears associated with the unfamiliar. Such activities provide new skills, information, social contacts, and prestige that may prove useful in the future. But with fewer years left, the balance shifts. The older one is, the less sense it makes to sacrifice present comforts and pleasures for possible future gain. According to Carstensen, this idea helps us understand many of the specific changes observed in the elderly.

44

How does the socioemotional selectivity theory account for elderly people's generally high satisfaction with life?

As people grow older, they devote less attention and energy to casual acquaintances and strangers and more to people with whom they already have close emotional ties (Fung & others, 1999, 2001; Löckenhoff & Carstensen, 2004). Long-married couples grow closer. Husbands and wives become more interested in enjoying each other and less interested in trying to improve, impress, or dominate each other, and satisfaction with marriage becomes greater (Henry & others, 2007; Levenson & others, 1993). Older adults typically show less anger than do younger adults, in response to similar provocations, and become better at preserving valued relationships (Blanchard-Fields, 2007). Ties with children, grandchildren, and long-time friends grow stronger and more valued with age, while broader social networks become less valued and shrink in size. Such changes have been observed not just among the elderly but also among younger people whose life expectancy is shortened by AIDS or other terminal illnesses (Carstensen & Fredrickson, 1998).

People who continue working into old age typically report that they enjoy their work more than they did when they were younger (Levinson, 1978; Rybash & others, 1995). They become, on average, less concerned with the rat race of advancement and impressing others and more concerned with the day-to-day work itself and the pleasant social relationships associated with it.

Socioemotional satisfaction As people grow older, they tend to become more interested in enjoying the present and less future-oriented than they were when they were younger.

Selective Attention to and Memory for the Positive

In several experiments, Carstensen and others have shown that older people, unlike younger people, attend more to emotionally positive stimuli than to emotionally negative stimuli and show better memory for the former than the latter (Kisley & others, 2007; Mather & Carstensen, 2003; St. Jacques & others, 2009). In one experiment (Charles & others, 2003), for example, young adults (aged 18–29), middle-aged adults (41–53), and old adults (65–80) were shown pictures of positive scenes (such as happy children and puppies), negative scenes (such as a plane crash and garbage), and neutral scenes (such as a runner and a truck). Then they were asked to recall and briefly describe, from memory, as many of the pictures as they could. One predictable result was that older people recalled fewer of the scenes, overall, than did younger people; memory for all information declines as we age (discussed in **Chapter 9**). The other, more interesting finding was that the decline in memory with age was much sharper for the negative scenes than for the positive scenes (see Figure 12.12). Apparently, selective attention and memory is one means by which older people regulate their emotions in a positive direction.

45

How might selective attention and selective memory contribute to satisfaction in old age?

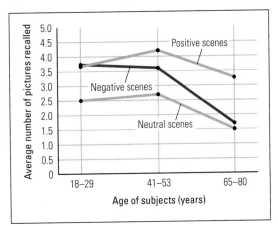

FIGURE 12.12 Effect of age on memory for positive, negative, and neutral scenes Memory for depictions of emotionally negative scenes declined much more sharply between middle age and old age than did memory for depictions of positive or neutral scenes. (Adapted from Charles & others, 2003.)

Approaching Death

The one certainty of life is that it ends in death. Surveys have shown that fear of death typically peaks in the person's fifties, which is when people often begin to see some of their peers dying from such causes as heart attack and cancer (Karp, 1988; Riley, 1970). Older people have less fear of death (Cicirelli, 2001). They are more likely to accept it as inevitable; and death in old age, when a person has lived a full life, seems less unfair than it did earlier.

Various theories have been offered regarding the stages or mental tasks involved in preparing for death. On the basis of her experience with caring for dying patients, Elisabeth Kübler-Ross (1969) proposed that people go through five stages when they hear that they are incurably ill and will soon die: (1) *denial*—"The diagnosis can't be right," or "I'll lick it"; (2) *anger*—"Why me?"; (3) *bargaining*—"If I do such-and-such, can I live longer?"; (4) *depression*—"All is lost"; and (5) *acceptance*—"I am prepared to die." Another theory is that preparation for death consists of reviewing one's life and trying to make sense of it (Butler, 1975).

As useful as such theories may be in understanding individual cases, research shows that there is no universal approach to death. Each person faces it differently. One person may review his or her life; another may not. One person may go through one or several of Kübler-Ross's stages but not all of them, and others may go through them in a different order (Kastenbaum, 1985). The people whom I have seen die all did it in pretty much the way they did other things in life. When my mother discovered that she would soon die—at the too-young age of 62—it was important to her that her four sons be around her so that she could tell us some of the things she had learned about life that we might want to know. She spent her time talking about what, from her present perspective, seemed important and what did not. She reviewed her life, not to justify it but to tell us why some things she did worked out and others didn't. She had been a teacher all her life, and she died one.

SECTION REVIEW

Love and work are the major themes of adulthood.

Love	Employment	Growing Old
➤ Romantic love has much in common with infant attachment to caregivers. The attachment style developed in infancy—secure, anxious, or avoidant—seems to carry forward into adult attachments.	➤ Jobs that permit considerable self-direction are enjoyed more than other jobs. Workers with such jobs become more self-directed in their overall approach to life and may, through their parenting, pass this trait on to their children.	➤ The elderly generally report greater life satisfaction than do middle-aged and young adults, despite the objective losses that accompany aging.
➤ Happy marriages are generally characterized by mutual liking and respect, individual commitment to the marriage, and constructive means of arguing.	➤ When husbands and wives both work outside the home, wives generally enjoy the out-of-home work more, and husbands enjoy the at-home work more. Perhaps the non-stereotypical task seems more a matter of choice, which promotes greater enjoyment.	➤ Elderly people focus more on the present and less on the future than do younger people. They also attend to and remember emotionally positive stimuli more than negative ones.
➤ Wives are generally better than husbands at perceiving and responding to their spouse's unspoken needs, so marital happiness often depends on the husband's developing those abilities.		➤ Though various theories make general statements about what people do as they approach death, it is really a highly individual matter.

Concluding Thoughts

This chapter has run the life course, from birth to death. As you review it, you might organize your thinking around the following two themes:

1. Development as a product of evolution The universal characteristics of human beings at each life phase are evolved adaptations that promote survival and reproduction, either immediately within that phase or through helping the individual prepare for challenges ahead. In your review, think about how this idea might apply to (a) the nature of infants' attachments to caregivers; (b) the characteristics of toddlers that influence their sharing, helping, and complying with requests; (c) the nature of children's play, including differences between girls' play and boys' play; (d) the tendency of children to attend to gender differences and to exaggerate them; (e) the heightened risk taking and, sometimes, aggressiveness of adolescence and youth; (f) the differences between young men and young women in courtship style; (g) the attachment bonds that form between adults in love; and (h) the changes in priorities that arise in old age.

As you think about each of these topics, you may well decide that the evolutionary accounts offered for some are more complete or compelling than those offered for others. You may think of alternative explanations, either founded in evolutionary theory or not.

2. Development as adaptation to the specifics of one's social environment Evolution has endowed us not with rigid instincts but with tendencies, drives, and alternative strategies that are facilitated, inhibited, selected, or redirected in accordance with our experiences in our social environments. Researchers have found many reliable correlations between aspects of a person's social environment and the person's development. How might these correlations be understood as adaptive changes that help the person to meet the specific social conditions of his or her life?

Think about this question as it might apply to behavioral changes or differences associated with (a) caregiver responsiveness or unresponsiveness to infants' signs of distress; (b) cultural and individual differences in sleeping arrangements for infants and young children; (c) differing styles of parental discipline of children; (d) age-mixed compared with age-segregated play environments; (e) cultural differences in the degree to which children witness violence among adults; (f) social-class differences that alter the chance of adolescents' achieving status through non-risky means; (g) good parental models for moral development in adolescence; (h) conditions that may alter sexual strategy toward either promiscuity or restraint; and (i) occupational self-direction in adulthood.

As you review, you may find that some of the explanations just called for are lacking or incomplete, or you may decide that the correlational evidence does not warrant the cause–effect inference implied. In such cases, how might future research fill the gaps and establish causal relationships?

Further Reading

Catherine Salmon (2008). *Family relationships: An evolutionary perspective.* Oxford, UK: Oxford University Press.

This is a scholarly book but still quite readable by the first-year student. Each chapter is written by a different expert or set of experts. The chapters bring an evolutionary perspective to bear on parent–child relationships, sibling relationships, domestic violence, and all aspects of family dynamics.

Barbara Rogoff (2003). *The cultural nature of human development.* Oxford, UK: Oxford University Press.

A thesis of this book, by a leading cross-cultural researcher, is that throughout development people look to others in their culture to see how to behave. The book examines cross-cultural differences in disciplinary styles, sleeping arrangements, children's segregation from or integration into the adult community, concepts of independence and interdependence, responsibilities at each life stage, concepts of adolescence, initiation into adulthood, and education.

Wendy Craig (2000). *Childhood social development: The essential readings.* Malden, MA: Blackwell.

The 13 articles in this collection are representative of theory and research about social development and are quite readable by the non-specialist. The topics include infant–mother attachment, parenting, friendships and peer relations, gender differences in development, moral reasoning, aggression, and development of antisocial behavior.

Robert Epstein (2007). *The case against adolescence: Rediscovering the adult in every teen.* Sanger, CA: Quill Driver Books

In this provocative book, Epstein argues—with considerable evidence—that young people, and our whole society, would be far better off if we treated adolescents more like adults than we currently do. He argues quite convincingly that most adolescents are fully capable of adult responsibilities. By infantilizing adolescents we deprive them of civil rights and frustrate their drives to behave in adultlike ways. Whether or not you agree with Epstein's thesis, the book will give you much to think about.

Elizabeth Marshall Thomas (2006). *The old way: A story of the first people.* New York: Farrar, Straus and Giroux.

Thomas was only 19 years old when she ventured into Africa's Kalahari Desert with the rest of her family in search of the !Kung hunter-gatherers. This book is a wonderfully written, vivid account of the lives and ways of these peaceful people. We can learn much about ourselves by examining our "old way"—our hunter-gatherer way—of living.

PART 7

The Person in a World of People

We humans are social beings through and through. We are motivated to understand others. We are concerned about what others think of us. Our understanding of ourselves is strongly affected by our perceptions of what others think of us. This two-chapter unit is on social psychology—the study of human thought and behavior in relation to the social contexts in which they occur. Chapter 13 is about the mental processes involved in understanding others, ourselves, and the social world in general. Chapter 14 is about some of the ways in which other people influence our behavior.

Social Perception and Attitudes

13

We are intensely social animals. We are designed, by natural selection, to depend on one another for even our most basic needs. We are not good, for example, at obtaining food alone; we need the help of others and the knowledge that is shared by members of a human community. Throughout our evolutionary history, to be thrown out of the tribe was tantamount to death. We are also thinking social animals. Most of what we think about is other people, ourselves, our relationships with other people, and the social conventions and norms that are essential aspects of life in any human society.

This is the first of a two-chapter sequence on **social psychology,** the subfield of psychology that deals most explicitly with how we view one another and are influenced by one another. This chapter focuses on *person perception*, the processes by which we perceive and understand one another and ourselves, and on *attitudes*, the evaluative beliefs that we have about our social world and the entities within it. The next chapter focuses on the effects that those perceptions and beliefs have on our emotions and actions.

■ Forming Impressions of Other People

One of social psychology's pioneers, Fritz Heider (1958), pointed out long ago that human beings are natural psychologists—or *naïve psychologists*, to use his term. Heider contended that humans are naturally interested in assessing the personality

1 ----------------------------------

In what sense are people natural psychologists?

characteristics and attitudes of other humans they encounter. From an evolutionary perspective, this drive to understand others has clear adaptive functions. Other people can help us or hurt us in our life endeavors. Understanding others helps us predict their behavior and decide how to interact with them. Consistent with Heider's general view, researchers have found that people untrained in psychology are nonetheless often remarkably accurate and quick at assessing others' personalities by observing their behavior (Ambady & others, 2000; Carney & others, 2007).

Yet, as Heider himself pointed out, the accuracy of our judgments of others sometimes suffers from certain consistent mistakes, or *biases*. These biases occur most often when we are not using our full mental resources, or have only limited information with which to reason, or have unconscious motives for reaching particular conclusions. Such biases interest social psychologists for two reasons. First, they provide clues about the mental processes that contribute to accurate as well as inaccurate perceptions and judgments. In this regard, social psychologists' interest in biases is analogous to perceptual psychologists' interest in visual illusions, which (as discussed in **Chapter 8**) provide clues to understanding normal, accurate visual perception. Second, an understanding of biases can promote social justice. By helping people understand the psychological tendencies that contribute to prejudice and unfair treatment of other people, social-psychological findings can help people overcome such biases.

Making Attributions from Observed Behavior

Actions are directly observable and thoughts are not. Therefore, our judgments about the personalities of people we encounter are based largely on what we observe of their actions. As "naïve psychologists" we intuitively, in our everyday experiences, form impressions of people's personalities on the basis of their actions.

For example, if a new acquaintance smiles at you, you do not simply register the fact that she smiled; rather, you interpret the smile's meaning and use that interpretation to infer something about her personality. Depending on the context, the precise form of the smile, and any prior information you have about her, you might decide that the smile represents friendliness, or smugness, or guile. What you carry away from the encounter is not so much a memory that the person smiled as a memory that she was friendly, smug, or deceitful. That memory is added to your growing impression of her and may affect—fairly or unfairly—your future interactions with her.

Is it the person or the situation? When we see someone behaving in a certain way, or expressing a particular emotion, we may attribute the behavior or emotion primarily to something unique about the person or to something about the situation. Here, we would need more information before making a confident judgment.

© Brooke Fasani/Corbis

Any such judgment about another person is, in essence, a claim about causation. It is an implicit claim that the person's behavior is caused in part by some more or less permanent characteristic of the person, such as friendliness or deceitfulness. In common English usage, any claim about causation is called an *attribution*. In the study of person perception, an **attribution** is a claim about the cause of someone's behavior. As Heider (1958) pointed out, we naturally make judgments about others' personalities on the basis of their behavior, but to do so meaningfully we must distinguish actions that tell us something lasting and unique about the person from those that do not.

The Logic of Attributing Behavior to the Person or the Situation

If you see a man running and screaming and then see that a tiger is chasing him, you might logically attribute his fear to the situation rather than to any special aspect of his personality; almost anyone would be afraid of a loose and charging tiger. To build a useful picture of a person on the basis of his or her actions, you must decide which actions imply something unique about the person and which actions would be expected of anyone under similar circumstances. Heider noted that when behavior is clearly appropriate to the environmental situation, people commonly attribute the behavior to the situation rather than to the behaving person's personality.

In line with Heider's general ideas about attributions, Harold Kelley (1967, 1973) developed a logical model for judging whether a particular action should be attributed to some characteristic of the acting person or to something about the immediate environment. The essence of the model is that we consider three questions in making an attribution:

1. *Does this person regularly behave this way in this situation?* If the answer is *yes,* we have grounds for attributing the behavior to some stable characteristic of either the person or the situation. If the answer is *no,* then this particular instance of the behavior may be a fluke that tells us little about either the person or the situation.

2. *Do many other people regularly behave this way in this situation?* If the answer is *yes,* we have grounds for attributing the behavior more to the situation than to the person. If the answer is *no,* then this behavior may tell us something unique about the person.

3. *Does this person behave this way in many other situations?* If the answer is *yes,* we have grounds for making a relatively general claim about the personality of the observed person. If the answer is *no,* then any personality claim we make about the person is limited to the particular situation.

As an illustration, imagine that we are caught in a traffic jam and Susan, our driver, is expressing a great deal of anger. Does her anger tell us something useful about her as a person? If we have observed that Susan regularly gets very angry in traffic jams (*yes* to Question 1) and that most other people don't get so angry in traffic jams (*no* to Question 2), then we might appropriately attribute her anger to something about her as a person. Given these answers to Questions 1 and 2, our answer to Question 3 will allow us to assess the generality of the personality attribute we can reasonably infer. If Susan also gets very angry in many other situations (*yes* to Question 3), we might logically conclude that she is an easily angered person and we should be careful around her in all situations. Conversely, if Susan rarely gets angry in other situations (*no* to Question 3), a reasonable conclusion would be that she is not generally an angry person but just cannot tolerate traffic jams.

Notice that there is nothing surprising in this model. It is simply a statement of the logic that you or I or anyone else—with sufficient motivation and information—would use in deciding whether or not an observed bit of behavior tells us something interesting about the person. It states explicitly the logic that leads us to conclude that a man's repeated fearful reaction to puppies and housecats tells us more about the man than does his fearful reaction to a loose and raging tiger.

Not surprisingly, a number of research studies have shown that when people are asked to explain the cause of a particular behavior and are given sufficient information to answer the three questions, they usually do make attributions that accord with the model just described (McArthur, 1972). But often people lack the information, the time, or the motivation to make a logical attribution. In that case they may take shortcuts in their reasoning, which may result in certain consistent errors, or biases.

The Person Bias in Attributions

In his original writings about attribution, Heider (1958) noted that people tend to give too much weight to personality and not enough to the environmental situation when they make attributions about others' actions. In our example of Susan and the traffic jam, people tend to ignore the traffic jam as cause and to attribute Susan's anger too heavily to her personality. Many researchers have confirmed the existence of this **person bias** in attribution.

Some of the most dramatic examples of the person bias occur in situations in which a person is socially pressured or required to behave in a certain way. In one experiment, for example, college students listened to a student who was assigned to read a political statement written by someone else (Gilbert & Jones, 1986). Even when the assignment was made by the observers themselves, so they could be sure that the reader had not chosen it himself, observers tended to rate the

2
According to Kelley's logical model, when should behavior be attributed to the person and when should it be attributed to the situation?

3
What evidence supports the existence of a person bias in attributions?

Do we assume he knows a lot? Long-time quiz game host Alex Trebek presents the questions and answers on *Jeopardy* and also at the *National Geographic Bee*. Even though everyone knows that the questions and answers don't come from Trebek's own fund of knowledge, people automatically view him as highly knowledgeable. This is an illustration of the person bias in attributions.

reader as politically liberal when the statement he read was liberal and as politically conservative when the statement was conservative. Although there was no logical reason to assume that the statement had anything to do with the reader's own political beliefs, the students made that attribution. Similar effects occur in judgments of the personalities of actors. In another experiment, people who saw an actor play the part of a kind person judged the actor himself as more kindly than did others who saw that same actor play the part of a villain (Tal-Or & Papirman, 2007).

Other research has shown that a person's social role can have undue effects on the attributions that others make about that person. When we observe a police officer, nurse, teacher, or student carrying out his or her duties, we tend—in accord with the person bias—to attribute the action to the individual's personality and to ignore the constraints that the role places on how the person can or must act. We might develop quite different impressions of the same person if we saw him or her in out-of-role situations.

In one experiment demonstrating this effect of roles, Ronald Humphrey (1985) set up a simulated corporate office and randomly assigned some volunteer subjects to the role of manager and others to that of clerk. The managers were given interesting tasks and responsibilities, and the clerks were given routine, boring tasks. At the end of the study, the subjects rated various aspects of the personalities of all subjects, including themselves. Compared with those in the clerk role, those in the manager role were judged by others more positively; they were rated higher in leadership, intelligence, assertiveness, supportiveness, and likelihood of future success. In keeping with the person bias, the subjects apparently ignored the fact that the role assignment, which they knew was random, had allowed one group to manifest characteristics that the other group could not. The bias did not hold when the subjects rated themselves, but it did hold when they rated others who had been assigned to the same role as themselves.

A recent analysis suggests that the CEOs (corporate executive officers) of large corporations in the United States are overrated, and overpaid, in part because of the person bias (Kolev, 2008). Shareholders attribute too much of the success or failure of a company to the most visible individual representative of the company, the CEO, and tend to ignore all of the other factors that influence the company's success or failure, such as the general state of the economy at the time. Because of the person bias, they are willing to pay top dollar to get or keep the "best" CEO available.

4

Why is the person bias often called the "fundamental attribution error"? In what conditions does the bias most often occur?

By the mid-1970s so much evidence appeared to support the person bias that Lee Ross (1977) called it the *fundamental attribution error,* a label designed to signify the pervasiveness and strength of the bias and to suggest that it underlies many other social-psychological phenomena. That label is still in use despite growing evidence that the bias may not be as fundamental as Ross and others thought (Uleman & others, 2008). People are much more likely to make this error if their minds are occupied by other tasks or if they are tired than if they devote their full attention to the task (Gilbert, 1989). Also, in many cases, the apparent demands of the experiment may artificially produce the person bias. Research subjects who are told that their task is to judge someone's personality are much more likely to exhibit the person bias than are those who are asked to explain the observed behavior in whatever terms they wish (Malle, 2006; Malle & others, 2000).

A Cross-Cultural Difference in Attributions

5

What logic and evidence suggest that the person bias may be a product of Western culture and may not exist in Eastern cultures?

Prior to the 1980s, social-psychological studies of attributions had been conducted only in Western cultures, mostly in North America and Western Europe. This observation led some to suggest that the person bias in attributions might be a product of a predominantly Western way of thinking. Western philosophies, religions, and political ideologies tend to emphasize the idea that people are in charge of their own destinies, so people growing up in Western cultures may learn to attribute behavior

Alexis C. Glenn / UPI / Landov

more to the person than to the situation (Jellison & Green, 1981). If so, then in Eastern cultures—such as those of India, China, and Japan, where philosophies and religions emphasize the role of fate or circumstances in controlling one's destiny—people might make relatively fewer person attributions and more situation attributions.

To test this theory, Joan Miller (1984) asked middle-class children and adults in the United States and in a Hindu community in India to think of an action by someone they knew and then to explain why the person had acted in that way. As predicted, the Americans made more attributions to personality and fewer to the situation than did the Indians. This difference was greater for adults—who would presumably have incorporated the cultural norms more strongly—than it was for children (see Figure 13.1).

In the years since Miller's pioneering work, similar results have been found in dozens of studies comparing attributions made by people raised in North America with those raised in various Far Eastern countries, including China, Japan, and Korea (Lehman & others, 2004; Norenzayan & Nisbett, 2000). The difference has been observed not just in the attributions made by research subjects in experiments, but also in attributions found in the literature and journalism of the different cultures.

In one study, for example, Michael Morris and Kaiping Peng (1994) analyzed the content of every article published in the *New York Times* and in the *World Journal*, a Chinese-language newspaper published in New York City, concerning two mass murders that took place in 1991. The researchers found that the articles in the *Times* focused most heavily on personality characteristics of the murderers—their traits, attitudes, character flaws, mental disorders, and so on. In contrast, the articles in the Chinese newspaper focused most heavily on the life situations of the murderers—their living conditions, social relationships, and frustrations that might have provoked their actions.

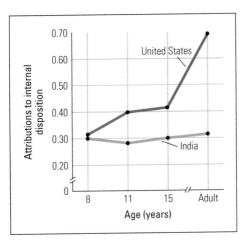

FIGURE 13.1 Cultural difference in making attributions When asked to explain another person's behavior, the proportion of attributions to internal disposition (personality or attitude) was greater among people in the United States than it was among Hindus in India, and this difference was greater for adults than for children. (The proportions were determined by dividing the number of person attributions by the total number of person plus situation attributions for each group. Data from Miller, 1984.)

Effects of Facial Features on Person Perceptions

"Don't judge a book by its cover" goes the saying, but we have the saying precisely because we know that people do often judge books by their covers. Similarly, we caution ourselves against judging people by their facial features, because we know that we do tend to make such judgments, often falsely and unfairly. The two most researched biases that derive from perceptions of facial features are the *attractiveness bias* and the *baby-face bias*.

The Attractiveness Bias

Consistent with folktales in which the good people (the princesses and princes) are beautiful and the bad people (the witches and ogres) are ugly, experiments have shown that physically attractive people are commonly judged as more intelligent, competent, sociable, and moral than less attractive people (Dion, 2002; Langlois & others, 2000).

In one experiment, fifth-grade teachers were given report cards and photographs of children whom they did not know and were asked to rate each child's intelligence and achievement. The teachers rated physically attractive children as brighter and more successful than unattractive children with identical report cards (Clifford & Walster, 1973). In a similar experiment, adults more frequently attributed a child's misbehavior to environmental circumstances if the child was physically attractive and to the child's personality if the child was not attractive (Dion, 1972). In yet another study, which analyzed actual court cases, judges regularly gave longer prison sentences to unattractive persons than to attractive persons convicted of comparable crimes (Stewart, 1985).

On the brighter side, there is evidence, too, that judgments of personality can affect judgments of physical appearance (Zebrowitz & Rhodes, 2002). In one experiment, an instructor who behaved in a warm and friendly way to one group of students

6

How have researchers documented biasing effects of physical attractiveness on perceptions of personality?

Luckily for them, they're cute
Researchers have found that good-looking children are less likely to be blamed for their misbehavior than are children who are not so good looking. The teacher here may be more inclined to attribute this disruptive behavior to the merriment of the situation than she would if the boys were not so cute.

Banana Stock / JupiterImages

and in a cold and aloof way to another group was judged as better looking by the first group than by the second (Nisbett & Wilson, 1977). There is also evidence that East Asians are less susceptible to the attractiveness bias than are Westerners (Dion, 2002). Just as they are less inclined than Westerners to judge a person's character from a brief glimpse of the person's behavior, they are also less inclined to judge it from the person's physical attractiveness. Apparently, the attractiveness bias is at least partly a result of an influence of Western culture.

The Baby-Face Bias

7
How have researchers documented biasing effects of a babyish versus a mature-looking face? What practical consequences have been shown to result from this bias?

Another pervasive, although less well-known, bias concerns a person's facial maturity. Some people, regardless of their age, have facial features that resemble those of a baby: a round rather than elongated head, a forehead protruding forward rather than sloping back, large eyes, and a small jawbone (see Figure 13.2). In a series of experiments conducted in both the United States and Korea, baby-faced adults were perceived as more naïve, honest, helpless, kind, and warm than mature-faced adults of the same age and sex, even though the perceivers could tell that the baby-faced persons were not really younger (McArthur & Berry, 1987; Zebrowitz & others, 1993).

In one study, Leslie Zebrowitz and Susan McDonald (1991) found that the baby-face bias influenced the outcomes of actual cases in a small-claims court. Baby-faced defendants were much more frequently found innocent in cases involving intentional wrongdoing than were mature-faced defendants, but they were neither more nor less frequently found innocent in cases involving negligence (such as performing a contracted job incompetently). Apparently, judges find it hard to think of baby-faced persons as deliberately causing harm but do not find it difficult to think of them as incompetent or forgetful.

FIGURE 13.2 Who would deceive you? Adults whose faces are babyish (left) are commonly seen as more naïve, honest, helpless, kind, and warm than are mature-faced adults (right). The characteristics of a baby face include a round head, large forehead, large eyes, short nose, and small chin.

© Frank Trapper / Corbis

Jemal Countess / WireImage / GettyImages

Another study, with enormous practical implications, showed that facial features play a big role in determining the results of U.S. Congressional elections. Alexander Todorov and his colleagues (2005) prepared black and white facial photographs of the two top candidates for each of 95 Senate races and 600 House of Representatives races, which took place between the year 2000 and the end of 2004. They showed each pair of photos for just 1 second to adult subjects, who were not familiar with the candidates, and asked them to judge, for each pair, which candidate looked more competent. The result was striking. The competence judgments, based on that 1-second viewing, correctly predicted the winner of 72% of the Senate races and 67% of the House races! Other evidence indicates that those judgments were probably founded primarily on assessments of facial maturity (Zebrowitz & Montepare, 2005). Apparently, people vote for the mature-faced person, who looks more competent, over the baby-faced person, who looks more naïve. Consistent with that interpretation, another research study showed that when photographs of former U.S. presidents Reagan and Kennedy were digitally altered to increase their baby-facedness, their perceived leadership qualities declined (Keating & others, 1999).

Konrad Lorenz (1943, 1971) suggested long ago that human beings instinctively respond to infants' facial features with feelings of compassion and care, a characteristic that helps promote the survival of our offspring. He also noted that the infant-like features of some animal species (such as rabbits and pandas) lead us to perceive them as particularly cute, innocent, and needing care, regardless of the animals' actual needs or behaviors. The work of Zebrowitz and others suggests that we generalize this response not just to babies and animals but also to adult humans whose faces resemble those of babies. We may want to cuddle and comfort the more baby-faced candidate, but we don't choose him or her as our leader. For another example of the relationship between baby-facedness and innocence, see Figure 13.3.

FIGURE 13.3 The evolution of innocence in Mickey Mouse
Mickey began life, in the 1928 cartoon *Steamboat Willie*, as a mischievous rodent who delighted in cranking a goat's tail and playing bagpipes on a pig's nipples. In response to social pressure from citizens concerned about Mickey's moral effects on children, the Walt Disney Company made him look and act increasingly innocent over the years. As part of this change, Disney artists augmented his juvenile features. Over a 50-year period Mickey's eye size increased markedly, and the apparent vault of his forehead increased as a result of the migration of his front ear toward the back of his head. (Based on S. J. Gould, 1980, pp. 96–97.)

© Disney Enterprises, Inc

Possible Evolutionary Consequences of the Baby-Face Bias

From an evolutionary perspective, it is noteworthy that human adults, overall, are much more baby-faced than the adults of our closest primate relatives. The typical adult human face looks much more like that of an infant chimpanzee than like that of an adult chimpanzee. This difference is generally attributed to the expanded cranial cavity that came with enlargement of the brain in humans. But I wonder if that is the whole explanation. In the course of human evolution, individuals who had babyish faces may have been treated more benignly than those who had more mature faces, and perhaps this helped promote our species' evolution toward baby-facedness. This is speculation, but it is supported by evidence that baby-faced children and adolescents are less often physically abused than are those who have more mature faces (McCabe, 1984) and by evidence that baby-faced adults receive more unsolicited help from strangers than do mature-faced adults (Keating & others, 2003).

As further speculation, perhaps the protective effect of a baby-face was of greater value for girls and women than for boys and men—for reasons having to do with the general sex differences in strength and aggressiveness. If so, that could account for the well-documented human sex difference in baby-facedness. By objective measures, women are, on average, more baby-faced than are men, and women are also universally judged to be kinder, more naïve, more in need of protection, and less socially dominant than men (Zebrowitz, 1996). In one research study, Heidi Friedman and Leslie Zebrowitz (1992) presented college students with schematic drawings of men's and women's faces in which facial maturity was varied by altering the size of the eyes and the length of the jaw. When the typical differences between men's and women's faces were present, students judged the men as more dominant and less warm than the women. But when the faces were equivalent on the maturity

8

From an evolutionary perspective, how might the baby-face bias have led to (a) the baby-faced appearance of human beings in general; (b) the tendency for women to be more baby-faced than men; and (c) the difference between fearful and angry facial expressions?

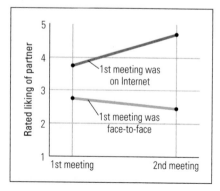

FIGURE 13.4 Fear expresses innocence, anger does not The fear expression, with eyes wide open, accents the baby-faced qualities of the face; the anger expression, with brows down, eyes less widely open, and jaw thrust forward, accents the mature qualities.

dimensions, the students judged the two as equal in dominance and warmth. So, our perception of sex differences in psychological traits might be at least partly the result of the baby-face bias.

Yet another possible evolutionary consequence of the baby-face bias is the manner in which we express fear and anger. Using both objective and subjective measurements, researchers have found that the facial expression of fear tends to enhance the babyish features of a face and the expression of anger tends to minimize those features (see Figure 13.4; Marsh & others, 2005; Zebrowitz & others, 2007). A major function of the human fear expression is to signal the need for protection and kind treatment from others, and the baby-faced aspect of the expression seems well designed for that (Marsh & Ambady, 2007). In contrast, a major function of the human anger expression is to instill a sense of dominance and competence—I *can* kill you if I choose!—and the mature-faced aspect of the anger expression may help convey that message. Consistent with these interpretations, the expression of fear is easier to perceive in baby-faced individuals than in mature-faced individuals, while the opposite is true for anger (Sacco & Hugenberg, 2009). Perhaps that helps explain why we tend to overestimate the degree of fear and underestimate the degree of anger shown in women and tend to do the opposite for men.

Forming Impressions on the Internet

The Internet, like the telephone before it and postal services before that, has added new dimensions to human communication. More than any other communication tool, the Internet allows people to locate and "meet" other people who have similar interests—through chat rooms, social networking sites, news groups, special-interest e-mail lists, dating services, and the like. While some research conducted in the early days of the Internet suggested that Internet use was socially detrimental, studies conducted more recently generally report positive correlations between Internet use and overall sociability and emotional well-being (Valkenburg & Peter, 2009). Here I will focus on the role of the Internet in meeting new people. Many friendships and valued acquaintanceships today involve people who first met in cyberspace. Some of these relationships remain confined to cyberspace, but in other cases Internet friends eventually meet in person and the friendship extends into the tangible world.

9
- - - - - - - - - - - - - - - - ◄ In several experiments, randomly formed pairs of opposite-sex college students

What evidence suggests that strangers who meet on the Internet like each other more than do strangers who meet in person? How might this phenomenon be explained?
- - - - - - - - - - - - - - - -

who did not know each other were assigned to participate in get-acquainted meetings, either on-line (through an Internet chat room) or in face-to-face encounters. The most striking general result is that those who had met on-line reported more liking of each other than did those who had met face-to-face (Bargh & McKenna, 2004). In one such experiment, this first meeting was followed by a second meeting, in which all pairs met face-to-face (McKenna & others, 2002). As you can see in Figure 13.5, the degree of liking between those who first met on the Internet increased even more in the face-to-face meeting, while the lesser degree of liking between those who first met face-to-face was not significantly affected by the second meeting.

FIGURE 13.5 Getting acquainted on the Internet Randomly selected opposite-sex pairs of students met for 20 minutes either on the Internet or face-to-face, and then all pairs met face-to-face for a second 20-minute period. After each meeting, subjects anonymously rated their liking of their partners using a scale in which 7 was maximal liking. (Data from McKenna & others, 2002, Study 3.)

How can such results be explained? Researchers have found that get-acquainted meetings over the Internet are more intimate, more revealing of what each person considers to be his or her "true self," than are such meetings conducted face-to-face (Bargh & McKenna, 2004; Valkenburg & Peter, 2009). Apparently, the relative anonymity of the Internet, along with the lack of visual and auditory contact, reduces social anxiety and frees people to reveal more about themselves than they would if they met face-to- face. Also, without knowledge of the physical features of the other person, the biasing effects of attractiveness, or lack thereof, are absent. Communication is not shut down by early negative judgments or anxieties based on physical features. When and if the two partners do meet, they already know a good deal about each other and may feel something of an emotional bond, which may lead them to see each other as more attractive than they would have if they were complete strangers.

Used wisely, the Internet apparently is a valuable tool for making friends. But, as is often pointed out, the Internet's seductive nature also creates potential dangers. People can easily create false impressions of themselves over the Internet, and early face-to-face meetings with Internet acquaintances should be held only in safe, public places.

SECTION REVIEW

We are constantly forming impressions of others and judging the causes of their behavior.

Basing Attributions on Observed Behavior	Effects of Physical Appearance	Forming Impressions on the Internet
➤ Logically, we might attribute a person's behavior primarily to characteristics of the person or the situation.	➤ A common bias is that we tend to see physically attractive people as more intelligent, social, competent, and moral than less attractive people.	➤ In experiments, people who met initially on the Internet liked each other more than people who initially met face-to-face.
➤ The person bias is the tendency to give undue weight to personality and not enough to the situation in making attributions.	➤ We tend to see baby-faced individuals as more honest, naïve, helpless, and warm—but less competent—than otherwise comparable people with mature faces. This may partly account for	➤ This tendency may result from people on the Internet being less anxious, more intimate, and freed from the biasing effects of physical appearance.
➤ The person bias appears not to hold true for East Asian cultures.	our differing perceptions of men's and women's personalities, and it may also help explain why fear and anger are expressed as they are.	

■ Perceiving and Evaluating the Self

Self-awareness is often described as one of the hallmarks of our species. At about 18 months of age, human infants stop reacting to their image in a mirror as if it were another child and begin to treat it as a reflection of themselves (Lewis & Brooks-Gunn, 1979; Lewis & Ramsay, 2004). If a researcher surreptitiously places a bright red spot of rouge on the child's nose or cheek before placing the child in front of the mirror, the 18-month-old responds by touching his or her own nose or cheek to feel or rub off the rouge; a younger child, by contrast, touches the mirror or tries to look behind it to find the child with the red spot.

────────10

How does the rouge test of self-recognition work? What has been learned from that test?

Chimpanzees also, at least in some cases, pass the rouge test. For that species, the capacity for self-recognition seems to depend on social interaction. In one study, chimps raised in isolation from others of their kind did not learn to make self-directed responses to their mirror images, whereas those raised with other chimps did (Gallup & others, 1971). Many psychologists and sociologists have argued that the self-concept, for humans as well as chimps, is fundamentally a *social* product. To become aware of yourself, you must first become aware of others of your species

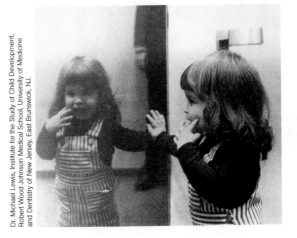

Dr. Michael Lewis, Institute for the Study of Child Development, Robert Wood Johnson Medical School, University of Medicine and Dentistry of New Jersey, East Brunswick, NJ.

It's me By pointing to the spot of rouge on her own cheek, this girl demonstrates her understanding that the mirror image is indeed of her. This photo is from the original study of mirror self-recognition by Lewis and Brooks-Gunn (1979).

and then become aware, perhaps from the way others treat you, that you are one of them. In humans, self-awareness includes awareness not just of the physical self, reflected in mirror images, but also of one's own personality and character, reflected psychologically in the reactions of other people.

Seeing Ourselves Through the Eyes of Others

11

According to Cooley, what is the "looking glass" with which we evaluate ourselves?

Many years ago the sociologist Charles Cooley (1902/1964) coined the term *looking-glass self* to describe what he considered to be a very large aspect of each person's self-concept. The "looking glass" to which he referred is not an actual mirror but other people who react to us. He suggested that we all naturally infer what others think of us from their reactions, and we use those inferences to build our own self-concepts. Cooley's basic idea has been supported by much research showing that people's opinions and attitudes about themselves are very much affected by the opinions and attitudes of others.

Effects of Others' Appraisals on Self-Understanding and Behavior

12

What are Pygmalion effects in psychology, and how were such effects demonstrated in elementary school classrooms?

The beliefs and expectations that others have of a person—whether they are initially true or false—can to some degree create reality by influencing that person's self-concept and behavior. Such effects are called *self-fulfilling prophecies* or *Pygmalion effects*.

Pygmalion was the mythical Roman sculptor, in Ovid's story, who created a statue of his ideal woman and then brought her to life by praying to Venus, the goddess of love. More relevant to the point being made here, however, is George Bernard Shaw's revision of the myth in his play *Pygmalion* (upon which the musical *My Fair Lady* was based). In the play, an impoverished Cockney flower seller, Eliza Doolittle, becomes a "fine lady" largely because of the expectations of others. Professor Higgins assumes that she is capable of talking and acting like a fine lady, and Colonel Pickering assumes that she is truly noble at heart. Their combined actions toward Eliza lead her to change her own understanding of herself, and therefore her behavior, so that the assumptions become reality. Psychological research indicates that such effects are not confined to fiction.

A Pygmalion effect In the movie *My Fair Lady*, based on the play *Pygmalion*, an impoverished Cockney woman begins to behave as an upper-class "fine lady" because she is treated as one.

Warner Bros./The Kobal Collection

Pygmalion in the Classroom In a classic experiment, Robert Rosenthal and Lenore Jacobson (1968) led elementary school teachers to believe that a special test had revealed that certain students would show a spurt in intellectual growth during the next few months. Only the teachers were told of the supposed test results, not the students. In reality, the students labeled as "spurters" had been selected not on the basis of a test score but at random. Yet, when all the students were tested 8 months later, the selected students showed significantly greater gains in IQ and academic performance than did their classmates. These were real gains, measured by objective tests, not just perceived gains. Somehow, the teachers' expectations that certain children would show more intellectual development than other children created its own reality.

Subsequent replications of this *Pygmalion in the classroom effect* provided clues concerning its mechanism. Teachers became warmer toward the selected students, gave them more time to answer difficult questions, gave them more challenging work, and noticed and reinforced more often their self-initiated efforts (Cooper & Good,

1983; Rosenthal, 1994). In short, either consciously or unconsciously, they created a better learning environment for the selected students than for other students. They also, through their treatment of them, changed the selected students' self-concepts. The students began to see themselves as more capable academically than they had before, and this led them to work harder to live up to that perception (Cole, 1991; Jussim, 1991).

More recently, many experiments have demonstrated the Pygmalion effect with adults as well as with children. When supervisors, in various business and management settings, are led to believe that some of their subordinates have "special promise," those randomly selected subordinates in fact do begin to perform better than they did before (Eden, 2003; Natanovich & Eden, 2008). Again, these effects appear to occur partly from the extra attention and encouragement that the selected subordinates get and partly from the change in the subordinates' self-concepts in relation to their work.

Changing Others' Behavior by Directly Altering Their Self-Concepts In the experiments just described, changes in subjects' self-concepts resulted from differences in the way that teachers or supervisors treated them. Other experiments have shown that simply telling others that they are a certain kind of person can, in some cases, lead them to behave in ways that are consistent with the attribute that they are told they have.

In one such experiment, some elementary school children were told in the course of classroom activity that they *were* neat and tidy (*attribution condition*); others were encouraged to become more neat and tidy (*persuasion condition*); and still others were given no special treatment (*control condition*). The result was that those in the attribution condition became significantly neater, as measured by the absence of littering, than did those in either of the other conditions (Miller & others, 1975). Similarly, children who were told that they were good at math showed greater subsequent improvements in math scores than did those who were told that they should try to become good at math (see Figure 13.6). In these experiments the change in behavior presumably occurred because of a direct effect of the appraisals on the children's self-concepts, which they then strove to live up to.

Of course, people's self-concepts are not always as moldable as the experiments just cited might suggest. In cases where an attribution runs directly counter to a person's strong beliefs about himself, the attributions can backfire. In some experiments, people have been observed to respond in ways that seem designed to correct what they believed to be mistaken perceptions of them—Pygmalion in reverse (Swann, 1987). For example, a person who has a strong self-image of being an artistic type, and not a scientific type, may counter an attribution that he is good at science by performing more poorly on the next science test than he did before.

> **13**
> What evidence supports the idea that simply attributing some characteristic to a person can, in some cases, lead that person to take on that characteristic?

FIGURE 13.6 Effect of attribution compared with persuasion (a) Fifth graders who were repeatedly told that they were neat and tidy (attribution condition) showed greater gain in use of the wastebasket than did those in the other conditions. (b) Second graders who were repeatedly told that they were good at math (attribution condition) showed greater improvement in math scores than did those in the other conditions. The delayed posttests were conducted several weeks after the pretests. (Adapted from Miller & others, 1975.)

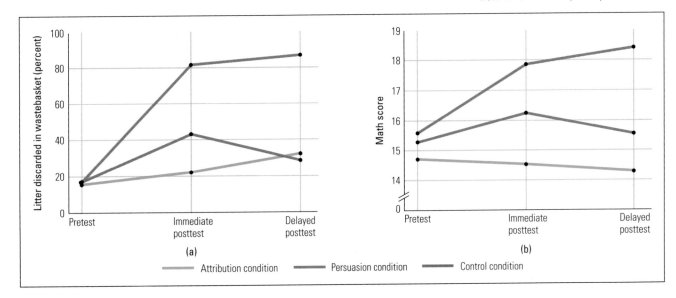

Self-Esteem as an Index of Others' Approval and Acceptance

Our self-concepts have a strong evaluative component, which psychologists refer to as self-esteem. ***Self-esteem,*** by definition, is one's feeling of approval, acceptance, and liking of oneself. It is usually measured with questionnaires in which people rate the degree to which they agree or disagree with such statements as, "On the whole, I am satisfied with myself" and "I feel that I have a number of good qualities" (Tafarodi & Milne, 2002).

14 ─────────────────────
What is the sociometer theory of self-esteem, and what evidence supports it?
─ ─ ─ ─ ─ ─ ─ ─ ─ ─ ─ ─ ─ ─ ─ ─ ─

◄ We experience self-esteem as deriving from our own judgments about ourselves, but, according to an influential theory proposed by Mark Leary (1999, 2005), these judgments derive primarily from our perceptions of others' attitudes toward us. The theory is referred to as the *sociometer theory,* because it proposes that self-esteem acts like a meter to inform us, at any given time, of the degree to which we are likely to be accepted or rejected by others. According to the sociometer theory, what you experience as your self-esteem at this very moment largely reflects your best guess about the degree to which other people, whom you care about, respect and accept you. As partial support of the sociometer theory, Leary and others have cited the following lines of evidence:

- Individual differences in self-esteem correlate strongly with individual differences in the degree to which people believe that they are generally accepted or rejected by others (Leary & others, 2001).

- When people were asked to rate the degree to which particular real or hypothetical occurrences in their lives (such as rescuing a child, winning an award, or failing a course) would raise or lower their self-esteem, and also to rate the degree to which those same occurrences would raise or lower other people's opinions of them, the two sets of ratings were essentially identical (Leary & others, 1995).

- In experiments, and in correlational studies involving real-life experiences, people's self-esteem increased after praise, social acceptance, or other satisfying social experiences and decreased after evidence of social rejection (Baumeister & others, 1998; Denissen & others, 2008; Leary & others, 2001).

- Feedback about success or failure on a test had greater effects on self-esteem if the person was led to believe that others would hear of this success or failure than if the person was led to believe that the feedback was private and confidential (Leary & Baumeister, 2000). This may be the most compelling line of evidence for the theory, because if self-esteem depended just on our own judgments about ourselves, then it shouldn't matter whether or not others knew how well we did.

The sociometer theory was designed to offer an evolutionary explanation of the function of self-esteem. From an evolutionary perspective, other people's views of us matter a great deal. Our survival depends on others' acceptance of us and willingness to cooperate with us. A self-view that is greatly out of sync with how others see us could be harmful. If I see myself as highly capable and trustworthy, but nobody else sees me that way, then my own high self-esteem will seem foolish to others and will not help me in my dealings with them. A major evolutionary purpose of our capacity for self-esteem, according to the sociometer theory, is to motivate us to act in ways that promote our acceptance by others. A decline in self-esteem may lead us to change our ways in order to become more socially acceptable, or it may lead us to seek a more compatible social group that approves of our ways. Conversely, an increase in self-esteem may lead us to continue on our present path, perhaps even more vigorously than before.

Actively Constructing Our Self-Perceptions

Although other people's views of us play a large role in our perceptions of ourselves, we do not just passively accept those views. We actively try to influence others' views of us, and in that way we also influence our own self-perceptions. In addition, we compare ourselves to others as a way of defining and evaluating ourselves, and we often bias those comparisons by giving more weight to some pieces of evidence than to others.

Social Comparison: Effects of the Reference Group

In perception everything is relative to some frame of reference, and in self-perception the frame of reference is other people. To see oneself as short, or conscientious, or good at math, is to see oneself as that *compared with other people*. The process of comparing ourselves with others in order to identify our unique characteristics and evaluate our abilities is called *social comparison.* A direct consequence of social comparison is that the self-concept varies depending on the *reference group,* the group against whom the comparison is made. If the reference group against which I evaluated my height were made up of professional basketball players, I would see myself as short, but if it were made up of jockeys, I would see myself as very tall.

Effect of the Reference Group on Self-Descriptions In one series of studies illustrating the role of the reference group, children's self-descriptions were found to focus on traits that most distinguished them from others in their group (McGuire & McGuire, 1988). Thus, children in racially homogeneous classrooms rarely mentioned their race, but those in racially mixed classrooms quite commonly did, especially if their race was in the minority. Children who were unusually tall or short compared with others in their group mentioned their height, and children with opposite-gender siblings mentioned their own gender more frequently than did other children (see Figure 13.7). Such evidence suggests that people identify themselves largely in terms of the ways in which they perceive themselves to be different from those around them.

▶ - - - - - - - - - - - - - - - - **15**

What is some evidence that people construct a self-concept by comparing themselves with a reference group? How can a change in reference group alter self-esteem?

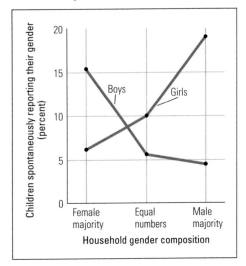

FIGURE 13.7 Evidence that children define themselves in terms of differences from their reference group As shown here, children were more likely to mention their gender when describing themselves if their gender was in the minority in their household than they were if it was in the majority. (Adapted from McGuire & McGuire, 1988.)

Effect of the Reference Group on Self-Evaluations The evaluative aspect of social comparison can be charged with emotion. We are pleased with ourselves when we feel that we measure up to the reference group and distressed when we don't. A change of reference group, therefore, can dramatically affect our self-esteem. Many first-year college students who earned high grades in high school feel crushed when their marks are only average or less compared with those of their new, more selective reference group of college classmates. Research conducted in many different countries has shown that academically able students at nonselective schools typically have higher academic self-concepts than do equally able students at very selective schools (Marsh & others, 2008), a phenomenon aptly called the *big-fish-in-little-pond effect.* The difference reflects the difference in the students' reference groups.

William James (1890/1950), reflecting on extreme instances of selective comparison, wrote: "So we have the paradox of the man shamed to death because he is only the second pugilist [boxer] or second oarsman in the world. That he is able to beat the whole population of the globe minus one is nothing; he has 'pitted' himself to beat that one and as long as he doesn't do that nothing else counts."

In a follow-up of James's century-old idea, Victoria Medvec and her colleagues (1995) analyzed the televised broadcasts of the 1992 Summer Olympics for the amounts of joy and agony expressed by the silver and bronze medalists after each event. The main finding was that the silver medalists (the second-place finishers)

The agony of being second best in the world Kristy Coventry (on the left), the silver medalist in the 200-meter individual medley swim of the 2008 World Olympics, seems much less happy about her medal than does bronze medalist Natalie Coughlin (on the right). Possible explanations are offered in the text.

showed, on average, less joy and more agony than did the bronze medalists (the third-place finishers), whom they had defeated. The researchers explained this finding by suggesting that the groups were implicitly making different comparisons. The silver medalists had almost come in first, so the prominent comparison to them was between themselves and the gold medalists, and in that comparison they were losers. In contrast, the bronze medalists had barely made it into the group that received a medal at all, so the prominent comparison in their minds was between themselves and the non-medalists, and in that comparison they were winners.

"Of course you're going to be depressed if you keep comparing yourself with successful people."

A subsequent study of medalists in the 2000 Summer Olympics, by other researchers, produced a somewhat different result (McGraw & others, 2005). That study took account of how well each medalist had *expected* to perform, and the main finding was that those who performed better than expected were happier than those who performed worse than expected, regardless of which medal they won. Bronze medalists who had expected to win no medal were happier than silver medalists who had expected to win the gold. But bronze medalists who had expected either gold or silver were less happy than silver medalists who had expected either bronze or no medal.

James (1890/1950) wrote that a person's self-esteem is equal to his achievements divided by his pretensions. By pretensions, he was referring to the person's self-chosen goals and reference groups. This formula nicely explains why high achievers typically do not have markedly higher levels of self-esteem than do people who achieve much less (Crocker & Wolfe, 2001). With greater achievements come greater aspirations and ever more elite reference groups for social comparison.

Enhancing Our Views of Ourselves

The radio humorist Garrison Keillor describes his mythical town of Lake Wobegon as a place where "all the children are above average." We smile at this statistical impossibility because we recognize the same bias in those around us and may vaguely recognize it in ourselves. Repeated surveys have found that most college students rate themselves as better students than the average college student, and in one survey 94 percent of college instructors rated themselves as better teachers than the average college instructor (Alicke & others, 1995; Cross, 1977). Indeed, at least in North America and Western Europe, people tend to rate themselves unduly high on practically every dimension that they value (Roese & Olson, 2007). It is useful to have relatively accurate views of ourselves, but it feels good to think well of ourselves, so most of us skew our self-evaluations in positive directions. We maintain our unduly high self-evaluations by treating evidence about ourselves differently from the way we treat evidence about others. Here are four means by which we do that.

Attributing Our Successes to Ourselves, Our Failures to Something Else One way that we maintain a high view of ourselves is to systematically skew the attributions we make about our successes and failures. Earlier in this chapter you read of the *person bias*—the general tendency to attribute people's actions, whether good or bad, to internal qualities of the person and to ignore external circumstances that constrained or promoted the actions. That bias applies when we think about other people's actions, but not when we think about our own actions. When we think about our own actions a different bias takes over, the ***self-serving attributional bias,*** defined as a tendency to attribute our *successes* to our own inner qualities and our *failures* to external circumstances. This bias has been demonstrated in countless experiments, with a wide variety of different kinds of tasks (Mezulis & others, 2004).

In one demonstration of this bias, students who performed well on an examination attributed their high grades to their own ability and hard work, whereas those who performed poorly attributed their low grades to bad luck, the unfairness of the test, or other factors beyond their control (Bernstein & others, 1979). In another study, essentially the same result was found for college professors who were asked to explain why a paper they had submitted to a scholarly journal had been either accepted or rejected (Wiley & others, 1979). My favorite examples of the self-serving attributional bias come from people's formal reports of automobile accidents, such as the following (quoted by Greenwald, 1980): "The telephone pole was approaching. I was attempting to swerve out of its way when it struck my front end." Clearly, a reckless telephone pole caused this accident; the skillful driver just couldn't get out of its way in time.

Accepting Praise at Face Value Most of us hear many more positive statements about ourselves than negative statements. Norms of politeness as well as considerations of self-interest encourage people to praise each other and inhibit even constructive criticism. "If you can't say something nice, say nothing at all" is one of our mores. Since we build our self-concepts at least partly from others' appraisals, we are likely to construct positively biased self-concepts to the degree that we believe the praise we hear from others. A number of experiments have shown that most people tend to discount praise directed toward others as insincere flattery or ingratiation, but accept the same type of praise directed toward themselves as honest reporting (Vonk, 2002).

Remembering Successes, Forgetting Failures Another means by which most of us maintain inflated views of ourselves involves selective memory. Research has shown that people generally exhibit better long-term memory for positive events and successes in their lives than for negative events and failures (D'Argembeau & Van der Linden, 2008). The same bias does not occur in memory for the successes and failures of other people.

Defining Our Own Unique Criteria for Success In many realms of activity the criteria for success are vague, and people may evaluate themselves by those measures that are most favorable to themselves (Suls & others, 2002). The majority of people may truly be "above average" if the criteria are allowed to vary from person to person in accordance with each person's unique view of the task. One student considers himself an above-average scholar because he plays such a constructive role in class discussions, another because she relates what she learns in class to practical problems in her life, another because he gets high scores on tests, and yet another because she disdains "grubbing for grades" and spends time reading books that are not assigned. One instructor sees herself as better than average because she treats her students as individuals, another because he explains the subject matter

16
What are four means by which people build and maintain inflated views of themselves?

The self-serving attributional bias
When people make a serious mistake, they tend to blame the situation—or someone else—rather than attribute the error to their own misjudgment.

clearly, another because she has high standards and is the toughest grader in her department, and yet another because he has never failed anyone.

Consistent with this interpretation of people's inflated self-ratings, researchers have found that such inflation is stronger for endeavors in which the criteria for success are not well defined than for those (such as running speed in the 100-meter dash) in which the criteria are more uniform and objectively measurable (Dunning & others, 1989). It is hard to know to what degree people define their criteria differently in order to view themselves in a better light, or to what extent their differing goals and criteria stem from truly differing conceptions of the task. Although psychologists have tended to focus mostly on the former possibility, it seems likely that both factors are involved.

East–West Differences in Self-Perceptions

As noted earlier in this chapter, the psychology of North Americans and Western Europeans is not necessarily the psychology of people everywhere. This appears to be particularly true in relation to people's perceptions of themselves. Much research indicates that people in East Asian countries—including Japan, Korea, and China—conceive of the self quite differently from the way people do in the West.

Greater Focus in the East on Relationships and Roles, Less on the Independent Self

17 – – – – – – – – – – – – – – – – – – ◄

How does Triandis characterize individualist and collectivist cultures? What differences have been found between the two in people's self-descriptions?

– –

Harry Triandis (1995), one of the pioneers of cross-cultural research in psychology, has drawn a rough distinction between two categories of cultures: individualist and collectivist. *Individualist cultures* predominate in North America, Western Europe, and Australia, where philosophical and political traditions emphasize personal freedom, self-determination, and individual competition. *Collectivist cultures* exist in much of Africa and Latin America, but have been most fully studied in East Asia. While individualist cultures emphasize the independence of each person, collectivist cultures emphasize the interdependence of people with others in their families, communities, and social groups.

Consistent with Triandis's view are numerous studies indicating that East Asians describe themselves differently from the way North Americans do (Kanagawa & others, 2001; Markus & Kitayama, 1991, 1994). The former describe themselves more often in terms of their social groups and roles and less often in terms of consistent personality traits that cut across their groups and roles. Asked to describe themselves, they are more likely to make such statements as "I am a student at University X" or "I am the eldest daughter in my family" and less likely to make such statements as "I am easygoing" or "I am ambitious." When they do describe themselves with personality traits, they typically restrict the traits to particular social contexts—"I am easygoing with my friends," "I am ambitious at work" (Cousins, 1989). They are more likely than are Westerners to see themselves as different in different social contexts (Kanagawa & others, 2001; Tafarodi & others, 2004). They are also more likely to attribute their achievements to their families or other social groups than to themselves as individuals (Chen & others, 1998). Such differences in self-descriptions are found even in young children (Wang, 2006).

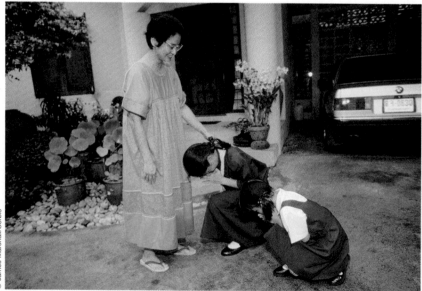

Respect your elders As part of their general emphasis on interdependence and proper social relationships, East Asian cultures encourage respectful behavior toward elders that is quite unlike that shown in the West. Here two children in Bangkok greet an adult acquaintance.

© James Marshall/Corbis

Less Self-Enhancement in the East, or Different Criteria for Self-Evaluation

Particularly in Japan, but also in other East Asian countries, the ideal person is a modest person. The ideal person is not someone who thinks highly of himself or herself, but someone who is aware of his or her deficiencies and is working hard to overcome them (Heine & others, 1999). Consistent with this observation are research findings indicating that self-enhancing biases are small or nonexistent in East Asia and may even be reversed in Japan (Heine & Hamamura, 2007; Lehman & others, 2004).

In one classic study, for example, Michael Bond and Tak-Sing Cheung (1983) asked university students in the United States, Hong Kong, and Japan to describe themselves in an open-ended way by creating 20 statements about themselves, each of which had to begin with the words *I am*. They then analyzed the statements for evaluative content and found that the ratio of positive to negative self-statements was nearly 2 to 1 for the American students, 1 to 1 for the Hong Kong students, and 1 to 2 for the Japanese students. In other words, the Japanese students showed a *self-effacing bias* that was as strong as the Americans' self-enhancing bias.

Such findings are apparently not just the result of Easterners' attempts to *appear* modest to others. In most studies, the questionnaires are filled out anonymously in such a way that it is clear that nobody, including the researchers, can know whose questionnaire is whose. Moreover, similar results are found in tests of implicit modesty, in which subtle behavioral measures are used in such a way that the subjects do not know that modesty is being assessed. In one experiment, Japanese students revealed, through various nonverbal behavioral indices, more surprise and disbelief upon hearing that they had performed better than the average student at their university on a test of intelligence than upon hearing that they had performed worse than average, while the opposite was true for Canadian students (Heine & others, 2000).

Several studies, however, indicate that on certain traits—traits that are particularly valued in collectivist cultures—Japanese and other East Asians do show self-enhancing biases. The typical East Asian does not rate himself or herself as more intelligent or physically skilled than average, but does rate himself or herself above average in such traits as agreeableness, cooperativeness, respectfulness to others, modesty, loyalty, and being a good listener (Gaertner & others, 2008; Sedikides & others, 2003). Such findings have led some researchers to suggest that self-enhancing biases are universal, but the traits that people most value, and on which they self-enhance, vary across cultures.

> ------------- **18**
> **What evidence suggests that East Asians generally show less self-enhancement than Westerners do, but may self-enhance on characteristics that are most valued in collectivist cultures?**

SECTION REVIEW

The social world around us profoundly affects our understanding of ourselves.

Seeing Ourselves Through Others' Eyes

➤ Classroom experiments have demonstrated Pygmalion effects, in which adults' expectations about children's behavior created the expected behavior. Such effects occur at least partly by altering the children's self-concepts.

➤ A variety of evidence supports the sociometer theory, which states that self-esteem reflects the level of acceptance or rejection we believe we can expect from others.

Active Construction of Self-Perceptions

➤ We perceive ourselves largely through social comparison—comparing ourselves to others. Our judgments and feelings about ourselves depend on the reference group to which we compare ourselves, as illustrated by the big-fish-in-little-pond effect.

➤ At least in North America and Western Europe, people tend to enhance their views of themselves through such means as making self-serving attributions (attributing success to the self and failure to the situation), accepting praise at face value, remembering successes more than failures, and defining their own criteria for success.

East–West Differences in Self-Perception

➤ In the collectivist cultures of East Asia, people tend to describe themselves more in terms of their social groups and roles than in terms of individual personality traits.

➤ East Asians are less likely than Westerners to self-enhance; the Japanese may even show a self-effacing bias. However, East Asians may still self-enhance on traits that they value highly, such as modesty itself.

◼ Perceiving Ourselves and Others as Members of Groups

In the previous section you read of evidence that the self-concept is social in that others are involved in its construction: We see ourselves reflected in others' reactions to us, and we understand ourselves by comparing our attributes with other people's. But the self-concept is social in another sense as well: Others are not just involved in its construction; they are also part of its contents. We describe and think of ourselves not just in terms of our individual characteristics—*I am short, adventurous, somewhat shy*—but also in terms of the groups to which we belong and with which we identify—*I am a French Canadian, Roman Catholic, member of the university marching band.* Self-descriptions that pertain to the person as a separate individual are referred to as ***personal identity,*** and those that pertain to the social categories or groups to which the person belongs are referred to as ***social identity*** (Tajfel, 1972). In this section we examine some consequences of viewing ourselves and others in terms of the groups to which we and they belong.

William Thomas Cain/Getty Images

Social identity can alter self-esteem When the Philadelphia Phillies won the baseball World Series, Philadelphians, including those who had nothing to do with the victory, felt good about themselves. Our self-esteem is affected by the successes and failures of groups with which we identify, even if we are not actually members of those groups.

Shifting Between Personal and Social Identities

19 ┈┈┈┈┈┈┈┈┈┈┈

What value might lie in our flexible capacity to think of ourselves in terms of both personal and social identities?

◀ Our self-concepts are relatively consistent from situation to situation, but not rigid (Oakes & others, 1994). We think of ourselves differently at different times, in ways that help us meet the ever-changing challenges of social life. Sometimes, for some purposes, we find it most useful to think of our unique characteristics and motives: our personal identity. At other times, for other purposes, we find it more useful to think of ourselves as components of a larger unit, a group to which we belong: our social identity. Our evolution as a species has entailed a continuous balance between the need to assert ourselves as individuals and the need to cooperate with others (Guisinger & Blatt, 1994). To enable us to walk that tightrope, without falling into isolation on the one side or complete self-sacrifice to the group on the other, natural selection apparently endowed us with the capacity to hold both personal and social identities and to switch between them to meet our needs for survival.

In evolutionary history the groups with which people cooperated included some that were lifelong, such as the family and tribe, and others that were more short-lived, such as a hunting party organized to track down a particular antelope. Today the relatively permanent groups with which we identify may include our family, ethnic group, co-religionists, and occupational colleagues. The temporary groups include the various teams and coalitions with which we affiliate for particular ends, for periods ranging from minutes to years.

Different cultures in today's world tend to vary in the relative weights they give to personal and social identity. As you might expect, individualist cultures emphasize personal identity, and collectivist cultures emphasize social identity. But the difference is relative. People everywhere can think of themselves in terms of both types of identity, to degrees that depend on the specific context and the problems they are dealing with at the time (Oyserman & Lee, 2008).

Consequences of Personal and Social Identity for Self-Esteem

Our feelings about ourselves depend not just on our personal achievements but also on the achievements of the groups with which we identify, even when we ourselves play little or no role in those achievements. Sports fans' feelings about themselves rise and fall as "their" team wins and loses (Hirt & others, 1992). Similarly, people feel good about themselves when their town, university, or place of employment achieves high rank or praise.

In some situations, the very same event—high achievement by other members of our group—can temporarily raise or lower our self-esteem, depending on whether our social identity or personal identity is more active. When our social identity predominates, our group-mates are part of us and we experience their success as ours. When our personal identity predominates, our group-mates are the reference group against which we measure our own accomplishments, so their success may diminish our view of ourselves. Social psychologists have demonstrated both these effects by priming people to think in terms of either their social or personal identities as they hear of high accomplishments by others in their group (Brewer & Weber, 1994; Gardner & others, 2002).

> **20**
> **Why is it that excellent performance by other members of our group can either lower or raise our self-esteem?**

You read previously that students at highly selective schools think worse of themselves as scholars than do equally able students at less selective schools because of the difference in their relative standing in their reference group. At least one study indicates that this is true for those who think primarily in terms of their personal identities but not for those who think primarily in terms of their social identities (McFarland & Buehler, 1995). When the social identity is foremost, self-feelings are elevated, not diminished, by the excellent performance of group-mates. Graceful winners of individual achievement awards know this intuitively, and to promote good feelings and not incur jealousy, they activate their group-mates' social identities by describing the award as belonging properly to the group as a whole.

Group-Enhancing Biases

Other studies reveal that our bias to think highly of ourselves applies to our social identity as well as to our personal identity. In some conditions our group-enhancing biases are at least as strong as our self-enhancing biases (Bettencourt & others, 2001; Rubin & Hewstone, 1998). In fact, the concept of social identity first became prominent in social psychology when Henri Tajfel (1972, 1982) used it to explain people's strong bias in favor of their own groups over other groups in all sorts of judgments. He argued that we exaggerate the virtues of our own groups to build up the part of our self-esteem that derives from our social identity.

> **21**
> **According to Tajfel, why do we inflate our view of the groups to which we belong? How does a study of members of volleyball teams support Tajfel's theory?**

Tajfel and others showed that group-enhancing biases occur even when there is no realistic basis for assuming that one group differs from another. In one laboratory experiment, people who knew they had been assigned to one of two groups by a purely random process—a coin toss—nevertheless rated their own group more positively than they did the other group (Locksley & others, 1980). You don't need a degree in psychology to know that the fans of opposing baseball teams see the same plays differently, in ways that allow them all to leave the game believing that theirs was the better team, regardless of the score. Strike three is attributed by one group to the pitcher's dazzling fastball and by the other to the umpire's unacknowledged need for eyeglasses.

Some research has shown that group-enhancing biases increase when people are primed to think of their social identities and decline when people are primed to

think of their personal identities. In one study, volleyball players attributed their team's victories to their team's great skill and their losses to external circumstances such as poor luck or bad officiating. This group-enhancing attributional bias disappeared, however, when the players underwent a self-affirmation procedure in which they listed their personal accomplishments in realms other than volleyball (Sherman & Kim, 2005). The self-affirmation presumably raised their self-esteem and primed them to think in terms of their personal rather than social identities, so they no longer felt motivated to think so highly of their team.

Stereotypes and Their Automatic Effects on Perception and Behavior

We can switch between personal and social identities in our perceptions of others as well as ourselves. When we view others in terms of their personal identities, we see them as unique individuals. When we view others in terms of their social identities, we gloss over individual differences and see all members of a group as similar to one another. This is particularly true when we view members of out-groups—that is, members of groups to which we do not belong.

The schema, or organized set of knowledge or beliefs, that we carry in our heads about any group of people is referred to as a **stereotype.** The first person to use the term *stereotype* in this way was the journalist Walter Lippmann (1922/1960), who defined it as "the picture in the head" that a person may have of a particular group or category of people. You may have stereotypes for men, women, Asians, African Americans, Californians, Catholics, and college professors. We gain our stereotypes largely from the ways our culture as a whole depicts and describes each social category. A stereotype may accurately portray typical characteristics of a group, or exaggerate those characteristics, or be a complete fabrication based on culture-wide misconceptions.

Stereotypes are useful to the degree that they provide us with some initial, valid information about a person, but they are also sources of prejudice and social injustice. Our stereotypes can lead us to pre-judge others on the basis of the group to which they belong, without seeing their qualities as individuals. In the United States, research on stereotyping has focused primarily on European Americans' stereotypes of African-Americans, which are part and parcel of a long history of racial bias that began with the institution of slavery.

"Actually, Lou, I think it was more than just my being in the right place at the right time. I think it was my being the right race, the right religion, the right sex, the right socioeconomic group, having the right accent, the right clothes, going to the right schools . . ."

Distinction Between Implicit and Explicit Stereotypes

Many people in our culture today, particularly college students, are sensitized to the harmful effects of stereotypes, especially negative stereotypes about socially oppressed groups, and are reluctant to admit to holding them. Partly for that reason, social psychologists find it useful to distinguish among three levels of stereotypes: public, private, and implicit (Dovidio & others, 1994). The *public* level is what we say to others about a group. The *private* level is what we consciously believe but generally do not say to others. Both public and private stereotypes are referred to as **explicit stereotypes,** because the person consciously uses them in judging other people. Such stereotypes are measured by questionnaires on which people are asked, in various ways, to state their views about a particular group, such as African Americans, women, or old people. Responses on such questionnaires are easy to fake, but the hope is that research subjects who fill them out anonymously will fill them out honestly.

Implicit stereotypes, in contrast, are sets of mental associations that operate more or less automatically to guide our judgments and actions toward members of the group in question, even if those associations run counter to our conscious beliefs. Most psychological research on stereotyping today has to do with implicit stereotypes. These stereotypes are measured with tests in which the person's attention is focused not on the stereotyped group per se, but on performing quickly and accurately an objective task that makes use of stimuli associated with the stereotype. Two types of tests commonly used in this way are *priming tests* and *implicit association tests*.

Priming as a Means of Assessing Implicit Stereotypes As discussed in Chapter 9, *priming* is a general method for measuring the strengths of mental associations. The premise underlying this method is that any concept presented to a person primes (activates) in the person's mind the entire set of concepts that are closely associated with that concept. Priming the mind with one concept makes the related concepts more quickly retrievable from long-term memory into working memory.

In a test of implicit stereotypes about black people compared to white people, for example, subjects might, on each trial, be presented with a picture of either a black face or a white face and then with some adjective to which the person must respond as quickly as possible in a way that demonstrates understanding of the adjective's meaning (Dovidio & others, 1996; Kawakami & Dovidio, 2001). For example, the required response might be to press one button if the adjective could describe a person and another button if it could describe a house but not a person. In some of these experiments the priming stimulus (the black or white face) that precedes the adjective is flashed very quickly on a screen—too quickly to be identified consciously but slowly enough that it can register in the subject's unconscious mind and affect his or her thought processes.

Experiments of this sort have shown that white U.S. college students respond especially quickly to such words as *lazy, hostile, musical,* and *athletic* when primed with a black face, and especially quickly to such words as *conventional, materialistic, ambitious,* and *intelligent* when primed with a white face. Although positive and negative traits appear in both stereotypes, the experiments reveal that the implicit stereotypes that white students have of blacks are significantly more negative than the ones they have of whites (Dovidio & others, 1986; Olson & Fazio, 2003).

Implicit Association Tests *Implicit association tests,* developed initially by Anthony Greenwald and his colleagues (1998, 2002), take advantage of the fact that people can classify two concepts together more quickly if they are already strongly associated in their minds than if they are not strongly associated. To get an idea of how such a test works, complete the paper-and-pencil

Beyond stereotypes Oprah Winfrey, Barack Obama, and Michelle Obama are among the most respected people in the United States. Their popularity is no doubt helping to modify the implicit as well as explicit stereotypes that white Americans have long held toward black Americans.

> 22
> **What is the distinction among public, private, and implicit stereotypes? What are two means by which researchers identify implicit stereotypes?**

A		B		C	
Male	Female	Male or Violent	Female or Nonviolent	Male or Nonviolent	Female or Violent
____ John ____		____ Henry ____		____ Jill ____	
____ Hank ____		____ War ____		____ Hug ____	
____ Joan ____		____ Fight ____		____ Punch ____	
____ David ____		____ Joan ____		____ Bill ____	
____ Mary ____		____ Help ____		____ Hank ____	
____ Jill ____		____ Mary ____		____ Fight ____	
____ Susan ____		____ David ____		____ Susan ____	
____ Bill ____		____ Hank ____		____ Help ____	
____ Henry ____		____ Love ____		____ Joan ____	
____ Amy ____		____ Jill ____		____ Kill ____	
____ David ____		____ Punch ____		____ John ____	
____ Hank ____		____ John ____		____ David ____	
____ Joan ____		____ Susan ____		____ Hit ____	
____ Jill ____		____ Care ____		____ Care ____	
____ John ____		____ Hit ____		____ War ____	
____ Mary ____		____ Bill ____		____ Henry ____	
____ Amy ____		____ Amy ____		____ Amy ____	
____ Bill ____		____ Peace ____		____ Love ____	
____ Susan ____		____ Kill ____		____ Mary ____	

FIGURE 13.8 An implicit association test How long does it take you to classify the items in each of these columns? Time yourself, in seconds, separately on each column. For column A, place a check to the left of each male name and to the right of each female name. For column B, place a check to the left of each male name or term that has to do with violence, and place a check to the right of each female name or term that has to do with nonviolence. For column C, place a check to the left of each male name or term that has to do with nonviolence, and place a check to the right of each female name or term that has to do with violence. (Modeled after an example in Gladwell, 2005.)

version that is presented in Figure 13.8, following the instructions in the caption. You will need a watch or clock that can count seconds to time yourself.

How did you perform? If you are like everyone I know who has taken this test, it took you longer to go through List C, where nonviolent terms are classified with male names and violent terms with female names, than it took you to go through List B, where violent terms go with male names and nonviolent terms with female names. Nearly everyone shares the stereotype that males are relatively violent and females are relatively nonviolent. Implicit association tests used in research are usually presented on a computer. Each individual stimulus appears on the screen, one at a time, and the person must respond by pressing one of two keys on the keyboard, depending on the category of the stimulus. If you wish to take such a test, you might find examples on the Internet at *https://implicit.harvard. edu/implicit*, where you can take part in an ongoing experiment involving implicit associations. (This site has been active for several years and may or may not still be active at the time that you are reading this.)

In implicit association tests having to do with race, a typical procedure is to use photographs of white and black faces, along with "good" words (such as love, happy, truth, terrific) and "bad" words (such as poison, hatred, agony, terrible) as the stimuli. In one condition, the job is to categorize white faces and "good" words together by pressing one key on the keyboard whenever one of them appears, and to classify black faces and "bad" words together by pressing another key whenever one of those appears. In the other condition, the job is to classify white faces and "bad" words together and black faces and "good" words together. The typical result is that white college students take about 200 milliseconds longer per key press, on average, in the latter condition than in the former (Aberson & others, 2004; Cunningham & others, 2001).

Implicit Stereotypes and Unconscious Discrimination

23
How have researchers shown that implicit stereotypes can lead to prejudicial behavior even in the absence of conscious prejudice?

◄ Implicit stereotypes can lead people who are not consciously prejudiced to behave in prejudicial ways, despite their best intentions. In one series of studies, for example, white students' scores on a test of implicit prejudice toward blacks correlated quite strongly with their subsequent reactions toward black conversation partners with whom they were paired (Dovidio & others, 1997, 2002). Those who scored highest in implicit prejudice spoke friendly words toward their black partners and believed they were behaving in a friendly way, but showed nonverbal signs of negativity or apprehension, which made them come across as unfriendly. They were less likely to make eye contact with their black partners, showed more rapid eye blinking, and were rated by their black partners and other observers as less friendly, despite their words, than were the students whose implicit prejudice scores were lower. None of these effects occurred when the conversation partners were white instead of black. In other studies, whites with high implicit prejudice toward blacks exhibited neural and

A possibly tense interview White interviewers, including those who are not explicitly prejudiced, tend to react to black interviewees in ways that provoke discomfort. The reaction derives from implicit stereotypes, which nearly everyone holds.

© John Birdsall/The Image Works

hormonal responses indicative of stress when interacting with a black partner, but not when interacting with a white partner (Mendes & others, 2007).

It is not hard to imagine how such reactions can have real-world consequences. A white employer, who thinks of himself as not prejudiced against black people, interviews several applicants for a job in his company. Some of the applicants are white, others black. Because of the employer's implicit negative stereotype of blacks, his interviews with black candidates come across as strained. He appears unfriendly to them, and they, in consequence, respond in a less friendly way toward him than they otherwise would. The result is that the employer concludes that none of the black candidates has quite the personality required for the job, and he selects one of the white applicants. All this may happen despite the employer's sincere intention to be unbiased in his selection.

Implicit Stereotypes Can Be Deadly

Around midnight, on February 3, 1999, four plainclothes policemen saw a young black man, Amadou Diallo, standing on the stoop of his apartment building in the South Bronx, in New York City (Gladwell, 2005). He looked suspicious to them, so they stopped their unmarked cruiser and approached him. As they approached, he drew something from his pocket that looked to one of the officers like a gun. Reacting quickly, in self-defense, that officer shouted "gun" and all of the officers opened fire on Diallo and killed him instantly. When the officers looked more closely at the dead man they discovered that what he had drawn from his pocket was not a gun but his wallet. Diallo had apparently assumed that the four large, white, non-uniformed men approaching him with guns were intent on robbing him, so, seeing no route for escape, he had taken out his wallet.

Would Diallo have been shot if he had been white? If he had been white, would he have been seen as suspicious and been approached by the police officers, and if he had been approached, would his wallet have been seen as a gun? We can never know the answers as applied to this individual case, but there are grounds for believing that skin color can play a large role in such cases. Many research studies have shown that whites implicitly view unfamiliar blacks as more hostile, violent, and suspicious-looking than unfamiliar whites, and several experiments, inspired by the Diallo case and others like it, reveal that whites implicitly associate black faces more strongly with guns than they do white faces (Correll & others, 2002; Payne, 2006; Plant & Peruche, 2005).

Most such experiments have used college students as subjects, but one was conducted with actual police officers (Plant & Peruche, 2005). In this experiment, which involved computer simulations of self-defense situations, the instructions to each officer included the following words:

> Today your task is to determine whether or not to shoot your gun. Pictures of people with objects will appear at various positions on the screen. . . . Some of the pictures will have the face of a person and a gun. These people are the criminals, and you are supposed to shoot at these people. Some of the pictures will have a face of a person and some other object (e.g., a wallet). These people are not criminals and you should not shoot at them. Press the "A" key for "shoot" and press the "L" key on the keyboard for "don't shoot."

During the experiment, each picture appeared on the screen until the officer responded or until a 630-millisecond time limit had elapsed. As shown in Figure 13.9, during the first 80 trials the officers mistakenly shot unarmed black suspects significantly more often than they shot unarmed white suspects. With practice, during which they received immediate feedback as to whether they had shot an armed or unarmed person, they gradually

▶- - - - - - - - - - - - - - - - - -**24**

What evidence suggests that implicit prejudice can cause police officers to shoot at black suspects more readily than at white suspects?

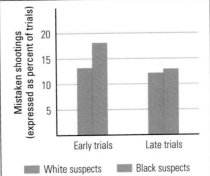

FIGURE 13.9 Race of suspect affects decision to shoot in computer simulations During the first 80 trials of a computer simulation game, police officers who had to make split-second decisions "shot" more often at unarmed black suspects than at unarmed white suspects. With practice, however, this bias disappeared. (Based on data in Plant & Peruche, 2005.)

overcame this bias. They did not show the bias during the final 80 trials of the 160-trial game. The researchers hope that such training will reduce officers' bias in real-life encounters with criminal suspects.

Defeating Explicit and Implicit Negative Stereotypes

25
What sorts of learning experiences are most effective in reducing (a) explicit and (b) implicit prejudice?

◄ Explicit and implicit stereotypes are psychologically quite different from each other. As you have seen, people often hold implicit stereotypes that do not coincide with their explicit beliefs about the stereotyped group. Whereas explicit stereotypes are products of conscious thought processes, modifiable by deliberate learning and logic, implicit stereotypes appear to be products of more primitive emotional processes, modifiable by such means as classical conditioning (Livingston & Drwecki, 2007). White people who have close black friends exhibit less implicit prejudice than do those without black friends (Aberson & others, 2004), and there is evidence that exposure to admirable black characters in literature, movies, and television programs can reduce implicit prejudice in white people (Rudman, 2004). Apparently, the association of positive feelings with individual members of the stereotyped group helps reduce automatic negative responses toward the group as a whole.

© Corbis

Happy conditioning Experiences such as that depicted here help to counter the development of implicit negative racial stereotypes.

In one long-term study, Laurie Rudman and her colleagues (2001) found that white students who volunteered for a diversity-training course showed, by the end of the course, significant reductions in both explicit and implicit prejudice toward black people, but the two reductions correlated only weakly with each other. Those students who showed the greatest decline in explicit prejudice did not necessarily show much decline in implicit prejudice, and vice versa. Further analysis revealed that those students who felt most enlightened by the verbal information presented in the course, and who reported the greatest conscious desire to overcome their prejudice, showed the greatest declines in explicit prejudice. In contrast, those who made new black friends during the course, or who most liked the African American professor who taught it, showed the greatest declines in implicit prejudice.

SECTION REVIEW

Social identity can be a major determinant of how we perceive ourselves and others.

Personal and Social Self-Identities

➤ We view ourselves in terms of both personal identity and social identity (the social categories or groups to which we belong). Individualist cultures emphasize personal identity, and collectivist cultures emphasize social identity.

➤ When social identity is uppermost in our minds, the success of others in our group boosts our self-esteem. When personal identity is uppermost, members of our group become our reference group, and their success can lower our self-esteem.

➤ Just as we have a self-enhancing bias, we have a group-enhancing bias, especially when our social identity predominates.

Implicit and Explicit Stereotypes

➤ Stereotypes—the schemas that we have about groups of people—can be explicit (available to consciousness) or implicit (unconscious but able to affect our thoughts, feelings, and actions). Implicit stereotypes are measured through priming and implicit association tests.

➤ Studies reveal that negative implicit stereotypes can promote prejudiced behavior even without conscious prejudice.

➤ Implicit prejudices are based on primitive emotional processes, modifiable by classical conditioning. Positive associations with members of the stereotyped group can help to reduce implicit prejudice.

▮ Attitudes: Their Origins and Their Effects on Behavior

Thus far in this chapter we have been discussing the ways in which people evaluate other people and themselves. In doing so, we have been implicitly discussing attitudes. An *attitude* is any belief or opinion that has an evaluative component—a judgment or feeling that something is good or bad, likable or unlikable, moral or immoral, attractive or repulsive. Our attitudes tie us both cognitively and emotionally to our entire social world. We all have attitudes about countless objects, people, events, and ideas, ranging from our feelings about a particular brand of toothpaste to those about democracy or religion. Our most central attitudes, referred to as *values*, help us judge the appropriateness of whole categories of actions. In this final section of the chapter we examine some ideas about the effects and origins of attitudes.

Relationships of Attitudes to Behavior: Distinction Between Explicit and Implicit Attitudes

Social psychologists first began to study attitudes as part of their attempts to predict how individuals would behave in specific situations. They conceived of attitudes as mental guides that people use to make behavioral choices (Allport, 1935). Over the years much research has been conducted to determine the degree to which people's attitudes do relate to their actual behavior and to understand the conditions in which that relationship is strong or weak. One clear finding is that the attitude–behavior relationship depends very much upon the way in which the attitude is assessed.

Earlier in this chapter, in the discussion of stereotypes, I distinguished between *explicit* and *implicit* racial attitudes. The same distinction applies to attitudes concerning all sorts of objects. **Explicit attitudes** are conscious, verbally stated evaluations. They are measured by traditional attitude tests in which people are asked, in various ways, to state their evaluation of some object or form of behavior. Until relatively recently, all attitude measures in psychology were of explicit attitudes. For example, to assess explicit attitudes about eating meat, people might be asked to respond, on a scale ranging from *strongly agree* to *strongly disagree*, to items such as "In general, I like to eat meat."

Implicit attitudes, by definition, are attitudes that are manifested in automatic mental associations (Fazio & Olson, 2003; Nosek, 2007). They are measured by implicit association tests, of the sort that I already described for assessing attitudes toward particular groups of people (look back at Figure 13.8). If you can more quickly associate *meat* and meat-related words or pictures with good terms (such as *wonderful*) than with bad terms (such as *terrible*), then you have a positive implicit attitude toward meat. If the opposite is true, then you have a negative implicit attitude toward meat.

Implicit Attitudes Automatically Influence Behavior

Implicit attitudes are gut-level attitudes. The object of the attitude automatically elicits mental associations that connote "good" or "bad," and these influence our bodily emotional reactions. In this sense, implicit attitudes automatically influence our behavior. The *less* we think about what we are doing, the more influence our implicit attitudes have. In contrast, our explicit attitudes require thought; the *more* we think about what we are doing, the more influence our explicit attitudes have. In many cases, people's implicit and explicit attitudes coincide, and in those cases behavior generally corresponds well with attitude. But quite often, as we discussed in the case of racial attitudes, implicit and explicit attitudes do not coincide (Nosek, 2007).

Suppose you have become convinced that eating meat is a bad thing—bad for animals, bad for the planet, maybe bad for your health. You have developed, therefore,

> ◢ - - - - - - - - - - - - - - - - - - - **26**
>
> **What is the difference between implicit and explicit attitudes in their manner of influencing behavior?**

a *negative explicit* attitude toward eating meat. But suppose, from your long history of enjoying meat, you have a *positive implicit* attitude toward eating meat. If meat is put before you, your implicit attitude will win out unless you consciously think about your explicit attitude and use restraint. Your implicit attitude automatically makes you want to eat the meat. Not surprisingly, people who successfully maintain a vegetarian diet generally have negative implicit as well as negative explicit attitudes toward eating meat, and positive implicit as well as positive explicit attitudes toward eating vegetables (De Houwer & De Bruycker, 2007).

Experiments using fMRI have shown that people's implicit attitudes are reflected directly in portions of the brain's limbic system that are involved in emotions and drives. In contrast, explicit attitudes are reflected in portions of the prefrontal cortex that are concerned with conscious control. In cases where an explicit attitude counters an implicit attitude, the subcortical areas respond immediately to the relevant stimuli, in accordance with the implicit attitude, but then downward connections from the prefrontal cortex may dampen that response (Stanley & others, 2008). If you have a positive implicit but negative explicit attitude about eating meat, pleasure and appetite centers might respond immediately to meat put before you, but then, if you think about your explicit attitude, those responses might be overcome through connections from your prefrontal cortex.

Early Findings of Lack of Correlations Between Explicit Attitudes and Behavior

27

What early evidence and reasoning led some psychologists to suggest that attitudes have little effect on behavior?

Until relatively recently, all studies of attitudes in social psychology were studies of explicit attitudes. Many of the earliest studies revealed a remarkable *lack* of correlation between measures of attitudes and measures of behavior. In one classic study, for instance, students in a college course filled out a questionnaire aimed at assessing their attitudes toward cheating, and later in the semester they were asked to grade their own true–false tests (Corey, 1937). The tests had already been graded secretly by the instructor, so cheating could be detected. The result was that a great deal of cheating occurred and no correlation at all was found between the attitude assessments and the cheating. Those who had expressed the strongest anti-cheating attitudes on the questionnaire were just as likely to cheat in grading their own tests as were those who had expressed weaker anti-cheating attitudes. A strong correlation was found, however, between cheating and students' true scores on the test: The lower the true score, the more likely the student was to try to raise it by cheating.

A number of findings such as this led some psychologists to conclude that attitudes play little or no role in guiding behavior (Wicker, 1969). Behavioral psychologists, such as B. F. Skinner (1957), who were already disposed to deny much relationship between thought and behavior, used such evidence to argue that attitudes are simply verbal habits, which influence what people say but are largely irrelevant to what they do. According to this view, people learn to say things like, "Honesty is the best policy," because they are rewarded for such words by their social group. But when confronted by an inducement to cheat—such as the opportunity to raise a test score—their behavior is controlled by a new set of rewards and punishments that can lead to an action completely contrary to the attitude they profess.

Explicit Attitudes Must Be Retrieved from Memory to Affect Behavior

28

How might people improve their abilities to behave in accordance with their explicit attitudes?

A good deal of research has shown that people are most likely to behave in accordance with an explicit attitude if they are reminded of that attitude just before the behavioral test (Aronson, 1992; Glasman & Albarracín, 2006). In the experiment on cheating, those who cheated may have been immediately overwhelmed by their poor test performance, which reminded them strongly of their negative attitude toward getting a bad grade but did not remind them of their negative attitude toward cheating. Subsequent research suggests that with more time to think about their attitudes, or with more inducement to think about them, fewer students would have

You promised yourself you'd
do something, someday.

Promise kept.

Call 1-800-614-7979.

Save the Children

Translating attitudes into actions
Ads such as this aim at promoting
behavioral change by reminding
people of their values.

cheated and a correlation may have been found between their anti-cheating attitudes and their behavior.

If you are trying to behave in accordance with some newly formed explicit attitude, then you may need to exert considerable mental effort, at least for a while, to keep reminding yourself of your attitude. If you are a recent convert to vegetarianism, but have a positive implicit attitude toward meat, you may need to remind yourself regularly of your explicit anti-meat attitude until your implicit attitude begins to change. With time, if you continue consciously to associate meat with negative images—perhaps images of cholesterol accumulating in your bloodstream or cattle being slaughtered—your implicit attitude may become more consistent with your explicit attitude. Then your chosen path will be easier.

The Origins of Attitudes, and Methods of Persuasion

People in our society devote enormous efforts and billions of dollars toward modifying other people's attitudes. Advertising, political campaigning, and the democratic process itself (in which people speak freely in support of their views) are, in essence, attempts to change others' attitudes—attitudes about everything from a brand of toothpaste to a war we are waging somewhere in the world. Here we shall examine some ideas about how attitudes are formed and how they are changed.

To a considerable degree, our attitudes are products of learning. Through direct experience or from information that others convey to us, we learn to like some objects, events, and concepts and to dislike others. Such learning can be automatic, involving no conscious thought, or, at the other extreme, it can be highly controlled, involving deliberate searches for relevant information and rational analysis of that information.

Attitudes Through Classical Conditioning: No Thought

Classical conditioning, a basic learning process discussed in **Chapter 4,** can be thought of as an automatic attitude generator. A new stimulus (the conditioned stimulus) is paired with a stimulus that already elicits a particular reaction (the unconditioned stimulus), and, as a result, the new stimulus comes to elicit, by itself, a reaction similar to that elicited by the original stimulus. Using the language of the present chapter, we can say that Pavlov's dog entered the experiment with a preexisting positive attitude toward meat. When Pavlov preceded the meat on several occasions with the sound of a bell, the dog acquired a positive attitude toward that sound. The dog now salivated and wagged its tail when the bell rang, and if given a chance, it would have learned to ring the bell itself.

◄ Classical conditioning leads us to feel positive about objects and events that have been linked in our experience to pleasant, life-promoting occurrences and to feel negative about those that have been linked to unpleasant, life-threatening occurrences. In today's world, however, where many of the stimulus links we experience are the creations of advertisers and others who want to manipulate us, classical conditioning can have maladaptive consequences. All those ads in which cigarettes, beer, and expensive gas-guzzling cars are paired with beautiful people, happy scenes, and enjoyable music are designed to exploit our most thoughtless attitude-forming system, classical conditioning. The advertisers want us to salivate, wag our tails, and run out and buy their products.

Controlled experiments have shown that it is relatively easy to condition positive or negative attitudes to such products as a brand of mouthwash by pairing the product with positive or negative scenes or words (Grossman & Till, 1998). In some experiments, such conditioning has been demonstrated even when the subjects are not aware of the pairing of the conditioned and unconditioned stimuli (De Houwer & others, 2001; Olson & Fazio, 2001). Not surprisingly, such conditioning generally affects people's implicit attitudes more than their explicit attitudes. In fact, some experiments have shown that it is possible to generate either a positive or negative implicit attitude through conditioning while, at the very same time, generating an opposite attitude through the presentation of evaluative statements. Here's an example of such an experiment (Rydell & others, 2006).

Subjects were presented, over a series of conditioning trials, with a photograph of a man named Bob, which appeared on a screen in front of them. Immediately before each presentation of Bob, a word was flashed on the screen, for just 25 milliseconds, too rapidly to read consciously but capable of being read at an unconscious level. For some subjects, each flashed word was negative, such as *hate* or *death*. For other subjects, the each flashed word was positive, such as *love* or *party*. In addition, on each trial, a verbal statement was presented along with the picture, which described something that Bob had done. This statement was on the screen long enough for subjects to read it consciously, and subjects had to respond to the statement in a manner showing that they had read it and understood it. For subjects who were presented with negative conditioning words the statement about Bob's behavior was always positive, and for subjects who were presented with positive conditioning words the statement about his behavior was always negative. Then the subjects were given both an implicit test and an explicit test of their attitudes toward Bob. In the implicit test they had to respond as quickly as possible in categorizing pictures of Bob with "good" terms on some trials and with "bad" terms on other trials. In the explicit test they rated how likeable Bob is, on a scale running from *very unlikeable* to *very likeable*.

The result, as predicted, was that the subjects manifested opposite implicit and explicit attitudes toward Bob. Their implicit attitudes were determined by the words flashed quickly on the screen, which unconsciously affected their mental associations about Bob. Their explicit attitudes were determined by the statements about Bob's behavior, which they had read and thought about consciously.

Other experiments have shown that classical conditioning, when its effects aren't countered with opposite statements, can affect explicit attitudes in the same direction as the implicit effects (Gawronski & Bodenhausen, 2006; Li & others, 2007). When positive or negative images, words, or even smells are consistently paired with a photograph of a particular person or object, people develop a positive or negative implicit attitude toward that person or object. If they have no conscious information

29

How do advertisers use classical conditioning to influence people's attitudes? How have researchers demonstrated effects of classical conditioning on implicit and explicit attitudes?

countering that attitude, the implicit attitude affects their explicit attitude. Other things being equal, we consciously like people and objects that elicit positive associations in our minds and consciously dislike those that elicit negative associations in our minds.

Attitudes Through Heuristics: Superficial Thought

Beyond simple classical conditioning is the more sophisticated but still relatively automatic process of using certain decision rules, or heuristics, to evaluate information and develop attitudes (Chen & Chaiken, 1999). Heuristics provide shortcuts to a full, logical elaboration of the information in a message. They are believed to affect primarily our explicit attitudes, but they can affect our implicit attitudes as well (Evans, 2008). Examples of such rules include the following:

1. If there are lots of numbers and big words in the message, it must be well documented.

2. If the message is phrased in terms of values that I believe in, it is probably right.

3. Famous or successful people are more likely than unknown or unsuccessful people to be correct.

4. If most people believe this message, it is probably true. (This heuristic has to do with effects of social norms on attitudes, discussed extensively in **Chapter 14.**)

We learn to use such rules, presumably, because they often allow us to make useful judgments with minimal expenditures of time and mental energy. The rules become mental habits, which we use implicitly, without awareness that we are using them. Advertisers, of course, exploit these mental habits, just as they exploit the process of classical conditioning.

30
What are some examples of decision rules (heuristics) that people use with minimal thought to evaluate messages?

H·M·VICTORIA EUGENIA *Queen of Spain*

A recent portrait of Her Majesty. Victoria Eugenia, Queen of Spain, here reproduced by gracious permission of Her Majesty to the Pond's Extract Company

Her royal pleasure
John B. Watson, the founder of behaviorism (discussed in **Chapter 4**), became an advertising specialist after leaving academia. This ad, created by Watson, helped sell a skin cream by associating it with the wealth and beauty of the queen of Spain. According to the fine print, the queen uses Pond's vanishing and cold creams and "has expressed her royal pleasure in them."

Courtesy of The J. Walter Thompson Archive, Duke University

They sprinkle their ads with irrelevant data and high-sounding words such as *integrity,* and they pay celebrities huge sums of money to endorse their products.

Attitudes Through Logical Analysis of the Message: Systematic Thought

Sometimes, of course, we think logically, in ways that produce rational effects on our explicit attitudes. Generally, we are most likely to do so for issues that really matter to us. In a theory of persuasion called the **elaboration likelihood model,** Richard Petty and John Cacioppo (1986) proposed that a major determinant of whether a message will be processed systematically (through logical analysis of the content) or superficially is the personal relevance of the message. According to Petty and Cacioppo, we tend to be *cognitive misers;* we reserve our elaborative reasoning powers for messages that seem most relevant to us, and we rely on mental shortcuts to evaluate messages that seem less relevant. Much research supports this proposition (Petty & Wegener, 1999; Pierro & others, 2004).

In one experiment on the role of personal relevance in persuasion, Petty and his colleagues (1981) presented college students with messages in favor of requiring students to pass a set of comprehensive examinations in order to graduate. Different groups of students received different messages, which varied in (a) the *strength* of the arguments, (b) the alleged *source* of the arguments, and (c) the *personal relevance* of the message. The weak arguments consisted of slightly relevant quotations,

31
How did an experiment support the idea that people tend to reserve systematic thought for messages that are personally relevant to them and to use heuristics for other messages?

FIGURE 13.10 Effect of persuasive arguments on attitude under various experimental conditions In this graph, protrusion above the horizontal axis indicates agreement with the persuasive message, and protrusion below the axis indicates disagreement. When the issue was of high personal relevance (left half of graph), the strength or weakness of the arguments had more impact than did the source of the arguments; but when the issue was of low personal relevance (right half of graph), the reverse was true. (Adapted from Petty & others, 1981.)

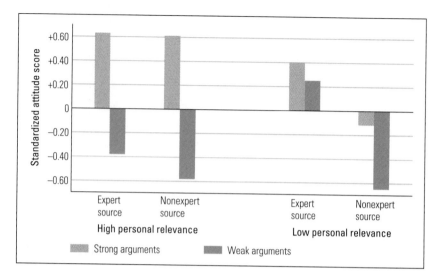

personal opinions, and anecdotal observations; the strong arguments contained well-structured statistical evidence that the proposed policy would improve the reputation of the university and its graduates. In some cases the arguments were said to have been prepared by high school students and in other cases by the Carnegie Commission on Higher Education. Finally, the personal relevance was varied by stating in the high-relevance condition that the proposed policy would take effect the following year, so current students would be subject to it, and in the low-relevance condition that it would begin in 10 years.

After hearing the message, students in each condition were asked to rate the extent to which they agreed or disagreed with the proposal. Figure 13.10 shows the results. As you can see, in the high-relevance condition the quality of the arguments was most important. Students in that condition tended to be persuaded by strong arguments and not by weak ones, regardless of the alleged source. Thus, in that condition, students must have listened to and evaluated the arguments. In the low-relevance condition, the quality of the arguments had much less effect, and the source of the arguments had much more. Apparently, when the policy was not going to affect them, students did not attend carefully to the arguments but, instead, relied on the simple decision rule that experts (members of the Carnegie Commission) are more likely to be right than are non-experts (high school students).

There is no surprise in Petty and Cacioppo's theory or in the results supporting it. The idea that people think more logically about issues that directly affect them than about those that don't was a basic premise of philosophers who laid the foundations for democratic forms of government. And, to repeat what is by now a familiar refrain, our mental apparatus evolved to keep us alive and promote our welfare in our social communities; it is no wonder that we use our minds more fully for those purposes than for purposes that have little effect on our well-being.

Attitudes as Rationalizations to Attain Cognitive Consistency

A century ago, Sigmund Freud began developing his controversial theory that human beings are fundamentally irrational. What pass for reasons, according to Freud, are most often rationalizations designed to calm our anxieties and boost our self-esteem. You will read more about Freud's view in **Chapter 15.** A more moderate view, to be pursued here, is that we are rational but the machinery that makes us so is far from perfect. The same mental machinery that produces logic can produce pseudo-logic.

In the 1950s, Leon Festinger (1957) proposed what he called the ***cognitive dissonance theory,*** which ever since has been one of social psychology's most central ideas. According to the theory, we have, built into the workings of our mind, a mechanism that creates an uncomfortable feeling of dissonance, or lack of harmony, when we sense some inconsistency among the various explicit attitudes, beliefs, and items of knowledge that constitute our mental store. Just as the discomfort of hunger motivates us to seek food, the discomfort of cognitive dissonance motivates us to seek ways to resolve contradictions or inconsistencies among our conscious cognitions.

Such a mechanism could well have evolved to serve adaptive functions related to logic. Inconsistencies imply that we are mistaken about something, and mistakes can lead to danger. Suppose you have a favorable attitude about sunbathing, but you learn that overexposure to the sun's ultraviolet rays is the leading cause of skin cancer. The discrepancy between your preexisting attitude and your new knowledge may create a state of cognitive dissonance. To resolve the dissonance, you might change your attitude about sunbathing from positive to negative or you might bring in a third cognition: "Sunbathing is relatively safe, in moderation, if I use a sunscreen lotion." But the dissonance-reducing drive, like other drives, does not always function adaptively. Just as our hunger can lead us to eat things that aren't good for us, our dissonance-reducing drive can lead us to reduce dissonance in illogical and maladaptive ways. Those are the effects that particularly intrigued Festinger and many subsequent social psychologists.

Avoiding Dissonant Information

I once heard someone cut off a political discussion with the words, "I'm sorry, but I refuse to listen to something I disagree with." People don't usually come right out and say that, but have you noticed how often they seem to behave that way? Given a choice of books or articles to read, lectures to attend, or documentaries to watch, people generally choose those that they believe will support their existing views. That observation is consistent with the cognitive dissonance theory. One way to avoid dissonance is to avoid situations in which we might discover facts or ideas that run counter to our current views. If we avoid listening to or reading about the evidence that ultraviolet rays can cause skin cancer, we can blithely continue to enjoy sunbathing. People don't always avoid dissonant information, but a considerable body of research indicates that they very often do (Frey, 1986; Jonas & others, 2001).

A good, real-world illustration of the avoidance of dissonant information is found in a research study conducted in 1973, the year of the Senate Watergate hearings, which uncovered illegal activities associated with then-President Richard Nixon's re-election campaign against George McGovern (Sweeney & Gruber, 1984). The hearings were extensively covered in all of the news media at that time. By interviewing a sample of voters before, during, and after the hearings, Sweeney and Gruber discovered that (a) Nixon supporters avoided news about the hearings (but not other political news) and were as strongly supportive of Nixon after the hearings as they had been before; (b) McGovern supporters eagerly sought out information about the hearings and were as strongly opposed to Nixon afterward as they had been before; and (c) previously undecided voters paid moderate attention to the hearings and were the only group whose attitude toward Nixon was significantly influenced (in a negative direction) by the hearings. So, consistent with the cognitive dissonance theory, all but the undecideds approached the hearings in a way that seemed designed to protect or strengthen, rather than challenge, their existing views.

> **32**
> How does the cognitive dissonance theory explain people's attraction to some information and avoidance of other information?

Firming Up an Attitude to Be Consistent with an Action

We make most of our choices in life with less-than-absolute certainty. We vote for a candidate not knowing for sure if he or she is best, buy one car even though some of the evidence favors another, or choose to major in psychology even though some other fields have their attractions. After we have irrevocably made one choice or another—after we have cast our ballot, made our down payment, or registered for our courses and let the deadline for schedule changes pass—any lingering doubts would be discordant with our knowledge of what we have done. So, according to

> **33**
> How does the cognitive dissonance theory explain why people are more confident of a decision just after they have made it than just before?

Dissonance abolished This couple may have agonized long and hard before signing on the dotted line, but once they signed, they set their doubts aside and focused on the positive qualities of their new home. According to the cognitive dissonance theory, people are generally more confident about the correctness of their choices after those choices are made than before.

34 ------------------------------
How is the insufficient-justification effect illustrated by Benjamin Franklin's story?
----

the cognitive dissonance theory, we should be motivated to set those doubts aside.

Many studies have shown that people do tend to set their doubts aside after making an irrevocable decision. Even in the absence of new information, people suddenly become more confident of their choice after acting on it than they were before. For example, in one study, bettors at a horse race were more confident that their horse would win if they were asked immediately after they had placed their bet than if they were asked immediately before (Knox & Inkster, 1968). In another study, voters who were leaving the polling place spoke more positively about their favored candidate than did those who were entering (Frenkel & Doob, 1976). In still another study, photography students who were allowed to choose one photographic print to keep as their own liked their chosen photograph better, several days later, if they were not allowed to revise their choice than if they were allowed to revise it (Gilbert & Ebert, 2002). In the reversible-choice condition, they could reduce dissonance by saying to themselves that they could exchange the photograph for a different one if they wanted to, so they had less need to bolster their attitude toward the one they had chosen.

Changing an Attitude to Justify an Action: The Insufficient-Justification Effect

Sometimes people behave in ways that run counter to their attitudes and then are faced with the dissonant cognitions, "I believe *this*, but I did *that*." They can't undo their deed, but they can relieve dissonance by modifying—maybe even reversing—their attitudes. This change in attitude is called the ***insufficient-justification effect,*** because it occurs only if the person has no easy way to justify the behavior, given his or her previous attitude.

Example from the Autobiography of Benjamin Franklin More than 200 years ago, the great inventor, statesman, and master of practical psychology Benjamin Franklin recognized what we now call the insufficient-justification effect and used it to his advantage. In his autobiography, Franklin (1818/1949) describes how he changed the attitude of a political opponent who was trying to block his appointment to a high office:

> I did not like the opposition of this new member, who was a gentleman of fortune and education with talents that were likely to give him in time great influence. . . . I did not, however, aim at gaining his favour by paying any servile respect to him, but after some time took this other method. Having heard that he had in his library a certain very scarce and curious book, I wrote a note to him expressing my desire of perusing that book and requesting he do me the favour of lending it to me for a few days. He sent it immediately. . . . When we next met in the House, he spoke to me (which he had never done before), and with great civility. And he ever afterwards manifested a readiness to serve me on all occasions, so that we became great friends. . . . This is another instance of the truth of an old maxim I had learned, which says, "He that has once done you a kindness will be more ready to do you another than he whom you yourself have obliged."

How would the cognitive dissonance theory explain why Franklin's former opponent changed his attitude toward Franklin? The opponent received Franklin's request to borrow the book, and for reasons of which he may not have been fully aware, such as the simple habit of courtesy, he did not turn it down. But once he sent the book to Franklin, he was thrown into a state of cognitive dissonance. One thought, *I do not like Ben Franklin,* was discordant with another, *I have just lent Franklin a very valuable book.* The second of these could not be denied, since that was an objective fact, so dissonance could best be relieved by changing the first: *Ben Franklin isn't really a bad sort. At least I know he's honest. If he weren't honest, I certainly wouldn't have lent him that valuable book.* Such thinking reduced or erased the dissonance and set the stage for new, friendlier behaviors toward Franklin in the future.

Conditions That Optimize the Insufficient-Justification Effect: Low Incentive and Free Choice One requirement for the insufficient-justification effect to occur is that there be no obvious, high incentive for performing the counter-attitudinal action. If Franklin had offered to do a large favor for his opponent in exchange for borrowing the book, the opponent could have maintained his dislike for Franklin by saying, "I lent him the book only to get him to do me that favor."

35

In theory, why should the insufficient-justification effect work best when there is minimal incentive for the action and the action is freely chosen? How was this theory verified by two classic experiments?

In a classic experiment that demonstrates the low-incentive requirement, Festinger and James Carlsmith (1959) gave college students a boring task (loading spools into trays and turning pegs in a pegboard) and then offered to "hire" them to tell another student that the task was exciting and enjoyable. Some students were offered $1 for their role in recruiting the other student, and others were offered $20 (a princely sum at a time when the minimum wage in the United States was $1 an hour). The result was that those in the $1 condition changed their attitude toward the task and later recalled it as truly enjoyable, whereas those in the $20 condition continued to recall it as boring. Presumably, students in the $1 condition could not justify their lie to the other student on the basis of the little they were promised, so they convinced themselves that they were not lying. Those in the $20 condition, in contrast, could justify their lie: *I said the task was enjoyable when it was actually boring, but who wouldn't tell such a small lie for $20?*

Another essential condition for the insufficient-justification effect is that subjects must perceive their action as stemming from their own free choice. Otherwise, they could justify the action—and relieve dissonance—simply by saying, "I was forced to do it."

In an experiment demonstrating the free-choice requirement, students were asked to write essays expressing support for a bill in the state legislature that most students personally opposed (Linder & others, 1967). Students in the free-choice condition were told clearly that they didn't have to write the essays, but they were encouraged to do so and none refused. Students in the no-choice condition were

simply told to write the essays, and all complied. After writing the essays, all students were asked to describe their personal attitudes toward the bill. Only those in the free-choice condition showed a significant shift in the direction of favoring the bill; those in the no-choice condition remained as opposed to it as did students who had not been asked to write essays at all.

In this case, attitude change in the free-choice condition apparently occurred because the students could justify their choice to write the essays only by deciding that they did, after all, favor the bill. Subsequent experiments, using essentially the same procedure, showed that students in the free-choice condition also exhibited more psychological discomfort and physiological arousal, compared to those in the no-choice condition, as they wrote their essays (Elkin & Leippe, 1986; Elliot & Devine, 1994). This finding is consistent with the view that they were experiencing greater dissonance.

SECTION REVIEW

An attitude is a belief or opinion that includes an evaluative component.

Attitudes and Behavior	Sources of Attitudes	Attitudes and Cognitive Dissonance
➤ Implicit attitudes—those formed through direct experience or repeated associations—influence behavior automatically.	➤ Implicit attitudes can be created or altered through classical conditioning, with no thought required and even without awareness.	➤ We are motivated to reduce cognitive dissonance—a discomforting lack of accord among our explicit beliefs, knowledge, attitudes, and actions.
➤ Early research suggested that explicit attitudes correlate little if at all with actual behavior. Subsequent research indicates that explicit attitudes must be recalled and thought about before they can affect behavior.	➤ By using heuristics (e.g., "If most people believe this, it is probably true"), people can arrive at attitudes through superficial thought.	➤ The desire to prevent or reduce cognitive dissonance often leads people to avoid dissonant information and to set aside doubts about a decision once it has been made.
	➤ When a message is highly relevant to us, we tend to base our explicit attitudes on logical analysis of the content.	➤ When we freely and with little incentive do something contrary to an attitude, we may alter the attitude to better fit the action; this is called the insufficient-justification effect.

Concluding Thoughts

To organize your thoughts about this chapter, you might find it useful to reflect on four themes that ran through it: the themes of bias, function, cultural differences, and implicit versus explicit mental processes.

1. Biases in social perceptions and attitudes can lead people to make judgments that are objectively untrue and unfair. You might think about each bias discussed in the chapter with the following questions in mind: What evidence was presented for the existence of the bias? In what contexts does the bias seem to occur or not occur? What, if any, functions might the bias serve for the person manifesting it? What harm might result from this bias, either to the person who manifests it or to the objects of the biased perception or thought? You will not find the answers to all these questions for every bias described in the chapter, but in most cases you will at least find hints. Apply such questions to the person bias, attractiveness bias, baby-face bias, biasing effects of others' appraisals on self-concept, big-fish-in-little-pond effect, self-enhancing biases (including the self-serving attributional bias), group-enhancing biases, biasing effects of stereotypes, and insufficient-justification effect.

2. Social perceptions and attitudes serve life-promoting functions for the individual. From the functionalist perspective, the first question asked about any consistent human tendency is: How might it serve the needs of the individual who manifests that tendency? Some of the ideas in this chapter were presented quite explicitly from that perspective, and others were not. As you review each of the phenomena described, think about whether and how it serves the individual. Concerning the biases in person perception, you might well conclude that some do serve useful functions for the perceiver and that others may be non-adaptive side effects of the ways that our minds work. Concerning self-perception, think about the potential survival-promoting values of the looking-glass self, self-esteem (according to the sociometer theory), the use of social comparison to understand oneself, the self-enhancing biases, and the capacity to shift between personal identity and social identity. Think also about the functions of implicit and explicit attitudes for guiding behavior.

3. Culture plays a powerful role in shaping our social perceptions and attitudes. The human mind evolved to meet the social needs of our hunter-gatherer ancestors, but each individual person's mind is honed, through development, to meet the requirements of life within that person's culture. In this chapter you have read about some consistent differences between Westerners and East Asians, including differences in susceptibility to self-enhancement and differences in the balance between personal identity and social identity. How might these differences be explained in terms of the different philosophical traditions of the West and the East?

4. Social perceptions and attitudes may be implicit and automatic or explicit and controlled. The distinction between implicit and explicit mental processes was most directly discussed in the sections on stereotypes and on the relationship between attitudes and behavior. You saw how implicit stereotypes and attitudes affect judgments and actions automatically and unconsciously, while explicit stereotypes and attitudes operate through conscious, deliberate means. The implicit–explicit distinction is relevant to all the topics of this chapter. All the biases affecting the impressions we form of other people—including the person bias in attributions, the attractiveness bias, and the baby-face bias–operate implicitly; we are usually unaware of their effects on our judgments and actions. You also read of implicit and explicit processes in the section dealing with the roles of classical conditioning, heuristics, and rational thought in attitude formation. As you review each of the social perceptual and attitudinal phenomena discussed in this chapter, think about the degree to which it may arise from implicit or explicit mental processes. How might we bring explicit processes to bear in reducing or countering the irrational and unfair implicit judgments that we make?

Further Reading

Malcolm Gladwell (2005). *Blink: The power of thinking without thinking.* Boston: Little, Brown.

This is a beautifully written brief book about the beneficial and harmful effects of our capacity to make quick, implicit, relatively unconscious judgments about people and other objects. Gladwell is a professional writer who has thoroughly familiarized himself with contemporary social psychological research. Here he relates research on implicit judgments to such practical issues as speed dating, market research, advertising, and racial prejudice.

Mark Leary (2004). *The curse of the self: Self-awareness, egotism, and the quality of human life.* Oxford, UK: Oxford University Press.

Our capacity for self-reflection is a large part of what makes us human. It allows us to think about and learn from our past successes and failures, to see ourselves somewhat as others see us, and to contemplate and plan our futures. However, that same capacity also contributes to human misery. Overemphasis on the self can lead to fruitless rumination, crippling self-conscious anxiety, egocentric selfishness and narcissism, and life-threatening depression when the bubble of self-inflation breaks or fails to materialize. Leary is the social psychologist who developed the sociometer theory of self-esteem. In this book, for the general reader, he writes clearly and persuasively about the dark side of too much focus on the self and too little focus on the world outside ourselves.

Melinda Jones (2002). *Social psychology of prejudice.* Upper Saddle River, NJ: Prentice Hall.

This brief, easy-to-read paperback textbook summarizes much of the social-psychological research on stereotyping and prejudice. It includes chapters on racism, sexism, and antigay prejudice; the relationship between values and prejudice; the cognitive foundations of categorization and stereotyping; intergroup comparison and conflict; the experiences of victims of prejudice; and methods of reducing prejudice.

Dan Ariely (2008). *Predictably irrational: The hidden forces that shape our decisions.* New York, NY: HarperCollins.

Ariely is one of a new breed of economist who is bringing psychology to bear in understanding how people make economic decisions. With experiments, logic, and humor he explains here why we often work harder for nothing than for money, why our choices of what to buy often have little to do with their actual value, and why we sometimes do and sometimes don't behave in accordance with our moral values.

Roy Baumeister (2005). *The cultural animal: Human nature, meaning, and social life.* Oxford, UK: Oxford University Press.

In this intellectually stimulating book, Baumeister, an eminent contemporary social psychologist, develops the thesis that we have been cultural animals for a long time and that evolution has shaped us for culture. The book brings together much of what social scientists (economists, sociologists, and anthropologists as well as psychologists) have learned about human motivation, emotion, thought, and behavior.

Social Influences on Behavior 14

A central theme of social psychology is that human behavior is influenced powerfully by the social environment in which it occurs. We behave as we do—sometimes heroically, sometimes villainously, more often somewhere in between—not just because of who we are, but also because of the social situations in which we find ourselves. Social norms and the examples, expectations, requests, and demands of those around us influence our behavior essentially every waking moment of every day. None of us is such an individualist as to be uninfluenced by others.

This chapter is about the ways by which the social environment influences our behavior. It deals with such topics as evaluation anxiety, conformity, obedience, cooperation, and conflict. A very general concept that runs through the chapter is that of *social pressure,* which can be defined as the entire set of psychological forces that are exerted on us by others' judgments, examples, expectations, and demands, whether real or imagined. At any given moment, we are most strongly influenced by those people who are physically or psychologically closest to us.

Social pressure arises from the ways we interpret and respond emotionally to the social situations around us. It is a normal part of being human. Such pressure is useful because it promotes our social acceptability and helps create order and predictability in social interactions. But it can also lead us, in some situations, to behave in ways that are objectively foolish or morally repugnant.

■ Effects of Being Observed and Evaluated

Let us begin by considering what might seem to be the minimal form of social pressure—the mere presence of other people who can observe us perform. We do not behave in exactly the same way when others can see us as we do when we are alone. As thinking, social beings, we are concerned about the impressions we make on other people, and that concern influences our behavior.

Facilitating and Interfering Effects of an Audience

In some of the earliest experiments in social psychology, people performed various tasks better when one or more observers were present than they did when alone. In one experiment, for example, college students who had achieved skill at a task involving eye–hand coordination (moving a hand-held pointer to follow a moving target) subsequently performed it more accurately when observed by a group of graduate students than when tested alone (Travis, 1925). The enhancing effect of an audience on task performance was soon accepted as a general law of behavior and was given a name: ***social facilitation.***

Other early experiments, however, demonstrated an opposite effect: ***social interference*** (also called *social inhibition*), a decline in performance when observers are present. For example, students who were asked to develop arguments opposing the views of certain classical philosophers developed better arguments when they worked alone than when they worked in the presence of observers (Allport, 1920). The presence of observers also reduced performance in solving math problems (Moore, 1917), learning a finger maze (Husband, 1931), and memorizing lists of nonsense syllables (Pressin, 1933).

Facilitation of "Easy" Tasks, Interference with "Hard" Ones

1 ┈┈┈┈┈┈┈┈┈┈┈┈┈┈◁

How does Zajonc's theory explain both social facilitation and social interference? What evidence supports the theory?

Why does an audience sometimes improve a person's performance and other times worsen it? In reviewing the experiments, Robert Zajonc [pronounced **Zai**-yons] (1965) noticed that social facilitation usually occurred with relatively simple or well-learned tasks and that social interference usually occurred with complex tasks or tasks that involved new learning. From this observation, Zajonc proposed the following generalization: *The presence of others facilitates performance of dominant actions and interferes with performance of non-dominant actions.* In this statement, the term *dominant actions* refers to actions that are so simple, instinctive, or well learned that they can be produced automatically, with little conscious thought; and *non-dominant actions* refers to actions that require considerable conscious thought or attention.

To explain both effects, Zajonc further proposed that the presence of an audience increases a person's level of drive or arousal (Aiello & Douthitt, 2001; Zajonc, 1965). The heightened drive increases the person's effort, which facilitates dominant tasks, where the amount of effort determines degree of success. The heightened drive interferes, however, with controlled, calm, conscious thought and attention and thereby worsens performance of non-dominant actions (see Figure 14.1).

Much subsequent research has supported Zajonc's theory. The presence of observers does increase drive and arousal, as measured by self-reports and by physiological indices such as increased heart rate and muscle tension (Cacioppo & others, 1990; Zajonc, 1980). Other studies have shown, just as Zajonc had predicted, that either facilitation or interference can occur in the very same task, depending on the performers' skill. In one experiment, for example, expert pool players performed better when they were watched conspicuously by a group of four observers than when they thought they were not being observed, and the opposite occurred for novice pool players (Michaels & others, 1982).

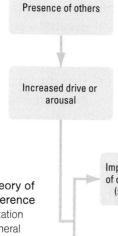

FIGURE 14.1 Zajonc's theory of social facilitation and interference This theory relates social facilitation and interference to a more general effect of high arousal or drive on dominant (habitual, cognitively easy) and non-dominant (nonhabitual, cognitively difficult) responses.

Presence of others

Increased drive or arousal

Improved performance of dominant responses (social facilitation)

Worsened performance of non-dominant responses (social interference)

Social facilitation When the performer is an expert, like Tiger Woods, the presence of an audience improves performance. Such an audience would worsen performance for a novice.

Evaluation Anxiety as a Basis for Social Interference

Zajonc did not explain why a state of high drive interferes with performance of novel or cognitively difficult tasks, but a good deal of research since his time suggests that the primary cause is evaluation anxiety. Social interference increases when the observers are high in status or expertise and are present explicitly to evaluate (Geen, 1980, 1991). It also increases when subjects are made to feel unconfident and more anxious about their ability, through negative feedback given just before the test; and it decreases or is abolished when subjects are made to feel very confident about their ability (Klehe & others, 2007). Moreover, people who have an optimistic, unflappable, low-anxiety personality are more likely to exhibit social facilitation and less likely to exhibit social inhibition than are the rest of us (Uziel, 2007).

> **2**
> What evidence suggests that evaluation anxiety is part of the causal chain of social interference?

Choking Under Pressure: The Working-Memory Explanation

Social interference can be thought of as a subcategory of a more general phenomenon commonly referred to as *choking under pressure*. The highly aroused mental state produced by any strong form of pressure to perform well can, ironically, cause performance to worsen.

Using the terminology of modern cognitive psychology, "choking" is especially likely to occur with tasks that make strong demands on working memory. Working memory, as described in **Chapter 9,** is the part of the mind that controls conscious attention and holds, in consciousness, those items of information that are needed to solve a problem. The kinds of tasks that Zajonc referred to as involving nondominant responses are, in general, tasks that make heavy demands on working memory. Pressure and accompanying anxiety can worsen performance of such tasks by creating distracting thoughts—thoughts about being evaluated, about the difficulty of the task, about the consequences of failing, and so on—which usurp much of the limited capacity of working memory and thereby interfere with concentration on the problem to be solved.

Choking on Academic Tests

Students who suffer from severe test anxiety report that distracting and disturbing thoughts flood their minds and interfere with their performance on important tests (Zeidner, 1998). With sufficient pressure, such choking can occur even in students who normally do not suffer from test anxiety, and researchers have found that it occurs specifically with test items that make the highest demands on working memory.

> **3**
> What evidence supports the view that choking on tests occurs because distracting thoughts interfere with working memory?

In one series of experiments, for example, students were given math problems that varied in difficulty and in the degree to which students had an opportunity to practice them in advance (Beilock & others, 2004). Pressure to perform well was manipulated by telling some students that they were part of a team and that if they failed to perform above a certain criterion neither they nor their team-mates—who had already performed above the criterion—would win a certain prize. They were also told that they would be videotaped as they worked on the problems, so that math teachers and professors could examine the problem-solving process. Students in the low-pressure group, in contrast, were simply asked to solve the problems as best they could. The result was that the high-pressure group performed significantly worse than the low-pressure group on the unpracticed difficult problems, but not on the easy or thoroughly practiced problems, which were less taxing on working memory.

Stereotype Threat as a Special Cause of Choking

4 ┄┄┄┄┄┄┄┄┄┄┄┄┄┄┄┄
How can the activation of a stereotype influence test performance? What evidence suggests that this effect, like other forms of choking, involves increased anxiety and interference with working memory?
┄┄┄┄┄┄┄┄┄┄┄┄┄┄┄┄

Stereotype threat, a particularly potent cause of choking on academic tests, was first described several years ago by Claude Steele (1997; Steele & others, 2002). It is threat that test-takers experience when they are reminded of the stereotypical belief that the group to which they belong is not expected to do well on the test. In a series of experiments, Steele found that African American college students, but not white college students, performed worse on various tests if the tests were referred to as "intelligence tests" than if the same tests were referred to by other labels. He found, further, that this drop in performance became even greater if the students were deliberately reminded of their race just before taking the test. The threat in this case came from the common stereotype that African Americans have lower intelligence than white Americans. Essentially all African American college students are painfully aware of this stereotype.

Subsequently, stereotype threat has been demonstrated with other stigmatized groups as well (Nguyen & Ryan, 2008; Schmader & others, 2008). For example, women consistently perform worse on problem-solving tests that are described as "math tests" than on the same tests when given other names, and this effect is magnified if attention is drawn to the stereotype that women have lower aptitude for math than do men (Johns & others, 2005; Wheeler & Petty, 2001). Even white males have been shown to exhibit stereotype threat in math, when the stereotype that whites have less math ability than do Asians is made salient to them (Aronson & others, 1999). The effect of stereotype threat is an example of what in **Chapter 13** were referred to as *self-fulfilling prophesies.* The expectation that you will perform badly in fact causes you to perform badly.

Stereotype threat If this is a mathematics quiz, the young woman's distraction may be a sign of stereotype threat. The confidence of the guy next to her, and his apparently rapid progress on the test, may remind her of the stereotype that women are less competent than men in mathematics.

As in the case of other examples of choking, stereotype threat seems to produce its effects by increasing anxiety and mental distraction. People report higher levels of felt anxiety and manifest greater physiological evidence of anxiety (such as heart-rate increase) when taking a test in the stereotype-threat condition than when taking the same test in the non-threat condition (Johns & others, 2008; Osborne, 2007). The threat seems to undermine confidence, while at the same time increasing motivation to do well (so as not to confirm the stereotype), resulting in increased anxiety. The increased anxiety apparently reduces performance at least in part by occupying working memory with worrisome thoughts, thereby reducing the amount of working memory capacity available to solve the problems. Researchers have found that stereotype threat reduces performance on problems that tax working memory more than on problems that can be answered largely through recall from long-term memory (Beilock & others, 2007).

Stockbyte/Getty Images

An example of an experiment showing a large effect of stereotype threat on working memory capacity is the following, which employed a standard test of working memory (Schmader & Johns, 2003). Each trial of the working-memory test requires subjects to hold a list of words in mind, and report them later, while solving simple arithmetic problems. In the experiment, men and women took this test under one of two conditions. In the *non-threat condition*, the test was described as a "test of memory" and no mention was made of gender differences. In the *stereotype-threat condition*, the test was described as a "mathematics test" and the students were informed that their gender might play a role in their performance. The results are shown in Figure 14.2. In the non-threat condition women and men performed equally, as measured by the number of words recalled correctly, but in the stereotype-threat condition women performed much worse than men.

In case you yourself have suffered from stereotype threat, you may be interested to know that simple awareness of the stereotype-threat phenomenon helps people overcome it (Johns & others, 2005). Apparently, such awareness leads test-takers to attribute their incipient anxiety to stereotype threat rather than to the difficulty of the problems or to some inadequacy in themselves, and this helps them to concentrate on the problems rather than on their own fears. Other research has shown that self-affirming thoughts before the test—such as thoughts created by listing your own strengths and values—can reduce or abolish stereotype threat, apparently by boosting confidence and/or by reducing the importance attributed to the test (Martens & others, 2006).

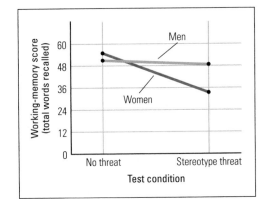

FIGURE 14.2 Stereotype threat reduces working-memory score in women When the test of working memory was described as a math test and attention was drawn to the stereotype that women do poorly in math (stereotype-threat condition), women scored much lower than men. In the non-threat condition, women and men scored equally well. (Data from Schmader & Johns, 2003. The maximum score on the test was 72.)

Impression Management: Behavior as Performance

Besides influencing our abilities to perform specific tasks, social pressures influence our choices of what to say and do in front of other people. Because we care what others think of us, we strive to influence their thoughts. To that end, we behave differently when witnesses are present than when we are alone, and differently in front of some witnesses than in front of others. Social psychologists use the term **impression management** to refer to the entire set of ways by which people consciously and unconsciously modify their behavior to influence others' impressions of them (Schlenker, 1980).

Humans as Actors and as Politicians

Poets and philosophers have always been aware of, and have frequently ridiculed, the human concern about appearances. As Shakespeare put it, "All the world's a stage, and all the men and women merely players." The sociologist Erving Goffman developed an entire approach to thinking about human behavior based on this metaphor. In a classic book titled *The Presentation of Self in Everyday Life*, Goffman (1959) portrayed us as actors, playing at different times on different stages to different audiences, always trying to convince our current audience that we are whom we are playing. In Goffman's view, we are not necessarily aware that we are performing. There need not be a division in our minds between the images we try to project and our sincere beliefs about ourselves (Schlenker & Pontari, 2000). At any given moment we may simply be trying to exhibit our best self, or those aspects of our self that seem most appropriate and useful to meet the moment's needs, which change with our audience.

An alternative metaphor, which captures long-range purposes of our performances, is that we are *intuitive politicians* (suggested by Tetlock, 1991, 2002). We perform in front of others not just to tell a good story or portray a character but to achieve real-life ends that may be selfish or noble, or to some degree both. To do what we want to do in life, we need the approval and cooperation of other people—their votes, as it were—and to secure those votes, we perform and compromise in various ways. We are intuitive politicians in that we campaign for ourselves and our interests quite naturally, often without consciousness of our political ingenuity and strategies.

5

How do certain theatrical and political metaphors apply to impression management? Why do we, as intuitive politicians, want to look "good" to other people?

FIVE DISTINGUISHED PROFESSORS, EACH TRYING TO LOOK LIKE A MORE DISTINGUISHED PROFESSOR THAN THE OTHER FOUR

© Sidney Harris

Depending on our needs, our capacities, and our audience, we may at any given time portray ourselves as pitiful, enraged, stern, or even irrational and unpredictable. These can be effective strategies for certain ends. For some people these strategies may even become regular ploys. But most of us, most of the time, try to make ourselves look *good* to other people. We want to come across as attractive, friendly, competent, rational, trustworthy, and moral, because we know that others will be more inclined to collaborate with us·if they see those qualities in us than if they don't. We also want to look modest, so people will think we are understating, not overstating, our virtues. And we want to look sincere, not as if we are putting on a show or trying to ingratiate ourselves. We may or may not be conscious of our delicate balancing act between showing off and appearing modest, or between sincerity and ingratiation, but the act requires effort nevertheless (Vohs & others, 2005).

Impressing Acquaintances More Than Close Friends

In general, we are more concerned with impression management with new acquaintances than with familiar friends and companions (Leary & Kowalski, 1995; Tice & others, 1995). That concern makes sense in light of our understanding that first impressions can have long-lasting effects. We have less need to manage impressions with close friends because they already know us well. A slip will not so seriously harm our reputation with friends as it will with strangers, and friends may see through our act no matter how clever the performance.

Other research shows, not surprisingly, that dating partners are much more concerned with making good impressions on each other than are married partners. Dating partners rate themselves as most intimate and secure in their relationship when they have highly favorable impressions of each other, but married partners rate themselves as most intimate and secure when they have "true" impressions of each other—that is, when each sees the other as the other sees himself or herself (Swann & others, 1994). To feel comfortable in marriage, the two partners must feel that they can "be themselves," warts and all, and not be rejected for it.

SECTION REVIEW

Social pressure affects our performance and leads us to try to control how others see us.

Effects of Having an Audience	Choking Under Pressure	Impression Management
➤ The presence of others can cause either social facilitation (improved performance) or social interference (worsened performance).	➤ Pressure to perform well, on an academic test for example, can cause a decline in performance (choking).	➤ Because of social pressure, we consciously or unconsciously modify our behavior in order to influence others' perceptions of us.
➤ The presence of others leads to heightened drive and arousal, which—in line with Zajonc's theory—improves performance on dominant tasks and worsens performance on non-dominant tasks.	➤ Choking occurs because pressure produces distracting thoughts that compete with the task itself for limited-capacity working memory.	➤ This tendency to manage impressions has led social scientists to characterize us as actors, playing roles, or as politicians, promoting ourselves and our agendas.
➤ Evaluation anxiety is at least part of the cause of social interference.	➤ Stereotype threat is a powerful form of choking that occurs when members of a stigmatized group are reminded of stereotypes about their group before performing a relevant task.	

■ Effects of Others' Examples and Opinions

Other people influence our behavior not just through their roles as observers and evaluators but also through the examples they set. There are two general reasons why we tend to conform to others' examples.

One reason has to do with information and pragmatics. If other people cross bridge A and avoid bridge B, they may know something about the bridges that we don't know. To be safe, we had better stick with bridge A too. If other people say rhubarb leaves are poisonous, then to be safe, in the absence of better information, we shouldn't eat them, and we should probably tell our children they are poisonous. One of the great advantages of social life lies in the sharing of information. We don't all have to learn everything from scratch, by trial and error. Rather, we can follow the examples of others and profit from trials and errors that may have occurred generations ago. Social influence that works through providing clues about the objective nature of an event or situation is referred to as *informational influence.*

The other general reason for conforming is to promote group cohesion and acceptance by the group. Social groups can exist only if some degree of behavioral coordination exists among the group members. Conformity allows a group to act as a coordinated unit rather than as a set of separate individuals. We tend to adopt the ideas, myths, and habits of our group because doing so generates a sense of closeness with others, promotes our acceptance by them, and enables the group to function as a unit. We all cross bridge A because we are the bridge A people, and proud of it! If you cross bridge B, you may look like you don't want to be one of us or you may look strange to us. Social influence that works through the person's desire to be part of a group or to be approved of by others is called *normative influence.*

6

What are two classes of reasons why people tend to conform to examples set by others?

Asch's Classic Conformity Experiments

Under some conditions, conformity can lead people to say or do things that are objectively ridiculous, as demonstrated in a famous series of experiments conducted by Solomon Asch in the 1950s. Asch's original purpose was to demonstrate the limits of conformity (Asch, 1952). Previous research had shown that people conform to others' judgments when the objective evidence is ambiguous (Sherif, 1936), and Asch expected to demonstrate that they would not conform when the evidence is clear-cut. But his results surprised him and changed the direction of his research.

Basic Procedure and Finding

Asch's (1956) procedure was as follows: A college-student volunteer was brought into the lab and seated with six to eight other students, and the group was told that their task was to judge the lengths of lines. On each trial they were shown one standard line and three comparison lines and were asked to judge which comparison line was identical in length to the standard (see Figure 14.3 on the next page). As a perceptual task, this was absurdly easy; in previous tests, subjects performing the task alone almost never made mistakes. But, of course, this was not really a perceptual task; it was a test of conformity. Unbeknown to the real subject, the others in the group were confederates of the experimenter and had been instructed to give a specific wrong answer on certain prearranged "critical" trials. Choices were stated

7

How did Asch demonstrate that a tendency to conform can lead people to disclaim the evidence of their own eyes?

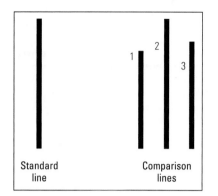

FIGURE 14.3 Sample stimuli used by Asch to study conformity The task on each trial was to select the comparison line that was identical in length to the standard. On critical trials, the confederates unanimously made a specific wrong choice (either 1 or 3, in this example). (Adapted from Asch, 1956.)

FIGURE 14.4 A perplexed subject in Asch's experiment It is not hard to tell who the real subject is in this photograph taken during a critical trial in one of Asch's experiments.

out loud by the group members, one at a time in the order of seating, and seating had been arranged so that the real subject was always the next to last to respond (see Figure 14.4). The question of interest was this: On the critical trials, would subjects be swayed by the confederates' wrong answers?

Of more than 100 subjects tested, 75 percent were swayed by the confederates on at least one of the 12 critical trials in the experiment. Some of the subjects conformed on every trial, others on only one or two. On average, subjects conformed on 37 percent of the critical trials. That is, on more than one third of the trials on which the confederates gave a wrong answer, the subject also gave a wrong answer, usually the same wrong answer as the confederates had given. Asch's experiment has since been replicated dozens of times, in at least 17 different countries (Bond & Smith, 1996). The results reveal some decline in conformity in North America after the 1950s and some variation across cultures, but they still reveal a considerable amount of conformity whenever and wherever the experiment is conducted.

William Vandivert/Scientific American

Was the Influence Informational or Normative?

8 ─ ─ ─ ─ ─ ─ ─ ─ ─ ─ ─ ─ ─ ─ ─ ─ ◀
What evidence led Asch to conclude that conformity in his experiments was caused more by normative than by informational influences?
─ ─ ─ ─ ─ ─ ─ ─ ─ ─ ─ ─ ─ ─ ─ ─

Did Asch's subjects conform as a result of *informational* or *normative* influence? That is, did the subjects use the majority response as evidence regarding the objective lengths of the lines, or did they conform out of fear of looking different (non-normative) to the others present? When Asch (1956) questioned the subjects after the experiment, very few said that they had actually seen the lines as the confederates had seemed to see them, but many said that they had been led to doubt their own perceptual ability. They made such comments as: "I thought that maybe because I wore glasses there was some defect"; "At first I thought I had the wrong instructions, then that something was wrong with my eyes and my head"; and "There's a greater probability of eight being right [than one]." Such statements suggest that to some degree the subjects did yield because of informational influence; they may have believed that the majority was right.

But maybe these comments were, to some degree, rationalizations. Maybe the main reasons for conformity had more to do with a desire to be liked or accepted by the others (normative influence) than with a desire to be right. To test this possibility, Asch (1956) repeated the experiment under conditions in which the confederates responded out loud as before, but the subjects responded privately in writing. To accomplish this, Asch arranged to have the real subjects arrive "late" to the experiment and be told that although no more subjects were needed, they might participate in a different way by listening to the others and then writing down, rather than voicing aloud, the answer they believed to be correct. In this condition, the amount of conformity dropped to about one third of that in the earlier experiments. This indicates that the social influence on Asch's original subjects was partly informational but

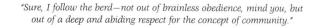

"Sure, I follow the berd—not out of brainless obedience, mind you, but out of a deep and abiding respect for the concept of community."

GREGORY

mostly normative. When subjects did not have to respond publicly, so that there was no fear of appearing odd to the other subjects, or of acting like they were rejecting the others' views, their degree of conformity dropped sharply. Many similar experiments, since Asch's, have likewise shown that conformity decreases when subjects can respond privately rather than publicly (Bond, 2005).

It's interesting to note that the majority of Asch's subjects conformed on some trials but not on others. One interpretation is that they were hedging their bets. On trials in which they answered as they saw it, they were portraying themselves as independent truth-tellers; and on trials in which they conformed they were informing the others in the group that they were not against them—they were trying to see things as the others saw them (Hodges & Geyer, 2006).

The Liberating and Thought-Provoking Influence of a Nonconformist

When Asch (1956) changed his procedure so that a single confederate gave a different answer from the others, the amount of conformity on the line-judging task dropped dramatically—to about one fourth of that in the unanimous condition. This effect occurred regardless of how many other confederates there were (from 2 to 14) and regardless of whether the dissenter gave the right answer or a different wrong answer from the others. Any response that differed from the majority encouraged the real subject to resist the majority's influence and to give the correct answer.

Since Asch's time, other experiments, using more difficult tasks or problems than Asch's, have shown that a single dissension from the majority can have beneficial effects not just through reducing normative pressure to conform but also through informational means, by shaking people out of their complacent view that the majority must be right (Nemeth, 1986). When people hear a dissenting opinion, they become motivated to examine the evidence more closely, and that can lead to a better solution.

> **9**
> What valuable effects can a single nonconformist have on others in the group?

Norms as Forces for Helpful and Harmful Actions

In Asch's experiments, the social context was provided by the artificial situation of a group of people misjudging the length of a line. In everyday life, the social context consists not just of what we hear others say or see them do, but also of the various telltale signs that inform us implicitly about which behaviors are normal and which are not in the setting in which we find ourselves. The norms established by such signs can have serious consequences for all of us.

The "Broken Windows" Theory of Crime

During the 1990s, New York City saw a precipitous drop in crime. The rates of murders and felonies dropped, respectively, to one third and one half of what they had been in the 1980s. A number of social forces contributed to the change, no doubt, but according to some analyses, at least some of the credit goes to the adoption of new law-enforcement policies recommended by George Kelling, a criminologist who was hired by the city as a consultant (Gladwell, 2000).

Kelling was already known as a developer of the *broken windows theory of crime* (Kelling & Coles, 1996). According to this theory, crime is encouraged by physical evidence of chaos and lack of care. Broken windows, litter, graffiti, and the like send signals that disrespect for law, order, and the rights of residents is normal. People regularly exposed to such an environment can develop a "law of the jungle" mentality, which leads not just to more petty crime but to thefts and murders as well. By physically cleaning up the subways, streets, and vacant buildings and by cracking down on petty crime, New York City authorities helped create a social environment that signaled that law and order are normal and law-breaking is abnormal. That signal may have helped to reduce crimes of all sorts, ranging from littering to murder. People are motivated to behave in ways they see as normal.

> **10**
> According to the "broken windows" theory, how do normative influences alter the crime rate? How was the theory tested with field experiments?

Kees Keizer

Kees Keizer

FIGURE 14.5 Spreading disorder
Here are the "ordered" and "disordered" conditions for one of the public areas observed by researchers in the Netherlands. People were much more likely to litter in the disordered condition than in the ordered condition. (From Keizer & others, 2008.)

More recently, researchers in Groningen, Netherlands, tested the broken windows theory with a series of field experiments (Keizer & others, 2008). In each experiment, they observed a public area in the city in each of two conditions. In one condition, the *order condition,* they made certain that the area was cleaned up of all litter and graffiti. In the other condition, the *disorder condition,* they deliberately spread litter or graffiti around that same area (for example, see Figure 14.5). In each condition, they observed inconspicuously for instances of littering or petty crime by people passing through. In one experiment, for example, they set up the possibility of stealing by placing a partly opened envelope with a 5-euro note sticking out of the opening of a mailbox. They found that 27% of passersby stole the money from the mailbox if there was graffiti on the mailbox, but only 13% stole it if there was no graffiti. In another experiment, 82% of passersby ignored an official-looking sign telling them not to walk along a particular path in the disordered condition, compared to 27% in the ordered condition. Of course, the researchers couldn't study major crimes in this way, but it is not hard to imagine how a proliferation of minor crimes and the attitude that they are normal could escalate into larger crimes.

Effects of Implicit Norms in Public-Service Messages

11

According to Cialdini, how can public-service messages best capitalize on normative influences? What evidence does he provide for this idea?

Many public-service messages include statements about the large number of people who engage in some undesirable behavior, such as smoking, drunk driving, or littering. According to Robert Cialdini, an expert on persuasion, such messages may undermine themselves. At the same time that they are urging people not to behave in a certain way, they are sending the implicit message that behaving in that way is normal—many people do behave in that way. Cialdini suggests that public-service messages would be more effective if they emphasized that the majority of people behave in the desired way, not the undesired way, and implicitly portrayed the undesired behavior as abnormal.

As a demonstration of this principle, Cialdini (2003) developed a public-service message designed to increase household recycling, and aired it on local radio and TV stations in four Arizona communities. The message depicted a group of people all recycling and speaking disapprovingly of a lone person who did not recycle. The result was a 25 percent increase in recycling in those communities—a far bigger effect than is usually achieved by public-service messages.

In another study, Cialdini (2003) and his colleagues created two signs aimed at decreasing the pilfering of petrified wood from Petrified Forest National Park. One sign read, "Many past visitors have removed petrified wood from the Park, changing the natural state of the Petrified Forest," and depicted three visitors taking petrified wood. The other sign depicted a single visitor taking a piece of wood, with a red circle-and-bar symbol superimposed over his hand, along with the message, "Please do not remove the petrified wood from the Park, in order to preserve the natural state of the Petrified Forest." On alternate weekends, one or the other of these signs was placed near the beginning of each path in the park. To measure theft, marked pieces of petrified wood were placed along each path. The dramatic result was that 7.92 percent of visitors tried to steal marked pieces on the days when the first sign was present, compared with only 1.67 percent on the days when the second sign was present. Previous research had shown that, with neither of these signs present but only the usual park injunctions against stealing, approximately 3 percent of visitors stole petrified wood from the park. Apparently, by emphasizing that many people steal, the first sign increased the amount of stealing sharply above the baseline rate; and the second sign, by implying that stealing is rare as well as wrong, decreased it to well below the baseline rate.

Conformity as a Basis for Failure to Help: The Passive Bystander Effect

A man lies ill on the sidewalk in full view of hundreds of passersby, all of whom fail to stop and ask if he needs help. A woman is brutally beaten in front of witnesses who fail to come to her aid or even to call the police. How can such incidents occur?

In many experiments, social psychologists have found that a person is much more likely to help in an emergency if he or she is the only witness than if other witnesses are also present (Latané & Nida, 1981). In one experiment, for example, college students filling out a questionnaire were interrupted by the sound of the researcher, behind a screen, falling and crying out, "Oh . . . my foot . . . I . . . can't move it; oh . . . my ankle . . . I can't get this thing off me" (Latané & Rodin, 1969). In some cases the student was alone, and in other cases two students sat together filling out questionnaires. The remarkable result was that 70 percent of those who were alone went to the aid of the researcher, but only 20 percent of those who were in pairs did so. Apparently an accident victim is better off with just one potential helper present than with two! Why? Part of the answer probably has to do with diffusion of responsibility. The more people present, the less any one person feels it is his or her responsibility to help (Schwartz & Gottlieb, 1980). But conformity also seems to contribute.

If you are the only witness to an incident, you decide whether it is an emergency or not, and whether you can help or not, on the basis of your assessment of the victim's situation. But if other witnesses are present, you look also at them. You wait just a bit to see what they are going to do, and chances are you find that they do nothing (because they are waiting to see what you are going to do). Their inaction is a source of information that may lead you to question your initial judgment: Maybe this is not an emergency, or if it is, maybe nothing can be done. Their inaction also establishes an implicit social norm. If you spring into action, you might look foolish to the others, who seem so complacent. Thus, each person's inaction can promote inaction in others through both informational and normative influences.

These interpretations are supported by experiments showing that the inhibiting effect of others' presence is reduced or abolished by circumstances that alter the informational and normative influences

> ---------- **12**
> **How can the failure of multiple bystanders to help a person in need be explained in terms of informational and normative influences?**

David McNew/Liaison/Newsmakers

Passing by The presence of other witnesses decreases each witness's likelihood of helping.

of the other bystanders. If the bystanders indicate, by voice or facial expressions, that they do interpret the situation as an emergency, then their presence has a much smaller or no inhibiting effect on the target person's likelihood of helping (Bickman, 1972). If the bystanders know one another well—and thus have less need to manage their impressions in front of one another, or know that each shares a norm of helping—they are more likely to help than if they don't know one another well (Rutkowski & others, 1983; Schwartz & Gottlieb, 1980).

Social Pressure in Group Discussions

When people get together to discuss an idea or make a decision, their explicit goal usually is to share information. But whether they want to or not, group members also influence one another through normative social pressure. Such pressure can occur whenever one person expresses an opinion or takes a position on an issue in front of another: Are you with me or against me? It feels good to be with, uncomfortable to be against. There is unstated pressure to agree.

Group Discussion Can Make Attitudes More Extreme

When a group is evenly split on an issue, the result is often a compromise (Burnstein & Vinokur, 1977). Each side partially convinces the other, so the majority leave the room with a more moderate view on the issue than they had when they entered. However, if the group is not evenly split—if all or a large majority of the members argue on the same side of the issue—discussion typically pushes that majority toward a more extreme view in the same direction as their initial view. This phenomenon is called **_group polarization._**

13

How has group polarization been demonstrated?

◀ Group polarization has been demonstrated in many experiments, with a wide variety of problems or issues for discussion. In one experiment, mock juries evaluated traffic-violation cases that had been constructed to produce either high or low initial judgments of guilt. After group discussion the jurors rated the high-guilt cases as indicating even higher levels of guilt, and the low-guilt cases as indicating even lower levels of guilt, than they had before the discussion (Myers & Kaplan, 1976). In other experiments, researchers divided people into groups on the basis of their initial views on a controversial issue and found that discussions held separately by each group widened the gaps between the groups (see Figure 14.6). In one experiment, for example, discussion caused groups favoring a strengthening of the military to favor it even more strongly and groups favoring a paring down of the military to favor that more strongly (Minix, 1976; Semmel, 1976).

FIGURE 14.6 Schematic illustration of group polarization Each circle represents the opinion of one individual. When the individuals are divided into two groups on the basis of the direction of their initial position (a) and then discuss the issue with other members of their group, most shift toward a more extreme position than they held before (b).

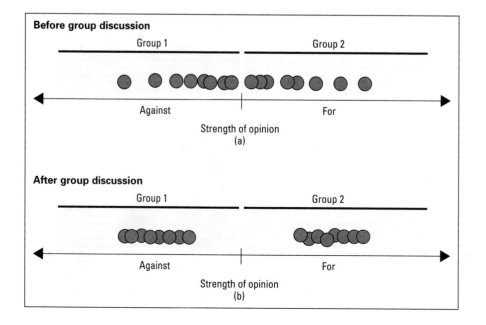

Group polarization can have socially serious consequences. When students whose political views are barely to the right of center get together to form a Young Conservatives club, their views are likely to shift further toward the right. Similarly, a Young Liberals club is likely to shift to the left. Prisoners who enter prison with little respect for the law and spend their time talking with other prisoners who share that view are likely to leave prison with even less respect for the law than they had before. Systematic studies of naturally occurring social groups suggest that such shifts are indeed quite common (Sunstein, 2003).

What Causes Group Polarization?

By now it should be no surprise to you that social psychologists have proposed two classes of explanations for group polarization: informational and normative. *Informational* explanations focus on the pooling of arguments that occurs during group discussion. People vigorously put forth arguments favoring the side toward which they lean and tend to withhold arguments that favor the other side. As a result, the group members hear a disproportionate number of arguments on the side of their initial leaning, which may persuade them to lean further in that direction (Kaplan, 1987; Vinokur & Burnstein, 1974). Moreover, simply hearing others repeat one's own arguments in the course of discussion can have a validating effect. People become more convinced of the soundness of their own logic and the truth of the "facts" they know when they hear the logic and facts repeated by another person (Brauer & others, 1995).

Normative explanations attribute group polarization to people's concerns about being approved of by other group members. One might expect normative influences to cause opinions within a group to become more similar to one another, but not more extreme. In fact, as illustrated in Figure 14.6 (on page 522), they do become more similar as well as, on average, more extreme.

Several normative hypotheses have been offered to explain why opinions within a like-minded group become more extreme. According to one, which we can call the *one-upmanship hypothesis*, group members vie with one another to become the most vigorous supporter of the position that most people favor, and this competition pushes the group as a whole toward an increasingly extreme position (Levinger & Schneider, 1969; Myers, 1982). According to another hypothesis, which we can call the *group differentiation hypothesis,* people who see themselves as a group often exaggerate their shared group opinions as a way of clearly distinguishing themselves from other groups (Hogg & others, 1990; Keltner & Robinson, 1996). The Young Liberals become more liberal to show clearly that they are not like those hard-hearted conservatives in the other club, and the Young Conservatives become more conservative to show that they are not like those soft-headed liberals.

As is so often the case in psychology, the hypotheses developed by different researchers are all probably valid, to differing degrees, depending on conditions. Group polarization in most instances probably results from a combination of normative and informational influences.

> ----------------------**14**
> **How might group polarization be explained in terms of (a) informational and (b) normative influences?**

Conditions That Lead to Good or Bad Group Decisions

Decisions made by groups are sometimes better and sometimes worse than decisions made by individuals working alone. To the degree that the group decision arises from the sharing of the best available evidence and logic, it is likely to be better (Surowiecki, 2004b). To the degree that it arises from shared misinformation, selective withholding of arguments on the less-favored side, and participants' attempts to please or impress one another rather than to arrive at the best decision, the group decision is likely to be worse than the decision most group members would have made alone.

In a now-classic book titled *Groupthink,* Irving Janis (1982) analyzed some of the most misguided policy decisions made in the U.S. White House. Among them were the decisions to sponsor the Bay of Pigs invasion of Cuba in 1961 (an invasion that failed disastrously); to escalate the Vietnam War during the late 1960s; and to cover

> ----------------------**15**
> **How did Janis explain some White House policy blunders with his groupthink theory? How can the tendency toward groupthink be countered?**

up the Watergate burglary in the early 1970s. Janis contends that each of these decisions came about because a tightly knit clique of presidential advisers, whose principal concerns were upholding group unity and pleasing their leader (Presidents Kennedy, Johnson, and Nixon, respectively), failed to examine critically the choice that their leader seemed to favor and instead devoted their energy to defending that choice and suppressing criticisms of it.

The Challenger explosion The flawed decision-making that Irving Janis called groupthink has been implicated in the 1986 explosion of the U.S. space shuttle Challenger. In striving for unanimity in the decision to launch, managers ignored engineers' warnings about the dangers of launching after a night of freezing temperatures.

To refer to such processes, Janis coined the term ***groupthink,*** which he defined as "a mode of thinking that people engage in when they are deeply involved in a cohesive ingroup, when the members' striving for unanimity overrides their motivation to realistically appraise alternative courses of action." More recently, many other ill-advised decisions, including the decision by NASA to launch the U.S. space shuttle Challenger in below-freezing weather (Moorhead & others, 1991), the endorsements by corporate boards of shady accounting practices, which led to the recent downfalls of Enron and several other large corporations (Postmes & others, 2001; Surowiecki, 2004a), and various ill-fated decisions by the G. W. Bush administration concerning the invasion and occupation of Iraq (Houghton, 2008) have been attributed to groupthink.

A number of experiments have aimed at understanding the conditions that promote or prevent groupthink. Overall, the results suggest that the ability of groups to solve problems and make effective decisions is improved if (a) the leaders refrain from advocating a view themselves and instead encourage group members to present their own views and challenge one another (Leana, 1985; Neck & Moorhead, 1995) and (b) the groups focus on the problem to be solved rather than on developing group cohesion (Mullen & others, 1994; Quinn & Schlenker, 2002). It is hard to learn this lesson, but a group that values the dissenter rather than ostracizes that person is a group that has the potential to make fully informed, rational decisions.

SECTION REVIEW

The opinions and examples of others can have strong effects on what we say and do.

Conformity Experiments

➤ Asch found that subjects often stated agreement to the majority view in judging the lengths of lines, even if it meant contradicting the evidence of their own eyes.

➤ Social influence leading to conformity can be normative (motivated by a desire to be accepted) or informational (motivated by a desire to be correct). In Asch's experiments the influence appeared to be largely normative.

➤ Even a single dissenting opinion can sharply reduce the tendency of others to conform.

Helpful and Harmful Norms

➤ According to the broken windows theory of crime, cues suggesting that disrespect for the law is normal can lead to an escalation in crime.

➤ Public-service messages can be made more effective if they portray the undesirable behavior (e.g., smoking or pilfering) as abnormal—that is, non-normative.

➤ The more bystanders present at an emergency, the less likely any of them are to help. This may result from both informational and normative influences.

Social Pressure Within Groups

➤ When most or all the people in a group initially agree, group discussion typically moves them toward a more extreme version of their initial view—a phenomenon called group polarization.

➤ Both informational and normative influences may contribute to group polarization.

➤ Groupthink occurs when group members are more concerned with group cohesion and unanimity than with genuine appraisal of various approaches to a problem. When this occurs at high levels of government or business, it can lead to disastrous decisions.

■ Effects of Others' Requests

One of the least subtle yet most potent forms of social influence is the direct request. If the request is small and made politely, we tend to comply automatically (Langer & others, 1978), and this tendency increases when our attention is otherwise occupied (Cialdini, 1993). But even if the request is onerous or offensive, people often find it hard to look a requester in the eye and say no. The tendency to comply usually serves us well. Most requests are reasonable, and we know that in the long run doing things for others pays off, as others in turn do things for us. But there are people who—out of selfishness, or because their jobs demand it, or because they are working for causes in which they sincerely believe—will exploit our tendency to comply. It is useful to know their techniques so that, instead of succumbing to pressure, we give when we want to give and buy what we want to buy.

Sales Pressure: Some Principles of Compliance

Robert Cialdini (1987, 2001) is a social psychologist who has devoted more than lip service to the idea of combining real-world observations with laboratory studies. To learn about compliance from the real-world experts, he took training in how to sell encyclopedias, automobiles, and insurance; infiltrated advertising agencies and fund-raising organizations; and interviewed recruiters, public-relations specialists, and political lobbyists. He learned their techniques, extracted what seemed to be basic principles, and tested those principles in controlled experiments. The following paragraphs describe a sample of compliance principles taken largely from Cialdini's work but also much studied by other social psychologists.

Cognitive Dissonance as a Force for Compliance

Chapter 13 contains an extensive discussion of the theory of cognitive dissonance. The basic idea of the theory, as you may recall, is that people are made uncomfortable by contradictions among their beliefs, or between their beliefs and their actions, and their discomfort motivates them to change their beliefs or actions to maintain consistency. According to Cialdini's analysis, a number of standard sales tricks make use of cognitive dissonance to elicit compliance. Here are two of them.

Throwing the Low Ball: Increasing the Price After Commitment to Buy One of the most underhanded sales tricks is the *low-ball technique.* The essence of this technique is that the customer first agrees to buy a product at a low price and then, after a delay, the salesperson "discovers" that the low price isn't possible and the product must be sold for more. Experiments conducted by Cialdini and others (1978) suggest that the trick works because customers, after agreeing to the initial deal, are motivated to reduce cognitive dissonance by setting aside any lingering doubts they may have about the product. During the delay between the low-ball offer and the real offer, they mentally exaggerate the product's value; they set their heart on the house, or car, or ice cream treat that they had agreed to purchase. Having done this, they are now primed to pay more than they would have initially.

Consistent with this interpretation, researchers have found that the low-ball technique works only if the customer makes a verbal commitment to the original, low-ball deal (Burger & Cornelius, 2003). If the initial offer is withdrawn and a worse offer is proposed *before* the person agrees verbally to the initial offer, the result is a *reduction* in compliance rather than an increase. With no verbal commitment, the customer has no need to reduce dissonance, no need to exaggerate mentally the value of the purchase, and in that case the low-ball offer just makes the final, real offer look bad by comparison.

Putting a Foot in the Door: Making a Small Request to Prepare the Ground for a Large One With some chagrin, I can introduce this topic with a true story in which I was outwitted by a clever gang of driveway sealers. While I was raking leaves in

16

How can the low-ball sales technique be explained in terms of cognitive dissonance? What evidence supports this explanation?

front of my house, these men pulled up in their truck and asked if they could have a drink of water. I, of course, said yes; how could I say no to a request like that? Then they got out of the truck and one said, "Oh, if you have some lemonade or soda, that would be even better; we'd really appreciate that." Well, all right, I did have some lemonade. As I brought it to them, one of the men pointed to the cracks in my driveway and commented that they had just enough sealing material and time to do my driveway that afternoon, and they could give me a special deal. Normally, I would never have agreed to a bargain like that on the spot; but I found myself unable to say no. I ended up paying far more than I should have, and they did a very poor job. I had been taken in by what I now see to be a novel twist on the foot-in-the-door sales technique.

A foot in the door By agreeing to the young man's first request (to sign a petition) this homeowner may find it more difficult to disagree to his next request, that she donate money or time to the cause.

17

How can the foot-in-the-door sales technique be explained in terms of cognitive dissonance?

◄ The basis of the ***foot-in-the-door technique*** is that people are more likely to agree to a large request if they have already agreed to a small one (Pascual & Guaguen, 2005). The driveway sealers got me twice on that: Their request for water primed me to agree to their request for lemonade, and their request for lemonade primed me to agree to their offer to seal my driveway. Cialdini (1987) has argued that the foot-in-the-door technique works largely through the principle of cognitive dissonance. Having agreed, apparently of my own free will, to give the men lemonade, I must have justified that action to myself by thinking, *These are a pretty good bunch of guys,* and that thought was dissonant with any temptation I might have had a few moments later, when they proposed the driveway deal, to think, *These people may be overcharging me.* So I pushed the latter thought out of my mind before it fully registered.

In situations like my encounter with the driveway sealers, the foot-in-the-door technique may work because compliance with the first request induces a sense of trust, commitment, or compassion toward the person making that request. In other situations it may work by inducing a sense of commitment toward a particular product or cause (Burger, 1999). The technique has proved to be especially effective in soliciting donations for political causes and charities. People who first agree to make a small gesture of support, such as by signing a petition or giving a few minutes of their time, are subsequently more willing than they otherwise would be to make a much larger contribution (Bell & others, 1994; Cialdini, 2001; Freedman & Fraser, 1966). Apparently the small donation leads the person to develop a firmer sense of support for the cause—"I contributed to it, so I must believe in it"—which in turn promotes willingness to make a larger donation.

The Reciprocity Norm as a Force for Compliance

18

How can the effectiveness of pregiving be explained in terms of the reciprocity norm?

◄ Anthropologists and sociologists have found that people all over the world abide by a ***reciprocity norm*** (Gouldner, 1960; Whatley & others, 1999)—that is, people everywhere feel obliged to return favors. This norm is so ingrained that people may even feel driven to reciprocate favors that they didn't want in the first place. Cialdini (1993) suggests that this is why the technique known as *pregiving*—such as pinning a flower on the lapel of an unwary stranger before asking for a donation or giving a free bottle of furniture polish to a potential vacuum-cleaner customer—is effective. Having received the gift, the victim finds it hard to turn away without giving something in return.

The reciprocity norm at Christmas The felt need to reciprocate can make the Christmas season quite burdensome. When we receive Christmas cards from others, we feel compelled to send cards back to them, so each year we send more and more cards. For many people, the same principle also applies to the exchange of Christmas gifts.

Notice that pregiving works through a means that is opposite to that proposed for the foot-in-the-door technique. The foot-in-the-door target is first led to make a small contribution, which induces a sense of commitment and thereafter a larger contribution. The reciprocity target, in contrast, is first presented with a gift, which leads to a felt need to give something back. If the two procedures were combined, they should tend to cancel each other out. The contribution would be seen as payment for the gift, reducing any further need to reciprocate, and the gift would be seen as justification for the contribution, reducing cognitive dissonance and thereby reducing the psychological drive to become more committed to the cause.

An experiment involving actual door-to-door solicitation of funds for a local AIDS foundation showed that in fact the two techniques do cancel each other out (Bell & others, 1994). Each person who was solicited first heard the same standard spiel about the foundation's good work. Some were then immediately asked for a donation (*control condition*). Others were given an attractive brochure containing "life-saving information about AIDS" (*pregiving condition*), or were asked to sign a petition supporting AIDS education (*foot-in-the-door condition*), or both (*combined condition*), before they were asked for a donation. As shown in Figure 14.7, the pregiving and foot-in-the-door techniques markedly increased the frequency of giving

> ━━━━━━━━━━━━━━━━━**19**
>
> **Logically, why should the pregiving and foot-in-the-door techniques be ineffective if combined? What evidence supports this logic?**
> ━━━━━━━━━━━━━━━━━

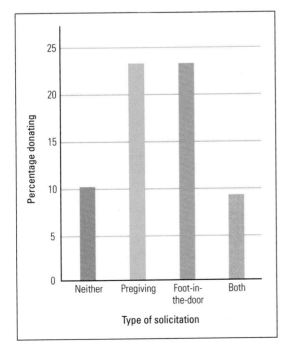

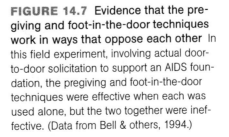

FIGURE 14.7 Evidence that the pregiving and foot-in-the-door techniques work in ways that oppose each other In this field experiment, involving actual door-to-door solicitation to support an AIDS foundation, the pregiving and foot-in-the-door techniques were effective when each was used alone, but the two together were ineffective. (Data from Bell & others, 1994.)

when either was used alone but had no effect beyond that of the control condition when the two were combined. This finding not only provides practical information for fund-raisers but also supports the proposed theories about the mechanisms of the two effects. If the two techniques operated simply by increasing the amount of interaction between the solicitor and the person being solicited, then the combined condition should have been most effective.

Shared Identity, or Friendship, as a Force for Compliance

20
- ◄
What evidence suggests that even trivial connections between a sales person and potential customers can increase sales?
- - - - - - - - - - - - - - - - - - - -

Great salespeople are skilled at identifying quickly the things they have in common with potential customers and at developing a sense of friendship or connectedness: "What a coincidence, my Aunt Millie lives in the same town where you were born." We automatically tend to like and trust people who have something in common with us or with whom we have enjoyed some friendly conversation, and we are inclined to do business with those people. In one series of experiments, compliance to various requests increased greatly when the targets of the requests were led to believe that the requester had the same birthday as they or the same first name or even a similar-looking fingerprint (Burger, 2007; Burger & others, 2004). In other experiments, people were much more likely to comply with a request if they had spent a few minutes sitting quietly in the same room with the requester than if they had never seen that person before (Burger & others, 2001). Apparently, even a brief period of silent exposure makes the person seem familiar and therefore trustworthy.

Conditions That Promote Obedience: Milgram's Experiments

Obedience refers to those cases of compliance in which the requester is perceived as an authority figure or leader and the request is perceived as an order. Obedience is often a good thing. Obedience to parents and teachers is part of nearly everyone's social training. Running an army, an orchestra, a hospital, or any enterprise involving large numbers of people would be almost impossible if people did not routinely carry out the instructions given to them by their leaders or bosses. But obedience also has a dark side. Most tragic are the cases in which people obey a leader who is malevolent, unreasonable, or sadly mistaken. Cases in which people, in response to others' orders, carry out unethical or illegal actions have been referred to as *crimes of obedience* (Hinrichs, 2007; Kelman & Hamilton, 1989).

Sometimes crimes of obedience occur because the order is backed up by threats; the subordinate's job or life may be at stake. In other cases, they occur because the subordinate accepts the authority's cause and doesn't interpret the action as wrong. In still other cases, however, people follow orders that they believe are wrong, even when there would be no punishment for disobeying. Those are the cases that interest us here, because they are the cases that must be understood in terms of psychological pressures. When social psychologists think of such cases, they relate them to a series of experiments performed by Stanley Milgram at Yale University in the early 1960s, which rank among the most famous of all experiments in social psychology. Milgram's goal was to identify some of the psychological pressures that underlie a person's willingness to follow a malevolent order.

Milgram's Basic Procedure and Finding

21
- ◄
How did Milgram demonstrate that a remarkably high percentage of people would follow a series of orders to hurt another person?
- - - - - - - - - - - - - - - - - - - -

To understand Milgram's experiments emotionally as well as intellectually, it is useful to imagine yourself as one of his subjects. You enter the laboratory and meet the experimenter and another person, who is introduced to you as a volunteer subject like yourself. The experimenter, a stern and expressionless man, explains that this is a study of the effects of punishment on learning and that one of you will serve as teacher and the other as learner. You draw slips of paper to see who will play which role and find that your slip says "teacher." The other subject, a pleasant middle-aged man, will be the learner.

You watch while the learner's arms are strapped to his chair and electrodes are taped to his wrist (see Figure 14.8). The experimenter explains that the straps will prevent excessive movement while the learner is shocked and that the electrode paste on the skin has been applied "to avoid blisters and burns." While he is being strapped in, the learner expresses some apprehension, saying that he is concerned because he has a heart condition.

After observing this part of the procedure, you—the teacher—are taken to an adjoining room, from which you can communicate with the learner through an intercom. Your job is to read off the questions on a test of verbal memory and to give the learner an electric shock whenever he gives a wrong answer. The shock generator in front of you has 30 switches, labeled with voltage designations from 15 to 450 volts. Additional labels next to the switches describe the shocks as ranging from "Slight shock" to "Danger, severe shock," followed by two switches labeled "XXX."

As the experiment progresses, the learner makes frequent mistakes, and at each mistake you give him a stronger shock than you gave before. The learner receives the early shocks silently, but when you get to 75 volts, he responds with an audible "unghh," and at stronger shocks his protests become more vehement. At 150 volts he cries out, "Experimenter, get me out of here! I won't be in the experiment any more! I refuse to go on!" At 180 volts he hollers, "I can't stand the pain!" By 270 volts his response to each shock is an agonized scream, and at 300 volts he shouts in desperation that he will no longer provide answers in the memory test. The experimenter instructs you to continue anyway and to treat each nonresponse as a wrong answer. At 315 and 330 volts the learner screams violently, and then, most frightening of all, from 345 volts on, the learner makes no sound at all. He does not respond to your questions, and he does not react to the shock.

At various points you look to the experimenter and ask if he should check on the learner or if the experiment should be terminated. You might even plead with the experimenter to let you quit giving shocks. At each of these junctures, the experimenter responds firmly with well-rehearsed prompts. First, he says, "Please continue." If you still protest, he responds, "The experiment requires that you continue." This is followed, if necessary, by "It is absolutely essential that you continue" and "You have no other choice; you must go on." These prompts are always used in the sequence given. If you still refuse to go on after the last prompt, the experiment is discontinued.

In reality—as you, serenely reading this book, have probably figured out—the learner receives no shocks. He is a confederate of the experimenter, trained to play his role. But you, as a subject in the experiment, do not know that. You believe that the learner is suffering, and at some point you begin to think that his life may be in danger. What do you do? If you are like the majority of people, you will go on with the experiment to the very end and eventually give the learner the strongest shock on the board—450 volts, "XXX." In a typical rendition of this experiment, 65 percent (26 out of 40) of the subjects continued to the very end of the series. They did not find this easy to do. Many pleaded with the experimenter to let them stop, and almost all of them showed signs of great tension, such as sweating and nervous tics, yet they went on.

Why didn't they quit? There was no reason to fear retribution for halting the experiment. The experimenter, although stern, did not look physically aggressive. He did not make any threats. The $5 pay (worth about $50 in today's money) for participating was so small as to be irrelevant; and all subjects had been told that the $5 was theirs just for showing up. So why didn't they quit?

Explaining the Finding

Upon first hearing about the results of Milgram's experiment, people are tempted to ▷ suggest that the volunteers must have been in some way abnormal to give painful, perhaps deadly, shocks to a middle-aged man with a heart condition. But that explanation

FIGURE 14.8 The "learner" in Milgram's obedience experiments While being strapped into a chair and fitted with electrodes, this pleasant man—the "learner"—mentioned that he had a heart condition.

22
Why does Milgram's finding call for an explanation in terms of the social situation rather than in terms of unique characteristics of the subjects?

doesn't hold up. The experiment was replicated dozens of times, using many different groups of subjects, and yielded essentially the same results each time. Milgram (1974) himself found the same results for women as for men and the same results for college students, professionals, and workers of a wide range of ages and backgrounds. Others repeated the experiment outside the United States, and the consistency from group to group was far more striking than the differences (A. G. Miller, 1986). It is tempting to believe that fewer people would obey today than in Milgram's time, but a recent partial replication casts doubt on that belief (Burger, 2009). In the replication, the experiment stopped, for ethical reasons, right after the 150-volt point for each subject, but nearly as many went to that point as had in Milgram's original experiments.

Another temptation is to interpret the results as evidence that people in general are sadistic. But nobody who has seen Milgram's film of subjects actually giving the shocks would conclude that. The subjects showed no pleasure in what they were doing, and they were obviously upset by their belief that the learner was in pain. How, then, can the results be explained? By varying the conditions of the experiment, Milgram (1974) and other social psychologists (A. G. Miller, 1986) identified a number of factors that contributed, in these experiments, to the psychological pressure to obey:

23

How might the high rate of obedience in Milgram's experiments be explained in terms of (a) the norm of obedience, (b) the experimenter's acceptance of responsibility, (c) the proximity of the experimenter, (d) the lack of a model for rebellion, and (e) the incremental nature of the requests?

- ● *The norm of obedience to legitimate authorities* The volunteer comes to the laboratory as a product of a social world that effectively, and usually for beneficent reasons, trains people to obey legitimate authorities and to play by the rules. Social psychologists refer to this as the *norm of obedience* (Cialdini & Goldstein, 2004). An experimenter, especially one at such a reputable institution as Yale University, must surely be a legitimate authority in the context of the laboratory, a context that the subject respects but doesn't fully understand. Thus, the person enters the laboratory highly prepared to do what the experimenter asks. Consistent with the idea that the perceived legitimacy of the authority contributed to this obedience, Milgram found that when he moved the experiment from Yale to a downtown office building, under the auspices of a fictitious organization, Research Associates of Bridgeport, the percentage who were fully obedient dropped somewhat—from 65 to 48 percent. Presumably, it was easier to doubt the legitimacy of a researcher at this unknown office than that of a social scientist at Yale.

- ● *The experimenter's self-assurance and acceptance of responsibility* Obedience is predicated on the assumption that the person giving orders is in control and responsible and that your role is essentially that of a cog in a machine. The preexisting beliefs mentioned earlier helped prepare subjects to accept the cog's role, but the experimenter's unruffled self-confidence during what seemed to be a time of crisis no doubt helped subjects to continue accepting that role as the experiment progressed. To reassure themselves, they often asked the experimenter questions like "Who is responsible if that man is hurt?" and the experimenter routinely answered that he was responsible for anything that might happen. The importance of attributing responsibility to the experimenter was shown directly in an experiment conducted by another researcher (Tilker, 1970), patterned after Milgram's. Obedience dropped sharply when subjects were told beforehand that they, the subjects, were responsible for the learner's well-being.

- ● *The proximity of the experimenter and the distance of the learner* We can picture Milgram's subjects as caught between two conflicting social forces. On one side was the experimenter demanding that the experiment be continued, and on the other was the learner pleading that it be stopped. Not only did the experimenter have the greater initial authority, but he was also physically closer and perceptually more prominent. He was standing in the same room with the subject, while the learner was in another room, out of sight. To test the importance of physical closeness, Milgram (1974) varied the placement of the experimenter or the learner.

In one variation, the experimenter left the room when the experiment began and communicated with the subject by telephone, using the same verbal prompts as in the original study; in this case, only 23 percent obeyed to the end, compared with 65 percent in the original condition. In another variation, the experimenter remained in the room with the subject, but the learner was also brought into that room; in this case, 40 percent obeyed to the end. In still another variation, the subject was required to hold the learner's arm on the shock plate while the shock was administered (see Figure 14.9), with the result that 30 percent obeyed to the end. Thus, any change that moved the experimenter farther away from the subject, or the learner closer to the subject, tended to tip the balance away from obedience.

- ***The absence of an alternative model of how to behave*** Milgram's subjects were in a novel situation. Unlike the subjects in Asch's experiments, those in most variations of Milgram's experiment saw no other subjects who were in the same situation as they, so there were no examples of how to respond to the experimenter's orders. In two variations, however, a model was provided in the form of another ostensible subject, actually a confederate of the experimenter, who shared with the real subject the task of giving shocks (Milgram, 1974). When the confederate refused to continue at a specific point and the experimenter asked the real subject to take over the whole job, only 10 percent of the real subjects obeyed to the end. When the confederate continued to the end, 93 percent of the real subjects did too. In an unfamiliar and stressful situation, having a model to follow has a potent effect. (For a summary of the results of the variations in Milgram's experiments, see Figure 14.10.)

- ***The incremental nature of the requests*** At the very beginning of the experiment, Milgram's subjects had no compelling reason to quit. After all, the first few shocks were very weak, and subjects had no way of knowing how many errors the learner would make or how strong the shocks would become before the experiment ended. Although Milgram did not use the term, we might think of his method as a very effective version of the foot-in-the-door technique. Having complied with earlier, smaller requests (giving weaker shocks), subjects found it hard to refuse new, larger requests (giving stronger shocks). The technique was especially effective in this case because each shock was only a little stronger than the previous one. At no point were subjects asked to do something radically

FIGURE 14.9 Giving a shock while in close proximity to the learner In one of Milgram's experiments, subjects were required to hold the learner's arm on the shock plate each time a shock was given. Fewer obeyed in this condition than when the learner received shocks in another room, out of sight of the subjects.

From the film *Obedience* distributed by New York University Film Library

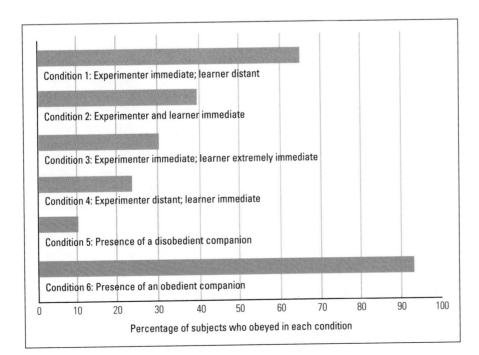

Percentage of subjects who obeyed in each condition

FIGURE 14.10 Results of Milgram's obedience experiments In the first four conditions of the experiment, the greatest degree of obedience occurred when the experimenter and the subject were in the same room and the learner was out of sight in another room. Obedience dropped with decreased proximity of the experimenter and increased proximity of the learner. In conditions 5 and 6, the presence of a disobedient or obedient confederate, masquerading as another subject, dramatically altered the tendency to obey. In each condition, obedience is defined as continuing to give shocks, up through the highest shock level.

different from what they had already done. To refuse to give the next shock would be to admit that it was probably also wrong to have given the previous shocks—a thought that would be dissonant with subjects' knowledge that they indeed had given those shocks.

Critiques of Milgram's Experiments

24 - - - - - - - - - - - - - - - - - - - ◄
How has Milgram's research been criticized on grounds of ethics and real-world validity, and how has the research been defended?

Because of their dramatic results, Milgram's experiments immediately attracted much attention and criticism from psychologists and other scholars.

The Ethical Critique Some of Milgram's critics focused on ethics (for example, Baumrind, 1964). They were disturbed by such statements as this one made in Milgram's (1963) initial report: "I observed a mature and initially poised businessman enter the laboratory smiling and confident. Within 20 minutes he was reduced to a twitching, stuttering wreck, who was rapidly approaching a point of nervous collapse." Was the study of sufficient scientific merit to warrant inflicting such stress on subjects, leading some to believe that they might have killed a man?

Milgram took great care to protect his subjects from psychological harm. Before leaving the lab, they were fully informed of the real nature and purpose of the experiment; they were informed that most people in this situation obey the orders to the end; they were reminded of how reluctant they had been to give shocks; and they were reintroduced to the learner, who offered further reassurance that he was fine and felt well disposed toward them. In a survey made a year after their participation, 84 percent of Milgram's subjects said they were glad to have participated, and fewer than 2 percent said they were sorry (Milgram, 1964). Psychiatric interviews of 40 of the former subjects revealed no evidence of harm (Errera, 1972). Still, because of concern for possible harm, a full replication of Milgram's experiments would not be approved today by the ethics review boards at any major research institution.

The Question of Generalizability to Real-World Crimes of Obedience Other critics have suggested that Milgram's results may be unique to the artificial conditions of the laboratory and have little to tell us about crimes of obedience in the real world, such as the Nazi Holocaust (Miller, 2004). Some of these argued that Milgram's subjects must have known, at some level of their consciousness, that they could not really be hurting the learner, because no sane experimenter would allow that to happen (Orne & Holland, 1968). From that perspective, the subjects' real conflict may have been between the belief that they weren't hurting the learner and the possibility that they were. Unlike subjects in Milgram's experiments, Nazis who were gassing people could have had no doubt about the effects of their actions. Another difference is that Milgram's subjects had no opportunity, outside the stressful situation in which the orders were given, to reflect on what they were doing. In contrast, Nazis who were murdering people would go home at night and then return to the gas chambers and kill more people the next day. Historians have pointed to motives for obedience on the part of Hitler's followers—including rampant anti-Semitism and nationalism (Goldhagen, 1996; Miller, 2004)—that are unlike any motives that Milgram's subjects had.

Most social psychologists would agree that Milgram's findings do not provide full explanations of real-world crimes of obedience, but do shed light on some general principles that apply, in varying degrees, to such crimes. Preexisting beliefs about the legitimacy of the endeavor, the authority's confident manner, the immediacy of authority figures, the lack of alternative models of how to behave, and the incremental nature of the requests or orders may contribute to real crimes of obedience in much the same way that they contributed to obedience in Milgram's studies, even when the motives are very different. This may be true for crimes ranging from acts of genocide on down to the illegal "cooking of books" by lower-level corporate executives responding to orders from higher-ups (Hinrichs, 2007).

"First of all, forget everything you learned in obedience school."

Our tendency to comply can be exploited by others.

Sales Pressure and Compliance	Conditions That Promote Obedience
➤ Salespersons can manipulate us into making purchases through the low-ball and foot-in-the-door techniques, both of which depend on our tendency to reduce cognitive dissonance.	➤ In his studies of obedience, Milgram found that most subjects obeyed commands to harm another person, even though it distressed them to do so and there was no real threat or reward involved.
➤ Pregiving—such as handing someone a free calendar before requesting a donation—takes advantage of the reciprocity norm, the universal tendency to return favors.	➤ Factors that help to explain the high rate of obedience in Milgram's experiments include the prevailing norm of obedience to legitimate authorities, the authority's acceptance of responsibility, the proximity of the authority figure, the incremental nature of the requests, and the lack of a model for disobeying.
➤ A sense of having something in common with the salesperson—even something quite trivial—can make us more likely to comply with the sales pitch.	➤ Though Milgram took precautions to protect his subjects from psychological harm, some critics object to the studies on ethical grounds. Others question whether the results can be generalized to real crimes of obedience, such as the Nazi Holocaust.

■ To Cooperate or Not: The Dilemma of Social Life

From an evolutionary perspective, the fundamental purpose of sociability is cooperation. Individual ants, wolves, chimpanzees, and humans live and work with others of their kind because they can fulfill certain life-sustaining needs better through cooperation than they could alone. At the same time that they are teammates working for common ends, however, the members of a group are also individuals with self-interests that can run counter to those of the group as a whole. The tension between acting for the good of the group (cooperation) and acting for one's own selfish good at the expense of the others (defection) is epitomized in **social dilemmas**. A social dilemma exists whenever a particular course of action or inaction will benefit the individual but harm the others in the group and cause more harm than good to everyone if everyone takes that course.

The Tragedy of the Commons: A Social-Dilemma Allegory

The significance of social dilemmas for human survival was dramatically illustrated by the ecologist Garrett Hardin (1968) with an allegory that he called *the tragedy of the commons*. Hardin compared our whole planet with the common grazing land that used to lie at the center of New England towns. When the number of cattle grazing the pasture began to reach the limit that the pasture could support, each farmer was faced with a dilemma: "Should I add another cow to my herd? One more cow will only slightly hurt the pasture and my neighbors, and it will significantly increase my profits. But if everyone adds a cow, the pasture will fail and all the cattle will die." The dilemma becomes a tragedy if all the farmers reason: "It is not my increase in cattle, but the combined increase by everyone, that will determine the fate of the commons. I will lose if others as well as I increase their herd, but I will lose even more if others increase their herd and I do not." So they all add a cow, the pasture gives out, the cattle die, and the townspeople all suffer the loss.

We are all constantly involved in social dilemmas, some so grand in scale as to encompass all members of our species as a single group and others much smaller in scale. Here's a grand one: Sound logic tells me that the pollution I personally add to the Earth's atmosphere by driving a gasoline-burning automobile does not seriously

25

How does "the tragedy of the commons" illustrate the critical importance of social dilemmas to human survival? What are some examples of real-world social dilemmas?

A modern tragedy of the commons
The oceans are common fishing grounds where thousands of people make their living. When too many fish are caught, the supply diminishes and valued species may even become extinct. Each fisherman can reason, logically, that his catch contributes very little to the problem; the diminished supply of fish is caused by the thousands of other fishermen.

damage the air. It is the pollution of the millions of cars driven by others that causes the serious damage. So I keep driving, everyone else does too, and the pollution keeps getting worse.

Here's a social dilemma of smaller scale, more typical of the kind that most of us actually experience as a dilemma: If you are part of a team of students working on a project to which everyone is supposed to contribute and for which everyone will receive the same grade, you might benefit by slacking off and letting others do the work. That way you could spend your time on other courses, where your grade depends only on your own effort. But if everyone in your group reasoned that way, the group project would not get done and you, along with the others in your group, would fail.

Another example, intermediate in scale, is that of public radio, which depends on voluntary contributions from its listeners. Any individual listener might reason that his or her contribution or lack of it won't make or break the station and might decide, therefore, to leave the contributing to others. If everyone reasoned that way, the station would disappear.

Every project that depends on group effort or voluntary contributions poses a social dilemma. In each case, *social working*, or *contributing*, is the individual's cooperative solution, and *social loafing*, or *free riding*, is the noncooperative solution. We are all involved in social dilemmas every day. What are the factors that lead us to cooperate or not in any given instance? Let's first look more closely at the logic of social dilemmas, as exemplified in laboratory games, and then at some conditions that promote cooperation in real-life social dilemmas.

The Logic of Social Dilemmas Exemplified in Games

To study the logic of social dilemmas, stripped of some of their real-world complexity, social scientists have invented a variety of social-dilemma games. Going further—stripping away also the emotions, values, and norms that human subjects carry with them—some social scientists use computer programs rather than humans as the players. Such studies help researchers understand the underlying logic of the dilemmas and develop hypotheses about real-life conditions that would tip the balance, logically, toward or away from cooperation.

The One-Trial Prisoner's Dilemma Game

26
What are the defining features of prisoner's dilemma games, and how do they put each player into a social dilemma?

The most common social-dilemma games used by researchers are two-person games called **prisoner's dilemma games.** They are called that because of their historical origin in a hypothetical dilemma in which each of two prisoners must choose between remaining silent and confessing. If both remain silent, both will get a short prison sentence based on other charges. If both confess, they will both get a moderately long sentence. If only one confesses, that one will be granted immunity and get no sentence but the partner will get a very long sentence. They can neither communicate nor learn the other's choice until both have chosen.

In prisoner's dilemma games played in the psychology laboratory, the consequence for one choice or the other is not a reduced or increased prison sentence but a lower or greater monetary reward. Figure 14.11 shows a typical payoff matrix for a two-person game. On each trial, each player can choose either to

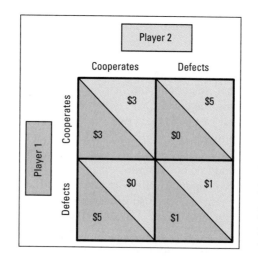

FIGURE 14.11 Sample payoff matrix for a prisoner's dilemma game On each trial, each player must decide whether to cooperate or defect, without knowing in advance what the other player will do. The payoff to each player depends on the combination of the two players' decisions. In this example, the possible payoffs to player 1 are shown in the blue portions of the matrix, and the possible payoffs to player 2 are shown in the green portions.

cooperate for the common good or to defect. Neither learns of the other's choice until both have responded, and the payoff to each player depends on the combination of their two responses. As in all prisoner's dilemma games, the payoff matrix has the following characteristics:

- The *highest individual payoff* goes to the player who defects while the other cooperates ($5 in the example in Figure 14.11).
- The *lowest individual payoff* goes to the player who cooperates while the other defects ($0 in the example).
- The *highest total payoff* to the two players combined occurs if both cooperate ($3 + $3 = $6 in the example).
- The *lowest total payoff* occurs if they both defect ($1 + $1 = $2 in the example).

Both players are informed of the payoff matrix and have adequate time to think about their choice. The game is a social dilemma because the highest individual payoff to either player comes from defecting, but the highest total payoff to the two combined comes from cooperating. If the other player defects, you will get more for defecting ($1) than for cooperating ($0); if the other cooperates, you will still get more for defecting ($5) than for cooperating ($3); but if you both defect, you will each get less ($1) than you would if you had both cooperated ($3).

In the *one-trial* version of the game, each player plays only once with a given other player. When the players are anonymous to each other, are not allowed to discuss their choices, and see their task as winning as much for themselves as they can, they usually defect. A person who always defects on one-trial prisoner's dilemma games will necessarily win more money than a person who sometimes or always cooperates. Logic tells both players to defect, so they both do and get $1 each. What a pity they are so logical! If they were illogical, they might have both cooperated and received $3 each.

The Iterative Prisoner's Dilemma Game: The Power of Reciprocity

If two players play the same prisoner's dilemma game repeatedly (iteratively) with each other for a series of trials rather than just once, the logic changes. Cooperation becomes a reasonable choice even when the only goal is to maximize one's own profits. Each player might now reason: "If I cooperate on this trial, maybe that will convince the other player to cooperate on the next. We'll both do a lot better over time if we cooperate and get $3 each per trial than if we defect and get $1 each per trial." In other words, logic and selfishness, which lead players to defect in the one-trial game, can lead them to cooperate in the iterative game.

In order to identify the best strategy in an iterative prisoner's dilemma game (the strategy that maximizes one's own earnings), Robert Axelrod (1984) held two round-robin tournaments played by computer programs rather than by human subjects. The programs were submitted by various experts on game strategy, including social scientists, mathematicians, and teenage computer experts. Each program was made to play a series of trials with each other program, using the payoff system shown in Figure 14.11. The objective was to see which program would accumulate the greatest number of points in the tournament. Some of the programs were very complicated, able to remember all the previous plays of the other player and take them into account in deciding on the next play. But in the end, the simplest program won both tournaments.

The winning program, sent in by psychologist Anatol Rapoport, was called *Tit-for-Tat* (or *TFT*). It consisted of just two rules: (1) The first time you meet a new program, cooperate with it. (2) After that, do on each trial what the other program did on its most recent previous trial with you.

Notice that TFT is incapable of "beating" any other program in head-to-head competition. It never cooperates less often than the other program does, and therefore it can never win more points in play with another program than that program wins in play with it. The TFT program won the tournament not by beating other

> ------- **27**
> **Why are players more likely to cooperate in an iterative (repeated) prisoner's dilemma game than in a one-trial game?**

> ------- **28**
> **What computer program won Axelrod's prisoner's dilemma tournaments, and why was it so successful?**

programs in individual encounters but by getting them to cooperate with it. Other programs earned at least as many points as TFT in their games with TFT, but they did not do so well in their games with each other, and that is why TFT earned the most points in the end.

Why is TFT so effective in eliciting cooperation? According to Axelrod's analysis, there are four reasons:

1. *TFT is nice.* By cooperating from the start, it encourages the other player to cooperate.

2. *TFT is not exploitable.* By reciprocating every failure to cooperate with its own failure to cooperate on the next turn, it discourages the other player from defecting.

3. *TFT is forgiving.* It resumes cooperating with any program as soon as that program begins to cooperate with it.

4. *TFT is transparent.* It is so simple that other programs quickly figure out its strategy and learn that they are best off cooperating with it.

Studies since Axelrod's have shown that TFT is highly effective in eliciting cooperation not just from other computer programs but also from human subjects in the laboratory (Komorita & Parks, 1999; Sheldon, 1999). People, like computer programs, figure out rather quickly that their best strategy when playing with TFT is to cooperate.

Decline in Cooperation as the Number of Players Increases

29
Why might we logically expect small groups to cooperate more than large ones? What evidence indicates that indeed they do?

Prisoner's dilemma games involve just two players, but other social-dilemma games—including those called *public-goods games*—can involve any number. In a typical public-goods game, each player is given a sum of money and then, under conditions of anonymity, must choose whether to keep the money or contribute it to a common pool (the public good). Then, if and only if at least a certain percentage of players (say, 75 percent) have contributed, all players, including those who haven't contributed, receive a reward that is substantially greater than the amount each person was asked to contribute.

In such games, each individual player's choice to contribute or not has a bigger impact on the whole group effort if the number of players is small than if it is large, so the temptation to refrain from contributing becomes greater as the number of players increases. With few players, each one might logically reason: "I'd better contribute or we won't reach the needed percentage to win the reward." But with many players, each might logically reason: "My contribution will have little effect on the total pool of contributions, so my best strategy is to keep my money and hope enough others will contribute to produce the reward."

The result is that far fewer rewards are won in such games when group size is large than when it is small (Alencar & others, 2008; Glance & Huberman, 1994). The same thing happens in experiments in which groups of people are asked to exert effort for a common goal. People work harder in small groups than in large ones (Karau & Williams, 1995, 2001). You are more likely to contribute to a course project for a common grade if you are one member on a team of 3 than if you are one on a team of 30. The larger the group, the greater is the diffusion of responsibility, and the less is the likelihood that a given individual will contribute.

BananaStock /Jupiterimagesca

A social dilemma in dining out
When diners agree before a meal to split the bill equally, a temptation may be created in each one to "cheat" by ordering a more expensive meal than he or she normally would. Since the added expense created by any one person's expensive meal is shared by the whole group, the temptation to order an expensive meal increases as the number of diners increases. But if everyone orders an expensive meal, then everyone pays dearly in the end.

Conditions That Promote Cooperation

In real life, and even in laboratory games, people cooperate more in social dilemmas than would be expected if their choices were based solely on immediate self-interest (Fehr & Fischbacher, 2003, 2004). Many people work hard on group projects even in large groups. Many people contribute to public television. Some people (though not nearly enough) even choose to ride a bicycle or use public transportation, rather than drive a car, to reduce pollution and help save the planet. What are the forces that lead us to cooperate in such "illogical" ways?

Evolution, cultural history, and our own individual experiences have combined to produce in us decision-making mechanisms that are not confined to an immediate cost–benefit analysis. Consciously or unconsciously, thoughtfully or automatically, we take into account factors that have to do with not just our short-term interests but also our long-term interests, which often reside in maintaining good relationships with other people. Many aspects of our social nature can be thought of as adaptations for cooperating in social dilemmas.

Accountability, Reputation, and Reciprocity as Forces for Cooperation

In the iterative prisoner's dilemma game, people and computer programs using the TFT strategy do well by cooperating because that encourages other players to cooperate in return. By cooperating, players greatly increase their long-term earnings at the expense of slightly reduced short-term earnings on any given play. The strategy works only because the other players can identify who did or did not cooperate, can remember that information from one trial to the next, and are inclined to respond to each player in accordance with that player's previous action toward them. In human terms, we would say that TFT is successful because each player is *accountable* for his or her actions. Through that accountability, TFT establishes a *reputation* as one who helps others and *reciprocates* help given by others but who won't be exploited by those who fail to reciprocate.

When players of laboratory social-dilemma games believe that others, who can identify them, will learn about their choices, they behave more generously, or more cooperatively, than they do in anonymous conditions (Piazza & Bering, 2008). When the players are free to choose the partners with whom they play, they favor those who have already developed a reputation for cooperation (Sheldon & others, 2000). The TFT strategy does especially well in this situation, because it attracts partners who seek to cooperate and repels potential partners who seek to compete (Van Lange & Visser, 1999).

In laboratory games, the factors that foster cooperation—accountability, reputation, and reciprocity—are neatly confined to the specific actions allowed by the game. But in real life they are not confined; they spill out everywhere. If I help a person today, that person and others who hear of my help may be disposed to help me in the future, in ways that I cannot even guess at today. Stories of long-range, unanticipated reciprocity are easy to find in everyone's autobiography. Research studies, in various cultures, suggest that people everywhere tend to keep track of the degree to which others are helpful and to offer the greatest help to those who have themselves been most helpful in the past (Fehr, 2004; Gurven, 2004; Price, 2003).

────────────────────────► **30**

Why is TFT especially successful in situations where players can choose their partners? How do real-life social dilemmas differ from laboratory games with respect to accountability, reputation, and reciprocity?

Norms of Fairness and Punishment of Cheaters as Forces for Cooperation

People everywhere seem to have a strong sense of fairness, which goes beyond immediate self-interest. In many situations, people would rather gain nothing than enter into an unfair agreement by which they gain a little and another person gains a lot (Fehr & Fischbacher, 2003, 2004; Tabibnia & others, 2008). This sense of fairness has been illustrated using laboratory games called *ultimatum games.*

B. Smaller

"O.K., if you can't see your way to giving me a pay raise, how about giving Parkerson a pay cut?"

31
How have laboratory games demonstrated the human sense of justice and willingness to punish even at a personal cost? How does such behavior promote long-term cooperation?

◀ In a typical ultimatum game, two players are told that a certain amount of money, say $100, will be divided between them. One player, the *proposer,* is allowed to propose how to divide the money, and the other player, the *responder,* has the choice of accepting or rejecting the offer. If the offer is accepted, the two players keep the amounts of money proposed by the proposer; if the offer is rejected, nobody gets anything. When this game is played in a one-shot manner (meaning that there will be no future games) under conditions of complete anonymity, it is irrational, from an economic point of view, for the responder to reject any offer above $0. Yet, the repeated result, wherever this game is played, is that responders typically reject any offer that is considerably less than half of the total money. In one experiment, this was true even when the amount of money to be divided was sufficiently substantial that the smaller (rejected) portion would pay the player's living expenses for several weeks (Cameron, 1999).

Other experiments show that in public-goods games with more than two players, people are willing to give up some of their own earnings in order to punish a

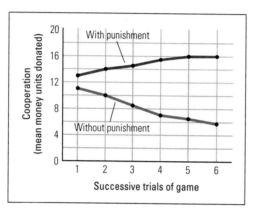

FIGURE 14.12 Altruistic punishment increases cooperation In each trial of this social-dilemma game, each player was given 20 money units and could contribute any amount of that to a common pool. The money contributed was then multiplied by 1.4 and redistributed evenly among the four players. In one condition, players could punish low contributors by giving up one of their own money units to have three units taken away from the punished player. With the punishment option, cooperation increased from trial to trial. Without that option, it decreased from trial to trial. At the end of all trials, the players could exchange the money units they had accumulated for real money. (Data from Fehr & Gächter, 2002.)

player who has contributed substantially less than his or her share to the public good (Fehr & Fishbacher, 2004; Gächter & others, 2008). The punishment, in such cases, involves removing some of the winnings that the "cheater" has garnered. As Figure 14.12 shows, when the opportunity to punish cheaters is introduced into the rules of such a game, most people stop cheating, so the total amount of cooperation—and thus, the total amount earned by all players combined—increases.

The fact that people are willing to go out of their way and pay a cost to punish cheaters may be a fact of human nature—and/or a norm resulting from cultural training—that helps maintain cooperation in human societies. Such behavior is mediated by emotions. Neuroimaging studies of people in ultimatum and public-goods games have shown that when people are cheated, brain areas associated with anger become active (Sanfey & others, 2003), and when people punish cheaters, brain areas associated with pleasure become active (de Quervain & others, 2004). Apparently, we are emotionally wired to get mad at cheaters and to enjoy revenge, even when that revenge entails an economic cost to ourselves.

Social Identity Promotes Cooperation Within Groups and Competition Across Groups

As discussed in **Chapter 13,** people everywhere have two different ways of thinking about themselves, which serve different functions. One is *personal identity,* which entails thought of oneself as an independent person with self-interests distinct from those of other people. The other is *social identity,* which entails thought of oneself as a more or less interchangeable member of a larger entity, the group, whose interests are shared by all members. Evolutionarily, the two modes of self-thought may have arisen from our need to survive both as individuals and as groups (Guisinger & Blatt, 1994). If I save myself but destroy the group on which I depend, I will, in the long run,

Should I drive or cycle to work? For some people it is easy to resolve this dilemma in the cooperative direction. Bicycle commuting not only helps preserve the earth's atmosphere but is also good exercise and more fun than driving.

Lorne Resnick/Stone

destroy myself. We don't logically think the issue through each time but, rather, tend automatically to cooperate more when we think of the others as members of our group than when we don't.

Many experiments have shown that people in all types of social-dilemma games cooperate much more when they think of the other players as group-mates than when they think of them as separate individuals or as members of other groups (Dawes & Messick, 2000; Van Vugt & Hart, 2004; Yamagishi & Mifune, 2008). In one study, for example, players differing in age cooperated much more if they were introduced to one another as citizens of the same town than if they were introduced as representatives of different age groups (Kramer & Brewer, 1984). In studies, simply referring to a set of unacquainted players as a "group," or allowing them to shake hands and introduce themselves before starting the game, increased their cooperation (Boone & others, 2008; Wit & Wilke, 1992).

Identification with a group increases people's willingness to help members of their own group but decreases their willingness to help members of another group. Groups playing social-dilemma games with other groups are far more likely to defect than are individuals playing with other individuals, even when the payoffs to individuals for cooperating or defecting are identical in the two conditions (Wildschut & others, 2007). People are much less likely to trust others and more likely to cheat others when they view those others as part of another group than when they view them as individuals. In real life, as in the laboratory, interactions between groups are typically more hostile than interactions between individuals (Hoyle & others, 1989). All too often the hostility becomes extreme.

> **32**
> What is some evidence that social identity can lead to helping group-mates and hurting those who are not group-mates?

Group Against Group: Lessons from Robbers Cave

The most vicious and tragic side of our nature seems to emerge when we see ourselves as part of a group united against some other group. Perhaps because of an evolutionary history of intertribal warfare, we can be easily provoked into thinking of other groups as enemies and as inferior beings, unworthy of respectful treatment. The history of humankind can be read as a sad, continuing tale of intergroup strife that often becomes intergroup atrocity.

There are limits to the degree to which researchers can, ethically, create the conditions that bring out intergroup hostility for the purpose of study. Muzafer Sherif and his colleagues (1961, 1966) approached those limits in a now-famous study, conducted in the 1950s, with 11- and 12-year-old boys at a 3-week camping program in Oklahoma's Robbers Cave Park (so named because it was once used as a hideout by the famous outlaw Jesse James). The researchers were interested in understanding how hostility between groups develops and how it can be resolved.

The Escalation of Conflict

To establish two groups of campers, Sherif and his colleagues divided the boys into two separate cabins and assigned separate tasks to each group, such as setting up camping equipment and improving the swimming area. Within a few days, with little adult intervention, each cabin of boys acquired the characteristics of a distinct social group. Each group established its own leaders, its own rules and norms of behavior, and its own name—the Eagles and the Rattlers.

When the groups were well established, the researchers proposed a series of competitions, and the boys eagerly accepted the suggestion. They would compete for valued prizes in such games as baseball, touch football, and tug-of-war. As Sherif had predicted from previous research, the competitions promoted three changes in the relationships among the boys within and between groups:

> **33**
> What changes occurred within and between two groups of boys as a result of intergroup competitions at a summer camp?

1. **Within-group solidarity** As the boys worked on plans to defeat the other group, they set aside their internal squabbles and differences, and their loyalty to their own group became even stronger than it was before.

2. **Negative stereotyping of the other group** Even though the boys had all come from the same background (white, Protestant, and middle class) and had been assigned to the groups on a purely random basis, they began to see members of the other group as very different from themselves and as very similar to one another in negative ways. For example, the Eagles began to see the Rattlers as dirty and rough, and in order to distinguish themselves from that group they adopted a "goodness" norm and a "holier-than-thou" attitude.

3. **Hostile between-group interactions** Initial good sportsmanship collapsed. The boys began to call their rivals names, accuse them of cheating, and cheat in retaliation. After being defeated in one game, the Eagles burned one of the Rattlers' banners, which led to an escalating series of raids and other hostilities. What at first was a peaceful camping experience turned gradually into something verging on intertribal warfare.

Resolving the Conflict by Creating Common Goals

In the final phase of their study, Sherif and his colleagues tried to reduce hostility between the two groups, a more difficult task than provoking it had been. In two previous studies similar to the one at Robbers Cave, Sherif had tried a number of procedures to reduce hostility, all of which had failed. Peace meetings between leaders failed because those who agreed to meet lost status within their own groups for conceding to the enemy. Individual competitions (similar to the Olympic Games) failed because the boys turned them into group competitions by tallying the total victories for each group (just as we find with the International Olympics). Sermons on brotherly love and forgiveness failed because, while claiming to agree with the messages, the boys simply did not apply them to their own actions.

Rattlers versus Eagles What at first were friendly competitions, such as the tug-of-war shown here, degenerated into serious hostility and aggression between the two groups of boys in Sherif's field study at Robbers Cave.

34 ─ ─ ─ ─ ─ ─ ─ ─ ─ ─ ─ ◄

How did Sherif and his colleagues succeed in promoting peace between the two groups of boys?
─ ─ ─ ─ ─ ─ ─ ─ ─ ─

At Robbers Cave, the researchers tried two new strategies. The first involved joint participation in pleasant activities. Hoping that mutual enjoyment of noncompetitive activities would lead the boys to forget their hostility, the researchers brought the two groups together for such activities as meals, movies, and shooting firecrackers. This didn't work either. It merely provided opportunities for further hostilities. Meals were transformed into what the boys called "garbage wars."

The second new strategy, however, was successful. This involved the establishment of ***superordinate goals,*** defined as goals that were desired by both groups and could be achieved best through cooperation between the groups. The researchers created one such goal by staging a breakdown in the camp's water supply. In response to this crisis, boys in both groups volunteered to explore the mile-long water line to find the break, and together they worked out a strategy to divide their efforts in doing so. Two other staged events similarly elicited cooperation. By the end of this series of cooperative adventures, hostilities had nearly ceased, and the two groups were arranging friendly encounters on their own initiative, including a campfire meeting at which they took turns presenting skits and singing songs. On their way home, one group treated the other to milkshakes with money left from its prizes.

Research since Sherif's suggests that the intergroup harmony brought on by superordinate goals involves the fading of group boundaries (Bodenhausen, 1991; Gaertner & others, 1990). The groups merge into one, and each person's social identity expands to encompass those who were formerly excluded. The boys at Robbers Cave might say, "I am an Eagle [or a Rattler], but I am also a member of the larger camp group of Eagles plus Rattlers—the group that found the leak in the camp's water supply."

If there is hope for a better human future, one not fraught with wars, it may lie in an increased understanding of the common needs of people everywhere and the establishment of superordinate goals. Such goals might include those of stopping the pollution of our shared atmosphere and oceans, the international drug trade, diseases such as AIDS that spread worldwide, and the famines that strike periodically and disrupt the world. Is it possible that we can conceive of all humanity as one group, spinning together on a small and fragile planet, dependent on the cooperation of all to find and stop the leaks?

REUTERS/Eric Miller

A superordinate task brings people together
When the Red River overflowed in Fargo, North Dakota, the local people worked together to create and stack sandbags to save homes from flooding. None of them could succeed at this task alone; they need one another. Social-psychological theory predicts that this experience will create positive bonds among the volunteers and promote their future cooperation.

SECTION REVIEW

Social dilemmas require individuals to decide whether or not to act for the common good.

The Tragedy of the Commons	Social-Dilemma Games	Roles of Accountability and Social Identity	Group Against Group
➤ In a social dilemma, the choice to behave in a certain way produces personal benefit at the expense of the group and leads to greater harm than good for all if everyone chooses that option. ➤ In the illustration called the tragedy of the commons, each individual puts one extra cow on the common pasture, thinking his or her cow will make little difference; but the collective effect is disastrous to all.	➤ Social-dilemma games, including prisoner's dilemma games, are used to study the conditions that promote cooperation. ➤ Players tend to defect in one-shot prisoner's dilemma games. When players can play each other repeatedly, however, a tit-for-tat strategy can promote cooperation. ➤ In social-dilemma games with multiple players, cooperation generally declines as the number of players increases.	➤ Cooperation increases when players are accountable for their actions and can develop reputations as cooperators or cheaters. ➤ The tendency for people to reject unfair offers and to punish cheaters, even at their own expense, is a force for cooperation. ➤ Shared social identity among group members increases cooperation within the group but decreases cooperation with other groups.	➤ In the Robbers Cave experiment, competition between the two groups of boys led to solidarity within groups, negative stereotyping of the other group, and hostile interactions between groups. ➤ Hostility was greatly reduced by superordinate goals that required the two groups to cooperate.

■ Emotional Foundations of Our Social Nature

All the social influences that you have been reading about in this chapter involve emotions. Our social situations affect our emotions, and our emotions affect our behavior. As social beings, we are endowed with emotions that help us to keep connected with others, to coordinate our behavior with that of others, to gain and retain social acceptance, and, at the same time, to avoid being exploited by others.

Emotions Help Keep Us Together and Coordinate Our Actions

The Pain of Exclusion and Social Loss

When we are excluded by others, we say that our "feelings are hurt." When we lose, through whatever means, a lover, dear friend, or family member, we say our "heart is broken." In many different languages, people describe social loss and exclusion using the same terms as those used for physical pain (Eisenberger & Lieberman, 2004). Psychologists use the term ***social pain*** to refer to the discomfort that people feel when they are socially rejected or when they lose a valued companion. There is reason to believe that the similarity between social pain and physical pain is not just metaphorical.

◄ Social pain and physical pain overlap in many ways (Eisenberger & others, 2006; MacDonald & Leary, 2005). Social pain magnifies physical pain, and vice versa. People who are experiencing a social loss suffer more from physical pain than do people who are not experiencing such a loss. People suffering from physical pain find relief in social companionship. Drugs that reduce physical pain also reduce social pain.

Neuroimaging research indicates that social pain involves some of the same brain areas that are involved in physical pain. As discussed in **Chapter 7,** the discomforting, aversive quality of physical pain, as opposed to its sensory quality, derives from activity in specific portions of the limbic system, notably the anterior cingulate cortex and the anterior insula. Nancy Eisenberger (2006) and her colleagues found that these same areas of the brain became unusually active when subjects in an fMRI scanner were led to believe that other subjects in the experiment had excluded them from a game. Moreover, the degree of activity in one of these areas, the anterior cingulate cortex, correlated positively with the amount of distress that the subjects reported feeling when they learned that they had been excluded. This, along with other evidence, suggests that the social pain system uses parts of the same neural system that evolved originally to serve the function of physical pain (MacDonald & Leary, 2005).

While the purpose of physical pain is to motivate us to avoid physical harm, the purpose of social pain—from an evolutionary perspective—is to motivate us to avoid social rejection and to maintain close social ties with other people. As social beings, the loss of people with whom we can cooperate is as detrimental to our well-being and survival as is serious damage to our bodily tissues.

Emotional Contagion as a Force for Group Cohesion

A social group is not just a collection of individuals. It is a *unified* collection. People in a social group behave, in many ways, more like one another than the same people would if they were not in a group. They tend automatically to mimic one another's postures, mannerisms, and styles of speech, and this imitation contributes to their sense of rapport (Lakin & Chartrand, 2003; van Baaren & others, 2004). They also tend to take on the same emotions.

◄ As noted in **Chapter 3,** people everywhere express emotions in relatively similar ways. Such expressions help members of a group know how to interact with one another. By seeing others' emotional expressions, group members know who needs help, who should be avoided, and who is most approachable at the moment for help. In addition, people tend automatically to adopt the emotions that they perceive in those around them, and this helps the group to function as a unit (Hatfield & others, 1994; Wild & others, 2001). Sadness in one person tends to induce sadness in others nearby, and that is part of the mechanism of empathy by which others become motivated to help the one in distress (discussed in **Chapter 12**). Anger expressed in the presence of potential allies may lead to shared anger that promotes their recruitment into a common cause. Likewise, fear in one person tends to induce fear in others nearby, placing them all in a state of heightened vigilance and thereby adding a measure of protection for the whole group.

One of the most contagious of all emotional signals is laughter, as evidenced by the regularity of mutual laughter in everyday interactions and the effectiveness of laugh tracks (often added to recorded comedy) in inducing laughter in audiences (Provine, 1996, 2004). The easy spread of laughter apparently helps put a group into a shared mood of playfulness, which reduces the chance that one person will be offended by the remarks or actions of another.

35
What is known about the neural basis of social pain? What, presumably, is the evolutionary function of social pain?

36
What is the value, for group life, of the spread of sadness, anger, fear, and laughter from person to person? How might emotional contagion figure into the rise of a group leader?

Researchers have found that the spread of emotions can occur completely unconsciously. Facial expressions of emotions flashed on a screen too quickly for conscious recognition can cause subjects to express the same emotion on their own faces and/or to experience brief changes in feeling compatible with that emotion (Dimberg & others, 2000; Ruys & Stapel, 2008).

Political leaders often achieve their status at least partly through their ability to manipulate others' emotions, and their own emotional expressions are part of that process. Former U.S. presidents Ronald Reagan and Bill Clinton were both known as "great communicators," and much of their communication occurred through their persuasive facial expressions. In a research study conducted shortly after Reagan was elected president, university students watched film clips of Reagan expressing happiness, anger, or fear as he spoke to the American public about events that faced the nation (McHugo & others, 1985). In some cases the sound track was kept on, in others it was turned off, and in all cases the students' own emotional reactions were recorded by measuring their heart rates, their sweating, and the movements of particular facial muscles. Regardless of whether they claimed to be his supporters or opponents, and regardless of whether they could or could not hear what he was saying, the students' bodily changes indicated that they were responding to Reagan's performance with emotions similar to those he was displaying.

A poker face is hard to keep We tend automatically to signal our emotions when in the company of others. Only through conscious effort can we refrain from giving away our hand.

Emotional contagion Many American citizens, regardless of their political views, found it hard not to feel good when they saw Ronald Reagan looking like this.

Our Self-Conscious Emotions Make Us Socially Acceptable

Our emotions not only help us coordinate our actions with those of others, they also help to make us socially acceptable. This is particularly true of *guilt, shame, embarrassment,* and *pride,* when they function as they have evolved to function. These four emotions are called the **self-conscious emotions,** because they are linked to thoughts about the self or one's own actions (Tangney & others, 2007). The feelings of guilt, shame, and embarrassment are painful, and the pain may motivate us to make amends when we have offended others or been ineffective in some way. Conversely, the feeling of pride rewards us for behaving effectively and gaining others' approval.

The self-conscious emotions have been studied primarily by two means. One is to observe them in very young children, who are less adept than older children or adults at hiding them and whose emotions can be manipulated relatively easily in the laboratory. The other means is to ask adults to describe one or more of their previous experiences with a particular emotion: What brought it on? What effects did it have on your behavior and that of others? How was the emotion resolved?

37 _ _ _ _ _ _ _ _ _ _ _ _ _ _ _ ◄
What differing functions are proposed for (a) guilt, (b) shame, and (c) embarrassment, and what evidence supports each function?
_ _ _ _ _ _ _ _ _ _ _ _ _ _ _

Guilt as a Motivator of Relationship Repair

When adults are asked to describe episodes in their lives that led them to experience guilt, they most often tell about hurting or disappointing someone they care about (Smith & others, 2002; Tangney, 1995). Typical guilt stories involve neglecting, offending, or being disloyal to a friend or partner.

In one study, Roy Baumeister and his colleagues (1995) asked university students to write out two episodes in which they caused someone else to become angry at them, one in which they responded with guilt and one in which they didn't. Compared with the non-guilt stories, the guilt stories were far more likely to involve selfish behavior toward someone whom they respected and with whom they had a mutually giving relationship. The guilt stories were also far more likely than the non-guilt stories to end with an apology or with a behavioral change designed to correct or prevent recurrence of the offense. Another study revealed that people who are most able to perceive events from another person's perspective are also most prone to experience guilt after an interpersonal conflict (Leith & Baumeister, 1998). When people perceive that they have hurt a valued partner, they experience guilt, which motivates them to behave in ways that bring the relationship back into balance.

Shame as a Motivator of Social Withdrawal

While guilt focuses our attention on another person's feelings and our role in causing those feelings, shame focuses our attention on some real or imagined flaw in ourselves—a flaw in appearance, ability, or moral character (Dost & Yagmurlu, 2008; Smith & others, 2002). In one research study, 3-year-olds manifested more evidence of shame in response to failing an easy task than to failing a difficult one, already showing a link between shame and perceived incompetence (Lewis, 1991). In other studies, university students were asked to describe one episode in which they had experienced shame and another in which they had experienced guilt (Tangney, 1995; Tracy & Robins, 2006). Compared with the guilt stories, the shame stories expressed more deeply felt pain and were more difficult for the students to tell. In the guilt episodes students saw themselves as relatively powerful—capable of either hurting or helping another person and motivated now to help. In the shame stories they saw themselves as blemished and powerless, motivated not to help but to disappear or hide.

Stories of shame suggest that it most often occurs when the person's failings have been publicly exposed (Smith & others, 2002), when it may truly be in the person's best interest to hide from negative judgment. Expressions of shame may also help communicate the person's feelings of self-derogation and powerlessness, which may induce compassion, perhaps even guilt, in those who would judge or punish the person (Giner-Sorolla & others, 2008).

Embarrassment as a Rectifier of Awkward Situations

When undergraduates were asked to write separate essays describing their experiences of embarrassment, shame, and guilt, the embarrassment essays far more often than the others focused on trivial or humorous incidents, not serious misconduct or deeply negative self-evaluations (Tangney & others, 1996). Embarrassment most often follows the inadvertent violation of a social norm or the receipt of unexpected or undesired attention from others. A house guest walks into the bathroom and finds it occupied; an after-dinner speaker notices that he has gravy on his necktie; a young girl is asked by her grandmother to sing in front of strangers; a student is complimented too effusively by a professor in front of classmates.

Unlike guilt, embarrassment most often involves acquaintances or strangers, whose reactions are not predictable, rather than close friends or family. Even toddlers as young as 15 months old have been observed to show signs of embarrassment when made the center of attention (Lewis, 1995).

The function of embarrassment appears to lie primarily in its communicative value. The blush and the sheepish grin, which crest just after the head and eyes have turned aside, are clear and immediate signals that what just happened is the result of circumstance or blunder or someone else's doing and is not a deliberate attempt by the self to disrupt the others' activities or become the center of attention (Miller, 1995). The sheepish or silly grin of embarrassment seems to say, nonverbally, "How silly of me" or "What a foolish thing this is that happened" (see Figure 14.13). The human display of embarrassment is similar in form and function to the appeasement displays shown by other primates (Keltner & Anderson, 2000). As noted in **Chapter 3,** apes and monkeys grin and turn their heads away or down as a nonverbal way of saying, "No offense was meant; please don't attack me."

Ondrea Barbe/Corbis

FIGURE 14.13 Embarrassment Blushing, grinning sheepishly, looking down to one side, and touching one's own face (as if symbolically hiding behind the hand) are common components of the human display of embarrassment.

Some people try to hide their embarrassment, but others—who know its power— may cultivate it and use it more or less deliberately for good effect. Several studies have shown that people are more attracted to those who manifest embarrassment in awkward situations than to those who don't (Keltner & Buswell, 1997). Embarrassment indicates concern for others' reactions and lack of haughtiness. In one experiment, subjects saw a video depicting a shopper bumping into a grocery display and then either expressing embarrassment or not as he began to pick up what he had knocked down (Semin & Manstead, 1982). The viewers who saw the embarrassment version rated the shopper as more likable than those who saw the calm, non-embarrassment version.

Pride as an Index of Social Acceptability

In the dance of social life, we experience guilt at ignoring our partner too long, shame at our awkward way of moving, and embarrassment when we accidentally bump a person we don't know very well. These reactions are useful; they help keep others from throwing us out despite our flaws. But sometimes we seem to do everything right, and then we experience pride. We throw our shoulders back, hold our heads high, speak in richer tones, and strut a little as the dance goes on, inviting others to admire us. As long as those others do indeed admire us, this drawing of attention to ourselves is useful; it adds to the cohort who may wish to make alliances with us for mutual benefit in the future.

Pride seems to be the direct opposite of shame. While shame is the emotional component of low self-esteem, pride is the emotional component of high self-esteem (Tracy & Robins, 2007). While shame focuses our attention on our own flaws and failures, pride focuses it on our own strengths and successes. While shame is felt and manifested as a desire to shrivel up and disappear, pride is felt and manifested as a desire to swell up and be seen by as many others as possible (Mascolo & Fischer, 1995; Tracy & Robins, 2007). Just as 2-year-olds react with shame when they fail at a task or are criticized, they react with pride when they succeed or are praised (Stipek, 1995).

38

When is it safe to express pride? What differing functions may be served by the feeling and expression of pride?

FIGURE 14.14 Pride The expression of pride is easy to recognize. Congenitally blind people, who have never seen the expression, express pride in the same way as do sighted people. When the expression is too extreme or occurs in inappropriate situations, it draws criticism, such as "She's got her nose in the air." When used more moderately, in situations where others are likely to admire us, however, it can draw positive attention to our accomplishments and confidence.

© Tracy, J. L., & Robins, R. W. (2004). Show your pride: Evidence for a discrete emotion expression. *Psychological Science, 15*, 194–197.

The good feeling of pride is a self-reward for virtuous, diligent, or skillful behavior. People who experience pride at a task are more likely to persevere and work hard at that task than are people who don't (Williams & DeSteno, 2008). The bodily expression of pride, which is universal and apparently does not require learning (Tracy & Matsumoto, 2008), is perhaps best understood functionally as an advertisement of self-confidence that invites others to feel confident in us also (see Figure 14.14). One must be careful about expressing pride, however. If shown too often, or in the wrong contexts, or with the wrong people, or in amounts that are disproportionate to the actual accomplishment, it is perceived as arrogance and can lead to derision and rejection.

SECTION REVIEW

Social influences on our behavior are mediated by our emotions.

Emotions Can Promote Group Cohesion

➤ Social pain—the discomfort we feel when we are socially rejected or lose a valued relationship—involves some of the same brain areas as physical pain. It motivates us to avoid situations that could lead to social isolation.

➤ Emotional contagion acts to unite the members of a group, coordinating their actions and promoting bonds of attachment. Successful leaders are often particularly good at expressing emotions in ways that lead others to share those emotions.

Functions of the Self-Conscious Emotions

➤ The self-conscious emotions—guilt, shame, embarrassment, and pride—serve to make us more socially acceptable to others.

➤ Guilt is typically felt when we have hurt someone we value. It motivates us to behave so as to bring the relationship back into balance.

➤ Shame—the emotional response to a real or imagined flaw in ourselves—often produces deeper pain than guilt, including a sense of powerlessness. It motivates us to withdraw, and it may evoke compassion if others witness it.

➤ Embarrassment is generally felt after we inadvertently breach a social norm or receive unwanted or unexpected attention. Embarrassment reveals our concern for others' feelings and can make us more likable.

➤ Pride is the emotional component of high self-esteem. In the right circumstances its expression can focus attention on our strengths and successes and lead others to ally themselves with us.

Concluding Thoughts

1. The desire to be accepted by others underlies much of social influence In surveying the body of research and theory on social influence, one cannot help being struck by the frequent recurrence of a single, simple idea: Human beings have a remarkably strong desire to be approved of by other human beings nearby.

Why do people experience arousal and a strong drive to do well—leading to either social interference or facilitation—when they know that their performance is being evaluated, even if the evaluator is a stranger and the evaluation doesn't count for anything? Why are people so concerned with impression management? Why did subjects in Asch's experiments deny the clear evidence of their own two eyes when it ran counter to what others were saying? Why are people so motivated to abide by social norms? Why do group polarization and groupthink

occur? Why do people find it hard to refuse a direct request? Why do people find it hard not to reciprocate a favor, even one that they did not want in the first place? Why did Milgram's subjects find it hard to tell the experimenter that he was asking them to do a terrible thing and that they would not do it? Why do subjects in prisoner's dilemma games find it much easier to take a competitive stance if they have colleagues (a group) on their side than if they play alone? Why do group polarization and groupthink occur? Why is social rejection painful? Why do we tend to adopt the emotions of those around us? Why do people respond with guilt, shame, or embarrassment when they feel they might have hurt or offended someone, even slightly?

I don't want to oversimplify. The desire to be accepted is surely not the *whole* answer to these questions, but it seems to be a big part of it. As you review each of the phenomena and experiments described in the chapter, you might ask yourself: To what extent (if at all) can this be explained by the desire for acceptance, and what additional explanatory principles seem to be needed?

2. Conformity derives from both normative and informational influences Normative social influences reflect people's desire to behave in accordance with group norms so as to be accepted or liked by the group. Informational social influences reflect people's use of others' responses as information to be included in solving a problem, so as to arrive at the objectively best solution. The difference between these two types of social influence was discussed explicitly in relation to (a) Asch's conformity experiments, (b) the effect that other bystanders have on any one bystander's willingness to help a person in distress, and (c) the polarizing effect that group discussion has on people's opinions or attitudes. As you review the chapter, you might think about how these two types of influence may apply to other phenomena as well. For example, how might both sorts of influence be involved in obedience, as observed by Milgram's experiments, and in cooperation, as studied in social-dilemma games?

3. Much of human nature can be understood as adaptation for group living As social beings, we are endowed with characteristics that draw us to other members of our species and help us to function effectively in groups. We feel lonely when separated from companions, pained when rejected, and satisfied or proud when accepted. Our self-conscious emotions help to dissuade others from rejecting us. We tend to adopt the attitudes, behavioral styles, and emotions of others in our group, which helps the group to function as a unit. We also have characteristics that keep us from being exploited by others in the group, as demonstrated by our concern for fairness and our tendency to either punish or avoid those who treat us unfairly. As you review each social-influence phenomenon discussed in this chapter, you might think about the aspects of human nature that underlie it and help to make group living possible and beneficial.

Further Reading

Noah Goldstein, Steve Martin, & Robert Cialdini (2008). *Yes! 50 scientifically proven ways to be persuasive.*

As the title suggests, this book consists of 50 short chapters (3 to 6 pages each), each describing a different idea about how to be persuasive. Each idea is supported by social psychological research, and each is accompanied by a little story illustrating its use. You will recognize some of the ideas that have to do with normative influences, uses of cognitive dissonance, making connections (however trivial), and reciprocity. The book is a treat to read and it may help you become more influential.

James Surowiecki (2004). *The wisdom of crowds.* New York: Doubleday.

Traditionally, social scientists have emphasized the irrationality of group thinking. This book, in contrast, emphasizes its rationality. Surowiecki, a professional writer, has delved into a diverse literature—in psychology, history, economics, politics, and business management—to support his thesis that groups, when they function well, make better decisions than even the most informed individuals in the group would make alone. To function well, however, groups must avoid the pitfalls of group polarization and groupthink, which are also discussed and exemplified in this delightful book.

Stanley Milgram (1974). *Obedience to authority: An experimental view.* New York: Harper & Row.

This is a fascinating, firsthand account of one of the most famous series of experiments in social psychology. Milgram describes his reasons for initiating the research, his findings in many variations of the basic experiment, and his interpretations of and reactions to the findings.

James Waller (2002). *Becoming evil: How ordinary people commit genocide and mass killing.* Oxford, UK: Oxford University Press.

Millions of people have played active roles in the massacres of millions of others. How can we explain the willingness, even eagerness, of ordinary people to partake in such genocides as those committed by European colonists against Native Americans, Turks against Armenians, Christians against Jews, and various tribes in Africa, the Near East, Eastern Europe, and Asia against closely related other tribes? In this book, a social psychologist brings together various explanations of those aspects of human nature and cultural conditioning that make such atrocities possible.

Natalie Henrich & Joseph Henrich (2007). *Why humans cooperate: A cultural and evolutionary explanation.* Oxford, UK: Oxford University Press.

This scholarly but highly readable book makes use of Nancy Henrich's in-depth study of cooperation in the Chaldean community of greater Detroit to shed light on general principles of human cooperation. The book deftly integrates the field research with laboratory studies involving social-dilemma and public-goods games to show how kinship, reciprocity, tit-for-tat strategy, social norms, social punishment (for violating norms), and concern for reputation all contribute to the high level of cooperation observed in this community of immigrants from Iraq.

PART 8

Personality and Disorders

We do not all approach life in the same way. We vary in our emotions, motives, and styles of thinking and behaving, and these differences give each of us a unique personality. Most of these differences are healthy and add spice to life, but some create problems and are classed as mental disorders. This final unit has three chapters. Chapter 15 is about ways of describing and explaining normal personality differences. Chapter 16 is about identifying mental disorders and understanding their origins. And Chapter 17 is about methods to help people overcome or cope with their mental problems and disorders.

Personality

Personality refers to a person's general style of interacting with the world, especially with other people—whether one is withdrawn or outgoing, excitable or placid, conscientious or careless, kind or stern. Most chapters of this book emphasize the ways in which we are similar to one another, but in this chapter we turn explicitly to differences among us. A basic assumption of the personality concept is that people do differ from one another in their styles of behavior in ways that are fairly consistent across time and place.

Most people are fascinated by human differences. Such fascination is natural and useful. In everyday life we take for granted those aspects of a person that are common to all people, and we focus, instead, on aspects that distinguish one person from another. Attention to differences helps us decide whom we want for partners and friends and how to deal with the different people that we know. *Personality psychologists* make a scientific study of such differences. Using questionnaires and other assessment tools, they conduct research to measure personality differences and explain their origins. They try to relate personality to the varying roles and habitats that people occupy in the social world, and they try to understand the mental processes that underlie the differences. Here we shall examine such endeavors.

The chapter is divided into four main sections. The first is concerned with the basic concept of personality traits and with questions about their validity, stability, and biological bases. The second is concerned with the adaptive functions of personality: How might individual differences prepare people for life within different niches of the social environment? The third and fourth sections are about the unconscious and conscious mental processes that may underlie and help explain behavioral differences among individuals. There you will read of psychodynamic, humanistic, and social-cognitive theories of personality.

Personality as Behavioral Dispositions, or Traits

What are the first three adjectives that come to mind concerning your own personality? Do they apply to you in all settings, or only in some? How clearly do they distinguish you from other people you know? Do you have any idea why you have those characteristics?

1 ----------------------------
What is a trait, and how do traits differ from states? What does it mean to say that a trait is a dimension rather than an all-or-none characteristic?

◄ The most central concept in personality psychology is the *trait,* which can be defined as a relatively stable predisposition to behave in a certain way. Traits are considered to be part of the person, not part of the environment. People carry their traits with them from one environment to another, although the actual manifestation of a trait in the form of behavior usually requires some perceived cue or trigger in the environment. For example, the trait of *aggressiveness* might be defined as an inner predisposition to argue or fight. That predisposition is presumed to stay with the person in all environments, but actual arguing or fighting is unlikely to occur unless the person perceives provocations in the environment. Aggressiveness or kindness or any other personality trait is, in that sense, analogous to the physical trait of "meltability" in margarine. Margarine melts only when subjected to heat (a characteristic of the environment); but some brands need less heat to melt than others do, and that difference lies in the margarine, not in the environment.

It is useful to distinguish traits from states. States of motivation and emotion (discussed in **Chapter 6**) are, like traits, defined as inner entities that can be inferred from observed behavior. But while traits are enduring, states are temporary. In fact, a trait might be defined as an enduring attribute that describes one's likelihood of entering temporarily into a particular state. The personality trait of aggressiveness describes the likelihood that a person will enter a belligerent state, much as the physical trait of meltability describes the likelihood that a brand of margarine will enter a liquid state.

Traits are not characteristics that people have or lack in all-or-none fashion but, rather, are dimensions (continuous, measurable characteristics) along which people differ by degree. If we measured aggressiveness or any other trait in a large number of people, our results would approximate a normal distribution, in which the majority are near the middle of the range and few are at the extremes (see Figure 15.1).

A state is not a trait This woman is clearly in a state of anger. However, before we judge her as having an aggressive or hostile personality we would have to know how easily she is provoked into anger.

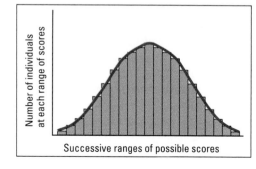

FIGURE 15.1 Typical distribution of scores measuring a personality trait When many individuals are tested for a personality trait—such as boldness versus shyness—the majority generally fall in the middle of the range and the frequency tapers off toward zero at the extremes, in a manner that approximates the bell-shaped *normal distribution* depicted here. (For a more complete description of normal distributions, see the Statistical Appendix at the end of the book.)

Number of individuals at each range of scores

Successive ranges of possible scores

Traits describe differences among people in their tendencies to behave in certain ways, but they are not themselves explanations of those differences. To say that a person is high in aggressiveness simply means that the person tends to argue or fight a lot, in situations that would not provoke such behavior in most people. The trait is inferred from the behavior. It would be meaningless, then, for me to say that Harry argues and fights a lot because he is highly aggressive. That would be essentially the same as saying, "Harry argues and fights a lot because he argues and fights a lot."

2

Why are traits considered to be descriptions rather than explanations of behavior?

Trait Theories: Efficient Systems for Describing Personalities

In everyday life we use an enormous number of personality descriptors. Gordon Allport (1937), one of the pioneers of personality psychology, identified 17,953 such terms in a standard English dictionary. Most of them have varying meanings, many of which overlap with the meanings of other terms. Consider, for example, the various connotations and overlapping meanings of *affable, agreeable, amiable, amicable, companionable, congenial, convivial, cordial, friendly, genial, gracious, hospitable, kind, sociable, warmhearted,* and *welcoming.* Personality psychologists have long been interested in devising a more efficient vocabulary for describing personality. The goal of any **trait theory** of personality is to specify a manageable set of distinct personality dimensions that can be used to summarize the fundamental psychological differences among individuals.

Factor Analysis as a Tool for Identifying an Efficient Set of Traits

In order to distill all the trait terms of everyday language down to a manageable number of meaningful, different dimensions of personality, trait theorists use a statistical technique called *factor analysis.* Factor analysis is a method of analyzing patterns of correlations in order to extract mathematically defined factors, which underlie and help make sense of those patterns. I will illustrate the technique here, with hypothetical data.

The first step in a factor-analytic study of personality is to collect data in the form of a set of personality measures taken across a large sampling of people. For example, the researcher might present a group of people with a set of adjectives and ask each person to indicate, on a scale of 1 to 5, the degree to which each adjective describes himself or herself. For the sake of simplicity, let us imagine a study in which just seven adjectives are used—*carefree, compliant, dependable, hardworking, kind, rude,* and *trusting.* To get a sense of what it is like to be a subject in such a study, you might rate yourself on each of these traits. For each term write a number from 1 to 5, depending on whether you think the term is (1) very untrue, (2) somewhat untrue, (3) neither true nor untrue, (4) somewhat true, or (5) very true of you as a person. Be honest in your ratings; you are doing this anonymously, as are the subjects in actual studies.

3

How is factor analysis used to identify trait dimensions that are not redundant with one another?

Once the data are collected, the researcher statistically correlates the scores for each adjective with those for each of the other adjectives, using the method of correlation described in **Chapter 2.** The result is a matrix of correlation coefficients, showing the correlation for every possible pair of scores (illustrated in Table 15.1 on the next page). As you may recall from **Chapter 2,** correlation coefficients can be positive or negative. A positive correlation between two measures means that people who score high on one measure tend to score high on the other. A negative correlation means that people who score high on one measure tend to score low on the other. The strength of either a positive or negative correlation is indicated by the absolute value of the correlation coefficient. The closer that value is to 1 (or the further it is from 0), the stronger is the correlation. Table 15.1 shows hypothetical correlation coefficients that might be obtained for the seven self-rating items of our imaginary study.

The next step in a factor analysis is a mathematically complex one called *factor extraction.* Through statistical means, the researcher identifies mathematical

TABLE 15.1 Hypothetical matrix of correlations among adjectives used as personality self-descriptions

Self-description	Compliant	Dependable	Hard-working	Kind	Rude	Trusting
Carefree	−.11	−.60	−.43	+.01	+.21	+.17
Compliant	—	+.29	+.13	+.39	−.70	+.53
Dependable		—	+.49	+.19	−.13	+.17
Hard-working			—	+.08	−.11	+.09
Kind				—	−.65	+.55
Rude					—	−.48
Trusting						—

factors that best account for the observed pattern of correlations. Roughly speaking, each factor corresponds to a cluster of measures that correlate relatively strongly (either positively or negatively) with one another and only weakly with items not in that cluster. For the data depicted in Table 15.1, such an analysis would identify two rather clear factors. One factor corresponds most closely with the adjectives *carefree, dependable,* and *hardworking;* and the other factor corresponds most closely with the adjectives *compliant, kind, rude,* and *trusting.* If you examine the table, you will see that within each of these two clusters of adjectives the correlations are relatively strong (the absolute values range from .39 to .70), and between clusters the correlations are relatively weak (the absolute values range from .01 to .29).

The final step is that of labeling the factors. This is a subjective process, based on the researcher's conception of the combined meanings of the cluster of items that contribute most heavily to the factor being named. In our hypothetical example, the factor that corresponds with *carefree, dependable,* and *hardworking* might be referred to as the *conscientiousness* dimension; and the factor that corresponds with *compliant, kind, rude,* and *trusting* might be referred to as the *agreeableness* dimension. Notice that each of these factor terms refers to a *dimension* of personality. The conscientiousness dimension runs from very low to very high conscientiousness, and the agreeableness dimension runs from very low to very high agreeableness. Items that contribute heavily to one of these trait factors may be at either the high end or the low end of the dimension. For example, *dependable* and *hardworking* represent the high end of the conscientiousness dimension, and *carefree,* which correlates negatively with the other two, represents the low end of that dimension.

What the factor analysis tells us is that these two dimensions of personality are relatively independent of each other. People who are high in conscientiousness are about equally likely to be either high or low in agreeableness, and vice versa. Thus, conscientiousness and agreeableness are useful, efficient trait dimensions because they are not redundant with each other and because each captures at least part of the essence of a set of more specific trait terms.

Cattell's Pioneering Use of Factor Analysis to Develop a Trait Theory

The first trait theory to be put to practical use was developed by Raymond Cattell (1950). Cattell's undergraduate degree was in chemistry, and his goal in psychology was to develop a sort of chemistry of personality. Cattell argued that just as an infinite number of different molecules can be formed from a finite number of atoms, an infinite number of different personalities can be formed from a finite number of traits. To pursue this idea, he needed to identify the elements of personality (trait dimensions) and develop a way to measure them.

◄ Cattell began his research by condensing Allport's 17,953 English adjectives describing personality down to 170 that he took to be logically different from one

Raymond Cattell Cattell (1905–1998) was a bold innovator in psychology who applied factor analysis to develop a two-factor theory of intelligence (discussed in **Chapter 10**) and a 16-factor theory of personality.

Courtesy of the University of Illinois Archives

4 - - - - - ▌ - - - - - - - - - - -

How did Cattell develop his trait theory?

another. He had large numbers of people rate themselves on each of these characteristics, and then he used factor analysis to account for patterns of correlation among the 170 different trait terms—a monumental task in the 1940s, before computers. Through this means, Cattell identified a preliminary set of traits and gave each a name. Then he developed various questionnaires aimed at assessing those traits in people and factor-analyzed the questionnaire results.

The upshot of his research, which spanned many years, was the identification of 16 basic trait dimensions, listed in Table 15.2, and a questionnaire called the *16 PF Questionnaire* to measure them (Cattell, 1950, 1973). (*PF* stands for *personality factors*.) The questionnaire consists of nearly 200 statements about specific aspects of behavior, such as "I like to go to parties." For each statement the respondent must select one of three possible answers—*yes, occasionally,* or *no*. The 16 PF Questionnaire is still sometimes used today, both as a clinical tool for assessing personality characteristics of clients in psychotherapy and as a research tool in studies of personality.

TABLE 15.2 Cattell's 16 source traits, or personality factors

1. Sociable–unsociable
2. Intelligent–unintelligent
3. Emotionally stable–unstable
4. Dominant–submissive
5. Cheerful–brooding
6. Conscientious–undependable
7. Bold–timid
8. Sensitive–insensitive
9. Suspicious–trusting
10. Imaginative–practical
11. Shrewd–naive
12. Guilt proclivity–guilt rejection
13. Radicalism–conservatism
14. Self-sufficiency–group adherence
15. Self-disciplined–uncontrolled will
16. Tense–relaxed

Note: In this table, descriptive terms have been substituted for the technical terms that Cattell coined for each trait.
Source: Adapted from *Personality and mood by questionnaire* (pp. 53–54) by R. B. Cattell, 1973, San Francisco: Jossey-Bass.

The Five-Factor Model of Personality

Many trait researchers find Cattell's 16-factor theory to be overly complex, with redundant factors. Indeed, even as Cattell was finalizing his theory, D. W. Fiske (1949) reported that many of Cattell's personality traits correlated rather strongly with one another. Fiske's reanalysis of Cattell's data resulted in a five-factor solution. Although Fiske's report lay in relative obscurity for many years, it was the first bit of evidence supporting a five-factor model of personality.

Today, with modern computers, it is much easier to perform large-scale factor-analytic studies than it was at the time of Cattell's early research. Over the past 40 years or so, hundreds of such studies have been done, with many different measures of personality and many different groups of subjects. Some studies have used self-ratings, based on adjectives or on responses to questions about behavior. Others have used ratings that people make of the personality of someone they know well rather than of themselves. Such studies have been conducted with children as well as with adults, and with people from many different cultures, using questionnaires translated into many different languages (McCrae & Allik, 2002; McCrae & Terracciano, 2005). Overall, the results have been fairly consistent in supporting what has become known as the ***five-factor model,*** or the *Big Five theory,* of personality.

According to the model, a person's personality is most efficiently described in terms of his or her score on each of five relatively independent global trait dimensions: *neuroticism* (vulnerability to emotional upset), *extraversion* (tendency to be socially outgoing), *openness to experience, agreeableness,* and *conscientiousness*. Nearly all of the thousands of adjectives commonly used to describe personalities correlate at least to some degree with one or another of these five traits. The model also posits that each global trait dimension encompasses six subordinate trait dimensions referred to as facets of that trait (Costa & McCrae, 1992; Paunonen & Ashton, 2001). The facets within any given trait dimension correlate with one another, but the correlations are far from perfect. Thus, a detailed description of someone's personality would include not just a score for each of the five global traits but also a score for each of the 30 facets. Table 15.3 on the next page, presents a brief description of each of the Big Five trait dimensions and a list of the six facets for each.

5 Why is the five-factor model of personality generally preferred over Cattell's trait theory today?

TABLE 15.3 The Big Five personality factors and their 30 facets

- **Neuroticism–stability (N):** *High end:* Experience many forms of emotional distress, have unrealistic ideas and troublesome urges. *Low end:* Emotionally stable, do not get upset easily, and are not prone to depression.
  Facets: Anxious–calm; Angry–placid; Depressed–not depressed; Self-conscious–not self-conscious; Impulsive–controlled; Vulnerable–secure.

- **Extraversion–introversion (E):** *High end:* Prefer intense and frequent interpersonal interactions; be energized and optimistic. *Low end:* Reserved and tend to prefer a few close friends to large groups of people.
  Facets: Warm–detached; Gregarious–withdrawn; Assertive–unassertive; Active–contemplative; Excitement-seeking–tranquility-seeking; Positive emotions–modulated emotions.

- **Openness to experience–non-openness (O):** *High end:* Seek out new experiences and have a fluid style of thought. *Low end:* Traditional, conservative, and prefer familiarity to novelty.
  Facets: The six facets refer to openness versus non-openness to experience in each of six realms: Fantasy, Aesthetics, Feelings, Actions, Ideas, and Values.

- **Agreeableness–antagonism (A):** *High end:* Regard others with sympathy and act unselfishly. *Low end:* Not concerned with other people and tend to be antagonistic and hostile.
  Facets: Trusting–suspicious; Straightforward–conniving; Altruistic–selfish; Compliant–noncompliant; Modest–self-aggrandizing; Tender-minded–hard-headed.

- **Conscientiousness–undirectedness (C):** *High end:* Control one's own behavior in the service of one's goals. *Low end:* Have a hard time keeping to a schedule, are disorganized, and are unreliable.
  Facets: Competent–incompetent; Ordered–disordered; Dutiful–neglectful; Achievement-striving–not achievement-striving; Self-disciplined–not self-disciplined; Deliberative–careless.

Note: In this table, the five major traits and the six facets of each trait are indicated as dimensions, using antonyms to indicate the two ends of each dimension. Usually the traits and facets are referred to using just the first term of each of the antonym pairs shown here. The descriptions in the table are from McCrae & Sutin (2007).

Measurement of the Big Five Traits and Their Facets

6

How are the Big Five traits and their facets measured in individuals?

Over the years, trait theorists have developed many different questionnaires to assess personality. The questionnaire most often used to measure the Big Five traits and their facets is the *NEO Personality Inventory* (where *N, E,* and *O* stand for three of the five major traits), developed by Paul Costa and Robert McCrae (1992). This questionnaire is now in its third revision, referred to as the *NEO-PI-3* (McCrae & others, 2005). In its full form, the person being tested rates 240 statements on a five-point scale ranging from "strongly disagree" to "strongly agree." Each statement is designed to assess one facet of one of the five major traits.

For example, here are two statements from the NEO-PI-3 designed to assess the sixth facet (values) of openness to experience:

118. *Our ideas of right and wrong may not be right for everyone in the world.*

238. *People should honor traditional values and not question them.*

Agreement with the first statement and disagreement with the second would count toward a high score on the *values* facet of *openness.* In the development of such tests, trait theorists submit the results of trial tests to factor analysis and use the results to eliminate items whose scores do not correlate strongly (positively or negatively) with the scores of other items designed to measure the same facet.

In recent years, shortened versions of the NEO-PI have been available on the Internet for self-testing. You can probably find one or more of these by searching "Big Five personality test" with Google or any other search engine. If you take such a test, you will get feedback regarding your results, and your data may also contribute to an ongoing research study. For one example of research findings using the NEO-PI, see Figure 15.2.

"When you lie about yourself, is it to appear closer to or farther away from the middle of the bell curve?"

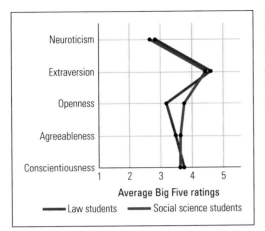

FIGURE 15.2 Personality profiles of law students and social science students at one university Shown here are the average Big Five personality ratings for students studying law and for students studying social sciences at Tel Aviv University, in Israel. The questionnaire used was a Hebrew version of the NEO Personality Inventory. The individual ratings could range from 1 to 5. The differences between the two groups on openness to experience and agreeableness were statistically significant. (Data from Rubinstein, 2005.)

One problem with almost all personality questionnaires, which you will discover if you take such a test, is that the questions are quite transparent. A person who wants to present himself as a particular kind of person can easily do so. The usefulness of the questionnaires depends on the honesty and insight of the respondent about his or her own behavior and emotions. In some research studies, and for some clinical purposes, personality inventories are filled out both by the person being evaluated and by others who know that person well. Agreement among the different ratings of the same person adds to the likelihood that the ratings are accurate.

The Relationship of Personality Measures to People's Actual Behavior

How *valid* are personality tests? As discussed in **Chapter 2,** a test is valid to the degree that its scores are true measures of the characteristics they are meant to measure. A personality test is valid to the degree that scores on each of its trait measures correlate with aspects of the person's real-world behavior that are relevant to that trait. Countless studies have shown that personality tests such as the NEO-PI are, to at least some degree, valid. Here are some examples of correlations—between Big-Five personality measures and actual behaviors—that demonstrate the validity of the personality measures:

How do researchers assess the validity of personality tests? What are some sample findings that show that measures of the Big Five personality traits are, to at least some degree, valid?

- People who score high on *neuroticism,* compared to those who score lower, have been found to (a) pay more attention to, and exhibit better memory of, threats and other unpleasant information (Matthews & others, 2000); (b) manifest more distress when given a surprise math test (Schneider, 2004); (c) experience less marital satisfaction and greater frequency of divorce (Roberts & others, 2007); and (d) be much more susceptible to mental disorders, especially depression and anxiety disorders (Hettema & others, 2004).

- People who score high on *extraversion,* compared to those who score as introverts, have been found to (a) attend more parties and be rated as more popular (Paunonen, 2003); (b) be more often seen as leaders and achieve leadership positions (Anderson & others, 2001; Roberts & others, 2007); (c) live with and work with more people (Diener & others, 1992); and (d) be less disturbed by sudden loud sounds or other intense stimuli (Eysenck, 1990; Geen, 1984; Stelmack, 1990).

- People who score high on *openness to experience,* when compared to those who score lower, have been found to (a) be more likely to enroll in liberal arts programs rather than professional training programs in college (Paunonen, 2003); (b) change careers more often in middle adulthood (McCrae & Costa, 1985); (c) perform better in job training programs (Goodstein & Lanyon, 1999); (d) be more likely to play a musical instrument (Paunonen, 2003); and (e) exhibit less racial prejudice (Flynn, 2005).

A stressful situation The first day on campus for first-year students is the kind of event that brings out personality differences.

- People who score high on *agreeableness*, compared to those who score lower, have been found to (a) be more willing to lend money (Paunonen & Ashton, 2001); (b) have fewer behavior problems during childhood (Laursen & others, 2002); (c) manifest less alcoholism or arrests in adulthood (Laursen & others, 2002); and (d) have more satisfying marriages and a lower divorce rate (Roberts & others, 2007).

- People who score high on *conscientiousness*, compared to those who score lower, have been found to (a) be more sexually faithful to their spouses (Buss, 1996); (b) receive higher ratings for job performance and higher grades in school (Ozer & Benet-Martínez, 2006); and (c) smoke less, drink less, drive more safely, follow more healthful diets, and live longer (Friedman & others, 1995; Roberts & others, 2007).

All such findings demonstrate that people's answers to personality test questions reflect, at least to some degree, the ways they actually behave and respond to challenges in the real world.

8

Why might personality traits be most apparent in novel situations or life transitions?

◀ Personality differences do not reveal themselves equally well in all settings. When you watch people in familiar roles and settings, conforming to well-learned social norms—at their jobs, in the classroom, or at formal functions such as weddings and funerals—the common influence of the situation may override individual personality styles. Personality differences may be most clearly revealed when people are in novel, ambiguous, stressful situations and in life transitions, where there are no or few cues as to what actions are appropriate (Caspi & Moffitt, 1991, 1993). As one pair of researchers put it, in the absence of cues as to how to behave, "the reticent become withdrawn, the irritable become aggressive, and the capable take charge" (Caspi & Moffitt, 1993).

Continuity and Change in Personality Over Time

Does personality change significantly over time in one's life, or is it stable?

If you ever have the opportunity to attend the 25th reunion of your high school class, don't miss it; it is bound to be a remarkable experience. Before you stands a person who claims to be your old friend Marty, whom you haven't seen for 25 years. The last time you saw Marty, he was a skinny kid with lots of hair, wearing floppy sneakers and a sweatshirt. What you notice first are the differences: This Marty has a potbelly and very little hair, and he is wearing a business suit. But after talking with him for a few minutes, you have the almost eerie knowledge that this is the same person you used to play basketball with behind the school. The voice is the same, the sparkle in the eyes, the quiet sense of humor, the way of walking. And when it is Marty's turn to stand up and speak to the group, he, who always was the most nervous about speaking before the class, is still most reluctant to do so. There's no doubt about it—this Marty, who now has two kids older than he was when you last saw him, is the same Marty you always knew.

But that is all impression. Is he really the same? Perhaps Marty is in some sense *your* construction, and it is your construction that has not changed over the years. Or maybe it's just the situation. This, after all, is a high school reunion held in your old school gymnasium, and maybe you've all been

Twenty-fifth reunion of the class of 1958 After 25 years, these women may not have recognized each other at first. But once they began talking and gesturing, so that their personalities came through, they most likely began to see each other as the same person they had known as an 18-year-old classmate.

transported back in your minds and are coming across much more like your old selves than you normally would. Maybe you're all trying to be the same kids you were 25 years ago, if only so that your former classmates will recognize you. Clearly, if we really want to answer the question of how consistent personality is over long periods, we've got to be more scientific.

The General Stability of Personality

Many studies have been conducted in which people fill out personality questionnaires, or are rated on personality characteristics by family members or friends, at widely separated times in their lives. The results indicate a rather high stability of personality throughout adulthood. Correlation coefficients on repeated measures of major traits (such as the Big Five) during adulthood typically range from .50 to .70, even with intervals of 30 or 40 years between the first and second tests (Costa & McCrae, 1994; Terracciano & others, 2006). Such stability apparently cannot be dismissed as resulting from a consistent bias in how individuals fill out personality questionnaires, as similar consistency is found even when the people rating the participants' personalities are not the same in the second test as in the first (Mussen & others, 1980).

Such studies also indicate that personality becomes increasingly stable with increasing age up to about age 50, and it remains at a relatively constant level of stability after age 50 (Caspi & others, 2005; Terracciano & others, 2006). One analysis of many studies, for example, revealed that the average test–retest correlation of personality measures across 7-year periods was .31 in childhood, .54 during young adulthood, .64 at around age 30, and .74 between ages 50 and 70 (Roberts & DelVecchio, 2000). Apparently, the older one gets, up to about age 50, the less one's personality is likely to change. But some degree of change can occur at any age.

> **9**
> **What is the evidence that personality is relatively stable throughout adulthood?**

Patterns of Change in Personality with Age

Some of the changes in personality that occur with age are relatively consistent across samplings of individuals and constitute what is commonly thought of as increased *maturity*. Studies in many different cultures on measures of the Big Five indicate that, over the adult years, neuroticism and openness to experience tend to decline somewhat, and conscientiousness and agreeableness tend to increase somewhat (Caspi & others, 2005; Srivastava & others, 2003). Data from one such study are shown in Figure 15.3. Other studies show similar results, but suggest, contrary to the data in the

> **10**
> **In what ways does personality tend to change with age?**

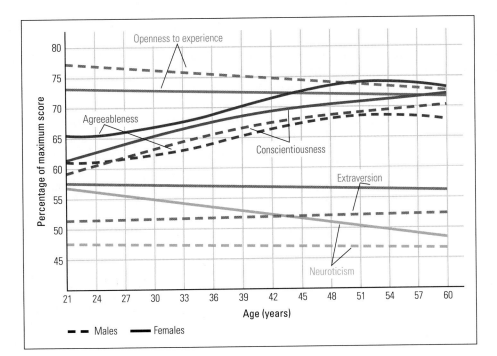

FIGURE 15.3 Average Big Five scores vary somewhat with age and sex This graph depicts the mean scores for men and women on each of the Big Five traits as a function of age. The results are derived from a sample of 132,515 adults, aged 21–60, who completed a version of the Big Five Personality Inventory that was posted on the Internet. Other studies, using more systematically chosen samples, have shown similar results. (Adapted from Srivastava & others, 2003, p. 1047.)

figure, that *agreeableness* continues to increase even into and possibly beyond one's 70s and 80s (Roberts & Mroczek, 2008; Weiss & others, 2005). Such findings are consistent with the general findings of increased life satisfaction in old age, discussed in **Chapter 12.**

In addition to the general age trends, other research indicates that an individual's personality can change, at least to some degree, in any direction, at any age, in response to a major life change, such as a new career, an altered marital status, or the onset of a chronic illness (Helson & Stewart, 1994; Roberts & Mroczek, 2008). Other studies suggest that people who have a particular personality characteristic often make life choices that alter their personality even further in the preexisting direction (Caspi & others, 2005; Roberts & Robins, 2004). For example, a highly extraverted person may choose a career that involves a lot of social activity, which may cause the person to become even more extraverted than before.

Genetic Foundations of Personality Traits

Where do traits come from? To some degree, at least, global traits such as the Big Five appear to derive from inherited physiological qualities of the nervous system.

The Heritability of Traits

11

How have researchers assessed the heritability of personality traits? What are the general results of such studies?

How heritable are personality traits? As discussed in **Chapter 10,** *heritability* refers to the degree to which individual differences derive from differences in genes rather than from differences in environmental experiences. Numerous research studies—using the behavior-genetics methods described in **Chapter 10**—have shown that the traits identified by trait theories are rather strongly heritable. The most common approach in these studies has been to administer standard personality questionnaires to pairs of identical twins and fraternal twins (who are no more similar genetically than are ordinary siblings). The usual finding is that identical twins are much more similar than are fraternal twins on every personality dimension measured, similar enough to lead to an average heritability estimate of roughly .50 for most traits, including all the Big Five (Bouchard, 2004; Loehlin, 1992). As explained in **Chapter 10,** a heritability of .50 means that about 50 percent of the variability among individuals results from genetic differences and the remaining 50 percent results from environmental differences.

In the past, such findings were criticized on the grounds that parents and others may treat identical twins more similarly than fraternal twins, and similar treatment may lead to similar personality. To get around that possibility, researchers at the University of Minnesota, led by David Lykken, gave personality tests to twins who had been separated in infancy and raised in different homes, as well as to twins raised in the same home (Bouchard, 1991, 1994; Tellegen & others, 1988). Their results were consistent with the previous studies: The identical twins were more similar to each other than were the fraternal twins on essentially every measure, whether they had been raised in the same home or in different homes, again leading to heritability scores averaging close to .50. Subsequent studies, by other researchers in several different countries, produced similar results (Plomin & Caspi, 1999).

"I was a good boy, grandpa was a good boy, his father was a good boy. In fact, since the dawn of history, there have only been good boys in this family. That's why you have to be a good boy."

Relative Lack of Shared Effects of the Family Environment

12

What evidence suggests that being raised in the same family does not promote similarity in personality?

In the past it was common for psychologists to attribute personality characteristics largely to the examples and training that people gain from their mothers and (to a lesser degree) their fathers (Harris, 1998). A common assumption was that people raised in the same family have similar personalities not just because of their shared genes but also because of their shared family environment. Perhaps the most surprising finding in the Minnesota study, confirmed since by other studies, is that this assumption is not true. Being raised in the same family has an almost negligible effect on measures of personality (Bouchard, 2004; Turkheimer & Waldron, 2000). Twin pairs who had been raised in different families were, on average, as similar to—and as different from—each other as were twin pairs who had been raised in the same family.

The contradiction between this finding and long-standing beliefs about the influence of parents is dramatically illustrated by some of the explanations that twins gave for their own behavioral traits (Neubauer & Neubauer, 1996). When one young man was asked to explain his almost pathological need to keep his environment neat and clean, he responded, "My mother. When I was growing up she always kept the house perfectly ordered. . . . I learned from her. What else could I do?" When his identical twin brother, who had grown up in a different home in a different country but was also compulsively neat and clean, was asked the same question, he said, "The reason is quite simple. I'm reacting to my mother, who was a complete slob!" In this case the similarity of the twins in their compulsive tendency was almost certainly the result of their shared genetic makeup, yet each one blamed this tendency on his adoptive mother.

The results of such studies of twins do not necessarily mean that the family environment has no influence on personality development. The results do imply, however, that those aspects of the family environment that contribute to personality differentiation are typically as different for people raised in the same family as they are for people raised in different families. Two children raised in the same family may experience that environment very differently from each other.

In work done before the Minnesota twin study, Sandra Scarr and her colleagues (1981) came to a similar conclusion concerning the family environment through a different route. They compared non-twin, adopted children with both their biological siblings (raised in a different home) and with their adoptive siblings (raised in the same home) and found that they were far more similar to their biological siblings than to their adoptive siblings. In fact, for most personality measures, the adoptive siblings, despite being raised in the same home, were on average no more similar to each other than were any two children chosen at random. Later in the chapter we will examine some possible causes of the large individual differences in personality found among children raised in the same family.

Single Genes and the Physiology of Traits

It is reasonable to assume that genes affect personality primarily by influencing physiological characteristics of the nervous system. One likely route by which they might do so is through their influence on neurotransmission in the brain. In line with that view, several laboratories have reported significant correlations between specific personality characteristics and specific genes that alter neurotransmission.

The most consistently replicated such finding concerns the relationship between *neuroticism* and a gene that influences the activity of the neurotransmitter serotonin in the brain. This particular gene (also discussed in **Chapter 12**) comes in two forms (alleles)—a short (*s*) form and a long (*l*) form. The general finding is that people who are homozygous for the *l* form (that is, have *l* on both paired chromosomes) are on average lower in neuroticism than are people who have at least one *s* allele (Gonda & others, 2009; Lesch, 2003; Schmitz & others, 2007). Serotonin is known to play a role in brain processes involved with emotional excitability, so it is not surprising that variations in serotonin might affect neuroticism.

Other researchers have found a significant relationship between the trait of *novelty seeking*—which includes elements of impulsiveness, excitability, and extravagance—and alleles that alter the action of the neurotransmitter dopamine (Benjamin & others, 1996, 1998; Lahti & others, 2006; Golimbet & others, 2007). As noted in **Chapter 6,** dopamine is involved in reward and pleasure systems in the brain, so it is not surprising that alterations in dopamine might affect behaviors that have to do with pleasure seeking.

Aaron Haupt/Stock, Boston

Identical twins To study the heritability of personality, researchers at the University of Minnesota located identical twins who had been adopted at an early age and raised in different homes, often in different parts of the country. They paid the twins to come to Minnesota for study, and, as a side effect of the study, reunited twins who had long been separated.

---13

How might variation in single genes influence personality?

Such effects are relatively small, and they are not seen in all populations. Variation in personality no doubt derives from the combined effects of many genes interacting with influences of the environment. The effect that any specific gene has on an individual's personality may depend on the mix of other genes that the person carries and on the person's environmental experiences.

SECTION REVIEW

The trait—a relatively stable behavioral predisposition—is a key concept in personality.

Trait Theories

➤ Factor analysis provides a mathematical means to identify an efficient, non-redundant set of personality traits based on correlations among larger sets of traits. Each trait is a continuous dimension: A person can score high, low, or anywhere in between on any given trait.

➤ Cattell pioneered this approach, producing a theory with 16 basic traits.

➤ The most widely accepted trait theory today posits five major traits (neuroticism, extraversion, openness to experience, agreeableness, and conscientiousness), each with six subordinate traits called facets.

➤ Questionnaires designed to measure individuals on the Big Five traits or other traits all require honesty and insight from the respondent to yield accurate results.

Predictive Value of Traits

➤ All of the Big Five traits have been shown to predict behavior at better-than-chance levels, which helps to establish the validity of the personality measures.

➤ Studies show that adult personality is relatively stable and becomes more stable with age. Correlation coefficients for repeated tests, even many years apart, range from .50 to .70.

➤ Personality does change, however. Increased age is typically accompanied by increased conscientiousness and agreeableness and decreased neuroticism and openness to experience.

➤ An individual's personality can change to some extent in any direction at any age in response to life changes.

Genetic Basis of Traits

➤ Studies comparing pairs of identical and fraternal twins yield heritability estimates for personality averaging about .50.

➤ The personalities of biological relatives raised in the same family are generally no more similar than those of equally related people raised apart.

➤ Researchers are searching, with moderate success, for specific gene alleles that contribute to particular traits.

▮ Personality as Adaptation to Life Conditions

14

How does an ultimate explanation of personality variability differ from a proximate one?

◄ *Why* are people different from one another in personality? As you may recall from **Chapter 3,** psychologists and biologists distinguish between two different types of answers to *why* questions. One type, referred to as *proximate explanation,* focuses on causal mechanisms that operate in the lifetime of the individual to produce the phenomenon in question. Proximate explanations of personality differences focus on ways by which differing genes and experiences work to make us different. The other type of answer, referred to as *ultimate explanation,* focuses on function, or evolutionary survival value, rather than mechanisms. How might personality differences help individuals survive longer and produce more offspring than they would if all individuals were identical in personality? Why were genetic, developmental, and learning mechanisms that ensure diversity in personality favored by natural selection over mechanisms that would have made us more uniform? These are the questions to which we turn now.

Advantages of Being Different from One Another

It is conceivable that variability in personality has no adaptive advantage. Perhaps the kinds of differences that personality theorists study simply represent a degree of randomness that could not be weeded out by natural selection. Perhaps; but I doubt it.

As noted in **Chapter 3,** sexual reproduction itself seems to be an adaptation that ensures the diversity of offspring. Mixing half of one parent's genes in a random manner with half of the other parent's genes leads to an essentially infinite number of possible new gene combinations in the offspring. From a purely biomechanical point of view, cloning is a far simpler and less costly form of reproduction than is sexual reproduction, so it is hard to imagine why sexual reproduction would have evolved and persisted if there were no advantage in diversity. It seems equally unlikely that learning mechanisms and other developmental mechanisms that lead us to become different in response to different environmental conditions would have evolved if they produced no survival advantage.

Research on dozens of species of other animals, ranging from ants to octopuses to chimpanzees, has revealed, in every species tested, individual differences in behavioral styles that can be described in terms similar to those that are used to describe human personality differences (Gosling, 2001; Uher, 2008). Personality appears to be a basic, biological aspect of animal life.

Diversifying One's Investment in Offspring

One way to think about the value of genetic diversity and personality differences is through an analogy between producing offspring and investing money (Miller, 1997). Investors who put all their money into one company risk going broke if that company suddenly collapses. Smart investors diversify: They invest in a variety of stocks, bonds, and other financial instruments, which are likely to respond differently to economic forces, so that when one goes down, another goes up or at least doesn't go down as rapidly as the first. Diversified investment greatly reduces the potential for dramatic loss while maintaining the potential for substantial gains over the long run.

From the perspective of evolution by natural selection, producing offspring is an investment, the goal of which is to send multiple copies of one's genes into future generations. Since conditions of survival and reproduction vary in unpredictable ways over time, the chance that an individual's genes will die out can be reduced if the offspring differ from one another in some of their characteristics, including their behavioral characteristics. Therefore, over the course of evolution, mechanisms that ensure diversity of personality in offspring—even the random diversity that results from genetic mixing in sexual reproduction—would be favored by natural selection.

> -------------------------15
> **How does an analogy to financial investment explain the value of producing offspring who differ from one another in personality?**

Studies of the Bold–Cautious Dimension in Fish

The most commonly studied dimension of personality in animals is that of boldness versus cautiousness (Gosling, 2001; Nettle, 2006). This dimension has been especially well documented and studied in various fish species, including pumpkinseed sunfish (Wilson, 1998), perch (Magnhagen & Staffan, 2005), and three-spined sticklebacks (Ward & others, 2004).

16

How has the bold–cautious dimension been studied in fish? What findings support the view that there is an evolutionary advantage in diversity?

A bold bear Animals of many species vary on a bold–cautious dimension. In places where wild animals are protected, such as Yosemite National Park, the bold individuals do especially well, resulting in a rather rapid evolution toward increased boldness. The increased boldness of some animals, especially bears, can create not just a nuisance but a danger for park visitors.

◀ In one series of studies, David Wilson and his colleagues (1993; Wilson, 1998) categorized pumpkinseed sunfish as bold or cautious on the basis of their tendency to approach (and get caught in) or to avoid wire traps placed in their habitat in a small experimental pond. Those caught by a trap were considered bold and those that avoided the traps (and were later caught by seining) were considered cautious. Subsequent study of the two groups of fish in laboratory tanks demonstrated the consistency and generality of the trait difference.

Compared with the cautious fish, the bold fish (a) adapted more readily to the tank, as shown by a quicker return to normal feeding, (b) more frequently swam off on their own rather than staying close to the other fish, and (c) were more likely to approach rather than avoid a human observer. In addition, analysis of the stomach contents of freshly caught bold and cautious fish revealed a striking difference in their diets. The bold fish had eaten far more copepods (tiny crustaceans), which were most plentiful in the areas of the pond where vegetation was least dense and the risk of predation by fish and birds was greatest.

One can well imagine the advantages and disadvantages of being either cautious or bold, among pumpkinseeds or any other vertebrate species. Caution reduces the risk of sudden death through predation or accident, but it also confines one's life to a relatively narrow portion of the available environment. Boldness allows one to explore new areas and locate foods that cautious individuals would not find, though at increased risk. Consistent with this view is the finding, with stickleback fish, that bold individuals eat more and grow more rapidly than do cautious individuals (Ward & others, 2004).

Boldness may be especially valuable when the narrow niche occupied by cautious individuals is nearly filled, so the risks entailed in exploring new objects, areas, and life strategies are offset by the potential for finding new, needed resources. Parents who produce offspring that differ from one another in their degree of caution or boldness are hedging their bets, much like investors who invest in a combination of conservative bonds and high-risk stocks.

There is also evidence that individual fish can become either bolder or more cautious, depending on the number of other bold or cautious fish in their environment. In one experiment, with perch, cautious fish became bolder when they were grouped, in large aquaria, only with other cautious fish; and bold fish became more cautious when grouped only with other bold fish (Magnhagen & Staffan, 2005). Such context-driven changes in personality are apparently adaptive: If the "cautious niche" is filled by many cautious individuals, then it is better to become bolder and explore new realms. Conversely, if the "bold niche" is filled by many bold individuals, who are spending little of their time in the relatively safe areas, so that food is still available in those areas, then it is better to be cautious and remain where it is safe.

The Big Five Traits as Alternative Problem-Solving Strategies

17

How might both heritable and non-heritable variations in the Big Five dimensions be explained in terms of alternative life strategies?

◀ From an evolutionary perspective, personality traits in humans—including the Big Five—can be thought of as alternative general strategies for solving problems related to survival and reproduction (Buss, 1996; Nettle, 2006). Consider, for example, the trait dimension of *extraversion–introversion*. Research has shown that extraverts are more likely than introverts to (a) have many sexual partners, (b) get divorced, and (c) become hospitalized because of accidents (Nettle, 2005). From these data alone, you can well imagine ways in which extraversion could, depending on environmental conditions, either increase or decrease the number of viable offspring a person produces. The extraversion–introversion dimension in people is in some ways comparable to the bold–cautious dimension in other species.

Getty Images/Altrendo

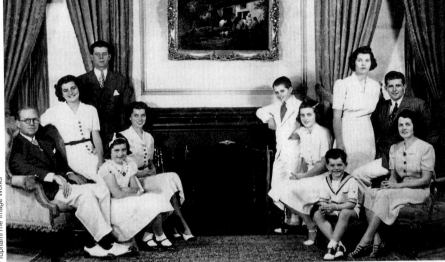

A family famous for boldness The members of the Kennedy clan are well known for their willingness to take risks in their political and personal lives. This photograph, taken in 1938, shows Joseph Kennedy (far left) with his wife Rose (far right) and their children (left to right): Patricia, John (who became the 35th president of the United States), Jean, Eunice, Robert, Kathleen, Edward, Rosemary, and Joseph. The subsequent histories of these people and of their own children offer repeated examples of triumphs and tragedies resulting from risky actions.

Similar analyses can be made of the other Big Five trait dimensions. In terms of psychological health and societal well-being, low *neuroticism* (high emotional stability), high *openness,* high *agreeableness,* and high *conscientiousness* seem to most of us to be more desirable than their opposites. However, you can imagine conditions in which the opposite ends of these dimensions might better promote survival and reproduction.

In truly dangerous conditions, the worry and vigilance shown by individuals high in *neuroticism* could save lives. In some social situations, the conservative values and closed-mindedness of those low in *openness* could lead to more stable family lives and more children than would be achieved by persons high in openness. Much as we all admire *agreeableness,* we must admit that disagreeable people sometimes do get their way, and in some life conditions this could happen often enough to make meanness more viable, in evolutionary terms, than niceness. *Conscientiousness* has to do with pursuing long-term goals and not being distracted by short-term impulses; but in some life conditions long-term goals are not likely to work out anyway and an opportunistic, impulsive approach to life could be more conducive to survival and reproduction.

The finding that individual differences on trait dimensions are partly heritable and partly the product of environmental experience is also consistent with the evolutionary perspective. In an environment that varies unpredictably, the chances that at least some offspring will survive are enhanced if the offspring are genetically inclined toward different life strategies. Genetic inclinations need to be flexible, however, so that individuals can move along a personality dimension in a direction compatible with their life situation. Perch that are genetically inclined to be cautious and people who are genetically inclined toward introversion can become more bold and extraverted if their condition of life promotes or requires such adaptation. (If I had to make my living selling books rather than writing them, then even I, a prototypical introvert, might become a bit less introverted.)

Adapting to the Family Environment

The first social environment to which most new human beings must adapt is that of the family into which they are born. The first view of other people, the first attempts at communication, the first emotional attachments, the first strivings for acceptance and approval, and the first competitions with others for resources occur most often within the context of the family. Children come into the world with nervous systems predisposed for behaving in certain ways, but those ways of behaving are first exercised and built upon within the family.

Yet, some psychologists contend that the family environment plays little or no role in shaping personality (Harris, 1998; Rowe, 1994). That contention stems primarily from the research indicating that people who were raised in the same home score, on average, just about as differently from one another on personality tests as do equally related people who were raised in different homes. To the degree that siblings are similar to one another in global personality traits, that similarity seems to come mainly from their shared genes, not from their shared home environment.

18

What are some ways by which the personality-forming experiences of children raised in the same family may differ?

One response to such findings and arguments has been to suggest that siblings raised in the same home, by the same parents, might nevertheless experience quite different environments (Dunn & Plomin, 1990; Vernon & others, 1997). The same family may influence two siblings in different ways, causing divergence in personalities as often as it causes convergence. Chance events may play a role. For example, one child may have an accident or extended illness that leads to extensive care from the parents, not given to the other child. In other cases preexisting differences between siblings may lead to differential parental responses, which magnify the pre-existing differences. For example, one child may become labeled as the "good child" and the other as the "problem child," and these may be associated with parental responses that cause the labels to become self-fulfilling prophesies. Preexisting personality differences might also lead siblings to interpret the same objective events quite differently, with different consequences for their further development. For example, a parent's persistent demands that chores be done might be understood by one child as a caring act designed to instill good work habits and by another as harsh discipline. There is evidence that siblings indeed do have different family experiences for all these kinds of reasons (Dunn & Plomin, 1990).

"And then, as soon as I had carved out my niche, they went and had another kid."

Sibling Contrast: Carving Out a Unique Niche Within the Family

Preexisting small differences between siblings may become exaggerated in part because siblings tend to define themselves as different from one another and tend to accentuate those differences through their own behavioral choices (Lalumière & others, 1996). When people are asked to describe their brother or sister, they commonly begin by saying, in effect, "Oh, he (or she) is entirely different from me," and then proceed to point out how (Dunn & Plomin, 1990). Parents likewise tend to focus more on differences than on similarities when they describe two or more of their children (Schachter, 1982). This within-family emphasis on the differences between siblings is referred to as ***sibling contrast.***

Possibly related to sibling contrast is ***split-parent identification,*** defined as a tendency for each of two siblings to identify with a different one of their two parents. If the first child identifies more strongly with the mother, the second typically identifies more strongly with the father, and vice versa. Sibling contrast and split-parent identification have been documented as highly reliable phenomena in questionnaires filled out by parents as well as in those filled out by the siblings themselves (Schachter, 1982).

19

How might sibling contrast and split-parent identification be useful in reducing sibling rivalry and diversifying parental investment?

Why do family members accentuate the differences rather than the similarities between siblings? A possible answer, proposed by Frances Schachter (1982), is that sibling contrast and split-parent identification are devices by which parents and children consciously or unconsciously strive to reduce sibling rivalry, which can be highly disruptive to family functioning. If siblings are seen by themselves and their parents as having very different abilities, needs, and dispositions, then the siblings are less likely to compete with one another and more likely to be valued and rewarded separately for their unique characteristics.

If Joan is understood to be reserved and scholarly and her sister Mary is understood to be outgoing and athletic, then Joan and Mary can be appreciated by their parents and by each other for their separate traits rather than viewed as competitors on the same dimension—a competition that one of them would have to lose. From an evolutionary perspective, such differentiation may promote the survival of the two siblings and other members of their family not only by reducing rivalry but also by diversifying the parental investment (Lalumière & others, 1996; Sulloway, 1996). To the degree that Joan and Mary move into different life niches, they will compete less with each other for limited resources both within the family and in the larger environment outside the family, and they may develop separate skills through which they can help each other and the family as a whole.

In support of the view that sibling contrast and split-parent identification serve to reduce sibling rivalry, Schachter (1982) found that both phenomena are much stronger for adjacent pairs of siblings than for pairs who are separated in birth order (see Figure 15.4) and stronger for same-sex pairs of siblings than for opposite-sex pairs. Other researchers have also found greater sibling contrast for siblings who are close in age than for those who are more distant in age (Feinberg & Hetherington, 2000). It seems reasonable that siblings who are the same sex, adjacent to each other in birth order, and close in age would be most subject to implicit comparisons and possible rivalries and would therefore have the greatest need to reduce rivalry through contrast and split-parent identification.

The observation that sibling contrast and split-parent identification are strongest for the first two children in a family (shown in Figure 15.4) is likewise consistent with the rivalry-reduction hypothesis. The first two children are likely to experience the greatest degree of sibling rivalry because, for a period of time, they are the only two children being compared. When third and subsequent children come along, multiple comparisons can be made, so the intensity of comparisons between any two, and the potential for rivalry between them, may be somewhat muted.

Influence of Birth Order on Personality

With the exception of twins, children within a family all differ from one another in one seemingly important way: birth order. Birth order certainly affects children's lives within the family. Earlier-born children, simply by virtue of being older, are, at least for most of their childhoods, bigger, stronger, more knowledgeable, and more competent than their later-born siblings. Because of this, earlier-born children are likely to dominate later-borns and may often be called upon to help care for them. Firstborns in particular occupy a special position. They are *first*: first in competitions, first in receiving new privileges and responsibilities, first to grow up. Do these differences in childhood experiences have lasting consequences for personality? One person who thinks they do is Frank Sulloway, a historian of science who became interested in this topic as a result of his interest in scientific revolutions.

Sulloway wondered why, at any given point in history, some people support and others oppose the new, revolutionary scientific theories of their time—theories such as Copernicus's idea that the earth revolves around the sun, Darwin's idea of evolution by natural selection, and Einstein's concept of special relativity. With the help of other historians of science, he identified hundreds of scientists and other intellectuals who, over the past 500 years of Western history, were on record as either supporting or opposing a particular revolutionary or innovative scientific idea of their time. He then classified these people according to birth order and found, overall, that later-borns were far more likely to support such ideas than were firstborns. For example, the odds that a later-born person relative to a firstborn supported the new scientific idea were 5.4 to 1 for Copernicus's theory and 4.6 to 1 for Darwin's theory. In a subsequent study, Sulloway also found that firstborns were disproportionately likely to support conservative political causes and later-borns were disproportionately likely to support liberal political causes.

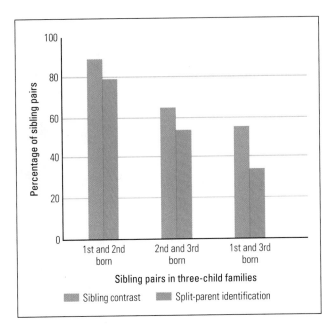

FIGURE 15.4 Sibling contrast and split-parent identification in three-child families Mothers were asked to compare pairs of their children by stating whether the two were similar or different on various personality dimensions and by stating which parent each child identified with more strongly. *Sibling contrast* (orange bars) refers to the percentage of times that the mothers said "different" rather than "alike" in response to personality questions. *Split-parent identification* (blue bars) refers to the percentage of times two siblings were said to identify with different parents rather than with the same parent. (Data from Schachter, 1982, pp. 128 and 141.)

20

What birth-order differences in personality did Sulloway find in his analyses of historical data? How did he explain these differences?

A brilliant, rebellious lastborn
Voltaire, the 18th-century satirist and leading critic of the Catholic Church—whose literary work sometimes led to periods of imprisonment or exile—was, according to Sulloway, reacting against his sanctimonious, pious eldest brother, his father's favorite son.

Archivo Iconografico, S. A./Corbis

Largely on the basis of these historical studies, Sulloway (1996) developed the theory that children's experiences within the family have long-lasting effects, such that firstborns tend to be conservative and traditional throughout their lives and later-borns tend to be more open to new ideas and more likely to rebel against established ways. Because firstborns are, for a while, the only child in their family, they identify strongly with their parents, and in doing so they develop strong respect for authority and for conventional ways of doing things. Later-born children enter a family that already has at least one older child. They cannot compete with the firstborn child at the activities that are most favored by their parents, so they are motivated to explore new activities and new ways of thinking. The status quo does not favor them, so they look for ways to shake things up. They also tend to identify with the underdog; they know what it is like to be dominated by their more powerful older siblings. Such forces, according to Sulloway, lead later-borns to be much more supportive than firstborns of new ideas and liberal political causes.

◀ Over the past several decades, psychologists have conducted dozens of research studies on the relationship between birth order and scores on standard personality tests. Most of the early studies revealed little or no evidence of any consistent effects of birth order on personality (Ernst & Angst, 1983). More recently, however, a number of studies, using methods aimed at minimizing confounding effects, have produced results that are consistent with Sulloway's theory (Beck & others, 2006; Healey & Ellis, 2007; Paulhus & others, 1999). These studies indicate that, overall, firstborns are higher in *conscientiousness,* lower in *openness,* higher in *dominance* (one aspect of extraversion), and lower in *sociability* (another aspect of extraversion) than are later-borns.

Although the results of these studies are in the direction predicted by Sulloway's theory, the effects tend to be modest in size, in contrast to the very large effects that Sulloway found in his historical study. How might this difference be explained?

One possibility is that the effects found by Sulloway depend on family practices that vary across place and time. Sulloway's historical study was primarily of famous men who grew up in upper-class homes a century or more ago. It is entirely possible that family practices that applied to those men—such as primogeniture (the practice of leaving most or all of the parents' wealth to the eldest son)—affected personality in ways that practices in most families today do not. It is also possible that people who eventually become famous are different from the rest of us, in ways that include a greater susceptibility to birth-order effects on personality. For example, they may be people who are strongly driven to high achievement, so birth-order effects on ways of competing and achieving may act more strongly on them than on the rest of us.

21
How have studies correlating personality with birth order in some cases cast doubt on and in some cases supported Sulloway's theory?

Adapting to One's Gender

Human beings, like other sexually reproducing animals, come in two varieties, female and male. If you have read the previous chapters of this book, you have already read a good deal about gender differences. For instance, in **Chapter 3** you read of the different problems that females and males must solve in mating and of their possible different strategies for solving them. In **Chapter 12** you read of differences in how the two sexes are treated, how they are expected to behave, and how they typically do behave at each life stage. As is pointed out in **Chapter 12,** psychologists generally use the word *sex* to refer to the clear-cut biological differences between males and females and the word *gender* to refer to the differences that may be heavily influenced by cultural forces and expectations.

One way to think about gender is in terms of niches to which we must adapt. The female and male niches are defined partly by biological sex: Females play one role in sexual reproduction, males another. The gender niches are further defined and elaborated upon socially in ways that vary at least somewhat from culture to culture. Females and males are viewed by the culture as having different attributes and being best suited for different social roles. We choose neither our sex nor our gender. Pure chance normally decides sex—X, you're a female; Y, you're a male. Then, throughout life, most of us live with that assignment. What consequences might all this have for personality?

Some Gender Differences in Personality

Standard personality tests do reveal relatively consistent differences, small to moderate in size, between men and women in average scores on many personality traits (Costa & others, 2001; Feingold, 1994; Schmitt & others, 2008). One of the largest and most consistent of such differences, found in essentially every culture where

Michelle D. Bridwell/Photo Edit

tests have been conducted, is that women score higher than men in agreeableness (look back at Figure 15.3 on page 557, for example). This result is in line with the results of many other studies, using a variety of measures, showing that women are, on average, more concerned than men with developing and maintaining positive social relationships (Kashima & others, 1995; Taylor & others, 2000).

Relatively consistent gender differences have also been observed in neuroticism, primarily because women report higher levels of anxiety and feelings of vulnerability than do men. Women also generally score slightly but significantly higher on conscientiousness. Results on the other two Big Five trait dimensions are more varied. Women tend to score considerably higher than men on the warmth and gregariousness facets of extraversion, but considerably lower on the excitement-seeking facet of that trait (McCrae & Terracciano, 2005). Women also tend to score considerably higher than men on the feelings and aesthetics facets of openness to experience, but not on the other four facets (fantasy, actions, ideas, and values) of that trait (McCrae & Terracciano, 2005).

Gender not only influences the kind of personality one develops but also affects the relationship of personality to life satisfaction (Rothbart & Bates, 1998). For example, researchers have found that shyness or behavioral inhibition correlates positively with feelings of emotional distress and unhappiness in young men but not in young women (Gest, 1997). That difference is not present in early childhood but seems to emerge in adolescence and reach a peak in young adulthood. A possible explanation lies in cultural expectations that make life more difficult for shy or inhibited young men than for similarly shy or inhibited young women. In our

"You've had to be kind to survive, and I've had to be nasty."

© The New Yorker Collection 2005 Victoria Roberts from cartoonbank.com. All rights reserved.

22
What differences have researchers found between women and men in personality traits?

Shyness may be harder on young men than on young women Shy men have been found to suffer more from their shyness, on average, than do shy women, apparently because men more than women are expected to be bold and assertive.

23
How might gender alter the relationship between personality and life satisfaction?

culture and all others that have been studied, men are expected to initiate romantic and sexual relationships and to be more assertive or dominant in social interactions of all types, and shyness or lack of assertion is considered more attractive in women than in men.

In other respects, too, personality dispositions that run counter to stereotypes can have social and emotional costs. Women who have a relatively competitive orientation toward others, rather than an orientation emphasizing similarity and agreeableness, typically score lower on measures of self-esteem than do other women, while the opposite is true for men (Josephs & others, 1992). Men who are high in neuroticism are viewed more negatively than are women who are high in that trait (Ozer & Benet-Martínez, 2006).

As noted earlier, personality measures are merely descriptions, not explanations, of psychological differences among people. What accounts for the just-described average differences between women and men on personality measures? In addressing that question, some psychologists focus on evolutionary history and others focus on the present-day pressures and expectations of the cultures in which we develop.

Evolutionary Foundations of Gender Differences

24

How might gender differences in personality be understood in terms of natural selection? What evidence suggests that hormones may provide a basis for such differences?

Personality theorists who favor evolutionary explanations of gender differences (such as Larsen & Buss, 2008) point to the universality of certain gender differences and to the long history of evolution in which males and females were subject, generation after generation, to different reproductive challenges. Females' greater role in child care, and perhaps a need for cooperative relationships with other adults in relation to child care, may have led to selection for personality qualities promoting nurturance, cooperation, and caution; and males' greater need to compete in order to reproduce may have led to selection for competitiveness, aggressiveness, and risk taking (as described in **Chapter 3**).

Consistent with this evolutionary perspective, Shelley Taylor and her colleagues (2000) have amassed considerable evidence that male and female mammals in general, including humans, tend to respond differently to stressful situations. Whereas males tend to respond to stress by becoming more aggressive, females tend to respond by becoming more nurturant and more motivated to strengthen social connections. According to Taylor, females are more likely than males to attempt to placate their rivals rather than intimidate them and more likely to seek comfort and support from friends. This difference, of course, is not all-or-none, but a matter of degree, and there is considerable overlap between the sexes. Taylor also summarizes evidence that sex differences in hormones contribute to these differences in personality (Taylor, 2006; Taylor & others, 2000). Oxytocin, which is at higher levels in females than in males, tends to promote affiliation; and testosterone, which is at higher levels in males, tends to promote aggression.

Cultural Foundations of Gender Differences

Cultural theorists, in contrast, point to the different experiences, expectations, role models, and opportunities provided by the culture for girls and boys—all the differences discussed in **Chapter 12.** From the cultural perspective, the most relevant niches to think about are not those existing in past generations of humans and prehumans but are those in existence right now (Bussey & Bandura, 1999; Wood & Eagly, 2002). The immediate causes of gender differences in personality are social forces that encourage girls to develop the nurturant, agreeable, and conscientious aspects of their nature and boys to develop their competitive, aggressive, and risk-taking aspects.

25

What evidence supports the view that gender differences in personality are at least partly shaped by cultural expectations?

Consistent with the cultural explanation is evidence that some gender differences in personality have changed, over historical time, in keeping with changing social roles and expectations. In particular, a systematic analysis of scores on various tests of *assertiveness*, given to men and women in the United States between 1931 and 1993, revealed that gender differences in this trait changed over time in

© Sean Gardner/Reuters/Corbis

Becoming assertive In the 30 years from 1970 to 2000, girls' and women's participation in formal sports increased by nearly tenfold (Twenge, 2001). Perhaps such cultural changes help to explain the increased assertiveness of women, as measured by personality tests, that occurred over that same period.

keeping with changes in the culture (Twenge, 2001). During the Great Depression and World War II, when women were generally expected to be self-sufficient, personality tests revealed relatively small gender differences in assertiveness. After the war, and through the 1950s and early 1960s, however, women were generally expected to be passive and domestic, and during those years women's scores on assertiveness tests declined considerably while men's scores remained relatively constant. Beginning in the mid-1960s, however, women entered the workforce in ever-increasing numbers and took on roles previously considered to be masculine, and their assertiveness scores subsequently increased. In fact, some studies suggest that by the end of the 20th century women's average assertiveness scores were as high as men's (Twenge, 2001).

Another route to assessing the role of culture in male–female personality differences is to examine gender differences cross-culturally. In an analysis of Big Five personality scores for men and women in 55 different countries, David Schmitt and his colleagues (2008) found—contrary to what you might expect—that gender differences in personality were *greater* in developed, prosperous, egalitarian countries than in relatively undeveloped, poor, traditional cultures. Overall, women tended to score higher than men in neuroticism, extraversion, agreeableness, and conscientiousness, and this difference was significantly greater in countries like France, the Netherlands, Canada, and the United States than in countries like Ethiopia, Malaysia, Botswana, and Indonesia. How might this finding be explained?

Schmitt and his colleagues interpret the results as support for the idea of inherent biological personality differences between men and women. They suggest that in wealthier, more egalitarian countries, where people are freer to choose their own routes in life, men and women choose ways of life that are consistent with and reinforce their inborn personality traits. Consistent with this interpretation is evidence that as women have become more accepted in traditionally male roles in developed countries, women have brought a more feminine orientation to those roles. Women business leaders, for example, are on average more likely to lead through nurturance and encouragement, and to exert greater conscientiousness and less aggressiveness, than men occupying similar positions (Eagly, 2007). Thus, increased freedom of occupational choice in wealthier countries may be accompanied by increased flexibility within each occupational role, so that people of either gender can bring their personality strengths to bear rather than modify their personalities to fit the job. This explanation of the cross-cultural findings is speculation, but interesting speculation.

26
How might increased occupational freedom *increase* gender differences in personality?

Personality differences may represent alternative adaptations to life's variable conditions.

Advantages of Being Different

➤ Just as diversified investments help protect one's financial future in a world of unpredictable change, diverse personalities may protect one's genetic investment.

➤ Fish (including pumpkinseeds and perch) can be bold or cautious; each tendency has benefits and risks. Such variation is affected by the environment (including the number of other bold or cautious fish present) as well as by heredity.

➤ Human variations in the Big Five traits can, likewise, be viewed as alternative strategies for survival and reproduction.

Adapting to the Family Environment

➤ Siblings raised together may experience quite different environments, for reasons that include chance events, consequences of their own choices, and differences in how they interpret the same occurrences.

➤ The tendency to exaggerate differences between siblings (sibling contrast) and the tendency for siblings to identify with different parents (split-parent identification) may reduce sibling rivalry and diversify parental investment.

➤ A historical analysis suggested that firstborns are more conservative and traditional, while later-borns are more open to new ideas and more likely to rebel against established ways. Contemporary studies of birth order have produced less dramatic, less consistent results.

Adapting to One's Gender

➤ On average, women score slightly to moderately higher than men on agreeableness, neuroticism, and conscientiousness.

➤ Apparently because of cultural pressures, some personality characteristics that run counter to gender stereotypes correlate with unhappiness. For example, shy young men are generally less happy than shy young women.

➤ Both evolutionary and cultural forces may help to account for gender differences in personality. There is evidence that these differences are greater in modern Western cultures than in more traditional cultures.

▇ Personality as Mental Processes I: Psychodynamic and Humanistic Views

Trait theories, such as the five-factor model, are useful as general schemes for describing human psychological differences and for thinking about possible functions of those differences. Such theories have little to say, however, about the internal mental processes that lead people to behave in particular ways. The rest of this chapter is devoted to ideas about the mental underpinnings of personality.

We begin by examining two very general, classic theoretical perspectives on personality: the psychodynamic and humanistic perspectives. These two perspectives derive largely from the observations and speculations of clinical psychologists, who were attempting to make sense of the symptoms and statements of their clients or patients. These two perspectives also provide much of the basis for the general public's understanding of psychology.

Elements of the Psychodynamic Perspective

The pioneer of clinical psychology, and of the clinical approach to understanding personality, was Sigmund Freud (1856–1939). Freud was a physician who specialized in neurology and, from 1886 on, worked with patients at his private office in Vienna. He found that many people who came to him had no detectable medical problems; their suffering seemed to derive from their memories, especially their memories of disturbing events in their childhoods. In many cases, they could not recall such memories consciously, but clues in their behavior led Freud to believe that disturbing memories were present nevertheless, buried in what he referred to as the *unconscious mind*. From this insight, Freud developed a method of treatment in which his patients would talk freely about themselves and he would analyze what they said in order to uncover buried memories and hidden emotions and motives. The goal was to make the patient conscious of his or her unconscious memories, motives, and emotions, so that the patient's conscious mind could work out ways of dealing with them.

Sigmund Freud The founder of psychoanalysis viewed himself as a detective whose task was to use cues in people's behavior to uncover the secrets of their unconscious minds.

Keystone/The Image Works

Freud coined the term *psychoanalysis* to refer both to his method of treatment (discussed in **Chapter 17**) and to his theory of personality. Freud's psychoanalytic theory was the first of what today are called *psychodynamic theories*—personality theories that emphasize the interplay of mental forces (the word *dynamic* refers to energy or force and *psycho* refers to mind). Two guiding premises of psychodynamic theories are that (a) people are often unconscious of their motives and (b) processes called *defense mechanisms* work within the mind to keep unacceptable or anxiety-producing motives and thoughts out of consciousness. According to psychodynamic theories, personality differences lie in variations in people's unconscious motives, in how those motives are manifested, and in the ways that people defend themselves from anxiety.

27
What characteristics of the mind underlie personality differences, according to the psychodynamic perspective?

The Concept of Unconscious Motivation

Freud proposed that the main causes of behavior lie deeply buried in the unconscious mind—that is, in the part of the mind that affects the individual's conscious thought and action but is not itself open to conscious inspection. The reasons people give to explain their behavior often are not the true causes. To illustrate this idea, Freud (1912/1932) drew an analogy between everyday behavior and the phenomenon of posthypnotic suggestion.

In a demonstration of posthypnotic suggestion, a person is hypnotized and given an instruction such as "When you awake, you will not remember what happened during hypnosis. However, when the clock chimes, you will walk across the room, pick up the umbrella lying there, and open it." When awakened, the subject appears to behave in a perfectly normal, self-directed way until the clock chimes. At this signal the subject consciously senses an irresistible impulse to perform the commanded action, and consciously performs it, but has no conscious memory of the origin of the impulse (the hypnotist's command). If asked why he or she is opening the umbrella, the subject may come up with a plausible though clearly false reason, such as "I thought I should test it because it may rain later." According to Freud, the real reasons behind our everyday actions are likewise hidden in our unconscious minds, and our conscious reasons are cover-ups, plausible but false rationalizations that we believe to be true.

28
How is the concept of unconscious motivation illustrated by posthypnotic suggestion?

Freud believed that to understand his patients' actions, problems, and personalities, he had to learn about the contents of their unconscious minds. But how could he do that when the unconscious, by definition, consists only of information that the patient cannot talk about? He claimed that he could do it by analyzing certain aspects of their speech and other observable behavior to draw inferences about their unconscious motives. This is where the term *psychoanalysis* comes from. His technique was to sift the patient's behavior for clues to the unconscious. Like a detective, he collected clues and tried to piece them together into a coherent story about the unconscious causes of the person's conscious thoughts and actions.

29
How did Freud draw inferences about the content of his clients' unconscious minds?

Because the conscious mind always attempts to act in ways that are consistent with conventional logic, Freud reasoned that the elements of thought and behavior that are least logical would provide the best clues to the unconscious. They would represent elements of the unconscious mind that leaked out relatively unmodified by consciousness. Freud therefore paid particular attention to his patients' slips of the tongue and other mistakes as clues to the unconscious. He also asked them to describe their dreams and to report in uncensored fashion whatever thoughts came to mind in response to particular words or phrases. These methods are described more fully, with examples, in **Chapter 17.**

Sex and Aggression as Motivating Forces in Freud's Theory

Unlike most modern psychologists, Freud considered drives to be analogous to physical forms of energy that build up over time and must somehow be released. To live peaceably in society (especially in the Victorian society that Freud grew up in), people must often inhibit direct expressions of the sexual and aggressive drives,

30
Why did Freud consider sex and aggression to be especially significant drives in personality formation?

so these are the drives that are most likely to build up and exert themselves in indirect ways. Freud concluded from his observations that much of human behavior consists of disguised manifestations of sex and aggression and that personality differences lie in the different ways that people disguise and channel these drives. Over time, Freud (1933/1964) came to define these drives increasingly broadly. He considered the sex drive to be the main pleasure-seeking and life-seeking drive and the aggressive drive to be the force that lies behind all sorts of destructive actions, including actions that harm oneself.

Social Drives as Motives in Other Psychodynamic Theories

Freud viewed people as basically asocial, forced to live in societies more by necessity than by desire, and whose social interactions derive primarily from sex, aggression, and displaced forms of these drives. In contrast, most psychodynamic theorists since Freud's time have viewed people as inherently social beings whose motives for interacting with others extend well beyond sex and aggression.

31 ------------------------------------
What drives or human needs provide bases for personality differences in Horney's and Adler's theories of personality?
-- -- -- -- -- -- -- -- -- -- -- -- --

◀ For example, Karen Horney developed a psychodynamic theory that focused on *security* as an inborn human need that can be filled only by other people. The most fundamental emotion in her theory is *basic anxiety,* defined as "the feeling a child has of being isolated and helpless in a potentially hostile world" (Horney, 1945). Parents influence a child's lifelong personality through the ways in which they succeed or fail in relieving the child's basic anxiety and helping the child feel secure.

Closely related to Horney's theory are more recent *object relations theories* of personality (Flanagan, 2008; Kernberg, 1976), which derive partly from John Bowlby's ideas concerning the emotional attachments that infants make with their caregivers (discussed in **Chapter 12**). The term *object relations,* in these theories, refers to the interactions between a child and the objects (people) to whom the child feels attached. According to these theories, the way people respond to others throughout life depends on the nature of their early attachments. For instance, inconsistent approval from attachment objects (typically parents) early in childhood—veering from fawning admiration to rejection—may result in an excessive need for others' approval later in life.

"Of course I'm feeling uncomfortable. I'm not allowed on the couch."

Hippocrates, March 2000

As another example, Alfred Adler developed a psychodynamic theory that centers on people's drive to feel competent. Adler (1930) contended that everyone begins life with a feeling of inferiority, which stems from the helpless and dependent nature of early childhood, and that the manner in which people learn to cope with or to overcome this feeling provides the basis for their lifelong personalities. While Horney emphasized emotional attachments as means of overcoming early anxieties, Adler emphasized the role of personal achievements. People who become overwhelmed by a sense of inferiority will develop either an *inferiority complex,* and go through life acting incompetent and dependent, or a *superiority complex,* and go through life trying to prove they are better than others as a means of masking their inferiority.

In all psychodynamic theories, including Freud's, the first few years of life are especially crucial in forming the personality. One's earliest attempts to satisfy drives result in positive or negative responses from others that, taken together, have lifelong effects on how those drives are subsequently manifested.

The Idea That the Mind Defends Itself Against Anxiety

A central idea in all psychodynamic theories is that mental processes of self-deception, referred to as **defense mechanisms,** operate to reduce one's consciousness of wishes, memories, and other thoughts that would threaten one's self-esteem or in other ways provoke a strong sense of insecurity, or anxiety. The theory of defense mechanisms was most thoroughly developed by Anna Freud (1936/1946), Sigmund's daughter, who was also a prominent psychoanalyst. Some examples of defense mechanisms are repression, displacement, reaction formation, projection, and rationalization.

Repression (discussed more fully in the next section) is the process by which
anxiety-producing thoughts are pushed out or kept out of the conscious mind. In
Freud's theory, repression provides the basis for most of the other defense mechanisms. Freud visualized repression as a damming up of mental energy. Just as water
will leak through any crack in a dam, repressed wishes and memories will leak
through the barriers separating the unconscious mind from the conscious mind. When
such thoughts leak through, however, the mind can still defend itself by distorting
the ideas in ways that make them less threatening. The other defense mechanisms
are the various means by which we create such distortions.

Displacement occurs when an unconscious wish or drive that would be unacceptable to the conscious mind is redirected toward a more acceptable alternative. For
example, a child long past infancy may still have a desire to suck at the mother's

────────────────── **32**

**How do repression, displacement,
reaction formation, projection, and
rationalization each serve to defend
against anxiety?**

breast—a desire that is now threatening and repressed,
because it violates the child's conscious understanding
of what is proper and possible. The desire might be displaced toward sucking on a lollipop, an action that is
symbolically equivalent to the original desire but more
acceptable and realistic.

In some cases, displacement may direct one's energies toward activities that are particularly valued by
society, such as artistic, scientific, or humanitarian endeavors. In these cases displacement is referred to as
sublimation. A highly aggressive person might perform
valuable service in a competitive profession, such as
being a trial lawyer, as sublimation of the drive to beat
others physically. As another example, Freud (1910/
1947) suggested that Leonardo da Vinci's fascination
with painting Madonnas was a sublimation of his desire
for his mother, which had been frustrated by his separation from her.

S. Gaboury/DMI/RexFeatures

Feeling good about feeling bad
Blues music, sung here by B.B. King,
may appeal to us because it turns our
unconscious as well as conscious pain
into something beautiful. In that sense,
it may be a form of sublimation.

Reaction formation is the conversion of a frightening wish into its safer opposite. For example, a young woman who unconsciously hates her mother and wishes
her dead may consciously experience these feelings as intense love for her mother
and strong concern for her safety. Psychodynamic theorists have long speculated
that *homophobia*—the irrational fear and hatred of homosexuals—may often stem
from reaction formation. People who have a tendency toward homosexuality, but
fear it, may protect themselves from recognizing it by vigorously separating themselves from homosexuals (West, 1977). In a study supporting that explanation, men
who scored as highly homophobic on a questionnaire were subsequently found,
through direct physical measurement, to show more penile erection while watching a male homosexual video than did other men, even though they denied experiencing any sexual arousal while watching the video (Adams & others, 1996).

Projection occurs when a person consciously experiences an unconscious drive
or wish as though it were someone else's. A person with intense, unconscious anger
may project that anger onto her friend—she may feel that it is her friend, not she,
who is angry. In an early study of projection conducted at college fraternity houses,
Robert Sears (1936) found that men who were rated by their fraternity brothers
as extreme on a particular characteristic, such as stinginess, but who denied
that trait in themselves tended to rate others as particularly high on that same
characteristic.

Rationalization is the use of conscious reasoning to explain away anxiety-provoking thoughts or feelings. A man who cannot face his own sadistic tendencies may
rationalize the beatings he gives his children by convincing himself that children
need to be beaten and that he is only carrying out his fatherly duty. Psychodynamic
theories encourage us to be wary of conscious logic, since it often serves to mask true
feelings and motives. (For discussion of the left-hemisphere interpreter, which seems
to be the source of rationalization, look back at **Chapter 5,** p. 136.)

Defensive Styles as Dimensions of Personality

Of all of Freud's big ideas about the mind, his concept of psychological defense has had the most lasting appeal in psychology and has generated the most research (Cramer, 2000). Some of the cognitive biases discussed in **Chapter 13,** by which people enhance their own perceptions of themselves and rationalize their own morally questionable actions, can be understood as defense mechanisms. These biased ways of thinking reduce anxiety by bolstering people's images of themselves as highly competent and ethical.

Much modern research on defense mechanisms focuses on individual differences in defensive styles. Some people habitually employ certain defenses as their routine modes of dealing with stressful situations in their lives, such that the defense mechanism can be thought of as a dimension of their personality. The most fully researched defensive style is that referred to as *repressive coping*.

Repressive Coping as a Personality Style

Freud's theory of repression centered on the idea that people often repress memories of traumatic or highly disturbing events so fully that they can be recalled only through psychotherapy, which uncovers them. Today this idea is still highly controversial. In cases where people claim to have recovered repressed memories of past events it is usually hard to verify that the events actually occurred (McNally, 2003). As described in **Chapter 9,** people often construct false memories of the past, based on cues in the present, and then cannot distinguish those memories from true memories. Most people who have suffered truly traumatic experiences wish they could forget them but cannot (Goodman & others, 2003). Repression of traumatic memories may well occur in some cases, but so far this has been difficult to document as a general phenomenon.

◄ In contrast, there is ample evidence that many people regularly repress the emotional *feelings* that accompany disturbing events in their lives. They are able to recall and describe the events, but they claim that such memories do not make them anxious or otherwise disturb them. Personality researchers refer to these people as *repressors*. For research purposes, repressors are identified by their scores on standardized questionnaires for assessing anxiety and defensiveness. They are people who report experiencing very little anxiety, but who answer other questions in ways that seem highly defensive (Weinberger, 1990). Their questionnaire responses indicate that they have an especially strong need to view themselves in a very favorable light; they do not admit to the foibles that characterize essentially all normal people.

Many research studies have compared repressors, identified in this way, with non-repressors in their reactions to moderately distressing situations in the laboratory. For example, subjects might be asked to complete sentences that contain sexual or aggressive themes, or to describe their least-desirable traits, or to recall fearful experiences that happened to them in the past, or to imagine some unhappy event that could afflict them in the future. The general finding is that repressors report much less psychological distress in these situations than do non-repressors; but, by physiological indices—such as heart rate, muscle tension, and sweating—they manifest *more* distress than do non-repressors (Derakshan & others, 2007; Weinberger, 1990). Research indicates that they are not lying when they say that they experience little anxiety; they apparently really believe what they are saying. Somehow they have banished anxious thoughts and feelings from their conscious minds, but have not banished the bodily reactions of anxiety.

In other experiments, repressors reported less anxiety or other unpleasant emotions in daily diaries, recalled fewer negative childhood experiences, and were less

33

What evidence exists that some people regularly repress anxious feelings? In general, how do such "repressors" differ from others in their reactions to stressful situations?

"The motion has been made and seconded that we stick our heads in the sand."

likely to notice consciously or remember emotion-arousing words or phrases presented during an experiment than was the case for non-repressors (Bonanno & others, 1991; Cutler & others, 1996; Davis & Schwartz, 1987; Fujiwara & others, 2008). They apparently avoid experiences of anxiety by diverting their conscious attention away from anxiety-arousing stimuli and by dwelling on pleasant rather than unpleasant thoughts.

A good deal of research has centered on the possible benefits and harm of the repressive style of coping. The repressive style may often originate, and be most helpful, at a time when the person is coping with a seriously disturbing life event. For example, this style is common among adolescent cancer survivors, and it seems to help them to maintain a remarkably positive outlook on life (Erickson & others, 2008). Other research indicates that the repressive style helps people who have had heart attacks, or who have lost loved ones to suicide, cope psychologically (Parker & McNally, 2008; Ginzburg & others, 2002). Laboratory studies suggest that repression may help people in these situations by preserving their conscious minds—their working memories—for rational planning and problem solving. As described in **Chapter 14,** anxious thoughts occupy space in working memory and thereby interfere with the person's ability to solve problems. Repressors are apparently much less affected by this than are the rest of us (Derakshan & Eysenck, 1998; Parker & McNally, 2008). They continue to function effectively, at work and elsewhere, despite events that would traumatize others.

On the other side of the coin, however, is evidence that repressors may develop more health problems and experience more chronic pain than do non-repressors (Burns, 2000; Schwartz, 1990). This is consistent with the idea that they experience stress physically rather than as conscious emotion. Repressors may be promoting their cognitive functioning at some cost to their bodies. One might expect also that the repressive style could lead people to overlook and fail to avoid real threats in their environments, but I don't know of any research demonstrating that. Like most personality dimensions, repressive coping has benefits and costs; the overall balance between the two depends on the environmental conditions to which the person must adapt.

▶----------------**34**

What benefit and harm might accrue from the repressive style of coping?

Distinction Between Mature and Immature Defensive Styles

Other research on defensive styles has focused on the idea that some defenses are more conducive to a person's long-term well-being than are others. The most ambitious and famous such study was begun in the 1930s, with male sophomores at Harvard University as subjects.

Each year until 1955, and less often after that, the Harvard men filled out an extensive questionnaire concerning such issues as their work, ambitions, social relationships, emotions, and health. Nearly 30 years after the study began, when the men were in their late forties, a research team led by George Vaillant (1995) interviewed

Lookalike Productions

A very healthy defense Alfred Adler claimed that people who have a handicap often work hard to compensate, sometimes to the point that they excel at the very activity that would otherwise be most difficult for them. Emmanual Osuff Yeboah of Ghana, shown here on his bicycle, may be an example. He was born with only one leg, but became an outstanding bicyclist. In Ghana people born with a handicap are greatly stigmatized; they are expected to become beggars. Yeboah was campaigning against that attitude by cycling through every part of his country to demonstrate what people with one leg can do.

in depth 95 of these men, randomly selected. By systematically analyzing the content and the style of their responses in the interview and on the previous questionnaires, the researchers rated the extent to which each man used specific defense mechanisms.

35

What relationships did Vaillant find between defensive styles and measures of life satisfaction?

◀ Vaillant divided the various defense mechanisms into categories according to his judgment of the degree to which they would seem to promote either ineffective or effective behavior. *Immature defenses* were those presumed to distort reality the most and to lead to the most ineffective actions. Projection was included in this category. *Intermediate defenses* (referred to by Vaillant as "neurotic defenses"), including repression and reaction formation, were presumed to involve less distortion of reality and to lead to somewhat more effective coping. *Mature defenses* were presumed to involve the least distortion of reality and to lead to the most adaptive behaviors. One of the most common of the mature defenses was *suppression,* which involves the conscious avoidance of negative thinking. Suppression differs from repression in that the person has more conscious control over the decision to think about, or not think about, the distressing experience. Another defense in the mature category was *humor,* which, according to Freud and other psychodynamic theorists, reduces fear by making fun of feared ideas. (For a compatible view, see the discussion of the evolution of laughter in **Chapter 3.**)

Consistent with Vaillant's expectations, the men who used the most mature defenses were the most successful on all measures of ability to love and work (Freud's criteria for mature adulthood). They were also, by their own reports, the happiest. Figure 15.5 depicts some of the comparisons between the men who used mainly mature defenses and those who used mainly immature defenses. Vaillant (1995) also found, not surprisingly, that as the Harvard men matured—from age 19 into their forties—the average maturity of their defenses increased. Immature defenses such as projection declined, and mature defenses such as suppression and humor increased.

FIGURE 15.5 Love, work, and happiness in men with mature and immature defensive styles Harvard alumni classified as using primarily mature defenses were more frequently rated as having rich friendships, a good marriage, satisfaction with their work, active involvement in public service, and a high degree of happiness than were those classified as using primarily immature defenses. (Data from Vaillant, 1977.)

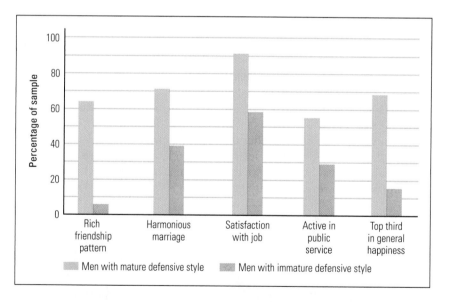

In subsequent research, using more diverse groups of subjects, including women as well as men, Vaillant and others found similar results (Cramer, 2008; Vaillant & Vaillant, 1992). As they grow older, from adolescence on, people rely less on defenses that deny or distort reality and more on defenses that allow them to accept reality. The use of mature rather than immature defenses correlates positively with measures of life satisfaction and success. Such correlations do not prove that mature defenses cause successful coping, but they do at least show that the two tend to go together.

The Humanistic Perspective: The Self and Life's Meanings

Humanistic theories of personality arose, in the mid-20th century, partly in reaction to the then-dominant psychodynamic theories. While psychodynamic theories emphasize unconscious motivation and defenses, humanistic theories emphasize people's conscious understanding of themselves and their capacity to choose their own paths to fulfillment. They are called *humanistic* because they center on an aspect of human nature that seems to distinguish us clearly from other animals—our tendency to create belief systems, to develop meaningful stories about ourselves and our world, and to govern our lives in accordance with those stories.

Phenomenology is the study of conscious perceptions and understandings, and humanistic theorists use the term ***phenomenological reality*** to refer to each person's conscious understanding of his or her world. Humanistic theorists commonly claim that one's phenomenological reality *is* one's real world; it provides the basis for the person's contentment or lack of contentment and for the meaning that he or she finds in life. In the words of

36
How, in general, do humanistic theories differ from psychodynamic theories?

Courtesy of Natalie Rogers/© Bob Van Doren

Carl Rogers Rogers (1902–1987) developed a humanistic theory of personality that centers on the self-concept and the ways in which it can be distorted by socially imposed conditions of worth.

one of the leaders of humanistic psychology, Carl Rogers (1980): "The only reality you can possibly know is the world as you perceive and experience it. . . . And the only certainty is that those perceived realities are different. There are as many 'real worlds' as there are people."

Being One's Self; Making One's Own Decisions

According to most humanistic theories, a central aspect of one's phenomenological reality is the *self-concept,* the person's understanding of who he or she is. Rogers referred to his own version of humanistic theory as *self theory.* He claimed that at first he avoided the construct of self because it seemed unscientific, but was forced to consider it through listening to his clients in therapy sessions. Person after person would say, in effect, "I feel I am not being my real self"; "I wouldn't want anyone to know the real me"; or "I wonder who I am." From such statements, Rogers (1959) gradually came to believe that a concept of self is a crucial part of a person's phenomenological reality and that a common goal of people is to "discover their real selves" and "become their real selves."

37
What human drive, or goal, characterizes healthy development in Rogers's self theory?

According to Rogers, people often are diverted from becoming themselves by the demands and judgments placed on them by other people, particularly by authority figures such as parents and teachers. To be oneself, according to Rogers, is to live life according to one's own wishes rather than someone else's. Thus, an important dimension of individual difference, in Rogers's theory, has to do with the degree to which a person feels in charge of his or her own life.

As would be predicted by Rogers's theory, researchers have found that people who feel as if a decision is fully their own, made freely by themselves, are more likely to follow through and act on it effectively than are people who feel that they are doing something because of social pressure or because an authority figure thinks they should do it. Those who think and talk about their intention to lose weight, stop smoking, exercise more, or take prescribed medicines on schedule as "following the doctor's orders" are less likely to succeed at such goals than are those who think and talk about the decision as their own (Ryan & Deci, 2000; Williams & others, 1995, 1996; Wilson & others, 2003). Employees who feel that their job is their own choice,

38
What research findings on self-determination appear to support Rogers's theory?

and that they are in charge of how they do the job, are happier and perform better than otherwise similar employees who feel that their work is dictated by other people or by necessity (Gagné & Deci, 2005). Other research—conducted in such diverse countries as Canada, Brazil, Russia, South Korea, Japan, and Turkey—has shown that people who feel that they are following their own desires are happier and more productive than those who feel that they are responding to social pressures (Chirkov & others, 2003, 2005; Ryan & Deci, 2006). In different cultures, people tend to have different values and to choose different activities, but in each culture those who see those choices as their own claim to be most satisfied with their lives.

Self-actualization Humanistic theorists draw an analogy between the self-actualization process in humans and the inner growth potential of all living things. This beech tree has long been using its environment to promote its own growth, and these children have for a much shorter time been doing the same.

Self-Actualization and Maslow's Hierarchy of Human Needs

Humanistic theorists use the term ***self-actualization*** to refer to the process of becoming one's full self—that is, of realizing one's dreams and capabilities. The specific route to self-actualization will vary from person to person and from time to time within a person's lifetime, but for each individual the route must be self-chosen.

Rogers (1963, 1977) often compared self-actualization in humans to physical growth in plants. A tree growing on a cliff by the sea must battle against the wind and saltwater and does not grow as well as it would in a more favorable setting, yet its inner potential continues to operate and it grows as well as it can under the circumstances. Nobody can tell the tree how to grow; its growth potential lies within itself. Humanistic theorists hold that full growth, full actualization, requires a fertile environment, but that the direction of actualization and the ways of using the environment must come from within the organism. In the course of evolution, organisms have acquired the capacity to use the environment in ways that maximize growth. In humans, the capacity to make free, conscious choices that promote positive psychological growth is the actualizing tendency. To grow best, individuals must be permitted to make those choices and must trust themselves to do so.

Courtesy of the Sudbury Valley School

39

What is Maslow's theory about the relationship among various human needs? How might the theory be reconciled with an evolutionary perspective?

Another pioneer of humanistic psychology, Abraham Maslow (1970), suggested that to self-actualize one must satisfy five sets of needs that can be arranged in a hierarchy (see Figure 15.6). From bottom to top, they are (1) *physiological needs* (the minimal essentials for life, such as food and water); (2) *safety needs* (protection from dangers in the environment); (3) *attachment needs* (acceptance and love); (4) *esteem needs* (competence, respect from others and the self); and (5) *self-actualization needs*. In Maslow's view, the self-actualization needs encompass the needs for self-expression, creativity, and "a sense of connectedness with the broader universe." Maslow argued that a person can focus on higher needs only if lower ones, which are more immediately linked to survival, are sufficiently satisfied so that they do not claim the person's full attention and energy.

Maslow's needs hierarchy makes some sense from an evolutionary perspective. The physiological and safety needs are most basic in that they are most immediately linked to survival. If one is starving or dehydrated, or if a tiger is charging, then

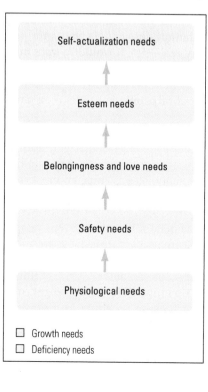

FIGURE 15.6 Maslow's hierarchy of human needs According to Maslow, needs at the lower portion of the hierarchy must be satisfied at least to some degree before people can focus on needs higher up. The most psychologically healthy people are those whose deficiency needs are sufficiently satisfied to free their energies for self-actualization.

Self-actualization needs

Esteem needs

Belongingness and love needs

Safety needs

Physiological needs

☐ Growth needs
☐ Deficiency needs

survival depends immediately upon devoting one's full resources to solving that problem. The social needs for acceptance, love, and esteem are also linked to survival, though not in quite as direct and immediate a fashion. We need to maintain good social relationships with others to ensure their future cooperation in meeting our physiological and safety needs and in helping us reproduce. Continuing in this line of thought, I would suggest that the self-actualization needs are best construed evolutionarily as *self-educative needs*. Playing, exploring, and creating can lead to the acquisition of skills and knowledge that help one later in such endeavors as obtaining food, fending off predators, attracting mates, and securing the goodwill and protection of the community. From this perspective, self-actualization is not in any ultimate sense "higher" than the other needs but is part of the long-term way of satisfying those needs.

The Life Story or Personal Myth as a Basis for Personality

People strive to make sense of their lives as a whole, and they may establish goals and make choices in accordance with that larger conception. One way to learn about individual people, which is gaining increasing acceptance among psychologists, is to ask them to tell their life stories. On the basis of his analysis of many such stories, Dan McAdams (1993, 2001) contends that the formats of the stories generally share certain characteristics, though the contents vary greatly. Each story contains themes and subthemes, morals, subordinate characters who influence the main character (the self), conflicts that get resolved, and a relatively consistent narrative tone (such as serious or lighthearted). The stories are not simply chronological chains of events, but are integrated wholes in which events are related to one another with themes pertaining to larger life purposes or a sense of personal destiny. The integrating themes are creations of the storyteller.

➤ ----------**40**

How is the life-story conception of personality consistent with the humanistic theorists' focus on phenomenology?

"*Look, making you happy is out the question, but I can give you a compelling narrative for your misery.*"

McAdams refers to the self-told story as a **personal myth,** because it seems to provide for the individual what religious myths provide for whole cultures. It gives a sense of direction and meaning to life (McAdams, 2006). People understand and explain individual events in their lives in terms of how those events fit into their larger life stories, and they make new decisions that are consistent with their stories. In their research, McAdams and his colleagues have found positive correlations between the coherence of people's life stories and measures of their mental health (Baerger & McAdams, 1999; Bauer & McAdams, 2004). They have also found that people who describe themselves as happiest are those whose stories tell of ways in which they overcame and learned from hardships and/or ways in which they are striving to give back to a society that has treated them well (Bauer & others, 2008; McAdams, 2006).

The personal myth changes with time and experience, usually gradually but sometimes dramatically and quickly. As circumstances change, the story may change to accommodate the new situation (Baumeister, 1994; McAdams, 1994). For instance, a couple's first meeting may be understood and described in romantic terms as part of their life destiny when the couple is happily married, but years later, when the couple is divorced, the same meeting might be described as an interfering accident, a digression from the true life path (Vaughan, 1986). From a phenomenological perspective, neither understanding is right or wrong; each is a way of making sense of one's current and ongoing life.

In a study of personal transformation, William Miller and Janet C'deBaca (1994) advertised for volunteers "who have been transformed in a relatively short period of time—who have had a deep shift in core values, feelings, attitudes, or actions." They had no trouble finding people who claimed to have had such an experience at some time in their lives, and they interviewed extensively 55 of them. Each story of

➤ ----------**41**

How does the life-story approach to personality differ from the trait approach in its conclusions about the modifiability of personality in adulthood?

change was different, but some common themes emerged. In general, these people saw themselves as acquiring over a short period of time, often less than 24 hours, a dramatic and lasting new insight, a new way of understanding themselves and their purposes in life. Usually they described themselves as emotionally distressed before the new insight and relieved and happy after it. Usually they described the change as liberating and involving a shift in values. Most often the shift was from worldly values—such as wealth, achievement, adventure, fitting in, and attractiveness—to social and spiritual values—such as honesty, generosity, personal peace, and obedience to God's will. Such changes occurred for different people at very different ages and in response to a wide variety of life events.

If personality is defined phenomenologically as one's self-told story, then personality can apparently change dramatically at any time in adulthood. Traits such as the Big Five, measured by standard personality tests, may not change much as people grow older and move from one life experience to another. But through their personal myths people can apparently acquire new ways of understanding and employing those traits at any time in life—new meanings, new self-definitions, and new life goals.

SECTION REVIEW

Psychodynamic and humanistic personality theories focus on mental processes.

The Psychodynamic Perspective	Defensive Styles as Personality Traits	The Humanistic Perspective
➤ Freud, whose psychoanalytic views originated this perspective, believed that the real causes of behavior lie in the unconscious mind, with sexual and aggressive motives being especially important.	➤ People classified as repressors routinely repress disturbing emotional feelings. Though they consciously experience little anxiety, their bodies react strongly to stressful situations. Such repression may help them cope cognitively in times of stress.	➤ Humanistic theories emphasize phenomenological reality (the self and world as perceived by the individual).
➤ Other psychodynamic theorists emphasized unconscious effects of other drives. Horney and Adler emphasized, respectively, the drives for security and competence.	➤ In a longitudinal study of men, Vaillant found that defensive styles that involved less distortion of reality and led to more effective behavior were correlated with greater success in all areas of life.	➤ Rogers proposed that individuals must move past social demands and judgments and make their own choices to become their real selves. Self-determination does correlate with greater life satisfaction.
➤ Defense mechanisms serve to reduce conscious awareness of unacceptable or emotionally threatening thoughts, wishes, and feelings.		➤ In Maslow's hierarchy of needs, self-actualization (becoming one's full self, living one's dreams) is addressed only when more basic needs are adequately met.
		➤ In the life-story approach to personality, a person's self-told story serves as a personal myth providing meaning and direction.

■ Personality as Mental Processes II: Social-Cognitive Views

42

How, in general, do social-cognitive theories differ from psychodynamic theories?

◄ *Social-cognitive theories* of personality, sometimes called *social-learning* or *social-cognitive-learning* theories, draw both from clinical psychologists' experiences with their clients and from academic psychologists' research on learning, cognition, and social influence. In place of the instinctive, unconscious motives posited by psychodynamic theories as the prime shapers of personality, social-cognitive theories emphasize the roles of *general beliefs* about the nature of the world, which are acquired through one's experiences in the social environment.

These beliefs may be conscious, but they may also be so ingrained and automatic that they exert their influence without the person's conscious awareness.

They can be thought of as automatic habits of thought, which can influence many aspects of a person's behavior. Thus, to social-cognitive theorists, the term *unconscious* generally refers to automatic mental processes, in the same sense as discussed in earlier chapters in this book, not to thoughts that are actively barred from consciousness by defense mechanisms. As you will see, social-cognitive ideas overlap very much with humanistic ideas about personality, but they are based more on laboratory research, and they have more to do with predicting people's behavior in specific situations, and less to do with global life choices, than is the case for humanistic theories.

Beliefs Viewed as Personality Traits

The kinds of beliefs that social-cognitive personality theorists have studied most frequently have to do, in one way or another, with the value or futility of action. Some beliefs tend to promote an affirmative, take-charge orientation toward the world, while their opposites tend to promote a more passive orientation. Here I describe the dimensions of belief that have been most thoroughly studied as personality traits. As you will see, these belief dimensions seem to overlap considerably with one another, but they have at least different shades of meaning, and some social-cognitive theorists think they are quite distinct from one another.

Beliefs About the Locus of Control over Desired Effects

If there is a principal founder of the social-cognitive perspective on personality, it is Julian Rotter, who wrote the first book explicitly describing a social-cognitive approach to personality (Rotter, 1954/1980). In his own early research, Rotter found that people behaved differently at various tasks or games in the laboratory, depending on whether they believed that success depended on skill or luck (Rotter & others, 1961). To the degree that they believed that success depended on skill (which it did), they worked hard and improved. To the degree that they believed that it depended on luck, they did not work hard and did not improve. Partly on the basis of these observations, Rotter argued that people's behavior depends not just on the objective relationship between their responses and rewards but also on their subjective beliefs about that relationship.

43

What, in Rotter's research, predicted people's improvement or failure to improve at various tasks? How did this lead to the concept of locus of control?

Photo Erich Lessing/Art Resource

Skill or luck? People approach an activity—such as a game of cards—very differently depending on whether they believe its potential rewards are controlled by skill or luck. This insight lay behind Rotter's concept of locus of control. Paul Cézanne, *The Card Players*, 1892. Paris, Musée d'Orsay.

In many life situations it is not clear to what degree we have control over rewards. For example, it is not completely clear that studying hard will lead to a good grade on an exam or that diet and exercise will prevent us from having a heart attack. Rotter (1966) suggested that in such situations people tend to behave according to a generalized disposition (a personality trait), acquired from past experience, to believe that rewards either are or are not usually controllable by people's own efforts. He referred to this disposition as **_locus_** (location) **_of control_** and developed a questionnaire designed to measure it. Table 15.4 shows sample test items from Rotter's locus-of-control questionnaire. People whose answers reflect a belief that individuals control their own rewards (and, by extension, their own fate) are said to have an *internal* locus of control. People whose answers reflect a belief that rewards (and fate) are controlled by factors outside themselves are said to have an *external* locus of control.

TABLE 15.4 Sample test items from Rotter's locus-of-control scale

The task on each item is to decide which alternative (*a* or *b*) seems more true. The actual test consists of 23 items similar to those shown here.

Item: a. In the long run, people get the respect they deserve in this world.

     b. Unfortunately, an individual's work often passes unrecognized, no matter how hard he or she tries.

Item: a. I have often found that what is going to happen will happen.

     b. Trusting to fate has never turned out as well for me as making a decision to take a definite course of action.

Item: a. In the case of the well-prepared student, there is rarely if ever such a thing as an unfair test.

     b. Many times exam questions tend to be so unrelated to course work that studying is really useless.

Note: For the items shown here, *internal* locus of control is indicated by choosing *a* for the first and third items and *b* for the second item.

Source: "Generalized expectancies for internal versus external locus of control of reinforcement" by J. B. Rotter, 1966, *Psychological Monographs: General and Applied, 80* (Whole no. 609), p. 11.

44

What sorts of behaviors correlate with an internal locus of control?

◄ Since its development, hundreds of studies have shown consistent, though usually not very high, correlations between scores on Rotter's locus-of-control scale and actual behavior in various situations. People who score toward the internal end of the scale are, on average, more likely than those who score toward the external end to try to control their own fate. They are more likely to take preventive health-care measures (Reich & others, 1997); to succeed in weight-loss programs (Adolfsson & others, 2005); to seek information on how to protect themselves during a tornado warning (Sims & Baumann, 1972); to resist group pressure in laboratory tests of conformity (Crowne & Liverant, 1963); and to prefer games of skill over games of chance (Schneider, 1972). Business leaders who have an internal locus of control implement more innovative, high-risk strategies for growing the business than do those who have an external locus of control, which can be good or bad depending on the economic climate (Wijbenga & van Witteloostuijn, 2007).

Other research indicates that people who score toward the internal end of the scale are, on average, less anxious and more content with life than those who score toward the external end (Phares, 1978, 1984). Apparently, the sense of control helps calm people's fears about potential mishaps and dangers.

Of course, as with all correlational research, we cannot be sure what is cause and what is effect. Does a sense of control promote hard work, responsible behavior, innovative action, and general satisfaction with life? Or do hard work, responsible behavior, innovative action, and general satisfaction promote a sense of control? Most social-cognitive theorists would contend that both of these causal hypotheses are correct to some degree. Successful action in any realm tends to lead to a stronger sense of control, which may promote further successful action; and vice versa. Most of us lie somewhere in the middle of the internal–external dimension because, truth be told, we really can control some things and not others, and it's not always clear which things lie in which category.

Beliefs About One's Own Ability to Perform Specific Tasks

Another pioneer of the social-cognitive perspective on personality is Albert Bandura, who, like Rotter, earned a degree in clinical psychology and then went on to a career of laboratory research. Much of Bandura's research centers on people's beliefs about their own abilities to perform specific tasks, which he refers to as ***self-efficacy***. People who expect that they can perform a certain task are said to have high self-efficacy about the task, and people who expect the opposite are said to have low self-efficacy about it.

Self-efficacy may seem similar to locus of control, but Bandura (1997) considers the two to be distinct. Self-efficacy refers to the person's sense of his or her own ability, while locus of control refers to the person's belief that ability will produce desired effects. Although self-efficacy and an internal locus of control usually go together, they do not always. If you believe, for example, that you are skilled at math but that the skill is worthless (perhaps because it is unrecognized by your math professor or others in society), then you have high self-efficacy but an external locus of control in that area. Conversely, if you believe that skill at math would bring rewards but that you don't have the skill, then you have low self-efficacy and an internal locus of control in that area. As is the case for locus of control, self-efficacy may be quite specific to a very narrow range of tasks or quite general over a broad range of tasks (Cervone, 1997; Welch & West, 1995).

> **45**
> How does self-efficacy differ from locus of control?

Bandura and his colleagues have repeatedly demonstrated that improved self-efficacy for a task predicts improvement in actual performance of the task. In one study, for example, various treatments were used to help people overcome their fear of snakes. The subjects who claimed after treatment that they now expected to be able to pick up and handle a large snake were indeed most likely to succeed at

> **46**
> What evidence supports the theory that high self-efficacy (a) predicts high performance and (b) may help cause high performance?

© Jim Arbogast/CORBIS

Self-efficacy According to Albert Bandura, the first step in acquiring a skill like this—or in doing anything that is difficult—is to believe you can do it.

the task, regardless of which treatment they had received (Bandura & others, 1977). Correlations between changes in self-efficacy and changes in performance have likewise been found in such diverse realms as mathematics, physical exertion, tolerance for pain, giving up smoking, and social skills (Bandura & Locke, 2003; Bandura & Cervone, 1983; Gwaltney & others, 2009; Schunk & Hanson, 1985).

Bandura believes that self-efficacy is not simply a correlate of good performance, but is also a cause of it (Bandura & Locke, 2003). As evidence, he cites experiments showing that false feedback, which raises or lowers a person's self-efficacy, can improve or worsen performance. In one experiment, for example, some subjects, randomly chosen, were told that, based on a previous measure, they had much higher than average pain tolerance, and others were told the opposite. When subsequently given a test of pain tolerance, those who were led to believe that they had excellent pain tolerance tolerated more pain than did those who were led to believe that they had poor pain tolerance (Litt, 1988). Another experiment showed similar results in the realm of problem solving. Those who were led to believe that they were good problem solvers worked more persistently, used better strategies, and were more successful at solving problems than were those who were led to believe that they were not so good (Bouffard-Bouchard, 1990).

Beliefs About the Possibility of Personal Improvement

Another dimension of belief explored by social-cognitive theorists concerns the degree of malleability of one's own personal qualities. Some people see themselves as rather *fixed* entities. They see themselves as having a certain degree of intelligence, a certain level of athletic ability, and certain rather unchangeable personality traits. They are inclined to agree with Popeye, famous for his saying, "I yam what I yam." In their minds they are what they are and they will always be that. People at the other end of this dimension have a relatively *malleable* view of themselves. They see themselves at any given point, even late in life, as changing, developing, improving. Their intelligence is not fixed, but is something that can grow or atrophy depending on their own efforts or lack of efforts. Their personality traits are moldable, not set in plaster. Carol Dweck, who has studied this belief dimension extensively, contends that your position on it makes a big difference in your approach to life.

47 - - - - - - - - - - - - - - - - - -
What is the benefit of the belief that the self is malleable? How can people's belief in their own malleability be enhanced, and what effects have been observed of such enhancement?
- - - - - - - - - - - - - - - - - - -

Dweck (2006, 2008) and her colleagues have found that people who view themselves as malleable are more likely to strive for self-improvement in all realms of life than are those who see themselves as fixed. They embrace education. They rebound from setbacks, which they interpret as growth experiences rather than failures. They seek out difficult problems to solve, so they can learn from them. They strive to improve their personal relationships with others, rather than accept them for what they are. Because of such efforts, they tend to succeed in life.

Several experiments have demonstrated that people can be taught to think of themselves as malleable and that such teaching can change their behavior. In one experiment, college students were shown a film depicting how neurons in the brain can make new connections throughout life and how the brain grows, like a muscle, with use. At the end of the semester, those students exhibited more enthusiasm for their academic work and had higher grade-point averages than did otherwise comparable students who had not seen the film (Aronson & others, 2002). Similar results were found, in another experiment, with students who had just entered junior high school (Blackwell & others, 2007). People also tend to develop either fixed or malleable views of themselves from the kinds of praise they hear (Mueller & Dweck, 1998). Global praise about attributes, such as "you are intelligent," tend to create a fixed, stagnant view of the self, while praise about effort or choice of strategy for specific tasks—such as "you worked hard and did a great job on that report"—tend to create a malleable, dynamic view of the self.

The Power of Positive Thinking

Much has been written, by psychologists and non-psychologists alike, about the benefits of a positive, optimistic outlook on life (Cousins, 1977; Peale, 1956; Seligman, 1990). You have just read about research indicating that people who believe in their own abilities (have high self-efficacy), believe that their abilities will be rewarded (have an internal locus of control), and believe in the possibility of personal improvement (have a malleable self-view) are generally happier and more successful than people who don't have those beliefs.

A number of psychologists have developed questionnaires designed to assess people's general tendency to think either positively or negatively. C. Rick Snyder (1994) and his colleagues developed a questionnaire to assess *hope,* which they construe as a belief in one's ability to solve solvable problems (generalized self-efficacy) combined with a belief that most problems in life are solvable. Martin Seligman (1990) and his colleagues developed a questionnaire to assess the degree to which people explain negative events in their lives in a pessimistic or optimistic manner (discussed in relation to theories of depression in **Chapter 16**). Michael Scheier and Charles Carver (1993) developed a questionnaire to assess *dispositional optimism,* the tendency to believe in a rosy future. On the questionnaire, people indicate the degree to which they agree or disagree with such statements as "In uncertain times, I usually expect the best."

Correlational studies using all these questionnaires have shown that, in general, people with an optimistic style of thought are happier and tend to cope more effectively with life's stressors than do people who have a pessimistic style (Bailey & others, 2007; Nes & Segerstrom, 2006; Peterson, 2000; Snyder, 1994; Taylor & others, 2003). In one such study, Scheier and his colleagues (1989) used

Optimism The belief that one can overcome adversity may become a self-fulfilling prophecy if that belief leads to effective actions. This young woman, the victim of a head-on automobile collision, works hard at strengthening her legs so she can walk again.

AP Photo/The Decatur Daily, Emily Saunders

their questionnaire to assess dispositional optimism in middle-aged men who were about to undergo coronary artery bypass surgery. They found that those who scored high on optimism before the surgery made quicker recoveries than did those who scored low, even when the medical conditions that led to surgery were equivalent. The optimists were quicker to sit up on their own, to walk, to resume vigorous exercise, and to get back to work full-time than were the pessimists.

The most likely explanation for this and other positive correlations with optimism is that optimistic thinking leads people to devote attention and energy to solving their problems or recovering from their disabilities, which in turn leads to positive results. Pessimists are relatively more likely to say, "It won't work out anyway, so why try?" A more controversial idea is that optimistic thinking may facilitate physical health and recovery through direct effects on body chemistry (discussed in **Chapter 16**).

Adaptive and Maladaptive Optimism and Pessimism

Before concluding that optimism is always best, before rushing out to trade the clear lenses on our glasses for rose-tinted ones, we should consider a potential hazard of optimism. Health psychologists have long pointed out the danger of unrealistic, self-delusional forms of optimism. Many people, especially adolescents and

48
What evidence supports the value of optimism? Through what mechanisms might optimism produce its beneficial effects?

49
What seems to differentiate adaptive from maladaptive optimism and adaptive from maladaptive pessimism?

young adults, optimistically believe that they are invulnerable to such catastrophes as AIDS, lung cancer, drug addiction, and automobile accidents and fail to take precautions to avoid such dangers (Schwarzer, 1994; Weinstein, 1980, 1982). Similarly, an optimistic, inflated belief in their academic or career abilities blinds some people to their own shortcomings and prevents them from taking steps to improve (Dunning & others, 2004). Optimism of this sort, which in the psychodynamic tradition is called *defensive optimism,* may reduce anxiety by diverting thoughts away from fearful possibilities, but it may also lead to serious harm. The optimistic belief that you can control your fate through active self-care and self-improvement usually leads to constructive behaviors, but the optimistic belief that fate will protect you without your participation can lead to dangerously imprudent behaviors.

Just as optimism can be adaptive or maladaptive, depending on whether or not it translates into constructive action, so can pessimism. In research on the cognitive underpinnings of success in college, Julie Norem and her colleagues found students who use apparently opposite mental strategies to perform well academically (Norem & Illingworth, 1993, 2004). Some students use an adaptive form of optimism. They believe they will do well, and that belief, coupled with their thoughts about the positive consequences of doing well, motivates them to work hard and actually do well. Other students, however, use an adaptive form of pessimism. They believe that there is a good chance that they will not do well, despite having done well in the past, and that belief, along with thoughts about the negative consequences of failure, motivates them to work hard to avoid failure. As a result, and apparently to their surprise, they not only pass but achieve high grades. Still, the optimists are probably better off in the long run than the pessimists. One study of adjustment to college life revealed that the pessimists' constant anxiety about failure led them to focus too narrowly on grades and lose the intrinsic pleasure of academic work (Cantor & Harlow, 1994).

My guess is that the difference between those who use either optimism or pessimism constructively and those who do not has to do with beliefs about locus of control and personal malleability. People who believe that rewards are controllable (internal locus of control) and that they themselves can improve through effort (malleable self-belief) are likely to work hard and do well regardless of whether or not their focus is on achieving anticipated success (the goal of optimists) or preventing anticipated failure (the goal of pessimists). Consistent with this view, Norem (2008) reports that the defensive pessimists she has studied believe more strongly than do other anxious people that they can improve themselves through effort.

The Idea of Situation-Specific Personality Traits

Social-cognitive theorists have long contended that global traits—such as those specified by the five-factor model—tell only part of the story of personality. To understand a person, according to these theorists, one must not only know that a person tends to be extraverted or introverted, for example, but must also know the contexts in which the person typically manifests those tendencies. One person might be shy (introverted) at parties but outspoken (extraverted) at formal meetings, while the opposite might be true of another person. One person who scores as disagreeable on the NEO-PI might be most disagreeable to subordinates while another, with the same score, might be most disagreeable to authority figures. The leading advocate for this contextual view of personality is social-cognitive theorist Walter Mischel (1984, 2007).

In one study, Mischel and Phillip Peake (1982) assessed repeatedly, by direct observation, 19 different forms of behavior presumed to be related to the trait of conscientiousness in a group of students at Carleton College in Minnesota. Included were measures of regularity of class attendance, promptness in completing assignments, bed neatness, and neatness of class notes. They found high consistency within any one of these measures but relatively low consistency across measures. For instance, students who kept neat notes for one class were very likely to keep neat notes for another class but only slightly more likely than average to keep their beds neat.

In another study, Mischel and his colleagues found that children with social adjustment problems at a summer camp were not well described by such global traits as "aggressive" or "withdrawn" but were quite well described and differentiated from one another by terms that referred to the social situations that prompted them to act aggressively or to withdraw (Mischel & Shoda, 1995; Shoda & others, 1994). Figure 15.7 shows sample results, from that study, for verbal aggressiveness for two children. As shown in the figure, both children were somewhat more verbally aggressive than the average child at the camp, but the two were very different from each other with regard to the situations in which they exhibited aggression. Child 28 was highly aggressive to peers who approached him in a friendly manner but not particularly aggressive in other situations, and child 9 was highly aggressive to adults but not to peers. Knowledge of that difference is essential to any clinically useful understanding of the children, but that knowledge would be obscured in a global rating of aggressiveness or disagreeableness for the two children.

> ►- - - - - - - - - - - - - - -**50**
>
> **What evidence supports Mischel's concept of situation-specific dispositions?**

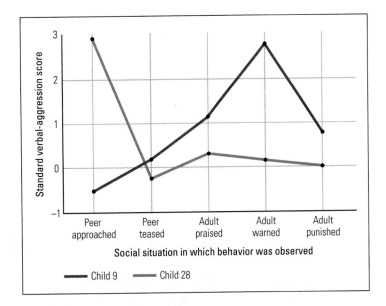

FIGURE 15.7 Situation-specific profiles of verbal aggression for two children Shoda, Mischel, and Wright (1994) recorded various categories of behaviors among emotionally disturbed children in various social situations at a summer camp. Shown here are results concerning verbal aggressiveness for two children. Zero on the *y* axis represents the average aggressiveness for all the children observed. In overall verbal aggressiveness, these two children were similar, but they were very different with respect to the situations that elicited their aggression.

Cross-Cultural Differences in Personality

If personality is, in part, ingrained beliefs and habits of thought that affect behavior, as social-cognitive theorists contend, then we should expect personality to vary across cultures. People growing up in different cultures are exposed to different values, philosophies, economic conditions, and models of how to behave.

Collectivism–Individualism as a Personality Dimension

As noted in **Chapter 13,** cultures vary in the degree to which they have a *collectivist* versus an *individualist* orientation. Collectivist cultures are those that emphasize the interdependence of people and the duties that people have to other members of their family and community. Individualist cultures, in contrast, place relatively more emphasis on personal freedom and rights, and relatively less emphasis on responsibilities to others. The cultures of North America, Australia, and Western Europe generally fall on the individualist side of this dimension, and the cultures of East Asia, Africa, and South America generally fall on the collectivist side. Many studies indicate that personalities of people in collectivist and individualist cultures differ from each other in predictable ways. Thus, collectivism and individualism can be thought of as personality traits as well as cultural characteristics (Heine & Buchtel, 2009; Triandis & Suh, 2002).

51
⟍ ⟍ ⟍ ⟍ ⟍ ⟍ ⟍ ⟍ ⟍ ⟍
In general, how do personalities in collectivist cultures differ from those in individualist cultures? What problems might arise in people whose personalities conflict with the norms of the culture in which they live?
━ ━ ━ ━ ━ ━ ━ ━ ━ ━ ━

◀ People with collectivist orientations are highly concerned with personal relationships and promoting the interests of the groups to which they belong. In contrast, those with individualist orientations focus more on their own interests and abilities and less on the interests of the group. While collectivists emphasize the similarities between themselves and other group members, individualists emphasize their own uniqueness. While collectivists see themselves as responding primarily to the conditions of their social environment, individualists see themselves as motivated by their own inner needs and aspirations. The humanistic concept of self-actualization, with its focus on resisting social pressures in order to "be yourself," is a quintessentially individualist concept.

As you would expect, personality tests that are aimed at assessing the collectivist–individualist personality dimension show that people in collectivist cultures generally score as collectivists in personality, and people in individualist cultures generally score as individualists. The differences, however, are by no means all-or-none; there is lots of overlap. In fact, according to data summarized by Harry Triandis and his colleagues, roughly 40 percent of people in collectivist cultures score on the individualist side of this personality dimension, and roughly 40 percent of people in individualist cultures score on the collectivist side (Triandis & Suh, 2002). Collectivists in individualist cultures tend to be loyal members of groups and avoid the "rat race" of individual competition; individualists in collectivist cultures often report feeling oppressed and held back by their culture's demands for conformity and obligations to the group (Triandis & Suh, 2002).

A study comparing personalities in Turkey (a collectivist culture) with those in the United States (an individualist culture) suggests that there is considerable cost to a personality that is too far out of sync with one's culture (Caldwell-Harris & Aycicegi, 2006). The researchers focused on people who scored at either extreme

Cultural differences in personality training In the American dance class (left-hand photo), a major goal is to allow children to express their individuality. In the Chinese dance class (right-hand photo), a major goal is to impart traditional Chinese methods so that the children's dancing will resemble the model. Such differences in expectations and training lead children in China and the United States to develop different personality styles.

of the collectivism–individualism dimension. Extreme collectivists in Turkey seemed to be well adjusted, but in the United States extreme collectivists tended to be anxious and depressed. Perhaps their strong need for community could not be satisfied in the individualist culture. In contrast, extreme individualists in the United States seemed to be well adjusted, but in Turkey extreme individualists scored high on measures of antisocial tendencies and paranoia (unwarranted suspicion of other people). Perhaps high individualism in a collectivist culture results in rejection by others, which may in turn promote paranoid thoughts and antisocial behavior. Or maybe only those people who for other reasons are paranoid or antisocial become extreme individualists in a collectivist culture. At any rate, the study nicely illustrates the point that the relationship between personality style and life satisfaction depends on the cultural context.

Cultural Differences in Conceptions of Personality

People in different cultures tend to differ not only in their average scores on various personality measures but also in their views about the significance of personality and the relative importance of particular traits. As discussed in **Chapter 13,** people in collectivist cultures, especially East Asian cultures, place less emphasis on personality than do people in individualist cultures. They are more likely to attribute individual differences in behavior to differences in the environmental situation than to personality differences. East Asians also generally see personality as more malleable than do Westerners (Heine & Buchtel, 2009). Consistent with the theory that belief in a malleable self leads to efforts toward self-improvement, that difference may help explain why East Asians tend to embrace schooling more fully than do Westerners and tend to learn more in school.

> **52**
> In what sense do Westerners give more weight to the concept of personality than do East Asians?

When East Asians do talk about personality, they tend to emphasize trait dimensions that are somewhat different from those emphasized in individualist cultures. For example, in China much emphasis is placed on such traits as *harmony* (inner peace of mind and a harmonious way of interacting with others), *face* (a concern with maintaining one's dignity or reputation in relationships with others), and *ren qing* (a relationship orientation that emphasizes the mutual exchange of favors) (Lin & Church, 2004). None of these traits quite matches any of the facets of Western psychologists' five-factor model (the model depicted in Table 15.3). When psychologists in China developed their own indigenous trait theory, using Chinese terms rather than translated versions of Western terms, their factor analysis produced factors that were in some ways quite different from those of Western psychologists' five-factor model. The most clearly different factor was one that they labeled *interpersonal relatedness,* which includes elements of harmony, concern for reciprocity, and concern for traditional Chinese ways of relating to others (Cheung, 2004; Cheung & others, 2008).

> **53**
> What sorts of trait dimensions are emphasized in China more than in Western cultures?

Even today, most personality tests used in non-Western cultures are translated versions of those developed in the West. As many cultural psychologists have pointed out, the results of such tests may often be misleading, because people in other cultures may interpret the questions differently than do people in the West and because the questions may not map well onto concepts and dimensions that are meaningful in their culture. Only recently have psychologists in non-Western cultures begun to develop their own personality tests, using their cultures' own terms and concepts. Such research promises to enrich our understanding of the potential ways that human beings can differ from one another and of the value of such differences.

Social-cognitive theorists stress the roles of beliefs and social contexts in personality.

Beliefs as Personality Traits	Domain-Specific and Situation-Specific Traits	Cross-Cultural Personality Differences
➤ People have an internal or external locus of control, depending on whether they do or do not believe that rewards are controlled by their own efforts.	➤ Locus of control and self-efficacy beliefs can be general, applying to many tasks, or domain-specific, applying to particular types of tasks. Domain-specific measures of these beliefs have the greatest predictive value.	➤ Because the social environment differs from one culture to another, social-cognitive theorists expect beliefs and habitual ways of thinking to differ cross-culturally.
➤ People have high or low self-efficacy, depending on whether they do or do not believe they can accomplish the relevant tasks.	➤ Social-cognitive theorists have also shown that traits such as conscientiousness and aggressiveness can vary across contexts, with the pattern of variation depending on the individual. They contend that situation-specific measures of traits have more predictive value than do global trait measures.	➤ In collectivist cultures, most people have collectivist personality styles, which focus on interdependence; in individualist cultures, most have individualist personality styles, which focus more on individuality and independence.
➤ People vary in the degree to which they see themselves as fixed entities or malleable.		➤ In non-Western cultures, the traits that are most useful in characterizing personality may not fully match the five-factor model.
➤ People with an internal locus of control, high self-efficacy, and malleable self-view tend to apply themselves more and to be more successful.		
➤ In general, people with optimistic styles of thought cope better than others with life's demands. However, defensive optimism can cause harm, and some people use pessimism adaptively.		

Concluding Thoughts

In this chapter you read about how personality can be described, why individuals differ in personality, and how such differences might be understood in terms of mental processes. Two general ideas might help you organize your thinking as you review the particular ideas of the chapter.

1. The varying purposes of personality theories Different personality theories have been developed to serve different purposes. Trait theorists try to distill the essential personality dimensions common to all people, while clinical theorists try to discover the mental processes and beliefs that help or hinder people in coping with life's demands.

Trait theories, such as the five-factor model, are attempts to describe the diversity of human personality objectively and efficiently, by identifying sets of non-redundant global traits and ways to measure them. The trait measures, usually made with questionnaires, are used in studies comparing one group of people with another, such as firstborns with later-borns, men with women, or people in one career with those in another. They are also used clinically (as explained in **Chapter 17**) as a first approximation to understanding individuals who seek help. Trait theories do not explain personality; they only describe its elements.

Psychodynamic, humanistic, and social-cognitive theories, in contrast, were designed to explain the particular behaviors, emotions, and thoughts of individual people, especially of people undergoing psychotherapy. Psychodynamic theories explain personality in terms of unconscious motives and defenses against anxiety. Humanistic theories explain personality in terms of people's subjective understanding of their world and themselves and their strivings for self-actualization. Social-cognitive theories also attempt to explain the behavior of individuals in terms of their beliefs but take a less holistic approach than do either humanistic or psychodynamic theories. Social-cognitive theorists are more often academic research psychologists than clinicians, and their interest tends to center more on a specific mental construct (such as locus of control) than on individuals as whole entities.

2. Adaptive functions of individual differences Because of the close tie between personality research and clinical research, personality theories have often been concerned with distinctions between healthy (or adaptive) and unhealthy (or maladaptive) personality styles. This concern is reflected in such distinctions as that between mature and immature defenses or between adaptive and maladaptive forms of optimism. An alternative way to think about personality differences, however, is to view them as adaptations to different niches or as different strategies for solving life's problems. In this way of thinking, two quite different styles might be equally healthy or adaptive. In this chapter you saw examples of this idea reflected especially in research and theories concerning animal personality and sibling and gender differences in personality.

As you review each of the dimensions of personality differences discussed in the chapter—including differences in defensive style, locus of control, optimism versus pessimism, and collectivism versus individualism, as well as the Big Five traits—think about ways in which variation in either direction could be either adaptive or maladaptive, depending on one's life circumstances.

Further Reading

David C. Funder & Daniel J. Ozer (Eds.) (2007). *Pieces of the personality puzzle: Readings in theory and research* (3rd ed.). New York: Norton.

This is a collection of articles that have helped to shape contemporary personality psychology. The authors include such well-known psychologists as Sigmund Freud and Karen Horney (on the psychoanalytic perspective); Abraham Maslow, Carl Rogers, and Dan McAdams (on the humanistic perspective); Walter Mischel and Albert Bandura (on the social-cognitive perspective); and Gordon Allport, Robert McCrae, and Paul Costa (on the trait perspective). There are also new articles on such topics as cross-cultural differences in personality, gender differences in personality, and the relation of personality to happiness.

Judith R. Harris (2006). *No two alike: Human nature and human individuality.* New York: Norton.

Harris is an independent thinker who loves to poke holes in the thinking and research of contemporary psychologists. Her primary objective in this book is to explain how people—even identical twins raised in the same home—grow to have different personalities. She shows how the brain systems that we all have in common can take different tracks in the course of development, producing different kinds of people. Perhaps the greatest value in reading this book, though, lies in learning how to think critically about psychological research. Harris is an expert at that.

Anneli Rufus (2003). *Party of one: The loners' manifesto.* New York: Marlow.

You have read repeatedly, in this textbook, about the social nature of human beings. But the truth is, some of us humans are much less social than others. In this beautifully written, often humorous book, Anneli Rufus, herself a happy, well-adjusted loner, writes about the struggles that loners often face in a world of people who try to convince them that there is something weird or sad about preferring to be alone. If you are by nature a loner, you will find comfort and good advice in this book; if you are not a loner, you may enjoy reading about the motives and feelings of people who are different from you.

Sigmund Freud (1901; reprinted 1960). *The psychopathology of everyday life* (J. Strachey, Ed.; A. Tyson, Trans.). New York: Norton.

This is one of Freud's most popular and fun-to-read books. It is full of anecdotes having to do with forgetting, slips of the tongue, and bungled actions. In each anecdote, Freud argues that an apparent mistake was really an expression of an unconscious wish.

Carol S. Dweck (2006). *Mindset: The new psychology of success.* New York: Random House.

In this book, written for the general public, Dweck presents her theory that people who have a malleable, or *growth,* mindset about themselves fare better in life than do those who have a *fixed* mindset about themselves. Using both research and anecdotes, she describes how the two mindsets influence people in schools, sports, business, and relationships, and she describes how people can acquire and benefit from a growth mindset. The book can be read for fun, for self-help, and for insight into a new way of thinking about personality.

Mental Disorders

A theme coursing through this book is that psychological processes are usually adaptive; they usually promote survival and well-being. Our drives and emotions, including those we experience as uncomfortable or painful, typically motivate survival-enhancing actions. Our perceptions usually provide useful information; and our thoughts usually produce effective plans.

But sometimes these processes, which normally work so well, break down and become maladaptive. Drives become too strong, too weak, or misdirected; emotions become overwhelming; perceptions become distorted; thoughts become confused; and behavior becomes ineffective. All of us experience such disturbances occasionally, to some degree, and accept them as a normal part of life. But sometimes such disturbances are so severe, prolonged, or recurrent that they seriously interfere with a person's ability to live a satisfying life. Then the person is said to have a *mental disorder*.

This chapter begins with general discussions of the nature and causes of mental disorders and then moves on to separate sections devoted to some of the most common classes of disorders—including anxiety disorders, mood disorders, and schizophrenia.

■ Problems in Identifying Mental Disorders

Human psychological misery comes in an infinite set of shades and intensities. In reality, it is better described in terms of dimensions rather than types. You might, for example, envision a three-dimensional model of mental disturbance, which includes intensity of felt misery as one dimension, degree of arousal versus despondency as another dimension, and degree of irrationality in the person's thinking as a third dimension. You might then imagine that any particular instance of psychological misery could be pinpointed to some place within that space, though even that model would be too simple. Such a model would help us understand, however, a couple of simple truths: (1) There is no sharp division between "abnormal" misery and "normal" misery—that is, between mental disorders and normal, run-of-the-mill psychological disturbances; and (2) there are no sharp divisions among different types of mental disorders.

Yet, psychiatrists and clinical psychologists regularly do make judgments about the presence or absence of a mental disorder, and they regularly distinguish among and give names to different types of mental disorders. How do they do it?

In an effort to bring consistency to the language used to talk about mental disorders, the American Psychiatric Association has developed a manual, called the *Diagnostic and Statistical Manual of Mental Disorders,* abbreviated *DSM.* The manual is continuously a work in progress. At the time that I am writing this, it is in its fourth edition, abbreviated **DSM-IV,** but teams of psychiatrists and clinical psychologists are already working on *DSM-V,* which is due to be published in 2012. The manual specifies criteria for deciding what is officially a "disorder" and what it not, and it lists many categories and sub-categories of disorders and criteria for identifying them. For better or worse, *DSM-IV* provides the current standard language for talking about mental disorders, so I almost necessarily must use that language in this chapter.

What Is a Mental Disorder?

As I have already implied, **mental disorder** has no really satisfying definition. It's a fuzzy concept. Everyone knows that, including the people who wrote *DSM-IV*. Yet, for various practical reasons, they had to come up with a definition. For one thing, insurance companies demand that patients be diagnosed as having a mental disorder if there is going to be reimbursement for treatment, so some sort of definition had to be laid out, no matter how fuzzy the concept.

◄ The definition of mental disorder in *DSM-IV* regards mental disorders as analogous to medical diseases and borrows from medicine the terms *symptom* and *syndrome*. A **symptom** is any characteristic of a person's actions, thoughts, or feelings that could be a potential indicator of a mental disorder, and a **syndrome** is a constellation of interrelated symptoms manifested by a given individual. According to *DSM-IV* (American Psychiatric Association, 2000), a syndrome is considered to be a mental disorder if, and only if, it satisfies the following three criteria:

- *It involves a clinically significant detriment.* The syndrome must involve *distress* (painful feelings) and/or *impairment of functioning* (interference with ability to work, play, or get along with people). The degree of distress or impairment must be *clinically significant,* meaning that it must be serious enough to warrant professional treatment.

- *It derives from an internal source.* The source of distress or impairment must be located within the person—that is, in the person's biology, mental structure (ways of perceiving, thinking, or feeling), or learned habits—and not in the person's immediate environment. The distress or impairment may have been prepared by past environmental circumstances and may be aggravated or triggered by present circumstances, but it cannot be simply an expectable reaction to present circumstances, such as despondency brought on by poverty or a period of grief brought on by the death of a loved one.

- *It is not subject to voluntary control.* The syndrome cannot be the result of a deliberate, voluntary decision to act in a manner contrary to the norms of society. Thus, a person who voluntarily undergoes starvation to protest a government policy, or who deliberately behaves in bizarre ways in order to amuse or shock others, is not considered to have a mental disorder.

Although these criteria are useful guidelines for thinking about and identifying mental disorders, they are by nature ambiguous, open to a wide range of interpretations; and in some cases they seem to be contradicted by the descriptions of particular disorders in *DSM-IV* (Widiger & Mullins-Sweatt, 2007).

1 -
How is *mental disorder* defined by the American Psychiatric Association? What ambiguities lie in that definition?

Cleo Freelance/Jeroboam, Inc.

Mental distress or mental disorder? Feelings of sadness, pessimism, and low self-esteem are evident here, but is the source of the distress the situation or something inside the person? This question is central to defining the concept of mental disorder.

Just how "distressing" or "impairing" must a syndrome be to be considered "clinically significant"? As all behavior involves an interaction between the person and the environment, how can we tell whether the impairment is really "within the person," rather than just in the environment? For example, in the case of someone living in poverty or experiencing discrimination, how can we tell if the person's actions are normal responses to those conditions or represent something more? When people claim that they are deliberately choosing to behave in a way that violates social norms and could behave normally if they wanted to, how do we know when to believe them? A person who starves to protest a government policy may not be mentally disordered, but what about a person who starves to protest the U.S. government's secret dealings with space aliens who may be planning an invasion? Who has the right to decide whether a person is or is not mentally disordered: the person, the person's family, a psychiatrist or psychologist, a court of law, a health insurance administrator who must approve or not approve payment for therapy?

These are tough questions that can never be answered strictly scientifically. The answers always represent human judgments, and they are always tinged by the social values and pragmatic concerns of those doing the judging.

Categorizing and Diagnosing Mental Disorders

The dividing lines among different mental disorders may be fuzzy, but in order to research and treat such disorders scientists and clinicians need a method for categorizing and labeling them. In keeping with the common Western practice of likening mental disorders to physical diseases, the process of assigning a label to a person's mental disorder is referred to as *diagnosis*. To be of value, any system of diagnosis must be *reliable* and *valid*.

The Quest for Reliability

The **reliability** of a diagnostic system refers to the extent to which different diagnosticians, all trained in the use of the system, reach the same conclusion when they independently diagnose the same individuals. If you have ever gone to two different doctors with a physical complaint and been given two different, non-synonymous labels for your disease, you know that, even in the realm of physical disorders, diagnosis is by no means completely reliable. Until relatively recently, psychiatrists and clinical psychologists had no reliable, agreed-upon method for diagnosing mental disorders. As a consequence, the same troubled person might be given a diagnosis of schizophrenia by one clinician, depression by another, and dementia by a third.

© Eve Vagg

As a step toward remedying this sort of problem, the American Psychiatric Association published the first edition of *DSM*, in 1952, as a standard system for labeling and diagnosing mental disorders. It and the second edition (published in 1968) were quite slim; diagnostic categories were defined briefly, in general terms, and much was left to the judgment of individual clinicians. The result was some degree of standardization in labeling, but still relatively little diagnostic reliability (Matarazzo, 1983; Spitzer & Fleiss, 1974). The third edition of the manual, *DSM-III,* which appeared in 1980, was much thicker, more detailed, and more useful.

The primary goal of the hundreds of psychiatrists, clinical psychologists, and other mental health professionals who produced *DSM-III* was to remove as much guesswork as possible from the task of diagnosis and thereby increase reliability. To

Leader of a revolution As head of the task force that created the third edition of the *Diagnostic and Statistical Manual of Mental Disorders* (*DSM-III*), Robert Spitzer, shown here, led a revolution in the manner by which mental disorders are diagnosed. He and those who worked with him created detailed checklists of objective symptoms for each disorder described in the manual. Spitzer views this and subsequent editions of the manual not as finished products but as steps in an ongoing process of creating more accurate labels and diagnostic guidelines. He refers to each edition of the manual as "a set of hypotheses to be tested."

- - - - - - - - - - - - - - - - 2

How did the developers of recent editions of the *DSM* strive to increase the reliability of the system for diagnosing mental disorders?

do this, they strove to define mental disorders as objectively as possible, in terms of symptoms that clinicians could observe or could assess by asking relatively simple, straightforward questions of the person being diagnosed or of those who knew that person well. To test alternative ways of diagnosing each disorder, they conducted field studies in which people who might have a particular disorder were diagnosed independently by a number of clinicians or researchers using each of several alternative diagnostic systems. In general, the systems that produced the greatest reliability—that is, the greatest agreement among the diagnosticians as to who had or did not have a particular disorder—were retained. As a result, the diagnostic reliability of *DSM-III* was quite high—comparable in many cases to the levels achieved in diagnosing physical disorders (Matarazzo, 1983; Segal & Coolidge, 2001). Further research and revision, to produce *DSM-IV*, made the manual even more reliable (Widiger, 2005). The main categories of disorders identified in *DSM-IV* are listed in Table 16.1. The first four categories in the list are the ones that we shall discuss in subsequent sections of this chapter.

TABLE 16.1 Summary of *DSM-IV* categories of mental disorders

Anxiety disorders* Disorders in which fear or anxiety is a prominent symptom. Examples: *generalized anxiety disorder, phobias, obsessive-compulsive disorder, panic disorder,* and *post-traumatic stress disorder.*

Mood disorders* Disorders marked by depression or mania. Examples: *major depression, dysthymia, bipolar I disorder,* and *bipolar II disorder.*

Somatoform disorders* Disorders involving physical (somatic) symptoms arising from unconscious psychological processes. Examples: *somatization disorder* and *conversion disorder.*

Schizophrenia and other psychotic disorders* *Schizophrenia* is marked by disorganized thought and speech, delusions, hallucinations, disorganized behavior, and flattened or inappropriate affect. Another psychotic disorder is *delusional disorder,* which involves persistent delusions (usually of persecution) not accompanied by other disruptions of thought or mood that would lead to a diagnosis of schizophrenia.

Dissociative disorders Disorders in which a part of one's experience is separated off (dissociated) from one's conscious memory or identity. Examples: *psychogenic amnesia, fugue states,* and *dissociative identity disorder.*

Disorders usually first diagnosed in infancy, childhood, or adolescence A diverse group of disorders that always or almost always first appear before adulthood. Included are *Down syndrome* and other forms of mental retardation, *autism,* and *ADHD (attention deficit/hyperactivity disorder).*

Delirium, dementia, amnesia, and other cognitive disorders A diverse group of disorders of perception, memory, and thought that stem from known damage to the brain. Included are disorders due to strokes, physical trauma to the brain, and degenerative brain diseases such as *Alzheimer's disease.*

Eating disorders Disorders marked by extreme undereating, overeating, or purging or by excessive concern about gaining weight. Examples: *anorexia nervosa* and *bulimia nervosa.*

Substance-related disorders Disorders brought on by drugs such as alcohol, cocaine, or opiates. Included are *dependence* (the intense craving for the substance), *abuse* (use of the substance in ways that harm the self or others), and effects of brain damage caused by prolonged use of the substance.

Sexual and gender identity disorders *Sexual disorders* are those of sexual functioning; they include *paraphilias* (in which bizarre imagery or acts are necessary for sexual excitement, such as *fetishism, exhibitionism,* and *sexual sadism*) and *psychosexual dysfunctions* (inability to become sexually aroused or to complete intercourse in a satisfying way). *Gender identity disorders* involve strong and persistent desires to be, or appear to be, a member of the other gender.

Impulse control disorders not elsewhere specified Disorders characterized by impulsive behaviors that are harmful to the self or others. Examples: *intermittent explosive disorder* (outbursts of aggression resulting in assault or property destruction), *kleptomania* (impulsive stealing), *pyromania* (impulsive setting of fires), and *pathological gambling.*

Sleep disorders Disorders include *insomnia* (too little sleep), *hypersomnia* (too much sleep), *sleep-wake disorder* (inability to establish a sleep-wake cycle corresponding with the 24-hour day), and disorders involving sleepwalking, fear of sleep, or fear of nightmares.

Adjustment disorder Maladaptive, excessive emotional reaction to an identified stressful event that occurred within the previous 6 months.

Personality disorders† Disorders involving inflexible, maladaptive personality traits. Examples: *antisocial personality disorder* (a history of antisocial acts and violation of others' rights, with no sense of guilt), *histrionic personality disorder* (excessively emotional, overly dramatic attention seeking), and *narcissistic personality disorder* (unwarranted sense of self-importance and demand for constant attention or admiration).

---

*The first four categories in the list correspond with major sections of this chapter. Throughout the table, all disorders that are referred to or described in the chapter are underlined.

†Because personality disorders involve a person's long-standing style of thinking and acting rather than a change in the person, they are categorized on a separate dimension, or axis (Axis II), from the other categories (which constitute Axis I).

Source: *Diagnostic and statistical manual of mental disorders* (4th, text-revised ed.). Washington, D.C.: American Psychiatric Association, 2000.

As an example of diagnostic criteria specified in *DSM-IV*, consider those for *anorexia nervosa,* an eating disorder that can result in self-starvation. The person must (a) refuse to maintain body weight at or above a minimally normal weight for age and height; (b) express an intense fear of gaining weight or becoming fat; (c) manifest a disturbance in the experience of her or his own body weight or shape, show an undue influence of body weight or shape on self-evaluation, or deny the seriousness of the current low body weight; and (d) if a postpubertal female, have missed at least three successive menstrual periods (a condition brought on by a lack of body fat). If any one of these criteria is not met, a diagnosis of anorexia nervosa would not be made. Notice that all these criteria are based on observable characteristics or self-descriptions by the person being diagnosed; none rely on inferences about underlying causes or unconscious symptoms that could easily result in disagreement among diagnosticians who have different perspectives.

The Question of Validity

The **validity** of a diagnostic system is an index of the extent to which the categories it identifies are clinically meaningful. (See Chapter 2, p. 43, for a more general discussion of both validity and reliability.) In theory, a diagnostic system could be highly reliable without being valid. For example, a system that reliably categorizes a group of people as suffering from Disorder X, on the basis of certain superficial characteristics, would not be valid if further work failed to reveal any clinical usefulness in that diagnosis. Do people with the same diagnosis truly suffer in similar ways? Does their suffering stem from similar causes? Does the label help predict the future course of the disorder and help in deciding on a beneficial treatment? To the degree that questions like these can be answered in the affirmative, a diagnostic system is valid.

The question of validity is much more complicated than that of reliability and must be based on extensive research. The developers of *DSM-III* and *DSM-IV* maintain that reliability is a prerequisite for validity (Spiegel, 2005; Wilson, 1993). In order to conduct the research needed to determine whether or not a diagnosis is valid, by the criteria listed earlier, one must first form a tentative, reliable diagnostic system. For example, the *DSM-IV* definition of anorexia nervosa can be used to identify a group of people whose disorder fits that definition, and then those people can be studied to see if their disorders have similar origins and courses of development and respond similarly to particular forms of treatment. The results of such studies may lead to new means of defining and diagnosing the disorder or to new subcategories of the disorder, leading to increased diagnostic validity. Research being conducted now will probably lead to refined definitions and new subcategories for many types of disorders in the next version of *DSM* (Maser & others, 2009).

> **3**
> How does validity differ from reliability? How can the validity of the *DSM* be improved through further research and revisions?

Possible Dangers in Labeling

Diagnosing and labeling may be essential for the scientific study of mental disorders, but labels can be harmful. A label implying mental disorder can blind clinicians and others to qualities of the person that are not captured by the label, can reduce the esteem accorded to the person by others, can reduce the labeled person's self-esteem, and, through these means, can interfere with the person's ability to cope well with his or her environment.

To reduce, at least somewhat, the likelihood of such effects, the American Psychiatric Association (2000) recommends that clinicians apply diagnostic labels only to people's disorders, not to people themselves. For example, a client or patient might be referred to as *a person who has schizophrenia* or *who suffers from alcoholism* but should not be referred to as *a schizophrenic* or *an alcoholic*. The distinction might at first seem subtle, but if you think about it, you may agree that it is not so subtle in psychological impact. If we say, "John has schizophrenia," we tend to be reminded that John is first and foremost a person, with qualities like those of other people, and that his having schizophrenia is just one of many things we could say about

> **4**
> What are some negative consequences of labeling a person as mentally disordered? What is recommended as a partial solution to this problem?

"You made that diagnosis just to be mean."

him. In contrast, the statement "John is a schizophrenic" tends to imply that everything about him is summed up by that label.

As I talk about specific disorders in the remainder of this chapter and the next, I will attempt to follow this advice even though it produces some awkward wording at times. I also urge you to add, in your mind, yet another step of linguistic complexity. When I refer to "a person who has schizophrenia," you should read this statement as "a person who has been diagnosed by someone as having schizophrenia," keeping in mind that diagnostic systems are never completely reliable.

Medical Students' Disease

The power of suggestion, which underlies the ability of labels to cause psychological harm, also underlies what is sometimes called *medical students' disease*. This disease, which could also be called *introductory psychology students' disease,* is characterized by a strong tendency to relate personally to, and to find in oneself, the symptoms of any disease or disorder described in a textbook. Medical students' disease was described by the 19th-century humorist Jerome K. Jerome (1889/1982) in an essay about his own discomfort upon reading a textbook of medical diagnoses. After explaining his discovery that he must have typhoid fever, St. Vitus's dance, and a multitude of diseases he had never heard of before, he wrote, "The only malady I concluded I had not got was housemaid's knee. . . . I had walked into that reading-room a happy, healthy man. I crawled out a decrepit wreck." As you read about specific disorders later in this chapter, brace yourself against medical students' disease. Everyone has at least some of the symptoms, to some degree, of essentially every disorder that can be found in this chapter, in *DSM-IV,* or in any other compendium.

Cultural Variations in Disorders and Diagnoses

Mental disorder is, to a considerable degree, a cultural construct. The kinds of distress that people experience, the ways in which they express that distress, and the ways in which other people respond to the distressed person vary from culture to culture and over time in any given culture. Moreover, cultural beliefs and values help determine whether particular syndromes are considered to be disorders or variations of normal behavior.

Culture-Bound Syndromes

The most striking evidence of cross-cultural variation in mental disorders can be found in *culture-bound syndromes*—expressions of mental distress that are almost completely limited to specific cultural groups (Tseng, 2006). In some cases, such syndromes represent exaggerated forms of behaviors that, in more moderate forms, are admired by the culture.

5
How do *taijin kyofusho* and eating disorders illustrate the role of culture in the mental disorders that people develop?

◄ An example of such a syndrome is *taijin kyofusho,* which is one of the most commonly diagnosed disorders in Japan but is almost unknown in other parts of the world (Dinnel & others, 2002; Kim & others, 2008). This disorder, which is diagnosed in men more often than in women, involves an incapacitating fear of offending or harming other people (Tarumi & others, 2004). In particular, the person may believe that he offends others through his own awkward social behavior or imagined physical defect, or through blushing or eye contact or a foul odor that he emits. Unlike the case for social phobias in the West, the conscious fear in *taijin kyofusho* centers on

Charles Gupton/Getty Images

Cultural foundation for taijin kyofusho Modesty and concern not to offend others are much valued in Japan. Such modesty and concern, when taken to the extreme, may provide the foundation for the mental disorder *taijin kyofusho*.

the possibility of harming others, not on possible harm to the self from others (such as being rejected or ridiculed). Japanese psychiatrists consider the disorder to be a pathological exaggeration of the modesty and sensitive regard for others that are considered proper in Japan (Kirmayer, 1991).

Examples of culture-related syndromes closer to home are the eating disorders *anorexia nervosa* and *bulimia nervosa*. Anorexia nervosa, as noted earlier, is characterized by an extraordinary preoccupation with thinness and a refusal to eat, sometimes to the point of death by starvation. Bulimia nervosa is characterized by periods of extreme binge eating followed by self-induced vomiting, misuse of laxatives or other drugs, or other means to undo the effects of a binge. It is probably not a coincidence that these disorders began to appear with some frequency in the 1970s in North America and Western Europe, primarily among adolescent girls and young women of the middle and upper classes, and that their prevalence increased through the remainder of the 20th century (Gordon, 1990; Hoek, 2002). During that period, Western culture became increasingly obsessed with dieting and an ideal of female thinness while, at the same time, weight control became more difficult because of the increased availability of high-calorie foods.

Until recently, these eating disorders were almost completely unknown in non-Western cultures. In recent years, however, with the increased globalization of Western media and values, anorexia nervosa and bulimia nervosa have begun to appear throughout the world. Studies in such places as the Pacific Islands and East Africa have shown that the incidence of these disorders correlates directly with the degree of Western media exposure (Becker & others, 2002; Eddy & others, 2007).

An example of a new culturally prepared psychological problem, appearing in various nations, is *Internet addiction*. This has been most fully documented in South Korea, where frighteningly large numbers of young people are dropping out of school or employment, and some are even starving, because of their compulsive game-playing and other uses of the Internet (Choi, 2007). To a lesser degree, Internet addiction appears to be a problem also in the United Sates, and some clinicians are advocating that *Internet addiction disorder* be added to the official list of mental disorders in *DSM-V* (Block, 2008).

Western values and abnormality Anorexia nervosa and bulimia nervosa are eating disorders found largely in Western countries. Many clinicians believe that these are culture-bound disorders caused in part by Western society's overemphasis on thinness as the aesthetic ideal for women, a preoccupation on display in Western ads, magazines, movies, and the like.

Joseph Neumayer/Design Conceptions

Role of Cultural Values in Determining What Is a Disorder

6

How does the example of homosexuality illustrate the role of culture in determining what is or is not a "disorder"?

◀ Culture does not affect just the types of behaviors and syndromes that people manifest; it also affects clinicians' decisions about what to label as disorders. A prime example has to do with homosexuality. Until 1973, homosexuality was officially—according to the American Psychiatric Association—a mental disorder in the United States; in that year, the association voted to drop homosexuality from its list of disorders (Minton, 2002). The vote was based partly on research showing that the suffering and impairment associated with homosexuality derived not from the condition itself but from social prejudice directed against homosexuals. The vote was also prompted by an increasingly vocal gay and lesbian community that objected to their sexual preferences being referred to as a disorder, and by gradual changes in attitudes among many in the straight community, who were beginning to accept the normality of homosexuality.

Cultural Values and the Diagnosis of ADHD

The American Psychiatric Association has added many more disorders to *DSM* over the past three or four decades than it has subtracted. The additions have come partly from increased understanding and partly from a general cultural shift toward seeing mental disorder where people previously saw normal human variation. An example that illustrates both of these trends is *attention-deficit/hyperactivity disorder,* more commonly known by its acronym **ADHD,** which in recent years has been the single most frequently diagnosed disorder among children in the United States (Bradley & Golden, 2001; Mayes & others, 2009).

7

How is ADHD identified and treated? How do critics of the high rate of diagnosis of ADHD explain the high rates?

◀ Most diagnoses of ADHD originate because of difficulties in school. Indeed, many of the *DSM-IV* symptoms of the disorder refer specifically to schoolwork (American Psychiatric Association, 2000). The manual describes three varieties of the disorder. The *predominantly inattentive type* is characterized by lack of attention to instructions, failure to concentrate on schoolwork or other such tasks, and carelessness in completing assignments. The *predominantly hyperactiveimpulsive type* is characterized by such behaviors as fidgeting, leaving one's seat without permission, talking excessively, interrupting others, and blurting out answers before the question is completed. The *combined type,* which is most common, is characterized by both sets of symptoms.

A prominent but still controversial theory of the neural basis of ADHD is that it involves deficits in, or a slower-than-average rate of maturation of, the prefrontal lobes of the cortex—a portion of the brain responsible for focusing attention on tasks and inhibiting spontaneous activities (Barkley, 2001; Halperin & Schulz, 2006). The most common treatment, by far, is the drug methylphenidate, sold in various short- and long-acting forms under such trade names as Ritalin and Concerta. Methylphenidate increases the activity of the neurotransmitters dopamine and norepinephrine in the brain, and its effectiveness may derive from its ability to boost neural activity in the prefrontal cortex. This drug reduces the immediate symptoms of ADHD in most diagnosed children, but there are as yet no long-term studies showing that the drug improves children's lives over the long run, or that it causes no long-term negative side effects (LeFever & others, 2003; Singh, 2008).

Anthony Strack/Gallo Images/Getty

Normal playfulness or ADHD?
There is no clear dividing line between normal rambunctious playfulness in children and ADHD. As a result, ADHD is diagnosed at much higher levels in some school districts than in others.

During the 1990s, the rate of diagnosis and treatment of ADHD in the United States increased eightfold (LeFever & others, 2003). Currently nearly 8 percent of all U.S. children and adolescents, age 7 to 17, are diagnosed with the disorder (Mayes & others, 2009). Since boys are diagnosed at rates that are at least three times those of girls, this means that the prevalence of ADHD diagnosis among boys is about 12 percent or more. The rate varies tremendously, however, depending on location. By actual count, in two middle-class school districts in Virginia, 33 percent of white boys were diagnosed with ADHD (LeFever & others, 2003). Whites, in general, are diagnosed with the disorder more frequently than are African Americans, not because they are more disruptive in school but because they are more often referred to clinicians for diagnosis and treatment (LeFever & others, 2003).

Many sociologists and a few psychologists have argued that the explosion in diagnosis of ADHD in the United States and other nations derives at least partly from the current obsession with school performance (Rafalovich, 2004). Children, especially boys, everywhere get into trouble in school because of their need for vigorous activity, their impulsiveness, their carelessness about schoolwork, and their willingness to defy teachers and other authority figures. These characteristics vary in a continuous manner, showing the typical bell-shaped distribution of any normal personality dimension (Nigg & others, 2002). Even defenders of the high rate of ADHD diagnosis acknowledge that the characteristics of this disorder exist to some degree in all children, more so in boys than in girls, and that children classed as having the disorder are simply those who have these characteristics to a greater extent than do other children (Maddux & others, 2005; Stevenson & others, 2005). In recent decades, the requirements of schools have become increasingly uniform and have demanded increased levels of docility on the part of children. The ADHD diagnosis and medication of children seems to be the culture's current preferred way of dealing with the lack of fit between the expectations of schooling and the natural activity level of many children. Consistent with this interpretation is the observation that many if not most diagnoses of ADHD originate with teachers' recommendations (Graham, 2007; Mayes & others, 2009).

Some critics of the high rate of ADHD diagnosis—including a prominent neuroscientist who has conducted research on brain systems involved in this condition (Panksepp, 1998, 2007)—contend that American society has made it increasingly difficult for children to engage in the sorts of vigorous free play needed by all young mammals, especially young males, for normal development. As a culture, they contend, we have chosen to treat many children with strong drugs, whose long-term consequences are still unknown, rather than to develop systems of schooling that can accommodate a wider range of personalities and neighborhood spaces that can accommodate children's needs for rough-and-tumble play.

SECTION REVIEW

Mental disorder presents numerous conceptual, diagnostic, and social challenges.

Categorizing and Diagnosing Mental Disorders

➤ To be considered a mental disorder by *DSM-IV* standards, a syndrome (set of interrelated symptoms) must involve a clinically significant detriment, derive from an internal source, and not be subject to voluntary control. Though these guidelines are useful, "mental disorder" is still a fuzzy concept.

➤ Classification and diagnosis (assigning a label to a person's mental disorder) are essential for clinical purposes and for scientific study of mental disorders.

➤ *DSM-III* and *DSM-IV* substantially increased reliability (the probability that independent diagnosticians would agree about a person's diagnosis) by using objective symptoms. Validity is a more complex issue.

➤ Because labeling a person can have negative consequences (e.g., lowering self-esteem or the esteem of others), labels should be applied only to the disorder, not to the person.

➤ Beware of medical students' disease.

Cultural Variations in Disorders and Diagnoses

➤ Culture-bound syndromes are expressions of mental distress limited to specific cultural groups. Examples are *taijin kyofusho* (in Japan) and bulimia nervosa (in cultures influenced by modern Western values).

➤ Culture also affects the types of behaviors or characteristics thought to warrant a diagnosis of mental disorder. Until 1973, homosexuality was officially classed as a mental disorder in the United States.

➤ The great increase in diagnosis of ADHD (attention-deficit/hyperactivity disorder) in the United States may result not just from increased understanding but also from the culture's increased emphasis on school performance and reduced opportunities for vigorous play.

■ Causes of Mental Disorders

Before moving on to discussions of major categories of mental disorders, it is worth spending a little time thinking about the general question of what causes mental disorders. In this section we look first at the brain, which is necessarily involved in *all* mental disorders. Then we consider a general framework for describing the ways that genes and environment can influence the incidence and onset of mental disorders. And finally we examine some possible reasons why some disorders occur more often in men than in women, or vice versa.

The Brain Is Involved in All Mental Disorders

As has been emphasized throughout this book, all thoughts, emotions, and actions—whether they are adaptive or maladaptive—are products of the brain. All the factors that contribute to the causation of mental disorders do so by acting, in one way or another, on the brain. These include genes that influence brain development; environmental assaults on the brain, such as those produced by a blow to the head, oxygen deprivation, viruses, or bacteria; and, more subtly, the effects of learning, which are consolidated in pathways in the brain.

Irreversible Mental Disorders Derive from Irreversible Characteristics of the Brain

The role of the brain is most obvious in certain chronic mental disorders—that is, in certain disorders that stay with a person for life once they appear. In these cases the brain deficits are irreversible—or at least cannot be reversed by any methods yet discovered. One example of such a disorder, discussed in **Chapter 11,** is *autism,* or *autistic disorder,* which corresponds with a brain abnormality that may be caused in some cases primarily by genes and in other cases primarily by prenatal toxins or birth complications that disrupt normal brain development (Kabot & others, 2003). Two other examples are Down syndrome and Alzheimer's disease. I describe them briefly here, because they are disorders linked to obvious brain deficits, for which the causes are reasonably well understood.

8 ─ ─ ─ ─ ─ ─ ─ ─ ─ ─ ─ ─ ─ ─ ─ ─ ─

How are Down syndrome and Alzheimer's disease characterized as brain diseases?

─ ─ ─ ─ ─ ─ ─ ─ ─ ─ ─ ─ ─ ─ ─ ─ ─ ─ ─

◄ *Down syndrome* is a congenital (present at birth) disorder that appears in about 1 out of every 800 newborn babies (American Psychiatric Association, 2000). It is caused by an error in meiosis, which results in an extra chromosome 21 in the egg cell or (less often) the sperm cell (the numbering of chromosomes is shown in Figure 3.3, p. 55). The extra chromosome is retained in all cells of the newly developing individual. Through a variety of means, it causes damage to many regions of the developing brain, such that the person goes through life with moderate to severe mental retardation and with difficulties in physical coordination.

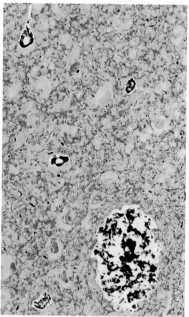

Alzheimer's brain This slice of brain tissue (magnified × 50), from a recently deceased person who suffered from Alzheimer's disease, reveals a large amyloid plaque—the yellow and black structure in the lower right-hand corner.

Simon Fraser/Photo Researchers, Inc.

Alzheimer's disease, found primarily in the elderly, has become increasingly prevalent as ever more people live into old age. It occurs in about 1 percent of people who are in their sixties, 3 percent of those in their seventies, 12 percent of those in their eighties, and 40 percent of those in their nineties (Nussbaum & Ellis, 2003). The disorder is characterized psychologically by a progressive deterioration, over the final years of the person's life, in all cognitive abilities—including memory, reasoning, spatial perception, and language—followed by deterioration in the brain's control of bodily functions.

Neurologically, Alzheimer's disease is characterized by certain physical disruptions in the brain, including the presence of *amyloid plaques.* The plaques are deposits of a particular protein, called *beta amyloid,* which form in the spaces between neurons and may disrupt neural communication (Nicoll & others, 2004). The disorder appears to be caused by a combination of genetic predisposition and general debilitating effects of old age. Among the genes that may contribute are those that affect the rate of production and breakdown of beta amyloid (Bertram & Tanzi, 2008). Age may contribute partly through the deterioration of blood vessels, which become ever less effective in carrying excess beta amyloid out of the brain (Nicoll & others, 2004).

Role of the Brain in Episodic Mental Disorders

Many disorders, including all the disorders discussed in the remaining sections of this chapter, are *episodic,* meaning that they are reversible. They may come and go, in episodes. Episodes of a disorder may be brought on by stressful environmental experiences, but the predisposition for the disorder nevertheless resides in one way or another in the brain.

Most mental disorders, including those that are episodic, are to some degree heritable. The more closely related two people are genetically, the more likely it is that they share the same mental disorder or disorders, regardless of whether or not they were raised in the same home (Howland, 2005; Rutter, 2002). In most cases it is not known just which genes are involved or how they influence the likelihood of developing the disorder, but it is reasonable to assume that such effects occur primarily through the genes' roles in altering the biology of the brain. Environmental assaults to the brain and the effects of learning can also contribute to the predisposition for episodic disorders.

A Framework for Thinking About Multiple Causes of Mental Disorders

Most mental disorders derive from the joint effects of more than one cause. Most disorders are not present at birth, but first appear at some point later in life, often in early adulthood. The subsequent course of a disorder—its persistence, its severity, its going and coming—is influenced by experiences that one has after the disorder first appears. It is useful, therefore, to distinguish among three categories of causes of mental disorders: predisposing, precipitating, and perpetuating causes—the *three Ps.*

Predisposing causes of mental disorders are those that were in place well before the onset of the disorder and make the person susceptible to the disorder. Genetically inherited characteristics that affect the brain are most often mentioned in this category. Predispositions for mental disorders can also arise from damaging environmental effects on the brain, including effects that occur before or during birth. Such environmental assaults as poisons (including alcohol or other drugs consumed by the mother during pregnancy), birth difficulties (such as oxygen deprivation during birth), and viruses or bacteria that attack the brain can predispose a child for the subsequent development of one or more mental disorders.

Prolonged psychologically distressing situations—such as living with abusive parents or an abusive spouse—can also predispose a person for one or another mental disorder. Other predisposing causes include certain types of learned beliefs and maladaptive patterns of reacting to or thinking about stressful situations. A young woman reared in upper-class Western society is more likely to acquire beliefs and values that predispose her for an eating disorder than is a young woman from a rural community in China. Highly pessimistic habits of thought, in which one regularly anticipates the worst and fails to think about reasons for hope, predispose people for mood disorders (particularly depression) and anxiety disorders.

Precipitating causes are the immediate events in a person's life that bring on the disorder. Any loss, such as the death of a loved one or the loss of a job; any real or perceived threat to one's well-being, such as physical disease; any new responsibility, such as might occur as a result of marriage or job promotion; or any large change in the day-to-day course of life can, in the sufficiently predisposed person, bring on the mood or behavioral change that leads to diagnosis of a mental disorder.

9

How can the causes of mental disorders be categorized into three types—"the three Ps"?

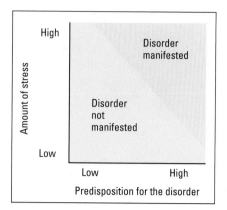

FIGURE 16.1 Relationship between predisposition and stress needed to trigger a mental disorder The amount of stress needed to bring on a mental disorder decreases as the predisposition for the disorder increases.

Precipitating causes are often talked about under the rubric of *stress,* a term that sometimes refers to the life event itself and sometimes to the worry, anxiety, hopelessness, or other negative experiences that accompany the life event (Lazarus, 1993). When the predisposition is very high, an event that seems trivial to others can be sufficiently stressful to bring on a mental disorder. When the predisposition is very low, even an extraordinarily high degree of loss, threat, or change may fail to bring on a mental disorder. Figure 16.1 depicts this inverse relationship.

Perpetuating causes are those consequences of a disorder that help keep it going once it begins. In some cases, a person may gain rewards, such as extra attention, which help perpetuate the maladaptive behavior. More often, the negative consequences of the disorder help perpetuate it. For example, a sufferer of depression may withdraw from friends, and lack of friends can perpetuate the depression. Behavioral changes brought on by a disorder, such as poor diet, irregular sleep, and lack of exercise, may also, through physiological means, help to prolong the disorder. Expectations associated with a particular disorder may play a perpetuating role as well. In a culture that regards a particular disorder as incurable, a person diagnosed with that disorder may simply give up trying to change for the better.

Possible Causes of Sex Differences in the Prevalence of Specific Disorders

Little difference occurs between men and women in the prevalence of mental disorder when all disorders are combined, but large differences are found for specific disorders (American Psychiatric Association, 2000). Women are diagnosed with *anxiety disorders* and *depression* at rates that are nearly twice as great as those for men. Men are diagnosed with *intermittent explosive disorder* (characterized by relatively unprovoked violent outbursts of anger) and with *antisocial personality disorder* (characterized by a history of antisocial acts with no sense of guilt) at rates that are three or four times those for women. Men are also diagnosed with *substance-use disorders* (including alcohol dependence and other drug dependence) at rates that are nearly twice as great as those for women. These differences may arise from a number of causes, including the following:

10

What are four possible ways of explaining sex differences in the prevalence of specific mental disorders?

- *Differences in reporting or suppressing psychological distress* Diagnoses of anxiety disorders and of depression necessarily depend to a great extent on self-reporting. Men, who are supposed to be the "stronger" sex, may be less inclined than women to admit to anxiety and despondency in interviews or questionnaires. Supporting

Hysterical or angry? Even today the word "hysterical" may come to mind more quickly when we view an angry woman than when we view an angry man. That same bias may contribute to the more frequent diagnosis of histrionic personality in women than in men.

this view, experiments have shown that when men and women are subjected to the same stressful situation, such as a school examination, men report less anxiety than do women even though they show physiological signs of distress that are as great as, or greater than, those shown by women (Polefrone & Manuck, 1987).

- *Clinicians' expectations* Diagnosticians may, to some degree, find a disorder more often in one sex than in the other because they *expect* to find it there. In an experiment demonstrating such an expectancy bias, several hundred clinical psychologists in the United States were asked to make diagnoses on the bases of written case histories that were mailed to them (Ford & Widiger, 1989). For some, the case history was constructed to resemble the *DSM-III* criteria for *antisocial personality disorder,* which is diagnosed more often in men than in women. For others it was constructed to resemble the *DSM-III* criteria for *histrionic personality disorder* (characterized by dramatic expressions of emotion to

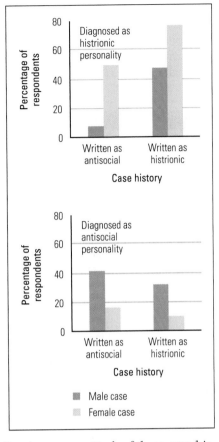

FIGURE 16.2 Evidence of a gender bias in diagnosis In this study, case histories were more likely to be diagnosed as antisocial personality if they described a fictitious male patient and as histrionic personality if they described a fictitious female patient, regardless of which disorder the case history was designed to portray. (Data from Ford & Widiger, 1989.)

seek attention), which is diagnosed more often in women. Each of these case histories was written in duplicate forms, for different clinicians, differing only in the sex of the person being described. As you can see in Figure 16.2, the diagnoses were strongly affected by the patient's sex. Given the exact same case histories, the man was far more likely than the woman to receive a diagnosis of antisocial personality, and the woman was far more likely than the man to receive a diagnosis of histrionic personality.

- *Differences in stressful experiences* A number of well-controlled studies indicate that at least some sex differences in the prevalence of disorders are real—they cannot be explained by sex differences in reporting or by biased diagnoses (Klose & Jacobi, 2004). One way to explain such actual differences is to search for differences in the social experiences of men and women. Women, throughout the world, are more likely than men to live in poverty, to experience discrimination, to have been sexually abused in childhood, and to be physically abused by their spouses—all of which can contribute to depression, anxiety, and various other disorders that occur more often in women than in men (Koss, 1990; Nolen-Hoeksema, 2001; Olff & others, 2007). There is also evidence that the typical responsibilities that women assume in the family, such as caring for children, are more conducive to anxiety and depression than are the typical roles that men assume (Almeida & Kessler, 1998; Barnett & Baruch, 1987).

- *Differences in ways of responding to stressful situations* The two sexes not only tend to experience different sorts of stressful situations, but also tend to respond differently to objectively similar situations (Kramer & others, 2008). Women tend to "internalize" their discomfort; they dwell mentally (ruminate) on their distress and seek causes within themselves. This manner of responding, in either sex, tends to promote both anxiety and depression (Kramer & others, 2008; Nolen-Hoeksema, 2001). Men, in contrast, more often "externalize" their discomfort; they tend to look for causes outside of themselves and to try to control those causes, sometimes in ways that involve aggression or violence. It is not clear what causes these differences in ways of responding, but it is reasonable to suppose that they are, in part, biologically predisposed. Such differences are observed throughout the world, and there is evidence that male and female hormones influence the typically male and female ways of reacting to stressful situations (Olff & others, 2007; Taylor & others, 2000).

SECTION REVIEW

Though mental disorders have many possible causes, all exert their effects via the brain.

The Brain's Role in Chronic and Episodic Mental Disorders	A Framework for Thinking About Multiple Causes	Causes of Sex Differences in Prevalence of Specific Disorders
➤ Chronic mental disorders such as Down syndrome and Alzheimer's disease arise from irreversible brain deficits.	➤ Predisposing causes, which make a person susceptible to a mental disorder, include genetic influences, early environmental effects on the brain, and learned beliefs.	➤ Some diagnoses (e.g., anxiety disorder) are much more prevalent in women, and some others (e.g., antisocial personality disorder) are much more prevalent in men.
➤ Down syndrome derives from an extra chromosome 21 that causes widespread brain damage and mental retardation.	➤ Precipitating causes, which bring on episodes of a disorder, are generally stressful life experiences or losses.	➤ Such differences may derive from (a) sex differences in the tendency to report or suppress psychological distress; (b) clinicians' expectations of seeing certain disorders more often in one sex than in the other; (c) sex differences in stress associated with differing social roles; or (d) sex differences in ways of responding to stress.
➤ Alzheimer's disease, which involves progressive decline in all cognitive functions, usually in old age, may result from disruptive effects of amyloid plaques in the brain.	➤ Perpetuating causes, which decrease the chance of recovery, include poor self-care, social withdrawal, and negative reactions from others.	
➤ All the other disorders discussed in the chapter are episodic, meaning that their active manifestations come and go. Causes may include hereditary influences on the brain's biology, environmental assaults on the brain, and effects of learning.		

▮ Anxiety Disorders

The rabbit crouches, frozen in the grass, minimizing its chance of being detected. Its sensory systems are at maximum alertness, all attuned to the approaching dog. With muscles tense, the rabbit is poised to leap away at the first sign that it has been detected; its heart races, and its adrenal glands secrete hormones that help prepare the body for extended flight if necessary. Here we see fear operating adaptively, as it was designed to operate by natural selection.

We humans differ from the rabbit on two counts: Our biological evolution added a massive, thinking cerebral cortex atop the more primitive structures that organize fear, and our cultural evolution led us to develop a habitat far different from that of our ancestors. Our pattern of fear is not unlike the rabbit's, but it can be triggered by an enormously greater variety of both real and imagined stimuli, and in many cases the fear is not adaptive. Fear is not adaptive when it causes a job candidate to freeze during an interview, or overwhelms a student's mind during an examination, or constricts the life of a person who can vividly imagine the worst possible consequence of every action.

The adaptive value of fear Fear causes this rabbit to remain motionless but highly alert to the nearby predator. The rabbit is hidden but ready to flee at the first indication of being detected.

Alamy

Anxiety disorders are those in which fear or anxiety is the most prominent disturbance. Although fear and anxiety can be used as synonyms, fear is more often used when the feared stimulus or event is specific and present, and anxiety is more often used when the stimulus or event is vague, not identifiable, or in the future. The major anxiety disorders recognized by *DSM-IV* are *generalized anxiety disorder, phobias, obsessive-compulsive disorder, panic disorder,* and *posttraumatic stress disorder*. Genetic differences play a considerable role in the predisposition for all these disorders. Research with twins indicates that roughly 30 to 50 percent of the individual variability in risk to develop any given anxiety disorder derives from genetic variability (Gelernter & Stein, 2009; Gordon & Hen, 2004). In what follows, I will describe the main diagnostic characteristics and precipitating causes of each of these common types of anxiety disorders.

Generalized Anxiety Disorder

Generalized anxiety is called *generalized* because it is not focused on any one specific threat; instead, it attaches itself to various threats, real or imagined. It manifests itself primarily as worry (Hazlett-Stevens & others, 2009). Sufferers of **generalized anxiety disorder** worry more or less continuously, about multiple issues, and they experience muscle tension, irritability, difficulty in sleeping, and sometimes gastrointestinal upset due to overactivity of the autonomic nervous system. They worry about the same kinds of issues that most of us worry about—family members, money, work, illness, daily hassles—but to a far greater extent and with much less provocation (Becker & others, 2003).

To receive a *DSM-IV* diagnosis of generalized anxiety disorder, such life-disrupting worry must occur on more days than not for at least 6 months and occur independently of other diagnosable mental disorders (American Psychiatric Association, 2000). By *DSM-IV* criteria, roughly 6 percent of people in North America could be diagnosed as having this disorder at some time in their lives (Kessler & others, 2005). In predisposed people, the disorder often first appears at a diagnosable level following a major life change in adulthood, such as getting a new job or having a baby, or after a disturbing event, such as an accident or illness (Blazer & others, 1987).

Laboratory research shows that people diagnosed with generalized anxiety disorder are particularly attuned to threatening stimuli. For example, they notice threatening words (such as "cancer" or "collapse"), but not unthreatening words, more quickly, reliably, and automatically than do other people (Mogg & Bradley, 2005). Such automatic attention to potential threat is referred to as *hypervigilance,* and there is evidence that such vigilance begins early in life and precedes the development of generalized anxiety disorder (Eysenck, 1992). Thus, hypervigilance may be a predisposing cause of generalized anxiety disorder as well as a symptom of the disorder.

Hypervigilance may result, in part, from genetic influences on brain development. As noted in **Chapter 6,** the brain's amygdala responds automatically to fearful stimuli, even when those stimuli don't reach the level of conscious awareness. In most of us, connections from the prefrontal lobe of the cortex help to control the fear reactions, but neuroimaging studies suggest that these inhibitory connections are less effective in people who are predisposed for generalized anxiety (Bishop, 2009). A lifelong tendency toward hypervigilance may also be brought on by unpredictable traumatic experiences in early childhood (Borkovec & others, 2004). In an environment where dangerous things can happen at any time, a high degree of vigilance is adaptive.

Surveys taken at various times, using comparable measures, indicate that the average level of generalized anxiety in Western cultures has increased sharply since the middle of the 20th century (Twenge, 2000). From a cultural perspective, that increase may be attributable to the reduced stability of the typical person's life. In a world of

> ---- **11**
>
> **How can generalized anxiety disorder be understood in terms of hypervigilance, genes, early traumatic experiences, and cultural conditions?**

© Hillary B. Price/King Features Syndicate.

rapid technological change, we can't be sure that today's job skills will still be useful tomorrow. In a world of frequent divorce and high mobility, we can't be sure that the people we are attached to now will be with us in the future. In a world of rapidly changing values and expectations, we have difficulty judging right from wrong or safe from unsafe. Such threats may be felt only dimly and lead not to conscious articulation of specific fears but to generalized anxiety. And, unlike the predator that scares the rabbit one minute and is gone the next, these threats are with us always.

Phobias

In contrast to generalized anxiety, a **phobia** is an intense, irrational fear that is very clearly related to a particular category of object or event. In *DSM-IV*, phobias are divided into two main types: social and specific. In a **social phobia,** the fear is of

© George D. Lepp/Corbis

A spider for the hypervigilant
People who suffer from a specific phobia tend to see the object of their fear even when it is so well camouflaged that most people would miss it. A sight such as this might cause someone with a spider phobia to avoid sunflowers forever after.

being scrutinized or evaluated by other people; included here are fears of public speaking, of eating in public places, and of meeting new people. In a **specific phobia,** the fear is of some specific, nonsocial category of object or situation. It may be of a particular type of animal (such as snakes), substance (such as blood), or situation (such as heights or being closed in). For a diagnosis to be given, the fear must be long-standing and sufficiently strong to disrupt everyday life in some way—such as causing one to leave a job or to refrain from leaving home in order to avoid encountering the feared object. Both categories of phobias are quite prevalent; surveys suggest that they are diagnosable, at some time in life, in somewhere between 7 and 13 percent of people in Western societies (Hofmann & others, 2009; Kessler & others, 2005).

Usually a phobia sufferer is aware that his or her fear is irrational but still cannot control it. The person knows well that the neighbor's kitten won't claw anyone to death, that common garter snakes aren't venomous, or that the crowd of 10-year-olds at the corner won't attack. People with phobias suffer doubly—from the fear itself and from knowing how irrational they are to have such a fear (Williams, 2005). Laboratory research shows that people with specific phobias are hypervigilant specifically for the category of object that they fear. For example, people with spider phobias can find spiders in photographs that contain many objects more quickly than can other people. Once they have spotted the object, however, they avert their eyes from it more quickly than do other people (Pflugshaupt & others, 2005).

The Relation of Phobias to Normal Fears

12

What evidence links phobias to the kinds of fears that most people have?

◀ Probably everyone has some irrational fears, and, as in all other anxiety disorders, the difference between the normal condition and the disorder is one of degree, not kind. Specific phobias are usually of things that many people fear to some extent, such as snakes, spiders, blood, darkness, or heights (Marks, 1987); and social phobias may simply be extreme forms of shyness (Rapee & Spence, 2004).

Also consistent with the idea that phobias lie on a continuum with normal fears is the observation that specific phobias are much more often diagnosed in women than in men, whereas social phobias are diagnosed about equally often in the two sexes (American Psychiatric Association, 2000). In the population as a whole, men and boys are much less likely than women and girls to report fears of such things as spiders and darkness but are about equally likely to report shyness. The sex difference in specific phobias could stem from the fact that boys are more strongly encouraged than are girls to overcome or to hide their childhood fears (Fodor, 1982).

Phobias Explained in Terms of Evolution and Learning

Relatively little is known about how phobias usually arise, but learning certainly plays some role in many if not most cases (Mineka & Zinbarg, 2006). Approximately 40 percent of people with specific phobias recall some specific traumatic situation in which they first acquired the fear (Hofmann & others, 2009). For example, people with dog phobias often recall an experience of being severely bitten by a dog. As described in **Chapter 4,** such experiences may be understood in terms of classical conditioning: The dog, in the example, is the conditioned stimulus for fear and the bite is the unconditioned stimulus. After the conditioning experience, the dog elicits fear even without a bite. In such trauma-producing situations, just one pairing of conditioned and unconditioned stimulus may be sufficient for strong conditioning to occur.

Contrary to a straightforward learning theory of phobias, however, is the observation that people often develop phobias of objects that have never inflicted damage or been a true threat to them. For example, a survey conducted many years ago in Burlington, Vermont, where there are no dangerous snakes, revealed that the single most common specific phobia there was of snakes (Agras & others, 1969). If phobias are acquired through traumatic experiences with the feared object, then why aren't phobias of such things as automobiles, electric outlets, or (in Burlington) icy sidewalks more common than phobias of harmless snakes?

According to an evolutionary account of phobias, first proposed by Martin Seligman (1971), people are genetically prepared to be wary of—and to learn easily to fear—objects and situations that would have posed realistic dangers during most of our evolutionary history (discussed in **Chapter 4**). This idea is helpful in understanding why phobias of snakes, spiders, darkness, and heights are more common than those of automobiles and electric outlets. Research has shown that people can acquire strong fears of such evolutionarily significant objects and situations more easily than they can acquire fears of other sorts of objects (Mineka & Zinbarg, 2006). Simply observing others respond fearfully to them, or reading or hearing fearful stories about them, can initiate or contribute to a phobia.

The fact that some people acquire phobias and others don't in the face of similar experiences probably stems from a variety of predisposing factors, including genetic temperament and prior experiences (Craske, 1999). People who have had a great deal of safe, prior experience with a type of object, such as snakes, are less likely to develop a phobia to that object type, after a traumatic experience with it, than are people whose traumatic experience accompanied their first exposure to that type of object (Field, 2006). As discussed in **Chapter 4,** classical conditioning of fears is reduced or blocked if the conditioned stimulus is first presented many times in the absence of the unconditioned stimulus.

The strong tendency of phobia sufferers to avoid looking at or being anywhere near the objects they fear is believed to be the primary perpetuating cause of the disorder. As discussed in **Chapter 17,** the best way to overcome an irrational fear is to expose oneself to the feared object or situation for increasingly long periods. Maybe the high rate of snake phobia in Burlington, Vermont, occurs because there are so few snakes of any kind there. Without exposure to snakes, there is little opportunity to overcome a fear of them.

> **13**
>
> How might phobias be explained in terms of learning that has been prepared by evolution?

Obsessive-Compulsive Disorder

An *obsession* is a disturbing thought that intrudes repeatedly on a person's consciousness even though the person recognizes it as irrational. A *compulsion* is a repetitive action that is usually performed in response to an obsession. Most people experience moderate forms of these, especially in childhood (Mathews, 2009). I remember a period in sixth grade when, while reading in school, the thought would repeatedly enter my

Reprinted from Health Magazine

mind that reading could make my eyes fall out. The only way I could banish this thought and go on reading was to close my eyelids down hard—a compulsive act that I fancied might push my eyes solidly back into their sockets. Of course, I knew that both the thought and the action were irrational, yet the thought kept intruding, and the only way I could abolish it for a while was to perform the action. Like most normal obsessions and compulsions, this one did not really disrupt my life, and it simply faded with time.

Characteristics of the Disorder

People who are diagnosed with ***obsessive-compulsive disorder*** are those for whom such thoughts and actions are severe, prolonged, and disruptive of normal life. To meet *DSM-IV* criteria for this disorder, the obsessions and compulsions must consume more than an hour per day of the person's time and seriously interfere with work or social relationships (American Psychiatric Association, 2000). By these criteria, the disorder occurs in roughly 1 to 2 percent of people at some time in their lives (Kessler & others, 2005).

14

How is an obsessive-compulsive disorder similar to and different from a phobia? What kinds of obsessions and compulsions are most common?

◀ Obsessive-compulsive disorder is similar to a phobia in that it involves a specific irrational fear. It is different from a phobia primarily in that the fear is of something that exists only as a thought and can be reduced only by performing some ritual. People with obsessive-compulsive disorder, like those with phobias, suffer also from their knowledge of the irrationality of their actions and go to great lengths to hide them from other people.

The obsessions experienced by people diagnosed with this disorder are similar to, but stronger and more persistent than, the kinds of obsessions experienced by people in the general population (Mathews, 2009; Rachman & DeSilva, 1978). The most common obsessions concern disease, disfigurement, or death, and the most common compulsions involve checking or cleaning. People with checking compulsions may spend hours each day repeatedly checking doors to be sure they are locked, the gas stove to be sure it is turned off, automobile wheels to be sure they are on tight, and so on. People with cleaning compulsions may wash their hands every few minutes, scrub everything they eat, and sterilize their dishes and clothes in response to their obsessions about disease-producing germs and dirt. Some compulsions, however, bear no apparent logical relationship to the obsession that triggers them. For example, a woman obsessed by the thought that her husband would die in an automobile accident could in fantasy protect him by dressing and undressing in a specific pattern 20 times every day (Marks, 1987).

Brain Abnormalities Related to the Disorder

15

How might damage to certain areas of the brain result in obsessive-compulsive disorder?

◀ More than is true for the other anxiety disorders, obsessive-compulsive disorder has been linked to observable damage in the brain. In some cases, the disorder first appears after known brain damage, from such causes as a blow to the head, poisons, or diseases (Berthier & others, 2001; Steketee & Barlow, 2002). Brain damage resulting from a difficult birth has also been shown to be a predisposing cause (Vasconcelos & others, 2007), and in many other cases, neural imaging has revealed brain abnormalities stemming from unknown causes (Szeszko & others, 2004).

The brain areas that seem to be particularly involved include portions of the frontal lobes of the cortex and parts of the underlying limbic system and basal ganglia (Britton & Rauch, 2009), which normally work together in a circuit to control voluntary actions, the kinds of actions that are controlled by conscious thoughts (as discussed in **Chapter 5**). One theory is that damage in these areas may produce obsessive-compulsive behavior by interfering with the brain's ability to produce the psychological sense of closure or safety that normally occurs when a protective action is completed. Consistent with this theory, people with obsessive-compulsive disorder often report that they do not experience the normal sense of task completion that should come after they have washed their hands or inspected the gas stove, so they feel an overwhelming need to perform the same action again (Szechtman & Woody, 2004).

Panic Disorder

Panic is a feeling of helpless terror, such as one might experience if cornered by a predator. In some people, this sense of terror comes at unpredictable times, unprovoked by any specific threat in the environment. Because the panic is unrelated to any specific situation or thought, the panic victim, unlike the victim of a phobia or an obsessive compulsion, cannot avoid it by avoiding certain situations or relieve it by engaging in certain rituals. Panic attacks usually last several minutes and are accompanied by high physiological arousal (including rapid heart rate and shortness of breath) and a fear of losing control and behaving in some frantic, desperate way (Barlow, 2002). People who have suffered such attacks often describe them as the worst experiences they have ever had—worse than the most severe physical pain they have felt.

To be diagnosed with ***panic disorder,*** by *DSM-IV* criteria, a person must have experienced at least two such attacks, each followed by at least 1 month of debilitating worry about having another attack or by life-constraining changes in behavior (such as quitting a job or refusing to travel) motivated by fear of another attack (American Psychiatric Association, 2000). By these criteria, roughly 2 percent of North Americans suffer from panic disorder at some time in their lives (Kessler & others, 2005). Most people diagnosed with panic disorder also suffer from a condition called *agoraphobia,* a fear of public places. The agoraphobia develops at least partly because panic victims fear the embarrassment and humiliation that might follow loss of control (panic) in front of others (Craske, 1999).

As is true with all other anxiety disorders, panic disorder often manifests itself shortly after some stressful event or life change (White & Barlow, 2002). Panic victims seem to be particularly attuned to, and afraid of, physiological changes that are similar to those involved in fearful arousal. In the laboratory or clinic, panic attacks can be brought on in people with the disorder by any of various procedures that increase heart rate and breathing rate—such as lactic acid injection, a high dose of caffeine, carbon dioxide inhalation, or intense physical exercise (Barlow, 2002). This has led to the view that a perpetuating cause, and possibly also predisposing cause, of the disorder is a learned tendency to interpret physiological arousal as catastrophic (Woody & Nosen, 2009). One treatment, used by cognitive therapists, is to help the person learn to interpret each attack as a temporary physiological condition rather than as a sign of mental derangement or impending doom.

Peter Cade/Getty Images

Panic This man has a reason to feel panic: He has just been attacked by a thief. People with panic disorder feel panic such as this at unpredictable times, without provocation.

> ------------------------**16**
>
> **What learned pattern of thought might be a perpetuating cause of panic disorder?**

Posttraumatic Stress Disorder

> ------------------------**17**
>
> **How does posttraumatic stress disorder differ from other anxiety disorders?**

All anxiety disorders can be brought on or exacerbated, to some degree, by stressful experiences, but ***posttraumatic stress disorder*** is the only anxiety disorder that is *necessarily* brought on by such experiences. By definition, the symptoms of posttraumatic stress disorder must be linked to one or more emotionally traumatic incidents that the affected person has experienced. The disorder is most common in torture victims, concentration camp survivors, people who have been raped or in other ways violently assaulted, people who have survived dreadful accidents, and soldiers who have experienced the horrors of battle.

The most characteristic features of this disorder, according to *DSM-IV,* are frightening, uncontrollable re-experiences of the traumatic events, in nightmares and in daytime thoughts or "flashbacks." Other common symptoms are sleeplessness, high arousal, irritability, guilt (perhaps for surviving when others didn't), emotional numbing, and depression (American Psychiatric Association, 2000). In an effort to relieve such symptoms, posttraumatic stress victims may turn to alcohol or street drugs, which often compound the problem.

Not surprisingly, the prevalence of this disorder depends very much on the population sampled. Surveys in the United States suggest that up to 7 percent of people may develop the disorder, by *DSM-IV* criteria, at some point in their lives (Kessler & others, 2005). In contrast, in Algeria, where nearly everyone has been a victim of terrorist attacks, 40 percent of a random sample of adults were found to suffer from this disorder (Khaled, 2004). Similarly, rates of posttraumatic distress disorder ranging from 15 to 30 percent have been found in war-torn regions of Cambodia, Ethiopia, and Palestine (de Jong & others, 2003).

18
What conditions are particularly conducive to development of posttraumatic stress disorder?

◄ People who are exposed repeatedly, or over long periods of time, to distressing conditions are much more likely to develop posttraumatic stress disorder than are those exposed to a single, short-term, highly traumatic incident. One study revealed that the incidence of posttraumatic stress disorder among Vietnam War veterans correlated more strongly with long-term exposure to the daily stressors and dangers of the war—such as heat, insects, loss of sleep, sight of dead bodies, and risk of capture by the enemy—than with exposure to a single atrocity (King & others, 1995). Another study, of 3000 war refugees, revealed that the percentage with posttraumatic stress disorder rose in direct proportion to the number of traumatic events they had experienced (Neuner & others, 2004). Likewise, children exposed to repeated abuse in their homes are particularly prone to the disorder (Roesler & McKenzie, 1994). Most people can rebound reasonably well from a single horrible event, but the repeated experience of such events seems to wear that resilience down, perhaps partly through long-term debilitating effects of stress hormones on the brain (Kolassa & Elbert, 2007).

Not everyone exposed to repeated highly stressful conditions develops posttraumatic stress disorder. Social support, both before and after the stressful experiences, seems to play a role in reducing the likelihood of the disorder (Ozer & others, 2003). Genes also play a role (Paris, 2000). One line of evidence for that comes from a study of twins who fought in Vietnam. Identical twins were considerably more similar to each other in the incidence of the disorder and in the types of symptoms they developed than were fraternal twins (True & others, 1993).

SECTION REVIEW

Anxiety disorders have fear or anxiety as their primary symptom.

Generalized Anxiety Disorder	Phobias	Obsessive-Compulsive Disorder	Panic Disorder	Posttraumatic Stress Disorder
➤ This disorder, characterized by excessive worry about real or imagined threats, may be predisposed by genes or childhood trauma and brought on by disturbing events in adulthood.	➤ Social phobias involve intense fear of evaluation by others. Specific phobias involve intense fear of specific nonsocial objects (e.g., spiders) or situations (e.g., heights).	➤ This disorder—involving repetitive, disturbing thoughts (obsessions) and repeated, ritualistic actions (compulsions)—is associated with abnormalities in an area of the brain that links conscious thought to action.	➤ People with this disorder experience bouts of helpless terror (panic attacks) unrelated to specific events in their environment.	➤ This disorder is characterized by the re-experiencing—in nightmares, daytime thoughts, and flashbacks—of an emotionally traumatic event or set of events that occurred in the person's life. Other symptoms include sleeplessness, irritability, guilt, and depression.
➤ Hypervigilance—automatic attention to possible threats—may stem from early trauma and may lead to generalized anxiety.	➤ Phobia sufferers usually know that the fear is irrational but still cannot control it.	➤ Obsessions and compulsions are often extreme versions of normal safety concerns and protective actions, which the sufferer cannot shut off despite being aware of their irrationality.	➤ The disorder may be predisposed and perpetuated by a learned tendency to regard physiological arousal as catastrophic.	➤ Genetic predisposition, repeated exposures to traumatic events, and inadequate social support increase the risk for the disorder.
➤ Levels of generalized anxiety have risen sharply in Western culture since the mid-20th century.	➤ The difference between a normal fear and a phobia is one of degree.		➤ Caffeine, exercise, or other ways of increasing heart and breathing rates can trigger panic attacks in susceptible people.	
	➤ Natural selection may have prepared us to fear some objects and situations more readily than others.			

◼ Mood Disorders

Mood refers to a prolonged emotional state that colors many, if not all, aspects of a person's thought and behavior. It is useful (though oversimplified) to think of a single dimension of mood, running from *depression* at one end to *elation* at the other. Because we all have tasted both, we have an idea of what they are like. Depression and elation are normal experiences, but at times either of them can become so intense or prolonged as to promote harmful, even life-threatening, actions. Extreme depression can keep a person from working, lead to withdrawal from friends, or even provoke suicide. Extreme elation, called *mania,* can lead to outrageous behaviors that turn other people away or to dangerous acts that stem from a false sense of security and bravado.

DSM-IV identifies two main categories of mood disorders: ***depressive disorders,*** characterized by prolonged or extreme depression, and ***bipolar disorders,*** characterized usually by alternating episodes of mania and depression. Here we shall examine the former quite fully and then take a briefer look at the latter.

Depression

Depression is characterized primarily by prolonged sadness, self-blame, a sense of worthlessness, and absence of pleasure. Other common symptoms include decreased or increased sleep, decreased or increased appetite, and either retarded or agitated motor symptoms. Retarded motor symptoms include slowed speech and slowed body movements. Agitated symptoms, which are less common than retarded symptoms, include repetitive, aimless movements such as hand wringing and pacing. To warrant a diagnosis of a depressive disorder, the symptoms must be either very severe or very prolonged and not attributable just to a specific life experience, though they may be triggered or exacerbated by such an experience.

Two main classes of depressive disorders are distinguished in *DSM-IV*. ***Major depression*** is characterized by very severe symptoms that last essentially without remission for at least 2 weeks. ***Dysthymia*** [dis-**thigh**-me-uh] is characterized by less severe symptoms that last for at least 2 years. Quite often, bouts of major depression are superimposed over a more chronic state of dysthymia, in which case the person is said to have *double depression*. Surveys in North America suggest that as many as 15 percent of people suffer from major depression, and 2 to 3 percent suffer from dysthymia, at some time in their lives (Kessler & others, 2005).

Depression This work, *Despair*, is by Edvard Munch, a Norwegian artist (1863–1944) who himself suffered from episodes of severe depression. Like many creative people who suffer from depression, Munch took much of his subject matter from his memories of his depressed mood, but created most of his works during periods of remission (Rothenberg, 2001).

SuperStock

Comparisons Between Depression and Generalized Anxiety

Much has been written about the similarities and differences between depression and generalized anxiety disorder. The two disorders are apparently predisposed by the same genes. The identical twins of people suffering from either generalized anxiety disorder or major depression exhibit equally enhanced rates of either disorder (Kendler & others, 2006). Other studies reveal that the two disorders often occur in the same individuals. Approximately 60 percent of people diagnosed with generalized anxiety disorder also suffer from a depressive disorder at some point in their lives (Hettema, 2008). Typically, generalized anxiety occurs before onset of major depression (Hunt & others, 2004; Wittchen & others, 2000).

One way to conceive of the difference between generalized anxiety and depression is to think of the former as a frantic, relatively ineffective attempt to cope with life's real and imagined threats, through worry and hypervigilance, and to think of the latter as a kind of giving up, which occurs when one has despaired of coping and concludes that life is not worth living. Cognitively, anxious individuals worry about what might happen in the future, while depressed individuals feel that all is

> **19**
> **What are some similarities and differences between depression and generalized anxiety?**

TABLE 16.2 Comparison of anxious thoughts with depressive thoughts

Anxious thoughts	Depressed thoughts
What if I get sick and become an invalid?	I'm worthless.
I might offend someone I care about.	I'm offensive to people.
Some might not like how I look.	I'm physically unattractive.
I could lose my job.	Nothing ever works out for me.
I could have a heart attack and die.	Life isn't worth living.

Modified and expanded from Beck & others, 1987.

already lost (see Table 16.2). Depressed individuals are much more likely than anxious individuals to stop caring for themselves and to stay in bed all day. The sense of giving up is commonly accompanied by strong feelings of self-blame, of not deserving to live. The feelings of worthlessness are captured in the following quotation from Norman Endler (1982), a highly respected psychologist describing his own bout with depression:

> I honestly felt subhuman, lower than the lowest vermin. . . . I could not understand why anyone would want to associate with me, let alone love me. . . . I was positive that I was a fraud and a phony. . . . I couldn't understand how I had written the books and journal articles that I had and how they had been accepted for publication. I must have conned a lot of people.

Negative Thought Pattern as a Cause of Depression

Negative thoughts are characteristic of people who are depressed, and they may also characterize people who are not depressed but are vulnerable to becoming so. Consider two non-depressed college students who have just taken and failed their first test in Introductory Psychology. One responds to the failure by thinking: "I'm stupid. I'm going to fail this course. I'm going to flunk out of college." The other responds by thinking: "Ouch. That was a tough test. I didn't study enough and I was up too late the night before." The first student illustrates a pattern of thought that is very likely to lead to depression, while the opposite is true of the second.

◀ A prominent modern theory of depression is the *hopelessness theory,* developed by Lyn Abramson and her colleagues (1989). According to this theory, depression results from a pattern of thinking about negative events that has the following three characteristics:

● The person assumes that the negative event will have disastrous consequences. (The failed test will lead to flunking out of college.)

● The person assumes that the negative event reflects something negative about himself or herself. (The failure is proof of stupidity, or some such personal inadequacy.)

● The person attributes the cause of the negative event to something that is *stable* (will not change) and *global* (capable of affecting many future events). (Stupidity is an unchangeable characteristic that will affect all realms of endeavor.)

20
According to the hopelessness theory, what pattern of thinking predisposes a person for depression? What is some evidence for the theory?

A major controversy concerning the hopelessness theory is whether the hopeless thought pattern merely *reflects* depression or is also a *cause* of depression (Joormann, 2009). Certainly, depressed people manifest this negative manner of thinking. By *DSM-IV* criteria or any other criteria, negative thinking is part of the definition of depression. But Abramson and her colleagues have shown that the hopeless manner of thinking about negative events can also occur, to varying degrees, in people who by other measures are not depressed, and in those people it is predictive of future depression.

In one study, first-year, non-depressed college students with no prior history of clinical depression filled out a questionnaire designed to measure the hopeless style of thinking about negative events and another questionnaire designed to assess their current level of mood. Then they were assessed at various times for depression over a 2.5-year follow-up period (Alloy & others, 2006). The result was that those who had scored high on the measure of negative thinking were over six times more likely to manifest an episode of major depression at some point during the follow-up period than were those who had scored low on that measure. This was true even when just those who were equivalent in mood level at the beginning of the study were compared.

Other evidence that negative thinking is a cause of depression comes from research showing that cognitive therapy, which is aimed at helping people change their habitual patterns of thinking, can help people overcome depression and can reduce the likelihood of its recurrence (discussed in **Chapter 17**). Moreover, several studies have shown that children and adolescents who have never been depressed can be at least partially inoculated against future depression by training in which they learn to interpret negative events in hope-promoting ways (Munoz & others, 2009).

Stressful Experiences Plus Genetic Predisposition as Cause of Depression

Many studies have shown that people who have recently suffered a severely stressful experience are much more likely to become depressed than are those who have not (Monroe & others, 2009; Kessler, 1997). The kinds of stressful events that are most strongly associated with depression are *losses* that alter the nature of one's life—such as loss of a spouse or other close daily companion, loss of a job that one has held for a long time, loss in social status, sharp loss in income, or permanent loss in health. Such events interrupt one's life routines and render ineffective well-established ways of satisfying one's needs and desires. They can promote the kind of hopeless thinking that corresponds with and predicts depression.

Yet, research has also shown very clearly that not everyone becomes depressed in response to such occurrences. Some people are resilient, even in the face of severe losses. They experience sadness, but not major depression, and they put their efforts effectively into restructuring their lives. The difference appears to reside largely in genes.

In a research study dramatically supporting this conclusion, Kenneth Kendler and his colleagues identified over 1000 women who had twin sisters (Kendler, 1998; Kendler & others, 1995). They studied each to identify (a) whether or not she had recently experienced a highly stressful life event (defined as assault, serious marital problems, divorce or breakup of a marriage or other romantic relationship, or death of a close relative), (b) whether or not a period of major depression began within a month after that stressful event (or within a comparable time period for those who had not experienced a serious stressor), and (c) her level of genetic predisposition for depression. The level of genetic predisposition was judged on the basis of whether or not the woman's twin sister (co-twin) did or did not have a history of major depression and whether she was an identical twin or a non-identical twin.

The results of the study are depicted in Figure 16.3 on the next page. Among women who had not recently experienced a highly stressful life event, the incidence of depression was very low regardless of level of genetic predisposition. However, among

> **21**
> How did Kendler demonstrate that the onset of major depression typically requires *both* genetic predisposition and a severely stressful life event?

FIGURE 16.3 Roles of genetic predisposition and stressful experiences in the incidence of depression Women who had recently experienced a severely stressful event were far more likely to experience the onset of major depression than were those who had not. This effect of stress was greater for those who were judged to be more genetically predisposed for depression (based on the status of their twin sisters, as shown in the key) than for those who were judged to be less genetically predisposed. (Adapted from Kendler & others, 1995, p. 837.)

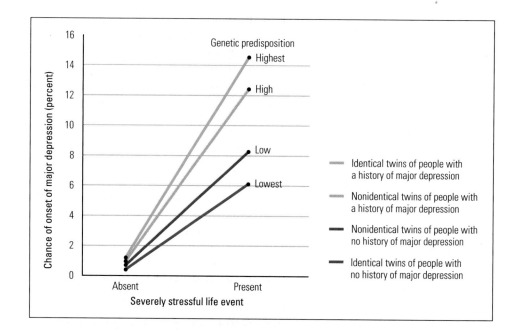

those who had recently experienced such an event, the incidence of depression was strongly related to the level of genetic predisposition. The results are quite consistent with the idea that major depression generally requires *both* a genetic predisposition for depression *and* some severely stressful event to bring it on.

More recently, research has focused on specific gene alleles that may be conducive to, or protective against, depression. The most consistent findings to date concern a gene that alters the effects of the neurotransmitter serotonin in the brain. As discussed in **Chapter 12,** this gene comes in two alleles—a *short* form and the *long* form. In **Chapter 12,** I describe research indicating that infants who have two copies of the long allele are protected from at least some of the negative effects of insensitive parenting. Several research studies suggest that this allele also tends to protect adults from becoming depressed in response to severe stressful events (Kendler & others, 2005; Levinson, 2009). At present, a number of researchers are working at replicating this effect and understanding it better.

Possible Brain Mechanisms of Depression

Depression, like every other psychological state, is a product of the brain. Thus, one route to understanding depression is to try to identify changes in the brain that might cause bouts of depression to appear and disappear.

◄ All the drugs that are used regularly to treat depression (discussed in **Chapter 17**) have the effect of increasing the amount or activity of one or both of two neurotransmitters in the brain: norepinephrine and serotonin. For that reason, an early theory of depression posited that the disorder results from a brain deficiency in either or both of these transmitters (Schildkraut, 1965). Today, however, that simple theory is much doubted (Krishnan & Nestler, 2008). One problem is that it does not explain the delayed effectiveness of drug treatments. Antidepressant drugs begin to enhance the activity of norepinephrine or serotonin (or both) in the brain immediately, yet they do not begin to relieve depression until at least 2 weeks of continuous treatment have elapsed. Moreover, by various measures, most depressed people do not appear to have unusually low levels of these neurotransmitters (Cowen, 2005).

◄ At present, many neuroscientists interested in depression are focusing on the ways that the brain changes during periods of psychological distress. Stress and worry are often associated with an increased release of cortisol, a hormone produced by the adrenal glands (discussed in **Chapter 5**). Research with animals shows that cortisol can act on the brain to shut off certain growth-promoting processes there. Over periods of weeks or months, a high level of cortisol can result in a small but measurable shrinkage in some portions of the brain, including portions of the prefrontal cortex and the

22
What early evidence supported the theory that depression results from a deficit in the neurotransmitters norepinephrine and serotonin? Why is that theory now doubted?

23
According to a new theory, how might stressful experiences alter the brain in a way that brings on depression?

hippocampus (Jacobs, 2004). These brain changes are reversible. During periods of reduced stress, the shrunken brain areas may regain their former size. Moreover, increases in norepinephrine and serotonin over periods of weeks can stimulate growth in these brain areas, and this observation may explain the delayed effects of drug treatments in relieving depression.

Thus, one current theory, which is far from proven, is that depression in humans results at least partly from a stress-induced loss of neurons or neural connections in certain parts of the brain and that recovery from depression results from regrowth in those brain areas (Jacobs, 2004; Martinowich & others, 2007; Perera & others, 2008). This theory is quite consistent with the evidence that depression often follows a rather prolonged period of anxiety. Anxiety stimulates production of the hormones that interfere with brain growth. The theory is also consistent with the idea that altered ways of thinking can alter one's predisposition for depression. Hopefulness reduces psychological distress, which reduces the production of the growth-inhibiting hormones and thereby protects the brain from the changes that lead to depression. It will be interesting to see how well this theory holds up to the tests of future research.

Thank God they have pills for that now.

Possible Evolutionary Bases for Depression

Psychologists viewing depression from an evolutionary perspective have suggested that it may be an exaggerated form of a response to loss that in less extreme form is adaptive (Allen & Badcock, 2006; Nesse, 2000). Only a minority of people develop clinically severe depression, but most of us, at some periods in our lives, experience a low mood or moderate depression. A depressed mood slows us down, makes us think realistically rather than optimistically, leads us to turn away from goals that we can no longer hope to achieve, and signals to others that we are no threat to them and need their help. The signals of helplessness by depressed persons resemble the appeasement displays used by other animals to signal submissiveness and need for care (Price & others, 2004). A depressed mood can also lead to a kind of soul-searching, the end result of which may be the establishment of new, more realistic goals and a new approach to life (Welling, 2003).

> **24**
> **How might moderate depression, following a loss, be adaptive?**

Matthew Keller and Randolph Nesse (2005, 2006) have suggested that depressed moods may come in a variety of different forms, each adapted for different survival purposes. Most people who live in northern latitudes experience some degree of depressed mood during the winter (Dam & others, 1998). When it occurs in extreme form, such winter-limited depression is diagnosed, according to *DSM-IV*, as *seasonal affective disorder,* or *SAD*. This form of depression is accompanied by increased appetite, increased sleepiness, and lethargy—all responses that, in less extreme form, may have been useful to our evolutionary ancestors for building layers of fat and conserving energy to survive the harsh winter. That form of depression is generally not accompanied by the degrees of sadness, crying, and self-reproach that occur in other forms of depression.

> **25**
> **According to Keller and Nesse, how might depressed moods vary, adaptively, depending on the situation?**

In their own research, Keller and Nesse (2006) found that depressed mood following the death of a loved one or the loss of a romantic partner is especially characterized by crying and other expressions of sadness, which may signal the need for help from others. In contrast, they found that depressed mood following repeated failure is especially characterized by self-blame and pessimism, which may motivate the person to withdraw from futile activities and begin a period of realistic reappraisal of life goals. It remains for future research to test further the idea that depressed moods come in different forms that serve different adaptive purposes.

A possible evolutionary precursor of depression The appeasement display, with bowed head and turned-away eyes, shown by the lower of these two mangabey monkeys, resembles the expression of a depressed person. One function of depression in humans may be to signal helplessness and lack of threat to others.

North Pole, South Pole, North Pole again. I just can't seem to settle down.

BI-POLAR BEAR

© Bizarro–Dan Piraro. King Features Syndicate

Dist. by Universal Press Synd.   www.uexpress.com   8-8 PIRARO

---

26 - - - - - - - - - - - - - - - - - - - ◄

How are manic states experienced? What is some evidence linking mild manic (hypomanic) episodes to heightened creativity?

- -

Bipolar Disorders

Major depression and dysthymia are sometimes called *unipolar disorders,* because they are characterized by mood changes in only one direction—downward from normal. Bipolar disorders (formerly called manic-depression) are characterized by mood swings in both directions: downward in depressive episodes and upward in manic episodes. Such episodes may last anywhere from a few days to several months, often separated by months or years of relatively normal mood.

DSM-IV identifies two main varieties of bipolar disorders. **Bipolar I disorder** is the classic type, characterized by at least one manic episode and at least one depressive episode. **Bipolar II disorder** is similar to bipolar I disorder except that its high phase is less extreme and is referred to as *hypomania* rather than mania. Bipolar I disorder occurs, at some time in life, in about 1 percent of the population, and bipolar II disorder occurs in about 2 to 3 percent of the population (Belmaker, 2004; Kessler & others, 2005). In some cases, episodes of mania may occur without intervening episodes of depression (Belmaker, 2004).

Research with twins and adoptees has shown that the predisposition for bipolar disorder is strongly heritable, more so than is unipolar depression or most other mental disorders (Johnson & others, 2009). Stressful life events may help bring on manic and depressive episodes in people who are predisposed (Ambelas, 1987; Hlastala & others, 2000), but the evidence for such effects is not as strong as it is for unipolar depression. Bipolar disorder, unlike unipolar depression, can usually be controlled with regular doses of the element *lithium,* used as a drug, but how lithium works is as yet unknown (Pilcher, 2003).

The Manic Condition

Manic episodes are typically characterized by expansive, euphoric feelings; elevated self-esteem; increased talkativeness; decreased need for sleep; and enhanced energy and enthusiasm, which may be focused on one or more grandiose projects or schemes (American Psychiatric Association, 2000). The inordinate feelings of power, confidence, and energy are illustrated by the following quotation from a woman describing her own disorder (Fieve, 1975):

> When I start going into a high, I no longer feel like an ordinary housewife. Instead, I feel organized and accomplished, and I begin to feel I am my most creative self. I can write poetry easily. I can compose melodies without effort. I can paint. . . . I have countless ideas about how the environmental problem could inspire a crusade for the health and betterment of everyone. . . . I don't seem to need much sleep. . . . I feel sexy and men stare at me. Maybe I'll have an affair, or perhaps several. I feel capable of speaking and doing good in politics.

During hypomania and the early stages of a manic episode, the high energy and confidence may lead to an increase in productive work, but, as a manic episode progresses, judgment becomes increasingly poor and behavior increasingly maladaptive. Full-blown mania may be accompanied by bizarre thoughts and dangerous behaviors, such as jumping off a building in the false belief that one can fly; and even hypomania may be accompanied by spending sprees, absence from work, or sexual escapades that the affected person later regrets (Akiskal, 2002). Moreover, not all people with bipolar disorders experience the manic state as euphoric: Some experience it as a time of extraordinary irritability, suspiciousness, or destructive rage (Carroll, 1991).

Possible Relation of Hypomania to Enhanced Creativity

Analyses of biographies and historical documents concerning eminently creative writers, artists, and musicians suggest that a disproportionate percentage of them suffered from a bipolar disorder (Andreasen, 1987; Jamison, 1995). The same studies suggest that those people were most productive during hypomanic phases of their illness—when their mood was elevated, but not to such an extreme as to prevent coherent thought and action. As one example, the composer Robert Schumann—who often suffered from severe depression—produced an extraordinary number of his valued musical works during two episodes of apparent hypomania, one in 1840 and the other in 1849 (Jamison, 1995). As another example, the poet Emily Dickinson wrote much of her best poetry during episodes of apparent hypomania that followed bouts of winter depression (Ramey & Weisberg, 2004).

Such analyses have been criticized on the grounds that the diagnoses of mood disorders and the judgments concerning hypomania were generally made after the fact, on the basis of written material that may not have been fully accurate (Rothenberg, 2001). It is also possible that hypomania in highly creative people is more a result of high creativity than a cause: People who become strongly absorbed in and excited by their work may, as a result, exhibit manic-like behaviors (Ramey & Weisberg, 2004). Still another possibility is that people who suffer from extremes of mood may not, on average, be naturally more creative than others, but may be more drawn to creative activities. Such activities may provide a means for them to deal with or express the unusual feelings and thoughts that accompany their low and high moods.

Further evidence for a correlation between creativity and hypomania—regardless of causal direction—comes from studies of creativity in people who are not famous for their creative accomplishments. In one study, people who manifested moderate mood swings—states of hypomania alternating with moderate levels of depression—were judged to be more creative in their regular work and home life than were those who exhibited greater stability in their moods (Richards & others, 1988). Another study, of 16-year-olds with no diagnosable mood disorders, revealed positive correlations between tendencies to experience hypomania and high scores on tests of creativity and of openness to experience, a personality trait (discussed in **Chapter 15**) that itself correlates positively with creativity (Furnham & others, 2008). People with bipolar disorder have also been found, on average, to score higher than others on tests of creativity and openness to experience (Nowakowska & others, 2005; Santosa & others, 2007). All in all, the weight of the evidence seems to favor the idea of a link between hypomanic mood states and heightened creativity, but the causal nature of that link has yet to be determined.

Corbis-Bettman

Ups and downs of a composer Like many highly creative people, composer Robert Schumann suffered from a mood disorder. He attempted suicide twice during bouts of severe depression and eventually died, in 1856, from self-starvation in an asylum. His depression waxed and waned over long cycles, and during two prolonged periods, in 1840 and 1849, he was hypomanic (exhibited moderate mania). Those were his most productive years by far: He composed 24 musical works in 1840 and 27 in 1849. (Jamison, 1995.)

SECTION REVIEW

Mood disorders involve intense, prolonged moods that can disrupt or threaten life.

Depression

➤ Prolonged sadness, self-blame, a sense of worthlessness, and an absence of pleasure are the hallmarks of depression.

➤ The same genes that predispose people for generalized anxiety also predispose them for depression. The two disorders often occur in the same person.

➤ According to the hopelessness theory, a negative thought pattern—which includes the attribution of negative experiences to stable, global causes—is a predisposing cause of depression.

➤ A study of twins revealed that major depression is generally brought on by severely stressful life events, in people who are genetically predisposed for depression.

➤ Depression may arise from reversible brain changes that occur during periods of psychological distress.

➤ Moderate depression may be adaptive, as exemplified by the different kinds of depressed reactions brought on by dark winters, lost loved ones, and repeated failure.

Bipolar Disorders

➤ Bipolar disorders—marked by mood changes in an upward (manic) as well as downward (depressive) direction—are highly heritable.

➤ Stressful life events may bring on episodes of bipolar disorder, but the evidence for this is not as clear as it is for unipolar depression.

➤ Manic episodes commonly involve expansive, euphoric feelings, high energy, extreme talkativeness, and abnormally high self-confidence.

➤ Full-blown mania involves poor judgment, bizarre thoughts, and self-harmful or dangerous actions; but milder mania (hypomania) may be a time of heightened creativity.

■ Psychological Influences on Physical Symptoms and Diseases

The brain is responsible not just for thoughts and emotion but also for sensation, movement, pain, and the regulation of many biological systems within the body. It is not surprising, therefore, that experiences that affect our thoughts and emotions can also affect our bodily functions and our manner of experiencing those functions.

Somatoform Disorders

Somatoform literally means "bodily form," and **somatoform disorders** are those in which the person experiences bodily ailments in the absence of any physical disease that could cause them. Such disorders are believed to result from psychological distress that manifests itself in the form of physical pain, discomfort, or interferences with normal bodily processes. *DSM-IV* distinguishes among a number of different categories of somatoform disorders. The two categories I will discuss here are *somatization disorder,* which is one of the most prevalent types, and *conversion disorder,* which is the most dramatic type.

Somatization Disorder, and the Role of Culture in Somatoform Disorders

Somatization disorder is characterized by a long history of dramatic complaints about many different medical conditions, most of which are vague and unverifiable, such as dizziness, general aching of the body, heart palpitations, and nausea. For a firm diagnosis of somatization disorder, there must be strong reason to believe that the symptoms stem from psychological distress and not from any physical disease or injury. The true prevalence of this disorder is unknown, as it is often difficult to know the true source of a patient's symptoms. From what data are available, the American Psychiatric Association (2000) estimates that the prevalence in the United States is somewhere between 0.2 and 1 percent of the population. The prevalence is reported to be much higher in some other cultures, particularly in China, other parts of Asia, and Latin America (Gureje, 2004; López & Guarnaccia, 2005).

Somatization appears, to many clinical researchers, to be closely related to depression. Indeed, somatization and depression may be alternative ways of feeling and expressing the same underlying problems. A sense of hopelessness is usually experienced as psychological depression in North America and Western Europe today but in the past was more often experienced as physical aches and pains, as it is still is today in many parts of the non-Western world (Kleinman, 2004; López & Guarnaccia, 2005). In China, throughout the 20th century, the most common psychiatric diagnosis by far was *neurasthenia,* characterized as aches, pains, weakness, and fatigue of unknown origin. Within the past decade or two, however, as China has increasingly adopted Western views concerning mental disorders, the diagnosis of neurasthenia has dropped sharply while that of depression has risen sharply (Lee & Kleinman, 2007). This change reflects not just changed diagnostic practices, but also changed attitudes and beliefs among the Chinese people. In general, as disorders purely of mood or emotion become more legitimized by a culture, the incidence of somatoform disorders of all types tends to go down and that of anxiety and mood disorders tends to go up.

Regardless of culture, it appears that a high percentage of people diagnosable with somatoform disorders of any type are people who find a psychological diagnosis unacceptable. Most people with these disorders seek help from general practice doctors, not from psychiatrists or psychologists, and a diagnosis implying that the discomfort is "all in their head" is often unacceptable or even insulting to

---

27
Why are somatoform disorders apparently more common in non-Western cultures than in Western cultures?

them (Sharpe & Mayou, 2004). For this reason, great tact is needed in helping people with somatoform disorders. The helpful clinician must keep in mind that, regardless of the source of suffering, the person really is suffering. Often such patients find explanations in terms of presumed brain pathways, which connect parts of the brain involved with emotion to other parts of the brain that produce their symptoms, to be more satisfying than purely psychological explanations (Sharpe & Mayou, 2004). The ability to see that there is no ultimate distinction between "physical" and "psychological" suffering, because all suffering involves the physical brain, helps patients accept the idea that psychological treatments might help.

Conversion Disorder

The most extreme and disabling category of somatoform disorder is **conversion disorder,** in which the person temporarily loses some bodily function, perhaps (in the most dramatic cases) becoming blind, deaf, or partially paralyzed, in a manner that cannot be explained in terms of physical damage to the affected organs or their neural connections (for example, see Figure 16.4). The term *conversion,* in this context, refers to the conversion of psychological distress into a physical disability.

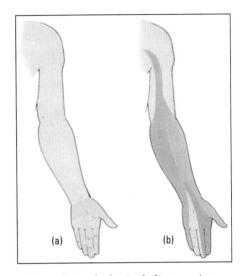

FIGURE 16.4 A conversion disorder Glove anesthesia—the experience of no sensation in the hand but continued sensation in all other parts of the arm, as shown in (a)—cannot result from nerve damage, because no nerves innervate the hand without innervating part of the arm. The actual areas of sensory loss that would occur if specific nerves were damaged are shown in (b). Thus, whenever glove anesthesia occurs, it is most likely a conversion disorder.

Conversion disorders are rare in North America and Western Europe today—with prevalence estimated at roughly 4 cases per 100,000 people (Krem, 2004)—but they were relatively common in those places 100 years ago and earlier. Such disorders were prominent in Sigmund Freud's practice in the late 19th and early 20th centuries, and they played a major role in his development of psychoanalytic theory. As a neurologist, Freud saw many patients with physical complaints and disabilities that appeared to have no medical explanation. He concluded that such symptoms were products of the patients' unconscious minds that served to protect them from anxiety-producing activities and experiences (discussed further in **Chapter 17**).

▶ – – – – – – – – – – – – – – – – **28**

How did Freud interpret conversion disorders? What conditions appeared to produce conversion reactions in Cambodian survivors of the Khmer Rouge and in certain children raised in dysfunctional families?

Today, the most dramatic examples of conversion disorder are generally found in people raised in non-Western cultures who have been exposed to highly traumatic events. An example is the relatively high rate of psychologically based blindness discovered among Cambodian women who managed to emigrate to the United States after the Khmer Rouge reign of terror in the 1970s (Rozée & Van Boemel, 1989). All these psychologically blind women manifested posttraumatic stress syndrome brought on by the tortures they had suffered and witnessed. Many of them had seen their own children being slowly tortured and murdered. One woman described the onset of her blindness in these words: "My family was killed in 1975 and I cried for 4 years. When I stopped crying I was blind." Another described becoming blind "from the smoke" as she was looking at the cooking pot in a forced-labor camp where she was held—a pot that, she knew, often contained human flesh, rats,

Traumatic blindness This woman is one of many Cambodian women whose acute vision problems have been tied to seeing atrocities committed by, and being tortured by, the Khmer Rouge.

Bart Bartholemew/NYT Pictures

and worms, which the women were forced to cook for themselves and other inmates to eat.

In Western countries, conversion disorder may be more common in children than is generally recognized. In Sydney, Australia, Kasia Kozlowska (2001, 2003) identified a number of children who suffered from partial paralysis, brought on, apparently unconsciously, as a way of protecting themselves from their overly demanding, abusive parents. Kozlowska describes these patients as "good children" who tried desperately to please their parents but who could not meet their parents' impossible demands and who, for relief, became partially paralyzed. The paralysis brought them to the hospital, where they felt safe. Treatment in these cases involved a combination of family counseling, aimed at improving the family environments, and psychotherapy for the children, aimed at helping them understand that their symptoms resulted from their stressful experiences at home and would subside as their homes became safer.

Brain Responses in Conversion Disorder

29

How might neuroimaging methods be used, in the future, to help identify true cases of conversion disorder?

To learn more about the neural pathways that may "convert" psychological distress into sensory or motor deficits, several neuroimaging studies have been conducted in recent years, using the fMRI and PET methods described in **Chapter 5** (Harvey & others, 2006; Stone & others, 2007; Vuilleumier & others, 2001). One clear finding is that the patterns of brain activity underlying conversion disorder are not mimicked in control subjects who are instructed to "pretend" that they are paralyzed, blind, or in some other way incapacitated. The brain activity patterns may, however, be at least partly mimicked in hypnotized subjects who are given the temporary suggestion that they have that disorder (Halligan & others, 2000; Ward & others, 2003).

Typically, both in hypnosis and in actual conversion disorder, relevant motor or sensory areas of the brain become less active than normal, and areas of the limbic system and prefrontal cortex that are known to inhibit those motor or sensory areas become unusually active. For example, one study of patients with medically unexplained partial blindness showed reduced neural activity in the visual cortex in response to light, but increased neural activity in portions of the limbic system, prefrontal cortex, and thalamus, all of which have inhibitory connections to the visual cortex (Werring & others, 2004). Such work has helped to demystify conversion disorder and may someday help clinicians distinguish true cases of conversion from other sources of motor and sensory impairment and from cases of malingering, in which the person consciously pretends to be incapacitated in some way.

Psychological Factors Affecting Medical Condition

You have just read of disorders in which bodily pain or disability is experienced in the absence of any medical explanation. We turn now to a different category of psychological effects on the body—cases in which one's behavior or emotions precipitate or influence the course of a disease that clearly does have a physical, medical basis. The harm-producing behaviors or emotions do not technically constitute mental disorders, but a category—called *psychological factors affecting medical condition*—is reserved for them in a section of *DSM-IV* devoted to clinically significant conditions other than mental disorders.

30

What evidence did a study of widows and widowers provide that a person's psychological state can affect his or her medical condition? What are possible mechanisms for such effects?

Typical of the evidence that psychological state can affect physical health are studies showing that recent widowers and widows are more vulnerable than others to essentially all types of physical diseases (Kaprio & others, 1987; Ray, 2004). In one study, 150 men and women whose spouses were terminally ill were assessed for their psychological state and physical health from the time just before they were widowed until 25 months afterward (Prigerson & others, 1997). On the basis of interviews conducted 6 months after their spouses died, a subgroup was identified whose members manifested what the researchers called *traumatic grief*—a syndrome similar to posttraumatic stress syndrome combined with extraordinary yearning for the deceased spouse. Although the members of this subgroup were not physically less healthy than the other subjects before the spouse's death or at the 6-month interview, by 25 months of widowhood they had developed significantly more incidences of flu, heart disease, and cancer than had the less-traumatized group.

It is not hard to imagine possible mechanisms through which traumatic grief or other disruptive psychological states can affect a person's health. The most obvious possibility is that the affected person may fail to take good physical care of himself or herself. Bereavement is often associated with poor diet, irregular sleep patterns, increased smoking, increased alcohol consumption, and failure to take prescribed medicines (Cohen & Herbert, 1996). Such decline in self-care typically occurs more strongly in men than in women, which may help explain why men, on average, exhibit more physical decline and higher rates of mortality after the death of their spouse than do women (Ray, 2004). There is also evidence, however, that psychological states can affect health directly, through the brain's effects on internal organs and the immune system.

Negative Emotions and Heart Disease

In the 1970s and 1980s a popular concept, supported by some research (Friedman & Rosenman, 1974), held that people with a *Type A personality* are at heightened risk for heart attacks and other cardiovascular disorders (disorders of the heart and its blood vessels). Type A people were identified as competitive, aggressive, easily irritated, impatient workaholics, constantly concerned with deadlines and getting ahead. In some corners, "I'm Type A" became a kind of boast, meaning "I'm so hard-working and competitive that I'm likely to have a heart attack."

Subsequent research has led to a modification of the original Type A theory. There is now strong evidence that people who frequently experience negative emotions—

31

How has the original "Type A" theory of heart disease been modified to accommodate research findings? Through what physiological means might negative emotions contribute to heart disease?

specifically, anger, anxiety, or sadness—have an enhanced risk for cardiovascular diseases, regardless of the degree to which they are competitive or work-oriented or have a hurried style of life (Stanley & Burrows, 2008; Suls & Bunde, 2005). The hard-working, constantly rushed person who enjoys what he or she is doing is apparently not at heightened risk for heart disease, but the emotionally distressed person is. This is confirmed in studies that control for other known risk factors, such as smoking and high cholesterol.

"I'm learning to relax, doctor—but I want to relax better and faster! I want to be on the cutting edge of relaxation!"

© Randy Glasbergen, 1997

Nobody knows for certain how negative emotions promote heart disease, but most researchers assume that the effect is mediated through the autonomic nervous system and endocrine system, both of which have direct influences on the circulatory system and are altered during emotional states. Negative emotions increase blood pressure, which can contribute to heart disease. The hormonal response to negative emotions also alters the activity of the immune system in ways that can promote inflammation in blood vessels in the heart, thereby contributing to heart disease (Miller & Blackwell, 2006). It is worth noting, in this regard, that the autonomic and hormonal responses to acutely stressful situations are generally larger in men than in women, which may help explain why, on average, men have more heart disease than do women (Kajantie, 2008).

Emotional Distress and Suppression of the Body's Defenses Against Disease

Emotional distress also tends to shut down some of the body's defenses against viruses and other pathogens, increasing our vulnerability to infectious diseases such as colds and flu (Kemeny & Schedlowski, 2007).

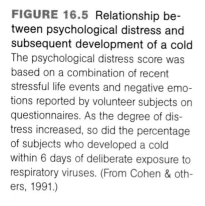

32

What is some evidence that one's emotional state can affect the immune system and alter one's chance of catching a cold?

◀ In one of the first studies to demonstrate such increased vulnerability, 394 healthy, rather heroic men and women agreed, for the sake of science, to have a fluid containing known respiratory viruses dribbled into their nostrils and then to remain quarantined for 6 days while researchers assessed their medical conditions (Cohen & others, 1991). At the outset of the study, each volunteer filled out a set of questionnaires to assess the degree of psychological distress he or she had experienced recently. The result was that the more distress people reported at the outset of the study, the more likely they were to develop a cold within the 6-day period (see Figure 16.5). The colds were real, not imagined; they were assessed by direct viral counts as well as by external symptoms. Moreover, the relation between distress and the incidence of colds could not be accounted for by any other risk factors the researchers measured, including smoking, alcohol consumption, diet, and quality of sleep.

FIGURE 16.5 Relationship between psychological distress and subsequent development of a cold The psychological distress score was based on a combination of recent stressful life events and negative emotions reported by volunteer subjects on questionnaires. As the degree of distress increased, so did the percentage of subjects who developed a cold within 6 days of deliberate exposure to respiratory viruses. (From Cohen & others, 1991.)

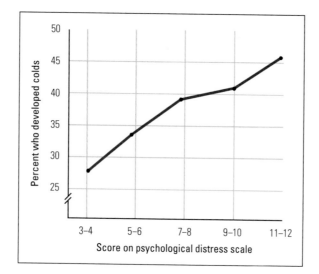

Subsequent studies have shown similar effects, not just with colds but also with flu and other ailments caused by viruses (Cohen & Pressman, 2006; Miller & others, 2009). Other studies, both with humans and with laboratory animals, have revealed some of the physiological mechanisms by which stress hormones can suppress portions of the body's immune response that are known to be involved in fighting viruses and other disease organisms (Ashcraft & others, 2008; Segerstrom & Miller, 2004).

33

From an evolutionary perspective, why might psychological distress inhibit immune function?

◀ You might wonder, from an evolutionary perspective, why we and other mammals are constructed in such a manner that our disease-fighting capacity is reduced in times of stress. A plausible answer (suggested by Maier & others, 1994, and Segerstrom, 2007) begins with a reminder that the body responds to stressful events in the environment by shifting its energy resources toward coping with the immediately threatening situation. To do so, the body partly shuts down many physiological functions that are not essential for dealing with the immediate emergency. The physiological mechanisms for resisting disease, including the production of new white blood cells, use a great deal of energy, so it makes sense that these would be suppressed when dealing with something like a charging tiger. The sympathetic nervous system and adrenal hormones mediate much of the body's response to stress, and, as part of that response, they inhibit energy-consuming aspects of the body's defense against disease. Unfortunately, that ancient stress response continues to be triggered by the anger, fear, or dread that we experience in response to situations or events that can't be dealt with by fight or flight, and that affect us for longer periods of time than a charging tiger would. The damage comes from long-term chronic distress, not from brief emergencies that are quickly resolved (Segerstrom & Miller, 2004).

■ Schizophrenia

John sits alone in his dismal room, surrounded by plastic bags of garbage that he has hoarded during late-night excursions onto the street. He is unkempt and scrawny. He has no appetite and hasn't eaten a proper meal in weeks. He lost his job months ago. He is afraid to go out during the day because he sees in every passing face a spy who is trying to learn, by reading his mind, the secret that will destroy him. He hears voices telling him that he must stay away from the spies, and he hears his own thoughts as if they were broadcast aloud for all to hear. He sits still, trying to keep calm, trying to reduce the volume of his thoughts. John's disorder is diagnosed as schizophrenia.

Schizophrenia is a serious disorder that is found in roughly 0.7 percent of people at some time in their lives (Tandon & others, 2008). It accounts for a higher percentage of the inpatient population of mental hospitals than do disorders in any other

Art by a person with schizophrenia This piece by Adolf Wölfi exemplifies the unusual personal symbolism and rhythmical forms that characterize the artwork of many people with schizophrenia.

Adolf wolfi, untitled (1915). The Prinzhorn Institute, University of Heidelberg.

diagnostic category. The disorder is somewhat more prevalent in men than in women, and it also typically strikes earlier and is more severe in men than in women (Taylor & Langdon, 2006). It usually first manifests itself in late adolescence or early adulthood, and the average age for first diagnosis is about 4 years later in women than in men (Riecher-Rossler & Hafner, 2000). Sometimes people make a full recovery from schizophrenia, sometimes they make a partial recovery, and sometimes the disorder takes a deteriorating course throughout the person's life.

The label *schizophrenia* was first used by the Swiss psychiatrist Eugen Bleuler (1911/1950), whose writings are still a valuable source of information and insight about the disorder. The term comes from the Greek words *schizo*, which means "split," and *phrenum*, which means "mind," so it literally means "split mind." Bleuler believed, as do many theorists today, that schizophrenia entails a split among such mental processes as attention, perception, emotion, motivation, and thought, such that these processes operate in relative isolation from one another, leading to bizarre and disorganized thoughts and actions.

Diagnostic Characteristics of Schizophrenia

No two sufferers of schizophrenia have quite the same symptoms. But to receive the *DSM-IV* diagnosis of **schizophrenia,** the person must manifest a serious decline in ability to work, care for himself or herself, and connect socially with others. The person must also manifest, for at least 1 month, two or more of the following five categories of symptoms: disorganized thought and speech, delusions, hallucinations, grossly disorganized or catatonic behavior, and negative symptoms—all described in this section. These symptoms are usually not continuously present; the person typically goes through episodes of active phases of the disorder, lasting for weeks or months, separated by periods of comparative normalcy.

34
What are the five main classes of symptoms of schizophrenia?

Disorganized Thought and Speech

Many people with schizophrenia show speech patterns that reflect an underlying deficit in the ability to think in a logical, coherent manner. In some cases, thought and speech are guided by loose word associations. A classic example is this greeting to Bleuler (1911/1950) from one of his patients: "I wish you a happy, joyful, healthy, blessed and fruitful year, and many good wine-years to come as well as a healthy and good apple-year, and sauerkraut and cabbage and squash and seed year." Once the patient's mind hooked onto fruit (in "fruitful year"), it entered into a chain of associations involving fruits and vegetables that had little to do with the original intent of the statement.

In all sorts of formal tests of logic, people with schizophrenia do poorly when in an active phase of their disorder (Docherty & others, 2003; Simpson & Done, 2004). They often encode the problem information incorrectly, fail to see meaningful connections, or base their reasoning on superficial connections having more to do with the sounds of words than with their meanings.

Delusions

A *delusion* is a false belief held in the face of compelling evidence to the contrary. Common types of delusions in schizophrenia are *delusions of persecution,* which are beliefs that others are plotting against one; *delusions of being controlled,* such as believing that one's thoughts or movements are being controlled in puppet-like fashion by radio waves or invisible wires; and *delusions of grandeur,* which are beliefs in one's own extraordinary importance—for example, that one is the queen of England or is the love object of a famous movie star.

Delusions may result, in part, from a fundamental difficulty in identifying and remembering the original source of ideas or actions (Moritz & others, 2005). For example, delusions of being controlled may derive from a failure to mentally separate voluntary actions from involuntary actions; people with schizophrenia may often find themselves performing actions without remembering that they willfully initiated those actions (Broome & others, 2005). Delusions of persecution may stem, in part, from attempts to make sense of their horrible feelings and confusion. Delusions of grandeur may derive from an inability to separate fantasies from real-world experiences. Moreover, all sorts of delusions may be buttressed by deficits in logical reasoning, as in the case of a woman who supported her claim to be the Virgin Mary this way: "The Virgin Mary is a virgin. I am a virgin. Therefore, I am the Virgin Mary" (Arieti, 1966).

Hallucinations

Hallucinations are false sensory perceptions—hearing or seeing things that aren't there. By far the most common hallucinations in schizophrenia are auditory, usually the hearing of voices. Hallucinations and delusions typically work together to support one another. For example, a man who has a delusion of persecution may repeatedly hear the voice of his persecutor insulting or threatening him.

A good deal of evidence supports the view that auditory hallucinations derive from the person's own intrusive verbal thoughts—thoughts that others of us would experience as disruptive but self-generated. People with schizophrenia apparently "hear" such thoughts as if they were broadcast aloud and controlled by someone else. When asked to describe the source of the voices, they typically say that they come from inside their own heads, and some even say that the voices are produced, against their will, by their own speech mechanisms (Smith, 1992). Consistent with these reports, people with schizophrenia can usually stop the voices by such procedures as humming, counting, or silently repeating a word—procedures that, in everyone, interfere with the ability to imagine vividly any sounds other than those that are being hummed or silently recited (Bick & Kinsbourne, 1987; Reisberg & others, 1989). In addition, brain-imaging research, using fMRI, has revealed that verbal hallucinations in people with schizophrenia are accompanied by neural activity in the same brain regions that are normally involved in subvocally generating and "hearing" one's own verbal statements (Allen & others, 2008; Shergill & others, 2004).

Grossly Disorganized Behavior and Catatonic Behavior

Not surprisingly, given their difficulties with thoughts and perceptions, people in the active phase of schizophrenia often behave in very disorganized ways. Many of their actions are strikingly inappropriate for the context—such as wearing many overcoats on a hot day or behaving in a silly manner at a solemn occasion. The inability to keep context in mind and to coordinate actions with it seems to be among the basic deficits in schizophrenia (Broome & others, 2005). Even when engaging in appropriate behaviors, such as preparing a simple meal, people with schizophrenia may fail because they are unable to generate or follow a coherent plan of action.

In some cases, schizophrenia is marked by *catatonic behavior,* defined as behavior that is unresponsive to the environment (American Psychiatric Association, 2000). Catatonic behavior may involve excited, restless motor activity that is not directed meaningfully toward the environment; or, at the other extreme, it may involve a complete lack of movement for long periods—a form referred to as a *catatonic stupor.* Such behaviors may be means of withdrawing from a world that seems frighteningly difficult to understand or control.

Negative Symptoms

The so-called *negative symptoms* of schizophrenia are those that involve a lack of, or reduction in, expected behaviors, thoughts, feelings, and drives (American Psychiatric Association, 2000). They include a general slowing down of bodily movements, poverty of speech (slow, labored, unspontaneous speech), flattened affect (reduction in or absence of emotional expression), loss of basic drives such as hunger, and loss of the pleasure that normally comes from fulfilling drives. Although you might expect

A person in a catatonic stupor
People with schizophrenia withdraw from their environment in various ways. One of the most extreme forms of withdrawal is the catatonic stupor, in which the person may remain motionless for hours in an uncomfortable position.

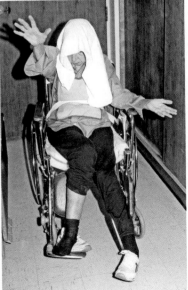

Grunnitus Studio

catatonic stupor to be included in the category of negative symptoms, it is usually not, because the stupor is believed to be actively maintained.

The majority of people with schizophrenia manifest negative symptoms to some degree, and for many these are the most prominent symptoms. I once asked a dear friend, who was suffering from schizophrenia and was starving himself, why he didn't eat. His answer, in labored but thoughtful speech, was essentially this: "I have no appetite. I feel no pleasure from eating or anything else. I keep thinking that if I go long enough without eating, food will taste good again and life might be worth living." For him, the most painful symptom of all was an inability to experience normal drives or the pleasure of satisfying them.

Variations of the Disorder

Two people diagnosed with schizophrenia may differ greatly from each other, with little overlap in the kinds of symptoms they show. Studies using factor analysis to determine which symptoms correlate most strongly with each other suggest three different clusters of symptoms: *positive symptoms* (primarily delusions and hallucinations), *disorganized symptoms* (disorganized thought, speech, and behavior), and *negative symptoms* (as defined earlier) (Toomey & others, 1997). Positive symptoms and, to a lesser degree, disorganized symptoms tend to come and go; patients often experience remission from them for many months between episodes (Docherty & others, 2003). These symptoms are also most responsive to antipsychotic drugs. The negative symptoms, in contrast, are more constant and less responsive to drugs.

Various subcategories of schizophrenia have been proposed, based on the prevalence of specific symptoms or symptom clusters. The subcategories described in *DSM-IV* include *paranoid type,* characterized mainly by delusions of persecution and grandeur and often by hallucinations; *catatonic type,* characterized mainly by non-reaction to the environment; and *disorganized type,* characterized by disorganized speech, disorganized behavior, and either inappropriate or flattened affect. However, no system of subcategories has proved very satisfactory. The symptoms appear in a huge number of different combinations and may change over time in a given person, thereby defying attempts at classification.

Underlying Cognitive and Neural Deficits in Schizophrenia

Schizophrenia is characterized primarily as a cognitive disorder, brought on by deleterious changes in the brain (Broome & others, 2005; Heinrichs, 2005). To say that it is a cognitive disorder is to say that the fundamental psychological deficits have to do with the ability to process information.

35

What general cognitive deficits have been observed in laboratory studies of people with schizophrenia?

Deficits in Information Processing

People with schizophrenia appear to suffer from deficits in essentially all the basic processes of attention and memory that were discussed in **Chapter 9** (Dickinson & others, 2008; Reichenberg & Harvey, 2007). They perform particularly poorly at tasks that require sustained attention over time or that require them to respond only to relevant information and to ignore irrelevant information (Bozikas & others, 2005; Nuechterlein & others, 1992; K. Wang & others, 2005). They are abnormally slow at bringing perceived information into their working-memory stores, and poor at holding onto the information once it is there (Barch, 2003; Fuller & others, 2005). They also perform more poorly than other subjects at encoding and recalling new long-term explicit memories, and they are especially deficient in remembering the source of new information (Kerns & Berenbaum, 2002; Moritz & others, 2005). Because of their failure to recall the source, they have difficulty knowing whether the information they recall was presented to them as truth or fiction or was something they merely imagined—a problem all of us occasionally experience to a much lesser degree. All these kinds of mental deficits appear to contribute to the whole set of diagnostic symptoms of schizophrenia—the disordered thought, delusions, hallucinations, disorganized behavior, and negative symptoms (Broome & others, 2005).

Such information-processing deficits are usually greatest during the active phase of the disorder, but they are also found in people who are in remission—that is, who are no longer manifesting the diagnostic symptoms (Green, 1993; Heinrichs, 2005). To a lesser degree, such deficits may also precede the onset of the disorder. In a long-term study of people known to be genetically at risk for schizophrenia, deficits in attention and memory in childhood correlated positively with the subsequent development of schizophrenia in adulthood (Erlenmeyer-Kimling & others, 2000). Such findings suggest that deficits in attention and memory are not just symptoms of schizophrenia, but are, to some degree, preexisting conditions that contribute to a person's vulnerability to the disorder.

Disruptions in Brain Chemistry

The mental problems observed in schizophrenia derive, presumably, from deficits in the brain. By the early 1970s evidence had accrued for the dopamine theory of schizophrenia—the theory that schizophrenia arises from too much activity at brain synapses where dopamine is the neurotransmitter. The most compelling evidence was the observation that the clinical effectiveness of drugs in reducing the positive symptoms of schizophrenia was directly proportional to the drug's effectiveness in blocking dopamine release at synaptic terminals (Seeman & Lee, 1975). Other support came from the finding that drugs such as cocaine and amphetamine, which increase the action of dopamine in the brain, can greatly exacerbate the symptoms of schizophrenia in people with the disorder (Davis, 1974) and, at higher doses, can even induce such symptoms in people who do not have the disorder (Griffith & others, 1972).

36 ▸

What early evidence supported the dopamine theory of schizophrenia? Why is the simple form of that theory doubted today?

Today, researchers continue to recognize the role of dopamine in schizophrenia but generally do not accept the original, simple form of the dopamine theory. One major flaw in the theory is that it does not explain the negative symptoms of schizophrenia, which are not well treated by drugs that act solely on dopamine and are not typically exacerbated by drugs that increase that action of dopamine. Modern theories suggest that schizophrenia may involve unusual patterns of dopamine activity. Overactivity of dopamine in some part of the brain, especially in the basal ganglia, may promote the positive symptoms of schizophrenia and *underactivity* of dopamine in the prefrontal cortex may promote the negative symptoms (Stone & others, 2007).

"We have pills for some of that."

Currently, a good deal of attention is being devoted to the role of *glutamate* in schizophrenia (Pomerantz, 2007). As is noted in **Chapter 5,** glutamate is the major excitatory neurotransmitter at fast synapses throughout the brain. Some research suggests that one of the major receptor molecules for glutamate is defective in people who have schizophrenia, resulting in a decline in the effectiveness of glutamate neurotransmission (Javitt & Coyle, 2004; Phillips & Silverstein, 2003). Such a decline could account for the general cognitive debilitation that characterizes the disorder. Consistent with this theory, the dangerous, often-abused drug phencyclidine (PCP)—known on the street as "angel dust"—interferes with glutamate neurotransmission and is capable of inducing, for varying periods of time, in otherwise normal people, the full range of schizophrenic symptoms, including the negative and disorganized symptoms as well as hallucinations and delusions (Javitt & Coyle, 2004).

37 ▸

What evidence supports the theory that a defect in glutamate neurotransmission may play a role in schizophrenia?

Alterations in Brain Structure

Studies using brain-imaging techniques have shown structural differences between the brains of people with schizophrenia and those of other people (Galderisi & others, 2008; Keshavan & others, 2008). The most common finding is enlargement of the cerebral ventricles (fluid-filled spaces in the brain) accompanied by a reduction in neural tissue surrounding the ventricles. Decreased neural mass has been found in various parts of the brain, especially the hippocampus (involved in memory) and the prefrontal cortex (involved in all sorts of conscious control of thought and behavior). These size differences are relatively small and vary from person to person; they are not sufficiently reliable to be useful in diagnosing the disorder (Heinrichs, 2005; Keshavan & others, 2008).

◄ Some researchers have attempted to explain the timing of the onset of schizophrenia in terms of maturational changes in the brain. During adolescence, the brain normally undergoes certain structural changes: Many neural cell bodies are lost, a process referred to as pruning, and many new neural connections grow. The result is a decrease in gray matter (masses of cell bodies) and an increase in white matter (bundles of axons running from one brain area to another). Some researchers have suggested that an abnormality in pruning, which leads to the loss of too many cell bodies, may underlie at least some cases of schizophrenia (Keshavan & others, 2006; Lewis & Levitt, 2002). Consistent with this view, neuroimaging studies of people at risk for schizophrenia revealed a larger decline in gray matter during adolescence or early adulthood in those who subsequently developed the disorder than in those who did not (Lawrie & others, 2008).

38

How might an exaggeration of a normal developmental change at adolescence help bring on schizophrenia?

Identical twins with nonidentical brains Steven, on the right, has schizophrenia. His genetically identical twin, on the left, does not. Brain scans revealed that Steven's brain has larger cerebral ventricles than does his brother's. Such discordance for schizophrenia in identical twins sometimes occurs when one of the two twins (usually the one born second) suffers from lack of oxygen during the birth process and the other does not.

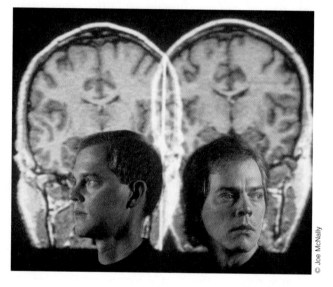

© Joe McNally

Genetic and Environmental Causes of Schizophrenia

Why do the neural and cognitive alterations that bring on and constitute schizophrenia occur in some people and not in others? Genetic differences certainly play a role, and environmental differences do, too.

Predisposing Effects of Genes

Schizophrenia was one of the first mental disorders to be studied extensively by behavior geneticists (Gottesman, 1991). In such studies, the first step is to identify a group of people, referred to as *index cases*, who have the disorder. Then the relatives of the index cases are studied to see what percentage of them have the disorder. This percentage is referred to as the **concordance** for the disorder, for the class of relatives studied. The average concordances found for schizophrenia in many such studies, for various classes of relatives, are shown in Table 16.3.

◄ All in all, the results indicate that genetic differences among individuals play a substantial role in the predisposition for schizophrenia. The more closely related a person is to an index case, the greater is the chance that he or she will develop schizophrenia. Other research, conducted with people who were adopted at an early age, shows high concordance for schizophrenia between biological relatives

39

How do the varying rates of concordance for schizophrenia among different classes of relatives support the idea that heredity influences one's susceptibility for the disorder?

TABLE 16.3 Concordance rates for schizophrenia

Relationship to a person who has schizophrenia	Average percentage found to have schizophrenia (concordance)
Relatives in same generation	
Identical twin	48%
Fraternal twin	17
Non-twin brother or sister	9
Half-sibling	6
First cousin	2
Relatives in later generation	
Child of two parents with schizophrenia	46
Child of one parent with schizophrenia	13
Grandchild of one person with schizophrenia	5
Niece or nephew of one person with schizophrenia	4

Sources: I. I. Gottesman, 1991. *Schizophrenia genesis: The origins of madness,* p. 96. New York: Freeman.

but not between adoptive relatives (Owen & O'Donovan, 2003). The results of one classic study of this type are shown in Figure 16.6. Such results indicate that it is the genetic similarity, not the environmental similarity, between relatives that produces high concordance for schizophrenia.

More recently a great deal of research has been aimed at identifying individual genes that contribute to the development of schizophrenia. Many different genes appear to be involved, and no single gene or small set of genes can account for most of the genetic influence in large samples of people with schizophrenia (Bertram, 2008). Consistent with current chemical theories of schizophrenia, at least some of the identified genes are known to influence dopamine neurotransmission and some are known to influence glutamate neurotransmission (Bertram, 2008; Broome & others, 2005).

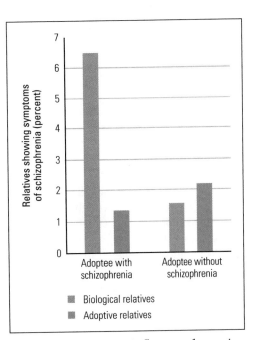

FIGURE 16.6 Results of a classic study of the heritability of schizophrenia The researchers looked for signs of schizophrenia in the biological and adoptive relatives of people who had been adopted at an early age and either did or did not subsequently develop schizophrenia. The results here are the percentage of relatives who showed either schizophrenia or a milder disorder now called schizotypal personality disorder. (Data from Kety & others, 1976.)

Effects of the Prenatal Environment and Early Brain Traumas

The data in Table 16.3 show that genes are heavily involved in the predisposition for schizophrenia, but they also show that genes are not the only determinants of the disorder. Of particular interest is the fact that the average concordance for schizophrenia for identical twins, 48 percent, is much less than the 100 percent that would be predicted if genes alone were involved. Another noteworthy observation, in the table, is that the concordance for schizophrenia in fraternal twins is considerably higher than that for non-twin pairs of full siblings—17 percent compared to 9 percent. This difference cannot be explained in terms of genes, as fraternal twins are no more similar to each other genetically than are other full siblings, but it is consistent with the possibility of a prenatal influence. Twins share the same womb at the same time, so they are exposed to the same prenatal stressors and toxins. That fact, of course, applies to identical twins as well as to fraternal twins, so some portion of the 48 percent concordance in identical twins may result not from shared genes but from shared prenatal environments.

◀ A number of studies have pointed to specific prenatal variables that can contribute to the likelihood of developing schizophrenia. One such variable is malnutrition (Brown & Susser, 2008). People born in the western Netherlands between October 15 and December 31, 1945, immediately following a severe famine brought on by a Nazi blockade of food supplies, are twice as likely as others born in the Netherlands to have developed schizophrenia (Susser & others, 1996). A more recent study, illustrated in Figure 16.7, revealed a similar effect for people who were born in China during or shortly after the Chinese famine of 1960–1961, which resulted from massive crop failures (St. Clair & others, 2005).

40

What sorts of early disruptions to brain development have been implicated as predisposing causes of schizophrenia?

FIGURE 16.7 Effect of malnutrition during pregnancy on rate of schizophrenia in offspring Children who were in their mothers' wombs during the period of great famine in China later developed schizophrenia at roughly twice the usual rate. (Data from St. Clair & others, 2005.)

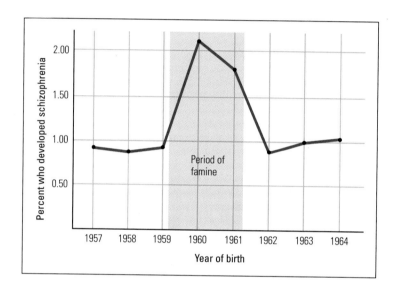

Prenatal viral infections and birth complications may also contribute to a predisposition for schizophrenia. Heightened rates of schizophrenia have been found in people whose mothers had rubella (also known as German measles) or certain other viral diseases during pregnancy and in people who had difficult births, involving oxygen deprivation or other trauma to the brain (Tandon & others, 2008). There is also evidence that head injury later on in childhood, before age 10, can increase the likelihood of developing schizophrenia (AbdelMalik & others, 2003).

Effects of Life Experiences

The effects discussed so far are predisposing effects. Given a certain level of predisposition, the actual manifestation and course of schizophrenia may be influenced by one's daily experiences. There is strong evidence that stressful life events of many sorts can precipitate schizophrenia and exacerbate its symptoms (Pallanti & others, 1997; van Os & others, 2008). Most research on such effects has focused on the family environment.

41

What evidence suggests that the family environment may promote schizophrenia, but only in those who are genetically predisposed for the disorder?

◀ The most thorough investigation, to date, of the effect of the family environment on schizophrenia is a 21-year-long study, in Finland, of two groups of adopted children (Tienari & others, 2004, 2006). One group of children was genetically at high genetic risk for schizophrenia because their biological mothers were diagnosed with either schizophrenia or a milder schizophrenia-like disorder, and the other group was at low risk because neither of their biological parents showed any evidence of schizophrenia or a related disorder. The main finding was that those high-risk children whose adoptive parents communicated in a relatively disorganized, hard-to-follow, or highly emotional manner were much more likely to develop schizophrenia or a milder disorder akin to schizophrenia than were high-risk children whose adoptive parents communicated in a calmer, more organized fashion. This relationship was not found among the low-risk children. The results suggest that a degree of disordered communication at home that does not harm most children may have damaging effects on those who are genetically predisposed for schizophrenia.

Other research has centered on a concept referred to as *expressed emotion,* defined as criticisms and negative attitudes or feelings expressed about and toward a person with a mental disorder by family members with whom that person lives. Families high in expressed emotion tend to blame the diagnosed person for his or her disruptive or ineffective behavior rather than seeing it as something that he or she cannot control. Many studies indicate that, other things being equal, the greater the expressed emotion, the greater the likelihood that the active symptoms will return or worsen and the person will require hospitalization (Hooley, 2004; Tienari & Wahlberg, 2008). Moreover, a number of experiments have shown that support and training for family members, aimed at creating a more stable and accepting home environment and reducing expressed emotion, may significantly reduce the rate of relapse (Askey & others, 2007; Hooley & Hiller, 2001).

42

What evidence suggests that a hostile family environment can be a perpetuating cause of schizophrenia?

Andrew Lepley/Redferns/Getty

Living and playing with schizophrenia Despite having schizophrenia since he was a young man, Tom Harrell has developed into one of the world's top jazz composers and trumpeters. According to his wife, composing and playing music help to focus Harrell's mind and to reduce the symptoms of schizophrenia.

A Cross-Cultural Study of the Course of Schizophrenia

In the 1970s, the World Health Organization (WHO) initiated an ambitious cross-cultural study of schizophrenia, involving, eventually, locations in 13 different nations. The nations included industrialized, *developed* countries, such as Germany, Japan, Ireland, and the United States, and relatively nonindustrialized, *developing* countries, such as India, Colombia, and Nigeria. Using agreed-upon criteria and cross-cultural reliability checks, the researchers diagnosed new cases of schizophrenia in each location, classed them according to symptom types and apparent severity, and reassessed each case through interviews conducted at various times in subsequent years. All in all, more than 1000 people with schizophrenia were identified and followed over periods of up to 26 years (Hopper & others, 2007).

The results showed considerable cross-cultural consistency. The relative prevalence of the various symptoms, the severity of the initial symptoms, the average age of onset of the disorder, and the sex difference in age of onset (later for women than for men) were similar from location to location despite wide variations in the ways that people lived. However, the study also led to two overall conclusions that were quite surprising to many schizophrenia experts. The first surprising finding was that quite a high percentage of people, in all locations, were found to *recover* from schizophrenia; and the second was that the rate of recovery was *greater* in the developing countries than in the developed countries.

43 ------------------------------
What cross-cultural difference has been observed in rate of recovery from schizophrenia? What are some possible explanations of that difference?

◄ At the two-year follow-up, for example, 63 percent of the patients in the developing countries, compared with 37 percent in the developed countries, showed full remission from schizophrenic symptoms (Jablensky & others, 1992). Subsequent follow-ups showed similar results and revealed that many of the originally recovered patients remained recovered over the entire study period (Hopper & others, 2007). Even among those who, on the basis of their initial symptoms, were identified as having a "poor prognosis," 42 percent recovered in the developing countries, compared to 33 percent in the developed countries, by the WHO criteria.

Why should people in the poorer countries, which have the poorest mental health facilities, fare better after developing schizophrenia than people in the richer countries? Nobody knows for sure, but some interesting hypotheses have been put forth (Jenkins & Karno, 1992; Lin & Kleinman, 1988; López & Guarnaccia, 2005). Family members in less industrialized countries generally place less value on personal independence and more on interdependence and family ties than do those in industrialized countries, which may lead them to feel less resentful and more nurturing toward a family member who needs extra care. They are more likely to live in large, extended families, which means that more people share in providing the extra care. Perhaps for these reasons, family members in less industrialized countries are more accepting and less critical of individuals diagnosed with schizophrenia than are those in industrialized countries. They show less expressed emotion, as defined earlier, which might account for the better recovery rate.

People in developing countries are also less likely to call the disorder "schizophrenia" or to think of it as permanent, and are more likely to refer to it as "a case of nerves," which sounds more benign and ties it to experiences that everyone has had. Finally, in less industrialized countries those with schizophrenia are more able to play an economically useful role. The same person who could not hold a nine-to-five job can perform useful chores on the family farm, or at the family trade, or at a local business where everyone knows the family. Being less stigmatized, less cut off from the normal course of human activity, and better cared for by close family members and neighbors may increase the chance of recovery.

Another possible explanation, rarely mentioned in the psychiatric literature, has to do with drugs. Over the course of the WHO study, patients in the developed countries were generally treated with antipsychotic drugs for prolonged periods, as they are today. In contrast, patients in the developing countries were more often not treated with drugs or were treated only for short periods to bring the initial symptoms under control (Jablensky & others, 1992). The authors of the WHO study (Hopper & others, 2007) devote no discussion to the possible role of drugs in promoting or inhibiting recovery, but they do mention, in passing, that the treatment center in Agra, India, which had the highest rate of recovery of all the centers studied, was the only center that used no drugs at all—because they could not afford them.

Some controversial studies in Europe and the United States, some years ago, suggested that prolonged use of antipsychotic drugs, while dampening the positive symptoms of schizophrenia, may impede full recovery (Warner, 1985). This ironic possibility—that the drugs we use to treat schizophrenia might prolong the disorder—has not been followed up with systematic research. Some critics of the Western mental health system have suggested that it is so invested in drugs, and so concerned with controlling immediate symptoms, that it has neglected to investigate seriously the possibility that patients might, over the long run, do better if they were not so heavily medicated (more on this can be found in **Chapter 17**).

A Developmental Model of Schizophrenia

The more scientists learn about schizophrenia, the more apparent it becomes that the disorder has no simple, unitary cause. Figure 16.8 provides a useful framework (similar to one developed by Tsuang & others, 2001) for thinking about the multiple causes. The disorder is brought on by some combination of genetic predisposition, early physical disruptions to normal brain development, and stressful life

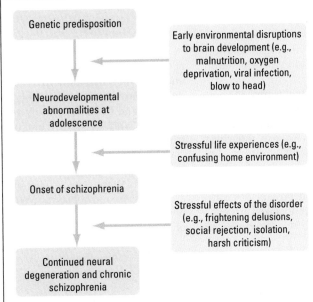

FIGURE 16.8 A developmental model of schizophrenia This model depicts researchers' understanding of the contributions of genes, environmental experiences, and the person's present neural and behavioral condition to the development of schizophrenia and, in some cases, its progression into a chronic condition. (Based on a model depicted by Tsuang & others, 2001, p. 22.)

experiences. Once the disorder begins, the disorder itself can have effects that help to prolong it, depending at least partly on how family members and others in one's community respond. Distressing effects of the disorder itself, or of others' reactions to it, can cause further deterioration of the brain and a more chronic course for the disorder.

SECTION REVIEW

Schizophrenia is a cognitive disorder with wide-ranging symptoms and multiple causes.

Diagnostic Characteristics

➤ Schizophrenia is characterized by various symptoms sometimes classified as positive, disorganized, and negative.

➤ Positive symptoms include delusions (false beliefs held despite compelling contrary evidence) and auditory hallucinations (which may come from the person's own intrusive verbal thoughts).

➤ Disorganized symptoms include illogical thought and speech, and behaviors that are inappropriate to the environmental context.

➤ Negative symptoms include slowed movement, poverty of speech, flattened affect, and the loss of basic drives and the pleasure that comes from fulfilling them.

➤ Symptoms occur in a great variety of combinations and may change over time in the same person.

Underlying Cognitive and Neural Deficits

➤ The fundamental deficits in schizophrenia are cognitive, including problems with attention, working memory, and long-term memory.

➤ Abnormalities in brain chemistry, such as a decline in the effectiveness of glutamate (the major excitatory neurotransmitter at fast synapses) or unusual patterns of dopamine activity, may help to explain the cognitive deficits.

➤ Structural differences in the brains of people with schizophrenia may include enlarged cerebral ventricles and reduced neural mass in some areas. Excessive pruning of neural cell bodies in adolescence may be a cause of some cases of schizophrenia.

Genetic and Environmental Causes

➤ Measures of concordance for schizophrenia in identical twins indicate substantial heritability. Some of the specific genes that appear to be involved have effects that are consistent with brain chemistry theories of the disorder.

➤ Predisposition may also arise from early environmental injury to the brain—including prenatal viruses or malnutrition, birth complications, or early childhood head injury.

➤ Stressful life experiences and aspects of the family environment can bring on the active phase of schizophrenia or worsen symptoms in predisposed people.

➤ Recovery from schizophrenia has been found to occur at higher rates in developing countries than in developed countries. Differences in living conditions and cultural attitudes and the lower use of antipsychotic drugs in developing countries may all play a role.

Concluding Thoughts

Here are three final ideas that may help you organize your thoughts as you reflect on what you have read in this chapter:

1. The multiple causes of mental disorders By this time in your study of psychology, you are no doubt used to the idea that human feelings, thoughts, and actions emerge from the interplay of many causes. This idea also applies to the feelings, thoughts, and actions that lead to the diagnosis of a mental disorder. The differences among us that are considered disorders—no less than the differences that are considered normal—are caused by differences in our genes and in our past and present environments. Any claim to have found *the* cause of generalized anxiety, depression, schizophrenia, or another major class of disorder is of doubtful validity.

One way to review this chapter would be to think about each disorder in relation to the three classes of causes—predisposing, precipitating, and perpetuating—that were introduced near the beginning of the chapter. How might genes and early physical assaults on the brain operate through the person's physiology to predispose him or her for the disorder? How might learned ways of thinking or acting predispose a person for the disorder? How might specific stressful events in life interact with the predisposition to precipitate the disorder? How might the disordered behavior itself, or people's reactions to it, help perpetuate the disorder once it begins? For each disorder, think about the relationship between the research or ideas described and the possible answers to these questions. Note, too, that similar stressful events can result in different kinds of symptoms—and different diagnosed disorders—for different individuals or at different times for any given individual.

2. The continuum between normality and abnormality Although a diagnosis of a mental disorder is categorical (all or none), the symptoms on which diagnoses are made are not; they vary in degree throughout the population. Thus, any decision as to whether a particular person does or does not have a mental disorder is based on arbitrary criteria describing how severe or prolonged each symptom must be in order to call the syndrome a disorder.

As you review each disorder described in the chapter, think about its symptoms in relation to the moods, emotions, thoughts, and behaviors that all of us manifest to some degree. Doing so helps remove some of the mystique from the concept of mental disorder and helps us identify with people whose troubles are like ours, only stronger. Thinking of disorders in terms of extremes of normal processes has also helped scientists understand them better. For example, in this chapter you read about evidence relating (a) the symptoms of ADHD to normal childhood impulsiveness and exuberance; (b) the symptoms of general anxiety disorder, phobias, and obsessive-compulsive disorders to normal worries, fears, thoughts, and actions; (c) the symptoms of depression to normal, possibly adaptive mood changes following loss or failure; and (d) the auditory hallucinations experienced in schizophrenia to the intrusive thoughts that all of us experience at times.

3. An evolutionary view of mental disorder The evolutionary theme running through this book maintains that behavior is generally functional: It promotes survival and reproduction. But mental disorder is dysfunctional: It reduces one's ability to work and interact with others effectively in survival-promoting ways. Why, then, do mental disorders exist?

One partial answer may be that mental disorders are a cost the species pays for the general advantages that come with diversity. The previous chapter, on personality, dealt with individual differences within the range generally considered healthy, or not disordered, and the case was made that natural selection may have favored diversity because those who are different from average can exploit unfilled niches and reap their rewards. Such diversity stems from variations in genes and from behavioral mechanisms that are capable of being modified through experience. Variation in capacity for anxiety, or compulsiveness, or sadness may be beneficial within a certain range; but the coin tosses that distribute genes and experiences will sometimes produce those characteristics at pathological levels.

Further Reading

Floyd Skloot (2005). *A world of light.* Lincoln: University of Nebraska Press.

In 1988, at age 41, Floyd Skloot lost much of his memory, linguistic ability, and ability for coherent thought as a result of a viral infection that destroyed parts of his brain. In 2003 he published a book, *In the Shadow of Memory*, describing his slow but active struggle to reconstruct his sense of self as he regained some of his mental capacities. Now, in *A World of Light*, he reconstructs some of his own past and describes his ongoing encounters with his mother, who is in her 90s and has Alzheimer's disease. The book offers a fascinating glimpse into the world of dementia, from a poetic soul who himself has experienced some of the effects of dementia.

Mathilde Monaque (2007). *Trouble in my head: A young girl's fight with depression.*

Mathilde Monaque became severely depressed at age 14 and was hospitalized. Within a year after emerging from her depression she began writing this compelling description of the despair, resignation, and wish to die—in her word, by "evaporation"—that characterized her disorder. The book is an excellent, first-hand account of depressive thoughts and feelings, and through her recovery the author provides hope for others who suffer similarly.

Kay Jamison (1995). *An unquiet mind.* New York: Knopf.

In this autobiography, Kay Jamison—a leading researcher of mood disorders—describes her own experiences as a sufferer of bipolar disorder. The book includes an especially vivid description of her first full-blown manic episode, which happened in her first year as an assistant professor, and a moving discussion of how she came to terms with the disorder and has managed to live with it.

Elyn Saks (2007). *The center cannot hold: My journey through madness.* New York: Hyperion.

Evelyn Saks is an accomplished scholar, an esteemed professor of law, who has suffered throughout her adult life from schizophrenia. In this remarkable autobiographical account she describes the terrors she has experienced during psychotic episodes. We learn here what it is like to experience commands coming from within, bizarre perceptual distortions, and periods of chaotic thoughts. We also learn about the high degree of support from others and determination from self that is required for a person with this disorder to live a productive and satisfying life, despite the continued disruptions.

Nancy C. Andreasen (2001). *Brave new brain: Conquering mental illness in the era of the genome.* Oxford, UK: Oxford University Press.

Andreasen is a leading researcher into the biological foundations of mental disorders and an excellent writer. Here, for nonspecialists, she conveys what it is like to have a serious mental disorder or to have a loved one with such a disorder, and she also describes how biological research is leading to new understandings of such disorders and new methods of treatment. She focuses particularly on schizophrenia, mood disorders, dementias (including Alzheimer's disease), and anxiety disorders.

Dale Peterson (Ed.) (1982). *A mad people's history of madness.* Pittsburgh: University of Pittsburgh Press.

In this fascinating collection of excerpts from autobiographies written over the past 500 years, people who either were, or were regarded as, seriously mentally disordered describe their suffering, the reactions of others, and their own efforts toward recovery. Some of the excerpts are from well-known books that have helped shape reforms in the understanding and treatment of people with mental disorders.

Treatment

Throughout this book you have read of psychology as a *science*. Perhaps you have discovered that psychology is a vast, complex, fascinating, and sometimes frustrating science in which every finding generates far more questions than it answers. If your experience in reading this book has been anything like mine in writing it, your attitude right now may be one of respect for what psychologists have discovered, combined with awe for the amount that is yet to be learned.

But psychology is not just a science; it is also a *practice*. Practitioners in psychology attempt to apply psychological ideas and findings in ways designed to make life more satisfying for individuals or society as a whole. This last chapter is about **clinical psychology,** the field of practice and research that is directed toward helping people who suffer from psychological problems and disorders. In this chapter you will see how some of the basic knowledge of the brain, mind, and behavior that you have read about in previous chapters has been applied in efforts to help people in psychological need.

The chapter begins with a section on the social problem of providing care for the seriously disturbed, and then it progresses through sections that deal with various biological and psychological treatments for mental disorders. The final section is concerned with questions about the effectiveness of psychotherapy.

■ Care as a Social Issue

The existence of mental suffering, like that of physical suffering, raises social and moral questions. Who, if anyone, is responsible for caring for those who cannot care for themselves?

What to Do with the Severely Disturbed? A Brief History

1

How has Western society's response to people with serious mental disorders changed since the Middle Ages? What were the goals of the moral-treatment and deinstitutionalization movements?

Through most of history, Western cultures felt little obligation toward people with mental disorders. During the Middle Ages, and even into the 17th century, people with serious mental disorders—the kind called "madness" or "lunacy" (and today most often diagnosed as schizophrenia)—were often considered to be in league with the devil, and "treatment" commonly consisted of torture, hanging, burning at the stake, or being sent to sea in "ships of fools" to drown or be saved, depending on divine Providence.

By the 18th century, such "religious" views had waned somewhat and a more secular attitude began to prevail, which attributed mental disorders not to supernatural powers but to the basic degeneracy and unworthiness of the disordered people themselves. The principal treatment for those who couldn't care for themselves

Life in a 19th-century mental hospital One source of pressure for mental hospital reform in early-19th-century England were portraits, such as this one, drawn by George Cruikshank. The man shown here had been bound to the wall by foot-long chains for 12 years at the time of the portrait.

was to put them out of the way of decent society in places that were called "hospitals" but in reality were dark, damp, miserable dungeons, where inmates were frequently kept chained to the walls, alive but in a state that was perhaps worse than death.

Early Attempts at Reform, and the Failure of Asylums

Not until the beginning of the 19th century did significant humanitarian reform begin to occur. The best-known leader of reform in Europe was Philippe Pinel (1745–1826), who, as director of a large mental hospital in Paris, unchained the inmates, transferred them to sunny and airy rooms, and gave them access to the hospital grounds for exercise. Under these conditions some inmates who had been deemed permanently and hopelessly deranged recovered sufficiently to be released from the hospital.

In the United States, the leading reformer was Dorothea Dix (1802–1887), a Boston schoolteacher who visited dozens of jails and almshouses where people with mental disorders were housed and who then publicized the appalling conditions she found. As this *moral-treatment movement* grew, it spurred the building of large, state-supported asylums for the mentally disordered. The idea behind such institutions was high-minded: to provide kindly care and protection for those unable to care for themselves. Unfortunately, public sympathy was rarely sustained at this high level, at least not in the tangible form of financial support. Almost invariably, the asylums became overcrowded and understaffed, and reverted to conditions not unlike those that had appalled Pinel and Dix. As recently as the 1940s, the following report could be written about a state mental institution in Philadelphia (Deutsch, 1948):

> The male "incontinent ward" was like a scene out of Dante's *Inferno*. Three hundred nude men stood, squatted and sprawled in this bare room. . . . Winter or summer, these creatures never were given any clothing at all. . . . Many patients [in another ward] had to eat their meals with their hands. . . . Four hundred patients were herded into a barn-like day room intended for only 80. There were only a few benches; most of the men had to stand all day or sit on the splintery floor. . . . The hogs in a nearby pigpen were far better fed, in far greater comfort than these human beings.

Dorothea Dix This Boston schoolteacher's crusade resulted in new asylums for the mentally ill and improved conditions in existing institutions.

Deinstitutionalization, and Continuing Deficits in Care

By the mid-1950s, disenchantment with large state institutions led to a new kind of reform movement in the United States—a movement to deinstitutionalize people with mental disorders, to get them back into the community. This new movement was inspired partly by the development of antipsychotic drugs and partly by a general mood of optimism in the nation, a feeling that everyone could "make it" if given the chance. President John F. Kennedy gave the movement a boost in 1961 by encouraging Congress to pass legislation to establish community-based mental health centers (Bassuk & Gerson, 1978). By the early 1970s, hundreds of such centers were in operation, offering transitional homes and outpatient care to patients who were capable of living in the community.

Unfortunately, the dream of the community mental health movement, like the earlier dream of asylums, has remained mostly unrealized. The number of chronic patients in state mental institutions has been greatly reduced—from about 600,000 in 1955 to about 60,000 in the early 21st century (Lamberg, 2004)—but it is debatable whether the quality of life of those who would formerly have been in asylums has been improved. They have generally not been integrated into the community but are living on its fringes. Roughly 200,000 of them are homeless, and a similar number are in prisons, usually for minor crimes such as trespassing or theft (Fleishman, 2004; Lamberg, 2004). Many thousands of others are living in rundown rooming houses and understaffed nursing homes (Lamb, 2000). The more fortunate minority are living in long-term residential-care facilities, or group homes, which provide room and board, supervise medication, and offer assistance with problems of daily living (Fleishman, 2004).

A Positive Development: Assertive Community Treatment

Over the past 35 years or so, an increasing number of communities have developed outreach programs, often referred to as *assertive community treatment* (ACT) programs, aimed at helping the severely mentally ill wherever they are in the community (DeLuca & others, 2008). Each mentally ill person in need is assigned to a multidisciplinary treatment team, which typically includes a case manager, psychiatrist, general physician, nurse, and social workers. Someone on the team is available at any time of day, seven days a week, to respond to crises. Each patient—whether living on the street or in a boarding house or with family—is visited at least twice a week by a team member, who checks on his or her health, sees if any services are needed, and offers counseling when that seems appropriate. In addition, the team meets frequently with family members who are involved with the patient, to support them in their care for the patient.

A number of well-designed research studies have shown that such programs can be highly effective in reducing the need for hospitalization and increasing patients' satisfaction with life (Coldwell & Bender, 2007; Nelson & others, 2007). Such programs are expensive to operate, but generally, in the long run, save money by keeping the mentally ill out of hospitals, where their care is much more expensive (Lehman & others, 1998). Despite such evidence, the majority of people with schizophrenia and their families in the United States do not receive such services.

> **2**
> How do assertive community treatment programs attempt to help the severely mentally disordered and their families?

Reaching out In some communities social workers and medical personnel seek out people who are in need, get to know them as individuals, and help them gain access to useful services and means of support.

Darren McCollester/Newsmakers/Getty

Structure of the Mental Health System

Public concern about mental health generally centers on the most severely disordered individuals, those who cannot care for themselves. But most people who seek mental health services have milder problems. The kinds of services they seek depend on such factors as the severity of their disorders, what they can afford, and the services available in their community. They may seek help from self-help groups organized by others who suffer from similar problems or disorders (such as Alcoholics Anonymous), from religious organizations, from general-practice physicians, or from mental health professionals.

Mental Health Professionals

3
What are the major categories of mental health providers?

Mental health professionals are those who have received special training and certification to work with people who have psychological problems or mental disorders. The primary categories of such professionals are the following:

- *Psychiatrists* have medical degrees, obtained through standard medical school training, followed by special training and residency in psychiatry. They are the only mental health specialists who can regularly prescribe drugs. They typically work in private offices, mental health clinics, and hospitals.

- *Clinical psychologists* usually have doctoral degrees in psychology, with training in research and clinical practice. Some are employed by universities as teachers and researchers in addition to having their own clinical practices. Like psychiatrists, they most often work in private offices, clinics, or hospitals.

- *Counseling psychologists* usually have doctoral degrees in counseling. Their training is similar to that of clinical psychologists but generally entails less emphasis on research and more on practice. In general, counseling psychologists are more likely than are psychiatrists or clinical psychologists to work with people who have problems of living that do not warrant a diagnosis of mental disorder.

- *Counselors* usually have master's degrees in counseling. They receive less training in research and psychological diagnostic procedures than do doctoral-level clinical or counseling psychologists. They often work in schools or other institutions, with people who are dealing with school- or job-related problems. They may also conduct psychotherapy in private practice.

- *Psychiatric social workers* usually have master's degrees in social work, followed by advanced training and experience working with people who have psychological problems. They are most often employed by public social-work agencies. They may conduct psychotherapy sessions or visit people in their homes to offer support and guidance.

- *Psychiatric nurses* usually have degrees in nursing, followed by advanced training in the care of mental patients. They usually work in hospitals and may conduct psychotherapy sessions as well as provide more typical nursing services.

Where People with Common Mental Disorders Go for Treatment

4
According to a survey conducted in the United States, where do people with mental disorders typically find treatment, and what types of treatment do they find?

A large-scale household survey was conducted several years ago, in the United States, to find out where people with mental disorders had sought treatment (P. S. Wang & others, 2005). The survey identified a representative sample of thousands of people who were suffering from clinically significant anxiety disorders, mood disorders (including major depression and bipolar disorders), substance use disorders (alcoholism and other drug abuse or dependence disorders), or intermittent explosive disorder (a disorder involving uncontrolled anger). Of these, 22 percent had received some form of treatment from a mental health professional within the past year, 59 percent had received no treatment at all, and most of the remainder had received treatment from a medical doctor or nurse who did not have a mental health specialty.

Mary Kate Denny/PhotoEdit, Inc.

Support for friends and family of alcohol and drug abusers
The family and friends of people with a debilitating mental or behavioral disorder often need psychological support themselves, in order to be helpful to their loved one while at the same time preserving their own well-being. Al-Anon is a self-help group run by and for people who have a friend or family member who is addicted to alcohol or another drug. Self-help groups are valuable components of the mental health system that are not directed by mental health professionals.

The survey also revealed that the typical person with a mental disorder who saw a general-practice physician saw that person just once or twice over the course of the year, usually to receive a prescription for drug treatment and/or a few minutes of counseling. In contrast, those who saw a mental health professional met with that person for an average of seven sessions of at least a half hour's length, mostly for counseling or psychotherapy. Not surprisingly, the wealthier and more educated a person with a mental disorder was, the more likely he or she was to have met for a series of sessions with a mental health professional for psychotherapy (P. S. Wang & others, 2005).

SECTION REVIEW

Caring for mentally suffering people raises moral, social, and practical issues.

How Society Has Responded to the Severely Disturbed

➤ Severely disturbed people were once considered to be allies of the devil or, later, degenerate and unworthy. They were often tortured, killed, or imprisoned in horrific so-called hospitals.

➤ In the early 19th century, reformers like Pinel in France and Dix in the United States successfully worked toward kindly treatment of the severely disturbed in large mental hospitals, but these soon returned to deplorable conditions.

➤ Deinstitutionalization, begun in the 1950s in the United States, was a response to both the gross failure of large mental institutions and the apparent success of antipsychotic drugs. The alternative envisioned, community-based care, was never fully realized.

➤ Some assertive community treatment programs, however, have offered extensive, well-integrated, effective multidisciplinary care on an ongoing basis.

Structure of the Mental Health System

➤ Mental health professionals include psychiatrists (the only category that regularly prescribes drugs), clinical psychologists, counseling psychologists, counselors, psychiatric social workers, and psychiatric nurses. They differ in level and type of training, in the severity of problems they deal with, and in work setting.

➤ A survey of people with mental disorders in the United States found that, in the previous year, 22 percent had received treatment from a mental health professional, 59 percent had received no treatment, and most others briefly saw a medical doctor or nurse.

■ Biological Treatments

A person diagnosed with a mental disorder might be treated by biological means (most often drugs), psychological means (psychotherapy of one form or another), or both. Biological treatments attempt to relieve the disorder by directly altering bodily processes. In the distant past, such treatments included drilling holes in the skull to let out bad spirits and bloodletting to drain diseased humors. Today, in decreasing order of extent of use, the three main types of biological treatments are drugs, electroconvulsive shock therapy, and psychosurgery.

Drugs

A new era in the treatment of mental disorders began in the early 1950s when two French psychiatrists, Jean Delay and Pierre Deniker (1952), reported that they had reduced or abolished the psychotic symptoms of schizophrenia with a drug called chlorpromazine. Today, a plethora of drugs is available for treating essentially all major varieties of mental disorders.

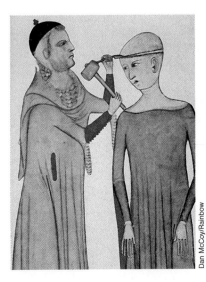

Madness as possession This 12th-century painting probably depicts trephination (piercing the skull to permit evil spirits to escape). With the revival of the medical model in the late Middle Ages, people gave up the use of trephination and other brutal treatments that were based on the belief that abnormal behavior indicates possession.

Drugs for mental disorders have been far from unmixed blessings, however. They are not magic bullets that zero in on and correct a disordered part of the mental machinery while leaving the rest of the machinery untouched. Drugs used to treat mental disorders nearly always produce undesirable side effects. Some of the drugs are also addictive, and the attempt to withdraw from them sometimes produces symptoms worse than those for which the drug was prescribed. As you read of the three categories of drugs described below, notice their drawbacks as well as their benefits.

5 ─ ─ ─ ─ ─ ─ ─ ─ ─ ─ ─ ─ ─ ─ ◀
What is known about the mechanisms, effectiveness, and limitations of drugs used to treat schizophrenia, generalized anxiety, and depression?

Antipsychotic Drugs

Antipsychotic drugs are used to treat schizophrenia and other disorders in which psychotic symptoms (such as hallucinations and delusions) predominate. Chlorpromazine (sold as Thorazine) was the first such drug, but now there are many others. Well-designed experiments have shown repeatedly that such drugs reduce and in some cases abolish the hallucinations, delusions, and bizarre actions that characterize the active phase of schizophrenia and that they reduce the need for hospitalization (Stroup & others, 2006). As noted in **Chapter 16,** all antipsychotic drugs in use today decrease the activity of the neurotransmitter dopamine at certain synapses in the brain, and that effect is believed to be responsible, directly or indirectly, for the reduction in psychotic symptoms.

Over the past two decades or so much research and discussion has centered on reputed differences between two classes of antipsychotic drugs—the so-called *typical* and *atypical* antipsychotics. The typical drugs—of which haloperidol is most used—were the ones first developed, and the atypical drugs—including olanzapine and risperidone—are newer. Early research on the atypical drugs, done mostly by the pharmaceutical companies themselves, suggested that they were more effective than the older drugs in reducing psychotic symptoms and that they produced fewer harmful side effects. Recent, unbiased, large-scale studies conducted with public funds, however, have questioned these contentions (Carpenter & Buchanan, 2008; Stargardt & others, 2008). At present there is no strong evidence that the atypical drugs are better overall than the less-expensive typical drugs. In terms of their biochemical mechanisms, both classes of drugs work primary by decreasing dopamine activity. Some of the atypical drugs may also alter activity of some other neurotransmitters in the brain, especially serotonin; but at present it is unknown if those effects play a useful therapeutic role.

All antipsychotic drugs have unpleasant and damaging side effects. They can produce dizziness, confusion, nausea, dry mouth, blurred vision, heart rate irregularities, constipation, weight gain, heightened risk for diabetes, sexual impotence in men, and disrupted menstrual cycles in women (Haddad & Sharma, 2007; McKim, 2006; Stroup & others, 2006). They also interfere with motor-control processes in the brain and sometimes produce symptoms akin to Parkinson's disease, including shaking and difficulty in controlling voluntary movements. Many patients who take such drugs for many years develop a serious and often irreversible motor disturbance called *tardive dyskinesia,* manifested as involuntary jerking of the tongue, face, and sometimes other muscles.

Given such effects, it is no wonder that many patients diagnosed with schizophrenia stop taking the drugs as soon as the psychotic symptoms decline, or sometimes even before. Clinicians usually regard such "failure to comply" as a serious problem, as there is indeed evidence that, for many patients, such noncompliance means that they are more likely to have another psychotic episode and require readmission to the hospital. A fact ignored by many clinicians, however, is that a significant number of patients who stop taking the drugs do quite well without them (Harrow & Jobe, 2007). These patients are frequently unknown to the clinicians because, not needing further treatment, they do not return to the clinic. As far I can tell—and I have looked—there have been no research studies designed to test the long-term consequences of living without the drugs compared to living with them, or to determine which patients really need the drugs and which ones can do without them, or to test the logically plausible hypothesis that long-term use of the drugs might alter the brain in ways that *prevent* eventual full recovery from schizophrenia. The mental health industry, whose research is financed mostly by pharmaceutical companies, has shown little interest in these questions.

Antianxiety Drugs

Drugs used primarily to treat anxiety are commonly referred to as *tranquilizers*. At one time, barbiturates such as phenobarbital were often prescribed as tranquilizers, and many people became seriously addicted to them. During the 1960s, barbiturates were replaced by a new, safer group of antianxiety drugs belonging to a chemical class called *benzodiazepines* [**ben**-zoh-di-**az**-uh-peens], including chlordiazepoxide (sold as Librium) and diazepam (sold as Valium). According to some estimates, by 1975 more than 10 percent of adults in the United States and Western Europe were taking these drugs on a regular basis (Lickey & Gordon, 1991; Lipman, 1989).

Biochemically, benzodiazepines appear to produce their tranquilizing effects by augmenting the action of the neurotransmitter GABA (gamma-aminobutyric acid) in the brain (Hefti, 2005). GABA is the brain's main inhibitory neurotransmitter, so its increased action decreases the excitability of neurons almost everywhere in the brain. Side effects of benzodiazepines at high doses include drowsiness, a decline in motor coordination, and a consequent increase in accidents. More important, the drugs enhance the action of alcohol; an amount of alcohol that would otherwise be safe can produce a coma or death in people taking a benzodiazepine. In addition, benzodiazepines are now known to be at least moderately addictive, and very unpleasant withdrawal symptoms—sleeplessness, shakiness, anxiety, headaches, and nausea—occur in those who stop taking them after having taken high doses for a long time (Bond & Lader, 1996).

Early research with benzodiazepines tended to show that they were highly effective in relieving generalized anxiety. More recent, more carefully controlled studies, however, have shown them to be of questionable effectiveness (Martin & others, 2007). Such studies have revealed that more than half of the people who were randomly assigned to the benzodiazepine condition dropped out either because of lack of anxiety relief or because of intolerance of the side effects (Martin & others, 2007). Overall, in the more recent studies, those on a placebo (a pill with no active chemicals) did nearly as well as those on a benzodiazepine.

Today benzodiazepines are still often used to treat generalized anxiety disorder and panic disorder, but are rarely used for other anxiety disorders. Their use for all anxiety disorders has declined partly because of growing recognition of their harmful side effects and partly because of evidence that anxiety may be better treated with antidepressant drugs, in the SSRI class, described below (Mathew & Hoffman, 2009). The effectiveness of antidepressant drugs in treating anxiety disorders is consistent with the evidence, discussed in **Chapter 16,** for a close biological relationship between anxiety and depression.

Antidepressant Drugs

From the 1960s into the mid-1980s, the drugs most commonly used to treat depression belonged to a chemical class referred to as *tricyclics,* of which imipramine (sold as Tofranil) and amitriptyline (sold as Elavil) are examples. Tricyclics block the normal reuptake of the neurotransmitters serotonin and norepinephrine into pre-synaptic neurons after their release into the synapse, thereby prolonging the action of the transmitter molecules on post-synaptic neurons (Hefti, 2005). Beginning in the mid-1980s, a newer class of antidepressants, referred to as *selective serotonin reuptake inhibitors (SSRIs),* which block the reuptake of serotonin but not

"...so I said," Hold on Doc, later for the family therapy. Let's just put the whole kit n'kaboodle on anti-depressants!"

SIPRESS

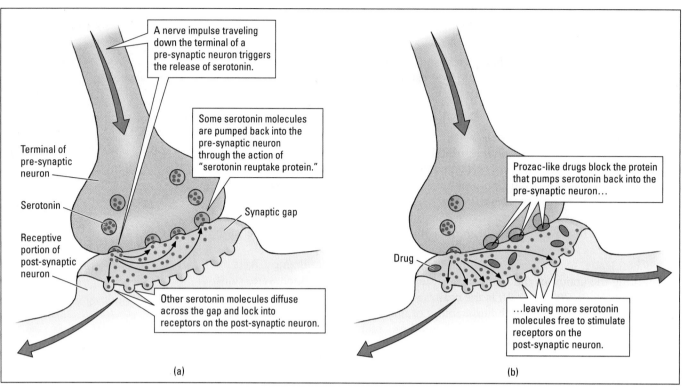

A nerve impulse traveling down the terminal of a pre-synaptic neuron triggers the release of serotonin.

Some serotonin molecules are pumped back into the pre-synaptic neuron through the action of "serotonin reuptake protein."

Terminal of pre-synaptic neuron

Serotonin

Synaptic gap

Receptive portion of post-synaptic neuron

Other serotonin molecules diffuse across the gap and lock into receptors on the post-synaptic neuron.

(a)

Prozac-like drugs block the protein that pumps serotonin back into the pre-synaptic neuron...

Drug

...leaving more serotonin molecules free to stimulate receptors on the post-synaptic neuron.

(b)

FIGURE 17.1 How Prozac and other SSRI antidepressant drugs work (a) When serotonin is released into a synapse, its action is normally cut short by reuptake into the pre-synaptic neuron. (b) Selective serotonin reuptake inhibitors block this reuptake and thereby increase the action of serotonin on the post-synaptic neuron.

of other monoamine transmitters, overtook the tricyclic drugs as the first line of treatment for depression (Gitlin, 2009). Among the most often prescribed of these drugs are fluoxetine (Prozac), citalopram (Celexa), and sertraline (Zoloft). To visualize how such drugs act at the synapse, see Figure 17.1.

Many research studies have demonstrated that the tricyclics and SSRIs are about equally effective in treating depression. With either type of drug, approximately 50 percent of people suffering from major depression show a clinically significant improvement in mood, compared with about 30 percent who improve over the same time period if given a placebo (inactive substance) instead (Hollon & others, 2002). The SSRIs are preferred because of their milder side effects. Tricyclics are much more likely to cause death if taken in overdose than are SSRIs, and they are also more likely to produce such disruptive and discomforting side effects as fatigue, dry mouth, and blurred vision. Still, in some people, the SSRIs do produce unwanted side effects, including reduced sexual drive, headache, nausea, and diarrhea (Gitlin, 2009; Hollon & others, 2002).

As noted in **Chapter 16,** the effects of antidepressant drugs on neurotransmitters occur immediately, but the antidepressant effects take several weeks to develop. This fact suggests that some gradual process—maybe including the growth of new neurons in the brain—underlies the therapeutic effect (Perera & others, 2008). However, despite many theories and much study, researchers still do not know just how antidepressants reduce depression.

Placebo Effects

When drugs are tested for their effectiveness in treating disorders, comparisons are made ideally among at least three different treatment conditions: *no treatment, placebo,* and *drug.* A *placebo* (discussed in **Chapter 2**) is an inactive substance that is indistinguishable in appearance from the drug. Such experiments are conducted in a double-blind manner (also discussed in **Chapter 2**)—that is, in such a way that neither the patients nor the researchers who evaluate them are told who is receiving the drug and who is receiving the placebo. Experiments of this sort allow researchers to separate out three different categories of effects through which people improve:

- *Spontaneous remission effect* refers to any improvement shown by those who receive no treatment.
- *Placebo effect* refers to any improvement shown by those receiving the placebo that goes beyond the improvement shown by those receiving no treatment.
- *Drug effect* refers to any improvement shown by those receiving the drug that goes beyond the improvement shown by those receiving the placebo.

When experiments of this sort are conducted with antianxiety or antidepressant drugs, the general finding is that most of the improvement results from the spontaneous remission and placebo effects; only a small amount of improvement can be attributed to the drug itself (Kirsch, 2000; Wampold & others, 2005). For example, in an analysis of such experiments for a variety of antidepressant drugs, Irving Kirsch concluded that about 25 percent of the improvement in those receiving the drug could be attributed to spontaneous remission, about 50 percent could be attributed to the placebo effect, and 25 percent could be attributed to the drug's chemical effects (Kirsch & Sapirstein, 1998).

Even this amount of drug effect, however, may be an overestimation, because the analysis was based only on experiments that had been published. Pharmaceutical companies sponsor most drug experiments, and the companies usually choose to publish only those that show significant effects of the drugs. In a later analysis, in which he managed to obtain data from unpublished as well as published experiments, Kirsch (2005) found that the drug effect was even smaller than in his earlier analysis. In fact, when all experiments were combined, the difference between the effects of the antidepressant drugs and the placebo was so small as to be considered clinically insignificant. Kirsch and others who reviewed these data have concluded that the millions of people who take antidepressant drugs and then feel better improve primarily because of the placebo effect—that is, primarily because they *expect* to feel better (Hammond, 2007).

Why is the placebo effect so powerful in treating depression? As discussed in **Chapter 16,** depression is characterized by feelings of helplessness and hopelessness. In fact, for some people those feelings *are* the disorder. Simply participating in a treatment program—meeting regularly with someone who seems to care and taking what is believed be a useful drug—may restore feelings of control and hope and produce expectations of improvement. These feelings and expectations may promote life changes, such as improved self-care and more involvement with friends, that lead to further improvement in mood. All such effects, which derive from the belief that one's disorder is being treated, contribute to the placebo effect. From this point of view it is really not surprising that a believable placebo may be the best treatment for depression.

6
What are three different reasons why symptoms of a disorder may decline after being treated with a drug? What evidence suggests that only a small percentage of the improvement following drug treatment for depression results from the chemical effects of the drug? Why might the power of suggestion, or expectancy, be especially effective in the treatment of depression?

"Play some Frisbee, chew on an old sock, bark at a squirrel. If that doesn't make you feel better, eat some cheese with a pill in it."

Other Biologically Based Treatments

The increased use of drugs, coupled with the increased understanding and acceptance of psychotherapy, has led to the abandonment of most non-drug biological therapies for mental disorders. Two such treatments still used, however, are electroconvulsive therapy and, in very rare cases, psychosurgery.

Electroconvulsive Therapy

Electroconvulsive therapy, or *ECT,* is used primarily in cases of severe depression that do not respond to psychotherapy or antidepressant drugs. To the general public this treatment often seems barbaric, a remnant of the days when victims of mental disorders were tortured to exorcise the demons, and indeed it once was a brutal treatment. The brain seizure induced by the shock would cause muscular

7
Under what conditions and how is ECT used to treat depression? Why is it often administered just to the right half of the brain?

Electroconvulsive therapy ECT is the treatment of choice for very severe depression that does not respond to drug therapy. This man has been anesthetized (so he will be unconscious), given a muscle relaxant (so he will not show muscle spasms when the shock is given), and provided with a tube so that his breathing will not be impeded. The shock will be applied to the right side of his brain through the two black leads shown in the photo. Unilateral right-hemisphere ECT disrupts memory much less than does ECT applied across the whole brain.

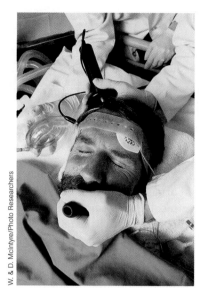

W. & D. McIntyre/Photo Researchers

contractions so violent that they sometimes broke bones. Today, however, ECT is administered in a way that is painless and quite safe (Keltner & Boschini, 2009; Lisanby, 2007). Before receiving the shock, the patient is put under general anesthesia and given a muscle-blocking drug, so that no pain will be felt and no damaging muscle contractions will occur. Then an electric current is passed through the patient's skull, triggering a seizure in the brain that lasts approximately one minute. Usually such treatments are given in a series, one every 2 or 3 days for about 2 weeks.

According to most estimates, somewhere between 50% and 80% of people who are suffering from major depression and have not been helped by other forms of treatment experience remission with ECT (Hollon & others, 2002; Lisanby, 2007). In some cases, the remission is permanent; in others, depression recurs after several months or more, and then another series of treatments may be given. Nobody knows how ECT produces its antidepressant effect. In nonhuman animals, such shocks cause immediate release of all varieties of neurotransmitters, followed by longer-lasting changes in transmitter production and in the sensitivity of post-synaptic receptors (Nutt & Glue, 1993). The shocks also stimulate the growth of new neurons in the brain, which some believe may contribute to their antidepressant effect (Jacobs, 2004).

Clinicians and researchers have long been concerned about the possibility that ECT can produce permanent brain damage. This concern is fueled by evidence of brain damage in laboratory animals subjected to intense electroconvulsive shocks. To date there is no evidence that such damage occurs with the shock levels used in clinical treatment, but temporary disruptions in cognition, especially in memory, do occur (Mathew & others, 2005). When ECT is applied in the traditional manner—*bilaterally,* so that the current runs across both of the brain's hemispheres—the patient typically loses memory for events that occurred a day or two before the treatment. With a series of such treatments, some memories for earlier events may also be lost, but these usually return within a month after the last treatment (Calev & others, 1993; Lisanby, 2007).

Many clinicians today apply ECT *unilaterally,* just to the right half of the brain. With a sufficiently high shock level, that procedure appears to be as effective, or nearly as effective, as the bilateral procedure in reducing depression, and it causes little or no loss of conscious, verbal memories (Sackeim & others, 2000; UK ECT Review Group, 2003). Unilateral right-brain treatment may, however, cause some loss of pictorial memories, as indexed by reduced recognition of geometric designs seen before the shocks (Sachs & Gelenberg, 1988). Such results are consistent with other findings (discussed in **Chapter 5**) showing that the left half of the brain is more involved than the right in verbal processes and the right half is more involved in visuospatial processes and emotion.

Psychosurgery and Deep Brain Stimulation

A treatment of last resort today is ***psychosurgery,*** which involves surgically cutting or producing lesions in portions of the brain to relieve a mental disorder. From the late 1930s into the early 1950s, tens of thousands of men and women were subjected to an operation called *prefrontal lobotomy,* in which the anterior (front) portions of the frontal lobes were surgically separated from the rest of the brain. Individuals with severe cases of schizophrenia, bipolar disorder, depression, obsessive-compulsive disorder, and pathological violence were subjected to the operation. Prefrontal lobotomy was so highly regarded that in 1949 the Portuguese neurologist who developed the technique, Egas Moniz, was awarded the Nobel Prize.

By the mid-1950s, however, prefrontal lobotomies had gone out of style, partly because newly developed drug treatments offered an alternative and partly because of mounting evidence that, although lobotomy relieved people of their incapacitating emotions, it left them severely incapacitated in new ways (Valenstein, 1986). The prefrontal lobes are a critical part of the brain's circuitry for integrating plans with action (discussed in **Chapter 5**), and lobotomized patients showed lifelong inabilities to make plans and behave according to them. As a consequence, they needed constant care.

Refined versions of psychosurgery were developed in the 1960s and continue to be used in rare cases today. The new procedures involve destruction of very small areas of the brain by applying radiofrequency current through fine wire electrodes implanted temporarily into the brain. Today this procedure is used primarily for treatment of highly incapacitating cases of obsessive-compulsive disorder that have proven, over many years, to be untreatable by any other means.

> ----------------------------- **8**
>
> **How are modern, refined forms of psychosurgery sometimes used today in the treatment of obsessive-compulsive disorder?**

As was noted in **Chapter 16,** obsessive-compulsive disorder is often associated with abnormal amounts of activity in a neural circuit that is involved in converting conscious thoughts into actions. This circuit includes a portion of the prefrontal cortex, a portion of the limbic system called the cingulum, and parts of the basal ganglia. Surgical destruction either of a portion of the cingulum or of a specific neural pathway that enters the basal ganglia reduces or abolishes obsessive-compulsive symptoms in about 50 percent of people who could not be successfully treated in any other way (Mashour & others, 2005). These procedures produce quite serious side effects in some patients, however, including confusion, weight gain, depression, and, very occasionally, epilepsy (Mashour & others, 2005; Trimble, 1996).

Since the mid 1990s, a number of brain surgeons have been experimenting with a new, safer procedure, called *deep brain stimulation,* for treating intractable cases of obsessive-compulsive disorder (Greenberg & others, 2006; Larson, 2008). In this procedure a hair-thin wire electrode is implanted permanently into the brain—usually in the cingulum or in a portion of the basal ganglia. The electrode can be activated in order to electrically stimulate, rather than destroy, the neurons lying near it. High-frequency but low-intensity stimulation through the electrode is believed to desynchronize and disrupt ongoing neural activity and in that way to have an effect comparable to producing a lesion. This effect, unlike that of a lesion, can be reversed just by turning off the electrical current. Trials with deep brain stimulation suggest that it may be as effective as psychosurgery, without the negative side effects (Husted & Shapira, 2004; Larson, 2008).

> ----------------------------- **9**
>
> **What is the advantage of deep brain stimulation over current forms of psychosurgery?**

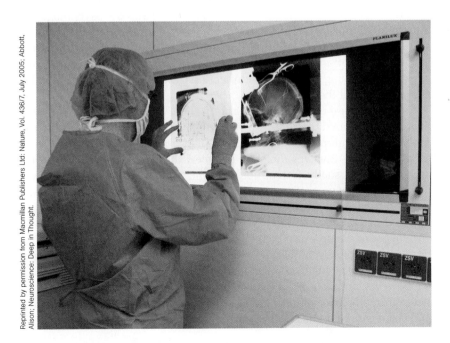

Reprinted by permission from Macmillan Publishers Ltd: Nature, Vol. 436/7, July 2005; Abbott, Alison; Neuroscience: Deep in Thought.

Preparation for deep brain stimulation As a thin wire electrode is inserted into the patient's brain, the surgeon keeps track of its position through brain imaging.

Biological treatments target the brain physically in order to alleviate mental disorders.

Drugs

➤ Antipsychotic drugs treat psychotic symptoms, but do not cure people. All such drugs decrease the effectiveness of the neurotransmitter dopamine, and the newer (atypical) drugs also affect other neurotransmitters. All have unpleasant side effects, some quite serious.

➤ Antianxiety drugs, in a chemical class called benzodiazepines, are used mainly for generalized anxiety disorder and panic disorder. They increase inhibitory activity in the brain, thus reducing excitability; but they are addictive, have potentially harmful side effects, and cause unpleasant withdrawal symptoms.

➤ Antidepressant drugs include tricyclics and selective serotonin reuptake inhibitors (SSRIs); the former prolong the action of serotonin and norepinephrine in the brain, while the latter affect only serotonin. They are equally effective in treating depression, but SSRIs have milder side effects and are therefore more often prescribed. The SSRIs are also used to treat anxiety disorders.

➤ Studies that break down patients' improvement after taking an antidepressant drug into three categories—spontaneous recovery, placebo effect, and drug effect—reveal that much if not most of the improvement is due to the placebo effect. Hope, provided by the sense of being treated, may be the principal ingredient of any treatment for depression.

Other Biological Treatments

➤ In electroconvulsive therapy (ECT), used to treat depression not helped by other means, electrical current is applied to the skull to induce brain seizures. It is quite safe and effective but causes some loss of recent memories when given across the whole brain rather than just across the right hemisphere.

➤ Prefrontal lobotomies, once common, are no longer performed. Today psychosurgery involving small, localized lesions is used occasionally for incapacitating obsessive-compulsive disorder. It is often effective but can produce harmful side effects.

➤ Deep brain stimulation, a possible alternative to psychosurgery, uses electrical current to disrupt activity rather than destroy tissue at specific brain locations.

◼ Psychotherapy I: Psychodynamic and Humanistic Therapies

While biological treatment for mental disorder is aimed at improving moods, thinking, and behavior through altering the chemistry and physiology of the brain, psychological treatment, referred to as *psychotherapy,* is aimed at improving the same through talk, reflection, learning, and practice.

The two approaches—biological and psychological—are not incompatible. Indeed, most clinicians believe that the best treatment for many people who suffer from serious mental disorders involves a combination of drug therapy and psychotherapy. In theory as well as in practice, the biological and the psychological are tightly entwined. Changes of any sort in the brain can alter the way a person feels, thinks, and behaves; and changes in feeling, thought, and behavior can alter the brain. The brain is not a "hard-wired" machine. It is a dynamic biological organ that is constantly growing new neural connections and losing old ones as it adapts to new experiences and thoughts.

Psychotherapy can be defined as any theory-based, systematic procedure, conducted by a trained therapist, for helping people to overcome or cope with mental problems through psychological rather than directly physiological means. Psychotherapy usually involves dialogue between the person in need and the therapist, and its aim is usually to restructure some aspect of the person's way of feeling, thinking, or behaving. If you have ever helped a child overcome a fear, encouraged a friend to give up a bad habit, or cheered up a despondent roommate, you have engaged in a process akin to psychotherapy, though less formal.

One count, made a number of years ago, identified more than 400 nominally different forms of psychotherapy (Karasu, 1986). Psychotherapists may work with groups of people, or with couples or families, as well as with individuals. In this chapter, however, our discussion is limited to four classic varieties of individual therapy. We examine *psychodynamic* and *humanistic* therapies in this section, and *cognitive* and *behavioral* therapies in the next.

There was a time when many psychotherapists believed that their own approach was "right" and other approaches "wrong." Today, however, most therapists recognize strengths and weaknesses in each of the classic schools of thought in psychotherapy. As shown in Figure 17.2, nearly 30 percent of contemporary psychotherapists consider themselves to be "eclectic" or "integrative" in orientation—that is, they do not identify with any one school of thought but use methods gleaned from various schools. Even among those who do identify with a particular school of thought, most borrow techniques and ideas from other schools.

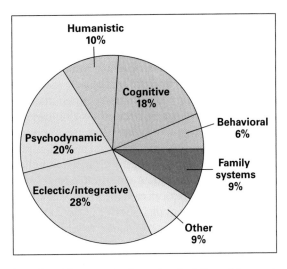

As you will discover as you read about them, each major approach in psychotherapy draws on a set of psychological principles and ideas that apply to adaptive as well as to maladaptive behavior.

- The psychodynamic approach focuses on the idea that unconscious memories and emotions influence our conscious thoughts and actions.

- The humanistic approach focuses on the value of self-esteem and self-direction, and on the idea that people often need psychological support from others in order to pursue freely their own chosen goals.

- The cognitive approach focuses on the idea that people's ingrained, habitual ways of thinking affect their moods and behavior.

- The behavioral approach focuses on the roles of basic learning processes in the development and maintenance of adaptive and maladaptive ways of responding to the environment.

Principles of Psychodynamic Therapies

Sigmund Freud, whose theory of personality was discussed in **Chapter 15,** was the primary founder of psychodynamic psychotherapy; indeed, he is widely regarded as the founder of all of psychotherapy. As noted in **Chapter 15,** Freud used the term *psychoanalysis* to refer to both his theory of personality and his methods of therapy. Today the term ***psychoanalysis*** is generally used to refer to those forms of therapy that adhere most closely to the ideas set forth by Freud, and the broader term ***psychodynamic therapy*** is used to include psychoanalysis and therapies that are more loosely based on Freud's ideas. In the survey depicted in Figure 17.2, only 10 percent of those who categorized their therapy as psychodynamic identified their specific method as psychoanalysis (Bechtoldt & others, 2001). In what follows, I set forth some of the main principles and methods that are common to most if not all psychodynamic therapies.

The Idea That Unconscious Conflicts, Often Deriving from Early Childhood Experiences, Underlie Mental Disorders

The most central, uniting idea of all psychodynamic theories is the idea that mental problems arise from unresolved mental conflicts, which themselves arise from the holding of contradictory motives and beliefs. The motives, beliefs, and conflicts may be unconscious, or partly so, but they nevertheless influence conscious thoughts and actions. The word *dynamic* refers to force, and *psychodynamic* refers to the forceful, generally unconscious influences that conflicting

FIGURE 17.2 Theoretical orientations of a sample of psychotherapists Shown here are the results of a survey in which North American clinical and counseling psychologists were asked to name the theoretical orientation with which they most closely identified (Bechtoldt & others, 2001). (Note: The "humanistic" category includes those who labeled their practice as humanistic, Rogerian, or existential; and the "psychodynamic" category includes those who labeled their practice as psychodynamic or psychoanalytic.)

Young Dr. Freud Sigmund Freud, shown here at age 29 (in 1885), started his career as a neurologist. He observed that many patients came to him with complaints for which there were no apparent medical causes, and this led him eventually to develop the method of therapy that he called *psychoanalysis*.

Rue des Archives/The Granger Collection, New York

10

According to psychodynamic therapists, what are the underlying sources of mental disorders?

motives and beliefs can have on a person's consciously experienced emotions, thoughts, and behavior.

Freud himself argued, in some of his writing (e.g., Freud, 1933/1964), that the unconscious conflicts that cause trouble always originate in the first five or six years of life and have to do with infantile sexual and aggressive wishes, but few psychodynamic therapists today have retained that view. Most psychodynamic therapists today are concerned with conflicts that can originate at any time in life and have to do with any drives or needs that are important to the person. Still, however, most such therapists tend to see sexual and aggressive drives as particularly important, as these drives often conflict with learned beliefs and societal constraints. They also tend to see childhood as a particularly vulnerable period during which frightening or confusing experiences can produce lasting marks on a person's ways of feeling, thinking, and behaving. Such experiences might derive from such sources as sexual or physical abuse, lack of security, or lack of consistent love from parents.

In general, psychodynamic theorists see their approach as tightly linked, theoretically, to the field of developmental psychology. In their view, growing up necessarily entails the facing and resolving of conflicts; conflicts that are not resolved can produce problems later in life (Thompson & Cotlove, 2005).

The Idea That Patients' Observable Speech and Behavior Provide Clues to Their Unconscious Conflicts

11

According to psychodynamic therapists, what is the relationship between symptoms and disorders?

To a psychodynamic therapist, the symptoms that bring a person in for therapy and that are used to label a disorder, using *DSM-IV* or any other diagnostic guide, are just that—*symptoms*. They are surface manifestations of the disorder; the disorder itself is buried in the person's unconscious mind and must be unearthed before it can be treated.

For example, consider a patient who is diagnosed as having anorexia nervosa (an eating disorder discussed in **Chapter 16**). To a psychodynamic therapist, the fundamental problem with the person is not the failure to eat but is something deeper and more hidden—some conflict that makes her want to starve herself. Two people who have similar symptoms and identical diagnoses of anorexia nervosa may suffer from quite different underlying conflicts. One might be starving herself because she fears sex, and starvation is a way of forestalling her sexual development; another might be starving herself because she feels unaccepted for who she is, so she is trying to disappear. To a psychodynamic therapist, the first step in treatment of either woman is finding out why she is starving herself; quite likely, she herself is not conscious of the real reason (Binder, 2004).

To learn about the content of a patient's unconscious mind, the psychodynamic therapist must, in detective-like fashion, analyze clues found in the patient's speech and other forms of observable behavior. This is where Freud's term *psychoanalysis* comes from. The symptoms that brought the patient in for help, and the unique ways those symptoms are manifested, are one source of clues that the therapist considers. What other clues might be useful? Since the conscious mind usually attempts to act in ways that are consistent with conventional logic, Freud reasoned that the elements of thought and behavior that are *least* logical would provide the most useful clues. They would represent elements of the unconscious mind that leaked out relatively unmodified by consciousness. This insight led Freud to suggest that the most useful clues to a patient's unconscious motives and beliefs are found in the patient's free associations, dreams, and slips of the tongue or behavioral errors. These sources of clues are still widely used by psychodynamic therapists.

12

How do psychodynamic therapists use patients' free associations, dreams, and "mistakes" as routes to learn about their unconscious minds?

Free Associations as Clues to the Unconscious The technique of *free association* is one in which the patient is encouraged to sit back (or, in traditional psychoanalysis, to lie down on a couch), relax, free his or her mind, refrain from trying to be logical or "correct," and report every image or idea that enters his or her awareness, usually in response to some word or picture that the therapist provides as an initial stimulus. You might try this exercise yourself: Relax, free your mind from what you have just been reading or thinking about, and write down the words or ideas that come immediately to your mind in response to each of the following: *liquid, horse, soft, potato.* Now, when you examine your set of responses to these words, do they make any sense that was not apparent when you produced them? Do you believe that they give you any clues to your unconscious mind?

Dreams as Clues to the Unconscious Freud believed that dreams are the purest exercises of free association, so he asked patients to try to remember their dreams, or to write them down upon awakening, and to describe them to him. During sleep, conventional logic is largely absent, and the forces that normally hold down unconscious ideas are weakened. Still, even in dreams, according to Freud and other psychodynamic therapists, the unconscious is partially disguised. Freud distinguished the underlying, unconscious meaning of the dream (the latent content) from the dream as it is consciously experienced and remembered by the dreamer (the manifest content). The analyst's task in interpreting a dream is the same as that in interpreting any other form of free association: to see through the disguises and uncover the latent content from the manifest content.

The original therapeutic couch This photograph of Freud's consulting room shows the couch on which patients reclined while he sat, out of their line of sight, listening to their free associations. Contemporary psychodynamic therapists have generally abandoned the couch in favor of a more egalitarian face-to-face encounter.

Psychodynamic therapists hold that the disguises in dreams come in various forms. Some are unique to a particular person, but some are common to many people. Freud himself looked especially for sexual themes in dreams, and the common disguises that he wrote about have become known as *Freudian symbols,* some of which he described as follows (from Freud, 1900/1953):

> The Emperor and Empress (or King and Queen) as a rule really represent the dreamer's parents; and a Prince or Princess represents the dreamer himself or herself. . . . All elongated objects, such as sticks, tree-trunks, and umbrellas (the opening of these last being comparable to an erection) may stand for the male organ—as well as all long, sharp weapons, such as knives, daggers, and pikes. . . . Boxes, cases, chests, cupboards, and ovens represent the uterus, and also hollow objects, ships, and vessels of all kinds. Rooms in dreams are usually women; if the various ways in and out of them are represented, this interpretation is scarcely open to doubt. In this connection interest in whether the room is open or locked is easily intelligible. There is no need to name explicitly the key that unlocks the room.

Mistakes and Slips of the Tongue as Clues to the Unconscious Still other clues to the unconscious mind, used by psychodynamic therapists, are found in the mistakes that patients make in their speech and actions. In Freud's rather extreme view, mistakes are never simply random accidents but are always expressions of unconscious wishes or conflicts. In one of his most popular books, *The Psychopathology of Everyday Life,* Freud (1901/1990) supported this claim with numerous, sometimes amusing examples of such errors, along with his interpretations.

Freudian symbols in a work of art painted four centuries before Freud This is a detail from *The Garden of Earthly Delights,* painted in the late 15th century by the Dutch artist Hieronymus Bosch. It is believed to represent Bosch's conception of decadence or Hell. Notice the dreamlike (nightmarish) quality and the numerous Freudian symbols—the protruding, phallic-like objects and the womb-like enclosures.

For example, he reported an incident in which a young woman, complaining about the disadvantages of being a woman, stated, "A woman must be pretty if she is to please the men. A man is much better off. As long as he has his *five straight limbs* he needs no more." According to Freud, this slip involved a fusion of two separate clichés, four straight limbs and five senses, which would not have occurred had it not expressed an idea that was on the woman's mind (either unconscious or conscious mind) that she consciously would have preferred to conceal. In another context the same statement could have been a deliberate, slightly off-color joke; but Freud claims that in this case it was an honest slip of the tongue, as evidenced by the woman's great embarrassment upon realizing what she had said.

The Roles of Resistance and Transference in the Therapeutic Process

13
In psychodynamic therapy, how do resistance and transference contribute to the therapeutic process?

Psychodynamic therapists, from Freud's time through today, have found that patients often resist the therapist's attempt to bring their unconscious memories or wishes into consciousness (Weiner & Bornstein, 2009). The **resistance** may manifest itself in such forms as refusing to talk about certain topics, "forgetting" to come to therapy sessions, or arguing incessantly in a way that subverts the therapeutic process. Freud assumed that resistance stems from the general defensive processes by which people protect themselves from becoming conscious of anxiety-provoking thoughts. Resistance provides clues that therapy is going in the right direction, toward critical unconscious material; but it can also slow down the course of therapy or even bring it to a halt. To avoid triggering too much resistance, the therapist must present interpretations gradually, when the patient is ready to accept them.

Freud also observed that patients often express strong emotional feelings—sometimes love, sometimes anger—toward the therapist. Freud believed that the true object of such feelings is usually not the therapist but some other significant person in the patient's life whom the therapist symbolizes. Thus, **transference** is the phenomenon by which the patient's unconscious feelings about a significant person in his or her life are experienced consciously as feelings about the therapist. Psychodynamic therapists to this day consider transference to be especially useful in psychotherapy because it provides an opportunity for the patient to become aware of his or her strong emotions (Weiner & Bornstein, 2009). With help from the analyst, the patient can gradually become aware of the origin of those feelings and their true target.

The Relationship Between Insight and Cure

14
According to psychodynamic theories, how do insights into the patient's unconscious conflicts bring about a cure?

Psychodynamic therapy is essentially a process in which the analyst makes inferences about the patient's unconscious conflicts and helps the patient become conscious of those conflicts. How does such consciousness help? According to psychodynamic therapists from Freud on, it helps because, once conscious, the conflicting beliefs and wishes can be experienced directly and acted upon or, if they are unrealistic, can be modified by the conscious mind into healthier, more appropriate beliefs and pursuits (Thompson & Cotlove, 2005). At the same time, the patient is freed of the defenses that had kept that material repressed and has more psychic energy for other activities. But for all this to happen, the patient must truly accept the

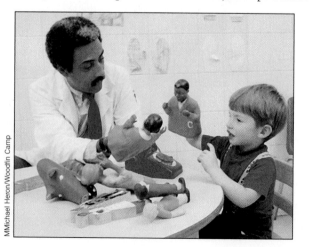

Play therapy In this extension of psychodynamic therapy, children use dolls and other toys to express their feelings. The therapist uses the child's actions as clues for understanding the child's feelings and motives. If the therapist joins in the play, as in this example, he must be careful to play only in a way that is responsive to and does not direct the child's actions.

MMichael Heron/Woodfin Camp

insights, viscerally as well as intellectually. The therapist cannot just tell the patient about the unconscious conflicts but must lead the patient gradually to actually experience the emotions and to arrive at the insights himself or herself.

A Case Example: Freud's Analysis of "the Rat Man"

All the just-described ideas about psychoanalysis can be made more vivid with a case example. Here, in much abbreviated form, is one of Freud's most famous and illustrative cases, that of a 29-year-old man referred to in the case history as "the Rat Man." This sketch necessarily leaves out many of the details and much of the subtlety of Freud's analysis, but it is useful nevertheless. You can decide for yourself from the sketch—or, better yet, from Freud's published report of the case (Freud, 1909/1963)—whether Freud's interpretation seems plausible or not.

The patient—I'll refer to him as RM—came to Freud complaining of various fears, obsessions, and compulsions that had begun 6 years earlier and had prevented him from completing his university studies and going on to a career. One of his most revealing symptoms—which gave the case its name—was an obsessive, extremely disturbing fantasy of a horrible torture applied both to RM's father and to the woman RM had been courting for the past 9 years, in which a pot of hungry rats strapped against the victims' buttocks would chew their way out through the only available opening. The fact that RM's father and beloved were both victims in this fantasy suggested to Freud that RM's problems lay in some conflict that had to do with both of these people and that elicited a great deal of unconscious anger in RM.

Freud's Analysis of the Immediate Cause of RM's Symptoms

Through dialogue in therapy, Freud learned that RM had, sometime before his symptoms had begun, expressed a desire to marry the woman he was courting, but his father had opposed this wish. This discovery led Freud to suppose that the man's conflict between his desire to marry his beloved and his desire to please his father was the immediate, precipitating cause of his symptoms. Unable to resolve this conflict consciously, he had allowed his unconscious mind to resolve it by making him too psychologically ill to complete his studies and start a career, which he viewed as a prerequisite for marriage. RM's psychological symptoms, according to Freud, protected him from having to choose between his own wish to marry the woman he loved and his father's wish that he not.

The relation between the rat fantasy and RM's father's opposition to the marriage was confirmed, in Freud's mind, by some of RM's free associations. For example, when Freud asked him to free-associate to the concept *rats* (*ratten* in German), RM immediately came up with *rates* (*raten* in German), meaning "installments" or "money." RM had previously mentioned that the woman had little money and that his father had wanted him to marry a certain wealthy relative.

Freud's Analysis of the Deeper, Childhood Cause of RM's Symptoms

Why was RM so reluctant to defy his father and proceed with a plan for marriage? By the time RM had started therapy, his father had already been dead for several years, so there was no realistic barrier to marriage. Freud guessed that the answer to this problem must lie in RM's early-childhood relationship with his father.

In one therapy session, RM described his mother's account of an event that took place when he was about 4 years old. RM's father had begun to beat him for having bitten his nurse, and RM had responded with such a torrent of angry words that his father, shaken, stopped the beating and never struck him again. In Freud's analysis, this incident had great significance. Freud assumed that biting the nurse was a sexual act for the boy and that the beating consolidated in RM a strong fear of his father's reactions to his sexual wishes—a fear that had lasted to that day and was preventing him from marrying the woman he loved.

> ---15
> **How did Freud's analysis explain the Rat Man's symptoms? How did free association and transference contribute to Freud's analysis?**

Moreover, according to Freud's analysis, RM's apparent power over his father at the age of 4—the fact that RM's anger had made his father stop the beating—helped stamp into RM the unconscious fear that he could kill his father through anger. From that time until his psychoanalysis, RM had never consciously experienced anger toward his father, and even now, with his father dead, he feared unconsciously that he could kill his father again if he expressed his anger. In addition, Freud saw direct symbolic links between this early childhood incident and the rat-torture obsession: Rats, biting into and destroying his woman friend and his father, symbolized another small, biting beast—RM himself, who had once bitten first his beloved nurse and then, with angry words, his father.

Transference also entered into Freud's analysis. At one point in therapy, RM reported a fantasy in which it was Freud, not RM's father, who was trying to control whom he married. At another point—which Freud regarded as the major breakthrough—RM became irrationally angry at Freud, jumping up from the couch and shouting abusive words at him. Reflecting on this incident later, RM recalled that his sudden anger was accompanied by a fear that Freud would beat him and that he had jumped up to defend himself. By this time in the analysis, it took little convincing for RM to share Freud's view that this was a reenactment of the incident in which his father had beaten him and he had responded so angrily.

According to Freud, this transference experience helped RM overcome his resistance to the idea that his problems arose from deep-seated fear and anger that he held toward his father. RM's conscious acceptance of those feelings led, according to Freud, to recovery from his symptoms. In a sad footnote to the case, Freud (1923/1963) added that after a short period as a healthy man, RM was killed as an officer in World War I.

Principles of Humanistic Therapy

Two fundamental psychological ideas that have been emphasized repeatedly in previous chapters of this book are these: (1) People have the capacity to make adaptive choices regarding their own behavior—choices that promote their survival and well-being. (2) In order to feel good about themselves and to feel motivated to move forward in life, people need to feel accepted and approved of by others. No approach to psychotherapy takes these two ideas more seriously than does the humanistic approach.

16

What is the primary goal of humanistic therapy? How does that goal relate to existentialist philosophy?

◄ As described in **Chapter 15,** the humanistic view of the person emphasizes the inner potential for positive growth—the so-called *actualizing potential.* For this potential to exert its effects, people must be conscious of their feelings and desires, not deny or distort them. Denial and distortion occur when people perceive that others who are important to them consistently disapprove of their feelings and desires. The goal of **humanistic therapy** is to help people regain awareness of their own desires and control of their own lives.

Carl Rogers The inventor of client-centered therapy (second from right) was a charismatic individual who personally embodied the empathy and genuineness that are the essence of his method of therapy.

Michael Rougier/LIFE Magazine, © Time Warner, Inc.

The humanistic movement in psychology originated in the mid-20th century. It grew partly out of existentialist philosophy, which focuses on the idea that human beings create their own life meanings (Hazler & Barwick, 2001). From an existentialist perspective, each person must decide for himself or herself what is true and worthwhile in order to live a full, meaningful life; meaning and purpose cannot be thrust upon a person from the outside.

The primary founder of humanistic psychotherapy was Carl Rogers, whose theory of personality was introduced in **Chapter 15.** Rogers (1951) called his therapeutic approach *client-centered therapy,* a term deliberately chosen to distinguish it from psychodynamic therapies. Client-centered therapy focuses on the abilities and insights of the client rather than those of the therapist. Practitioners of this approach today, however, more often refer to it as **person-centered therapy,** because they see the therapeutic process as involving a relationship between two unique persons— the client and the therapist (Mearns & Thorne, 2000; Wilkins, 2003). The therapist must attend to his or her own thoughts and feelings, as well as to those of the client, in order to respond in a supportive yet honest way to the client.

The core principles of person-centered therapy, elaborated upon below, all have to do with the relationship between the therapist and the client. The therapist lets the client take the lead in therapy, strives to understand and empathize with the client, and endeavors to think positively and genuinely of the client as a competent, valuable person. Through these means, the therapist tries to help the client regain the self-understanding and confidence necessary to control his or her own life.

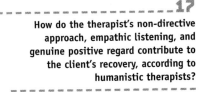

How do the therapist's non-directive approach, empathic listening, and genuine positive regard contribute to the client's recovery, according to humanistic therapists?

Allowing the Client to Take the Lead

Humanistic psychotherapists usually refer to those who come to them for help as *clients,* not as patients, because the latter term implies passivity and lack of ability. In humanistic therapy, at least in theory, the client is in charge; it is the therapist who must be "patient" enough to follow the client's lead. The therapist may take steps to encourage the client to start talking, to tell his or her story; but once the client has begun to talk it is the therapist's task to understand, not to direct it or interpret the client's words in ways that the client does not. While psychodynamic theorists may strain their patients' credulity with far-reaching interpretations, humanistic therapists more often just paraphrase what the client said, as a way of checking to be sure that they understood correctly.

Listening Carefully and Empathetically

The humanistic therapist tries to provide a context within which clients can become aware of and accept their own feelings and learn to trust their own decision-making abilities. To do so, the therapist must first and foremost truly listen to the client in an empathetic way (Raskin & Witty, 2007; Rogers, 1951). *Empathy* here refers to the therapist's attempt to comprehend what the client is saying or feeling at any given moment from the client's point of view rather than as an outsider. As part of the attempt to achieve and manifest such empathy, the therapist frequently reflects back the ideas and feelings that the client expresses. A typical exchange might go like this:

> **Client:** *My mother is a mean, horrible witch!*
>
> **Therapist:** *I guess you're feeling a lot of anger toward your mother right now.*

To an outsider, the therapist's response here might seem silly, a statement of the obvious. But to the client and therapist fully engaged in the process, the response serves several purposes. First, it shows the client that the therapist is listening and trying to understand. Second, it distills and reflects back to the client the feeling that seems to lie behind the client's words—a feeling of which the client may or may not have been fully aware at the moment. Third, it offers the client a chance to correct the therapist's understanding. By clarifying things to the therapist, the client clarifies them to himself or herself.

"Mom and Pop Psychology."
It'll make you feel like a kid again.

Providing Unconditional but Genuine Positive Regard

Unconditional positive regard implies a belief on the therapist's part that the client is worthy and capable even when the client may not feel or act that way. By expressing positive feelings about the client regardless of what the client says or does, the therapist creates a safe, nonjudgmental environment for the client to explore and express all of his or her thoughts and feelings. Through experiencing the therapist's positive regard, clients begin to feel more positive about themselves, an essential step if they are going to take charge of their lives. Unconditional positive regard does not imply agreement with everything the client says or approval of everything the client does, but it does imply faith in the client's underlying capacity to make appropriate decisions. Consider the following hypothetical exchange:

> **Client:** *Last semester in college I cheated on every test.*
>
> **Therapist:** *I guess what you're saying is that last semester you did something against your values.*

Notice that the therapist has said something positive about the client in relation to the misdeed without condoning the misdeed. The shift in focus from the negative act to the client's positive values affirms the client's inner worth and potential ability to make constructive decisions.

Humanistic therapists must work hard to be both positive and genuine in the feedback they supply to clients. They contend that it is impossible to fake empathy and positive regard, that the therapist must really experience them. If the therapist's words and true feelings don't match, the words will not be believable to the client. The capacity for genuine empathy and positive regard toward all clients might seem to be a rare quality, but Rogers suggests that it can be cultivated by deliberately trying to see things as the client sees them.

A Case Example: Rogers's Meetings with a Silent and Bitter Young Man

18 ◀ — — — — — — — — — — —

How did Rogers use empathy, unconditional positive regard, and genuineness to help a man who had been diagnosed with schizophrenia?

Rogers's greatest challenge as a therapist came when, as part of a research study, he conducted client-centered therapy with severely withdrawn inpatients in a state mental hospital (Rogers, 1967). One of these individuals was Jim, a 28-year-old man who had been hospitalized for 2 years with a diagnosis of schizophrenia. Prior to the two sessions excerpted below, Rogers had met with Jim once a week for months, and most of that time had been spent in silence. According to Rogers, these two sessions marked a turning point, because for the first time Jim began to express how he felt. As you read the exchange, notice the qualities of patience, empathy, and genuine positive regard reflected in Rogers's words.

> [At about 40 minutes into the session, marked mostly by silence.]
>
> **Jim:** *I just ain't no good to nobody, never was and never will be.*
>
> **Rogers:** *Feeling that now, hm? . . . Those really are lousy feelings. Just feel that you're no good at all, hm?*
>
> **Jim:** *Yeah.* [Muttering in a low, discouraged voice.] *That's what this guy I went to town with just the other day told me.*
>
> **Rogers:** *This guy that you went to town with really told you that you were no good? Is that what you're saying? Did I get that right?*
>
> **Jim:** *M-hm.*
>
> **Rogers:** *I guess the meaning of that, if I get it right, is that here's somebody that meant something to you and what does he think of you? Why, he's told you that he thinks you're no good at all. And that just really knocks the props out from under you.* [Jim weeps quietly.] *It just brings the tears.*

[Silence of 20 seconds.]

Jim: [Defiantly.] *I don't care though.*

Rogers: *You tell yourself you don't care at all, but somehow I guess some part of you cares because some part of you weeps over it.*

[This is followed by more silence, more weeping, and more reflection by Rogers on how it must hurt to feel that someone thinks you're no good. The next session also begins with lots of silence, punctuated by bitter statements in which Jim says that he wants to die. We pick up the conversation as Rogers breaks a long silence by asking whether Jim's wish to die is related to the comment discussed in the previous session.]

Rogers: *Can't help but wonder whether it's still true that some things this friend said to you—are those still part of the thing that makes you feel so awful?*

Jim: *In general, yes.*

Rogers: *M-hm.*

[Silence of 47 seconds, interrupted by another comment from Rogers. Then:]

Jim: *I ain't no good to nobody, or I ain't no good for nothin', so what's the use of living?*

Rogers: *M-hm. I guess a part of that is—here I'm kind of guessing and you can set me straight, I guess a part of that is that you felt, "I tried to be good for something as far as he was concerned. I really tried. And now—If I'm no good to him, if he feels I'm no good, then that proves I'm just no good to anybody." Is that, uh—anywhere near it?*

Jim: *Oh, well, other people have told me that, too.*

Rogers: *Yeah, m-hm. I see. So you feel if, if you go by what others—what several others have said, then, you are no good. No good to anybody.*

[This is followed by more silence, interrupted by a few comments along the same track. Then:]

Jim: [Muttering in discouraged tone.] *That's why I want to go, 'cause I don't care what happens.*

Rogers: *M-hm, m-hm . . . You don't care what happens. And I guess I'd just like to say—I care about you. And, I care what happens.*

[Silence of 30 seconds, and then Jim bursts into tears.]

Rogers: [Tenderly] *Somehow that just—makes the feelings pour out.* [Silence of 35 seconds.] *And you just weep and weep. And feel so badly.*

Commenting on this transaction, Rogers (1967) wrote:

Jim Brown, who sees himself as stubborn, bitter, mistreated, worthless, useless, hopeless, unloved, unlovable, experiences my caring. In that moment his defensive shell cracks wide open, and can never be quite the same. When someone cares for him, and when he feels and experiences this caring, he becomes a softer person whose years of stored-up hurt come pouring out in anguished sobs. He is not the shell of hardness and bitterness, the stranger to tenderness. He is a person hurt beyond words, and aching for the love and caring which alone can make him human. This is evident in his sobs. It is evident too in his returning to my office [shortly after the session], partly for a cigarette, partly to say spontaneously that he will return.

After this session, according to Rogers, Jim gradually became more open, spontaneous, and optimistic at their meetings. After several months, he was able to leave the hospital and support himself with a job. Eight years later, on his own initiative, Jim called Rogers to tell him that he was still employed, had friends, was content with life, and that his feelings toward Rogers were still important, even though they had not been in touch during all that time (Meador & Rogers, 1973).

Talk, reflection, learning, and practice are the tools psychotherapists use to help people.

Principles of Psychodynamic Therapies

➤ An assumption of this approach is that mental disorders arise from unresolved mental conflicts that, though unconscious, strongly influence conscious thought and action.

➤ The psychodynamic therapist's job is to identify the unconscious conflict from observable clues, such as dreams, free association, mistakes, and slips of the tongue. The goal is to help the patient become aware of the conflicting beliefs and wishes and thus be able to deal with them.

➤ The patient's resistance to the uncovering of unconscious material suggests that the therapist is on the right track. Transference of feelings about significant persons in the patient's life to the therapist helps the patient become aware of these strong emotions.

➤ The case of "the Rat Man" illustrates all the preceding principles, as well as Freud's belief that problematic conflicts generally originate in early childhood and involve sexual and aggressive wishes.

Principles of Humanistic Therapies

➤ Humanistic therapists strive to help clients accept their own feelings and desires, a prerequisite for self-actualization (positive, self-directed psychological growth).

➤ Clients may fail to accept (deny and distort) their feelings and desires because they perceive that these are disapproved of by valued others.

➤ The humanistic therapist lets clients take the lead, listens carefully and empathetically, and provides unconditional but genuine positive regard.

➤ A case example shows Carl Rogers, the founder of this approach, helping a client diagnosed with schizophrenia emerge from silence, pain, and bitterness to live a satisfying life.

▮ Psychotherapy II: Cognitive and Behavioral Therapies

19

In what ways are cognitive and behavioral therapies similar to each other?

Cognitive and behavioral therapies are in many ways similar. Whereas psychodynamic and humanistic therapies tend to be holistic in their approach, focusing on the whole person, cognitive and behavioral therapies typically focus more directly and narrowly on the specific symptoms and problems that the client presents. Cognitive and behavioral therapists both are also very much concerned with data; they use objective measures to assess whether or not the treatment given is helping the client overcome the problem that is being treated. Many therapists today combine cognitive and behavioral methods, in what they call **cognitive-behavioral therapy.** Here, however, we will discuss the two separately, as they involve distinct assumptions and methods.

Principles of Cognitive Therapy

20

According to cognitive therapists, what is the source of clients' behavioral and emotional problems?

Cognitive therapy arose in the 1960s as part of a shift in the overall field of psychology toward greater focus on the roles of thoughts, beliefs, and attitudes in controlling behavior. In previous chapters (especially **Chapters 13 and 15**) you have read of evidence that people's beliefs and ingrained, habitual ways of thinking affect their behavior and emotions. Cognitive therapy begins with the assumption that people disturb themselves through their own, often illogical beliefs and thoughts. Maladaptive beliefs and thoughts make reality seem worse than it is and in that way produce anxiety or depression. The goal of cognitive therapy is to identify maladaptive ways of thinking and replace them with adaptive ways that provide a base for more effective coping with the real world. Unlike psychoanalysis, cognitive therapy generally centers on conscious thoughts, though such thoughts may be so ingrained and automatic that they occur with little conscious effort.

Founder of rational-emotive therapy Albert Ellis, who died in 2007 at age 93, was a colorful individual who, in his practice, took a highly assertive role with clients. He would refer to their maladaptive, irrational thoughts with such terms as "musturbation" and "awfulizing."

Courtesy of Albert Ellis Institute

The two best-known pioneers of cognitive therapy are Albert Ellis and Aaron Beck. Both started their careers in the 1950s as psychodynamic therapists but became disenchanted with that approach (Bowles, 2004; Ellis, 1986). Each was impressed by the observation that clients seemed to distort, mentally, their experiences in ways that quite directly produced their problems or symptoms. Ellis (who died in 2007) referred to his specific brand of cognitive therapy as *rational-emotive therapy*, highlighting his belief that rational thought will improve clients' emotions.

Here we will look briefly at three general principles of cognitive therapy: the identification and correction of maladaptive beliefs and thoughts; the establishment of clear-cut goals and steps for achieving them; and the changing role of the therapist, from that of teacher early in the process to that of consultant later on.

Identifying and Correcting Maladaptive Beliefs and Habits of Thought

Different cognitive therapists take different approaches to pointing out their patients' irrational ways of thinking. Beck, as you will see later (in the case example), tends to take a Socratic approach, in which, through questioning, he gets the patient himself or herself to discover and correct the irrational thought (Beck & Weishaar, 2007). Ellis, in contrast, took a more direct and blunt approach. He gave humorous names to certain styles of irrational thinking. Thus, *musturbation* is the irrational belief that one must have some particular thing or must act in some particular way in order to be happy or worthwhile. If a client said, "I have to get all A's this semester in college," Ellis might respond, "You're musturbating again." *Awfulizing*, in Ellis's vocabulary, is the mental exaggeration of setbacks or inconveniences. A client who felt bad for a whole week because of a dent in her new car might be told, "Stop awfulizing."

21
How did Ellis explain people's negative emotions in terms of their irrational beliefs?

The following dialogue between Ellis (1962) and a client not only illustrates Ellis's blunt style but also makes explicit his theory of the relationship between thoughts and emotions—a theory shared by most cognitive therapists. The client began the session by complaining that he was unhappy because some men with whom he played golf didn't like him. Ellis, in response, claimed that the client's reasoning was illogical—the men's not liking him couldn't make him unhappy.

> **Client:** *Well, why was I unhappy then?*
>
> **Ellis:** *It's very simple—as simple as A, B, C, I might say. A in this case is the fact that these men didn't like you. Let's assume that you observed their attitude correctly and were not merely imagining they didn't like you.*
>
> **Client:** *I assure you that they didn't. I could see that very clearly.*
>
> **Ellis:** *Very well, let's assume they didn't like you and call that A. Now, C is your unhappiness—which we'll definitely have to assume is a fact, since you felt it.*
>
> **Client:** *Damn right I did!*
>
> **Ellis:** *All right, then: A is the fact that the men didn't like you, and C is your unhappiness. You see A and C and you assume that A, their not liking you, caused your unhappiness. But it didn't.*
>
> **Client:** *It didn't? What did, then?*
>
> **Ellis:** *B did.*
>
> **Client:** *What's B?*
>
> **Ellis:** *B is what you said to yourself while you were playing golf with those men.*
>
> **Client:** *What I said to myself? But I didn't say anything.*
>
> **Ellis:** *You did. You couldn't possibly be unhappy if you didn't. The only thing that could possibly make you unhappy that occurs from without is a brick falling on your head, or some such equivalent. But no brick fell. Obviously, therefore, you must have told yourself something to make you unhappy.*

FIGURE 17.3 The ABCs of Ellis's theory Ellis and other cognitive therapists contend that our emotional feelings stem not directly from events that happen to us, but from our interpretation of those events. By changing our beliefs—the cognitions we use for interpreting what happens—we can alter our emotional reactions.

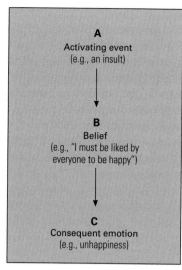

A
Activating event
(e.g., an insult)

B
Belief
(e.g., "I must be liked by everyone to be happy")

C
Consequent emotion
(e.g., unhappiness)

In this dialogue, Ellis invokes his famous *ABC theory of emotions*: *A* is the *activating event* in the environment, *B* is the *belief* that is triggered in the client's mind when the event occurs, and *C* is the emotional *consequence* of the triggered belief (illustrated in Figure 17.3). Therapy proceeds by changing B, the belief. In this particular example, the man suffers because he believes irrationally that he must be liked by everyone (an example of musturbation), so if someone doesn't like him, he is unhappy. The first step will be to convince the man that it is irrational to expect everyone to like him and that there is little or no harm in not being liked by some people.

Establishing Clear-Cut Goals and Steps for Achieving Them

22

What is the purpose of homework in cognitive therapy?

Once a client admits to the irrational and self-injurious nature of some belief or habit of thought, the next step is to help the client get rid of that belief or habit and replace it with a more rational and adaptive way of thinking. That takes hard work. Long-held beliefs and thoughts do not simply disappear once they are recognized as irrational. They occur automatically unless they are actively resisted.

To help clients overcome their self-injurious ways of thinking, cognitive therapists often assign homework. For example, clients might be asked to keep a diary, or to fill out a form every day such as that depicted in Figure 17.4 (on p. 664), in which they record the negative emotions they felt that day, describe the situations and automatic thoughts that accompanied those emotions, and describe a rational alternative thought that might make them feel less upset. Such exercises help train clients to become more aware of their automatic thoughts and, through awareness, change them. The diaries or charts also become a record of progress, by which the therapist and client can see if positive ways of thinking are increasing over time and negative emotions are decreasing.

Moving from a Teaching Role to a Consulting Role with the Client

23

In what sense is a cognitive therapist initially a teacher and later a consultant?

Cognitive therapists, unlike humanistic therapists, are quite directive in their approach. At least at the beginning, the relationship between cognitive therapist and client is fundamentally like that of a teacher and student. The therapist helps the client identify a set of goals, develops a curriculum for achieving those goals, assigns homework, and assesses the client's progress using the most objective measures available. With time, however, as the client becomes increasingly expert in spotting and correcting his or her own maladaptive thoughts, the client becomes increasingly self-directive in the therapy, and the therapist begins to act more like a consultant and less like a teacher (Hazler & Barwick, 2001). Eventually, the client may meet with the therapist just occasionally to describe continued progress and to ask for advice when needed. When such advice is no longer needed, the therapy has achieved its goals and is over.

Although cognitive therapists are directive with clients, most of them acknowledge the value of some of the other tenets of humanistic therapy, particularly the value of maintaining a warm, genuine, and empathic relationship with their clients (Beck & Weishaar, 2007). In fact, increasingly, psychotherapists of all theoretical persuasions are acknowledging that empathy and understanding of the patient are an essential part of the therapeutic process (Hazler & Barwick, 2001; Weiner & Bornstein, 2009).

A Case Example: Beck's Cognitive Treatment of a Depressed Young Woman

Aaron Beck, who at this writing has been applying and researching cognitive therapy for more than 50 years, is by far the most influential cognitive therapist. His earliest and best-known work was with depressed patients, but he has also developed cognitive therapy methods for treating anxiety, uncontrollable anger, and schizophrenia (Bowles, 2004). In the dialogue that follows (from Beck & Young, 1985) we see him at work with a client referred to as Irene—a 29-year-old woman with two young children who was diagnosed with major depression.

Irene had not been employed outside her home since marriage, and her husband, who had been in and out of drug-treatment centers, was also unemployed. She was socially isolated and felt that people looked down on her because of her poor control over her children and her husband's drug record. She was treated for three sessions by Beck and then was treated for a longer period by another cognitive therapist.

During the first session, Beck helped Irene to identify a number of her automatic negative beliefs, including: *things won't get better; nobody cares for me;* and *I am stupid.* By the end of the session, she accepted Beck's suggestion to try to invalidate the first of those thoughts by doing certain things for herself, before the next session, that might make life more fun. She agreed to take the children on an outing, visit her mother, go shopping, read a book, and find out about joining a tennis group—all things that she claimed she would like to do. Having completed that homework, she came to the second session feeling more hopeful. However, she began to feel depressed again when, during the session, she misunderstood a question that Beck asked her, which, she said, made her "look dumb." Beck responded with a questioning strategy that helped her to distinguish between the *fact* of what happened (not understanding a question) and her *belief* about it (looking dumb):

> **Beck:** *OK, what is a rational answer* [to why you didn't answer the question]? *A realistic answer?*
>
> **Irene:** *I didn't hear the question right; that is why I didn't answer it right.*
>
> **Beck:** *OK, so that is the fact situation. And so, is the fact situation that you look dumb or you just didn't hear the question right?*
>
> **Irene:** *I didn't hear the question right.*
>
> **Beck:** *Or is it possible that I didn't say the question in such a way that it was clear?*
>
> **Irene:** *Possible.*
>
> **Beck:** *Very possible. I'm not perfect so it's very possible that I didn't express the question properly.*
>
> **Irene:** *But instead of saying you made a mistake, I would still say I made a mistake.*
>
> **Beck:** *We'll have to watch the video to see. Whichever. Does it mean if I didn't express the question, if I made the mistake, does it make me dumb?*
>
> **Irene:** *No.*
>
> **Beck:** *And if you made the mistake, does it make you dumb?*
>
> **Irene:** *No, not really.*
>
> **Beck:** *But you felt dumb?*
>
> **Irene:** *But I did, yeah.*
>
> **Beck:** *Do you still feel dumb?*
>
> **Irene:** *No. Right now I feel glad. I'm feeling a little better that at least somebody is pointing all these things out to me because I have never seen this before. I never knew that I thought that I was that dumb.*

24

How does Beck's treatment of a depressed woman illustrate his approach to identifying and correcting maladaptive, automatic thoughts?

A pioneer of cognitive therapy
Aaron Beck's approach to therapy is gentler than Ellis's, but not less teacher-like. Beck typically leads clients, through a Socratic style of questioning, to discover the irrationality of their thoughts. In this photo (taken in 2008), Beck, at age 87, addresses participants in a training program at the Beck Institute for Cognitive Therapy and Research.

Clem Murray/Philadelphia Inquirer/MCT/Newscom

	SITUATION	EMOTION(S)	AUTOMATIC THOUGHT(S)	RATIONAL RESPONSE	OUTCOME
DATE	Describe: 1. Actual event leading to unpleasant emotion, or 2. Stream of thoughts, daydream, or recollection, leading to unpleasant emotion.	1. Specify sad/ anxious/ angry, etc. 2. Rate degree of emotion, 1–100.	1. Write automatic thought(s) that preceded emotion(s). 2. Rate belief in automatic thought(s), 0–100%.	1. Write rational response to automatic thought(s). 2. Rate belief in rational response, 0–100%.	1. Rerate belief in automatic thought(s), 0–100%. 2. Specify and rate subsequent emotions, 0–100.
7/15	Store clerk didn't smile at me when I paid for purchase.	Sad – 60 Anxious – 40	Nobody likes me – 70% I look awful – 80%	Maybe the clerk was having a bad day or maybe she never smiles at customers – 70%	1. 20% 30% 2. Pleasure – 25

Explanation: When you experience an unpleasant emotion, note the situation that seemed to stimulate the emotion. (If the emotion occurred while you were thinking, daydreaming, etc., please note this.) Then note the automatic thought associated with the emotion. Record the degree to which you believe this thought: 0% = not at all, 100% = completely. In rating degree of emotion: 1 = a trace, 100 = the most intense possible.

FIGURE 17.4 Homework sheet for cognitive therapy The purpose of this homework is to enable clients to become aware of and correct the automatic thoughts that contribute to their emotional difficulties. (Adapted from Beck & Young, 1985.)

As homework between the second and third sessions, Beck gave Irene the assignment of catching, writing down, and correcting her own dysfunctional thoughts, using the form shown in Figure 17.4. Subsequent sessions were aimed at eradicating each of her depressive thoughts, one by one, and reinforcing the steps she was taking to improve her life. Progress was rapid. Irene felt increasingly better about herself. During the next several months, she joined a tennis league, got a job, took a college course in sociology, and left her husband after trying and failing to get him to develop a better attitude toward her or to join her in couples therapy. By this time, according to Beck, she was cured of her depression, had created for herself a healthy environment, and no longer needed therapy.

Principles of Behavior Therapy

25
How is behavior therapy distinguished from cognitive therapy?

◀ If a cognitive therapist is a teacher, a behavior therapist is a trainer. While cognitive therapy deals with maladaptive habits of thought, behavior therapy deals directly with maladaptive behaviors. **Behavior therapy** is rooted in the research on basic learning processes initiated by such pioneers as Ivan Pavlov, John B. Watson, and B. F. Skinner (discussed in **Chapter 4**). Unlike all the other psychotherapy approaches we have discussed, behavior therapy is not fundamentally talk therapy. Rather, in behavior therapy clients are exposed by the therapist to new environmental conditions that are designed to retrain them, so that maladaptive habitual or reflexive ways of responding become extinguished and new, healthier habits and reflexes are conditioned.

In other regards, behavior therapy is much like cognitive therapy, and, as I noted earlier, the approaches are often combined, in cognitive-behavioral therapy. Behavior therapy, like cognitive therapy, is very much symptom-oriented and concerned with immediate, measurable results. Two of the most common types of treatment in behavior therapy, discussed below, are *contingency management therapy* to modify habits and *exposure therapy* to overcome unwanted fears.

Contingency Management: Altering the Relationship Between Actions and Rewards

The basic principle of operant conditioning, discussed in **Chapter 4,** is that behavioral actions are reinforced by their consequences. People, like other animals, learn to behave in ways that bring desired consequences and to avoid behaving in ways that do not. When a behavior therapist learns that a client is behaving in ways that are harmful to himself or herself, or to others, the first question the therapist might ask is this: *What reward is this person getting for this behavior, which leads him or her to continue it?* The next step, once the reward is understood, is to modify the behavior–reward contingency, so that desired actions are rewarded and undesired ones are not. The broad term for all therapy programs that alter the contingency between actions and rewards is ***contingency management.***

For example, if parents complain to a behavior therapist that their child is acting in aggressive and disruptive ways at home, the therapist might ask the parents to keep a record, for a week or more, of each instance of such misbehavior and of how they or others in the family responded. From that record, the therapist might learn that the child is gaining desired attention through misbehavior. The therapist might then work out a training program in which the parents agree to attend more to the child when he is behaving in desired ways and to ignore the child, or provide some clearly negative consequence (such as withdrawing some privilege), when he is behaving in undesired ways. This sort of behavioral work with families, aimed at altering the contingencies between actions and rewards at home, is referred to as *parent management training* (Kazdin, 2003).

Contingency management is also sometimes used, in programs referred to as *token economies,* in mental hospitals and group homes for people with schizophrenia or other serious mental disorders (Ayllon & Azrin, 1968; Dickerson & others, 2005). Patients may receive tokens for such activities as making their beds, helping out in the kitchen, or helping other patients in specific ways, and they can cash in the tokens for desired privileges, such as movies or treats at the hospital commissary. This technique not only helps build desired habits but also helps combat the lethargy, boredom, and dependence that are so common in mental institutions. In a number of controlled studies, patients in token economy programs improved more quickly, and were able to leave the institutions sooner, than otherwise similar patients who were not in such programs (Dickerson & others, 2005).

In recent years, contingency management has been instituted in many community drug rehabilitation programs. In these programs, patients who remain drug-free for specified periods of time, as measured by regular urine tests, receive vouchers that they can turn in for valued prizes. Such programs have proven quite successful in encouraging cocaine and heroin abusers to go many weeks without taking drugs, and in at least some cases these programs are less expensive than other, more standard treatments (Barry & others, 2009; Higgins & others, 2007).

▶ -------------------------------- 26

How has contingency management been used to improve children's behavior, promote self-care in residents of mental institutions, and motivate abstinence in drug abusers?

Jon Feingersh/Jupiterimages

Contingency management at home In some cases "contingency management" is simply pay for a job well done.

Exposure Treatments for Unwanted Fears

27

What is the theoretical rationale for treating specific phobias by exposing clients to the feared objects or situations?

Behavior therapy has proven especially successful in treating specific phobias, in which the person fears something well defined, such as high places or a particular type of animal (Emmelkamp, 2004). From a behavioral perspective, fear is a reflexive response, which through classical conditioning (discussed in **Chapter 4**) can come to be triggered by various non-dangerous as well as dangerous stimuli. An unconditioned stimulus for fear is one that elicits the response even if the individual has had no previous experience with the stimulus; a conditioned stimulus for fear is one that elicits the response only because the stimulus was previously paired with some fearful event in the person's experience. Opinions may differ as to whether a particular fear, such as a fear of snakes, is unconditioned or conditioned (unlearned or learned), but in practice this does not matter because the treatment is the same in either case.

A characteristic of the fear reflex, whether conditioned or unconditioned, is that it declines and gradually disappears if the eliciting stimulus is presented many times or over a prolonged period in a context where no harm comes to the person. In the case of an unconditioned fear reflex—such as the startle response to a sudden noise—the decline is called *habituation*. In the case of a conditioned fear reflex, the decline that occurs when the conditioned stimulus is presented repeatedly without the unconditioned stimulus is called *extinction* (discussed in **Chapter 4**). For example, if a person fears all dogs because of once having been bitten, then prolonged exposure to various dogs (the conditioned stimuli) in the absence of being bitten (the unconditioned stimulus) will result in reduction or eradication of the fear. Any treatment for an unwanted fear or phobia that involves exposure to the feared stimulus in order to habituate or extinguish the fear response is referred to as an **exposure treatment** (Moscovitch & others, 2009). Behavior therapists have developed three different means to present feared stimuli to clients in such treatments (Krijn & others, 2004).

28

What are three ways of exposing clients to feared objects or situations, and what are the advantages of each?

One means is *imaginative exposure*. A client in this form of treatment is instructed to imagine a particular, moderately fearful scene as vividly as possible, until it no longer seems frightening. Then the client is instructed to imagine a somewhat more fearful scene, until that no longer seems frightening. In this way the client gradually works up to the most feared scene. For example, a woman afraid of heights might be asked first to imagine that she is looking out a second-floor window, then a third-floor window, and so on, until she can imagine, without strong fear, that she is looking down from the top of a skyscraper. An assumption here is that the ability to remain calm while imagining the previously feared situation will generalize, so that the person will be able to remain calm in the actual situation. Research involving long-term follow-up has shown that imaginative exposure techniques can be quite effective in treating specific phobias (Zinbarg & others, 1992).

The most direct exposure technique is *in vivo exposure*—that is, real-life exposure. With this technique the client, usually accompanied by the therapist or by some other comforting and encouraging helper, must force himself or herself to confront the feared situation in reality. For example, to overcome a fear of flying, the client might, as a first assignment, go to the airport and watch planes take off and land until that can be done without fear. Then, through a special arrangement with an airline, the client might enter a stationary plane and sit in it for a while, until that can be done without fear. Finally, the

Virtual reality exposure treatment As treatment for her spider phobia, this woman wears a headset that allows her to walk through a virtual environment in which she confronts spiders, some of which are monstrously large. The screen in the background depicts the scene that she is currently seeing, but her view is three-dimensional. The fuzzy object held in front of her will add a tactile component to her spider experience; she will be asked to touch it with her real hand as she touches the virtual spider with her virtual hand.

client goes on an actual flight—perhaps just a short one the first time. Research suggests that in vivo exposure is generally more effective than imaginative exposure when both are possible (Emmelkamp, 2004). However, in vivo exposure is usually more time-consuming and expensive, and is often not practical because the feared situation is difficult to arrange for the purpose of therapy.

Today, with advanced computer technology, a third means of exposure is possible and is rapidly growing in use—*virtual reality exposure*. With this technique, the client wears a helmet that contains two goggle-sized TV screens, one in front of each eye. A slightly different image of the virtual environment is sent to each eye, such that the client sees that environment in three dimensions and experiences it as if he or she were truly immersed in it. The helmet contains sensors that track head movements, and these sensors control the display in the TV screens so that the view of the virtual environment changes, in appropriate ways, as the client's head moves. Thus the client can scan the virtual environment, seeing different parts of it, by rotating his or her head left and right or up and down. The client can also experience himself or herself as moving through the virtual environment, either through actually walking or through use of a joystick. At the same time, sound effects that add to the reality of the client's experience can be played through speakers in the helmet.

Virtual worlds have been developed for exposure treatments for many different phobias, including fear of heights, fear of flying, claustrophobia (fear of being in small, enclosed spaces), spider phobia, and fear of public speaking (Krijn & others, 2004). Results to date suggest that virtual reality exposure is quite effective (Krijn & others, 2004; Parsons & Rizzo, 2008). In one research study, for example, all nine participants, who came with strong fears of flying, overcame their fears within six 1-hour sessions of virtual exposure—exposure in which they progressed gradually through virtual experiences of going to an airport, entering a plane, flying, looking out the plane window, and feeling and hearing turbulence while flying (Botella & others, 2004). After the therapy, all of them were able to take an actual plane fight with relatively little fear.

THE FAR SIDE® By GARY LARSON

Professor Gallagher and his controversial technique of simultaneously confronting the fear of heights, snakes, and the dark.

A Case Example: Miss Muffet Overcomes Her Spider Phobia

Our case example of behavior therapy is that of a woman nicknamed Miss Muffet by her therapists (Hoffman, 2004). For 20 years prior to her behavioral treatment, Miss Muffet had suffered from an extraordinary fear of spiders, a fear that had led to a diagnosis not just of spider phobia but also obsessive-compulsive disorder. Her obsessive fear of spiders prompted her to engage in such compulsive rituals as regularly fumigating her car with smoke and pesticides, sealing her bedroom windows with duct tape every night, and sealing her clothes in plastic bags immediately after washing them. She scanned constantly for spiders wherever she went, and she avoided places where she had ever encountered spiders. By the time she came for behavior therapy her spider fear was so intense that she found it difficult to leave home at all.

Miss Muffet's therapy, conducted by Hunter Hoffman (2004) and his colleagues, consisted of ten 1-hour sessions of virtual reality exposure, using the helmet system described earlier. In the first session she navigated through a virtual kitchen, where she encountered a huge virtual tarantula. She was asked to approach this spider as closely as she could, using a handheld joystick to move forward in the three-dimensional scene. In later sessions, as she became less fearful of approaching the virtual tarantula, she was instructed to reach out and "touch" it. To create the tactile effect of actually touching the spider, the therapist held out a fuzzy toy spider, which she felt with her real hand as she saw her virtual hand touch the virtual spider.

In other sessions, she encountered other spiders of various shapes and sizes. On one occasion she was instructed to pick up a virtual vase, out of which wriggled a virtual spider. On another, a virtual spider dropped slowly to the floor of the virtual

------29
How did virtual exposure treatment help Miss Muffet overcome her fear of spiders?

kitchen, directly in front of her, as sound effects from the horror movie *Psycho* were played through her headphones. The goal of the therapy was to create spider experiences that were more frightening than any she would encounter in the real world, so as to convince her, at a gut emotional level, that encountering real spiders would not cause her to panic or go crazy. As a test, after the ten virtual reality sessions, Miss Muffet was asked to hold a live tarantula (a large, hairy, fearsome looking, but harmless spider), which she did with little fear, even while the creature crawled partway up her arm.

SECTION REVIEW

Cognitive and behavioral therapy—both problem-centered—are often combined.

Principles of Cognitive Therapy

➤ Cognitive therapy is based on the idea that psychological distress results from maladaptive beliefs and thoughts.

➤ The cognitive therapist works to identify the maladaptive thoughts and beliefs, convince the client of their irrationality, and help the client eliminate them along with the unpleasant emotions they provoke.

➤ To help the client replace the old, habitual ways of thinking with more adaptive ways, cognitive therapists often assign homework (e.g., writing down and correcting irrational thoughts). Progress is objectively measured. As the client can assume more of the responsibility, the therapist becomes less directive.

➤ A case example shows Aaron Beck's cognitive treatment of a depressed young woman who came to see how her automatic negative thoughts (e.g., "I am stupid") were affecting her.

Principles of Behavior Therapy

➤ The goals of behavior therapy are to extinguish maladaptive responses and to condition healthier responses by exposing clients to new environmental conditions.

➤ Contingency management programs (such as the token economies used in some mental institutions) are based on operant-conditioning principles. They modify behavior by modifying behavior–reward contingencies.

➤ Exposure treatments, based on classical conditioning, are used to habituate or extinguish reflexive fear responses in phobias. Three techniques are imaginative exposure, in vivo (real-life) exposure, and virtual reality exposure.

➤ In a case example, virtual reality exposure therapy helped "Miss Muffet" overcome a debilitating fear of spiders.

▉ Evaluating Psychotherapies

30
Why must we rely on experiments rather than case studies to assess the effectiveness of psychotherapy?

You have just read about four major varieties of psychotherapy. Do they work? That might seem like an odd question at this point. After all, didn't Freud cure the Rat Man; didn't Rogers help the silent young man; didn't Beck and his associates cure the depressed young woman; and didn't behavior therapy cure Miss Muffet? But case studies—even thousands of them—showing that people are better off at the end of therapy than at the beginning cannot tell us for sure that therapy works. Maybe those people would have improved anyway, without therapy.

An adage about the common cold goes like this: "Treat a cold with the latest remedy and you'll get rid of it in 7 days; leave it untreated and it'll hang on for a week." Maybe psychological problems or disorders are often like colds in this respect. Everyone has peaks and valleys in life, and people are most likely to start therapy while in one of the valleys (see Figure 17.5). Thus, even if therapy has no effect, most people will feel better at some time after entering it than they did when they began (a point that was made earlier in this chapter in the discussion of drug treatments). The natural tendency for both therapist and client is to attribute the improvement to the therapy, but that attribution may often be wrong.

The only way to know if psychotherapy really works is to perform controlled experiments, in which groups of people undergoing therapy are compared with otherwise-similar control groups who are not undergoing therapy.

FIGURE 17.5 The peaks and valleys of life If a person enters psychotherapy while in a valley, he or she is likely to feel better after a time even if the therapy is ineffective.

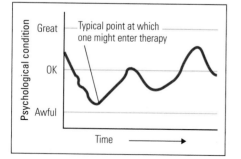

Is Psychotherapy Helpful, and Are Some Types of It More Helpful Than Others?

A Classic Example of a Therapy-Outcome Experiment

One of the earliest well-controlled experiments on therapy outcome was conducted at a psychiatric outpatient clinic in Philadelphia (Sloane & others, 1975). The subjects were 94 men and women, ages 18 to 45, who sought psychotherapy at the clinic. Most of them suffered from diffuse anxiety, the type that today would probably be diagnosed as generalized anxiety disorder. Each was assigned by a random procedure to one of three groups. Members of one group received once-a-week sessions of *behavior therapy* for 4 months (including such procedures as imaginative exposure to various feared situations and training in assertiveness) from one of three highly experienced behavior therapists. Members of the second group received the same amount of *psychodynamic therapy* (including such procedures as probing into childhood memories, dream analysis, and interpretation of resistance) from one of three highly experienced psychodynamic therapists. The members of the third group, the *no-therapy group,* were placed on a waiting list and given no treatment during the 4-month period but were called periodically to let them know that they would eventually be accepted for therapy.

To measure treatment effectiveness, all subjects, including those in the no-therapy group, were assessed both before and after the 4-month period by psychiatrists who were not informed of the groups to which the subjects had been assigned. As illustrated in Figure 17.6, all three groups improved during the 4-month period, but the treatment groups improved significantly more than did the no-treatment group. Moreover, the two treatment groups did not differ significantly from each other in degree of improvement.

This early study anticipated the result of hundreds of other psychotherapy-outcome experiments that have followed it. Overall, such research provides compelling evidence that psychotherapy works, but little if any evidence that one variety of therapy is regularly better than any other standard variety (Lambert & Ogles, 2004; Staines, 2008).

▶ – – – – – – – – – – – – – –31

How did an experiment in Philadelphia demonstrate the effectiveness of behavior therapy and psychodynamic therapy?

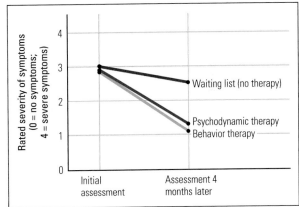

FIGURE 17.6 Results of the Philadelphia experiment
Psychiatrists rated the severity of each subject's symptoms before and after a 4-month treatment period. As shown here, those in the two therapy groups improved more than did those who were placed on the waiting list.

Evidence That Psychotherapy Helps

When hundreds of separate therapy-outcome experiments are combined, the results indicate, very clearly, that therapy helps. In fact, about 75 to 80 percent of people in the psychotherapy condition in such experiments improved more than did the average person in a non-therapy condition (Lambert & Ogles, 2004). Experiments comparing the effectiveness of psychotherapy with standard drug therapies indicate, overall, that psychotherapy is at least as effective as drug therapy in treating depression and generalized anxiety disorder and is more effective than drug therapy in treating panic disorder (Imel & others, 2008; Gould & others, 1995; Mitte, 2005).

A note of caution should be added, however, for interpreting such findings. Psychotherapy-outcome experiments are usually carried out at clinics associated with major research centers. The therapists are normally highly experienced and, since they know that their work is being evaluated, they are presumably functioning at maximal capacity. It is quite possible that the outcomes in these experiments are more positive than are the average therapy outcomes, where therapists are not always so experienced or so motivated (Lambert & Ogles, 2004). Moreover, just as in the case of drug studies, there is a bias for researchers to publish results that show significant positive effects of psychotherapy and not to publish results that show no effects. This, too, would lead to an overestimation of therapy effectiveness, since the analyses are usually based only on the published findings (Staines, 2008).

▶ – – – – – – – – – – – – – –32

What is the evidence that psychotherapy works and that for some disorders it works as well as, or better than, standard drug treatments?

Evidence That No Type of Therapy Is Clearly Better, Overall, Than Other Standard Types

33

What general conclusions have been drawn from research comparing different forms of psychotherapy?

There was a time when psychotherapists who adhered to one variety of therapy argued strongly that their variety was greatly superior to others. Such arguments have largely been quelled by the results of psychotherapy-outcome experiments. Taken as a whole, such experiments provide no convincing evidence that any of the major types of psychotherapy is superior to any other for treating the kinds of problems—such as depression and generalized anxiety—for which people most often seek treatment (Lambert & Ogles, 2004; Staines, 2008; Wampold, 2001). Most such experiments have pitted some form of cognitive or cognitive-behavioral therapy against some form of psychodynamic therapy. When the two forms of therapy are given in equal numbers of sessions, by therapists who are equally well trained and equally passionate about the value of the therapy they administer, the usual result is no difference in outcome; people treated by either therapy get better at about the same rate. Relatively few studies have compared humanistic forms of therapy with others, but the results of those few suggest that humanistic therapy works as well as the others (Lambert & Ogles, 2004; Smith & others, 1980).

There are some exceptions to the generalization that all types of therapy are equally effective. Most experts agree that behavioral exposure treatment is the most effective treatment for specific phobias (Antony & Barlow, 2002). There is also some reason to believe that cognitive and behavior therapies generally work best for clients who have rather specific problems—problems that can be zeroed in on by the specific techniques of those therapies—and that psychodynamic and humanistic therapies may be most effective for clients who have multiple or diffuse problems or problems related to their personalities (Lambert & Ogles, 2004; Weston & others, 2004).

One reason for the general equivalence in effectiveness of different therapies may be that they are not as different in practice as they are in theory. Analyses of recorded therapy sessions have revealed that good therapists, regardless of the type of therapy they claim to practice, often use methods that overlap with other types of therapy. For example, effective cognitive and behavior therapists, who are normally quite directive, tend to become non-directive—more like humanistic therapists—when working with clients who seem unmotivated to follow their lead (Barlow, 2004; Beutler & Harwood, 2000). Similarly, psychodynamic therapists often use cognitive methods (such as correcting maladaptive automatic thoughts), and cognitive therapists often use psychodynamic methods (such as asking clients to talk about childhood experiences), to degrees that seem to depend on the client's personality and the type of problem to be solved (Weston & others, 2004).

The Role of Common Factors in Therapy Outcome

Ostensibly different types of psychotherapy are similar to one another not just because the therapists borrow one another's methods but also because all or at least most therapies, regardless of theoretical orientation, share certain *common factors*. These factors may be more important to the effectiveness of therapy than are the specific, theory-derived factors that differentiate therapies from one another (Lambert & Ogles, 2004; Wampold, 2001). Many common factors have been proposed, but I find it useful to distill them into three fundamental categories: *support, hope,* and *motivation.*

34

How might support, hope, and motivation be provided within the framework of every standard type of psychotherapy? What evidence suggests that these common factors may be crucial to the therapy's effectiveness?

Support

Support includes acceptance, empathy, and encouragement. By devoting time to the client, listening warmly and respectfully, and not being shocked at the client's statements or actions, any good psychotherapist communicates the attitude that the client is a worthwhile human being. This support may directly enhance the client's self-esteem and indirectly lead to other improvements as well.

Many therapy studies have demonstrated the value of such support. One long-term study, for example, revealed that psychodynamic therapists provide more support and less insight to their clients than would be expected from psychoanalytic theory (Wallerstein, 1989). The same study also showed that support, even without insight, seemed to produce stable therapeutic gains. Another study, of cognitive-behavioral therapy for depression, revealed that the bond of rapport that clients felt with their therapists early in treatment was a good predictor of their subsequent improvement (Klein & others, 2003). In yet another study, college professors with no training in psychology or methods of therapy, but with reputations for good rapport with students, proved able to help depressed college students in twice-a-week therapy sessions as effectively as did highly trained and experienced clinical psychologists (Strupp & Hadley, 1979).

Results such as these led one prominent psychodynamic therapist, Hans Strupp (1989), to the following conclusion: "The first and foremost task for the therapist is to create an accepting and empathic context, which in itself has great therapeutic value because for many people it is a novel and deeply gratifying experience to be accepted and listened to respectfully."

Hope

Hope, for a suffering person, is the expectation that things will get better, that life will become more enjoyable. In psychotherapy, hope may come partly from the sense of support, but it may also come from faith in the therapy process.

Most psychotherapists believe in what they do. They speak with authority and confidence about their methods, and they offer scientific-sounding theories or even data to back up their confidence. Thus, clients also come to believe that their therapy will work. Many studies have shown that people who believe they will get better have an improved chance of getting better, even if the specific reason for the belief is false. As was discussed earlier in the chapter, patients who take an inactive placebo pill are likely to improve if they believe that they are taking a drug that will help them. Belief in the process is at least as important for improvement in psychotherapy as it is in drug therapy (Wampold & others, 2005). Hope derived from faith in the process is an element that all sought-after healing procedures have in common, whether provided by psychotherapists, medical doctors, faith healers, or folk healers.

Many psychotherapy-outcome experiments have compared accepted forms of psychotherapy with made-up, "false" forms of psychotherapy—forms that lack the specific ingredients that mark any well-accepted type of therapy. For example, in one such study, cognitive-behavioral therapy for problems of anxiety was compared with a made-up treatment called "systematic ventilation," in which clients talked about their fears in a systematic manner (Kirsch & others, 1983). A general problem with such studies is that it is hard for therapists to present the "false" therapy to clients in a convincing manner, especially if the therapists themselves don't believe it will work. Yet, analyses of many such studies indicate that when the "false" therapy is equivalent to the "real" therapy in credibility to the client, it is also generally equivalent in effectiveness (Ahn & Wampold, 2001; Baskin & others, 2003).

Motivation

Psychotherapy is not a passive process; it is not something "done to" the client by the therapist. The active agent of change in psychotherapy is the client himself or herself. This is an explicit tenet of humanistic therapy and an implicit tenet of other therapies (Hazler & Barwick, 2001). To change, the client must work at changing, and such work requires strong motivation. Motivation for change comes partly from the support and hope engendered by the therapist, which make change seem worthwhile and feasible, but it also comes from other common aspects of the psychotherapy process.

Every form of psychotherapy operates in part by motivating the client to confront his or her problems directly, to think about them in new ways, and, in so doing, to take charge of them and work at resolving them. Almost any caring therapist, regardless of theoretical orientation, will start sessions by asking the client how things have gone since the last meeting. The anticipation of such reporting may cause

Group support In group therapy, the therapeutic elements of support, hope, and motivation may derive not just from the therapist but also from all of the other participants.

clients to go through life, between therapy sessions, with more conscious attention to their actions and feelings than they otherwise would, so that they can give a full report. Such attention leads them to think more consciously, fully, and constructively about their problems, which enhances their motivation to improve and may also lead to new insights about how to improve. Such reporting may also make the client aware of progress, and progress engenders a desire for more progress.

A Final Comment

Through most of this book our main concern has been with normal, healthy, adaptive human behavior. It is perhaps fitting, though, and certainly humbling, to end on this note concerning psychotherapy:

We are *social animals* who need positive regard from other people in order to function well, but sometimes that regard is lacking. We are *thinking animals,* but sometimes our emotions and disappointments get in the way of our thinking. We are *self-motivated and self-directed creatures,* but sometimes we lose our motivation and direction. In these cases, a supportive, hope-inspiring, and motivating psychotherapist can help. The therapist helps not by solving our problems for us, but by providing a context in which we can solve them ourselves.

SECTION REVIEW

Psychotherapy's effectiveness, and reasons for its effectiveness, have been widely researched.

Determining the Effectiveness of Psychotherapy	The Role of Common Factors in Therapy Outcome
➤ Many controlled experiments, comparing patients in psychotherapy with comparable others not in psychotherapy, have shown that psychotherapy helps.	➤ Common factors, shared by all standard psychotherapies, may account for much of the effectiveness of psychotherapy. These include support, hope, and motivation.
➤ Research also indicates that no form of therapy is more effective overall than any other, perhaps because they differ less in practice than in theory.	➤ Support (acceptance, empathy, and encouragement) helps to build the client's confidence. Research suggests that support, in and of itself, has considerable therapeutic value.
➤ Some therapies are better than others for particular situations, however. For example, behavioral exposure therapy is more effective than other treatments for specific phobias.	➤ Hope comes in part from faith in the process, bolstered by the therapist's own faith in it. People who believe they will get better have a greater chance of getting better.
	➤ The support, hope, and regular reporting of experiences in therapy help to motivate clients toward self-improvement.

Concluding Thoughts

The best way to review this chapter is to think about the principles underlying each approach to treatment, about the potential problems of each approach, and about the evidence concerning its effectiveness. As a start in that review, the following ideas may be useful.

1. Self-knowledge and self-acceptance as goals of psychodynamic and humanistic therapies The psychodynamic and humanistic approaches to treatment focus less on the person's specific symptoms or problems, and more on the person as a whole, than do the other approaches. A psychoanalyst or other psychodynamic therapist who is asked to describe the purpose of therapy might well respond with the Socratic dictum: *Know thyself.* A goal of such therapies is to enable clients to learn about aspects of themselves that were previously unconscious, so that they can think and behave in more rational and integrated ways.

Most humanistic therapists would agree with the Socratic dictum, but they would add, and place greater emphasis on, a second dictum: *Accept thyself.* Humanistic therapists argue that people often learn to dislike or deny important aspects of themselves because of real or imagined criticism from other people. A major task for the humanistic therapist is to help clients regain their self-esteem, so that they can regain control of their lives.

2. Biological, behavioral, and cognitive therapies as derivatives of basic approaches to psychological research Biological, behavioral, and cognitive therapies focus more closely on clients' specific symptoms than do psychodynamic and humanistic therapies. These three approaches differ from one another, however, in that they emphasize different levels of causation of behavior. In that respect, they mirror the approaches taken by research psychologists who focus on (a) physiological mechanisms, (b) the role of environmental stimuli and learned habits, and (c) the role of cognitive mediators of behavior.

Biological treatments are founded on the knowledge that everything psychological is a product of the nervous system. Drugs, electroconvulsive therapy, psychosurgery, and deep brain stimulation all involve attempts to help a person overcome psychological problems or disorders by altering the nervous system in some direct way. Behavioral treatments are founded on the knowledge that people acquire, through conditioning, automatic and sometimes maladaptive ways of responding to stimuli in the world around them. The goal of behavior therapy is to eliminate the maladaptive responses and replace them with useful responses. Cognitive treatments are founded on the knowledge that people interpret and think about stimuli in their environments and that those interpretations and thoughts affect the way they feel and behave. The goal of cognitive therapy is to replace maladaptive ways of thinking with useful ways of thinking.

3. Psychotherapy and science Two questions can be asked about the relationship between psychotherapy and science: (a) Is psychotherapy a science? (b) Has science shown that psychotherapy works?

The first question concerns the degree to which the techniques used in psychotherapy are based on scientific principles and can be described objectively. Most psychotherapists would respond that their practice is a blend of science and art—that it is based on theories that stem from scientific research but that it also involves a great deal of intuition, not unlike the sort of intuition that is critical to any prolonged interaction between two human beings. Each client is a distinct individual with distinct problems and needs, who does not necessarily fit snugly with the statistically derived principles that have emerged from scientific research. One way to compare the various psychotherapy approaches is on the degree to which they explicitly, as part of the theories behind them, emphasize the roles of empathy and intuition compared with the rigorous application of laboratory-derived principles. Rogers's humanistic therapy lies at one end of this spectrum and behavior therapy lies at the other.

The second question concerns the use of scientific methods to evaluate psychotherapy. Carefully controlled therapy-outcome experiments suggest that all the well-established psychotherapies work about equally well, on a statistical basis, though some may be more effective than others in treating certain kinds of problems. Such findings have led to increased recognition of the nonspecific therapeutic factors shared by the various approaches and have also inspired a movement toward eclecticism, in which therapists draw from each tradition those methods that seem most appropriate to the client's specific needs.

Further Reading

Raymond J. Corsini & Danny Wedding (2007). *Current psychotherapies* (8th ed.). Belmont, CA: Brooks/Cole.

This is an excellent source for learning more about the main varieties of psychotherapies in use today. There are chapters on psychoanalysis, Adlerian and analytical psychodynamic psychotherapy, person-centered therapy, rational emotive therapy (by Ellis himself), cognitive therapy (by Beck and Weishaar), behavior therapy, and several others. Each chapter is by a different expert or pair of experts and discusses the therapy's history, theory, and application.

Irving B. Weiner & Robert F. Bornstein (2009). *Principles of psychotherapy: Promoting evidence-based psychodynamic practice* (3rd ed.). Hoboken, NJ: Wiley.

If you are thinking of psychotherapy as a career, this highly readable textbook, dealing with all phases of the therapy process, will give you a realistic picture of what the job entails. The book begins with chapters on assessment and initial interviews; continues with chapters on treatment, including chapters on resistance and transference; and ends with a chapter on termination of therapy. The authors represent well the evidence-based, non-doctrinaire spirit of modern-day psychodynamic psychotherapy.

James Bailey (2007). *Man interrupted: Welcome to the bizarre world of OCD, where once more is never enough*. Edinburgh: Mainstream Publishing.

Bailey has obsessive-compulsive disorder coupled with a terrific sense of humor. His main obsession concerns drugs: He fears constantly that someone has put drugs in his food, and he needs repeated reassurances that they have not. The book centers on his treatment at a center where the primary treatment is exposure; he must expose himself regularly to the conditions that frighten him, and he must learn to accept them without following through on his compulsion. His descriptions of his own reactions and that of his fellow patients are laugh-out-loud funny. Yet, they portray the terror and the extraordinary life restrictions that accompany this very serious disorder.

David Healy (2008). *Psychiatric drugs explained* (5th ed.). London: Elsevier.

This is a straightforward, balanced account of the uses, benefits, mechanisms of action, and adverse effects of each of the major categories of drugs used in modern psychiatric medicine. It is designed to be used as a handbook for service providers and users, but it can also serve well as an authoritative yet easy-to-read resource for students who wish to know more about current drug therapies.

Robert Whitaker (2002). *Mad in America: Bad science, bad medicine, and the enduring mistreatment of the mentally ill*. Cambridge, MA: Perseus.

Whitaker, a science reporter, begins this book by reviewing the neglect and brutal treatment of people with schizophrenia from the mid-18th to the mid-20th century. Through the rest of the book he argues that the neglect and brutality continue. His most controversial claim is that an unholy alliance between the pharmaceutical industry and the medical research community has suppressed evidence concerning the harmful effects of antipsychotic drugs, including evidence that the drugs may prevent full recovery from schizophrenia. Whitaker may overstate the case, but his argument deserves serious consideration.

Statistical Appendix

TABLE A.1 Twenty scores unranked and ranked

Scores in the order they were collected	The same scores ranked
58	17
45	23
23	31
71	36
49	37
36	41
61	43
41	45
37	45
75	49
91	50
54	54
43	57
17	58
63	61
73	63
31	71
50	73
45	75
57	91

Statistical procedures are tools for dealing with data. Some people find them fascinating for their own sake, just as some become intrigued by the beauty of a saw or a hammer. But most of us, most of the time, care about statistics only to the extent that they help us answer questions. Statistics become interesting when we want to know our batting average, or the chance that our favorite candidate will be elected, or how much money we'll have left after taxes. In psychology, statistics are interesting when they are used to analyze data in ways that help answer important psychological questions.

Some of the basics of statistics are described in Chapter 2. The main purpose of the first three sections of this appendix is to supplement that discussion and make it more concrete by providing some examples of statistical calculations. The fourth section (Supplement on Psychophysical Scaling) supplements the discussion of Fechner's and Stevens's work in the section on psychophysics in Chapter 7.

■ Organizing and Summarizing a Set of Scores

This section describes some basic elements of descriptive statistics: the construction of frequency distributions, the measurement of central tendency, and the measurement of variability.

Ranking the Scores and Depicting a Frequency Distribution

Suppose you gave a group of people a psychological test of introversion-extroversion, structured such that a low score indicates introversion (a tendency to withdraw from the social environment) and a high score indicates extroversion (a tendency to be socially outgoing). Suppose further that the possible range of scores is from 0 to 99, that you gave the test to 20 people, and that you obtained the scores shown in the left-hand column of Table A.1. As presented in that column, the scores are hard to describe in a meaningful way; they are just a list of numbers. As a first step toward making some sense of them, you might rearrange the scores in rank order, from lowest to highest, as shown in the right-hand column of the table. Notice how the ranking facilitates your ability to describe the set of numbers.

TABLE A.2 Frequency distribution formed from scores in Table A.1

Interval	Frequency
0–9	0
10–19	1
20–29	1
30–39	3
40–49	5
50–59	4
60–69	2
70–79	3
80–89	0
90–99	1

You can now see that the scores range from a low of 17 to a high of 91 and that the two middle scores are 49 and 50.

A second useful step in summarizing the data is to divide the entire range of possible scores into equal intervals and determine how many scores fall in each interval. Table A.2 presents the results of this process, using intervals of 10. A table of this sort, showing the number of scores that occurred in each interval of possible scores, is called a ***frequency distribution.*** Frequency distributions can also be represented graphically, as shown in Figure A.1. Here, each bar along the horizontal axis represents a different interval, and the height of the bar represents the frequency (number of scores) that occurred in that interval.

As you examine Figure A.1, notice that the scores are not evenly distributed across the various intervals. Rather, most of them fall in the middle intervals (centering around 50), and they taper off toward the extremes. This pattern would have been hard to see in the original, unorganized set of numbers.

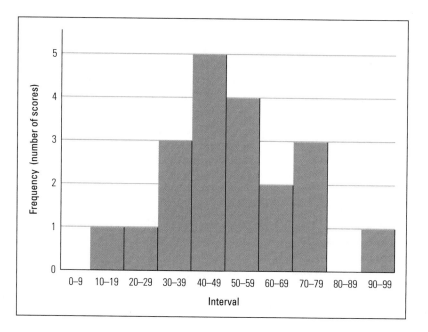

FIGURE A.1 A frequency distribution depicted by a bar graph This graph depicts the frequency distribution shown in Table A.2. Each bar represents a different interval of possible scores, and the height of each bar represents the number of scores that occurred in that interval.

Shapes of Frequency Distributions

The frequency distribution in Figure A.1 roughly approximates a shape that is referred to as a ***normal distribution*** or *normal curve.* A perfect normal distribution (which can be expressed by a mathematical equation) is illustrated in Figure A.2a. Notice that the maximum frequency lies in the center of the range of scores and that the frequency tapers off—first gradually, then more rapidly, and then gradually again—symmetrically on the two sides, forming a bell-shaped curve. Many measures in nature are distributed in accordance with a normal distribution. Height (for people of a given age and sex) is one example. A variety of different factors (different genes and nutritional factors) go into determining a person's height. In most cases, these different factors—some promoting tallness and some shortness—average themselves out, so that most people are roughly average in height (accounting for the peak frequency in the middle of the distribution). A small proportion of people, however, will have just the right combination of factors to be much taller or much shorter than average (accounting for the tails at the high and low ends of the distribution). In general, when a measure is determined by several independent factors, the frequency distribution for that measure at least approximates the normal curve. The results of most psychological tests also form a normal distribution if the test is given to a sufficiently large group of people.

But not all measures are distributed in accordance with the normal curve. Consider, for example, the set of scores that would be obtained on a test of English vocabulary if some of the people tested were native speakers of English and others were not. You would expect in this case to find two separate groupings of scores. The native speakers would score high and the others would score low, with relatively few scores in between. A distribution of this sort, illustrated in Figure A.2b, is referred to as a *bimodal distribution*. The **mode** is the most frequently occurring score or range of scores in a frequency distribution; thus, a bimodal distribution is one that has two separate areas of peak frequencies. The normal curve is a *unimodal distribution*, because it has only one peak in frequency.

Some distributions are unimodal, like the normal distribution, but are not symmetrical. Consider, for example, the shape of a frequency distribution of annual incomes for any randomly selected group of people. Most of the incomes might center around, let's say, $20,000. Some would be higher and some lower, but the spread of higher incomes would be much greater than that of lower incomes. No income can be less than $0, but no limit exists to the high ones. Thus, the frequency distribution might look like that shown in Figure A.2c. A distribution of this sort, in which the spread of scores above the mode is greater than that below, is referred to as a *positively skewed distribution*. The long tail of the distribution extends in the direction of high scores.

As an opposite example, consider the distribution of scores on a relatively easy examination. If the highest possible score is 100 points and most people score around 85, the highest score can only be 15 points above the mode, but the lowest score can be as much as 85 points below it. A typical distribution obtained from such a test is shown in Figure A.2d. A distribution of this sort, in which the long tail extends toward low scores, is called a *negatively skewed distribution*.

Measures of Central Tendency

Perhaps the most useful way to summarize a set of scores is to identify a number that represents the center of the distribution. Two different centers can be determined—the median and the mean (both described in Chapter 2). The **median** is the middle score in a set of ranked scores. Thus, in a ranked set of nine scores, the fifth score in the ranking (counting in either direction) is the median. If the data set consists of an even number of scores, determining the median is slightly more complicated because two middle scores exist rather than one. In this case, the median is simply the midpoint between the two middle scores. If you look back at the list of twenty ranked scores in Table A.1, you will see that the two middle scores are 49 and 50; the median in this case is 49.5. The **mean** (also called the *arithmetic average*) is found simply by adding up all of the scores and dividing by the total number of scores. Thus, to calculate the mean of the twenty introversion-extroversion scores in Table A.1, simply add them (the sum is 1020) and divide by 20, obtaining 51.0 as the mean.

Notice that the mean and median of the set of introversion-extroversion scores are quite close to one another. In a perfect normal distribution, these two measures of central tendency are identical. For a skewed distribution, on the other hand, they can be quite different. Consider, for example, the set of incomes shown in Table A.3 on page A-4. The median is $19,500, and all but one of the other incomes are rather close to the median. But the set contains one income of $900,000, which is wildly different from the others. The size of this income does not affect the median. Whether the highest income were $19,501 (just above the median) or a trillion dollars, it still counts as just one income in the ranking that determines the median. But this income has a dramatic effect on the mean. As shown in the table, the mean of these incomes is $116,911. Because the mean is most affected by extreme scores, it will usually be higher than the median in a positively skewed distribution and lower than the median in a negatively skewed distribution. In a positively skewed distribution the most extreme scores are high scores (which

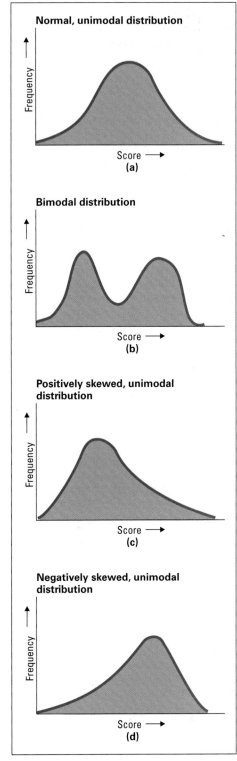

FIGURE A.2 Four differently shaped frequency distributions You can imagine that each of these curves was formed from a set of bars similar to those in Figure A.1, but the bars would be narrower and more numerous (the intervals would be smaller) and the data sets would be much larger.

TABLE A.3 Sample incomes, illustrating how the mean can differ greatly from the median

Rank	Income
1	$15,000
2	16,400
3	16,500
4	17,700
5	(19,500)
6	21,200
7	22,300
8	23,600
9	900,000
	Total: $1,052,200

Mean = $1,052,200 ÷ 9 = $116,911

Median = $19,500

raise the mean above the median), and in a negatively skewed distribution they are low scores (which lower the mean below the median).

Which is more useful, the mean or the median? The answer depends on one's purpose, but in general the mean is preferred when scores are at least roughly normally distributed, and the median is preferred when scores are highly skewed. In Table A.3 the median is certainly a better representation of the set of incomes than is the mean, because it is typical of almost all of the incomes listed. In contrast, the mean is typical of none of the incomes; it is much lower than the highest income and much higher than all the rest. This, of course, is an extreme example, but it illustrates the sort of biasing effect that skewed data can have on a mean. Still, for certain purposes, the mean might be the preferred measure even if the data are highly skewed. For example, if you wanted to determine the revenue that could be gained by a 5 percent local income tax, the mean income (or the total income) would be more useful than the median.

Measures of Variability

The mean or median tells us about the central value of a set of numbers, but not about how widely they are spread out around the center. Look at the two frequency distributions depicted in Figure A.3. They are both normal and have the same mean, but they differ greatly in their degree of spread or variability. In one case the scores are clustered near the mean (low variability), and in the other they are spread farther apart (high variability). How might we measure the variability of scores in a distribution?

One possibility would be to use the *range*—that is, simply the difference between the highest and lowest scores in the distribution—as a measure of variability. For the scores listed in Table A.1, the range is 91 − 17 = 74 points. A problem with the range, however, is that it depends on just two scores, the highest and lowest. A better measure of variability would take into account the extent to which all of the scores in the distribution differ from each other.

One measure of variability that takes all of the scores into account is the **variance.** The variance is calculated by the following four steps: (1) Determine the mean of the set of scores. (2) Determine the difference between each score and the mean; this difference is called the *deviation*. (3) Square each deviation (multiply it by itself). (4) Calculate the mean of the squared deviations (by adding them up and dividing by the total number of scores). The result—the mean of the squared deviations—is the variance. This method is illustrated for two different sets of scores in Table A.4. Notice that the two sets each have the same mean (50), but

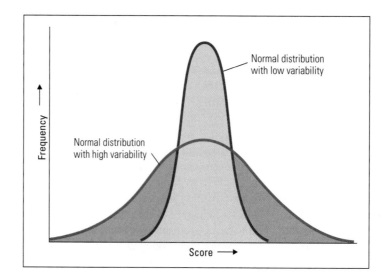

FIGURE A.3 Two normal distributions These normal distributions, superimposed on one another, have identical means but different degrees of variability.

TABLE A.4 Calculation of the variance and standard deviation for two sets of scores that have identical means

First set of scores			*Second set of scores*		
Score	**Deviation (Score − 50)**	**Squared deviation**	**Score**	**Deviation (Score − 50)**	**Squared deviation**
42	−8	64	9	−41	1681
44	−6	36	19	−31	961
47	−3	9	31	−19	361
49	−1	1	47	−3	9
52	+2	4	56	+6	36
54	+4	16	70	+20	400
55	+5	25	78	+28	784
57	+7	49	90	+40	1600
Total = 400		Total = 204	Total = 400		Total = 5832
Mean = 400/8 = 50		Mean = 204/8 = 25.5	Mean = 400/8 = 50		Mean = 5832/8 = 729

Variance = **Mean squared deviation = 25.5**

Standard deviation = $\sqrt{\text{Variance}} = \sqrt{25.5} = 5.0$

Variance = **Mean squared deviation = 729**

Standard deviation = $\sqrt{\text{Variance}} = \sqrt{729} = 27.0$

most of the scores in the first set are much closer to the mean than are those in the second set. The result is that the variance of the first set (25.5) is much smaller than that of the second set (729).

Because the variance is based on the squares of the deviations, the units of variance are not the same as those of the original measure. If the original measure is points on a test, then the variance is in units of squared points on the test (whatever on earth that might mean). To bring the units to their original form, all we need to do is take the square root of the variance. The square root of the variance is the ***standard deviation,*** which is the measure of variability that is most commonly used. Thus, for the first set of scores in Table A.4, the standard deviation = $\sqrt{25.5}$ = 5.0; for the second set, the standard deviation = $\sqrt{729}$ = 27.0.

◼ Converting Scores for Purposes of Comparison

Are you taller than you are heavy? That sounds like a silly question, and it is. Height and weight are two entirely different measures, and comparing them is like the proverbial comparison of apples and oranges. But suppose I worded the question this way: Relative to other people of your gender and age group, do you rank higher in height or in weight? Now that is an answerable question. Similarly, consider this question: Are you better at mathematical or at verbal tasks? This, too, is meaningful only if your mathematical and verbal skills are judged relative to those of other people. Compared to other people, do you rank higher in mathematical or in verbal skills? To compare different kinds of scores with each other, we must convert each score into a form that directly expresses its relationship to the whole distribution of scores from which it came.

Percentile Rank

The most straightforward way to see how one person compares to others on a given measure is to determine the person's ***percentile rank*** for that measure. The percentile rank of a given score is simply the percentage of scores that are equal to that score or lower, out of the whole set of scores obtained on a given measure. For example, in the distribution of scores in Table A.1, the score of 37 is at the 25th percentile, because five of the twenty scores are at 37 or lower ($^5/_{20} = ^1/_4 = 25\%$). As another example in the same distribution, the score of 73 is at the 90th percentile because eighteen of the twenty scores are lower ($^{18}/_{20} = ^9/_{10} = 90\%$). If you had available the heights and weights of a large number of people of your age and gender, you could answer the question about your height compared to your weight by determining your percentile rank on each. If you were at the 39th percentile in height and the 25th percentile in weight, then, relative to others in your group, you would be taller than you were heavy. Similarly, if you were at the 94th percentile on a test of math skills and the 72nd percentile on a test of verbal skills, then, relative to the group who took both tests, your math skills would be better than your verbal skills.

Standardized Scores

Another way to convert scores for purposes of comparison is to *standardize* them. A **standardized score** is one that is expressed in terms of the number of standard deviations that the original score is from the mean of original scores. The simplest form of a standardized score is called a **z score**. To convert any score to a z score, you first determine its deviation from the mean (subtract the mean from it), and then divide the deviation by the standard deviation of the distribution. Thus,

$$z = \frac{\text{score} - \text{mean}}{\text{standard deviation}}$$

For example, suppose you wanted to calculate the z score that would correspond to the test score of 54 in the first set of scores in Table A.4. The mean of the distribution is 50, so the deviation is $54 - 50 = +4$. The standard deviation is 5.0. Thus, $z = ^4/_5 = +0.80$. Similarly, the z score for a score of 42 in that distribution would be $^{(42 - 50)}/_5 = -^8/_5 = -1.60$. Remember, the z score is simply the number of standard deviations that the original score is away from the mean. A positive z score indicates that the original score is above the mean, and a negative z score indicates that it is below the mean. A z score of +0.80 is 0.80 standard deviation above the mean, and a z score of −1.60 is 1.60 standard deviations below the mean.

Other forms of standardized scores are based directly on z scores. For example, College Board (SAT) scores were originally (in 1941) determined by calculating each person's z score, then multiplying the z score by 100 and adding the result to 500 (DuBois, 1972). That is,

$$\text{SAT score} = 500 + 100(z)$$

Thus, a person who was directly at the mean on the test ($z = 0$) would have an SAT score of 500; a person who was 1 standard deviation above the mean ($z = +1$) would have an SAT score of 600; a person who was 2 standard deviations above the mean would have 700; and a person who was 3 standard deviations above the mean would have 800. (Very few people would score beyond 3 standard deviations from the mean, so 800 was set as the highest possible score.) Going the other way, a person who was 1 standard deviation below the mean ($z = -1$) would have an SAT score of 400, and so on. (Today, a much broader range of people take the SAT tests than in 1941, when only a relatively elite group applied to colleges, and the scoring system has not been restandardized to maintain 500 as the average score. The result is that average SAT scores are now considerably less than 500.)

Wechsler IQ scores (discussed in Chapter 10) are also based on z scores. They were standardized—separately for each age group—by calculating each person's z score on the test, multiplying that by 15, and adding the product to 100. Thus,

$$\text{IQ} = 100 + 15(z)$$

This process guarantees that a person who scores at the exact mean achieved by people in the standardization group will have an IQ score of 100, that one who scores 1 standard deviation above that mean will have a score of 115, that one who scores 2 standard deviations above that mean will have a score of 130, and so on.

Relationship of Standardized Scores to Percentile Ranks

If a distribution of scores precisely matches a normal distribution, one can determine percentile rank from the standardized score, or vice versa. As you recall, in a normal distribution the highest frequency of scores occurs in intervals close to the mean, and the frequency declines with each successive interval away from the mean in either direction. As illustrated in Figure A.4, a precise relationship exists between any given z score and the percentage of scores that fall between that score and the mean.

As you can see in the figure, slightly more than 34.1% of all scores in a normal distribution will be between a z score of +1 and the mean. Since another 50% will fall below the mean, a total of slightly more than 84.1% of the scores in a normal distribution will be below a z score of +1. By using similar logic and examining the figure, you should be able to see why z scores of −3, −2, −1, 0, +1, +2, and +3, respectively, correspond to percentile ranks of about 0.1, 2.3, 15.9, 50, 84.1, 97.7, and 99.9, respectively. Detailed tables have been made that permit the conversion of any possible z score in a perfect normal distribution to a percentile rank.

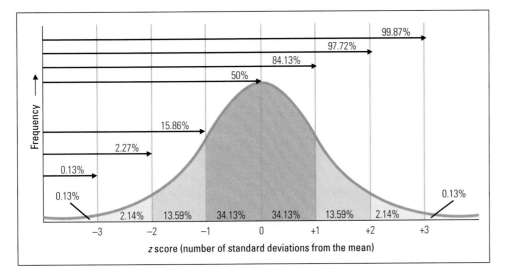

FIGURE A.4 Relationship between z score and percentile rank for a normal distribution

Because the percentage of scores that fall between any given z score and the mean is a fixed value for data that fit a normal distribution, it is possible to calculate what percentage of individuals would score less than or equal to any given z score. In this diagram, the percentages above each arrow indicate the percentile rank for z scores of -3, -2, -1, 0, +1, +2, and +3. Each percentage is the sum of the percentages within the portions of the curve that lie under the arrow.

■ Calculating a Correlation Coefficient

The basic meaning of the term *correlation* and how to interpret a correlation coefficient are described in Chapter 2. As explained there, the correlation coefficient is a mathematical means of describing the strength and direction of the relationship between two variables that have been measured mathematically. The sign (+ or −) of the correlation coefficient indicates the direction (positive or negative) of the relationship; and the absolute value of the correlation coefficient (from 0 to 1.00, irrespective of sign) indicates the strength of the correlation. To review the difference between a positive and negative correlation, and between a weak and strong correlation, look back at Figure 2.3 and the accompanying text on p. 36. Here, as a supplement to the discussion in Chapter 2, is the mathematical means for calculating

TABLE A.5 Calculation of a correlation coefficient (r)

Students (ranked by IQ)	IQ score	GPA	z_{IQ}	z_{GPA}	Cross-products $(z_{IQ}) \times (z_{GPA})$
1	82	2.0	−1.77	−0.66	1.17
2	91	1.2	−1.01	−1.71	1.73
3	93	2.3	−0.84	−0.26	0.22
4	97	2.2	−0.51	−0.39	0.20
5	104	3.0	+0.08	+0.66	0.05
6	105	1.8	+0.17	−0.92	−0.16
7	108	3.5	+0.42	+1.32	0.55
8	109	2.6	+0.51	+0.13	0.07
9	118	2.5	+1.26	0.00	0.00
10	123	3.9	+1.68	+1.84	3.09

Sum = 1030   Sum = 25.0   Sum = 6.92

Mean = 103   Mean = 2.5   Mean = 0.69 = r

SD = 11.88   SD = 0.76

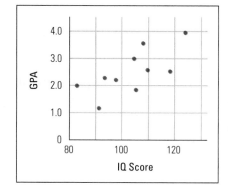

FIGURE A.5 Scatter plots relating GPA to IQ

Each point represents the IQ and the GPA for one of the ten students whose scores are shown in Table A.5. (For further explanation, refer to Figure 2.3 in Chapter 2.)

the most common type of correlation coefficient, called the *product-moment correlation coefficient.*

To continue the example described in Chapter 2, suppose you collected both the IQ score and GPA (grade-point average) for each of ten different high school students and obtained the results shown in the "IQ score" and "GPA" columns of Table A.5. As a first step in determining the direction and strength of correlation between the two sets of scores, you might graph each pair of points in a *scatter plot*, as shown in Figure A.5 (compare this figure to Figure 2.3). The scatter plot makes it clear that, in general, the students with higher IQs tended to have higher GPAs, so you know that the correlation coefficient will be positive. However, the relationship between IQ and GPA is by no means perfect (the plot does not form a straight line), so you know that the correlation coefficient will be less than 1.00.

The first step in calculating a correlation coefficient is to convert each score to a z score, using the method described in the section on standardizing scores. Each z score, remember, is the number of standard deviations that the original score is away from the mean of the original scores. The standard deviation for the ten IQ scores in Table A.5 is 11.88, so the z scores for IQ (shown in the column marked z_{IQ}) were calculated by subtracting the mean IQ score (103) from each IQ and dividing by 11.88. The standard deviation for the ten GPA scores in Table A.5 is 0.76, so the z scores for GPA (shown in the column marked z_{GPA}) were calculated by subtracting the mean GPA (2.5) from each GPA and dividing by 0.76.

To complete the calculation of the correlation coefficient, you multiply each pair of z scores together, obtaining what are called the *z-score cross-products*, and then determine the mean of those cross-products. The product-moment correlation coefficient, r, is, by definition, the mean of the z-score cross-products. In Table A.5, the z-score cross-products are shown in the right-hand column, and the mean of them is shown at the bottom of that column. As you can see, the correlation coefficient in this case is +0.69—a rather strong positive correlation.

■ Supplement on Psychophysical Scaling

This section should *not* be read as a supplement to Chapter 2. It concerns two issues discussed in the section on psychophysical scaling in Chapter 7.

Derivation of Fechner's Law from Weber's Law

In Chapter 7, I described Ernst Weber's law, according to which the just-noticeable difference (jnd) between a comparison stimulus and a standard stimulus is directly proportional to the physical magnitude of the standard stimulus (M). As a formula, this is

$$jnd = kM$$

I then noted that Gustav Fechner used Weber's law to derive a law of psychophysical scaling, according to which the magnitude of a sensory experience (S) is directly proportional to the logarithm of the physical magnitude of the stimulus (M). As a formula, this is

$$S = c \log M$$

Here I will use the numbers shown in Table A.6 to demonstrate the logic of Fechner's derivation of his law from Weber's. The logic begins with the assumption that every jnd is subjectively equal to every other jnd. Thus, the sensory scale in the left-hand column of the table is a jnd scale, and each step in that scale produces an equal change in the magnitude of sensory experience (S). The example is for loudness of a 2000-Hz sound, for which the Weber fraction (k) is $1/10$ and the minimal intensity that can be heard is 1 sound-pressure unit. With these assumptions, Weber's law predicts that the intensity that will be 1 jnd above the minimum will be 1.10 units ($1 + 1/10$th of $1 = 1.10$). Similarly, the intensity that will be 2 jnd's above threshold will be 1.21 units ($1.10 + 1/10$th of $1.10 = 1.21$).

Continuing in this way, it is possible to derive the physical intensity of the stimulus that would be any given number of jnd's above threshold. The results, for 5 jnd's, are shown in the middle column of the table. Notice that each successive jnd step involves a greater increase in the physical intensity than did the step before. For example, going from 0 to 1 jnd above threshold requires an addition of 0.10 physical unit, whereas going from 4 to 5 jnd's requires an addition of 0.15 physical unit ($1.61 - 1.46 = 0.15$). Thus, the relationship between the first and second columns is not linear. The third column of the table shows the logarithms (to base 10) of the numbers in the middle column. (If you have a calculator, you can check them yourself. The logarithm of

TABLE A.6 Demonstration that a jnd sensory scale is linearly related to the logarithm of the physical stimulus (log *M*)		
S in jnd units	M in sound-pressure units if k = 1/10	Log M
0	1.00	0
1	1.10	0.041
2	1.21	0.082
3	1.33	0.123
4	1.46	0.164
5	1.61	0.205

1 is 0, that of 1.1 is 0.041, and so on.) Notice that now, after the logarithmic transformation, the numbers do form a linear relationship with the numbers in the first column. Each jnd step corresponds with an increase of approximately 0.041 log unit. Thus, in line with Fechner's law, each constant step in sensory magnitude corresponds with a constant step in the logarithm of the physical intensity of the stimulus.

Illustration Showing That Stevens's Power Law Preserves Sensory Ratios

At the end of Chapter 7, I described Stevens's power law, which states that the magnitude of a sensory experience (S) is directly proportional to the physical magnitude of the stimulus (M) raised by a constant power (p). As a formula, this is

$$S = cM^p$$

I then pointed out (as had Stevens) that our sensory systems may have evolved to operate according to a power law because such a law preserves constant sensory ratios as the overall physical intensity of stimulation waxes or wanes. For example, as a sound becomes closer (and therefore more intense), we hear its various pitches as maintaining the same ratios of intensity to each other as before, and thus we hear it as the same sound. As another example, as light fades in the evening, the relative brightness of one object compared to another in the visual scene remains constant. To make this more concrete, I mentioned in Chapter 7 that, according to Stevens's power law, every eightfold change in light intensity causes a twofold change in apparent brightness, no matter where on the intensity continuum we start from. Following are calculations proving that point.

For brightness estimations, $p = \frac{1}{3}$ (as shown in Table 7.4). Let S_1 be the sensory magnitude for a stimulus whose physical magnitude is M, and let S_2 be the sensory magnitude for a stimulus that is physically eight times as intense as S_1 (that is, whose physical magnitude is $8M$). In accordance with the power law,

$$S_1 = cM^{1/3} \text{ and } S_2 = c(8M)^{1/3}$$

The ratio of S_2/S_1 can now be calculated as follows:

$$\frac{S_2}{S_1} = \frac{c(8M)^{1/3}}{cM^{1/3}} = \frac{(8M)^{1/3}}{M^{1/3}} = (8M/M)^{1/3} = 8^{1/3} = 2$$

Thus, regardless of the value of the original stimulus magnitude (M), an eightfold increase in that magnitude will produce a doubling of the sensory magnitude, or an eightfold decrease will produce a halving of the sensory magnitude. So, if the physical intensity of each part of a visual scene decreases to one-eighth what it was before, the sensory intensity experienced from each part of the scene will be cut in half and each part of the scene will maintain the same ratio of sensory intensity to each other part as it had before.

Glossary

absolute threshold In psychophysics, the faintest (lowest-intensity) stimulus of a given sensation (such as sound or light) that an individual can detect. For contrast, see *difference threshold.* (p. 262)

accommodation In Piaget's theory of cognitive development, the change that occurs in an existing mental scheme or set of schemes as a result of the assimilation of the experience of a new event or object. See also *assimilation.* (p. 405)

action potentials Neural impulses; the all-or-nothing electrical bursts that begin at one end of the axon of a neuron and move along the axon to the other end. (p. 140)

activating effects of sex hormones Temporary, reversible effects that sex hormones have on sexual drive. Contrast to *differentiating effects* of sex hormones. (p. 205)

additive color mixing The mixing of colored lights (lights containing limited ranges of wavelengths) by superimposing them to reflect off the same surface. It is called *additive* because each light adds to the total set of wavelengths that are reflected to the eye. For contrast, see *subtractive color mixing.* (p. 276)

ADHD Common acronym for *attention deficit/hyperactivity disorder,* a frequently diagnosed disorder in children, characterized by impulsiveness and difficulties in focusing attention on tasks. (p. 600)

affect Pronounced **aph**-ect, a noun referring to any emotional feeling. (p. 220)

aggression Fighting and threats of fighting among members of the same species. (p. 84)

alleles Different genes that can occupy the same locus on a pair of chromosomes and thus can potentially pair with one another. (p. 56)

altruism In sociobiology, a type of helping behavior in which an individual increases the survival chance or reproductive capacity of another individual while *decreasing* its own survival chance or reproductive capacity. For contrast, see *cooperation.* (p. 87)

Alzheimer's disease A disorder found primarily in the elderly, characterized by progressive deterioration in cognitive functioning and the presence of deposits in the brain referred to as amyloid plaques. (p. 602)

amplitude The amount of physical energy or force exerted by a physical stimulus at any given moment. For sound, this physical measure is related to the psychological experience of loudness. (p. 252)

amygdala A brain structure that is part of the limbic system and is particularly important for evaluating the emotional and motivational significance of stimuli and generating emotional responses. (pp. 158, 226)

analogy In ethology and comparative psychology, any similarity among species that is not due to common ancestry but has evolved independently because of some similarity in their habitats or lifestyles. For contrast, see *homology.* (pp. 75, 352)

androgen A category of hormones, including testosterone, which are produced by the testes in male animals and are normally thought of as "male hormones." These hormones are also produced at lower levels by the adrenal glands, in females as well as in males. (p. 204)

anterograde amnesia Loss, due to injury to the brain, in ability to form new long-term memories for events that occur after the injury. Contrast to *retrograde amnesia.* (p. 332)

anxiety disorders The class of mental disorders in which fear or anxiety is the most prominent symptom. It includes *generalized anxiety disorder, obsessive-compulsive disorder, panic disorder, phobias,* and *posttraumatic stress disorder.* (p. 606)

aphasia Any loss in language ability due to brain damage. See also *Broca's aphasia, Wernicke's aphasia.* (p. 169)

arcuate nucleus A nucleus (cluster of neural cell bodies) in the hypothalamus of the brain that plays a critical role in the control of appetite. (p. 196)

arousability In discussions of sexuality, refers to the capacity to become sexually aroused in response to sexually relevant stimuli. For contrast, see *proceptivity.* (p. 204)

artificial selection The deliberate selective breeding of animals or plants by humans for the purpose of modifying the genetic makeup of future generations. See *selective breeding.* For contrast, see *natural selection.* (pp. 63–64)

assimilation In Piaget's theory of cognitive development, the process by which experiences are incorporated into the mind or, more specifically, into mental schemes. See also *accommodation.* (p. 404)

association Concerning the mind, a link between two memories or mental concepts, such that recall of one tends to promote recall of the other. (p. 335)

association areas Areas of the cerebral cortex that receive input from the primary or secondary sensory areas for more than one sensory modality (such as vision and hearing) and are involved in associating this input with stored memories, in the processes of perception, thought, and decision making. (p. 159)

association by contiguity Aristotle's principle that if two environmental events (stimuli) occur at the same time or one right after the other (contiguously), those events will be linked together in the mind. (p. 335)

association by similarity Aristotle's principle that objects, events, or ideas that are similar to one another become linked (associated) in the person's mind (structure of memory), such that the thought of one tends to elicit the thought of the other. (p. 335)

attachment The long-lasting emotional bonds that infants develop toward their principal caregivers. More broadly, the long-lasting emotional bonds that any individual develops toward any other individual or object. (p. 436)

attention In the modal model of the mind, the process that controls the flow of information from the sensory store into working memory. More broadly, any focusing of mental activity along a specific track, whether that track consists purely of inner memories and knowledge or is based on external stimuli. (p. 312)

attitude Any belief or opinion that has an evaluative component—a belief that something is good or bad, likable or unlikable, attractive or repulsive. (p. 499)

attribution In social cognition, any inference about the cause of a person's behavioral action or set of actions. More generally, any inference about the cause of any observed action or event. (p. 476)

auditory masking The phenomenon by which one sound (usually a lower-frequency sound) tends to prevent the hearing of another sound (usually a higher-frequency sound). (p. 258)

autism A congenital (present-at-birth) disorder, typically marked by severe deficits in social interaction, severe deficits in language acquisition, a tendency to perform repetitive actions, and a restricted focus of attention and interest. (pp. 44, 417)

autonomic portion of the peripheral motor system The set of motor neurons that act upon visceral muscles and glands. (p. 153)

availability bias Tendency, in reasoning, to rely too much on information that is readily available to us and to ignore information that is less available. (p. 356)

axon A thin, tubelike extension from a neuron that is specialized to carry neural impulses (action potentials) to other cells. (p. 140)

axon terminal A swelling at the end of an axon that is designed to release a chemical substance (neurotransmitter) onto another neuron, muscle cell, or gland cell. (p. 140)

basal ganglia The large masses of gray matter in the brain that lie on each side of the thalamus; they are especially important for the initiation and coordination of deliberate movements. (p. 156)

basilar membrane A flexible membrane in the cochlea of the inner ear; the wavelike movement of this structure in response to sound stimulates the receptor cells for hearing. See also *hair cells*. (p. 254)

behavior The observable actions of an individual person or animal. (p. 1)

behavior therapy Category of treatment methods that use basic principles of learning in order to weaken unwanted behavioral responses or strengthen desired behavioral responses. (p. 664)

behavioral genetics Research specialty that attempts to explain psychological differences among individuals in terms of differences in their genes. (p. 12)

behavioral neuroscience Research specialty that attempts to explain behavior in terms of processes occurring within the nervous system. (p. 11)

behaviorism A school of psychological thought that holds that the proper subject of study is observable behavior, not the mind, and that behavior should be understood in terms of its relationship to observable events in the environment rather than in terms of hypothetical events within the individual. (p. 99)

bias A technical term referring to nonrandom (directed) effects on research results, caused by some factor or factors extraneous to the research hypothesis. For contrast, see *error*. (p. 41)

biased sample A subset of the population under study that is not representative of the population as a whole. (p. 42)

binocular disparity The cue for depth perception that stems from the separate (disparate) views that the two eyes have of any given visual object or scene. The farther away the object is, the more similar are the two views of it. (p. 299)

bipolar cells The class of neurons in the retina that receive input from the receptor cells (rods and cones) and form synapses on ganglion cells (which form the optic nerve). (p. 273)

bipolar disorders Mood disorders that are characterized by episodes of abnormally high mood (mania) and abnormally low mood (depression). See *bipolar I disorder* and *bipolar II disorder*. (p. 613)

bipolar I disorder The most severe type of bipolar disorder, characterized by at least one episode of mania and one episode of major depression. See *bipolar disorder*. For contrast, see *bipolar II disorder*. (p. 618)

bipolar II disorder The type of bipolar disorder in which the manic phase is less extreme than it is in Bipolar I disorder and is referred to as hypomania rather than mania. See *bipolar disorder*. For contrast, see *bipolar I disorder*. (p. 618)

blind In scientific research, the condition in which those who collect the data are deliberately kept uninformed about aspects of the study's design (such as which subjects have had which treatment) that could lead them either unconsciously or consciously to bias the results. See also *bias, observer-expectancy effect*. (p. 45)

blind spot The place in the retina of the eye where the axons of visual sensory neurons come together to form the optic nerve. Because the blind spot lacks receptor cells, light that strikes it is not seen. (p. 272)

blood-brain barrier The tight capillary walls and the surrounding glial cells that prevent many chemical substances from entering the brain from the blood. (p. 180)

bottom-up control In theories of perception, mental processes that bring the individual stimulus features recorded by the senses together to form a perception of the larger object or scene. For contrast, see *top-down processes*. (p. 291)

brainstem The primitive, stalklike portion of the brain that can be thought of as an extension of the spinal cord into the head; it consists of the medulla, pons, and midbrain. (p. 155)

Broca's aphasia A specific syndrome of loss in language ability that occurs due to damage in a particular part of the brain called *Broca's area*; it is characterized by telegraphic speech in which the meaning is usually clear but the small words and word endings that serve grammatical purposes are missing; also called *nonfluent aphasia*. For contrast, see *Wernicke's aphasia*. (p. 169)

cell body The widest part of a neuron, which contains the cell nucleus and the other basic machinery common to all cells. (p. 139)

cell membrane The thin, porous outer covering of a neuron or other cell that separates the cell's intracellular fluid from extracellular fluid. (p. 141)

central drive system According to the central-state theory of drives, a set of neurons in the brain that, when active, most directly promotes a specific motivational state, or drive. (p. 189)

central executive In Baddeley's theory, a component of the mind responsible for coordinating all the activities of working memory and for bringing new information into working memory. (p. 321)

central nervous system The brain and spinal cord. (p. 138)

central-state theory of drives The theory that the most direct physiological bases for motivational states, or drives, lie in neural activity in the brain. According to most versions of this theory, different drives correspond to activity in different, localizable sets of neurons. See also *central drive system*. (p. 189)

cerebellum The relatively large, conspicuous, convoluted portion of the brain attached to the rear side of the brainstem; it is especially important for the coordination of rapid movements. (p. 156)

cerebral cortex The outermost, evolutionarily newest, and (in humans) by far the largest portion of the brain; it is divisible into two hemispheres (right and left), and each hemisphere is divisible into four lobes—the occipital, temporal, parietal, and frontal. (p. 159)

chromosomes The structures within the cell nucleus that contain the genetic material (DNA). (p. 54)

chunking A strategy for improving the ability to remember a set of items by grouping them mentally to form fewer items. (p. 327)

circadian rhythm Any cyclic physiological or behavioral change in a person or other living thing that has a period of about 1 day even in the absence of external cues signaling the time of day. (p. 217)

classical conditioning A training procedure or learning experience in which a neutral stimulus (the conditioned stimulus) comes to elicit a reflexive response through its being paired with another stimulus (usually an unconditioned stimulus) that already elicits that reflexive response; originally studied by Pavlov. See also *conditioned response, conditioned stimulus, unconditioned response, unconditioned stimulus*. (p. 95)

clinical psychology The field of practice and research that is directed toward helping people who suffer from psychological problems and disorders. (p. 639)

closure principle See *Gestalt principles of grouping*.

cochlea A coiled structure in the inner ear in which the receptor cells for hearing are located. (p. 254)

cognitive-behavior therapy The psychotherapy approach that stems from a union of cognitive and behavioral theory; it usually characterizes psychological problems as learned habits of thought and action, and its approach to treatment is to help people change those habits. See also *behavior therapy, cognitive therapy*. (p. 660)

cognitive dissonance theory Festinger's theory that people seek to relieve the discomfort associated with the awareness of inconsistency between two or more of one's own cognitions (beliefs or bits of knowledge). (p. 504)

cognitive psychology Research specialty that attempts to explain behavior or mental experiences in terms of the cognitions (items of mental information or knowledge) that underlie the behavior or experience. (p. 14)

cognitive therapy An approach to psychotherapy that begins with the assumption that people disturb themselves through their own thoughts and that they can overcome their problems through changing the way they think about their experiences. (p. 660)

common movement principle See *Gestalt principles of grouping*.

concept A rule or other form of mental information for categorizing stimuli into groups. (p. 116)

concordance In behavioral genetics research, an index of heritability that is found by identifying a set of individuals who have a particular trait or disorder and then determining the percentage of some specific class of their relatives (such as identical twins) who have the same trait or disorder. (p. 630)

concrete-operational scheme In Piaget's theory, the type of mental stimulus that allows a child to think logically about reversible actions (operations) but only when applied to objects with which the child has had direct (concrete) experience. See also *operation*. (p. 407)

conditioned reflex In classical conditioning, a reflex that occurs only because of previous conditions in the individual's experience; a learned reflex. For contrast, see *unconditioned reflex*. (p. 95)

conditioned response In classical conditioning, a reflexive response that is elicited by a stimulus (the conditioned stimulus) because of the previous pairing of that stimulus with another stimulus (the unconditioned stimulus) that already elicits a reflexive response. For contrast, see *unconditioned response*. (p. 95)

conditioned stimulus In classical conditioning, a stimulus that comes to elicit a reflexive response (the conditioned response) because of its previous pairing with another stimulus (the unconditioned stimulus) that already elicits a reflexive response. For contrast, see *unconditioned stimulus*. (p. 95)

cones The class of receptor cells for vision that are located in and near the fovea of the retina, operate in moderate to bright light, and are most important for the perception of color and fine detail. For contrast, see *rods*. (p. 271)

cone vision The high-acuity color vision that occurs in moderate to bright light and is mediated by cones in the retina; also called *photopic* or *bright-light vision*. See *cones*. For contrast, see *rod vision*. (p. 272)

confirmation bias Tendency of people to seek evidence that confirms, rather than disconfirms, their current hypotheses. (p. 356)

consciousness In perception, the experiencing of percepts or other mental events in such a manner that one can report on them to others. (p. 309)

consolidation The process by which a new memory becomes solidified in the brain, such that it is not easily forgotten. (p. 332)

content morphemes Words, including nouns, verbs, adjectives, and adverbs, that are most essential to the meaning of a sentence. For contrast, see *grammatical morphemes*. (p. 419)

contingency management In behavior therapy, any systematic alteration in the relationship (contingency) between actions and rewards that is designed to alter the client's behavior in a desired direction. See *behavior therapy*. (p. 665)

control processes In the modal model of the mind, the mental processes that operate on information in the memory stores and move information from one store to another. See *attention, encoding, retrieval*. (p. 311)

conversion disorder A category of somatoform disorder in which the person, for psychological reasons, loses some bodily function. (p. 621)

cooperation In sociobiology, a type of helping behavior in which interaction among two or more individuals increases the survival chance or reproductive capacity of each individual involved in the interaction. For contrast, see *altruism*. (p. 86)

cornea The curved, transparent tissue at the front of the eyeball that helps to focus light rays as they first enter the eye. (p. 270)

corpus callosum A massive bundle of axons connecting the right and left hemispheres of the higher parts of the brain, including the cerebral cortex. (p. 165)

correlation coefficient A numerical measure of the strength and direction of the relationship between two variables. (p. 38)

correlational study Any scientific study in which the researcher observes or measures (without directly manipulating) two or more variables to find relationships between them. Such studies can identify lawful relationships but cannot determine whether change in one variable is the cause of change in another. (p. 33)

cranial nerve A nerve that extends directly from the brain. See *nerves*. For contrast, see *spinal nerve*. (p. 152)

creole language A new language, with grammatical rules, that develops from a pidgin language in colonies established by people who had different native languages. See *pidgin language*. (p. 427)

critical period A relatively restricted time period in an individual's development during which a particular form of learning can best occur. See *imprinting*. (p. 132)

crystallized intelligence In Cattell's theory, the variety of intelligence that derives directly from previous experience. It includes one's accumulated knowledge and verbal skills. For contrast, see *fluid intelligence*. (p. 380)

cultural psychology Research specialty that attempts to explain mental experiences and behavior in terms of the culture in which the person developed. (p. 15)

dark adaptation The increased visual sensitivity that occurs when the eyes are exposed for a period of time to dimmer light than was present before the adaptation period. For contrast, see *light adaptation*. (p. 272)

deductive reasoning Logical reasoning from the general to the specific; the reasoner begins by accepting the truth of one or more general premises or axioms and uses them to assert whether a specific conclusion is true, false, or indeterminate. For contrast, see *inductive reasoning*. (p. 359)

defense mechanisms In psychoanalytic theory, self-deceptive means by which the mind defends itself against anxiety. See *displacement, projection, rationalization, reaction formation, repression, sublimation*. (p. 572)

dendrites The thin, tubelike extensions of a neuron that typically branch repeatedly near the neuron's cell body and are specialized for receiving signals from other neurons. (p. 140)

dependent variable In an experiment, the variable that is believed to be dependent upon (affected by) another variable (the independent variable). In psychological experiments, it is usually some measure of behavior. (p. 31)

depressive disorders The class of mood disorders characterized by prolonged or frequent bouts of depression. See *dysthymia, major depression*. (p. 613)

descriptive statistics Mathematical methods for summarizing sets of data. (p. 37)

descriptive study Any study in which the researcher describes the behavior of an individual or set of individuals without systematically investigating relationships between specific variables. (p. 34)

deterministic fallacy The mistaken belief that genes control, or determine, behavior in a manner that is independent of environmental influences. (p. 89)

developmental psychology The branch of psychology that charts changes in people's abilities and styles of behaving as they get older and tries to understand the factors that produce or influence those changes. (pp. 16, 397)

difference threshold In psychophysics, the minimal difference that must exist between two otherwise similar stimuli for an individual to detect them as different; also called the *just-noticeable difference (jnd)*. (p. 262)

differential lighting of surfaces A pictorial cue for perceiving depth in which the amount of light reflecting on different surfaces indicates the position of objects relative to the light source. (p. 302)

differentiating effects of sex hormones Effects of sex hormones that create the long-lasting structural differences between males and females of a species. Contrast to *activating effects of sex hormones*. (p. 205)

discrimination training The procedure, in both classical and operant conditioning, by which generalization between two stimuli is diminished or abolished by reinforcing the response to one stimulus and extinguishing the response to the other. See *extinction, generalization, reinforcement*. (p. 97)

discriminative stimulus In operant conditioning, a stimulus that serves as a signal that a particular response will produce a particular reinforcer. (p. 115)

displacement The defense mechanism by which a drive is diverted from one goal to another that is more realistic or acceptable. Also called *sublimation* in cases where the goal toward which the drive is diverted is highly valued by society. (p. 573)

dominant gene A gene that produces its observable effects even if the person is heterozygous for that gene (that is, has that gene allele on only one of the two paired chromosomes). Contrast to *recessive gene*. (p. 56)

dopamine One of many neurotransmitter substances in the brain. It is, among other things, crucial for the "wanting" component of reward. (p. 192)

double-blind experiment An experiment in which both the observer and the subjects are blind with respect to the subjects' treatment conditions. See also *blind*. (p. 46)

Down syndrome A disorder that results from having an extra chromosome 21, characterized by a specific set of physical symptoms and moderate to severe retardation in intellectual functioning. (p. 602)

drive See *motivational state*.

drug tolerance The phenomenon by which a drug produces successively smaller physiological and behavioral effects, at any given dose, if it is taken repeatedly. (p. 106)

DSM-IV Commonly used abbreviation for the *Diagnostic and Statistical Manual of Mental Disorders*, Fourth Edition, published by the American Psychiatric Association, which defines a wide variety of mental disorders and establishes criteria for diagnosing them. (p. 594)

dualism The philosophical theory that two distinct systems—the material body and the immaterial soul—are involved in the control of behavior. For contrast, see *materialism*. (p. 3)

dysthymia A mental disorder characterized by feelings of depression that are less severe than those in major depression but which last for at least a 2-year period. See also *major depression*. (p. 613)

echoic memory Sensory memory for the sense of hearing. (p. 316)

ECT See *electroconvulsive therapy*.

elaboration The process of thinking about an item of information in such a way as to tie the item mentally to other information in memory, which helps to encode the item into long-term memory; also called *elaborative rehearsal*. (p. 326)

elaboration likelihood model A theory of persuasion postulating that people are more likely to think logically about a message (that is, elaborate upon the message) if it is personally relevant than if it is not. (p. 503)

electroconvulsive therapy (ECT) A procedure for treating severe depression, in which a patient is anesthetized and given a muscle relaxant, and then an electric current is passed through the patient's skull in such a way as to set up a seizure either in one hemisphere of the brain (unilateral ECT) or in both hemispheres (bilateral ECT). (p. 647)

electroencephalogram (EEG) A record of the electrical activity of the brain that can be obtained by amplifying the weak electrical signals picked up by recording electrodes pasted to the person's scalp. It is usually described in terms of wave patterns. (p. 148)

emotion A subjective feeling that is experienced as directed toward some particular object or event. Contrast to *mood*. (p. 220)

empiricism The idea that all human knowledge and thought ultimately come from sensory experience; the philosophical approach to understanding the mind that is based on that idea. For contrast, see *nativism*. (p. 6)

encoding In the modal model of the mind, the mental process by which long-term memories are formed. See also *long-term memory*. (p. 313)

encoding rehearsal Any active mental process by which a person strives to encode information into long-term memory. For contrast, see *maintenance rehearsal*. (p. 325)

endorphins Chemicals produced in the body that act like morphine in inhibiting pain. (pp. 193, 250)

episodic memory Explicit memory of past events (episodes) in one's own life. For contrast, see *semantic memory, implicit memory*. (p. 343)

error A technical term referring to random variability in research results. For contrast, see *bias*. (p. 41)

evolutionary psychology Research specialty that attempts to explain how or why specific behavioral characteristics would have come about, by natural selection, in the course of evolution. (p. 13)

excitatory synapse A synapse at which the neurotransmitter increases the likelihood that an action potential will occur, or increases the rate at which they are already occurring, in the neuron on which it acts. For contrast, see *inhibitory synapse*. (p. 144)

experiment A research design for testing hypotheses about cause-effect relationships, in which the researcher manipulates one variable (the independent variable) in order to assess its effect on another variable (the dependent variable). (p. 31)

explicit attitudes Conscious attitudes; that is, attitudes that people are aware of holding and can state verbally. For contrast, see *implicit attitudes*. (p. 499)

explicit memory The class of memory that can be consciously recalled and used to answer explicit questions about what one knows or remembers. See *episodic memory, semantic memory*. For contrast, see *implicit memory*. (p. 342)

explicit stereotypes Stereotypes that people hold consciously. See *stereotypes*. For contrast, see *implicit stereotypes*. (p. 495)

exposure treatment Any method of treating fears—including flooding and systematic desensitization—that involves exposing the client to the feared object or situation (either in reality or imagination) so that the process of extinction or habituation of the fear response can occur. (p. 666)

extinction In classical conditioning, the gradual disappearance of a conditioned reflex that results when a conditioned stimulus occurs repeatedly without the unconditioned stimulus. (p. 97) In operant conditioning, the decline in response rate that results when an operant response is no longer followed by a reinforcer. (p. 112) See *classical conditioning, operant conditioning*.

fact An objective statement, usually based on direct observation, that reasonable observers agree is true. In psychology, facts are usually particular behaviors, or reliable patterns of behaviors, of persons or animals. (p. 29)

factor analysis A statistical procedure for analyzing the correlations among various measurements (such as test scores) taken from a given set of individuals; it identifies hypothetical, underlying variables called *factors* that could account for the observed pattern of correlations and assesses the degree to which each factor is adequately measured by each of the measurements that was used in the analysis. (p. 551)

feature detector In vision, any neuron in the brain that responds to a specific property of a visual stimulus, such as its color, orientation, movement, or shape of its contour. More generally, any neuron in the brain that responds to a particular property (feature) of any sensory stimulus. (p. 284)

Fechner's law The idea that the magnitude of the sensory experience of a stimulus is directly proportional to the logarithm of the physical magnitude of the stimulus. For contrast, see *power law*. (p. 264)

field study Any scientific research study in which data are collected in a setting other than the laboratory. (p. 35)

figure In perception, the portion of a visual scene that draws the perceiver's attention and is interpreted as an object rather than as the background. For contrast, see *ground*. (p. 288)

five-factor model of personality Model holding that a person's personality is most efficiently described in terms of his or her score on each of five relatively independent global trait dimensions: *neuroticism, extraversion, openness to experience, agreeableness*, and *conscientiousness*. (p. 553)

fixed-interval (FI) schedule In operant conditioning, a schedule of reinforcement in which a fixed period of time must elapse after each reinforced response before it produces a reinforcer. (p. 553)

fixed-ratio (FR) schedule In operant conditioning, a schedule of reinforcement in which a response must be produced a certain fixed number of times (more than once) before it produces a reinforcer. (p. 113)

fluid intelligence In Cattell's theory, the variety of intelligence that enables one to perceive relationships independent of previous specific practice or instruction concerning those relationships. For contrast, see *crystallized intelligence*. (p. 380)

fMRI See *functional magnetic resonance imaging*.

foot-in-the-door technique A technique for gaining compliance in which one first asks for some relatively small contribution or favor before asking for a larger one. Complying with the first request predisposes the person to comply with the second. (p. 526)

formal-operational scheme In Piaget's theory, the type of mental stimulus that allows a person to reason about abstract concepts and hypothetical ideas. See also *operation, schemes*. (p. 407)

fovea The pinhead-size area of the retina of the eye in which the cones are concentrated and that is specialized for high visual acuity. (p. 271)

fraternal twins Two individuals who developed simultaneously in the same womb, but who originated from separate zygotes (fertilized eggs) and are therefore no more genetically similar to one another than are nontwin siblings; also called *dizygotic twins*. For contrast, see *identical twins*. (p. 56)

free association In psychoanalysis, the procedure in which a patient relaxes, frees his or her mind from the constraints of conscious logic, and reports every image and idea that enters his or her awareness. (p. 652)

frequency For any form of energy that changes in a cyclic or wave-like way, the number of cycles or waves that occur during a standard unit of time. For sound, this physical measure is related to the psychological experience of pitch. (p. 253)

frequency distribution A table or graph depicting the number of individual scores, in a set of scores, that fall within each of a set of equal intervals. (p. A-2)

frontal lobe The frontmost lobe of the cerebral cortex, bounded in the rear by the parietal and temporal lobes; it contains the motor area and parts of the association areas involved in planning and making judgments. (p. 159)

functionalism A school of psychological thought, founded by William James and others, that focuses on understanding the functions, or adaptive purposes, of mental processes. For contrast, see *structuralism*. (p. 67)

functional magnetic resonance imagining (fMRI) A method for visually displaying brain activity that is based on the fact that protons in certain molecules can be made to resonate and give off radio waves indicating relative amounts of neural activity in each portion of the brain. (p. 149)

ganglion cells The sensory neurons for vision; their cell bodies are located in the retina, and their axons run by way of the optic nerve into the brain. (p. 273)

gate-control theory Melzack and Wall's theory that pain will be experienced only if the input from peripheral pain neurons passes through a "gate" located at the point that the pain-carrying neurons enter the spinal cord or lower brainstem. (p. 248)

gaze following The automatic, reflexive action by which one individual's eyes move when another individual's eyes move, so that both end up looking at the same object. (p. 127)

gender identity A person's subjective sense of being male or female. (p. 454)

general intelligence In Spearman's theory of intelligence (and in other theories based on Spearman's), the underlying mental ability that affects performance on a wide variety of mental tests and accounts for the statistical correlation among scores on such tests; also called *g*. (p. 379)

generalization In classical conditioning, the phenomenon by which a stimulus that resembles a conditioned stimulus will elicit the conditioned response even though it has never been paired with the unconditioned stimulus. (p. 104) In operant conditioning, the phenomenon by which a stimulus that resembles a discriminative stimulus will increase the rate at which the animal produces the operant response, even though the response has never been reinforced in the presence of that stimulus. (p. 97)

generalized anxiety disorder A mental disorder characterized by prolonged, severe anxiety that is not consistently associated in the person's mind with any particular object or event in the environment or any specific life experience. (p. 607)

genotype The set of genes inherited by the individual. See also *phenotype*. (p. 54)

Gestalt principles of grouping The rules, proposed by Gestalt psychologists, concerning the manner by which the perceptual system groups sensory elements together to produce organized perceptions of whole objects and scenes. They include the principles of (a) *proximity* (nearby elements are grouped together), (b) *similarity* (elements that resemble one another are grouped together), (c) *closure* (gaps in what would otherwise be a continuous border are ignored), (d) *good continuation* (when lines intersect, those segments that would form a continuous line with minimal change in direction are grouped together), (e) *common movement* (elements moving in the same direction and velocity are grouped together), and (f) *good form* (elements are grouped in such a way as to form percepts that are simple and symmetrical). (p. 287)

Gestalt psychology A school of psychological thought, founded in Germany, which emphasizes the idea that the mind must be understood in terms of organized wholes, not elementary parts. For contrast, see *structuralism*. (p. 286)

good continuation principle See *Gestalt principles of grouping*.

good form principle See *Gestalt principles of grouping*.

grammar The entire set of rules that specify the permissible ways that smaller units can be arranged to form morphemes, words, phrases, and sentences in a language. (p. 420)

grammatical morphemes The class of words, suffixes, and prefixes that serve primarily to fill out the grammatical structure of a sentence rather than to carry its main meaning. For contrast, see *content morphemes*. (p. 419)

ground In perception, the portion of a visual scene that is interpreted as the background rather than as the object of attention. For contrast, see *figure*. (p. 288)

group polarization The tendency for a group of people who already share a particular opinion to hold that opinion more strongly—or in a more extreme form—after discussing the issue among themselves. (p. 522)

groupthink A model of thinking in which members of a group are more concerned with group cohesiveness and unanimity than with realistic appraisal of the actions being considered. (p. 524)

habituation The decline in the magnitude or likelihood of a reflexive response that occurs when the stimulus is repeated several or many times in succession. (p. 94)

hair cells The receptor cells for hearing, which are arranged in rows along the basilar membrane of the cochlea in the inner ear. (p. 254)

helping In sociobiology, any behavior that increases the survival chance or reproductive capacity of another individual. See also *altruism, cooperation*. (p. 86)

heritability The proportion of the variability in a particular characteristic, in a particular group of individuals, that is due to genetic rather than environmental differences among the individuals. For contrast, see *environmentality*. (p. 385)

heritability coefficient A measure of heritability, which can vary from 0 (no heritability) to 1 (complete heritability); specifically, variance due to genes divided by total variance. See *heritability*. (p. 385)

heterozygous The condition in which a pair of genes occupying the same locus on a pair of chromosomes are different from one another. For contrast, see *homozygous*. (p. 56)

hippocampus A structure in the limbic system of the brain that is essential for encoding explicit memories for long-term storage. (p. 158)

homeostasis The constancy in the body's internal environment that must be maintained through the expenditure of energy. (p. 187)

homology In ethology and comparative psychology, any similarity among species that exists because of the species' common ancestry. For contrast, see *analogy*. (p. 74)

homozygous The condition in which a pair of genes occupying the same locus on a pair of chromosomes are identical to one another. For contrast, see *heterozygous*. (p. 56)

hormone Any chemical substance that is secreted naturally by the body into the blood and can influence physiological processes at specific target tissues (such as the brain) and thereby influence behavior. (p. 177)

humanistic theories Personality theories that attempt to focus attention on the whole, unique person, especially on the person's conscious understanding of his or her self and the world. (p. 577)

humanistic therapy Any of several types of psychotherapy that emerged from humanistic personality theories, usually emphasizing the client's own constructions of his or her reality. See *humanistic personality theories* and *person-centered therapy*. (p. 656)

hypothalamus A small brain structure lying just below the thalamus, connected directly to the pituitary gland and to the limbic system, that is especially important for the regulation of motivation, emotion, and the internal physiological conditions of the body. (p. 158)

hypothesis A specific prediction about what will be observed in a research study, usually derived from a more general conception or theory. See also *theory*. (p. 29)

iconic memory Sensory memory for the sense of vision. (p. 316)

identical twins Two individuals who are genetically identical to one another because they originated from a single zygote (fertilized egg); also called monozygotic twins. For contrast, see *fraternal twins*. (p. 56)

implicit association tests Tests of a person's automatic, unconscious mental associations, designed to assess implicit stereotypes or other implicit attitudes. See *implicit stereotypes*. (p. 495)

implicit attitudes Attitudes that are manifested in a person's behavior or automatic mental associations, even though the person may not be conscious of holding those attitudes. For contrast, see *explicit attitudes*. (p. 499)

implicit memory Memory that influences one's behavior or thought but does not itself enter consciousness. See *priming, procedural memory*. For contrast, see *explicit memory*. (p. 342)

implicit stereotypes Stereotypes that automatically, unconsciously influence people's judgments and actions toward others. See *stereotypes*. For contrast, see *explicit stereotypes*. (p. 495)

impression management The entire set of ways by which people either consciously or unconsciously attempt to influence other people's impressions (perceptions and judgments) of them. (p. 515)

imprinting Ethologists' term for a relatively sudden and irreversible form of learning that can occur only during some critical period of the individual's development. See *critical period*. (p. 132)

independent variable In an experiment, the condition that the researcher varies in order to assess its effect upon some other variable (the dependent variable). In psychology, it is usually some condition of the environment or of the organism's physiology that is hypothesized to affect the individual's behavior. (p. 31)

inductive reasoning Logical reasoning from the specific to the general; the reasoner begins with a set of specific observations or facts and uses them to infer a more general rule to account for those observations or facts; also called *hypothesis construction*. For contrast, see *deductive reasoning*. (p. 355)

inferential statistics Mathematical methods for helping researchers determine how confident they can be in drawing general conclusions (inferences) from specific sets of data. (p. 37)

informational influence The class of social influence that derives from the use of others' behavior or opinions as information in forming one's own judgment about the objective nature of an event or situation. For contrast, see *normative influence*. (p. 517)

inhibitory synapse A synapse at which the neurotransmitter decreases the likelihood that an action potential will occur, or decreases the rate at which they are already occurring, in the neuron upon which it acts. For contrast, see *excitatory synapse*. (p. 144)

inner ear The portion of the ear lying farthest inward in the head; it contains the cochlea (for hearing) and the vestibular apparatus (for the sense of balance). (p. 254)

insight problem A problem that is difficult to solve until it is viewed in a new way, involving a different mental set from that originally taken. See *mental set*. (p. 362)

insufficient-justification effect A change in attitude that serves to justify an action that seems unjustified in the light of the previously held attitude. (p. 506)

intelligence The variable mental capacity that underlies individual differences in reasoning, solving problems, and acquiring new knowledge. (p. 375)

interneuron A neuron that exists entirely within the brain or spinal cord and carries messages from one set of neurons to another. (p. 139)

IQ Abbreviation for *intelligence quotient*, defined as a score on a test of intelligence that is standardized in such a way that the average score for the population is 100 and the distribution of scores around that average matches a normal distribution. See *standardized score* and *normal distribution*. (p. 377)

iris The colored (usually brown or blue), doughnut-shaped, muscular structure in the eye, located behind the cornea and in front of the lens, that controls the size of the pupil and in that way controls the amount of light that can enter the eye's interior. (p. 270)

just-noticeable difference (jnd) See *difference threshold*.

kin selection theory of altruism The sociobiological theory that apparent acts of altruism have come about through natural selection because such actions are disproportionately directed toward close genetic relatives and thus promote the survival of others who have the same genes. See also *altruism*. (p. 87)

laboratory study Any research study in which the subjects are brought to a specially designated area (laboratory) that has been set up to facilitate the researcher's ability to control the environment or collect data. (p. 35)

language-acquisition device (LAD) Chomsky's term for the special, innate characteristics of the human mind that allow children to learn their native language; it includes innate knowledge of basic aspects of grammar that are common to all languages and an innate predisposition to attend to and remember the critical, unique aspects of the language. (p. 427)

language-acquisition support system (LASS) The term used by social-learning theorists to refer to the simplification of language and the use of gestures that occur when parents or other language users speak to young children, which helps children learn language; developed as a complement to Chomsky's concept of the LAD (language-acquisition device). (p. 429)

latent learning Learning that is not demonstrated in the subject's behavior at the time that the learning occurs but can be inferred from its effect on the subject's behavior at some later time. (p. 124)

law of complementarity The observation that certain pairs of limited-wavelength lights that produce different colors (such as red and green) alone will produce the perception of white (no color) when mixed. See also *additive color mixing*. (p. 276)

law of effect Thorndike's principle that responses that produce a satisfying effect in a particular situation become more likely to recur in that situation, and responses that produce a discomforting effect become less likely to recur in that situation. (p. 109)

learning The process or set of processes through which sensory experience at one time can affect an individual's behavior at a future time. (p. 93)

learning psychology Research specialty, in psychology, that attempts to understand how the behavior of individuals is shaped through basic learning processes. (p. 13)

lens In the eye, the transparent structure behind the iris that helps focus light that passes through the pupil. (p. 270)

leptin A hormone produced by fat cells that acts in the brain to inhibit hunger and regulate body weight. (p. 198)

level of analysis The type ("level") of causal process that is referred to in explaining some phenomenon. In psychology, a given type of behavior might be explained at the neural, genetic, evolutionary, learning, cognitive, social, cultural, or developmental level of analysis. (p. 10)

light adaptation The decreased visual sensitivity that occurs when the eyes are exposed for a period of time to brighter light than was present before the adaptation period. For contrast, see *dark adaptation.* (p. 272)

limbic system An interconnected set of brain structures (including the amygdala and hippocampus) that form a circuit wrapped around the thalamus and basal ganglia, underneath the cerebral cortex. These structures are especially important for the regulation of emotion and motivation and are involved in the formation of long-term memories. (p. 158)

linear perspective A pictorial cue for perceiving depth in which the convergence of parallel lines indicates the distance of objects. Parallel lines appear to converge as they become more distant. (p. 302)

linguistic relativity Whorf's theory that people who have different native languages perceive the world differently and think differently from each other because of their different languages. (p. 370)

locus In genetics, a position on a chromosome that contains the DNA of a single gene. (p. 56)

locus of control According to Rotter, a person's perception of the typical source of control over rewards. *Internal locus of control* refers to the perception that people control their own rewards through their own behavior, and *external locus of control* refers to the perception that rewards are controlled by external circumstances or fate. (p. 582)

long-term memory In the modal model of the mind, information that is retained in the mind for long periods (often throughout life). For contrasts, see *sensory memory, working memory.* (p. 312)

long-term potentiation (LTP) A process by which repeated activation of synapses results in strengthening of those synapses. (p. 175)

loudness The quality of the psychological experience (sensation) of a sound that is most directly related to the amplitude of the physical sound stimulus. (p. 253)

low-ball technique A sales trick in which the salesperson suggests a low price for the item being sold, and then, when the potential customer has agreed to buy it at that price, pretends to discover that the item cannot be sold for that price. (p. 525)

LTP See *long-term potentiation.*

maintenance rehearsal Any active mental process by which a person strives to hold information in short-term memory for a period of time. For contrast, see *encoding rehearsal.* (p. 325)

major depression A mental disorder characterized by severe depression that lasts essentially without remission for at least 2 weeks. (p. 613)

materialism Hobbes's theory that nothing exists but matter and energy. For contrast, see *dualism.* (p. 4)

mean The arithmetic average of a set of scores, determined by adding the scores and dividing the sum by the number of scores. (pp. 37, A-3)

medial forebrain bundle A bundle of neurons that runs from the midbrain to the basal ganglia and other forebrain areas. (p. 191)

median The center score in a set of scores that have been rank-ordered. (pp. 37, A-3)

medulla The lowest portion of the brainstem, bounded at one end by the spinal cord and at the other by the pons. It is responsible, with the pons, for organizing reflexes more complex than spinal reflexes. (p. 155)

meiosis The form of cell division involved in producing egg or sperm cells, which results in cells that are genetically dissimilar and that each have half the number of chromosomes of the original cell. (p. 55)

memory 1. The mind's ability to retain information over time. 2. Information retained in the mind over time. (p. 310)

memory stores In cognitive psychology, hypothetical constructs that are conceived of as places where information is held in the mind. (p. 311)

mental disorder A disturbance in a person's emotions, drives, thought processes, or behavior that (a) involves serious and relatively prolonged distress and/or impairment in ability to function, (b) is not simply a normal response to some event or set of events in the person's environment, and (c) is not explainable as an effect of poverty, prejudice, or other social forces that prevent the person from behaving adaptively, nor as a deliberate decision to act in a way that is contrary to the norms of society. (p. 594)

mental set A habit of perception or thought, stemming from previous experience, that can either help or hinder a person in solving a new problem. (p. 364)

midbrain The upper portion of the brainstem, bounded at its lower end by the pons and at its upper end by the thalamus, that contains neural centers that organize basic movement patterns. (p. 155)

middle ear The air-filled cavity separated from the outer ear by the eardrum; its main structures are three ossicles (tiny bones) that vibrate in response to sound waves and stimulate the inner ear. (p. 254)

mind The entire set of an individual's sensations, perceptions, memories, thoughts, dreams, motives, emotional feelings, and other subjective experiences. (p. 1) 2. In cognitive psychology, the set of hypothesized information-processing steps that analyze stimulus information and organize behavioral responses. (p. 1)

mirror neurons Neurons in the brain that become active both when the individual makes a particular motion and when the individual sees another individual making that same motion. These neurons are believed to facilitate observational learning. (p. 125)

mitosis The form of cell division involved in normal body growth, which produces cells that are genetically identical to each other. (p. 55)

modal model of the mind A depiction of the mind as a set of memory storage compartments and control processes for manipulating and moving information. It has long served as the standard framework for thinking about the human mind. (p. 310)

mode The most frequently occurring score in a set of scores; in a frequency distribution, the interval that contains the highest frequency of scores. (p. A-3)

monogamy A mating system in which one female and one male bond only with each other. For contrast, see *polyandry, polygyny, polygynandry.* (p. 78)

mood A free-floating emotional feeling, not directed at a specific object. Contrast to *emotion.* (p. 220)

moon illusion The illusion by which the moon appears larger when seen near the horizon and smaller when seen near the zenith, even though it is objectively the same size and distance from the viewer in either location. (p. 305)

morphemes The smallest meaningful units of a verbal language; words, prefixes, or suffixes that have discrete meanings. (p. 419)

motion parallax The cue for depth perception that stems from the changed view one has of a scene or object when one's head moves sideways to the scene or object; the farther away an object is, the smaller is the change in view. (p. 301)

motivation The entire constellation of factors, some inside the organism and some outside, that cause an individual to behave in a particular way at a particular time. See also *incentive, motivational state.* (p. 186)

motivational state An internal, reversible condition in an individual that orients the individual toward one or another type of goal (such as food or water). This condition is not observed directly but is inferred from the individual's behavior; also called a *drive.* (p. 186)

motor neuron A neuron that carries messages from the brain or spinal cord, through a nerve, to a muscle or gland. (p. 139)

Müller-Lyer illusion A visual size illusion in which a horizontal line looks longer if attached at each end to an outward-extending, V-shaped object, and looks shorter if attached at each end to an inward-extending, V-shaped object. (p. 304)

mutations Errors that occasionally and unpredictably occur during DNA replication, producing a "replica" that is different from the original. Mutations are believed to be the original source of all genetic variability. (p. 64)

myelin sheath A casing of fatty cells wrapped tightly around the axon of some neurons. (p. 140)

nativism The idea that certain elementary ideas are innate to the human mind and do not need to be gained through experience; the philosophical approach to understanding the mind that is based on that idea. For contrast, see *empiricism*. (p. 7)

natural selection The selective breeding that results from the obstacles to reproduction that are imposed by the natural environment; it is the driving force of evolution. See *selective breeding*. (p. 64)

naturalistic fallacy The mistaken belief that whatever is natural (and particularly whatever is a product of natural selection) is right, good, or moral. (p. 89)

naturalistic observation Any data-collection procedure in which the researcher records subjects' ongoing behavior in a natural setting, without interfering with that behavior. (p. 36)

nature–nurture debate The long-standing controversy as to whether the differences among people are principally due to their genetic differences (nature) or differences in their past and present environment (nurture). (p. 384)

negative contrast effect In operant conditioning, the decline in response rate, when the size of a reinforcer (or reward) is reduced, to a rate below that which occurs for subjects that had been receiving the smaller reinforcer all along. For contrast, see *positive contrast effect*. (p. 118)

negative punishment In operant conditioning, the type of punishment in which the *removal* of a stimulus (such as taking food or money) when a response occurs decreases the likelihood that the response will recur. For contrast, see *positive punishment*. (p. 114)

negative reinforcement In operant conditioning, the condition in which a response results in *removal* of a negative reinforcer. See *negative reinforcer*. (p. 114)

negative reinforcer In operant conditioning, a stimulus (such as electric shock or loud noise) that is *removed* after a response and whose removal increases the likelihood that the response will recur. (p. 114)

nerve A large bundle containing the axons of many neurons. Located in the peripheral nervous system, nerves connect the central nervous system with muscles, glands, and sensory organs. (p. 138)

neurohormone A chemical substance that is similar to a neuro-transmitter in that it is secreted from the axon terminals of neurons but is classed as a hormone because it is secreted into blood vessels rather than onto other neurons. (p. 178)

neuromodulators Slow-acting neurotransmitters that do not directly alter the electrical charges across post-synaptic neurons, but, instead, alter the manner by which post-synaptic neurons respond to fast-acting neurotransmitters. (p. 145)

neurons Single cells in the nervous system that are specialized for carrying information rapidly from one place to another and/or integrating information from various sources; also called *nerve cells*. (p. 138)

neuropeptide Y Neurotransmitter that acts in the brain to stimulate appetite. (p. 196)

neurotransmitter A chemical substance released from the axon terminal of a neuron, at a synapse, that influences the activity of another neuron, a muscle cell, or a glandular cell; also called a *transmitter*. (p. 143)

nonregulatory drive Any motivational state (such as the sex drive) that serves some function *other than* that of preserving some constancy of the body's internal environment. For contrast, see *regulatory drive*. (p. 188)

non-REM sleep Stages 2, 3, and 4 of sleep, characterized by the occurrence of slow (delta) waves in the EEG and the lack of rapid eye movements. Contrast to *REM sleep*. (p. 210)

normal distribution A bell-shaped frequency distribution in which the mean, median, and mode are identical and the frequency of scores tapers off symmetrically on both sides, as defined by a specific mathematical equation. See *frequency distribution*. (pp. 60, A-2)

normative influence The class of social influence that derives from people's concern about what others will think of them if they behave in a certain way or express a certain belief. For contrast, see *informational influence*. (p. 517)

nucleus In neuroanatomy, a cluster of cell bodies of neurons within the central nervous system (not to be confused with the cell nucleus within each cell). (p. 146)

nucleus accumbens A nucleus (center of neural cell bodies) in the basal ganglia that is a crucial part of the brain's reward mechanism. (p. 191)

object permanence Piaget's term for the understanding that an object still exists even when it is out of view. (p. 402)

observational learning Learning by watching others. See also *modeling*. (p. 124)

observational method Any data-collection procedure in which the researcher directly observes the behavior of interest rather than relying on subjects' self-descriptions. (p. 36)

observer-expectancy effect Any bias in research results that derives from the researcher's desire or expectation that a subject or set of subjects will behave in a certain way. See *bias, subject-expectancy effect*. (p. 43)

obsessive-compulsive disorder A mental disorder characterized by a repeated, disturbing, irrational thought (the *obsession*) that can only be terminated (temporarily) by performing some action (the *compulsion*). (p. 610)

occipital lobe The rearmost lobe of the cerebral cortex, bounded in front by the temporal and parietal lobes; it contains the visual area of the brain. (p. 159)

occlusion A pictorial cue for perceiving depth in which the closer object occludes (cuts off) part of the view of the more distant object. (p. 301)

operant conditioning A training or learning process by which the consequence of a behavioral response affects the likelihood that the individual will produce that response again; also called *instrumental conditioning*. (p. 108)

operant response Any behavioral response that produces some reliable effect on the environment that influences the likelihood that the individual will produce that response again; also called *instrumental response*. (p. 108)

operation Piaget's term for a reversible action that can be performed either in reality or mentally upon some object or set of objects. For example, rolling a clay ball into a clay sausage is an operation, because the sausage can be rolled back again to form the ball. (p. 406)

opponent-process theory of color vision A theory designed by Hering to explain the law of complementarity, it holds that units (neurons) that mediate the perception of color are excited by one range of wavelengths and inhibited by another (complementary) range of wavelengths. According to the theory, such units cancel out the perception of color when two complementary wavelength ranges are superimposed. See also *law of complementarity*. (p. 280)

optic nerve The cranial nerve that contains the sensory neurons for vision, which run from the eye's retina into the brain. (p. 271)

outer ear The pinna (the visible, external portion of the ear) and the auditory canal (the air-filled opening that extends inward from the pinna to the middle ear). (p. 253)

overjustification effect The phenomenon in which a person who initially performs a task for no reward (except the enjoyment of the task) becomes less likely to perform that task for no reward after a period during which he or she has been rewarded for performing it. (p. 119)

panic disorder A mental disorder characterized by the repeated occurrence of panic attacks at unpredictable times and with no clear relationship to environmental events. Each attack involves an intense feeling of terror, which usually lasts several minutes and is accompanied by signs of high physiological arousal. (p. 611)

parallel processing In perception, the early (unconscious) steps in the analysis of sensory information that act simultaneously on all (or at least many) of the stimulus elements that are available at any given moment. For contrast, see *serial processing*. (p. 284)

parasympathetic division of the autonomic motor system The set of motor neurons that act upon visceral muscles and glands and mediate many of the body's regenerative, growth-promoting, and energy-conserving functions. For contrast, see *sympathetic division of the autonomic motor system*. (p. 154)

parental investment The time, energy, and risk to survival involved in producing, feeding, and otherwise caring for each offspring. (p. 78)

parietal lobe The lobe of the cerebral cortex that lies in front of the occipital lobe, above the temporal lobe, and behind the frontal lobe; it contains the somatosensory area of the brain. (p. 159)

partial reinforcement In operant conditioning, any condition in which the response sometimes produces a reinforcer and sometimes does not. See *reinforcer*. (p. 112)

pattern generators Networks of neurons that stimulate one another in a cyclic manner and thereby produce bursts of action potentials that wax and wane in a regular, repeating rhythm. They help to control rhythmic sequences of muscle movements, such as those involved in walking, running, flying (in birds), or swimming (in fish). (p. 155)

percentile rank For any single score in a set of scores, the percentage of scores in the set that are equal to or lower than that score. (p. A-5)

perception The recognition, organization, and meaningful interpretation of sensory stimuli. For contrast, see *sensation*. (p. 232)

peripheral nervous system The entire set of cranial and spinal nerves that connect the central nervous system (brain and spinal cord) to the body's sensory organs, muscles, and glands. (p. 138)

perpetuating causes of a mental disorder Those consequences of a mental disorder—such as the way other people treat the person who has it—that help keep the disorder going once it begins. See *precipitating* and *predisposing causes of a mental disorder*. (p. 604)

person bias The tendency to attribute a person's behavior too much to the person's inner characteristics (personality) and not enough to the environmental situation. Sometimes called the fundamental attribution error. For contrast, see *situation bias*. (p. 477)

person-centered therapy The humanistic approach to psychotherapy (also called *client-centered therapy*) developed by Carl Rogers, in which the therapist generally refrains from offering advice or leading the course of therapy, but rather listens to the client with empathy and respect and reflects the client's thoughts and feelings back to him or her. See *humanistic therapy* and *humanistic personality theories*. (p. 657)

personal identity The portion of the self-concept that pertains to the self as a distinct, separate individual. For contrast, see *social identity*. (p. 492)

personal myth The ever-changing self-told story of an individual that gives a sense of direction and meaning to one's life. (p. 579)

personality The relatively consistent patterns of thought, feeling, and behavior that characterize each person as a unique individual. (p. 549)

PET See *positron emission tomography*.

phenomenological reality Humanistic theorists' term for each person's conscious understanding of his or her world. (p. 577)

phenotype The observable properties of an individual's body and behavior. See also *genotype*. (p. 54)

pheromone A chemical that is released by an animal and that acts on other members of the species to promote some specific behavioral or physiological response. (p. 241)

phobia Any mental disorder characterized by a strong, irrational fear of some particular category of object or event. (p. 608)

phonemes The various vowel and consonant sounds that provide the basis for a spoken language. (pp. 260, 420)

phonological loop In Baddeley's theory, a component of working memory responsible for holding verbal information. (p. 321)

photoreceptors Specialized light-detecting cells connected to the nervous system in many multicellular animals. (p. 269) In humans and other vertebrates, the photoreceptors are rods and cones. (p. 269)

pictorial cues for depth perception The depth cues that operate not only when viewing real scenes but also when viewing pictures. They include *occlusion, relative image size for familiar objects, linear perspective, texture gradient, differential lighting of surfaces*, and (for outdoor scenes) *position relative to the horizon*. (p. 301)

pidgin language A primitive system of communication that emerges when people with different native languages colonize the same region; it uses words from the various native languages and has either no or minimal grammatical structure. See also *creole language*. (p. 427)

pitch The quality of the psychological experience (sensation) of a sound that is most related to the frequency of the physical sound stimulus. (p. 253)

placebo In drug studies, an inactive substance given to subjects assigned to the nondrug group. More generally, any treatment that alters a person's behavior or feelings through the power of suggestion. (p. 46)

polyandry A mating system in which one female bonds with more than one male. For contrast, see *monogamy, polygyny, polygynandry*. (p. 78)

polygenic characteristic Any trait or characteristic for which the observed variation is affected by many genes. (p. 60)

polygynandry A mating system in which members of a group consisting of more than one male and more than one female mate with one another. For contrast, see *monogamy, polygyny, polyandry*. (p. 78)

polygyny A mating system in which one male bonds with more than one female. For contrast, see *monogamy, polyandry, polygynandry*. (p. 78)

pons The portion of the brainstem that is bounded at its lower end by the medulla and its upper end by the midbrain and is responsible, with the medulla, for organizing reflexes more complex than spinal reflexes. (p. 155)

Ponzo illusion A visual size illusion in which two converging lines cause objects between the two lines to look larger near the converging ends of the lines and smaller near the diverging ends. (p. 304)

position relative to the horizon A pictorial cue for perceiving depth in which objects nearer the horizon seem farther away than objects displaced from the horizon. (p. 302)

positive contrast effect In operant conditioning, the increase in response rate, when the size of the reinforcer (or reward) is increased, to a rate that increases above that which occurs for subjects that had been receiving the larger reinforcer all along. For contrast, see *negative contrast effect*. (p. 118)

positive punishment In operant conditioning, the type of punishment in which the *presentation* of a stimulus (such as an electric shock or scolding) when a response occurs decreases the likelihood that the response will recur. For contrast, see *negative punishment*. (p. 114)

positive reinforcement In operant conditioning, the condition in which a response results in a positive reinforcer. (p. 114)

positive reinforcer In operant conditioning, a stimulus (such as food or money) that is presented after a response and that increases the likelihood that the response will recur. (p. 114)

positron emission tomography (PET) A method for visually displaying brain activity that is based upon the uptake of a radioactive form of oxygen into active areas of the brain. (p. 149)

posttraumatic stress disorder A mental disorder that is directly and explicitly tied to a particular traumatic incident or set of incidents (such as torture) that the affected person has experienced. (p. 611)

preattentive processing The analysis, at an unconscious level, in which the mind determines which stimuli are worth passing into working memory. (p. 314)

precipitating causes of a mental disorder The events that most immediately bring on a mental disorder in a person who is sufficiently predisposed for the disorder. See also *maintaining* and *predisposing causes of a mental disorder*. (p. 603)

predictable-world bias Tendency to believe that events are more predictable than they actually are. (p. 357)

predisposing causes of a mental disorder Those conditions that are in place well before the onset of a mental disorder and that make the person susceptible to the disorder. They may include genetic predisposition, early childhood experiences, and the sociocultural environment in which one develops. See also *maintaining* and *precipitating causes of a mental disorder.* (p. 603)

prefrontal cortex The front-most portion of the frontal lobe of the brain's cerebral cortex. (pp. 162, 227)

premotor areas Portions of the brain's cerebral cortex that lie directly anterior to (in front of) the motor area. They provide neural programs for producing organized movements. (p. 161)

preoperational scheme In Piaget's theory, mental structures that permit the child to symbolize objects and events that are absent, but do not permit the child to think about the operations that can be performed on objects. See also *operation, schemes.* (p. 406)

primary motor area An area in the rear part of the frontal lobe of the cerebral cortex that is directly involved in the control of movements, especially finely coordinated movements of small muscles, as in the fingers and vocal apparatus. (p. 159)

primary sensory areas Specialized areas of the cerebral cortex that receive input from sensory nerves and tracts by way of the relay nuclei in the thalamus. They include the visual area (in the occipital lobe), auditory area (in the temporal lobe), and somatosensory area (in the parietal lobe). (p. 159)

primary visual area The area in the rearmost part of the occipital lobe that receives input from the optic nerves (by way of the thalamus) and sends output to other visual-processing areas of the brain. (p. 283)

priming The implicit memory process by which a stimulus (the priming stimulus) activates (makes more retrievable) one or more memories that already exist in a person's mind. See *implicit memory.* (p. 317)

prisoner's dilemma games A class of laboratory games in which the tendency to compete can be pitted against the tendency to cooperate. In such games, the highest combined payoff to the two players occurs if both choose the cooperative response, but the highest individual payoff goes to a player who chooses the competitive response on a play in which the other chooses the cooperative response. (p. 534)

procedural memory The class of implicit memory that enables a person to perform specific learned skills or habitual responses. See *implicit memory.* (p. 344)

proceptivity In discussions of sexuality, refers to one's motivation to seek out and initiate sexual activity, even when sexually arousing stimuli are not already present. For contrast, see *arousability.* (p. 204)

projection The defense mechanism by which a person consciously experiences his or her own unconscious emotion or wish as though it belongs to someone else or to some part of the environment. (p. 573)

proximate explanations Explanations of behavior that state the immediate environmental conditions or the mechanisms within the individual that cause the behavior to occur. For contrast, see *ultimate explanations.* (p. 67)

proximity principle See *Gestalt principles of grouping.*

psychoanalysis 1. The theory of the mind developed by Freud, which emphasizes the roles of unconscious mental processes, early childhood experiences, and the drives of sex and aggression in personality formation; also called *psychoanalytic theory.* (p. 571) 2. Freud's therapy technique in which such methods as free association, dream analysis, and analysis of transference are used to learn about the person's unconscious mind; the goal is to make the unconscious conscious. (p. 651)

psychodynamic theories of personality Any theory that describes personality and its development in terms of inner mental forces that are often in conflict with one another and are shaped by experiences in early childhood. (p. 571)

psychodynamic therapy Any approach to psychotherapy that is based on the premise that psychological problems are manifestations of inner mental conflicts and that conscious awareness of those conflicts is a key to recovery. See also *psychoanalysis.* (p. 651)

psychology The science of behavior and the mind. (p. 1)

psychophysics The scientific study of the relationship between physical characteristics of stimuli and the psychological (sensory) experiences that the stimuli produce. (p. 262)

psychosurgery The surgical cutting or production of lesions in a portion of the brain to relieve a mental disorder. (p. 648)

psychotherapy Any formal, theory-based, systematic treatment for mental problems or disorders that uses psychological means (such as dialogue or training) rather than physiological means (such as drugs) and is conducted by a trained therapist. (p. 650)

punishment In operant conditioning, the process through which the consequence of a response *decreases* the likelihood that the response will recur. For contrast, see *reinforcement.* (p. 114)

pupil The hole in the center of the iris of the eye through which light passes. See *iris.* (p. 270)

PYY Abbreviation for *peptide YY_{3-36}*, which is an appetite-suppressing hormone produced by cells in the small intestine. (p. 197)

rationalization The defense mechanism by which a person uses conscious reasoning to justify or explain away his or her harmful or irrational behaviors or thoughts. (p. 573)

reaction formation The defense mechanism by which the mind turns a frightening wish into its safer opposite. (p. 573)

receptor potential The electrical change that occurs in a receptor cell (such as a rod or cone in the eye, or a hair cell in the inner ear) in response to the energy of a physical stimulus (such as light or sound). (p. 234)

recessive gene A gene that produces its observable effects only if the individual is homozygous for that gene (that is, has that gene allele on both of the two paired chromosomes). Contrast to *dominant gene.* (p. 56)

reciprocity norm The widespread sense of obligation that people have to return favors. (p. 526)

reciprocity theory of altruism The sociobiological theory that apparent acts of altruism have come about through natural selection because they are actually forms of long-term cooperation rather than true altruism. See also *altruism, cooperation.* (p. 88)

reference group A group of people with whom an individual compares himself or herself for the purpose of self-evaluation. See also *social comparison.* (p. 487)

reflex A simple, relatively automatic, stimulus-response sequence mediated by the nervous system. (p. 94)

regulatory drive Any motivational state (such as hunger or thirst) that helps maintain some constancy of the body's internal environment that is necessary for survival. For contrast, see *nonregulatory drive.* (p. 188)

reinforcement In operant conditioning, the presentation of a positive reinforcer or removal of a negative reinforcer when a response occurs, which increases the likelihood that the subject will repeat the response. See *negative reinforcer, positive reinforcer.* For contrast, see *punishment.* (p. 114)

reinforcer In operant conditioning, any stimulus change that occurs after a response and tends to *increase* the likelihood that the response will be repeated. See *negative reinforcer, positive reinforcer.* (p. 110)

relative image size for familiar objects A pictorial cue for perceiving depth in which one infers the distance of familiar objects on the basis of their known actual sizes and the size of their retinal images. (p. 301)

reliability Degree to which a measurement system produces similar results each time it is used with a particular subject or set of subjects under a particular set of conditions (p. xx). Regarding diagnoses of disorders, the degree to which different diagnosticians, all trained in the use of the diagnostic system, reach the same conclusions when they independently diagnose the same individuals. (p. 595).

REM (rapid-eye-movement) sleep The recurring stage of sleep during which the EEG resembles that of an alert person, rapid eye movements occur, the large muscles of the body are most relaxed, and true dreams are most likely to occur. It is sometimes called *emergent stage 1*. For contrast, see *slow-wave sleep*. (p. 210)

repression The defense mechanism by which the mind prevents anxiety-provoking ideas from becoming conscious. (p. 573)

resistance Attempts by a patient to avoid bringing unconscious memories or wishes into consciousness. (p. 654)

response Any well-defined behavioral action, especially one that is elicited by some form of environmental stimulation or provocation. (p. 94)

resting potential The constant electrical charge that exists across the membrane of an inactive neuron. (p. 141)

retina A thin membrane of cells that lines the rear interior of the eyeball; it contains the receptor cells for vision (rods and cones). (p. 270)

retrieval In the modal model of the mind, the mental process by which long-term memories are brought into working memory, where they become part of the flow of thought. See also *long-term memory, working memory*. (p. 313)

retrieval cue A word, phrase, or other stimulus that helps one retrieve a specific item of information from long-term memory. (p. 335)

retrograde amnesia Loss, due to injury to the brain, of long-term memories that had been formed before the injury. Contrast to *anterograde amnesia*. (p. 332)

reversible figure A visual stimulus (usually a picture) in which any given part is seen sometimes as the *figure* and other times as the *ground*. (p. 288)

rhodopsin The photochemical in rods that undergoes structural changes in response to light and thereby initiates the transduction process for rod vision. (p. 271)

rods The class of receptor cells for vision that are located in the peripheral portions of the retina (away from the fovea) and are most important for seeing in very dim light. For contrast, see *cones*. (p. 271)

rod vision The low-acuity, high-sensitivity, noncolor vision that occurs in dim light and is mediated by rods in the retina of the eye. For contrast, see *cone vision*. (p. 272)

schema The mental representation of a concept; the information stored in long-term memory that allows a person to identify a group of different events or items as members of the same category. (p. 338)

schemes Piaget's term for the mental entities that provide the basis for thought and that change in a stagelike way through development. They contain information about the actions that one can perform on objects, either in reality or symbolically in the mind. (p. 404)

schizophrenia A serious class of mental disorder that is characterized by disrupted perceptual and thought processes, often including hallucinations and delusions. (p. 626)

science An approach to answering questions that is based on the systematic collection and logical analysis of objectively observable data. (p. 1)

script A variety of schema that represents in memory the temporal organization of a category of event (such as the sequence of occurrences at a typical birthday party). (p. 338)

selective breeding The mating of those members of a strain of animals or plants that manifest a particular characteristic, which may or may not be done deliberately, to affect the genetic makeup of future generations of that strain; can be used to assess *heritability*. (p. 61)

self-actualization In humanistic psychology, the fulfillment of drives that go beyond one's survival needs and pertain to psychological growth, creativity, and self-expression. (p. 578)

self-conscious emotions The feelings of guilt, shame, embarrassment, and pride, which are linked to thoughts about the self or one's own actions. (p. 543)

self-efficacy A person's subjective sense of his or her own ability to perform a particular task or set of tasks. (p. 583)

self-esteem A person's feeling of approval and acceptance of himself or herself. (p. 486)

self-report method A data-collection method in which the people being studied are asked to rate or describe their own behaviors or mental states. See also *interview, questionnaire*. (p. 35)

self-serving attributional bias The tendency of people to attribute their successes to their own qualities and their failures to the situation. (p. 489)

semantic memory One's storehouse of explicit general knowledge, that is, of knowledge that can be expressed in words and is not mentally tied to specific experiences in one's own life. Semantic memory includes, but is not limited to, one's knowledge of word meanings. For contrasts, see *episodic memory, implicit memory*. (p. 343)

sensation The psychological experience associated with a sound, light, or other simple stimulus and the initial information-processing steps by which sense organs and neural pathways take in stimulus information from the environment. For contrast, see *perception*. (p. 232)

sensorimotor scheme In Piaget's theory, the type of mental structure that enables an infant to act on objects that are immediately present but does not permit thought about objects that are absent. See also *schemes*. (p. 406)

sensory adaptation The temporary decrease in sensitivity to sensory stimulation that occurs when a sensory system is stimulated for a period of time, and the temporary increase in sensitivity that occurs when a sensory system is not stimulated for a period of time. See also *dark adaptation, light adaptation*. (p. 235)

sensory areas of the cerebral cortex Areas of the brain's cerebral cortex that receive and analyze input from the body's senses. Separate sensory areas exist for each distinct sense. See *primary sensory areas*. (p. 233)

sensory coding The process by which information about the quality and quantity of a stimulus is preserved in the pattern of action potentials sent through sensory neurons to the central nervous system. (p. 234)

sensory memory In the modal model of the mind, the memory trace that preserves the original information in a sensory stimulus for a brief period (less than 1 second for sights and up to 3 seconds for sounds) following the termination of the stimulus; it is experienced as if one is still sensing the original stimulus. For contrasts, see *long-term memory, working memory*. (p. 311)

sensory neuron A neuron that carries messages from a sensory organ, through a nerve, into the brain or spinal cord. (pp. 138, 233)

sensory receptors Specialized biological structures—which in some cases are separate cells and in other cases are the sensitive tips of sensory neurons—that respond to physical stimuli by producing electrical changes that can initiate neural impulses (action potentials) in sensory neurons. (p. 233)

sensory-specific satiety The phenomenon by which a person or animal who is satiated on one food still has an appetite for another food that has a different taste. (p. 199)

serial processing The steps in the processing of sensory information that operate sequentially, an item at a time, on the available sensory information. For contrast, see *parallel processing*. (p. 284)

shaping An operant-conditioning procedure in which successively closer approximations to the desired response are reinforced until the response finally occurs. See *reinforcement*. (p. 112)

short-term memory See *working memory*. (p. 311)

sibling contrast Tendency to emphasize and exaggerate the differences between siblings. (p. 564)

similarity principle See *Gestalt principles of grouping*.

size constancy The perceptual ability to see an object as the same size despite change in image size as it moves farther away or closer. (p. 303)

skeletal portion of the peripheral motor system The set of peripheral motor neurons that act upon skeletal muscles. (p. 153)

social-cognitive theories of personality Theories of personality that emphasize the roles of beliefs and habits of thought that are acquired through one's unique experiences in the social environment. Also called *social-learning* or *social-cognitive-learning theories*. (p. 580)

social comparison Any process in which an individual evaluates his or her own abilities, characteristics, ideas, or achievements by comparing them with those of other people. See also *reference group*. (p. 487)

social dilemma A situation in which a particular action will (a) benefit the individual who takes it, (b) harm the individuals who don't, and (c) cause more harm than benefit to everyone if everyone takes it. See *prisoner's dilemma games.* (p. 533)

social facilitation The tendency to perform a task better in front of others than when alone. For contrast, see *social interference.* (p. 512)

social identity The portion of the self-concept that pertains to the social categories or groups of which the person is a part. For contrast, see *personal identity.* (p. 492)

social interference The tendency to perform a task worse in front of others than when alone. For contrast, see *social facilitation.* (p. 512)

social pain The discomfort that people feel when they are socially rejected or when they lose a valued companion. (p. 542)

social phobia Any phobia in which the basic fear is of being scrutinized or evaluated by other people. For contrast, see *specific phobia.* (p. 608)

social pressure The entire set of psychological forces that are exerted on an individual by other people or by the individual's beliefs about other people. (p. 511)

social psychology The branch of psychology that attempts to understand how the behavior and subjective experiences of individuals are influenced by the actual or imagined presence of other people. (pp. 14, 475)

social referencing The process by which infants use the nonverbal emotional expressions of a caregiver as cues to guide their behavior. (p. 400)

somatization disorder A category of somatoform disorder that is characterized by vague, unverifiable complaints about many different medical conditions. (p. 620)

somatoform disorders The class of mental disorders in which the person experiences bodily ailments in the absence of any physical disease that could cause them. It includes *conversion disorder* and *somatization disorder.* (p. 620)

somatosensation The set of senses that derive from the whole body—such as from the skin, muscles, and tendons—as opposed to those senses that come from the special sensory organs of the head. (p. 152)

span of short-term memory The number of pronounceable items of information (such as single, randomly chosen digits) that a person can retain in short-term (working) memory at any given time through rote rehearsal. (p. 321)

species-typical behavior Any behavior pattern that is so characteristic of a given species of animal that it can be used to help identify that species. (p. 70)

specific phobia Any phobia in which the feared object is a well-defined category of object (such as snakes) or environmental situa-

tions (such as heights) other than other people. See also *phobia.* For contrast, see *social phobia.* (p. 608)

spinal nerve A nerve that extends directly from the spinal cord. See *nerve.* For contrast, see *cranial nerve.* (p. 152)

split-parent identification Tendency for each of two siblings to identify with a different one of their two parents. (p. 564)

spontaneous recovery In both classical and operant conditioning, the return—due to passage of time with no further testing or training—of a conditioned response that had previously undergone extinction. (p. 97)

standard deviation A measure of the variability in a set of scores, determined by taking the square root of the variance. (pp. 38, A-5)

standardized score A score that is expressed in terms of the number of standard deviations the original score is from the mean of the original scores. (p. A-6)

statistical significance A statistical statement of how small the likelihood is that an obtained result occurred by chance. By convention, research findings are said to be *statistically significant* if the probability is less than 5 percent that the data could have come out as they did if the research hypothesis were wrong. (p. 40)

stereotypes Mental concepts by which people characterize specific groups or categories of people. (p. 494)

stereotype threat The threatened feeling that occurs, during the taking of a test, when a person is reminded of the fact that he or she belongs to a group that, according to a culturally prominent stereotype, is expected to perform poorly on the test. See *stereotype.* (p. 514)

Stevens's power law In psychophysics, S. S. Stevens's idea that the intensity of a sensation is directly proportional to the intensity of the physical stimulus raised by a constant power. For contrast, see *Fechner's law.* (p. 265)

stimulus A well-defined element of the environment that can potentially act on an individual's nervous system and thereby influence the individual's behavior. (p. 94)

strange-situation test A test of an infant's attachment to a particular familiar person, in which the infant's behavior is observed in an unfamiliar room while the familiar person and a stranger move in and out of the room in a preplanned way. (p. 438)

stress-induced analgesia The reduced sensitivity to pain that occurs when one is subjected to highly arousing (stressful) conditions. (p. 250)

Stroop interference effect Named after J. Ridley Stroop, the effect by which a printed color word (such as the word *red*) interferes with a person's ability to name the color of ink in which the word is printed if the ink color is not the same as the color named by the word. (p. 319)

subject-expectancy effect Any bias in research results that derives from subjects' expectations or beliefs about how they should feel or behave in response to the variables imposed in the study. See also *bias, observer-expectancy effect.* (p. 46)

sublimation See *displacement.*

subtractive color mixing The mixing of pigments whereby each pigment absorbs a different set of wavelengths of light that would otherwise be reflected to the eye. For contrast, see *additive color mixing.* (p. 275)

superordinate goals The goals shared by two or more groups, which tend to foster cooperation among the groups. (p. 540)

suprachiasmatic nucleus Nucleus (cluster of neurons) in the brain's hypothalamus that controls circadian rhythms of sleep and arousal. (p. 218)

sympathetic division of the autonomic motor system The set of motor neurons that act upon visceral muscles and glands and mediate many of the body's responses to stressful stimulation, preparing the body for possible "fight or flight." For contrast, see *parasympathetic division of the autonomic motor system.* (p. 153)

symptom In clinical psychology or psychiatry, any characteristic of a person's actions, thoughts, or feelings that could be a potential indicator of a mental disorder. (p. 594)

synapse The functional connection through which neural activity in the axon of one neuron influences the action of another neuron, a muscle cell, or a glandular cell. (p. 143)

syndrome In clinical psychology or psychiatry, the entire pattern of symptoms manifested in an individual's behavior and self-statements, which, collectively, may constitute evidence of a mental disorder. (p. 594)

syntax The set of grammatical rules for a given language that specifies how words can be arranged to produce phrases and sentences. (p. 420)

temporal lobe The lobe of the cerebral cortex that lies in front of the occipital lobe and below the parietal and frontal lobes and that contains the auditory area of the brain. (p. 159)

temporal-lobe amnesia The loss in memory abilities that occurs as a result of damage to structures in the limbic system that lie under the temporal lobe of the cerebral cortex. (p. 331)

test In psychology, a data collection method in which stimuli or problems are deliberately presented by the researcher for the subject to respond to. (p. 36)

texture gradient A pictorial cue for perceiving depth in which the gradual change in size and density of textured elements (such as pebbles or blades of grass) indicates depth. (p. 302)

thalamus The brain structure that sits directly atop the brainstem; it functions as a sensory relay station, connecting incoming sensory tracts to special sensory areas of the cerebral cortex. (p. 156)

theory A belief or set of interrelated beliefs that one has about some aspect of the universe, which is used to explain observed facts and to predict new ones. See also *hypothesis*. (p. 29)

three-primaries law The observation that one can choose three limited-wavelength lights (called *primaries*) and, by mixing them in differing proportions, match any color that the human eye can see. See also *additive color mixing*. (p. 276)

TMS See *Transcranial magnetic stimulation*.

tolerance See *drug tolerance*.

tonotopic organization Refers to the manner by which neural cells in the primary auditory area of the cerebral cortex are organized. Each neuron is maximally responsive to sounds of a particular frequency, and the neurons are systematically arranged such that high-frequency tones activate neurons at one end of this cortical area and low-frequency tones activate neurons at the other end. (p. 259)

top-down control In theories of perception, mental processes that bring preexisting knowledge or expectations about an object or scene to bear upon the perception of that object or scene. For contrast, see *bottom-up processes*. (p. 291)

tract A bundle of neural axons coursing together within the central nervous system; analogous to a *nerve* in the peripheral nervous system. (p. 146)

trait A hypothetical, relatively stable, inner characteristic that influences the way a person responds to various environmental situations. (p. 550)

trait theories of personality Theories of personality that are based on the idea that people can be described and differentiated in terms of hypothetical underlying personality dimensions, called *traits,* which can be measured by questionnaires or other quantitative means. (p. 551)

transcranial magnetic stimulation A procedure for temporarily altering the responsiveness of a localized area of the cerebral cortex by creating a magnetic field over that brain area. (p. 147)

transduction The process by which a receptor cell (such as a rod or cone in the eye, or a hair cell in the inner ear) produces an electrical change in response to the energy of a physical stimulus (such as light or sound). (p. 234)

transference The phenomenon by which a patient's unconscious feelings about a significant person in his or her life are experienced consciously as feelings about the therapist. (p. 654)

trichromatic theory of color vision Theory proposed independently by Young and

Helmholtz to explain the three-primaries law of color vision; it holds that the human ability to perceive color is mediated by three different types of receptors, each of which is most sensitive to a different range of wavelengths. See also *three-primaries law.* (p. 278)

ultimate explanations Functional explanations of behavior that state the role that the behavior plays or once played in survival and reproduction, that is, explanations of why the potential for the behavior was favored by natural selection. For contrast, see *proximate explanations.* (p. 67)

unconditioned reflex A reflex that does not depend upon previous conditions in the individual's experience; an unlearned reflex. For contrast, see *conditioned reflex.* (p. 95)

unconditioned response A reflexive response that does not depend upon previous conditioning or learning. For contrast, see *conditioned response.* (p. 95)

unconditioned stimulus A stimulus that elicits a reflexive response without any previous training or conditioning. For contrast, see *conditioned stimulus.* (p. 95)

unconscious inference With respect to vision, the process by which the brain uses sensory input as clues in order to perceive whole patterns or objects. (p. 289)

validity Degree to which a measurement system actually measures the characteristic that it is supposed to measure (p. xx). Regarding diagnoses of mental disorders, the degree to which the disorders identified are clinically meaningful; that is, the degree to which the diagnostic labels predict real-world behaviors and treatment outcomes. (p. 597).

variability The degree to which the individual numbers in a set of numbers differ from one another or from their mean. See *variance* and *standard deviation*, which are common measures of variability. (p. 38)

variable-interval (VI) schedule In operant conditioning, a schedule of reinforcement in which an unpredictable period of time, varying around some average, must elapse between the receipt of one reinforcer and the availability of another. (p. 113)

variable-ratio (VR) schedule In operant conditioning, a schedule of reinforcement in which the response must be produced a certain *average* number of times before a reinforcer will appear, but the number needed on any given instance varies randomly around that average. (p. 113)

variance A measure of the variability of a set of scores, determined by obtaining the

difference (deviation) between each score and the mean, squaring each deviation, and calculating the mean of the squared deviations. (p. A-4)

vestigial characteristics Inherited characteristics of anatomy or behavior that are no longer useful to the species but were presumably useful at an earlier time in evolution. (p. 68)

visual agnosia A condition caused by damage to specific portions of the occipital and temporal lobes of the cortex, in which people cannot make sense of what they see. (p. 295)

visual form agnosia A variety of agnosia in which people can identify some elements of what they see but cannot perceive an object's shape. (p. 295)

visual object agnosia A variety of agnosia in which people can identify and draw the shapes of objects but cannot identify the objects. (p. 295)

visuospatial sketchpad In Baddeley's theory, a component of working memory responsible for holding visual and spatial information. (p. 321)

Weber's law The idea that, within a given sensory modality (such as vision), the difference threshold (amount that the stimulus must be changed in magnitude to be perceived as different) is a constant proportion of the magnitude of the original stimulus. (p. 263)

Wernicke's aphasia A specific syndrome of loss of language ability that occurs due to damage in a particular part of the brain called Wernicke's area. Speech in a person with this disorder typically retains its grammatical structure but loses its meaning due to the speaker's failure to provide meaningful content words (nouns, verbs, adjectives, and adverbs); also called fluent aphasia. For contrast, see Broca's aphasia. (p. 170)

working memory In the modal model, the memory store that is considered to be the main workplace of the mind. Among other things, it is the seat of conscious thought and reasoning. For contrast, see *sensory memory, long-term memory.* (p. 311)

z score The simplest form of a standardized score; it is the score minus the mean divided by the standard deviation. (p. A-6)

zone of proximal development The range or set of activities that a child can do in collaboration with more competent others but cannot yet do alone. (p. 410)

zygote The single cell that is formed when an egg and sperm cell unite; the first, single-cell form of a newly developing individual. (p. 56)

References

AbdelMalik, P., Husted, J., Chow, E., & Bassett, A. (2003). Childhood head injury and expression of schizophrenia in multiply affected families. *Archives of General Psychiatry, 60,* 231–236.

Aberson, C. L., Shoemaker, C., & Tomolillo, C. (2004). Implicit bias and contact: The role of interethnic friendships. *Journal of Social Psychology, 144,* 335–347.

Abma, J. C., Martinez, G. M., Mosher, W. D., Dawson, B. S. (2004). Teenagers in the United States: Sexual activity, contraceptive use, and childbearing, 2002. National Center for Health Statistics. *Vital Health Statistics, 23, #24.*

Abramson, L. Y., Matelsky, G. I., & Alloy, L. B. (1989). Hopelessness depression: A theory-based subtype of depression. *Psychological Review, 96,* 358–372.

Ackerman, P. L., & Heggestad, E. D. (1997). Intelligence, personality, and interests: Evidence for overlapping traits. *Psychological Bulletin, 121,* 219–245.

Adams, D. B., Gold, A. R., & Burt, A. D. (1978). Rise in female-initiated sexual activity at ovulation and its suppression by oral contraceptives. *The New England Journal of Medicine, 299,* 1145–1150.

Adams, H. E., Wright, L. W., & Lohr, B. A. (1996). Is homophobia associated with homosexual arousal? *Journal of Abnormal Psychology, 105,* 440–445.

Adamson, R. E. (1952). Functional fixedness as related to problem solving. *Journal of Experimental Psychology, 44,* 288–291.

Adkins-Regan, E. (1981). Early organizational effects of hormones: An evolutionary perspective. In N. T. Adler (Ed.), *Neuroendocrinology of reproduction.* New York: Plenum Press.

Adler, A. (1930). Individual psychology. In C. Murchison (Ed.), *Psychologies of 1930.* Worcester, MA: Clark University Press.

Adolfsson, B., Andersson, I., Elofsson, S., Rössner, S., & Undén, A. (2005). Locus of control and weight reduction. *Patient Education & Counseling, 56,* 55–56.

Adolph, K. E., Vereijken, B., & Shrout, P. E. (2003). What changes in infant walking and why? *Child Development, 74,* 475–497.

Agras, S., Sylvester, D., & Oliveau, D. (1969). The epidemiology of common fears and phobias. *Comprehensive Psychiatry, 10,* 151–156.

Ahluvalia, T., & Schaefer, C. E. (1994). Implications of transitional object use: A review of empirical findings. *Psychology, a Journal of Human Behavior, 31* (2), 45–57.

Ahn, H., & Wampold, B. E. (2001). Where oh where are the specific ingredients? A meta-analysis of component studies in counseling and psychotherapy. *Journal of Counseling Psychology, 48,* 251–257.

Aiello, J. R., & Douthitt, E. A. (2001). Social facilitation from Triplett to electronic performance monitoring. *Group Dynamics: Theory, Research, and Practice, 5,* 163–180.

Ainsworth, M. D. S. (1979). Attachment as related to mother-infant interaction. *Advances in the Study of Behaviour, 9,* 2–52.

Ainsworth, M. D. S. (1989). Attachments beyond infancy. *American Psychologist, 44,* 709–716.

Ainsworth, M. D. S., Blehar, M. C., Waters, E., & Wall, S. (1978). *Patterns of attachment: A psychological study of the strange situation.* Hillsdale, NJ: Erlbaum.

Akiskal, H. S. (2002). Classification, diagnosis and boundaries of bipolar disorders: A review. In M. Mario, H. S. Akiskal, J. J. López-Ibor, & N. Sartorius (Eds.), *Bipolar disorder.* West Sussex, England: Wiley.

Albert, M. K. (2007). Mechanisms of modal and amodal interpolation. *Psychological Review, 114,* 455–469.

Alencar, A. I., Siqueira, J. de O., & Yamamoto, M. E. (2008). Does group size matter? Cheating and cooperation in Brazilian school children. *Evolution and Human Behavior, 29,* 42–48.

Alicke, M. D., Klotz, M. L., Breitenbecher, D. L., Yurak, T. J., & Vredenburg, D. S. (1995). Personal contact, individuation, and the better-than-average effect. *Journal of Personality and Social Psychology, 68,* 804–825.

Allen, N. B., & Badcock, P. B. T. (2006). Darwinian models of depression: A review of evolutionary accounts of mood and mood disorders. *Progress in Neuro-Psychopharmacology & Biological Psychiatry, 30,* 815–826.

Allen, P., Laroi, F., McGuire, P. K., & Aleman, A. (2008). The hallucinating brain: A review of structural and functional neuroimaging studies of hallucinations. *Neuroscience & Biobehavioral Reviews, 32,* 175–191.

Allison, T., & Cicchetti, D. V. (1976). Sleep in mammals: Ecological and constitutional correlates. *Science, 194,* 732–734.

Allman, J., & Brothers, L. (1994). Faces, fear and the amygdala. *Nature, 372,* 613–614.

Alloy, L. B., Abramson, L. Y., Whitehouse, W. G., Hogan, M. E., Panzarella, C., & Rose, D. T. (2006). Prospective incidence of first onsets and recurrence of depression in individuals at high and low cognitive risk for depression. *Journal of Abnormal Psychology, 115,* 145–156.

Allport, F. H. (1920). The influence of the group upon association and thought. *Journal of Experimental Psychology, 3,* 159–182.

Allport, G. W. (1935). Attitudes. In C. Murchison (Ed.), *Handbook of social psychology.* Worcester, MA: Clark University Press.

Allport, G. W. (1937). *Personality: A psychological interpretation.* New York: Holt.

Allport, G. W. (1968). The historical background of modern social psychology. In G. Lindzey & E. Aronson (Eds.), *The handbook of social psychology* (2nd ed., Vol. 1). Reading, MA: Addison-Wesley.

Almeida, D. M., & Kessler, R. C. (1998). Everyday stressors and gender differences in daily distress. *Journal of Personality and Social Psychology, 75,* 670–680.

Altmann, E. M., & Gray, W. D. (2002). Forgetting to remember: The functional relationship of decay to interference. *Psychological Science, 13,* 27–33.

Ambady, N., Bernieri, F. J., & Richeson, J. A. (2000). Toward a histology of social behavior: Judgmental accuracy from thin slices of the behavioral stream. *Advances in Experimental Social Psychology, 32,* 201–271.

Ambelas, A. (1987). Life events and mania: A special relationship? *British Journal of Psychiatry, 150,* 235–240.

Amedi, A., Raz, N., Pianka, P., Malach, R., & Zohary, E. (2003). Early 'visual' cortex activation correlates with superior verbal memory performance in the blind. *Nature Neuroscience, 6,* 758–766.

American Psychiatric Association (2000). *Diagnostic and statistical manual of mental disorders* (4th ed., text-revised). Washington, DC: Author.

American Psychological Association (2002). Ethical principles of psychologists and a code of conduct. *American Psychologist, 57,* 1060–1073.

Anders, S., Birbaumer, N., Sadowski, B., Erb, M., Mader, I., Grodd, W., et al. (2004). Parietal somatosensory association cortex mediates affective blindsight. *Nature Neuroscience, 7,* 339–340.

Anderson, C. A., Lindsay, J. J., & Bushman, B. J. (1999). Research in the psychological laboratory: Truth or triviality? *Current Directions in Psychological Science, 8,* 3–9.

Anderson, C., John, O. P., Keltner, D., & Kring, A. M. (2001). Who attains social status? Effects of personality and physical attractiveness in social groups. *Journal of Personality and Social Psychology, 81,* 116–132.

Anderson, J. R. (2000). *Learning and memory* (2nd ed.). New York: Wiley.

Andersson, M. (2005). Evolution of classical polyandry: Three steps to female emancipation. *Ethology, 111,* 1–23.

Andreasen, N. C. (1987). Creativity and mental illness: Prevalence rates in writers and their first-degree relatives. *American Journal of Psychiatry, 144,* 1288–1292.

Antony, M. M., & Barlow, D. H. (2002). Specific phobias. In D. H. Barlow, *Anxiety and its disorders: The nature and treatment of anxiety and panic* (2nd ed.). New York: Guilford.

Antrobus, J. (2000). Theories of dreaming. In M. H. Kryger, T. Roth, & W. C. Dement (Eds.), *Principles and practice of sleep medicine* (3rd ed.). Philadelphia: W. B. Saunders.

Anzai, A., Peng, X., & Van Essen, D. C. (2007). Neurons in monkey visual area V2 encode combinations of orientations. *Nature Neuroscience, 10,* 1313–1321.

Archer, J. (2004). Sex differences in aggression in real-world settings: A meta-analytic review. *Review of General Psychology, 8,* 291–322.

Archer, J. (2006). Testosterone and human aggression: An evaluation of the challenge hypothesis. *Neuroscience and Biobehavioral Reviews, 30,* 319–345.

Arditi, A. (1986). Binocular vision. In K. R. Boff, L. Kaufman, & J. P. Thomas (Eds.), *Handbook of perception and human performance.* New York: Wiley.

Arieti, S. (1966). Schizophrenic cognition. In P. Hook & J. Zubin (Eds.), *Psychopathology of schizophrenia.* New York: Grune & Stratton.

Arnett, J. J. (1992). Reckless behavior in adolescence: A developmental perspective. *Developmental Review, 12,* 339–373.

Arnett, J. J. (1995). The young and the reckless: Adolescent reckless behavior. *Current Directions in Psychological Science, 4,* 67–71.

Arnett, J. J. (2000). Emerging adulthood: A theory of development from the late teens through the twenties. *American Psychologist, 55,* 469–480.

Aronson, E. (1992). The return of the repressed: Dissonance theory makes a comeback. *Psychological Inquiry, 3,* 303–311.

Aronson, J., Fried, C., & Good, C. (2002). Reducing the effects of stereotype threat on African American college students by shaping theories of intelligence. *Journal of Experimental Social Psychology, 38,* 113–125.

Aronson, J., Lustina, M. J., Good, C., Keough, K., Steele, C. M., & Brown, J. (1999). When white men can't do math: Necessary and sufficient factors in stereotype threat. *Journal of Experimental Social Psychology, 35,* 29–46.

Asch, S. E. (1952). *Social psychology.* Englewood Cliffs, NJ: Prentice-Hall.

Asch, S. E. (1956). Studies of independence and conformity: I. A minority of one against a unanimous majority. *Psychological Monographs: General and Applied, 70*(9, Whole No. 416).

Ash, I. K., & Wiley J. (2006). The nature of restructuring in insight: An individual-differences approach. *Psychonomic Bulletin & Review, 13,* 66–73.

Ashcraft, K. A., Hunzeker, J., & Bonneau, R. H. (2008). Psychological stress impairs the local CD8 + T cell response to mucosal HSV-1 infection and allows for increased pathogenicity via a glucocorticoid receptor-mediated mechanism. *Psychoneuroendocrinology, 33,* 951–963.

Askey, R., Gamble, C., & Gray, R. (2007). Family work in first-onset psychosis: A literature review. *Journal of Psychiatric and Mental Health Nursing, 14,* 356–365.

Atance, C. M., & O'Neill, D. K. (2004). Acting and planning on the basis of a false belief: Its effects on 3-year-old children's reasoning about their own false beliefs. *Developmental Psychology, 40,* 953–964.

Atkin, O. (1980). *Models of architectural knowledge.* London: Pion.

Atkinson, R. C., & Shiffrin, R. M. (1968). Human memory: A proposed system and its control processes. In K. W. Spence & J. T. Spence (Eds.), *The psychology of learning and motivation: Advances in research and theory* (Vol. 2). New York: Academic Press.

Au, T. K., Knightly, L. M., Jun, S-A., & Oh, J. S. (2002). Overhearing a language during childhood. *Psychological Science, 13,* 238–243.

Axelrod, R. (1984). *The evolution of cooperation.* New York: Basic Books.

Ayllon, T., & Azrin, N. H. (1968). *The token economy: A motivational system for therapy and rehabilitation.* New York: Appleton-Century-Crofts.

Baars, B. J., & Franklin, S. (2003). How conscious experience and working memory interact. *Trends in Cognitive Sciences, 7,* 166–172.

Backhaus, J., Hoeckesfeld, R., Born, J., Hohagen, F., & Junghanns, K. (2008). Immediate as well as delayed post learning sleep but not wakefulness enhances declarative memory consolidation in children. *Neurobiology of Learning and Memory, 89,* 76–80.

Baddeley, A. (1986). *Working memory.* Oxford: Clarendon.

Baddeley, A. (2003). Working memory: Looking back and looking forward. *Nature Reviews Neuroscience, 4,* 829–839.

Baddeley, A. (2006). Working memory: An overview. In S. J. Pickering (Ed.), *Working memory and education.* New York: Academic Press.

Baddeley, A., Thomson, N., & Buchanan, M. (1975). Word length and the structure of short-term memory. *Journal of Verbal Learning and Verbal Behavior, 14,* 575–589.

Baerger, D. R., & McAdams, D. P. (1999). Life story coherence and its relation to psychological well-being. *Narrative Inquiry, 9,* 69–96.

Bagger, J., Li, An. & Gutek, B. A. (2008). How much do you value your family and does it matter? The joint effects of family identity salience, family-interference-with-work, and gender. *Human Relations, 61,* 187–211.

Bailey, T. C., Eng, W., Frisch, M. B., & Snyder, C. R. (2007). Hope and optimism as related to life satisfaction. *Journal of Positive Psychology, 2,* 168–175.

Baillargeon, R. (1987). Object permanence in 3 1/2- and 4 1/2-month-old infants. *Developmental Psychology, 23,* 655–664.

Baillargeon, R. (1994). How do infants learn about the physical world? *Current Directions in Psychological Science, 3,* 133–140.

Baillargeon, R. (1998). Infants' understanding of the physical world. In M. Sabourin, F. Craik, & M. Robert (Eds.), *Advances in psychological science* (Vol. 2). Hove, England: Psychology Press.

Baillargeon, R. (2004). Infants' physical world. *Current Directions in Psychological Science, 13,* 89–94.

Baillargeon, R. (2008). Innate ideas revisited. *Perspectives in Psychological Science, 3,* 2–13.

Baillargeon, R. H., Zoccolillo, M., Keenan, K., Côté, S., Pérusse, D., Wu, H-X, Boivin, M., & Tremblay, R. E. (2007). Gender differences in physical aggression: A prospective population-based survey of children before and after 2 years of age. *Developmental Psychology, 43,* 12–26.

Bakeman, R., Adamson, L. B., Konner, M., & Barr, R. (1990). !Kung infancy: The social context of object exploration. *Child Development, 61,* 794–809.

Bakermans-Kranenburg, M. J., & van Ijzendoorn, M. H. (2007). Research review: Genetic vulnerability or differential susceptibility in child development: The case of attachment. *Journal of Child Psychology and Psychiatry, 48,* 1160–1173.

Bakermans-Kranenburg, M. J., van IJzendoorn, M. H., & Juffer, F. (2003). Less is more: Meta-analysis of sensitivity and attachment interventions in early childhood. *Psychological Bulletin, 129,* 195–215.

Bakin, J. S., South, D. A., & Weinberger, N. M. (1996). Induction of receptive field plasticity in the auditory cortex of the guinea pig during instrumental avoidance conditioning. *Behavioral Neuroscience, 110,* 905–913.

Balaban, M. T., & Waxman, S. R. (1997). Do words facilitate object categorization in 9-month-old infants? *Journal of Experimental Child Psychology, 64,* 3–26.

Baldwin, D. A. (2000). Interpersonal understanding fuels knowledge acquisition. *Current Directions in Psychological Science, 9,* 40–45.

Baldwin, D. A., Markman, E. M., & Melartin, R. L. (1993). Infants' ability to draw inferences about nonobvious object properties: Evidence from exploratory play. *Child Development, 64,* 711–728.

Ball, G. F., & Hulse, S. H. (1998). Birdsong. *American Psychologist, 53,* 37–58.

Banarjee, S., & Bhat, M. (2007). Neuron-glial interactions in blood-brain barrier formation. *Annual Review of Neuroscience, 30,* 235–258.

Bandura, A. (1997). *Self-efficacy: The exercise of control.* New York: Freeman.

Bandura, A., & Cervone, D. (1983). Self-evaluative and self-efficacy mechanisms governing the motivational effects of goal systems. *Journal of Personality and Social Psychology, 45,* 1017–1028.

Bandura, A., & Locke, E. A. (2003). Negative self-efficacy and goal effects revisited. *Journal of Applied Psychology, 88,* 87–99.

Bandura, A., Adams, N. E., & Beyer, J. (1977). Cognitive processes mediating behavioral change. *Journal of Personality and Social Psychology, 35,* 125–139.

Bandura, A., Cioffi, D., Taylor, C. B., & Brouillard, M. E. (1988). Perceived self-efficacy in coping with cognitive stressors and opioid activation. *Journal of Personality and Social Psychology, 55,* 479–488.

Bandura, A., O'Leary, A., Taylor, C. B., Gauthier, J., & Gossard, D. (1987). Perceived self-efficacy and pain control: Opioid and nonopioid mechanisms. *Journal of Personality and Social Psychology, 53,* 563–571.

Barber, N. (2003). Paternal investment prospects and cross-national differences in single parenthood. *Cross-Cultural Research, 37,* 163–177.

Barch, D. M. (2003). Cognition in schizophrenia: Does working memory work? *Current Directions in Psychological Science, 12,* 146–150.

Bargh, J. A., & McKenna, K. Y. A. (2004). The internet in social life. *Annual Review of Psychology, 55,* 573–590.

Barkley, R. A. (2001). Executive function and ADHD: A reply. *Journal of the American Academy of Child and Adolescent Psychiatry, 40,* 501–502.

Barlow, D. H. (2002). The nature of anxious apprehension. In D. H. Barlow, *Anxiety and its disorders* (2nd ed.). New York: Guilford.

Barlow, D. H. (2004). Psychological treatments. *American Psychologist, 9,* 869–877.

Barnett, R. C., & Baruch, G. K. (1987). Social roles, gender, and psychological distress. In R. C. Barnett, L. B. Biener, & G. K. Baruch (Eds.), *Gender and stress.* New York: Free Press.

Barnett, R. C., & Hyde, J. S. (2001). Women, men, work, and family: An expansionist theory. *American Psychologist, 56,* 781–796.

Baron-Cohen, S. (1995). *Mindblindness: An essay on autism and theory of mind.* Cambridge, MA: Bradford Books/MIT Press.

Baron-Cohen, S., Leslie, A. M., & Frith, U. (1985). Does the autistic child have a "theory of mind"? *Cognition, 21,* 37–46.

Barrett, L. F. (2006) Emotions as natural kinds? *Perspectives on Psychological Science, 1,* 28–58.

Barry, D., Sullivan, B., & Petry, N. M. (2009). Comparable efficacy of contingent management for cocaine dependence among African American, Hispanic, and White methadone maintenance clients. *Psychology of Addictive Behaviors, 23,* 168–174.

Barry, H., III, & Paxson, L. (1971). Infancy and early childhood: Cross-cultural codes, 2. *Ethnology, 10,* 466–508.

Barry, R. A., Kochanska, G., & Philibert, R. A. (2008). G x E interaction in the organization of attachment: Mother's responsiveness as a moderator of children's genotypes. *Journal of Child Psychology and Psychiatry, 49,* 1313–1320.

Barsh, G. S., Farooqi, S., & O'Rahilly, S. (2000). Genetics of body-weight regulation. *Nature, 404,* 644–651.

Bartlett, F. C. (1932). *Remembering: A study in experimental and social psychology.* Cambridge, England: Cambridge University Press.

Bartoshuk, L. M., & Beauchamp, G. K. (1994). Chemical senses. *Annual Review of Psychology, 45,* 419–449.

Basbaum, A. I., & Fields, H. L. (1984). Endogenous pain control systems: Brainstem spinal pathways and endorphin circuitry. *Annual Review of Neuroscience, 7,* 309–338.

Basbaum, A. I., & Jessell, T. M. (2000). The perception of pain. In E. R. Kandel, J. H. Schwartz, & T. M. Jessell (Eds.), *Principles of neuroscience* (4th ed.). New York: McGraw-Hill.

Baskin, T. W., Tierney, S. C., Minami, T., & Wampold, B. E. (2003). Establishing specificity in psychotherapy: A meta-analysis of structural equivalence of placebo controls. *Journal of Consulting and Clinical Psychology, 71,* 973–979.

Bassuk, E. L., & Gerson, S. (1978, February). Deinstitutionalization and mental health services. *Scientific American,* pp. 46–53.

Bateson, P. (2000). What must be known in order to understand imprinting? In C. Heyes & L. Huber (Eds.), *The evolution of cognition.* Cambridge, MA: MIT Press.

Batterham, R. L., Cohen, M. A., Ellis, S. M., Le Roux, C. W., Withers, D. J., Frost, G. S., et al. (2003). Inhibition of food intake in obese subjects by peptide YY_{3-36}. *New England Journal of Medicine, 349,* 941–948.

Bauer, J. J., & McAdams, D. P. (2004). Personal growth in adults' stories of life transitions. *Journal of Personality, 72,* 573–602.

Bauer, J. J., McAdams, D. P., & Pals, J. L. (2008). Narrative identity and eudaimonic well-being. *Journal of Happiness Studies, 9,* 81–104.

Bauer, P. J., & Coyne, M. J. (1997). When the name says it all: Preschoolers' recognition and use of the gendered nature of common proper names. *Social Development, 6,* 271–291.

Baumeister, R. F. (1994). The crystallization of discontent in the process of major life change. In T. F. Heatherton & J. L. Weinberger (Eds.), *Can personality change?* Washington, DC: American Psychological Association.

Baumeister, R. F., Dori, G. A., & Hastings, S. (1998). Belongingness and temporal bracketing in personal accounts of changes in self-esteem. *Journal of Research in Personality, 32,* 222–235.

Baumeister, R. F., Stillwell, A. M., & Heatherton, T. F. (1995). Personal narratives about guilt: Role of action control and interpersonal relationships. *Basic and Applied Social Psychology, 17,* 173–198.

Baumgart, F., Gaschler-Markefski, B., Woldorff, M. G., Heinze, H., & Scheich, H. (1999). A movement-sensitive area in auditory cortex. *Nature, 400,* 724–726.

Baumrind, D. (1964). Some thoughts on ethics of research: After reading Milgram's "Behavioral study of obedience." *American Psychologist, 19,* 421–423.

Baumrind, D. (1967). Child care practices anteceding three patterns of preschool behavior. *Genetic Psychology Monographs, 75,* 43–88.

Baumrind, D. (1971). Current patterns of parental authority. *Developmental Psychology Monograph, 4,* 1–103.

Baumrind, D. (1986). *Familial antecedents of social competence in middle childhood.* Unpublished monograph, University of California, Institute of Human Development, Berkeley.

Bayley, P. J., O'Reilly, R. C., Curran, T., & Squire, L. R. (2008). New semantic learning in patients with large medial temporal lobe lesions. *Hippocampus, 18,* 575–583.

Bechtoldt, H., Norcross, J. C., Wyckoff, L. A., Pokrywa, M. L., & Campbell, L. F. (2001). Theoretical orientations and employment settings of clinical and counseling psychologists: A comparative study. *The Clinical Psychologist, 54(1),* 3–6.

Beck, A. T., & Weishaar, M. (2007). Cognitive therapy. In R. J. Corsini & D. Wedding (eds.), *Current psychotherapies* (8th ed.). Belmont, CA: Brooks-Cole.

Beck, A. T., Brown, G., Eidelson, J. I., Steer, R. A., & Riskind, J. H. (1987). Differentiating anxiety and depression: A test of the cognitive content-specificity hypothesis. *Journal of Abnormal Psychology, 96,* 179–183.

Beck, A. T., & Young, J. E. (1985). Depression. In D. H. Barlow (Ed.), *Clinical handbook of psychological disorders: A step-by-step treatment manual.* New York: Guilford.

Beck, E., Burnet, K. L., & Vosper, J. (2006). Birth-order effects on facets of extraversion. *Personality and Individual Differences, 40,* 953–959.

Beck, M., & Galef, B. G. (1989). Social influences on the selection of a protein-sufficient diet by Norway rats (*Rattus norvegicus*). *Journal of Comparative Psychology, 103,* 132–139.

Becker, A. E., Burwell, R. A., Gilman, S. E., Herzog, D. B., & Hamburg, P. (2002). Eating behaviors and attitudes following prolonged exposure to television among ethnic Fijian adolescent girls. *British Journal of Psychiatry, 180,* 509–514.

Becker, E. S., Goodwin, R., Hölting, C., Hoyer, J., & Margraf, J. (2003). Content of worry in the community: What do people with generalized anxiety disorder or other disorders worry about? *Journal of Nervous and Mental Disease, 191,* 688–691.

Behrens, M., Foerster, S., Staehler, F., Raguse, J-D., & Meyerhof, W. (2007). Gustatory expression pattern of the human TAS2R bitter receptor gene family reveals a heterogeneous population of bitter taste receptor cells. *Journal of Neuroscience, 27,* 12630–12640.

Beilock, S. L., Kulp, C. A., Holt, L. E., & Carr, T. H. (2004). More on the fragility of performance: Choking under pressure in mathematical problem solving. *Journal of Experimental Psychology: General, 133,* 584–600.

Beilock, S. L., Rydell, R. J., & McConnell, A. R. (2007). Stereotype threat and working memory: Mechanisms, alleviation, and spillover. *Journal of Experimental Psychology: General, 136,* 256–276.

Bell, A. P., Weinberg, M. S., & Hammersmith, S. K. (1981). *Sexual preference: Its development in men and women.* Bloomington: Indiana University Press.

Bell, R. A., Cholerton, M., Fraczek, K. E., Rohlfs, G. S., & Smith, B. A. (1994). Encouraging donations to charity: A field study of competing and complementary factors in tactic sequencing. *Western Journal of Communication, 58,* 98–115.

Belleine, B. W., & Dickinson, A. (2006). Motivational control of blocking. *Journal of Experimental Psychology: Animal Behavior Processes, 32,* 33–43.

Belmaker, R. (2004). Bipolar disorder. *New England Journal of Medicine, 351,* 476–486.

Belsky, J. (2007). Experience in childhood and the development of reproductive strategies. *Acta Psychologica Sinica, 39,* 454–468.

Belsky, J., Bakermans-Kranenburg, M. J., & van Ijzendoorn, M. H. (2007). For better *and* for worse: Differential susceptibility and environmental influences. *Current Directions in Psychological Science, 16,* 300–303.

Belsky, J., Steinberg, L., & Draper, P. (1991). Childhood experience, interpersonal development, and reproductive strategy: An evolutionary theory of socialization. *Child Development, 62,* 647–670.

Benedict, H. (1979). Early lexical development A: Comprehension and production. *Journal of Child Language, 6,* 183–200.

Benham, B. (2008). The ubiquity of deception and the ethics of deceptive research. *Bioethics, 22,* 147–156.

Benjamin, J., Ebstein, R. P., & Lesch, K. (1998). Genes for personality traits: Implications for psychology. *International Journal of Neuropsychopharmacology, 1,* 153–168.

Benjamin, J., Li, L., Patterson, C., Greenberg, B. D., Murphy, D. L., & Hamer, D. H. (1996). Population and familial association between the D4 dopamine receptor gene and measures of novelty seeking. *Nature Genetics, 12,* 81–84.

Berglund, A., & Rosenqvist, G. (2001). Male pipefish prefer ornamental females. *Animal Behaviour, 61,* 345–350.

Berk, L. E. (1994, November). Why children talk to themselves. *Scientific American,* pp. 78–83.

Berk, L. E., & Lewis, N. G. (1977). Sex role and social behavior in four school environments. *The Elementary School Journal, 77,* 205–217.

Berkeley, G. (1710; reprinted 1820). *A treatise concerning the principles of human knowledge.* In *The works of George Berkeley* (3 vols.). London: Richard Priestley.

Berko, J. (1958). The child's learning of English morphology. *Word, 14,* 150–177.

Bernal, S., Lidz, J., Millotte, S., & Christophe, A. (2007). Syntax constrains the acquisition of verb meaning. *Language Learning and Development, 3,* 325–341.

Berndt, T. J. (1992). Friendship and friends' influence in adolescence. *Current Directions in Psychological Science, 1,* 156–159.

Bernstein, I. L. (1991). Flavor aversion. In R. C. Doty, L. M. Bartoshuk, & J. B. Snow (Eds.), *Smell and taste in health and disease.* New York: Raven.

Bernstein, W. M., Stephan, W. G., & Davis, M. H. (1979). Explaining attributions for achievement: A path analytic approach. *Journal of Personality and Social Psychology, 37,* 1810–1821.

Berntson, G. G., Bechara, A., Damasio, H., Tranel, D., & Cacioppo, J. T. (2007). Amygdala contribution to selective dimensions of emotion. *Social Cognitive and Affective Neuroscience, 2,* 123–129.

Berridge, K. C. (2003). Comparing the emotional brains of humans and other animals. In R. J. Davidson, K. R. Scherer, & H. Hill Goldsmith (Eds.), *Handbook of affective sciences.* Oxford: Oxford University Press.

Berridge, K. C., & Kringelbach, M. L. (2008). Affective neuroscience of pleasure: Reward in humans and animals. *Psychopharmacology, 199,* 457–480.

Berridge, K. C., & Robinson, T. E. (2003). Parsing reward. *Trends in Neurosciences, 26,* 507–513.

Berthier, M. L., Kulisevsky, J., Gironell, A., & López, O. L. (2001). Obsessive-compulsive disorder and traumatic brain injury: Behavioral, cognitive, and neuroimaging findings. *Neuropsychiatry, Neuropsychology, and Behavioral Neurology, 14,* 23–31.

Berthoud, H-R., & Morrison, C. (2008). The brain, appetite, and obesity. *Annual Review of Psychology, 59,* 55–92.

Bertram, L. (2008). Genetic research in schizophrenia: New tools and future perspectives. *Schizophrenia Bulletin, 34,* 806–812.

Bertram, L., & Tanzi, R. E. (2008). Thirty years of Alzheimer's disease genetics: The implications of systematic meta-analysis. *Nature Reviews Neuroscience, 9,* 768–778.

Best, P. J., White, A. M., & Minai, A. (2001). Spatial processing in the brain: The activity of hippocampal place cells. *Annual Review of Neuroscience, 24,* 459–486.

Bettencourt, B. A., Dorr, N., Charlton, K., & Hume, D. L. (2001). Status differences in in-group bias: A meta-analytic examination of the effects of status stability, status legitimacy, and group permeability. *Psychological Bulletin, 127,* 520–542.

Beutler, L. E., & Harwood, M. T. (2000). *Prescriptive therapy: A practical guide to systematic treatment selection.* New York: Oxford University Press.

Bhugra, D. (1993). Cross-cultural aspects of jealousy. *International Review of Psychiatry, 5,* 271–280.

Bi, G., & Poo, M. (2001). Synaptic modification by correlated activity: Hebb's postulate revisited. *Annual Review of Neuroscience, 24,* 139–166.

Bick, P. A., & Kinsbourne, M. (1987). Auditory hallucinations and subvocal speech in schizophrenic patients. *American Journal of Psychiatry, 144,* 222–225.

Bickerton, D. (1984). The language bioprogram hypothesis. *Behavioral and Brain Sciences, 7,* 173–221.

Bickman, L. (1972). Social influence and diffusion of responsibility in an emergency. *Journal of Experimental Social Psychology, 8,* 438–445.

Biederman, I. (1987). Recognition-by-components: A theory of human image understanding. *Psychological Review, 94(2),* 115–147.

Biklen, D. (1990). Communication unbound: Autism and praxis. *Harvard Educational Review, 60,* 291–314.

Binder, J. L. (2004). *Key competencies in brief dynamic psychotherapy: Clinical practice beyond the manual.* New York: Guilford.

Binet, A., & Henri, V. (1896). La psychologie individuelle. *Année Psychologie, 11,* 163–169.

Binet, A., & Simon, T. (1916; reprinted 1973). *The development of intelligence in children.* New York: Arno Press.

Birkhead, T. R., & Moller, A. P. (1992). *Sperm competition in birds: Evolutionary causes and consequences.* London: Academic Press.

Bishay, N. R., Tarrier, N., Dolan, M., & Beckett, R. (1996). Morbid jealousy: A cognitive outlook. *Journal of Cognitive Psychotherapy, 10,* 9–22.

Bishop, S. J. (2009). Trait anxiety and impoverished prefrontal control of attention. *Nature Neuroscience, 12,* 92–98.

Bivens, J. A., & Berk, L. E. (1990). A longitudinal study of the development of elementary school children's private speech. *Merrill-Palmer Quarterly, 36,* 443–463.

Bjorklund, D. F., & Pellegrini, A. D. (2002). *The origins of human nature: Evolutionary developmental psychology.* Washington, DC: American Psychological Association.

Blackwell, L., Trzesniewski, K., & Dwick, C. S. (2007). Implicit theories of intelligence predict achievement across an adolescent transition: A longitudinal study and an intervention. *Child Development, 78,* 246–263.

Blanchard, R. (2001). Fraternal birth order and the maternal immune hypothesis of male homosexuality. *Hormones and Behavior, 40,* 105–114.

Blanchard, R. (2008). Review and theory of handedness, birth order, and homosexuality in men. *Laterality: Assymmetries of body, brain, and cognition, 13,* 51–70. I have abstract.

Blanchard-Fields, F. (2007). Everyday problem solving and emotion: An adult developmental perspective. *Current Directions in Psychological Science, 16,* 26–31.

Blanchette, I., & Dunbar, K. (2000). How analogies are generated: The roles of structural and superficial similarity. *Memory and Cognition, 28,* 108–124.

Blaustein, J. D. (2008). Neuroendocrine regulation of feminine sexual behavior: Lessons from rodent models and thoughts about humans. *Annual Review of Psychology, 59,* 93-118.

Blazer, D., Hughes, D., & George, L. D. (1987). Stressful life events and the onset of a generalized anxiety syndrome. *American Journal of Psychiatry, 144,* 1178–1183.

Bleuler, E. P. (1911; reprinted 1950). *Dementia praecox, or the group of schizophrenias* (J. Zinkin, Trans.). New York: International Universities Press.

Bligh, S., & Kupperman, P. (1993). Facilitated communication evaluation procedure accepted in a court case. *Journal of Autism and Developmental Disorders, 23,* 553–557.

Bliss, T. V. P., & Lømo, T. (1973). Long-lasting potentiation of synaptic transmission in the dentate area of the anaesthetized rabbit following stimulation of the perforant path. *Journal of Physiology (London), 232,* 331–356.

Block, J. J. (2008). Issues for DSM-V: Internet addiction. *American Journal of Psychiatry, 165,* 306–307.

Bloom, L. M., & Lahey, M. (1978). *Language development and language disorders.* New York: Wiley.

Bloom, P. (2001). Précis of *How children learn the meanings of words. Behavioral and Brain Sciences, 24,* 1095–1103.

Blurton-Jones, N. G. (1967). An ethological study of some aspects of social behavior of children in nursery school. In D. Morris (Ed.), *Primate ethology.* Chicago: Aldine.

Blurton-Jones, N. G., & Konner, M. J. (1973). Sex differences in the behavior of Bushman and London two- to five-year-olds. In J. Crook & R. Michael (Eds.), *Comparative ecology and behavior of primates.* New York: Academic Press.

Bodenhausen, G. V. (1991). Identity and cooperative social behavior: Pseudospeciation or human integration? *World Futures, 31,* 95–106.

Bogaert, A. F. (2006). Biological versus nonbiological older brothers and men's sexual orientation. *Proceedings of the National Academy of Sciences, 103,* 10771–10774.

Bolles, R. (1993). *The story of psychology: A thematic history.* Pacific Grove, CA: Brooks/Cole.

Bonanno, G. A., Davis, P. J., Singer, J. L., & Schwartz, G. E. (1991). The repressor personality and avoidant information processing: A dichotic listening study. *Journal of Research in Personality, 25,* 386–401.

Bond, A. J., & Lader, M. H. (1996). *Understanding drug treatment in mental health care.* New York: Wiley.

Bond, M. H., & Cheung, T. (1983). College students' spontaneous self-concept: The effect of culture among respondents in Hong Kong, Japan, and the United States. *Journal of Cross-Cultural Psychology, 14,* 153–171.

Bond, R. (2005). Group size and conformity. *Group Processes & Intergroup Relations, 8,* 331–354.

Bond, R., & Smith, P. B. (1996). Culture and conformity: A meta-analysis of studies using Asch's (1952b, 1956) line judgment task. *Psychological Bulletin, 119,* 111–137.

Bookheimer, S. (2002). Functional MRI of language: new approaches to understanding the cortical organization of semantic processing. *Annual Review of Neuroscience, 25,* 151–188.

Boone, C., Declerck, C. H., & Suetens, S. (2008). Subtle social cues, explicit incentives and cooperation in social dilemmas. *Evolution and Human Behavior, 29,* 179–188.

Borbély, A. (1986). *The secrets of sleep.* New York: Basic Books.

Borges, M. A., & Dutton, L. J. (1976). Attitudes toward aging. *The Gerontologist, 16,* 220–224.

Borkovec, T. D., Alcaine, O., & Behar, E. (2004). Avoidance theory of worry and generalized anxiety disorder. In R. G. Heimberg, C. L. Turk, & D. S. Mennin (Eds.), *Generalized anxiety disorder: Advances in research and practice.* New York: Guilford.

Botella, C., Osma, J., Garcia-Palacios, A., Quero, S., & Banos, R. M. (2004). Treatment of flying phobia using virtual reality: Data from a 1-year follow-up using a multiple baseline design. *Clinical Psychology and Psychotherapy, 11,* 311–323.

Both, S., Laan, E., Spiering, M., Nilsson, T., Oomans, S., & Everaerd, W. (2008). Appetitive and aversive conditioning of female sexual response. *Journal of Sexual Medicine, 5,* 1386–1401.

Bouchard, T. J. (1991). A twice-told tale: Twins reared apart. In W. M. Gove & D. Cicchetti (Eds.), *Thinking clearly about psychology: Vol. 2. Personality and psychopathology.* Minneapolis: University of Minnesota Press.

Bouchard, T. J. (1994). Genes, environment, and personality. *Science, 264,* 1700–1701.

Bouchard, T. J. (2004). Genetic influence on human psychological traits: A survey. *Current Directions in Psychological Science, 13,* 148–151.

Bouffard-Bouchard, T. (1990). Influence of self-efficacy on performance in a cognitive task. *Journal of Social Psychology, 130,* 353–363.

Boulkroune, N., Wang, L., March, A., Walker, N., & Jacob, T. J. (2007). Repetitive olfactory exposure to the biologically significant steroid androstadienone causes a hedonic shift and gender dimorphic changes in olfactory-evoked potentials. *Neuropsychopharmacology, 32,* 1822–1829.

Bourgeois, K. S., Khawar, A. W., Neal, S. A., & Lockman, J. J. (2005). Infant manual exploration of objects, surfaces, and their interrelations. *Infancy, 8,* 233–252.

Bouton, M. E., Westbrook, R. F., Corcoran, K. A., & Maren, S. (2006). Contextual and temporal modulation of extinction: Behavioral and biological mechanisms. *Biological Psychiatry, 60,* 352–360.

Bowlby, J. (1958). The nature of the child's tie to his mother. *International Journal of Psychoanalysis, 39,* 350–373.

Bowlby, J. (1973). *Attachment and loss: Vol. 2. Separation: Anxiety and anger.* New York: Basic Books.

Bowlby, J. (1982). *Attachment and loss* (2nd ed.). New York: Basic Books.

Bowles, A. (2004). Beck in action: Grawemeyer-winning psychiatrist influential in psychology. *APS Observer, 17(3),* 7–8.

Bowmaker, J. K., & Dartnall, H. J. A. (1980). Visual pigments of rods and cones in a human retina. *Journal of Physiology (London), 298,* 501–511.

Bozikas, V. P., Andreou, C., Giannakou, M., Tonia, T., Anezoulaki, D., Karavatos, A., et al. (2005). Deficits in sustained attention in schizophrenia but not in bipolar disorder. *Schizophrenia Research, 78,* 225–233.

Bradfield, L., & McNally, G. P. (2008). Unblocking in Pavlovian fear conditioning. *Journal of Experimental Psychology: Animal Behavior Processes, 34,* 256–265.

Bradley, G., & Wildman, K. (2002). Psychosocial predictors of emerging adults' risk and reckless behaviors. *Journal of Youth and Adolescence, 31,* 253–265.

Bradley, J. D. D., & Golden, C. J. (2001). Biological contributions to the presentation and understanding of attention-deficit/hyperactivity disorder: A review. *Clinical Psychology Review, 21,* 907–929.

Bramlett, M. D., & Mosher, W. D. (2002). *Cohabitation, marriage, divorce, and remarriage in the United States* (Vital Health Statistics, Series 23, Number 22). Hyattsville, MD: National Center for Health Statistics.

Brand, P., & Yancey, P. (1993). *Pain: The gift nobody wants.* New York: HarperCollins.

Bransford, J. D., Stein, B. S., Vye, N. J., Franks, J. J., Auble, P. M., Mezynski, K. J., & Perfetto, G. A. (1982). Different approaches in learning: An overview. *Journal of Experimental Psychology: General, 111,* 390–398.

Brase, G. (2003). The allocation system: Using signal detection processes to regulate representations in a multimodular mind. In D. E. Over (Ed.), *Evolution and the psychology of thinking: The debate.* New York: Psychology Press.

Brauer, M., Judd, C. M., & Gliner, M. D. (1995). The effects of repeated expressions on attitude polarization during group discussions. *Journal of Personality and Social Psychology, 68,* 1014–1029.

Bregman, E. (1934). An attempt to modify emotional attitude of infants by the conditioned response technique. *Journal of Genetic Psychology, 45,* 169–198.

Breiter, H. C., Aharon, I., Kahnaman, D., Dale, A., & Shizgal, P. (2001). Functional imaging of neural responses to expectancy and experience of monetary gains and losses. *Neuron, 30,* 619–639.

Brennan, P. A., & Zufall, F. (2006). Pheromonal communication in vertebrates. *Nature, 444,* 308–315.

Bretherton, I., Golby, B., & Cho, E. (1997). Attachment and the transmission of values. In J. E. Grusec & L. Kuczynski (Eds.), *Parenting and children's internalization of values: A handbook of contemporary theory.* New York: Wiley.

Brewer, M. B., & Weber, J. G. (1994). Self-evaluation effects of interpersonal versus intergroup social comparison. *Journal of Personality and Social Psychology, 66,* 268–275.

Britton, J. C., & Rauch, S. L. (2009). Neuroanatomy and neuroimaging of anxiety disorders. In M. M. Antony & M. B. Stein (Eds.), *Oxford handbook of anxiety related disorders.* Oxford, UK: Oxford University Press.

Broca, P. (1861; reprinted 1965). Paul Broca on the speech centers (M. D. Boring, Trans.). In R. J. Herrnstein & E. G. Boring (Eds.), *A source book in the history of psychology.* Cambridge, MA: Harvard University Press.

Broccia, M., & Campos, J. J. (1989). Maternal emotional signals, social referencing, and infants' reactions to strangers. In N. Eisenberg (Ed.), *Empathy and related emotional responses* (New Directions for Child Development, No. 44). San Francisco: Jossey-Bass.

Brody, G. H. (2004). Siblings' direct and indirect contributions to child development. *Current Directions in Psychological Science, 13,* 124–126.

Brody, N. (1992). *Intelligence* (2nd ed.). San Diego, CA: Academic Press.

Brooks, R., & Meltzoff, A. N. (2002). The importance of eyes: How infants interpret adult looking behavior. *Developmental Psychology, 38,* 958–966.

Brooks, R., & Meltzoff, A. N. (2008). Infant gaze following and pointing predict accelerated vocabulary growth through two years of age: A longitudinal, growth curve modeling study. *Journal of Child Language, 5,* 207–220.

Brown, A. S., & Susser, E. S. (2008). Prenatal nutritional deficiency and risk of adult schizophrenia. *Schizophrenia Bulletin, 34,* 1054–1063.

Brown, J., Cooper-Kuhn, C. M., Kempermann, G., Van Praag, H., Winkler, J., Gage, F. H., et al. (2003). Enriched environment and physical activity stimulate hippocampal but not olfactory bulb neurogenesis. *European Journal of Neuroscience, 17,* 2042–2046.

Brown, J. R., Ye, H., Bronson, R. T., Dikkes, P., & Greenberg, M. E. (1996). A defect in nurturing in mice lacking the immediate early gene fosB. *Cell, 86,* 297–309.

Brown, R. (1973). *A first language.* Cambridge, MA: Harvard University Press.

Brown, R., & Hanlon, C. (1970). Derivational complexity and order of acquisition in child speech. In J. R. Hayes (Ed.), *Cognition and the development of language.* New York: Wiley.

Bruce, V., & Young, A. (1998). *In the eye of the beholder: The science of face perception.* Oxford: Oxford University Press.

Bruner, J. S. (1983). *Child's talk: Learning to use language.* New York: Norton.

Brunstrom, J. M. (2005). Dietary learning in humans: Directions for further research. *Physiology and Behavior, 85,* 57–65.

Brunstrom, J. M., & Mitchell, G. L. (2007). Flavor-nutrient learning in restrained and unrestrained eaters. *Physiology and Behavior, 90,* 133–141.

Buchsbaum, B. R., & D'Esposito, M. (2008). The search for the phonological store: From loop to convolution. *Journal of Cognitive Neuroscience, 20,* 762–778.

Buck, L. B. (2000a). The molecular architecture of odor and pheromone sensing in mammals. *Cell, 100,* 611–618.

Buck, L. B. (2000b). Smell and taste: The chemical senses. In E. R. Kandel, J. H. Schwartz, & T. M. Jessell (Eds.), *Principles of neuroscience* (4th ed.). New York: McGraw-Hill.

Buehlman, K. T., Gottman, J. M., & Katz, L. F. (1992). How a couple views their past predicts their future: Predicting divorce from an oral history interview. *Journal of Family Psychology, 5,* 295–318.

Bugliosi, V. (1978). *Till death do us part.* New York: Bantam Books.

Burger, J. M. (1999). The foot-in-the-door compliance procedure: A multiple-process analysis and review. *Personality and Social Psychology Review, 3,* 303–325.

Burger, J. M. (2007). Fleeting attraction and compliance with requests. In A. R. Pratkanis (Ed.), *The science of social influence: Advances and future progress.* New York: Psychology Press.

Burger, J. M. (2009). Replicating Milgram: Would people still obey today? *American Psychologist, 64,* 1–11.

Burger, J. M., & Cornelius, T. (2003). Raising the price of agreement: Public commitment and the lowball compliance procedure. *Journal of Applied Social Psychology, 33,* 923–934.

Burger, J. M., Messian, N., Patel, S., del Prado, A., & Anderson, C. (2004). What a coincidence! The effects of incidental similarity on compliance. *Personality and Social Psychology Bulletin, 30,* 35–43.

Burger, J. M., Soroka, S., Gonzago, K., Murphy, E., & Somervell, E. (2001). The effect of fleeting attraction on compliance requests. *Personality and Social Psychology Bulletin, 27,* 1578–1586.

Burns, J. W. (2000). Repression predicts outcome following multidisciplinary treatment of chronic pain. *Health Psychology, 19,* 75–84.

Burnstein, E., & Vinokur, A. (1977). Persuasive argumentation and social comparison as determinants of attitude polarization. *Journal of Social Psychology, 13,* 315–332.

Bushnell, I. W. R., Sai, F., & Mullin, J. T. (1989). Neonatal recognition of the mother's face. *British Journal of Developmental Psychology, 7,* 3–15.

Buss, D. M. (1994). *The evolution of desire: Strategies of human mating.* New York: Basic Books.

Buss, D. M. (1995). Psychological sex differences: Origins through sexual selection. *American Psychologist, 50,* 164–168.

Buss, D. M. (1996). Social adaptation and five major factors of personality. In J. S. Wiggins (Ed.), *The five-factor model of personality: Theoretical perspectives.* New York: Guilford.

Buss, D. M. (2000a). Desires in human mating. *Annals of the New York Academy of Sciences, 907,* 39–49.

Buss, D. M. (2000b). *The dangerous passion: Why jealousy is as necessary as love and sex.* New York: The Free Press.

Bussey, K., & Bandura, A. (1999). Social cognitive theory of gender development and differentiation. *Psychological Review, 106,* 676–713.

Butler, D. (2004). Slim pickings. *Nature, 428,* 252–254.

Butler, R. N. (1975). *Why survive?* New York: Harper & Row.

Butterfield, E. C., & Siperstein, G. N. (1974). Influence of contingent auditory stimulation upon non-nutritional suckle. *In Proceedings of the third symposium on oral sensation and perception: The mouth of the infant.* Springfield, IL: Charles C. Thomas.

Byers, J. A. (1977). Terrain preferences in the play behavior of Siberian ibex kids (*Capra ibex sibirica*). *Zeitschrift fur Tierpsychologie, 45,* 199–209.

Byers, J. A. (1998). Biological effects of locomotor play: Getting into shape, or something more specific? In M. Bekoff & J. A. Byers (Eds.), *Animal play: Evolutionary, comparative, and ecological perspectives.* Cambridge University Press.

Byrne, J. H. (2003). Postsynaptic potentials and synaptic integration. In L. R. Squire, F. L. Bloom, S. K. McConnell, J. L. Roberts, N. C. Spitzer, & M. J. Zigmond (Eds.), *Fundamental neuroscience* (2nd ed.). San Diego, CA: Academic Press.

Byrne, J. H. (2008). Learning and memory. In L. Squire, D. Berg, F. Bloom, S. du Lac, A. Ghosh, & N. Spitzer (Eds.), *Fundamental neuroscience.* New York: Elsevier.

Byrne, R. W., & Russon, A. E. (1998). Learning by imitation: A hierarchical approach. *Behavioral and Brain Sciences, 21,* 667–721.

Cabib, S., Orsini, C., Le Moal, M., & Piazza, P. V. (2000). Abolition and reversal of strain differences in behavioral responses to drugs of abuse after a brief experience. *Science, 289,* 463–465.

Cacioppo, J. T., Berntson, G. G., & Klein, D. J. (1992). What is an emotion? The role of somatovisceral afference, with special emphasis on somatovisceral "illusions." *Review of Personality and Social Psychology,* Vol. 13.

Cacioppo, J. T., Rourke, P. A., Marshall-Goodell, B. S., Tassinary, L. G., & Baron, R. S. (1990). Rudimentary physiological effects of mere observation. *Psychophysiology, 27,* 177–186.

Caldwell-Harris, C. L., & Aycicegi, A. (2006). When personality and culture clash: The psychological distress of allocentrics in an individualist culture and idiocentrics in a collectivist culture. *Transcultural Psychiatry, 43,* 331–361.

Calev, A., Pass, H. L., Shapira, B., Fink, M., Tubi, N., & Lerer, B. (1993). ECT and memory. In C. E. Coffey (Ed.), *The clinical science of electroconvulsive therapy.* Washington, DC: American Psychiatric Press.

Cameron, L. A. (1999). Raising the stakes in the ultimatum game: Experimental evidence from Indonesia. *Economic Inquiry, 37,* 47–59.

Campbell, A. (1995). A few good men: Evolutionary psychology and female adolescent aggression. *Ethology and Sociobiology, 16,* 99–123.

Campbell, A. (2002). *A mind of her own: The evolutionary psychology of women.* Oxford: Oxford University Press.

Campbell, K. (1970). *Body and mind.* Notre Dame, IN: University of Notre Dame Press.

Campbell, S. S., & Tobler, I. (1984). Animals sleep: A review of sleep duration across phylogeny. *Neuroscience and Biobehavioral Review, 8,* 269–300.

Campos, J. J., Anderson, D. I., Barbu-Roth, M. A., Hubbard, E. M., Hertenstein, M. J., & Witherington, D. (2000). Travel broadens the mind. *Infancy, 1,* 149–219.

Cannon, W. B. (1932; reprinted 1963). *The wisdom of the body.* New York: Norton.

Cantor, N., & Harlow, R. E. (1994). Personality, strategic behavior, and daily-life problem solving. *Current Directions in Psychological Science, 3,* 169–172.

Cao, X., Cui, Z., Feng, R., Tang, Y-P., Qin, Z., Mei, B., & Tsien, J. Z. (2007). Maintenance of superior learning and memory function in NR2B transgenic mice during aging. *European Journal of Neuroscience, 25,* 1815–1822.

Capaldi, D. M., Crosby, L., & Stoolmiller, M. (1996). Predicting the timing of first sexual intercourse for at-risk adolescent males. *Child Development, 67,* 344–359.

Carlier, P., & Jamon, M. (2006). Observational learning in C57BL/6j mice. *Behavioural Brain Research, 174,* 125–131.

Carlson, S. M., Taylor, M., & Levin, G. (1998). The influence of culture on pretend play: The case of Mennonite children. *Merrill-Palmer Quarterly, 44,* 538–565.

Carney, D. R., Colvin, C. R., & Hall, J. A. (2007). A thin slice perspective on the accuracy of first impressions. *Journal of Research in Personality, 41,* 1054–1072.

Caro, T. M. (1995). Short-term costs and correlates of play in Cheetahs. *Animal Behaviour, 49,* 333–345.

Carpenter, P. A., Just, M. A., & Shell, P. (1990). What one intelligence test measures: A theoretical account of the processing in the Raven Progressive Matrices Test. *Psychological Review, 97,* 404–431.

Carpenter, W. T., & Buchanan, R. W. (2008). Lessons to take home from CATIE. *Psychiatric Services, 59,* 523–525.

Carr, S., Dabbs, J., & Carr, T. (1975). Mother-infant attachment: The importance of the mother's visual field. *Child Development, 46,* 331–338.

Carroll, B. J. (1991). Psychopathology and neurobiology of manic-depressive disorders. In B. J. Carroll & J. E. Barrett (Eds.), *Psychopathology and the brain.* New York: Raven Press.

Carroll, J. L., Shmidt, J. L., & Sorensen, R. (1992). Careers in psychology: Or what can I do with a bachelor's degree? *Psychological Reports, 71,* 1151–1154.

Carroll, M. A., Schneider, H. G., & Wesley, G. R. (1985). *Ethics in the practice of psychology.* Englewood Cliffs, NJ: Prentice-Hall.

Carstensen, L. L. (1992). Social and emotional patterns in adulthood: Support for socioemotional selectivity theory. *Psychology and Aging, 7,* 331–338.

Carstensen, L. L., & Fredrickson, B. L. (1998). Influence of HIV status and age on cognitive representations of others. *Health Psychology, 17,* 494–503.

Carstensen, L. L., & Mikels, J. A. (2005). At the intersection of emotion and cognition: Aging and the positivity effect. *Current Directions in Psychological Science, 14,* 117–121.

Cashdan, E. (1994). A sensitive period for learning about food. *Human Nature, 5,* 279–291.

Caspi, A., & Moffitt, T. E. (1991). Individual differences are accentuated during periods of social change: The sample case of girls at puberty. *Journal of Personality and Social Psychology, 61,* 157–168.

Caspi, A., & Moffitt, T. E. (1993). When do individual differences matter? A paradoxical theory of personality coherence. *Psychological Inquiry, 4,* 247–271.

Caspi, A., Roberts, B. W., & Shiner, R. L. (2005). Personality development: Stability and change. *Annual Review of Psychology, 56,* 453–484.

Cattell, R. B. (1943). The measurement of adult intelligence. *Psychological Bulletin, 40,* 153–193.

Cattell, R. B. (1950). *Personality: A systematic, theoretical, and factual study.* New York: McGraw-Hill.

Cattell, R. B. (1971). *Abilities: Their structure, growth, and action.* Boston: Houghton Mifflin. (Revised edition: Amsterdam: North-Holland, 1987.)

Cattell, R. B. (1973). *Personality and mood by questionnaire.* San Francisco: Jossey-Bass.

Ceci, S. J. (1996). *On intelligence: A bioecological treatise on intellectual development.* Cambridge, MA: Harvard University Press.

Cervone, D. (1997). Social-cognitive mechanisms and personality coherence: Self-knowledge, situational beliefs, and cross-situational coherence in perceived self-efficacy. *Psychological Science, 8,* 43–50.

Cézilly, F., & Zayan, R. (2000). Integrating different levels of analysis in the study of mate choice and mating systems in vertebrates. *Behavioural Processes, 51,* 1–5.

Chagnon, N. A. (1979). Mate competition, favoring close kin, and village fissioning among the Yanomamö Indians. In N. A. Chagnon & W. Irons (Eds.), *Evolutionary biology and human social behavior: An anthropological perspective.* North Scituate, MA: Duxbury Press.

Chandrashekar, J., Hoon, M. A., Ryba, N. J. P., & Zuker, C. S. (2006). The receptors and cells for mammalian taste. *Nature, 444,* 288–294.

Charles, S. T., Mather, M., & Carstensen, L. L. (2003). Aging and emotional memory: The forgettable nature of negative images for older adults. *Journal of Experimental Psychology: General, 132,* 310–324.

Chater, N. (1996). Reconciling simplicity and likelihood principles in perceptual organization. *Psychological Review, 103,* 566–581.

Chen, S., & Chaiken, S. (1999). The heuristic-systematic model in its broader context. In A. Chaiken & Y. Trope (Eds.), *Dual-process theories in social psychology.* New York: Guilford.

Chen, X., Chang, L., & He, Y. (2003). The peer group as a context: Mediating and moderating effects of relations between academic and social functioning in Chinese children. *Child Development, 74,* 710–727.

Chen, Y., Brockner, J., & Katz, T. (1998). Toward an explanation of cultural differences in in-group favoritism: The role of individual versus collective primacy. *Journal of Personality and Social Psychology, 75,* 1490–1502.

Cherry, E. C. (1953). Some experiments on the recognition of speech, with one and with two ears. *Journal of the Acoustical Society of America, 25,* 975–979.

Cherry, E. C., & Taylor, W. K. (1954). Some further experiments on the recognition of speech with one and two ears. *Journal of the Acoustical Society of America, 26,* 554–559.

Chesler, P. (1969). Maternal influence in learning by observation in kittens. *Science, 166,* 901–903.

Cheung, F. M. (2004). Use of Western and indigenously developed personality tests in Asia. *Applied Psychology: An International Review, 53,* 173–191.

Cheung, F., Weigiao, F., & To, C. (2008). The Chinese Personality Assessment Inventory as a culturally relevant personality measure in applied settings. *Social and Personality Psychology Compass, 2,* 74–89.

Chi, M. T. H., Bassok, M., Lewis, M. W., Reimann, P., & Glaser, R. (1989). Self-explanations: How students study and use examples in learning to solve problems. *Cognitive Science, 13,* 145–182.

Chi, M. T. H., de Leeuw, N., Chiu, M., & LaVancher, C. (1994). Eliciting self-explanations improves understanding. *Cognitive Science, 18,* 439–477.

Chirkov, V., Ryan, R. M., Kim, Y., & Kaplan, U. (2003). Differentiating autonomy from individualism and independence: A self-determination theory perspective on internalization of cultural orientations and well-being. *Journal of Personality and Social Psychology, 84,* 97–110.

Chirkov, V., Ryan, R. M., & Willness, C. (2005). Cultural context and psychological needs in Canada and Brazil: Testing a self-determination approach to the internalization of cultural practices, identity, and well-being. *Journal of Cross-Cultural Psychology, 36,* 423–443.

Chivers, M. L., Rieger, G., Latty, E., & Bailey, J. M. (2004). A sex difference in the specificity of sexual arousal. *Psychological Science, 15,* 736–744.

Choi, Y. H. (2007). Advancement of IT and seriousness of youth Internet addiction. In *2007 International Symposium on Counseling and Treatment of Youth Internet Addiction.* Seoul, Korea: National Youth Commission.

Chomsky, N. (1957). *Syntactic structures.* The Hague: Mouton.

Chomsky, N. (1965). *Aspects of a theory of syntax.* Cambridge, MA: MIT Press.

Chomsky, N. (1968). *Language and mind.* New York: Harcourt Brace Jovanovich.

Cialdini, R. B. (1987). Compliance principles of compliance professionals: Psychologists of necessity. In M. Zanna, J. M. Olson, & C. P. Herman (Eds.), *Social influence: The Ontario symposium* (Vol. 5). Hillsdale, NJ: Erlbaum.

Cialdini, R. B. (1993). *Influence: Science and practice* (3rd ed.). New York: HarperCollins.

Cialdini, R. B. (2001). *Influence: Science and practice* (4th ed.). Boston: Allyn & Bacon.

Cialdini, R. B. (2003). Crafting normative messages to protect the environment. *Current Directions in Psychological Science, 12,* 105–109.

Cialdini, R. B., Cacioppo, J. T., Bassett, R., & Miller, J. A. (1978). The lowball procedure for producing compliance: Commitment then cost. *Journal of Personality and Social Psychology, 36,* 463–476.

Cialdini, R. B., & Goldstein, N. J. (2004). Social influence: Compliance and conformity. *Annual Review of Psychology, 55,* 591–621.

Cicirelli, V. G. (2001). Personal meanings of death in older adults and young adults in relation to their fears of death. *Death Studies, 25*, 663–683.

Cisek, P., & Kalaska, J. F. (2004). Neural correlates of mental rehearsal in dorsal premotor cortex. *Nature, 431*, 993–996.

Clark, E. (1973). What's in a word? On the child's acquisition of semantics in his first language. In T. Moore (Ed.), *Cognitive development and the acquisition of language*. New York: Academic Press.

Clark, E. (1987). The principle of contrast: A constraint on language acquisition. In B. MacWhinney (Ed.), *Mechanisms of language acquisition*. Hillsdale, NJ: Erlbaum.

Clark, E. V. (1995). Language acquisition: The lexicon and syntax. In J. L. Miller & P. D. Eimas (Eds.), *Speech, language, and communication*. San Diego, CA: Academic Press.

Clearfield, M. W., & Nelson, N. M. (2006). Sex differences in mothers' speech and play behavior with 6-, 9-, and 14-month-old infants. *Sex Roles, 54*, 127–137.

Clifford, M. M., & Walster, E. (1973). The effects of physical attractiveness on teacher expectation. *Sociology of Education, 46*, 248–258.

Cocchini, G., Logie, R. H., Della Sala, S., MacPherson, S. E., & Baddeley, A. D. (2002). Concurrent performance of two memory tasks: Evidence for domain-specific working memory systems. *Memory and Cognition, 30(7)*, 1086–1095.

Cohen, R. A., & Albers, H. E. (1991). Disruption of human circadian and cognitive regulation following a discrete hypothalamic lesion: A case study. *Neurology, 41*, 726–729.

Cohen, S., & Herbert, T. B. (1996). Health psychology: Psychological factors and physical disease from the perspective of human psychoneuroendocrinology. *Annual Review of Psychology, 47*, 113–142.

Cohen, S., & Pressman, S. D. (2006). Positive affect and health. *Current Directions in Psychological Science, 15*, 122–125.

Cohen, S., Tyrrell, D. A. J., & Smith, A. P. (1991). Psychological stress and susceptibility to the common cold. *New England Journal of Medicine, 325*, 606–612.

Colby, A., & Damon, W. (1995). The development of extraordinary moral commitment. In M. Killen & D. Hart (Eds.), *Morality in everyday life: Developmental perspectives*. Cambridge, England: Cambridge University Press.

Colby, A., Kohlberg, L., Gibbs, J., & Lieberman, M. (1983). A longitudinal study of moral judgment. *Monographs of the Society for Research in Child Development, 148*(Whole Nos. 1 & 2).

Coldwell, G. M., & Bender, W. S. (2007). The effectiveness of assertive community treatment for homeless populations with severe mental illness: A meta-analysis. *American Journal of Psychiatry, 164*, 393–399.

Cole, D. A. (1991). Change in self-perceived competence as a function of peer and teacher evaluation. *Developmental Psychology, 27*, 682–688.

Cole, M., Gay, J., Glick, J., & Sharp, D. W. (1971). *The cultural context of learning and thinking*. New York: Basic Books.

Cole, M., & Means, B. (1981). *Comparative studies of how people think*. Cambridge, MA: Harvard University Press.

Collins, A., & Loftus, E. (1975). A spreading-activation theory of semantic processing. *Psychological Review, 82*, 407–428.

Collins, W. A., Welsh, D. P., & Furman, W. (2009). Adolescent romantic relationships. *Annual Review of Psychology, 60*, 631–652.

Colonnesi, C., Koops, & Terwogt, M. M. (2008). Young children's psychological explanations and their relationship to perception- and intention-understanding. *Infant and Child Development, 17*, 163–179.

Connolly, J. A., & Doyle, A. (1984). Relation of social fantasy play to social competence in preschoolers. *Developmental Psychology, 20*, 797–806.

Conway, A. R. A., Kane, M. J., & Engle, R. W. (2003). Working memory capacity and its relation to general intelligence. *Trends in Cognitive Sciences, 7*, 547–552.

Cook, M., & Mineka, S. (1989). Observational conditioning of fear to fear-relevant versus fear-irrelevant stimuli in rhesus monkeys. *Journal of Abnormal Psychology, 98*, 448–459.

Cook, M., & Mineka, S. (1990). Selective associations in the observational conditioning of fear in rhesus monkeys. *Journal of Experimental Psychology: Animal Behavior Processes, 16*, 372–389.

Cook, R. G., & Smith, J. D. (2006). Stages of abstraction and exemplar memorization in pigeon category learning. *Psychological Science, 17*, 1059–1066.

Cooley, C. H. (1902; reprinted 1964). *Human nature and the social order*. New York: Schocken Books.

Cooper, H. M., & Good, T. L. (1983). *Pygmalion grows up: Studies in the expectation communication process*. New York: Longman.

Corballis, P. M. (2003). Visuospatial processing and the right-hemisphere interpreter. *Brain and Cognition, 53*, 171–176.

Coren, S., & Ward, L. M. (1989). *Sensation and perception* (3rd ed.). New York: Harcourt Brace Jovanovich.

Corey, D. P. (2007). Stringing the fiddle: The inner ear's two-part invention. *Nature Neuroscience, 10*, 1232–1233.

Corey, S. M. (1937). Professed attitudes and actual behavior. *Journal of Educational Psychology, 28*, 271–280.

Corkin, S. (2002). What's new with the amnesic patient H. M.? *Nature Reviews Neuroscience, 3*, 153–160.

Correll, J., Park, B., Judd, C. M., & Wittenbrink, B. (2002). The police officer's dilemma: Using ethnicity to disambiguate potentially threatening individuals. *Journal of Personality and Social Psychology, 83*, 1314–1329.

Costa, P. T., & McCrae, R. R. (1992). *The NEO-PI-R professional manual*. Odessa, FL: Psychological Assessment Resources.

Costa, P. T., & McCrae, R. R. (1994). Set like plaster? Evidence for the stability of adult personality. In T. F. Heatherton & J. L. Weinberger (Eds.), *Can personality change?* Washington, DC: American Psychological Association.

Costa, P. T., Terracciano, A., & McCrae, R. R. (2001). Gender differences in personality traits across cultures: Robust and surprising findings. *Journal of Personality and Social Psychology, 81*, 322–331.

Coughlin, L. D., & Patel, V. L. (1987). Processing of critical information by physicians and medical students. *Journal of Medical Education, 62*, 818–828.

Cousins, N. (1977, May 23). Anatomy of an illness (as perceived by the patient). *Saturday Review*, Nos. 4–6, pp. 48–51.

Cousins, S. D. (1989). Culture and self-perception in Japan and the United States. *Journal of Personality and Social Psychology, 56*, 124–131.

Cowan, N., Nugent, L. D., Elliott, E. M., & Saults, J. S. (2000). Persistence of memory for ignored lists of digits: Areas of developmental constancy and change. *Journal of Experimental Child Psychology, 76*, 151–172.

Cowart, B. J. (1981). Development of taste perception in humans: Sensitivity and preference throughout the life span. *Psychological Bulletin, 90*, 43–73.

Cowen, P. J. (2005). The neurobiology of depression. In E. J. L. Griez, C. Faravelli, J. J. Nutt, & J. Zohar (Eds.), *Mood disorders: Clinical management issues*. West Sussex, England: Wiley.

Cowlishaw, G., & Dunbar, R. I. M. (1991). Dominance rank and mating success in male primates. *Animal Behaviour, 41*, 1045–1056.

Cox, J. J., Reimann, F., Nicholas, A. K., Thornton, G., Roberts, E., Springell, K., Karbani, G., Jafri, H., Mannan, J., Raashid, Y., Al-Gazali, L., Hamamy, H., Valente, E. M., Gorman, S., Williams, R., McHale, D., Wood, J. N., Gribble, F. M., & Woods, C. G. (2006). An *SCN9A* channelopathy causes congenital inability to experience pain. *Nature, 444*, 894–898.

Cox, M. J., Owen, M. T., Henderson, V. K., & Margand, N. A. (1992). Prediction of infant-father and infant-mother attachment. *Developmental Psychology, 28,* 474–483.

Crabbe, J. C., Phillips, T. J., Buck, K. J. Cunningham, C. L., & Belknap, J. K. (1999a). Identifying genes for alcohol and drug sensitivity: Recent progress and future directions. *Trends in Neuroscience, 22,* 173–179.

Crabbe, J. C., Wahlsten D., & Dudek, B. C. (1999b). Genetics of mouse behavior: Interactions with the laboratory environment. *Science, 284,* 1670–1672.

Craik, F. I., & Tulving, E. (1975). Depth of processing and the retention of words in episodic memory. *Journal of Experimental Psychology: General, 104,* 268–294.

Cramer, P. (2000). Defense mechanisms in psychology today: Further processes for adaptation. *American Psychologist, 55,* 637–646.

Cramer, P. (2008). Identification and the development of competence: A 44-year longitudinal study from late adolescence to late middle age. *Psychology and Aging, 23,* 410–421.

Craske, M. G. (1999). *Anxiety disorders: Psychological approaches to theory and treatment.* Boulder, CO: Westview.

Crawford, C. J. (1994). Parenting in the Basque country: Implications of infant and childhood sleeping location for personality development. *Ethos, 22,* 42–82.

Critchley, H. D., Wiens, S., Rotschtein, P., Öhman, A., & Dolan, R. J. (2004). Neural systems supporting interoceptive awareness. *Nature Neuroscience, 7,* 189–195.

Crittenden, P. M., & Claussen, A. H. (Eds.). (2003). *The organization of attachment relationships: Maturation, culture, and context.* Cambridge, England: Cambridge University Press.

Crocker, J., & Wolfe, C. T. (2001). Contingencies of self-worth. *Psychological Review, 108,* 593–623.

Cross, P. (1977). Not *can* but *will* college teachers be improved? *New Directions for Higher Education, 17,* 1–15.

Crowley, K., Callanan, M. A., Tenenbaum, H. R., & Allen, E. (2001). Parents explain more often to boys than to girls during shared scientific thinking. *Psychological Science, 12,* 258–261.

Crowne, D. P., & Liverant, S. (1963). Conformity under varying conditions of personal commitment. *Journal of Abnormal and Social Psychology, 66,* 547–555.

Cudjoe, S., Moss, S., & Nguyen, L. (2007). How do exercise and diet compare for weight loss? *Journal of Family Practice, 56,* 841–843.

Culp, R. E., Cook, A. S., & Housley, P. C. (1983). A comparison of observed and reported adult-infant interactions: Effects of perceived sex. *Sex Roles, 9,* 475–479.

Cunningham, W. A., Preacher, K. J., & Banaji, M. R. (2001). Implicit attitude measures: Consistency, stability, and convergent validity. *Psychological Science, 12,* 163–170.

Curran, P., Stice, E., & Chassin, L. (1997). The relation between adolescent alcohol use and peer alcohol use: A longitudinal random coefficients model. *Journal of Consulting and Clinical Psychology, 65,* 130–140.

Curtiss, S. (1977). *Genie: A psycholinguistic study of a modern-day "wild child."* New York: Academic Press.

Curtiss, S. (1989). The independence and task-specificity of language. In M. H. Bornstein & J. S. Bruner (Eds.), *Interaction in human development.* Hillsdale, NJ: Erlbaum.

Cutler, S. S., Larsen, R. J., & Bunce, S. C. (1996). Repressive coping style and the experience and recall of emotion: A naturalistic study of daily affect. *Journal of Personality, 65,* 379–405.

Cyranoski, D. (2002). Almost human. *Nature, 418,* 910–912.

Czeisler, C. A., Johnson, M. P., Duffy, J. E., Brown, E. N., Ronda, J. M., & Kronauer, R. E. (1990). Exposure to bright light and darkness to treat physiologic maladaptation to night work. *New England Journal of Medicine, 322,* 1253–1259.

Czeisler, C. A., Kronauer, R. E., Allen, J. S., Duffy, J. F., Jewett, M. E., Brown, E. N., & Ronda, J. M. (1989). Bright light induction of strong (type O) resetting of the human circadian pacemaker. *Science, 244,* 1328–1333.

D'Argembeau, A., & Van der Linden, M. (2008). Remembering pride and shame: Self-enhancement and the phenomenology of autobiographical memory. *Memory, 16,* 538–547.

Dacey, D. M. (2000). Parallel pathways for spectral coding in primate retina. *Annual Review of Neuroscience, 23,* 743–775.

Daley, T. C., Whaley, S. E., Sigman, M. D., Espinosa, M. P., & Neumann, C. (2003). IQ on the rise: The Flynn effect in rural Kenyan children. *Psychological Science, 14,* 215–219.

Dalton, P., Doolittle, N., & Breslin, P. A. S. (2002). Gender-specific induction of enhanced sensitivity to odors. *Nature Neuroscience, 5,* 199–200.

Dalton, R. (2004). True colours. *Nature, 428,* 596–597.

Daly, M., & Wilson, M. (1988). *Homicide.* New York: de Gruyter.

Daly, M., & Wilson, M. (1990). Killing the competition. *Human Nature, 1,* 81–107.

Dam, H., Jakobsen, K., & Mellerup, E. (1998). Prevalence of winter depression in Denmark. *Acta Psychiatrica Scandinavica, 97,* 104.

Damasio, A. (2001). Fundamental feelings. *Nature, 413,* 781.

Damon, W., & Hart, D. (1992). Self-understanding and its role in social and moral development. In M. H. Bornstein & M. E. Lamb (Eds.), *Developmental psychology: An advanced textbook* (3rd ed.). Hillsdale, NJ: Erlbaum.

Damsma, G., Pfaus, J. G., Wenkstern, D., Phillips, A. G., & Fibiger, H. C. (1992). Sexual behavior increases dopamine transmission in the nucleus accumbens and striatum of male rats: Comparison with novelty and locomotion. *Behavioral Neurosciences, 106,* 181–191.

Darwin, C. (1859; reprinted 1963). *The origin of species.* New York: Washington Square Press.

Darwin, C. (1872; reprinted 1965). *The expression of the emotions in man and animals.* Chicago: University of Chicago Press.

Daum, I., Channon, S., & Canavar, A. (1989). Classical conditioning in patients with severe memory problems. *Journal of Neurology and Neurosurgery Psychiatry, 52,* 47–51.

Davidson, J. M. (1980). Hormones and sexual behavior in the male. In D. T. Krieger & J. C. Hughes (Eds.), *Neuroendocrinology.* Sunderland, MA: Sinauer.

Davidson, J. M., Camargo, C. A., & Smith, E. R. (1979). Effects of androgen on sexual behavior in hypogonadal men. *Journal of Clinical Endocrinology and Metabolism, 48,* 955–958.

Davidson, J. M., & Myers, L. S. (1988). Endocrine factors in sexual psychophysiology. In R. C. Rosen & J. G. Beck (Eds.), *Patterns of sexual arousal: Psychophysiological processes and clinical applications.* New York: Guilford.

Davidson, R. J., Pizzagalli, D., Nitschke, J. B., & Kalin, N. H. (2003). Parsing the subcomponents of emotion and disorders of emotion: Perspectives from affective neuroscience. In R. J. Davidson, K. R. Scherer, & H. H. Goldsmith (Eds.), *Handbook of affective sciences.* Oxford: Oxford University Press.

Davis, J. M. (1974). A two-factor theory of schizophrenia. *Journal of Psychiatric Research, 11,* 25–30.

Davis, M. (1992). The role of the amygdala in fear and anxiety. *Annual Review of Neuroscience, 15,* 353–375.

Davis, O. S. P., Arden, R., & Plomin, R. (2008). *g* in middle childhood: Moderate genetic and shared environmental influence using diverse measures of general cognitive ability at 7, 9 and 10 years in a large population sample of twins. *Intelligence, 36,* 68–80.

Davis, P. J., & Schwartz, G. E. (1987). Repression and the inaccessibility of affective memories. *Journal of Personality and Social Psychology, 52,* 155–162.

Dawes, R. M., & Messick, D. M. (2000). Social dilemmas. *International Journal of Psychology, 35,* 111–116.

Dawood, K., Pillard, R. C., Horvath, C., Revelle, W., & Bailey, J. M. (2000). Familial aspects of male homosexuality. *Archives of Sexual Behavior, 29,* 155–163.

Day, J. J., Roitman, M. F., Wightman, R. M. & Carelli, R. M. (2007). Associative learning mediates dynamic shifts in dopamine signaling in the nucleus accumbens. *Nature Neuroscience, 10,* 1020–1028.

de Boysson-Bardies, B. (1999). *How language comes to children.* Cambridge, MA: MIT Press.

de Groot, A. D. (1965). *Thought and choice in chess.* The Hague: Mouton.

De Houwer, J., & De Bruycker, E. (2007). Implicit attitudes towards meat and vegetables in vegetarians and nonvegetarians. *International Journal of Psychology, 42,* 158–165.

De Houwer, J., Thomas, S., & Baeyens, F. (2001). Associative learning of likes and dislikes: A review of 25 years of research on human evaluative conditioning. *Psychological Bulletin, 127,* 853–869.

de Jong, J. T. V. M., Komproe, I. H., & Ommeren, M. V. (2003). Common mental disorders in postconflict settings. *The Lancet, 361,* 2128–2130.

de Paula, F., Soares, J. M., Haider, M. A., de Lima, G. R., & Baracat, E. C. (2007). The benefits of androgens combined with hormone replacement therapy regarding to patients with postmenopausal sexual symptoms. *Maturitas, 56,* 69–77.

de Quervain, D. J.-F., Fischbacher, U., Treyer, V., Schellhammer, M., Schnyder, U., Buck, A., et al. (2004). The neural basis of altruistic punishment. *Science, 305,* 1254–1258.

De Valois, R. L., Abramov, I., & Jacobs, G. H. (1966). Analysis of response patterns of LGN cells. *Journal of the Optical Society of America, 56,* 96–97.

de Villiers, J. G., & de Villiers, P. A. (1979). *Language acquisition.* Cambridge, MA: Harvard University Press.

de Waal, F. (1997). *Bonobo: The forgotten ape.* Berkeley: University of California Press.

De Waal, F. (2005). *Our inner ape: A leading primatologist explains why we are who we are.* New York: Riverhead Books.

Deary, I. (2008). Why do intelligent people live longer? *Nature, 456,* 175–176.

Deary, I. J., & Der, G. (2005). Reaction time explains IQ's association with death. *Psychological Science, 16,* 64–69.

Deaux, K. (1985). Sex and gender. *Annual Review of Psychology, 36,* 49–81.

DeCasper, A. J., & Fifer, W. P. (1980). Of human bonding: Newborns prefer their mothers' voices. *Science, 208,* 1174–1176.

Dehaene, S., Jobert, A., Naccache, L., Ciuciu, P., Poline, J.-B., Le Bihan, D., et al. (2004). Letter binding and invariant recognition of masked words. *Psychological Science, 15,* 307–314.

Dehaene, S., Naccache, L., Cohen, L., Le Bihan, D., Mangin, J.-F., Poline, J.-B., et al. (2001). Cerebral mechanisms of word masking and unconscious repetition priming. *Nature Neuroscience, 4,* 752–758.

DeJonge, F. H., Louwerse, A. L., Ooms, M. P., Evers, P., Endert, E., & Van de Poll, N. E. (1989). Lesions of the SDN-POA inhibit sexual behavior of male Wistar rats. *Brain Research Bulletin, 23,* 483–492.

Delay, J., & Deniker, P. (1952). Trente-huit cas de psychoses traitées par la cure prolongée et continué de 4560 RP. *Comptes Rendus Congrès des Médecins Aliénistes et Neurologistes de France et des Pays de Langue Française, 50,* 497–502.

DeLuca, N. L., Moser, L. L., & Bond, G. R. (2008). Assertive community treatment. In K. T. Mueser & D. V. Jeste (eds.), *Clinical handbook of schizophrenia.* New York: Guilford.

Dember, W. N., & Fowler, H. (1958). Spontaneous alternation behavior. *Psychological Bulletin, 53,* 412–428.

Denissen, J. J. A., Penke, L., Schmitt, D. P., & Van Aken, M. A. G. (2008). Self-esteem reactions to social interactions: Evidence for sociometer mechanisms across days, people, and nations. *Journal of Personality and Social Psychology, 95,* 181–196.

Dennett, D. C. (1994). Language and intelligence. In J. Khalfa (Ed.), *What is intelligence?* Cambridge, England: Cambridge University Press.

Derakshan, N., & Eysenck, M. W. (1998). Working memory capacity in high trait-anxious and repressor groups. *Cognition and Emotion, 12,* 697–613.

Derakshan, N., Eysenck, M. W., & Myers, L. B. (2007). Emotional information processing in repressors: The vigilance-avoidance hypothesis. *Cognition and Emotion, 21,* 1585–1614.

Descartes, R. (1637; reprinted 1972). *Treatise of man* (T. S. Hall, Trans.). Cambridge, MA: Harvard University Press.

Descartes, R. (1649; reprinted 1985). *The passions of the soul.* In J. Cottingham, R. Stoothoff, & D. Murdoch (Eds. and Trans.), *The philosophical writings of Descartes* (Vol. 1, pp. 324–404). Cambridge, England: Cambridge University Press.

Deutch, A. Y., & Roth, R. H. (2008). Neurotransmitters. In L. Squire, D. Berg, F. Bloom, S. du Lac, A. Ghosh, & N. Spitzer (Eds.), *Fundamental neuroscience.* New York: Elsevier.

Deutsch, A. (1948). *The shame of the states.* New York: Harcourt, Brace.

Deutsch, F. M. (2001). Equally shared parenting. *Current Directions in Psychological Science, 10,* 25–28.

DeWitt, L. A., & Samuel, A. G. (1990). The role of knowledge-based expectations in music perception: Evidence from musical restoration. *Journal of Experimental Psychology: General, 119,* 123–144.

Dewsbury, D. A. (1988). The comparative psychology of monogamy. In D. W. Leger (Ed.), *Comparative perspectives in modern psychology. Nebraska Symposium on Motivation, 1987.* Lincoln: University of Nebraska Press.

Diamond, L. M. (2004). Emerging perspectives on distinctions between romantic love and sexual desire. *Current Directions in Psychological Science, 13,* 116–119.

Diamond, L. M. (2006). The evolution of plasticity in female-female desire. *Journal of Psychology and Human Sexuality, 18,* 245–247.

Dias, M. G., & Harris, P. L. (1988). The effect of make-believe play on deductive reasoning. *British Journal of Developmental Psychology, 6,* 207–221.

Dickens, W. T., & Flynn, J. R. (2006). Black Americans reduce the racial IQ gap: Evidence from standardized samples. *Psychological Science, 17,* 913–924.

Dickerson, F. B., Tenhula, W. N., & Green-Paden, L. D. (2005). The token economy for schizophrenia: Review of the literature and recommendations for future research. *Schizophrenia Research, 75,* 405–416.

Dickinson, A., & Balleine, B. W. (2000). Causal cognition and goal-directed action. In C. Heyes & L. Huber (Eds.), *The evolution of cognition.* Cambridge, MA: MIT Press.

Dickinson, A., & Dawson, G. R. (1987). The role of the instrumental contingency in motivational control of performance. *Quarterly Journal of Experimental Psychology, 39B,* 77–93.

Dickinson, D., Ragland, J. D., Gold, J. M., & Gur, R. C. (2008). General and specific cognitive deficits in schizophrenia: Goliath defeats David? *Biological Psychiatry, 64,* 823–827.

Diener, E., Sandvik, E., Pavot, W., & Fujita, F. (1992). Extraversion and subjective well-being in a U.S. national probability sample. *Journal of Research in Personality, 26,* 205–215.

Dillon, K. M. (1993). Facilitated communication, autism, and Ouija. *Skeptical Inquirer, 17,* 281–287.

DiMascio, A., Weissman, M. M., Prusoff, B. A., Neu, C., Zwilling, M., & Klerman, G. L. (1979). Differential symptom reduction by drugs and psychotherapy in acute depression. *Archives of General Psychiatry, 36,* 1450–1456.

Dimberg, U., Thunberg, M., & Elmehed, K. (2000). Unconscious facial reactions to emotional facial expressions. *Psychological Science, 11,* 86–89.

Dinnel, D. L., Kleinknecht, R. A., & Tanaka-Matsumi, J. (2002). A cross-cultural comparison of social phobia symptoms. *Journal of Psychopathology and Behavioral Assessment, 24,* 75–82.

Dion, K. K. (1972). Physical attractiveness and evaluation of children's transgressions. *Journal of Personality and Social Psychology, 24,* 207–213.

Dion, K. K. (2002). Cultural perspectives on facial attractiveness. In G. Rhodes & L. A. Zebrowitz (Eds.), *Facial attractiveness: Evolutionary, cognitive, and social perspectives.* Westport, CT: Ablex.

Docherty, N. M., Cohen, A. S., Nienow, T. M., Dinzeo, T. J., & Dangelmaier, R. E. (2003). Stability of formal thought disorder and referential communication disturbances in schizophrenia. *Journal of Abnormal Psychology, 112,* 469–475.

Domhoff, G. W. (2003). *The scientific study of dreams: Network analysis, cognitive development, and content analysis.* Washington, DC: American Psychological Association.

Domjan, M. (2003). *The principles of learning and behavior* (5th ed.). Belmont, CA: Wadsworth.

Donenberg, G. R. (1998). Guilt and abnormal aspects of parent-child interactions. In J. Bybee (Ed.), *Guilt and children.* San Diego, CA: Academic Press.

Dorman, M. F., & Wilson, B. S. (2004). The design and function of cochlear implants. *American Scientist, 92,* 436–445.

Dost, A., & Yagmurlu, B. (2008). Are constructiveness and destructiveness essential features of guilt and shame feelings respectively? *Journal for the Theory of Social Behaviour, 38,* 109–129.

Doty, R. L. (2001). Olfaction. *Annual Review of Psychology, 52,* 423–452.

Douglas, K. M., & Bilkey, D. K. (2007). Amusia is associated with deficits in spatial processing. *Nature Neuroscience, 10,* 915–921.

Douglas, N. J. (2002). *Clinician's guide to sleep medicine.* London: Arnold.

Dovidio, J. F., Brigham, J. C., Johnson, B. T., & Gaertner, S. L. (1996). Stereotyping, prejudice, and discrimination. In C. N. Macrae, C. Stangor, & M. Hewstone (Eds.), *Stereotypes and stereotyping.* New York: Guilford.

Dovidio, J. F., Evans, N., & Tyler, R. B. (1986). Racial stereotypes: The contents of their cognitive representations. *Journal of Experimental Social Psychology, 22,* 22–37.

Dovidio, J. F., Johnson, C., Gaertner, S. L., Validzic, A., Howard, A., & Eisinger, N. (1994, April). *Racial bias and the role of implicit and explicit attitudes.* Paper presented at the annual meeting of the Eastern Psychological Association, Providence, RI.

Dovidio, J. F., Kawakami, K., & Gaertner, S. L. (2002). Implicit and explicit prejudice and interracial interaction. *Journal of Personality and Social Psychology, 82,* 62–68.

Dovidio, J., Kawakami, K., Johnson, C., Johnson, B., & Howard, A. (1997). On the nature of prejudice: Automatic and controlled processes. *Journal of Experimental Social Psychology, 33,* 510–540.

Dozier, M., Peloso, E., Lindhiem, O., Gordon, M. K., Manni, M., Sepulveda, S., & Ackerman, J. (2006). Developing evidence-based interventions for foster children: An example of a randomized clinical trial with infants and toddlers. *Journal of Social Issues, 62,* 767–785.

Draper, P., & Harpending, H. (1982). Father absence and reproductive strategy: An evolutionary perspective. *Journal of Anthropological Research, 38,* 255–273.

Draper, P., & Harpending, H. (1988). A sociobiological perspective on the development of human reproductive strategies. In K. B. MacDonald (Ed.), *Sociobiological perspectives on human development.* New York: Springer-Verlag.

Dronkers, N. F., Pinker, S., & Damasio, A. (2000). Language and the aphasias. In E. R. Kandel, J. H. Schwartz, & T. M. Jessell (Eds.), *Principles of neural science* (4th ed.). New York: McGraw-Hill.

Duffy, V. B., & Bartoshuk, L. M. (1996). Sensory factors in feeding. In E. D. Capaldi (Ed.), *Why we eat what we eat: The psychology of eating.* Washington, DC: American Psychological Association.

Dumont, M., & Beaulieu, C. (2007). Light exposure in the natural environment: Relevance to mood and sleep disorders. *Sleep Medicine, 8,* 557–565.

Dunbar, K. (1999). The scientist in vivo: How scientists think and reason in the laboratory. In L. Magnani, N. Nersessian, & P. Thatard (Eds.), *Model-based reasoning in scientific discovery.* New York: Plenum Press.

Dunbar, K. (2001). The analogical paradox: Why analogy is so easy in naturalistic settings, yet so difficult in the psychology laboratory. In D. Gentner, K. J. Holyoak, & B. N. Kokinov (Eds.), *The analogical mind: Perspectives from cognitive science.* Cambridge, MA: MIT Press.

Duncan, J., Seitz, R. J., Kolodny, J., Bor, D., Herzog, H., Ahmed, A., Newell, F. N., & Emslie, H. (2000). A neural basis for general intelligence. *Science, 289,* 457–460.

Duncker, K. (1945). On problem-solving. *Psychological Monographs, 58* (Whole No. 270).

Dunn, F. A., Lankheet, M. J., & Rieke, F. (2007). Light adaptation in cone vision involves switching between receptor and post-receptor sites. *Nature, 449,* 603–607.

Dunn, J., & Plomin, R. (1990). *Separate lives: Why siblings are so different.* New York: Basic Books.

Dunning, D., Heath, C., & Suls, J. M. (2004). Flawed self-assessment: Implications for health, education, and the workplace. *Psychological Science in the Public Interest, 5,* 69–106.

Dunning, D., Meyerowitz, J. A., & Holzberg, A. D. (1989). Ambiguity and self-evaluation: The role of idiosyncratic trait definitions in self-serving assessments of ability. *Journal of Personality and Social Psychology, 57,* 1082–1090.

Dweck, C. S. (2006). *Mindset: The new psychology of success.* New York: Random House.

Dweck, C. S. (2008). Can personality be changed? The role of beliefs in personality change. *Current Directions in Psychological Science, 17,* 391–394.

Dweck, C. S., Davidson, W., Nelson, S., & Enna, B. (1978). Sex differences in learned helplessness: II. The contingencies of evaluative feedback in the classroom. III. An experimental analysis. *Developmental Psychology, 14,* 268–276.

Eacott, M. J. (1999). Memory for events in early childhood. *Current Directions in Psychological Science, 8,* 46–49.

Eagle, M., Wolitzky, D. L., & Klein, G. S. (1966). Imagery: Effect of a concealed figure in a stimulus. *Science, 151,* 837–839.

Eagly, A. H. (2007). Female leadership advantage and disadvantage: Resolving the contradictions. *Psychology of Women Quarterly, 31,* 1–12.

Eaton, W. O., & Ritchot, K. F. M. (1995). Physical maturation and information-processing speed in middle childhood. *Developmental Psychology, 31,* 967–972.

Eddy, K. T., Hennessey, M., & Thompson-Brenner, H. (2007). Eating pathology in East African women. *Journal of Nervous and Mental Disease, 195,* 196–202.

Edelman, G. M. (1987). *Neural Darwinism*. New York: Basic Books.

Eden, D. (2003). Self-fulfilling prophesies in organizations. In J. Greenberg (Ed.), *Organizational behavior: The state of the science* (2nd ed.). Mahwah, NJ: Erlbaum.

Eibl-Eibesfeldt, I. (1975). *Ethology: The biology of behavior* (2nd ed.). New York: Holt, Rinehart & Winston.

Eibl-Eibesfeldt, I. (1989). *Human ethology*. New York: de Gruyter.

Eichenbaum, H. (2001). The long and winding road to memory consolidation. *Nature Neuroscience, 4*, 1057–1058.

Eichenbaum, H. (2003). How does the hippocampus contribute to memory? *Trends in Cognitive Sciences, 7*, 427–429.

Eisenberg, N. (2000). Emotion, regulation, and moral development. *Annual Review of Psychology, 51*, 665–697.

Eisenberger, N. I. (2006). Identifying the neural correlates underlying social pain: Implications for developmental processes. *Human Development, 49*, 273–293.

Eisenberger, N. I., & Lieberman, M. D. (2004). Why rejection hurts: A common neural alarm system for physical and social pain. *Trends in Cognitive Sciences, 8*, 294–300.

Eisenberger, N. I., Jarcho, J. M., Lieberman, M. D., & Naliboff, B. D. (2006). An experimental study of shared sensitivity to physical pain and social rejection. *Pain, 126*, 132–138.

Ekman, P. (1984). Expression and the nature of emotion. In K. R. Scherer & P. Ekman (Eds.), *Approaches to emotion*. Hillsdale, NJ: Erlbaum.

Ekman, P. (1992). Facial expressions of emotion: New findings, new questions. *Psychological Science, 3*, 34–38.

Ekman, P., & Friesen, W. V. (1975). *Unmasking the face*. Englewood Cliffs, NJ: Prentice-Hall.

Ekman, P., & Friesen, W. V. (1982). Measuring facial movements with the facial action coding system. In P. Ekman (Ed.), *Emotion in the human face*. Cambridge, England: Cambridge University Press.

Ekman, P., Friesen, W. V., O'Sullivan, M., Chan, A., et al. (1987). Universals and cultural differences in the judgments of facial expressions of emotion. *Journal of Personality and Social Psychology, 53*, 712–717.

Ekman, P., Levenson, R. W., & Friesen, W. V. (1983). Autonomic nervous system activity distinguishes among emotions. *Science, 221*, 1208–1210.

Elbert, T., Pantev, C., Wienbruch, C., Rockstroh, B., & Taub, E. (1995). Increased cortical representation of the fingers of the left hand in string players. *Science, 270*, 305–307.

Elfenbein, H. A., & Ambady, N. (2003). Universals and cultural differences in recognizing emotions. *Current Directions in Psychological Science, 12*, 159–164.

Elfenbein, H. A., Beaupré, M., Lévesque, M., & Hess, U. (2007). Toward a dialect theory: Cultural differences in the expression and recognition of posed expressions. *Emotion, 7*, 131–146.

Elias, C. L, & Berk, L. E. (2002). Self-regulation in young children: Is there a role for sociodramatic play? *Early Childhood Research Quarterly, 17*, 216–238.

Elkin, R., & Leippe, M. (1986). Physiological arousal, dissonance, and attitude change: Evidence for a dissonance-arousal link and a "don't remind me" effect. *Journal of Personality and Social Psychology, 51*, 55–65.

Elkind, D. (1978). Understanding the young adolescent. *Adolescence, 13*, 127–134.

Elliot, A. J., & Devine, P. G. (1994). On the motivational nature of cognitive dissonance: Dissonance as psychological discomfort. *Journal of Personality and Social Psychology, 67*, 382–394.

Ellis, A. (1962). *Reason and emotion in psychotherapy*. New York: Lyle Stuart.

Ellis, A. (1986). Rational-emotive therapy. In I. L. Kutash & A. Wolf (Eds.), *Psychotherapist's casebook*. San Francisco: Jossey-Bass.

Ellis, B. J. (2004). Timing of pubertal maturation in girls: An integrated life history approach. *Psychological Bulletin, 130*, 920–958.

Ellis, B. J., Bates, J. E., Dodge, K. A., Fergusson, D. M., Horwood, L. J., Pettit, G. S., et al. (2003). Does father absence place daughters at special risk for early sexual activity and teenage pregnancy? *Child Development, 74*, 801–821.

Ellis, L, & Hellberg, J. (2005). Fetal exposure to prescription drugs and adult sexual orientation. *Personality and Individual Differences, 38*, 225–236.

Ellis, L., & Cole-Harding, S. (2001). The effects of prenatal stress, and of prenatal alcohol and nicotine exposure, on human sexual orientation. *Physiology and Behavior, 74*, 213–226.

Ellis, S., Rogoff, B., & Cromer, C. (1981). Age segregation in children's social interactions. *Developmental Psychology, 17*, 399–406.

Else-Quest, N. M., Hyde, J. S., Goldsmith, H. H., & Hulle, C. A. (2006). Gender differences in temperament: A meta-analysis. *Psychological Bulletin, 132*, 33–72.

Emmelkamp, P. M. G. (2004). Behavior therapy with adults. In M. J. Lambert (Ed.), *Bergin and Garfield's handbook of psychotherapy and behavior change* (5th ed.). New York: Wiley.

Endler, J. A. (1986). *Natural selection in the wild*. Princeton, NJ: Princeton University Press.

Endler, N. S. (1982). *Holiday of darkness: A psychologist's personal journey out of his depression*. New York: Wiley.

Engle, R. W. (2002). Working memory capacity as executive attention. *Current Directions in Psychological Science, 11*, 19–23.

Erickson, S. J., Gersle, M., & Montague, E. Q. (2008). Repressive adaptive style and self-reported psychological functioning in adolescent cancer survivors. *Child Psychiatry and Human Development, 39*, 247–260.

Ericsson, K. A., & Delaney, P. F. (1999). Long-term working memory as an alternative to capacity models of working memory in everyday skilled performance. In A. Miyake & P. Shah (Eds.), *Models of working memory: Mechanisms of active maintenance and executive control*. Cambridge, England: Cambridge University Press.

Ericsson, K. A., & Kintsch, W. (1995). Long-term working memory. *Psychological Review, 102*, 211–245.

Erikson, E. H. (1963). *Childhood and society* (2nd ed.). New York: Norton.

Erikson, E. H. (1968). *Identity: Youth and crisis*. New York: Norton.

Erlenmeyer-Kimling, L., Rock, D., Roberts, S. A., Janal, M., Kestenbaum, C., Cornblatt, B., Adamo, U. H., & Gottesman, I. I. (2000). Attention, memory, and motor skills as childhood predictors of schizophrenia-related psychoses: The New York high-risk project. *American Journal of Psychiatry, 157*, 1416–1422.

Ernst, C., & Angst, J. (1983). *Birth order: Its influence on personality*. Berlin: Springer-Verlag.

Errera, P. (1972). Statement based on interviews with forty "worst cases" in the Milgram obedience experiments. In J. Katz (Ed.), *Experimentation with human beings: The authority of the investigator, subject, professions, and state in the human experimentation process*. New York: Russell Sage Foundation.

Ertmer, D. J. (2007). Speech intelligibility in young cochlear implant recipients: Gains during year three. *Volta Review, 107*, 85–99.

Essock-Vitale, S. M., & McGuire, M. T. (1980). Predictions derived from the theories of kin selection and reciprocation assessed by anthropological data. *Ethology and Sociobiology, 1*, 233–243.

Estrada, C. A., Isen, A. M., & Young, M. J. (1997). Positive affect facilitates integration of information and decreases anchoring in reasoning among physicians. *Organizational Behavior and Human Decision Processes, 72*, 117–135.

Etscorn, F., & Stephens R. (1973). Establishment of conditioned taste aversions with a 24-hour CS-US interval. *Physiological Psychology, 1*, 251–253.

Evans, J. (2005). Deductive reasoning. In K. J. Holyoak & R. G. Morrison (Eds.), *Cambridge handbook of thinking and reasoning.* Cambridge, UK: Cambridge University Press.

Evans, J. St. B. T. (2008). Dual-process accounts of reasoning, judgment, and social cognition. *Annual Review of Psychology, 59,* 255–278.

Evarts, E. V. (1979, September). Brain mechanisms in movement. *Scientific American,* pp. 164–179.

Eveleth, P. B., & Tanner, J. M. (1990). *Worldwide variation in human growth* (2nd ed.). Cambridge, England: Cambridge University Press.

Everson, C. A. (1993). Sustained sleep deprivation impairs host defense. *American Journal of Physiology, 265,* R1148–R1154.

Everson, C. A., Bergmann, B. M., & Rechtschaffen, A. (1989). Sleep deprivation in the rat: III. Total sleep deprivation. *Sleep, 12,* 13–21.

Eysenck, H. J. (1990). Biological dimensions of personality. In L. A. Pervin (Ed.), *Handbook of personality: Theory and research.* New York: Guilford.

Eysenck, M. W. (1992). *Anxiety: The cognitive perspective.* Hillsdale, NJ: Erlbaum.

Fancher, R. E. (1985). *The intelligence men: Makers of the IQ controversy.* New York: Norton.

Fangmeier, T., Knauff, M., Ruff, C. C., & Sloutsky, V. (2006). fMRI evidence for a three-stage model of deductive reasoning. *Journal of Cognitive Neuroscience, 18,* 320–334.

Farah, M. J. (1989a). The neuropsychology of mental imagery. In J. W. Brown (Ed.), *Neuropsychology of visual perception.* Hillsdale, NJ: Erlbaum.

Farah, M. J. (1989b). *Visual agnosia.* Cambridge, MA: MIT Press.

Farooqi, S., Matarese, G., Lord, G. M., Keogh, J. M., Lawrence, E., Agwu, C., et al. (2002). Beneficial effects of leptin on obesity, T cell hyporesponsiveness, and neuroendocrine/metabolic dysfunction of human congenital leptin deficiency. *Journal of Clinical Investigation, 110,* 1093–1103.

Fazio, R. H., & Olson, M. A. (2003). Implicit measures in social cognition research: Their meaning and use. *Annual Review of Psychology, 54,* 297–327.

Fechner, G. T. (1860; translated edition 1966). *Elements of psychophysics.* (H. E. Alder, Trans.). New York: Holt, Rinehart & Winston.

Feder, H. H. (1984). Hormones and sexual behavior. *Annual Review of Psychology, 35,* 165–200.

Feeney, B. C., & Kirkpatrick, L. A. (1996). Effects of adult attachment and presence of romantic partners on physiological responses to stress. *Journal of Personality and Social Psychology, 70,* 255–270.

Fehr, E. (2004). Don't lose your reputation. *Nature, 423,* 449.

Fehr, E., & Fischbacher, U. (2003). The nature of human altruism. *Nature, 425,* 785–791.

Fehr, E., & Fischbacher, U. (2004). Social norms and human cooperation. *Trends in Cognitive Sciences, 8,* 185–190.

Fehr, E., & Gächter, S. (2002). Altruistic punishment in humans. *Nature, 415,* 137–140.

Feinberg, M., & Hetherington, E. M. (2000). Sibling differentiation in adolescence: Implications for behavioral genetic theory. *Child Development, 71,* 1512–1524.

Feingold, A. (1994). Gender differences in personality: A meta-analysis. *Psychological Bulletin, 116,* 429–456.

Feldman, J. (1997). *The educational opportunities that lie in self-directed age mixing among children and adolescents.* Unpublished doctoral dissertation, Department of Psychology, Boston College, Chestnut Hill, MA.

Feldman, J., & Gray, P. (1999). Some educational benefits of freely chosen age mixing among children and adolescents. *Phi Delta Kappan, 80,* 507–512.

Feng, A. S., & Ratnam, R. (2000). Neural basis of hearing in real-world situations. *Annual Review of Psychology, 51,* 699–725.

Feng, J., Spence, I., & Pratt, J. (2007). Playing an action video game reduces gender differences in spatial cognition. *Psychological Science, 18,* 850–855.

Festinger, L. (1957). *A theory of cognitive dissonance.* Stanford, CA: Stanford University Press.

Festinger, L., & Carlsmith, J. M. (1959). Cognitive consequences of forced compliance. *Journal of Abnormal and Social Psychology, 58,* 203–210.

Field, A. P. (2006). Is conditioning a useful framework for understanding development and treatment of phobias? *Clinical Psychological Review, 26,* 857–875.

Field, T. (1996). Attachment and separation in young children. *Annual Review of Psychology, 47,* 541–561.

Fieve, R. R. (1975). *Mood swing.* New York: W. Morrow.

Fiorello, C. D., Tobler, P. N., & Schultz, W. (2003). Discrete coding of reward probability and uncertainty by dopamine neurons. *Science, 299,* 1898–1902.

Fisher, C. (2000). From form to meaning: A role for structural alignment in the acquisition of language. *Advances in Child Development and Behavior, 27,* 1–53.

Fisher, H. (2004). *Why we love: The nature and chemistry of romantic love.* New York: Henry Holt.

Fisher, H. E. (1992). *Anatomy of love: The natural history of monogamy, adultery, and divorce.* New York: Norton.

Fisher, P., Gunner, M., Dozier, M., Bruce, J., & Pears, K. (2006). Effects of therapeutic interventions for foster children on behavioral problems, caregiver attachment, and stress regulatory neural systems. *Annals of the New York Academy of Sciences, 1094,* 215–225.

Fisher, S. E. (2003). Isolation of the genetic factors underlying speech and language disorders. In R. Plomin, J. C. Defries, I. W. Craig, & P. McGuffin (Eds.), *Behavioral genetics in the postgenomic era.* Washington, DC: American Psychological Association.

Fiske, D. W. (1949). Consistency of the factorial structures of personality rating from different sources. *Journal of Abnormal and Social Psychology, 44,* 329–344.

Flack, W. F. (2006). Peripheral feedback effects of facial expressions, bodily postures, and vocal expressions on emotional feelings. *Cognition and Emotion, 20,* 177–195.

Flaherty, C. F. (1996). *Incentive relativity.* New York: Cambridge University Press.

Flanagan, L. M. (2008). Object relations theory. In J. Berzoff, L. M. Flanagan, & P. Hertz (Eds.), *Inside out and outside in: Psychodynamic clinical theory and psychopathology in contemporary multicultural contexts* (2nd ed.). Lanham, MD: Jason Aronson.

Flaten, M. A., & Blumenthal, T. D. (1999). Caffeine-associated stimuli elicit conditioned responses: An experimental model of the placebo effect. *Psychopharmacology, 145,* 105–112.

Fleishman, M. (2004). The problem: How many patients live in residential care facilities? *Psychiatric Services, 55,* 620–622.

Flor, H., Nikolajsen, L., & Jensen, T. S. (2006). Phantom limb pain: A case of maladaptive CNS plasticity. *Nature Reviews Neuroscience, 7,* 873–881.

Flourens, P. J. M. (1824; reprinted 1965). *Pierre Jean Marie Flourens on the functions of the brain* (M. D. Boring, Trans.). In R. J. Herrnstein & E. G. Boring (Eds.), *A source book in the history of psychology.* Cambridge, MA: Harvard University Press.

Flynn, F. J. (2005). Having an open mind: The impact of openness to experience on interracial attitudes and impression formation. *Journal of Personality and Social Psychology, 88,* 816–826.

Flynn, J. R. (1987). Massive IQ gains in 14 nations: What IQ tests really measure. *Psychological Bulletin, 101,* 171–191.

Flynn, J. R. (1999). Searching for justice: The discovery of IQ gains over time. *American Psychologist, 54,* 5–20.

Flynn, J. R. (2003). Movies about intelligence: The limitations of *g. Current Directions in Psychological Science, 12,* 95–99.

Flynn, J. R. (2007). *What is intelligence? Beyond the Flynn effect.* Cambridge, UK: Cambridge University Press.

Fodor, I. G. (1982). Gender and phobia. In I. Al-Issa (Ed.), *Gender and psychopathology.* New York: Academic Press.

Foltz, E. L, & White, L. E. (1968). The role of rostral cingulotomy in 'pain' relief. *International Journal of Neurology, 6,* 353–373.

Fontaine, J. R. J., Scherer, K.R., Roesch, E. B., & Ellsworth, P. C. (2007). The world of emotions is not two-dimensional. *Psychological Science, 18,* 1050–1058.

Fontaine, R. P. (1994). Play as physical flexibility training in five Ceboid primates. *Journal of Comparative Psychology, 108,* 203–212.

Forbes, J. F., & Weiss, D. S. (1992). The cosleeping habits of military children. *Military Medicine, 157,* 196–200.

Ford, M. R., & Widiger, T. A. (1989). Sex bias in the diagnosis of histrionic and antisocial personality disorders. *Journal of Consulting and Clinical Psychology, 57,* 301–305.

Forgatch, M. S., & DeGarmo, D. S. (1999). Parenting through change: An effective prevention program for single mothers. *Journal of Consulting and Clinical Psychology, 67,* 711–724.

Foulkes, D. (1985). *Dreaming: A cognitive-psychological analysis.* Hillsdale, NJ: Erlbaum.

Fowler, S., Ogston, K., Roberts, G., & Swenson, A. (2006). The effects of early language enrichment. *Early Child Development and Care, 176,* 777–815.

Fox, N. A., & Davidson, R. J. (1988). Patterns of brain electrical activity during facial signs of emotion in 10-month-old infants. *Developmental Psychology, 24,* 230–236.

Fraley, R. C. (2002). Attachment stability from infancy to adulthood: Meta-analysis and dynamic modeling of developmental mechanisms. *Personality and Social Psychology Review, 6,* 123–151.

Fraley, R. C., & Brumbaugh, C. C. (2004). A dynamical systems approach to conceptualizing and studying stability and change in attachment security. In W. S. Rholes & J. A. Simpson (Eds.), *Adult attachment: Theory, research, and clinical implications.* New York: Guilford.

Frandsen, A. N., & Holder, J. R. (1969). Spatial visualization in solving complex verbal problems. *Journal of Psychology, 73,* 229–233.

Franklin, B. (1818; reprinted 1949). *The autobiography of Benjamin Franklin.* Berkeley: University of California Press.

Frederickson, B. L. (2006). The broaden-and-build theory of positive emotions. In M. Csikszentmihalyi & I. S. Csikszentmihalyi (Eds.), *A life worth living: Contributions to positive psychology.* Oxford: Oxford University Press.

Fredrickson, B. L. (2001). The role of positive emotions in positive psychology: The broaden-and-build theory of positive emotions. *American Psychologist, 56,* 218–226.

Fredrickson, B. L. (2003). The value of positive emotions. *American Scientist, 91,* 330–335.

Freedman, J. L, & Fraser, S. C. (1966). Compliance without pressure: The foot-in-the-door technique. *Journal of Personality and Social Psychology, 4,* 195–202.

Frenkel, O. J., & Doob, A. N. (1976). Post-decision dissonance at the polling booth. *Canadian Journal of Behavioural Science, 8,* 347–350.

Frensch, P. A., & Rünger, D. (2003). Implicit learning. *Current Directions in Psychological Science, 12,* 13–18.

Freud, A. (1936; reprinted 1946). *The ego and the mechanisms of defense* (C. Baines, Trans.). New York: International Universities Press.

Freud, S. (1900; reprinted 1953). *The interpretation of dreams* (J. Strachey, Ed. & Trans.). London: Hogarth Press.

Freud, S. (1901; reprinted 1990). *The psychopathology of everyday life* (A. Tyson, Trans.). In J. Strachey (Ed.), *The standard edition of the complete psychological works of Sigmund Freud.* New York: Norton.

Freud, S. (1909; reprinted 1963). Notes upon a case of obsessional neurosis. In P. Rieff (Ed.), *Three case histories.* New York: Collier Books.

Freud, S. (1910; reprinted 1947). *Leonardo da Vinci: A study in psychosexuality.* New York: Random House.

Freud, S. (1912; reprinted 1932). A note on the unconscious in psychoanalysis. In J. Rickman (Ed.), *A general selection from the works of Sigmund Freud.* London: Hogarth Press.

Freud, S. (1923; reprinted 1963). [Note appended to the 1963 reprint of "Notes upon a case of obsession neurosis."] In P. Rieff (Ed.), *Three case histories.* New York: Collier Books.

Freud, S. (1933; reprinted 1964). *New introductory lectures on psychoanalysis.* In J. Strachey (Ed. & Trans.), *The standard edition of the complete works of Sigmund Freud* (Vol. 20). London: Hogarth Press.

Freud, S. (1935; reprinted 1960). *A general introduction to psychoanalysis.* New York: Washington Square Press.

Frey, D. (1986). Recent research on selective exposure to information. *Advances in Experimental Social Psychology, 19,* 41–80.

Friedman, H. S., Tucker, J. S., Schwartz, J. E., Martin, L. R., Tomlinson-Keasey, C., Wingard, D. L., & Criqui, M. H. (1995). Childhood conscientiousness and longevity: Health behaviors and cause of death. *Journal of Personality and Social Psychology, 68,* 696–703.

Friedman, H., & Zebrowitz, L. A. (1992). The contribution of typical sex differences in facial maturity to sex role stereotypes. *Personality and Social Psychology Bulletin, 18,* 430–438.

Friedman, J. M. (1997). The alphabet of weight control. *Nature, 385,* 119–120.

Friedman, J. M. (2003). A war on obesity, not the obese. *Science, 299,* 856–858.

Friedman, M., & Rosenman, R. H. (1974). *Type A behavior and your heart.* New York: Knopf.

Friedman, S. (1972). Habituation and recovery of visual response in the alert human newborn. *Journal of Experimental Child Psychology, 13,* 339–349.

Frings, C. (2006). Relevant distractors do not cause negative priming. *Psychonomic Bulletin & Review, 13,* 322–327.

Fry, D. P. (1992). "Respect for the rights of others is peace": Learning aggression versus nonaggression among the Zapotec. *American Anthropologist, 94,* 621–639.

Fujiwara, E., Levine, B., & Anderson, A. K. (2008). Intact implicit and reduced explicit memory for negative self-related information in repressive coping. *Cognitive, Affective, & Behavioral Neuroscience, 8,* 254–263.

Fuller, R. L., Luck, S. J., McMahon, R. P., & Gold, J. M. (2005). Working memory consolidation is abnormally slow in schizophrenia. *Journal of Abnormal Psychology, 114,* 279–290.

Fung, H. H., Carstensen, L. L., & Lutz, A. M. (1999). Influence of time on social preferences: Implications for life-span development. *Psychology & Aging, 14,* 595–604.

Fung, H. H., Lai, P., & Ng, R. (2001). Age differences in social preferences among Taiwanese and mainland Chinese: The role of perceived time. *Psychology & Aging, 16,* 351–356.

Furman, W., & Buhrmester, D. (1992). Age and sex differences in perceptions of networks of personal relationships. *Child Development, 63,* 103–115.

Furman, W., & Shomaker, L. (2008). Patterns of interaction in adolescent romantic relationships: Distinct features and links to other close relationships. *Journal of Adolescence, 31,* 771–788.

Furnham, A., Batey, M., Anand, K., & Manfield, J. (2008). Personality, hypomania, intelligence, and creativity. *Personality and Individual Differences, 44,* 1060–1069.

Furrow, D., Nelson, K., & Benedict, H. (1979). Mothers' speech to children and syntactic development: Some simple relationships. *Journal of Child Language, 6,* 423–442.

Furth, H. G. (1996). *Desire for society: Children's knowledge as social imagination.* New York: Plenum.

Fuson, K. C., & Kwon, Y. (1992). Learning addition and subtraction: Effects of number words and other cultural tools. In J. Bideaud, C. Meljac, & J. Fischer (Eds.), *Pathways to number: Children's developing numerical abilities.* Hillsdale, NJ: Erlbaum.

Fuster, J. M. (2006). The cognit: A network model of cortical representation. *International Journal of Psychophysiology, 60,* 25–132.

Futuyma, D. J. (1997). *Evolutionary biology* (3rd ed.). Sunderland, MA: Sinauer.

Gabrieli, J. D. E. (1998). Cognitive neuroscience of human memory. *Annual Review of Psychology, 49,* 87–115.

Gabrieli, J. D. E., Corkin, S., Mickel, S. F., & Growdon, J. H. (1993). Intact acquisition and long-term retention of mirror-tracing skill in Alzheimer's disease and in global amnesia. *Behavioral Neuroscience, 107,* 899–910.

Gächter, S., Renner, E., & Sefton, M. (2008). The long-run benefits of punishment. *Science, 332,* 1510.

Gaertner, L., Sedikides, C., & Chang, K. (2008). On pancultural self-enhancement: Well-adjusted Taiwanese self-enhance on personally valued traits. *Journal of Cross-Cultural Psychology, 39,* 463–477.

Gaertner, S. L., Mann, J. A., Dovidio, J. F., Murrell, A. J., & Pomare, M. (1990). How does cooperation reduce intergroup bias? *Journal of Personality and Social Psychology, 59,* 692–704.

Gagné, M., & Deci, E. L. (2005). Self-determination theory and work motivation. *Journal of Organizational Behavior, 26,* 331–362.

Galanter, E. (1962). Contemporary psychophysics. In R. Brown, E. Galanter, E. Hess, & G. Mandler (Eds.), *New directions in psychology.* New York: Holt, Rinehart & Winston.

Galderisi, S., Quarantelli, M., Volpe, U., Mucci, A., Cassano, G. B., Invernizzi, G., Rossi, A., Vita, A., Pini, S., Cassano, P., Daneluzzo, E., De Peri, L., Stratta, P., Brunetti, A., & Maj, M. (2008). Patterns of structural MRI abnormalities in deficit and nondeficit schizophrenia. *Schizophrenia Bulletin, 34,* 393–401.

Galef, B. G. (1990). An adaptationist perspective on social learning, social feeding, and social foraging in Norway rats. In D. A. Dewsbury (Ed.), *Contemporary issues in comparative psychology.* Sunderland, MA: Sinauer.

Galef, B. G. (2002). Social influences on food choices of Norway rats and mate choices of Japanese quail. *Appetite, 39,* 179–180.

Galef, B. G., & Giraldeau, L. (2001). Social influences on foraging in vertebrates: Causal mechanisms and adaptive functions. *Animal Behaviour, 61,* 3–15.

Galef, B. G., Jr., & Clark, M. M. (1971). Social factors in the poison avoidance and feeding behavior of wild and domesticated rat pups. *Journal of Comparative and Physiological Psychology, 75,* 341–357.

Galinsky, E., Bond, J. T., & Friedman, D. E. (1993). *The changing workforce: Highlights of the national study.* New York: Families and Work Institute.

Gallup, G. G., McClure, M. K., Hill, S. D., & Bundy, R. A. (1971). Capacity for self-recognition in differentially reared chimpanzees. *Psychological Record, 21,* 69–74.

Gantt, W. H. (1975, April 25). Unpublished lecture on Pavlov given at Ohio State University, Columbus.

Gangestad, S. W., Simpson, J. A., Cousins, A. J., Garver-Apgar, C. E., & Christensen, P. N. (2004). Women's preference for male

behavioral displays change across the menstrual cycle. *Psychological Science, 15,* 203–207.

Garcia, J., Brett, L. P., & Rusiniak, K. W. (1989). Limits of Darwinian conditioning. In S. B. Klein & R. R. Mowrer (Eds.), *Contemporary learning theories: Instrumental conditioning theory and the impact of biological constraints on learning.* Hillsdale, NJ: Erlbaum.

Garcia, J., McGowan, B. K., & Green, K. F. (1972). Biological constraints on conditioning. In A. H. Black & W. G. Prokasy (Eds.), *Classical conditioning II: Current research and theory.* New York: Appleton-Century-Crofts.

Garcia, J., McGowan, B. K., Ervin, F. R., & Koelling, R. A. (1968). Cues—their relative effectiveness as a function of the reinforcer. *Science, 160,* 794–795.

Gardiner, J. M., Brandt, K. R., Baddeley, A. D., Vargha-Khadem, F., & Mishkin, M. (2008). Charting the acquisition of semantic knowledge in the case of developmental amnesia. *Neuropsychologia, 46,* 2865–2868.

Gardiner, J. V., Jayasena, C. N., & Bloom, S. R. (2008). Gut hormones: A weight off your mind. *Journal of Neuroendocrinology, 20,* 834–841.

Gardner, R. A., & Gardner, B. T. (1978). Comparative psychology and language acquisition. In K. Slazinger & F. L. Denmark (Eds.), Psychology: The state of the art. *Annals of the New York Academy of Sciences, 309,* 37–76.

Gardner, R. A., & Gardner, B. T. (1989). A cross-fostering laboratory. In R. A. Gardner, B. T. Gardner, & T. E. Van Cantfort (Eds.), *Teaching sign language to chimpanzees.* Albany: State University of New York Press.

Gardner, W. L., Gabriel, S., & Hochschild, L. (2002). When you and I are "we," you are not threatening: The role of self-expansion in social comparison. *Journal of Personality and Social Psychology, 82,* 239–251.

Garland, D. J., & Barry, J. R. (1991). Cognitive advantage in sports: The nature of perceptual structures. *American Journal of Psychology, 104,* 211–228.

Garver-Apgar, C. E., Gangestad, S. W., Thornhill, R., Miller, R. D., & Olp, J. J. (2006). Major histocompatibility complex alleles, sexual responsivity, and unfaithfulness in romantic couples. *Psychological Science, 17,* 830–835.

Garvey, C. (1990). *Play* (enlarged ed.). Cambridge, MA: Harvard University Press.

Gathercole, S. E., Pickering, S. J., Ambridge, B., & Wearing, H. (2004). The structure of working memory from 4 to 15 years of age. *Developmental Psychology, 40,* 177–190.

Gawronski, B., & Bodenhausen, G. V. (2006). Associative and propositional processes in evaluation: An integrative review of implicit and explicit attitude change. *Psychological Bulletin, 132,* 692–731.

Gazzaniga, M. S. (1967, August). The split brain in man. *Scientific American,* pp. 24–29.

Gazzaniga, M. S. (1970). *The bisected brain.* New York: Appleton-Century-Crofts.

Gazzaniga, M. S. (1998, July). The split brain revisited. *Scientific American,* pp. 50–55.

Gazzaniga, M. S. (2000). Cerebral specialization and interhemispheric communication: Does the corpus callosum enable the human condition? *Brain, 123,* 1293–1326.

Ge, S., Yang, C. H., Hsu, K. S., Ming, G. L., & Song, H. (2007). A critical period for enhanced synaptic plasticity in newly generated neurons of the adult brain. *Neuron, 54,* 559–566.

Gee, H. (2002). Aspirational thinking. *Nature, 420,* 611.

Geen, R. G. (1980). The effects of being observed on performance. In P. B. Paulus (Ed.), *Psychology of group influence.* Hillsdale, NJ: Erlbaum.

Geen, R. G. (1984). Preferred stimulation levels in introverts and extraverts: Effects on arousal and performance. *Journal of Personality and Social Psychology, 45,* 1303–1312.

Geen, R. G. (1991). Social motivation. *Annual Review of Psychology, 42,* 377–399.

Géléoc, G. S. G., & Holt, J. R. (2003). Auditory amplification: Outer hair cells *pres* the issue. *Trends in Neurosciences, 26,* 115–117.

Gelernter, J., & Stein, M. B. (2009). Heritability and genetics of anxiety disorders. In M. M. Antony & M. B. Stein (Eds.), *Oxford handbook of anxiety related disorders.* Oxford, UK: Oxford University Press.

Gentner, D. (2003). Why we're so smart. In D. Gentner & S. Goldin-Meadow (Eds.), *Language in mind: Advances in the study of language and thought.* Cambridge, MA: MIT Press.

Gentner, D., & Gentner, D. R. (1983). Flowing waters or teeming crowds: Mental models of electricity. In D. Gentner & A. L. Stevens (Eds.), *Mental models.* Hillsdale, NJ: Erlbaum.

Gentner, D., & Kurtz, K. J. (2006). Relations, objects, and the composition of analogies. *Cognitive Science 30,* 609–642.

Gentner, D., & Markman, A. B. (1997). Structure mapping in analogy and similarity. *American Psychologist, 52,* 45–56.

Gerstein, M. B., Bruce, C., Rozowsky, J. S., Zheng, D., Du, J., Korbel, J. O., Emanuelsson, O., Zhang, Z. D., Weissman, S., & Snyder, M. (2007). What is a gene, post-ENCODE? History and updated definition. *Genomic Research, 17,* 669–681.

Gescheider, G. A. (1976). *Psychophysics: Methods and theory.* Hillsdale, NJ: Erlbaum.

Geschwind, N. (1972, April). Language and the brain. *Scientific American,* pp. 76–83.

Gest, S. D. (1997). Behavioral inhibition: Stability and associations with adaptation from childhood to early adulthood. *Journal of Personality and Social Psychology, 72,* 467–475.

Ghez, C., & Krakauer, J. (2000). The organization of movement. In E. R. Kandel, J. H. Schwartz, & T. M. Jessell (Eds.), *Principles of neural science* (4th ed.). New York: McGraw-Hill.

Gibbs, W. W. (1996, August). Gaining on fat. *Scientific American,* pp. 88–94.

Gifford, R., Shallop, J. K., & Peterson, A. M. (2008). Speech recognition materials and ceiling effects: Considerations for cochlear implant programs. *Audiology and Neurotology, 13,* 193–205.

Gignac, G., Staough, C., & Loukomitis, S. (2004). Openness, intelligence, and self-reported intelligence. *Intelligence, 32,* 133–143.

Giladi, N., Weitzman, N., Schreiber, S., Shabtai, H., & Peretz, C. (2007). *Journal of Psychopharamacology, 21,* 501–506.

Gilbert, D. T. (1989). Thinking lightly about others: Automatic components of the social inference process. In J. S. Uleman & J. A. Bargh (Eds.), *Unintended thought.* New York: Guilford.

Gilbert, D. T., & Ebert, J. E. J. (2002). Decisions and revisions: The affective forecasting of changeable outcomes. *Journal of Personality and Social Psychology, 82,* 503–514.

Gilbert, D. T., & Jones, E. E. (1986). Perceiver-induced constraint: Interpretations of self-generated reality. *Journal of Personality and Social Psychology, 50,* 269–280.

Gillam, B., & Chan, W. M. (2002). Grouping has a negative effect on both subjective contours and perceived occlusion at T-junctions. *Psychological Science, 13,* 279–283.

Giner-Sorolla, R., Castano, E., Espinosa, P., & Brown, R. (2008). Shame expressions reduce the recipient's insult from outgroup reparations. *Journal of Experimental Social Psychology, 44,* 519–526.

Ginzburg, K., Solomon, Z., & Bleich, A. (2002). Repressive coping style, acute stress disorder, and posttraumatic stress disorder after myocardial infarction. *Psychosomatic Medicine, 64,* 748–757.

Gitlin, M. J. (2009). Pharmacotherapy and other somatic treatments for depression. In I. H. Gotlib & C. L. Hammen (Eds.), *Handbook of depression* (2nd ed.). New York: Guilford.

Gladwell, M. (2000). *The tipping point: How little things can make a big difference.* Boston: Little, Brown and Company.

Gladwell, M. (2005). *Blink: The power of thinking without thinking.* Boston: Little, Brown and Company.

Glance, N. S., & Huberman, B. A. (1994, March). The dynamics of social dilemmas. *Scientific American,* pp. 76–81.

Glasman, L. R., & Albarracin, E. (2006). Forming attitudes that predict behavior: A meta-analysis of the attitude-behavior relation. *Psychological Bulletin, 132,* 778–822.

Glisky, E. L., Schacter, D. L., & Tulving, E. (1986). Computer learning by memory-impaired patients: Acquisition and retention of complex knowledge. *Neuropsychologia, 24,* 313–328.

Gobet, F., Lane, P. C. R., Croker, S., Cheng, P. C.-H., Jones, G., Oliver, I., et al. (2001). Chunking mechanisms in human learning. *Trends in Cognitive Sciences, 5,* 236–243.

Goel, V. (2007). Anatomy of deductive reasoning. *Trends in Cognitive Neurosciences, 11,* 435–441.

Goetz, A. T. (2008). Violence and abuse in families: The consequences of paternal uncertainty. In C. A. Salmon & T. K. Shackelford (Eds.), *Family relationships: An evolutionary perspective* (pp. 259–274). Oxford: Oxford University Press.

Goffman, E. (1959). *The presentation of self in everyday life.* Garden City, NY: Doubleday.

Gold, J. J., & Squire, L. R. (2006). The anatomy of amnesia: Neurohistological analysis of three new cases. *Learning & Memory, 13,* 699–710.

Goldenthal, P., Johnston, R. E., & Kraut, R. E. (1981). Smiling, appeasement, and the silent bared-teeth display. *Ethology and Sociobiology, 2,* 127–133.

Goldhagen, D. J. (1996). *Hitler's willing executioners: Ordinary Germans and the Holocaust.* New York: Knopf.

Golimbet, V. E., Alfimova, M. V., Gritsenko, I. K., & Ebstein, R. P. (2007). Relationship between dopamine system genes and extraversion and novelty seeking. *Neuroscience and Behavioral Physiology, 37,* 601–606.

Golinkoff, R. M., Mervis, C. B., & Hirsh-Pasek, K. (1994). Early object labels: The case for a developmental lexical principles framework. *Journal of Child Language, 21,* 125–155.

Golinkoff, R. M., Shuff-Bailey, M., Olguin, R., & Ruan, W. (1995). Young children extend novel words at the basic level: Evidence for the principle of categorical scope. *Developmental Psychology, 31,* 494–507.

Gomes, H., Sussman, E., Ritter, W., Kurtzberg, D., Cowan, N., & Vaughan, H. G. (1999). Electrophysiological evidence for developmental changes in the duration of sensory memory. *Developmental Psychology, 35,* 294–302.

Gonda, X., Fountoulakis, K. N., Rihmer, Z., Lazary, J., Laszik, A., Akiskal, K. K., Akiskal, H. S., & Bagdy, G. (2009). Towards a genetically validated new affective temperament scale: A delineation of the temperament 'phenotype' of 5-HTTLPR using the TEMPS-A. *Journal of Affective Disorders, 112,* 19–29.

Goodale, M. A. (2007). Duplex vision: Separate cortical pathways for conscious perception and control of action. In M. Velmans & S. Schneider (Eds.), *The Blackwell companion to consciousness.* Malen, MA: Blackwell.

Goodale, M. A., & Milner, A. D. (2004). *Sight unseen: An exploration of conscious and unconscious vision.* Oxford: Oxford University Press.

Goodale, M. A., & Murphy, K. (1997). Action and perception in the visual periphery. In P. Their & H. O. Karnath (Eds.), *Parietal lobe contributions to orientation in 3D space.* Heidelberg: Springer-Verlag.

Goodall, J. (1986). *The chimpanzees of Gombe.* Cambridge, MA: Harvard University Press.

Goodall, J. (1988). *In the shadow of man* (Rev. ed.). Boston: Houghton Mifflin.

Goodman, G. S., Ghetti, S., Quas, J. A., Edelstein, R. S., Alexander, K. W., Redlich, A. D., et al. (2003). A prospective study of memory for child sexual abuse: New findings relevant to the repressed-memory controversy. *Psychological Science, 14,* 113–118.

Goodman, J. C., McDonough, L., & Brown, N. B. (1998). The role of semantic context and memory in the acquisition of novel nouns. *Child Development, 69,* 1330–1344.

Goodstein, L. D., & Lanyon, R. I. (1999). Applications of personality assessment to the workplace: A review. *Journal of Business and Psychology, 13,* 291–322.

Goossens, F. A., & van Ijzendoorn, M. H. (1990). Quality of infants' attachments to professional caregivers: Relation to infant-parent attachment and day-care characteristics. *Child Development, 61,* 550–567.

Gopnik, M. (1999). Familial language impairment: More English evidence. *Folia Phoniatrica et Logopaedica, 51,* 5–19.

Gopnik, M., & Crago, M. B. (1991). Familial aggregation of a developmental language disorder. *Cognition, 39,* 1–50.

Gordon, D. M. (1995). The expandable network of ant exploration. *Animal Behaviour, 50,* 995–1007.

Gordon, J. A., & Hen, R. (2004). Genetic approaches to the study of anxiety. *Annual Review of Neuroscience, 27,* 193–222.

Gordon, P. (2004). Numerical cognition without words: Evidence from Amazonia. *Science, 306,* 496–499.

Gordon, R. A. (1990). *Anorexia and bulimia: Anatomy of a social epidemic.* Cambridge, MA: Basil Blackwell.

Gordon, S., & Gilgun, J. F. (1987). *Adolescent sexuality.* In V. B. Van Hasselt & M. Hersen (Eds.), *Handbook of adolescent psychology.* New York: Pergamon Press.

Gorski, R. A. (1996). Gonadal hormones and the organization of brain structure and function. In D. Magnusson (Ed.), *The lifespan development of individuals: Behavioral, neurobiological, and psychosocial perspectives.* Cambridge, England: Cambridge University Press.

Gorski, R. A., Harlan, R. E., Jacobson, C. D., Shryne, J. E., & Southham, A. M. (1980). Evidence for the existence of a sexually dimorphic nucleus in the preoptic area of the rat. *Journal of Comparative Neurology, 193,* 529–539.

Gosling, S. D. (2001). From mice to men: What can we learn about personality from animal research? *Psychological Bulletin, 127,* 45–86.

Gottesman, I. I. (1991). *Schizophrenia genesis: The origins of madness.* New York: Freeman.

Gottfredson, L. S. (2002). Where and why g matters: Not a mystery. *Human Performance, 15,* 25–46.

Gottfredson, L. S., & Deary, I. J. (2004). Intelligence predicts health and longevity, but why? *Current Directions in Psychological Science, 13,* 1–4.

Gottman, J. M. (1994). *What predicts divorce? The relationship between marital processes and marital outcomes.* Hillsdale, NJ: Erlbaum.

Gottman, J. M. (1998). Psychology and the study of marital processes. *Annual Review of Psychology, 49,* 169–197.

Gottman, J. M., & Krokoff, L. J. (1989). Marital interaction and satisfaction: A longitudinal view. *Journal of Consulting and Clinical Psychology, 57,* 47–52.

Goudie, A. J. (1990). Conditioned opponent processes in the development of tolerance to psychoactive drugs. *Progress in Neuro-Psychopharmacology and Biological Psychiatry, 14,* 675–688.

Gougoux, F., Zatorre, R. J., Lassonde, M., Voss, P., & Lepore, F. (2005). A functional neuroimaging study of sound localization: Visual cortex activity predicts performance in early-blind individuals. *PloS Biology, 3,* 324–333.

Gould, R. A., Otto, M. W., & Pollack, M. H. (1995). A meta-analysis of treatment outcome for panic disorder. *Clinical Psychology Review, 15,* 819–844.

Gould, S. J. (1980). A biological homage to Mickey Mouse. In *The panda's thumb: More reflections in natural history.* New York: Norton.

Gould, S. J., & Eldredge, N. (1993). Punctuate equilibrium comes of age. *Nature, 366,* 223–227.

Gould-Beierle, K. L., & Kamil, A. C. (1999). The effect of proximity on landmark use in Clark's nutcrackers. *Animal Behaviour, 58,* 477–488.

Gouldner, A. W. (1960). The norm of reciprocity: A preliminary statement. *American Sociological Review, 25,* 161–178.

Graham, L. J. (2007). Out of sight, out of mind, out of site: Schooling and attention-deficit/hyperactivity disorder. *International Journal of Qualitative Studies in Education, 20,* 585–602.

Grandin, T. (2006). *Thinking in pictures: and other reports from my life with autism* (2nd ed.). New York: Vintage Books.

Grant, J. E., Kim, S. W., & Kuskowki, M. (2004). Retrospective review of treatment retention in pathological gambling. *Comprehensive Psychiatry, 45,* 83–87.

Grant, P. R., & Grant, R. (2006). Evolution of character displacement in Darwin's finches. *Science, 313,* 224–226.

Grant, P. R., & Grant, R. (2008). *How and why species multiply: The radiation of Darwin's finches.* Princeton, NJ: Princeton University Press.

Gray, J. R., Chabris, C. F., & Braver, T. S. (2003). Neural mechanisms of general fluid intelligence. *Nature Neuroscience, 6,* 316–322.

Gray, P. (2008). The value of Psychology 101 in liberal arts education: A psychocentric theory of the university. *APS Observer,* in press.

Gray, P. (2009). Play as a foundation for hunter-gatherer social existence. *American Journal of Play, 1,* 476–522.

Gray, P., & Chanoff, D. (1984). When play is learning: A school designed for self-directed education. *Phi Delta Kappan, 65,* 608–611.

Gray, P., & Feldman, J. (1997). Patterns of age mixing and gender mixing among children and adolescents at an ungraded democratic school. *Merrill-Palmer Quarterly, 43,* 67–86.

Gray, P., & Feldman, J. (2004). Playing in the zone of proximal development: Qualities of self-directed age mixing between adolescents and young children at a democratic school. *American Journal of Education, 110,* 108–145.

Graziano, M. (2006). The organization of behavioral repertoire in motor cortex. *Annual Review of Neuroscience, 29,* 105-134.

Green, C. S., & Bavelier, D. (2006). Enumeration versus multiple object tracking: The case of action video game players. *Cognition, 101,* 217–245.

Green, C. S., & Baveller, D. (2003). Action video game modifies visual selective attention. *Nature, 423,* 534–537.

Green, M. F. (1993). Cognitive remediation in schizophrenia: Is it time yet? *American Journal of Psychiatry, 150,* 178–187.

Greenberg, B. D., Malone, D. A., Friehs, G. M., Rezai, A. R., Kubu, C. S., Malloy, P. F., Salloway, S. P., Okun, M. S., Goodman, W. K., & Rasmussen, S. A. (2006). Three-year outcomes of deep brain stimulation for highly resistant obsessive-compulsive disorder. *Neuropsychopharmacology, 31,* 2384–2393.

Greenberg, D. (1992). Sudbury Valley's secret weapon: Allowing people of different ages to mix freely at school. In *The Sudbury Valley School experience* (3rd ed.). Framingham, MA: Sudbury Valley School Press.

Greenfield, P., & Lyn, H. (2007). Symbol combination in Pan: Language, action, and culture. In D. A. Washburn (Ed.), *Primate perspectives on behavior and cognition.* Washington DC: American Psychological Association.

Greengard, P. (2001). The neurobiology of slow synaptic transmission. *Science, 294,* 1024–1030.

Greenough, W. T., & Black, J. E. (1992). Induction of brain structure by experience: Substrate for cognitive development. In M. R. Gunnar & C. A. Nelson (Eds.), *Developmental behavioral neuroscience: The Minnesota Symposia on Child Psychology* (Vol. 24). Hillsdale, NJ: Erlbaum.

Greenwald, A. G. (1980). The totalitarian ego: Fabrication and revision of personal history. *American Psychologist, 35*, 603–618.

Greenwald, A. G. (1992). New look 3: Unconscious cognition reclaimed. *American Psychologist, 47*, 766–779.

Greenwald, A. G., Banaji, M. R., Rudman, L. A., Farnham, S. D., Nosek, B. A., & Mellott, D. S. (2002). A unified theory of implicit attitudes, stereotypes, self-esteem, and self-concept. *Psychological Review, 109*, 3–25.

Greenwald, A. G., McGhee, D. E., & Schwartz, J. L. K. (1998). Measuring individual differences in implicit cognition: The Implicit Association Test. *Journal of Personality and Social Psychology, 74*, 1464–1480.

Gregory, R. L. (1968, November). Visual illusions. *Scientific American*, pp. 66–76.

Gregory, R. L. (1996). *Eye and brain: The psychology of seeing* (5th ed.). Princeton, NJ: Princeton University Press.

Greulich. W. W. (1957). A comparison of the physical growth and development of American-born and native Japanese children. *American Journal of Physical Anthropology, 15*, 489–515.

Griffin, D. R. (1986). *Listening in the dark: The acoustic orientation of bats and men.* Ithaca, NY: Cornell University Press.

Griffith, J. D., Cavanaugh, J., Held, N. N., & Oates, J. A. (1972). Dextroamphetamine: Evaluation of psychotomimetic properties in man. *Archives of General Psychiatry, 26*, 97–100.

Griffiths, T. L., Steyvers, M., & Firl, A. (2007). Google and the mind. *Psychological Science, 18*, 1069–1076.

Grill-Spector, K., & Sayres, R. (2008). Object recognition: Insights from advances in fMRI methods. *Current Directions in Psychological Science, s17*, 73–79.

Grilo, C. M., & Pogue-Geile, M. F. (1991). The nature of environmental influences on weight and obesity: A behavior genetic analysis. *Psychological Bulletin, 110*, 520–537.

Grimes, B. F. (Ed.) (2000). *Ethnologue: Languages of the world* (14th ed.). Dallas, TX: SIL International.

Grodzinsky, Y. (2000). The neurology of syntax: Language use without Broca's area. *Behavioral and Brain Sciences, 23*, 1–71.

Grodzinsky, Y., & Friederici, A. D. (2006). Neuroimaging of syntax and syntactic processing. *Current Opinion in Neurobiology, 16*, 240–246.

Groeger, J. A., Clegg, B. A., & O'Shea, G. (2005). Conjunction in simulated railway signals: A cautionary note. *Applied Cognitive Psychology, 19*, 973–984.

Groopman, J. (2007). *How doctors think.* Boston: Houghton Mifflin.

Gross, C. G. (1998). *Brain, vision, memory: Tales in the history of neuroscience.* Cambridge, MA: MIT Press.

Groos, K. (1898). *The play of animals.* New York: Appleton.

Groos, K. (1901). *The play of man.* New York: Appleton.

Grossman, R. P., & Till, B. D. (1998). The persistence of classically conditioned brand attitudes. *Journal of Advertising, 27*, 23–31.

Grossman, S. P. (1979). The biology of motivation. *Annual Review of Psychology, 30*, 209–242.

Guay, A. T. (2001). Decreased testosterone in regularly menstruating women with decreased libido: A clinical observation. *Journal of Sex and Marital Therapy, 27*, 513–519.

Guerrero, L. K. (1998). Attachment-style differences in the expression of romantic jealousy. *Personal Relationships, 5*, 273–291.

Guerrero, L. K., Trost, M. R., & Yoshimura, S. M. (2005). Romantic jealousy: Emotions and communicative responses. *Personal Relationships, 12*, 233–252.

Guisinger, S., & Blatt, S. J. (1994). Individuality and relatedness: Evolution of a fundamental dialectic. *American Psychologist, 49*, 104–111.

Gureje, O. (2004). What can we learn from a cross-national study of somatic distress? *Journal of Psychosomatic Research, 56*, 409–412.

Gurven, M. (2004). Reciprocal altruism and food sharing decisions among Hiwi and Ache hunter-gatherers. *Behavioral Ecology and Sociobiology, 56*, 366–380.

Guthrie, E. R. (1952). *The psychology of learning.* New York: Harper & Row.

Guttmacher Institute. (2004). *U.S. teenage pregnancy statistics: Overall trends, trends by race and ethnicity and state-by-state information.* New York: Alan Guttmacher Institute.

Guyote, M. J., & Sternberg, R. J. (1981). A transitive-chain theory of syllogistic reasoning. *Cognitive Psychology, 13*, 461–525.

Gwaltney, C. J., Meltrik, J., Shiffman, S., & Kahler, C. W. (2009). Self-efficacy and smoking cessation: A meta-analysis. *Psychology of Addictive Behavior, 23*, 56–66.

Haan, N., Smith, M. B., & Block, J. (1968). The moral reasoning of young adults: Political-social behaviour, family background and personality correlated. *Journal of Personality and Social Psychology, 10*, 183–201.

Haddad, P. M., & Sharma, S. G. (2007). Adverse effects of atypical antipsychotics: Differential risk and clinical implications. *CNS Drugs, 21*, 911–936.

Haist, F., Gore, J. B., & Mao, H. (2001). Consolidation of human memory over decades revealed by functional magnetic resonance imaging. *Nature Neuroscience, 11*, 1139–1145.

Hall, D. G., Lee, S. C., & Bélanger, J. (2001). Young children's use of syntactic cues to learn proper names and count nouns. *Developmental Psychology, 37*, 298–307.

Haller, W., Nitschke, J. B., & Miller, G. A. (1998). Lateralization in emotion and emotional disorders. *Current Directions in Psychological Science, 7*, 26–32.

Halligan, P. W., Athwal, B. S., Oakley, D. A., & Frackowlak, R. S. J. (2000). Imaging hypnotic paralysis: Implications for conversion hysteria. *The Lancet, 355*, 986–987.

Halperin, J. M., & Schulz, K. P. (2006). Revisiting the role of the prefrontal cortex in the pathophysiology of attention-deficit/hyperactivity disorder. *Psychological Bulletin, 132*, 560–581.

Halpern, A. R. (1986). Memory for tune titles after organized or unorganized presentation. *American Journal of Psychology, 99*, 57–70.

Halpern, D. F. (1996). *Thought and knowledge: An introduction to critical thinking* (3rd ed.). Hove, England: Erlbaum.

Hamann, S. B., Ely, T. D., Hoffman, J. M., & Kilts, C. D. (2002). Activation of the human amygdala in positive and negative emotion. *Psychological Science, 13*, 135–141.

Hamill, J. F. (1990). *Ethno-logic: The anthropology of human reasoning.* Urbana and Chicago: University of Illinois Press.

Hamilton, W. D. (1964). The genetical theory of social behaviour, I, II. *Journal of Theoretical Biology, 12*, 12–45.

Hammond, D. C. (2007). Hypnosis, placebos, and systematic research bias in biological psychiatry. *American Journal of Clinical Hypnosis, 50*, 37–47.

Hara, T. J. (1994). Olfaction and gustation in fish: An overview. *Acta Physiologica Scandinavica, 152*, 207–217.

Hardin, G. (1968). The tragedy of the commons. *Science, 162*, 1243–1248.

Hardy-Brown, K., Plomin, R., & DeFries, J. C. (1981). Genetic and environmental influences on the rate of communicative development in the first year of life. *Developmental Psychology, 17*, 704–717.

Harlow, H. F. (1959, June). Love in infant monkeys. *Scientific American*, pp. 68–74.

Harmon-Jones, E., Lueck, L., Fearn, M., & Harmon-Jones, C. (2006). The effect of personal relevance and approach-related action expectation on relative left frontal cortical activity. *Psychological Science, 17*, 434–439.

Harper, L. V., & Sanders, K. M. (1975). The effect of adults' eating on young children's acceptance of unfamiliar foods. *Journal of Experimental Child Psychology, 20,* 206–214.

Harris, J. R. (1995). Where is the child's environment? A group socialization theory of development. *Psychological Review, 102,* 458–489.

Harris, J. R. (1998). *The nurture assumption: Why children turn out the way they do.* New York: Simon & Schuster.

Harrison, L. (1975). Cro-magnon woman—in eclipse. *Science Teacher, 42,* 8–10.

Harrow, M., & Jobe, T. H. (2007). Factors involved in outcome and recovery in schizophrenia patients not on antipsychotic medications: A 15-year multifollow-up study. *Journal of Nervous and Mental Disease, 195,* 406–414.

Hart, D., Yates, M., Fegley, S., & Wilson, G. (1995). Moral commitment in inner-city adolescents. In M. Killen & D. Hart (Eds.), *Morality in everyday life: Developmental perspectives.* Cambridge, England: Cambridge University Press.

Hart, S., & Carrington, H. (2002). Jealousy in 6-month-old infants. *Infancy, 3,* 395–402.

Hartup, W. W. (1983). Peer relations. In E. M. Hetherington (Ed.), P. H. Mussen (Series Ed.), *Handbook of child psychology, Vol. 4: Socialization, personality, and social development.* New York: Wiley.

Harvey, S. B., Stanton, B.R., & David, A. S. (2006). Conversion disorder: Towards a neurobiological understanding. *Neuropsychiatric Disease and Treatment, 2,* 13–20.

Hasler, A. D., & Larsen, J. A. (1955, August). The homing salmon. *Scientific American,* pp. 72–76.

Hatfield, E., Cacioppo, J. T., & Rapson, R. L. (1994). *Emotional contagion.* Cambridge, England: Cambridge University Press.

Hawkins, H. L., & Presson J. C. (1986). Auditory information processing. In K. R. Boff, L. Kaufman, & J. P. Thomas (Eds.), *Handbook of perception and human performance: Vol. II. Cognitive processes and performance.* New York: Wiley.

Hay, D. F., & Murray, P. (1982). Giving and requesting: Social facilitation of infants' offers to adults. *Infant Behavior and Development, 5,* 301–310.

Haykin, S., & Chen, Z. (2005). The cocktail party problem. *Neural Computation, 17,* 1875–1902.

Hays, W. T. (2003). Human pheromones: Have they been demonstrated? *Behavioral Ecology and Sociobiology, 54,* 89–97.

Hazan, C., & Shaver, P. R. (1987). Romantic love conceptualized as an attachment process. *Journal of Personality and Social Psychology, 52,* 511–524.

Hazan, C., & Shaver, P. R. (1994). Attachment as an organizational framework for research on close relationships. *Psychological Inquiry, 5,* 1–22.

Hazler, R. J., & Barwick, N. (2001). *The therapeutic environment: Core conditions for facilitating therapy.* Philadelphia: Open University Press.

Hazlett-Stevens, H., Pruitt, L. D., & Collins, A. (2009). Phenomenology of generalized anxiety disorder. In M. M. Antony & M. B. Stein (Eds.), *Oxford handbook of anxiety related disorders.* Oxford, UK: Oxford University Press.

Healey, M. D., & Ellis, B. (2007). Birth order, conscientiousness, and openness to experience: Tests of the family-niche model of personality using a within-family methodology. *Evolution and Human Behavior, 28,* 55–59.

Hebb, D. (1958a). *A textbook of psychology.* Philadelphia: Saunders.

Hebb, D. (1958b). *The organization of behavior: A neuropsychological theory.* New York: Wiley.

Hécaen, H., & Albert, M. L. (1978). *Human neuropsychology.* New York: Wiley.

Heckler, S. (1994). Facilitated communication: A response by child protection. *Child Abuse and Neglect, 18,* 495–503.

Hefferline, R. F., Keenan, B., & Harford, R. A. (1959). Escape and avoidance conditioning of human subjects without their observation of the response. *Science, 130,* 1338–1339.

Hefti, F. F. (2005). *Drug discovery for nervous system diseases.* Hoboken, NJ: Wiley.

Hegdé, J., & Van Essen, D. C. (2003). Strategies of shape representation in macaque visual area V2. *Visual Neuroscience, 20,* 313–328.

Hehdta, P. H., & Josephs, R. A. (2006). Testosterone change after losing predicts the decision to compete again. *Hormones and Behavior, 50,* 684–692.

Heider, F. (1958). *The psychology of interpersonal relations.* New York: Wiley.

Heiman, M. (1987). Learning to learn: A behavioral approach to improving thinking. In D. N. Perkins, J. Lockhead, & J. Bishop (Eds.), *Thinking: The Second International Conference.* Hillsdale, NJ: Erlbaum.

Heine, S. J., & Buchtel, E. E. (2009). Personality: The universal and the culturally specific. *Annual Review of Psychology, 60,* 369–394.

Heine, S. J., & Hamamura, T. (2007). In search of Asian self-enhancement. *Personality and Social Psychology Review, 11,* 4–27.

Heine, S. J., Lehman, D. R., Markus, H. R., & Kitayama, S. (1999). Is there a universal need for positive self-regard? *Psychological Review, 106,* 766–794.

Heine, S. J., Takata, T., & Lehman, D. R. (2000). Beyond self-presentation: Evidence for self-criticism among Japanese. *Personality and Social Psychology Bulletin, 26,* 71–78.

Heinrichs, R. W. (2005). The primacy of cognition in schizophrenia. *American Psychologist, 60,* 229–242.

Helmholtz, H. von (1962; originally published in the *Handbuch der physiologischen optik,* 1867). *Helmholtz's treatise on physiological optics* (J. P. C. Southall, Ed. and Trans.). New York: Dover.

Helmholtz, H. von (1852). On the theory of compound colors. *Philosophical Magazine, 4,* 519–534.

Helmuth, L. (2003). Fear and trembling in the amygdala. *Science, 300,* 568–569.

Helson, R., & Stewart, A. (1994). Personality change in adulthood. In T. F. Heatherton & J. L. Weinberger (Eds.), *Can personality change?* Washington, DC: American Psychological Association.

Hendricks, B., Marvel, M. K., & Barrington, B. L. (1990). The dimensions of psychological research. *Teaching of Psychology, 17,* 76–82.

Henry, J. L. (1986). Role of circulating opioids in the modulation of pain. In D. D. Kelly (Ed.), *Stress-induced analgesia* (Vol. 467 of the *Annals of the New York Academy of Sciences*). New York: New York Academy of Sciences.

Henry, N. J., M., Berg, C. A., Smith, T. W., & Florsheim, P. (2007). Positive and negative characteristics of marital interaction and their association with marital satisfaction in middle-aged and older couples. *Psychology and Aging, 22,* 428–441.

Hepper, P. G., Scott, D., & Shahidullah, S. (1993). Newborn and fetal response to maternal voice. *Journal of Reproductive and Infant Psychology, 11,* 147–153

Herdt, G., & Boxer, A. (1993). *Children of horizons.* New York: Beacon Press.

Hering, E. (1878; translated edition 1964). *Outlines of a theory of the light sense* (L. M. Hurvich and D. Jameson, Trans.). Cambridge, MA: Harvard University Press.

Herness, M. S., & Gilbertson, T. A. (1999). Cellular mechanisms of taste transduction. *Annual Review of Physiology, 61,* 837–900.

Herrnstein, R. J. (1979). Acquisition, generalization, and discrimination reversal of a natural concept. *Journal of Experimental Psychology: Animal Behavior Processes, 5,* 116–129.

Herrnstein, R. J. (1990). Levels of stimulus control: A functional approach. *Cognition, 37,* 133–166.

Herrnstein, R. J., & Murray, C. (1994). *The bell curve: Intelligence and class structure in American life.* New York: Free Press.

Hershenson, M. (1989). The most puzzling illusion. In M. Hershenson (Ed.), *The moon illusion.* Hillsdale, NJ: Erlbaum.

Hershenson, M. (2003). A trick of moonlight. *Nature, 421,* 695.

Herzog, E. D. (2007). Neurons and networks in daily rhythms. *Nature Reviews Neuroscience, 8,* 790–802.

Hess, E. H. (1958, March). "Imprinting" in animals. *Scientific American,* pp. 81–90.

Hess, E. H. (1972, August). "Imprinting" in a natural laboratory. *Scientific American,* pp. 24–31.

Hetherington, E. M. (1972). Effects of father absence on personality development in adolescent daughters. *Developmental Psychology, 7,* 313–326.

Hettema, J. M. (2008). The nosologic relationship between generalized anxiety disorder and major depression. *Depression and Anxiety, 25,* 300–316.

Hettema, J. M., Prescott, C. A., & Kendler, K. S. (2004). Genetic and environmental sources of covariation between generalized anxiety disorder and neuroticism. *American Journal of Psychiatry, 161,* 1581–1587.

Hewlett, B. S. (1988). Sexual selection and paternal investment among Aka pygmies. In L. Betzig, M. B. Mulder, & P. Turke (Eds.), *Human reproductive behavior: A Darwinian perspective.* Cambridge, England: Cambridge University Press.

Hickling, A. K., & Wellman, H. M. (2001). The emergence of children's causal explanations and theories: Evidence from everyday conversation. *Developmental Psychology, 37,* 668–683.

Higgins, S. T., Sliverman, K., & Heil, S. H. (eds.) (2007). *Contingency management in substance abuse treatment.* New York: Guildford.

Hill, J. O., Wyatt, H. R., Reed, G. W., & Peters, J. C. (2003). Obesity and the environment: Where do we go from here? *Science, 299,* 853–855.

Hill, K. (2002). Altruistic cooperation during foraging by the Ache, and the evolved human predisposition to cooperate. *Human Nature, 13,* 105–128.

Hill, P. M., & McCune-Nicolich, L. (1981). Pretend play and patterns of cognition in Down's syndrome children. *Child Development, 52,* 217–250.

Hilts, P. J. (1995). *Memory's ghost.* New York: Simon & Schuster.

Himelein, M. J., Vogel, R. E., & Wachowiak, D. G. (1994). Nonconsensual sexual experience in precollege women: Prevalence and risk factors. *Journal of Counseling and Development, 72,* 411–415.

Hines, M., Brook, C., & Conway, G. S. (2004). Androgen and psychosexual development: Core gender identity, sexual orientation, and recalled childhood gender role behavior in women and men with congenital adrenal hyperplasia (CAH). *Journal of Sex Research, 41,* 75–81.

Hines, T. (2003). *Pseudoscience and the paranormal* (2nd ed.). Amherst, NY: Prometheus Books.

Hinrichs, K. T. (2007). Follower propensity to commit crimes of obedience: The role of leadership belief. *Journal of Leadership and Organizational Studies, 14,* 69–76.

Hinson, R. E., Poulos, C. X., Thomas, W., & Cappell, H. (1986). Pavlovian conditioning and addictive behavior: Relapse to oral self-administration of morphine. *Behavioral Neuroscience, 100,* 368–375.

Hippocrates. (1923). The sacred disease. In W. H. S. Jones (Trans.), *Hippocrates* (Vol. 2). London: Heinemann.

Hirata, S., & Morimura, N. (2000). Naive chimpanzees' (*Pan troglodytes*) observation of experienced conspecifics in a tool-using task. *Journal of Comparative Psychology, 114,* 291–296.

Hirt, E. R., Zillman, D., Erickson, G. A., & Kennedy, C. (1992). The costs and benefits of allegiance: Changes in fans' self-described competence after team victory versus team defeat. *Journal of Personality and Social Psychology, 63,* 724–738.

Hittelman, J. H., & Dickes, R. (1979). Sex differences in neonatal eye contact time. *Merrill-Palmer Quarterly, 25,* 171–184.

Hlastala, S. A., Frank, E., Kowalski, K., Sherrill, J. T., Tu, X. M., Anderson, B., & Kupfer, D. J. (2000). Stressful life events, bipolar disorder, and the "kindling model." *Journal of Abnormal Psychology, 109,* 777–786.

Hobson, J. A. (1987). (1) Sleep, (2) Sleep, functional theories of, (3) Dreaming. All in G. Adelman (Ed.), *Encyclopedia of neuroscience.* Boston: Birkhäuser.

Hobson, J. A. (1988). *The dreaming brain.* New York: Basic Books.

Hobson, J. A. (1995). *Sleep.* New York: Scientific American Library.

Hobson, J. A. (2002). *Dreaming: An introduction to the science of sleep.* New York: Oxford University Press.

Hobson, J. A. (2004). A model for madness? Dream consciousness: Our understanding of the neurobiology of sleep offers insight into abnormalities in the waking brain. *Nature, 430,* 21.

Hochberg, J. (1971). Perception II: Space and movement. In J. W. Kling & L. A. Riggs (Eds.), *Woodworth & Schlosberg's experimental psychology* (3rd ed.). New York: Holt, Rinehart & Winston.

Hodges, B. H., & Geyer, A. L. (2006). A nonconformist account of the Asch experiments: Value, pragmatics, and moral dilemmas. *Personality and Social Psychological Review, 10,* 2–19.

Hoebel, B. G., Monaco, A. P., Hernandez, L., Aulisi, E. F., Stanley, B. G., & Lenard, L. G. (1983). Self-injection of amphetamine directly into the brain. *Psychopharmacology, 81,* 158–163.

Hoek, H. W. (2002). The distribution of eating disorders. In K. D. Brownell & C. G. Fairburn (Eds.), *Eating disorders and obesity: A comprehensive handbook* (2nd ed.). New York: Guilford.

Hoelzel, A. R., Le Boeuf, B. J., Reiter, J., & Campagna, C. (1999). Alpha-male paternity in elephant seals. *Behavioral Ecology and Sociobiology, 46,* 298–306.

Hoffman, D. D. (1998). *Visual intelligence: How we create what we see.* New York: Norton.

Hoffman, H. (2007). The role of classical conditioning in sexual arousal. pp. 261–273 in E. Janssen (Ed.), *The psychology of sex. The Kinsey Institute series.* Bloomington, IN: Indiana University Press.

Hoffman, H. G. (2004, August). Virtual-reality therapy. *Scientific American, 291,* pp. 58–65.

Hoffman, M. L. (1982). Development of prosocial motivation: Empathy and guilt. In N. Eisenberg (Ed.), *The development of prosocial behavior.* New York: Academic Press.

Hoffman, M. L. (1983). Affective and cognitive processes in moral internalization. In E. T. Higgins, D. N. Ruble, & W. W. Hartup (Eds.), *Social cognition and social development.* Cambridge, England: Cambridge University Press.

Hoffman, M. L. (1998). Varieties of empathy-based guilt. In J. Bybee (Ed.), *Guilt and children.* San Diego: Academic Press.

Hoffman, M. L. (2000). *Empathy and moral development: Implications for caring and justice.* Cambridge, England: Cambridge University Press.

Hoffman, M. L. (2007). The origins of empathic morality in toddlerhood. In C. A. Brownell & C. B. Kopp (Eds.), *Socioemotional development in the toddler years: Transitions and transformations.* New York: Guilford.

Hofmann, S. G., Alpers, G. W., & Paul, P. (2009). Phenomenology of panic and phobic disosrders. In M. M. Antony & M. B. Stein (Eds.), *Oxford handbook of anxiety related disorders.* Oxford, UK: Oxford University Press.

Hofstadter, D. R. (2001). Epilogue: Analogy as the core of cognition. In D. Gentner, K. J. Holyoak, & B. N. Kokinov (Eds.), *The analogical mind: Perspectives from cognitive science.* Cambridge, MA: MIT Press.

Hofsten, C. von, & Siddiqui, A. (1993). Using the mother's actions as a reference for object exploration in 6- and 12-month-old infants. *British Journal of Developmental Psychology, 11,* 61–74.

Hogg, M. A., Turner, J. C., & Davidson, B. (1990). Polarized norms and social frames of reference: A test of the self-categorization theory of group polarization. *Basic and Applied Social Psychology, 11*, 77–100.

Hohmann, G., & Fruth, B. (2000). Use and function of genital contacts among female bonobos. *Animal Behaviour, 60*, 107–120.

Hohmann, G., & Fruth, B. (2003). Intra- and inter-sexual aggression by bonobos in the context of mating. *Behaviour, 140*, 1389–1413.

Holden, C. (2001). Behavioral addictions: Do they exist? *Science, 294*, 980–982.

Hollis, K. L., Pharr, V. L., Dumas, M. J., Britton, G. B., & Field, J. (1997). Classical conditioning provides paternity advantage for territorial male blue gouramis (*Trichogaster trichopterus*). *Journal of Comparative Psychology, 111*, 219–225.

Hollon, S. D., Thase, M. E., & Markowitz, J. C. (2002). Treatment and prevention of depression. *Psychological Science in the Public Interest, 3*, 39–77.

Honig, K. M., & Townes, B. D. (1976). Infants' attachment to inanimate objects: A cross-cultural study. *American Academy of Child Psychiatry Journal, 15*, 49–61.

Hooley, J. M. (2004). Do psychiatric patients do better clinically if they live with certain kinds of families? *Current Directions in Psychological Science, 13*, 202–205.

Hooley, J. M., & Hiller, J. B. (2001). Family relationships and major mental disorder: Risk factors and preventive strategies. In B. R. Sarason & S. Duck (Eds.), *Personal relationships: Implications for clinical and community psychology.* Chichester, England: Wiley.

Hopper, K., Harrison, G., Janca, A., & Sartorius, N. (Eds.) (2007). *Recovery from schizophrenia: An international perspective. A report from the WHO Collaborative Project, the International Study of Schizophrenia.* Oxford, UK: Oxford University Press.

Hopper, L. M., Spiteri, A., Lambeth, S. P., Schapiro, S. J., Horner, V., & Whiten, A. (2007). Experimental studies of traditions and underlying transmission processes in chimpanzees. *Animal Behavior, 73*, 1021–1032.

Horn, J. L. (1985). Remodeling old models of intelligence. In B. B. Wolman (Ed.), *Handbook of intelligence: Theories, measurements, and applications.* New York: Wiley.

Horne, J. A. (1979). Restitution and human sleep: A critical review. *Physiological Psychology, 7*, 115–125.

Horne, J. A. (1988). *Why we sleep: The functions of sleep in humans and other mammals.* Oxford: Oxford University Press.

Horne, J. A., & Reyner, L. A. (1995). Sleep related vehicle accidents. *British Medical Journal, 310*, 565–567.

Horne, J. A., & Reyner, L. A. (2001). Sleep-related vehicle accidents: Some guides for road safety policies. *Transportation Research Part F: Traffic Psychology & Behaviour, 4*, 63–74.

Horney, K. (1945). *Our inner conflicts.* New York: Norton.

Hornik, R., Risenhoover, N., & Gunnar, M. (1987). The effects of maternal positive, neutral, and negative affective communications on infant responses to new toys. *Child Development, 58*, 937–944.

Hosobuchi, Y., Rossier, J., Bloom, F. E., & Guillemin, R. (1979). Stimulation of human periaqueductal gray for pain relief increases immunoreactive beta-endorphin in ventricular fluid. *Science, 203*, 279–281.

Hothersall, D. (1995). *History of psychology* (3rd ed.). New York: McGraw-Hill.

Houghton, D. P. (2008). Invading and occupying Iraq: Some insights from political psychology. *Peace and Conflict, 14*, 169–192.

Houk, J. C., & Mugnaini, E. (2003). Cerebellum. In L. R. Squire, F. L. Bloom, S. K. McConnell, J. L. Roberts, N. C. Spitzer, & M. J. Zigmond (Eds.), *Fundamental neuroscience* (2nd ed.). San Diego, CA: Academic Press.

Howland, R. H. (2005). Biological base in psychopathology. In J. Maddux & B. Winstead (Eds.), *Psychopathology: Foundations for a contemporary understanding.* Mahwah, NJ: Erlbaum.

Hoyle, R. H., Pinkley, R. L., & Insko, C. A. (1989). Perceptions of social behavior: Evidence for differing expectations for interpersonal and intergroup interactions. *Personality and Social Psychology Bulletin, 15*, 365–376.

Hrdy, S. B. (1981). *The woman that never evolved.* Cambridge, MA: Harvard University Press.

Hrdy, S. B. (2000). The optimal number of fathers: Evolution, demography, and history in the shaping of female mate preferences. *Annals of the New York Academy of Sciences, 907*, 75–96.

Hrdy, S. B. (2005). On why it takes a village: Cooperative breeders, infant needs, and the future. In R. L. Burgess & K. MacDonald (Eds.), *Evolutionary perspectives on human development* (2nd ed.). Thousand Oaks, CA: Sage.

Hron-Stewart, K. M. (1988, April). *Gender differences in mothers' strategies for helping toddlers solve problems.* Paper presented at the biennial International Conference on Infancy Studies, Washington, DC.

Hubel, D. H., & Wiesel, T. N. (1962). Receptive fields, binocular interaction, and functional architecture of the cat's visual cortex. *Journal of Physiology* (London), *160*, 106–154.

Hubel, D. H., & Wiesel, T. N. (1979, September). Brain mechanisms of vision. *Scientific American*, pp. 150–162.

Hudspeth, A. J. (2000a). Hearing. In E. R. Kandel, J. H. Schwartz, & T. M. Jessell (Eds.), *Principles of neuroscience* (4th ed). New York: McGraw-Hill.

Hudspeth, A. J. (2000b). Sensory transduction in the ear. In E. R. Kandel, J. H. Schwartz, & T. M. Jessell (Eds.), *Principles of neuroscience* (4th ed). New York: McGraw-Hill.

Huey, E. D., Krueger, F., & Grafman, J. (2006). Representations in the human prefrontal cortex. *Current Directions in Psychological Science, 15*, 167–171.

Huff, D. (1954). *How to lie with statistics.* New York: Norton.

Hughes, H. C. (1999). *Sensory exotica: A world beyond human experience.* Cambridge, MA: MIT Press.

Huizinga, J. (1944; reprinted 1970). *Homo ludens: A study of the play-element in culture.* London: Paladin.

Humphrey, R. (1985). How work roles influence perception: Structural-cognitive processes and organizational behavior. *American Sociological Review, 50*, 242–252.

Hunt, C., Slade, T., & Andrews, G. (2004). Generalized anxiety disorder and major depressive disorder comorbidity in the national survey of mental health and well-being. *Depression and Anxiety, 20*, 23–31.

Hunt, M. (1993). *The story of psychology.* New York: Doubleday.

Hurvich, L. M., & Jameson, D. (1957). An opponent-process theory of color vision. *Psychological Review, 64*, 384–404.

Husband, R. W. (1931). Analysis of methods in human maze learning. *Journal of Genetic Psychology, 39*, 258–278.

Husted, D. S., & Shapira, N. A. (2004). A review of treatment for refractory obsessive-compulsive disorder: From medicine to deep brain stimulation. *CNS Spectrums, 9*, 833–847.

Huxley, J. H., Mayr, E., Osmond, H., & Hoffer, A. (1964). Schizophrenia as a genetic morphism. *Nature, 204*, pp. 220–221.

Hyde, J. S. (2005). The genetics of sexual orientation. In J. S. Hyde (Ed.), *Biological substrates of human sexuality.* Washington, DC: American Psychological Association.

Hyman, I. E., & Pentland, J. (1996). The role of mental imagery in the creation of false childhood memories. *Journal of Memory and Language, 35*, 101–117.

Hyman, S. E., Malenka, R. C., & Nestler, E. J. (2006). Neural mechanisms of addiction: The role of reward-related learning and memory. *Annual Review of Neuroscience, 29,* 565–598.

Iacoboni, M., & Dapretto, M. (2006). The mirror system and the consequences of its dysfunction. *Nature Reviews Neuroscience, 7,* 942–951.

Imel, Z. E., Malterer, M. B., McKay, K. M., & Wampold, B. E. (2008). A meta-analysis of psychotherapy and medication in unipolar depression and dysthymia. *Journal of Affective Disorders, 110,* 197–206.

Inglis, I. R., Langton, S., Forkman, B., & Lazarus, J. (2001). An information primacy model of exploratory and foraging behaviour. *Animal Behaviour, 62,* 543–557.

Inhelder, B., & Piaget, J. (1958). *The growth of logical thinking from childhood to adolescence.* New York: Basic Books.

Inoue-Nakamura, N., & Matsuzawa, T. (1997). Development of stone tool use by wild chimpanzees (*Pan troglodytes*). *Journal of Comparative Psychology, 111,* 159–173.

Isen, A. M. (2001). An influence of positive affect on decision making in complex situations: Theoretical issues with practical implications. *Journal of Consumer Psychology, 11,* 75–85.

Isen, A. M., Daubman, K. A., & Nowicki, G. P. (1987). Positive effect facilitates creative problem solving. *Journal of Personality and Social Psychology, 52,* 1122–1131.

Ivey Henry, P., Morelli, G. A., & Tronick, E. Z. (2005). Child caretakers among Efe foragers of the Ituri Forest. In B. S. Hewlett & M. E. Lamb (Eds.), *Hunter-gatherer childhoods: Evolutionary, developmental, and cultural perspectives.* New Brunswick, NJ: Transaction Publishers.

Izard, C. E., Fantauzzo, C. A., Castle, J. M., Haynes, O. M., Rayias, M. F., & Putnam, P. H. (1995). The ontogeny and significance of infants' facial expressions in the first 9 months of life. *Developmental Psychology, 31,* 997–1013.

Jablensky, A., Sartorius, N., Ernberg, G., Anker, M., Korten, A., Cooper, J. E., Day, R., & Bertelsen, A. (1992). Schizophrenia: Manifestations, incidence and course in different cultures. A World Health Organization ten-country study. *Psychological Medicine, Monograph Supplements* (Whole Vol. 20).

Jaccard, J., Blanton, H., & Dodge, T. (2005). Peer influence on risk behavior: An analysis of the effects of a close friend. *Developmental Psychology, 41,* 135–147.

Jackendoff, R. (2003). Précis of *Foundations of language: brain, meaning, grammar, evolution. Behavioral and Brain Sciences, 26,* 651–707.

Jackson, T. T., & Gray, M. (1976). Field study of risk-taking behavior of automobile drivers. *Perceptual and Motor Skills, 43,* 471–474.

Jacobs, B. L. (2004). Depression: The brain finally gets into the act. *Current Directions in Psychological Science, 13,* 103–106.

Jacobson, J. W., Mulick, J. A., & Schwartz, A. A. (1995). A history of facilitated communication: Science, pseudoscience, and antiscience. *American Psychologist, 50,* 750–765.

Jaffe, E. (2007). Mirror neurons: How we reflect on behavior. *American Psychological Society Observer, 20,* 20–25.

Jaffee, S. R., Caspi, A., Moffitt, T. E., Polo-Tomas, M., Price, T. S., & Taylor, A. (2004). The limits of child effects: Evidence for genetically mediated child effects on corporal punishment but not on physical maltreatment. *Developmental Psychology, 40,* 1047–1058.

James, W. (1890; reprinted 1950). *The principles of psychology.* New York: Dover.

James, W. H. (2005). Biological and psychological determinants of male and female sexual orientation. *Journal of Biosocial Science, 37,* 555–567.

Jamison, K. R. (1995, February). Manic-depressive illness and creativity. *Scientific American,* pp. 62–67.

Janal, M. N., Colt, E. W. D., Clark, W. C., & Glusman, M. (1984). Pain sensitivity, mood and plasma endocrine levels in man following long-distance running: Effects of naloxone. *Pain, 19,* 13–25.

Janis, I. (1982). *Groupthink: Psychological studies of policy decisions and fiascoes* (2nd ed.). Boston: Houghton Mifflin.

Jankowiak, W. R., & Fischer, E. F. (1991). A cross-cultural perspective on romantic love. *Ethnology, 31,* 149–155.

Javitt, D. C., & Coyle, J. T. (2004, January). Decoding schizophrenia. *Scientific American, 290,* pp. 48–55.

Jellison, J. M., & Green, J. (1981). A self-presentation approach to the fundamental attribution error: The norm of internality. *Journal of Personality and Social Psychology, 40,* 643–649.

Jenkins, H. M., Barrera, F. J., Ireland, C., & Woodside, B. (1978). Signal-centered action patterns of dogs in appetitive classical conditioning. *Learning and Motivation, 9,* 272–296.

Jenkins, J. H., & Karno, M. (1992). The meaning of expressed emotion: Theoretical issues raised by cross-cultural research. *American Journal of Psychiatry, 149,* 9–21.

Jenkins, J. M., & Astington, J. W. (1996). Cognitive factors and family structure associated with theory of mind development in young children. *Developmental Psychology, 32,* 70–78.

Jennings, J. R., Monk, T. H., & van der Molen, M. W. (2003). Sleep deprivation influences some but not all processes of supervisory attention. *Psychological Science, 14,* 473–479.

Jensen, A. R. (1980). *Bias in mental testing.* New York: Free Press.

Jerome, J. K. (1889; reprinted 1982). *Three men in a boat (to say nothing of the dog).* London: Pavilion Books.

Ji, R., Kohno, T., Moore, K. A., & Woolf, C. J. (2003). Central sensitization and LTP: Do pain and memory share similar mechanisms? *Trends in Neurosciences, 26,* 96–705.

Johns, M., Inzlicht, M., & Schmader, T. (2008). Stereotype threat and executive resource depletion: Examining the influence of emotion regulation. *Journal of Experimental Psychology: General, 137,* 691–705.

Johns, M., Schmader, T., & Martens, A. (2005). Knowing is half the battle: Teaching stereotype threat as a means of improving women's math performance. *Psychological Science, 16,* 175–180.

Johnson, G. R. (1987). In the name of the fatherland: An analysis of kin term usage in patriotic speech and literature. *International Political Science Review, 8,* 165–174.

Johnson, J. S., & Newport, E. L. (1989). Critical period effects in second-language learning: The influence of maturational state on the acquisition of English as a second language. *Cognitive Psychology, 21,* 60–99.

Johnson, M. H., & Horn, G. (1988). Development of filial preferences in dark-reared chicks. *Animal Behaviour, 36,* 675–783.

Johnson, M. K., Hashtroudi, S., & Lindsay, D. S. (1993). Source monitoring. *Psychological Bulletin, 114,* 3–28.

Johnson, S. (2005). *Everything bad for you is good for you: How today's popular culture is actually making us smarter.* New York: Riverhead Books.

Johnson, S. L., Cuellar, A. K., & Miller, C. (2009). Bipolar and unipolar depression: A comparison of clinical phenomenology, biological vulnerability, and psychosocial predictors. In I. H. Gotlib & C. L. Hammen (Eds.), *Handbook of depression* (2nd ed.). New York: Guilford.

Johnston, T. D., & Edwards, L. (2002). Genes, interactions, and development of behavior. *Psychological Review, 109,* 26–34.

Johnson-Laird, P. N. (1983). *Mental models: Towards a cognitive science of language, inference, and consciousness.* Cambridge, MA: Harvard University Press.

Johnson-Laird, P. N. (1985). Deductive reasoning ability. In R. J. Sternberg (Ed.), *Human abilities: An information-processing approach.* New York: Freeman.

Johnson-Laird, P. N. (2006). *How we reason.* Oxford, UK: Oxford University Press.

Johnson-Laird, P. N., Byrne, R. M. J., & Schaeken, W. (1994). Why models rather than rules give a better account of propositional reasoning: A reply to Bonatti and to O'Brien, Braine, and Yang. *Psychological Review, 101,* 734–739.

Johnson-Laird, P. N., Legrenzi, P., Girotto, V., & Legrenzi, M. S. (2000). Illusions in reasoning about consistency. *Science, 288,* 531–532.

Jonas, E., Schulz-Hardt, S., Frey, D., & Thelen, N. (2001). Confirmation bias in sequential information search after primary decisions: An expansion of dissonance theoretical research on selective exposure to information. *Journal of Personality and Social Psychology, 80,* 557–571.

Jonides, J., Lacey, S. C., & Nee, D. E. (2005). Processes of working memory in mind and brain. *Current Directions in Psychological Science, 14,* 2–5.

Joormann, J. (2009). Cognitive aspects of depression. In I. H. Gotlib & C. L. Hammen (Eds.), *Handbook of depression* (2nd ed.). New York: Guilford.

Josephs, R. A., Markus, H. R., & Tafarodi, R. W. (1992). Gender and self-esteem. *Journal of Personality and Social Psychology, 63,* 391–402.

Jussim, L. (1991). Social perception and social reality: A reflection-construction model. *Psychological Review, 98,* 54–73.

Kabot, S., Masi, W., & Segal, M. (2003). Advances in the diagnosis and treatment of autism spectrum disorders. *Professional Psychology: Research and Practice, 34,* 26–33.

Kagan, J. (1976). Emergent themes in human development. *American Scientist, 64,* 186–196.

Kail, R. (1993). The role of a global mechanism in developmental change in speed of processing. In M. L. Howe & R. Pasnak (Eds.), *Emerging themes in cognitive development: Vol. 1. Foundations.* New York: Springer-Verlag.

Kail, R. V. (2007). Longitudinal evidence that increases in processing speed and working memory enhance children's reasoning. *Psychological Science, 18,* 312–313.

Kaitz, M., Good, A., Rokem, A. M., & Eidelman, A. I. (1987). Mothers' recognition of their newborns by olfactory cues. *Developmental Psychobiology, 20,* 587–591.

Kajantie, E. (2008). Physiological stress response, estrogen, and the male-female mortality gap. *Current Directions in Psychological Science, 17,* 348–352.

Kamei, N. (2005). Play among Baka children in Camaroon. In B. S. Hewlett & M. E. Lamb (Eds.), *Hunter-gatherer childhoods: Evolutionary, developmental, and cultural perspectives.* New Brunswick, NJ: Transaction Publishers.

Kamil, A. C., & Balda, R. P. (1985). Cache recovery and spatial memory in Clark's nutcrackers (*Nucifraga Columbiana*). *Journal of Experimental Psychology: Animal Behavior Processes, 11,* 95–111.

Kamin, L. J. (1969). Predictability, surprise, attention, and conditioning. In B. A. Campbell & R. M. Church (Eds.), *Punishment and aversive behavior.* New York: Appleton-Century-Crofts.

Kaminski, J., Call, J., & Fischer, J. (2004). Word learning in a domestic dog: Evidence for "fast mapping." *Science, 304,* 1682–1683.

Kanagawa, C., Cross, S. E., & Markus, H. R. (2001). "Who am I?" The cultural psychology of the conceptual self. *Personality and Social Psychology Bulletin, 27,* 90–103.

Kanazawa, S. (2004). General intelligence as a domain-specific adaptation. *Psychological Review, 111,* 512–523.

Kane, M. J., & Engle, R. W. (2002). The role of the prefrontal cortex in working-memory capacity, executive attention, and general fluid intelligence: An individual-differences perspective. *Psychonomic Bulletin & Review, 9,* 637–671.

Kano, T. (1992). *The last ape: Pygmy chimpanzee behavior and ecology.* Stanford, CA: Stanford University Press.

Kano, T. (1998). Comment on Stanford, C. B., 1998, "The social behavior of chimpanzees and bonobos: Empirical evidence and shifting assumptions". *Current Anthropology, 39,* 399–420.

Kant, I. (1781; reprinted 1965). *Critique of pure reason* (J. Watson, Trans.). In B. Rand (Ed.), *Modern classical philosophers.* Boston: Houghton Mifflin.

Kaplan, G. A., & Simon, H. A. (1990). In search of insight. *Cognitive Psychology, 22,* 374–419.

Kaplan, M. F. (1987). The influencing process in group decision making. In C. Hendrick (Ed.), *Review of personality and social psychology: Vol. 8. Group processes.* Newbury Park, CA: Sage.

Kaprio, J., Koskenvuo, M., & Rita, H. (1987). Mortality after bereavement: A prospective study of 95,647 widowed persons. *American Journal of Public Health, 77,* 283–287.

Karasu, T. B. (1986). The specificity versus nonspecificity dilemma: Toward identifying therapeutic change agents. *American Journal of Psychiatry, 143,* 687–695.

Karau, S. J., & Williams, K. D. (1995). Social loafing: Research findings, implications, and future directions. *Current Directions in Psychological Science, 4,* 134–140.

Karau, S. J., & Williams, K. D. (2001). Understanding individual motivation in groups: The collective effort model. In M. E. Turner (Ed.), *Groups at work: Theory and research.* Mahwah, NJ: Erlbaum.

Karney, B. R., Beckett, M. K., Collins, R. L., & Shaw, R. (2007). *Adolescent romantic relationships as precursors of healthy adult marriages: A review of theory, research, and programs.* Santa Monica, CA: RAND Corporation.

Karp, D. (1988). A decade of reminders: Changing age consciousness between fifty and sixty years old. *The Gerontologist, 28,* 727–738.

Kashima, Y., Yamaguchi, S., Kim, U., Choi, S., Gelfand, M. J., & Yuki, M. (1995). Culture, gender, and self: A perspective from individualism-collectivism research. *Journal of Personality and Social Psychology, 69,* 925–937.

Kastenbaum, R. (1985). Dying and death. In J. E. Birren & K. W. Schaie (Eds.), *Handbook of the psychology of aging* (2nd ed.). New York: Van Nostrand-Reinhold.

Kaufman, A. S., & Lichetenberger, E. O. (1999). *Essentials of WAIS-III assessment.* New York: Wiley.

Kaufman, J., Yang, B., Douglas-Palumberi, H., Grasso, D., Lipschitz, D., Houshyar, S., et al., (2006). Brain-derived neurotrophic factor-5-HTTLPR gene interactions and environmental modifiers of depression in children. *Biological Psychiatry, 59,* 673–680.

Kaufman, J., Yang, B., Douglas-Palumberi, H., Houshyar, S., Lipschitz, D., Krystal, J. H., et al., (2004). Social supports and serotonin transporter gene moderate depression in maltreated children. *Proceedings of the National Academy of Sciences, 101,* 17316–17321.

Kaufman, L., & Kaufman, J. H. (2000). Explaining the moon illusion. *Proceedings of the National Academy of Sciences (USA), 97,* 500–505.

Kaufman, L., & Rock, I. (1962, July). The moon illusion. *Scientific American,* pp. 120–130.

Kaufman, L., & Rock, I. (1989). The moon illusion thirty years later. In M. Hershenson (Ed.), *The moon illusion.* Hillsdale, NJ: Erlbaum.

Kaufman, L., Vassiliades, V., Noble, R., Alexander, R., Kaufman, J., & Edlund, S. (2007). Perceptual distance and the moon illusion. *Spatial Vision, 20,* 155–175.

Kavaliers, M., Choleris, E., Colwell, D. D., & Ossenkopp, K. (1999). Learning to cope with biting flies: Rapid NMDA-mediated acquisition of conditioned analgesia. *Behavioral Neuroscience, 113,* 126–135.

Kawakami, K., & Dovidio, J. (2001). The reliability of implicit stereotyping. *Personality and Social Psychology Bulletin, 27,* 212–225.

Kazdin, A. E. (2003). Psychotherapy for children and adolescents. *Annual Review of Psychology, 54,* 253–276.

Keating, C. F., Randall, D. W., Kendrick, T., & Gutshall, K. A. (2003). Do babyfaced adults receive more help? The (cross-cultural) case of the lost resume. *Journal of Nonverbal Behavior, 27,* 89–109.

Keating, C. F., Randall, D., & Kendrick, T. (1999). Presidential physiognomies: Altered images, altered perceptions. *Political Psychology, 20,* 593–610.

Keen, R. (2003). Representation of objects and events: Why do infants look so smart and toddlers look so dumb? *Current Directions in Psychological Science, 12,* 79–82.

Keesey, R. E., & Corbett, S. W. (1984). Metabolic defense of the body weight set-point. In A. J. Stunkard & E. Stellar (Eds.), *Eating and its disorders.* New York: Raven Press.

Kefalov, V., Fu, Y., March-Armstrong, N., & Yau, K. (2003). Role of visual pigment properties in rod and cone phototransduction. *Nature, 425,* 526–531.

Keizer, K., Lindenberg, S., & Steg, L. (2008). The spreading of disorder. *Science, 322,* 1681–1685.

Keller, A., Zhuang, H., Chi, Q., Vosshall, L. B., & Matsunami, H. (2007). Genetic variation in a human odorant receptor alters odour perception. *Nature, 449,* 468–472.

Keller, M. A., & Goldberg, W. A. (2004). Co-sleeping: Help or hindrance for young children's independence? *Infant and Child Development, 13,* 369–388.

Keller, M. C., & Nesse, R. M. (2005). Is low mood an adaptation? Evidence for subtypes with symptoms that match precipitants. *Journal of Affective Disorders, 86,* 27–35.

Keller, M. C., & Nesse, R. M. (2006). The evolutionary significance of depressive symptoms: Different adverse situations lead to different depressive symptom patterns. *Journal of Personality and Social Psychology, 91,* 316–330.

Kelley, A. E., & Berridge, K. C. (2002). The neuroscience of natural rewards: Relevance to addictive drugs. *The Journal of Neuroscience, 22,* 3306–3311.

Kelley, H. H. (1967). Attribution theory in social psychology. In D. Levine (Ed.), *Nebraska Symposium on Motivation, 1967.* Lincoln: University of Nebraska Press.

Kelley, H. H. (1973). The process of causal attribution. *American Psychologist, 28,* 107–128.

Kelling, G. L., & Coles, C. M. (1996). *Fixing broken windows.* New York: Touchstone.

Kelly, S., & Dunbar, R. I. M. (2001). Who dares, wins: Heroism versus altruism in women's mate choice. *Human Nature, 12,* 89–105.

Kelman, H. C., & Hamilton, V. L. (1989). *Crimes of obedience.* New Haven, CT: Yale University Press.

Keltner, D., & Anderson, C. (2000). Saving face for Darwin: The functions and uses of embarrassment. *Current Directions in Psychological Science, 9,* 187–192.

Keltner, D., & Buswell, B. N. (1997). Embarrassment: Its distinct form and appeasement functions. *Psychological Bulletin, 122,* 250–270.

Keltner, D., & Robinson, R. J. (1996). Extremism, power, and the imagined basis of social conflict. *Current Directions in Psychological Science, 5,* 101–105.

Keltner, N. L., & Boschini, D. J. (2009). Electroconvulsive therapy. *Perspectives in Psychiatric Care, 45,* 66–70.

Kemeny, M. E., & Schedlowski, M. (2007). Understanding the interaction between psychosocial stress and immune-related diseases: A stepwise progression. *Brain, Behavior, and Immunity, 21,* 1009–1018.

Kempermann, G., & Gage, F. H. (1999, May). New nerve cells for the adult brain. *Scientific American,* pp. 48–53.

Kendler, K. S. (1998). Major depression and the environment: A psychiatric genetic perspective. *Pharmacopsychiatry, 31,* 5–9.

Kendler, K. S., Gardner, C. O., & Pedersen, G. M. (2006). The sources of co-morbidity between major depression and generalized anxiety disorder in a Swedish national twin sample. *Psychological Medicine, 37,* 453–462.

Kendler, K. S., Kessler, R. C., Walters, E. E., MacLean, C., Neale, M. C., Heath, A., C., & Eaves, L. J. (1995). Stressful life events, genetic liability, and the onset of an episode of major depression in women. *American Journal of Psychiatry, 152,* 833–842.

Kendler, K. S., Kuhn, J. W., Vittum, J., Prescott, C. A., & Riley, B. (2005). The interaction of stressful life events and serotonin transporter polymorphism in the prediction of episodes of major depression. *Archives of General Psychiatry, 62,* 529–535.

Kendler, T. S. (1972). An ontogeny of mediational deficiency. *Child Development, 43,* 1–17.

Kendrick, K. M., Lévy, F., & Keverne, E. B. (1992). Changes in sensory processing of olfactory signals induced by birth in sheep. *Science, 256,* 833–836.

Kermoian, R., & Campos, J. J. (1988). Locomotor experience: A facilitator of spatial cognitive development. *Child Development, 59,* 908–917.

Kernberg, O. (1976). *Object relations theory and clinical psychoanalysis.* New York: Jason Aronson.

Kerns, J. G., & Berenbaum, H. (2002). Cognitive impairments associated with formal thought disorder in people with schizophrenia. *Journal of Abnormal Psychology, 111,* 211–224.

Keshavan, M. S., Gilbert, A. R., & Diwadkar, V. A. (2006). Neurodevelopmental theories. In J. A. Lieberman, T. S. Stroup, & D. O. Perkins (Eds.), *The American Psychiatric Publishing textbook of schizophrenia.* Washington, DC: American Psychiatric Publishing.

Keshavan, M. S., Tandon, R., Boutros, N. N., & Nasrallah, H. A. (2008). Schizophrenia, "just the facts": What we know in 2008. Part 3: Neurobiology. *Schizophrenia Research, 106,* 89–107.

Kessler, R. C. (1997). The effects of stressful life events on depression. *Annual Review of Psychology, 48,* 191–214.

Kessler, R. C., Berglund, P., Demler, O., Jin, R., Merikangas, K. R., & Walters, E. E. (2005). Lifetime prevalence and age-of-onset distributions of *DSM-IV* disorders in the national comorbidity survey replication. *Archives of General Psychiatry, 62,* 593–602.

Kety, S. S., Rosenthal, D., Wender, P. H., Schulsigner, F., & Jacobson, B. (1976). Mental illness in the biological and adoptive families of adopted individuals who have become schizophrenic. *Behavior Genetics, 6,* 219–225.

Khaled, N. (2004). Psychological effects of terrorist attacks in Algeria. *Journal of Aggression, Maltreatment & Trauma, 9,* 201–212.

Khorsroshahi, F. (1989). Penguins don't care, but women do: A social identity analysis of a Whorfian problem. *Language in Society, 18,* 505–525.

Kiang, L., Moreno, A. J., & Robinson, J. L. (2004). Maternal preconceptions about parenting predict child temperament, maternal sensitivity, and children's empathy. *Developmental Psychology, 40,* 1081–1092.

Kiehn, O. (2006). Locomotor circuits in the mammalian spinal cord. *Annual Review of Neuroscience, 29,* 279–306.

Kim, J., Rapee, R. M., & Gaston, J. E. (2008). Symptoms of offensive type *taijin-kyofusho* among Australian social phobics. *Depression and Anxiety, 25,* 601–608.

Kimberg, D. Y., D'Esposito, M., & Farah, M. J. (1997). Cognitive functions in the prefrontal cortex—working memory and executive control. *Current Directions in Psychological Science, 6,* 185–192.

King, D. W., King, L. A., Gudanowski, D. M., & Vreven, D. L. (1995). Alternative representations of war zone stressors: Relationships to posttraumatic stress disorder in male and female Vietnam veterans. *Journal of Abnormal Psychology, 104,* 184–196.

Kirmayer, L. J. (1991). The place of culture in psychiatric nosology: *Taijin kyofusho* and DSM-III-R. *Journal of Nervous and Mental Disease, 179,* 19–28.

Kirsch, I. (2000). Are drug and placebo effects in depression additive? *Biological Psychiatry, 47*, 733–735.

Kirsch, I. (2005). Medication and suggestion in the treatment of depression. *Contemporary Hypnosis, 22*, 59–66.

Kirsch, I., & Sapirstein, G. (1998). Listening to Prozac but hearing placebo: A meta-analysis of antidepressant medication. *Prevention and Treatment, 1*, Article 0002a.

Kirsch, I., Moore, T. J., Scoboria, A., & Nicholls, S. S. (2002). The emperor's new drugs: An analysis of antidepressant medication data submitted to the U.S. Food and Drug Administration. *Prevention & Treatment, 5.* Retrieved July 2005 from http://journals.apa.org/prevention.

Kirsch, I., Tennen, H., Wickless, C., Saccone, A. J., & Cody, S. (1983). The role of expectancy in fear reduction. *Behavior Therapy, 14*, 520–533.

Kisley, M. A., Wood, S., & Burrows, C. L. (2007). Looking at the sunny side of life: Age-related change in an event-related potential measure of the negativity bias. *Psychological Science, 18*, 838–843.

Kiuken, T., Miller, L. A., Lipschutz, R. D., Lock, B. A., Stubblefield, K., Marasco, P. D., Zhou, P., & Dumanian, G. A. (2007). Targeted reinnervation for enhanced prosthetic arm function in a woman with a proximal amputation: A case study. *Lancet, 369*, 371–380.

Klehe, U-C., Anderson, N., & Hoefnagels, E. A. (2007). Social facilitation and inhibition during maximal versus typical performance situations. *Human Performance, 20*, 223–239.

Klein, D. N., Schwartz, J. E., Santiago, N. J., Vivian, D., Vocisano, C., Castonguay, L. G., et al. (2003). Therapeutic alliance in depression treatment: Controlling for prior change and patient characteristics. *Journal of Consulting and Clinical Psychology, 71*, 997–1006.

Kleinman, A. (2004). Culture and depression. *New England Journal of Medicine, 351*, 951–954.

Klemm, W. R. (1990). Historical and introductory perspectives on brainstem-mediated behaviors. In W. R. Klemm & R. P. Vertes (Eds.), *Brainstem mechanisms of behavior.* New York: Wiley.

Klinke, R. (1986). Physiology of hearing. In R. F. Schmidt (Ed.), *Fundamentals of sensory physiology.* New York: Springer-Verlag.

Klose, M., & Jacobi, F. (2004). Can gender differences in the prevalence of mental disorders be explained by sociodemographic factors? *Archives of Women's Mental Health, 7*, 133–148.

Kluger, M. J. (1991). Fever: Role of pyrogens and cryogens. *Physiological Reviews, 71*, 93–127.

Klüver H., & Bucy, P. C. (1937). "Psychic blindness" and other symptoms following temporal lobectomy in rhesus monkeys. *American Journal of Physiology, 119*, 352–353.

Knafo, A., Zahn-Waxler, C., Hulle, C. V., Robinson, J. L., & Rhee, S. H. (2008). The developmental origins of a disposition toward empathy: Genetic and environmental contributions. *Emotion, 8*, 737–752.

Knowlton, B. J., Ramus, S. J., & Squire, L. R. (1992). Intact artificial grammar learning in amnesia: Dissociation of classification learning and explicit memory for specific instances. *Psychological Science, 3*, 172–179.

Knox, R. E., & Inkster, J. A. (1968). Postdecision dissonance at post time. *Journal of Personality and Social Psychology, 8*, 319–323.

Knudsen, E. I. (2007). Fundamental components of attention. *Annual Review of Neuroscience, 30*, 57–78.

Knutson, B., Adams, C. M., Fong, G. W., & Hommer, D. (2001). Anticipation of increasing monetary reward selectively recruits nucleus accumbens. *The Journal of Neuroscience, 21:RC159*, 1–5.

Kobayashi, M. (2006). Functional organization of the human gustatory cortex. *Journal of Oral Biosciences, 48*, 244–260.

Kochanska, G., Aksan, N., Prisco, T. R., & Adams, E. E. (2008). Mother-child and father-child mutually responsive orientation in the first 2 years and children's outcomes at preschool age: Mechanisms of influence. *Child Development, 79*, 30–44.

Kochanska, G., Gross, J. N., Lin, M., & Nichols, K. E. (2002). Guilt in young children: Development, determinants, and relations with a broader system of standards. *Child Development, 73*, 461–482.

Kochanska, G., Tjebkes, T. L., & Forman, D. R. (1998). Children's emerging regulation of conduct: Restraint, compliance, and internalization from infancy to the second year. *Child Development, 69*, 1378–1389.

Koffka, K. (1935). *Principles of Gestalt psychology.* New York: Harcourt Brace Jovanovich.

Kohlberg, L. (1966). A cognitive-developmental analysis of children's sex-role concepts and attitudes. In E. E. Maccoby (Ed.), *The development of sex differences.* Stanford, CA: Stanford University Press.

Kohlberg, L. (1984). *The psychology of moral development.* San Francisco: Harper & Row.

Kohlberg, L., Yaeger, J., & Hjertholm, E. (1968). Private speech: Four studies and a review of theories. *Child Development, 39*, 691–736.

Kohler, R. (2008). *Jean Piaget.* New York: Continuum International Publishing Group.

Kohn, M. L. (1980). Job complexity and adult personality. In N. J. Smelser & E. H. Erikson (Eds.), *Theories of work and love in adulthood.* Cambridge, MA: Harvard University Press.

Kohn, M. L., & Slomczynski, K. M. (1990). *Social structure and self-direction: A comparative analysis of the United States and Poland.* Cambridge, MA: Basil Blackwell.

Koivisto, M., & Revonsuo, A. (2007). How meaning shapes seeing. *Psychological Science, 18*, 845–849.

Kolassa, I-T., & Elbert, T. (2007). Structural and functional neuroplasticity in relation to traumatic stress. *Current Trends in Psychological Science, 16*, 321–325.

Kolb, B., & Whishaw, I. Q. (2003). *Fundamentals of human neuropsychology* (5th ed.). New York: Worth.

Kolb, B., & Whishaw, I. Q. (2009). *Fundamentals of human neuropsychology* (6th ed.). New York: Worth.

Kolev, G. (2008). The stock market bubble, shareholders' attribution bias and excessive top CEO pay. *Journal of Behavioral Finance, 9*, 62–71.

Komorita, S. S., & Parks, C. D. (1999). Reciprocity and cooperation in social dilemmas: Review and future directions. In D. B. Budescu, I. Erev, & R. Zwick (Eds.), *Games and human behavior: Essays in honor of Amnon Rapaport.* Mahwah, NJ: Erlbaum.

Konen, C. S., & Kastner, S. (2008). Two hierarchically organized neural systems for object information in human visual cortex. *Nature Neuroscience, 11*, 224–231.

Konner, M. (1972). Aspects of the developmental ethology of a foraging people. In N. G. Blurton-Jones (Ed.), *Ethological studies of child behavior.* Cambridge, England: Cambridge University Press.

Konner, M. (2005). Hunter-gatherer infancy and childhood: The !Kung and others. In B. S. Hewlett & M. E. Lamb (Eds.), *Hunter-gatherer childhoods: Evolutionary, developmental, and cultural perspectives.* New Brunswick, NJ: Transaction Publishers.

Konner, M. J. (1975). Relations among infants and juveniles in comparative perspective. In M. Lewis & L. A. Rosenblum (Eds.), *The origins of behavior: Vol. 4. Friendship and peer relations.* New York: Wiley.

Konner, M. J. (1976). Maternal care, infant behavior and development among the !Kung. In R. B. Lee & I. DeVore (Eds.), *Kalahari hunter-gatherers: Studies of the !Kung San and their neighbors.* Cambridge, MA: Harvard University Press.

Konner, M. J. (2002). *The tangled wing: Biological constraints on the human spirit* (2nd ed.). New York: Henry Holt.

Koodsma, D. E., & Byers, B. E. (1991). The functions of bird song. *American Zoologist, 31*, 318–328.

Koop, G. F., Everitt, B. J., & Robbins, T. W. (2008). Reward, motivation, and addiction. In L. Squire, D. Berg, F. Bloom, S. du Lac, A. Ghosh, & N. Spitzer (Eds.), *Fundamental neuroscience,* 3rd ed. Boston: Elsevier.

Korner, J., & Leibel, R. L. (2003). To eat or not to eat—how the gut talks to the brain. *New England Journal of Medicine, 349,* 926–928.

Kornhuber, H. H. (1974). Cerebral cortex, cerebellum and basal ganglia: An introduction to their motor functions. In F. O. Schmitt & F. G. Worden (Eds.), *The neurosciences: Third study program.* Cambridge, MA: MIT Press.

Koss, M. P. (1990). The women's mental health research agenda: Violence against women. *American Psychologist, 45,* 374–380.

Kosslyn, S. M. (1973). Scanning visual images: Some structural implications. *Perception and Psychophysics, 14,* 90–94.

Kosslyn, S. M. (1980). *Image and mind.* Cambridge, MA: Harvard University Press.

Kosslyn, S. M., & Koenig, O. (1992). *Wet mind: The new cognitive neuroscience.* New York: Free Press.

Kozlowska, K. (2001). Good children presenting with conversion disorder. *Clinical Child Psychology and Psychiatry, 6,* 575–591.

Kozlowska, K. (2003). Good children with conversion disorder: Breaking the silence. *Clinical Child Psychology and Psychiatry, 8,* 73–90.

Kraemer, G. W. (1992). A psychobiological theory of attachment. *Behavioral and Brain Sciences, 15,* 493–541.

Kramer, M. D., Krueger, R. F., & Hicks, B. M. (2008). The role of internalizing and externalizing liability factors in accounting for gender differences in the prevalence of common psychopathological syndromes. *Psychological Medicine, 38,* 51–61.

Kramer, R. M., & Brewer, M. B. (1984). Effect of group identity on resource use in a simulated common dilemma. *Journal of Personality and Social Psychology, 46,* 1044–1057.

Kraus, N., & Banai, K. (2007). Auditory-processing malleability. *Current Directions in Psychological Science, 16,* 105–110.

Krem, M. M. (2004). Motor conversion disorders reviewed from a neuropsychiatric perspective. *Journal of Clinical Psychiatry, 65,* 783–790.

Krijn, M., Emmelkamp, P. M. G., Olafsson, R. P., & Biemond, R. (2004). Virtual reality exposure therapy of anxiety disorders: A review. *Clinical Psychology Review, 24,* 259–281.

Krishnan, V., & Nestler, E. J. (2008). The molecular neurobiology of depression. *Nature, 455,* 894–902.

Kruger, A. C. (1992). The effect of peer and adult-child transactive discussions on moral reasoning. *Merrill-Palmer Quarterly, 38,* 191–211.

Kruger, D. J., Fisher, M., & Jobling, I. (2003). Proper and dark heroes as dads and cads: Alternative mating strategies in British romantic literature. *Human Nature, 14,* 305–317.

Kryter, K. D. (1985). *The effects of noise on man* (2nd ed.). Orlando, FL: Academic Press.

Kübler-Ross, E. (1969). *On death and dying.* New York: Macmillan.

Kuczaj, S. A. (1977). The acquisition of regular and irregular past tense forms. *Journal of Verbal Learning and Verbal Behavior, 16,* 589–600.

Kuhl, P. K., Conboy, B. T., Coffey-Corina, S., Padden, D., Rivera-Gaxiola, M., & Nelson, T. (2008). Phonetic learning as a pathway to language: New data and native language magnet theory expanded (NLM-e). *Philosophical Transactions of the Royal Society B, 363,* 979–1000.

Kuhl, P. K., Conboy, B. T., Padden, D., Nelson, T., & Pruitt, J. (2005). Early speech perception and later language development: Implications for the "critical period." *Language Learning and Development, 1,* 237–264.

Kukekova, A., Trut, L. N., Chase, K., Shepeleva, D. V., Vladimirova, A. V., Kharlamova, A. V., Oskina, I. N., Stepika, A., Klebanov, S., Erb, H. N., & Acland, G. M. (2008). Measurement of segregating behaviors in experimental silver fox pedigrees. *Behavior Genetics, 38,* 185–194.

Kuncel, N. R., & Hezlett, S. A. (2007). Standardized tests predict graduate students' success. *Science, 315,* 1080–1081.

Kuncel, N. R., Hezlett, S. A., & Ones, D. S. (2004). Academic performance, career potential, creativity, and job performance: Can one construct predict them all? *Journal of Personality and Social Psychology, 86,* 148–161.

Kurihara, K., & Kashiwayanagi, M. (1998). Introductory remarks on umami taste. *Annals of the New York Academy of Sciences, 855,* 393–397.

Kurland, J. A. (1979). Paternity, mother's brother, and human sociality. In N. A. Chagnon & W. Irons (Eds.), *Evolutionary biology and human social behavior: An anthropological perspective.* North Scituate, MA: Duxbury Press.

Kuther, T. L., & Higgins-D'Alessandro, A. (2000). Bridging the gap between moral reasoning and adolescent engagement in risky behavior. *Journal of Adolescence, 23,* 409–422.

Lachter, J., Forster, K. I., & Ruthruff, E. (2004). Forty-five years after Broadbent (1958): Still no identification without attention. *Psychological Review, 111,* 880–913.

Lack, D. (1968). *Ecological adaptations for breeding in birds.* London: Methuen.

Lack, L., Wright, H., & Paynter, D. (2007). The treatment of sleep onset insomnia with bright morning light. *Sleep and Biological Rhythms, 5,* 173–179.

Laeng, B., & Teodorescu, D.-S. (2002). Eye scanpaths during visual imagery reenact those of perception of the same scene. *Cognitive Science, 26,* 207–231.

Lahti, J., Räikkönen, K., Ekelund, J., Peltonen, L., Raitakari, O. T., & Keltikangas-Järvinen, L. (2006). Socio-demographic characteristics moderate the association between DRD4 and novelty seeking. *Personality and Individual Differences, 40,* 533–543.

Lakin, J. L., & Chartrand, T. L. (2003). Using nonconscious behavioral mimicry to create affiliation and rapport. *Psychological Science, 14,* 334–339.

Lalumière, M. L., Quinsey, V. L., & Craig, W. M. (1996). Why children from the same family are so different from one another: A Darwinian note. *Human Nature, 7,* 281–290.

Lamb, H. R. (2000). Deinstitutionalization and public policy. In R. W. Menninger & J. C. Nemiah (Eds.), *American psychiatry after World War II.* Washington, DC: American Psychiatric Press.

Lamb, M. E., & Hewlett, B. S. (2005). Reflections on hunter-gatherer childhoos. In B. S. Hewlett & M. E. Lamb (Eds.), *Hunter-gatherer childhoods: Evolutionary, developmental, and cultural perspectives.* New Brunswick, NJ: Transaction Publishers.

Lamb, T. D., Collin, S. P., & Pugh, E. N. (2007). Evolution of the vertebrate eye: Opsins, photoreceptors, retina and eye cup. *Nature Reviews Neuroscience, 8,* 960–975.

Lamberg, L. (2004). Efforts to keep mentally ill out of jails. *Journal of the American Medical Association, 292,* 555–556.

Lambert, M. J., & Ogles, B. M. (2004). The efficacy and effectiveness of psychotherapy. In M. J. Lambert (Ed.), *Bergin and Garfield's handbook of psychotherapy and change* (5th ed.). New York: Wiley.

Lancaster, J. B. (1971). Play-mothering: The relations between juvenile females and young infants among free-ranging vervet monkeys (*Cercopithecus aethiops*). *Folia Primatologica, 15,* 161–182.

Land, M. F., & Furnald, R. D. (1992). The evolution of eyes. *Annual Review of Neuroscience, 15,* 1–29.

Landrum, E., Davis, S., & Landrum, T. (2007). *The psychology major: Career options and strategies for success* (3rd ed.). Upper Saddle River, NJ: Prentice-Hall.

Langer, E. J., Blank, A., & Chanowitz, B. (1978). The mindlessness of ostensibly thoughtful action. *Journal of Personality and Social Psychology, 36,* 635–642.

Langlois, J. H., Kalakanis, L., Rubenstein, J., Larson, A., Hallam, M., & Smoot, M. (2000). Maxims or myths of beauty? A meta-analytic and theoretical review. *Psychological Bulletin, 126,* 390–423.

Larsen, R. J., & Buss, D. M. (2008). *Personality psychology: Domains of knowledge about human nature* (3rd ed.). New York: McGraw-Hill.

Larson, P. S. (2008). Deep brain stimulation for psychiatric disorders. *Neurotherapeutics, 5,* 50–58.

Larson, R. W., Richards, M. H., & Perry-Jenkins M. (1994). Divergent worlds: The daily and emotional experience of mothers and fathers in the domestic and public spheres. *Journal of Personality and Social Psychology, 67,* 1034–1046.

Latané, B., & Nida, S. (1981). Ten years of research on group size and helping. *Psychological Bulletin, 89,* 308–324.

Latané, B., & Rodin, J. (1969). A lady in distress: Inhibiting effects of friends and strangers on bystander intervention. *Journal of Experimental Social Psychology, 5,* 189–202.

Lauer, J., & Lauer, R. (1985, June). Marriages made to last. *Psychology Today,* pp. 22–26.

Laursen, B., Pulkkinen, L., & Adams, R. (2002). The antecedents and correlates of agreeableness in adulthood. *Developmental Psychology, 38,* 591–603.

Lavelli, M., & Fogel, A. (2005). Developmental changes in the relationship between the infant's attention and emotion during early face-to-face communication: The 2-month transition. *Developmental Psychology, 41,* 265–280.

Lawrie, S. M., McIntosh, A. M., Hall, J., Owens, D. G. C., & Johnstone, E. C. (2008). Brain structure and function changes during the development of schizophrenia: The evidence from studies of subjects at increased genetic risk. *Schizophrenia Bulletin, 34,* 330–340.

Lazarus, J., Inglis, I. R., & Torrance, R. L. L. F. (2004). Mate guarding conflict, extra-pair courtship and signaling in the harlequin duck. *Histrionicus histrionicus. Behaviour, 141,* 1061–1078.

Lazarus, R. S. (1993). From psychological stress to the emotions: A history of changing outlooks. *Annual Review of Psychology, 44,* 1–21.

Leana, C. R. (1985). A partial test of Janis' groupthink model. Effects of group cohesiveness and leader behavior on defective decision making. *Journal of Management, 11,* 5–17.

Leary, M. R. (1999). Making sense of self-esteem. *Current Directions in Psychological Science, 8,* 32–35.

Leary, M. R. (2005). Sociometer theory and the pursuit of relational value: Getting to the root of self-esteem. *European Review of Social Psychology, 16,* 75–111.

Leary, M. R., & Baumeister, R. F. (2000). The nature and function of self-esteem: Sociometer theory. In M. Zanna (Ed.), *Advances in experimental social psychology* (Vol. 32, pp. 1–62). San Diego, CA: Academic Press.

Leary, M. R., Cottrell, C. A., & Phillips, M. (2001). Deconfounding the effects of dominance and social acceptance on self-esteem. *Journal of Personality and Social Psychology, 81,* 898–909.

Leary, M. R., & Kowalski, R. M. (1995). *Social anxiety.* New York: Guilford.

LeDoux, J. E. (1996). *The emotional brain: The mysterious underpinnings of emotional life.* New York: Simon & Schuster.

LeDoux, J. E., Romanski, L., & Xagoraris, A. (1989). Indelibility of subcortical emotional memories. *Journal of Cognitive Neuroscience, 1,* 238–243.

Lee, J. L. C. (2008). Memory reconsolidation mediates the strengthening of memories by additional learning. *Nature Neuroscience, 11,* 1264–1266.

Lee, S., & Kleinman, A. (2007). Are somatoform disorders changing with time? The case of neurasthenia in China. *Psychosomatic Medicine, 69,* 846–849.

Lee, T. S. (2002). Top-down influence in early visual processing: A Bayesian perspective. *Physiology and Behavior, 77,* 645–650.

LeFever, G. B., Arcone, A. P., & Antonuccio, D. O. (2003). ADHD among American schoolchildren. *The Scientific Review of Mental Health Practice, 2,* 49–60.

Lehman, A. F., Steinwachs, D. M., & survey co-investigators of the PORT project. (1998). Patterns of usual care for schizophrenia: Initial results from the schizophrenia patient outcomes research team (PORT) client survey. *Schizophrenia Bulletin, 24,* 11–20.

Lehman, D. R., Chiu, C., & Schaller, M. (2004). Psychology and culture. *Annual Review of Psychology, 55,* 689–714.

Leibel, R. L., Rosenbaum, M., & Hirsch, J. (1995). Changes in energy expenditure resulting from altered body weight. *New England Journal of Medicine, 332,* 621–628.

Leith, K. P., & Baumeister, R. F. (1998). Empathy, shame, guilt, and narratives of interpersonal conflicts: Guilt-prone people are better at perspective taking. *Journal of Personality, 66,* 1–37.

Lemon, R. N. (2008). Descending pathways in motor cortex. *Annual Review of Neuroscience, 31,* 195–218.

Lenneberg, E. H. (1969). *Biological foundations of language.* New York: Wiley.

Leonard, B., & McNaughton, B. L. (1990). Spatial representation in the rat: Conceptual, behavioral and neurophysiological perspectives. In R. P. Kenser & D. S. Olton (Eds.), *Neurobiology of comparative cognition.* Hillsdale, NJ: Erlbaum.

Lepper, M. R., & Greene, D. (1978). Overjustification research and beyond: Toward a means-end analysis of intrinsic and extrinsic motivation. In M. R. Lepper & D. Greene (Eds.), *The hidden costs of reward: New perspectives on the psychology of human motivation.* New York: Wiley.

Lerner, M. R., Gyorgyi, T. K., Reagan, J., Roby-Shemkovitz, A., Rybczynski, R., & Vogt, R. (1990). Peripheral events in moth olfaction. *Chemical Senses, 15,* 191–198.

Lesch, K. P. (2003). Neuroticism and serotonin: A developmental genetic perspective. In R. Plomin, J. C. Defries, I. W. Craig, & P. McGuffin (Eds.), *Behavioral genetics in the postgenomic era.* Washington, DC: American Psychological Association.

Leslie, A. M. (1987). Pretense and representation: The origins of "theory of mind." *Psychological Review, 94,* 412–426.

Leslie, A. M. (1991). The theory of mind impairment in autism: Evidence for a modular mechanism of development? In A. Whiten (Ed.), *Natural theories of mind: Evolution, development and simulation of everyday mindreading.* Cambridge, MA: Basil Blackwell.

Leslie, A. M. (1994). Pretending and believing: Issues in the theory of ToMM. *Cognition, 50,* 211–238.

Leslie, A. M., & Thaiss, L. (1992). Domain specificity in conceptual development: Neuropsychological evidence from autism. *Cognition, 43,* 225–251.

Levenson, R. W. (1992). Autonomic nervous system differences among emotions. *Psychological Science, 3,* 23–27.

Levenson, R. W., Carstensen, L. L., & Gottman, J. M. (1993). Long-term marriage: Age, gender, and satisfaction. *Psychology and Aging, 8,* 301–313.

Levenson, R. W., Ekman, P., Heider, K., & Friesen, W. V. (1992). Emotion and autonomic nervous system activity in the Minangkabau of West Sumatra. *Journal of Personality and Social Psychology, 62,* 972–988.

Levine, J. D., Gordon, N. C., & Fields, H. L., (1979). The role of endorphins in placebo analgesia. *Advances in Pain Research and Therapy, 3,* 547–550.

Levine, K., Shane, H. C., & Wharton, R. H. (1994). What if . . . : A plea to professionals to consider the risk-benefit ratio of facilitated communication. *Mental Retardation, 31,* 300–307.

Levinger, G., & Schneider, D. J. (1969). Test of the "risk is a value" hypothesis. *Journal of Personality and Social Psychology, 11*, 165–169.

Levinson, D. F. (2009). Genetics of major depression. In I. H. Gotlib & C. L. Hammen (Eds.), *Handbook of depression* (2nd ed.). New York: Guilford.

Levinson, D. J. (1978). *The seasons of a man's life.* New York: Ballantine.

Levinson, D. J. (1986). The conception of adult development. *American Psychologist, 41*, 3–13.

Levinson, S. C. (1997). Language and cognition: The cognitive consequences of spatial description in Guugu Yimithirr. *Journal of Linguistic Anthropology, 7*, 98–131.

Levinson, S. C. (2003). *Space in language and cognition: Explorations in cognitive diversity.* Cambridge, England: Cambridge University Press.

Levy, D. A., Stark, C. E. L., & Squire, L. R. (2004). Intact conceptual priming in the absence of declarative memory. *Psychological Science, 15*, 680–683.

Lewicka, M. (1998). Confirmation bias: Cognitive error or adaptive strategy of action control? In M. Kofta, G. Weary, & G. Sedek (Eds.), *Personal control in action: Cognitive and motivational mechanisms.* New York: Plenum.

Lewis, D. A., & Levitt, P. (2002). Schizophrenia as a disorder of neurodevelopment. *Annual Review of Neuroscience, 25*, 409–432.

Lewis, J. W., Cannon, J. T., & Liebeskind, J. C. (1980). Opioid and nonopioid mechanisms of stress analgesia. *Science, 208*, 623–625.

Lewis, M. (1991). Self-conscious emotions and the development of self. *Journal of the American Psychoanalytic Association (Supplement), 39*, 45–73.

Lewis, M. (1995). Embarrassment: The emotion of self-exposure and evaluation. In J. P. Tangney & K. W. Fischer (Eds.), *Self-conscious emotions: The psychology of shame, guilt, embarrassment, and pride.* New York: Guilford.

Lewis, M., & Brooks-Gunn, J. (1979). *Social cognition and the acquisition of self.* New York: Plenum Press.

Lewis, M., & Ramsay, D. (2004). Development of self-recognition, personal pronoun use, and pretend play during the 2nd year. *Child Development, 75*, 1821–1831.

Lewis, M., Alessandri, S. M., & Sullivan, M. W. (1990). Violation of expectancy, loss of control, and anger expressions in young infants. *Developmental Psychology, 26*, 745–751.

Li, S., Naveh-Benjamin, M., & Lindenberger, U. (2005). Aging neuromodulation impairs associative binding: A neurocomputational account. *Psychological Science, 16*, 445–450.

Li, W. Moallem, I., Paller, K. A., & Gottfried, J. A. (2007). Subliminal smells can guide social preferences. *Psychological Science, 18*, 1044–1049.

Li, W., Howard, J. D., Parrish, T. B., & Gottfried, J. A. (2008). Aversive learning enhances perceptual and cortical discrimination of indiscriminable odor cues. *Science, 319*, 1842–1845.

Lichtman, A. H., & Fanselow, M. S. (1990). Cats produce analgesia in rats on the tail-flick test: Naltrexone sensitivity is determined by the nociceptive test stimulus. *Brain Research, 553*, 91–94.

Lickey, M. E., & Gordon, B. (1991). *Medicine and mental illness: The use of drugs in psychiatry.* New York: Freeman.

Lieberman, D. A. (2000). *Learning: Behavior and cognition* (3rd. ed.). Belmont, CA: Wadsworth.

Lieberman, P. (2007). The evolution of human speech: Its anatomical and neural bases. *Current Anthropology, 48*, 39–66.

Lillard, A. S., & Flavell, J. H. (1990). Young children's preference for mental state versus behavioral descriptions of human action. *Child Development, 61*, 731–741.

Lillard, A. S., & Flavell, J. H. (1992). Young children's understanding of different mental states. *Developmental Psychology, 28*, 626–634.

Lima, S. L., Rattenborg, N. C., Lesku, J. A., & Amlaner, C. J. (2005). Sleeping under the risk of predation. *Animal Behaviour, 70*, 723–736.

Lin, E. H., & Church, A. T. (2004). Are indigenous Chinese personality dimensions culture-specific? An investigation of the Chinese Personality Assessment Inventory in Chinese American and European American samples. *Journal of Cross-Cultural Psychology, 35*, 586–605.

Lin, K., & Kleinman, A. M. (1988). Psychopathology and clinical course of schizophrenia: A cross-cultural perspective. *Schizophrenia Bulletin, 14*, 555–567.

Lindberg, S. M., Hyde, J. S., & Hirsch, L. M. (2008). Gender and mother-child interactions during mathematics homework: The importance of individual differences. *Merrill-Palmer Quarterly, 54*, 232–255.

Linder, D. E., Cooper, J., & Jones, E. E. (1967). Decision freedom as a determinant of the role of incentive magnitude in attitude change. *Journal of Personality and Social Psychology, 6*, 245–254.

Lindsay, D. S. (2008). Source monitoring. In J. Byrne (Series Ed.) & H. L. Roediger, III (Vol. Ed.), *Learning and memory: A comprehensive reference: Vol. 2. Cognitive psychology of memory.* Oxford, England: Elsevier.

Lindsay, P. H., & Norman, D. A. (1977). *Human information processing* (2nd ed.). New York: Academic Press.

Lipman, R. S. (1989). Pharmacotherapy of the anxiety disorders. In S. Fischer & R. P. Greenberg (Eds.), *The limits of biological treatments for psychological distress: Comparisons with psychotherapy and placebo.* Hillsdale, NJ: Erlbaum.

Lippmann, W. (1922; reprinted 1960). *Public opinion.* New York: Macmillan.

Lisanby, S. H. (2007). Electroconvulsive therapy for depression. *New England Journal of Medicine, 357*, 1939–1945.

Litt, M. D. (1988). Self-efficacy and perceived control: Cognitive mediators of pain tolerance. *Journal of Personality and Social Psychology, 54*, 149–160.

Livingston, R. W., & Drwecki, B. B. (2007). Why are some individuals not racially biased? *Psychological Science, 18*, 816–823.

Livingstone, D. (1857). *Missionary travels and researches in South Africa.* London: John Murray.

Locke, J. (1690; reprinted 1975). *An essay concerning human understanding* (P. Nidditch, Ed.). Oxford: Clarendon.

Locke, J. L. (1983). *Phonological acquisition and change.* New York: Academic Press.

Löckenhoff, C. E., & Carstensen, L. L. (2004). Socioemotional selectivity theory, aging, and health: The increasingly delicate balance between regulating emotions and making tough choices. *Journal of Personality, 72*, 1395–1424.

Lockman, J. J., & McHale, J. P. (1989). Object manipulation in infancy: Developmental and contextual determinants. In J. L. Lockman & N. Hazen (Eds.), *Action in social context: Perspectives on early development.* New York: Plenum Press.

Locksley, A., Ortiz, V., & Hepburn, C. (1980). Social categorization and discriminatory behavior: Extinguishing the minimal intergroup discrimination effect. *Journal of Personality and Social Psychology, 39*, 773–783.

Loehlin, J. C. (1992). *Genes and environment in personality development.* Newbury Park, CA: Sage.

Loehlin, J. C., Vandenberg, S., & Osborne, R. (1973). Blood group genes and Negro-White ability differences. *Behavior Genetics, 3*, 263–270.

Loehlin, J. C., Willerman, L., & Horn, J. M. (1988). Human behavior genetics. *Annual Review of Psychology, 39*, 101–133.

Loftus, E. F. (1992). When a lie becomes memory's truth: Memory distortion after exposure to misinformation. *Current Directions in Psychological Science, 1*, 121–123.

Loftus, E. F. (1997). Memory for a past that never was. *Current Directions in Psychological Science, 6*, 60–65.

Loftus, E. F. (2004). Memories for things unseen. *Current Directions in Psychological Science, 13*, 145–147.

Loftus, E. F., & Palmer, J. C. (1974). Reconstruction of automobile destruction: An example of the interaction between language and memory. *Journal of Verbal Learning and Verbal Behavior, 13*, 585–589.

Loftus, E. F., & Pickrell, J. E. (1995). The formation of false memories. *Psychiatric Annals, 25*, 720–725.

Logothetis, N. K. (2008). What we can and what we cannot do with fMRI. *Nature, 453*, 869–878.

Logue, A. W. (1988). A comparison of taste aversion learning in humans and other vertebrates: Evolutionary pressures in common. In R. C. Bolles & M. D. Beecher (Eds.), *Evolution and learning.* Hillsdale, NJ: Erlbaum.

Loidolt, M., Aust, U., Meran, I., & Huber, L. (2003). Pigeons use item-specific and category-level information in the identification and categorization of human faces. *Journal of Experimental Psychology: Animal Behavior Processes, 29*, 261–276.

Lombar, S. G., & Malhotra, S. (2008). Double dissociation of 'what' and 'where' processing in auditory cortex. *Nature Neuroscience, 11*, 609–616.

López, H. H., & Ettenberg, A. (2002). Sexually conditioned incentives: Attenuation of motivational impact during dopamine receptor antagonism. *Pharmacology, Biochemistry, and Behavior, 72*, 65–72.

López, S. R., & Guarnaccia, P. J. (2005). Cultural dimensions of psychopathology: The social world's impact on mental illness. In J. Maddux & B. Winstead (Eds.), *Psychopathology: Foundations for a contemporary understanding.* Mahwah, NJ: Erlbaum.

Lorenz, K. (1935; reprinted 1970). Companions as factors in the bird's environment (R. Martin, Trans.). In K. Lorenz (Ed.), *Studies in animal and human behavior* (Vol. 1). Cambridge, MA: Harvard University Press.

Lorenz, K. Z. (1943). Die angeborenen Formen möglicher Erfahrung. *Zeitschrift für Tierpsychologie, 5*, 235–409.

Lorenz, K. Z. (1971). *Studies in animal and human behavior* (Vol. 2). Cambridge, MA: Harvard University Press.

Lorenz, K. Z. (1974). Analogy as a source of knowledge. *Science, 185*, 229–234.

Lozoff, B., Wolf, A. W., & Davis, N. S. (1984). Cosleeping in urban families with young children in the United States. *Pediatrics, 74*, 171–182.

Luo, C. R. (1999). Semantic competition as the basis of Stroop Interference: Evidence from color-word matching tasks. *Psychological Science, 10*, 35–40.

Luria, A. R. (1971). Towards the problem of the historical nature of psychological processes. *International Journal of Psychology, 6*, 259–272.

Lyn, H. (2007). Mental representation of symbols as revealed by vocabulary errors in two bonobos (*Pan paniscus*). *Animal Cognition, 10*, 461–475.

Lynn, B. L., & Perl, E. R. (1996). Afferent mechanisms of pain. In L. Kruger (Ed.), *Pain and touch.* San Diego, CA: Academic Press.

Lynn, S. J., Lock, T. G., Myers, B., & Payne, D. G. (1997). Recalling the unrecallable: Should hypnosis be used to recover memories in psychotherapy? *Current Directions in Psychological Science, 6*, 79–83.

Maccoby, E. E. (1990). Gender and relationships: A developmental account. *American Psychologist, 45*, 513–520.

Maccoby, E. E. (1998). *The two sexes: Growing up apart, coming together.* Cambridge, MA: Harvard University Press.

Maccoby, E. E. (2002). Gender and group process: A developmental perspective. *Current Directions in Psychological Science, 11*, 54–58.

Maccoby, E. E., & Jacklin, C. N. (1987). Gender segregation in childhood. In H. W. Reese (Ed.), *Advances in child development and behavior* (Vol. 20). Orlando, FL: Academic Press.

MacDonald, G., & Leary, M. R. (2005). Why does social exclusion hurt? The relationship between social and physical pain. *Psychological Bulletin, 131*, 202–223.

MacDonald, K. (1992). Warmth as a developmental construct: An evolutionary analysis. *Child Development, 63*, 753–773.

Macfarlane, A. J. (1975). Olfaction in the development of social preferences in the human neonate. *Ciba Foundation Symposium, 33*, 103–117.

Mack, A., Pappas, Z., Silverman, M., & Gay, R. (2002). What we see: Inattention and the capture of attention by meaning. *Consciousness and Cognition, 11*, 488–506.

MacKay, D. G. (1973). Aspects of the theory of comprehension, memory and attention. *Quarterly Journal of Experimental Psychology, 25*, 22–40.

MacKay, D. G. (1980). Psychology, prescriptive grammar, and the pronoun problem. *American Psychologist, 35*, 444–449.

Mackintosh, N. J., & Dickinson, A. (1979). Instrumental (Type II) conditioning. In A. Dickinson & R. A. Boakes (Eds.), *Mechanisms of learning and motivation.* Hillsdale, NJ: Erlbaum.

Macknik, S. L., King, M., Randi, J., Robbins, A., Teller, Thompson, J., & Martinez-Conde, S. (2008). Attention and awareness in stage magic: Turning tricks into research. *Nature Reviews Neuroscience, 9*, 871–879.

MacWhinney, B. (1998). Models of the emergence of language. *Annual Review of Psychology, 49*, 1999–2227.

Maddux, J. E., Gosselin, J. T., & Winstead, B. A. (2005). Conceptions of psychopathology: A social constructionist perspective. In J. Maddux & B. Winstead (Eds.), *Psychopathology: Foundations for a contemporary understanding.* Mahwah, NJ: Erlbaum.

Magendie, F. (1822). Expériences sur les fonctions des racines des nerfs rachidiens. *Journal de Physiologie Expérimentale et Pathologique, 2*, 276–279.

Magistretti, P. J. (2008). Brain energy metabolism. In L. Squire, D. Berg, F. Bloom, S. du Lac, A. Ghosh, & N. Spitzer (Eds.), *Fundamental neuroscience.* New York: Elsevier.

Magnhagen, C., & Staffan, F. (2005). Is boldness affected by group composition in young-of-the-year perch (*Perca fluviatilis*)? *Behavioral Ecology and Sociobiology, 57*, 295–303.

Maguire, E. A., Gadian, D. G., Johnsrude, I. S., Good, C. D., Ashburner, J., Frackowiak, R. S. J., et al. (2000). Navigation-related structural change in the hippocampi of taxi drivers. *Proceedings of the National Academy of Sciences, 97*, 4398–4403.

Maguire, E. A., Valentine, E. R., Wilding, J. M., & Kapur, N. (2003). Routes to remembering: The brains behind superior memory. *Nature Neuroscience, 6*, 90–95.

Maier, S. F., Watkins, L. R., & Fleshner, M. (1994). Psychoneuroimmunology: The interface between behavior, brain, and immunity. *American Psychologist, 49*, 1004–1017.

Majid, A., Bowerman, M., Kita, S., Haun, D. B. M., & Levinson, S. C. (2004). Can language restructure cognition? The case for space. *Trends in Cognitive Sciences, 8*, 108–114.

Malcolm, J. R. (1985). Paternal care in Canids. *American Zoologist, 25*, 853–859.

Malle, B. F. (2006). The actor-observer asymmetry in attribution: A (surprising) meta-analysis. *Psychological Bulletin, 132*, 895–919.

Malle, B. F., Knobe, J., O'Laughlin, M. J., Pearce, G. E., & Nelson, S. E. (2000). Conceptual structure and social functions of behavioral explanations: Beyond person-situation attributions. *Journal of Personality and Social Psychology, 79*, 309–326.

Maltz, D. N., & Borker, R. A. (1982). A cultural approach to male-female miscommunication. In J. J. Gumperz (Ed.), *Language and social identify.* Cambridge, England: Cambridge University Press.

Maner, J. K., & Shackelford, T. K. (2008). The basic cognition of jealousy: An evolutionary perspective. *European Journal of Personality, 22*, 31–36.

Mäntylä, T. (1986). Optimizing cue effectiveness: Recall of 500 and 600 incidentally learned words. *Journal of Experimental Psychology: Learning, Memory, and Cognition, 12*, 66–71.

Marcus, G. F., & Fisher, S. E. (2003). *FOXP2* in focus: What can genes tell us about speech and language? *Trends in Cognitive Science, 7,* 257–262.

Marcus, G. F., Pinker, S., Ullman, M., Hollander, M., Rosen, T. J., & Xu, F. (1992). Overregularization in language acquisition. *Monographs of the Society for Research in Child Development, 57.*

Maren, S. (1999). Long-term potentiation in the amygdala: A mechanism for emotional learning and memory. *Trends in Neuroscience, 22,* 561–567.

Marks, I. M. (1987). *Fears, phobias, and rituals: Panic, anxiety, and their disorders.* New York: Oxford University Press.

Markus, H. R., & Kitayama, S. (1991). Culture and the self: Implications for cognition, emotion and motivation. *Psychological Review, 98,* 224–253.

Markus, H. R., & Kitayama, S. (1994). A collective fear of the collective: Implications for selves and theories of selves. *Personality and Social Psychology Bulletin, 20,* 568–579.

Marler, P. (1970). A comparative approach to vocal learning. Song development in white-crowned sparrows. *Journal of Comparative and Physiological Psychology, 7,* 1–25.

Marlowe, F. (2000). Paternal investment and the human mating system. *Behavioural Processes, 51,* 45–61.

Marlowe, F. W. (2003). The mating system of foragers in the Standard Cross-Cultural Sample. *Cross-Cultural Research: The Journal of Comparative Social Science, 37,* 282–306.

Marsh, A. A., & Ambady, N. (2007). The influence of fear facial expression on prosocial responding. *Cognition and Emotion, 21,* 225–247.

Marsh, A. A., Adams, R. B., & Kleck, R. E. (2005). Why do fear and anger look the way they do? Form and social function in facial expressions. *Personality and Social Psychology Bulletin, 31,* 73–86.

Marsh, H. W., Seaton, M., Trautwein, U., Ladtke, O., Hau, K. T., O'Mara, A. J., & Craven, R. G. (2008). The big-fish-little-pond-effect stands up to critical scrutiny: Implications for theory, methodology, and future research. *Educational Psychology Review, 20,* 319–350.

Marshall, N. L. (2004). The quality of early child care and children's development. *Current Directions in Psychological Science, 13,* 165–168.

Marshall-Pescini, S., & Whiten, A. (2008). Social learning and nutcracking behavior in East African sanctuary-living chimpanzees (*Pan troglodytes schweinfurthii*). *Journal of Comparative Psychology, 122,* 186–194.

Martens, A., Johns, M., Greenberg, J., & Schimel, J. (2006). Combating stereotype threat: The effect of self-affirmation on women's intellectual performance. *Journal of Experimental Social Psychology, 42,* 236–243.

Martin, C. A., Kelly, T. H., Rayens, M. K., Brogli, B., Himelreich, K., Brenzel, A., et al. (2004). Sensation seeking and symptoms of disruptive disorder: Association with nicotine, alcohol, and marijuana use in early and mid-adolescence. *Psychological Reports, 94,* 1075–1082.

Martin, C. L. (1990). Attitudes and expectations about children with nontraditional and traditional gender roles. *Sex Roles, 22,* 151–165.

Martin, C. L., & Ruble, D. (2004). Children's search for gender cues: Cognitive perspectives on gender development. *Current Directions in Psychological Science, 13,* 67–70.

Martin, C. L., Ruble, D. N., & Szkrybalo, J. (2002). Cognitive theories of early gender development. *Psychological Bulletin, 128,* 903–933.

Martin, J. L. R., Sainz-Pardo, M., Furukawa, T. A., Martin-Sánchez, E., Seoane, T., & Galán, C. (2007). Benzodiazepines in generalized anxiety disorder: Heterogeneity of outcomes based on a systematic review and meta-analysis of clinical trials. *Journal of Psychopharmacology, 21,* 774–782.

Martinowich, K., Manji, H., & Lu, B. (2007). New insights into BDNF function in depression and anxiety. *Nature Neuroscience, 10,* 1089–1093.

Marx, J. (2003). Cellular warriors at the battle of the bulge. *Science, 299,* 846–849.

Masataka, N. (2003). *On the onset of language.* Cambridge, England: Cambridge University Press.

Mascolo, M. F., & Fischer, K. W. (1995). Developmental transformations in appraisals for pride, shame, and guilt. In J. P. Tangney & K. W. Fischer (Eds.), *Self-conscious emotions: The psychology of shame, guilt, embarrassment, and pride.* New York: Guilford.

Maser, J. D., Norman, S. B., Zisook, S., Everall, I. P., Stein, M. B., Schettler, P. J., & Judd, L. L. (2009). Psychiatric nosology is ready for a paradigm shift in DSM-V. *Clinical Psychology: Science and Practice, 16,* 24–40.

Mashour, G. A., Walker, E. E., & Martuza, R. L. (2005). Psychosurgery: Past, present, and future. *Brain Research Reviews, 48,* 409–419.

Masland, R. H. (2001). The fundamental plan of the retina. *Nature Neuroscience, 4,* 877–886.

Maslow, A. H. (1970). *Motivation and personality* (2nd ed.). New York: Harper & Row.

Mason, P. (2001). Contributions of the medullary raphe and ventromedial reticular region to pain modulation and other homeostatic functions. *Annual Review of Neuroscience, 24,* 737–777.

Masters, W. H., Johnson, V. E., & Kolodny, R. C. (1992). *Human sexuality* (4th ed.). New York: HarperCollins.

Mastrangelo, S. (2009). Play and the child with autism spectrum disorder: From possibilities to practice. *International Journal of Play Therapy, 18,* 13–30.

Masuda, T., & Nisbett, R. E. (2001). Attending holistically versus analytically: Comparing the context sensitivity of Japanese and Americans. *Journal of Personality and Social Psychology, 81,* 922–934.

Masuda, T., & Nisbett, R. E. (2006). Culture and change blindness. *Cognitive Science: A Multidisciplinary Journal, 30,* 381–399.

Matarazzo, J. D. (1983). The reliability of psychiatric and psychological diagnosis. *Clinical Psychology Review, 3,* 103–145.

Mather, M., & Carstensen, L. L. (2003). Aging and attentional biases for emotional faces. *Psychological Science, 14,* 409–415.

Mathew, S. J., & Hoffman, E. J. (2009). Pharmacotherapy for generalized anxiety disorder. In M. M. Antony & M. B. Stein (Eds.), *Oxford handbook of anxiety related disorders.* Oxford, UK: Oxford University Press.

Mathew, S. J., Amiel, J. M., & Sackeim, H. A. (2005). Electroconvulsive therapy in treatment-resistant depression. *Primary Psychiatry, 12,* 52–56.

Mathews, C. A. (2009) Phenomenology of obsessive-compulsive disorder. In M. M. Antony & M. B. Stein (Eds.), *Oxford handbook of anxiety related disorders.* Oxford, UK: Oxford University Press.

Matlin, M. W., & Foley, H. J. (1997). *Sensation and perception* (4th ed.). Boston: Allyn & Bacon.

Matthews, G., Derryberry, D., & Siegle, G. J. (2000). Personality and emotion: Cognitive science perspectives. In S. E. Hampson (Ed.), *Advances in personality psychology* (Vol. 1, pp. 199–237). Philadelphia: Taylor & Francis.

Matthews, R. N., Domjam, M., Ramsey, M., & Crews, D. (2007). Learning effects on sperm competition and reproductive fitness. *Psychological Science, 18,* 758–762.

Matzel, L, Townsend, D. A., Grossman, H., Han, Y. R., Hale, G., Zappulla, M., Light, K., & Kolata, S. (2006). Exploration in outbred mice covaries with general learning abilities irrespective of stress reactivity, emotionality, and physical attributes. *Neurobiology of Learning and Memory, 86,* 228–240.

Maurer, D., & Maurer, C. (1988). *The world of the newborn.* New York: Basic Books.

Maxwell, J. S., & Davidson, R. J. (2007). Emotion and motion: Asymmetries in approach and avoidant actions. *Psychological Science, 18,* 1113–1119.

Mayberry, R. I., Lock, E., & Kazmi, H. (2002). Linguistic ability and early language exposure. *Nature, 417,* 38.

Mayes, R., Bagwell, C., & Erkulwater, J. (2009). *Medicating children: ADHD and pediatric mental health.* Cambridge, MA: Harvard University Press.

Mazoni, G., & Memon, A. (2003). Imagination can create false autobiographical memories. *Psychological Science, 14,* 186–188.

McAdams, D. (1993). *The stories we live by: Personal myths and the making of the self.* New York: Morrow.

McAdams, D. (1994). Can personality change? Levels of stability and growth in personality across the life span. In T. F. Heatherton & J. L. Weinberger (Eds.), *Can personality change?* Washington, DC: American Psychological Association.

McAdams, D. P. (2001). The psychology of life stories. *Review of General Psychology, 5,* 100–122.

McAdams, D. P. (2006). The role of narrative in personality psychology today. *Narrative Inquiry, 16,* 11–18.

McAlister, A., & Peterson, C. (2007). A longitudinal study of child siblings and theory of mind development. *Cognitive Development, 22,* 258–270.

McArthur, L. Z. (1972). The how and what of why: Some determinants and consequences of causal attribution. *Journal of Personality and Social Psychology, 22,* 171–193.

McArthur, L. Z., & Berry, D. S. (1987). Cross-cultural agreement in perceptions of babyfaced adults. *Journal of Cross-Cultural Psychology, 18,* 165–192.

McCabe, V. (1984). Abstract perceptual information for age level: A risk factor for maltreatment? *Child Development, 55,* 267–276.

McCrae, R. R., & Allik, J. (Eds.) (2002). *The five-factor model of personality across cultures.* New York: Klewer Academic/Plenum Publishers.

McCrae, R. R., & Costa, P. T. (1985). Openness to experience. In R. Hogan & W. H. Jones (Eds.), *Perspectives in personality* (Vol. 1). Greenwich, CT: JAI Press.

McCrae, R. R., & Sutin, A. R. (2007). Frontiers for the five-factor model: Preview of the literature. *Social and Personality Psychology Compass, 1,* 423–440.

McCrae, R. R., & Terracciano, A. (2005). Universal features of personality traits from the observer's perspective: Data from 50 cultures. *Journal of Personality and Social Psychology, 88,* 547–561.

McCrae, R. R., Costa, P. T., & Martin, T. A. (2005). The NEO-PI-3: A more readable revised NEO personality inventory. *Journal of Personality Assessment, 84,* 261–270.

McElwain, A. K., Korabik, K., & Rosin, H. M. (2005). An examination of gender differences in work-family conflict. *Canadian Journal of Behavioral Sciences 37,* 283–298.

McEwen, B. S. (1989). Endocrine effects on the brain and their relationship to behavior. In G. J. Siegel, B. W. Agranoff, R. W. Albers, & P. B. Molinoff (Eds.), *Basic neurochemistry: Molecular, cellular, and medical aspects* (4th ed.). New York: Raven Press.

McFarland, C., & Buehler, R. (1995). Collective self-esteem as a moderator of the frog-pond effect in reactions to performance feedback. *Journal of Personality and Social Psychology, 68,* 1055–1070.

McGarrigle, J., & Donaldson, M. (1975). Conservation accidents. *Cognition, 3,* 341–350.

McGraw, A. P., Mellers, B. A., & Tetlock, P. E. (2005). Expectations and emotions of Olympic athletes. *Journal of Experimental Social Psychology, 41,* 438–446.

McGue, M., Bouchard, T. J., Iacono, W. G., & Lykken, D. T. (1993). Behavioral genetics of cognitive ability: A life-span perspective. In R. Plomin & G. E. McClearn (Eds.), *Nature, nurture, and psychology.* Washington, DC: American Psychological Association.

McGuire, W. J., & McGuire, C. V. (1988). Content and process in the experience of self. In L. Berkowitz (Ed.), *Advances in experimental social psychology* (Vol. 21). Orlando, FL: Academic Press.

McHugo, G. J., Lanzetta, J. T., Sullivan, D. G., Masters, R. D., & Englis, B. G. (1985). Emotional reactions to a political leader's expressive displays. *Journal of Personality and Social Psychology, 49,* 1513–1529.

McKenna, K. Y. A., Green, A. S., & Gleason, M. E. J. (2002). Relationship formation on the Internet: What's the big attraction? *Journal of Social Issues, 58,* 9–31.

McKim, W. A. (2006). *Drugs and behavior: An introduction to behavioral pharmacology* (6th ed.). Upper Saddle River, NJ: Prentice Hall.

McNally, R. J. (2003). *Remembering trauma.* Cambridge, MA: Harvard University Press.

Mead, M. (1935). *Sex and temperament in three primitive societies.* New York: Wm. Morrow.

Meador, B. D., & Rogers, C. R. (1973). Client-centered therapy. In R. Corsini (Ed.), *Current psychotherapies.* Itasca, IL: Peacock.

Meaney, M. J., Stewart, J., & Beatty, W. W. (1985). Sex difference in social play: The socialization of sex roles. *Advances in the Study of Behavior, 15,* 1–58.

Mearns, D., & Thorne, B. (2000). *Person-centred therapy today: New frontiers in theory and practice.* London: Sage.

Meddis, R. (1977). *The sleep instinct.* London: Routledge & Kegan Paul.

Medina, J. F., Nores, W. L., & Mauk, M. D. (2002). Inhibition of climbing fibers is a signal for the extinction of conditioned eyelid responses. *Nature, 416,* 330–333.

Medina, J. H., Bekinschtein, P., Cammarota, M., & Izquierdo, I. (2008). Do memories consolidate to persist or do they persist to consolidate? *Behavioural Brain Research, 192,* 61–69.

Medvec, V. H., Madey, S., & Gilovich, T. (1995). When less is more: Counterfactual thinking and satisfaction among Olympic medalists. *Journal of Personality and Social Psychology, 69,* 603–610.

Mehta, P. H., & Josephs, R. A. (2006). Testosterone change after losing predicts the decision to compete again. *Hormones and Behavior, 50,* 684–692.

Meisel, R. L., & Sachs, B. D. (1994). The physiology of male sexual behavior. In E. Knobil & J. Neill (Eds.), *The physiology of reproduction.* New York: Raven Press.

Melara, R. D., & Algom, D. (2003). Driven by information: A tectonic theory of Stroop Effects. *Psychological Review, 110,* 422–471.

Melchior, C. L. (1990). Conditioned tolerance provides protection against ethanol lethality. *Pharmacology Biochemistry and Behavior, 37,* 205–206.

Melzack, R. (1992, April). Phantom limbs. *Scientific American,* pp. 120–126.

Melzack, R., & Wall, P. D. (1965). Pain mechanisms: A new theory. *Science, 150,* 971–979.

Melzack, R., & Wall, P. D. (1996). *The challenge of pain: Updated second edition.* New York: Penguin.

Mendes, W. B., Gray, H. M., Mendoza-Denton, R., Major, B., & Epel, E. S. (2007). Why egalitarianism might be good for your health: Physiological thriving during stressful intergroup encounters. *Psychological Science, 18,* 991–998.

Merbs, S. L., & Nathans, J. (1992). Absorption spectra of human cone pigments. *Nature, 356,* 433–435.

Mercader, J., Panger, M., & Boesch, C. (2002). Excavation of a chimpanzee stone tool site in the African rainforest. *Science, 296,* 1452–1455.

Mercer, N., & Littleton, K. (2007). *Dialogue and the development of children's thinking: A sociocultural approach.* New York: Routledge.

Mervis, C. M., & Bertrand, J. (1994). Acquisition of the novel name-nameless category (N3C) principle. *Child Development, 65,* 1646–1662.

Mesich, H. M. (2005). Mother-infant co-sleeping. *American Journal of Maternal/Child Nursing, 30,* 30–37.

Mezulis, A. H., Abramson, L. Y., Hyde, J. S., & Hankin, B. L. (2004). Is there a universal positivity bias in attributions? A meta-analytic review of individual, developmental, and cultural differences in self-serving attributional bias. *Psychological Bulletin, 130,* 711–747.

Michael, R. T., Gagnon, J. H., Laumann, E. O., & Kolata, G. (1994). *Sex in America: A definitive survey.* Boston: Little, Brown and Company.

Michaels, J. W., Blommel, J. M., Brocato, R. M., Linkous, R. A., & Rowe, J. S. (1982). Social facilitation and inhibition in a natural setting. *Replications in Social Psychology, 2,* 21–24.

Mikulincer, M., & Shaver, P. R. (2007). *Attachment in adulthood: Structure, dynamics, and change.* New York: Guilford.

Miles, L. (1983). Apes and language: The search for communicative competence. In J. de Luce & H. T. Wilder (Eds.), *Language in primates.* New York: Springer-Verlag.

Milgram, S. (1963). Behavioral study of obedience. *Journal of Abnormal and Social Psychology, 67,* 371–378.

Milgram, S. (1964). Issues in the study of obedience: A reply to Baumrind. *American Psychologist, 19,* 848–852.

Milgram, S. (1974). *Obedience to authority: An experimental view.* New York: Harper & Row.

Mill, J. S. (1875). *A system of logic* (9th ed.). London: Longmans, Green, Reader & Dyer. (Original work published 1843.)

Miller, A. G. (1986). *The obedience experiments: A case study of controversy in social science.* New York: Praeger.

Miller, A. G. (2004). What can the Milgram obedience experiments tell us about the Holocaust? In A. G. Miller (Ed.), *The social psychology of good and evil.* New York: Guilford.

Miller, E. M. (1997). Could nonshared environmental variance have evolved to assure diversification through randomness? *Evolution and Human Behavior, 18,* 195–221.

Miller, G. E. (1956). The magic number seven plus or minus two: Some limits on our capacity for processing information. *Psychological Review, 63,* 81–97.

Miller, G., & Blackwell, E. (2006). Turning up the heat: Inflammation as a mechanism linking chronic stress, depression, and heart disease. *Current Directions in Psychological Science, 15,* 269–272.

Miller, G., Chen, E., & Cole, S. W. (2009). Health psychology: Developing biologically plausible models linking the social world and physical health. *Annual Review of Psychology, 60,* 501–524.

Miller, J. G. (1984). Culture and the development of everyday social explanations. *Journal of Personality and Social Psychology, 46,* 961–978.

Miller, K. F., Smith, C. M., Zhu, J., & Zhang, H. (1995). Preschool origins of cross-national differences in mathematical competence: The role of number-naming systems. *Psychological Science, 6,* 56–60.

Miller, L. T., & Vernon, P. A. (1992). The general factor in short-term memory, intelligence, and reaction time. *Intelligence, 16,* 5–29.

Miller, R. (1995). Embarrassment and social behavior. In J. P. Tangney & K. W. Fischer (Eds.), *Self-conscious emotions: The psychology of shame, guilt, embarrassment, and pride.* New York: Guilford.

Miller, R. L., Brickman, P., & Bolen, D. (1975). Attribution versus persuasion as a means for modifying behavior. *Journal of Personality and Social Psychology, 31,* 430–441.

Miller, W. R., & C'deBaca, J. (1994). Quantum change: Toward a psychology of transformation. In T. F. Heatherton & J. L. Weinberger (Eds.), *Can personality change?* Washington, DC: American Psychological Association.

Milner, A. D., & Goodale, M. A. (1995). *The visual brain in action.* Oxford: Oxford University Press.

Milner, B. (1965). Memory disturbance after bilateral hippocampal lesions. In P. Milner & S. Glickman (Eds.), *Cognitive processes and the brain.* Princeton, NJ: Van Nostrand.

Milner, B. (1970). Memory and the medial temporal regions of the brain. In K. H. Pribram & D. E. Broadbent (Eds.), *Biology of memory.* New York: Academic Press.

Milner, B. (1984). *Temporal lobes and memory disorders.* Paper presented at the American Psychological Association Convention, Toronto, Canada.

Mineka, S., & Öhman, A. (2002). Phobias and preparedness: The selective, automatic, and encapsulated nature of fear. *Biological Psychiatry, 52,* 927–937.

Mineka, S., & Zinbarg, R. (2006). A contemporary learning theory perspective on the etiology of anxiety disorders: It's not what you thought it was. *American Psychologist, 61,* 10–26.

Mineka, S., Davidson, M., Cook, M., & Keir, R. (1984). Observational conditional of snake fear in rhesus monkeys. *Journal of Abnormal Psychology, 93,* 355–372.

Ming, G., & Song, H. (2005). Adult neurogenesis in the mammalian central nervous system. *Annual Review of Neuroscience, 28,* 223–250.

Minix, D. A. (1976). *The rule of the small group in foreign policy decision making: A potential pathology in crisis decisions?* Paper presented to the Southern Political Science Association. (For description, see D. G. Myers, 1982.)

Minton, H. L. (2002). *Departing from deviance: A history of homosexual rights and emancipatory science in America.* Chicago: University of Chicago Press.

Mirgain, S. A., & Cordova, J. V. (2007). Emotion skills and marital health: The association between observed and self-reported emotion skills, intimacy, and marital satisfaction. *Journal of Social and Clinical Psychology, 9,* 983–1009.

Mischel, W. (1984). Convergences and challenges in the search for consistency. *American Psychologist, 39,* 351–364.

Mischel, W., & Peake, P. K. (1982). Beyond déjà vu in the search for cross-situational consistency. *Psychological Review, 89,* 730–755.

Mischel, W., & Shoda, Y. (1995). A cognitive-affective system theory of personality: Reconceptualizing situations, dispositions, dynamics, and invariance in personality structure. *Psychological Review, 102,* 246–268.

Mischell, W. (2007). Toward a cognitive social learning reconceptualization of personality. In Y. Shoda, D. Cervone, & G. Downey (Eds.), *Persons in context: Buildindg a science of the individual.* New York: Guilford.

Mitte, K. (2005). Meta-analysis of cognitive-behavioral treatments for generalized anxiety disorder: A comparison with pharmacotherapy. *Psychological Bulletin, 131,* 785–795.

Miura, I. T., & Okamoto, Y. (2003). In A. J. Baroody & A. Dowker (Eds.), *The development of arithmetic concepts and skills: Constructing adaptive expertise. Studies in mathematical learning.* Mahwah, NJ: Erlbaum.

Miura, I. T., Okamoto, Y., Kim, C. C., Chang, C., Steere, M., & Fayol, M. (1994). Comparisons of children's cognitive representation of number: China, France, Japan, Korea, Sweden, and the United States. *International Journal of Behavioral Development, 17,* 401–411.

Moffitt, T. E. (1993). Adolescence-limited and life-course-persistent antisocial behavior: A developmental taxonomy. *Psychological Review, 100,* 674–701.

Mogg, K., & Bradley, B. P. (2005). Attentional bias in generalized anxiety disorder versus depressive disorder. *Cognitive Therapy and Research, 29,* 29–45.

Money, J., & Ehrhardt, A. (1972). *Man and woman, boy and girl.* Baltimore: Johns Hopkins University Press.

Monk, T. H., Buysse, D. J., Welsh, D. K., Kennedy, K. S., & Rose, L. R. (2001). A sleep diary and questionnaire study of naturally short sleepers. *Journal of Sleep Research, 10,* 173–179.

Monroe, S. M., Slavich, G. M., & Georgiades, K. (2009). The social environment and life stress in depression. In I. H. Gotlib & C. L. Hammen (Eds.), *Handbook of depression* (2nd ed.). New York: Guilford.

Moore, B. C. J. (1997). *An introduction to the psychology of hearing.* San Diego, CA: Academic Press.

Moore, G. E. (1903). *Principia ethica.* Cambridge, England: Cambridge University Press.

Moore, H. T. (1917). Laboratory tests of anger, fear, and sex interests. *American Journal of Psychology, 28,* 390–395.

Moorhead, G., Ference, R., & Neck, C. P. (1991). Group decision fiascoes continue: Space shuttle *Challenger* and a revised groupthink framework. *Human Relations, 44,* 539–550.

Moray, N. (1959). Attention in dichotic listening: Effective cues and the influence of instructions. *Quarterly Journal of Experimental Psychology, 11,* 56–60.

Mordkoff, J. T., & Halterman, R. (2008). Feature integration without visual attention: Evidence from the correlated flankers task. *Psychonomic Bulletin & Review, 15,* 385–389.

Morelli, G. A., & Tronick, E. Z. (1991). Parenting and child development in the Efe foragers and the Lese farmers of Zaïre. In M. H. Bornstein (Ed.), *Cultural approaches to parenting.* Hillsdale, NJ: Erlbaum.

Morelli, G. A., Rogoff, B., Oppenheim, D., & Goldsmith, D. (1992). Cultural variation in infants' sleeping arrangements: Questions of independence. *Developmental Psychology, 28,* 604–613.

Moritz, S., Woodward, T. S., Whitman, J. C., & Cuttler, C. (2005). Confidence in errors as a possible basis for delusions in schizophrenia. *Journal of Nervous and Mental Disease, 193,* 9–16.

Morris, M. W., & Peng, K. (1994). Culture and cause: American and Chinese attributions for social and physical events. *Journal of Personality and Social Psychology, 67,* 949–971.

Moscovitch, D. A., Antony, M. M., & Swinson, R. P. (2009). In M. M. Antony & M. B. Stein (Eds.), *Oxford handbook of anxiety related disorders.* Oxford, UK: Oxford University Press.

Moser, E. I., Kropff, E., & Moser, M-B. (2008). Place cells, grid cells, and the brain's spatial representation system. *Annual Review of Neuroscience, 31,* 69–89.

Mosko, S., McKenna, J., Dickel, M., & Hunt, L. (1993). Parent-infant cosleeping: The appropriate context for the study of infant sleep and implications for sudden infant death syndrome (SIDS) research. *Journal of Behavioral Medicine, 16,* 589–610.

Mostert, M. P. (2001). Facilitated communication since 1995: A review of published studies. *Journal of Autism and Developmental Disorders, 31,* 287–313.

Mowrer, O. H. (1960). *Learning theory and behavior.* New York: Wiley.

Mroczek, D. K. (2001). Age and emotion in adulthood. *Current Directions in Psychological Science, 10,* 87–90.

Mueller, C. M., & Dweck, C. S. (1998). Intelligence praise can undermine motivation and performance. *Journal of Personality and Social Psychology, 75,* 33–52.

Muhlberger, P. (2000). Moral reasoning effects on political participation. *Political Psychology, 21,* 667–695.

Muir, D., & Field, J. (1979). Newborn infants orient to sounds. *Child Development, 50,* 431–436.

Mulder, R. A. (1994, November). Faithful philanderers. *Natural History, 103,* pp. 57–62.

Mullen, B., Anthony, T., Salas, E., & Driskell, J. E. (1994). Group cohesiveness and quality of decision making: An integration of tests of the groupthink hypothesis. *Small Group Research, 25,* 189–204.

Müller, J. (1838; reprinted 1965). *Elements of physiology* (Vol. 2) (W. Baly, Trans.). Excerpted in R. J. Herrnstein & E. G. Boring (Eds.), *A source book in the history of psychology.* Cambridge, MA: Harvard University Press.

Mundy, P., Sigman, M., & Kasari, C. (1990). A longitudinal study of joint attention and language development in autistic children. *Journal of Autism and Developmental Disorders, 20,* 115–128.

Munoz, R. F., Le, H-N., Clarke, G. N., Barrera, A. Z., & Torres, L. D. (2009). In I. H. Gotlib & C. L. Hammen (Eds.), *Handbook of depression* (2nd ed.). New York: Guilford.

Muntz, W. R. A. (1964, May). Vision in frogs. *Scientific American,* pp. 110–119.

Murdock, G. P. (1981). *Atlas of world cultures.* Pittsburgh, PA: University of Pittsburgh Press.

Murphy, C., Schubert, C. R., Cruickshanks, K. J., Klein, B. E. K., Klein, R., & Nondahl, D. M. (2002). Prevalence of olfactory impairment in older adults. *Journal of the American Medical Association, 288,* 2307–2312.

Murray, S. L., Bellavia, G. M., Rose, P., & Griffin, D. W. (2003). Once hurt, twice hurtful: How perceived regard regulates daily marital interactions. *Journal of Personality and Social Psychology, 84,* 126–147.

Mussen, P., Eichorn, D. H., Honzik, M. P., Bieher, S. L., & Meredith, W. (1980). Continuity and change in women's characteristics over four decades. *International Journal of Behavioral Development, 3,* 333–347.

Myers, D. G. (1982). Polarizing effects of social interaction. In H. Brandstatter, J. H. Davis, & G. Stocker-Kreichgauer (Eds.), *Group decision making.* New York: Academic Press.

Myers, D. G., & Kaplan, M. F. (1976). Group-induced polarization in simulated juries. *Personality and Social Psychology Bulletin, 2,* 63–66.

Naigles, L. (1990). Children use syntax to learn verb meanings. *Journal of Child Language, 17,* 357–374.

Nairne, J. S., Pandeirada, J. N. S., & Thompson, S. R. (2008). Adaptive memory. *Psychological Science, 19,* 176–180.

Natanovich, G., & Eden, D. (2008). Pygmalion effects among outreach supervisors and tutors: Extending sex generalizability. *Journal of Applied Psychology, 93,* 1382–1389.

Nature Neuroscience editorial (2007). More noise than signal. *Nature Neuroscience, 10,* 799.

Navitt, G. A., Dittman, A. H., Wuinn, T. P., & Moody, W. J. (1994). Evidence for peripheral olfactory memory in imprinting in salmon. *Proceedings of the National Academy of Sciences, USA, 91,* 4288–4292.

Neck, C. P., & Moorhead, G. (1995). Groupthink remodeled: The importance of leadership, time pressure, and methodical decision-making procedures. *Human Relations, 48,* 537–557.

Nee, D. E., Berman, M. G., Moore, K. S., & Jonides, J. (2008). Neuroscientific evidence about the distinction between short-term and long-term memory. *Current Directions in Psychological Science, 17,* 102–106.

Neisser, U. (1976). *Cognition and reality.* San Francisco: Freeman.

Neitz, J., Neitz, M., & Kainz, P. M. (1996). Visual pigment gene structure and the severity of color vision defects. *Science, 274,* 801–804.

Nelson, D. A., Hallberg, K. I., & Soha, J. A. (2004). Cultural evolution of Puget white-crowned sparrow song dialects. *Ethology, 110,* 879–908.

Nelson, G., Aubry, T., & Lafrance, A. (2007). A review of the literature on the effectiveness of housing and support, assertive community treatment, and intensive care management interventions for persons with mental illness who have been homeless. *American Journal of Orthopsychology, 77,* 350–361.

Nelson, K., & Fivush, R. (2004). The emergence of autobiographical memory: A social cultural developmental theory. *Psychological Review, 111,* 486–511.

Nemeth, C. J. (1986). Differential contributions of majority and minority influence. *Psychological Review, 93,* 23–32.

Nes, L. S., & Segerstrom, S. C. (2006). Dispositional optimism and coping: A meta-analytic review. *Personality and Social Psychology Review, 10,* 235–251.

Nesse, R. M. (2000). Is depression an adaptation? *Archives of General Psychiatry, 57,* 14–20.

Nestler, E., & Malenka, R. C. (2004, March). The addicted brain. *Scientific American, 290,* pp. 78–85.

Nettle, D. (2005). An evolutionary approach to the extraversion continuum. *Evolution and Human Behavior, 26,* 363–373.

Nettle, D. (2006). The evolution of personality variation in humans and other animals. *American Psychologist, 61,* 622–631.

Neubauer, P. B., & Neubauer, A. (1996). *Nature's thumbprint: The new genetics of personality* (2nd ed.). New York: Columbia University Press.

Neugarten, B. L. (1979). Time, age, and the life cycle. *American Journal of Psychiatry, 136,* 887–894.

Neugarten, B. L. (1984). Interpretive social science and research on aging. In A. Rossi (Ed.), *Gender and the life course.* Chicago: Aldine.

Neuner, F., Schauer, M., Klaschik, C., Karunakara, U., Elbert, T. (2004). Comparison of narrative exposure therapy, supportive counseling, and psychoeducation for treating posttraumatic stress disorder in an African refugee settlement. *Journal of Consulting and Clinical Psychology, 74,* 579–587.

Newman, L. S., & Baumeister, R. F. (1996). Toward an explanation of UFO abduction phenomenon: Hypnotic elaboration, extraterrestrial sadomasochism, and spurious memories. *Psychological Inquiry, 7,* 99–126.

Neyer, F., & Lang, F. R. (2003). Blood is thicker than water: Kinship orientation across adulthood. *Journal of Personality and Social Psychology, 84,* 310–321.

Nguyen, H-H. D., & Ryan, A. M. (2008). Does stereotype threat affect test performance of minorities and women? A meta-analysis of experimental evidence. *Journal of Applied Psychology, 93,* 1314–1334.

NICHD Early Child Care Research Network (2006). Child-care effect sizes for the NICHD study of early child care and youth development. *American Psychologist, 61,* 99–116.

Nicoll, J. A. R., Yamada, M., Frackowiak, J., Mazur-Kolecka, B., & Weller, R. O. (2004). Cerebral amyloid angiopathy plays a direct role in the pathogenesis of Alzheimer's disease: Pro-CAA position statement. *Neurobiology of Aging, 25,* 589–597.

Nigg, J. T., John, O. P., Blasky, L. G., Huang-Pollock, C. L., Willcutt, E. G., Hinshaw, S. P., & Pennington, B. (2002). Big Five dimensions and ADHD symptoms: Links between personality traits and clinical symptoms. *Journal of Personality and Social Psychology, 83,* 451–469.

Nisbett, R. E., & Masuda, T. (2007). Culture and point of view. *Intellectica, 46-47,* 143–172.

Nisbett, R. E., & Wilson, T. D. (1977). The halo effect: Evidence for unconscious alteration of judgments. *Journal of Personality and Social Psychology, 35,* 250–256.

Nisbett, R. E., Peng, K., Choi, I., & Norenzayan, A. (2001). Culture and systems of thought: Holistic versus analytic cognition. *Psychological Review, 108,* 291–310.

Nishida, T. (Ed.) (1990). *The chimpanzees of the Mahale Mountains: Sexual and life history strategies.* Tokyo: University of Tokyo Press.

Niu, W., Zhang, J. X., & Yang, Y. (2007). Deductive reasoning and creativity: A cross-cultural study. *Psychological Reports, 100,* 509–519.

Noice, H., & Noice, T. (2006). What studies of actors and acting can tell us about memory and cognitive functioning. *Current Directions in Psychological Science, 15,* 14–18.

Nolen-Hoeksema, S. (2001). Gender differences in depression. *Current Directions in Psychological Science, 10,* 173–176.

Nordin, S., Broman, D. A., Olofsson, J. K., & Wulff, M. (2004). A longitudinal study of self-reported abnormal smell and taste perception in pregnant women. *Chemical Senses, 29,* 391–402.

Norem, J. K. (2008). Defensive pessimism, anxiety, and the complexity of evaluating self-regulation. *Social and Personality Compass, 2,* 121–134.

Norem, J. K., & Illingworth, K. S. S. (1993). Strategy-dependent effects of reflecting on self and tasks: Some implications of optimism and defensive pessimism. *Journal of Personality and Social Psychology, 65,* 822–835.

Norem, J. K., & Illingworth, K. S. S. (2004). Mood and performance among defensive pessimists and strategic optimists. *Journal of Research in Personality, 38,* 351–366.

Norenzayan, A., & Nisbett, R. E. (2000). Culture and cognition. *Current Directions in Psychological Science, 9,* 132–135.

Nosek, B. A. (2007). Implicit-explicit relations. *Current Directions in Psychological Science, 16,* 65–70.

Nowakowska, C., Strong, C. M., Santosa, C. M., Want, P. W., & Ketter, T. A. (2005). Temperamental commonalities and differences in euthymic mood disorder patients, creative controls, and healthy controls. *Journal of Affective Disorders, 85,* 207–215.

Nowlis, G. H., & Frank, M. (1977). Qualities in hamster taste: Behavioral and neural evidence. In J. LeMagnen & P. MacLeod (Eds.), *Olfaction and taste* (Vol. 6). Washington, DC: Information Retrieval.

Nuechterlein, K. H., Dawson, M. E., Gitlin, M., Ventura, J., Goldstein, M. J., Snyder, K. S., Yee, C. M., & Mintz, J. (1992). Developmental processes in schizophrenic disorders: Longitudinal studies of vulnerability and stress. *Schizophrenia Bulletin, 18,* 387–425.

Numan, M. (2007). Motivational systems and neural circuitry in maternal behavior in the rat. *Developmental Psychobiology, 49,* 12–21.

Nussbaum, R. L., & Ellis, C. E. (2003). Alzheimer's disease and Parkinson's disease. *New England Journal of Medicine, 348,* 1356–1364.

Nutt, D. J., & Glue, P. (1993). The neurobiology of ECT: Animal studies. In C. E. Coffee (Ed.), *The clinical science of electroconvulsive therapy.* Washington, DC: American Psychiatric Press.

Oakes, L. M., & Tellinghuisen, D. J. (1994). Examining in infancy: Does it reflect active processing? *Developmental Psychology, 30,* 748–756.

Oakes, P. J., Halsam, S. A., & Turner, J. C. (1994). *Stereotyping and social reality.* Oxford: Blackwell.

Oberauer, K., Weidenfeld, A., & Hörnig, R. (2006). Working memory capacity and the construction of spatial mental models in comprehension and deductive reasoning. *Quarterly Journal of Experimental Psychology, 59,* 426–447.

Ochs, E., & Schieffelin, B. (1995). The impact of language socialization on grammatical development. In P. Fletcher & B. MacWhinney (Eds.), *The handbook of child language.* Cambridge, MA: Basil Blackwell.

O'Connor, T. G., Deater-Deckard, K., Fulker, D., Rutter, M., & Plomin, R. (1998). Genotype-environment correlations in late childhood and early adolescence: Antisocial behavioral problems and coercive parenting. *Developmental Psychology, 34,* 970–981.

Ofen, N., Kao, Y-C., Sokol-Hessner, P., Kim, H., Whitfield-Gabrieli, S., & Gavrieli, J. D. E. (2007). Development of the declarative memory system in the human brain. *Nature Neuroscience, 9,* 1198–1205.

Offer, D., & Schonert-Reichl, K. A. (1992). Debunking the myths of adolescence: Findings from recent research. *Journal of the American Academy of Child and Adolescent Psychiatry, 31,* 1003–1013.

Ogbu, J. U. (1986). The consequences of the American caste system. In U. Neisser (Ed.), *The school achievement of minority children: New perspectives.* Hillsdale, NJ: Erlbaum.

Ogbu, J. U., & Stern, P. (2001). Caste status and intellectual development. In R. J. Sternberg & E. L. Grigorenko (Eds.), *Environmental effects on cognitive abilities.* Mahwah, NJ: Erlbaum.

Ogden, C. L., Carroll, M. D., Curtin, L. R., McDowell, M. A., Tabak, C. J., & Flegal, K. M. (2006). Prevalence of overweight and obesity in the United States, 1999-2004. *Journal of the American Medical Association, 295,* 1549–1555.

Öhman, A. (1999). Distinguishing unconscious from conscious emotional processes: Methodological considerations and theoretical implications. In T. Dalgleish & M. Power (Eds.), *Handbook of cognition and emotion.* Chichester, England: Wiley.

Ohyama, T., Nores, W. L., Murphy, M., & Mauk, M. D. (2003). What the cerebellum computes. *Trends in Neurosciences, 26,* 222–227.

Okamoto-Barth, S., Call, J., & Tomasello, M. (2007). Great apes' understanding of other individuals' line of sight. *Psychological Science, 18,* 462–468.

Olds, J. (1956, October). Pleasure centers in the brain. *Scientific American,* pp. 105–116.

Olds, J., & Milner, P. (1954). Positive reinforcement produced by electrical stimulation of the septal area and other regions of the rat brain. *Journal of Comparative and Physiological Psychology, 47,* 419–427.

Olff, M., Langeland, W., Draijer, N. & Gersons, B. P. R. (2007). Gender differences in posttraumatic stress disorder. *Psychological Bulletin, 133,* 183–204.

Olson, M. A., & Fazio, R. H. (2001). Implicit attitude formation through classical conditioning. *Psychological Science, 12,* 413–417.

Olson, M. A., & Fazio, R. H. (2003). Relations between implicit measures of prejudice: What are we measuring? *Psychological Science, 14,* 636–639.

Oring, L. W. (1995, August). The early bird gives the sperm: Spotted sandpipers on a Minnesota lake reveal the secrets of their breeding success. *Natural History, 104,* pp. 58–61.

Orne, M. T., & Holland, C. G. (1968). On the ecological validity of laboratory deception. *International Journal of Psychiatry, 6,* 282–293.

Ornstein, R. (1991). *The evolution of consciousness.* Englewood Cliffs, NJ: Prentice-Hall.

Osborne, J. W. (2007). Linking stereotype threat and anxiety. *Educational Psychology, 27,* 135–154.

Osofsky, J. D., & O'Connell, E. J. (1977). Patterning of newborn behavior in an urban population. *Child Development, 48,* 532–536.

Otten, L. J., Henson, R. N. A., & Rugg, M. D. (2001). Depth of processing effects on neural correlates of memory encoding: Relationship between findings from across- and within-task comparisons. *Brain, 124,* 399–412.

Oulasvirta, A., & Saariluoma, P. (2006). Surviving task interruptions: Investigating the implications of long-term memory theory. *International Journal of Human-Computer Studies, 64,* 941–961.

Overmann, S. R. (1976). Dietary self-selection by animals. *Psychological Bulletin, 83,* 218–235.

Owen, A. M., & Coleman, M. R. (2008). Functional neuroimaging of the vegetative state. *Nature Reviews Neuroscience, 9,* 235–243.

Owen, M. J., & O'Donovan, M. C. (2003). Schizophrenia and genetics. In R. Plomin, J. C. DeFries, I. W. Craig, & P. McGuffin (Eds.), *Behavioral genetics in the postgenomic era.* Washington, DC: American Psychological Association.

Oyserman, D., & Lee, S. W. S. (2008). Does culture influence what and how we think? Effects of priming individualism and collectivism. *Psychological Bulletin, 134,* 311–342.

Ozer, D. J., & Benet-Martínez, V. (2006). Personality and the prediction of consequential outcomes. *Annual Review of Psychology, 57,* 401–421.

Ozer, E. J., Best, S. R., Lipsey, T. L., & Weiss, D. S. (2003). Predictors of posttraumatic stress disorder and symptoms in adults: A meta-analysis. *Psychological Bulletin, 129,* 52–73.

Packard, M. G., & Knowlton, B. J. (2002). Learning and memory functions of the basal ganglia. *Annual Review of Neuroscience, 25,* 563–593.

Page, D., Mosher, R., Simpson, E. M., Fisher, E. M. C., Mardon, G., Pollack, J., McGillivray, B., Chapelle, A., & Brown, L. (1987). The sex-determining region of the human Y chromosome encodes a finger protein. *Cell, 51,* 1091–1104.

Pagel, M., Venditti, C., & Meade, A. (2006). Large punctuational contribution of speciation to evolutionary divergence at the molecular level. *Science, 314,* 119–121.

Paivio, A. (1986). *Mental representations: A dual coding approach.* New York: Oxford University Press.

Palagi, E., Paoli, T., & Tarli, S. B. (2006). Short-term benefits of play behavior and conflict prevention in *Pan paniscus. International Journal of Primatology, 27,* 1257–1269.

Pallanti, S., Quercioli, L., & Pazzagli, A. (1997). Relapse in young paranoid schizophrenic patients: A prospective study of stressful life events, P300 measures, and coping. *American Journal of Psychiatry, 154,* 792–798.

Panksepp, J. (1998). Attention deficit/hyperactivity disorders, psychostimulants, and intolerance of childhood playfulness: A tragedy in the making? *Current Directions in Psychological Science, 7,* 91–98.

Panksepp, J. (2007). Can PLAY diminish ADHD and facilitate the construction of the social brain? *Journal of the Canadian Academy of Child and Adolescent Psychiatry, 16,* 57–66.

Papini, M. R. (2002). Pattern and process in the evolution of learning. *Psychological Review, 109,* 186–201.

Papousek, H. (1969). Individual variability in learned responses in human infants. In R. J. Robinson (Ed.), *Brain and early behavior.* New York: Academic Press.

Paris, J. (2000). Predispositions, personality traits, and posttraumatic stress disorder. *Harvard Review of Psychiatry, 8,* 175–183.

Parish, A. R. (1996). Female relationships in bonobos (*Pan Paniscus*): Evidence for bonding, cooperation, and female dominance in a male-philopatric species. *Human Nature, 7,* 61–96.

Parish, A. R., & de Waal, F. B. (2000). The other "closest living relative": How bonobos (*Pan paniscus*) challenge traditional assumptions about females, dominance, intra- and intersexual interactions, and hominid evolution. *Annals of the New York Academy of Sciences, 907,* 96–113.

Parker, H. A., & McNally, R. J. (2008). Regressive coping, emotional adjustment, and cognition in people who have lost loved ones to suicide. *Suicide and Life-Threatening Behavior, 38,* 676–687.

Parker, J. G., Low, C. M., Walker, A. R., & Gamm, B. K. (2005). Friendship jealousy in young adolescents: Individual differences and links to sex, self-esteem, aggression, and social adjustment. *Developmental Psychology, 41,* 235–250.

Parks, T. E., & Rock, I. (1990). Illusory contours from pictorially three-dimensional inducing elements. *Perception, 19,* 119–121.

Parr, L. A., Waller, B. M., Vick, S. J., & Bard, K. A. (2007). Classifying chimpanzee facial expressions using muscle action. *Emotion, 7,* 172–181.

Parsons, T. D., & Rizzo, A. A. (2008). Affective outcomes of virtual reality exposure therapy for anxiety and specific phobias: A meta-analysis. *Journal of Behavior Therapy and Experimental Psychiatry, 39,* 250–261.

Pascual, A., & Guaguen, N. (2005). Foot-in-the-door and door-in-the-face: A comparative meta-analytic study. *Psychological Reports, 96,* 122–128.

Pascual-Leone, A., Amedi, A., Fregni, F., & Merabet, L. B. (2005). *Annual Review of Neuroscience, 28,* 377–401.

Pashler, H. E. (1998). *The psychology of attention.* Cambridge, MA: MIT Press.

Passingham, R. E., Perry, V. H., & Wilkinson, F. (1983). The long-term effects of removal of sensorimotor cortex in infant and adult rhesus monkeys. *Brain, 106,* 675–705.

Pasterski, V., Hindmarsh, P., Geffner, M., Brook, C., Brain, C., & Hines, M. (2007). Increased aggression and activity level in 3- to 11-year-old girls with congenital adrenal hyperplasia (CAH). *Hormones and Behavior, 52,* 368–374.

Patterson, F., & Linden, E. (1981). *The education of Koko.* New York: Holt, Rinehart & Winston.

Patterson, K., Nestor, P. J., & Rogers, T. T. (2007). Where do you know what you know? The representation of semantic knowledge in the human brain. *Nature Reviews Neuroscience, 8,* 976–987.

Paulesu, E., Frith, C. D., & Frackowiak, R. S. J. (1993). The neural correlates of the verbal components of working memory. *Nature, 362,* 342–345.

Paulhus, D. L., Trapnell, P. D., & Chen, D. (1999). Birth order effects on personality and achievement within families. *Psychological Science, 10,* 482–488.

Paunonen, S. V. (2003). Big Five factors of personality and replicated predictions of behavior. *Journal of Personality and Social Psychology, 84,* 411–424.

Paunonen, S. V., & Ashton, M. C. (2001). Big Five factors and facets and the prediction of behavior. *Journal of Personality and Social Psychology, 81,* 524–539.

Pavlov, I. P. (1927; reprinted 1960). *Conditioned reflexes* (G. V. Anrep, Ed. & Trans.). New York: Dover.

Pawlowski, B. (1999). Loss of oestrus and concealed ovulation in human evolution: The case against the sexual-selection hypothesis. *Current Anthropology, 40,* 257–275.

Payne, B. K. (2006). Weapon bias: Split-decisions and unintended stereotyping. *Current Directions in Psychological Science, 15,* 287–291.

Peale, N. V. (1956). *The power of positive thinking.* Englewood Cliffs, NJ: Prentice-Hall.

Pearson, K. & Gordon, J. (2000). Locomotion. In E. R. Kandel, J. H. Schwartz, & T. M. Jessell (Eds.), *Principles of neural science* (4th ed.). New York: McGraw-Hill.

Pearson, K. (1920). Notes on the history of correlation. *Biometrika, 13,* 25–45.

Pecoraro, N. C., Timberlake, W. D., & Tinsley, M. (1999). Incentive downshifts evoke search repertoires in rats. *Journal of Experimental Psychology: Animal Behavior Processes, 25,* 153–167.

Peissig, J. J., & Tarr, M. J. (2007). Visual object recognition: Do we know more now than we did 20 years ago? *Annual Review of Psychology, 58,* 75–96.

Pellegrini, A. D., & Bjorklund, D. F. (2004). The ontogeny and phylogeny of children's object and fantasy play. *Human Nature, 15,* 23–43.

Pellegrini, A. D., Long, J. D., Roseth, C. J., Bohn, C. M., & Van Ryzin, M. (2007). A short-term longitudinal study of preschoolers' (*Homo sapiens*) sex segregation: The role of physical activity, sex, and time. *Journal of Comparative Psychology, 121,* 282–289.

Pendergrast, M. (1995). *Victims of memory: Incest accusations and scattered lives.* Hinesburg, VT: Upper Access.

Penfield, W., & Faulk, M. E. (1955). The insula: Further observation on its function. *Brain, 78,* 445–470.

Penfield, W., & Perot, P. (1963). The brain's record of auditory and visual experience. *Brain, 86,* 595–696.

Penke, L., & Asendorpf, J. B. (2008). Evidence for conditional sex differences in emotional but not in sexual jealousy at the autonomic level of cognitive processing. *European Journal of Personality, 22,* 3–30.

Penn, D. (2002). The scent of genetic compatibility: Sexual selection and the major histocompatibility complex. *Ethology, 108,* 1–21.

Perera, T. D., Park, S., & Nemirovskaya, Y. (2008). Cognitive role of neurogenesis in depression and antidepressant treatment. *The Neuroscientist, 14,* 326–338.

Perlmutter, J. S., & Mink, J. W. (2006). Deep brain stimulation. *Annual Review of Neuroscience, 29,* 229–257.

Peters, J., Shackelford, T. K., & Buss, D. M. (2002). Understanding domestic violence against women: Using evolutionary psychology to extend the feminist functional analysis. *Violence and Victims, 17,* 255–264.

Petersen, S. E., Fox, P. T., Posner, M. I., Mintun, M., & Raichle, M. E. (1989). Positron emission tomographic studies of the processing of single words. *Journal of Cognitive Neuroscience, 1,* 153–170.

Peterson, C. (2000). The future of optimism. *American Psychologist, 55,* 44–55.

Petitpas, A. J., & Champagne, D. E. (2000). Sports and social competence. In S. Danish & T. P. Gullotta (Eds.), *Developing competent youth and strong communities through after-school programming.* Washington, DC: Child Welfare League of America.

Petitto, L. A., Holowka, S., Serio, L. E., & Ostry, D. (2001). Language rhythms in baby hand movements. *Nature, 413,* 35–36.

Petrovich, G. D., & Gallagher, M. (2007). Control of food consumption by learned cues: A forebrain-hypothalamic network. *Physiology & Behavior, 91,* 397–403.

Petty, R. E., & Cacioppo, J. T. (1986). The elaboration likelihood model of persuasion. In L. Berkowitz (Ed.), *Advances in experimental social psychology* (Vol. 19). New York: Academic Press.

Petty, R. E., & Wegener, D. T. (1999). The elaboration likelihood model: Current status and controversies. In S. Chaiken & Y. Trope (Eds.), *Dual-process theories in social psychology.* New York: Guilford.

Petty, R. E., Cacioppo, J. T., & Goldman, R. (1981). Personal involvement as a determinant of argument-based persuasion. *Journal of Personality and Social Psychology, 41,* 847–855.

Pfaus, J. G., Kippin, T. E., & Ceneno, S. (2001). Conditioning and sexual behavior: A review. *Hormones and Behavior, 40,* 291–321.

Pfennig, D. W., & Sherman, P. W. (1995, June). Kin recognition. *Scientific American,* pp. 98–103.

Pflugshaupt, T., Mosimann, U. P., von Wartburg, R., Schmitt, W., Nyffeler, T., & Müri, R. M. (2005). Hypervigilance-avoidance pattern in spider phobia. *Journal of Anxiety Disorders, 19,* 105–116.

Pfungst, O. (1911, reprinted 1965). *Clever Hans: The horse of Mr. von Osten* (C. L. Rahn, Trans.). New York: Holt, Rinehart & Winston.

Phares, E. J. (1978). Locus of control. In H. London & J. E. Exner (Eds.), *Dimensions of personality.* New York: Wiley.

Phares, E. J. (1984). *Introduction to personality.* Columbus, OH: Merrill.

Phillips, D. P. (1989). The neural coding of simple and complex sounds in the auditory cortex. In J. S. Lund (Ed.), *Sensory processing in the mammalian brain: Neural substrates and experimental strategies.* Oxford: Oxford University Press.

Phillips, P. E. M., Stuber, G. D., Helen, M. L. A. V., Wightman, R. M., & Carelli, R. M. (2003). Subsecond dopamine release promotes cocaine seeking. *Nature, 422,* 614–618.

Phillips, W. A., & Silverstein, S. M. (2003). Convergence of biological and psychological perspectives on cognitive coordination in schizophrenia. *Behavioral and Brain Sciences, 26,* 65–138.

Piaget, J. (1927). *The child's conception of physical causality* (M. Worden, Trans.). New York: Harcourt, Brace & World.

Piaget, J. (1932; reprinted 1965). *The moral judgment of the child.* New York: Free Press.

Piaget, J. (1936; reprinted 1963). *The origins of intelligence in the child.* New York: Norton.

Piaget, J. (1962). *Play, dreams and imitation in childhood.* New York: Norton.

Piaget, J. (1970). *Genetic epistemology* (E. Duckworth, Trans.). New York: Norton.

Piazza, J., & Bering, J. M. (2008). Concerns about reputation via gossip promote generous allocations in an economic game. *Evolution and Human Behavior, 29,* 172–178.

Pierce, J. D., Cohen, A. B., & Ulrich, P. M. (2004). Responsivity to two odorants, androstenone and amyl acetate, and the affective impact of odors on interpersonal relationships. *Journal of Comparative Psychology, 118,* 14–19.

Pierro, A., Mannetti, L., Kruglanski, A. W., & Sleeth-Keppler, D. (2004). Relevance override: On the reduced impact of "cues" under high-motivation conditions of persuasion studies. *Journal of Personality and Social Psychology, 86,* 251–264.

Pilcher, H. R. (2003). The ups and downs of lithium. *Nature, 425,* 118–120.

Pinker, S. (1994). *The language instinct.* New York: Morrow.

Pinker, S. (1997). *How the mind works.* New York: Norton.

Pinker, S., & Bloom, P. (1992). Natural language and natural selection. In J. H. Barkow, L. Cosmides, & J. Tooby (Eds.), *The adapted mind: Evolutionary psychology and the generation of culture.* New York: Oxford University Press.

Pinker, S., & Jackendoff, R. (2005). The faculty of language: What's special about it? *Cognition, 95,* 201–236.

Piolino, P., Hisland, M., Ruffeveille, I., Matuszewski, V., Jambaqué, I., & Eustache, F. (2007). Do school-age children remember or know the personal past? *Consciousness and Cognition, 16,* 84–101.

Pipitone, R. N., & Gallup, G. G. (2008). Women's voice attractiveness varies across the menstrual cycle. *Evolution and Human Behavior, 29,* 268–274.

Pitman, R. K., van der Kolk, B. A., Orr, S. P., & Greenberg, M. S. (1990). Naloxone-reversible analgesic response to combat-related stimuli in posttraumatic stress disorder. *Archives of General Psychiatry, 47,* 541–544.

Plant, E. A., & Peruche, B. M. (2005). The consequences of race for police officers' responses to criminal suspects. *Psychological Science, 16,* 180–183.

Plaud, J. J., & Martini, J. R. (1999). The respondent conditioning of male sexual arousal. *Behavior Modification, 23,* 254–268.

Pleim, E. T., & Barfield, R. J. (1988). Progesterone versus estrogen facilitation of female sexual behavior by intracranial administration to female rats. *Hormones and Behavior, 22,* 150–159.

Plomin, R., & Caspi, A. (1999). Behavioral genetics and personality. In L. A. Pervin & O. John (Eds.), *Handbook of personality: Theory and research* (2nd ed.). New York: Guilford.

Plomin, R., & Daniels, D. (1987). Why are children in the same family so different from one another? *Behavioral and Brain Sciences, 10,* 1–60.

Plomin, R., DeFries, J. C., & McClearan, G. E. (1990). *Behavioral genetics: A primer* (2nd ed.). New York: Freeman.

Plutchik, R. (2001). The nature of emotions. *American Scientist, 89,* 344–350.

Poldrack, R. A., & Foerde, K. (2008). Category learning and the memory systems debate. *Neuroscience and Biobehavioral Reviews, 32,* 197–205.

Polefrone, J., & Manuck, S. (1987). Gender differences in cardiovascular and neuroendocrine response to stressors. In R. C. Barnett, L. Biener, & G. K. Baruch (Eds.), *Gender and stress.* New York: Free Press.

Pollick, A. S., & de Waal, F. B. M. (2007). Ape gestures and language evolution. *Proceedings of the National Academy of Sciences, 104,* 8184–8189.

Pomerantz, J. M. (2007). Glutamate hypofunction and schizophrenia: A new theory. *Drug Benefit Trends, 19,* 290–293.

Pongrácz, P., Vida, V., Bánhegyi, P., & Miklósa, A. (2008). How does dominance rank status affect individual and social learning performance in the dog (*Canis familiaris*)? *Animal Cognition, 11,* 75–82.

Poremba, A., Saunders, R. C., Crane, A. M., Cook, M., Sokoloff, L., & Mishkin, M. (2003). Functional mapping of the primate auditory system. *Science, 299,* 568–572.

Portas, C. M., Krakow, K., Allen, P., Josephs, O., Armony, J. L., & Frith, C. D. (2000). Auditory processing across the sleep-wake cycle: Simultaneous EEG and fMRI monitoring in humans. *Neuron, 28,* 991–999.

Porter, R. H. (1991). Human reproduction and the mother-infant relationship: The role of odors. In T. V. Getchell, R. L. Doty, L. M. Bartoshuk, & J. B. Snow (Eds.), *Smell and taste in health and disease.* New York: Raven Press.

Posada, G., Carbonell, O. A., Alzate, G., & Plata, S. J. (2004). Through Colombian lenses: Ethnographic and conventional analyses of maternal care and their associations with secure base behavior. *Developmental Psychology, 40,* 508–518.

Postmes, T., Spears, R., & Sezgin, C. (2001). Quality of decision making and group norms. *Journal of Personality and Social Psychology, 80,* 918–930.

Potts, W. K., Manning, C. J., & Wakeland, E. K. (1991). Mating patterns in seminatural populations of mice influenced by MHC genotype. *Nature, 352,* 619–621.

Poulos, C. X., & Cappell, H. (1991). Homeostatic theory of drug tolerance: A general model of physiological adaptation. *Psychological Review, 98,* 390–408.

Power, T. G. (2000). *Play and exploration in children and animals.* Mahwah, NJ: Erlbaum.

Prabhakar, S., Noonan, J. P., Pääbo, S., & Rubin, E. M. (2006). Accelerated evolution of conserved noncoding sequences in humans. *Science, 314,* 786.

Prabu, D. (1998). News concreteness and visual-verbal association: Do news pictures narrow the recall gap between concrete and abstract news? *Human Communication Research, 25,* 180–201.

Premack, D. (1990). The infant's theory of self-propelled objects. *Cognition, 36,* 1–16.

Pressin, J. (1933). The comparative effects of social and mechanical stimulation on memorizing. *American Journal of Psychology, 45,* 263–270.

Preuschoft, S., & van Hooff, J. (1997). The social function of "smile" and "laughter": Variations across primate species and societies. In U. Segerstrale & P. Molnar (Eds.), *Nonverbal communication: Where nature meets culture.* Mahwah, NJ: Erlbaum.

Price, D. D. (2000). Psychological and neural mechanisms of the affective dimension of pain. *Science, 288,* 1769–1772.

Price, D. D., Finniss, D. G., & Benedetti, F. (2008). A comprehensive review of the placebo effect: Recent advances and current thought. *Annual Review of Psychology, 59,* 565–590.

Price, J. S., Gardner, R., Jr., & Erickson, M. (2004). Can depression, anxiety, and somatization be understood as appeasement displays? *Journal of Affective Disorders, 79,* 1–11.

Price, M. E. (2003). Pro-community altruism and social status in a Shuar village. *Human Nature, 14,* 191–208.

Prickaerts, J., Koopmans, G., Blokland, A., & Arjan, S. (2004). Learning and adult neurogenesis: Survival with or without proliferation? *Neurobiology of Learning and Memory, 81,* 1–11.

Prigerson, H. G., Bierhals, A. J., Stanislav, V. K., Reynolds, C. F., Shear, M. K., Day, N., Beery, L. C., Newsom, J. T., & Jacobs, S. (1997). Traumatic grief is a risk factor for mental and physical morbidity. *American Journal of Psychiatry, 154,* 616–623.

Pritchard, T. C. (1991). The primate gustatory system. In T. V. Getchell, R. L. Doty, L. M. Bartoshuk, & J. B. Snow (Eds.), *Smell and taste in health and disease.* New York: Raven Press.

Profet, M. (1992). Pregnancy sickness as adaptation: A deterrent to maternal ingestion of teratogens. In J. H. Barkow, L. Cosmides, & J. Tooby (Eds.), *The adapted mind: Evolutionary psychology and the generation of culture.* Oxford: Oxford University Press.

Provine, R. R. (1996). Laughter. *American Scientist, 84,* 38–45.

Provine, R. R. (2004). Laughing, tickling, and the evolution of speech and self. *Current Directions in Psychological Science, 13,* 215–218.

Pryor, K. (1985). *Don't shoot the dog: The new art of teaching and training.* New York: Bantam.

Purves, D., Williams, S. M., Nundy, S., & Lotto, R. B. (2004). Perceiving the intensity of light. *Psychological Review, 111,* 142–158.

Querleu, D., Lefebvre, C., Renard, X., Titran, M., Morillion, M., & Crepin, G. (1984). Réactivité du nouveau né de moins de deux heures de vie à la voix maternelle. *Journal de Gynecologie, Obstétrique et Biologie de la Reproduction, 13,* 125–134.

Quickfall, J., & Suchowersky, O. (2007). Pathological gambling associated with dopamine agonist use in restless legs syndrome. *Parkinsonism and Related Disorders, 13,* 535–536.

Quinn, A., & Schlenker, B. R. (2002). Can accountability produce independence? Goals as determinants of the impact of accountability on conformity. *Personality and Social Psychology Bulletin, 28,* 472–483.

Rachels, J. (1990). *Created from animals: The moral implications of Darwinism.* Oxford: Oxford University Press.

Rachlin, H. (1990). Why do people gamble and keep gambling despite heavy losses? *Psychological Science, 1,* 249–297.

Rachman, S. J., & DeSilva, P. (1978). Abnormal and normal obsessions. *Behavioral Research and Therapy, 16,* 223–248.

Rafalovich, A. (2004). *Framing ADHD children: A critical examination of the history, discourse, and everyday experience of attention deficit/hyperactivity disorder.* Lanham, MD: Lexington Books.

Rahman, Q., & Wilson, G. D. (2003). Born gay? The psychobiology of human sexual orientation. *Personality and Individual Differences, 34,* 1337–1382.

Raikes, H. A., & Thompson, R. A. (2008). Attachment security and parenting quality predict children's problem-solving, attributions, and loneliness with peers. *Attachment and Human Development, 10,* 319–344.

Rakoczy. H. (2008). Pretense as individual and collective intentionality. *Mind and Language, 23,* 499–517.

Ramey, C. H., & Weisberg, R. W. (2004). The "poetical activity" of Emily Dickinson: A further test of the hypothesis that affective disorders foster creativity. *Creativity Research Journal, 16,* 173–185.

Randall, M., & Haskell, L. (1995). Sexual violence in women's lives: Findings from the Women's Safety Project, a community-based survey. *Violence Against Women, 1,* 6–31.

Rapee, R. M., & Spence, S. H. (2004). The etiology of social phobia: Empirical evidence and an initial model. *Clinical Psychology Review, 24,* 737–767.

Rasch, B., & Born, J. (2008). Reactivation and consolidation of memory during sleep. *Current Directions in Psychological Science, 17,* 188–192.

Raskin, N. J., & Witty, M. (2007). Person-centered therapy. In R. J. Corsini & D. Wedding (eds.), *Current psychotherapies* (8th ed.). Belmont, CA: Brooks-Cole.

Rasmussen, T., & Milner, B. (1977). The role of early left brain injury in determinating lateralization of cerebral speech functions. *Annals of the New York Academy of Sciences, 299,* 355–369.

Rauschecker, J. P., Tian, B., & Hauser, M. (1995). Processing of complex sounds in the macaque nonprimary auditory cortex. *Science, 268,* 111–114.

Ray, O. (2004). How the mind hurts and heals the body. *American Psychologist, 59,* 29–40.

Raynor, H. A., & Epstein, L. H. (2001). Dietary variety, energy regulation, and obesity. *Psychological Bulletin, 127,* 325–341.

Razran, G. A. (1939). A quantitative study of meaning by a conditioned salivary technique (semantic conditioning). *Science, 90,* 89–91.

Reber, A. S. (1989). Implicit learning and tacit knowledge. *Journal of Experimental Psychology: General, 118,* 219–235.

Reber, P. J., Siwiec, R. M., Gitleman, D. R., Parrish, T. B., Mesulam, M.-M., & Paller, K. A. (2002). Neural correlates of successful encoding identified using functional magnetic resonance imaging. *Journal of Neuroscience, 22,* 9541–9548.

Recanzone, G. H., & Sutter, M. L. (2008). The biological basis of audition. *Annual Review of Psychology, 59,* 119–142.

Recanzone, G. H., Merzenich, M. M., Jenkins, W. M., Grajski, K. A. & Dinse, H. R. (1992). Topographic reorganization of the hand representation in cortical area 3b of owl monkeys trained in a frequency-discrimination task. *Journal of Neurophysiology, 67,* 1031–1056.

Redelmeier, M. D., & Tibshirani, R. J. (1997). Association between cellular-telephone calls and motor vehicle collisions. *New England Journal of Medicine, 336,* 453–457.

Redican, W. K. (1982). An evolutionary perspective on human facial displays. In P. Ekman (Ed.), *Emotion in the human face.* Cambridge, England: Cambridge University Press.

Rees, J. A., & Harvey, P. H. (1991). The evolution of mating systems. In V. Reynolds & J. Kellett (Eds.), *Mating and marriage.* Oxford: Oxford University Press.

Regier, T. (2003). Emergent constraints on word-learning: A computational perspective. *Trends in Cognitive Sciences, 7,* 263–268.

Reich, J. W., Erdal, K. J., & Zautra, A. (1997). Beliefs about control and health behaviors. In D. S. Gochman (Ed.), *Handbook of health behavior research: I. Personal and social determinants.* New York: Plenum.

Reichenberg, A., & Harvey, P. D. (2007). Neuropsychological impairments in schizophrenia: Integration of performance-based brain imaging findings. *Psychological Bulletin, 133,* 833–858.

Reisberg, D., Smith, J. D., Baxter, D. A., & Sonenshine, M. (1989). "Enacted" auditory images are ambiguous; "pure" auditory images are not. *Quarterly Journal of Experimental Psychology: Human Experimental Psychology, 41,* 619–641.

Reiser, M. F. (1991). *Memory in mind and brain: What dream imagery reveals.* New York: Basic Books.

Renner, M. J. (1988). Learning during exploration: The role of behavioral topography during exploration in determining subsequent adaptive behavior. *The International Journal of Comparative Psychology, 2,* 43–56.

Renner, M. J., & Seltzer, C. P. (1991). Molar characteristics of exploratory and investigatory behavior in the rat (*Rattus norvegicus*). *Journal of Comparative Psychology, 105,* 326–339.

Repacholi, B. M., & Gopnick, A. (1997). Early reasoning about desires: Evidence from 14- and 18-month-olds. *Developmental Psychology, 33,* 12–21.

Rescorla, R. A. (1973). Effect of US habituation following conditioning. *Journal of Comparative and Physiological Psychology, 82,* 137–143.

Rescorla, R. A. (1988). Pavlovian conditioning: It's not what you think it is. *American Psychologist, 43,* 151–160.

Rescorla, R. A., & Wagner, A. R. (1972). A theory of Pavlovian conditioning: Variations in effectiveness of reinforcement and nonreinforcement. In A. Black & W. F. Prokasky, Jr. (Eds.), *Classical conditioning II.* New York: Appleton-Century-Crofts.

Reuter-Lorenz, P. A., & Miller, A. C. (1998). The cognitive neuroscience of human laterality: Lessons from the bisected brain. *Current Directions in Psychological Science, 7,* 15–20.

Reyes-Vallejo, L, Lazarou, S., & Morgentaler, A. (2007). Subjective sexual response to testosterone replacement therapy based on initial serum levels of total testosterone. *Journal of Sexual Medicine, 4,* 1757–1762.

Reynolds, D. V. (1969). Surgery in the rat during electrical analgesia induced by focal brain stimulation. *Science, 164,* 444–445.

Reynolds, J. H. (2008). Mapping the microcircuitry of attention. *Nature Neuroscience, 11,* 861–862.

Reynolds, J. N. J., Hyland, B., & Wickens, J. R. (2001). A cellular mechanism of reward-related learning. *Nature, 413,* 67–70.

Rheingold, H. L. (1982). Little children's participation in the work of adults, a nascent prosocial behavior. *Child Development, 53,* 114–125.

Rheingold, H. L., Hay, D. F., & West, M. J. (1976). Sharing in the second year of life. *Child Development, 47,* 1148–1158.

Richards, C. A., & Sanderson, J. A. (1999). The role of imagination in facilitating deductive reasoning in 2-, 3-, and 4-year-olds. *Cognition, 72,* B1–B9.

Richards, R., Kinney, D. K., Lunde, I., Benet, M., & Merzel, A. P. C. (1988). Creativity in manic-depressives, cyclothymes, their normal relatives and control subjects. *Journal of Abnormal Psychology, 97,* 281–288.

Richardson, D. C., Dale, R., & Kirkham, N. Z. (2007). The art of conversation is coordination. *Psychological Science, 18,* 407–413.

Richardson, R., & Hayne, H. (2007). You can't take it with you: The translation of memory across development. *Current Directions in Psychological Science, 16,* 223–227.

Rickert, V. I., Wiemann, C. M., Vaughan, R. D., & White, J. W. (2004). Rates and risk factors for sexual violence among an ethnically diverse sample of adolescents. *Archives of Pediatric Adolescent Medicine, 158,* 1132–1139.

Riecher-Rossler, A., & Hafner, H. (2000). Gender aspects in schizophrenia: Bridging the border between social and biological psychiatry. *Acta Psychiatrica Scandinavica Supplement, 102,* 58–62.

Riggs, L. A. (1965). Visual acuity. In C. H. Graham (Ed.), *Vision and visual perception.* New York: Wiley.

Riley, J. W., Jr. (1970). What people think about death. In O. B. Brim, Jr., H. E. Freeman, S. Levine, & N. A. Scotch (Eds.), *The dying patient.* New York: Russell Sage Foundation.

Rilling, J. K., Winslow, J. T., & Kilts, C. D. (2004). The neural correlates of mate competition in dominant male rhesus macaques. *Biological Psychiatry, 56,* 364–375.

Rime, B., Philippot, P., & Cisamolo, D. (1990). Social schemata of peripheral changes in emotion. *Journal of Personality and Social Psychology, 59,* 38–49.

Roberts, B. W., & DelVecchio, W. F. (2000). The rank-order consistency of personality traits from childhood to old age: A quantitative review of longitudinal studies. *Psychological Bulletin, 126,* 3–25.

Roberts, B. W., & Mroczek, D. (2008). Personality trait change in adulthood. *Current Directions in Psychological Science, 17,* 31–34.

Roberts, B. W., & Robins, R. W. (2004). A longitudinal study of person-environment fit and personality development. *Journal of Personality, 72,* 89–110.

Roberts, B. W., Kuncel, N. R., Shiner, R., Caspi, A., & Goldberg, L. R. (2007). The power of personality: The comparative validity of personality traits, socioeconomic status, and cognitive ability for predicting important life outcomes. *Perspectives on Psychological Science, 2,* 313–345.

Roberts, W. A., Cruz, C., & Tremblay, J. (2007). Rats take correct novel routes and shortcuts in an enclosed maze. *Journal of Experimental Psychology: Animal Behavior Processes, 33,* 79-91.

Robertson, S. I. (2001). *Problem solving.* Hove, England: Psychology Press.

Robins, L. N., Helzer, J. E., & Davis, D. H. (1975). Narcotic use in Southeast Asia and afterwards. *Archives of General Psychiatry, 32,* 955–961.

Rochat, P. (1989). Object manipulation and exploration in 2- to 5-month-old infants. *Developmental Psychology, 25,* 871–884.

Rock, I., & Gutman, D. (1981). The effect of inattention on form perception. *Journal of Experimental Psychology: Human Perception and Performance, 7,* 275–285.

Rodier, P. M. (2000, February). The early origins of autism. *Scientific American,* 56–63.

Rodin, J., Schank, D., & Striegel-Moore, R. (1989). Psychological features of obesity. *Medical Clinics of North America, 73,* 47–66.

Rodseth, L., Wrangham, R. W., Harrigan, A. M., & Smuts, B. B. (1991). The human community as a primate society. *Current Anthropology, 32,* 221–252.

Roelfsema, P. R. (2006). Cortical algorithms for perceptual grouping. *Annual Review of Neuroscience, 29,* 203–227.

Roesch, M. R., Calu, D. J., & Schoenbaum, G. (2007). Dopamine neurons encode the better option in rats deciding between differently delayed or sized rewards. *Nature Neuroscience, 10,* 1615–1624.

Roese, N. J., & Olson, J. M. (2007). Better, stronger, faster: Self-serving judgment, affect regulation, and the optimal vigilance hypothesis. *Perspectives in Psychological Science, 2,* 124–141.

Roesler, T. A., & McKenzie, N. (1994). Effects of childhood trauma on psychological functioning in adults sexually abused as children. *Journal of Nervous and Mental Disease, 182,* 145–150.

Rogers, C. R. (1951). *Client-centered therapy: Its current practice, implications, and theory.* Boston: Houghton Mifflin.

Rogers, C. R. (1959). A theory of therapy, personality, and interpersonal relationships, as developed in the client-centered frame-work. In S. Koch (Ed.), *Psychology: A study of a science* (Vol. 3). New York: McGraw-Hill.

Rogers, C. R. (1963). The actualizing tendency in relation to "motives" and to consciousness. In M. R. Jones (Ed.), *Nebraska Symposium on Motivation.* Lincoln: University of Nebraska Press.

Rogers, C. R. (1977). *Carl Rogers on personal power.* New York: Delacorte Press.

Rogers, C. R. (1980). *A way of being.* Boston: Houghton Mifflin.

Rogers, C. R. (Ed.) (1967). *The therapeutic relationship and its impact: A study of psychotherapy with schizophrenics.* Madison: University of Wisconsin Press.

Rogoff, B. (1990). *Apprenticeship in thinking: Cognitive development in social context.* New York: Oxford University Press.

Rogoff, B. (1993). Children's guided participation and participatory appropriation in sociocultural activity. In R. H. Wozniak & K. W. Fisher (Eds.), *Development in context: Acting and thinking in specific environments.* Hillsdale, NJ: Erlbaum.

Rogoff, B. (2003). *The cultural nature of human development.* Oxford: Oxford University Press.

Rolls, E. T. (2004). The functions of the orbitofrontal cortex. *Brain and Cognition, 55,* 11–29.

Rolls, E. T., Murzi, E., Yaxley, S., Thorpe, S. J., & Simpson, S. J. (1986). Sensory-specific satiety: Food-specific reduction in responsiveness of ventral forebrain neurons after feeding in the monkey. *Brain Research, 368,* 79–86.

Roney, J. R., Lukaszewski, A. W., & Simmons, Z. L. (2007). Rapid endocrine responses of young men to social interactions with young women. *Hormones and Behavior, 52,* 326-333.

Rose, A., J., & Rudolph, K. D. (2006). A review of sex differences in peer relationship processes: Potential trade-offs for the emotional and behavioral development of girls and boys. *Psychological Bulletin, 132,* 98–131.

Rosenthal, R. (1994). Interpersonal expectancy effects: A 30-year perspective. *Current Directions in Psychological Science, 3,* 176–179.

Rosenthal, R., & Jacobson, L. (1968). *Pygmalion in the classroom.* New York: Holt, Rinehart & Winston.

Rosenzweig, M. R., Bennett, E. L., & Diamond, M. C. (1972, February). Brain changes in response to experience. *Scientific American,* pp. 22–29.

Ross, H. E., & Plug, C. (2002). *The mystery of the moon illusion: Exploring size perception.* Oxford: Oxford University Press.

Ross, L. (1977). The intuitive psychologist and his shortcomings: Distortions in the attribution process. In L. Berkowitz (Ed.), *Advances in experimental social psychology.* New York: Academic Press.

Roth, T. C., Lesku, J. A., Amlaner, C. J., & Lima, S. L. (2006). A phylogenetic analysis of the correlates of sleep in birds. *Journal of Sleep Research, 15,* 395–402.

Rothbart, M. K., & Bates, J. (1998). Temperament. In N. Eisenberg (Ed.), *Handbook of child psychology* (5th ed.). Vol. 3, *Social, emotional, and personality development.* New York: Wiley.

Rothenberg, A. (2001). Bipolar illness, creativity, and treatment. *Psychiatric Quarterly, 72,* 131–147.

Rotter, J. B. (1954; reprinted 1973, 1980). *Social learning and clinical psychology.* New York: Johnson Reprint Co.

Rotter, J. B. (1966). Generalized expectancies for internal versus external locus of control of reinforcement. *Psychological Monographs: General and Applied, 80* (Whole No. 609).

Rotter, J. B., Liverant, S., & Crowne, D. P. (1961). The growth and extinction of expectancies in change of controlled and skilled tasks. *Journal of Psychology, 52,* 161–177.

Rovee-Collier, C., & Cuevas, K. (2009). Multiple memory systems are unnecessary to account for infant memory development: An ecological model. *Developmental Psychology, 45,* 160–174.

Rowe, D. C. (1994). *The limits of family influence: Genes, experience, and behavior.* New York: Guilford.

Rozée, P. D., & Van Boemel, G. V. (1989). The psychological effects of war trauma and abuse on older Cambodian refugee women. *Women & Therapy, 8,* 23–50.

Rozin, P., & Kalat, J. (1971). Specific hungers and poison avoidance as adaptive specializations of learning. *Psychological Review, 78,* 459–486.

Rozin, P., & Schull, J. (1988). The adaptive-evolutionary point of view in experimental psychology. In R. L. Atkinson, R. J. Herrnstein, G. Lindzey, & R. D. Luce (Eds.), *Steven's Handbook of Experimental Psychology* (2nd ed.). New York: Wiley.

Rubin, E. (1915; reprinted 1958). Figure and ground. In D. C. Beardslee & M. Wertheimer (Eds.), *Readings in perception.* Princeton, NJ: Van Nostrand.

Rubin, M., & Hewstone, M. (1998). Social identity theory's self-esteem hypothesis: A review and some suggestions for clarification. *Review of Personality and Social Psychology, 2,* 40–62.

Rubinstein, G. (2005). The Big Five among male and female students of different faculties. *Personality and Individual Differences, 38,* 1495–1503.

Rudman, L. A. (2004). Sources of implicit attitudes. *Current Directions in Psychological Science, 13,* 79–82.

Rudman, L. A., Ashmore, R. D., & Gary, M. L. (2001). "Unlearning" automatic biases: The malleability of implicit stereotypes and prejudice. *Journal of Personality and Social Psychology, 81,* 856–868.

Ruff, C. C., Kristjánsson, Á., & Driver, J. (2007). Readout from iconic memory and selective spatial attention involve similar neural processes. *Psychological Science, 18,* 901–909.

Ruff, H. A. (1986). Components of attention during infants' manipulative exploration. *Child Development, 75,* 105–114.

Ruff, H. A. (1989). The infant's use of visual and haptic information in the perception and recognition of objects. *Canadian Journal of Psychology, 43,* 302–319.

Ruffman, T., Perner, J., Naito, M., Parkin, L., & Clements, W. A. (1998). Older (but not younger) siblings facilitate false belief understanding. *Developmental Psychology, 34,* 161–174.

Ruffman, T., Slade, L., & Redman, J. (2005). Young infants' expectations about hidden objects. *Cognition, 97,* B35–B43.

Russell, J. (2003). Core affect and the psychological construction of emotion. *Psychological Review, 110,* 145–172.

Rutkowski, G. K., Gruder, C. L., & Romer, D. (1983). Group cohesiveness, social norms, and bystander intervention. *Journal of Personality and Social Psychology, 44,* 545–552.

Rutter, M. (2002). Nature, nurture, and development: From evangelism through science toward policy and practice. *Child Development, 73,* 1–21.

Rutter, M. (2007). Proceeding from observed correlation to causal inference: The use of natural experiments. *Perspectives in Psychological Science, 2,* 377–408.

Ruys, K. I., & Stapel, D. A. (2008). Emotion elicitor or emotion messenger? Subliminal priming reveals two faces of facial expressions. *Psychological Science, 19,* 593–600.

Ruys, K. I., & Stapel, D. A. (2008). The secret life of emotions. *Psychological Science, 19,* 385–391.

Ryan, R. M., & Deci, E. L. (2000). Self-determination theory and the facilitation of intrinsic motivation, social development, and well-being. *American Psychologist, 55,* 68–78.

Ryan, R. M., & Deci, E. L. (2006). Self-regulation and the problem of human autonomy: Does psychology need choice, self-determination, and will? *Journal of Personality, 74,* 1557–1585.

Rybash, J. M., Roodin, P. A., & Hoyer, W. J. (1995). *Adult development and aging* (3rd ed.). Dubuque, IA: Brown & Benchmark.

Rydell, R. J., McConnell, A. R., Mackie, D. M., & Strain, L. M. (2006). Of two minds: Forming and changing valence-inconsistent implicit and explicit attitudes. *Psychological Science, 17,* 954–958.

Rymer, R. (1993). *Genie: An abused child's flight from silence.* New York: HarperCollins.

Sabbatini da Silva Lobo, D., Vallada, H. P., Knight, J., Martins, S. S., Tavares, H., Gentil, V., & Kennedy, J. L. (2007). Dopamine genes and pathological gambling in discordant sib-pairs. *Journal of Gambling Studies, 23,* 421–433.

Sacco, D. F., & Hugenberg, K. (2009). The look of fear and anger: Facial maturity modulates recognition of fearful and angry expressions. *Emotion, 9,* 39–49.

Sachs, G. S., & Gelenberg, A. J. (1988). Adverse effects of electroconvulsive therapy. In A. J. Frances & R. E. Hales (Eds.), *Review of psychiartry* (Vol. 7). Washington, DC: American Psychiatric Press.

Sackeim, H. A., Prudic, J., Devanand, D. P., Nobler, M. S., Lisanby, S. H., Peyser, S, et al. (2000). A prospective, randomized, double-blind comparison of bilateral and right unilateral electroconvulsive therapy at different stimulus intensities. *Archives of General Psychiatry, 57,* 425–534.

Sacks, O. (1995). *An anthropologist on Mars: Seven paradoxical tales.* New York: Knopf.

Sakai, K., Rowe, J. B., & Passingham, R. E. (2002). Active maintenance in prefrontal area 46 creates distractor-resistant memory. *Nature Neuroscience, 5,* 479–484.

Sakurai, T. (2007). The neural circuit of orexin (hypocretin): Maintaining sleep and wakefulness. *Nature Reviews Neuroscience, 8,* 171–181.

Salonia, A., Pontillo, M., Nappi, R. A., Zanni, G., Fabbri, F., Scavini, M., Daverio,R., Gallina, A., Rigatti, P., Bosi, E., Bonini, P. A., & Montorsi, F. (2008). Menstrual cycle-related changes in circulating androgens in healthy women with self-reported normal sexual function. *Journal of Sexual Medicine, 5,* 854–863.

Salthouse, T. A. (2004). What and when of cognitive aging. *American Psychological Society, 13,* 140–144.

Samuel, A. G. (1991). A further examination of attentional effects in the phonemic restoration illusion. *Quarterly Journal of Experimental Psychology, 43A,* 679–699.

Sanfey, A. G., Rilling, J. K., Aronson, J. A., Nystrom, L. E., & Cohen, J. D. (2003). The neural basis of economic decision-making in the ultimatum game. *Science, 300,* 1755–1758.

Sanford, E. C. (1982; originally written as a letter in 1917). Professor Sanford's morning prayer. In U. Neisser (Ed.), *Memory observed: Remembering in natural contexts.* New York: Freeman.

Santosa, C. M., Strong, C. M., Nowakowska, C., Wang, P. W., Rennicke, C. M., & Ketter, T. A. (2007). Enhanced creativity in bipolar disorder patients: A controlled study. *Journal of Affective Disorders, 100,* 31–39.

Saper, C. B., Chou, T. C., & Scammell, T. E. (2001). The sleep switch: Hypothalamic control of sleep and wakefulness. *Trends in Neurosciences, 24,* 726–731.

Sapir, E. (1941; reprinted 1964). *Culture, language, and personality.* Berkeley: University of California Press.

Sarra, S., & Otta, E. (2001). Different types of smiles and laughter in preschool children. *Psychological Reports, 89,* 547–558.

Savage-Rumbaugh, E. S., & Fields, W. M. (2000). Linguistic, cultural, and cognitive capacities of bonobos (*Pan paniscus*). *Culture and Psychology, 6,* 131–153.

Savage-Rumbaugh, E. S., McDonald, K., Sevcik, R. A., Hopkins, B., & Rupert, E. (1986). Spontaneous symbol acquisition and communicative use by pygmy chimpanzees. *Journal of Experimental Psychology: General, 115,* 211–235.

Savage-Rumbaugh, S., Murphy, J., Sevcik, R. A., Brakke, K. E., Williams, S., & Rumbaugh, D. M. (1993). Language comprehension in ape and child. *Monographs of the Society for Research on Child Development* (3 & 4).

Saxe, R., Carey, S., & Kanwisher, N. (2004). Understanding other minds: Linking developmental psychology and functional neuroimaging. *Annual Review of Psychology, 55,* 87–124.

Scarr, S., & Carter-Saltzman, L. (1983). Genetics and intelligence. In J. L. Fuller & E. C. Simmel (Eds.), *Behavior genetics: Principles and applications.* Hillsdale, NJ: Erlbaum.

Scarr, S., & McCartney, K. (1983). How people make their own environments: A theory of genotype–environment effects. *Child Development, 54,* 424–435.

Scarr, S., Weber, P. L., Weinberg, R. A., & Wittig, M. A. (1981). Personality resemblance among adolescents and their parents in biologically related and adoptive families. *Journal of Personality and Social Psychology, 40,* 885–898.

Schab, F. R. (1990). Odors and remembrance of things past. *Journal of Experimental Psychology: Learning, Memory, and Cognition, 16,* 648–655.

Schachter, F. F. (1982). Sibling deidentification and split-parent identification: A family tetrad. In M. E. Lamb & B. Sutton-Smith (Eds.), *Sibling relationships: Their nature and significance across the lifespan.* Hillsdale, NJ: Erlbaum.

Schachter, S. (1971). *Emotion, obesity, and crime.* New York: Academic Press.

Schacter, D. L., Addis, D.R., & Buckner, R. L. (2007). Remembering the past to imagine the future: The prospective brain. *Nature Reviews Neuroscience, 9,* 657–661.

Schafe, G. E., Sollars, S. I., & Bernstein, I. L. (1995). The CS-US interval and taste aversion learning: A brief look. *Behavioral Neuroscience, 109,* 799–802.

Schaller, George B. (1972). *The Serengeti lion: A study of predator-prey relations.* Chicago: University of Chicago Press.

Schank, R. C., & Abelson, R. P. (1977). *Scripts, plans, goals and understanding.* Hillsdale, NJ: Erlbaum.

Scharf, B. (1964). Partial masking. *Acustica, 14,* 16–23.

Scheers, N. J., Rutherford, M. S., & Kemp, J. S. (2003). Where should infants sleep? A comparison of risk for suffocation of infants sleeping in cribs, adult beds, and other sleeping locations. *Pediatrics, 112,* 883–889.

Scheier, M. F., & Carver, C. S. (1993). On the power of positive thinking: The benefits of being optimistic. *Current Directions in Psychological Science, 2,* 26–30.

Scheier, M. F., Matthews, K. A., Owens, J. F., Magovern, G. J., Lefebvre, R., Abbott, R. C., & Carver, C. S. (1989). Dispositional optimism and recovery from coronary artery bypass surgery: The beneficial effects of optimism on physical and psychological well-being. *Journal of Personality and Social Psychology, 57,* 1024–1040.

Schiff, N. D., Giacino, J. T., Kalmar, K., Victor, J. D., Baker, K., Gerber, M., Fritz, B., Eisenberg, B., O'Connor, J., Kobylarz, E. J., Farris, S., Machado, A., McCagg, C., Plum, F., Fins, J. J., & Rezai, A. R. (2007). Behavioural improvements with thalamic stimulation after severe traumatic brain injury. *Nature, 448,* 600–604.

Schiffman, H. R. (1996). *Sensation and perception: An integrated approach* (4th ed.). Hoboken, NJ: Wiley.

Schildkraut, J. J. (1965). The catecholamine hypothesis of affective disorders: A review of supporting evidence. *American Journal of Psychiatry, 122,* 509–522.

Schindler, I., Rice, N. J., McIntosh, R. D., Rossetti, Y., Vighetto, A., & Milner, A. D. (2004). Automatic avoidance of obstacles is a dorsal stream function: Evidence from optic ataxia. *Nature Neuroscience, 7,* 779–784.

Schlenker, B. R. (1980). *Impression management: The self-concept, social identity, and interpersonal relations.* Monterey, CA: Brooks/Cole.

Schlenker, B. R., & Pontari, B. A. (2000). The strategic control of information: Impression management and self-presentation in daily life. In A. Tesser, R. B. Felson, & J. M. Suls (Eds.), *Psychological perspectives on self and identity.* Washington, DC: American Psychological Association.

Schmader, T., & Johns, M. (2003). Converging evidence that stereotype threat reduces working memory capacity. *Journal of Personality and Social Psychology, 85,* 440–452.

Schmader, T., Johns, M., & Forbes, C. (2008). An integrated process model of stereotype threat effects on performance. *Psychological Review, 115,* 336–356.

Schmidt, F. L., & Hunter, J. (2004). General mental ability in the world of work: Occupational attainment and job performance. *Journal of Personality and Social Psychology, 86,* 162–173.

Schmidt, R. F. (1986). Motor systems. In R. F. Schmidt (Ed.), *Fundamentals of neurophysiology* (3rd ed.). New York: Springer-Verlag.

Schmitt, D. P. (2003). Universal sex differences in the desire for sexual variety: Tests from 52 nations, 6 continents, and 13 islands. *Journal of Personality & Social Psychology, 85,* 85–104.

Schmitt, D. P., Realo, A., Voracek, M., & Allik, J. (2008). Why can't a man be more like a woman? Sex differences in big five personality traits across 55 cultures. *Journal of Personality and Social Psychology, 94,* 168–182.

Schmitz, A., Hennig, J., Kuepper, Y., & Reuter, M. (2007). The association between neuroticism and the serotonin transporter polymorphism depends on structural differences between personality measures. *Personality and Individual Differences, 42,* 789–799.

Schnapf, J. L., & Baylor, D. A. (1987, April). How photoreceptor cells respond to light. *Scientific American,* pp. 40–47.

Schneider, B. H., Atkinson, L., & Tardif, C. (2001). Child-parent attachment and children's peer relations: A quantitative review. *Developmental Psychology, 37,* 86–100.

Schneider, J. M. (1972). Relationship between locus of control and activity preferences: Effects of masculinity, activity, and skill. *Journal of Consulting and Clinical Psychology, 38,* 225–230.

Schneider, J. W., & Hacker, S. L. (1973). Sex role imagery and use of the generic "man" in introductory texts: A case of the sociology of sociology. *The American Sociologists, 8,* 12–18.

Schneider, T. R. (2004). The role of neuroticism on psychological and physiological stress responses. *Journal of Experimental Social Psychology, 40*, 795–804.

Schooler, C. & Mulatu, M. S. (2001). The reciprocal effects of leisure time activities and intellectual functioning in older people: A longitudinal analysis. *Psychology and Aging, 16*, 466–482.

Schooler, C. (2001). The intellectual effects of the demands of the work environment. In R. J. Sternberg & E. L. Grigorenko (Eds.), *Environmental effects on cognitive abilities.* Mahwah, NJ: Erlbaum.

Schooler, C. (2007). Use it—and keep it, longer, probably. *Perspectives in Psychological Science, 2*, 24–29.

Schultz, W. (1998). Predictive signal of dopamine neurons. *Journal of Neurophysiology, 80*, 1–27.

Schulz, L. E., & Bonawitz, E. B. (2007). Serious fun: Preschoolers engage in more exploratory play when evidence is confounded. *Developmental Psychology, 43*, 1045–1050.

Schunk, D. H., & Hanson, A. R. (1985). Peer models: Influence on children's self-efficacy and achievement. *Journal of Educational Psychology, 77*, 313–322.

Schwartz, G. E. (1990). Psychobiology of repression and health: A systems approach. In J. L. Singer (Ed.), *Repression and dissociation: Implications for personality theory, psychopathology, and health.* Chicago: University of Chicago Press.

Schwartz, M. F. (1987). Patterns of speech production of deficit within and across aphasia syndromes: Application of a psycholinguistic model. In M. Coltheart, G. Sartori, & R. Job (Eds.), *The cognitive neuropsychology of language.* Hillsdale, NJ: Erlbaum.

Schwartz, S. H., & Gottlieb, A. (1980). Bystander anonymity and reactions to emergencies. *Journal of Personality and Social Psychology, 39*, 418–430.

Schwartz-Giblin, S., McEwen, B. S., & Pfaff, D. W. (1989). Mechanisms of female reproductive behavior. In F. R. Brush & S. Levine (Eds.), *Psychoendocrinology.* San Diego, CA: Academic Press.

Schwartzman, H. (1978). *Transformations: The anthropology of children's play.* New York: Plenum Press.

Schwarz, S., & Hassebrauck, M. (2008). Self-perceived and observed variations in women's attractiveness throughout the menstrual cycle—a diary study. *Evolution and Human Behavior, 29*, 282–288.

Schwarzer, R. (1994). Optimism, vulnerability, and self-beliefs as health-related cognitions: A systematic overview. *Psychology and Health, 9*, 161–180.

Schweizer, K. (2007). Investigating the relationship of working memory tasks and fluid intelligence tests by means of the fixed-links model in considering the impurity problem. *Intelligence, 35*, 591–604.

Scotko, B. G., Rubin, D. C., & Tupler, L. A. (2008). H. M.'s personal crossword puzzles: Understanding memory and language. *Memory, 16*, 89–96.

Scott, J. P. (1963). The process of primary socialization in canine and human infants. *Monograph of the Society for Research in Child Development, 28*, 1–47.

Scott, J. P., & Fuller, J. L. (1965). *Genetics and the social behavior of the dog.* Chicago: University of Chicago Press.

Scribner, S. (1977). Modes of thinking and ways of speaking: Culture and logic reconsidered. In P. N. Johnson-Laird & P. C. Wason (Eds.), *Thinking: Readings in cognitive science.* Cambridge, England: Cambridge University Press.

Searle, L. V. (1949). The organization of hereditary maze-brightness and maze-dullness. *Genetic Psychology Monographs, 39*, 279–325.

Sears, R. R. (1936). Experimental studies of projection: I. Attributions of traits. *Journal of Social Psychology, 7*, 151–163.

Sechenov, I. M. (1863; reprinted 1935). Reflexes of the brain. In A. A. Subkow (Ed. & Trans.), *I. M. Sechenov: Selected works.* Moscow: State Publishing House for Biological and Medical Literature.

Sedikides, C., Gaertner, L., & Goguchi, Y. (2003). Pancultural self-enhancement. *Journal of Personality and Social Psychology, 84*, 60–79.

Seeman, P., & Lee, T. (1975). Antipsychotic drugs: Direct correlation between clinical potency and presynaptic action on dopamine neurons. *Science, 188*, 1271–1219.

Segal, D. L., & Coolidge, F. L. (2001). Diagnosis and classification. In M. Hersen & V. B. Van Hasselt (Eds.), *Advanced abnormal psychology* (2nd ed.). New York: Klewer Academic/Plenum.

Segerstrom, S. C. (2007). Stress, energy, and immunity. *Current Directions in Psychological Science, 16*, 326–330.

Segerstrom, S. C., & Miller, G. E. (2004). Psychological stress and the human immune system: A meta-analytic study of 30 years of inquiry. *Psychological Bulletin, 130*, 601–630.

Seifer, R., Schiller, M., Sameroff, A. J., Resnick, S., & Riordan, K. (1996). Attachment, maternal sensitivity, and infant temperament during the first year of life. *Developmental Psychology, 32*, 12–25.

Self, D. (2003). Dopamine as chicken and egg. *Nature, 422*, 573–574.

Seligman, M. E. P. (1971). Phobias and preparedness. *Behavior Therapy, 2*, 307–320.

Seligman, M. E. P. (1990). *Learned optimism.* New York: Knopf.

Semin, G. R., & Manstead, A. S. R. (1982). The social implications of embarrassment displays and restitution behavior. *European Journal of Social Psychology, 12*, 367–377.

Semmel, A. K. (1976). *Group dynamics and foreign policy process: The choice-shift phenomenon.* Paper presented to the Southern Political Science Association. (For description, see D. G. Myers, 1982.)

Senghas, A., & Coppola, M. (2001). Children creating language: How Nicaraguan sign language acquired a spatial grammar. *Psychological Science, 12*, 323–328.

Senghas, A., Kita, S., & Özyürek, A. (2004). Children creating core properties of language: Evidence from an emerging sign language in Nicaragua. *Science, 305*, 1779–1782.

Sereno, M. I., Dale, A. M., Reppas, J. B., Kwong, K. K., Belliveau, J. W., Brady, T. J., Rosen, B. R., & Tootell, R. B. H. (1995). Borders of multiple visual areas in humans revealed by functional magnetic imaging. *Science, 268*, 889–892.

Sevcik, R. A., & Savage-Rumbaugh, E. S. (1994). Language comprehension and use by great apes. *Language and Communication, 14*, 37–58.

Shadan, S. (2009). A taste of umami. *Nature, 457*, 160.

Shanker, S. G., & King, B. J. (2002). The emergence of a new paradigm in ape language research. *Behavioral and Brain Sciences, 25*, 605–656.

Sharpe, M., & Mayou, R. (2004). Somatoform disorders: A help or a hindrance to good patient care? *British Journal of Psychiatry, 184*, 465–467.

Sheldon, K. M. (1999). Learning the lessons of tit-for-tat: Even competitors can get the message. *Journal of Personality and Social Psychology, 77*, 1245–1253.

Sheldon, K. M., & Kasser, T. (2001). Getting older, getting better? Personal strivings and psychological maturity across the life span. *Developmental Psychology, 37*, 491–501.

Sheldon, K. M., Sheldon, M. S., & Osbaldiston, R. (2000). Prosocial values and group assortation within an *N*-person Prisoner's Dilemma Game. *Human Nature, 11*, 387–404.

Shepherd, G. M. (2006). Smell images and the flavour system in the human brain. *Nature, 444*, 316–321.

Sheppard, L. D., & Vernon, P. A. (2008). Intelligence and speed of information-processing: A review of 50 years of research. *Personality and Individual Differences, 44*, 535–551.

Shergill, S. S., Brammer, M. J., Amaro, E., Williams, S. C. R., Murray, R. M., & McGuire, P. K. (2004). Temporal course of auditory hallucinations. *British Journal of Psychiatry, 185*, 516–517.

Sherif, M. (1936). *The psychology of social norms.* New York: Harper.

Sherif, M. (1966). *In common predicament: Social psychology of inter-group conflict and cooperation.* Boston: Houghton Mifflin.

Sherif, M., Harvey, O. J., White, B. J., Hood, W. E., & Sherif, C. S. (1961). *Intergroup conflict and cooperation: The Robbers Cave experiment.* Norman: University of Oklahoma Book Exchange.

Sherman, D. K., & Kim, H. S. (2005). Is there an "I" in "team"? The role of self in group-serving judgments. *Journal of Personality and Social Psychology, 88,* 108–120.

Sherman, P. W. (1977). Nepotism and the evolution of alarm calls. *Science, 197,* 1246–1253.

Sherrington, C. (1906). *The integrative action of the nervous system.* Cambridge, England: Cambridge University Press.

Sherwin, B. B., & Gelfand, M. M. (1987). Androgen enhances sexual motivation in females: A prospective cross-study of sex hormone administration in the surgical menopause. *Psychosomatic Medicine, 47,* 339–351.

Shettleworth, S. J. (1983, March). Memory in food-hoarding birds. *Scientific American,* pp. 102–110.

Shettleworth, S. J., & Westwood, R. P. (2002). Divided attention, memory, and spatial discrimination in food-storing and nonstoring birds, black-capped chickadees (*Poecile atricapilla*) and dark-eyed juncos (*Junco hyemalis*). *Journal of Experimental Psychology: Animal Behavior Processes, 28,* 227–241.

Shipp, S. (2004). The brain circuitry of attention. *Trends in Cognitive Sciences, 8,* 223–230.

Shoda, Y., Mischel, W., & Wright, J. C. (1994). Intraindividual stability in organization and patterning of behavior: Incorporating psychological situations into the idiographic analysis of personality. *Journal of Personality and Social Psychology, 67,* 674–687.

Siegel, J. M. (2003, October). Why we sleep. *Scientific American, 289,* pp. 92–97.

Siegel, J. M. (2005). Sleep phylogeny: Clues to the evolution and function of sleep. In P-H. Luppi (Ed.), *Sleep: Circuits and functions.* Boca Raton, FL: CRC Press.

Siegel, S. (1976). Morphine analgesia tolerance: Its situation specificity supports a Pavlovian conditioning model. *Science, 193,* 323–325.

Siegel, S. (1984). Pavlovian conditioning and heroin overdose: Reports by overdose victims. *Bulletin of the Psychonomic Society, 22,* 428–430.

Siegel, S. (1999). Drug anticipation and drug addiction. The 1998 H. David Archibald Lecture. *Addiction, 94,* 1113–1124.

Siegel, S. (2005). Drug tolerance, drug addiction, and drug anticipation. *Current Directions in Psychological Science, 14,* 296–300.

Siegel, S., & Ramos, B. M. C. (2002). Applying laboratory research: Drug anticipation and the treatment of drug addiction. *Experimental and Clinical Psychopharmacology, 10,* 162–183.

Siegler, R. S., & Svetina, M. (2006). What leads children to adopt new strategies? A microgenetic/cross-sectional study of class inclusion. *Child Development, 77,* 997–1015.

Silk, J. B. (2002). Kin selection in primate groups. *International Journal of Primatology, 23,* 849–875.

Simerly, R. B. (2002). Wired for reproduction: Organization and development of sexually dimorphic circuits in the mammalian forebrain. *Annual Review of Neuroscience, 25,* 507–536.

Simons, D. J., & Chabris, C. F. (1999). Gorillas in our midst: Sustained inattentional blindness for dynamic events. *Perception, 28,* 1059–1074.

Simpson, J., & Done, D. J. (2004). Analogical reasoning in schizophrenic delusions. *European Psychiatry, 19,* 344–348.

Sims, J. H., & Baumann, D. D. (1972). The tornado threat: Coping styles of the north and south. *Science, 176,* 1386–1392.

Singh, I. (2008). Beyond polemics: Science and the ethics of ADHD. *Nature Reviews Neuroscience, 9,* 957–964.

Sio, U. N., & Ormerod, T. C. (2009). Does incubation enhance problem solving? A meta-analytic review. *Psychological Bulletin, 135,* 94–120.

Siqueland, R. R., & Lipsitt, L. P. (1966). Conditioned headturning in human newborns. *Journal of Experimental Child Psychology, 3,* 356–376.

Sivonen, P., Maess, B., Lattner, S., & Friederici, A. D. (2006). Phonemic restoration in a sentence context: Evidence from early and late ERP effects. *Brain Research, 1121,* 177–189.

Skinner, B. F. (1938). *The behavior of organisms.* New York: Appleton-Century-Crofts.

Skinner, B. F. (1953). *Science and human behavior.* New York: Macmillan.

Skinner, B. F. (1957). *Verbal behavior.* New York: Appleton-Century-Crofts.

Skinner, B. F. (1966). The phylogeny and ontogeny of behavior. *Science, 153,* 1205–1213.

Skov, R. B., & Sherman, S. J. (1986). Information-gathering processes: Diagnosticity, hypothesis confirmation strategies and perceived hypothesis confirmation. *Journal of Experimental Social Psychology, 22,* 93–121.

Slagsvold, T., Svein, D., & Lampe, H. M. (1999). Does female aggression prevent polygyny? An experiment with pied flycatchers (*Ficedula hypoleuca*). *Behavioral Ecology and Sociobiology, 45,* 403–410.

Sloane, R. B., Staples, F. R., Cristo, A. H., Yorkston, N. J., & Whipple, K. (1975). *Psychotherapy versus behavior therapy.* Cambridge, MA: Harvard University Press.

Small, M. F. (1993). *Female choices: Sexual behavior of female primates.* Ithaca, NY: Cornell University Press.

Smith, J. D. (1992). The auditory hallucinations of schizophrenia. D. Reisberg (Ed.), *Auditory imagery.* Hillsdale, NJ: Erlbaum.

Smith, K. (2006). Homing in on the genes for humanity. *Nature, 442,* 725.

Smith, K. S., & Berridge, K. C. (2007). Opioid limbic circuit for reward: Interaction between hedonic hotspots of nucleus accumbens and ventral pallidum. *Journal of Neuroscience, 27,* 1594–1605.

Smith, M. L., Glass, G. V., & Miller, T. I. (1980). *The benefits of psychotherapy.* Baltimore: Johns Hopkins University Press.

Smith, R. H., Webster, J. M., Parrot, W. G., & Eyre, H. L. (2002). The role of public exposure in moral and nonmoral shame and guilt. *Journal of Personality and Social Psychology, 83,* 138–159.

Smith, S. M., & Vela, E. (2001). Environmental context-dependent memory: A review and meta-analysis. *Psychonomic Bulletin and Review, 8,* 203–220.

Smuts, B. (1992). Male aggression against women. An evolutionary perspective. *Human Nature, 3,* 1–44.

Snow, C. E. (1984). Parent-child interaction and the development of communicative ability. In R. L. Schiefelbusch & J. Pickar (Eds.), *The acquisition of communicative competence.* Baltimore: University Park Press.

Snyder, C. R. (1994). *The psychology of hope: You can get there from here.* New York: Free Press.

Snyder, M. (1981). Seek and ye shall find: Testing hypotheses about other people. In E. T. Higgins, C. P. Herman, & M. P. Zanna (Eds.), *Social cognition: The Ontario symposium on personality and social psychology* (pp. 277–303). Hillsdale, NJ: Erlbaum.

Snyder, M., & Omoto, A. M. (1992). Volunteerism and society's response to the HIV epidemic. *Current Directions in Psychological Science, 1,* 113–116.

Snyder, S. H. (1985, October). The molecular basis of communication between cells. *Scientific American,* pp. 132–141.

Snyderman, M., & Rothman, S. (1987). Survey of expert opinion on intelligence and aptitude testing. *American Psychologist, 42,* 137–144.

Soderstrom, M. (2007). Beyond babytalk: Re-evaluating the nature and content of speech input to preverbal infants. *Developmental Review, 27,* 501–532.

Solomon, S. G., & Lennie, P. (2007). The machinery of colour vision. *Nature Reviews Neuroscience, 8*, 267–277.

Sommer, S. (2000). Sex-specific predation on a monogamous rat, *Hypogeomys antimena* (Muridae: Nesomyinae). *Animal Behaviour, 59*, 1087–1094.

Sorce, J. F., Emde, R. N., Campos, J., & Klinnert, M. D. (1985). Maternal emotional signaling: Its effect on the visual cliff behavior of 1-year-olds. *Developmental Psychology, 21*, 195–200.

Soussignan, R. (2002). Duchenne smile, emotional experience, and autonomic reactivity: A test of the facial feedback hypothesis. *Emotion, 2*, 52–74.

Spalding, D. A. (1873; reprinted 1954). Instinct with original observations on young animals. *British Journal of Animal Behavior, 2*, 2–11.

Spearman, C. (1927). *The abilities of man.* New York: Macmillan.

Spector, P. E. (2002). Employee control and occupational stress. *Current Directions in Psychological Science, 11*, 133–136.

Spelke, E. S. (2000). Core knowledge. *American Psychologist, 55*, 1233–1243.

Spelke, E. S., Breinlinger, K., Macomber, J., & Jacobson, K. (1992). Origins of knowledge. *Psychological Review, 99*, 605–632.

Spelke, E. S., Katz, G., Purcell, S., Ehrlich, S., & Breinlinger, K. (1994). Early knowledge of object motion: Continuity and inertia. *Cognition, 51*, 131–176.

Spencer, H. (1879). *The data of ethics.* New York: Crowell.

Sperling, G. (1960). The information available in brief visual presentations. *Psychological Monographs, 74* (Whole No. 498).

Spiegel, A. (2005, January 3). The dictionary of disorder. *The New Yorker,* pp. 56–63.

Spinka, M., Newberry, R. C., & Bekoff, M. (2001). Mammalian play: Training for the unexpected. *Quarterly Review of Biology, 76*, 141–168.

Spinney, L. (2008). Line-ups on trial. *Nature, 453*, 442–444.

Spitzer, R. L., & Fleiss, J. L. (1974). A reanalysis of the reliability of psychiatric diagnosis. *British Journal of Psychiatry, 125*, 341–347.

Spock, B., & Rothenberg, M. B. (1985). *Dr. Spock's baby and child care* (Rev. & updated ed.). New York: Pocket Books.

Squire, L. R. (1992). Memory and the hippocampus: A synthesis from findings with rats, monkeys, and humans. *Psychological Review, 99*, 195–231.

Squire, L. R., Knowlton, B., & Musen, G. (1993). The structure and organization of memory. *Annual Review of Psychology, 44*, 453–495.

Srivastava, S., John, O. P., Gosling, S. D., & Potter, J. (2003). Development of personality in early and middle adulthood: Set like plaster or persistent change? *Journal of Personality and Social Psychology, 84*, 1041–1053.

St. Clair, D., Xu, M., Wang, P., Yu, Y., Fang, Y., Zhang, F., et al. (2005). Rates of adult schizophrenia following prenatal exposure to the Chinese famine of 1959–1961. *Journal of the American Medical Association, 294*, 557–562.

St. Jacques, P. L., Dolcos, F., & Cabeza, R. (2009). Effects of aging on functional connectivity of the amygdala for subsequent memory of negative pictures. *Psychological Science, 20*, 74–84.

Staines, G. L. (2008). The relative efficacy of psychotherapy: Reassessing the methods-based paradigm. *Review of General Psychology, 12*, 330–342.

Stanley, B. G., & Gillard, E. R. (1994). Hypothalamic neuropeptide Y and the regulation of eating behavior and body weight. *Current Directions in Psychological Science, 3*, 9–15.

Stanley, D., Phelps, E., & Banaji, M. (2008). The neural basis if implicit attitudes. *Current Directions in Psychological Science, 17*, 164–170.

Stanley, R. O., & Burrows, G. D. (2008). Psychogenic heart disease—stress and the heart: A historical perspective. *Stress and Health, 24*, 181–187.

Stanovich, K. E. (2003). The fundamental computational biases of human cognition. In J. E. Davidson & R. J. Sternberg (Eds.), *The psychology of problem solving.* Cambridge, England: Cambridge University Press.

Stanovich, K. E., & West, R. F. (2003). Evolutionary versus instrumental goals: How evolutionary psychology misconceives human rationality. In D. E. Over (Ed.), *Evolution and the psychology of thinking: The debate.* New York: Psychology Press.

Stanovich, K. E., & West, R. F. (2008). On the relative independence of thinking biases and cognitive ability. *Journal of Personality and Social Psychology, 94*, 672–695.

Stargardt, T., Weinbrenner, S., Reinhard, B., Juckel, G., & Gericke, C. A. (2008). Effectiveness and cost of atypical versus typical antipsychotic treatment for schizophrenia in routine care. *Journal of Mental Health Policy and Economics, 11*, 89–97.

Steblay, N. M., & Bothwell, R. K. (1994). Evidence for hypnotically refreshed testimony: The view from the laboratory. *Law and Human Behavior, 18*, 635–651.

Steele, C. M. (1997). A threat in the air: How stereotypes shape intellectual identity and performance. *American Psychologist, 52*, 613–629.

Steele, C. M., Spencer, S. J., & Aronson, J. (2002). Contending with group image: The psychology of stereotype and social identity threat. *Advances in Experimental Social Psychology, 34*, 369–440.

Steinberg, L, & Monahan, K. C. (2007). Age differences in resistance to peer influence. *Developmental Psychology, 43*, 1531–1543.

Steinberg, L. (1989). Pubertal maturation and parent-adolescent distance: An evolutionary perspective. In G. R. Adams, R. Montemayor, & T. P. Gullota (Eds.), *Biology of adolescent behavior and development.* Newbury Park, CA: Sage.

Steinberg, L. (1996). *Beyond the classroom: Why school reform has failed and what parents need to do.* New York: Simon & Schuster.

Steinberg, L. (2001). We know some things: Adolescent-parent relationships in retrospect and prospect. *Journal of Research on Adolescence, 11*, 1–20.

Steinberg, L. (2008a). *Adolescence* (8th ed.) New York: McGraw-Hill.

Steinberg, L. (2008b). A social neuroscience perspective on adolescent risk-taking. *Developmental Review, 28*, 78–106.

Steketee, G., & Barlow, D. H. (2002). Obsessive-compulsive disorder. In D. H. Barlow, *Anxiety and its disorders* (2nd ed.). New York: Guilford.

Stelmack, R. M. (1990). Biological bases of extraversion: Psychophysiological evidence. *Journal of Personality, 58*, 293–311.

Steriade, M., McCormick, D. A., & Sejnowski, T. J. (1993). Thalamocortical oscillations in the sleeping and aroused brain. *Science, 262*, 679–685.

Sternberg, R. J. (1985). *Beyond IQ: A triarchic theory of human intelligence.* Cambridge, England: Cambridge University Press.

Sternberg, R. J. (1986). Intelligence is mental self-government. In R. J. Sternberg & D. K. Detterman (Eds.), *What is intelligence? Contemporary viewpoints on its nature and definition.* Norwood, NJ: Ablex.

Stevens, S. S. (1975). *Psychophysics: Introduction to its perceptual, neural, and social prospects.* New York: Wiley.

Stevenson, J., Asherson, P., Hay, D., Levy, F., Swanson, J., Thapar, A., et al. (2005). Characterizing the ADHD phenotype for genetic studies. *Developmental Science, 8*, 115–121.

Stewart, J. E., II (1985). Appearance and punishment: The attraction-leniency effect in the courtroom. *Journal of Social Psychology, 125*, 373–378.

Stickgold, R. (2005). Sleep-dependent memory consolidation. *Nature, 437*, 1272–1278.

Stoddart, D. M. (1990). *The scented ape.* Cambridge, England: Cambridge University Press.

Stone, A., & Valentine, T. (2007). The categorical structure of knowledge for famous people (and a novel application of centre-surround theory). *Cognition, 104*, 535–564.

Stone, J., Morrison, P., & Pilowsky, L. (2007). Glutamate and dopamine dysregulation in schizophrenia—a synthesis and selective review. *Journal of Psychopharmacology, 21,* 440–452.

Stone, J., Zeman, A., Simonotto, E., Meyer, M., Azuma, R., Flett, S., & Sharpe, M. (2007). fMRI in patients with motor conversion symptoms and controls with simulated weakness. *Psychosomatic Medicine, 69,* 961–969.

Stoolmiller, M. (1999). Implications of the restricted range of family environments for estimates of heritability and nonshared environment in behavior-genetic adoption studies. *Psychological Bulletin, 125,* 392–409.

Strayer, D. L., & Drews, F. A. (2007). Cell-phone-induced driver distraction. *Current Directions in Psychological Science, 16,* 128–131.

Strayer, D. L., & Johnston, W. A. (2001). Driven to distraction: Dual-task studies of simulated driving and conversing on a cellular telephone. *Psychological Science, 12,* 462–466.

Stricker, E. M. (1973). Thirst, sodium appetite, and complementary physiological contributions to the regulation of intravascular fluid volume. In A. N. Epstein, H. R. Kissileff, & E. Stellar (Eds.), *The neuropsychology of thirst: New findings and advances in concepts.* Washington, DC: Winston.

Stroebe, W., Stroebe, M., Abakoumkin, G., & Schut, H. (1996). The role of loneliness and social support in adjustment to loss: A test of attachment versus stress theory. *Journal of Personality and Social Psychology, 70,* 1241–1249.

Stroop, J. R. (1935). Studies of interference in serial verbal reactions. *Journal of Experimental Psychology, 18,* 643–662.

Stroup, T. S., Kraus, J. E., & Marder, S. R. (2006). Pharmacotherapies. In J. A. Lieberman, T. S. Stroup, & D. O. Perkins (Eds.), *The American Psychiatric Publishing textbook of schizophrenia.* Washington, DC: American Psychiatric Publishing.

Strupp, H. H. (1989). Psychotherapy: Can the practitioner learn from the researcher? *American Psychologist, 44,* 717–724.

Strupp, H. H., & Hadley, S. W. (1979). Specific vs. nonspecific factors in psychotherapy: A controlled study of outcome. *Archives of General Psychiatry, 36,* 1125–1136.

Stumpf, R. M., & Boesch, C. (2006). The efficacy of female choice in chimpanzees of the Taï Forest, Côte d'Ivoire. *Behavioral Ecology and Sociobiology, 60,* 749–765.

Stunkard, A., Sorensen, T., Hanis, C., Teasdale, T., Chakraborty, R., Schull, W., & Schulsinger, F. (1986). An adoption study of human obesity. *New England Journal of Medicine, 314,* 193–198.

Stylianou, D. A. (2002). On the interaction of visualization and analysis: The negotiation of a visual representation in expert problem solving. *Journal of Mathematical Behavior, 21,* 303–317.

Sullivan, M. W., & Lewis, M. (2003). Contextual determinants of anger and other negative expressions in young infants. *Developmental Psychology, 39,* 693–705.

Sulloway, F. J. (1996). *Born to rebel: Birth order, family dynamics, and creative lives.* Pantheon Books: New York.

Suls, J., & Bunde, J. (2005). Anger, anxiety, and depression as risk factors for cardiovascular disease: The problems and implications of overlapping affective dispositions. *Psychological Bulletin, 131,* 260–300.

Suls, J., Lemos, K., & Stewart, L. (2002). Self-esteem, construal, and comparisons with the self, friends, and peers. *Journal of Personality and Social Psychology, 82,* 252–261.

Sunstein, C. (2003). *Why societies need dissent.* Cambridge, MA: Harvard University Press.

Surowiecki, J. (2004a, March 8). Board stiffs. *The New Yorker,* p. 30.

Surowiecki, J. (2004b). *The wisdom of crowds.* New York: Doubleday.

Susser, E., Neugebauer, R., Hoek, H. W., Brown, A. S., Lin, S., Labovitz, D., & Gorman, J. M. (1996). Schizophrenia after prenatal famine. *Archives of General Psychiatry, 53,* 25–31.

Susskind, J. M., Lee, D. H., Cusi, A., Feiman, R., Grabksi, W., & Anderson, A. K. (2008). Expressing fear enhances sensory acquisition. *Nature Neuroscience, 11,* 843–850.

Svirsky, M. A., Robbins, A. M., Kirk, K. I., Pisoni, D. B., & Miyamoto, R. T. (2000). Language development in profoundly deaf children with cochlear implants. *Psychological Science, 11,* 153–158.

Swann, W. B. (1987). Identity negotiation: Where two roads meet. *Journal of Social Psychology, 53,* 1038–1051.

Swann, W. B., De La Ronde, C., & Hixon, J. G. (1994). Authenticity and positivity strivings in marriage and courtship. *Journal of Personality and Social Psychology, 66,* 857–869.

Swanson, H. L. (2008). Working memory and intelligence in children: What develops? *Journal of Educational Psychology, 100,* 581–602.

Sweeney, P. D., & Gruber, K. L. (1984). Selective exposure: Voter information preferences and the Watergate affair. *Journal of Personality and Social Psychology, 46,* 1208–1221.

Swingley, D. (2008). The roots of the early vocabulary in infants' learning from speech. *Current Directions in Psychological Science, 17,* 308–312.

Symons, D. (1978). *Play and aggression: A study of rhesus monkeys.* New York: Columbia University Press.

Symons, D. (1979). *The evolution of human sexuality.* Oxford: Oxford University Press.

Szechtman, H., & Woody, E. (2004). Obsessive-compulsive disorder as a disturbance of security motivation. *Psychological Review, 111,* 111–127.

Szeszko, P. R., MacMillan, S., McMeniman, M., Chen, S., Baribault, K., Lim, K. O., et al. (2004). Brain structural abnormalities in psychotropic drug-naïve pediatric patients with obsessive-compulsive disorder. *American Journal of Psychiatry, 161,* 1049–1056.

Tabibnia, G., Satpute, A. B., & Lieberman, M. D. (2008). The sunny side of fairness: Preference for fairness activates reward circuitry. *Psychological Science, 19,* 339–347.

Tafarodi, R. W., & Milne, A. B. (2002). Decomposing global self-esteem. *Journal of Personality, 70,* 443–483.

Tafarodi, R. W., Lo, C., Yamaguchi, S., Lee, W. W.-S., & Katsura, H. (2004). The inner self in three countries. *Journal of Cross-Cultural Psychology, 35,* 97–117.

Tager-Flusberg, H. (2007). Evaluating the theory-of-mind hypothesis of autism. *Current Directions in Psychological Science, 16,* 311–315.

Tajfel, H. (1972). Social categorization. In S. Moscovici (Ed.), *Introduction à la psychologie sociale* [Introduction to social psychology] (Vol. 1). Paris: Larousse.

Tajfel, H. (1982). Social psychology of intergroup relations. *Annual Review of Psychology, 33,* 1–39.

Tal-Or, N., & Papirman, Y. (2007). The fundamental attribution error in attributing fictional figures' characteristics to the actor. *Media Psychology, 9,* 331–345.

Tamez, E., Myerson, J., & Hale, S. (2008). Learning, working memory, and intelligence revisited. *Behavioural Processes, 27,* 240–245.

Tamis-LeMonda, C. S., Bornstein, M. H., & Baumwell, L. (2001). Maternal responsiveness and children's achievement of language milestones. *Child Development, 72,* 748–767.

Tandon, R., Keshavan, M. S., & Nasrallah, H. A. (2008). Schizophrenia, "just the facts": What we know in 2008. 2. Epidemiology and etiology. *Schizophrenia Research, 102,* 2–18.

Tang, Y., Shimizu, E., Dube, G. R., Rampon, C., Kerchner, G. A., Zhou, M., Liu, G., & Tsien, G. Z. (1999). Genetic enhancement of learning and memory in mice. *Nature, 401,* 63–69.

Tangney, J. P. (1995). Shame and guilt in interpersonal relationships. In J. P. Tangney & K. W. Fischer (Eds.), *Self-conscious emotions: The psychology of shame, guilt, embarrassment, and pride.* New York: Guilford.

Tangney, J. P., Miller, R. S., Flicker, L., & Barlow, D. H. (1996). Are shame, guilt, and embarrassment distinct emotions? *Journal of Personality and Social Psychology, 70,* 1256–1269.

Tangney, J. P., Stuewig, J., & Mashek, D. J. (2007). Moral emotions and moral behavior. *Annual Review of Psychology, 58,* 345–372.

Tarumi, S., Ichimiya, A., Yamada, S., Umesue, M., & Kuroki, T. (2004). Taijin Kyofusho in university students: Patterns of fear and pre-dispositions to the offensive variant. *Transcultural Psychiatry, 41,* 533–546.

Taylor, R., & Langdon, R. (2006). Understanding gender differences in schizophrenia: A review of the literature. *Current Psychiatry Reviews, 2,* 255–265.

Taylor, S. E. (2006). Tend and befriend: Biobehavioral bases of affiliation under stress. *Current Directions in Psychological Science, 15,* 273–277.

Taylor, S. E., Klein, L. C., Lewis, B. P., Gruenewald, T. L., Gurung, R. A. R., & Updegraff, J. A. (2000). Biobehavioral responses to stress in females: Tend-and-befriend, not fight-or-flight. *Psychological Review, 107,* 411–429.

Taylor, S. E., Lerner, J. S., Sherman, D. K., Sage, R. M., & McDowell, N. K. (2003). Are self-enhancing cognitions associated with healthy or unhealthy biological profiles? *Journal of Personality and Social Psychology, 85,* 605–615.

Tecott, L. H. (2003). The genes and brains of mice and men. *American Journal of Psychiatry, 160,* 646–656.

Tellegen, A., Lykken, D. T., Bouchard, T. J., Wilcox, K. J., Segal, N. L., & Rich, S. (1988). Personality similarity in twins reared apart and together. *Journal of Personality and Social Psychology, 54,* 1031–1039.

Temple, J. L., Giacomelli, A. M., Roemmich, J. N., & Epstein, L. H. (2008). Dietary variety impairs habituation in children. *Health Psychology, 27,* S10–S19.

Tenenbaum, H. R., & Leaper, C. (2003). Parent-child conversations about science: The socialization of gender inequities? *Developmental Psychology, 39,* 34–47.

Terracciano, A., Costa, P. T., & McCrae, R. R. (2006). Personality plasticity after age 30. *Personality and Social Psychology Bulletin, 32,* 999–1009.

Terrace, H. S. (1985). In the beginning was the "name." *American Psychologist, 40,* 1011–1028.

Tessler, M., & Nelson, K. (1994). Making memories: The influence of joint encoding on later recall by young children. *Consciousness and Cognition, 3,* 307–326.

Tetlock, P. E. (1991). An alternative metaphor in the study of judgment and choice: People as politicians. *Theory and Psychology, 1,* 451–475.

Tetlock, P. E. (2002). Social functionalist framework for judgment and choice: Intuitive politicians, theologians, and prosecutors. *Psychological Review, 109,* 451–471.

Thiessen, E. D., Hill, E. A., & Saffran, J. R. (2005). Infant-directed speech facilitates word segmentation. *Infancy, 7,* 53–71.

Thomas, G., & Fletcher, G. J. O. (2003). Mind-reading accuracy in intimate relationships: Assessing the roles of the relationship, the target, and the judge. *Journal of Personality and Social Psychology, 85,* 1079–1094.

Thomas, O. M., Cumming, B. G., & Parker, A. J. (2002). A special-ization for relative disparity in V2. *Nature Neuroscience, 50,* 472–478.

Thompson, J. M., & Cotlove, C. (2005). *The therapeutic process: A clin-ical introduction to psychodynamic psychotherapy.* Lanham, MD: Rowman & Littlefield.

Thompson, R. F. (1985). *The brain: An introduction to neuroscience.* New York: Freeman.

Thompson, S. K., von Kriegstein K., Deane-Pratt, A., Marquardt, T., Deichmann, R., Griffiths, T. D., & McAlpine, D. (2006). Representation of interaural time delay in the human auditory mid-brain. *Nature Neuroscience, 9,* 1006-1008.

Thomson, J. R., & Chapman, R. S. (1977). Who is "Daddy" revisited: The status of two-year-olds' over-extended words in use and compre-hension. *Journal of Child Language, 4,* 359–375.

Thorndike, E. L. (1898). Animal intelligence: An experimental study of associative processes in animals. *Psychological Review Monograph Supplements, 2,* 4–160.

Thorne, B. (1993). *Gender play: Girls and boys in school.* New Brunswick, NJ: Rutgers University Press.

Tice, D. M., Butler, J. L., Muraven, M. B., & Stillwell, A. M. (1995). When modesty prevails: Differential favorability of self-presentation to friends and strangers. *Journal of Personality and Social Psychology, 69,* 1120–1138.

Tienari, P., & Wahlberg, K-E. (2008). Family environment and psy-chosis. In C. Morgan, K. McKenzie, & P. Fearon (Eds.), *Society and psy-chosis.* New York: Cambridge University Press.

Tienari, P., Wahlberg, K-E., & Wynne, L. C. (2006). Finnish adoption study of schizophrenia: Implications for family interventions. *Families, Systems, & Health, 24,* 442–451.

Tienari, P., Wynne, L. C., Sorri, A., Lahti, I., Läksy, K., Moring, J., et al. (2004). Genotype-environment interaction in schizophrenia-spectrum disorder: Long-term follow-up study of Finnish adoptees. *British Journal of Psychiatry, 184,* 216–222.

Tilker, H. A. (1970). Socially responsible behavior as a function of ob-server responsibility and victim feedback. *Journal of Personality and Social Psychology, 14,* 95–100.

Tincoff, R., & Jusczyk, P. W. (1999). Some beginnings of word com-prehension in 6-month-olds. *Psychological Science, 10,* 172–175.

Tither, J. M., & Ellis, B. J. (2008). Impact of fathers on daughters' age at menarche: A genetically and environmentally controlled sibling study. *Developmental Psychology, 44,* 1409–1420.

Tobias, J., & Seddon, N. (2000). Territoriality as a paternity guard in the European robin, *Erithacus rubecula. Animal Behaviour, 60,* 165–173.

Todorov, A., Mandisodza, A. N., Goren, A., & Hall, C. C. (2005). Inferences of competence from faces predict election outcomes. *Science, 308,* 1623–1626.

Tolman, E. C. (1948). Cognitive maps in rats and men. *The Psycho-logical Review, 55,* 189–208.

Tolman, E. C. (1959). Principles of purposive behavior. In S. Koch (Ed.), *Psychology: A study of a science* (Vol. 2). New York: McGraw-Hill.

Tolman, E. C., & Honzik, C. H. (1930). "Insight" in rats. *University of California Publications in Psychology, 4,* 215–232.

Tomasello, M. (2007). For human eyes only. *New York Times,* Jan. 13, 2007, op ed page.

Tomasello, M., & Haberl, K. (2003). Understanding attention: 12- and 18-month-olds know what is new for other persons. *Developmental Psychology, 39,* 906–912.

Tomonaga, M. (2007). Is chimpanzee (*Pan troglodytes*) spatial attention reflexively triggered by gaze cue? *Journal of Comparative Psychology, 121,* 156–170.

Toni, N., Teng, E. M., Bushong, E. A., Aimone, J. B., Zhao, C., Consiglio, A., van Praag, H., Martone, M. E., Ellisman, M. H., & Gage, F. H. (2007). Synapse formation on neurons born in the hip-pocampus. *Nature Neuroscience, 10,* 727–734.

Toomey, R., Kremen, W. S., Simpson, J. C., Samson, J. A., Seidman, L. J., Lyons, M. J., Faraone, S. V., & Tsuang, M. T. (1997). Revisiting the factor structure for positive and negative symptoms: Evidence from a large heterogeneous group of psychiatric patients. *American Journal of Psychiatry, 154,* 371–377.

Toplak, M. E., Liu, E., MacPherson, R., Toneatto, T., & Stanovich, K. E. (2007). The reasoning skills and thinking dispositions of problem gamblers: A dual-process taxonomy. *Journal of Behavioral Decision Making, 20,* 103–124.

Tordoff, M. G. (2002). Intragastric calcium infusions support flavor preference learning by calcium-deprived rats. *Physiology and Behavior, 76,* 521–529.

Torriero, S., Oliveri, M., Koch, G., Caltagirone, C., & Petrosini, L. (2007). The what and how of observational learning. *Journal of Cognitive Neuroscience, 19,* 1656–1663.

Tracy, J. L., & Matsumoto, D. (2008). The spontaneous expression of pride and shame: Evidence for biologically innate nonverbal displays. *Proceedings of the National Academy of Sciences of the USA, 105,* 11655–11660.

Tracy, J. L., & Robins, R. W. (2006). Appraisal antecedents of shame and guilt: Support for a theoretical model. *Personality and Social Psychology Bulletin, 32,* 1339–1351.

Tracy, J. L., & Robins, R. W. (2007). Emerging insights into the nature and functions of pride. *Current Directions in Psychological Science, 16,* 147–150.

Travis, L. E. (1925). The effect of a small audience upon eye-hand coordination. *Journal of Abnormal and Social Psychology, 20,* 142–146.

Treisman, A. (1986, November). Features and objects in visual processing. *Scientific American,* pp. 114B–125B.

Treisman, A. (1998). Feature binding, attention and object perception. *Philosophical Transactions of the Royal Society of London, Series B, 353,* 1295–1306.

Treisman, A., & Gormican, S. (1988). Feature analysis in early vision: Evidence from search asymmetries. *Psychological Review, 95,* 15–48.

Treue, S. (2001). Neural correlates of attention in primate visual cortex. *Trends in Neurosciences, 24,* 295–300.

Triandis, H. C. (1995). *Individualism and collectivism.* Boulder, CO: Westview.

Triandis, H. C., & Suh, E. M. (2002). Cultural influence on personality. *Annual Review of Psychology, 53,* 133–160.

Trimble, M. R. (1996). *Biological psychiatry* (2nd ed.). New York: Wiley.

Trivers, R. L. (1971). The evolution of reciprocal altruism. *Quarterly Review of Biology, 46,* 35–57.

Trivers, R. L. (1972). Parental investment and sexual selection. In B. Campbell (Ed.), *Sexual selection and the descent of man.* Chicago: Aldine.

Tronick, E. Z., Morelli, G. A., & Ivey, P. K. (1992). The Efe forager infant and toddler's pattern of social relationships: Multiple and simultaneous. *Developmental Psychology, 28,* 568–577.

Tronson, N. C., & Taylor, J. R. (2007). Molecular mechanisms of memory reconsolidation. *Nature Reviews Neuroscience, 8,* 262–275.

True, W. R., Rice, J., Eisen, S. A., Heath, A. C., Goldberg, J., Lyons, M. J., & Nowak, J. (1993). A twin study of genetic and environmental contributions to liability for posttraumatic stress symptoms. *Archives of General Psychiatry, 50,* 257–264.

Trut, L. N. (1999). Early canid domestication: The farm-fox experiment. *American Scientist, 87,* 160–169.

Tryon, R. C. (1942). Individual differences. In F. A. Moss (Ed.), *Comparative psychology* (Rev. ed.). New York: Prentice-Hall.

Tseng, W-S. (2006). From peculiar psychiatric disorders through culture-bound syndromes to culture-related specific syndromes. *Transcultural Psychiatry, 43,* 554–576.

Tsien, J. Z. (2000, April). Building a brainier mouse. *Scientific American,* pp. 62–68.

Tsuang, M. T., Stone, W. S., & Faraone, S. V. (2001). Genes, environment, and schizophrenia. *British Journal of Psychiatry, 178,* s18–s24.

Tulving, E. (1985). How many memory systems are there? *American Psychologist, 40,* 385–398.

Tulving, E. (2000). Concepts of memory. In E. Tulving & F. I. M. Craik (Eds.), *The Oxford handbook of memory.* New York: Oxford University Press.

Tulving, E. (2002). Episodic memory: From mind to brain. *Annual Review of Psychology, 53,* 1–25.

Turkheimer, E., & Waldron, M. (2000). Nonshared environment: A theoretical, methodological, and quantitative review. *Psychological Bulletin, 126,* 78–108.

Tversky, A., & Kahneman, D. (1973). Availability: A heuristic for judging frequency and probability. *Cognitive Psychology, 5,* 207–232.

Twenge, J. M. (2000). The age of anxiety? Birth cohort change in anxiety and neuroticism, 1952–1993. *Journal of Personality and Social Psychology, 79,* 1007–1021.

Twenge, J. M. (2001). Changes in women's and men's assertiveness in response to status and roles: A cross-temporal meta-analysis, 1931–1993. *Journal of Personality and Social Psychology, 81,* 133–145.

Uher, J. (2008). Comparative personality research: Methodological approaches. *European Journal of Personality, 22,* 427–455.

UK ECT Review Group (2003). Efficacy and safety of electroconvulsive therapy in depressive disorders: A systematic review and meta-analysis. *The Lancet, 361,* 799–808.

Uleman, J. S., Saribay, S. A., & Gonzalez, C. M. (2008). Spontaneous inferences, implicit impressions, and implicit theories. *Annual Review of Psychology, 59,* 329–360.

Uziel, L. (2007). Individual differences in the social facilitation effect: A review and meta-analysis. *Journal of Research in Personality, 41,* 579–601.

Vaillant, G. E. (1977). *Adaptation to life.* Boston: Little, Brown and Company.

Vaillant, G. E. (1995). *Adaptation to life* (2nd ed.). Cambridge, MA: Harvard University Press.

Vaillant, G. E., & Vaillant, C. O. (1992). Empirical evidence that defensive styles are independent of environmental influence. In G. E. Vaillant (Ed.), *Ego mechanisms of defense: A guide for clinicians and researchers.* Washington, DC: American Psychiatric Press.

Valenstein, E. S. (1986). *Great and desperate cures: The rise and decline of psychosurgery and other radical treatments for mental illness.* New York: Basic Books.

Valkenburg, P. M., & Peter, J. (2009). Social consequences of the Internet for adolescents. *Current Directions in Psychological Science, 18,* 1–5.

Valli, K., Standholm, T., Sillanmäki, L., & Revonsuo, A. (2008). Dreams are more negative than real life: Implications for the function of dreaming. *Cognition and Emotion, 22,* 833–861.

van Baaren, R. B., Holland, R. W., Kawakami, K., & van Knippenberg, A. (2004). Mimicry and prosocial behavior. *Psychological Science, 15,* 71–74.

van den Boom, D. C. (1991). The influence of infant irritability on the development of the mother-infant relationship in the first six months of life. In J. K. Nugent, M. M. Lester, & T. B. Brazelton (Eds.), *The cultural context of infancy* (Vol. 2). Norwood, NJ: Ablex.

van den Boom, D. C. (1994). The influence of temperament and mothering on attachment and exploration: An experimental manipulation of sensitive responsiveness among lower-class mothers with irritable infants. *Child Development, 65,* 1457–1477.

Van Doesum, K. T., M., Riksen-Walraven, J. M., Hosman, C. M. H., & Hoefnagels, C. (2008). A randomized controlled trial of a home-visiting intervention aimed at preventing relationship problems in depressed mothers and their infants. *Child Development, 79,* 547–561.

Van Gelder, R. N. (2008). How the clock sees the light. *Nature Neuroscience, 11,* 628–630.

van Hooff, J. A. (1972). A comparative approach to the phylogeny of laughter and smiling. In R. A. Hinde (Ed.), *Nonverbal communication.* Cambridge, England: Cambridge University Press.

van Hooff, J. A. (1976). The comparison of facial expression in man and higher primates. In M. von Cranach (Ed.), *Methods of inference from animal to human behaviour.* Chicago: Aldine.

Van Itallie, T. B., & Kissileff, H. R. (1990). Human obesity: A problem in body energy economics. In E. M. Stricker (Ed.), *Handbook of* *behavioral neurobiology: Vol. 10. Neurobiology of food and fluid intake.* New York: Plenum Press.

Van Lange, P. A. M., & Visser, K. (1999). Locomotion in social dilemmas: How people adapt to cooperative, tit-for-tat, and noncooperative partners. *Journal of Personality and Social Psychology, 77,* 762–773.

van Os, J., Rutten, B. P. F., & Poulton, R. (2008). Gene-environment interactions in schizophrenia: Review of epidemiological findings and future directions. *Schizophrenia Bulletin, 34,* 1066–1082.

van Veen, V., & Carter, C. S. (2006). Conflict and cognitive control in the brain. *Current Directions in Psychological Science, 15,* 237–240.

Van Vugt, M., & Hart, C. M. (2004). Social identity as social glue: The origins of group loyalty. *Journal of Personality and Social Psychology, 86,* 585–598.

Vance, E. B., & Wagner, N. N. (1976). Written descriptions of orgasm: A study of sex differences. *Archives of Sexual Behavior, 5,* 87–98.

Vandello, J. A., & Cohen, D. (2008). Culture, gender, and men's intimate partner violence. *Social and Personality Psychology Compass, 2,* 652–667.

Varendi, H., Porter, R. H., & Winberg, J. (2002). The effect of labor on olfactory exposure learning within the first postnatal hour. *Behavioral Neuroscience, 116,* 206–211.

Vargha-Khadem, F., & Liégeois, F. (2007). From speech to gene: The KE family and the FOXP2. In B. Stein (Ed.), *On being moved: From mirror neurons to empathy,* pp. 137–146. Amsterdam, Netherlands: John Benjamins Publishing.

Vargha-Khadem, F., Gadian, D. G., & Mishkin, M. (2002). Dissociation in cognitive memory: The syndrome of developmental amnesia. In A. Baddeley, J. P. Aggleton, & M. A. Conway (Eds.), *Episodic memory: New directions in research.* Oxford: Oxford University Press.

Vargha-Khadem, F., Gadian, D. G., Watkins, K. E., Connelly, A., Van Paesschen, W., & Mishkin, M. (1997). Differential effects of early hippocampal pathology on episodic and semantic memory. *Science, 277,* 376–380.

Vasconcelos, M. S., Sampaio, A. S., Hounie, A. G., Akkerman, F., Curi, M., Lopes, A. C., & Miguel, E. C. (2007). Prenatal, perinatal, and postnatal risk factors in obsessive-compulsive disorder. *Biological Psychiatry, 61,* 301–307.

Vaughan, D. (1986). *Uncoupling.* New York: Oxford University Press.

Vernon, P. A., Jang, K. L., Harris, J. A., & McCarthy, J. M. (1997). Environmental predictors of personality differences: A twin and sibling study. *Journal of Personality and Social Psychology, 72,* 177–183.

Vernon, P. A., & Kantor, L. (1986). Reaction time correlations with intelligence test scores obtained under either timed or untimed conditions. *Intelligence, 9,* 357–374.

Vicente, K. J., & Wang, J. H. (1998). An ecological theory of expertise in memory recall. *Psychological Review, 105,* 33–37.

Vinokur, A., & Burnstein, E. (1974). Effects of partially shared persuasive arguments on group-induced shifts: A group problem-solving approach. *Journal of Personality and Social Psychology, 29,* 305–315.

Vohs, K. D., Baumeiter, R. F., & Ciarocco, N. J. (2005). Self-regulation and self-presentation: Regulatory resource depletion impairs impression management and effortful self-presentation depletes regulatory resources. *Journal of Personality and Social Psychology, 88,* 632–657.

Volkova, V. D. (1953). On certain characteristics of the formation of conditioned reflexes to speech stimuli in children. *Fiziologicheskii Zhurnal USSR, 39,* 540–548.

Vonk, R. (2002). Self-serving interpretations of flattery: Why ingratiation works. *Journal of Personality and Social Psychology, 82,* 515–526.

Vouloumanos, A., & Werker, J. F. (2007). Listening to language at birth: Evidence for a bias for speech in neonates. *Developmental Science, 10,* 159–171.

Vuilleumier, P., Chicherio, C., Assal, F., Schwartz, S., Slosman, D., & Landis, T. (2001). Functional neuroanatomical correlates of hysterical sensorimotor loss. *Brain, 124,* 1077–1099.

Vygotsky, L. S. (1933; reprinted 1978). Play and its role in the mental development of the child. In M. Cole, V. John-Steiner, S. Scribner, & E. Sourberman (Eds.), *Mind in society.* Cambridge, MA: Harvard University Press.

Vygotsky, L. S. (1934; reprinted 1962). *Thought and language* (E. Haufmann & G. Vaker, Eds. & Trans.). Cambridge, MA: MIT Press.

Vygotsky, L. S. (1935; reprinted 1978). Interaction between learning and development. In M. Cole, V. John-Steiner, S. Scribner, & E. Souberman (Eds.), *Mind in society: The development of higher psychological processes.* Cambridge, MA: Harvard University Press.

Wade, N. J., & Swanston, M. (1991). *Visual perception: An introduction.* London: Routledge.

Wagner, U., Gals, S., Halder, H., Verleger, R., & Born, J. (2004). Sleep inspires insight. *Nature, 427,* 352–355.

Walden, T. A. (1991). Infant social referencing. In J. Garber & K. A. Dodge (Eds.), *The development of emotion regulation and dysregulation.* Cambridge, England: Cambridge University Press.

Walker, W. I. (1973). Principles of organization of the ventrobasal complex in mammals. *Brain Behavior and Evolution, 7,* 253–336.

Wallace, P. (1977). Individual discrimination of humans by odor. *Physiology and Behavior, 19,* 577–579.

Wallen, K. (2001). Risky business: Social context and hormonal modulation of primate sexual desire. In W. Everaerd & E. Laan (Eds.), *Sexual appetite, desire and motivation: Energetics of the sexual system.* Amsterdam, Netherlands: Koninklijke Nederlandse Akademie van Wetenschappen.

Wallerstein, R. S. (1989). The psychotherapy research project of the Menninger Foundation: An overview. *Journal of Consulting and Clinical Psychology, 57,* 195–205.

Wampold, B. E. (2001). *The great psychotherapy debate: Models, methods, and findings.* Mahwah, NJ: Erlbaum.

Wampold, B. E., Minami, T., Tierney, S. C., Baskin, T. W., & Bhati, K. S. (2005). The placebo is powerful: Estimating effects in medicine and psychotherapy from randomized clinical trials. *Journal of Clinical Psychology, 61,* 835–854.

Wang, K., Fan, J., Dong, Y., Wang, C., Lee, T. M. C., & Posner, M. I. (2005). Selective impairment of attentional networks of orienting and executive control in schizophrenia. *Schizophrenia Research, 78,* 235–241.

Wang, P. S., Lane, M., Olfson, M., Pincus, H. A., Wells, K. B., & Kessler, R. C. (2005). Twelve-month use of mental health services in the United States: Results from the national comorbidity survey replication. *Archives of General Psychiatry, 62,* 629–640.

Wang, Q. (2006). Cultural knowledge and the development of self-knowledge. *Current Directions in Psychological Science, 15,* 182–187.

Ward, A. J. W., Thomas, P., Hart, P. J. B., & Krause, J. (2004). Correlates of boldness in three-spined sticklebacks (*Gasterosteus aculeatus*). *Behavioral Ecology and Sociobiology, 55,* 561–568.

Ward, I. L. (1992). Sexual behavior: The product of perinatal hormonal and prepubertal social factors. In A. A. Gerall, H. Moltz, & I. L. Ward (Eds.), *Handbook of behavioral neurobiology: Vol. 11. Sexual differentiation,* New York: Plenum Press.

Ward, N. S., Oakley, D. A., Frackowiak, R. S. J., & Halligan, P. W. (2003). Differential brain activations during intentionally simulated and subjectively experienced paralysis. *Cognitive Neuropsychiatry, 8,* 295–312.

Warner, R. (1985). *Recovery from schizophrenia.* London: Routledge & Kegan Paul.

Warren, R. M. (1970). Perceptual restoration of missing speech sounds. *Science, 167,* 392–393.

Warren, R. M. (1984). Perceptual restoration of obliterated sounds. *Psychological Bulletin, 96,* 371–383.

Wason, P. C. (1960). On the failure to eliminate hypotheses in a conceptual task. *Quarterly Journal of Experimental Psychology, 12,* 129–140.

Wassenberg, R., Hendricksen, J. G. M., Hurks, P. P. M., Feron, F. J. M., Keulers, E. H. H., Vles, J. S. H., & Jolles, J. (2008). Development of inattention, impulsivity, and processing speed as measured by the d2 test: Results of a large cross-sectional study in children aged 7–13. *Child Neuropsychology, 14,* 195–210.

Wasserman, E. A. (1995). The conceptual abilities of pigeons. *American Scientist, 83,* 246–255.

Waters, E., Hamilton, C. E., & Weinfield, N. S. (2000). The stability of attachment security from infancy to adolescence and early adulthood: General introduction. *Child Development, 71,* 678–683.

Watkins, L. R., & Maier, S. F. (2000). The pain of being sick: Implications of immune-to-brain communication for understanding pain. *Annual Review of Psychology, 51,* 29–57.

Watkins, L. R., Hutchinson, M. R., Milligan, E. D., & Maier, S. (2007). "Listening" and "talking" to neurons: Implications of immune activation for pain control and increasing efficacy of opioids. *Brain Research Reviews, 56,* 148–169.

Watson, J. B. (1913). Psychology as the behaviorist views it. *Psychological Review, 20,* 158–177.

Watson, J. B. (1924). *Behaviorism.* Chicago: University of Chicago Press.

Watson, J. B., & Rayner, R. (1920). Conditioned emotional reactions. *Journal of Experimental Psychology, 3,* 1–14.

Watson, J. S. (1972). Smiling, cooing, and "the game." *Merrill-Palmer Quarterly, 18,* 323–339.

Waugh, N. C., & Norman, D. A. (1965). Primary memory. *Psychological Review, 72,* 89–104.

Waxman, S. R., & Markow, D. B. (1995). Words as invitations to form categories: Evidence from 12- to 13-month-old infants. *Cognitive Psychology, 29,* 257–302.

Weber, E. H. (1834). *De pulen, resorptione, auditu et tactu: Annotationes anatomicae et physiologicae.* Leipzig: Koehler.

Weber, N., & Brewer, N. (2003). Expert memory: The interaction of stimulus structure, attention, and expertise. *Applied Cognitive Psychology, 17,* 295–308.

Wedekind, C., & Füri, S. (1997). Body odour preferences in men and women: Do they aim for specific MHC combinations or simply heterozygosity? *Proceedings of the Royal Society of London, Series B, 264,* 1471–1479.

Wedekind, C., Seebeck, T., Bettens, F., & Paepke, A. J. (1995). MHC-dependent mate preference in humans. *Proceedings of the Royal Society of London, Series B, 260,* 245–249.

Wegner, D. M., Fuller, V. A., & Sparrow, B. (2003). Clever hands: Uncontrolled intelligence in facilitated communication. *Journal of Personality and Social Psychology, 85,* 5–19.

Wegner, D. M., Wenzlaff, R. M., & Kozak, M. (2004). Dream rebound: The return of suppressed thoughts in dreams. *Psychological Science, 15,* 232–236.

Weinberg, M. K., Tronick, E. Z., Cohn, J. F., & Olson, K. L. (1999). Gender differences in emotional expressivity and self-regulation during early infancy. *Developmental Psychology, 35,* 175–188.

Weinberger, D. A. (1990). The construct validity of the repressive coping style. In J. L. Singer (Ed.), *Repression and dissociation: Implications for personality theory, psychopathology, and health.* Chicago: University of Chicago Press.

Weiner, J. (1994). *The beak of the finch: A story of evolution in our time.* New York: Knopf.

Weiner, R. B., & Bornstein, R. F. (2009). *Principles of psychotherapy: Promoting evidence-based psychodynamic practice* (3rd ed.). Hoboken, NJ: Wiley.

Weinstein, N. D. (1980). Unrealistic optimism about future events. *Journal of Personality and Social Psychology, 39,* 806–820.

Weinstein, N. D. (1982). Unrealistic optimism about susceptibility to health problems. *Journal of Behavioral Medicine, 5,* 441–460.

Weiskrantz, L. (1956). Behavioral changes associated with ablation of the amygdaloid complex in monkeys. *Journal of Comparative Physiology and Psychology, 49,* 381–391.

Weiss, A., Costa, P. T., Karuza, J., Duberstein, P. R., Friedman, B., & McCrae, R. R. (2005). Cross-sectional age differences in personality among Medicare patients aged 65 to 100. *Psychology of Aging, 20,* 182–185.

Weiss, R. S. (1975). *Marital separation.* New York: Basic Books.

Welch, D. C., & West, R. L. (1995). Self-efficacy and mastery: Its application to issues of environmental control, cognition, and aging. *Developmental Review, 15,* 150–171.

Welling, H. (2003). An evolutionary function of the depressive reaction: The cognitive mapping hypothesis. *New Ideas in Psychology, 21,* 147–156.

Wellman, H. M., Cross, D., & Watson, J. (2001). Meta-analysis of theory-of-mind development: The truth about false-belief. *Child Development, 72,* 655–684.

Wells, G. L., & Bradfield, A. L. (1999). Distortions in eyewitnesses' recollections: Can the postidentification-feedback effect be moderated? *Psychological Science, 10,* 138–144.

Wells, G. L., Memon, A., & Penrod, S. D. (2006). Eyewitness evidence: Improving its probative value. *Psychological Science in the Public Interest, 7,* 45–73.

Wells, G. L., Olson, E. A., & Charman, S. D. (2002). The confidence of eyewitnesses in their identifications from lineups. *Current Directions in Psychological Science, 11,* 151–154.

Werker, J. F., & Tees, R. C. (1992). The organization and reorganization of human speech perception. *Annual Review of Neuroscience, 15,* 377–402.

Werker, J. F., & Tees, R. C. (1999). Influences on infant speech processing: Toward a new synthesis. *Annual Review of Psychology, 50,* 509–535.

Wernicke, C. (1874; reprinted 1977). The aphasia symptom complex: A psychological study on an anatomical basis. In G. H. Eggard (Ed. & Trans.), *Wernicke's works on aphasia.* The Hague: Mouton.

Werring, D. J., Weston, L., Bullmore, E. G., Plant, G. T., & Ron, M. A. (2004). Functional magnetic resonance imaging of the cerebral response to visual stimulation in medically unexplained visual loss. *Psychological Medicine, 34,* 583–589.

Wertheimer, M. (1923; reprinted 1938). Principles of perceptual organization. In W. D. Ellis (Ed. & Trans.), *A source-book of Gestalt psychology.* New York: Harcourt Brace.

Wesensten, N. J., Belenky, G., Kautz, M. A., Thorne, D. R., Reichardt, R., M., & Balkin, T. J. (2002). Maintaining alertness and performance during sleep deprivation: Modafinil versus caffeine. *Psychopharmacology, 159,* 238–247.

West, D. J. (1977). *Homosexuality re-examined.* Minneapolis: University of Minnesota Press.

Weston, D., Novotny, C. M., & Thompson-Brenner, H. (2004). The empirical status of empirically supported psychotherapies: Assumptions, findings, and reporting in controlled clinical trials. *Psychological Bulletin, 130,* 631–663.

Whalen, P. J. (1998). Fear, vigilance, and ambiguity: Initial neuroimaging studies of the human amygdala. *Current Directions in Psychological Science, 7,* 177–188.

Whatley, M. A., Webster, J. M., Smith, R. H., & Rhodes, A. (1999). The effect of a favor on public and private compliance: How internalized is the norm of reciprocity? *Basic and Applied Social Psychology, 21,* 251–259.

Wheeler, M. A. (2000). Episodic memory and autonoetic awareness. In E. Tulving & F. I. M. Craik (Eds.), *The Oxford handbook of memory.* New York: Oxford University Press.

Wheeler, M. A., Stuss, D. T., & Tulving, E. (1997). Toward a theory of episodic memory: The frontal lobes and autonoetic consciousness. *Psychological Bulletin, 121,* 331–354.

Wheeler, S. C., & Petty, R. E. (2001). The effects of stereotype activation on behavior: A review of possible mechanisms. *Psychological Bulletin, 127,* 797–826.

White, F. A., & Matawie, K. M. (2004). Prenatal morality and family processes as predictors of adolescent morality. *Journal of Child and Family Studies, 13,* 219–233.

White, F. J., & Wood, K. D. (2007). Female feeding priority in bonobos, *Pan paniscus,* and the question of female dominance. *American Journal of Primatology, 69,* 837–850.

White, K. S., & Barlow, D. H. (2002). Panic disorder and agoraphobia. In D. H. Barlow, *Anxiety and its disorders* (2nd ed.). New York: Guilford.

Whiten, A. (1998). Imitation of the sequential structure of actions by chimpanzees (*Pan troglodytes*). *Journal of Comparative Psychology, 112,* 270–281.

Whiten, A., Goodall, J., McGrew, W. C., Nishida, T., Reynolds, V., Sugiyama, Y., Tutin, C. E. G., Wrangham, R. W., & Boesch, C. (1999). Culture in chimpanzees. *Nature, 399,* 682–685.

Whiting, B. B., & Edwards, C. P. (1988). *Children of different worlds: The formation of social behavior.* Cambridge, MA: Harvard University Press.

Whiting, J. W. M. (1971). *Causes and consequences of the amount of body contact between mother and infant.* Paper read at the annual meeting of the American Anthropological Association, New York.

Whorf, B. (1956). *Language, thought, and reality.* New York: Wiley.

Wicker, A. W. (1969). Attitude versus actions: The relationship of verbal and overt behavioral responses to attitude objects. *Journal of Social Issues, 25,* 41–78.

Widiger, T. A. (2005). Classification and diagnosis: Historical development and contemporary issues. In J. Maddux & B. Winstead (Eds.), *Psychopathology: Foundations for a contemporary understanding.* Mahwah, NJ: Erlbaum.

Widiger, T. A., & Mullins-Sweatt, S. (2007). Mental disorders as discrete clinical conditions: Dimensional versus categorical classification. In M. Hersen, S. M. Turner, & D. C. Beidel (Eds.), *Adult psychopathology and diagnosis* (5th ed.). Hoboken, NJ: Wiley.

Wiens, S., Mezzacappa, E., & Katkin, E. S. (2000). Heartbeat detection and the experience of emotions. *Cognition and Emotion, 14,* 417–427.

Wiessner, P. (1982). Risk, reciprocity and social influences on !Kung San economics. In E. Leacock & R. Lee (Eds.), *Politics and history in band societies.* Cambridge, England: Cambridge University Press.

Wijbenga, F. H., & van Witteloostruijn, A. (2007). Entrepreneurial locus of control and competitive strategies—the moderating effect of environmental dynamism. *Journal of Economic Psychology, 28,* 566–589.

Wild, B., Erb, M., & Bartels, M. (2001). Are emotions contagious? Evoked emotions while viewing emotionally expressive faces: Quality, quantity, time course and gender differences. *Psychiatry Research, 102,* 109–124.

Wildschut, T., Insko, C. A., & Pinter, B. (2007). Interindividual-intergroup discontinuity as a joint function of acting as a group and interacting with a group. *European Journal of Social Psychology, 37,* 390–399.

Wiley, M. G., Crittenden, K. S., & Birg, L. D. (1979). Why a rejection? Causal attributions of a career achievement event. *Social Psychology Quarterly, 42,* 214–222.

Wilkins, L., & Richter, C. P. (1940). A great craving for salt by a child with cortico-adrenal insufficiency. *JAMA, Journal of the American Medical Association, 114,* 866–868.

Wilkins, P. (2003). *Person-centred therapy in focus.* London: Sage.

Wilkinson, G. S. (1988). Reciprocal altruism in bats and other mammals. *Ethology and Sociobiology, 9,* 85–100.

Williams, A. C. (2002). Facial expression of pain: An evolutionary account. *Behavioral and Brain Sciences, 25,* 439–488.

Williams, G. C., Grow, V. M., Freedman, Z. R., Ryan, R. M., & Deci, E. L. (1996). Motivational predictors of weight loss and weight-loss maintenance. *Journal of Personality and Social Psychology, 70,* 115–126.

Williams, G. C., Rodin, G. C., Ryan, R. M., Grolnick, W. S., & Deci, E. L. (1995). Compliance or autonomous regulation: New insights about adherence to medical regimens. *Journal of General Internal Medicine, Supplement, 10(4),* 116.

Williams, J. E., & Best, D. L. (1990). *Measuring sex stereotypes: A multination study, revised edition.* Newbury Park, CA: Sage.

Williams, K. R., & Hawkins, R. (1989). The meaning of arrest for wife assault. *Criminology, 27,* 163–181.

Williams, S. L. (2005). Anxiety disorders. In J. Maddux & B. Winstead (Eds.), *Psychopathology: Foundations for a contemporary understanding.* Mahwah, NJ: Erlbaum.

Williams, L. A., & DeSteno, D. (2008). Pride and perseverance: The motivational role of pride. *Journal of Personality and Social Psychology, 94,* 1007–1017.

Wilson, D. S. (1998). Adaptive individual differences within single populations. *Philosophical Transactions of the Royal Society of London, 353,* 199–205.

Wilson, D. S., Coleman, K., Clark, A. B., & Biederman, L. (1993). Shy-bold continuum in pumpkinseed sunfish (*Lepomis gibbosus*): An ecological study of a psychological trait. *Journal of Comparative Psychology, 70,* 250–260.

Wilson, M. (1993). DSM-III and the transformation of American psychiatry: A history. *American Journal of Psychiatry, 150,* 399–410.

Wilson, M. (2001). The case for sensorimotor coding in working memory. *Psychonomic Bulletin & Review, 8,* 44–57.

Wilson, M., & Daly, M. (1985). Competitiveness, risk taking, and violence: The young male syndrome. *Ethology and Sociobiology, 6,* 59–73.

Wilson, P. M., Rodgers, W. M., Blanchard, C. M., & Gessell, J. (2003). The relationship between psychological needs, self-determined motivation, exercise attitudes, and physical fitness. *Journal of Applied Social Psychology, 33,* 2373–2392.

Wilson, R. I., & Mainen, Z. F. (2006). Early events in olfactory processing. *Annual Review of Neuroscience, 29,* 161–201.

Wimer, R. E., & Wimer, C. C. (1985). Animal behavior genetics: A search for the biological foundations of behavior. *Annual Review of Psychology, 36,* 171–218.

Winfield, R. C., & Dennis, W. (1934). The dependence of the rat's choice of pathways upon the length of the daily trial series. *Journal of Comparative Psychology, 18,* 135–147.

Wing, R., & Hill, J. (2004). *National weight control registry Web site.* http://www.lifespan.org/services/bmed/wt_loss/nwcr/

Winsler, A., de León, J. R., Wallace, B. A., Carlton, M. P., & Willson-Quayle, A. (2003). Private speech in preschool children: Developmental stability and change, across-task consistency, and relations with classroom behaviour. *Journal of Child Language, 30,* 583–608.

Wise, R. A. (1996). Addictive drugs and brain stimulation reward. *Annual Review of Neuroscience, 19,* 319–340.

Wishart, J. G., & Bower, T. G. R. (1984). Spatial relations and the object concept: A normative study. In L. P. Lipsitt & C. Rovee-Collier (Eds.), *Advances in infancy research* (Vol. 3). Norwood, NJ: Ablex.

Wissler, C. (1901). The correlation of mental and physical tests. *Psychological Review, 3*(Whole No. 6).

Wit, A. P., & Wilke, H. A. M. (1992). The effect of social categorization on cooperation in three types of social dilemmas. *Journal of Economic Psychology, 13,* 135–151.

Wittchen, H. U., Kessler, R. C., Pfister, H., & Lieb, M. (2000). Why do people with anxiety disorders get depressed? A prospective-longitudinal community study. *Acta Psychiatrica Scandinavica, 406,* 14–23.

Wittig, R. M., & Boesch, C. (2003). "Decision-making" in conflicts of wild chimpanzees (*Pan troglodytes*): An extension of the relational model. *Behavioral Ecology and Sociobiology, 54,* 491–504.

Witty, P. A., & Jenkins, M. D. (1935). Intra-race testing and Negro intelligence. *Journal of Psychology, 1,* 179–192.

Wixted, J. T. (2004). The psychology and neuroscience of forgetting. *Annual Review of Psychology, 55,* 235–269.

Wixted, J. T. (2005). A theory about why we forget what we once knew. *Current Directions in Psychological Science, 14,* 6–9.

Wolf, A. W., & Lozoff, B. (1989). Object attachment, thumbsucking, and passage to sleep. *Journal of the American Academy of Child and Adolescent Psychiatry, 28,* 287–292.

Wood, D. M., & Emmett-Oglesby, M. W. (1989). Mediation in the nucleus accumbens of the discriminative stimulus produced by cocaine. *Pharmacology, Biochemistry, and Behavior, 33,* 453–457.

Wood, W., & Eagly, A. H. (2002). A cross-cultural analysis of the behavior of women and men: Implications for the origins of sex differences. *Psychological Bulletin, 128,* 699–727.

Woods, S. C., Schwartz, M. W., Baskin, D. G., & Seeley, R. J. (2000). Food intake and the regulation of body weight. *Annual Review of Psychology, 51,* 255–277.

Woodward, A. L. (2003). Infants' developing understanding of the link between looker and object. *Developmental Science 6,* 297–311.

Woody, S. R., & Nosen, E. (2009). Psychological models of phobic disorders and panic. In M. M. Antony & M. B. Stein (Eds.), *Oxford handbook of anxiety related disorders.* Oxford, UK: Oxford University Press.

Woolf, C. J., & Salter, M. W. (2000). Neuronal plasticity: Increasing the gain in pain. *Science, 288,* 1765–1768.

Woolley, J. D. (1995). Young children's understanding of fictional versus epistemic mental representations: Imagination and belief. *Child Development, 66,* 1011–1021.

Worthman, C. M. (1999). Evolutionary perspectives on the onset of puberty. In W. Trevethan, E. O. Smith, & J. J. McKenna (Eds.), *Evolutionary medicine.* New York: Oxford University Press.

Wrangham, R. W. (1993). The evolution of sexuality in chimpanzees and bonobos. *Human Nature, 4,* 47–79.

Wulff, S. B. (1985). The symbolic and object play of children with autism: A review. *Journal of Autism and Developmental Disorders, 15,* 139–148.

Wyatt, T. D. (2009). Fifty years of pheromones. *Nature, 457,* 262–263.

Wyrwicka, W. (1996). *Imitation in human and animal behavior.* New Brunswick, NJ: Transaction Books.

Yamagishi, T., & Mifune, N. (2008). Does shared group membership promote altruism? *Rationality and Society, 20,* 5–30.

Yamane, Y., Carlson, E. T., Bowman, K. C., Wang, Z., & Connor, C. E. (2008). A neural code for three-dimensional object shape in macaque inferotemporal cortex. *Nature Neuroscience, 11,* 1352–1360.

Yamazaki, K., Beauchamp, G. K., Fung-Win, S., Bard, J., & Boyse, E. A. (1994). Discrimination of odor types determined by the major histocompatibility complex among outbred mice. *Proceedings of the National Academy of Sciences (USA), 91,* 3735–3738.

Yamazaki, K., Beauchamp, G. K., Kupniewski, D., Bard, J., Thomas, L., & Boyse, E. A. (1988). Familial imprinting determines H-2 selective mating preferences. *Science, 240,* 1331–1332.

Yanca, C., & Low, B. S. (2004). Female allies and female power: A cross-cultural analysis. *Evolution and Human Behavior, 25,* 9–23.

Yantis, S. (2008). The neural basis of selective attention. *Current Directions in Psychological Science, 17,* 86–90.

Yeomans, M. R., & Gray, R. W. (1996). Selective effects of naltrexone on food pleasantness and intake. *Physiology and Behavior, 60,* 439–446.

Yirmiya, N., Solomonica-Levi, D., & Shulman, C. (1996). The ability to manipulate behavior and to understand manipulation of beliefs: A comparison of individuals with autism, mental retardation, and normal development. *Developmental Psychology, 32,* 62–69.

Youngblade, L. M., & Dunn, J. (1995). Individual differences in young children's pretend play with mother and sibling: Links to relationships and understanding of other people's feelings and beliefs. *Child Development, 66,* 1472–1492.

Zacharias, I., & Wurtman, R. J. (1969). Age at menarche: Genetic and environmental influences. *New England Journal of Medicine, 280,* 868–875.

Zahn-Waxler, C., & Radke-Yarrow, M. (1990). The origins of empathic concern. *Motivation and Emotion, 14,* 107–130.

Zajonc, R. B. (1965). Social facilitation. *Science, 149,* 269–274.

Zajonc, R. B. (1980). Compresence. In P. B. Paulus (Ed.), *Psychology of group influence.* Hillsdale, NJ: Erlbaum.

Zantell, T. R. (2006). Imitation: definitions, evidence, and mechanisms. *Animal Cognition, 9,* 3335–353.

Zaragoza, M. S., & Mitchell, K. J. (1996). Repeated exposure to suggestion and the creation of false memories. *Psychological Science, 7,* 294–300.

Zebrowitz, L. A. (1996). Physical appearance as a basis of stereotyping. In C. N. Macrae, C. Stangor, & M. Hewstone (Eds.), *Stereotypes and stereotyping.* New York: Guilford.

Zebrowitz, L. A., & McDonald, S. M. (1991). The impact of litigants' baby-facedness and attractiveness on adjudications in small claims courts. *Law and Human Behavior, 15,* 603–623.

Zebrowitz, L. A., & Montepare, J. M. (2005). Appearance DOES matter. *Science, 308,* 1565–1566.

Zebrowitz, L. A., & Rhodes, G. (2002). Nature let a hundred flowers bloom: The multiple ways and wherefores of attractiveness. In G. Rhodes & L. A. Zebrowitz (Eds.), *Facial attractiveness: Evolutionary, cognitive, and social perspectives.* Westport, CT: Ablex.

Zebrowitz, L. A., Kikuchi, M., & Fellous, J-M. (2007). Are effects of emotion expression on trait impressions mediated by babyfacedness? Evidence from connectionist modeling. *Personality and Social Psychology Bulletin, 33,* 648–662.

Zebrowitz, L. A., Montepare, J. M., & Lee, H. K. (1993). They don't all look alike: Individuated impressions of other racial groups. *Journal of Personality and Social Psychology, 65,* 85–101.

Zeh, J. A., & Zeh, D. W. (2001). Reproductive mode and the genetic benefits of polyandry. *Animal Behaviour, 61,* 1051–1063.

Zeidner, M. (1998). *Test anxiety: The state of the art.* New York: Plenum.

Zentall, T. R. (2003). Imitation in animals: How do they do it? *Current Directions in Psychological Science, 12,* 91–95.

Zhang, M., & Kelley, A. E. (2000). Enhanced intake of high-fat food after striatal mu-opioid stimulation: microinjection mapping and fos expression. *Neurocience, 99,* 267–272.

Zhang, M., Balmadrid, C., & Kelley, A. E. (2003). Nucleus accumbens opioid, GABAergic, and dopaminergic modulation of palatable food motivation: Contrasting effects revealed by a progressive ratio study in the rat. *Behavioral Neuroscience, 117,* 202–211.

Zinbarg, R. E., Barlow, D. H., Brown, T. A., & Hertz, R. M. (1992). Cognitive-behavioral approaches to the nature and treatment of anxiety disorders. *Annual Review of Psychology, 43,* 235–267.

Zohary, E., Celebrini, S., Britten, K. H., & Newsome, W. T. (1994). Neuronal plasticity that underlies improvement in perceptual performance. *Science, 263,* 1289–1292.

Zurif, E. G. (1990). Language and the brain. In D. N. Osherson & H. Lasnik (Eds.), *Language: An invitation to cognitive science* (Vol. 1). Cambridge, MA: MIT Press.

Name Index

Subject Index